# Geometric Programming
# for Computer-Aided Design

# Geometric Programming for Computer-Aided Design

Alberto Paoluzzi
Dip. Informatica e Automazione, Università Roma Tre, Rome, Italy

with contributions from

Valerio Pascucci
Center for Applied Scientific Computing, L. Livermore National Laboratory, California, USA

Michele Vicentino
Wind Telecomunicazioni Spa, Services Architecture Management, Rome, Italy

Claudio Baldazzi
IT Telecom Spa, Internet Services Design, Pomezia, Rome, Italy

and

Simone Portuesi
Dip. Informatica e Automazione, Università Roma Tre, Rome, Italy

WILEY

Copyright © 2003     John Wiley & Sons Ltd, The Atrium, Southern Gate, Chichester, West Sussex PO19 8SQ, England

Telephone (+44) 1243 779777

Email (for orders and customer service enquiries): cs-books@wiley.co.uk
Visit our Home Page on www.wileyeurope.com or www.wiley.com

*Other Wiley Editorial Offices*

John Wiley & Sons Inc., 111 River Street, Hoboken, NJ 07030, USA

Jossey-Bass, 989 Market Street, San Francisco, CA 94103-1741, USA

Wiley-VCH Verlag GmbH, Boschstr. 12, D-69469 Weinheim, Germany

John Wiley & Sons Australia Ltd, 33 Park Road, Milton, Queensland 4064, Australia

John Wiley & Sons (Asia) Pte Ltd, 2 Clementi Loop #02-01, Jin Xing Distripark, Singapore 129809

John Wiley & Sons Canada Ltd, 22 Worcester Road, Etobicoke, Ontario, Canada M9W 1L1

Wiley also publishes its books in a variety of electronic formats. Some content that appears in print may not be available in electronic books.

*Library of Congress Cataloging-in-Publication Data*

Paoluzzi, Alberto.
  Geometric programming for computer aided design / Alberto Paoluzzi ; with
  Contributions from Valerio Pascucci, Michele Vicentino, Claudio Baldazzi and Simone Portuesi.
    p. cm.
  Includes bibliographic references and index.
  ISBN 0-471-89942-9 (alk. paper)
    1. Geometric programming. 2. Computer-aided design. I. Title.

T57.825 .P36 2003
620'.0042'0285dc21

                                            2002191056

*British Library Cataloguing in Publication Data*

A catalogue record for this book is available from the British Library

ISBN 0-471-89942-9

Typeset by the author on Mac OS X using OzTeX, Alpha, BBEdit, Adobe Illustrator and PLaSM

This book is printed on acid-free paper responsibly manufactured from Sustainable forestry in which at least two trees are planted for each one used for paper production.

Son of man, ... show them
the design and plan of the Temple, its exits and
entrances, its shape, how all of it is arranged, the
entire design and all its principles.

Give them all this in writing so that they can see
and take note of its design and the way it is all
arranged and carry it out.

(Ezekiel 43, 10–11)

# Contents

# Preface

This book is about design, programming and geometry, or, better, about design programming using geometry. These three worlds meet and communicate with each other using computer graphics. Therefore, this book is also about computer graphics, but its first aim is to discuss a functional approach to geometric programming that supports the rapid prototyping of design applications.

It is our experience that some great people (at *Spatial, Dassault, Autodesk, EDS, PTS*, etc.) have spent a lot of time and effort programming great geometric tools so that the rest of us may make better designs. The results of their work are the powerful computer-aided design systems that some readers may have on their desk. But such systems, even when they offer an application programming interface, hide the power and the beauty of geometric methods behind the scenes. My opinion is that we need to gain full control of what we do when we develop new design methods or applications, not least for æstetic reasons.

In particular, to teach (and learn) computer-aided design and graphics methods using a standard programming approach, say one based on imperative languages and on some kernel APIs, may be quite difficult. To explain, and display, how to stack three cubes of varying dimensions requires a substantial programming effort, that might be measured in several lines of code. Even worse, the majority of such a code may have nothing to do with the problem, but with the computational framework, the user interface, the display method, and so on. My hope, about 12 years ago, was to devise some symbolic design approach, where an assembly made by three parametrized cubes could be defined by writing one line of code.

About one decade ago, after having taught computer graphics and geometric modeling for several years, I learned some functional programming and discovered the Backus' FL language and its algebra of programs. I suddenly realized that an algebraic calculus oriented to geometric expressions could be established upon this language. We only needed to add to FL some specialized data structure to represent geometric objects and their properties and some fundamental geometric algorithms.

PLaSM is the result of this addition. It provides a specialized design environment where complex geometric objects and methods may be defined, abstracted, parametrized and combined by writing one or, more rarely, a few lines of code, thus giving a very powerful and terse geometric calculus under direct user control.

*Geometric Programming for Computer-Aided Design*  Alberto Paoluzzi
© 2003 John Wiley & Sons, Ltd  ISBN 0-471-89942-9

The author's hope is that this language may became useful for geometric design applications, as *Mathematica* or *MathLab* are for symbolic or numeric applications, by offering the user a programming environment where geometric objects and methods may be prototyped and visualized with the minimal development effort.

This book is also the product of 25 years of teaching practice in computer graphics and geometric modeling with engineering students at various curricula levels, giving courses that in the past six years have been successfully based on PLaSM examples and implementations. I hope the book will help the reader to learn that programming with geometry, and the development of customized computer-aided design tools, may be very easy and fast, and great fun.

**Book roadmap**

This book contains three parts, dedicated to: (a) providing an introduction to functional programming with PLaSM and covering the mathematical background needed to work with geometric applications; (b) teaching some basic techniques of graphics programming; and (c) discussing some basic and advanced geometric modeling, including motion modeling and animation. A useful appendix is dedicated to documenting both the built-in operators of the language and the libraries that can be loaded at run time in its computational environment.

Each of the three parts is relatively self-contained, provided that a working introduction to the language is obtained by reading some sections of Chapter 1. One part can therefore be used to teach one semester courses in functional programming and geometry, in basic graphics programming and in geometric modeling, respectively. An advanced graphics course could also add the motion modeling chapter. Conversely, a geometric modeling course could find useful additions from materials located in Chapters 6 and 8, which are more dedicated to affine transformations and to hierarchical assemblies, respectively.

The more advanced sections can be skipped both by those on a beginner's or undergraduate course. They may possibly integrate the teaching materials for courses at graduate level.

To gain a deep understanding of graphics and modeling issues is not easy, because it requires being able to know, appreciate and combine several topics from different areas of mathematics, engineering, computer science and arts. In writing this book, we made an attempt to show some of these connections. As a consequence we had to collect quite different materials that do not necessarily require to be read by the casual user of the book. Conversely, we hope that some book sections are likely to be appreciated by different audiences, and in particular by people with a background in mathematics or mechanical engineering or architecture.

Finally, we would like to remark that, since the book presents the reader with methodological issues, the central role that we assigned to PLaSM should be considered the assessment of an interpreted RAD (rapid application development) environment for graphics, modeling and animation, that allows both the teacher and the student to generate examples and prototypes with the minimal programming effort and using free software. When a PLaSM prototype is ready, it is usually a fast and error-free task to deploy an efficient version of a design application making use of the best libraries and geometric kernels available.

The more recent versions of the opensource and multiplatform PLaSM environment are available at the web site www.plasm.net, where several programming and teaching resources are also available, including most examples and pictures given in the following chapters, and up-to-date software sources, binaries and documentation.

## Acknowledgements

My first acknowledgement is for Gianfranco Carrara, who, several years ago, proposed I create a language for architectural design, and suggested I read Ferdinand de Saussure and Noam Chomsky, as well as the design theorists of seventies, the Negroponte's *Architecture Machine* [Neg70] and the Mitchell's *Computer Aided Architectural Design* [Mit77]. The present book describes the result of two and half decades of research following his initial suggestion.

Then, my most grateful thanks go to the memory of Antonio Ruberti, who gave me a position in the Computer Science Department at "La Sapienza" University in Rome, and as the Italian Ministry of Research (later the European Commissary for Research) liked the PLaSM project and helped to get it funded. Without his insight, this language and this book would not exist.

Great thanks to John E. Hopcroft, who invited me to visit his Robotics Group at Cornell University during my sabbatical in 1986. He posed some challenging problems and offered me the opportunity to learn doing research in a highly competitive academic environment. My first work with simplicial geometric complexes is dated to the last weeks of my stay at Cornell.

The PLaSM project started in 1990, funded by a pluriannual grant from the "PF Edilizia" Project of Italian National Research Council. At about the same time, I encountered the algebraic approach to functional programming carried out by the Backus' and Williams' Functional Programming Group at IBM Almaden. Their FL language, with its unique compositional semantics, strongly inspired the PLaSM design. I never met John Backus, although I visited his group at Almaden, but I hope that he would appreciate the demonstration of the FL expressive power given by PLaSM.

To acknowledge all people that contributed to this project is quite impossible. Important contributions came from Carlo Cattani, Vincenzo Ferrucci and Fausto Bernardini, who contributed to the seminal work on multidimensional geometric computing with simplicial complexes; later Claudio Sansoni collaborated with the initial language design; Valerio Pascucci, Michele Vicentino and Giuseppe Proietti developed the first PLaSM interpreter and kernel based on hierarchical polyhedral complexes of convex cells; Claudio Baldazzi contributed the implementation of Boolean operations with multidimensional BSP trees. More recently, Simone Portuesi, Giorgio Scorzelli, Stefano Francesi and Glauco Cenciotti have developed the current interpreter and geometric kernel written respectively in Scheme and C++; Franco Milicchio has developed the specialized editor XPLODE. Giorgio Marzano is using the language for knowledge representation and interaction with a reasoning engine. Several students gave us useful feedback by developing PLaSM-based projects and applications. Also, I am grateful to the many hundreds of students which experimented with the various versions of the language, and pained over preliminary teaching materials and drafts of some chapters of this book.

I'm also most grateful to the friends and collegues that gave encouragement, advice and comments during the long development of this book. In particular, I was greatly helped by the very useful comments and suggestions by Ralph Martin and Antonio Di Carlo, that greatly improved several chapters. Useful suggestions and friendly encouragement came from Chandrajit Bajaj, Fausto Bernardini, Hanspeter Bieri, Leila De Floriani, Vincenzo Ferrucci, Joe Kearney, Antonio Sassano, Vadim Shapiro and Ernesto Staffetti. Several useful comments and constructive criticism came from the anonymous book referees and from the friends that contributed both to the PLaSM language and to this book. Also, I would like to thank the editors at Wiley, and in particular Birgit Gruber, Sally Mortimore, Zoë Pinnock and Martin Tribe, who with the greatest patience and professional ability guided me along the long path of preparing this book. Clearly, I am solely responsible for the errors it contains.

Finally, I would like to acknowledge the great, warm and continuous support given by Father Isidoro Del Lungo, who also provided the rare book [San70] used to model the basilica of S. Stefano Rotondo displayed on the book cover, and give grateful thanks to my wife Anna and sons Claudio and Francesco for the understanding and love they demonstrated during the long years of this writing.

*Alberto Paoluzzi*
Rome

# Part I

# Programming and Geometry

# 1

# Introduction to FL and PLaSM

A *statement* is a programming language construct that is evaluated only for its effect. Examples include assignment, input/output statements, and control statements. Programs in most languages are composed primarily of statements; such languages are said to be *statement oriented*.

Programming language constructs that are evaluated to obtain values are called *expressions*. Arithmetic expressions are the most common example. Expressions may occur as parts of statements, as in the right-hand side of an assignment statement. Expressions that are evaluated solely for their value, and not for any other effects of the computation, are said to be *functional*.

Some programming languages, such as Scheme, are *expression oriented*; their programs are constructed of definitions and expressions; there are no statements.

(D. P. Friedman, M. Wand, and C. T. Haynes
*Essentials of Programming Languages*
The MIT Press and McGraw-Hill, 1992)

The *design language* PLaSM, which this book aims to describe, is a geometry-oriented extension of a subset of FL, an advanced language for programming at *Function Level*, developed by the Functional Programming Group of IBM Research Division at Almaden [BWW90, BWW+89]. The design language PLaSM, whose name stands for "Programming LAnguage for Symbolic Modeling", was developed [PPV95] by the CAD Group at the University "La Sapienza" and then supported and further developed at "Roma Tre" University in Rome. Such language is strongly influenced by FL; actually, it can be considered a geometry-oriented extension of a FL subset, with only a few small syntactical differences. In the present chapter a short outline of the FL approach to functional programming is given, together with an introduction to PLaSM and to its geometric operators. The chapter is aimed at discussing the language

*Geometric Programming for Computer-Aided Design*  Alberto Paoluzzi
© 2003 John Wiley & Sons, Ltd  ISBN 0-471-89942-9

syntax and at getting started with a working system. In the last part of the chapter we introduce the first examples of *geometric programming*. The main goal of the chapter is to give the flavor of language style and expressive power. Therefore, many concepts are introduced informally here and defined carefully in later chapters.

## 1.1   Introduction to symbolic design programming

The FL language, on the line traced by the Backus' Turing lecture [Bac78], introduces an algebra over programs, where a set of algebraic identities between functional expressions is established. Such an algebraic approach to programming allows, among several other interesting features, formal reasoning about computer programs. Furthermore, programs are easily combined, so that new programs are obtained from simpler ones in a easy and elegant way. Also, it is possible to find simpler equivalent programs, both at the design and at compiling stages. Great advantages are thus obtained in the style and efficiency of program prototyping.

   More generally, it is well known that functional programming enjoys several good properties:

1. The set of syntax rules of a functional language is very small.
2. Each rule is very simple.
3. The program code is terse and clear.
4. The meaning of a program is well understood, since there is no state.
5. Functions may be used both as programs and as data.
6. Programs are easily connected by concatenation and nesting.

   The PLaSM language was designed upon the main assumption that a functional computing environment is *the* natural environment for geometric computations and generation of geometric models of shape. In fact, a complex geometric shape is often constituted by an assembly of components, which are highly dependent on each other. In particular:

1. Components may result from computations invoking other components.
2. Parameterized generating functions may be associated with each component.
3. Geometric expressions are the best candidates to produce actual parameter values when generating assembly components.

   Our design language, strongly inspired from FL, can therefore evaluate *geometric expressions*, that are expressions whose value is a polyhedral complex, i.e. a set of polyhedral point sets. It is also able to combine functions to produce higher-level functions in the FL style. Beyond the adopted approach to programming at *Function Level*, which allows computing with functions as well as with numbers, we note the unique design choice of dealing only with a *dimension-independent* implementation of geometric data structures and algorithms. The first feature results in a very natural approach to parametric geometry. The second feature, coupled with the "combinatorial engine" of FL, gives the language an amazing descriptive power in computing with geometry.

### 1.1.1 Computational model

In this section a first introduction to our approach to symbolic design programming is given. A more detailed discussion of language syntax and semantics is left to the following sections and chapters.

**Programs are functions** Generally speaking, a program is a *function*. When *applied* to some input *argument*, a program produces some output *value*. Two programs are usually connected by using functional composition, so that the output of the first program is used as input to the second program.

**Program composition and application** The composition of PLaSM programs behaves exactly as the standard composition of mathematical functions. For example, the application of the compound mathematical function $f \circ g$ to the $x$ argument

$$(f \circ g)(x) \equiv f(g(x))$$

means that the function $g$ is first applied to $x$ and that the function $f$ is then applied to the value $g(x)$. The PLaSM notation for the previous expressions will be

$$(\mathtt{f} \sim \mathtt{g}) : \mathtt{x} \equiv \mathtt{f} : (\mathtt{g} : \mathtt{x})$$

where $\sim$ stands for function *composition* and where g:x stands for *application* of the function g to the argument x.

**Naming objects** In PLaSM, a name can be assigned to every value generated by the language, by using a DEF construct, either with or without explicit parameters. In both cases the so-called *body* of the definition, i.e. the expression which follows the definition *head*, at the right hand of the "=" symbol, will describe the computational process which generates the value produced by the computation. The parameters which it implicitly/explicitly depends on may be embedded in such a definition.

For example we may have

```
DEF object = (Fun3 ~ Fun2 ~ Fun1):parameters;
```

The computational process which produces the object value can be thought as the computational pipeline shown in Figure 1.1.

**Figure 1.1**  Example of computational pipeline

In the previous example the dependence of the model upon the parameters is implicit. In order to modify the generated object value it is necessary (a) to change the source code in either the body or the local environment of its generating function; (b) to compile the new definition; and (c) to evaluate again the object identifier.

**Parametrized objects**  A *parametric* geometric model can be defined, and easily combined with other such models, by using a generating function with formal *parameters*. Such kind of function may be instanciated with different actual *arguments*, thus obtaining different output values. For example, we may have

```
DEF object (params::IsSeq) = (Fun3 ∼ Fun2 ∼ Fun1):params;

DEF obj1 = object:< p₁, p₂, ... , pₙ >;
DEF obj2 = object:< q₁, q₂, ... , qₙ >;
```

It is interesting to note that the generating function of a geometric model may accept parameters of *any* type, including other geometric objects.


## 1.2   Getting started with PLaSM

When taking the first steps with a new computer language, it is useful to carefully introduce the operations to start. In particular, in this section we discuss step-by-step how to download the PLaSM design environment from the web, its installation on the desktop machine, and the first computational experiences with it.


### 1.2.1   Installing the language

The integrated PLaSM "design environment" consists at least of a language *interpreter*, and may contain a source *editor*, a local or remote language *server*, and the preferred web *browser* enriched with one or more graphics plug-ins. PLaSM is available for all the *Windows* versions, all the brands of *GNU/Linux*, and the Apple's *Mac OS X* operating system.


**Software download**

The current PLaSM interpreter is written in Scheme and C++, by using a first-class multi-platform Scheme implementation called PLT Scheme.[1] The first task for the user is to download the PLaSM interpreter and, possibly, other useful softwares from the web sites they reside on.

1. *Interpreter*

   The PLaSM interpreter is located at the web address

   > http://www.plasm.net/download/

   The typical user may like to get the binary executables for the preferred computational environment. Conversely, the advanced user might prefer to get the sources and to recompile and build the interpreter.

2. *Editor*

   An integrated language editor is not strictly required, since a standard text editor would be sufficient, but it may be very useful. The specialized PLaSM

---

[1] The common page of the PLT Group (Programming Language Team Group), currently disseminated in several universities, is http://www.plt-scheme.org/.

editor *Xplode*, which stands for *"Is a PLasm Open Design Environment"*, will provide for syntax coloring, tab completion, menus of available libraries and functions, quick documentation and direct evaluation of every sub-expression. A standard version is already integrated in the interpreter package. [2]

3. *Browser plug-ins*

The PLaSM environment does not currently offer an integrated viewer for graphics data. Conversely, it allows the user to export the geometric objects generated by the language into some largely diffused web standard formats, including VRML (Virtual Reality Modeling Language) for 3D graphics, as well as *SVG* (Scalable Vector Graphics) and Flash for 2D graphics. The reader may find large collections of VRML resources on the web.[3] The browser plug-ins for .svg (*SVG*) and .swf (Flash) files can be downloaded from the *Adobe*[4], and the *Macromedia*[5] web sites, respectively.

**Software installation**

A minimal PLaSM system is constituted by a language client connected to a remote server and by a web browser with a VRML viewer installed. A full PLaSM environment contains a local language server, an integrated editor and more plug-ins for supported graphics formats.

The following instructions are for all *Windows* environments. For other platforms follow the installation guidelines given on the language site.

1. *Language server*

The installation on the local machine is very simple: double-click on the file plasm.exe[6] and answer the installer requests.

2. *Language client and editor*

The language client and integrated editor *Xplode* are already installed automatically in the previous step. Launch *Start* → *Programs* → *Plasm* → *Xplode* to start working. If some problems arise, the editor will ask to browse within the disk and to show where the server is located.

3. *Plug-ins*

Follow the installation instructions given at the web sites of the graphics plug-ins used, normally to be installed within a web browser.

---

[2]  The PLaSM editor can be also downloaded separately, for each of the supported platforms.
[3]  http://www.web3d.org/vrml/vrml.htm
[4]  http://www.adobe.com/svg/viewer/install/
[5]  http://www.macromedia.com/software/flash/download/
[6]  In *Mac OS X* and *Linux*, the installation packge is called plasm.pkg and plasm.rpm, respectively.

*1.2.2   Using the language*

A typical PLaSM session consists in reading/writing/editing definitions, evaluating definitions and/or expressions, exporting geometric values to external files, saving/restoring geometries to/from XML files, and in visualizing the contents of graphic files.

**Getting started**

In order to check if the language environment has been installed correctly, try generating a red cube and displaying it within your web browser. To do this:

1. Launch the *Xplode* editor from either the *Start → Programs → Plasm → Xplode* menu (on *Windows*) or from the *Applications* folder (on *MacOS X*).
2. Write on the superior editor window the following code:

   ```
   DEF mycube = CUBOID:<1,1,1> COLOR RED;
   mycube;
   ```

   then either launch the menu item *PLaSM → Evaluate Buffer* or hit <ctrl>B (on *Windows*) or <cmmd>B (on *MacOS X*).
3. The listener should write, on the inferior window, the message:

   ```
   ==================
   mycube DEFINED
   ==================
   '
   PolComplex < 3 , 3 >
      $ < < 'RGBcolor' , < 1 , 0 , 0 > > >
   ```

   that acknowledges the correct definition of the mycube symbol and tell the user about the type of the expression evaluated on the last input line.
4. Select the mycube symbol using the mouse.
5. Either launch the menu item *PLaSM → Vrml Export* or hit <ctrl>M (on *Windows*) or <cmmd>M (on *MacOS X*). Answer *OK* to the dialog window asking for confirmation on the symbol/expression to evaluate and export.
6. Insert, in the exporting dialog window the filename mycube.wrl and select the directory where to export the generated file. You should own the writing permissions on such directory.
7. Load the mycube.wrl file within your browser, where you must have previously installed and configured a VRML plug-in.
8. Enjoy rotating and scaling your first geometric model!

   The remainder of this section is quite technical, and can be avoided at a first reading by a non-computer science-oriented reader. That kind of reader can go directly to Section 1.3. He or she will go back when willing to understand what is going on within the language design environment and exporter.

**Interacting with the language**

First of all, the reader must understand that every PLaSM source program is a *string*, i.e. a sequence of characters enclosed between (double) quotes, that must be processed by the language interpreter.

The PLaSM interpreter was previously written in Common Lisp, and is currently implemented in MzScheme ("Miss Scheme"), a first-class implementation [FFFK98] of Scheme, which is a simple, powerful and beatiful Lisp dialect [SF97, FH92].

**Evaluating expressions** The processing of every PLaSM program requires the evaluation of a Scheme expression. For example, the evaluation of the PLaSM expression

```
(SQRT:3 + 10) / (3.5 * COS:(PI/4))
```

where SQRT:3 stands for $\sqrt{3}$ and COS:(PI/4) stands for $\cos\frac{\pi}{4}$, as well as the evaluation of *every* other PLaSM program, requires the processing of a source string, in this case

```
"(SQRT:3 + 10) / (3.5 * COS:(PI/4))"
```

The translation of such a source string into some machine-executable code is done by asking the language interpreter to evaluate a Scheme form (plasm " ... "). Here, we must evaluate the Scheme expression:

```
(plasm "(SQRT:3 + 10) / (3.5 * COS:(PI/4))")
```

The wrapping of a PLaSM expression as a string within a Scheme expression is not needed when an integrated PLaSM editor is available. Only in that case, can the user write some PLaSM code and directly evaluate every expression or sub-expression in it, simply by:

1. Selecting the text portion he or she wants to evaluate.
2. Executing the menu item *PLaSM → Evaluate expression*, or by pressing the corresponding keyboard shortcut.

Clearly the completion of the PLaSM expression as one of the two equivalent Scheme expressions

```
(plasm " ...  ")
(eval-plasm " ...  ")
```

will in this case be automatically performed by the editor.[7]

**Scripting** A source program, or *script*, is constituted by one or more PLaSM definitions and expressions. A script is normally stored in a file with suffix .psm, that stands for "plasm".

A script is loaded within the run-time environment as the result of the application of the load operator on the PLaSM string that contains the name, and possibly the path, of the script file. For example, the script contained within the file example.psm of the subdirectory path of the current directory is loaded as result of the evaluation of

```
(plasm " LOAD:'path/example.psm' ")
```

Notice that a PLaSM string, and in particular a file name, is a sequence of characters enclosed between *single* quotes.

---

[7] The two forms are needed for backward compatibility with former interpreter versions.

Several interpreter actions may be requested by the user, by just including the
(plasm " ...  ") expressions within a (begin ...  ) environment. For example,
we may write:

```
(begin
    (plasm " LOAD:'script1.psm' ")
    (plasm " DEF fun1 (a::Isreal) = (SIN * COS):a ")
    (plasm " fun1:(PI/6) + fun1:(PI/4) ")
)
```

In order to be *loadable* as described above, a script file must contain a Scheme
expression, i.e. it should contain either (plasm " ... ") or (begin ... ). Scheme
expressions like the above one will be usually substituted by simpler equivalent
expressions, which contain a *unique* source string. Therefore, in order to write a
loadable file, the user must type within the file:

---

**Script 1.2.1**
```
    (plasm "
       LOAD:'script1.psm' ;
       DEF fun1 (a::Isreal) = (SIN * COS):a ;
       fun1:(PI/6) + fun1:(PI/4)
    ")
```

---

Conversely, when using the integrated PLaSM editor, the previous Scheme expression
is substituted by the *contents* of the source string, i.e. by a set of PLaSM definitions
and/or expressions. So, within *Xplode*, the user must write and evaluate the following
code:

---

**Script 1.2.2**
```
    LOAD:'script1.psm' ;
    DEF fun1 (a::Isreal) = (SIN * COS):a ;
    fun1:(PI/6) + fun1:(PI/4)
```

---

In the remainder of the book we normally make use of this simpler approach. Only
occasionally, some PLaSM expressions will be embedded in their ground Scheme forms.
   The reader should notice that every pair of adjacent definitions and/or expressions
— within the same source string — is separated by a semicolon. A final semicolon to
terminate the last expression or definition is optional. It may be useful to insert such
a final semicolon when the program script is still under development, in order to avoid
the compilation error generated when two subsequent expressions are not separated
by a semicolon.

**Listener**  Every time the user requires the evaluation of some PLaSM code, the
interpreter generates an internal value for each of the processed definitions and
expressions, and at the same time produces some log on the screen of the action,
type or value generated. If the specialized *Xplode* editor is available, such a screen

echo is sent into a separate window, called the *listener*; otherwise, the log messages are sent to the window of the language server.

**Libraries**  A predefined set of function definitions, when recognized to have some general utility, may be defined as a *library*. Libraries are .psm files stored in the special subdirectory plasm/psmlib and are loaded by using either the Scheme form

```
(plasm " LOADLIB:'libname' ")
```

in the PLaSM interpreter, or the PLaSM expression

```
LOADLIB:'libname';
```

in the integrated editor. In both cases the library name is given without file path and suffix. The remarkable difference between libraries and standard script files concerns the symbols defined in libraries, which — after the library loading — become *protected* by the language environment, and cannot be changed nor redefined by the user. This design choice is supposed to help avoiding naming conflicts, which might produce unpredictable mistakes. Currently, all libraries are loaded when starting the interpreter. The user may easily change this behavior, by either preventing the loading of some libraries, or by loading them as non protected at set-up, or by loading some libraries only on request during a work session.

## Exporting graphics

The PLaSM environment does not currently contain an integrated viewer of graphics data, but may export geometric objects as data files to various well-known graphics formats, as summarized below. In general, PLaSM is committed to support graphics web standards.

**VRML**  The *Virtual Reality Modeling Language* (VRML) is the ISO standard for 3D graphics on the *World-Wide Web*. [8] In particular, the geometric value of the PLaSM object named out can be exported to the file out.wrl, using the current VRML standard coding, as the effect of evaluating the statement

```
VRML: out: 'out.wrl';
```

**Flash**  The .swf file format by *Macromedia*'s Flash is the *de facto* industrial standard for 2D vector graphics animation and streaming on the World-Wide Web. A .swf file with the contents of the out object, reversed into a draving area wide 150 pixels, may by produced as:

```
... some PLaSM code ...
DEF out = ...

flash: out: 150: 'out.swf' ;
```

---

[8] New updated versions of VRML are currently under development by the W3C consortium, and are called VRML2000 and X3D, which stands for "VRML coded in XML".

**SVG**   The *Scalable Vector Graphics* (SVG) is the ISO draft proposal developed by W3C for 2D vector graphics on the web. The exporting into the out.svg file of the geometric value of the 2D PLaSM object named out, assuming a drawing area with 15 centimeters of width, is obtained by

```
svg: out: 15: 'out.svg';
```

### Saving/restoring geometry

A very useful feature of the current PLaSM version is the ability to save and restore geometric objects into/from external files by using a XML coding. The XML (Extensible Markup Language), can be considered the best method known today for putting structured data in a text file. It is a subset of the text processing international standard SGML (Standard Generalized Markup Language) (ISO 8879), specialized for use on the World-Wide Web.

Thus, large and computing intensive models can be generated only once, stored in external files and directly restored in memory in subsequent work sessions with PLaSM. Even more, the XML coding can be very useful when storing geometric objects in a database or when exchanging geometries across a computer network, within a collaborative and spatially distributed design environment.

The syntax to save/restore the geometric value associated to the object symbol is

```
DEF object = ...  ;
save: object:'path/object.xml';
```

in the saving session, whereas in the restoring session the saved object must be defined as:

```
DEF object = open:'path/object.xml';
```

### 1.3   Programming at Function Level

PLaSM can be considered a geometry-oriented extension of a subset of the FL language [BWW90, BWW+89], which is a pure functional language based on combinatorial logic. In particular, the FL language makes use of both pre-defined and user-defined *combinators*, i.e. higher-order functions which are applied to functions to produce new functions. The small but very significant FL subset which is used as the base environment of PLaSM is summarized in this section.

Notice that here and in the remainder of this book the infix symbol $\equiv$ is normally used to tell the reader that the *expression* on its left side evaluates to the *value* on its right side. Sometimes this symbol is also used to denote an equivalence between syntactical forms.

#### 1.3.1   *Elements of* FL *syntax*

Primitive FL *objects* are characters, numbers and truth values. Primitive objects, functions, applications and sequences are *expressions*. *Sequences* are expressions separated by commas and contained within a pair of angle brackets:

```
<5, fun>
```

An *application* expression `exp1:exp2` applies the *function* resulting from the evaluation of `exp1` on the *argument* resulting from the evaluation of `exp2`. Notice that binary functions can also be used in infix form:

```
1 + 3 ≡ +:<1,3> ≡ 4
```

Application associates to left, i.e. a sequence of repeated applications is evaluated from left to right. Notice that this is only possible if all the applications, but possibly the last one, generate a new function to be applied to the next argument:

```
f:g:h ≡ (f:g):h
```

Application binds stronger than composition, i.e. applications are evaluated first before compositions, as is shown in the following example:

```
f:g ~ h ≡ (f:g) ~ h
```

### 1.3.2  Combining forms and functions

The function level approach to programming of FL emphasizes the definition of new functions by combining existing functions in various ways. The result of this approach is a programming style based on function-valued expressions. Some more important FL *combining forms* and functions follow.

**Construction**  The combining form `CONS` allows application of a sequence of functions to an argument producing the sequence of applications:

```
CONS:<f₁,...,fₙ>:x ≡ [f₁,...,fₙ]:x ≡ <f₁:x,...,fₙ:x>
```

A CONSed sequence of functions is a sort of *vector function*, that can be composed with other functions and that can be applied to data. E.g. `cons:<+,->`, written also `[+,-]`, when applied to the argument `<3,2>` returns the sequence of applications

```
[+,-]:<3,2> ≡ <+:<3,2>,-:<3,2>> ≡ <5,1>
```

**Apply-to-all**  The combining form `AA` has a symmetric effect, i.e. it applies a function to a sequence of arguments giving a sequence of applications

```
AA:f:<x₁,...,xₙ> ≡ <f:x₁,...,f:xₙ>
```

For example, we may apply the `SIN` function to all the elements of a list of numeric expressions:

```
AA:SIN:< 0, PI/3, PI/6, PI/2 >
    ≡ < SIN:0, SIN:(PI/3), SIN:(PI/6), SIN:(PI/2) >
    ≡ < 0 , 0.8660254037844382 , 0.49999999999999956 , 1.0 >;
```

The reader should notice that numeric computations often introduce round-off and approximation errors. Just remember that $\pi$ is an irrational number and cannot be represented exactly by using finite precision arithmetic. Also, functions like `SIN` are computed by using some truncated series expansion.

**Identity**    The function ID returns its argument unchanged

```
ID:x ≡ x
```

In other words, the application of the identity function to *any* argument, gives back the same argument:

```
ID:0.5 ≡ 0.5
ID:SIN ≡ SIN
ID:SIN:0 ≡ SIN:0 ≡ 0
ID:'out.wrl' ≡ 'out.wrl'
```

**Constant**    The combining form K is evaluated as follows, for whatever $x_2$:

```
K:x₁:x₂ ≡ x₁;
```

In other words, the first application returns a constant function of value $x_1$, i.e. such that when applied to *any* argument $x_2$, *always* returns $x_1$. Some concrete examples follow:

```
K:0.5 ≡ Anonymous-Function
K:0.5:10 ≡ 0.5
K:0.5:100 ≡ 0.5
K:0.5:SIN ≡ 0.5
```

**Composition**    The binary composition of functions, denoted by the symbol "$\sim$", is defined in the standard mathematical way:

```
(f ∼ g):x ≡ f:(g:x)
```

$n$-ary composition of functions is also allowed:

```
COMP:< f, g, h >:x ≡ (f ∼ g ∼ h):x ≡ f:(g:(h:x))
```

In this case we have, where PI, COS and ACOS are the PLaSM denotations for $\pi$, cos and arccos, respectively:

```
(ACOS ∼ COS):PI ≡ ACOS:(COS:PI) ≡ ACOS:-1 ≡ 3.141592653589793
(COS ∼ ACOS):-1 ≡ COS:(ACOS:-1) ≡ COS:3.141592653589793 ≡ -1
(ACOS ∼ COS ∼ ACOS):-1 ≡ (ACOS:(COS:(ACOS:-1))) ≡ 3.141592653589793
```

**Conditional**    The conditional form IF:< p, f, g > is evaluated as follows:

```
IF:< p, f, g >:x ≡ f:x   if   p:x ≡ TRUE
                ≡ g:x   if   p:x ≡ FALSE
```

Notice that both the predicate[9] p, as well as f and g, to be alternatively executed depending on the truth value of the expression p:x, must be all *functions*. E.g., we have:

```
IF:< IsIntPos, K:True, K:False >:1000 ≡ True
IF:< IsIntPos, K:True, K:False >:-1000 ≡ False
```

where IsIntPos is a predefined predicate that returns True when applied to some positive integer.

---

[9] A *predicate* is a function p : Dom $\longrightarrow$ { True, False }, where Dom is any set. Both True and False are called *truth values,* and also *Boolean* values.

**Insert Right/Left**   The combining forms INSR and INSL allow the user to apply a
*binary* function f, with signature[10] f : $D \times D \to D$, on a sequence of arguments of
*any* length $n$. Notice that in the right-hand expressions below, f is applied to a *pair*
of arguments:

INSR:f:< $x_1$, $x_2$, ... , $x_n$ > ≡ f:< $x_1$, INSR:f:< $x_2$, ... , $x_n$ > >

INSL:f:< $x_1$, ... , $x_{n-1}$, $x_n$ > ≡ f:< INSL:f:< $x_1$, ... , $x_{n-1}$ >, $x_n$ >,

where INSR:f:<x> ≡ INSL:f:<x> ≡ x.

An interesting example of use of the INSL combinator is given below, where the
function bigger : Num × Num → Num is defined, being the syntax of definitions explained
in detail in the next section. Notice that IsNum is a predicate used to check at run-time
if the arguments of function application are of the correct type. The bigger function
returns the one of its *two* arguments with maximum value; the biggest function does
the same from a list of arguments of *arbitrary length*:

```
DEF bigger  (a,b::IsNum) = IF:< GT:a, K:b, K:a >:b;
DEF biggest = INSL:bigger;

bigger:<-10, 0> ≡ 0
biggest:<-10, 0, -100, 4, 22, -3, 88, 11 > ≡ 88
```

**Catenate**   The CAT function appends any number of input sequences creating a single
output sequence:

CAT:<<a,b,c>,<d,e>,...,<x,y,z>> ≡ <a,b,c,d,e,...,x,y,z>

A pair of concrete examples of how the CAT function is used follows. The second one
is quite interesting: it gives a *filter* function used to select the non-negative elements
of a number sequence:

```
CAT:<<1,2,3>,<11,12,13>,<21,22,23>> ≡ <1,2,3,11,12,13,21,22,23>

(CAT ∼ AA:(IF:< LT:0, K:<>, [ID] >)):< -101, 23, -37.02, 0.1, 84 >
≡ CAT:<<>, <23>, <>, <0.1>, <84>>
≡ <23, 0.1, 84>
```

It may be very useful to *abstract* a filter function with respect to a generic predicate
and to a generic argument sequence, by giving a function *definition*:

---

**Script 1.3.1 (Filter function)**
```
DEF filter (predicate::IsFun) (sequence::IsSeq) =
    (CAT ∼ AA:(IF:< predicate, K:<>, [ID] >)):sequence;
```

---

Two examples of application of the filter function to actual arguments follow.
Notice that the two applications respectively return the positive and the negative
elements of the input sequence. Remember that a sequence of applications is *left-
associative*:

---

[10] The *signature* of a function $f$ from a *domain* $A$ to a *codomain* $B$ is the ordered pair of sets
$(A, B)$. It is normally associated to $f$ by writing $f : A \to B$.

```
filter:(LE:0):< -101, 23, 0, -37.02, 0.1, 84 >
    ≡ (filter:(LE:0)):< -101, 23, 0, -37.02, 0.1, 84 >
    ≡ Anonymous-Function:< -101, 23, 0, -37.02, 0.1, 84 >
    ≡ <23, 0.1, 84>

filter:(GE:0):< -101, 23, 0, -37.02, 0.1, 84 >
    ≡ (filter:(GE:0)):< -101, 23, 0, -37.02, 0.1, 84 >
    ≡ Anonymous-Function:< -101, 23, 0, -37.02, 0.1, 84 >
    ≡ <-101, -37.02>
```

**Distribute Right/Left**   The functions DISTR and DISTL are defined as:

```
DISTR:<<a,b,c>, x> ≡ <<a,x>, <b,x>, <c,x>>
DISTL:<x, <a,b,c>> ≡ <<x,a>, <x,b>, <x,c>>
```

They accordingly transform a *pair*, constituted by an arbitrary expression x and by an arbitrary sequence, into a *sequence of pairs*.

Let us give an example of use. The Euler number $e$ is defined as the sum of a series of numbers. In particular:

$$e = \frac{1}{0!} + \frac{1}{1!} + \frac{1}{2!} + \cdots + \frac{1}{n!} + \cdots$$

We compute an *approximation* of $e$, named `euler`, as the sum of the first 21 terms of the series above. The definition of the factorial function `fact` is given in Script 2.1.6. Notice that the + operator may be applied to a sequence of numeric arguments and remember that $0! = 1$.

```
DEF euler = (+ ~ AA:/ ~ DISTL):< 1.0, AA:fact:(0..20) >;

euler ≡ (+ ~ AA:/ ~ DISTL):< 1.0, AA:fact:(0..20) >
    ≡ (+ ~ AA:/ ~ DISTL):< 1.0, AA:fact:< 0, 1, 2, ... , 8, 9 > >
    ≡ (+ ~ AA:/ ~ DISTL):< 1.0, < fact:0, fact:1, ... , fact:8, fact:9 > >
    ≡ (+ ~ AA:/ ~ DISTL):< 1.0, < 1, 1, 2, 6, ... , 40320, 362880 > >
    ≡ (+ ~ AA:/): (DISTL:< 1.0, < 1, 1, 2, 6, ... , 40320, 362880 > >)
    ≡ (+ : (AA:/: < <1.0, 1>, <1.0, 1>, ... , <1.0, 40320>, <1.0, 362880> >))
    ≡ + : < 1.0/1, 1.0/1, 1.0/2, 1.0/6, ... , 1.0/40320, 1/362880 >
    ≡ 2.7182815255731922
```

Above we have seen our first important example of FL computation as a sequence of expression transformations using the defining rules of the combinators. The order of transformations is induced by the parenthesis included into an expression. The sub-expressions nested more deeply are transformed first.

A simpler and more elegant implementation of the Euler number is given in Script 1.3.2, where C is the currifier combinator discussed in Section 1.4.3.

---

**Script 1.3.2 (Euler number)**
```
DEF euler = (+ ~ AA:(C:/:1.0 ~ fact)):(0..20)
```

---

**Example 1.3.1 (Conditional operator)**
As we have seen, the conditional form IF:<p,f,g>:data has the following semantic:
"IF the predicate p applied to data is true, THEN apply f to data; ELSE apply g to
data". This construct is very useful when it is necessary to apply different actions
to input data depending on the value of some predicate evaluated on them, and is
probably more "natural" than the conditional statements available in other languages.

From a syntactical viewpoint, notice that the IF operator is a higher-order function
that *must* be applied to a *triplet of functions* in order to return a function which is in
turn applied to the input data.

Such a syntax and semantics of the IF operator can be demonstrated by the following
code, where a string is generated depending on the truth value of a simple predicate.
The reader should notice that the result of evaluating both the expressions K:'True'
and K:'False' is a (constant) function.

```
IF:< EQ, K:'True', K:'False' >:<10, 20> ≡ 'False'
IF:< EQ, K:'True', K:'False' >:<20, 20> ≡ 'True'
```

## 1.4   Basics of PLaSM programming

The PLaSM language was designed to introduce a well-founded programming approach
to *generative modeling*, where geometric objects are generated by invoking the
generating functions with *geometric expressions* as actual parameters. This is achieved
by allowing for a sort of *geometric calculus* over embedded polyhedra. For this
purpose the language contains in its kernel a *dimension-independent* approach to the
representation of geometric data structures and algorithms.

The programming approach to geometric design enforced by PLaSM makes it possible
to manage a sort of extended *variational geometry* [LG82], where classes of objects
with varying topology and shape are parametrized by some language function and
handled and combined as a whole. The language can be considered a *geometry-oriented
extension* of a quite small subset of the functional language FL, where the *validity* of
geometry is always syntactically guaranteed. In other words it is guaranteed that any
well-formed language expression which generates a polyhedrally-typed data object
always corresponds to some valid internal data structure.

Such a functional and dimension-independent approach to geometric design achieves
a *representation domain* broader than usually done by standard solid modelers, so
that points, wire-frames, surfaces, solids and even higher dimensional manifolds can
be suitably combined or blended altogether.

### 1.4.1   Expressions

The syntax of PLaSM is very similar to the syntax of FL (see Section 1.3.1). For the
reader experienced in FL we may say that the differences mainly concern the meaning
of few symbols (composition and constant operators) and the lack of pattern matching
in the definition of type predicates. In particular, the PLaSM language:

1. uses a case-insensitive alphabet;
2. allows for overloading of some (pre-defined) operators;
3. evaluates expressions which return a polyhedral complex as value;

4. produces higher-level functions in the FL style;
5. allows for partially specified (curried) functions.
6. introduces two new combining forms AC (*apply-in-composition*) and AS (*apply-in-sequence*) to use a function with a number of specification parameters greater than the number used in its definition.

Unlike FL, the PLaSM language does allow the use of identifiers for any language object, including numbers, strings and polyhedral complexes, but does not provide pattern matching to identify the sub-components of a data structure. The current PLaSM implementation also provides free nesting of local functional environments.

### 1.4.2  *User-defined functions*

User-defined functions as recognized by PLaSM are either *global* or *local*. Global functions are also called top-level functions.

**Global functions**  A global function definition always contains a *function head* separated from the *function body* by the = character. The body is optionally followed by a *local environment*, which contains one or more local function definitions separated by commas and enclosed between a pair of WHERE and END keywords. Global functions are allowed to contain formal parameters in the head. Formal parameters are specified together with a predicate which is used to perform dynamic type checking at run-time.

Global function definitions are separated by ";" (semicolon) punctuation.

**Local functions**  The visibility of local functions is restricted to the scope of a global function. No formal parameters are allowed in a local function definition. In such a case an identifier is associated by equality to an expression. The value resulting from the expression evaluation is returned by invoking the name. Such a value may be any PLaSM object, including numbers, functions, sequences, polyhedral complexes, etc.

Local function definitions are separated by "," (comma) punctuation.

A top-level function template in the general case is the following:

```
DEF global (p1::IsType1; p2::IsType2) (q1,q2::IsType3) = Body
WHERE
    local1 = body1,
    local2 = body2
    WHERE local21 = body21 END
END;
```

where DEF, WHERE and END are reserved keywords; global is the name of the top-level function; Body is any PLaSM expression which is used to compute the function values; p1, p2 and q1, q2 are formal parameters; IsType1, IsType2 and IsType3 are predicates used for dynamic type checking of actual values of parameters at function invocation time; local1 and local2 are the names of two local functions; body1 and body2 are any PLaSM expression used for computing their values.

Notice that local function definitions are separated by commas. Formal parameters to be checked by the same predicate are separated by commas. The triplet "parameters", "::", "IsType", where IsType is any PLaSM predicate, is called *parameter sublist*. A *parameter list* contain one or more parameter sublists separated by semicolons and enclosed in round brackets.

A global function head may contain zero, one or more parameter lists. Correspondingly, the function is invoked with zero, one or more applications to *actual arguments*. The presence of more than one parameter list is allowed to permit specification of *partial functions*.

**Function definition**    It is useful to look at some different global function definitions, given for the sake of simplicity without any local functional environment.

```
DEF f (a::type1) = bodyF;
DEF g (a1,...,an::type2) = bodyG;
DEF h (a1::type1)(a2::type2) = bodyH;
DEF l (a1::type1; a2,a3::type2) = bodyL;
DEF m = bodyM;
```

**Function invocation**    The functions previously defined are correspondingly invoked with one, more or zero application to actual arguments, depending on the number of parameter lists in their definition:

```
f:x ;
g:<y1, ... , yn > ;
h:x1:y2 ;
l:<x1, y2,y3 > ;
m ;
```

### Example 1.4.1 (Function definition and invocation)

As simple and useful examples of function definitions, we give in Script 1.4.1 two predicates IsEven and IsOdd that return True when applied to some even or odd argument, respectively, and False otherwise. Examples of function application using the CONS combinator are given in the last two rows of the script.

---

### Script 1.4.1 (IsEven and IsOdd predicates)

```
DEF IsEven (n::IsInt) = IsInt:(n / 2);
DEF IsOdd = NOT ~ IsEven;

[IsEven, IsOdd]: 100 ≡ < True , False >
[IsEven, IsOdd]: 101 ≡ < False , True >
```

---

### 1.4.3    Built-in functions

Several non-geometric functions and combining forms are predefined in PLaSM, and are introduced in this section. Various simple examples are also given. The reader is strongly encouraged to explore the language by trying similar examples, possibly with the insertion of small changes.

**Type predicates**   A *predicate* is a function which returns either True or False when applied to actual arguments. We conventionally start the name of most predicates with the "Is" substring. A quite large set of predefined predicates to be used for dynamic type checking is available. For example:

    IsInt, IsIntPos, IsReal, IsRealPos, IsSeq, IsFun, IsPol, IsChar, IsString

return True when applied to integers, positive integers, reals, positive reals, sequences, functions, polyhedra, characters and strings, respectively.

    IsInt:1000 ≡ True
    IsIntPos: -123 ≡ False
    IsReal: 345.28 ≡ True
    IsReal: 3.4528E+2 ≡ True
    IsRealPos: 3.4528E-2 ≡ True
    IsSeq: < 345.28, -123, SQRT, 'aaaaa' > ≡ True
    IsFun: ID ≡ True
    IsPol: (CUBOID:<1,1,1>) ≡ True
    IsChar: 'a' ≡ True
    IsString: 'Alberto' ≡ True

A second-order function IsSeqOf must be applied to a predicate and then to a sequence of objects or expressions. For example:

    IsSeqOf: IsInt: < 10, 2, (12 - 8)/2, 99 + 100, 0 > ≡ True
    IsSeqOf: IsInt: < 10, 2, (11 - 8)/2, 99 + 100, 0 > ≡ False

The following equivalence holds:

    IsSeqOf:*predicate* ≡ AND ∼ AA:*predicate*

**Logical functions and constants**   The truth values *True* and *False* are respectively denoted as TRUE and FALSE. According to the Lisp approach, the empty sequence <> may be also used for *False*. The available logical operators are the standard ones:

    AND, OR, NOT

Some examples of logical expressions follows:

    AND: < True, True, True, True > ≡ True
    AND: < True, True, False > ≡ False
    OR:  < True, False, True > ≡ True
    OR:  < False, False, False, False > ≡ False
    NOT: False ≡ True
    AND: < True OR NOT:True, NOT:False > ≡ True

**Comparison functions**   A standard set of comparison predicates between numeric expressions is given, where

    GT, GE, LT, LE, EQ

respectively stand for "greater than", "greater or equal", "less than", "less or equal", "equal".

All such operators compare two arguments, but there is a significant difference in their use. The first four are second-order predicates. EQ is conversely a standard binary predicate. Hence they must be used as follows:

```
GT:1:2 ≡ True              to read: "is 'greater than 1' 2 ?"
GE:1:2 ≡ True
LE:1:2 ≡ False
LE:2:( 20 / 10 ) ≡ True
EQ:< 1, 5 - 3 > ≡ False
EQ:< 6 / 3, 2 > ≡ True
```

Comparison functions are often used together with logical operators to construct logical expressions. Syntactically equivalent forms of same logical expressions or functions follow:

```
GE:0:0.5 AND LE:1:0.5 ≡ True
(GE:0 AND LE:1): 0.5 ≡ True
(GE:0 AND LE:1): -0.5 ≡ False
(AND ~ [GE:0, LE:1]): 0.5 ≡ True
(NOT ~ AND ~ [GE:0, LE:1]): 0.5 ≡ False
(IsIntPos AND GT:10): 5 ≡ False
(AND ~ [IsIntPos, GT:10]): 50.001 ≡ False
(AND ~ [IsIntPos, GT:10]): 50.0 ≡ True
```

**Mathematical functions**  The standard mathematical functions on numbers are also available. For example

```
+, -, *, /, **, SIN, COS, TAN, ATAN, LN, EXP, SQRT, ...
```

denote respectively the algebraic operators, the power raising, the trigonometric functions sin, cos, tan, the arc associated with a given tangent, the logarithm in basis $e$, the $e^x$ function, the square root, etc. The symbol PI is the PLaSM denotation of the $\pi$ number. The ** operator denotes power raising. In other words, the x ** y expression stands for $x^y$. The reader should notice that every arithmetic operator, except **, are $n$-ary, i.e. may be applied to non-empty sequences of arguments. Some examples of use follow. Notice also their *overloading* as algebraic operator between functions.

```
3 + 4 ≡ 7
+:< 1,2,3,4 > ≡ 10
-:< 1,2,3,4 > ≡ -8
*:< 1,2,3,4 > ≡ 24
/:< 2,2,3,4 > ≡ 1/12
PI ≡ 3.14159265358979
SIN:PI ≡ 0.0
COS:PI ≡ -1.0
ACOS:-1 ≡ 3.141592653589793
SQRT:(9 * 9) ≡ 9
(9 * 9) ** (1/2) ≡ 9.0
(9 * 9) ** (-1/2) ≡ 0.1111111111111111
1 / 0.1111111111111111 ≡ 9.0
COS + SIN ≡ Anonymous-Function
(COS + SIN):PI ≡ -1.0
```

**Sequence functions**  Several operations on sequence are built in. In particular:

```
AL, AR, FIRST, LAST, TAIL, CAT, SEL, LEN, LIST
```

stand respectively for append left, append right, return the first element, return the last element, return the subsequence from the second to the last element, catenate a sequence of sequences, and select a specified element of a sequence. LEN returns the integer length of the input sequence. LIST encloses its input into a pair of angle brackets.

```
AL:< 99,< 1,2,3,4,5 > > ≡ < 99,1,2,3,4,5 >
99 AL < 1,2,3,4,5 > ≡ < 99,1,2,3,4,5 >
AR:< < 1,2,3,4,5 >,99 > ≡ < 1,2,3,4,5,99 >
< 1,2,3,4,5 > AR 99 ≡ < 1,2,3,4,5,99 >
CAT:<< 101,102 >,< 901,902,903 >> ≡ < 101,102,901,902,903 >
SEL:4:< 101,102,901,902,903 > ≡ 902
(SEL:4 ~ CAT):<< 101,102 >,< 901,902,903 >> ≡ 902
(SEL:4 ~ CAT):<< ID,K >,< COS,SIN,TAN >> ≡ Anonymous-Function
((SEL:4 ~ CAT):<< ID,K >,< COS,SIN,TAN >>):(PI/2) ≡ 1.0
LIST:10 ≡ [ID]:10 ≡ < 10 >
```

**String functions**  The *string*, i.e. an ordered set of characters used as an atomic value, is a primitive data type in PLaSM. A *char* (character) is a string with only one character. Some predefined functions on chars and strings are

```
ISCHAR, ISSTRING, ORD, CHAR, CHARSEQ, STRING, LT, LE, EQ, GE, GT
```

whose use is summarized by the following examples. They are further discussed in Section 2.1.4.

```
ISCHAR:'p' ≡ True
ISSTRING:'abcdefghijk' ≡ True
ORD:'p' ≡ 112
CHAR:112 ≡ 'p'
CHARSEQ:'Homer' ≡ < 'H','o','m','e','r' >
STRING:< 'H','o','m','e','r' > ≡ 'Homer'
LT:'a':'b' ≡ False
GT:'a':'b' ≡ True
```

**Sequence generators**  The FROMTO operator generates integer sequences between two given extreme integers. It is also denoted by an infix double period as an equivalent syntactical form:

```
2..5 ≡ FROMTO:<2,5> ≡ <2,3,4,5>
```

Similarly, the unary INTSTO (*Integers to*) operator generates integer sequences starting from 1:

```
INTSTO:5 ≡ <1,2,3,4,5>
```

Some further examples are:

```
CAT:< 20..22, 40..42, 60..62 > ≡ < 20,21,22, 40,41,42, 60,61,62 >
(AA:SEL:(5..8)):(CAT:< 20..22, 40..42, 60..62 >) ≡ < 41,42, 60,61 >
(INTSTO ~ LEN ~ CAT):< 20..22, 40..42, 60..62 > ≡ < 1,2,3,4,5,6,7,8,9 >
(STRING ~ AA:CHAR):(65..70) ≡ 'ABCDEF'
```

**Repeated instancing** The repetitition operator # allows for instancing $n$ times any given expression:

    #:3:expr ≡ < expr,expr,expr >

Similarly, the catenation of repeated sequences ## repeats and catenates a given sequence:

    ##:3:<a,b,c > ≡ < a,b,c, a,b,c, a,b,c >

**Selector functions** The selector functions, as introduced by FL, are used to respectively select the first, second, or $n$-th element of a sequence:

    S1, S2, S3, ... , S$n$

SEL is a primitive (second-order) operator with a specification parameter i, such that when applied to a sequence, the $i$-th sequence element is returned:

    SEL:2:<13, 4.5, ID> ≡ 4.5.

**Extended application** Two new useful combining forms AC, AS are introduced, which respectively stand for *apply-in-composition* and for *apply-in-sequence*, and are defined as follows:

$$AC:f:<x_1, \ldots ,x_n> \equiv f:x_1\sim \cdots \sim f:x_n$$
$$AS:f:<x_1, \ldots ,x_n> = [f:x_1, \ldots ,f:x_n]$$

They have several interesting geometric uses. When combined with AC or AS, the SEL operator is modified as follows:

    AC:SEL:<3, 1>:<<1,3,8,7>, 89, fun> ≡
        (SEL:3 ∼ SEL:1):<<1,3,8,7>, 89, fun> ≡ 8

    AS:SEL:<3, 1>:<<1,3,8,7>, 89, fun> ≡
        [SEL:3, SEL:1]:<<1,3,8,7>, 89, fun> ≡ <fun, <1,3,8,7>>

**Higher-order functions**

A function with $n$ parameter lists is called a function of $n$-th *order*. Such a function, when applied to actual arguments for the first parameter list, returns a function of order $(n-1)$. This one, when further applied to actual arguments for the second parameter list, returns a function of order $(n-2)$, and so on. Finally, when all the parameter lists are *bound* to actual arguments, the function returns the value generated by the evaluation of its body. Functions of order higher than one are called *higher-order* functions. The functions returned from the application of higher-order functions to some (ordered) *subset* of their parameter lists are called *partial* functions.

**Example 1.4.2 (Partial functions)**
The primitive predicates LT (Less Than) and GT (Greater Than) are defined as second-order functions. Therefore, to test if $a < b$, the user may write one of the two expressions:

```
LT:b:a
GT:a:b
```

In both cases, the first application returns a partial function, i.e. LT:b and GT:a, to read "Is Less Than b ?" and "Is Greater Than a ?", respectively. The second application (clearly on the second argument) conversely returns a truth value, i.e. either True or False.

The possibility of producing partial functions may be very useful. For example, in order to count the number of positive numbers in a sequence of real numbers, we might write:

```
DEF CountPositive = + ~ AA:(IF:< GT:0, K:1, K:0 >);
CountPositive:< 6, -22, 0, 4.25, 999, -33, 0 > ≡ 3
```

**Curried functions**

An higher-order function $g$ is said to be *curried*, from the name of logician Haskell B. Curry, who introduced this technique, when the following equivalence with a function $f$ exists:

$$f(x_1, x_2, \ldots, x_n) \equiv g(x_1)(x_2) \cdots (x_n).$$

In this case $g$ is called a curried version of $f$, which can be used also when only a subset of $f$ arguments is available. If we look at the *signatures* of the two functions, i.e. to their domain and range sets, then we may write:

$$f \; : \; \mathcal{A}_1 \times \mathcal{A}_2 \times \cdots \times \mathcal{A}_n \to \mathcal{B}$$
$$g \; : \; \mathcal{A}_1 \to \mathcal{A}_2 \to \cdots \to \mathcal{A}_n \to \mathcal{B}$$

The FL language gives a predefined combinator C to currying any function with arguments:

```
f:< x1,x2,...,xn > ≡ C:f:x1:x2:  ⋯  :xn
```

**Example 1.4.3 (Curried equality)**

The comparison predicate EQ is normally used as a binary predicate, i.e. is normally applied to a pair of arguments.[11] It can sometimes be very useful to have a partial function to test the equality of a variable argument with a fixed one. This test could be done, e.g., by using the curried function C:EQ.

For example, we may write:

```
DEF CountZero = + ~ AA:(IF:< C:EQ:0, K:1, K:0 >);
CountZero:< 6, -22, 0, 4.25, 999, -33, 0 > ≡ 2
```

---

[11] Actually, it can be applied to any $n$-tuple of arguments, with $n \geq 1$.

## 1.5  Geometric operators

In this section we introduce the built-in geometric operators. Therefore, here we enumerate the predefined operations available in the language, by giving some very simple examples. In the next chapter some more interesting programs are discussed, to introduce the reader to the language flavour and methods.

### 1.5.1  Pre-defined geometric operators

The PLaSM language is characterized by a small number of pre-defined geometric operators that allow to easily implement several geometric operations useful in generative modeling. Most geometric operators are *dimension-independent*, i.e. can be applied to 2D objects as well as to 3D objects, and even to higher dimensional objects.

Our geometric operations are *closed* in the space of polyhedral complexes. This implies that sub-expressions which contain operators, arguments and parentheses can be combined into more complex expressions, thus giving a well-founded generative *geometric calculus*.

In this section such operators are briefly introduced, together with some simple examples of use. In later sections and chapters they are all described in much greater detail.

### Elementary shape constructors

A small set of geometric primitives is provided, including

> CUBOID and SIMPLEX

which respectively allow for generating $d$-dimensional cuboids, i.e. 1D segments, 2D *rectangles*, 3D *parallelepipeds*, 4D *hyper-parallelepipeds*, etc., and $d$-dimensional simplices, i.e. 1D *segments*, 2D *triangles*, 3D *tetrahedra*, etc.

**CUBOID primitive**  The CUBOID primitive generates $d$-dimensional intervals of intrinsic dimension given by the number of actual parameters, which ordinately correspond to the sizes of sides. Such intervals always have a vertex on the origin and edges parallel to the axes of the reference frame. For example:

> CUBOID:5 $\equiv$ 1D segment of length 5
> CUBOID:<5,10> $\equiv$ 2D rectangle of area 5 × 10
> CUBOID:<5,10,5> $\equiv$ 3D parallelepiped of volume 5 × 10 × 5
> CUBOID:<1,1,1,1> $\equiv$ 4D hypercuboid of volume 1

**SIMPLEX primitive**  The SIMPLEX primitive generates simplices of different intrinsic dimension. For instance:

> SIMPLEX:5 $\equiv$ 1D segment of length 5;
> SIMPLEX:<1,1> $\equiv$ 2D standard triangle of area $\frac{1}{2!}$;
> SIMPLEX:<1,a,1> $\equiv$ 3D standard tetrahedron of volume $\frac{a}{3!}$;
> SIMPLEX:<1,a,b,1> $\equiv$ 4D simplex of volume $\frac{ab}{4!}$.

**Polyhedral complex handlers**

Polyhedral complexes are *the* geometric objects used by the language and discussed in Section 4.6. Each cell of such a complex is a polyhedron, which can be further subdivided into convex cells. Some primitives that work on polyhedral complexes are the following:

    MKPOL, UKPOL, JOIN, EMBED

The MKPOL constructor is the most powerful geometric primitive, which provides a very high geometric covering to the language. This constructor allows for easily implementing *polylines, polymarkers, triangle stripes, quadrilateral meshes*, various kinds of *solid meshes*, and so on. The UKPOL primitive is conversely used to unpack the internal data structure and return an external representation of a polyhedral complex. The JOIN function is applied to a sequence of polyhedral complexes, embedded in the same space $\mathbb{E}^d$, and returns their convex hull.[12] The EMBED operator is used to give a higher number of coordinates to its argument, i.e. to *embed* a polyhedron or a complex into some Euclidean space of higher dimension. For example EMBED:1:polygon is used to embed a 2D polygon in the $z = 0$ subspace of the 3D space, by adding 1 more coordinate (with 0 value) to its points.

MKPOL **primitive**   The "Make polyhedron" constructor MKPOL generates polyhedral complexes of any dimension. It is the basic geometry constructor in PLaSM. The MKPOL operator is a mapping from triples of sequences to polyhedral complexes:

    MKPOL:< verts, cells, pols >

where verts is a sequence of points in the same space $\mathbb{E}^d$; cells is a sequence of convex cells (given as sequences of point indices); pols is a sequence of polyhedra (given as sequences of cell indices). Each cell is defined as the convex hull of its vertices, each polyhedron is defined as the union set of its convex cells. This definition is quite general, and may include (complexes of) polylines, plane and space polygons, 3D polyhedra and higher dimensional geometric objects, both solid and embedded.

**Example 1.5.1 (Polyhedral complex)**
Two slightly different models of a 2D L-shaped polygon are given as *polyhedral complexes* in Script 1.5.1, by using the MKPOL primitive. At this point the sequence of polygon *vertices* is associated with the symbol verts, then two convex cells are given as sequences of indices of vertices, and associated with the cells symbol. Finally, a set of polyhedral cells, each one defined as a sequence of cell indices, is associated with the pols symbol.

Notice that L_shape1 is defined by using two polyhedral cells, each one associated with a convex cell. Conversely, L_shape2 contains only one polyhedral cell, defined by two convex cells, that meet along a common face. The important difference between the two definitions can be observed by looking at Figures 1.2b and 1.2c. An explanation of this behavior requires concepts on *polytopal subdivisions* discussed in Section 4.6. The skeletons of a polyhedral complex are introduced on page 28.

---

[12] The minimum convex set that contains them. Alternate definitions of this concept are given in Section 4.2.

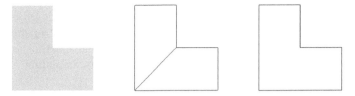

**Figure 1.2** (a) L-shaped *polyhedral complex* produced by the MKPOL primitive (b) 1-skeleton of the definition with 2 polyhedral cells (c) 1-skeleton of the definition with 1 polyhedral cell

**Script 1.5.1**
```
DEF L_shape1 = MKPOL:< verts, cells, pols >
WHERE
   verts = <<0,0>,<2,0>,<2,1>,<1,1>,<1,2>,<0,2>>,
   cells = <<1,2,3,4>,<4,5,6,1>>,
   pols = <<1>,<2>>
END;

DEF L_shape2 = MKPOL:< verts, cells, pols >
WHERE
   verts = <<0,0>,<2,0>,<2,1>,<1,1>,<1,2>,<0,2>>,
   cells = <<1,2,3,4>,<4,5,6,1>>,
   pols = <<1,2>>
END;
```

**UKPOL primitive** As we already said, the UKPOL primitive is exactly the inverse function of the MKPOL constructor. So it can be applied to any geometric object and returns the triplet of its vertices, convex cells and polyhedral cells. A simple example is given in Script 1.5.2, where a parallelepiped with sides of measure 1, 2 and 3, respectively, is *unpacked* as a triplet of vertices, cells and polyhedra.

**Script 1.5.2 (Unpacked parallelepiped)**
```
UKPOL:(CUBOID:<1,2,3>) ≡ <
   < < 0.0,2.0,3.0 >,< 1.0,2.0,3.0 >,< 0.0,0.0,3.0 >,< 1.0,0.0,3.0 >,
     < 0.0,2.0,0.0 >,< 1.0,2.0,0.0 >,< 0.0,0.0,0.0 >,< 1.0,0.0,0.0 > >,
   < < 1,2,3,4,5,6,7,8 > >,
   < < 1 > > >
```

**Affine transformations**

Affine transformations, i.e. the elementary translation, rotation, scaling, reflexions and shearing, as well the general bijective transformations of an Euclidean space, are fundamental tools in graphics and modeling. PLaSM provides both specific operators

```
T, S, R, H, MAT
```

for dimension-independent elementary transformations and a `MAT` operator which returns the transformation associated to any given non singular matrix.

PLaSM gives as pre-definite some elementary affine operators, including

```
T:coords:parameters ≡ translation
R:coords:parameters ≡ rotation
S:coords:parameters ≡ scaling
```

where `coords` denotes the coordinates affected by the transformation, and `parameters` denotes its parameters.

For efficiency reasons, a special form for parameter specification has been used for some frequently found elementary geometric functions. In particular, the affine transformation functions `T`, `S`, `R`, `H` can be specified both on a single value and on a sequence of values. E.g., `T` denotes translation, `T:1` denotes translation on the first coordinate direction, and `T:1:2.5` means translation of `2.5` units on the first coordinate. For a translation on more than one coordinate we can write, e.g., `T:<1, 3>:<2.5, 6/1.5>`. When evaluated, this functional expression returns the *translation tensor* that translates the geometric objects it is applied to, by `2.5` units on the first coordinate direction (i.e. on the $x$ axis) and by $6/1.5 \equiv 4.0$ units on the second coordinate direction (i.e. on the $y$ axis). Note that several equivalences hold for such *functions*. For instance:

```
T:<1, 3>:<2.5, 6/1.5> ≡ T:1:2.5 ~ T:3:(6/1.5)
```

Since they are functions, affine transformations can be composed and applied to polyhedra. In such a case they are equivalent to the application of a `STRUCT` operator, described in the following subsection. Below we show how to generate a unit cube with a vertex on the origin, move its basis center to the origin and rotate it by 45 degrees about $z$.

```
(R:<1,2>:(PI/4) ~ T:<1,2>:<-0.5,-0.5>): (CUBOID:<1,1,1>)
   ≡ STRUCT:< R:<1,2>:(PI/4), T:<1,2>:<-0.5,-0.5>, CUBOID:<1,1,1> >
   ≡ STRUCT:< Anonymous-Function, Anonymous-Function, PolComplex<3,3> >
   ≡ PolComplex<3,3>
```

## Hierarchical assemblies

According to modern high-level graphics systems, e.g. to *PHIGS*, *Inventor* or VRML, PLaSM provides an easy tool to build hierarchical assemblies, where each component or sub-assembly is defined in its local coordinate frame. This task is performed by the

```
STRUCT
```

operator. This function can only be applied to sequences containing polyhedral complexes, affine transformations and other invocations of the `STRUCT` function.

**STRUCT primitive**  The constructor `STRUCT` is used to generate hierarchical assemblies of objects defined in local coordinates. It is applied to sequences of polyhedra, affine transformations and STRUCT invocations. At traversal time (at evaluation time, in our case) each occurrence of an object in a hierarchical network of structures is transformed from local coordinates into the coordinates of the root of the network. Such world coordinates coincide with those of the first polyhedral complex in the structure argument sequence. Its semantics, discussed in Chapter 8, is very close to the one of ISO PHIGS graphics standard.

**Example 1.5.2 (Table assembly)**
In Script 1.5.3 two alternate equivalent definitions of the Table model displayed in Figure 1.3 are given. Both Table and Table1 definitions use local coordinates for the assembly components (four Leg instances and one Plane instance). The reader is advised to analyze the differences between the two definitions, and to make some hybrid attempts, while looking at the obtained results.

---

**Script 1.5.3 (Table model)**
```
DEF Leg = CUBOID:< 0.1,0.1,0.7 >;
DEF Plane = CUBOID:< 1, 1, 0.2>;

DEF Table = STRUCT:<
    Leg, T:1:0.9, Leg, T:2:0.9, Leg, T:1:-0.9, Leg,
    T:<2,3>:<-0.9,0.7>, Plane >;

DEF Table1 = STRUCT:<
    Leg, T:1:0.9:Leg, T:<1,2>:<0.9,0.9>:Leg, T:2:0.9:Leg,
    T:3:0.7:Plane >;

VRML: Table:'out.wrl';
```

---

 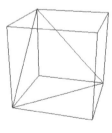

**Figure 1.3**   (a) Table model (b) 1-skeletons of the unit 3D cube and the unit 3-simplex

**Skeletons of a complex**

The cells of a polyhedral complex have different dimensions. In particular, the boundary of a $d$-dimensional cell, or $d$-cell, contains cells of dimension between 0 and $(d-1)$. PLaSM provides a set of extractor operators

```
@0, @1, @2, @3, ...
```

of the $d$-dimensional skeletons of a complex, i.e. of the sub-complex of cells of dimension less or equal to a given integer.

**SKELETONS primitives**  In PLaSM are called *skeleton extractors* operators, or $r$-skeletons, the mappings

$$@r : \mathcal{P}^{d,n} \to \mathcal{P}^{r,n}, \qquad 0 < r < d,$$

such that @r:Pol is the $r$-skeleton of the polyhedral complex Pol. Notice that @0:Pol returns the polyhedral complex of Pol vertices; @1:Pol returns the polyhedral complex of vertices and edges; @2:P returns the polyhedral complex of vertices, edges and faces. When exporting a polyhedral complex from the language environment, the 2-skeleton is automatically extracted if the object dimension is greater than 2.

### Example 1.5.3 (1-skeleton of 3-cube and 3-simplex)

The 1-skeletons of both the 3D cube and the tetrahedon (3-simplex) are extracted and assembled togheter in Script 1.5.4 and displayed in Figure 1.3b. The reader should notice here the infix use of the STRUCT aggregation operator, and is asked to discover in Figure 1.3b the (common) position of the origin of the local reference frames of the cube and the tetrahedron.

---

**Script 1.5.4 (1-skeleton)**
```
DEF out = @1:(CUBOID:<1,1,1> STRUCT SIMPLEX:3);

VRML: out:'out.wrl';
```

---

### Constructor of 1D polyhedra

A constructor of 1D polyhedra is extensively used in PLaSM programs. It is denoted as

QUOTE

and transforms non-empty sequences of non-zero reals into 1D polyhedra. In particular, positive numbers are transformed into solid segments, whereas negative numbers are used to translate the solid ones along the 1D line. Consecutive numbers along the input sequence correspond to adjacent segments along the output polyhedral complex.

**QUOTE primitive**  The QUOTE operator is used in PLaSM to define 1-polyhedra embedded in 1D space. Such $(1,1)$-polyhedra are often used by other PLaSM functions. The range of this operator is the set of sequences of non-zero reals:

$$\text{QUOTE} : (\mathbb{R} - \{0\})^* \to \mathcal{P}^{1,1}$$

Negative elements in the sequence argument are used to denote empty intervals in the complex.

**Example 1.5.4 (User-defined operator)**
Let us introduce in Script 1.5.5 our first user-defined geometric operator. This one will
be called Q and defined as follows:

---

**Script 1.5.5 (Q operator)**
```
DEF Q = QUOTE ∼ IF:< IsSeQ, ID, [ID] >
```

---

which is the PLaSM composition of the simpler functions QUOTE and IF:< IsSeQ,
ID, [ID] >. The reader should notice that such functions are applied in reverse order
to the input. In particular, when Q is applied to some number x, first the

```
IF:<IsSeq,ID,[ID]>:x
```

expression is evaluated. The resulting value is then passed to the QUOTE function.

According to the semantics of the IF conditional construct, the predicate IsSeq:x is
tested to check if x is either a sequence or not. Since the predicate *"Is x a sequence?"*
is false, the expression [ID]:x is evaluated and <x> is returned. Such a sequence is
passed to the QUOTE operator, and further transformed into a 1D line segment of $x$
size.

Also, any sequence of non-zero numbers will be transformed by the Q function into
a *complex* of segments on the real line. For example, the evaluation of the expression

```
Q:<5,-2,5,-2,5>
```

will return the complex of 1D segments shown in Figure 1.4. Most of figures in this
chapter are generated by grabbing the screen during the browsing of a VRML file
generated by the PLaSM interpreter.

---

**Figure 1.4**   The complex of segments generated by evaluating the expression
```
Q:<5,-2,5,-2,5>
```

The application of Q to a negative number or to a sequence of negative numbers
will produce a language *exception*, i.e. the capture of a run-time error.

**Cartesian product**

An important operator on polyhedral complexes of any dimension is their Cartesian
product, denoted in PLaSM by the standard product symbol

*

According to the standard FL syntax, such operation symbol can be used either infix
in an argument pair or as prefix to a sequence of arguments. From both a formal and
an algorithmic viewpoint, it is a special case of the "generalized product" introduced
in [BFPP93].

PRODUCT **primitive**   The Product operator is defined as a mapping from pairs of polyhedra to polyhedra, where the cells in the polyhedral output are generated by pair-wise Cartesian products of the cells in the polyhedral input pair. Algorithms for dimension-independent "generalized" product of both polyhedra and polyhedral complexes are given in [BFPP93] and [PFP96], respectively. A detailed discussion of the meaning and algorithmic implementation of this important operator is deferred until Chapter 14. Anyway, it is so easy and natural to use, that we will make great use of it through the whole book.

**Example 1.5.5 ($d$-dimensional (multiple) intervals)**
The geometric objects generated by the following expressions, which contain the Cartesian product and the user-defined Q operation discussed above, are shown in Figure 1.5.

```
Q:<10,-10,10> ≡ PolComplex{1,1}
Q:<10,-10,10> * Q:<10,-10,10> ≡ PolComplex{2,2}
Q:<10,-10,10> * Q:<10,-10,10> * Q:3 ≡ PolComplex{3,3}
```

**Figure 1.5**   1-, 2- and 3-dimensional complexes generated by Q and * operators

**Example 1.5.6 (Building facade)**
An example is given in Script 1.5.6, and shown in Figure 1.6a, where a 2D complex is generated by Cartesian product of 1D complexes produced by the QUOTE operator. Several other examples of the QUOTE operator are given in Section 1.6.2.

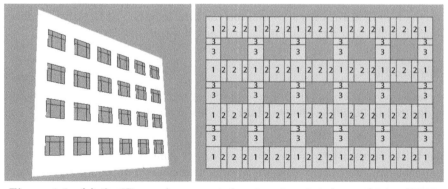

**Figure 1.6**   (a) the 2D complex generated as `facade:<6,4>` by combining QUOTE, product and 1-skeleton operators (b) the generating scheme of `facade` panels

The `facade` generating function works by assembling three 2D Cartesian products of alternating 1D complexes, produced by `Q:xRithm`, `Q:xVoid` and by `Q:yRithm`, `Q:yVoid`, respectively. In particular, the `xRithm` sequence contains the numeric series used in the $x$ direction; analogously `yRithm` for the $y$ direction. Conversely, `xVoid` and `yVoid` host the series with opposite signs of elements. So, the first three Cartesian products in the `STRUCT` sequence produce a sort of checkboard covering that follows the scheme given in Figure 1.6b.

---

**Script 1.5.6 (Building facade)**

```
DEF facade (n,m::IsIntPos) = STRUCT:<
    Q:xRithm * Q:yRithm,
    Q:xVoid * Q:yRithm,
    Q:xRithm * Q:yVoid ,
    @1:(Q:xVoid * Q:yVoid) >
WHERE
    xRithm = ##:n:<5,-2,-5,-2> AR 5,
    yRithm = ##:m:<7,-5,-2> AR 7,
    xVoid = AA:-:xRithm,
    yVoid = AA:-:yRithm
END;
```

---

**Intersection of extrusions**

Another special case of the generalized product of polyhedra [BFPP93] gives an operation where the arguments are first properly embedded into coordinate subspaces of the space of the result, then are subject to indefinite orthogonal extrusions, and are finally pair-wise intersected. Such operation is denoted (in the 3D case) as

$$\&\&:<<i_0,i_1,i_2>,<j_0,j_1,j_2>>$$

where both $<i_0,i_1,i_2>$ and $<j_0,j_1,j_2>$ are permutations of the sequence $<0,1,2>$. Such permutations are needed to specify how to embed the arguments into the coordinate subspaces of the result. The `&&` operation, combined with the 2-skeleton extractor `@2`, is the perfect solution to automatically generate a 3D model of a building starting from its 2D plans and sections.

**Example 1.5.7 (Intersection of extrusions operator)**
In this example a building `plan` is defined as a 2D assembly, and it is used both to generate a $(2,3)$-dimensional `House`, shown in Figure 1.7a, and a $(2,3)$-dimensional apartment `Block`, shown in Figure 1.7b. To generate the house a 2D `section` is also defined, which is combined with `plan` by using the infix operator

```
<1,2,0> && <1,0,2>
```

To generate the block a Cartesian product with the 1D polyhedron `Q:<3,3,3>` is conversely sufficient.

A solid offset version of the 1-skeleton of the `House` object is shown in Figure 1.8.

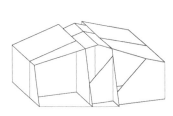 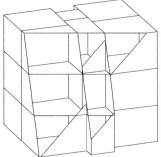

**Figure 1.7**  Polyhedral product of a 2D plan times a $(1,1)$-complex: (a) clipped view of the House (b) clipped view of the Block

---

**Script 1.5.7**

```
DEF plan = STRUCT:< Q:<4,-2,4> * Q:<4,4>, T:<1,2>:<4,1>, Q:2 * Q:<2,4,2> >;
DEF section = MKPOL:<<<0,0>,<10,0>,<10,3>,<5,4.5>,<0,3>>,<1..5>,<<1>>>;

DEF House = @2:(plan (<1,2,0> && <1,0,2>) section)
DEF Block = @2:(plan * Q:<3,3,3>)
```

---

## Parametric mapping

The MAP operator applies a vector-valued function to the vertices of a suitable cell decomposition[13] of a polyhedron embedded in the mapping domain, thus returning a curved or deformed instance of it without changing its topology. The MAP operator is used with a double application

    MAP:VectorFunction:Domain

where VectorFunction is a CONSed sequence of coordinate functions and Domain is any polyhedral complex. Such operator is used to generate curves, surfaces, splines and in general to generate any kind of parametric geometry, including transfinite approaches like Coons-Gordon's surfaces or meshes. It is also used in PLaSM for simpler tasks, like the generation of an arc of circumference.

MAP **primitive**   The "Parametric mapping" constructor MAP allows for simplicial mapping of polyhedral domains. The syntax is:

    MAP:vfun:domain

where vfun is a vector function (written using the FL selectors) and domain is a polyhedral complex. The semantics is very simple: MAP applies vfun to all vertices of a simplicial decomposition of the polyhedral cells of domain.

Usually vfun is the CONS of a sequence of $d$ coordinate functions which are applied to the vertices of the simplicial decomposition to generate their images in target space $E^d$. Notice that the dimension $d$ of such space will equate the number $d$ of coordinate functions in the CONSed vfun.

---

[13] Actually, a so-called *simplicial complex*, discussed in Section 4.5.

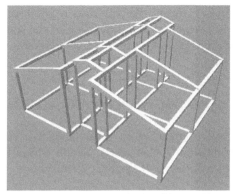

**Figure 1.8**   Solid frame generated by the expression (`OffSet:<0.2,0.2,0.2>` ∼
`@1):House`. The `OffSet` function is discussed in Section 14.6.3

**Example 1.5.8 (Graph of the `SIN` function)**
A piecewise linear approximation with 32 segments of graph of the sin function in the
interval $[0, 2\pi]$, where `PI` is the `PLaSM` denotation for $\pi$, is generated in Script 1.5.8
and shown in Figure 1.9. Notice the mandatory use of the `FL` selector `S1`, which is
used to select the needed coordinate of vertices of `domain` decomposition. Vertices are
in fact represented as sequences of coordinates.

**Figure 1.9**   Polyhedral approximation of `MAP` of the `[ID, SIN]` function on the
$[0, 2\pi]$ `domain`

---

**Script 1.5.8**
```
DEF sinFun = [ID, SIN] ∼ S1;
DEF domain (n::IsIntPos) = (QUOTE ∼ #:n):(2*PI/n);

MAP: sinFun: (domain:32);
```

---

**Regularized Booleans**

Set-theoretic operations like *union*, *intersection* and *difference* of solid models, also
called Boolean operations, are very useful in a geometric modeling system. Actually,
a modified definition of such operations is normally used (see p. 585), where the
resulting sets are *regularized*, i.e. are generated with removal of dangling parts of
lower dimensions.

In the geometric calculus allowed by `PLaSM`, regularized Boolean operators can
be currently applied only to pairs of polyhedrally valued expressions of the same
dimension, i.e. which are both 2D, or 3D, and so on. Also, a further requirement

concern the *solidity* of both arguments. We say that a polyhedral complex is *solid* when its *intrinsic* dimension is equal to the dimension of the space that contains it, that we call the *embedding* dimension. For example, a polygon is solid in 2D but not in 3D. The operation symbols

+, &, ∧, -

respectively denote union, intersection, symmetric difference (XOR) and difference of polyhedral complexes.

According to the standard approaches in solid modeling, the built-in Boolean operators in PLaSM are regularized.[14] Conversely, PLaSM currently includes the first dimension-independent implementation of Boolean operations.

**Example 1.5.9 (Boolean operations between cubes)**
In Script 1.5.9 a composite geometric value is produced, that contains the union, intersection, xor and difference of two rotated unit cubes a and b. It is displayed in Figure 1.10. As the reader will notice, at least after reading Section 13.1.1, the results of the xor and difference operations are *non-manifold* and *unconnected*, respectively.

---

**Script 1.5.9 (Boolean example)**
```
DEF a = T:<1,2>:<-0.5,-0.5>:(CUBOID:<1,1,1>);
DEF b = R:<1,2>:(PI/4):a;

STRUCT:< a + b, T:1:2, a & b, T:1:2, a ∧ b, T:1:2, a - b >;
```

---

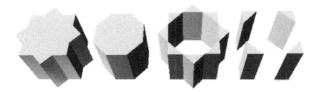

**Figure 1.10**   From left to right: (a) union (b) intersection (d) XOR and (e) difference of two rotated cubes

**Relative positioning operators**

To help the user in positioning a polyhedral complex with respect to another, PLaSM provides the functions

ALIGN, TOP, BOTTOM, LEFT, RIGHT, ...

where ALIGN is truly dimension-independent, whereas TOP, BOTTOM, LEFT, RIGHT are some shortcuts usable only in relative positioning of 3D objects. Several examples are

---

[14] Anyway, a non-regularized implementation of Booleans is under study, and will be enclosed in some future release of the language.

given in the next chapter.

An alternative (and much easier) definition of the Table model already discussed in Script 1.5.3 is given in Script 1.5.10. The new definition uses a suitable combination of the Q, * and TOP operators. In particular, the Legs object is produced as Cartesian product of three sets of intervals along the $x$, $y$ and $z$ coordinate directions. The Plane object is generated analogously. The Table value is the assembly produced by the binary TOP operator described above. The Chair object is produced by suitably scaling the Table.

---

**Script 1.5.10 (Table model (2))**

```
DEF legs = Q:< 0.1,-0.8,0.1 > * Q:< 0.1,-0.8,0.1 > * Q:0.7;
DEF plane = Q:1 * Q:1 * Q:0.2;
DEF table = Legs TOP Plane;
DEF chair = S:<1,2,3>:<0.4,0.4,0.5>:Table;

DEF assembly = chair RIGHT table RIGHT chair UP chair DOWN chair
VRML:assembly:'out.wrl'
```

---

**Figure 1.11**  assembly using positioning operators

**Note**  The more interesting line of code is the assembly definition. It is written by sequencing several infix instances of binary positioning operators. The language syntax states that all operators, when used infix, are left-associative. This rule implies that the above expression is actually evaluated as follows:

```
(((chair RIGHT table) RIGHT chair) UP chair) DOWN chair
```

Therefore, the table is put RIGHT the first chair instance; the second chair instance is put RIGHT the previous *sub-assembly*, the third chair instance is put UP the previous sub-assembly, and so on.

**Note**  A further remark upon the code given in Script 1.5.10 may be interesting. By changing some arbitrary parameters in the definition of some assembly component, the whole assembly construction continues to work!

**Sizing functions**

A set of pre-defined functions is also provided, including

        SIZE, BOX, MAX, MIN, MED

where SIZE:<$i_1$, ... ,$i_n$>:pol returns the sequence of sizes of the projection of the polyhedral argument along the specified coordinate directions. The expression BOX:<$i_1$, ... ,$i_n$>:pol returns the containment box of the pol projection into the subspace of the specified coordinates. Conversely, MAX:<$i_1$, ... ,$i_n$>:pol return the maximum values achieved on pol by the same coordinates. The behavior of MIN and MED is similar.

An example of use of the BOX primitive is given in Figure 1.12, that shows the geometric result of the following computation:

        (STRUCT ~ [ID, BOX:<1,2>]):assembly
          ≡ STRUCT:([ID, BOX:<1,2>]:assembly)
          ≡ STRUCT:([ID, Anonymous-Function]:assembly)
          ≡ STRUCT:< ID:assembly, Anonymous-Function:assembly >
          ≡ STRUCT:< assembly, PolComplex<2,3> >
          ≡ PolComplex<3,3>

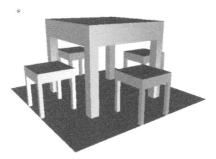

**Figure 1.12**  Geometric value of the expression (STRUCT ~ [ID,
BOX:<1,2>]):assembly

**Parametric vs implicit geometry**

Some further explanation should be addressed to the PLaSM representation and treatment of *curved* objects (curves, surfaces, solids, and so on). They are always represented in a *parametric* form, as the mapping of an appropriate set of coordinate functions over a suitable cell decomposition of some polyhedral domain, as discussed in following sections of this book.

Mostly it is possible to delay the evaluation of such mapping as late as possible, i.e. until the exporting of the geometry to some external viewer, as well as linking it with appropriate rendering properties (like color or normal shading) to recover a curved appearance of the exported object. Other times such delayed mapping evaluation is not possible, as when performing Boolean operations between curved objects, so that the user is in this case obliged to work with some faceted approximation of the Boolean result.

The impossibility of dealing with *implicit* representations of curved geometry is probably the weakest aspect of the PLaSM approach. Conversely, the language gives exact (i.e. symbolic) and very high level support to the parametric representation, which is the "natural" representation in differential geometry and mechanics.

A quite detailed discussion of the possible representations of "curved" geometry is given in Section 11.1.


## 1.6 Examples

In this section some non-trivial examples of the PLaSM programming approach to geometric design are given. The aim is both to transmit the flavour of the language and to allow the reader to build some geometric models of encreasing complexity.


### 1.6.1 First programs

First, we go to generate a simple 2D Flash artwork, shown in Figure 1.14. For this purpose we start by defining a `circle` generating function. Then we construct an assembly of 3D cubes, and make some simple variations to the PLaSM code, thus generating the pictures given in Figure 1.15, produced by grabbing a portion of the screen during the browsing of the exported VRML files.

In the sequel, the pre-defined PLaSM functions are written by using all capital letters. The user-defined functions will be normally written by capitalizing only the first letter of each word included in their names, like e.g. in `MyFirstFunction`.


### Circle

A piecewise linear approximation of the circle of variable radius and centered at the origin is discussed here. For this purpose we need a parametric representation. *parametric representation* of a plane curve is a *function* $D \to \mathbb{E}^2$, with $D \subset \mathbb{R}$, such that for each value of the parameter $u$ in the curve *domain* $D \subset \mathbb{R}$, a point $(x(u), y(u))$ of the curve is generated. The parametric equations of the 2D circle boundary with $r$ radius and centered at the origin are:

$$x(u) = r \cos u, \qquad y(u) = r \sin u, \qquad u \in [0, 2\pi].$$

The generating functions of a polygonal approximation with $n$ sides of the Circumference and Circle are given in Script 1.6.1. We notice that:

1. the parameter interval $[0, 2\pi]$ is decomposed into $n$ subintervals of equal size $2\pi/n$, by the expression `Intervals:(2*pi):n ;`
2. the 1D polyhedral approximation of circle boundary so generated is curved by the `mapping:r` function;
3. the 2D circle is generated as a mapping of two real parameters from the 2D domain `Intervals:(2*PI):n * Intervals:r:m`, where `*` is a Cartesian product of point sets.

A detailed discussion of the geometric approach used is deferred to later sections, and in particular to Chapter 5.

**Script 1.6.1 (Circle)**

```
DEF mapping (r::IsRealPos) = [K:r * COS, K:r * SIN] ~ S1;
DEF Intervals (a::IsRealPos)(n::IsIntPos) = (QUOTE ~ #:n):(a/n);
DEF Circumference (r::IsRealpos)(n::IsIntPos) = MAP:(mapping:r):(domain:n);
DEF Circle (r::IsReal)(n,m::IsIntPos) = MAP:
   <S2 * COS ~ S1, S2 * SIN ~ S1>:(Intervals:(2*PI):n * Intervals:r:m);

Circumference:1:48 RIGHT circle:1:<48,1>
```

The geometric value generated by last expression is shown in Figure 1.13. Several other examples of PLaSM scripts that make use of the MAP operator can be found in subsequent chapters.

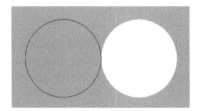

**Figure 1.13**    Assembly of circumference and circle of unit radiuses

**Flash 2D artwork**

The objects c1, c2 and c3 given in Script 1.6.2 are generated by applying the circle operator to actual arguments, i.e. to the radius values 1, 0.7 and 0.4, and to the number 48 of sides of the approximating polygon. ACOLOR is a pre-defined operator contained in the flash library; expressions like rgbacolor:<0,1,0,1> produce an object with value in the RGB$\alpha$ color space used by flash, where $\alpha$ stands for *transparency*. Later in this chapter we will learn that STRUCT is the operator frequently used to aggregate simpler objects into a composite geometric object.

**Script 1.6.2 (Italy's Football Cup)**

```
DEF c1 = circle:1:<48,1> ACOLOR rgbacolor:<0,1,0,1>;
DEF c2 = circle:0.7:<48,1> ACOLOR rgbacolor:<1,1,1,1>;
DEF c3 = circle:0.4:<48,1> ACOLOR rgbacolor:<1,0,0,1>;

DEF out = STRUCT:< c1, c2, c3 >;

flash:out:100:'/path/out.swf';
```

As the reader already experienced with graphics knows, Flash may only manage 2D graphics and animations. The last expression of Script 1.6.2 has the effect of exporting the value of out object to the file 'out.swf' using a graphics *canvas* wide 100 *pixels*. The reader may check the result by just opening the file with the preferred web browser.

**Figure 1.14**   The symbol of the Italy's Football Cup, exported as Flash file by the PLaSM script 1.6.3

### VRML assembly of 3D cubes

A simple assembly of colored cubes is produced in Script 1.6.3, and exported as VRML file 'out.wrl'. In this case the unit cube object is produced by the CUBOID primitive applied to the sequence of object lengths in the $e_i$ directions ($1 \leq i \leq 3$) of the reference axes. Such object is then *instanced* three times, associated to predefined color constants CYAN, MAGENTA and YELLOW. The assembly composite object contains the result of the repeated (infix) application of the binary operator TOP to the cube1, cube2 and cube3 arguments. Conversely, the basis object is defined as the 2D square of side length 3, embedded in the coordinate subspace $z = 0$ of 3D space. Finally, the object named out contains the geometric value exported to the VRML file and visualized in Figure 1.6.3.

---

**Script 1.6.3 (Assembly of colored cubes)**

```
(plasm "
    DEF cube = CUBOID:<1,1,1>;
    DEF cube1 = cube COLOR CYAN;
    DEF cube2 = cube COLOR MAGENTA;
    DEF cube3 = cube COLOR YELLOW;
    DEF basis = (EMBED:1 ~ CUBOID):<3,3>;
    DEF assembly = cube1 TOP cube2 TOP cube3;

    DEF out = basis TOP assembly;
")
```

---

### Interaction with the design environment

We continue now by introducing small variations to the code of Script 1.6.3. The PLaSM *design environment* allows the user to build complex models incrementally, by introducing new objects and definitions, and by re-defining operators and/or objects already defined or evaluated. The design environment will automatically take care of tracing the user actions, and will maintain continuously updated and consistent the internal geometric data base.

In the remainder of this book we do not further display the embedding Scheme forms of type (plasm " ...   ... "). As the reader already knows, they are not necessary when using a PLaSM specialized *editor*.

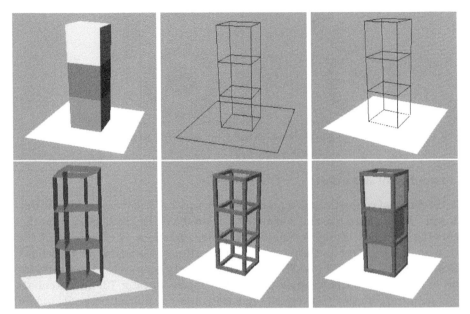

**Figure 1.15**   Small variations of the source Script 1.6.3

a. First, we export the geometric content of the out object to the external VRML file 'out.wrl'. The result is shown in Figure 1.15a. The pictures are ordered from top to bottom, and from left to right.

```
VRML:out:'out.wrl';
```

b. Then we export the 1-*skeleton* of the out object, i.e. the set of boundary edges of all the *polyhedral cells* it is composed of. Such concepts will be clearly detailed in the rest of the book. The result is shown in Figure 1.15b. We are used to export to the same output file, because in this way only one click on the Refresh (*MS Explorer*) or the Reload (*Netscape Navigator*) button is sufficient to display the result.

```
VRML:(@1:out):'out.wrl';
```

c. Here we return to give a more solid aspect to the out object, and redefine it as compound by the 2D basis and by the @1-skeleton ot the assembly object. Then we export the new out value, displayed in Figure 1.15c.

```
DEF out = basis TOP @1:assembly;
VRML:out:'out.wrl';
```

d. We use the SWEEP operator to transform every segment of the 1-skeleton of the assembly object into the polygon generated by translation with vector < 0.2, 0.2, 0.2 >. Clearly enough, the result of the evaluation of the expression SWEEP:< 0.2, 0.2, 0.2 > is a *function*, in order to be composed with the @1 function. Notice that only the sub-expression on the right-hand of TOP operator is affected by the binary operator COLOR. This fact is obtained by proper use of parenthesis. The resulting geometric value is shown in Figure 1.15d.

```
DEF out = basis TOP ((SWEEP:< 0.2, 0.2, 0.2 > ~ @1):assembly COLOR RED);
```

```
VRML:out:'out.wrl';
```

e. A better *solidification* of the 1-skeleton of `assembly` is provided by the functional value of the `OFFSET:< 0.1, 0.1, 0.1 >` expression. The result is given in Figure 1.15e.

```
DEF out = basis TOP ((OFFSET:< 0.1, 0.1, 0.1 > ~ @1):assembly COLOR RED);
VRML:out:'out.wrl';
```

f. Finally, the `assembly` object is aggregated with the "solidified" instance of its 1-skeleton. The geometric result is displayed in Figure 1.15f.

```
DEF out = basis TOP
    ((STRUCT ~ [ID, OFFSET:< 0.1, 0.1, 0.1 > ~ @1]):assembly COLOR RED);
VRML:out:'out.wrl';
```

In order to see the generated geometric model, it is required that either your web *browser* is already equipped with a VRML *plug-in*, or your machine contains a separate VRML *viewer*. Therefore, let point your browser to the `out.wrl` file on your machine, open it and look at the result.

At this point, we strongly hope that both the novice and the experienced user have appreciated how easy is to produce quite complex models with PLaSM. So, don't wait: try PLaSM and enjoy!

*1.6.2  Further examples*

A sequence of integer numbers is generated by evaluting some PLaSM expression like the following one:

```
5 .. 10
```

which produces as the output of its evaluation the sequence:

```
<5, 6, 7, 8, 9, 10>
```

The `InsertSpace` function of Script 1.6.4 allows the introduction of a negative number x between any pair of consecutive numbers of the input sequence `seq`.

---

**Script 1.6.4**
```
DEF InsertSpace (seq::IsSeqOf:IsReal) (x::IsRealNeg) =
    (CAT ~ TRANS):< seq, #:(LEN:seq):x >

DEF Xdims = InsertSpace:(2..10):-2;
DEF Ydims = InsertSpace:(3..8):-2;
```

---

Notice that it results, respectively:

```
Xdims ≡ <2,-2,3,-2,4,-2,5,-2,6,-2,7,-2,8,-2,9,-2,10,-2>
Ydims ≡ <3,-2,4,-2,5,-2,6,-2,7,-2,8,-2>
```

The previous sequences of number are so transformed into 1D polyhedra by the `Q` operator of Script 1.5.5, and multiplied by Cartesian product to give the 2D and 3D models shown in Figures 1.16a and 1.16b, respectively:

```
Q:Xdims * Q:Ydims;
Q:Xdims * Q:Ydims * Q:<4,-20,4>;
```

**Figure 1.16**   (a) Cartesian product of two 1D polyhedral complexes (b) Cartesian product of three 1D polyhedral complexes

A user-defined `Extrude` function is given in Script 1.6.5 to extrude with height `h` the n-th polyhedral cell of the polyhedral complex `p`. Such a result is simply obtained by Cartesian product of the n-th cell with the 1D segment `Q:h`. The n-th cell of the `p` polyhedral complex is extracted by first unpacking (`UKPOL`) the `p`'s internal data structure, then by `SEL`ecting the appropriate data components and finally by recostructing (`MKPOL`) the internal representation of the complex.

---

**Script 1.6.5**

```
DEF Extrude (n::IsIntPos; p::IsPol; h::IsRealPos) =
    (MKPOL ~ [S1,S2,LIST~SEL:n~S3] ~ UKPOL):p * Q:h

DEF plan2D = Q:Xdims * Q:Ydims;
DEF building1 = Extrude:<10,plan2D, 12>;
DEF building2 = Extrude:<25,plan2D, 20>;

STRUCT:< EMBED:1:plan2D, building1, building2 >;
```

---

A 2D complex `plan2D` is so defined, together with two 3D polyhedra `building1` and `building2`, which are obtained by extruding with heights 12 and 20, respectively, the 10-th and 25-th polyhedral cells of `plan2D`. The model in Figure 1.17 is finally generated by evaluating the last line of Script 1.6.5, where `plan2D` (a) is `EMBED`ded in 3D by adding 1 more coordinate, and (b) is aggregated into a 3D `STRUCT`ure together with the polyhedra `building1` and `building2`.

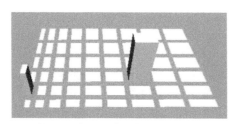

**Figure 1.17**   2D complex with selective extrusion of two cells

### 1.6.3 Virtual Manhattan

A more realistic Mahattan-like 2D complex of polyhedra is defined in Script 1.6.6 by using the MKPOL basic geometric constructor and by explicitly giving vertices, convex cells and polyhedral cells of the object to be generated. The resulting 2D polyhedral complex is shown in Figure 1.18.

---

**Script 1.6.6**

```
DEF Manhattan2D = MKPOL:< verts, cells, pols >
WHERE
    verts = < <0,0>,<3,0>,<5,0>,<7,0>,<8,0>,<9.5,1>,<10,1.5>,<0,3>,<3,3>,<5,3>,
        <7,3>,<8,3>,<9.5,3>,<0,4>,<3,4>,<5,4>,<9.5,4>,<12,4>,<9.5,5>,<10,5>,
        <12,5>,<0,6>,<3,6>,<5,6>,<0,7>,<3,7>,<5,7>,<9.5,7>,<12,7>,<9.5,8>,
        <12,8>,<0,9>,<3,9>,<5,9>,<8,9>,<9,9>,<12,9>,<0,10>,<3,10>,<5,10>,
        <8,10>,<9,10>,<9.5,10>,<10,10>,<12,10>,<6,11>,<7,11>,<0,12>,<3,12>,<9,12>,
        <9.5,12>,<0,13>,<3,13>,<6,13>,<7,13>,<9,13>,<9.5,13>,<0,14>,<3,14>,<5,14>,
        <8,14>,<9,14>,<9.5,14>,<10,14>,<12,14>,<0,15>,<3,15>,<5,15>,<8,15>,<0,16>,
        <6,16>,<7,16>,<9,17>,<9.5,17>,<10,17>,<12,17>,<6,18>,<7,18>,<9,18>,<9.5,18>,
        <10,18>,<12,18>,<2,19>,<3,19>,<5,19>,<8,19>,<9,19>,<9.5,19>,<10,19>,<12,19>,
        <5,20>,<12,20>,<7,22>,<10,22>,<9,6>,<12,6>,<9,15>,<9.5,15>,<10,15>,<12,15> >,
    cells = < <1,2,9,8>,<3,4,11,10>,<5,6,13,12>,<14,15,23,22>, <16,17,19,24>,
        <7,18,21,20>,<25,26,33,32>,<27,95,28,35,34>,<95,96,29,28>, <30,31,37,36>,
        <38,39,49,48>,<40,41,47,46>,<41,61,55,47>,<55,61,60,54>, <54,60,40,46>,
        <42,43,51,50>,<44,45,65,64>,<52,53,59,58>,<56,57,63,62>, <66,67,84,83,70>,
        <68,69,72,71>,<69,86,78,72>,<78,86,85,77>,<71,77,85,68>, <97,98,74,73>,
        <99,100,76,75>,<79,80,88,87>,<81,82,90,89>, <91,92,94,93> >,
    pols = AA:LIST:(1..29)
END;
```

---

**Figure 1.18** Polyhedral complex generated by evaluating the object Manhattan2D

The *cells* of the Manhattan2D complex are finally extruded to produce a 3D virtual environment. For this purpose the MultExtrude function is given, which accepts as input a polyhedral complex p and a sequence h of real numbers. The multiple extrusion is thus performed by the Cartesian product of each cell of p with one of elements of the h sequence, properly transformed into a 1D segment.

Two sequences GrowingH and ManhattanH of heights are also given in Script 1.6.7. The two geometric assemblies of Figure 1.19 are finally generated by respectively evaluating the two PLaSM expressions:

```
MultExtrude:Manhattan2D:GrowingH;
MultExtrude:Manhattan2D:ManhattanH;
```

---

**Script 1.6.7**
```
    DEF MultExtrude (p::IsPol) (h::IsSeqOf:IsReal) =
        (STRUCT ~ AA:* ~ TRANS):< ThePolSeq, AA:Q:h >
    WHERE
        ThePolSeq = (REVERSE ~ AA:MKPOL ~ AA:CAT ~ DISTR):
            < DISTL:< MyVerts, MyCells >, <<<1>>> >,
        MyVerts = (S1 ~ UKPOL):P,
        MyCells = (AA:LIST ~ S2 ~ UKPOL):P
    END;

    DEF GrowingH = 1..29;
    DEF ManhattanH = <1,3,1,11,1,0.2,1,0.1,1,8,15,1,
        1,1,1,8,1,15,8,1,2,2,2,2,5,9,1,1,1>;
```

---

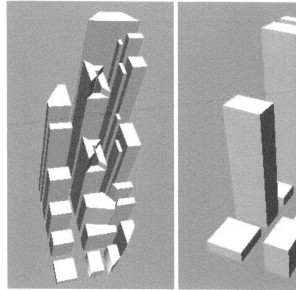

**Figure 1.19** (a) 3D complex generated from Manhattan2D with increasing heights of ordered cells (b) A more realistic model of our simplified virtual Manhattan

*1.6.4   Virtual skyscraper*

At this point we want to generate the geometric model of a skyscraper, to be put into our virtual Manhattan. For this purpose we start to generate a possible external envelope.

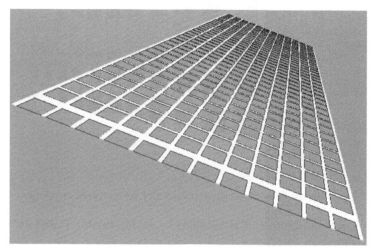

**Figure 1.20**   2D complex to be used as facade of a virtual skyscraper

The 2D facade with 12 bays and 36 floors of Figure 1.20 is generated by Script 1.6.8, and in particular by evaluating the expression

```
BuildingFront:<1,0.5,0.2>:<12,36>;
```

where a function `BuildingFront` is used with three real parameters `a,b,c` to set the geometric rythm of the facade and with two integer parameters `n,m` to set the numbers of bays and floors, respectively. The infix function `AR` (`AL`) is used to "append right" ("append left") one more object to a sequence.

---

**Script 1.6.8**
```
DEF BuildingFront (a,b,c::IsRealPos)(n,m::IsIntPos) = STRUCT:<
    Q:xFull * Q:yFull,
    Q:xVoid * Q:yFull,
    Q:xFull * Q:yVoid,
    @1:(Q:xVoid * Q:yVoid) >
WHERE
    xFull = ##:n:< c,-:a > AR c,
    yFull = -:a AL (b AL ##:m:< -:a,c > AR b),
    xVoid = AA:-:xFull,
    yVoid = AA:-:yFull
END;
```

---

Geometric models of a parametric skyscraper with **m** floors and **n1 × n2** boundary bays are generated by Script 1.6.9. In particular, the model with 36 floors and 12 × 6

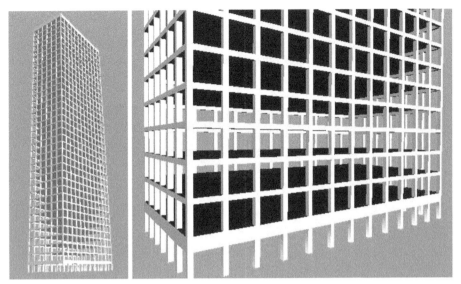

**Figure 1.21**   (a) Virtual skyscraper (b) Particular of the external envelope

boundary bays shown in Figure 1.21 is obtained by evaluating the PLaSM expression

```
Skyscraper:<1,0.5,0.2>:<12,6,36>;
```

Notice that such a model includes also the floor surfaces, generated by the 6-th source line of the Skyscraper function.

---

**Script 1.6.9**
```
DEF Skyscraper (a,b,c::IsReal)(n1,n2,m::IsIntPos) = STRUCT:<
   front1,
   front2,
   T:3:(-:side2):front1,
   T:1:(side1 - 0.2):front2,
   T:3:(-:side2):(Q:side1 * (@0 ~ Q):(-:(a+b) AL #:m:(a+c)) * Q:side2) >
WHERE
   front1 = BuildingFront:<1,0.5,0.2>:<n1,m> * Q:0.2,
   front2 = R:<1,3>:(PI/-2):(BuildingFront:<1,0.5,0.2>:<n2,m> * Q:0.2),
   side2 = SIZE:3:front2,
   side1 = SIZE:1:front1
END;
```

---

### 1.6.5   Roof of S. Stefano Rotondo

A different example of generation of a quite complex geometric assembly is given in Script 1.6.10, where the PLaSM code necessary to the generation of the trellis of the central roof of the old basilica of S. Stefano Rotondo in Rome is shown. Such a complex trellis is generated by first modeling the 2D wire-frame of the single beam, then by properly embedding it in 3D, then by automatically transforming it into a solid model using an `OffSet` with parameters `<1,0.5,1>`. The dimension-independent `OffSet` function, which implements the *Minkowski sum* of a polyhdral *d*-complex with a *n*-dimensional interval, is described in Section 14.6.3. The rotational assembly of **n** instances of either a wire-frame or a solid element is finally performed by the function `Radial`.

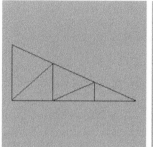 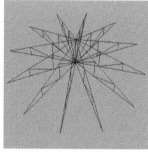 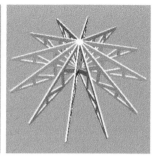

**Figure 1.22** (a) 2D model generated by `Trellis2D:<12,23>` (b) 3D model generated by `Radial:12:Trellis3D` (c) Solid model generated by `Radial:12:SolidTrellis`

---

**Script 1.6.10**

```
DEF Trellis2D (H,L::IsRealPos) = MKPOL:
    <<<0,0>,<L/3,0>,<2*L/3,0>,<L,0>,<2*L/3,H/3>,<L/3,2*H/3>,<0,H>>,
    <<1,2>,<2,3>,<3,4>,<4,5>,<5,6>,<6,7>,<7,1>,<1,6>,<6,2>,<2,5>,
    <5,3>>,<1..11> > ;

DEF Trellis3D = (R:<2,3>:(PI/2) ~ EMBED:1 ~ Trellis2D):<12,23>;
DEF SolidTrellis = OffSet:<1,0.5,1>:Trellis3D;
DEF Radial (n::IsIntPos)(obj::IsPol) =
    (STRUCT ~ ##:n):< obj, R:<1,2>:(2*PI/n) >;

VRML: (Radial:12:Trellis3D):'out.wrl';
VRML: (Radial:12: SolidTrellis):'out.wrl';
```

---

The whole basilica of S. Stefano Rotondo in Rome has been implemented in **PLaSM** with few pages of source code. Two views of the resulting **VRML** model, to be experimented on the web with any browser for virtual reality, are given in Figures 1.23 and 1.24.

## 1.7  Annotated references

The interested reader is referred to the Backus' Turing lecture [Bac78] for motivation of programming at function level, to [Wil82, BWW90] for a more introductory treatment of the topic, and to [BWW+89] for a complete description of FL syntax and semantics.

A discussion on program optimization using program transformation in the context of a programming language designed to facilitate writing high level programs that are

**Figure 1.23**   External view of basilica of S. Stefano Rotondo in Rome

**Figure 1.24**   Internal view of one of the cross-chapels

clear and concise can be found in [WW91]. A very interesting approach to 2D graphics
with functional programming can be found in [LZ88, ZLL$^+$88] where a functional
system equivalent to *Postscript* is described.

The PLaSM language design was introduced in [PS92] and later presented and
discussed on [PPV95]. The generalized product operation has been introduced
in [BFPP93] on polyhedra defined as omplexes of convex cells, and discussed in its
generalization to hierarchical polyhedral complexes in [PFP96]. The design of the HPC
data structure is also discussed in [PFP96]. The dimension-independent approach to
geometric data structures and algorithms extensively adopted in the language has
been introduced in [PBCF93].

# 2

# Geometric programming

In this chapter the reader is introduced to the PLaSM programming by discussing first some examples from number and set theory. Other basic programming examples come from character coding and text processing, and from fundamental algorithms like sorting and merging. Then some elements of geometric programming are discussed, by introducing the reader to the generation of polyhedral approximation of curved manifolds by parametric maps. Also some primitive operators for aggregation of component objects into an assembly are discussed. The aim is both to introduce the reader to basic programming with a very simple but powerful functional language, and to discuss the generation of first non-trivial geometric models.

## 2.1 Basic programming

In this section some programming problems are discussed of very basic type, with the aim of showing that a PLaSM program is, in most cases, a sort of computational pipeline between the input data and the output results. We begin by computing, in various ways, standard functions on natural numbers like the factorial or the binomial function. Other basic examples are given from set theory. Then we discuss the implementation of simple programs for computing the Cartesian product of two sets and the Cartesian product of several sets, or for computing the power set of a given set, i.e. the collection of all its subsets, and so on. Programming problems of increasing complexity work with characters, strings and the contents of the ASCII character table. This direction is pursued until the implementation of a simple parser of strings. In this section we also discuss the important functions SORT and MERGE, for ordering and merging unordered and ordered sequences, respectively.

**A first example** The length of a sequence is computed by the predefined function LEN. As a programming exercise, we give here an equivalent function length, defined by the composition of two simpler programs (i.e. functions). In particular, we implement this program by first applying to the input sequence a function AA:(K:1), which transforms each sequence element into the number 1, thus transforming the input sequence into a sequence of ones with the same length. Such a sequence of

*Geometric Programming for Computer-Aided Design*  Alberto Paoluzzi
© 2003 John Wiley & Sons, Ltd  ISBN 0-471-89942-9

ones is then summed, generating the actual sequence length. The implementation of such an algorithmic approach, together with an example of computation, are given in Script 2.1.1. Remember that AA and K are predefined combinators; see Section 1.3.2.

---

**Script 2.1.1**

```
DEF length = + ~ AA:(K:1)

length:<3,*,1,AA>
    ≡ (+ ~ AA:(K:1)):<3,*,1,AA>
    ≡ +:(AA:(K:1):<3,*,1,AA>)
    ≡ +:<(K:1):3, (K:1):*, (K:1):1, (K:1):AA>
    ≡ +:<1,1,1,1> ≡ 4
```

---

### 2.1.1  Some operations on numbers

In several books on basic programming the user is rapidly introduced to writing simple programs to compute basic functions on natural numbers like the factorial function and the binomial function. Here we follow the same approach.

**Arithmetic operations**  A very simple program, called prog1, may be given by applying the arithmetic operators of sum, product and division to the same pair of arguments, thus producing a sequence of results. For this purpose the combining form called *construction* is used. As we already know, the operation symbols may be inserted between braces (square parenthesis), and the resulting vector function, having the arithmetic operators as components, may so be applied to data. Notice that the expression [+, *, /] is a function.[1] Hence it is meaningful to apply it to some arguments. An example of such a computation is given in the following script.

---

**Script 2.1.2**

```
DEF prog1 = [+, *, /];

prog1:<10, 5>
    ≡ [+, *, /]:<10, 5>
    ≡ <+:<10, 5>, *:<10, 5>, /:<10, 5>>
    ≡ <15, 50, 2>
```

---

**Infix expressions**  It may be interesting to compare the program given in Script 2.1.2 with the one shown in Script 2.1.3. It is worth noting that the "body" of prog2 is an infix expression of the kind *expr1 expr2 expr3*, where the parentheses are actually optional and can be safely omitted. In PLaSM every infix expression is

---

[1] Remember the difference between the vector function [f,g,h], whose components must be all functions, and the sequence <a,b,c>, that is a useful data structure, whose element may have any type. See Section 1.3.2.

evaluated as follows:

```
expr1 expr2 expr3 ≡ expr2 ~ [expr1, expr3]
```

when the following conditions apply:

1. both `expr1` and `expr3` evaluate to a function value;
2. `expr2` evaluates to a higher-order binary function value, i.e. to some function which can be applied to two functions and returns a function.

Otherwise, the infix expression is evaluated in the following way:

```
expr1 expr2 expr3 ≡ expr2 : < expr1, expr3 >
```

---

**Script 2.1.3**
```
    DEF prog2 = (+ * /);

    prog2:<10, 5>
        ≡ (+ * /):<10, 5>
        ≡ (* ~ [+, /]):<10, 5>
        ≡ * : <+:<10, 5>, /:<10, 5>>
        ≡ * : <15, 2>
        ≡ 30
```

---

**Lambda-style and FL-style**  The lambda calculus, or $\lambda$-calculus, from the Greek letter $\lambda$, is a formal language introduced in the thirties by the logician Church to study the calculus with functions. All the functional languages can be considered equivalent to some (specialized) $\lambda$-calculus.

In the basic $\lambda$-calculus a function with parameter $x$ and rule $M$ (usually called *body*), to compute the function values, is denoted as $\lambda x.M$. The *application* of a function $f$ to an argument $a$ is written $fa$. E.g., the application of the function $\lambda x.x * x$, which returns its squared argument, to the number 8, would be written $(\lambda x.x * x)8$. Such an expression let 8 correspond to $8 \times 8$.

In $\lambda$-calculus a *term*, or $\lambda$-term, is either a *variable* $x$, or an *application* $MN$ of the $M$ function to the $N$ term, or an *abstraction* $\lambda x.M$. The variable $x$ is said *bound* in $M$. The variables unbound in $M$ are said to be *free* in $M$. A *combinator* is a $\lambda$-term without free variables. The combinatoric logic, i.e. the use of combinators for the study of functions, started also in the thirties with the work of Schönfinkel and Curry.

We say "$\lambda$-style" to indicate the writing of definitions of functions (i.e. the ability to make abstractions) by giving a list of variables, and where the body expression makes explicit reference to such variables. In this book we also call "FL-style" the making of abstractions using only combinators, and therefore without variables. A discussion of pros and cons of both styles is beyond the scope of this book. In order to see a variable-free notation to denote mathematical functions, the reader is referred to Section 5.1.1.

**Even and odd numbers**   Even numbers are, by definitions, those natural numbers (non negative integers) that are divisible by 2, i.e. such that the remainder of their division by 2 is zero. It follows that if a natural is multipied by 2, then the result is *even*. Also, by adding 1 to an even number, a *odd* number is generated.

In Script 2.1.4 two very simple programs Even and Odd are given, to generate the first $n$ even and odd numbers, respectively. Notice that the first one is built by multiplying times 2 each element of the integer sequence from 0 to $n-1$. Analogously, the second one works by adding one to each element of the sequence generated by the expression Even:n.

---

**Script 2.1.4 (Even and odd numbers)**

```
DEF Even (n::IsInt) = AA:(C:*:2):(0..(n - 1));
DEF Odd  (n::IsInt) = AA:(C:+:1):(Even:n);

Even:10 ≡ < 0 , 2 , 4 , 6 , 8 , 10 , 12 , 14 , 16 , 18 >
Odd :10 ≡ < 1 , 3 , 5 , 7 , 9 , 11 , 13 , 15 , 17 , 19 >
```

---

The reader should notice that the *curried* (see Section 1.4.3) function C:*:2 doubles the value it is applied to, as well as C:+:1 adds one to its argument.


**Factorial function**   The factorial of $n$ is defined as

$$n! = 1 \times 2 \times \cdots \times (n-1) \times n,$$

with $n$ non-negative integer. In many programming languages, both functional and imperative, such a function is normally computed using either an iterative or a recursive approach. In PLaSM (i.e in FL) it is more "natural" to compute the function by directly implementing the above definition. The result is hence generated by multiplying each term of the sequence from 1 to $n$, as shown by Script 2.1.8. Notice that the application INTSTO:n generates the sequence of first $n$ positive integers, and that the * operator, when applied to a number sequence, returns the product of sequence elements.

---

**Script 2.1.5 (Factorial of a positive number)**

```
DEF fact = * ~ INTSTO

fact:n ≡ (* ~ INTSTO):n
       ≡ *:(INTSTO:n)
       ≡ *:<1,2,...,n>
```

---

The previous definition computes only the factorial of positive numbers. Actually, such a function should also return a value for zero value of the argument, with $0! = 1$ by definition. The implementation of such extended definition is given in Script 2.1.6, by using both a FL style and a $\lambda$-style of programming, discussed in the above paragraph. Notice that the curried expression (Section 1.4.3)

```
C:EQ:0
```

returns a function such that

```
C:EQ:0:0 ≡ True
C:EQ:0:x ≡ False                    x ≠ 0
```

Notice also that, when using a λ-style of programming, the actual arguments are checked for validity according to the type predicate specified in the list of formal parameters of the function. In this case the type predicate is given as AND ∼ [IsInt, GE:0]. Such a data typing is called *dynamic typing*, since the type predicate is applied to the input data only at run time. Two equivalent definitions of the fact function are given below, using both a proper FL style and a λ-style.

---

**Script 2.1.6 (Factorial of a non-negative number)**
```
DEF fact = IF:< C:EQ:0, K:1, * ∼ INTSTO >;

DEF fact (n::(AND ∼ [IsInt, GE:0])) = IF:< C:EQ:0, K:1, * ∼ INTSTO >:n;

AA:fact:< 0,1,2,3 > ≡ < 1,1,2,6 >
```

---

A recursive implementation of the factorial function is given in the Script 2.1.7, according to the definition

$$n! = \begin{array}{ll} 1, & n = 0 \\ n \times (n-1)! & n > 0 \end{array}$$

and using both a proper FL style and a λ programming style. In this case let us notice that the "∗" and "−" symbols denote arithmetic operations between functions. The pred function (*predecessor*) is defined as pred : $Int \to Int$ such that $n \mapsto n - 1$.

---

**Script 2.1.7 (Recursive factorial)**
```
DEF pred = ID - K:1;

DEF fact = IF:< C:EQ:0, K:1, ID * fact ∼ pred >;

DEF fact (n::(AND ∼ [IsInt, GE:0])) =
    IF:< C:EQ:0, K:1, ID * fact ∼ pred >:n;
```

---

To understand the behavior of Script 2.1.7 we should remember that the IF combinator must be applied to a triplet of functions. So, when the integer input to the fact function is positive, the function ID * fact ∼ pred is applied to it. Therefore we have, for example:

```
fact:4
    ≡ (IF:< C:EQ:0, K:1, ID * fact ∼ pred >): 4
    ≡ (ID * fact ∼ pred):4
    ≡ (* ∼ [ID, fact ∼ pred]): 4
    ≡ *: < 4, fact:(pred:4) >
```

**Table 2.1**   The Pascal triangle of binomial coefficients $\binom{n}{k}$

| $n$ \ $k$ | 0 | 1 | 2 | 3 | 4 | 5 |
|---|---|---|---|---|---|---|
| 0 | 1 | | | | | |
| 1 | 1 | 1 | | | | |
| 2 | 1 | 2 | 1 | | | |
| 3 | 1 | 3 | 3 | 1 | | |
| 4 | 1 | 4 | 6 | 4 | 1 | |
| 5 | 1 | 5 | 10 | 10 | 5 | 1 |

```
≡ 4 * fact:3
```

and so on, recursively, until we have:

```
fact:4
   ≡ 4 * fact:3
   ≡ 4 * 3 * fact:2
   ≡ 4 * 3 * 2 * fact:1
   ≡ 4 * 3 * 2 * 1 * fact:0
   ≡ 4 * 3 * 2 * 1 * 1 ≡ 24
```

**Binomial function**   The *binomial* function goes from pairs of natural (i.e. non-negative integer) numbers to natural numbers. The binomial number $\binom{n}{k}$ denotes the number of different ways to choose a subset of $k$ elements from a set of $n$ elements. As is well known, the first binomial numbers may be ordered within a lower-triangular matrix, called *Pascal triangle* in English,[2] according to Table 2.1.

A standard formula for the computation of binomial numbers is

$$\binom{n}{k} = \frac{n!}{k!\,(n-k)!}.$$

A direct implementation of this formula is given in Script 2.1.8, where the values of the binomial function, called **choose** in the following, are also shown for some values of the input pair.

---

**Script 2.1.8 (Binomial by factorial)**
```
DEF choose (n,k::IsInt) = Fact:n / (Fact:k * Fact:(n-k));

AA:choose:( 4 DISTL (0..4) )  ≡  < 1 , 4 , 6 , 4 , 1 >
```

---

A recursive function to compute the binomial numbers according to the well-known formula

$$\binom{n}{k} = \binom{n-1}{k-1} + \binom{n-1}{k}, \qquad 0 < k < n \tag{2.1}$$

---

[2] Actually, the triangle of binomial numbers was discovered by the Italian matematician Nicolò Tartaglia (1499–1557), and not by Blaise Pascal (1623–1662). Nicolò Tartaglia also discovered the resolution formula for the algebraic equations of degree 3.

depicted by boxes in Table 2.1 is given in Script 2.1.9. Notice, from Table 2.1, that such formula may only work when $0 < k < n$. Conversely we have, for the binomial numbers on the border of the triangle:

$$\binom{n}{k} = 1, \qquad k = 0, k = n. \tag{2.2}$$

The function Choose in Script 2.1.9 is written by using a proper FL style, i.e. without formal parameters. According to the IF semantics, there are three functions within its argument sequence. The first one is the predicate used to verify if the computation must proceed according to either the basis case of equation (2.2) or the inductive case of equation (2.1). As usual, the arithmetic operators between function-valued expressions denote operations which return a function as value. The predefined selectors S1 and S2 are used to extract the first and the second element, respectively, from the input pair $< n, k >$.

---

**Script 2.1.9 (Binomial by recursion)**
```
    DEF Choose = IF:<
       OR ~ [C:EQ:0 ~ S2, EQ],
       K:1,
       Choose ~ [S1 - K:1, S2 - K:1] + Choose ~ [S1 - K:1, S2]
    >;
```

---

The previous implementation, which makes use of the equations 2.1 and 2.2, is highly inefficient. In fact, the computation of a single binomial number requires the computation of very many such numbers and, even worse, computes most of them again and again many times.

A much better solution, given in Script 2.3, is obtained by using the following equation:

$$\binom{n}{k} = \binom{n-1}{k-1} \frac{n}{k}, \qquad 0 < k < n. \tag{2.3}$$

In this case, the function Choose makes only one call to itself in the recursive case instead than two. An approach of this kind, where a recursive function calls itself at most one time, is called *linear recursion*. It is easy to see, looking at Table 2.1, that to compute $\binom{n}{k}$ in the worst case needs a total number of function calls which is of the same magnitude of $n$.

Computer scientists would say that this algorithm has linear complexity, denoted as $O(n)$ (to read as "Order of $n$"), in the worst case. Conversely, the algorithm implemented by Script 2.1.9 has worst case exponential complexity $O(2^n)$.

Notice that the implementation in Script 2.1.10 uses the infix notation for the function to be applied in the recursive case. The meaning of infix functional expressions like

```
    expr * /
```

where expr evaluates to some functional value, is discussed in Section 2.1. Notice also the meaning of the function AA:(C:+:-1); when applied to a number sequence, it decrements by one each element.

## Script 2.1.10 (Binomial by linear recursion)

```
DEF Choose = IF:<
    OR ~ [C:EQ:0 ~ S2, EQ], K:1, Choose ~ AA:(C:+:-1) * /
>;
```

## Example 2.1.1 (Pascal triangle)

A simple script, to generate the Pascal triangle of any size, is step-wise discussed in this example. First, a matrix of index pairs, with both row and column indices ranging from 0 to $n$, is generated by the function pairs when applied to the natural number $n$. In Script 2.1.11 two further predicates IsNat and IsNum are given, to test if the input is a natural number (say, it is an integer AND is greater or equal to zero) or simply a number (say, it is an integer OR a real).

## Script 2.1.11 (Pairs of matrix indices)

```
DEF IsNat = AND ~ [IsInt, GE:0];
DEF IsNum = OR ~ [IsInt, IsReal];

DEF pairs (n::IsNat) =
    (AA:DISTL ~ DISTR ~ [ID,ID] ~ FROMTO ~ [K:0, ID]):n ;

pairs:5 ≡ <
    <<0, 0>, <0, 1>, <0, 2>, <0, 3>, <0, 4>, <0, 5>>,
    <<1, 0>, <1, 1>, <1, 2>, <1, 3>, <1, 4>, <1, 5>>,
    <<2, 0>, <2, 1>, <2, 2>, <2, 3>, <2, 4>, <2, 5>>,
    <<3, 0>, <3, 1>, <3, 2>, <3, 3>, <3, 4>, <3, 5>>,
    <<4, 0>, <4, 1>, <4, 2>, <4, 3>, <4, 4>, <4, 5>>,
    <<5, 0>, <5, 1>, <5, 2>, <5, 3>, <5, 4>, <5, 5>>>
```

Then, a matrix of binomial coefficients is generated, by applying the choose function to each pair in the lower-triangular submatrix of the matrix generated by pairs:$n$, and by writing 0 in the upper triangular submatrix. In order to penetrate a *double* sequence (a matrix is a sequence of rows, which are also sequences) to reach the pair elements to whom apply either the choose or the K:0 function, the AA ~ AA operator is used.

## Script 2.1.12 (Pascal's matrix)

```
DEF IsLE (a,b::IsNum) = LE:a:b;
DEF Pascal = (AA ~ AA):(IF:< IsLE, choose, K:0 >);

(Pascal ~ pairs):5 ≡ <
    <1, 0, 0, 0, 0, 0>,
    <1, 1, 0, 0, 0, 0>,
    <1, 2, 1, 0, 0, 0>,
    <1, 3, 3, 1, 0, 0>,
    <1, 4, 6, 4, 1, 0>,
    <1, 5, 10, 10, 5, 1>>
```

Finally, the `filter` function introduced in Script 1.3.1 is applied in Script 2.1.13 to the matrix generated by the function `Pascal` $\sim$ `pairs`, giving as output only its non-zero elements. The resulting output is the *Pascal's triangle* of any size, organized by rows. Such computation works by applying the function `filter:(C:EQ:0)` is applied to each matrix row.

---

**Script 2.1.13 (Pascal triangle)**

```
DEF PascalTriangle (n::IsIntPos) =
    (AA:(filter:(C:EQ:0)) ~ Pascal ~ pairs):n;

PascalTriangle:5 ≡ <
    <1>,
    <1, 1>,
    <1, 2, 1>,
    <1, 3, 3, 1>,
    <1, 4, 6, 4, 1>,
    <1, 5, 10, 10, 5, 1>>
```

---

It is easy to see, by using the `Choose` implementation given in Script 2.1.10, that the complexity of the computation of the Pascal triangle with $n$ rows is $O(n^3)$. In fact, the number of terms to be computed is $O(n^2)$, and each term is computed with time and space complexity $O(n)$.

**Pascal triangle in optimal time**   The computation of the Pascal triangle with $n + 1$ rows can be computed in $O(n^2)$ time by using a proper FL style, say, without neither iteration nor recursion, but using a computational pipelining of data across a series of compositions of the same function. A time $O(n^2)$ is optimal, because it is of the same order of magnitude of the output results.

The terse implementation given in Script 2.1.14 relies on the fact that a new triangle row can be obtained by adding termwise two instances of the previous row, with a 0 element appended at the left and at the right, respectively. As a matter of fact, we have:

$$
\begin{array}{ccccccc}
(0, & 1, & 4, & 6, & 4, & 1) & + \\
(1, & 4, & 6, & 4, & 1, & 0) & = \\
(1, & 5, & 10, & 10, & 5, & 1) &
\end{array}
$$

The program's building block, to be composed $n$ times with itself, is the function `addrow`, whose effect is to add a $(i + 1)$ row to its input sequence with $i$ rows. The computation of the new row according with the above scheme is performed by the `row` function. The `vectsum` function, used for termwise addition of two sequences of numbers, is given in Script 2.1.19. Notice that `C:AL:0` is a *curried* version of the `AL` combinator, that appends a 0 element on the left of its input sequence.

**Script 2.1.14 (Pascal triangle (2))**

```
DEF pascalTriangle (n::IsIntPos) = (REVERSE ~ COMP:(#:n:addrow)):<<1>>
WHERE
    addrow = AL ~ [row ~ S1, ID],
    row = vectsum ~ [ID, REVERSE] ~ C:AL:0
END;

pascalTriangle:20
```

### 2.1.2  Set operations

In this section we introduce some basic operations on sets with elements of arbitrary type, including the generation of the Cartesian product set of two or more sets and the power set of a given set. Let notice that the PLaSM representation of any set is the *sequence* of the set elements.

**Cartesian product of two sets**   Given two sets $A = \{a_i\}$ and $B = \{b_j\}$, their *Cartesian product* is defined as the set $A \times B = \{(a_i, b_j)|\ a_i \in A, b_j \in B\}$ of all ordered pairs of elements from $A$ and $B$.

A PLaSM function, denoted as cart2, which generates the Cartesian product of any two sets, i.e. of any two sequences, is given in Script 2.1.15. Its body is defined as the composition of three functions DISTR, AA:DISTL and CAT, to be orderly applied to the pair of set arguments, as shown in the example of computation given in the script. In particular, the function cart2 is applied to the pair <1, 2, 3> and <'a', 'b'>, generating the sequence of pairs <<1, 'a'>, <1, 'b'>, <2, 'a'>, <2, 'b'>, <3, 'a'>, <3, 'b'>>.

**Script 2.1.15 (Binary Cartesian product)**

```
DEF cart2 = CAT ~ AA:DISTL ~ DISTR

cart2:<<1, 2, 3>, <'a', 'b'>>
   ≡ <<1, 'a'>, <1, 'b'>, <2, 'a'>,<2, 'b'>, <3, 'a'>, <3, 'b'>>
```

**Example 2.1.2 (Debugging by PRINT)**

For purpose of debugging, the language offers an useful PRINT function, which is equivalent to ID, with the additional *side effect* of printing in the listener window the value of its input. Hence a new implementation of the cart2 function is given in Script 2.1.16, which allows the intermediate results of the computation to be known.

**Cartesian product of several sets**   The Cartesian product of $n$ sets is defined as the set of ordered $n$-tuples, obtained by choosing an element from each set in every possible way.

This operation is implemented very simply in Script 2.1.17 by using the proper FL programming style. In particular, we use here the primitive combining form TREE, which allows for recursive application of a *binary* function f to a sequence of $n$ arguments. Such a primitive form is defined as follows:

**Script 2.1.16**

```
DEF cart2 = CAT ~ PRINT ~ AA:DISTL ~ PRINT ~ DISTR

cart2:<<1, 2, 3>, <'a', 'b'>>
    ≡ (CAT ~ PRINT ~ AA:DISTL):
        <<1, <'a', 'b'>>, <2, <'a', 'b'>>, <3, <'a', 'b'>>>
    ≡ CAT:
        <<<1, 'a'>, <1, 'b'>>, <<2, 'a'>, <2, 'b'>>, <<3, 'a'>, <3, 'b'>>>
    ≡ <<1, 'a'>, <1, 'b'>, <2, 'a'>, <2, 'b'>, <3, 'a'>, <3, 'b'>>
```

$$\texttt{TREE:f}:<x_1, x_2, \dots, x_n> \equiv$$
$$\texttt{f}:< \texttt{TREE:f}:<x_1, \dots, x_k>, \texttt{TREE:f}:<x_{k+1}, \dots, x_n> > \quad \text{where } k = \lceil n/2 \rceil,$$

$$\texttt{TREE:f}:<x_1> \equiv x_1.$$

We already know two similar combining forms, named `INSR` and `INSL`, respectively. They execute the same reduction by applying the argument function from either the right or the left of the sequence argument, as seen in Section 1.3.2. Conversely, the `TREE` combining form executes a similar recursive reduction, but subdividing the argument sequence in two subsets of nearly equal length. Notice that the `cart2` function is the one defined in Script 2.1.15.

**Script 2.1.17 ($n$-ary Cartesian product)**

```
DEF cart = TREE:f2 ~ f1
WHERE
    f2 = AA:CAT ~ cart2,
    f1 = AA:(AA:[ID])
END;

cart:<<1,2>, <3>, <4,5>>
    ≡ <<1,3,4>, <1,3,5>, <2,3,4>, <2,3,5>>
```

**Power set**    An implementation of the `power_set` function, which computes the *power set* of any given set, is discussed here. It is worth remembering that the power set of a set $A = \{a_i\}$ is defined as the collection of all subsets of $A$, including the empty set and $A$ itself. Notice that if $A$ has $n$ elements, then the power set of $A$ has $2^n$ elements. For this reason, the notation $2^A$ is often used to denote this set. Sometimes the notation $\mathcal{P}(A)$ is instead used. The generating function `power_set` is given in Script 2.1.18.

The used algorithm can be summarized as follows:

1. the $n$ input elements $a_i$ are transformed into $n$ pairs $<<a_i>, <>>$;
2. the Cartesian product of such pairs is computed, producing $2^n$ $n$-tuples;
3. all such $n$-tuples are catenated, to eliminate the empty elements;

As a further example we can see that:

```
powerSet:< 1, 2, 3, 4 >
    ≡ < <1,2,3,4>, <1,2,3>, <1,2,4>, <1,2>, <1,3,4>, <1,3>, <1,4>, <1>,
        <2,3,4>, <2,3>, <2,4>, <2>, <3,4>, <3>, <4>, <> >
```

**Script 2.1.18**

```
DEF power_set = AA:CAT ~ cart ~ AA:([[ID], K:<>])
power_set:< 1, ID, 4 >
   ≡ (AA:CAT ~ cart ~ AA:([[ID], K:<>])):<1,ID,4>
   ≡ AA:CAT:(cart:(AA:([[ID], K:<>]):<1,ID,4>))
   ≡ AA:CAT:(cart:<[[ID], K:<>]:1,
                   [[ID], K:<>]:ID,
                   [[ID], K:<>]):4>
   ≡ AA:CAT:(cart:<<<1>,<>>, <<ID>,<>>, <<4>,<>>>)
   ≡ AA:CAT:<<<1>, <ID>, <4>>,
             <<1>, <ID>, <>>,
             <<1>, <>, <4>>,
             <<1>, <>, <>>,
             <<>, <ID>, <4>>,
             <<>, <ID>, <>>,
             <<>, <>, <4>>,
             <<>, <>, <>>>
   ≡ < <1, ID, 4>, <1, ID>, <1, 4>, <1>, <ID, 4>, <ID>, <4>, <> >
```

*2.1.3   Vector and matrix operations*

Here we introduce the basic vector operations of sum of two or more vectors of arbitrary dimensions, the product of a scalar times a vector and the sum of compatible matrices. A vector is represented as the sequence of its components, and a matrix as the sequence of its row vectors.

**Addition element-wise of two sequences**   A vector $v \in \mathbb{R}^d$ is represented in PLaSM as a sequence of $d$ numbers. The PLaSM program to add two vectors, i.e. to add component-wise two sequences of the same length, can be defined as follows, by first transposing the input sequences, and then by adding each generated pair.

**Script 2.1.19**

```
DEF vectSum = AA:+ ~ TRANS;

vectSum:<<1, 2, 3, 4>, <11, 12, 13, 14>>
   ≡ (AA:+ ~ TRANS):<<1, 2, 3, 4>, <11, 12, 13, 14>>
   ≡ (AA:+:(TRANS:<<1, 2, 3, 4>, <11, 12, 13, 14>>)
   ≡ AA:+:<<1, 11>, <2, 12>, <3, 13>, <4, 14>>
   ≡ <+:<1, 11>, +:<2, 12>, +:<3, 13>, +:<4, 14>>
   ≡ <12, 14, 16, 18>
```

It might be interesting to notice, as a further example of the amazing power of the combinatorial logic underlying FL, that the same vectSum function may also be used to add *any set* of vectors in the same vector space, i.e. with the same number of components. E.g.

```
vectSum:<<1,2,3,4>, <11,12,13,14>, <21,22,23,24>, <31,32,33,34>>
   ≡ <64, 68, 72, 76>
```

**Product of a scalar times a vector**  The product of a scalar times a vector, represented as a sequence of numbers, returns a sequence of the same length where each element is the product of the scalar times an element of the original sequence. The realization of a PLaSM function for this operation is very easy. First, the scalar is left-distributed on the sequence; then, the product operation is applied to all the pairs so generated.

---

**Script 2.1.20**
```
DEF scalarVectProd = AA:* ~ DISTL

scalarVectProd:<2, <1, 2, 3, 4>>
    ≡ (AA:* ~ DISTL):<2, <1, 2, 3, 4>>
    ≡ AA:*:( DISTL:<2, <1, 2, 3, 4>> )
    ≡ AA:* :<<2, 1>, <2, 2>, <2, 3>, <2, 4>>
    ≡ <*:<2, 1>, *:<2, 2>, *:<2, 3>, *:<2, 4>>
    ≡ <2, 4, 6, 8>
```

---

The `scalarVectProd` operator given in Script 2.1.20 may be only used with an ordered pair *<scalar, vector>*. A useful generalization of such operation, which is also able to manage the converse case *<vector, scalar>*, is given in Script 2.1.21.

---

**Script 2.1.21**
```
DEF scalarVectProd = AA:* ~ IF:< IsReal ~ S1, DISTL, DISTR >

scalarVectProd:<2, <1, 2, 3, 4>>
    ≡ scalarVectProd:<<1, 2, 3, 4>, 2>
    ≡ <2, 4, 6, 8>
```

---

**Addition of compatible matrices**  Two matrices of numbers are said to be *compatible* when they have the same number of rows and column, i.e. when they belong to the same space $\mathcal{M}_n^m$. The *sum* of two compatible matrices $A = (a_{ij})$ and $B = (b_{ij})$ is the matrix $A + B = (a_{ij} + b_{ij})$ obtained by component-wise addition of matrix elements.

In PLaSM a matrix is represented as a *sequence of rows*, in turn represented as sequences of elements. Notice that all the rows *must* have the same length, which equates the number of matrix columns. The type of the matrix is that of its elements.

A function `matSum` to add two compatible matrices is given in Script 2.1.22. To add two compatible matrices we must start by producing a sequence of pairs of corresponding rows, then transpose all such (row) pairs, thus producing sequences of element pairs, and finally applying the sum operation to all such pairs. This last step is performed by the operation (`AA ~ AA`):+, since two levels of parentheses must be penetrated.

**Script 2.1.22**

```
DEF matSum = (AA ~ AA):+ ~ AA:TRANS ~ TRANS;

matSum:<<<1,2,3>,<4,5,6>>,
       <<11,12,13>,<14,15,16>>>
   ≡ <<12,14,16>,<18,20,22>>
```

### 2.1.4  String and character operations

In PLaSM there are some predefined *string operations*, which allow for manipulation of strings as sequences of characters. In particular:

1. ISSTRING predicate tests if its input is a string;
2. ISCHAR predicate tests if its input is a string of unit length, i.e. constituted by a single character;
3. STRING function maps a sequence of characters into a string;
4. CHARSEQ function maps a string into a sequence of characters;
5. ORD function maps an ASCII character into its ordinal value, i.e. into the integer associated to the character in the ASCII table;
6. CHAR function maps an integer from the interval $[0, 255]$ into the corresponding ASCII character;
7. comparison predicates LT (less than), LE (less or equal), EQ (equal), GE (greater or equal) and GT (greater than) are used to compare characters and strings in *lexicographic order*, as discussed in a following paragraph, as well as to compare numbers.

### Example 2.1.3 (Printable ASCII)

It is very easy to transform any string into the sequence of ordinal values of its characters, and vice versa. The following Script 2.1.23 shows the PLaSM generation of the subset of printable ASCII characters, with ordinal value in the interval $[32, 126]$. Let us notice that the expression (STRING ~ AA:CHAR):(32..126) maps the sequence of numbers into a unique string.

### Example 2.1.4 (Natural numbers as binary strings)

An useful function nat2string is given in Script 2.1.24 to transform a natural number to a binary string, i.e. to a string containing only the two symbols $'0'$ and $'1'$, corresponding to the binary representation of the number. The binary string is generated by the standard algorithm of successive divisions by 2. In particular, the recursive function dec2binSeq generates a nested sequence of binary digits. For example:

```
dec2binSeq:10 ≡ <<<1, 0>, 1>, 0>
```

The output of dec2binSeq is then modified by the recursive function flatten:

```
(flatten ~ dec2binSeq):10 ≡ <1, 0, 1, 0>
```

Such number sequence is transformed into the sequence of ordinal values of characters $'0'$ and $'1'$ by adding 48 to each element via the curried + operator:

**Script 2.1.23** (ASCII table)

```
AA:[ID, CHAR]:(32..126) ≡ <
  < 32, '⊔'>, < 33, '!'>, < 34, '"'>, < 35, '#'>, < 36, '/'>,
  < 37, '%'>, < 38, '&'>, < 39, '''>, < 40, '('>, < 41, ')'>,
  < 42, '*'>, < 43, '+'>, < 44, ','>, < 45, '-'>, < 46, '.'>,
  < 47, '/'>, < 48, '0'>, < 49, '1'>, < 50, '2'>, < 51, '3'>,
  < 52, '4'>, < 53, '5'>, < 54, '6'>, < 55, '7'>, < 56, '8'>,
  < 57, '9'>, < 58, ':'>, < 59, ';'>, < 60, '<'>, < 61, '='>,
  < 62, '>'>, < 63, '?'>, < 64, '@'>, < 65, 'A'>, < 66, 'B'>,
  < 67, 'C'>, < 68, 'D'>, < 69, 'E'>, < 70, 'F'>, < 71, 'G'>,
  < 72, 'H'>, < 73, 'I'>, < 74, 'J'>, < 75, 'K'>, < 76, 'L'>,
  < 77, 'M'>, < 78, 'N'>, < 79, 'O'>, < 80, 'P'>, < 81, 'Q'>,
  < 82, 'R'>, < 83, 'S'>, < 84, 'T'>, < 85, 'U'>, < 86, 'V'>,
  < 87, 'W'>, < 88, 'X'>, < 89, 'Y'>, < 90, 'Z'>, < 91, '['>,
  < 92, '\'>, < 93, ']'>, < 94, '^'>, < 95, '_'>, < 96, '`'>,
  < 97, 'a'>, < 98, 'b'>, < 99, 'c'>, <100, 'd'>, <101, 'e'>,
  <102, 'f'>, <103, 'g'>, <104, 'h'>, <105, 'i'>, <106, 'j'>,
  <107, 'k'>, <108, 'l'>, <109, 'm'>, <110, 'n'>, <111, 'o'>,
  <112, 'p'>, <113, 'q'>, <114, 'r'>, <115, 's'>, <116, 't'>,
  <117, 'u'>, <118, 'v'>, <119, 'w'>, <120, 'x'>, <121, 'y'>,
  <122, 'z'>, <123, '{'>, <124, '|'>, <125, '}'>, <126, '~'>>
```

```
(AA:(C:+:48) ~ flatten ~ dec2binSeq):10 ≡ <49, 48, 49, 48>
```

and this one is mapped to a sequence of characters:

```
(AA:(CHAR ~ C:+:48) ~ flatten ~ dec2binSeq):10 ≡ <'1', '0', '1', '0'>
```

The last step is quite obvious:

```
(STRING ~ AA:(CHAR ~ C:+:48) ~ flatten ~ dec2binSeq):10 ≡ '1010'
```

Notice that the MOD function given in Script 2.1.24 must be applied to a pair of integers and returns the remainder of their division. E.g. MOD:<7,2> ≡ 1. The IsNat predicate, to test if the input of the nat2string function is a natural number, is defined in Script 2.1.11.

**Example 2.1.5 (String to tokens)**
In this example a second order function StringTokens is given, which is first applied to a sequence of separators and then to a string. It returns the sequence of so-called *tokens* contained in the input string, i.e. the sequence of substrings separated by the elements of the given set of separators. The example is aimed at discussing a non-trivial exercise of non-geometric PLaSM programming.

In order to reach our goal we start by defining a IN predicate used to test the *set-membership* property for a generic set and a generic element. Clearly this predicate will return TRUE if the element is contained in the set and will return FALSE otherwise.

The algorithm used in implementing the StringTokens function is very simple (and quite inefficient). In particular, the value of type STRING contained in the formal parameter input is preliminarily transformed into a CHAR sequence. Such a sequence is then transformed into a sequence of pairs, where each character is coupled with its

**Script 2.1.24 (Number to binary string)**

```
DEF MOD = - ~ [S1, S2 * FLOOR ~ /];

DEF flatten =
    IF:< IsSeq, IF:< IsSeq ~ S1, AR, ID > ~ [flatten ~ FIRST, LAST], ID >;

DEF dec2binSeq =
    IF:< GE:2, [dec2binSeq ~ FLOOR ~ /, MOD] ~ [ID, K:2], ID >;

DEF nat2string (n::IsNat) = ( STRING
    ~ AA:(CHAR ~ C:+:48)
    ~ IF:<IsSeq, ID, [ID]>
    ~ flatten
    ~ dec2binSeq ):n;

AA:nat2string:< 0,1,10,14,255,256 >
    ≡ < '0' , '1' , '1010' , '1110' , '11111111' , '100000000' >
```

position in the **input** string. Then all the positions of separators constituted by a single character are selected. Such positions are used to build the pairs of indices associated with each sub-string. The pairs then properly generate the selector functions used to extract the various substrings.

Finally, an internal **filter** function is applied to eliminate the empty sequences and the substrings possibly contained in the separator set **separators**, which may contain both single characters and substrings. It is worth noting that such a formal variable is defined of type **IsSeqOf:IsString**.

Notice also that the **TT** predefined symbol denotes a predicate which returns **TRUE** for every input, and is used to leave *undefined* the type of a formal parameter. It is actually equivalent to the function **K:TRUE**.

**Example 2.1.6 (String parsing)**

Some examples of application of the token extractor **StringTokens** are given in Script 2.1.26. In particular, in the first PLaSM expression, the only defined separator is the *blank* character '⊔'; in the second expression three separators are given, corresponding to the characters '⊔', ',' and to the word 'and'.

**Example 2.1.7 (Parsing of source code)**

A further and more interesting example with the **StringTokens** operator is shown in Script 2.1.27, where tokens are extracted from a fragment of source code, given as the input string of the **StringTokens** function.

In this case it is useful to insert in the set of separators both the language keywords, and some single and double separators. Notice also that the ASCII character denoted as CR (*Carriage Return*) is inserted in such a set, by using its generating expression CHAR:13. The second part of Script 2.1.27 shows the output generated by applying the **StringTokens** operation to the fragment of source code where the IN function is defined.

**Script 2.1.25 (Tokens extraction from a string)**
```
DEF IN (set::IsSeq)(element::TT) = (OR ~ AA:EQ ~ DISTR):< set, element >;

DEF StringTokens (separators::IsSeqOf:IsString) (input::IsString) =
   ( filter ~ AA:(IF:< NOT ~ ISNULL, [STRING], ID >) ~ APPLY
   ~ [ CONS
      ~ AA:CONS
      ~ (AA ~ AA):SEL
      ~ AA:FROMTO
      ~ TRANS
      ~ start_stop_pos, ID
      ] ~ CHARSEQ ):input
WHERE
   separator_pos = CAT ~ AA:(IF:< IN:separators ~ S1, [S2], K:<> >)
      ~ TRANS ~ [ID, INTSTO ~ LEN],
   start_stop_pos = [
      AA:(ID + K:1) ~ AL ~ [K:0, separator_pos],
      AA:(ID - K:1) ~ AR ~ [separator_pos, LEN + K:1]
      ],
   filter = CAT ~ AA:(IF:< IN:separators, K:<>, [ID] >) ~ CAT
END;
```

**Script 2.1.26 (String parsing)**
```
StringTokens:<'⊔'>:'hello PLaSM world' ≡ <'hello', 'PLaSM', 'world'>

StringTokens:< '⊔', 'and', ',' >:'Fred, Wilma, Barney and Lucy' ≡
   < 'Fred', 'Wilma', 'Barney', 'Lucy' >
```

*2.1.5  Other examples*

Some further examples of basic data structures and algorithms are given here, including fundamental list operations like sorting and merging, the construction and quick search of associative lists, and the set operations of union, intersection and difference.

**List operation**  The function butFirstButLast given in Script 2.1.28 may only operate on sequences. In particular such a program returns the input sequence but without the first and last element. The implementation makes use of the primitive operations TAIL and REVERSE. The first one returns the input sequence without the

**Script 2.1.27 (Parsing)**
```
DEF separators = < 'DEF', 'WHERE', 'END',
   '(', ')', '::', ':', '⊔', '=', ' ~ ', ',', ';', '<', '>', CHAR:13 >;

StringTokens:separators: 'DEF IN (set::IsSeq) (element::K:TRUE) =
   (OR ~ AA:EQ ~ DISTR):< set, element >;'

≡ < 'IN', 'set', 'IsSeq', 'element', 'K', 'TRUE', 'OR',
    'AA', 'EQ', 'DISTR', 'set', 'element' >
```

first element; the second one reverses the order of its input.

---

**Script 2.1.28**
```
DEF butFirstButLast = REVERSE ~ TAIL ~ REVERSE ~ TAIL

butFirstButLast:<10, 30, 50, 70> = <30, 50>
butFirstButLast:(15..20) = <16, 17, 18, 19>
butFirstButLast:<ID, *, AA, K, (ID * ID)> = <*, AA, K>
```

---

**Merge of ordered sequences**  A primitive FL combining form is used to merge two ordered sequences $x = \langle x_1, \ldots, x_n \rangle$ and $y = \langle y_1, \ldots, y_m \rangle$. As usual, the combining form MERGE is defined in a very general way, i.e. with respect to every binary predicate f:

```
MERGE:f:<x,y> =
    x or y if either y = <> or x = <>
    AL:<x₁, MERGE:f:<TAIL:x,y>> if f:<x₁,y₁> ≡ true
    AL:<y₁, MERGE:f:<x,TAIL:y>> if f:<x₁,y₁> ≡ false
```

The MERGE operator was conceived to work with binary predicates of the kind $op:\langle x_i, y_j \rangle$, which return a truth value when applied to the pair of their arguments. Actually, the current implementation of PLaSM uses a curried version of the comparison predicates GE, GT, LE and LT, making impossible their direct use with the MERGE operator.

In order to use the MERGE combining form with the comparison operators it is necessary to transform expressions like GT:a:b into expressions like IsGT:<a,b>. Hence a complete set of un-curried comparison operators is also given.

Such a transformation can be executed by some very simple function like the one given in Script 2.1.29, so that we can finally write, to merge two or more ordered sequences:

---

**Script 2.1.29 (Merge of number sequences)**
```
DEF IsGT (a,b::TT) = GT:a:b;
DEF IsLT (a,b::TT) = LT:a:b;
DEF IsGE (a,b::TT) = GE:a:b;
DEF IsLE (a,b::TT) = LE:a:b;

MERGE:IsGT: <<1,3,4,5,5.15,7,9,10>,<2,4,6,8>>
    ≡ <1, 2, 3, 4, 4, 5, 5.15, 6, 7, 8, 9, 10>

(INSL:(MERGE:IsGT)): <<1,3,4,5,5.15,7,9,10>,<2,4,6,8>,<-4,8.2,20,61>>
    ≡ <-4, 1, 2, 3, 4, 4, 5, 5.15, 6, 7, 8, 8.2, 9, 10, 20, 61>
```

---

**Sort of unordered sequences**  By using few FL combining forms and the predefined operator MERGE it is possible to give an amazingly simple implementation of the well-known *merge-sort* algorithm (see, e.g. [AU92]), which executes the sorting of unordered sequences by recursively merging ordered sub-sequences.

The function SORT, given in Script 2.1.30, depends also on a `predicate` used to compare a pair of elements to be ordered. By using either the predicate IsGT or the predicate IsLT, both given in Script 2.1.29, the output sequence will contain an increasing or decreasing ordering, respectively.

---

**Script 2.1.30 (Sort of numbers)**

```
DEF SORT (predicate::IsFun) = TREE:(MERGE:predicate) ~ AA:[ID];

SORT:IsGT:<8, 2, 4, 2, 3, 11, -5> ≡ <-5, 2, 2, 3, 4, 8, 11>
SORT:IsLT:<8, 2, 4, 2, 3, 11, -5> ≡ <11, 8, 4, 3, 2, 2, -5>
```

---

The algorithm used by SORT works as follows:

1. First, the input number sequence is transformed into a sequence of sequences with only one element by the AA:[ID] function.
2. Then, the TREE operator[3] applies *recursively* the MERGE:predicate operator to both half sub-sequences of its unorderd input, and merges their ordered results;
3. The recursive application of MERGE:predicate continues until a sub-sequence is split into two parts of length either two or one;

   (a) in the former case each sub-sequence is ordered (since it contains only one element), and the MERGE operator can be applied, returning an ordered sequence;

   (b) in the latter case the unique sub-sequence with one element is already ordered, and is directly returned.

**Lexicographic ordering** The same function SORT may be used to compute the ordering of a sequence of strings. We only need a predicate able to compare any pair of strings and answer the question if the pair is either ordered or not.

The ordering normally used for strings is said to be *lexicographic*. It is used, e.g., to order the user names in a phone directory. In such ordering, given any two strings, considered as arrays of characters:

$$a = a[i] \quad \text{and} \quad b = b[j], \qquad 1 \leq i \leq m,\ 1 \leq j \leq n,$$

we say that $a < b$ if either

$$\text{ord}(a[1]) < \text{ord}(b[1])$$

or

$$\text{ord}(a[k]) < \text{ord}(b[k]) \quad \text{and} \quad \text{ord}(a[j]) = \text{ord}(b[j]), \qquad 1 \leq j < k.$$

Where the value of the function ord applied to a character is the corresponding index in the ASCII table. For example, ord('a') = 97. The ord value of a character is also

---

[3] See Section 2.1.2.

called its *ordinal value*. The ordinal values of the printable subset of ASCII characters are given by Script 2.1.23.

The standard PLaSM comparison predicates LT (less than), LE (less or equal), EQ (equal), GE (greater or equal) and GT (greater than) are applicable to a pair of strings $a$ and $b$, and return TRUE if either $a$ pred $b$ in lexicographic ordering, or FALSE otherwise. Some examples follows. Remember that all such predicates but EQ are second-order functions, i.e. must be applied twice to their arguments. The function EQ can by used at the same way if curried:

$$
\begin{aligned}
\text{LT: 'Barney': 'Fred'} &\equiv \quad \text{FALSE} \\
\text{LE: 'Barney': 'Fred'} &\equiv \quad \text{FALSE} \\
\text{C:EQ: 'Barney': 'Fred'} &\equiv \text{FALSE} \\
\text{GE: 'Barney': 'Fred'} &\equiv \quad \text{TRUE} \\
\text{GT: 'Barney': 'Fred'} &\equiv \quad \text{TRUE}
\end{aligned}
$$

### Example 2.1.8 (Sort and merge of strings)

Some examples of sorting unordered sequences and merging ordered sequences of strings are given in the following. Notice that both the SORT and the MERGE functions are the same for sorting and merging numbers, respectively.

```
SORT:IsGT:< 'Fred', 'Wilma', 'Barney', 'Lucy' > ≡
    <'Barney', 'Fred', 'Lucy', 'Wilma'>

SORT:IsGT:< 'Homer', 'Margie', 'Bart', 'Lisa', 'Maggie' > ≡
    <'Bart', 'Homer', 'Lisa', 'Maggie', 'Margie'>

MERGE:IsGT: < <'Barney', 'Fred', 'Lucy', 'Wilma'>,
    <'Bart', 'Homer', 'Lisa', 'Margie'> > ≡
    <'Barney', 'Bart', 'Fred', 'Homer', 'Lisa', 'Lucy',
    'Maggie', 'Margie', 'Wilma'>
```

**Associative lists**  An associative list is a data structure often used in programming languages. It is defined as a sequence of pairs <key, data>, where the first element is an integer and the second element may be in our case any language expression. It is used to execute a quick search of some information depending on the value of the *key*.

In Script 2.1.31 we give a function alias used to return the data value paired to an integer key in an associative list. In particular it returns the data value if the key value is found in the list; otherwise it returns the null value, i.e. the empty sequence. This function is implemented using the function assoc, which returns the nearest pair, say, the pair whose key has smallest distance from the input key. It is supposed that the pairs are mantained in increasing order of the key. In case of multiple pairs with the same key, the last associated pair is returned by alloc.

Both the expressions assoc:$n$ and alias:$n$, where $n$ is an integer, return a function that must be applied to an ordered sequence of pairs, where the first element is an integer, and the second one may be any PLaSM expression, as in the following examples:

```
alias:0:
    <<-1,35>, <2,1..3>, <5,41>, <7,43>, <8,44>> ≡ <>;
```

**Script 2.1.31** (alias and alloc)

```
DEF nearest (key::IsInt)(p1,p2::IsPair) =
   IF:< K:(GT:d1:d2), S1, S2 >:<p1,p2>
WHERE
   d1 = ABS:(key - S1:p1),
   d2 = ABS:(key - S1:p2)
END;

DEF assoc (key::IsInt) = TREE:(nearest:key);
DEF alias (key::IsInt) = IF:< C:EQ:key ~ S1, S2, K:<> > ~ assoc:key;
```

```
alias:2:
   <<-1,35>, <2,1..3>, <5,41>, <7,43>, <18,44>> ≡ <1,2,3>;

alias:3:
   <<1,'dog'>, <2,37>, <3,'cat'>, <4,ID>, <6,<11,2>>> ≡ 'cat';
```

**Set operations**   A quite natural representation of sets is given in PLaSM by using sequences. In Script 2.1.25 we have given an implementation of the set-membership predicate, which allows testing if an element $e$ belongs to a set $S$, by returning TRUE if and only if $e \in S$, and returning FALSE otherwise. In the following Script 2.1.32 the four operations of set union, intersection, difference and symmetric difference are given, respectively denoted as setOR, setAND, setDIFF and setXOR.

The algorithm used is quadratic, since we stress here the code simplicity and compactness, and is similar for each operation. Hence the common part of the code is abstracted as an external function InSet. For example, the expression

```
InSet:NOT:set_b: set_a
```

returns the subset of set_a whose elements are not contained in set_b.

**Script 2.1.32** (Set operations)

```
DEF InSet (p::IsFun)(set::IsSeq) = CAT ~ AA:(IF:<p ~ IN:set, [ID], K:<>>);

DEF setOR (set_a, set_b::IsSEq) = InSet:NOT:set_b: set_a CAT set_b;
DEF setAND (set_a, set_b::IsSEq) = InSet:ID:set_b: set_a;
DEF setDIFF (set_a, set_b::IsSEq) = InSet:NOT:set_b: set_a;
DEF setXOR = CAT ~ AA:setDIFF ~ [[S1,S2], [S2,S1]];
```

**Example 2.1.9**

The four set operations defined above are contemporarily applied to two sequences of strings, numbers and functions, using an infix style. The sequence of results of the operations is given below.

```
DEF A = <ID, 11, 'Lucy', 12, 'Bart', 'Albert'>;
DEF B = <'Bart', 'Homer', 11, ID>

A setOR   B ≡ <'Lucy', 12, 'Albert', 'Bart', 'Homer', 11, ID>,
```

```
A setAND  B ≡ <ID, 11, 'Bart'>,
A setDIFF B ≡ <'Lucy', 12, 'Albert'>,
A setXOR  B ≡ <'Lucy', 12, 'Albert', 'Homer'>
```

### 2.1.6  Pipeline paradigm

In this book we will often use the algorithmic scheme[4] based on the *pipelining* of data across repeated instances of a function with equal domain and codomain, so that the computational machinery

$$\texttt{prog} : \text{Dom} \rightarrow \text{Dom},$$

is applied $n$ times to its own output. For example, this paradigm was used in the optimal time generation of the Pascal triangle in Script 2.1.14, in the following computation of the `ProgressiveSum` function, as well as for generating the *fractal simplex* given in Script 4.5.3. Such pipeline paradigm is depicted in Figure 2.1, where input $\in$ Dom.

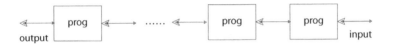

**Figure 2.1**   Pictorial representation of the pipeline paradigm

**Progressive sums**   As our last example of FL computation with numbers, we give a function `ProgressiveSum` from sequences of reals to sequences of reals of the same length, which returns for each $x_k$ input value the sum of the first $k$ terms of the sequence. Formally we can write:

$$\texttt{ProgressiveSum} : \mathbb{R}^d \rightarrow \mathbb{R}^d : (x_k) \mapsto (\textstyle\sum_{i=1}^{k} x_i), \qquad 1 \leq d$$

A good example of pipelined computation is given in Script 2.1.33, where we have a computational `pipeline` made by n repeated applications of the `block` function, followed by a `finish` function to perform some final housekeeping. The behavior of the `block` function is represented in Figure 2.2.

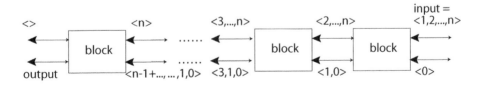

**Figure 2.2**   Computational pipeline of `ProgressiveSum` function

---

[4] Also called *paradigm*.

**Script 2.1.33 (Pipeline paradigm example)**

```
DEF ProgressiveSum (input::IsSeqOf:isNum) = (finish ~ pipeline):<input,<0>>
WHERE
    n = LEN:input,
    block = [TAIL ~ S1, AL ~ [FIRST ~ S1 + FIRST ~ S2, S2]],
    pipeline = (COMP ~ #:n):block,
    finish = TAIL ~ REVERSE ~ S2
END;
```

```
ProgressiveSum:<1,2,3,4,5,6,7,8,9,10> ≡ <1,3,6,10,15,21,28,36,45,55>
ProgressiveSum:<1,-1,0,1.5,2.5,10,0.5> ≡ <1,0,0,1.5,4.0,14.0,14.5>
```

**Example 2.1.10 (Squares of first integers)**
It may be interesting to notice that the sequence of squares of the first $n$ integers can be computed by evaluating the ProgressiveSum function on the sequence of the first $n$ *odd* numbers. E.g.:

```
ProgressiveSum:<1,3,5,7,9,11,13,15,17,19> ≡ <1,4,9,16,25,36,49,64,81,100>
```

## 2.2   Basic geometric programming

In this section we systematically present the geometric primitives of the PLaSM language. We begin by showing the very few constructors of primitive shapes, and continue by discussing the powerful MAP construct, used to generate any user-defined parametric map, which allow building of circumferences, spheres, toruses, as well as any kind of manifold of dimension 1, 2, 3 and even of higher dimension. The basic geometric concepts used here are discussed with much greater detail in Chapter 4.

### 2.2.1   Primitive shapes

Only three primitive shape constructors SIMPLEX, CUBOID and CYLINDER are predefined in PLaSM, for building dimension-independent simplices and cuboids and for 3D cylinders, respectively. The very powerful basic generator MKPOL of polyhedral complexes is also discussed here.

**Simplex**   The *convex hull* of a set of points of $\mathbb{E}^n$ is the smallest convex set of $\mathbb{E}^n$ which contains all the points.

The *simplex* of dimension $d$, or *d-simplex*, is defined as the *convex hull* of $d + 1$ *affinely independent* points of Euclidean space of dimension $n$, with $d \leq n$. Two such points are affinely independent when they are non-coincident, three points are a.i. when non-aligned, four points are a.i. when non-coplanar, and so on.

In particular, in $\mathbb{E}^3$, 0-simplex is a single point, 1-simplex is a segment, 2-simplex is a triangle, 3-simplex is a tetrahedron.

A primitive function SIMPLEX is available in PLaSM, to be applied to an integer parameter $d$, which returns the *standard d-simplex* of Euclidean $d$-space. This one is the convex hull generated by the origin $o$ and by the $d$ points $o + e_i$, where $(o, \{e_i\})$ is a Cartesian frame of $\mathbb{E}^d$. In Figure 2.3 the show the standard $d$-simplices of $\mathbb{E}^3$, with $d = 0, 1, 2, 3$.

**Figure 2.3**   Standard $d$-simplices of dimension $0, 1, 2$ and $3$ embedded in $\mathbb{E}^3$

**Cuboid**   A primitive PLaSM function named CUBOID is used to generate the geometric model of hyper-parallelopipeds of dimension $n$, depending on the number of arguments passed when invoking the function. This function allows generation of line segments, plane rectangles, space parallelepipeds, and even hyper-parallelopipeds of intrinsic dimension higher than three.

---

**Script 2.2.1 (Unit hyper-parallelopipeds)**

```
DEF Segment   = CUBOID:<1>;
DEF Square    = CUBOID:<1,1>;
DEF Cube      = CUBOID:<1,1,1>;
DEF Hypercube = CUBOID:<1,1,1,1>;
```

---

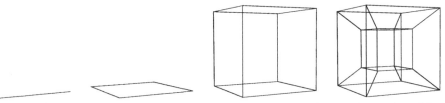

**Figure 2.4**   Unit segment, unit square, unit cube, unit 4D hypercube projected in 3D space

**Example 2.2.1 ($d$-dimensional cuboid)**
A function to generate 1D segments, 2D rectangles, 3D parallelepipeds and higher dimensional hypercubes, shown in Figure 2.4, is quite easy to define in PLaSM. It is sufficient to transform the sequence of numeric arguments into a sequence of 1D polyhedra, and then to apply to this sequence — via the INSR combining form — the binary product operation between polyhedra defined in [BFPP93], and implemented as * operation in PLaSM. Both such user-specified definition of the cuboid function and an example of computation are given in the following.

**Cylinder**   A predefined function CYLINDER generates 3D cylinder of variable radius and height, polyhedrally approximated with a variable number of side facets. The CYLINDER function has two real arguments and one integer arguments.

Remember that the geometric kernel of the language is able to work only with linear polyhedra, i.e. geometric object with no curved faces.

**Script 2.2.2**

```
DEF cuboid = (INSR:*) ~ (AA:(QUOTE ~ [ID]))

cuboid:<x₁, x₂, ..., xd>
    = (INSR:* ~ AA:(QUOTE ~ [ID])):<x₁, ..., xd>
    = (INSR:*):((AA:(QUOTE ~ [ID])):<x₁, ..., xd> )
    = (INSR:*):< (QUOTE ~ [ID]):x₁, ..., (QUOTE ~ [ID]):xd >
    = (INSR:*):< QUOTE:<x₁>, ..., QUOTE:<xd> >
    = (INSR:*):< p₁, ..., pd >
```

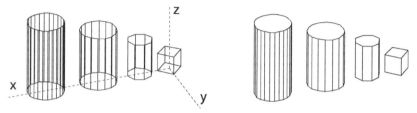

**Figure 2.5**   Cylinders with different radius, height and number of side faces

The cylinders in Figure 2.5 are generated by the following PLaSM expression, where each cylinder is moved by a translation along the $x$ axis.

```
STRUCT:<
    CYLINDER:<1, 1>:4, T:1:2.5,
    CYLINDER:<1, 2>:8, T:1:3.5,
    CYLINDER:<1.5, 3>:16, T:1:4.5,
    CYLINDER:<1.5, 4>:24
>;
```

**Basic polyhedral constructor**   The PLaSM language contains only one basic constructor, named MKPOL, of geometric objects. The type of geometric objects is called *polyhedral complex*. As we discuss in Chapter 4, this kind of complex can be seen as a set of convex cells, grouped into subsets called polyhedral cells. Each cell is obtained as the convex hull of a discrete subset of points. Therefore there are three ingredients in a *polyhedral complex*:

1. a discrete set of points, called *vertices*;
2. a discrete set of convex cells, called *cells*;
3. a discrete set of collections of cells, called *polyhedra*.

All vertices must have the same number of coordinates, i.e. must belong to the same Euclidean space. Depending on the number of coordinates, the resulting object may be either 1D, or 2D, or 3D or even higher-dimensional.

   Each cells is defined as the convex hull of a subset of vertices. The various cells give a cell *covering* of the resulting object. The cells may have any intrinsic dimension, i.e. may be topologically equivalent to either a point, a curve, a surface, a solid and so on.

   Each polyhedron in a complex is in turn defined as the union of a subset of convex cells, possibly embedded in different affine subspaces of the Euclidean space. When

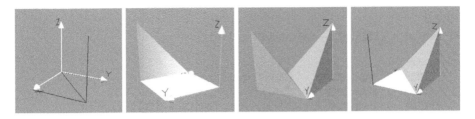

**Figure 2.6**   Polyhedral complexes of dimension 1,2,3 and of mixed dimensionality,
drawn with a model of reference frame

the affine hulls of all cells of a polyhedron are coincident, the polyhedron is said to be *regular* or homogeneously dimensional. When all the polyhedra in a complex are regular and have the same dimension of the embedding space, the complex is *solid*.

A polyhedral complex is produced in PLaSM by applying the basic constructor MKPOL to a triplet of *vertices, cells* and *polyhedra*. Vertices are specified as sequences of coordinates, cells and polyhedra are given as sequences of indices of vertices and cells, respectively.

### Example 2.2.2 (Polyhedral complexes)
Some complexes of different dimensionality are defined in Script 2.2.3 and are shown in Figure 2.6. All examples rely on the same set, named verts, of vertices in $\mathbb{E}^3$. In particular, the object named pol_1D generates a 1D complex with three convex cells (segments) defined by pairs of vertices with indices <1,4>, <2,4> and <4,8>, respectively. Analogously, the pol_2D object has two convex cells with four and three vertices, respectively. The pol_3D object is a solid complex with two convex cells of four vertices. Finally, the mixed_D object, of mixed dimensionality, contains three cells, of dimension 3, 2 and 1, respectively. The generated objects are combined with the model of the reference frame given by the symbol MKframe, that is defined in Script 6.5.3.

### Script 2.2.3

```
DEF verts =
    <<0,0,0>,<1,0,0>,<0,1,0>,<1,1,0>,<0,0,1>,<1,0,1>, <0,1,1>,<1,1,1>>;

DEF pol_1D = MKPOL:< verts, cells, pols > STRUCT MKframe
WHERE
    cells = <<1,4>,<2,4>,<4,8>>,
    pols = <<1,2,3>>
END;

DEF pol_2D = MKPOL:<verts, <<1,2,3,4>,<2,4,8>>, <<1>,<2>>> STRUCT MKframe
DEF pol_3D = MKPOL:<verts, <<1,2,3,5>,<2,3,4,8>>, <<1,2>>> STRUCT MKframe
DEF mixed_D = MKPOL:<verts, <<1,2,3,5>,<2,3,4>,<4,8>>, <<1,2,3>> >
    STRUCT MKframe
```

## 2.2.2  Non-primitive shapes (simplicial maps)

As we already said, the geometric kernel of the language gives support only for modeling linear polyhedra. Curved objects are always approximated — with user-defined precision — by linear polyhedra. This is actually the standard approach in computer graphics, where every curved line is drawn as a polygonal line made of many small segments, and every surface is rendered as faceted by a great number of small triangles. Analogously, a curved solid may be approximated by a number of small tetrahedra.

All such approximations can be seen as resulting from the application of a so-called *simplicial mapping* to some properly decomposed *domain*. The domain image in such a mapping gives a polyhedral approximation of the curved object. The finer the domain decomposition, the better is the linear approximation of the object. A well-known example is the circle approximation by regular polygons with increasing number of sides.

**Parametric MAP operator**  The very useful primitive operator MAP allows for generating curves and surfaces — as well as higher-dimensional manifolds — via parametric maps from a simplicial decomposition of a polyhedral complex. The predefined operator MAP is used at this purpose as

```
MAP:f:domain
```

where

- the mapping f is either the *construction* [$f_1$, $f_2$, ... , $f_n$] of a number $n$ of *coordinate functions* or is their *sequence* <$f_1$, $f_2$, ... , $f_n$>. Notice that $n$ is the dimension of the *target space* of the mapping, where the domain is embedded and (usually) incurved, and
- domain is a *polyhedral complex*. A commonly enforced requirement is that the intrinsic dimension of domain is either less or equal than the dimension of the target space of the mapping.

The operational semantics of the MAP operator can be briefly described as follows:

1. compute a simplicial decomposition of the convex cells of the polyhedral domain;
2. apply to each vertex of such a decomposition the coordinate functions $f_1$, $f_2$, ... , $f_n$, in order to generate the vertex image in the target space $\mathbb{E}^n$.

Notice that each *coordinate function* will produce one of the $n$ coordinates of vertices in target space, by properly combining vertex coordinates in domain space. Since vertices are internally seen as sequences of coordinates, these *must* be extracted, in the formal definition of the coordinate functions, by using the standard FL selector functions S1, S2, ... , S$n$. This is a strict *semantic requirement* when using the MAP operator. We hope the examples will clarify this point.

**Circumference**  A polygonal line with $n$ segments which approximates the boundary of the unit circle can easily be generated as discussed in the following.

Our aim is to implement the trigonometric parametrization of circumference with unit radius given by equations:

$$x(u) = \cos u$$
$$y(u) = \sin u$$

where $u \in [0, 2\pi]$.

First, we decompose the $[0, 2\pi]$ interval into $n$ parts of equal size. For this purpose we generate the sequence of $n$ numbers $\frac{2\pi}{n}$. This sequence is then transformed into a 1D polyhedron by the PLaSM primitive QUOTE. Finally, on such domain decomposition we apply the trigonometric mapping $\mathtt{f} \colon \mathbb{R} \to \mathbb{R}^2$, where

    f = [cos, sin] ~ S1

As we already noticed, the primitive selector S1 must be used to extract the first (and unique) coordinate from vertices of the domain decomposition into small segments. In particular, a polygonal approximation with 24 line segments of the circumference is obtained as done in Script 2.2.4 and shown in Figure 2.7. Notice that Circumference is a function in proper FL style, that returns a polyhedral complex when applied to some positive integer.

---

**Script 2.2.4 (Circumference)**
```
DEF Domain (a::IsReal)(n::IsIntPos) = (QUOTE ~ #:n):(a/n);
DEF Circumference = MAP:([COS, SIN] ~ S1) ~ Domain:(2*PI);

Circumference:24
```

---

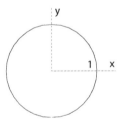

**Figure 2.7**    Unit circumference centered in the origin, as generated by the function
Circumference

**Circle**    A polyhedral approximation of the unit circle can be easily obtained as the JOIN of the circle boundary. We remember that this function generates the convex hull of its polyhedral argument:

    (JOIN ~ Circumference:1):24;

Actually, a finer decomposition of the circle of radius $r$ can be obtained by using the parametric equations

$$x(u) = v \cos u$$
$$y(u) = v \sin u$$

where $\leq u \leq 2\pi$, $0 \leq v \leq r$, or better, $(u,v) \in [0, 2\pi] \times [0, r]$. Hence the polyhedral approximation of the circle is obtained by the map $\gamma : \mathbb{R}^2 \to \mathbb{R}^2$ such that

$$\gamma = [\texttt{S2} * \texttt{COS} \sim \texttt{S1}, \texttt{S2} * \texttt{SIN} \sim \texttt{S1}]$$

Notice, according to Script 2.2.5, that the $\gamma$ function will be applied by the MAP operator to all vertices of the simplicial decomposition of the complex generated by the function-valued expression `Domain2D:<2*PI,1>`. Notice also that `Domain2D` is a second-order function which produces a decomposition into n×m sub-intervals of the 2D domain produced by Cartesian product of the intervals $[0, \texttt{a}]$ and $[0, \texttt{b}]$.

---

**Script 2.2.5 (Circle)**

```
DEF Domain2D (a,b::IsReal)(n,m::IsIntPos) = Domain:a:n * Domain:b:m;
DEF Circle (r::IsReal) =
    MAP:[S2 * COS ~ S1, S2 * SIN ~ S1] ~ Domain2D:<2*PI,r>;

Domain2D:<2*PI,1>:<24,4>;
Circle:1:<24,4>;
```

---

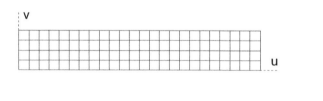 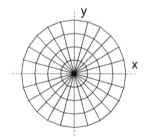

**Figure 2.8**   Domain and range decomposition associated with `Circle:1:<24,4>`

In Figure 2.8 there are actually represented the polyhedral domains generated by evaluating the following PLaSM expressions, where the @1 operator executes the extraction of the 1-skeleton of the the resulting object, i.e. the set of its 1-cells (see Chapter 4 for a definition):

```
(@1 ~ Domain2D:<2*PI,1>):<24,4>;
(@1 ~ Circle:1):<24,4>
```

The generating code can be further specialized to produce circles with a hole, called *rings*, and circular segments with either a filled or an empty hole, by just modifying the limits of the domain interval in parameter space. The definition of a function Ring in proper FL style is given in Script 2.2.6. The Ring function actually depends also (implicitly) on two integer parameters, needed by the partially specified function Interval2D in its body. A picture of the object generated by the last expression of the Script is shown in Figure 2.9.

**Script 2.2.6**

```
DEF Interval (x1,x2::IsReal)(n::IsIntPos) =
    (T:1:x1 ~ QUOTE ~ #:n):((x2-x1)/n);

DEF Interval2D (a1,a2,b1,b2::IsReal)(n,m::IsIntPos) =
    Interval:<a1,a2>:n * Interval:<b1,b2>:m;

DEF Ring (r1,r2::IsReal) =
    MAP:[s2 * cos ~ S1, s2 * sin ~ S1] ~ Interval2D:<0,2*PI, r1,r2>;

(@1 ~ Ring:<0.5,1>):<24,4>;
```

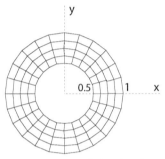

**Figure 2.9**  Polyhedral approximation of the circular ring by a decomposition of
domain directions into 24 and 4 parts

**Sphere**  The trigonometric parametrization of the spherical surface with radius $r$
and center in the origin has equations:

$$
\begin{aligned}
x(u,v) &= -r \cos u \sin v, \\
y(u,v) &= r \cos u \cos v, \\
z(u,v) &= r \sin u,
\end{aligned}
$$

where $(u,v) \in [-\frac{\pi}{2}, \frac{\pi}{2}] \times [0, 2\pi]$.

A second-order function **Sphere** is given in Script 2.2.7, which must be applied
first to a real positive **radius** parameter. The resulting partial function must then be
applied to a pair of integers **n** and **m**, used to specify the "grain" of the polyhedral
approximation of the surface, i.e. of its domain decomposition.

**Figure 2.10**  Unit spherical surface: (a) polyhedral approximation of the surface
(b) smooth rendering via color shading

**Script 2.2.7 (Spherical surface)**

```
DEF Sphere (radius::IsRealPos)(n,m::IsIntPos) = MAP:[fx,fy,fz]:domain
WHERE
    fx = K:radius * - ~ SIN ~ S2 * COS ~ S1,
    fy = K:radius * COS ~ S1 * COS ~ S2,
    fz = K:radius * SIN ~ S1,
    domain = Interval:<PI/-2,PI/2>:n * Interval:<0,2*PI>:m
END;

(STRUCT ~ [ID, @1] ~ Sphere:1):<12,24>;
Sphere:1:<12,24> CREASE (PI/2);
```

The result of the evaluation of the last two expressions of Script 2.2.7 is shown in Figures 2.10a and 2.10b. Notice that both the spherical surface and its 1-skeleton are aggregated in the resulting object of Figure 2.10a, in order to better highlight the facets of the approximating polyhedron. Conversely, a *color shading* is used when browsing the VRML file generated when exporting the geometric object produced by the last PLaSM expression. In particular, the surface facets are rendered on the screen by using a color interpolation tecnique, according with the value of the *crease angle* between adjacent facets. This smooth rendering technique, which is very frequently used in computer graphics, is discussed in Section 10.6. The reader should notice that *both* images are produced by using the *same* (polyhedral) geometric model.

**Cone**    A very different constructive method is used in Script 2.2.8 to generate a solid model of the 3D cone with assigned **radius** and **height**. In particular we generate the cone as the *convex hull* of the **basis** and the **apex**, represented as polyhedra of dimension 2 and 0, respectively. The predefined PLaSM operator **JOIN** is used at this purpose. Notice that, once more, the generated object is a polyhedral approximation of the curved solid.

The function **basis** is the composition of two functions. The **Circle:radius** function generates a 2D circle of proper **radius** centered in the origin, whereas the **EMBED:1** function embed this circle in 3D, actually putting it in the coordinate subspace $z = 0$. The **apex** object is a 0D polyhedron constituted by a single point, which is embedded in 3D by the function **EMBED:3** and then is translated along the $z$ coordinate by the function **T:3:height**.

Notice that the integer parameter of the **EMBED:$d'$** unary operator must be the *codimension* (see Section 3.1) of the geometric object returned by the operator, with $d + d' = n$, where $d$ and $n$ are the *intrinsic* and the *embedding* dimensions, respectively.

**Script 2.2.8**

```
DEF Cone (radius, height::IsReal)(n::IsInt) = JOIN:< basis:<n,1>, apex >
WHERE
    basis = EMBED:1 ~ Circle:radius,
    apex = (T:3:height ~ EMBED:3 ~ SIMPLEX):0
END;
```

An equivalent definition for the `apex` object, as a 0D polyhedral complex made by a single cell, in turn consisting in only one 3D point, could be given as

```
apex = MKPOL:< <<0,0,height>>, <<1>>, <<1>> >
```

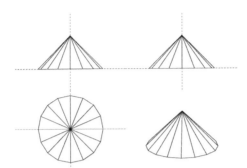

**Figure 2.11**   Orthographic and dimetric projections of the faceted cone with unit radius and height generated by `Cone:<1,1>:16`

**Cylinder and tube**   A primitive `CYLINDER` generator is predefined in PLaSM. A possible implementation is given by the `Cylnder` function in Script 2.2.9. It works by computing the Cartesian product of a circle of radius $r$ times a 1D segment of length $h$. The same approach is used to compute the empty cylinder with the function `Tube`, as a Cartesian product of a 2D object generated by the `Ring` function, times a 1D segment of proper length. In both cases the formal parameter n denotes the number of facets in the polyhedral approximation of the side surface. Pictures of the object generated by last expressions of Script 2.2.9 are given in Figure 2.12. Notice the graphical smoothing of adjacent facets is performed only when their common angle is *greater* than $\frac{\pi}{2}$.

---

**Script 2.2.9**
```
DEF Cylnder (r,h::IsReal)(n::IsInt) = Circle:r:<n,1> * QUOTE:<h>;
DEF Tube (r1,r2,h::IsReal)(n::IsInt) = Ring:<r1,r2>:<n,1> * QUOTE:<h>;

Tube:<0.8, 1, 2>:24
Tube:<0.8, 1, 2>:24 CREASE (PI/2)
```

---

**Torus**   A *torus* is a 3D surface with the characteristic shape of a doughnut. Such a surface can be thought of as being generated by rotating with angle $2\pi$ a circumference about an axis of its plane, providing that the rotation axis does not intersect the circumference.

In particular, the torus surface may be generated by rotating, about the $z$ axis, a circle on the plane $y = 0$, with center $(0, 0, R)$ and radius $r$. In this case the parametric equations of the surface are:

**Figure 2.12**   Geometric object generated by expression `Tube:<0.8,1,2>:24`
(a) standard rendering (b) smooth rendering via color shading

$$
\begin{aligned}
x(u,v) &= (r\cos u + R)\cos v, \\
y(u,v) &= (r\cos u + R)\sin v, \qquad (u,v) \in [0,2\pi]^2 \\
z(u,v) &= r\sin u
\end{aligned}
\tag{2.4}
$$

Such equations are directly translated in PLaSM to the function `torus` given in Script 2.2.10. In this case the symbol `domain2D` is redefined locally, to take into account the new domain limits of $u$ and $v$ parameters. Notice once more that the coordinate functions `fx`, `fy` and `fz` are written by using the FL selectors `S1` and `S2`. Their aim is to properly select the coordinates of vertices of the simplicial decomposition of the mapping domain generated by the `MAP` operator.

---

**Script 2.2.10**

```
DEF torus (r1,R2::IsReal) (n,m::IsIntPos) = MAP:[fx,fy,fz]:domain
WHERE
    fx = (K:r1 * COS ~ S1 + K:R2) * COS ~ S2,
    fy = (K:r1 * COS ~ S1 + K:R2) * SIN ~ S2,
    fz = (K:r1 * SIN ~ S1),
    domain = Interval:<0,2*PI>:n * Interval:<0,2*PI>:m
END;

torus:<1,3>:<12,24>
torus:<1,3>:<12,24> CREASE PI/2
```

---

A different method of generating the torus as the manifold product of 2D circles will be given in Example 5.4.2.

**Figure 2.13**   Polyhedral approximation of torus surface produced by
`torus:<1,3>:<12,24>` (a) standard rendering (b) smooth rendering

## 2.3    Assembling shapes

In geometric modeling of complex assemblies the geometric and graphics programmer makes wide use of the so-called *hierarchical scene graphs* [WO94, SRD00] or hierarchical structures [Gas92], where sub-assemblies are defined in local coordinates, and are transformed into the coordinate frame of the calling assembly by explicitly using proper coordinate transformations. Such "modeling transformations" are left entirely to the programmer's responsibility. To this topic we dedicate the whole of Chapter 8. In the present section we conversely discuss some simplified assembly operators, where the coordinate transformations are computed automatically by the language.

### 2.3.1    Primitive alignments

**Measuring**    A primitive function SIZE of second order provides support for computing the size of the projection of any polyhedral complex along any coordinate subspace. The result of a double application of the SIZE function to either a coordinate index or a sequence of indices, followed by the application to the polyhedral argument, will accordingly return either a single positive number or a sequence of positive numbers. For example:

```
(SIZE:1 ~ T:1:PI ~ CYLINDER):<1,1,24> ≡ 2.0
(SIZE:<1,2,3> ~ CYLINDER):<1,1,24> ≡ <2.0, 2.0, 1.0>
(SIZE:<1,2,3> ~ R:<2,3>:(PI/2) ~ CYLINDER):<1,1,24> ≡ <2.0, 1.0, 2.0>
```

**Pointing**    Three specialized functions MIN, MED and MAX may be used to compute the corresponding extreme (or middle) values within the coordinate interval projected by a given polyhedral complex on each coordinate axis. For example:

```
DEF TheCylinder = CYLINDER:<1,2>:24

MIN:3:TheCylinder ≡ 0.0;
MED:3:TheCylinder ≡ 1.0;
MAX:3:TheCylinder ≡ 2.0;

MIN:<1,2>:TheCylinder ≡ <-1.0, -1.0>;
MED:<1,2>:TheCylinder ≡ <0.0, 0.0>;
MAX:<1,2>:TheCylinder ≡ <1.0, 1.0>;
```

**Boxing**    Similarly, a predefined function BOX of second order returns the containment box of a proper projection of the polyhedral argument. The result of a double application of the BOX function to a sequence of indices, followed by the application to a polyhedral complex, is the minimal hyper-parallelepiped parallel to the reference frame which contains the polyhedral argument in its interior. The results of the evaluation of the three examples given in the following are shown in Figure 2.14.

```
(@1 ~ STRUCT ~ [ID, BOX:<1,2>] ~ CYLINDER):<1,1,24>;
(@1 ~ STRUCT ~ [ID, BOX:<1,2,3>] ~ CYLINDER):<1,1,24>;
(STRUCT ~ [ID, @1 ~ BOX:<1,2,3>] ~ CYLINDER):<1,1,24>;
```

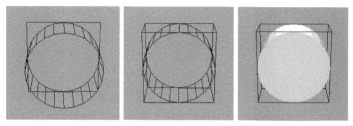

**Figure 2.14**   (a) Containment box of the cylinder projection in a coordinate plane
(b, c) Containment box of the cylinder

**Aligning**   Every pair of polyhedral complexes may be aligned along any given subset
of coordinates by using the primitive binary function `ALIGN`. Such a second-order
operator must be applied to a sequence of triples which define a specialized behavior
for each affected coordinate. The resulting specialized operator is then applied to a
pair of polyhedral complex, and returns a single polyhedral complex. Each alignment
directive along a coordinate must belong to the set

$$\{1, \dots, n\} \times \{\text{MIN, MED, MAX, K}:\alpha\} \times \{\text{MIN, MED, MAX, K}:\alpha\}$$

where $n$ is the dimension of the embedding space of the two polyhedral arguments,
and $\alpha \in \mathbb{R}$.

**Example 2.3.1 (Diagram)**
The simple diagram of Figure 2.15 is produced by Script 2.3.1. The *circle*,
*square* and *segment* symbols are named a, b and l, respectively. Then the
sequence of symbols < a,l,b,l,a > is pairwise aligned according to the directives
<<1,MAX,MIN>,<2,MED,MED>>. Therefore, *each* consecutive pair, say <p1,p2>, is
aligned so that:

1. the `MAX` value of coord 1 of p1 coincides with the `MIN` value of coord 1 of p2;
2. the `MED` value of coord 2 of p1 coincides with the `MED` value of coord 2 of p2.

---

**Script 2.3.1**
```
    DEF a = Circle:0.75:<24,1>;
    DEF b = CUBOID:< 1,1 >;
    DEF l = (EMBED:1 ~ CUBOID):< 1 >;

    INSL:(ALIGN:<<1,MAX,MIN>,<2,MED,MED>>):< a,l,b,l,a >;
```

---

**Example 2.3.2 (Histogram)**
A very simple implementation of various kind of histogram generating functions is
given in Script 2.3.2. The three definitions correspond to a 2D histogram and to a 3D
histogram of a single sequence of data, and to a 3D histogram of a double sequence of
data, respectively. The histograms of the number series given in the script are shown
in Figure 2.16.

**Figure 2.15**   Simple diagram generated by alignment operators

---

**Script 2.3.2 (Histograms)**

```
DEF histogram1 = INSR:(ALIGN:<<1,MAX,MIN>>) ~ AA:(CUBOID ~ [K:1,ID]);
DEF histogram2 = INSR:(ALIGN:<<1,MAX,MIN>>) ~ AA:(CUBOID ~ [K:1,K:1,ID]);
DEF histogram3 = INSR:(ALIGN:<<2,MAX,MIN>>) ~ AA:histogram2;

histogram1:<3,5,4,6.5,2.34,6,7>;
histogram2:<3,5,4,6.5,2.34,6,7>;
histogram3:<
    <3,5,5,6.5,2.34,6,7>,
    <2,5,4,3.6,3,4,2>,
    <4,5,6,1.5,4,1,0.5>,
    <1,5,3,4.2,2.5,5,1>,
    <0.5,3,2,3.5,1,6,2>,
    <0.1,5,4,1.5,2.4,1,4> >;
```

---

*2.3.2   Relative arrangements*

The PLaSM language has some predefined binary functions used to relatively locate two complexes with respect each other. In particular, the second argument of such functions will be positioned either TOP the first one, or ABOVE, or LEFT, or RIGHT, or UP, or DOWN, respectively, according to the alignment semantics given in Script 2.3.3, where the definitions of such primitive functions are reported.

As we show in this section, such relative positioning operator allows for the easy construction of quite complex assemblies, without taking explicitly into account the local coordinate frames where the sub-assemblies and the elementary parts are defined. With an approach of this kind we avoid applying affine transformations explicitly parametrized on the dimensions of the arguments objects, as it is conversely needed in hierarchical scene graphs.

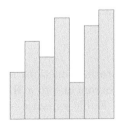
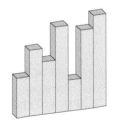

**Figure 2.16**   (a) 2D histogram (b) 3D histogram (c) 3D histogram of a double sequence of values

**Binary placements**   The predefined binary function TOP, given in Script 2.3.3, locates the second argument on top of the first, by making also coincident the centers of their projection extents on the $xy$ plane. In particular, a proper translation is applied to the second object, with translation vector (see Section 6.2.1) produced by the difference of points generated by the expressions

$$[\texttt{MED,MED,MIN}]\texttt{:pol2} \quad \text{and} \quad [\texttt{MED,MED,MAX}]\texttt{:pol1}$$

   The resulting complex is defined in the local frame of the first argument (i.e. pol1). Similar placements are produced by the other operators BOTTOM, LEFT, RIGHT, UP and DOWN.

---

**Script 2.3.3 (Relative arrangements)**

```
DEF TOP (pol1, pol2 ::IsPol) =
   ALIGN:<<3,MAX,MIN>,<1,MED,MED>,<2,MED,MED>>:<pol1, pol2>

DEF BOTTOM (pol1, pol2 ::IsPol) =
   ALIGN:<<3,MIN,MAX>,<1,MED,MED>,<2,MED,MED>>:<pol1, pol2>

DEF LEFT (pol1, pol2 ::IsPol) =
   ALIGN:<<1,MIN,MAX>,<3,MIN,MIN>>:<pol1, pol2>

DEF RIGHT (pol1, pol2 ::IsPol) =
   ALIGN:<<1,MAX,MIN>,<3,MIN,MIN>>:<pol1, pol2>

DEF UP (pol1, pol2 ::IsPol) =
   ALIGN:<<2,MAX,MIN>,<3,MIN,MIN>>:<pol1, pol2>

DEF DOWN (pol1, pol2 ::IsPol) =
   ALIGN:<<2,MIN,MAX>,<3,MIN,MIN>>:<pol1, pol2>
```

---

**Example 2.3.3 (Single placement)**
Let us consider the standard unit cube and the cylinder with unit radius and height generated by PLaSM expressions

```
DEF Cube = CUBOID:<1,1,1>;
DEF Cyl = CYLINDER:<1,1>:16;
```

The result of the relative placement produced by the expression

```
Cube TOP Cyl;
```

is graphically shown in Figure 2.17.

**Example 2.3.4 (Multiple placement)**
The TOP operator may be used more times in the same expression, both with and without parentheses, since it is left- and right-associative. Anyway, the reader should remember that every multiple infix expression in PLaSM is left-associative. The result of each expression in Script 2.3.4 is shown in Figure 2.18a.

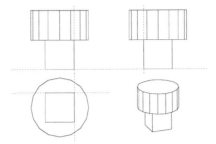

**Figure 2.17**   Monge's projections and dimetric projection of the result of the expression `Cube TOP Cyl`

---

**Script 2.3.4 (Associative property)**
```
(Cube TOP Cyl) TOP Simplex:3; ≡
Cube TOP (Cyl TOP Simplex:3); ≡
Cube TOP Cyl TOP Simplex:3;
```

---

The aggregation by `TOP` of several instances of two objects may be defined by exploiting the combinatorial features of the language. For example, four instances of the pair `<Cube, Cyl>` may be vertically aggregated as shown in Script 2.3.5.

where the binary operator `TOP` is applied to a sequence of eight arguments by using the `FL` combinator `INSL`. The result of the evaluation of this expression is shown in Figure 2.18b.

## 2.4   Examples

Two examples of assembly by relative location operators are given in this section. The first one is a mechanical example where a parametrized assembly of two different families of nuts is discussed. In the second example we generate a simplified model of a Greek temple. A programming example concludes this section, aiming at showing the great difference in making geometric programming by using the standard iteration of functional programming, based on recursion, and the proper `FL` approach based on combinators.

### 2.4.1   Parametric nut stack

We define here a parametric model of a mechanical assembly constituted by alternate cylindric and cubic nuts, with a variable number of such parts, each one with a variable width. In particular our aim is to write a generating function depending on the numeric sequence of nut widths.

Let us start by giving two generating functions `Nut_1` and `Nut_2` which produce a squared and hexagonal nut model, respectively, when applied to the h parameter.

Notice that both the `Nut_1` and the `Nut_2` partial function must be further applied

---

**Script 2.3.5 (*n*-ary usage of the operator)**
```
(INSL:TOP ~ ##:4):<Cube, Cyl>
```

---

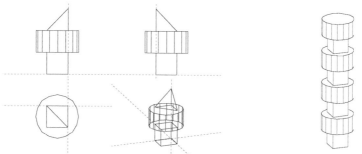

**Figure 2.18**  (a) Cube, cylinder and 3D simplex (b) multiple aggregation

---

**Script 2.4.1 (Nut stack)**

```
DEF Nut (radius::IsReal; nstep::IsIntPos) (h::IsReal) =
    CYLINDER:<radius,h>:nstep;

DEF Nut_1 = Nut:<0.5, 4>;
DEF Nut_2 = Nut:<0.5, 6>;

(INSR:TOP ~ AA:APPLY ~ TRANS):
    < ##:4:< Nut_1, Nut_2 >, <0.1, 1, 0.3, 0.3, 1, 0.4, 2, 0.2> >
```

---

to a real **h** parameter to generate a geometrical object.

**Figure 2.19**  Composite nut assembled from parts of various heights

The following functions are orderly applied to the pair constituted by the function sequence ##:4:< Nut_1, Nut_2 > and by the sequence of numbers:

1. the function TRANS returns a sequence of pairs <*function, number*>;
2. to each such pairs is applied the primitive FL function APPLY, thus generating a sequence of nuts, each one defined in a local coordinate system;
3. the function INSR:TOP is finally applied to the nut sequence, so producing the geometric model of the whole assembly, which is shown in Figure 2.19.

### 2.4.2  Hierarchical temple

In this section we discuss the hierarchical modeling of a simplified Greek temple. The construction will proceed bottom-up by generating:

1. the single column with a beam;
2. a row of columns;

3. the gable;
4. a row of columns with gable;
5. a first temple version;
6. the arrangement of secondary beams;
7. the final temple version.


**Column definition**  A simplified column model may be defined as shown in Figure 2.20, where a parallelepiped `basis` and `capital` are separated by the cylinder `trunk` of the column, approximated by 12 rectangular facets. On the column top is centered a `beam` obtained by scaling three times in the direction of the first coordinate the parallelepiped model of the capital. The model generated by the `column` function is parametrized by positive real formal parameters `r` and `h`, corresponding to the `trunk` radius and to the vertical size of the aggregation of `basis`, `trunk` and `capital`. Both `basis` and `capital` are defined with side `1.2 * r`.

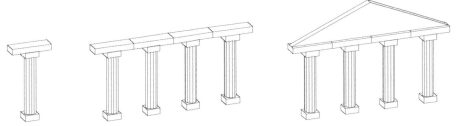

**Figure 2.20**  Projections of the models generated by `Column:<1,12>`, by `ColRow:4` and by `ColRowAndGable`, respectively


---

**Script 2.4.2 (Column)**

```
DEF Column (r,h::IsRealPos) = basis TOP trunk TOP capital TOP beam
WHERE
    basis = CUBOID:< 2*r*1.2, 2*r*1.2, h/12 >,
    trunk = CYLINDER:< r, (10/12)*h >:12,
    capital = basis,
    beam = S:1:3:capital
END;

DEF col = Column:<1, 12>
```

---

For the sake of computational efficiency it is useful to invoke the `Column` function through the definition of a constant symbol, say, the symbol `col` in Script 2.4.2. When such a symbol is evaluated the first time, its value is computed by evaluating the *body* of its definition and it is stored as associated to the symbol. In every subsequent invocation of the symbol such value is just referred to, and is neither computed nor stored again.

**Column row**   A row of $n$ columns, with $n$ positive integer, is generated by the
ColRow function of Script 2.4.3, where the `column` value memorized in the constant
col is instanced $n$ times and located each time on the RIGHT of the previous instancing.
The model generated by `ColRow:4` expression is shown in Figure 2.20b.

---

**Script 2.4.3**

```
DEF ColRow (n::IsIntPos) = (INSR:RIGHT ~ #:n):col;

ColRow:4
```

---

**Gable**   A simplified temple's `Gable` is defined here. Later on it will be positioned on
top of first and last column rows. This is not historically correct, but helps to give
a "temple" aspect to our simplified model. The shape chosen for the gable is that
of a vertical solid triangle. Such geometric model can be generated in several ways.
We choose one geometric construction which uses only geometric operators that we
already encountered in this chapter. In particular we generate the `Gable` of Script 2.4.4
by JOIN of basis and apex of the solid triangle. Notice that apex is given as a 3D
segment in its proper position.

---

**Script 2.4.4 (Gable)**

```
DEF Gable (radius,h::IsReal; n::IsInt) = JOIN:<basis, apex>
WHERE
    basis = (EMBED:1 ~ CUBOID):<1, w>,
    apex = MKPOL:<<<1/2,0,h/2>,<1/2,w,h/2>>,<<1,2>>,<<1>>>,
    l = 3*n*(2*w),
    w = 1.2*radius
END;

DEF ColRowAndGable = ColRow:4 TOP Gable:<1,12,4>;
```

---

**Column row and gable**   The location of the gable over the row of four columns is
produced by using the relative positioning operator TOP. The result of the evaluation
of the `ColRowAndGable` symbol, defined in Script 2.4.4, is shown in Figure 2.20c.

**First temple version**   At this point we are able to generate the first quite complete
version of the temple model, by aggregation of four rows of columns without gable
with two `ColRowAndGable` positioned at model extremes in the direction of second
coordinate axis.

For this purpose we use, in Script 2.4.5, the predefined function STRUCT, which allows
for hierarchical *aggregation* of sub-assemblies. In particular we catenate three partial
sequences: (a) a first `ColRowAndGable` instance, together with the translation function
which is applied to the subsequent column rows; (b) four catenated pairs *<row,
translation>*; and (c) the final `ColRowAndGable` instance. The actual mechanism of

composition of sub-assemblies given in local coordinate frames by means of intermixed affine transformations will be discussed in Chapter 8.

---

**Script 2.4.5**
```
DEF myColRow = ColRow:4

DEF Temple1 = (STRUCT ~ CAT):<
    <ColRowAndGable, T:2:6>,##:4:<myColRow, T:2:6>,<ColRowAndGable> >
```

---

In Figure 2.21 we can see a projection of the geometric model generated by evaluation of the symbol `Temple1`.

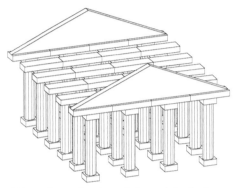

**Figure 2.21**   Dimetric projection of the polyhedral complex `Temple1`

**Secondary beams**   The geometric model of the grid of secondary beams is defined in a very compact way by making use of the Cartesian product operator uniquely provided [BFPP93, PFP96] by the PLaSM language.

Depending on the regularity of repetition of secondary beams in the three coordinate directions, we can build three 1D polyhedral complexes, orderly named `Xsizes`, `Ysizes` and `Zsizes` in Script 2.4.6, and compute their Cartesian product, so generating a lattice of 3D parallelepipeds.

The 1D polyhedral arguments are generated by applying the primitive operator `QUOTE` to three non-empty sequences of non-zero reals. In such sequences, positive numbers correspond to the material cells, whereas negative numbers correspond to the empty space between cells. Notice that negative parameters, to be interpreted as *displacements*, are also used here to locate the complex in the coordinate frame of the temple.

**Final model**   The complete geometric model associated in Script 2.4.6 to the `FinalTemple` symbol is just the aggregation of `Temple1` and `SecondaryBeams` in the same reference frame. In Figure 2.22. three views of the VRML file generated by PLaSM are reported. It would also be possible to easily apply some texture mapping on such a generated model, as discussed in Chapter 10.

**Script 2.4.6**

```
DEF SecondaryBeams = Xsizes * Ysizes * Zsizes
WHERE
    Xsizes = QUOTE:( ##:14:<0.6,-1.2> ),
    Ysizes = QUOTE:( AL:< -0.7, ##:5:<-1,5> > ),
    Zsizes = QUOTE:< -13,0.6 >
END;

DEF FinalTemple = STRUCT: < Temple1, SecondaryBeams >
```

**Figure 2.22**   Three views from the VRML file of the temple generated by PLaSM

# 3

# Elements of linear algebra

A few important concepts of linear algebra are rapidly recalled in this chapter, mostly
without proofs. Our goal is to recall the algebraic framework of computer graphics
and geometric modeling, as well as to discuss the algebraic concepts underlying
the geometric calculus with PLaSM. In particular, we show in this chapter how
PLaSM represents vectors and vector operations. Also, we introduce its functional
representation of linear (invertible) transformations as vector space automorphisms.
This approach is quite different from what is usually done in computer graphics, where
linear transformations of vector spaces are most often represented by normalized
homogeneous matrices. We only assume that the reader is already acquainted with
some matrix calculus.

## 3.1   Vector spaces

A vector space $\mathcal{V}$ over a field $\mathcal{F}$ is a set with two composition rules

$$+ \quad : \mathcal{V} \times \mathcal{V} \to \mathcal{V} \text{ (addition)}$$
$$\cdot \quad : \mathcal{F} \times \mathcal{V} \to \mathcal{V} \text{ (product by a scalar)}$$

such that, for each $\boldsymbol{u}, \boldsymbol{v}, \boldsymbol{w} \in \mathcal{V}$ and for each $\alpha, \beta \in \mathcal{F}$, the rules $+, \cdot$ satisfy the following
axioms:

1. $\boldsymbol{v} + \boldsymbol{w} = \boldsymbol{w} + \boldsymbol{v}$;                                    (commutativity of addition)
2. $\boldsymbol{u} + (\boldsymbol{v} + \boldsymbol{w}) = (\boldsymbol{u} + \boldsymbol{v}) + \boldsymbol{w}$;                         (associativity of addition)
3. there is a $\boldsymbol{0} \in \mathcal{V}$ such that $\boldsymbol{v} + \boldsymbol{0} = \boldsymbol{v}$;             (neutral element of addition)
4. there is a $-\boldsymbol{v} \in \mathcal{V}$ such that $\boldsymbol{v} + (-\boldsymbol{v}) = \boldsymbol{0}$;         (inverse of addition)
5. $\alpha \cdot (\boldsymbol{v} + \boldsymbol{w}) = \alpha \cdot \boldsymbol{v} + \alpha \cdot \boldsymbol{w}$;       (distributivity of addition w.r.t. product)
6. $(\alpha + \beta) \cdot \boldsymbol{v} = \alpha \cdot \boldsymbol{v} + \alpha \cdot \boldsymbol{v}$;       (distributivity of product w.r.t. addition)
7. $\alpha \cdot (\beta \cdot \boldsymbol{v}) = (\alpha\beta) \cdot \boldsymbol{v}$;                        (associativity of product)
8. $1 \cdot \boldsymbol{v} = \boldsymbol{v}$.                                             (neutral element of product)

The dot operator to multiply a vector by a scalar will be dropped in the remainder of
this book, so that the operation will be denoted by the juxtaposition of the arguments.
Hence we write $\alpha(\beta\boldsymbol{v})$ instead of $\alpha \cdot (\beta \cdot \boldsymbol{v})$.

*Geometric Programming for Computer-Aided Design*   Alberto Paoluzzi
© 2003 John Wiley & Sons, Ltd  ISBN 0-471-89942-9

**Example 3.1.1 (Vector space of real matrices)**
Let $\mathcal{M}_n^m(\mathbb{R})$ be the set of $m \times n$ matrices with elements in the field $\mathbb{R}$. An element $A$ in such a set is denoted as

$$A = (\alpha_{ij})$$

Addition and multiplication by a scalar are defined component-wise:

$$A + B = (\alpha_{ij}) + (\beta_{ij}) = (\alpha_{ij} + \beta_{ij})$$

$$\gamma A = \gamma(\alpha_{ij}) = (\gamma\alpha_{ij})$$

To indicate the vector space of matrices with either only one column or only one row, we write, respectively

$$
\begin{aligned}
\mathcal{M}_1^m(\mathbb{R}) &= \mathbb{R}^m &&\text{(column vectors)} \\
\mathcal{M}_n^1(\mathbb{R}) &= \mathbb{R}_n &&\text{(row vectors)} \\
\mathcal{M}_n^m(\mathbb{R}) &= \mathbb{R}_n^m &&\text{(matrices)}
\end{aligned}
$$

**Subspace**   Let $(\mathcal{V}, +, \cdot)$ be a vector space on the field $\mathcal{F}$. We say that $\mathcal{U} \subset \mathcal{V}$ is a *subspace* of $\mathcal{V}$ if $(\mathcal{U}, +, \cdot)$ is a vector space with respect to the same operations. In particular, $\mathcal{U} \subset \mathcal{V}$ is a *subspace* of $\mathcal{V}$ if and only if:

1. $\mathcal{U} \neq \emptyset$;
2. for each $\alpha \in \mathcal{F}$ and $\boldsymbol{u}_1, \boldsymbol{u}_2 \in \mathcal{U}$, $\alpha\boldsymbol{u}_1 + \boldsymbol{u}_2 \in \mathcal{U}$

The *codimension* of a subspace $\mathcal{U} \subset \mathcal{V}$ is defined as $\dim \mathcal{V} - \dim \mathcal{U}$. It is useful to note that the intersection of subspaces is a subspace. In particular, if $\mathcal{U}_1, \mathcal{U}_2$ are subspaces of $\mathcal{V}$, then $\mathcal{U}_1 \cap \mathcal{U}_2$ is a subspace of $\mathcal{V}$.

**Linear combination**   Let $\boldsymbol{v}_1, \boldsymbol{v}_2, \ldots, \boldsymbol{v}_n \in \mathcal{V}$ and $\alpha_1, \alpha_2, \ldots, \alpha_n \in \mathcal{F}$, ($\mathcal{V}$ a vector space on the field $\mathcal{F}$). The vector

$$\alpha_1 \boldsymbol{v}_1 + \cdots + \alpha_n \boldsymbol{v}_n = \sum_{i=1}^{n} \alpha_i \boldsymbol{v}_i \in \mathcal{V}$$

is called a *linear combination* of vectors $\boldsymbol{v}_1, \boldsymbol{v}_2, \ldots, \boldsymbol{v}_n$.

The set of all linear combinations of elements of a set $S \subset \mathcal{V}$ is a subspace of $\mathcal{V}$. Such a subspace is called the *span* of $S$ and is denoted as $\lim S$. If a subspace $\mathcal{U}$ of $\mathcal{V}$ can be generated as the span of a set $S$ of vectors in $\mathcal{V}$, then $S$ is called a *generating set* or a *spanning set* for $\mathcal{U}$.

A set of vectors $\{\boldsymbol{v}_1, \boldsymbol{v}_2, \ldots, \boldsymbol{v}_n\}$ is *linearly independent* if $\sum_{i=1}^{n} \alpha_i \boldsymbol{v}_i = \boldsymbol{0}$ implies that $\alpha_i = 0$ for each $i$. As a consequence, a set of vectors is linearly independent when none of them belongs to the span of the others.

*3.1.1   Bases and coordinates*

When working with vector spaces, the concept of *basis*, a discrete subset of linearly independent elements, is probably the most useful to deal with. In fact, each element of the space can be represented uniquely as linear combination of basis elements. This leads to a *parametrization* of the space, i.e. to representing each element by using a sequence of scalars, called its *coordinates* with respect to the chosen basis.

**Basis**   A set of vectors $\{e_1, e_2, \ldots, e_n\}$ is a *basis* for the vector space $\mathcal{V}$ if the set is linearly independent, and $\mathcal{V} = \text{lin}\{e_1, e_2, \ldots, e_n\}$.

   Some important properties of the bases of a vector space are listed below:

1. each spanning set for $\mathcal{V}$ contains a basis;
2. each minimal spanning set is a basis;
3. each linearly independent set of vectors is contained in a basis;
4. each maximal set[1] of linearly independent vectors is a basis;
5. two bases of $\mathcal{V}$ have the same number $(\dim \mathcal{V})$ of elements, that is called the *dimension* of $\mathcal{V}$.

**Components**   If $(e_1, e_2, \ldots, e_n)$ is an ordered basis for $\mathcal{V}$, then for each $v \in \mathcal{V}$ there exists a *unique* $n$-tuple of scalars $\alpha_1, \alpha_2, \ldots, \alpha_n \in \mathcal{F}$ such that

$$v = \sum_{i=1}^{n} \alpha_i e_i.$$

   The $n$-tuple of scalars $(\alpha_i)$ is called the *components* of $v$ with respect to the ordered basis $(e_1, e_2, \ldots, e_n)$. If such a $n$-tuple were not unique, then $v = \sum \alpha_i e_i = \sum \beta_i e_i$. But this one would imply $\sum (\alpha_i - \beta_i) e_i = 0$, hence $(\alpha_i - \beta_i) = 0$, i.e. $\alpha_i = \beta_i$, for each $i$.

*3.1.2   PLaSM representation of vectors*

An element of a vector space on a field will be represented in PLaSM as a *sequence* of field elements. In this book we usually consider sequences of either real numbers or polynomial functions of bounded degree.

   It is very useful to start our computer representation of a vector space by defining a predicate, i.e. a PLaSM function which returns a truth value, in order to test if the value returned by a language expression is a vector. First, we define a vector as a sequence of real numbers.

```
DEF IsVect = IsSeqOf:IsReal;
```

A more general set of definitions is given in Script 3.1.1, that allows us to consider a sequence of either real numbers or functions as a vector. The PLaSM representation of matrices will be shown in Script 3.3.3.

---

[1]  A set $S$ is said to be *maximal* with respect to some property $\mathcal{P}$ when $S$ satisfies $\mathcal{P}$ and $S$ is not a proper subset of any other set which satisfies $\mathcal{P}$.

**Script 3.1.1** (IsVect predicate definition)
```
DEF IsRealVect = IsSeqOf:IsReal;
DEF IsFunVect = IsSeqOf:IsFun;
DEF IsVect = OR~[IsRealVect,IsFunVect];
```

**Example 3.1.2** (IsVect predicate application)
With the last definition for IsVect the right-hand values will be returned by the
interpreter when evaluating the left-hand expressions. Remember that $\equiv$ means that
the *expression* on the left-hand side evaluates to the *value* on the right-hand side.

```
IsVect:<1.0,2.0,3.0> ≡ TRUE
IsVect:<1,2,3,4,5,6> ≡ TRUE
IsVect:<SIN,COS,TAN> ≡ TRUE
IsVect:<+,-,*,ID,TRANS> ≡ TRUE
IsVect:<+,-,*,1,2,3> ≡ FALSE
```

**Vector operations**    Below the PLaSM implementation of the most common vector
operations in $\mathcal{V}^n$ is given. Notice that the language allows us to work indifferently with
real vectors and with function vectors. Also, most of the following operations work in
vector spaces of any dimension.

In particular, the VectSum and VectDiff, respectively for *vector sum* and *vector
difference*, transpose the argument pair, and finally apply to each generated pair
of numbers either the sum or difference operator, respectively. The operation
ScalarVectProd multiplies a scalar times a vector. To better understand the meaning
of such definitions, the reader should look again at Script 2.1.19.

**Script 3.1.2** (Vector sum, vector difference and product times a scalar)
```
DEF VectSum = AA:+ ~ TRANS;
DEF VectDiff = AA:- ~ TRANS;
DEF ScalarVectProd = AA:* ~ IF:< IsNum ~ S1, DISTL, DISTR >;
```

As always in PLaSM, binary operators can be applied to both prefix and infix. Let
us notice that ScalarVectProd can be indifferently applied to the pair $(\alpha, v)$ and to
the input pair $(v, \alpha)$. If the first element of the pair argument is a number, then the
DISTL operator is applied to the input, else the DISTR operator is used.

```
VectSum:  <<11,12,13>,<4,5,6>> ≡ <15, 17, 19>
VectDiff: <<11,12,13>,<4,5,6>> ≡ <7, 7, 7>
<11,12,13> VectSum  <4,5,6> ≡ <15, 17, 19>
<11,12,13> VectDiff <4,5,6> ≡ <7, 7, 7>
ScalarVectProd:<10, <1,2,3>> ≡ <10, 20, 30>
ScalarVectProd:<<1,2,3>, 10> ≡ <10, 20, 30>
```

**Example 3.1.3** (Vector product in 3D)
Let us compute the vector product of $u, v \in \mathbb{R}^3$. The PLaSM implementation is

straightforward if you remember that $\boldsymbol{u} \times \boldsymbol{v}$ is defined as the determinant of a matrix:

$$\boldsymbol{w} = \boldsymbol{u} \times \boldsymbol{v} = \det \begin{pmatrix} \boldsymbol{e}_1 & \boldsymbol{e}_2 & \boldsymbol{e}_3 \\ u_1 & u_2 & u_3 \\ v_1 & v_2 & v_3 \end{pmatrix} = \begin{vmatrix} \boldsymbol{e}_1 & \boldsymbol{e}_2 & \boldsymbol{e}_3 \\ u_1 & u_2 & u_3 \\ v_1 & v_2 & v_3 \end{vmatrix}.$$

Hence we have:

$$\boldsymbol{w} = \begin{vmatrix} u_2 & u_3 \\ v_2 & v_3 \end{vmatrix} \boldsymbol{e}_1 - \begin{vmatrix} u_1 & u_3 \\ v_1 & v_3 \end{vmatrix} \boldsymbol{e}_2 + \begin{vmatrix} u_1 & u_2 \\ v_1 & v_2 \end{vmatrix} \boldsymbol{e}_3$$

---

**Script 3.1.3**

```
DEF vectProd (u,v::IsVect) = <w1, w2, w3>
    WHERE
        w1 = (u2 * v3) - (u3 * v2),
        w2 = (u3 * v1) - (u1 * v3),
        w3 = (u1 * v2) - (u2 * v1),
        u1 = s1:u, u2 = s2:u, u3 = s3:u,
        v1 = s1:v, v2 = s2:v, v3 = s3:v
    END;

vectProd:<<1,0,0>,<1,1,0>> ≡ <0, 0, 1>
```

---

## 3.2   Affine spaces

The idea of affine space corresponds to that of a set of points where the *displacement* from a point $\boldsymbol{x}$ to another point $\boldsymbol{y}$ is obtained by summing a vector $\boldsymbol{v}$ to the $\boldsymbol{x}$ point.

**Affine space**   A set $\mathcal{A}$ of points is called an *affine space* modeled on the vector space $\mathcal{V}$ if there is a function

$$\mathcal{A} \times \mathcal{V} \to \mathcal{A} : (\boldsymbol{x}, \boldsymbol{v}) \mapsto \boldsymbol{x} + \boldsymbol{v}$$

called *affine action*, with the properties:

1. $(\boldsymbol{x} + \boldsymbol{v}) + \boldsymbol{w} = \boldsymbol{x} + (\boldsymbol{v} + \boldsymbol{w})$   for each $\boldsymbol{x} \in \mathcal{A}$ and each $\boldsymbol{v}, \boldsymbol{w} \in \mathcal{V}$;
2. $\boldsymbol{x} + \boldsymbol{0} = \boldsymbol{x}$ for each $\boldsymbol{x} \in \mathcal{A}$,   where $\boldsymbol{0} \in \mathcal{V}$ is the null vector;
3. for each pair $\boldsymbol{x}, \boldsymbol{y} \in \mathcal{A}$ there is a unique $(\boldsymbol{y} - \boldsymbol{x}) \in \mathcal{V}$ such that

$$\boldsymbol{x} + (\boldsymbol{y} - \boldsymbol{x}) = \boldsymbol{y}.$$

**Dimension**   The affine space $\mathcal{A}$ is said of *dimension* $n$ if modeled on a vector space $\mathcal{V}$ of dimension $n$.

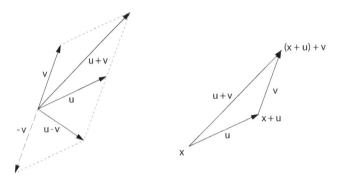

**Figure 3.1**   (a) Vector sum and difference are given by the parallelogram rule
(b) associativity of displacement (point and vector sum) in an affine space

### 3.2.1   Operations on vectors and points

The *addition* of vectors is a primitive operation in a vector space. The *difference* of
vectors is defined through the two primitive operations:

$$v_1 - v_2 = v_1 + (-1)v_2.$$

Addition and difference of vectors are geometrically produced by the parallelogram
rule, shown in Figure 3.1a. Figure 3.1b shows the associative property of the affine
action on a point space. Notice also that:

1. the addition of points is *not* defined;
2. the difference of two points is a vector;
3. the sum of a point and a vector is a point.

The sum of a set $\{v_i\}$ of vectors ($i = 1, \ldots, n$) can be geometrically obtained, in
an affine space, by setting $p_0 = 0$ and $p_i = p_{i-1} + v_i$, so that $\sum_i v_i = p_n - p_0$.

### 3.2.2   Positive, affine and convex combinations

Three types of combinations of vectors or points can be defined. They lead to the
concepts of cones, hyperplanes and convex set, respectively.

**Positive combination**   Let $v_0, \ldots, v_d \in \mathbb{R}^n$ and $\alpha_0, \ldots, \alpha_d \in \mathbb{R}^+ \cup \{0\}$. The vector

$$\alpha_0 v_0 + \cdots + \alpha_d v_d = \sum_{i=0}^{d} \alpha_i v_i$$

is called a *positive combination* of such vectors. The set of all the positive combinations
of $\{v_0, \ldots, v_d\}$ is called the *positive hull* of $\{v_0, \ldots, v_d\}$ and denoted pos $\{v_0, \ldots, v_d\}$.
This set is also called the *cone* generated by the given elements.

**Affine combination** Let $\boldsymbol{p}_0, \ldots, \boldsymbol{p}_d \in \mathbb{E}^n$ and $\alpha_0, \ldots, \alpha_d \in \mathbb{R}$, such that $\alpha_0 + \cdots + \alpha_d = 1$. The point

$$\sum_{i=0}^{d} \alpha_i \boldsymbol{p}_i := \boldsymbol{p}_0 + \sum_{i=1}^{d} \alpha_i (\boldsymbol{p}_i - \boldsymbol{p}_0) \tag{3.1}$$

is called an *affine combination* of the points $\boldsymbol{p}_0, \ldots, \boldsymbol{p}_d$.

The set of all affine combinations of $\{\boldsymbol{p}_0, \ldots, \boldsymbol{p}_d\}$ is an affine subspace, denoted by aff$\{\boldsymbol{p}_0, \ldots, \boldsymbol{p}_d\}$. It is easy to verify that:

$$\text{aff}\,\{\boldsymbol{p}_0, \ldots, \boldsymbol{p}_d\} = \boldsymbol{p}_0 + \text{lin}\,\{\boldsymbol{p}_1 - \boldsymbol{p}_0, \ldots, \boldsymbol{p}_d - \boldsymbol{p}_0\}.$$

The *dimension* of an affine subspace is the dimension of the corresponding linear vector space. Affine subspaces of $\mathbb{E}^d$ with dimensions 0, 1, 2 and $d-1$ are called *points*, *lines*, *planes* and *hyperplanes*, respectively. Affine subspaces are also called *flats*.

Every affine subspace can be described either as the intersection of affine hyperplanes, or as the affine hull of a finite set of points.

**Convex combination** Let $\boldsymbol{p}_0, \ldots, \boldsymbol{p}_d \in \mathbb{E}^n$ and $\alpha_0, \ldots, \alpha_d \in \mathbb{R}^+ \cup \{0\}$, with $\alpha_0 + \cdots + \alpha_d = 1$. The point

$$\alpha_0 \boldsymbol{p}_0 + \cdots + \alpha_d \boldsymbol{p}_d = \sum_{i=0}^{d} \alpha_i \boldsymbol{p}_i$$

is called a *convex combination* of points $\boldsymbol{p}_0, \ldots, \boldsymbol{p}_d$.

A convex combinations is both affine and positive. The set of all convex combinations of $\{\boldsymbol{p}_0, \ldots, \boldsymbol{p}_d\}$ is a convex set, called *convex hull* of $\{\boldsymbol{p}_0, \ldots, \boldsymbol{p}_d\}$, and is denoted by conv$\{\boldsymbol{p}_0, \ldots, \boldsymbol{p}_d\}$.

**Example 3.2.1 (Convex hull)**
In PLaSM, an operator which generates the convex hull of a discrete set of points can be easily defined by using the primitive function MKPOL. We remember (see Section 1.5.1) that this one needs as input a triplet < points, cells, polyhedra >, with a sequence of points, a sequence of convex cells and a sequence of polyhedral cells, respectively.

In order to generate the set

$$\text{conv}\,\{\boldsymbol{p}_i \in \mathbb{E}^d | i = 1, \ldots, n\}$$

of a discrete set of points, a ConvexHull operator can be defined in a very straightforward way, as done in Script 3.2.1. We like to note that the *beneath-beyond* algorithm [Ede87], used by PLaSM to compute the convex hull, is actually hidden from the user by the language interface.

According with the *dimension-independent* nature of the language, the ConvexHull function may be applied to sequences of points in Euclidean spaces of arbitrary finite dimension. In Figure 3.2 are shown the Monge projections of the convex hull generated by the last row of Script 3.2.1.

**Script 3.2.1**

```
DEF ConvexHull (points::IsSeq) = MKPOL:< points, <1..LEN:points>, <<1>> >

ConvexHull:<<0,0>,<1,0>,<0,1>,<1,1>,<2,3>,<0.5,4>>
ConvexHull:<<0,0,2>,<1,0,-1>,<0,1,1>,<1,1,0.5>,<2,3,0>,<0.5,4,-1.5>>
```

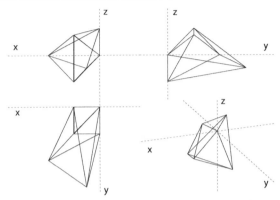

**Figure 3.2**  Monge projections of the convex hull of the set of points of $\mathbb{E}^3$ given in Script 3.2.1

*3.2.3  Linear, affine and convex independence*

A set of *vectors* is said to be *linearly independent* if none of them can be obtained as a linear combination of the other ones.

Analogously, a set of *points* is said *affinely/convexely independent* if none of them can be obtained as an affine/convex combination of the other ones, respectively.

**Example 3.2.2 (Affine combination)**
The set of affine combinations of two affinely independent (i.e. distinct) points $p_0, p_1 \in \mathbb{E}^n$, $p_0 \neq p_1$, is the line through them:

$$
\begin{aligned}
\alpha_0 p_0 + \alpha_1 p_1 &:= (1 - \alpha_1)p_0 + \alpha_1 p_1 \\
&= p_0 + \alpha_1(p_1 - p_0)
\end{aligned}
$$

Remember that a difference of points is a vector, and that the sum of a point and a vector is a point.

**Example 3.2.3 (Convex combination)**
The set of convex combinations of two affinely independent (i.e. distinct) points $p_0, p_1 \in \mathbb{E}^n$, $p_0 \neq p_1$, is the line segment joining $p_0$ with $p_1$:

$$
\begin{aligned}
p(\beta) &= (1 - \beta)p_0 + \beta p_1 \\
&= p_0 + \beta(p_1 - p_0), \qquad 0 \leq \beta \leq 1
\end{aligned}
$$

Notice that:

$$
p(0) = p_0, \quad \text{and} \quad p(1) = p_1.
$$

The set of affine combinations of three affinely independent (i.e. not aligned) points is their plane. The set of convex combinations of three affinely independent points is their triangle, i.e. the triangle whose vertices are those points.

**Example 3.2.4 (Plane for three points)**
A non-trivial geometric construction is done in Script 3.2.2 using quite typical graphics methods. The resulting object is shown in Figure 3.3. In particular, we give the definition of a `plane` function, with with parameters `point0`, `point1` and `point2`. This function returns as output a triplet constituted by the `normal` vector, by `point0` and by a transparent rectangle representing the plane `geometry`. We leave to the reader the task of reading and interpreting the given PLaSM code. We notice that (a) the `optimize` function, given in Script 6.5.2, that actually performs some "flattening" of the internal data structure, is needed to correctly export to VRML the generated rectangle, and (b) that the PLaSM libraries `'colors'` and `'vectors'` must firstly be loaded in the PLaSM environment.[2]

---

**Script 3.2.2 (2-plane in $\mathbb{E}^3$)**

```
DEF plane (point0, point1, point2::IsPoint) = < normal, point0, geometry >
WHERE
    normal = (unitVect ~ vectProd):< v1, v2 >,
    v1 = point1 vectDiff point0,   v2 = point2 vectDiff point0,
    axis = <0,0,1> vectProd normal,
    side1 = vectNorm:v1,   side2 = vectNorm:v2,
    angle = ACOS:(<0,0,1> innerProd unitVect:normal),
    geometry = (Optimize
        ~ T:<1,2,3>:point0
        ~ Rotn:< angle, axis >
        ~ EMBED:1
        ~ T:<1,2>:< -1*side1,-1*side2 >
        ~ CUBOID): <2*side1, 2*side2 >
    MATERIAL Transparentmaterial:<GREEN, 0.8>
END;

DEF out = (S3 ~ plane):<<0,0,0>,<1,0,0>,<1,1,1>> STRUCT MKframe;
```

---

The functions for vector calculus named `unitVect`, `vectProd`, `vectDiff`, `vectNorm`, `innerProd` and `Rotn` are given in following examples of this chapter, but their meaning can easily be forecast by their name. `MKframe` is the constructor of the model of the 3D standard basis, and is given in Script 6.5.3. The `MATERIAL`, `GREEN` and `Transparentmaterial` symbols are defined in the `'colors'` library.

---

[2] Currently, this loading is automatically done at the starting of the interpreter.

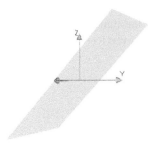

**Figure 3.3**  Plane passing for $(0,0,0)$, $(1,0,0)$ and $(1,1,1)$

### *3.2.4  Convex coordinates*

Given a point $\boldsymbol{p} \in \operatorname{conv}\{\boldsymbol{p_0}, \ldots, \boldsymbol{p_d}\}$, the scalars $\alpha_0, \ldots, \alpha_d$ such that:

$$\boldsymbol{p} = \alpha_0 \boldsymbol{p_0} + \cdots + \alpha_d \boldsymbol{p_d}.$$

are called *convex coordinates* of $\boldsymbol{p}$. Convex coordinates are *unique* if the points $\boldsymbol{p_0}, \ldots, \boldsymbol{p_d}$ are affinely independent.

### Example 3.2.5 (Triangle through 3 points)

Given four points $\boldsymbol{p}, \boldsymbol{q}, \boldsymbol{r}, \boldsymbol{s} \in \mathbb{E}^2$, with $\boldsymbol{p}, \boldsymbol{q}, \boldsymbol{r}$ non-colinear, there are two disjoint possibilities:

$$\boldsymbol{s} \in \operatorname{conv}\{\boldsymbol{p}, \boldsymbol{q}, \boldsymbol{r}\}, \qquad \boldsymbol{s} \notin \operatorname{conv}\{\boldsymbol{p}, \boldsymbol{q}, \boldsymbol{r}\}.$$

In the first case there exists a triplet of numbers $(\alpha, \beta, \gamma)$, with $\alpha + \beta + \gamma = 1$ and $0 \leq \alpha, \beta, \gamma \leq 1$, such that:

$$\boldsymbol{s} = \alpha \boldsymbol{p} + \beta \boldsymbol{q} + \gamma \boldsymbol{r}. \tag{3.2}$$

Notice that the product of a point by a scalar has not been defined. However, equation (3.2) may be given meaning as follows:

$$
\begin{aligned}
\boldsymbol{s} &= \alpha \boldsymbol{p} + \beta \boldsymbol{q} + \gamma \boldsymbol{r} \\
&= (1 - \beta - \gamma)\boldsymbol{p} + \beta \boldsymbol{q} + \gamma \boldsymbol{r} \\
&= \boldsymbol{p} + \beta(\boldsymbol{q} - \boldsymbol{p}) + \gamma(\boldsymbol{r} - \boldsymbol{p})
\end{aligned}
$$

Notice also that the three vertices $\boldsymbol{p}, \boldsymbol{q}, \boldsymbol{r}$ are associated with convex coordinates $(1,0,0)$, $(0,1,0)$ and $(0,0,1)$, respectively.

### Example 3.2.6 (Convex coordinates and volume)

The convex coordinates $(\alpha, \beta, \gamma)$ of a point $\boldsymbol{s} \in \operatorname{conv}(\boldsymbol{p}, \boldsymbol{q}, \boldsymbol{r}) \subset \mathbb{E}^d$ can be defined as the ratios between the areas of suitable triangles. In particular:

$$\alpha = \frac{\operatorname{area}(\boldsymbol{s}, \boldsymbol{q}, \boldsymbol{r})}{\operatorname{area}(\boldsymbol{p}, \boldsymbol{q}, \boldsymbol{r})}, \quad \beta = \frac{\operatorname{area}(\boldsymbol{p}, \boldsymbol{s}, \boldsymbol{r})}{\operatorname{area}(\boldsymbol{p}, \boldsymbol{q}, \boldsymbol{r})}, \quad \gamma = \frac{\operatorname{area}(\boldsymbol{p}, \boldsymbol{q}, \boldsymbol{s})}{\operatorname{area}(\boldsymbol{p}, \boldsymbol{q}, \boldsymbol{r})}.$$

as shown in Figure 3.4.

This property immediately generalizes to any convex set in any $d$-dimensional space, by using ratios of volumes of $d$-simplices.

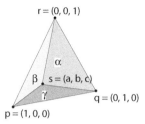

**Figure 3.4**   Interpretation of convex coordinates as ratios of triangle areas

A few examples of both affine or convex independence follow:

1. two distinct points are independent in any $\mathbb{E}^d$, $d \geq 1$;
2. three non-colinear points are independent in any $\mathbb{E}^d$, $d \geq 2$;
3. four non-coplanar points are independent in any $\mathbb{E}^d$, $d \geq 3$;
4. $d+1$ points not belonging to the same affine subspace of codimension 1
   (i.e. dimension $d-1$) are independent in any $\mathbb{E}^D$, $D \geq d$;
5. $m$ points are convexely independent if none of them is in the convex hull of
   the other $m-1$ points.

**Example 3.2.7 (Convex polygon)**
The vertices of a convex polygon in $\mathbb{E}^2$ are convexly independent, as none of them
can be generated as a convex combination of the others. This is easy to see, since each
vertex is external to the convex hull of the other vertices (see Figure 3.5a). All of the
vertices of a convex polyhedron in $\mathbb{E}^d$ are convexely independent for the same reason.
Notice that points in conv $\{p_0, \ldots, p_n\}$, with $p_0, \ldots, p_n \in \mathbb{E}^d$, have *non unique*
convex coordinates when $d < n$ (see, e.g. Figure 3.5b).

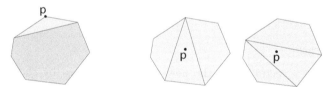

**Figure 3.5**   (a) Each vertex of a convex polygon is external to the convex hull of
the others (b) Convex coordinates of an internal point are not unique when the point
is contained in more than one simplex

**Parametric form of affine sets**   The affine subspace generated by $d+1$ affinely
independent points $p_0, p_1, \ldots, p_d \in \mathbb{E}^n$, also called a *d-flat*, can be written in
*parametric form* as an affine function of $d$ independent real parameters:

$$S(\alpha_1, \ldots, \alpha_d) = \{p \in \mathbb{E}^n \mid p = p_0 + \alpha_1(p_1 - p_0) + \cdots + \alpha_d(p_d - p_0)\}$$

**Example 3.2.8 (Parametric segment)**
Consider the segment in $\mathbb{E}^2$ joining $p_0 = (p_{0x}, p_{0y})$ with $p_1 = (p_{1x}, p_{1y})$:

$$L(\alpha) = \{p \in \mathbb{E}^2 \mid p = p_0 + \alpha(p_1 - p_0)\}.$$

**Example 3.2.9 (Parametric plane)**
A plane (or "2-flat") in $\mathbb{E}^n$ generated by points $q, r, s$ is defined as:

$$P(\alpha, \beta) = \{p \in \mathbb{E}^n \mid p = (1 - \beta)((1 - \alpha)q + \alpha r) + \beta s\} \qquad (3.3)$$

A direct implementation of definition (3.3) is given in Script 3.2.3. It is a quite advanced example (for *advanced readers* only) that makes use of bilinear *transfinite interpolation* (see Section 12.5). It is interesting to notice that it generates a 2-flat in $\mathbb{E}^d$, depending on the number $d$ of coordinates of the actual values for p0, p1 and p2 parameters. Notice also that the vector calculus functions scalarVectProd and vectSum, defined in this chapter, are now working in a functional vector space. The IsPoint predicate is just an alias for IsVect. The geometric object generated in $\mathbb{E}^3$ is quite similar to the one generated by Script 3.2.2.

---

**Script 3.2.3 (2-plane in $\mathbb{E}^d$, $2 \leq d$)**
```
DEF IsPoint = IsVect;

DEF mapping (p0,p1,p2::IsPoint) = CONS:(
   ((K:1 - S2) scalarVectProd (term0 vectSum term1)) vectSum term2)
WHERE
   term0 = (K:1 - S1) scalarVectProd AA:K:p0,
   term1 = S1 scalarVectProd AA:K:p1,
   term2 = S2 scalarVectProd AA:K:p2
END;

DEF out = MAP:(mapping:<<0,0,0>,<1,0,0>,<1,1,1>>):(CUBOID:<1,1>)
   MATERIAL Transparentmaterial:< GREEN, 0.8>
   STRUCT MKframe
```

---

*3.2.5   Euclidean spaces*

Let now introduce in a vector space the new structure induced by the functions of *norm* and *inner product*, also called *scalar product*, which generalize the concepts of length and angle, respectively. A (real) vector space equipped with norm and inner product is said to be a *Euclidean space*.

**Norm**   Let $\mathcal{V}$ be a real vector space. A *norm* on $\mathcal{V}$ is defined as a function $\mathcal{V} \to \mathbb{R} : u \mapsto \|u\|$, which satisfies the following axioms for each $u, v \in \mathcal{V}$ and $\alpha \in \mathbb{R}$:

1. $\|u\| \geq 0$,   with $\|u\| = 0$ if and only if $u = 0$;   (positivity)
2. $\|\alpha u\| = |\alpha|\|u\|$   (scalar multiple)
3. $\|u\| + \|v\| \geq \|u + v\|$   (triangle inequality)

**Inner product**   A *Euclidean inner product* on $\mathcal{V}$ is a bilinear function $\cdot : \mathcal{V} \times \mathcal{V} \to \mathbb{R}$ which satisfies the following properties for each $u, v, w \in \mathcal{V}$ and $\alpha \in \mathbb{R}$:

1. $v \cdot (u + w) = v \cdot u + v \cdot w$   (distributivity w.r.t. vector addition)

2. $(\alpha v) \cdot u = \alpha(v \cdot u)$            (associativity w.r.t. scalar product)
3. $v \cdot w = w \cdot v$                   (commutativity)
4. $u \cdot u \geq 0$, with $u \cdot u = 0$ iff $u = 0$.     (positivity)

The inner product of vectors $u$ and $v$ is defined so that the inner product and norm functions are linked by the equality:

$$u \cdot u =: \|u\|^2$$

**Orthogonal vectors**   Let $u, v \in \mathcal{V}$, where $\mathcal{V}$ is an inner product space. We say that $u$ is orthogonal to $v$ when

$$u \cdot v = 0$$

Notice that the null vector is orthogonal to all vectors, since $0 \cdot u = 0$ for each $u \in \mathcal{V}$. Two subspaces $U, V$ of a vector space $\mathcal{V}$ equipped with an inner product are said to be *orthogonal* if each vector in $U$ is orthogonal to each vector in $V$. A set of vectors $(e_i)$ is said to be *orthonormal* when

$$e_i \cdot e_j = \begin{array}{ll} 1 & \text{if } i = j, \\ 0 & \text{if } i \neq j. \end{array}$$

Each set of orthonormal vectors in an inner product space $\mathcal{V}$ is linearly independent. Hence, there is no orthonormal set having more than $n = \dim \mathcal{V}$ elements.

**Euclidean point space**   An affine space modeled on the vector space $\mathbb{R}^n$ and equipped with the standard inner product is called *Euclidean space* $\mathbb{E}^n$. It can be proved (see e.g. [LD93], pages 122–133) that a two dimensional affine space with the additional structure given by an Euclidean inner product on the underlying vector space satisfies the congruence postulates and Hilbert's parallel postulate. Such an affine space is hence a good algebraic model for the Euclidean plane.

**Cartesian coordinates**   A *Cartesian coordinate system* in an Euclidean space $\mathbb{E}^n$ modeled on a vector space $\mathbb{R}^n$ consists of a *orthonormal basis*

$$(e_i) = (e_1, \ldots, e_n)$$

in $\mathbb{R}^n$, together with a point $o \in \mathbb{E}^n$ called the *origin*. In such a system the components of a vector $u$ are $u_i = u \cdot e_i$. Analogously, the coordinates of a point $x$ are:

$$x_i = (x - o) \cdot e_i.$$

**Linear forms and the dual space**

The linear functions from a vector space $\mathcal{V}$ into $\mathbb{R}$ are called *linear forms*. A linear form $\psi : \mathcal{V} \to \mathbb{R}$ satisfies the following properties for each $u, w \in \mathcal{V}$ and $\alpha \in \mathbb{R}$. Notice that the operations on the left-hand side are in $\mathcal{V}$, whereas the operations on the right-hand side are in $\mathbb{R}$:

1. $\psi(\boldsymbol{u} + \boldsymbol{w}) = \psi(\boldsymbol{u}) + \psi(\boldsymbol{w})$,                    (addition)
2. $\psi(\alpha\boldsymbol{u}) = \alpha\psi(\boldsymbol{u})$                              (product by a scalar)

The vector space $\operatorname{lin}(\mathcal{V}; \mathbb{R})$ of linear forms on $\mathcal{V}$ is called the *dual space* of $\mathcal{V}$ and is denoted as $\mathcal{V}^*$. The elements of this space are also called *covectors*. It is easy to see that $\mathcal{V}^*$ is isomorphic to $\mathcal{V}$. The duality relationship is symmetric, i.e. $(\mathcal{V}^*)^* = \mathcal{V}$.

**Representation theorem**    Let $\psi \in \mathcal{V}^*$, i.e. let $\psi : \mathcal{V} \to \mathbb{R}$ be a linear form. Then there exists a unique vector $\boldsymbol{a} \in \mathcal{V}$ such that

$$\psi(\boldsymbol{v}) = \boldsymbol{a} \cdot \boldsymbol{v} \qquad (3.4)$$

for each vector $\boldsymbol{v} \in \mathcal{V}$. In other words, it is possible to represent a linear mapping $\psi \in \mathcal{V}^*$ by means of the scalar product with its image $\boldsymbol{a} \in \mathcal{V}$ in the space isomorphism $\mathcal{V}^* \to \mathcal{V}$.

**Example 3.2.10 (Plane in 3D space)**
A plane $P$ in $\mathbb{E}^3$, defined by the Cartesian equation

$$ax + by + cz + d = 0,$$

can be seen as the set of points defined by

$$P = \boldsymbol{o} - \nu^{-1}(d),$$

where $\boldsymbol{o}$ is is the origin of the Cartesian reference system, and $\nu$ is a covector in $\operatorname{lin}(\mathbb{R}^3; \mathbb{R})$. With a more explicit notation we also have:

$$P = \{\boldsymbol{p} \in \mathbb{E}^3 | \ \nu(\boldsymbol{p} - \boldsymbol{o}) = -d\},$$

where $\nu(\boldsymbol{p} - \boldsymbol{o}) = \boldsymbol{n} \cdot (\boldsymbol{p} - \boldsymbol{o})$, by the representation theorem above. The vector $\boldsymbol{n} = (a, b, c)$ is said to be the *normal vector* to the $P$ plane.

**Example 3.2.11**
To compute the norm $\|\boldsymbol{v}\|$ of a vector $\boldsymbol{v}$ we need to define a "square" function, denoted as SQR, which is not predefined in PLaSM. A function SQRT for computing the square root is instead predefined. A UnitVect function is given to normalize a given non-zero vector. The ScalarVectProd, given in Script 3.1.2, computes the scalar product of a scalar times a vector. Some examples of computation are also given in the following script. In particular, the InnerProd function is used both prefix and infix.

## 3.3    Linear transformations and tensors

The concept of tensor is very important for the PLaSM language described in this book. In such a language a geometric transformation (e.g. a rotation, a translation, a scaling) of an Euclidean space is just represented as a tensor. Tensors are applied to geometric objects and assemblies as functions; last but not least, pipelines of different transformations can be transformed into a single function by functional composition.

**Script 3.2.4**

```
DEF SQR = ID * ID;
DEF VectNorm = SQRT ~ + ~ AA:Sqr;
DEF UnitVect (v::IsVect) = ScalarVectProd:<1 / VectNorm:v, v>;
DEF InnerProd = + ~ AA:* ~ TRANS;

UnitVect:<10,20,30> ≡ < 0.26726124191242434, 0.5345224838248487,
    0.8017837257372731 >
(VectNorm ~ UnitVect):<10,20,30> ≡ 0.9999999999999999
InnerProd:<<11,12,13>,<4,5,6>> ≡ 182
<11,12,13> InnerProd <4,5,6> ≡ 182
```

**Linear transformation**   A *linear transformation* $T : \mathcal{V}_1 \to \mathcal{V}_2$ is a function between vector spaces that preserves the linear combinations:

$$T(\alpha_1 v_1 + \cdots + \alpha_n v_n) = \alpha_1 T v_1 + \cdots + \alpha_n T v_n.$$

**Affine transformation**   A *affine transformation* $T : \mathbb{E}_1 \to \mathbb{E}_2$ is a function between affine spaces that preserves the affine action:

$$T(x + \alpha(y - x)) = Tx + \alpha(Ty - Tx)$$

An affine transformation extends naturally to the underlying vector space, by defining

$$Tv = Ty - Tx, \quad \text{where} \quad v = y - x.$$

**Tensors**   The term *tensor* is here used as a synonym of *invertible linear transformation* $T$ from a vector space $\mathcal{V}$ to itself. In other words, a tensor is a linear function $T$ which maps the vector $u$ to the vector $Tu$.

The set of all tensors on $\mathcal{V}$ is a vector space, denoted as $\lin \mathcal{V}$, if addition of tensors and product of a tensor by a scalar are defined as:

$$\begin{aligned} (S + T)v &= Sv + Tv, \\ (\alpha S)v &= \alpha(Sv). \end{aligned}$$

The *null tensor* $0$ and the *identity tensor* $I$ map each vector $v \in \mathcal{V}$ to the null vector and to itself, respectively:

$$\begin{aligned} 0v &= 0, \\ Iv &= v. \end{aligned}$$

*3.3.1   Tensor operations*

**Product**   The *product* of tensors $S, T \in \lin \mathcal{V}$ is defined as *composition* of functions:

$$ST = S \circ T.$$

Hence $(ST)v = S(Tv)$ for each $v \in \mathcal{V}$.

For the products of a tensor $S$ with itself we have

$$S^2 := SS, \qquad S^3 := S^2 S, \qquad \text{etc.}$$

### Example 3.3.1 (Tensor product)

In PLaSM, invertible linear and affine transformations are represented, in a very natural way, as space automorphism, i.e. as invertible transformations of a space into itself. Therefore the *product* of tensors is given as *composition* of functions. In Script 3.3.1 we show that a rotation with axis parallel to the $z$ axis and passing for $(0.5, 0.5, 0)$ can be espressed as the composition of elementary transformations of translation and rotation about the $z$ axis.

---

### Script 3.3.1 (Tensor product)

```
DEF tensor = T:<1,2>:<0.5,0.5> ~ R:<1,2>:(PI/4) ~ T:<1,2>:<-0.5,-0.5>;

DEF rotatedCube = tensor:(CUBOID:<1,1,1>);

VRML:rotatedCube:'out.wrl'
```

---

**Transpose**  The *transpose* $S^T$ of $S \in \text{lin} \mathcal{V}$ is the unique tensor in $\text{lin} \mathcal{V}$ such that, for each $u, v \in \mathcal{V}$,

$$Su \cdot v = u \cdot S^T v$$

The transposition of tensors satisfies the properties:

$$
\begin{aligned}
(S + T)^T &= S^T + T^T, \\
(ST)^T &= T^T S^T, \\
(S^T)^T &= S.
\end{aligned}
$$

**Tensor decomposition**  A tensor $X$ is said *symmetric* if $X = X^T$. It is said to be *skew* if $X = -X^T$. Each tensor $X$ can be expressed *uniquely* as the sum of a symmetric and a skew part:

$$X = E + W$$

where

$$E = \frac{1}{2}(X + X^T), \qquad W = \frac{1}{2}(X - X^T).$$

A PLaSM implementation of the tensor decomposition in a symmetric and a skew part is given in Script ??.

**Tensor product of vectors**  The *tensor product* of two vectors $a, b \in \mathcal{V}$ is the tensor $a \otimes b \in \mathrm{lin}\,\mathcal{V}$ that maps a vector $v$ to the vector $(b \cdot v)a$. More formally:

$$\otimes : \mathcal{V}^2 \to \mathrm{lin}\,\mathcal{V} : (a, b) \mapsto a \otimes b$$

such that, for each $v \in \mathcal{V}$

$$(a \otimes b)v = (b \cdot v)a.$$

**Properties of tensor product of vectors**  A few important properties of tensor product follow:

1. $(a \otimes b)^T = (b \otimes a)$;
2. $(a \otimes b)(c \otimes d) = (b \cdot c)a \otimes d$;
3. $(e_i \otimes e_i)(e_j \otimes e_j) = \begin{array}{ll} \mathbf{0}, & i \neq j, \\ e_i \otimes e_i & i = j; \end{array}$
4. $\sum_i e_i \otimes e_i = I$.

**Directional decomposition of vectors**  Let $e, v \in \mathcal{V}$, with $e$ a unit vector. The tensor $e \otimes e$ applied to the vector $v$ gives the projection of $v$ onto the $e$ direction:

$$(e \otimes e)v = (e \cdot v)e$$

Conversely, the tensor $I - e \otimes e$, when applied to $v$, gives

$$(I - e \otimes e)v = v - (e \cdot v)e,$$

which is the projection of $v$ onto the linear subspace orthogonal to $e$.

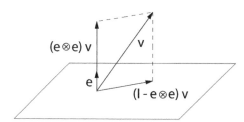

**Figure 3.6**  Directional and orthogonal projections of a vector

**Example 3.3.2 (Directional decomposition)**
The directional decomposition of a vector is implemented in Script 3.3.2, where a dimension-independent solution is given, according to the true nature of the PLaSM language. The VectDiff, VectSum and ScalarVectProd operations are given in Script 3.1.2. The InnerProd and UnitVect operations are defined in Script 3.2.4. The last PLaSM expression aims to show that the vector addition of the two generated vector projections returns the original vector.

---

**Script 3.3.2**

```
    DEF DirProject (e::Isvect)(v::Isvect) =
      (UnitVect:e InnerProd v) ScalarVectProd UnitVect:e;
    DEF OrthoProject (e::Isvect)(v::Isvect) =
      v VectDiff DirProject:(UnitVect:e):v;

    DirProject:<1,1,0,0>:<10,15,20,25>  ≡ <12.5, 12.5, 0.0, 0.0>;
    OrthoProject:<1,1,0,0>:<10,15,20,25> ≡ <-2.5, 2.5, 20.0, 25.0>;

    (VectSum ~ [DirProject:<1,1,0,0>, OrthoProject:<1,1,0,0>]):<10,15,20,25>
      ≡ <10.0, 15.0, 20.0, 25.0>;
```

---

*3.3.2   Coordinate representation*

When an orthonormal basis $(e_i)$ in $\mathcal{V}$ is given, the components $S_{ij}$ of a tensor $\boldsymbol{S} \in \operatorname{lin} \mathcal{V}$ are defined as

$$S_{ij} = e_i \cdot \boldsymbol{S} e_j.$$

By this definition, the vector $\boldsymbol{v} = \boldsymbol{S}\boldsymbol{u}$ can be represented component-wise with respect to the $(e_i)$ basis as $(v_i)$, with

$$v_i = \sum_j S_{ij} u_j.$$

As a matter of fact, by the expression of the component of $\boldsymbol{v}$ with respect to the basis and by the linearity of both the tensor $\boldsymbol{S}$ and the scalar product, we have

$$
\begin{aligned}
v_i &= e_i \cdot \boldsymbol{v} = e_i \cdot \boldsymbol{S}\boldsymbol{u} \\
&= e_i \cdot \boldsymbol{S} \sum_j (e_j \cdot \boldsymbol{u}) e_j = e_i \cdot \boldsymbol{S} \sum_j u_j e_j \\
&= \sum_j u_j (e_i \cdot \boldsymbol{S} e_j) = \sum_j S_{ij} u_j.
\end{aligned}
$$

It is also easy to give a coordinate decomposition of a tensor $\boldsymbol{S}$ as a combination of tensor components $S_{ij}$ with the basis $(e_i \otimes e_j)$ of $\operatorname{lin}\mathcal{V}$ induced by the basis $(e_i)$ of $\mathcal{V}$:

$$\boldsymbol{S} = \sum_{ij} S_{ij} e_i \otimes e_j$$

as well as to give the components of a tensor product of vectors

$$(\boldsymbol{a} \otimes \boldsymbol{b})_{ij} = a_i b_j. \tag{3.5}$$

equation 3.5 will be useful when deriving the tensor product expression of a surface in parametric form (see Section 12.3).

**Matrix of a tensor**   The components of a tensor $\boldsymbol{S} \in \operatorname{lin}\mathcal{V}$ can be assembled in a square matrix, denotated as $[\boldsymbol{S}]$. If $\mathcal{V} = \mathbb{R}^d$, then we have

$$
[\boldsymbol{S}] = \begin{bmatrix}
S_{11} & S_{12} & \cdots & S_{1d} \\
S_{21} & S_{22} & \cdots & S_{2d} \\
\cdots & \cdots & \cdots & \cdots \\
S_{d1} & S_{d2} & \cdots & S_{dd}
\end{bmatrix}
$$

A matrix $A = (a_{ij})$ is *transposed* when its rows are interchanged with its columns, and vice versa. The transposed matrix is denoted as $A^T = (a_{ji})$.

A few useful properties of tensor matrices follow:

1. $[S^T] = [S]^T$ (transposition)
2. $[ST] = [S][T]$ (product)

3. $[I] = \begin{bmatrix} 1 & 0 & \cdots & 0 \\ 0 & 1 & \cdots & 0 \\ \cdots & \cdots & \cdots & \cdots \\ 0 & 0 & \cdots & 1 \end{bmatrix}$ (identity)

*3.3.3 PLaSM matrix representation*

A matrix in $\mathcal{M}_m^n$ is represented in PLaSM as a sequence of $n$ sequences of length $m$. In other words, a matrix is represented by rows. A predicate IsMat is therefore given to verify if a data structure is a sequence of sequences of either real numbers or functions. The predicate also tests if all the component elements (rows) have the same length (number of columns). The predicates IsRealVect e IsFunVect, which test if an object is a sequence of reals or functions, respectively, were defined in Script 3.1.1.

---

**Script 3.3.3 (IsMat predicate)**

```
DEF IsMat = AND ~ [OR ~ [IsSeqOf:IsRealVect,
                         IsSeqOf:IsFunVect],
                  EQ ~ AA:LEN];
```

---

**Example 3.3.3 (PLaSM matrix)**
A matrix $A \in \mathbb{R}_3^3$ can be represented by a PLaSM symbol (name), as shown in Script 3.3.4.

---

**Script 3.3.4**

```
DEF A = <
   < 1.0, 2.0, 3.0 >,
   < 4.0, 5.0, 6.0 >,
   < 7.0, 8.0, 9.0 >>;

IsMat:A ≡ TRUE
```

---

For example, the identity matrix $[I] \in \mathbb{R}_3^3$ may be defined as:

```
DEF Identity = <<1, 0, 0>, <0, 1, 0>, <0, 0, 1>>
```

A matrix can also be directly used without being named, as we show in several examples in the remainder of this chapter.

**Example 3.3.4 (Identity matrix)**
A function IDNT is defined here. This function, when applied to an integer $n$, returns the identity matrix $I \in \mathbb{R}_n^n$. The function IDNT is defined in pure FL style, using

neither iteration nor recursion.

We utilize the following algorithmic scheme. First, the set $N^2 = N \times N$ is built, where $N = \{1, \dots, n\}$. Then we apply to each pair $(i, j) \in N^2$ the Kröneker's function, defined as

$$\delta : N^2 \to \{0, 1\} : (i, j) \mapsto \begin{array}{ll} 1 & \text{if } i = j \\ 0 & \text{if } i \neq j \end{array}$$

which returns either 0 or 1 depending on the identity of input pairs. The `cart` operator, that executes the Cartesian product of finite sets, is given in Script 2.1.17.

---

**Script 3.3.5 (Identity matrix (1))**

```
DEF IDNT (n::IsIntPos) = (AA~AA):Kroneker:(cart:<1..n,1..n>)
WHERE
    Kroneker = IF:<EQ, K:1, K:0>
END

IDNT:4 ≡ <
    <1, 0, 0, 0>,
    <0, 1, 0, 0>,
    <0, 0, 1, 0>,
    <0, 0, 0, 1> >
```

---

A simpler implementation of the `IDNT` operator is given in Script 3.3.6, where the strong connection between the vertices of a simplex (see Section 4.5) and the identity matrix as a set of unit vectors is exploited. The `RTAIL` function, which returns the elements of a sequence except the last one, is given in Script 4.2.5.

---

**Script 3.3.6 (Identity matrix (2))**

```
DEF IDNT (n::IsIntPos) = (RTAIL ~ S1 ~ UKPOL ~ SIMPLEX):n;
```

---

**Predefined matrix operators**    Some predefined matrix operators are available in PLaSM. In particular, the `TRANS` function is a unary operator that returns the transpose when applied to a matrix. Analogously, the `INV` unary operator returns the inverse of its argument when applied to an invertible square matrix. Otherwise it returns an exception.

```
TRANS:<<1,2,3>,<4,5,6>> ≡ <<1, 4>, <2, 5>, <3, 6>>

INV:<<2,0,0>,<0,2,0>,<0,0,2>> ≡
    <<0.5, 0.0, 0.0>, <0.0, 0.5, 0.0>, <0.0, 0.0, 0.5>>
```

Predefined binary operators are available for *addition*, *difference* and *product* of compatible matrices.

Let $A = (a_{ij})$ and $B = (b_{ij})$ in $\mathbb{R}_m^\ell$, and $C = (c_{ij})$ in $\mathbb{R}_n^m$. The binary matrix operations have the standard component-wise meaning

$$A + B = (a_{ij} + b_{ij}), \qquad A - B = (a_{ij} - b_{ij}), \qquad BC = \left(\sum_{k=1}^{m} b_{ik} c_{kj}\right)$$

Such operations are denoted in PLaSM with the symbols +, - and *, respectively. As always in the language, a binary operator can be used as either prefix or infix, as shown in the following examples. The function IDNT, when applied to an integer $n$, returns the identity matrix $[I] \in \mathbb{R}_n^n$. This function is not primitive in PLaSM. It is defined in Script 3.3.5. Notice that predefined algebraic operators are implicitly lifted (see below) when infix between functions: i.e.:

```
IDNT + IDNT ≡ + ~ [IDNT, IDNT]
```

**Function lifting and raising**    RAISE and LIFT are two primitive FL combining forms defined by the following equational semantics. The RAISE combining form is used to allow overloaded use of operators over both numbers and functions. For example, the PLaSM algebraic operators like "+" and "*", are actually *raised*-up versions of their numeric counterparts.

---

**Script 3.3.7** (LIFT and RAISE combining forms)
```
LIFT:f:<f₁,...,fₙ> ≡ f ~ [f₁,...,fₙ]

RAISE:f:seq ≡ IF:<IsSeqOf:IsFun, LIFT:f, f>:seq
```

---

**Example 3.3.5** (Matrix expressions)
Some interesting examples of calculus at function level with matrices are given in Script 3.3.8. For example, the **0** matrix $n \times n$ can be generated by applying the function IDNT - IDNT to an arbitrary positive integer $n$.

---

**Script 3.3.8** (Matrix calculus examples)
```
(IDNT - IDNT):3 ≡ <<0.0, 0.0, 0.0>,<0.0, 0.0, 0.0>,<0.0, 0.0, 0.0>>
(IDNT + IDNT):3 ≡ <<2.0, 0.0, 0.0>,<0.0, 2.0, 0.0>,<0.0, 0.0, 2.0>>

<<1,2,3>,<4,5,6>,<7,8,9>> * <<1,2,3>,<4,5,6>,<7,8,9>> ≡ <
    <30.0, 36.0, 42.0>,
    <66.0, 81.0, 96.0>,
    <102.0, 126.0, 150.0>>

<<1,2,3>,<4,5,6>> * TRANS:<<1,2,3>,<4,5,6>> ≡ <
    <14.0, 32.0>,
    <32.0, 77.0>>
```

---

Both matrix operators and data can be freely combined in writing matrix expressions, like in the following example, where A is the matrix defined in Example 3.3.3:

```
(TRANS ~ INV):(IDNT:3 - A) ≡ <
    <-0.5, 0.3125, 0.125>,
    <0.25, -0.65625, 0.4375>,
    <0.0, 0.375, -0.25> >
```

## Example 3.3.6 (Scalar multiple of a matrix)

Let us define a function `ScalarMatProd` which computes the product of a scalar $\alpha \in \mathbb{R}$ times a matrix $A = (a_{ij}) \in \mathbb{R}^n_n$, for the arbitrary positive integer $n$. The problem can be approached by first computing a matrix of pairs $(\alpha, a_{ij})$ and then by applying to each pair the operation of product between numbers. We use here a pure FL style, i.e. without formal parameters (see Section 2.1.1). `ScalarMatProd` can be used as either infix or prefix, but notice that the first argument must be the scalar one.

---

**Script 3.3.9**

```
DEF ScalarMatProd = (AA~AA):* ~ AA:DISTL ~ DISTL;

9 ScalarMatProd IDNT:3 ≡
    <<9, 0, 0>,
     <0, 9, 0>,
     <0, 0, 9>>;
```

---

**Trace of tensor**   The *trace* is the only linear form

$$tr : \text{lin } \mathcal{V} \to \mathbb{R}$$

satisfying

$$tr\,(\boldsymbol{u} \otimes \boldsymbol{v}) = \boldsymbol{u} \cdot \boldsymbol{v}$$

for each $\boldsymbol{u}, \boldsymbol{v} \in \mathcal{V}$.

The scalar $tr\,\boldsymbol{S}$ is easy to compute starting from the matrix $[\boldsymbol{S}]$. In fact, for the linearity of $tr$ we have:

$$
\begin{aligned}
tr\,\boldsymbol{S} &= tr\left(\sum_{i,j} S_{ij} e_i \otimes e_j\right) \\
&= \sum_{i,j} S_{ij} tr(e_i \otimes e_j) \\
&= \sum_{i,j} S_{ij} e_i \cdot e_j = \sum_i S_{ii}
\end{aligned}
$$

Henceforth, the trace of a square matrix is defined as the sum of diagonal elements. It is possible to verify that:

$$
\begin{aligned}
tr\,\boldsymbol{S}^T &= tr\,\boldsymbol{S}, \\
tr\,(\boldsymbol{S}\boldsymbol{T}) &= tr\,(\boldsymbol{T}\boldsymbol{S}).
\end{aligned}
$$

**Example 3.3.7 (Trace computation)**
A function `Trace` is here defined which computes the trace of a matrix $A \in \mathbb{R}_n^n$, for the arbitrary positive integer $n$. The algorithm coded by the function can be described as follows:

1. Compute the number $n$ of matrix rows.
2. Generate the integer sequence from 1 to $n$.
3. Produce the sequence of pairs $(i, A_i)$, where $A_i$ is the $i$-th row of $A$.
4. Apply to all pairs a function which select the $a_{ii}$ element.
5. Compute the sum of all selected elements.

---

**Script 3.3.10**
```
DEF Trace (matrix::IsMat) = (+ ~ AA:select ~ TRANS):< 1..n, matrix >
WHERE
    n = LEN:matrix,
    select = APPLY ~ [SEL~S1, S2]
END;

Trace:<<1,2,3>,<4,5,6>,<7,8,9>> ≡ 15
```

---

**Inner product of tensors** The space lin $\mathcal{V}$ of tensors on the $\mathcal{V}$ vector space has a natural *inner product*, that is defined as:

$$S \cdot T = tr \ (S^T T),$$

which component-wise becomes:

$$S \cdot T = \sum_{i,j} S_{ij} T_{ij}.$$

in the following example we extend this operations to compatible matrices.

**Example 3.3.8 (Inner product of matrices)**
The goal is to add all the products of corresponding elements in the argument matrices. This is obtained by the algorithm:

1. Generate a sequence of pairs of corresponding rows.
2. Transpose all such pairs of rows.
3. Catenate the result, so generating a single sequence of pairs of numbers.
4. Apply to all number pairs the product operator.
5. Add all the resulting numbers.

The function `matDotProd` computes the dot product of any two compatible matrices with any number of rows and columns, according to the algorithm described above. Script 3.3.11 also reports a step-wise example of computation, by showing the partial elaborations of an input instance.

**Script 3.3.11**

```
DEF matDotProd = + ~ AA:* ~ CAT ~ AA:TRANS ~ TRANS;
DEF A = <<1,2>,<3,4>,<5,6>>;
DEF B = <<10,20>,<30,40>,<50,60>>;

matDotProd:< A, B > ≡ 910
```

### 3.3.4  Determinant and inverse

**Determinant of a matrix**  A *permutation* is a one-to-one function on a finite set. A permutation $\pi : \{1, 2, \ldots, n\} \rightarrow \{1, 2, \ldots, n\}$ is usually denoted as

$$\pi = \left( \begin{array}{cccc} 1 & 2 & \cdots & n \\ \pi(1) & \pi(2) & \cdots & \pi(n) \end{array} \right).$$

The *determinant* of a square number matrix $A$ is a number $\det A$ such that

$$\det A = \det \left( \begin{array}{ccc} a_{11} & \cdots & a_{1n} \\ \vdots & \ddots & \vdots \\ a_{n1} & \cdots & a_{nn} \end{array} \right) = \left| \begin{array}{ccc} a_{11} & \cdots & a_{1n} \\ \vdots & \ddots & \vdots \\ a_{n1} & \cdots & a_{nn} \end{array} \right|$$

$$= \sum_{\pi} \text{sign}(\pi) a_{1\pi(1)} a_{2\pi(2)} \cdots a_{n\pi(n)}$$

where the sum is taken over all the $n!$ permutations $\pi$ of $\{1, \ldots, n\}$, and $\text{sign}(\pi)$ is either $+1$ or $-1$ according as $\pi$ is either an even or odd permutation. Notice that each product $a_{1\pi(1)} a_{2\pi(2)} \cdots a_{n\pi(n)}$ contains $n$ matrix elements such that no two of them belong to the same row or to the same column.

**Determinant of a tensor**  The determinant $det : \text{lin } \mathcal{V} \rightarrow \mathbb{R}$ of a tensor $\boldsymbol{S}$ is defined as the determinant of its matrix $[\boldsymbol{S}]$:

$$det \ \boldsymbol{S} = det \ [\boldsymbol{S}].$$

A tensor $\boldsymbol{S}$ is *invertible* if there exists a tensor $\boldsymbol{S}^{-1}$, called the *inverse* of $\boldsymbol{S}$, such that:

$$\boldsymbol{S}\boldsymbol{S}^{-1} = \boldsymbol{S}^{-1}\boldsymbol{S} = \boldsymbol{I}.$$

$\boldsymbol{S}$ is invertible if and only if $det \ \boldsymbol{S} \neq 0$

Some properties of determinants and inverse tensors follow:

1. $det \ (\boldsymbol{S}\boldsymbol{T}) = (det \ \boldsymbol{S})(det \ \boldsymbol{T})$
2. $det \ \boldsymbol{S}^{T} = det \ \boldsymbol{S}$
3. $det \ (\boldsymbol{S}^{-1}) = (det \ \boldsymbol{S})^{-1}$
4. $(\boldsymbol{S}\boldsymbol{T})^{-1} = \boldsymbol{T}^{-1}\boldsymbol{S}^{-1}$
5. $(\boldsymbol{S}^{-1})^{T} = (\boldsymbol{S}^{T})^{-1}$

*3.3.5   Orthogonal tensors*

A tensor $Q \in \text{lin } V$ is said to be *orthogonal* if it preserves the inner products, i.e. if for each $u, v \in V$:

$$Qu \cdot Qv = u \cdot v.$$

A necessary and sufficient condition for $Q$ be orthogonal is that

$$QQ^T = Q^T Q = I.$$

By properties of tensor matrices, we have in this case:

$$[Q][Q]^T = [Q]^T [Q] = [I]$$

For this reason, a matrix $A$ such that $AA^T = A^T A = I$ is also said *orthogonal*.

**Example 3.3.9**
We show that the one-parameter family of matrices $M : \mathbb{R} \to R_2^2$ defined as

$$M(u) = \begin{pmatrix} \cos u & -\sin u \\ \sin u & \cos u \end{pmatrix}$$

is orthogonal for each $u \in \mathbb{R}$:

$$
M(u)M^T(u) = \begin{pmatrix} \cos u & -\sin u \\ \sin u & \cos u \end{pmatrix} \begin{pmatrix} \cos u & \sin u \\ -\sin u & \cos u \end{pmatrix}
$$
$$
= \begin{pmatrix} \cos^2 u + \sin^2 u & 0 \\ 0 & \cos^2 u + \sin^2 u \end{pmatrix} = \begin{pmatrix} 1 & 0 \\ 0 & 1 \end{pmatrix}
$$

We also define the M function, and then execute various computations showing the orthogonality of $M(u)$ for different values of $u$. Remember that PI is the PLaSM denotation for $\pi$.

---

**Script 3.3.12**
```
DEF M (u::IsReal) = [[cos, -~sin],[sin, cos]]:u;
M:(PI/6)
    ≡ <<0.8660254037844387, -0.5>,
        <0.5, 0.8660254037844387>>
M:1
    ≡ <<0.5403023058681398, -0.8414709848078965>,
        <0.8414709848078965, 0.5403023058681398>>
(M * (TRANS~M)):(PI/6)
    ≡ <<1.0, 0.0>, <0.0, 1.0>>
(M * (TRANS~M)):1
    ≡ <<1.0, 0.0>, <0.0, 1.0>>
```

---

*3.3.6* PLaSM *representation of tensors*

Tensors are represented in PLaSM by applying the predefinite function MAT to the matrix of the tensor. This is clearly possible when a basis $(e_i)$ has been given for the underlying vector space. The reference frame for a Euclidean space is usually Cartesian. For example, we may define two tensors X and Y as follows:

```
DEF X = MAT:<<0,0,1>,<1,0,1>,<0,2,1>>;
DEF Y = MAT:<<0,1,1>,<,0,1>,<1,1,1>>;
```

Tensors defined as vector space endomorphisms have a first-class citizenship in PLaSM, so that they can be composed by generating new tensors. For instance:

```
DEF Z = Y ∼ X
```

**Application of PLaSM tensors**   Tensors can be applied to polyhedral complexes[3] of generic dimension $(d, n)$, where $d$ is the intric dimension of the complex (e.g. $d = 1$ for curves, $d = 2$ for surfaces, $d = 3$ for solids, etc.) and $n$ is the dimension of the embedding space, i.e. the number of point coordinates.

For this purpose, it is necessary to use a normalized homogeneous representation of the affine space $\mathbb{E}^n$, using $n + 1$ coordinates with the first one equal to 1. This allows the user, as we discuss in following chapters, and in particular in Section 6.1.4, to treat any affine mapping, including translations, as a linear mapping. For this purpose, see also Section 4.2.1. Two affine maps can be combined by matrix product of their matrix representations.

Hence we introduce here a useful function MatHom (for "Matrix Homogeneize"), which makes a square matrix homogeneous and normalized. This function, when applied to an actual parameter $M \in \mathbb{R}^n_n$, returns the matrix $M'$ obtained by embedding $M$ in the identity $I \in \mathbb{R}^{n+1}_{n+1}$, so that both the first column and the first row contain the unit vector.

---

**Script 3.3.13**

```
DEF IsSqrMat = AND ∼ [IsMat, EQ ∼ [LEN, LEN ∼ s1]];
DEF MatHom (m::IsSqrMat) = AL:< firstRow, (AA:AL ∼ DISTL):<0,m> >
WHERE
    firstRow = AL:<1,#:(LEN:m):0>
END;

MatHom:<<1,2,3>,<4,5,6>,<7,8,9>> ≡
    <<1, 0, 0, 0>,
     <0, 1, 2, 3>,
     <0, 4, 5, 6>,
     <0, 7, 8, 9>>
```

---

Both the MatHom definition and the result of its application to a $3 \times 3$ matrix are given in Script 3.3.13. Remember that the predefined function AL ("Append Left"),

---

[3] See Sections 4.6 and 14.1.

to be applied to pairs constituted by any element and by any sequence, appends the element as the first one of the output sequence.

Tensors in PLaSM can be applied only to expressions which denote polyhedral complexes. The evaluation of such applications return the polyhedral complex after the transformation of coordinates.

---

**Script 3.3.14 (User-defined PLaSM tensors)**

```
DEF Tensor = MAT ∼ MatHom;
DEF X = (Tensor ∼ TRANS):<<0,1,0>, <0,0,2>, <1,1,1>>;
DEF Y = (Tensor ∼ INV ∼ TRANS):<<0,1,0>, <0,0,2>, <1,1,1>>;
DEF Cube = CUBOID:<1,1,1>;

(STRUCT ∼ [ID, X]):Cube;
(STRUCT ∼ [ID, Y]):Cube;
(STRUCT ∼ [Y∼X, X∼Y]):Cube;
```

---

**Application of tensors to points**  As we have seen, PLaSM tensors can be applied only to polyhedral complexes. But it is also possible to apply a tensor to a point or to a discrete point set in $\mathbb{E}^d$, by transforming the argument into a polyhedral complex of dimension $(0, d)$, and by transforming back to points the complex mapped by the tensor.

Hence we give in Script 3.3.15 both the definition of two operators which execute the object conversion in both-ways, and an example of application of a tensor to either a point or to a set of points.

In particular, the MK (MaKe) function transforms a point in $\mathbb{E}^d$, i.e. a sequence of $d$ coordinates, into a polyhedron of intrinsic dimension 0. The UK (UnmaKe) function performs the inverse transformation. The following expressions show:

1. that UK∼MK equates the identity tensor (plus a casting to real coordinates);
2. how to apply an X tensor to a point (where X is defined in Script 3.3.14);
3. the type of the result of a MK application;
4. how to look for intrinsic and embedding dimensions of a polyhedral complex;
5. how to transform a sequence of $d$-points into a 0-dimensional polyhedral complex in $\mathbb{E}^d$.

---

**Script 3.3.15 (Point→polyhedron and vice versa)**

```
DEF MK = MKPOL∼[LIST,K:<<1>>,K:<<1>>];
DEF UK = S1∼S1∼UKPOL;

(UK∼MK):<0,0,0>        ≡ <0.0, 0.0, 0.0>
(UK∼X∼MK):<0,0,0>      ≡ <0.5, 1.0, 0.0>
MK:<0,1,2>             ≡ A-Polyhedral-Complex{0,3}
[DIM,RN]:(MK:<0,1,2>)  ≡ <0, 3>
(STRUCT∼AA:MK):<<0,1,1>,<0.5,0,2>,<1,4,0>> ≡ A-Polyhedral-Complex{0,3}
```

---

# 4

# Elements of polyhedral geometry

This chapter reviews the algebraic and geometric concepts which underlie the geometric kernel of the PLaSM language. The aim is both to collect concepts and tools from different fields, and to provide the reader with key ideas useful in understanding the behavior of basic operators of the language. For this purpose, the chapter contains some materials about convexity theory, double representation of polyhedral sets, polarity, the boundary structure of a polytope, simplicial and polyhedral complexes, Nef polyhedra and linear programming. At the same time, polyhedral geometry offers exciting opportunities to explore a programming language properly designed to support geometric calculus. The straighforward generation of $d$-dimensional permutahedra and the construction of Platonic solids inscribed in a unit sphere provide convincing examples.

## 4.1 Basic concepts

Let us first recall some basic topological concepts like *interior*, *boundary* and *closure*, and the basic elements, like *halfplanes*, *halfspaces* and *flats*, of the affine structure of Euclidean spaces.

**Topology**  A *topology* on a set $W$ is a family $\mathcal{T}$ of subsets, called *open sets*, of $W$ such that:

1. any union of elements of $\mathcal{T}$ belongs to $\mathcal{T}$;
2. the intersection of any two elements of $\mathcal{T}$ belongs to $\mathcal{T}$;
3. $\emptyset$ and $W$ belong to $\mathcal{T}$.

The pair $(W, \mathcal{T})$ is called a *topological space*. When no ambiguity arises about the chosen topology, $W$ itself is called a topological space. A *metric* topology on $W$ is the set of open balls centered at each $W$ element, whose points have distance from the center less than the radius. The *natural* topology, i.e. the metric topology induced by the Euclidean distance, is assumed when considering $\mathbb{E}^n$ as a topological space.

*Geometric Programming for Computer-Aided Design*  Alberto Paoluzzi
© 2003 John Wiley & Sons, Ltd  ISBN 0-471-89942-9

**Boundary, interior, closure**   Let $W$ be a topological space and $x \in W$. A subset $S \subset W$ is a *neighborhood* of $x$ if there exists an open set $V$ in the topology of $W$ such that $x \in V \subset S$.

A point $x \in W$ is a boundary point of $S$ if neither $S$ nor $W \backslash S$ is a neighborhood of $x$. The *boundary* $\partial S$ is the set of boundary points of $S$. A point $x \in W$ is an interior point of $S$ if $S$ is a neighborhood of $x$. The *interior* $\text{int}\, S$ is the set of interior points of $S$. The *closure* of $S$ is the set $\text{clos}\, S := S \cup \partial S$. $S$ is said to be *closed* (*open*) if and only if $S = \text{clos}\, S$ (respectively, $S = \text{int}\, S$).

A set $A \subset \mathbb{E}^n$ is *relatively closed* (relatively open) if it is closed (open) with respect to the *subspace topology* induced on aff $A$ by the natural topology of $\mathbb{E}^n$. Analogously, the *relative interior* relint $A$ is the set of interior points of $A$ with respect to the subspace topology of aff $A$.

The set $A$ is *bounded* when there exists $\kappa \in \mathbb{R}$ such that $\|x - y\| < \kappa$, for each $x, y \in A$. Also, the set $A$ is said to be *compact* if it is bounded and closed.

**Segments**   A *closed segment* $[x, y]$, with $x, y \in \mathbb{E}^n$, is defined as:

$$[x, y] := \{(1 - \lambda)x + \lambda y | 0 \leq \lambda \leq 1\}.$$

An *open* segment, and a right (left) *semi-closed* segment, denoted as $(x, y)$, $[x, y)$ and $(x, y]$ respectively, correspond to $0 < \lambda < 1$, to $0 \leq \lambda < 1$, and to $0 < \lambda \leq 1$. Notice that open, closed and semi-closed segments are well defined even with coinciding extremes. E.g.: $(x, x) = [x, x] = \{x\}$.

**Set operations**   Minkowski addition of sets $A, B \subset \mathbb{E}^n$ and Minkowski product of a set times a scalar $\lambda \in \mathbb{R}$ are defined respectively as:

$$A + B \quad := \quad \{a + b | a \in A, b \in B\},$$
$$\lambda A \quad := \quad \{\lambda a | a \in A\}.$$

An algorithm for Minkowski addition of a polyhedral complex with a special class of convex sets and its PLaSM implementation are provided in Section 14.6. This operation is used for translational *motion planning* of a robot moving amidst obstacles [LPW79]. See Section 15.6.4 for a description.

**Hyperplanes and half-spaces**   A *hyperplane* of $\mathbb{E}^n$ may be written as

$$H_{u, \alpha} := \{x \in \mathbb{E}^n | u^T x = \alpha\},$$

where $u \in \mathbb{E}^n \backslash \{o\}$ is the *normal vector* of $H_{u, \alpha}$ and $\alpha \in \mathbb{R}$.

A hyperplane may have several equivalent representations. In particular:

$$H_{u, \alpha} = H_{v, \beta}$$

if and only if $(v, \beta) = (\lambda u, \lambda \alpha)$, with $\lambda \in \mathbb{R}$. It follows that $H_{u, \alpha} = H_{u/|u|, \alpha/|u|}$, where $\alpha/|u|$ is the *signed distance* of $H_{u, \alpha}$ from the origin.

A hyperplane $H_{u, \alpha}$ is a translate of a parallel linear subspace $H_{u, 0}$, i.e. is an affine subspace:

$$H_{u, \alpha} = H_{u, 0} + \frac{\alpha}{|u|} \frac{u}{|u|} = H_{u, 0} + \frac{\alpha}{u \cdot u} u.$$

The *dimension* of $H_{\boldsymbol{u},\alpha}$ is the cardinality of a minimal subset of $\mathbb{E}^n$ which spans $H_{\boldsymbol{u},0}$. A hyperplane $H_{\boldsymbol{u},\alpha}$ subdivides the space $E^n$ into two *closed halfspaces*

$$
\begin{aligned}
H^-_{\boldsymbol{u},\alpha} &:= \{\boldsymbol{x} \in \mathbb{E}^n | \boldsymbol{u}^T\boldsymbol{x} \le \alpha\}, \\
H^+_{\boldsymbol{u},\alpha} &:= \{\boldsymbol{x} \in \mathbb{E}^n | \boldsymbol{u}^T\boldsymbol{x} \ge \alpha\},
\end{aligned}
$$

which will be occasionally named *below* and *above* halfspace, respectively.

**Flats and half-flats**  An affine subspace is also called a *flat*. A flat may be always represented as an intersection of hyperplanes. The intersection of an halfspace with a flat not completely contained in it is called *half-flat*. A *line* is a flat of dimension 1. A *ray* is a half-flat of dimension 1.

## 4.2   Convex sets

Convex sets are the main ingredient of our language for geometric design, since each geometric value in PLaSM is a covering of a compact point set with convex cells of appropriate dimension. It is hence very useful to reserve special attention to the theory of convex sets.

### 4.2.1   Positive, affine and convex hulls

Here we recall some concepts quickly introduced in Chapter 3, in order to make the present chapter more self-contained. In the remainder we do not distinguish between a Euclidean space as a set of points and the underlying vector space. Anyway, the terms vector and point are appropriately used when useful.

**Positive hulls and cones**  A *positive* (or *conical*) *combination* of a set of vectors $\{\boldsymbol{x}_i | i \in I\}$ is a linear combination with scalars $\alpha_i \ge 0, i \in I$.

A *cone* is a set $C \subseteq \mathbb{E}^n$ which is closed with respect to the positive combination of every subset of elements.

*Positive* (or *conical*) *hull* of a set $S \subset \mathbb{E}^n$ is the set cone $S$ of all positive combinations of $S$ elements. The set cone $S$ is the smallest cone which contains $S$. Since every positive hull contains the zero vector, it is customary to define cone $\emptyset = \{\boldsymbol{0}\}$.

**Example 4.2.1 (Finite cone generated by a convex set)**
In Script 4.2.1 the FiniteCone function generates the set conv $A \cup \{\boldsymbol{0}\}$, where A is any geometric value generated by PLaSM. The result of application to a translated cube skeleton is shown in Figure 4.1. Clearly, the set $(\texttt{Cone:A}) \cup \lambda\,(\texttt{Cone:A})$, $\lambda > 1$, is a cone. We call the set Cone:A a *finite cone*. Notice that $\texttt{FiniteCone:A} \equiv \lambda\,A$, $\lambda \in [0,1]$.

The FiniteCone generator function, depending on a formal parameter pol of polyhedral complex type, is produced by the JOIN of its argument $\texttt{pol} \in \mathcal{P}^{d,n}$ with the convex set $\{\boldsymbol{0}\}$, where $\boldsymbol{0} \in \mathbb{R}^n$. Let us remember that the built-in geometric operator RN returns the embedding dimension of the complex to which it is applied. Notice that both the MATERIAL and the STRUCT primitives are used infix within their arguments. To export the out object will require a preliminary loading of the 'colors' library.

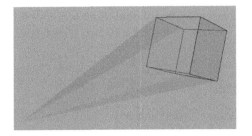

**Figure 4.1**    Finite cone

---

**Script 4.2.1** (Cone generator)

```
DEF FiniteCone (pol::IsPol) = pol JOIN (MK ~ #:(RN:pol)):0;
DEF complex = (T:<1,2,3>:<1,2,3> ~ @1 ~ CUBOID):<1,1,1>;

DEF out = FiniteCone:complex
    MATERIAL Transparentmaterial:<GREEN, 0.8>
    STRUCT complex
```

---

**Affine hulls and affine spaces**    An *affine combination* of a set of points $\{x_i | i \in I\}$ is a linear combination with scalars $\alpha_i$ such that $\sum_{i \in I} \alpha_i = 1$.

The *affine hull* of a set $S \subset \mathbb{E}^n$ is the set aff $S$ of all affine combinations of elements of $S$. Every affine hull, called also affine space, is the translate of a linear space:

$$\text{aff}\,\{x_0, x_1, \dots, x_d\} = x_0 + \text{lin}\,\{x_1 - x_0, \dots, x_d - x_0\}$$

Let $S \subset \mathbb{E}^n$, and $x \in S$. Then $\dim \text{aff}\, S = \dim \text{lin}\,(S - x)$.

A non-empty subset $U \subset \mathbb{E}^n$ is an *affine space* if and only if there exist suitable $A \in \mathbb{R}_n^m$ and $b \in \mathbb{R}^m$ such that

$$U = \{x \in \mathbb{E}^n | Ax = b\}.$$

**Convex hulls and convex sets**    A *convex combination* of a set of points $\{x_i | i \in I\}$ is a linear combination which is both positive and affine, i.e. with scalars $\alpha_i \geq 0$ such that $\sum_{i \in I} \alpha_i = 1$.

The *convex hull* of a set $S$ is the set conv $S$ of all convex combinations of $S$ elements. The set conv $S$ is the smallest convex set which contains $S$. A set $K \subset \mathbb{E}^n$ is *convex* if it contains the segment connecting any pair of points in it, i.e. if for $x, y \in K$ and $0 \leq \lambda \leq 1$

$$(1 - \lambda)x + \lambda y \in K.$$

In other words, a set is convex when it is closed with respect to convex combination of elements. Also, a set $K$ is *convex* if $K = \text{conv}\, K$.

A convex non-empty set $A \subset \mathbb{E}^n$ is said to be a *convex cone* if $x \in A$ implies $\lambda x \in A$, with $\lambda \geq 0$. Notice that, if $A$ is a convex cone, then $0 \in A$.

The *dimension* of a convex set $K$ is that of the affine hull: $\dim K = \dim \text{aff}\, K$.

Hyperplanes, halfspaces, affine subspaces, convex cones and polyhedra are convex sets, and so is the space $\mathbb{E}^n$. If $A, B \subset \mathbb{E}^n$ are convex, then $A + B$ and $\lambda A$, $\lambda \in \mathbb{R}$ are convex. Furthermore, the intersection and projection of convex sets are convex.

**Example 4.2.2 (Convex hull)**
In Script 4.2.2 a simple implementation of the `ConvexHull` operator is given, where
the function `MK`, introduced in Script 3.3.15, is defined as `MK` : $\mathbb{E}^n \to \mathcal{P}^{0,n}$. A different
implementation for the `ConvexHull` operator was provided in Script 3.2.1.

---

**Script 4.2.2** (`ConvexHull` operator)
```
DEF ConvexHull (points::IsSeqof:IsPoint) = (JOIN ∼ AA:MK): points;
```

---

**Homogenization**   A map

$$\text{homog} : \mathbb{E}^n \to \mathbb{E}^{n+1} : x \mapsto \begin{pmatrix} 1 \\ x \end{pmatrix}$$

is said to *homogenize* the points of a set $A \subset \mathbb{E}^n$. A set of points $A = \{x_0, x_1, \ldots, x_d\}$
is affinely independent if and only if the vector images of points in $\text{homog}(A)$ are
linearly independent.

**Barycentric coordinates**   Let $A = \{x_0, x_1, \ldots, x_n\}$ be affinely independent, and
$y \in \text{aff } A$, i.e.:

$$y = \sum_{i=0}^{n} \lambda_i x_i, \quad \text{with} \quad \sum_{i=0}^{n} \lambda_i = 1.$$

The (unique) coefficients $\lambda_0, \ldots, \lambda_d$ are called *barycentric coordinates* of $y$ in $A$.

**Carathéodory's theorem**   This important theorem states that if $A \subseteq \mathbb{E}^n$ and
$x \in \text{conv } A$, then $x$ can be expressed as the convex combination of at most $n + 1$
affinely independent points of $A$.

**Simplex and its interior**   The set $\text{conv} \{x_0, x_1, \ldots, x_d\}$ of $d + 1$ affinely
independent points of $\mathbb{E}^n$, $d \leq n$, is called *d-simplex*. Such points are called *vertices*.
     A consequence of Carathéodory's theorem is that a set $\text{conv } A$ is the union of all
simplices with vertices in $A$.
     Let $A := \{x_0, x_1, \ldots, x_n\}$ be affinely independent, i.e. $\text{conv } A$ be a simplex, and
$x \in \text{aff } A$. Then $x \in \text{relint conv } A$ if and only if all the barycentric coordinates of $x$ in
$A$ are positive.

**Example 4.2.3 (Barycentric coordinates)**
To compute the barycentric coordinates $\boldsymbol{\lambda} = (\lambda_0, \lambda_1, \ldots, \lambda_d)$ of a point $x \in \mathbb{E}^d$,
either internal or external to a simplex $\text{conv} \{x_0, x_1, \ldots, x_d\}$, it is sufficient to solve
the simultaneous set of $d + 1$ linear equations in $d + 1$ unknowns, whose first equation
codifies the constraint that $\boldsymbol{\lambda}$ must be a partition of the unity:

$$\begin{pmatrix} 1 \\ x \end{pmatrix} = \begin{pmatrix} 1 & 1 & \cdots & 1 \\ x_0 & x_1 & \cdots & x_d \end{pmatrix} \boldsymbol{\lambda},$$

so that

$$\boldsymbol{\lambda} = \begin{pmatrix} 1 & 1 & \cdots & 1 \\ \boldsymbol{x}_0 & \boldsymbol{x}_1 & \cdots & \boldsymbol{x}_d \end{pmatrix}^{-1} \begin{pmatrix} 1 \\ \boldsymbol{x} \end{pmatrix}.$$

The above method is equivalent to computing a coordinate transformation for $\mathrm{homog}\,(\boldsymbol{x}) \in \mathbb{E}^{d+1}$ with respect to the new basis $\mathrm{homog}\,\{\boldsymbol{x}_0, \boldsymbol{x}_1, \ldots \boldsymbol{x}_d\}$.

**Implementation**  A dimension-independent implementation of this approach is given by the `Convexcoords` function in Script 4.2.3, together with some examples of its use. Notice that the given implementation requires a Cartesian (say, without homogeneous coordinate) representation of the input point x. Notice also that the expression `AA:[ID]:(1 AL x)` generates a column matrix representation in $\mathbb{R}_1^d$ of the homogenized x point. For example:

> `AA:[ID]:(1 AL <0.5, 0, 0>)` $\equiv$ `< < 1 > , < 0.5 > , < 0 > , < 0 > >`

The overloaded * operator denotes here infix matrix multiplication. The `IsSimplex` predicate is given in Script 4.4.1.

---

**Script 4.2.3 (Barycentric coordinates)**

```
DEF Convexcoords (p::IsSimplex)(x::IsPoint) = CAT:(
    (INV ~ TRANS ~ AA:AL ~ DISTL ~ [K:1, S1] ~ UKPOL):p
    * AA:[ID]:(1 AL x)
);

Convexcoords:(SIMPLEX:3):< 1/3, 1/3, 1/3 > ≡
    < 0.3333333333333333 , 0.3333333333333333 , 0.3333333333333333 , 0,0 >
```

---

The above example shows that the point $\boldsymbol{x} = (1/3, 1/3, 1/3)$ belongs to one of external faces of the unit tetrahedron. The reader might find useful to look once more at Example 3.2.6.

**Example 4.2.4 (Hyperplane defined by $n$ points in $\mathbb{E}^n$)**
It is often necessary to get the Cartesian equation $ax_1 + bx_2 + cx_3 + d = 0$ of the plane passing through three affinely independent points $\boldsymbol{y}_0, \boldsymbol{y}_1, \boldsymbol{y}_2 \in \mathbb{E}^3$. This hyperplane is defined as the set

$$H \subset \mathbb{E}^3 = \mathrm{aff}\,\{\boldsymbol{y}_0, \boldsymbol{y}_1, \boldsymbol{y}_2\} = \boldsymbol{y}_0 + \mathrm{lin}\,\{\boldsymbol{y}_1 - \boldsymbol{y}_0, \boldsymbol{y}_2 - \boldsymbol{y}_0\},$$

so that $\dim H = 2$.

This set may be generated, by using homogeneous coordinates, as the projection of the linear subspace of $\mathbb{E}^4$ spanned by linearly independent vectors $(1, \boldsymbol{y}_i) \in \mathbb{E}^4$ $(0 \leq i \leq 2)$, i.e. as the set

$$H = \{\boldsymbol{x} | (1, \boldsymbol{x}) \in H'\},$$

with

$$H' = \mathrm{lin}\,\{(1, \boldsymbol{y}_0), (1, \boldsymbol{y}_1), (1, \boldsymbol{y}_2)\}$$

With matrix language, and by using the standard notation for determinants, i.e. $\det A = |A|$, the previous statement reduces to:

$$\det A = \begin{vmatrix} 1 & x_1 & x_2 & x_3 \\ 1 & y_{01} & y_{02} & y_{03} \\ 1 & y_{11} & y_{12} & y_{13} \\ 1 & y_{21} & y_{22} & y_{23} \end{vmatrix} = 0,$$

since the first row is a linear combination of the others. Notice that rank $A = 3$, by definition, since we supposed $\boldsymbol{y}_0, \boldsymbol{y}_1, \boldsymbol{y}_2$ affinely independent. By computing

$$\det A = \sum_{j=1}^{4} (-1)^{1+j} |A_{1j}| \, a_{1j} = ax_1 + bx_2 + cx_3 + d = 0$$

where $A_{1j}$ is the submatrix obtained by cancelling the first row and the $j$-th column from $A$, we get

$$a = |A_{11}|, \qquad b = -|A_{12}|, \qquad c = |A_{13}|, \qquad d = -|A_{14}|.$$

This approach is readily extended to the hyperplane $\boldsymbol{h}^T \boldsymbol{x} + h_0 = 0$ defined by $n$ affinely independent points in $\mathbb{E}^n$, so that $h_j = (-1)^{j+1}|A_{1j}|$.

For example, the line in $\mathbb{E}^2$ passing for $(1,0)$ and $(0,1)$ is

$$\begin{vmatrix} 0 & 1 \\ 1 & 1 \end{vmatrix} x_1 - \begin{vmatrix} 1 & 1 \\ 0 & 1 \end{vmatrix} x_2 + \begin{vmatrix} 1 & 0 \\ 0 & 1 \end{vmatrix} = -x_1 - x_2 + 1 = 0.$$

*4.2.2  Support, separation, extreme points*

The main source for this section, as well as for several concepts in this chapter, is Schneider's book [Sch93] on convex bodies and Brunn-Minkowski theory.

**Support hyperplanes and halfspaces**  Let $A \subset \mathbb{E}^n$, $H \subset \mathbb{E}^n$ be a set and a hyperplane, respectively, with $H^+$ and $H^-$ the two closed halfspaces bounded by $H$. Then $H$ *supports* $A$ *at* $x$ if $x \in A \cap H$ and either $A \subset H^+$ or $A \subset H^-$.

The hyperplane $H$ is called a *support hyperplane* of $A$ if $H$ supports some boundary point $x$ of $A$. If $A \subset H^+$ ($A \subset H^-$), then $H^+$ ($H^-$) is called a *support halfspace* of $A$.

The existence of support hyperplanes through *every boundary point* of a set $A \subset \mathbb{E}^n$ characterizes it as a *convex* set. In fact, it is possible to prove [Sch93] that if this existence is guaranteed, then the set is convex. Each non-empty closed convex set in $\mathbb{E}^n$ is the intersection of its supporting halfspaces.

**Separation**  The sets $A$ and $B$ are *separated* by an hyperplane $H$ if $A \subset H^+$ and $B \subset H^-$. non-empty convex sets $A$ and $B$ can be properly separated if and only if relint $A \cap$ relint $B = \emptyset$

**Extremal points**  An *extremal point* of a convex set $A$ is a point $z \in A$ that cannot be written in the form $z = (1 - \lambda)x + \lambda y$, for $x, y \in A$ and $\lambda \in (0, 1)$. If $\{z\} \subset A$ is a face (see Section 4.4.2), then $z$ is an extremal point.

It is very important to write a closed convex set as the convex hull of a much smaller finite set. *Minkowski's theorem* states that each convex body is the convex hull of its extremal points.

### 4.2.3  Duality

**Polar set of a convex**  Let $S \subset \mathbb{E}^n$ be a convex body with $o \in \operatorname{int} S$. The *polar set* of $S$ is properly defined as the subset of dual space $(\mathbb{E}^n)^*$:

$$S^* := \{y \in (\mathbb{E}^n)^* | y(x) \leq 1, \text{for all } x \in S\}.$$

By the canonical isomorphism between $(\mathbb{E}^n)^*$ and $\mathbb{E}^n$ induced by the Euclidean scalar product, and the representation theorem (3.4), the polar set can be directly given in $\mathbb{E}^n$, as

$$S^* := \{y \in \mathbb{E}^n | x \cdot y \leq 1, \text{for all } x \in S\}.$$

**Polarity is a duality**  It is possible to show that polarity is a true duality [Sch93], since: the polar $S^*$ of a convex $S$ is convex, satisfies the requirement that $o \in \operatorname{int} S^*$, and $S^{**} = S$.

The polarity relation is called *duality* in many books, so that we use occasionally the same word, mainly in Chapter 13. Notice that the polar set depends on the position of $o$. This could be avoided by defining "cone polarity" between linearized sets [Zie95].

**Example 4.2.5 (Polar sets of $d$-cubes)**
A $d$-cube $C_d$ is defined as a Cartesian product of $d$ closed intervals $[-1, 1] \subset \mathbb{E}$:

$$C_d := [-1, +1]^d = \{x \in \mathbb{E}^d | -1 \leq x_i \leq 1\},$$

The polar set of the standard square $C_2 \subset \mathbb{E}^2$ is the *rhombus* $C_2^*$. The polar set of the standard cube $C_3 \subset \mathbb{E}^3$ is the *octahedron* $C_3^*$. Both such cubes and their dual are shown in Figure 4.2. Notice that faces of a convex body correspond to vertices of its dual.

**Implementation**  In Script 4.2.4 some PLaSM functions are given, to generate both $d$-cubes and their polar sets.

In particular, DeHomog is the inverse of the homog operator of Section 4.2. In this case it is not sufficient to drop the first coordinate of $x = (x_0, x_1, \dots, x_d)$, because it may be $x_0 \neq 1$. In fact DeHomog is applied to covectors $x \in (\mathbb{E}^d)^*$ returned by PLaSM and these are stored in a normalized form such that $|x| = 1$.

The UKPOLF (UnmaKe POLyhedron by Faces) function, which is a predefined PLaSM operator, returns the internal representation *by faces* of a polyhedral complex as a triplet <covectors, cells, pols>, very similar to the triplet <vertices, cells, pols> returned by the UKPOL operator. For example, we have:

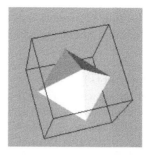

**Figure 4.2**   (a) $C_2$ cube and its polar set $C_2^*$, known as *rhombus*; (b) Octahedron
$C_3^*$, polar set of the $C_3$ cube

```
UKPOLF:(CUBOID:<1,1>) ≡ <
  < < 1.0, 0.0, 0.0 >,
    < -0.7071067811865475, 0.0, 0.7071067811865475 >,
    < 0.0, 1.0, 0.0 >,
    < 0.0, -0.7071067811865475, 0.7071067811865475 > >,
  < < 1,2,3,4 > >, < < 1 > > >
```

Thus, the `Polar` function just constructs a polyhedron by using as vertices the
(projected) face covectors of its dual.

Finally, notice that `Segment` produces a direct construction of the interval $[-1, 1]$
as a polyhedron in $\mathcal{P}^{1,1}$, whereas

$$\texttt{Cube} : \mathbf{Z}^+ \to \mathcal{P}^{d,d} : d \mapsto C_d,$$

with $\mathbf{Z}^+ = \{1, 2, \dots\}$, is the constructor function of $d$-cubes, via the Cartesian product
of $d$ `Segment` instances. The last two expressions of Script 4.2.4 produce the geometric
objects displayed in Figure 4.2.

---

**Script 4.2.4 (Polar sets of $d$-cubes)**
```
    DEF DeHomog = AA:/ ~ DISTR ~ [TAIL, FIRST];
    DEF Polar = MKPOL ~ [AA: DeHomog ~ S1,S2,S3] ~ UKPOLF;

    DEF Segment = MKPOL:<<<-1>,<1>>,<<1,2>>,<<1>>>;
    DEF Cube (d::IsIntPos) = (* ~ #:d): Segment;
    DEF Rhombus = (Polar ~ Cube):2;
    DEF Octahedron = (Polar ~ Cube):3;

    STRUCT:< (@1 ~ Cube):2, Rhombus >;
    STRUCT:< (@1 ~ Cube):3, Octahedron >;
```

---

No test for $x_0 = 0$ was actually performed before division in function `DeHomog`,
because we used the `Polar` function in the previous assumption that $o \in \operatorname{int} C$, where
$C$ is the input convex set.

A new implementation of `DeHomog` function is given in Script 4.2.5, where a test
for the null value of the homogeneous coordinate of covectors is performed. Such a
coordinate is simply dropped out when equal to zero, otherwise it is used to divide

the other ones. The `CLOSETO` function is used to test if the absolute value of difference of the input to some real `number` is smaller than some given `precision`.

---

**Script 4.2.5 (Polar sets)**

```
DEF CLOSETO (precision::IsRealPos)(number::IsReal) =
    IF:< LT: precision ~ ABS ~ - ~ [ID, K:number], K:True, K:False >;
DEF RTAIL = REVERSE ~ TAIL ~ REVERSE;
DEF DeHomog =
    IF:< CLOSETO:1E-12:0 ~ LAST, RTAIL , AA:/ ~ DISTR ~ [RTAIL, LAST] >;
DEF Polar = MKPOL ~ [AA: DeHomog ~ S1,S2,S3] ~ UKPOLF;
```

---

It is interesting to see in Script 4.2.6 that the *Platonic solids*, discussed in Section 4.9.1, are pairwise polar, with the `tetrahedron` being the polar of itself. Notice that in order to apply the `polar` function, the `dodecahedron` implementation given in Script 4.9.4 as a multicell polyhedral complex, must be preliminary transformed into a polyhedron constituted by a single cell. The single cell generated by the expression `JOIN:< dodecahedron >` could be used for this purpose. A *much* better programming strategy, which avoids the quite complex geometric construction of Script 4.9.4, is given below; the `icosahedron` implementation is given in Script 4.9.5.

---

**Script 4.2.6 (Polar of Platonic solids)**

```
(Polar):tetrahedron ≡ tetrahedron

(Polar ~ CUBOID):<1,1,1> ≡ octahedron
(Polar ~ Polar ~ CUBOID):<1,1,1> ≡ hexahedron

DEF dodecahedron1 = Polar:icosahedron;

(Polar):dodecahedron1 ≡ icosahedron
(Polar ~ Polar):dodecahedron1 ≡ dodecahedron
```

---

### 4.2.4   Boundary structure

Let us suppose in this section that $C \subset \mathbb{E}^n$ is a non-empty closed convex set.

**Faces**   A *face* of $C$ can be defined as a convex subset $F \subseteq C$ such that $x, y \in C$ and $(x+y)/2 \in F$ implies $x, y \in F$. Notice that both $C$ and $\emptyset$ are faces of $C$. A non-empty face $F$ is said to be *proper* when $F$ is a proper subset of $C$. The set of faces of $C$ will be denoted as $\mathcal{F}(C)$. A face of dimension $d$ will be called a $d$-face, and $\mathcal{F}_d(C) \subset \mathcal{F}(C)$ will denote the set of $d$-faces.

The relative interiors of any two faces in $\mathcal{F}(C)$ are disjointed. Thus, the family

$$\{\text{relint } F | F \in \mathcal{F}(C)\} \cup \mathcal{F}_0(C)$$

of relative interiors of faces of $C$, united with the set of 0-dimensional faces $\mathcal{F}_0(C)$, i.e. of faces $\{x\}$, where $x$ is an extreme point, gives a partition of $C$ into disjointed subsets.

**Skeletons**   The last property leads to a classification of a point $x \in C$ depending on the dimension of the uniquely determined face $F_x$ whose relative interior $x$ belongs to. The set $K_r(C)$ of all points $x$ belonging to faces of dimension $d \leq r$ will be called *r-skeleton* of $C$:

$$K_r(C) := \{x \in F_x | F_x \in \mathcal{F}_d(C), d \leq r\}.$$

Clearly for $0 \leq r < \dim C$, $K_r(C) \subseteq \partial C$, where the equality holds if and only if $r = \dim C - 1$.

## 4.3    Polyhedral sets

Polyhedra and cones are collectively called *polyhedral sets*. They are often referred to as $\mathcal{H}$-polyhedra, which means that they can be presented as the intersection of closed halfspaces.

**Definitions**   A set $P \in \mathbb{E}^n$ is a *polyhedron* if and only if it is the intersection of a finite number of closed halfspaces. So, we define:

$$\mathcal{H}(P) := P(\boldsymbol{A}, \boldsymbol{b}) := \{x \in \mathbb{E}^n | \boldsymbol{A}\boldsymbol{x} \leq \boldsymbol{b}\},$$

for some $\boldsymbol{A} \in \mathbb{R}^m_n$ and some $\boldsymbol{b} \in \mathbb{R}^m$.
    A set $C \in \mathbb{E}^n$ is said a *polyhedral cone* if and only if

$$\mathcal{H}(C) := C(\boldsymbol{A}, \boldsymbol{0}) := \{x \in \mathbb{E}^n | \boldsymbol{A}\boldsymbol{x} \leq \boldsymbol{0}\},$$

for some $\boldsymbol{A} \in \mathbb{R}^m_n$. Such a kind of set is both a cone and a polyhedron.

### 4.3.1    Extremal points

A point of a convex set $P$ is called an *extremal point* if it cannot be written as $(1 - \alpha)\boldsymbol{x} + \alpha\boldsymbol{y}$, with $\boldsymbol{x}, \boldsymbol{y} \in P$ and $0 < \alpha < 1$. The set of extremal points of $P$ is denoted as $\text{ext } P$.
    The inequality $\boldsymbol{a}\boldsymbol{x} \leq \beta$ is said to be *valid* with respect to the polyhedron $P$ if and only if $P \subseteq H^+_{\boldsymbol{a},\beta}$.
    The hyperplane $H_{\boldsymbol{a},\beta}$ is said to be a *support hyperplane* for the $P$ polyhedron if either $\boldsymbol{a}\boldsymbol{x} \leq \beta$ or $\boldsymbol{a}\boldsymbol{x} \geq \beta$ is valid and $H_{\boldsymbol{a},\beta} \cap P \neq \emptyset$.
    Let $P \subset \mathbb{E}^n$ be a polyhedron and $H$ a support hyperplane of $P$. The set $F = P \cap H$ is called a *face* of $P$. The $F$ face is a *vertex* if $\dim F = 0$; it is an *edge* if $\dim F = 1$, and it is a *facet* if $\dim F = n - 1$.

**Algebraic characterization of vertices**   Let $P = P(\boldsymbol{A}, \boldsymbol{b})$ be a polyhedron of $\mathbb{E}^n$, with $\boldsymbol{A} \in \mathbb{R}^m_n$ and $\boldsymbol{b} \in \mathbb{R}^m$. A point $\boldsymbol{x} \in P$ is an extreme of $P$ if and only if it satisfies as equations $n$ rows of the system $\boldsymbol{A}\boldsymbol{x} \leq \boldsymbol{b}$. It follows that a polyhedron $P(\boldsymbol{A}, \boldsymbol{b}) \subset \mathbb{E}^n$ contains extreme points if and only if $\text{rank } \boldsymbol{A} = n$.
    The extreme points of $P(\boldsymbol{A}, \boldsymbol{b}) \in \mathbb{E}^n$, if they exist, are a discrete set denoted $\text{ext } P(\boldsymbol{A})$, and their number at most equates the number $\binom{m}{n}$ of $\boldsymbol{A}$ minors with rank $n$. Such points are called polyhedron *vertices*.

*4.3.2   Double description*

The following *main theorems*[Zie95] give three pairs of alternative characterization of *polyhedra, polytopes,* and *cones,* respectively, that appear all to be very useful, maybe in different contexts. Notice that the same notation is used both for matrices, considered as sets of column vectors, and for sets of points in Euclidean space. For proofs, the reader is referred to [Zie95].

**Theorem 4.3.1 (Main theorem for polyhedra)** *A set $P \subseteq \mathbb{E}^d$ is the sum of a convex hull of a finite set of points plus a conical combination of vectors, say, a $\mathcal{V}$-polyhedron*

$$P = \operatorname{conv} V + \operatorname{cone} E, \qquad \text{for some } V \in \mathbb{E}_n^d, E \in \mathbb{R}_{n'}^d,$$

*if and only if it is an intersection of halfspaces, say a $\mathcal{H}$-polyhedron*

$$P = P(\boldsymbol{A}, \boldsymbol{b}), \qquad \text{for some } \boldsymbol{A} \in \mathbb{E}_d^m, \boldsymbol{b} \in \mathbb{E}^m,$$

*with $V = \operatorname{ext} P(\boldsymbol{A}, \boldsymbol{b})$ and $\operatorname{cone} E = P(\boldsymbol{A}, \boldsymbol{0})$.*

In other terms, a set $P \subseteq \mathbb{E}^d$ can be finitely generated either as a convex-conical combination of vectors ($\mathcal{V}$-polyhedron) or as the intersection of halfspaces ($\mathcal{H}$-polyhedron). If $P(\boldsymbol{A}, \boldsymbol{0}) = \{\boldsymbol{0}\}$, the $\mathcal{V}$-polyhedron is called *polytope* or $\mathcal{V}$-*polytope*, so that the previous theorem becomes the following one.

**Theorem 4.3.2 (Main theorem for polytopes)** *A set $P \subseteq \mathbb{E}^d$ is the convex hull of a finite set of points, say a $\mathcal{V}$-polytope*

$$P = \operatorname{conv} V, \qquad \text{for some } V \in \mathbb{E}_n^d$$

*if and only if it is a* bounded *intersection of halfspaces, say a $\mathcal{H}$-polytope*

$$P = P(\boldsymbol{A}, \boldsymbol{b}), \qquad \text{for some } \boldsymbol{A} \in \mathbb{E}_d^m, \boldsymbol{b} \in \mathbb{E}^m.$$

An alternate definition of a polytope $P$ is as a *bounded polyhedron*, i.e. such that there exists some $\kappa \in \mathbb{R}$ such that $|\boldsymbol{x} - \boldsymbol{y}| < \kappa$ for each $\boldsymbol{x}, \boldsymbol{y} \in P$. Finally, if $\operatorname{ext} P = \{\boldsymbol{0}\}$, then the $\mathcal{V}$-polyhedron is called a *polyhedral cone*. In this case we have:

**Theorem 4.3.3 (Main theorem for cones)** *A set $C \subseteq \mathbb{E}^d$ is the conical combination of a finite set of vectors*

$$C = \operatorname{cone} E, \qquad \text{for some } E \in \mathbb{E}_n^d$$

*if and only if it is a finite intersection of closed halfspaces containing the origin*

$$C = P(\boldsymbol{A}, \boldsymbol{0}), \qquad \text{for some } \boldsymbol{A} \in \mathbb{E}_d^m.$$

**Note**   The PLaSM kernel maintains both a $\mathcal{H}$- and a $\mathcal{V}$-representation of convex cells of a polyhedral complex. They are used as primary representations in the implementation of different operations. For example, the $\mathcal{H}$–representation is mainly useful with the Cartesian product and the Boolean operations, whereas the $\mathcal{V}$–representation is needed to generate the graphical output and to compute the inertial properties of a polyhedral complex.

## 4.4   Polytopes

We already know that a polyhedron is the solution set of a system of linear inequalities $Ax \le b$, and that a *polytope* is a bounded polyhedron. In particular we know that a polyhedron is a polytope when it does not contain a cone, i.e. when the associated homogeneous system $Ax \le 0$ has no solutions different from the zero vector.

**Properties**   Some useful properties of polytopes are listed below.

1. Each polytope is the intersection of finitely many closed halfspaces.
2. Each bounded intersection of finitely many closed halfspaces is a polytope.
3. The join, intersection, sum, product, projection of polytopes is a polytope.
4. The projection of a simplex is a polytope.
5. The polar body of a polytope is a polytope.
6. Each face of a polytope is a polytope.
7. Each proper face of a polytope $P$ is contained in some facet of $P$.

**Simplicial and simple polytopes**   A polytope $P \subset \mathbb{E}^d$ is said to be *simplicial* when all its facets are simplices. It is said to be *simple* when each vertex is generated as intersection of the minimal number $d$ of facets. Examples of simplicial polytopes are the octahedron and the icosahedron, where each face is a triangle. Examples of simple polytopes are the cube and the dodecahedron, where each vertex is the intersection of three facets. Simplicial and simple polytopes are linked by polarity: the polar of a simple polytope is a simplicial polytope, and vice versa. Simplices are the only polytopes which are both simple and simplicial.

### Example 4.4.1 (`IsPolytope` and `IsSimplex` predicates)
Two PLaSM predicates `IsPolytope` and `IsSimplex` are given in Script 4.4.1, in order to test if a geometric object is respectively a polytope or a simplex (of whatever dimensions) or not. Both predicates contain a logical `AND` of two component predicates. The predefined `IsPol` function is used to check if the function input is a polyhedral complex; the second predicate of `IsPolytope` just checks if the input contains a unique convex cell. The `IsSimplex` function aims to verify if the input is a polytope and if the number of vertices is $n + 1$, where $n$ is the dimension of the embedding space $\mathbb{E}^n$ of the input object.

### 4.4.1   Examples of polytopes

Some interesting and useful classes of polytopes are studied and implemented in this section. In particular, we give generative functions for *regular polygons* in 2D, the

**Script 4.4.1 (IsPolytope and IsSimplex)**

```
DEF IsPolytope = AND ~ [IsPol, EQ ~ [LEN ~ S2 ~ UKPOL, K:1]];
DEF IsSimplex = AND ~ [ IsPolytope, EQ ~ [LEN ~ S1 ~ UKPOL, RN + K:1] ];

IsSimplex:(CUBOID:<1>) ≡ True
IsSimplex:(SIMPLEX:3) ≡ True
IsSimplex:(CUBOID:<1,1>) ≡ False
IsPolytope:(CUBOID:<1,1>) ≡ True
```

standard *d-simplex*, the *d*-dimensional *crosspolytope*, the *pyramid* and the *prism* over a *d*-polytope, and the *d*-dimensional *permutahedron*, where *d* is an arbitrary positive integer.

## Regular polygons

2-polytopes with $n$ vertices are called *n-gons* or polygons. The word *polygon* is normally reserved to denote a larger class of 2D geometric objects, that are not necessarily convex. No ambiguity arises with *regular polygons*, which are *n*-gons with internal angles of equal size $\frac{2\pi}{n}$.

Regular polygons are easily generated by the ngon function of Script 4.4.2 as polyhedral approximation of the unit circle. The Circumference function given in Script 1.6.1 is used at this purpose. The last expression generates the compound geometric value with interposed translations shown in Figure 4.3.

**Script 4.4.2 (Regular polygons)**

```
DEF ngon (n::AND ~ [IsIntPos, GE:3]) = Circumference:1:n;

(STRUCT ~ CAT): (AA:ngon:(3..8) DISTR T:1:2.5)
```

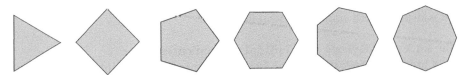

**Figure 4.3**   Regular polygons with a number of sides from 3 (triangle) to 8 (octagon)

## Standard *d*-simplex

In some books, including [Zie95], the standard *d*-simplex $\Delta_d$ is defined in $\mathbb{E}^{d+1}$ as the intersection of the hyperplane $\mathbb{1}x = 1$ with the standard cone $x \geq 0$, i.e.:

$$\Delta_d := \{x \in \mathbb{E}^{d+1} | \mathbb{1}x = 1, x \geq 0\} = \text{conv}\{e_1, \dots, e_{d+1}\}$$

Conversely, in PLaSM, the unit $d$-simplex is defined in $\mathbb{E}^d$ as

$$\texttt{SIMPLEX:d} \equiv \operatorname{conv}\{o, e_1, \dots, e_d\}.$$

Generating $\Delta_d$ is very simple. A direct generation method as convex hull of the extreme points of vectors $\{e_i\} \subset \mathbb{E}^{d+1}$ is given in Script 4.4.3 by the `Delta` function. The `IDNT` function, used to produce the sequence of $\{e_i\}$ vectors, is given in Script 3.3.5.

The `MyFrame` function simply produces a polyhedral complex in $\mathcal{P}^{1,d}$, whose cells are bijectively associated to vectors $e_i$, with $1 \leq i \leq d$. Each unit vector "image" is scaled to 1.5 size.

A picture of the generated $\Delta_2$, compared to a picture of `SIMPLEX:2`, is shown in Figure 4.4.1. The second one is clearly reducible to the first by an affine transformation. The associated geometric objects are produced by the last two expressions of Script 4.4.3.

---

**Script 4.4.3 (Standard $d$-simplex)**

```
DEF Delta (d::IsInt) = MKPOL:< IDNT:(d+1), <1..(d+1)>, <<1>> >;

DEF MyFrame (d::IsInt) = (S:(1..d):(#:d:1.5) ~ MKPOL):
   < #:d:0 AL IDNT:d, 1 DISTL (2..(d+1)), <1..d> >;

STRUCT:<Delta:2, MyFrame:3>;
STRUCT:<SIMPLEX:2, MyFrame:2>;
```

---

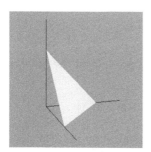 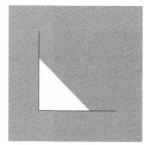

**Figure 4.4**   (a) Standard $d$-simplex $\Delta_2$; (b) Geometric value generated by `SIMPLEX:2`

### $d$-dimensional crosspolytope

A *crosspolytope* of dimension $d$, denoted $C_d^\Delta$, is the convex hull of the set $\{e_i\} \cup \{-e_i\}$, $1 \leq i \leq d$. Such polytopes are very easy to build with PLaSM, as the polyhedral complex whose vertices are generated by the expression

```
(CAT ~ [ID, (AA ~ AA):-] ~ IDNT):d
```

and having just one convex cell, i.e. the convex hull of the above $2d$ vertices. A generating function

$$\texttt{CrossPolytope}{:}Z^+ \to \mathcal{P}^{d,d} : d \mapsto C_d^\Delta,$$

with $Z^+ = \{1, 2, 3, \ldots\}$, is given in Script 4.4.4. The geometric constructions in Figure 4.5, with *rhombus* $\subset \mathbb{E}^2$, *octahedron* $\subset \mathbb{E}^3$ and their coordinate axes, are respectively generated by the last two PLaSM expressions.

---

**Script 4.4.4 (*d*-Crosspolytopes)**

```
DEF CrossPolytope (d::IsIntPos) = MKPOL:<
    (CAT ~ [ID, (AA ~ AA):-] ~ IDNT):d, <1..(2*d)>, <<1>> >;

(STRUCT ~ [CrossPolytope, Frame]):2;
(STRUCT ~ [CrossPolytope, Frame]):3;
```

---

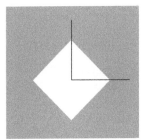 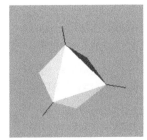

**Figure 4.5**   CrossPolytopes $C_2^\Delta$ and $C_3^\Delta$

## Prism over a polytope

A *prism* over a polytope $P$ is defined as a Cartesian product of the polytope times a unit interval $[0, 1] \subset \mathbb{R}$.

$$\texttt{Prism} : \mathcal{P}^{d,n} \to \mathcal{P}^{d+1,n+1} : P \mapsto P \times [0, 1]$$

The PLaSM implementation is extremely simple, because we may use the operation of *Cartesian product* (see Section 14.4) as a language primitive. The Prism definition is here usefully abstracted with respect to the basis object and to the height of the generated object. This operation is called *linear extrusion* in solid modeling.

---

**Script 4.4.5 (Prism over a polytope)**

```
DEF Prism (height::IsRealPos)(basis::IsPol) = basis * QUOTE:< height >;
```

---

Clearly, the basis object can be either a polytope or a polyhedral complex.

## Permutahedron

The permutahedron $\Pi_{d-1} \subset \mathbb{E}^d$ is defined as the convex hull of the permutations of the first $d$ integers, i.e.:

$$\Pi_{d-1} := \{ x \in \text{conv} \{ (\pi_i(1), \pi_i(2), \ldots, \pi_i(d)) \in \mathbb{E}^d \} \}, \qquad i \in \{1, \ldots, d!\}.$$

We remember that each permutation $\pi_i$ of a finite set is a bijective mapping on it, and in particular:

$$\pi_i : \{1, 2, \ldots, d\} \to \{1, 2, \ldots, d\}, \qquad \text{bijective.}$$

Clearly, each point $(\pi_i(1), \pi_i(2), \ldots, \pi_i(d))$ belongs to the sphere $S_{d-1} \subset \mathbb{E}^d$ of radius $(\pi_i(1)^2 + \pi_i(2)^2 + \cdots + \pi_i(d)^2)^{\frac{1}{2}}$. It is possible to show that $\dim(\text{aff } \Pi_{d-1}) = d-1$.

**Permutations**   The `permutations` function given in Script 4.4.6, is a general utility operator that allows generation of the (images of) the whole group of permutations of `<1,2, ... ,d>`.

The used algorithm starts with the pair `<<>,<1,2, ... ,d>>` and produces $d$ pairs `<<1>,<2, ... ,d>>`, `<<2>,<1,3, ... ,d>>`, `... ,<<d>,<1,2, ... ,d-1>>`; then from each `<<i>,<1, ... ,i-1,i+1, ... ,d>>` produces $d-1$ pairs `<<i,1>,<2, ... ,i-1,i+1, ... ,d>>`, `<<i,2>,<1,3, ... ,i-1,i+1, ... ,d>>`, `...`, and so on, until the second sequence of each pair becomes empty and is removed.

---

**Script 4.4.6 (Permutations)**

```
DEF remove (n::IsIntPos; seq::IsSeq) =
   (CONS ~ AA:SEL ~ CAT):< 1 .. n - 1, n + 1 .. LEN:seq >:seq;

DEF permutations (seq::IsSeq) =
   COMP:(AA:CAT AL #:n:(CAT ~ AA:permute)):<< <>, seq>>
WHERE
   n = LEN:seq,
   extract = AA: remove ~ DISTR ~ [INTSTO ~ LEN, ID],
   permute = TRANS ~ [ AA:AR ~ DISTL, extract ~ S2 ]
END;

permutations:<1,2,3> ≡ <<1,2,3>,<1,3,2>,<2,1,3>,<2,3,1>,<3,1,2>,<3,2,1>>

permutations:<1,2,3,4> ≡
   <<1,2,3,4>,<1,2,4,3>,<1,3,2,4>,<1,3,4,2>,<1,4,2,3>,<1,4,3,2>,<2,1,3,4>
   ,<2,1,4,3>,<2,3,1,4>,<2,3,4,1>,<2,4,1,3>,<2,4,3,1>,<3,1,2,4>,<3,1,4,2>
   ,<3,2,1,4>,<3,2,4,1>,<3,4,1,2>,<3,4,2,1>,<4,1,2,3>,<4,1,3,2>,<4,2,1,3>
   ,<4,2,3,1>,<4,3,1,2>,<4,3,2,1>>
```

---

**Permutahedron implementation**   As always in this book, a complete implementation of the studied object follows. In particular, the $\Pi_{d-1}$ permutahedron is implemented in a dimension-independent fashion in Script 4.4.7. Pictures of the objects generated by the last expressions are shown in Figure 4.6.

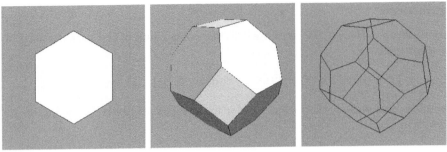

**Figure 4.6**   (a) Permutahedron $\Pi_2$ (b) Permutahedron $\Pi_3$ (c) 1-skeleton of $\Pi_3$

A $d$-dimensional `object` is first generated by `MKPOL` as the polytope with `vertices` given by `permutations:<1, ... ,d+1>`. The function `translation` is then applied to it, so moving its `Meanpoint` to the origin. Then a suitable sequence of `rotations` is applied, until the set aff `translation:object` is rotated to the coordinate subspace $\{x | x_{d+1} = 0\}$. The last (zero) coordinate is finally eliminated by application of the function `project:1`.

---

**Script 4.4.7 (Permutahedron)**

```
DEF permutahedron (d::IsIntPos) =
    ( project:1 ~ rotations ~ translation ):object
WHERE
    object = (MKPOL ~ [ID, [INTSTO ~ LEN], K:<<1>>]): vertices,
    vertices = permutations:(1 .. (d+1)),
    center = Meanpoint: vertices,
    translation = T:(1..(d+1)):(AA:-: center),
    rotations = COMP:(((CONS ~ AA:R):(1..d DISTR (d+1))):(PI/4))
END;

VRML: ((STRUCT ~ [ID, @1]):(permutahedron:2)):'out1.wrl';
VRML: ((STRUCT ~ [ID, @1]):(permutahedron:3)):'out2.wrl';
VRML: (@1:(permutahedron:3)):'out3.wrl';
```

---

It may be interesting to notice that polytopes $\Pi_2$ and $\Pi_3$ are subject to `rotations` tensors

$$(\text{COMP} \sim [\text{R:<1,3>, R:<2,3>}]):\tfrac{\pi}{4} ,$$
$$(\text{COMP} \sim [\text{R:<1,4>, R:<2,4>, R:<3,4>}]):\tfrac{\pi}{4}$$

respectively, before being projected, as they are generated in higher dimension. Analogously, for the $\Pi_d$ polytope we have:

$$(\text{COMP} \sim [\text{R:<1,d+1>, R:<2,d+1>, ... , R:<d,d+1>}]):\tfrac{\pi}{4}$$

The diligent reader might also like to know that the functions `Meanpoint` and `project` are defined in Scripts 4.4.8 and 4.4.9, respectively.

*4.4.2   Faces of polytopes*

Let $P = P(\boldsymbol{A}, \boldsymbol{b}) \subset \mathbb{E}^n$ be a polytope.

A set $F \subset P$ is called a *face* of $P$ if there exists a valid inequality $\boldsymbol{a}^T \boldsymbol{x} \leq \beta$ such that $F = \{\boldsymbol{x} \in P | \boldsymbol{a}^T \boldsymbol{x} = \beta\}$. $F$ is said to be the face induced by $\boldsymbol{a}^T \boldsymbol{x} \leq \beta$.

**Face lattice**  Both the sets $F = P$ and $F = \emptyset$ are faces of $P$, because the above definition is satisfied by the equalities $\boldsymbol{0}\boldsymbol{x} = 0$ and $\boldsymbol{0}\boldsymbol{x} = -1$, respectively.

Also, every intersection of faces is a face. In fact, let $F_i = \{\boldsymbol{x} \in P | \boldsymbol{a}_i^T \boldsymbol{x} = \beta_i\}$ and $F_j = \{\boldsymbol{x} \in P | \boldsymbol{a}_j^T \boldsymbol{x} = \beta_j\}$. Then we have that the set $F_i \cap F_j$ is induced by any linear combination of the equations of $F_i$ and $F_j$, for example:

$$F_i \cap F_j = \{\boldsymbol{x} \in P | (\boldsymbol{a}_j + \boldsymbol{a}_j)^T \boldsymbol{x} = (\beta_i + \beta_j)\},$$

and hence is a face.

It is possible to see [Zie95] that the set $\mathcal{F}(P)$ of faces of a polytope $P$ is a *lattice*, i.e. a partially ordered algebraic structure with unit $P$ and zero $\emptyset$, and with two operations *join* ($\vee$) and *meet* ($\wedge$) that satisfy the standard axioms of Boolean algebras. The two operations respectively return the unique minimal common ancestor and the unique maximal common descendant of any pair of faces, being the lattice partially ordered with respect to a containment relation.

Such algebraic structure is particularly easy to see in $\mathcal{F}(\sigma_d)$, where $\sigma_d$ is a simplex, and the face lattice is isomorphic to the family $2^{V(\sigma_d)}$ of subsets of $\sigma_d$ vertices.

**Dimension**  The *dimension* of a face $F$ is the dimension of aff $F$.

### Pyramid over a polytope

A *pyramid* is defined as the convex combination of a $d$-polytope $P \subset \mathbb{E}^n$ and a point $\boldsymbol{y} \notin \text{aff}\, P$:

$$\text{Pyramid} : \mathcal{P}^{d,n} \times \mathbb{E}^n \to \mathcal{P}^{d+1,n} : (P, \boldsymbol{y}) \mapsto \text{conv}\,(P \cup \{\boldsymbol{y}\}).$$

Polytope $P$ and point $\boldsymbol{y}$ are called the *basis* and *apex* of the pyramid, respectively.

**Faces of pyramid**  The set $\mathcal{F}(Q)$ of faces of $Q = \text{pyramid}(P, \boldsymbol{y})$ is easy to compute:

$$\mathcal{F}(Q) = \mathcal{F}(P) \cup \{F\boldsymbol{y} | F \in \mathcal{F}(P)\} \cup \{P\boldsymbol{y}\}.$$

where $A\boldsymbol{x}$ stands for the *join* of the set $A$ and the point $\boldsymbol{x}$.

**Implementation**  The implementation of Script 4.4.8 assumes $P$ to be full-dimensional, and embeds it so that aff $P := \{\boldsymbol{x} \in \mathbb{E}^{n+1} | x_{n+1} = 0\}$, and sets $\boldsymbol{y} :=$ (Meanpoint V($P$), $h$), $h \neq 0$, where Meanpoint $S = \frac{1}{|S|} \sum S$, with $S \subset \mathbb{E}^n$ a discrete set. Notice that Meanpoint $S \in \text{conv}\, S$, because it is a convex combination of points of $S$. The function

$$\text{MK} : \mathbb{E}^n \to \mathcal{P}^{0,n} : \boldsymbol{x} \mapsto \text{conv}\,\{\boldsymbol{x}\}$$

may be found in Script 3.3.15.

The geometric object generated by last expression of the script below is shown in Figure 4.7. The function SPLIT, to extract the sequence of convex cells from a polyhedral complex, is given in Script 10.8.4. The definition of the house2 object, entered as a triangleStrip, can be found in Script 7.2.19.

**Script 4.4.8** $((d+1)$-pyramid)

```
DEF mean = + / LEN;
DEF Meanpoint = AA:mean ~ TRANS;
DEF Pyramid (h::IsReal) = JOIN
    ~ [EMBED:1, MK ~ AR ~ [Meanpoint ~ S1 ~ UKPOL, K:h]];

(STRUCT ~ AA:(Pyramid:1) ~ SPLIT): house2;
```

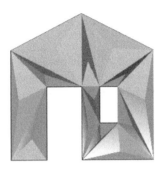

**Figure 4.7**   Pyramids over the convex cells of a polyhedral complex generated as a
triangle strip

*4.4.3  Projection*

Given two $\mathcal{H}$-polyhedra $P$ and $Q$, such that

$$P(\boldsymbol{A}, \boldsymbol{b}) \subset \mathbb{E}^n, \quad \text{and} \quad Q(\boldsymbol{A}', \boldsymbol{b}') \subset \mathbb{E}^q,$$

with $q \leq n$, we say that $Q$ is obtained by *projection* of $P$ if and only if:

$$\boldsymbol{y} \in Q \quad \Longleftrightarrow \quad \exists \boldsymbol{z} \in \mathbb{E}^{n-q} \text{ such that } \boldsymbol{x} = (\boldsymbol{y}, \boldsymbol{z}) \in P$$

Algebraically speaking, we say that the system of inequalities $\boldsymbol{A}' \boldsymbol{y} \leq \boldsymbol{b}'$ is derived from $\boldsymbol{A} \boldsymbol{x} \leq \boldsymbol{b}$ by *eliminating* the components of $\boldsymbol{z}$.

It turns out more useful to define a projection operator along a single coordinate direction. Let us start with $P(\boldsymbol{A}, \boldsymbol{b}) \subset \mathbb{E}^n$ and suppose we want to project on the coordinate hyperplane $\{\boldsymbol{x} \in \mathbb{E}^n | x_k = 0\}$. So we define, following Ziegler [Zie95], the *projection* of $P$ in the direction of $\boldsymbol{e}_k$ as:

$$\begin{aligned} \text{proj}_k P &:= \{\boldsymbol{x} - x_k \boldsymbol{e}_k | \boldsymbol{x} \in P\} \\ &= \{\boldsymbol{x} \in \mathbb{E}^n | x_k = 0, \exists y \in \mathbb{R} : \boldsymbol{x} + y\boldsymbol{e}_k \in P\}. \end{aligned}$$

A very similar set is the *elimination* of $x_k$ in P, defined as follows. Both $\text{proj}_k P$ and $\text{elim}_k P$ are shown in Figure 4.8.

$$\begin{aligned} \text{elim}_k P &:= \{\boldsymbol{x} - t\boldsymbol{e}_k | \boldsymbol{x} \in P\} \\ &= \{\boldsymbol{x} \in \mathbb{E}^n | \exists y \in \mathbb{R} : \boldsymbol{x} + y\boldsymbol{e}_k \in P\}. \end{aligned}$$

Clearly, given $P \subseteq \mathbb{E}^n$, there is an isomorphism

$$\text{elim}_k P \cong \text{proj}_k P \times \mathbb{E},$$

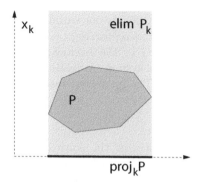

**Figure 4.8**  Polyhedron $P$ and associated set $\mathrm{proj}_k P$ and $\mathrm{elim}_k P$

which reduces to equality when $k = n$ and the last coordinate of points in $\mathrm{proj}_n P$ is dropped out:

$$\mathrm{elim}_n P = \{x \in \mathbb{E}^{n-1} | (x,0) \in \mathrm{proj}_n P\}) \times \mathbb{E}$$

### Example 4.4.2 (Projection operator)
A possible PLaSM implementation of a projection operator

$$\texttt{Project}: Z^+ \times \mathbb{E}^n \to \mathbb{E}^{n-m} : (m, P) \mapsto (\mathrm{proj}_{n-m} \circ \cdots \circ \mathrm{proj}_{n-1} \circ \mathrm{proj}_n )P,$$

where $Z^+$ is the set of positive integers, is given in Script 4.4.9. The last expression shows that `Project:2`, when applied to a 5-dimensional object, returns a 3-dimensional object. The implementation clearly exploits the property that the projection of a collection $\{P(V_i)\}$ of $\mathcal{V}$-polytopes is the collection of convex hulls of the projected vertices:

$$\mathrm{proj}_k \{P(V_i)\} = \{\mathrm{proj}_k P(V_i)\} = \{\mathrm{conv}\,(\mathrm{proj}_k V_i)\}$$

---

**Script 4.4.9 (Projection operator)**
```
DEF Project (m::IsIntPos)(pol::IsPol) =
    (MKPOL ~ [AA:CutCoords ~ S1, S2, S3] ~ UKPOL):pol
WHERE
    CutCoords = Reverse ~ (COMP ~ #:m):TAIL ~ Reverse
END;

Project:2:(CUBOID:<1,1,1,1,1>) ≡ CUBOID:<1,1,1>
```

---

**Fourier-Motzkin elimination**  The so-called *Fourier-Motzkin projection method*, also known as Fourier-Motzkin elimination, finds one solution, if it exists, of a system of simultaneous linear inequalities. In particular, this algorithm solves a system $A^{(1)}x^{(1)} \le b^{(1)}$ with $n$ variables, by projecting it onto a system $A^{(2)}x^{(2)} \le b^{(2)}$, with $n-1$ variables, and so on, until a final projected system $A^{(n)}x^{(n)} \le b^{(n)}$ with only one variable is obtained. A single inequality in only one variable is easy to study. If it cannot be solved, then the original system is *incompatible*, i.e. cannot be solved. Otherwise, a solution of $A^{(n)}x^{(n)} \leq b^{(n)}$ is used in the backward phase of the algorithm to reconstruct a solution $x$ to the original system. A detailed discussion of this algorithm is out the scope of the present book. The interested reader is referred to [DC73].

## 4.5   Simplicial complexes

We already met a definition of *simplex* as the convex hull of affinely independent points. A slightly different approach and notation are used in this section to discuss simplices and well-formed assemblies of simplices, called *simplicial complexes*, by using language and terminology from algebraic topology [Poi53]. At the end of this section we give a function to generate the so-called (after Maldelbrot [Man88]) *fractal simplex* of dimension $d$ and depth $n$, with $d, n$ arbitrary positive integers

### 4.5.1   Definitions

A notational warning is first needed. We use here simple subscripts both to denote dimension and indices. In case of possible confusion, parenthesized subscripts are used as indices.

**Join operation**   The *join* of two sets $P, Q \subset \mathbb{E}^n$ is the set

$$PQ = \{\alpha x + \beta y \mid x \in P, y \in Q\},$$

where $\alpha, \beta \in \mathbb{R}$, $\alpha, \beta \geq 0$ and $\alpha + \beta = 1$. The join operation is associative and commutative.

**Example 4.5.1 (JOIN primitive)**
PLaSM offers a primitive operator from sequences of polyhedra in $\mathbb{E}^n$ to polyhedra in $\mathbb{E}^n$:

$$\mathtt{JOIN} : (\mathcal{P}^{d_i, n})^* \to \mathcal{P}^{m,n} : \{P_1, \dots, P_s\} \mapsto \operatorname{conv} P_1 \cup \dots \cup P_s, \qquad i \in \{1, \dots, s\},$$

where $m = \dim \operatorname{conv} P_1 \cup \dots \cup P_s$. JOIN can be also applied to sequences of points in the same space, but they must be preliminarily transformed into 0-dimensional polyhedra.

**Simplex**   A *d-simplex* $\sigma_d \subset \mathbb{E}^n$ ($0 \leq d \leq n$) may be defined as the repeated join of $d + 1$ affinely independent points, called *vertices*. A $d$-simplex can be seen as a $d$-dimensional triangle: a 0-simplex is a *point*, a 1-simplex is a *segment*, a 2-simplex is a *triangle*, a 3-simplex is a *tetrahedron*, and so on.

The set $\{v_0, v_1, \dots, v_d\}$ of vertices of $\sigma_d$ is called the *0-skeleton* of $\sigma_d$. The $s$-simplex generated from *any* subset of $s + 1$ vertices ($0 \leq s \leq n$) of $\sigma_d$ is called an *s-face* of $\sigma_d$.

Let us notice, from the definition, that a simplex may be considered both as a purely combinatorial object and as a geometric object, i.e. as the compact point set defined by the convex hull of a discrete set of points.

**Complex**   A set $\Sigma$ of simplices is called a *triangulation*. A *simplicial complex*, often simply denoted as *complex*, is a triangulation $\Sigma$ that verifies the following conditions:

1. if $\sigma \in \Sigma$, then any face of $\sigma$ belongs to $\Sigma$;
2. if $\sigma, \tau \in \Sigma$, then either $\sigma \cap \tau = \emptyset$, or $\sigma \cap \tau$ is a face of both $\sigma$ and $\tau$.

A simplicial complex can be considered a "well-formed" triangulation. Such kind of triangulations are widely used in engineering analysis, e.g., in topography or in finite element methods.

The *order* of a complex is the maximum order of its simplices. A complex $\Sigma_d$ of order $d$ is also called a *d-complex*. A $d$-complex is said to be *regular* or *pure* if each simplex is a face of a $d$-simplex. A regular $d$-complex is homogeneously $d$-dimensional.

The *combinatorial boundary* $\Sigma_{d-1} = \partial \sigma_d$ of a simplex $\sigma_d$ is a simplicial complex consisting of all proper $s$-faces ($s < d$) of $\sigma_d$.

Two simplices $\sigma$ and $\tau$ in a complex $\Sigma$ are called *s-adjacent* if they have a common $s$-face. Hereafter, when we refer to adjacencies into a $d$-complex, we intend to refer to the maximum order adjacencies, i.e. to $(d-1)$-adjacencies. $\mathcal{K}_s$ ($s \leq d$) denotes the set of $s$-faces of $\Sigma_d$, and $|K_s|$ denotes the number of $s$-simplices.

With some abuse of language, we call (combinatorial) *s-skeletons* the sets $\mathcal{K}_s$ ($s \leq d$). *Geometric carrier* $|\Sigma|$, also called the *support space*, is the point set union of simplices in $\Sigma$.

**Orientation**   The ordering of the 0-skeleton of a simplex implies an *orientation* of it. The simplex can be oriented according to the even or odd permutation class of its 0-skeleton. The two opposite orientation of a simplex will be denoted as $+\sigma$ and $-\sigma$. Two simplices are *coherently oriented* when their common faces have opposite orientation. A complex is *orientable* when all its simplices can be coherently oriented. It is assumed that:

1. the two orientations of a simplex represent its relative interior and exterior;
2. the two orientations of an orientable simplicial complex analogously represent the relative interior and exterior of the complex, respectively;
3. the boundary of a complex maintains the same orientation of the complex.

The volume associated with an orientation of a simplex (or complex) is positive, while the one associated with the opposite orientation has the same absolute value and opposite sign. It is assumed that the bounded object has positive volume. It is also assumed that either a minus sign or a multiplying factor $-1$ denote a complementation, i.e. an opposite orientation of the simplex, which can be explicitly obtained by swapping two vertices in its ordered 0-skeleton. For example:

$$+\sigma_3 = \langle v_0, v_1, v_2, v_3 \rangle$$
$$-\sigma_3 = \langle v_1, v_0, v_2, v_3 \rangle$$

**Face extraction**   The oriented facets $\sigma_{d-1,(i)}$ ($0 \leq i \leq d$) of the oriented $d$-simplex $\sigma_d = +\langle v_0, v_1, \ldots, v_d \rangle$ are obtained by removing the $i$-th vertex $v_i$ from the 0-skeleton of $\sigma_d$:

$$\sigma_{d-1,(i)} = (-1)^i(\sigma_d - \langle v_i \rangle), \qquad 0 \leq i \leq d. \tag{4.1}$$

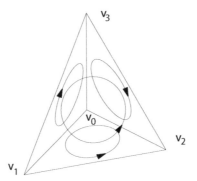

**Figure 4.9**   Coherent orientation of the faces of a 3-simplex

The 0-skeleton of $\sigma_{d-1,(i)}$ is therefore obtained by removing the $i$-th vertex from the 0-skeleton of $\sigma_d$ and either by swapping a pair of vertices or, better, by inverting the simplex sign, when $i$ is odd.

Finally, we will use the notation $\mathcal{A}(\sigma_{(i)})$ to denote the unique $d$-simplex which is $(d-1)$-adjacent to $\sigma$ along the face $\sigma_{(i)}$, if it exists. When $\sigma_{(i)}$ is a boundary simplex, $\mathcal{A}(\sigma_{(i)})$ is not defined, which we denote by $\mathcal{A}(\sigma_{(i)}) = \perp$.

**Oriented faces of a simplex**   According to equation (4.1), the set of 2-faces (see Figure 4.9) of the 3-simplex $\sigma_3 = +\langle v_0, v_1, v_2, v_3 \rangle$ is: $\mathcal{K}_2(\sigma_3) = \{\sigma_{2,(0)}, \sigma_{2,(1)}, \sigma_{2,(2)}, \sigma_{2,(3)}\}$, where

$$
\begin{aligned}
\sigma_{2,(0)} &= +\langle v_1, v_2, v_3 \rangle, \\
\sigma_{2,(1)} &= -\langle v_0, v_2, v_3 \rangle, \\
\sigma_{2,(2)} &= +\langle v_0, v_1, v_3 \rangle, \\
\sigma_{2,(3)} &= -\langle v_0, v_1, v_2 \rangle.
\end{aligned}
$$

Notice that all the triangle faces of the tetrahedron $\sigma_3$ are coherently oriented, and that, by using again the equation (4.1), the edges of triangles are generated coherently oriented.

For instance, taking $\sigma_{2,(0)} = +\langle v_1, v_2, v_3 \rangle$ and $\sigma_{2,(1)} = -\langle v_0, v_2, v_3 \rangle$, we see that their common faces $\sigma_{1,(0),(0)} = +\langle v_2, v_3 \rangle$ and $\sigma_{1,(1),(0)} = -\langle v_2, v_3 \rangle$, built according again to (4.1), have opposite orientations.

**Simplicial prism**   The prism over a simplex $\sigma_d = \langle v_0, \ldots, v_d \rangle$, defined as the set $P_{d+1} := \sigma_d \times [a, b]$, with $[a, b] \subset \mathbb{E}$, will be called *simplicial $(d+1)$-prism*. An oriented complex which triangulates $P_{d+1}$ can be defined combinatorially, by using a closed form formula for its $\mathcal{K}_{d+1}$ skeleton:

$$
\mathcal{K}_{d+1} = \{\sigma_{d+1,(i)} = (-1)^{id} \langle v_i^a, v_{i+1}^a, \ldots, v_d^a, v_0^b, v_1^b, \ldots, v_i^b \rangle | 0 \leq i \leq d\}
$$

where $v_i^a = (v_i, a)$ and $v_i^b = (v_i, b)$.

**Implementation**   To generate a triangulation of the simplicial $d$-prism is quite easy, by considering that the simplices in $\mathcal{K}_{d+1} = \{\sigma_{d+1,(i)} | 0 \leq i \leq d\}$ of the previous

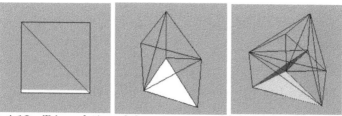

**Figure 4.10**    Triangulation of the prisms over: (a) 1-simplex (b) 2-simplex (c)
3-simplex, with the basis simplices highlighted.

formula can simply be obtained by extracting the adjacent $(d + 2)$-tuples from the
ordered set

$$(v_0^a, v_1^a, \ldots, v_d^a, v_0^b, v_1^b, \ldots, v_d^b)$$

with $2(d + 1)$ elements.

The geometric object in Figure 4.10b is generated by the last expression of
Script 4.5.1. The object shown in Figure 4.10c is first rotated in $\mathbb{E}^4$, then projected
in $\mathbb{E}^3$. The IsSimplex predicate is given in Script 4.4.1.

---

**Script 4.5.1 (Triangulation of simplicial $d$-prism)**

```
DEF simplexPile (cell::IsSimplex) = (MKPOL ~ [ID, cells, pols]):verts
WHERE
    cells = TRANS ~ AA:FROMTO ~ ((CONS ~ AA:CONS ~ TRANS):
        < AA:K:(1..(d+1)), (AA:(- ~ [K:LEN, K]) ~ reverse):(0..d) >),
    pols = AA:LIST ~ INTSTO ~ K:d,
    verts = (CAT ~ AA:(S1 ~ UKPOL) ~ [ID, T:n:1] ~ EMBED:1): cell,
    d = DIM: cell + 1,
    n = RN: cell + 1
END;

(STRUCT ~ [@1 ~ simplexPile, ID] ~ SIMPLEX):2
```

---

Closed formulas to triangulate the $(d + 1)$-prism over a $d$-complex in a time linear
with the size of the output, while computing also the $d$-adjacencies between the
resulting $(d + 1)$-simplices, can be found in [FP91].

### 4.5.2   Linear d-Polyhedra

In some algebraic topology books a definition of $d$-polyhedron is given, that is quite
different from the one discussed in Section 4.3.

In this case a *d-polyhedron* is defined as a compact set $P_d \subset \mathbb{E}^n$ for which at least
a pair $(\Sigma_d, h)$ exists, where $\Sigma_d$ $(d \leq n)$ is a simplicial $d$-complex, and $h : P_d \to |\Sigma_d|$
is a homeomorphic map.[1]

Following the above definition, polyhedra are not necessarily linear; for example, a
sphere or a torus or a free-form surface are polyhedra.

---

[1] A homeomorphic map is an invertible continuous topological transformation.

 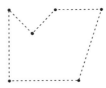

**Figure 4.11**   Skeletons $K_s(P_2)$, $(2 \geq s \geq 0)$

A polyhedron is *regular* if any associated complex is regular; it is *linear* if the map $h$ is the identity map. Hence, a *linear polyhedron coincides with the geometric carrier of a simplicial complex* (see Figure 4.11). Since we deal only with linear polyhedra, we may use equally the terms polyhedron and complex.

**Boundary**   If any $(d-1)$-simplex in $\Sigma$ is a face of exactly two $d$-simplices, then $\Sigma$ is said to be *closed*; otherwise it is said to be *open*. As an example, let us consider any 1-complex and any 2-complex which triangulate the circumference $S_1$ and the circle $S_2$, respectively: the first complex is closed; the second is open.

The *boundary* $\partial P_d$ of a polyhedron $P_d$ is the geometric carrier of the $(d-1)$-complex whose $(d-1)$-simplices are faces of exactly one $d$-simplex in a complex which triangulates $P_d$. An important theorem states that a closed complex has no boundary:

$$\partial \partial P_d = \emptyset.$$

A maximal $(d-1)$-connected component of a closed $d$-complex is called a *shell* of the complex.

### 4.5.3   Fractal d-simplex

We discuss in this section the generation of the *fractal d-simplex*, sometimes also called the *recursive d-simplex* or the *Sierpinski simplex*, that is generated by subtracting from the standard simplex of the same dimension a central portion defined by the convex hull of middle points of 1-faces.

This subtraction generates $d + 1$ new $d$-simplices, each one adjacent to one of the vertices of the original $d$-simplex. The 1-faces of the new simplices have half-length with respect to the original ones. This process may be repeated on each of the $d + 1$ $d$-simplices previously generated, so producing $(d + 1)^2$ $d$-simplices. The subdivision can be repeated several times, producing $(d+1)^n$ $d$-simplices after $n$ subdivision steps. They are spatially organized as a sort of $d$-dimensional fractal structure, as shown by Figures 4.12 and 4.13.

**Implementation**   We implement here a PLaSM function `fractalSimplex`, which is used to produce the fractal $d$-simplex of any depth $n$.

Let us first define a `component` function which transforms the sequence of vertices of a simplex into a new sequence where the $i$-th vertex, called the `pivot`, is fixed, whereas the other are moved to the `Meanpoint` between the `pivot` position and their old position. The script also shows two examples of use of the `component` function on the vertices of the standard $\mathbb{E}^2$ `triangle`.

A local function named `expand` is used to transform the sequence of the $d + 1$ vertices of a $d$-simplex into the sequence of sequences of vertices of the $d+1$ $d$-simplices

**Figure 4.12**  (a) Fractal triangle of depth 5 generated by `fractalSimplex:2:5` (b) Fractal tetrahedron of depth 3 generated by `fractalSimplex:3:3`

---

**Script 4.5.2**

```
DEF component (i::IsIntPos; seq::IsSeq) = CAT:< firstPart, <pivot>, lastPart >
WHERE
    firstSeq = AS:SEL:(1..(i - 1)):seq,
    pivot = SEL:i:seq,
    lastSeq = AS:SEL:((i + 1)..LEN:seq):seq,
    firstPart = (AA:Meanpoint ~ DISTR):< firstSeq, pivot >,
    lastPart  = (AA:Meanpoint ~ DISTR):< lastSeq,  pivot >
END;
DEF triangle = <<0.0, 0.0>, <0.0, 1.0>, <1.0, 0.0>>

component:<1, triangle> = <<0.0, 0.0>, <0.0, 0.5>, <0.5, 0.0>>
component:<3, triangle> = <<0.5, 0.0>, <0.5, 0.5>, <1.0, 0.0>>
```

---

generated by the `component` function, by using as pivot element each vertex of the input simplex.

We can finally define the operator `fractalSimplex`, shown in Script 4.5.3. This one will accept as input parameters the dimension $d$ and the depth $n$ of the fractal simplex to be generated. Notice that such a function is written in *pure* FL style, i.e. with neither recursion nor iteration. Conversely, a sort of *stream processing* is used here, where to all simplices generated at each step is applied a sort of *black box*, i.e. the `expand` function, that from each input simplex generates $(d + 1)$ smaller $d$-simplices suitably positioned on its interior.

---

**Script 4.5.3**

```
DEF fractalSimplex (d::IsIntPos)(n::IsIntPos) =
    (mkpols ~ splitting ~ [S1] ~ UKPOL ~ SIMPLEX):d
WHERE
    mkpols = STRUCT ~ AA:MKPOL ~ AA:AL ~ DISTR ~ [ID,K:<<1..d+1>,<<1>>>],
    splitting = (COMP ~ #:n):(CAT ~ AA: expand),
    expand = AA:component ~ DISTR ~ [INTSTO ~ LEN, ID]
END;
```

---

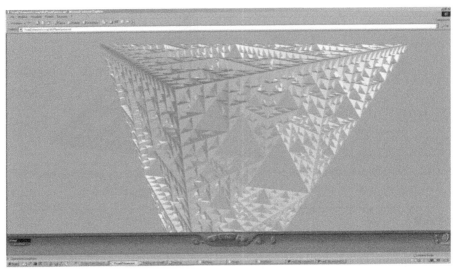

**Figure 4.13**   Polyhedral complex generated by `fractalSimplex:3:5`

## 4.6   Polyhedral complexes

Polyhedral complexes are very important in the context of geometric programming, since every object of geometric type in PLaSM is a polyhedral complex, possibly composed by just one convex cell, and (only implicitly) by all its faces.

**Definition**   A *polyhedral complex* $\mathcal{C}$ is a finite collection of polyhedra of $\mathbb{E}^n$ such that:

1. if $P \in \mathcal{C}$, then $\mathcal{F}(P) \subseteq \mathcal{C}$;
2. if $P, Q \in \mathcal{C}$, then $P \cap Q \in \mathcal{F}(P)$ and $P \cap Q \in \mathcal{F}(Q)$.

A polyhedral complex $\mathcal{C}$ such that every element $P \in \mathcal{C}$ is a polytope is also called a *polytopal complex*. Actually, the geometric data structure used by PLaSM, and named HPC (Hierarchical Polyhedral Complex), is a finite collection of polytopal complexes, each of which satisfies the properties 1. and 2. given above.

The *dimension* dim$\mathcal{C}$ of a polytopal complex is the highest dimension of its polytope elements. Analogously, the dimension of a collection $\mathcal{P} = \{\mathcal{C}_i\}$, made by polytopal complexes, is their highest dimension.

**Polytopal subdivision and triangulation**   A *polytopal subdivision* of a set $P \subset \mathbb{E}^n$ is a polytopal complex $\mathcal{C} = \{C_i\}$ such that:

1. $\cup_i |C_i| = P$;
2. all the cells $C_i \in \mathcal{C}$ are polytopes.

A polytopal subdivision $\mathcal{T}$ of a set $P \subset \mathbb{E}^n$ is called a (well-formed) *triangulation* when all the cells in $\mathcal{T}$ are simplices or, equivalently, $\mathcal{T}$ is a simplicial complex.

**Example 4.6.1 (Polytopal subdivision)**
The primitive constructor `MKPOL` of geometric objects in PLaSM requires, in order

to work correctly, that the convex cells define a polytopal subdivision of the linear polyhedron we want to represent.

**Figure 4.14**   (a) Linear polyhedron $P$ (b) Non-polytopal subdivision of $P$
(c) Polytopal subdivision of $P$

We leave as an exercise for the reader the task of coping with three different definitions of the `complex` object, until the three images of Figure 4.14 from the expression:

    (STRUCT $\sim$ [ID, @1]): complex

are achieved.

**Notational warning**   Through the whole book, we use the notation $\mathcal{P}^{d,n}$ to denote:

the *space* $\mathcal{P}^{d,n}$ of geometric objects with *intrinsic* dimension $d$ and *embedding* dimension $n$.

Now we are finally able to give a precise meaning to such expression:

1. "the *space* $\mathcal{P}^{d,n}$ of geometric objects" is the set of finite collections of polytopal subdivisions of linear polyhedra;
2. "with *intrinsic* dimension $d$" means that, if $P \in \mathcal{P}^{d,n}$, then $P = \{P_i\}$ is a collection of polytopal subdivisions $P_i$ such that

$$d = \max\{\dim(\text{aff } P_i) | P_i \in P\},$$

    where $\text{aff } P_i = \text{aff } |P_i|$;
3. "and *embedding* dimension $n$" means that, if $P \in \mathcal{P}^{d,n}$, then $|P| \subset \mathbb{E}^n$.

For sake of simplicity, we make a further distinction between a (combinatorial) complex $P \in \mathcal{P}^{d,n}$ as a family (of faces) of polytopes, and its (geometric) support space $|P| \subset \mathbb{E}^n$, only in case of need. In both meanings we will normally use the notation $P$. The distinction should usually be clear from the context.

Furthermore, in the current implementation of the PLaSM language, the constraint that each $P_i$ must constitute a polytopal subdivision is actually not enforced.

### 4.6.1   Schlegel diagrams

**Definition**   The *Schlegel diagram* of a polytope $P \subset \mathbb{E}^d$, with $\dim P = d$, is defined as the polytopal complex $\mathcal{S}(P, F, \boldsymbol{y})$, of dimension $d-1$, which is obtained by projecting $P$ onto a facet $F \in \mathcal{F}(P)$ from an external point $\boldsymbol{y}$.

In some sense, the Schlegel diagram $\mathcal{S}(P)$ encodes the combinatorial structure of a $d$-polytope $P$ into a $(d-1)$-complex $\mathcal{S}(P)$.

**Construction** Let us consider a facet $F \in \mathcal{F}(P)$, and let $H_F^+$ be its support hyperspace, such that $P \subset H_F^+$. Let us also consider a point $\boldsymbol{y} \in H_F^-$, with its orthogonal projection within $F$, i.e. such that $\pi(\boldsymbol{y}) \in F$.

Let $G\boldsymbol{y}$, i.e. the *join* of face $G \subset \mathcal{F}(P)$ and $\boldsymbol{y}$, be the pyramid with basis $G$ and apex $\boldsymbol{y}$. Then the *Schlegel diagram* of $P$ from $\boldsymbol{y}$ on $F \in \mathcal{F}(P)$ is precisely defined as the polytopal complex:

$$\mathcal{S}(P, F, \boldsymbol{y}) = \{G\boldsymbol{y} \cap H_F | G \in \mathcal{F}(P) \backslash \{F\}\}.$$

**Implementation** The easiest implementation is obtained by projecting the $P$ polytope from the point $(0, \ldots, 0, r) \in \mathbb{E}^d$ into the coordinate hyperplane $\{\boldsymbol{x}|x_d = 0\}$. This choice will require, in most of cases, the preliminary application of some affine transformation to $P$ to adjust its position and orientation in order to have some $F$ facet close and parallel to the hyperplane $\{\boldsymbol{x}|x_d = 0\}$.

Such projection $\pi_d : \mathbb{E}^d \to \mathbb{E}^d$ may be represented in homogeneous coordinates, using standard graphics techniques (see Foley *et al.* [FvDFH90], p. 256), as a matrix $\boldsymbol{M}'_{per}$ which differs from the identity $(d+1) \times (d+1)$ just for the elements of the last two rows, and such that:

$$\begin{pmatrix} 1 & & & & \\ & 1 & & & \\ & & \ddots & & \\ 0 & & & 0 & 0 \\ & & & 1/r & 1 \end{pmatrix} \begin{pmatrix} x_1 \\ \vdots \\ x_{d-1} \\ x_d \\ 1 \end{pmatrix} = \begin{pmatrix} x_1 \\ \vdots \\ x_{d-1} \\ 0 \\ x_d/r \end{pmatrix} \simeq \begin{pmatrix} \frac{x_1}{(x_d/r)} \\ \vdots \\ \frac{x_{d-1}}{(x_d/r)} \\ 0 \\ 1 \end{pmatrix}.$$

Such perspective transformation can be directly applied in PLaSM to a polyhedral domain by using the primitive operator MAP, as shown in Script 4.6.1, where two different operators schlegel2D and schlegel3D are given, to generate the diagrams of 3D and 4D polytopes, respectively. Notice that the center of projection is located at $(0, 0, 0.2)$ and at $(0, 0, 0, 0.2)$, respectively.

---

**Script 4.6.1 (Schlegel diagrams)**

```
DEF schlegel2D (d::isreal) = MAP:[s1/(s3/K:d), s2/(s3/K:d), K:0];
DEF schlegel3D (d::isreal) =
    project:1 ~ MAP:[s1/(s4/K:d), s2/(s4/K:d), s3/(s4/K:d), K:0];
```

---

The three Schlegel diagrams in Figure 4.15, with the 1-skeletons of the 4-simplex $\Delta_4$, of the 4-dimensional cube and of the 4-polytope $\Delta_2 \times \Delta_2$, are generated by the three expressions of Script 4.6.2, respectively.

---

**Script 4.6.2 (Schlegel diagrams examples (1))**

```
schlegel3D:0.2: ((@1 ~ T:<1,2,3,4>:<-1,-1,-1,1> ~ CUBOID):<2,2,2,2>);
schlegel3D:0.2: ((@1 ~ T:<1,2,3,4>:<-1/3,-1/3,-1,1>):(SIMPLEX:4));
schlegel3D:0.2: ((@1 ~ T:<1,2,3,4>:<-1/3,-1/3,-1,1>):(SIMPLEX:2 * SIMPLEX:2))
```

---

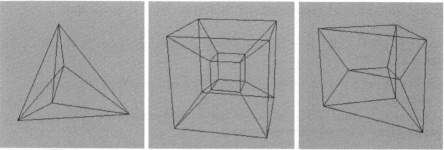

**Figure 4.15**   1-skeletons of Schlegel diagrams: (a) 4-simplex $\Delta_4$
(b) 4-dimensional cube (c) 4-polytope $\Delta_2 \times \Delta_2$

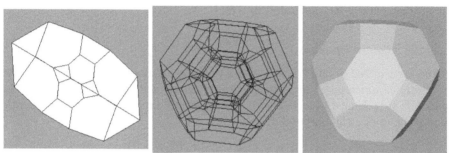

**Figure 4.16**   Schlegel diagrams: (a) 3-permutahedron $\Pi_3$ (b) 1-skeleton of $\Pi_4$
(c) 4-permutahedron $\Pi_4$

Analogously, the Schlegel diagrams of the 3- and 4-permutahedron given in Figure 4.16 are produced by the three expressions of Script 4.6.3.

---

**Script 4.6.3 (Schlegel diagrams examples (2))**

```
(STRUCT ~ [ID,@1] ~ schlegel2D):0.2:((@2 ~ T:3:2.5 ~ permutahedron):3);
schlegel3D:0.2: ((@1 ~ T:4:5):(permutahedron:4));
schlegel3D:0.2: ((@2 ~ T:4:5):(permutahedron:4));
```

---

## 4.7   Nef polyhedra

Nef polyhedra are introduced and shortly discussed in this section. This very general definition of polyhedra allows representation of a very large class of piecewise-linear point sets. Nef's concept of polyhedron appears to meet the needs of solid modeling surprisingly well: Nef polyhedra can have internal boundaries, they can be neither closed nor open, as well as non-regular and non-manifold (see Section 13.1.1). Moreover, a complete and mathematically sound theory is contained in the original Nef's work [Nef78]. Such point sets provide a a powerful modeling space for the purpose of (piecewise-linear) solid modeling and related applications (see Chapter 13). Our main references for the present section are Bieri [Bie94b, Bie94a] and Ferrucci [Fer95a, Fer95b].

A Nef polyhedron can be defined in several equivalent ways. In particular:

**Definition**   A set $P \subseteq \mathbb{E}^n$ is a *Nef polyhedron* if and only if one of the following properties is satisfied:

1. $P$ is obtainable by a finite number of intersections and complements of open affine halfspaces;
2. $P$ is generated by any finite number of union, intersection and difference operations between closed affine subspaces;
3. there exist finitely many relatively closed open sets $\{A_i\}$ and $\{B_j\}$ such that $P = \cup_i A_i$ and complement $P = \cup_j B_j$;
4. there exists a family $\{H_k\} \subset (\mathbb{E}^n)^*$ of hyperplanes such that $P$ is the union of the arrangement of $\mathbb{E}^n$ generated by $\{H_k\}$.

### 4.7.1   Locally adjoined pyramids

A central concept in Nef polyhedra is that of a pyramid around a point $x \in \mathbb{E}^n$, which is called *locally adjoined pyramid* to polyhedron $P$ in $x$, in short l.a. pyramid, and is denoted as $P^x$. It is defined as a cone with apex in $x$ and directions defined by vectors internal to some open neighborhood of $x$ in $P$:

$$P^x := \{x + \lambda(y - x) | y \in N_\epsilon(x, P), \lambda > 0\},$$

where $N_\epsilon(x, P) := \{y \in P | d(x, y) < \epsilon\}$ is an $\epsilon$-neighborhood of $x$ in $P$.

**Properties of pyramids**   Locally adjoined pyramids enjoy several interesting properties, that translate all topological tests on points and polyhedra, often called *point set membership* tests, into a suitable set-theoretical characterization of the pyramid adjoined to the considered point. In particular:

1. If a point $x$ is in $P$, then it is also in $P^x$:

$$x \in P \implies x \in P^x$$

2. The pyramid adjoined to an interior point is the whole space, in the hypothesis that $\dim P = n$:

$$x \in \operatorname{int} P \iff P^x = \mathbb{E}^n$$

3. Otherwise, if $\dim P < n$, then:

$$x \in \operatorname{relint} P \iff P^x = \operatorname{aff} P$$

4. The converse property states that the pyramid adjoined to exterior points is empty:

$$x \in \operatorname{ext} P \iff P^x = \emptyset$$

5. Also, the adjoined pyramid is neither empty nor the whole space when the point is on the boundary:

$$x \in \partial P \iff (P^x \neq \emptyset) \wedge (P^x \neq \mathbb{E}^n)$$

6. Finally, an adjoined pyramid is not empty if and only if the considered point is either on the boundary or on the interior of $P$:

$$x \in \operatorname{clos} P \quad \Longleftrightarrow \quad P^x \neq \emptyset$$

**Example 4.7.1 (Nef polyhedron)**
An example of Nef polyhedron is given by the geometric value generated by evaluating the nef_pol symbol in Script 4.7.1. The generated set is shown in Figure 4.17. The example is aimed to show that a Nef polyhedron may be non-regular, i.e. may be dimensionsionally unhomogeneous. In particular, it is easy to see that the following hold:

dim (basis JOIN apex) $= 3$,
dim (apex JOIN top) $= 1$,
dim (flag) $= 2$,

respectively.

---

**Script 4.7.1 (Example of Nef polyhedron)**
```
DEF basis = (T:<1,2>:<-1,-1> ~ CUBOID):<2,2,1>;
DEF apex  = MKPOL:<<<0,0,2>>,<<1>>,<<1>>>;
DEF top   = MKPOL:<<<0,0,3>>,<<1>>,<<1>>>;
DEF flag  = (T:3:2.5 ~ R:<2,3>:(PI/2) ~ EMBED:1 ~ MKPOL):<
    <<0,0>,<0.5,0>,<0.5,0.5>,<0,0.5>,<0.25,0.25>>,
    <<1,2,5>,<3,4,5>,<1,4,5>>, <1..3> >;

DEF nef_pol = STRUCT:< basis JOIN apex, apex JOIN top, flag >;
```

---

**Figure 4.17**   Example of Nef polyhedron

*4.7.2   Faces of Nef polyhedra*

The most interesting aspect of Nef polyhedra is probably that they support a definition of face which is both mathematically sound and intuitively appealing. In particular, faces are defined by Nef as equivalence classes of points with the same adjoined pyramid.

**Definition**   Let $P \subseteq \mathbb{E}^n$ be a Nef polyhedron. A *face* of P is an equivalence class of the relation $\sim$, where for every $x, y \in \mathbb{E}^n$:

$$x \sim y \quad \Longleftrightarrow \quad P^x = P^y.$$

**Closure of operations**   The class of Nef polyhedra is closed under the Boolean operations of *union, intersection, difference* and *complementation*. It is also closed under the topological operations of *interior, boundary* and *closure*. So, Nef polyhedra define the best class of mathematical models (see Chapter 13) for piecewise-linear solid modeling, and more in general for geometric objects generated by selecting some not necessarily regular or connected subset of cells from the arrangement, i.e. the space partition, generated by an arbitrary set of affine hyperplanes. Their great usefulness for applications in graphics and modeling has been recognized quite recently, so that general purpose C++ libraries are yet under development.

**Caveat**   The reader should notice that, whereas it is possible to generate with PLaSM the quite large class of non-regular and unconnected but *closed* Nef polyhedra, yet this class is currently not closed under Boolean set operations. The current PLaSM implementation of such operations (see Section 14.2) in fact requires the operand objects being regular and full dimensional. Anyway, both the algorithm and the data structures used to this purpose may be (hopefully) extended to process the whole class of Nef polyhedra in arbitrary dimensions, using two basic concepts of solid modeling, i.e. simplicial complexes and ternary space partitioning trees (extension of BSP-trees — see Section 13.3.2) like those used by Vaněček [Van91], enriched with a cell selector function, as suggested by Ferrucci [Fer95a, Fer95b].

## 4.8   Linear programming

Linear programming methods are extensively used in PLaSM, mainly in the implementation of dimension-independent Boolean operations, and in the internal conversions between facet-based and vertex-based representations of polyhedral complexes. So we give here a brief introduction to such methods. The interested reader is referred to [Chv83] and [Mur83]. A more abstract approach, devoted to proving the polynomial time solvability of geometric problems with combinatorial optimization is [GLS88].

**Mathematical programming**   A mathematical programming problem is formulated as the search for

$$\min\{f(x)|x \in X\}$$

where $X$ is the set of *feasible solutions*, and $f : X \to \mathbb{R}$ is called *objective function*. When $X = \emptyset$, the problem is said to be impossible or *unfeasible*; when the objective function is inferiorly unlimited, i.e. when $\min\{f(x)|x \in X\} = -\infty$, the problem is said *unbounded*. An *optimal solution* is a point $x^* \in X$ such that $f(x^*) \leq f(x)$ for every $x \in X$.

**LP problems**   A mathematical programming problem is called a *linear programming* (LP) problem when it is of the form

$$\min\{c^T x | Ax \geq b, x \geq 0\}.$$

The above form of the LP problem, where the feasible set is the intersection of the *convex polyhedron* $\{x | Ax \geq b\}$ with the cone $\{x \geq 0\}$, is called the *general form*. The LP problem can also be given in *standard form*

$$\min\{c^T x | Ax = b, x \geq 0\}.$$

where the feasible set is the intersection of the *affine manifold* $\{x | Ax = b\}$ with the cone $\{x \geq 0\}$, and in particular, is an intersection of half-flats.

Due to the economical interpretations of the LP problems, $c$ and $b$ are called *cost* and *resource* vector, respectively, $A$ is the matrix of (technological) *constraints*, and $x$ is the vector of *decision variables*.

**Equivalent formulations**   Several conversions between equivalent problems can be given. In particular:

1. from max to min:

$$\max d^T x \quad \Longrightarrow \quad -\min c^T x$$

   with $c = -d$;

2. from *below* ($\leq$) constraints to equality constraints, by introducing *slack* variables $s_i$:

$$a_i x \leq b_i \quad \Longrightarrow \quad \begin{cases} a_i x + s_i &= b_i \\ s_i &\geq 0 \end{cases}$$

3. from *above* ($\geq$) constraints to equality constraints, by introducing *surplus* variables $s_i$:

$$a_i x \geq b_i \quad \Longrightarrow \quad \begin{cases} a_i x - s_i &= b_i \\ s_i &\geq 0 \end{cases}$$

4. from equality constraints to *above* ($\geq$) constraints:

$$a_i x = b_i \quad \Longrightarrow \quad \begin{cases} a_i x &\geq b_i \\ -a_i x &\geq -b_i \end{cases}$$

5. from sign unconstrained variables to sign constrained variables:

$$x_i \gtrless 0 \quad \Longrightarrow \quad \begin{cases} x_i &= x_i^+ - x_i^- \\ x_i^+ &\geq 0 \\ x_i^- &\geq 0 \end{cases}$$

*4.8.1   Geometry of linear programming*

As we know, a (convex) *polyhedron* is defined as the intersection of finitely many affine subspaces and hyperplanes. A *polytope* is a bounded polyhedron. A *vertex* of a polyhedron $P$ is a point which cannot be obtained by convex combination of other points. The fundamental *theorem of Minkowski/Weil* states that each point of a polytope can be obtained by convex combination of its vertices. As an easy corollary, it is possible to show that if the feasible set $P$ is non-empty and inferiorly bounded, then there exists at least one optimal vertex, where the objective function gets its minimum value.

**Algebraic characterization of vertices**   Let us suppose $A \in \mathrm{I\!R}_n^m$, i.e. that there are $m$ constraints and $n$ variables, with $m < n$. So, it is possible to give an arbitrary value, zero in particular, to $n-m$ unknowns and to solve uniquely for the others, while at the same time guaranteeing that the solution, called the *basic feasible* solution, is a vertex of the feasible polyhedron $P$.

To characterize algebraically the vertices of $P = \{x \geq 0 | Ax = b\}$ is quite easy. Let us consider a collection $B$ of $m$ linearly independent columns of $A = (a_1, a_2, \dots, a_n)$, and suppose, for the sake of simplicity, that

$$A = (\;B\quad N\;), \quad B = (\;a_1, \dots, a_m\;), \quad N = (\;a_{m+1}, \dots, a_n\;).$$

The variables $x_B$ associated to $B$ are called *basic* variables; the others $x_N$ are said *non-basic*, and let

$$x = \begin{pmatrix} x_B \\ x_N \end{pmatrix} = \begin{pmatrix} B^{-1}(b - Nx_N) \\ x_N \end{pmatrix}$$

be a solution of $Ax = b$. The solution $x = (\;x_B\quad 0\;)^T$ is said to be the *basic solution* associated to the $B$ basis. A basic solution is *feasible* if

$$x_B = B^{-1}b \geq 0.$$

By extension, the $B$ basis associated with a basic feasible solution is also called a *feasible* basis.

A fundamental theorem states that $x$ is a vertex of the convex polyhedron $P := \{x \geq 0 | Ax = b\}$ if and only if $x$ is a *basic feasible solution* of $Ax = b$.

Also, each problem $\min\{c^T x | Ax = b, x \geq 0\}$ with a non-empty and bounded, say inferiorly limited, feasible set has at least one optimal solution that coincides with a basic feasible solution.

*4.8.2   Simplex method*

The well-known *simplex method* to solve LP problems is due to Dantzig [Dan51, Dan63]. The simplex method can be geometrically summarized as follows: in a first phase, a vertex $v$ of the feasible set is chosen; then, in a second phase, the algorithm moves stepwise to an adjacent vertex $w$ where $f(w)$ is less or equal to the previous value $f(v)$, and repeats the move until an optimal vertex is reached. The existence of a decreasing path from each vertex $v$ to the optimal face $F_0 = \{x^* | f(x^*) = z_0\}$, with $z_0 = \min\{c^T x | Ax = b, x \geq 0\}$, is always guaranteed.

**Tableau-based simplex algorithm**   The *simplex algorithm* is the most well known and practically efficient resolution procedure for linear programs in standard form.

There are several variations of the simplex algorithm [Mur83], to solve efficiently in practical cases very large-scale LP problems [Nem96], say, problems with hundreds of thousands, and even millions, variables and equations.

Some of such methods use the so-called *simplex tableau,* where the data of the problem are organized into a two-dimensional array, and where the main operation is the *pivot* operation, corresponding to Gauss' elimination of one variable. At each suitably performed pivot operation, one of the variables leaves the basis, and another one enters the basis, so moving the current basic feasible solution from the current $P$ vertex to one of its neighborhoods, until an optimal basic solution is found.

**Pivoting operation**   Let us suppose a matrix $A = ( a_{i,j} ) \in \mathbb{R}^m_n$ representing a linear system of $m$ equation in $n$ variables is given, and let $a_{h,k} \neq 0$. A pivoting operation on the matrix $A$, with *pivot element* of indices $(h, k)$ is aimed at eliminating the $k$-th variable from all equations, but not from the $h$-th one. The effect on the resulting matrix is the appearance of a unit $k$-th column, with the 1 element in position $(h, k)$, and with 0 elsewhere.

For this purpose, rows (i.e. equations) are summated to linear combinations of other rows, so that the solutions of the system do not change. In particular, the $h$-th row is divided for the pivot element $a_{h,k}$, supposed non-zero, while the other rows, for example the $i$-th, are subtracted by the *new* $h$-th row times the element on the $i$-th position of the pivot column. More formally, let denote as $A' = ( a'_{i,j} ) = ( a'_i )$ the resulting matrix after pivoting on the $(h, k)$ element. Then we have:

$$a'_h \quad := \quad \frac{1}{a_{h,k}} a_h, \tag{4.2}$$

$$a'_i \quad := \quad a_i - a_{i,k} a'_h, \qquad i \neq h \tag{4.3}$$

**Example 4.8.1 (Pivoting operation)**
Looking carefully at equations (4.2–4.3), it is easy to see that the result $A'$ of the pivot operation about the element $(h, k)$ on the matrix $A \in \mathbb{R}^m_n$ can be obtained as

$$A' = P(h, k)\, A$$

where the matrix $P(h, k) \in \mathbb{R}^m_m$ differs from the identity $m \times m$ only on the $h$-th column:

$$P(h,k) = \begin{pmatrix} 1 & & & -\frac{a_{1,k}}{a_{h,k}} & & \\ & 1 & & -\frac{a_{2,k}}{a_{h,k}} & & \\ & & \ddots & \vdots & & \\ & & & \frac{1}{a_{h,k}} & & \\ & & & \vdots & \ddots & \\ & & & -\frac{a_{m,k}}{a_{h,k}} & & 1 \end{pmatrix}$$

The pivoting matrix can be generated in PLaSM by using the Pivot function given in Script 4.8.1. The body of the function just substitutes the updated_column to the $h$-th column of the identity $m \times m$. The function IDNT used to generate the identity matrix is given in Script 3.3.5. The scalarVectProd operator, to execute a product of a scalar times a vector, is given in Script 2.1.20. Notice that the update function updates the n-th element of the seq sequence with the new value x, of any type. To understand the Pivot code, the reader should remember that a matrix in PLaSM is represented as a sequence of rows.

---

**Script 4.8.1 (Pivot matrix)**

```
DEF update (n::IsIntPos)(seq::IsSeq)(x::TT) = CAT:<
    (CONS ~ AA:SEL):(1..n - 1):seq,
    < x >,
    (CONS ~ AA:SEL):(n + 1..LEN:seq):seq
>;

DEF Pivot (h,k::IsIntPos) (mat:: IsMat) =
    (TRANS ~ update:h:(IDNT:m)): updated_column
WHERE
    pivot_column  = SEL:k: (TRANS:mat),
    pivot_element = SEL:h: pivot_column,
    m = LEN:mat,
    updated_column = (-1/pivot_element) scalarVectProd update:h:pivot_column:-1
END;
```

---

Notice that when computing $A' = P(h, k)\, A$, the matrix $A$ is not necessarily squared, whereas the pivot matrix $P(h, k)$ is squared. Two examples of the operator

$$\texttt{Pivot} : (Z^+ \times Z^+) \to (\mathbb{R}^m_n \to \mathbb{R}^m_m)$$

are given in Scripts 4.8.2 and 4.8.3.

---

**Script 4.8.2 (Pivot matrix)**

```
Pivot:<2,5>:
< < 11 , -12 ,  13 ,  14 ,  15 , 16 > ,
  < 21 ,  22 , -23 ,  24 ,  25 , 26 > ,
  < 31 ,  32 ,  33 , -34 ,  35 , 36 > ,
  < 41 ,  42 ,  43 ,  44 , -45 , 46 > >
≡
< < 1 , -3/5 , 0 , 0 > ,
  < 0 , 1/25 , 0 , 0 > ,
  < 0 , -7/5 , 1 , 0 > ,
  < 0 ,  9/5 , 0 , 1 > >
```

---

The effect of a double pivoting on an input matrix is shown in Script 4.8.3. Notice that an infix expression like (Pivot:<2,5> * ID) returns a function, which can be compound with other similar functions.

**Script 4.8.3 (Pivoting example)**

```
((Pivot:<3,1> * ID) ~ (Pivot:<2,5> * ID)):
< < 11 , -12 ,  13 ,  14 ,  15 , 16 > ,
  < 21 ,  22 , -23 ,  24 ,  25 , 26 > ,
  < 31 ,  32 ,  33 , -34 ,  35 , 36 > ,
  < 41 ,  42 ,  43 ,  44 , -45 , 46 > >

≡

< < 0 ,  -24 ,        92 ,    -68 , 0 ,      0 > ,
  < 0 ,   1/4 , -703/20 , 729/20 , 1 ,    5/4 > ,
  < 1 ,   3/4 ,   163/4 , -169/4 , 0 ,   -1/4 > ,
  < 0 , 45/2 , -6419/2 , 6833/2 , 0 , 225/2 > >
```

*4.8.3  Some polyhedral algorithms*

Two algorithmic problems are of major interest when using decompositions with $d$-dimensional polytopes, namely the *vertex enumeration* and the *facet enumeration* problem. We just address here the main coordinates of such problems. For a deep review and a wide survey of the field the interested reader is referred to Avis, Bremner and Seidel's article entitled "How good are convex hull algorithms?" [ABS97].

**Beneath/Beyond method**

The convex hull of a finite set of points in $\mathbb{E}^n$, for arbitrary positive integer $n$, can be computed by using Seidel's "Beneath Beyond" method [Sei81], described by Edelsbrunner in [Ede87]. This method is a well-known, simple and efficient algorithm implemented by several geometric codes. It is also used by the PLaSM geometric kernel in the implementation of the the the basic primitive MKPOL.

In an initialization step of the algorithm the input points are sorted lexicographically. Then the convex hull is incrementally built, starting from the empty set and adding a sorted point at a time. In doing so, a distinction is made between the cases where the affine hull of the previous points either contains or does not contain the added point.

The second case is much easier: the updated convex hull is a pyramid having the previous convex hull as the basis and the new point as the apex. All the faces of a pyramid are easily obtained by the join of the apex to all faces of the basis. The highest dimensional face is obtained by the join of the apex to the basis.

The second case, requiring a non-pyramidal update, is quite more complex. A detailed description can be found in Edelsbrunner [Ede87] and in Preparata and Shamos [PS85].

**Vertex enumeration problem**

Given a polytope $P$, represented as an intersection of halfspaces $\mathcal{H}(P) = P(\boldsymbol{A}, \boldsymbol{b}) = \{\boldsymbol{x} \in \mathbb{E}^n | \boldsymbol{A}\boldsymbol{x} \leq \boldsymbol{b}\}$, the generation of its representation as the convex hull of its vertices $\mathcal{V}(P)$, is called the *vertex enumeration problem*. Several solution algorithms exist for this problem, that can still be considered a research problem in computational geometry.

The solution algorithms can be classified as *pivotal* methods and *progressive* methods. The first class makes use of the pivot operation as the basic operation to move from one vertex to one of the vertices adjacent to it. Unfortunately, it is not possible to consider each vertex only one time. This is possible only if the graph associated with the polyhedron has a Hamiltonian cycle, and this is in general not true. Such algorithms may either pass more than one time on each vertex or visit points which are external to the polyhedron.

We discuss here both a basic trivial method and the solution currently implemented in PLaSM.

**Trivial approach**   The easiest way of solving the vertex enumeration problem consists in:

1. considering each $n$-tuple of boundary hyperplanes $H_{a_i, b_i} = \{x \in \mathbb{E}^n | a_i^T x = b_i\}$;
2. solving their squared system for the common point, say $y$;
3. checking for *feasibility*, i.e. if $y \in P(A, b)$. In other words, it is necessary to verify if $Ay \leq b$. Clearly, this is true if and only if $y$ is a vertex of $P$.

Let us suppose $A \in \mathbb{R}_n^m$, i.e. that there are $m$ inequalities in $\mathcal{H}(P)$, with $m \geq n$. This method requires the solution of a number $\binom{m}{n}$ of $n \times n$ systems of linear equations. A further computational cost is given by the feasibility check $Ay \leq b$ for each solution $y$. Such method may be acceptable only for very small values of both $m$ and $n$.

**Example 4.8.2 (Vertex enumeration)**
It is easy to see that the trivial generation of vertices of 3D tetrahedron would require $\binom{4}{3} = 4$ resolutions of $3 \times 3$ systems of linear equations, i.e. one for each vertex, because each triplet of face hyperplanes generates a vertex.

The vertex enumeration of the 3D cube would require solving $\binom{6}{3} = 20$ linear systems, and only 8 solutions would actually pass the feasibility test.

Conversely, the same operation for the 3D icosahedron (see Section 23) would require the resolution of $\binom{20}{3} = 1140$ linear systems of dimension $3 \times 3$. In this case only 12 solutions would be accepted as icosahedron vertices.

**Pivoting algorithms**   One of best known pivoting methods, named after its authors M. Manas and J. Nedoma [MN68], starts from the simplex tableau in canonical form, which gives the first vertex of the polyhedron, and explores the set of adjacent bases associated to basic feasible solutions, thus constructing a covering tree of the graph described below, until the set of all vertices has been built.

Let $P = \{x \geq 0 | Ax = b\}$ be in standard form. A graph $G = (N, A)$ with nodes corresponding to $m$-tuples of indices associated to feasible bases, and arcs between nodes which differ in just one component, can be built incrementally moving from each vertex to its adjacent vertices. Visiting a node corresponds to computing the Cartesian coordinates of the polyhedron vertex associated with a basic feasible solution of the LP problem. The algorithm is initialized by putting the simplex tableau in canonical form, thus achieving an initial node of the graph and a first polyhedron vertex.

David Avis's *lrslib* is a self-contained ANSI C implementation of the reverse search algorithm [AF92] for vertex enumeration/convex hull problems. A more efficient method of finding all the vertices of a polytope without using any slack/surplus variables is given in Arsham [Ars97].

**Progressive algorithms**  More recent and efficient algorithms make direct use of the polyhedron description as a set of inequalities, thus avoiding increasing the number of problem variables, and compute the set of vertices by repeatedly adding one inequality. Such algorithms often start from the simplex generated from the first $n$ inequalities, then update the current set of vertices by suitable comparisons to the boundary hyperplane associated to the added inequality. New vertices must obviously be added when such a new hyperplane cuts the current polyhedral set. A combined solution of both enumeration problems (say, of vertices and facets enumeration) is given by Bremner, Fukuda and Marzetta in [BFM98].

## 4.9 Examples

From the very first development of Greek geometry, some interesting solids intrigued the mathematicians because of the extreme perfection of their definition. In particular, five polyhedra, bounded by regular polygons which are all equal to each other, and are joined by equal internal angles, are cited in Plato's work *Timaeus*, so that they are collectively known as *Platonic solids*. The construction of Platonic solids is the last topic in Euclid's *Elements* of geometry book. We present in this section a straightforward PLaSM modeling of the five Platonic solids.

### 4.9.1 Platonic solids

We discuss here the construction of *tetrahedron, hexahedron, octahedron, dodecahedron* and *icosahedron,* all inscribed in a sphere of unit radius, following the lines developed in the second chapter of the beautiful and inspiring book *Polyhedra* by P. Cromwell [Cro97]. Such solids are illustrated in Figure 4.18.[2]

### Tetrahedron

The tetrahedron as a polytope, bounded by four triangle faces and having six edges and four vertices, is well known to our reader. Tetrahedra are commonly produced in PLaSM by the SIMPLEX primitive applied to the integer 3, and are generated as the convex hull of the set $\{o, e_1, e_2, e_3\}$. Such unit 3-simplex lacks the symmetries that the Platonic tetrahedron enjoys, and cannot be inscribed in the unit sphere.

Hence, the generation method of tetrahedron given in Script 4.9.1 closely resembles its construction in the Euclid's *Elements*, as reported by Cromwell [Cro97]. In particular, the solid is produced by the JOIN of the equilateral triangle of the basis, inscribed in the unit circle centered at the origin, with the apex vertex located perpendicularly along the $z$ axis, at a distance $\frac{4}{3}$ from the origin. The ngon function, used to generate regular polygons with any number of sides, is given in Script 4.4.2.

---

[2] The quality of images is quite poor, because they were produced by using a standard web browser, and not by using a raytracer.

**Figure 4.18**    *Tetrahedron, hexahedron, octahedron, dodecahedron* and *icosahedron* inscribed in a unit sphere

In order to inscribe the generated polyhedron in the unit sphere we need to move it in the reverse $z$ direction, with translation vector $(0, 0, -\frac{1}{3})$. The same effect is obtained by translating the basis, and joining it to the set conv $\{e_3\} \in \mathcal{P}^{0,3}$. The function $MK : \mathbb{E}^d \to \mathcal{P}^{0,d}$, with $d$ arbitrary positive integer, was given in Script 3.3.15.

---

**Script 4.9.1 (Tetrahedron)**

```
DEF tetrahedron = (T:3:(-1/3) ~ EMBED:1 ~ ngon):3 JOIN MK:<0,0,1> ;
```

---

## Hexahedron

The cube — bounded by six planes and hence called also a *hexahedron* — is generated, in Script 4.9.2, with center in the origin and inscribed in the unit sphere. Such an inscribed cube has edges of length $a = 2/\sqrt{3}$, as the reader may check by considering the great diagonal of the cube as the hypotenuse of a right-angled triangle whose cathetuses have lengths $a$ and $a\sqrt{2}$, respectively.

---

**Script 4.9.2 (Hexahedron)**

```
DEF hexahedron = (T:<1,2,3>:< a/-2,a/-2,a/-2 > ~ CUBOID):< a,a,a >
WHERE a = 2 / sqrt:3 END;
```

---

## Octahedron

The Platonic solid named *octahedron*, which is bounded by 8 triangular faces organized as a double squared pyramid, is simply the three-dimensional *CrossPolytope* defined in Section 4.4.1 as the set conv $\{e_i, -e_i\}$, $1 \leq i \leq 3$. The implementation given in Script 4.9.3 is consequently simple.

---

**Script 4.9.3 (Octahedron)**

```
DEF octahedron = CrossPolytope:3;
```

---

## Dodecahedron

The Platonic solid bounded by 12 pentagons is called *dodecahedron*. As suggested by [Cro97], this one can be constructed by glueing a properly defined "roof" to each face of a central cube, as shown by Figure 4.19a. A first roof is given by the convex set

$$R := \text{conv}\,(B \cup T)$$

i.e. as the convex hull of the embedded 2D *basis* interval $B := [0,1]^2 \times \{0\}$, join the embedded 1D *top* segment $T := \text{conv}\,\{p_1, p_2\}$, with $p_1 = (1 - g, 1, g)$ and $p_2 = (1 + g, 1, g)$, respectively, where $g$ is the golden ratio. The other roofs are defined by properly translating and rotating $R$.

**Golden ratio**   The *golden ratio* is defined as the ratio between the length $g$ of the interval $[0, g] \subset [0, 1]$, and the unit length of the $[0, 1]$ segment. The $g$ value must equate by definition the ratio between the length $1 - g$ of the $[g, 1]$ segment and $g$ itself. In other words, $g$ must satisfy the constraint:

$$g : 1 = (1 - g) : g.$$

It is very easy to see, by getting the positive root of equation $g^2 + g - 1 = 0$, that $g = \frac{1}{2}(\sqrt{5} - 1)$.

**Implementation**   The dodecahedron inscribed in the unit sphere is implemented in Script 4.9.4 by using the method described above. For sake of simplicity the primary construction is done using a central cube with edge length equal to 2. The assembled polytope generated by STRUCT is then properly scaled by a factor $1/\sqrt{3}$, so reducing the half-diagonal of the interior cube to the unit size of the inscribing sphere. The resulting solid is shown in Figure 4.19b.

The geometric value obtained when evaluating the last expression of Script 4.9.4 is displayed in Figure 4.19a. The SPLIT and explode operators, to extract the convex 3-cells of the dodecahedron complex and to produce a (controlled) "explosion" of cells about the origin, are given in Scripts 10.8.4 and 10.8.6, respectively.

To fully understand the STRUCT semantics and the implicit composition of sequences of affine transformations, some preliminary reading of Chapters 6 and 8 may be very useful.

**Script 4.9.4 (Dodecahedron)**

```
DEF dodecahedron = (S:<1,2,3>:< a,a,a > ~ STRUCT):<
    T:<1,2,3>:< -1,-1,-1 >:(CUBOID:<2,2,2>),
    roofpair, R:<1,3>:(PI/2), R:<1,2>:(PI/2), roofpair ,
    R:<1,2>:(PI/2), R:<2,3>:(PI/2), roofpair >
WHERE
    g = (SQRT:5 - 1)/2,
    top = MKPOL:< <<1-g,1,0-g>,<1+g,1,0-g>>, <<1,2>>, <<1>> >,
    basis = (EMBED:1 ~ CUBOID):<2,2>,
    roof = (T:<1,2,3>:< -1,-1,-1 > ~ JOIN):< basis, top >,
    roofpair = STRUCT:< roof, R:<2,3>:PI, roof >,
    a = 1 / sqrt:3
END;

(STRUCT ~ explode:<1.1,1.1,1.1> ~ SPLIT): dodecahedron
```

In order to obtain a more compact VRML output for the dodecahedron value, it might be preferable to insert a pair MKPOL ~ UKPOL on the top of the function body. As the reader already knows, this operator insertion flattens the hierarchy of the internal geometry representation, thus reducing the file size of deep hierarchical assemblies, and may eliminate some awkward rendering effects introduced by scaling with negative coefficients, which are formally not allowed by the VRML specification [ISO97].

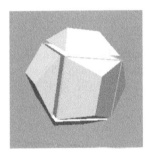 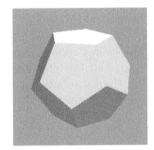

**Figure 4.19** (a) Exploded dodecahedron (b) Dodecahedron

## Icosahedron

The *icosahedron* is the Platonic solid bounded by 20 equilateral triangles. Its boundary can be seen as composed by threes layers, as shown by Figure 4.20c. The intermediate layer is produced by joining two parallel pentagons mutually rotated by $\pi$ radians. Since each of their $5 + 5$ sides is joined to one vertex in the opposite pentagon, this layer contains 10 triangles. Also, 5 triangles are contained in the top layer and 5 in the bottom layer.

**Implementation**  According to [Cro97], the solid is generated in Script 4.9.5 as the convex hull of three orthogonal rectangles whose sides are in the golden ratio each other. Such a convex hull is finally scaled to be inscribed in the unit circle. The scaling coefficient $b$ simply transforms the half-diagonal of such "golden rectangles" to the unit radius of the inscribing sphere.

---

**Script 4.9.5 (Icosahedron)**

```
DEF icosahedron = (S:<1,2,3>:<b,b,b> ~ JOIN):< rectx, recty, rectz >
WHERE
    rectx = (EMBED:1 ~ T:<1,2>:<-:g,-1> ~ CUBOID): < 2*g, 2>,
    recty = (R:<1,3>:(PI/2) ~ R:<1,2>:(PI/2)): rectx,
    rectz = (R:<2,3>:(PI/2) ~ R:<1,2>:(PI/2)): rectx,
    g = (SQRT:5 - 1)/2,
    b = 2 / sqrt:(10 - 2*sqrt:5)
END;
```

---

**Example 4.9.1 (Icosahedron constructions)**
The icosahedron images shown in Figures 4.9.5a and 4.9.5b are generated by evaluating the out1 and out2 symbols given in Script 4.9.6. In particular, the definition of the planes assembly is obtained from the icosahedron definition by just substituting the operator STRUCT to JOIN in the function body. Notice that the COLORS.psm package must be loaded into memory before evaluating the out1 symbol.

Figure 4.9.5b of the layered icosahedron structure is generated as value of the out2 object. In this case (a) the solid is rotated by $\pi/2$ about the $(-1, \frac{1-\sqrt{5}}{2}, 0)$ axis in order to move the diagonal of the rectangle located in the $z = 0$ plane to coincide with the $z$-axis; (b) the 2-skeleton is extracted; (c) the resulting complex is split into a sequence of convex cells; (d) this sequence is "exploded" along the $z$ direction, and finally (e) a single polyhedral assembly is generated.

---

**Script 4.9.6 (Icosahedron)**

```
DEF out1 = STRUCT:<
    icosahedron MATERIAL
        Transparentmaterial:< RGBCOLOR:<0.3, 0.7, 0.9>, 0.6>,
    planes COLOR red >;

DEF out2 = (STRUCT ~ explode:<1,1,1.3> ~ SPLIT ~ @2
    ~ Rot_n:< PI/2, <-1, (1-SQRT:5)/2, 0> >): icosahedron;
```

---

Notice that the function Rot_n for 3D rotation about an axis for the origin can be loaded from VECTORS.psm package, whereas the explode and SPLIT functions came from Scripts 10.8.6 and 10.8.4, respectively.

**Example 4.9.2 (Platonic solids in a unit sphere)**
The five pictures given in Figure 4.18 are generated from models defined in Script 4.9.7, where each of out$i$ objects correspond in order to Platonic solids inscribed in a transparent unit sphere centered in the origin of the $\mathbb{E}^3$ space. The Sphere generating function is given in Section 2.2.7. Notice that in order to generate colored or shaded or transparent objects, the PLaSM package named COLORS.psm must be loaded in memory

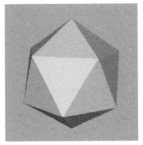

**Figure 4.20**    (a) Icosahedron (b) Generation of icosahedron as JOIN of three orthogonal rectangles with sides in the golden ratio (c) Layered structure of icosahedron

in advance. A quite detailed discussion of color and material properties, both in PLaSM and in VRML, may be found in the second part of Chapter 10.

---

**Script 4.9.7 (Platonic solids in a transparent sphere)**

```
DEF red = RGBCOLOR:< 1, 0, 0 >;
DEF white = RGBCOLOR:< 1, 1, 1 >;
DEF mymaterial = white Transparentmaterial 0.9;
DEF UnitSphere = Sphere:1:<18,24> CREASE (PI/2) MATERIAL mymaterial;

DEF out1 = STRUCT:< UnitSphere, tetrahedron COLOR red >;
DEF out2 = STRUCT:< UnitSphere, hexahedron COLOR red >;
DEF out3 = STRUCT:< UnitSphere, octahedron COLOR red >;
DEF out4 = STRUCT:< UnitSphere, dodecahedron COLOR red >;
DEF out5 = STRUCT:< UnitSphere, icosahedron COLOR red >;
```

---

## 4.10   References

The reader interested to some in-depth study of polyhedral geometry topics we introduced in this chapter, is referred to the following list of papers or books:

[Bal61, Bie95, Bie98, Bie94a, Bie94b, BN88, Bro83, Bro88, Bur74, CHJ90, Che65, Chv83, Cro97, Dan63, DP77a, DP77b, Dye83, Ede87, Fer95a, Fer95a, Gib77, GT87, Grü67, GS85, GW89, Hop83, BF89, Lef49, Lue84, LW69, MN68, MR77, MR80, Mun84, Mur83, Nak91, Nef78, PS85, Req77, RS72, RS89, Sch93, Sch86, Sob89, Sug93, Von81, Wen71, Yao90, Zie95]

# 5

# Elements of differential geometry

This chapter presents various concepts useful to fully understand curves and surfaces discussed in later sections. In particular, we introduce here the notion of a curve as a point-valued function of a real variable, the variable-free representation of functions and the Fréchet derivative for functions of one and several variables. This derivative gives the framework for introducing the concepts of manifold, tangent space and vector field from a geometrical perspective. Then, more standard topics on curves are briefly outlined, including tangent, curvature, centre of curvature and osculating circles. Finally, some elements of differential geometry of surfaces are discussed, including first and second fundamental forms and Gauss curvature. As usual in this book, the mathematics is normally given without proofs, but is often coupled with a PLaSM implementation of the important ideas. We hope that the implementation and the examples may help to clarify subtle mathematical details.

## 5.1  Curves

A *curve* in $\mathbb{E}^d$ is a point-valued mapping defined by summing to the origin of a Cartesian system $\{o, (e_i)\}$ a vector-valued function $\boldsymbol{\alpha} : \mathbb{R} \to \mathbb{R}^d$ of a real parameter, so that a point of the curve is generated as:

$$\boldsymbol{c}(u) = \boldsymbol{o} + \boldsymbol{\alpha}(u), \qquad u \in [a, b] \subset \mathbb{R}.$$

The *image* of the curve is the set $\boldsymbol{c}[a, b]$ of its $\mathbb{E}^d$ points. The *domain* of the curve is the parameter interval $[a, b]$, i.e. the set $\{u \in \mathbb{R} | a \leq u \leq b\}$, often normalized to the standard unit interval $[0, 1]$.

The important part of the curve definition is the vector-valued function $\boldsymbol{\alpha}$, so that sometimes we use the word "curve" for it. From a notational viewpoint, we normally use a bold Latin letter, say $\boldsymbol{a}$, $\boldsymbol{b}$ or $\boldsymbol{c}$, to indicate a map $\mathbb{R} \to \mathbb{E}^d$, and a bold Greek letter, say $\boldsymbol{\alpha}$, $\boldsymbol{\beta}$ or $\boldsymbol{\gamma}$, to indicate a map $\mathbb{R} \to \mathbb{R}^d$. This convention will sometimes be broken according to the standard usage of symbols, e.g. for the *intrinsic triplet* of vector functions $\mathbb{R} \to \mathbb{R}^3$, that are denoted by $\boldsymbol{t}$, $\boldsymbol{n}$ and $\boldsymbol{b}$, respectively.

### Example 5.1.1 (3D curve)
A curve $\boldsymbol{c}$ in three-dimensional space has 3 *coordinate functions*, and is often denoted

*Geometric Programming for Computer-Aided Design*  Alberto Paoluzzi
© 2003 John Wiley & Sons, Ltd  ISBN 0-471-89942-9

as

$$c(u) = (x(u), y(u), z(u))^T, \qquad u \in [a, b]$$

where $x(u) = \alpha(u) \cdot e_1$, $y(u) = \alpha(u) \cdot e_2$ and $z(u) = \alpha(u) \cdot e_3$. The *tangent* vector function $t$ is defined by

$$t(u) = \frac{d}{du} c(u) = \frac{d}{du} \alpha(u) = (x'(u), y'(u), z'(u))^T, \qquad u \in [a, b].$$

### 5.1.1   *Variable-free notation*

Accordingly with the functional approach of the PLaSM language, we often denote a 3D curve, as well as its derivative curves, by using the variable-free notation:

$$c = (x, y, z)^T$$

with $x = \alpha \cdot e_1$, $y = \alpha \cdot e_2$, and $z = \alpha \cdot e_3$.

It should be clearly understood that $x, y, z$ are here maps $\mathbb{R} \to \mathbb{R}$ and that each $e_i$ has the constant maps $\underline{0} : \mathbb{R} \to 0$ and $\underline{1} : \mathbb{R} \to 1$ as components.

Analogously, we write a curve $c : \mathbb{R} \to \mathbb{E}^d$, as $c = o + \alpha$, with $\alpha = (\alpha_i)$, where $\alpha_i : \mathbb{R} \to \mathbb{R}$, for all $i$. The variable-free notation, where functions are directly added and multiplied, exactly like numbers, is very useful for quickly and easily implementing curves and surfaces in our language.

**Useful maps**   Some special maps are needed to perform such variable-free calculus with functions. As the reader already knows, they have a direct translation in PLaSM.

1. $\text{id} : \mathbb{R} \to \mathbb{R}; x \mapsto x$                                      (identity)
2. $\underline{c} : \mathbb{R} \to \mathbb{R}; x \mapsto c$                                      (constant)
3. $\sigma : \{1, \ldots, d\} \times \mathbb{R}^d \to \mathbb{R}; (i, (x_1, \ldots, x_d)) \mapsto x_i$          (selection)

A computer scientist would probably prefer the following specification, just to point out that $\sigma$ is often used as a *partial* function, i.e. a function which may be applied to a subset of its arguments:

3. $\sigma : \{1, \ldots, d\} \to (\mathbb{R}^d \to \mathbb{R}); i \mapsto ((x_1, \ldots, x_d) \mapsto x_i)$          (selection)

Actually, the FL primitives ID, K and SEL used by the PLaSM language have no domain restrictions, and can be applied to any type of data objects.

**Algebraic operations**   We also need to recall how to perform algebraic operations in the linear algebra of maps $\mathbb{R} \to \mathbb{R}$. For each map $\alpha, \beta : \mathbb{R} \to \mathbb{R}$ and each scalar $a \in \mathbb{R}$

$$\alpha + \beta : u \mapsto \alpha(u) + \beta(u), \quad \alpha\beta : u \mapsto \alpha(u)\beta(u), \quad a\beta : u \mapsto a\beta(u).$$

Consequently we have that

$$\alpha - \beta : u \mapsto \alpha(u) - \beta(u), \quad \alpha/\beta : u \mapsto \alpha(u)/\beta(u).$$

**Coordinate representation**   Finally, remember that the coordinate functions of a curve $\alpha = (\alpha_i)$ are maps $\mathbb{R} \to \mathbb{R}$. The variable-free vector notation stands for the linear combination of coordinate functions with the basis vectors of the target space:

$$(\alpha_1, \cdots, \alpha_d)^T : \ \mathbb{R} \to \mathbb{R}^d; \ u \mapsto \sum_{i=1}^{d} \alpha_i e_i.$$

**Example 5.1.2 (Circular arc)**
Some different curves are given here. They have the same image in $\mathbb{E}^2$ but different coordinate representation in the space of functions $\mathbb{R} \to \mathbb{R}$. All such curves generate a circular arc of unit radius centered at the origin.

1. trigonometric representation:

$$\alpha(u) = \left( \cos \left( \frac{\pi}{2} u \right), \sin \left( \frac{\pi}{2} u \right) \right)^T \qquad u \in [0, 1]$$

2. rational representation:

$$\beta(u) = \left( \frac{1 - u^2}{1 + u^2}, \frac{2u}{1 + u^2} \right)^T \qquad u \in [0, 1]$$

3. Cartesian representation:

$$\gamma(u) = \left( u, \sqrt{1 - u^2} \right)^T \qquad u \in [0, 1]$$

It is possible to verify that the image sets of such curves coincide, i.e. that $\alpha[0, 1] = \beta[0, 1] = \gamma[0, 1]$.

**Example 5.1.3 (Variable-free circular arc)**
It may be useful to give the variable-free representation of the three maps on the $[0, 1]$ interval shown in Example 5.1.2, that is exactly the representation we need to give a PLaSM implementation of such maps, provided in Script 5.1.2:

$$\alpha \ = \ \left( \cos \circ \left( \frac{\pi}{2} \mathrm{id} \right), \ \sin \circ \left( \frac{\pi}{2} \mathrm{id} \right) \right)^T \tag{5.1}$$

$$\beta \ = \ \left( \frac{1 - \mathrm{id}^2}{1 + \mathrm{id}^2}, \ \frac{2 \, \mathrm{id}}{1 + \mathrm{id}^2} \right)^T \tag{5.2}$$

$$\gamma \ = \ \left( \mathrm{id}, \ \mathrm{id}^{\frac{1}{2}} \circ (1 - \mathrm{id}^2) \right)^T \tag{5.3}$$

**Script 5.1.1 (Toolbox)**

```
DEF interval (a,b::IsReal)(n::IsIntPos) = (T:1:a ~ QUOTE ~ #:n):((b-a)/n);
DEF interval2D (a1,a2,b1,b2::IsReal)(n1,n2::IsIntPos) =
    interval:<a1,b1>:n1 * interval:<a2,b2>:n2;
```

**Toolbox**  Some predicates and functions needed by the operators in this chapter are given in Script 5.1.1. In particular, the `interval` operator provides a simplicial decomposition with n elements of the real interval $[a, b]$, whereas the `interval2D` operator returns a decomposition with n1 × n2 subintervals of the domain $[a1, b1] \times [a2, b2] \subset \mathbb{R}^2$.

Few other functions of general utility are used in the remainder of this chapter. In particular, the `SQR` function, that returns its squared input, was defined in Script 3.2.4; the predicates `IsVect` and `IsPoint` were given in Script 3.1.1 and 3.2.3, respectively. The vector operations used here were defined in Chapter 3.

**Implementation**  The circle segment representations of Example 5.1.3 are directly used in the PLaSM implementation of curves in Script 5.1.2. To understand the implementation, notice that we generate a polyhedral complex by mapping the curve vector function (either $\alpha$, $\beta$ or $\gamma$ of Example 5.1.3) on the polyhedral representation of the $[0, 1] \subset \mathbb{R}$ domain.

According to the semantics of the `MAP` function, the curve mapping is applied to all vertices of a simplicial decomposition of the polyhedral domain. But all vertices are represented as *sequences* of coordinates, say *<u>* for a curve, so that in order to act on u the mapping must necessarily *select* it from the sequence.

Hence we might substitute each *id* function instance with the PLaSM denotation S1 for the $\sigma(1)$ selector function.

Exactly the same result is obtained by using either $\alpha \circ \sigma(1), \beta \circ \sigma(1)$ or $\gamma \circ \sigma(1)$, as done in the following code.

**Script 5.1.2 (Circular arc maps)**

```
DEF SQRT  = ID ** K:(1/2);

DEF alpha = < cos ~ (K:(PI/2) * ID), sin ~ (K:(PI/2) * ID) >;
DEF beta  = < (K:1 - SQR)/(K:1 + SQR), (K:2 * ID)/(K:1 + SQR) >;
DEF gamma = < ID, SQRT ~ (K:1 - SQR) >;

MAP:(CONS:alpha ~ S1):(interval:<0,1>:10);
MAP:(CONS:beta  ~ S1):(interval:<0,1>:10);
MAP:(CONS:gamma ~ S1):(interval:<0,1>:10);
```

**Remarks**  Let us note that, e.g., `alpha` is a *sequence* of coordinate functions. Conversely, `CONS:alpha` is the correct implementation of the *vector-valued* function $\alpha$, which only can be *composed* with other functions, say S1.

Notice also that `SQR` (square), given in Script 3.2.4, is the PLaSM implementation of the $id^2$ function and that the language explicitly requires the operator * to denote the product of functions.

Finally, we remark that SQRT (square root), which is actually primitive in PLaSM, can be also defined easily using standard algebraic rules, where ** is the predefined power operator.

### Example 5.1.4 (Comparing parametrizations)

The parametrizations of the arcs generated by maps $\alpha$, $\beta$ and $\gamma$ are quite different. It is possible to see this fact by looking at Figure 5.1, where the graphical markers associated with the mapped image of each point of a uniform sampling of the curve domain generated by Script 5.1.3 are shown. The polymarker and markerSize implementation is given in Script 7.2.9. Notice that the functional expression

```
polymarker:1 ~ S1 ~ UKPOL
```

converts its polyhedral input into a triplet of vertices, cells and polyhedra, then extracts the vertices, and finally gives them as arguments to the function polymarker:1, which attaches a marker of type 1 to each point.

---

### Script 5.1.3 (Curve sampling marking)

```
DEF markerSize = 0.05;
DEF markers = polymarker:1 ~ S1 ~ UKPOL;

(markers ~ MAP:(CONS:alpha ~ S1)):(interval:<0,1>:10);
(markers ~ MAP:(CONS:beta  ~ S1)):(interval:<0,1>:10);
(markers ~ MAP:(CONS:gamma ~ S1)):(interval:<0,1>:10);
```

---

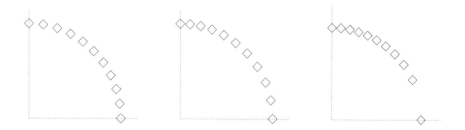

**Figure 5.1**   Trigonometric, rational and Cartesian parametrization

### Example 5.1.5 (Coordinate maps)

It should be remembered that curves, as $\alpha$, $\beta$ and $\gamma$ in the previous example, are vector-valued functions. In order to obtain their coordinate maps, say $\alpha_i : \mathbb{R} \to \mathbb{R}$, a composition with the appropriate selector function is needed:

$$\alpha_i = \sigma(i) \circ \alpha$$

The conversion from a 3D vector-valued function   curve := CONS:alpha   to the sequence of its coordinate functions may be obtained in PLaSM as:

```
< S1 ~ curve, S2 ~ curve, S3 ~ curve >;
```

Such an approach is quite expensive and inefficient, because the curve function is repeatedly evaluated on data points to get its three component functions. So, for the sake of efficiency, we suggest maintaining a coordinate representation as a *sequence* of scalar-valued functions, and then `CONS` it into a single *vector-valued* function only when it is strictly necessary.

Anyway, an operator `Curve2MapVect` is given in Script 5.1.4. This operator, when applied to a vector-valued map $\mathbb{R} \to \mathbb{E}^d$ with arbitrary $d$, will return the sequence of its $d$ coordinate functions.

---

**Script 5.1.4 (Curve to vector of maps)**

```
DEF Curve2MapVect (curve::IsFun) = AA:COMP:(selectors DISTR curve)
WHERE
    selectors = AA:SEL:(1..d),
    d = LEN:(curve:<0>)
END;

Curve2MapVect:curve ≡ < curve₁ , curve₂ >
```

---

### 5.1.2  Reparametrization

A *smooth curve* is defined as a curve whose coordinate functions are smooth (see Section 5.2) i.e. can be derived as many times it is needed. If $c : I \to \mathbb{E}^d$, with $I \subset \mathbb{R}$, is a smooth curve and $\rho : I \to I$ is a smooth invertible function, i.e. a *diffeomorphism*, then also

$$c_\rho = c \circ \rho$$

is a smooth curve. It is called a *reparametrization* of $c$.

A very simple reparametrization is the *change of origin*. For example $c_\rho$ is called a change of origin when

$$\rho = \mathrm{id} + \underline{c}.$$

A reparametrization $c_\tau$ by an affine function

$$\tau = \underline{a}\,\mathrm{id} + \underline{c},$$

with $a \neq 0$, is called an *affine reparametrization*.

**Example 5.1.6 (Circle reparametrization)**
The circle with the center in the origin and unit radius may be parametrized on different intervals:

$$
\begin{array}{rcll}
c_1(u) & = & (\ \cos u \quad \sin u\ ), & u \in [0, 2\pi] \\
c_2(u) & = & (\ \cos(2\pi u) \quad \sin(2\pi u)\ ), & u \in [0, 1]
\end{array}
$$

or with a different starting point:

$$\boldsymbol{c_3}(u) \;=\; (\; \cos(2\pi u + \tfrac{\pi}{2}) \quad \sin(2\pi u + \tfrac{\pi}{2}) \;), \qquad u \in [0,1]$$

The reparametrization becomes evident if we use a variable-free representation:

$$\begin{aligned}
\boldsymbol{c_1} &= (\; \cos \quad \sin \;), \\
\boldsymbol{c_2} &= (\; \cos \quad \sin \;) \circ (\underline{2\,\pi}\,\mathrm{id}), \\
\boldsymbol{c_3} &= (\; \cos \quad \sin \;) \circ (\underline{2\,\pi}\,\mathrm{id} + \underline{\pi/2}).
\end{aligned}$$

**Example 5.1.7 (Reparametrization of a parabola)**
Several curves may have the same image. Two different parametrizations of the same subset of parabola $y = x^2$ are given below:

$$\begin{aligned}
\boldsymbol{p_1}(u) &= (\; u \quad u^2 \;), & u \in [0,2], \\
\boldsymbol{p_2}(u) &= (\; 2u \quad 4u^2 \;), & u \in [0,1],
\end{aligned}$$

Using the variable-free notation, we have:

$$\begin{aligned}
\boldsymbol{p_1} &= (\; \mathrm{id} \quad \mathrm{id}^2 \;), \\
\boldsymbol{p_2} &= (\; \mathrm{id} \quad \mathrm{id}^2 \;) \circ \underline{2}\,\mathrm{id}.
\end{aligned}$$

A very similar PLaSM implementation of curve $\boldsymbol{p_2}$ follows. The `interval` function is defined in Script 5.1.1.

---

**Script 5.1.5 (Parabola)**

```
DEF p2 = [ID, ID * ID] ~ (K:2 * S1);

MAP:p2:(interval:<0,1>:30);
```

---

*5.1.3   Orientation*

Two curves with the same image can be distinguished by the sense in which the image is traversed for increasing values of the parameter. Two curves which are traversed in the same way are said to have the same *orientation*. Actually, an orientation is an equivalence class of parametrizations.

A *reversed orientation* of a curve $\boldsymbol{c} : \mathbb{R} \to \mathbb{E}^d$, with image $\boldsymbol{c}[a,b]$, is given by the affine reparametrization $\boldsymbol{c_\lambda} = \boldsymbol{c} \circ \lambda$, where $\lambda : \mathbb{R} \to \mathbb{R}$ such that $x \mapsto -x + (a+b)$. This map can be written as:

$$\lambda = \underline{-1}\,\mathrm{id} + \underline{(a+b)}.$$

**Example 5.1.8 (Reversing orientation)**

It is useful to have a PLaSM function REV, which reverses the orientation of any curve parametrized on the interval $[a, b] \subset \mathbb{R}$. The REV function will therefore be abstracted with respect to the bounds a and b, which are real numbers.

In Script 5.1.6 we also give a polyhedral approximation of the boundary of unit circle centered in the origin, as seen from the angle interval $[0, \frac{\pi}{2}]$. The curve is a map from $[0, 1]$ with reversed orientation.

---

**Script 5.1.6**

```
DEF REV (a,b::IsReal) = K:-1 * ID + K:(a+b);
DEF alpha = [ COS, SIN ] ~ (K:(PI/2) * ID);

MAP:(alpha ~ REV:<0,1> ~ S1):(interval:<0,1>:20);
```

---

## 5.2   Differentiation

Let $\phi : U \to F$ be a *continuous* map, with $E, F$ normed linear spaces, $U \subset E$ open set, and $x \in U$.

**Definition 5.2.1** *The map $\phi$ is* differentiable *at $x$ if there is a* linear *map $L_x : E \to F$ which approximates $\phi$ at $x$, i.e. such that*

$$(\phi(x + h) - \phi(x)) - L_x(h) = o(\|h\|)$$

where $o(\|h\|)$ means that the left-hand side approaches zero faster than $\|h\|$. In general, $L_x$ depends on $x$. When it exists, it is unique. If $\phi$ is differentiable at every $x \in U$ we say that $\phi$ is differentiable in $U$.

$L_x$ is a linear map in $\lin(E; F)$. It is called the *(Fréchet-)derivative of $\phi$ at $x$* and is denoted as $D\phi(x)$. Hence we can write:

$$\phi(x + h) - \phi(x) = D\phi(x)(h) + o(h)$$

The map $D\phi : U \to \lin(E; F)$ is called the *derivative of $\phi$*.

A map $\phi : U \to F$ is *continuously differentiable* if it is differentiable and $D\phi \in C^0(U; \lin(E, F))$. We also say that $\phi$ is of class $C^1$. Analogously,

$$C^n = \{\phi \in C^{n-1} : D\phi \in C^{n-1}\}.$$

is the class of functions which are $n$-times differentiable. A *smooth* function is a function of class $C^\infty$.

### 5.2.1   Real-valued maps of a real variable

For real maps of a single real variable we have $E = F = \mathbb{R}$. In this case the elementary notion of derivative can be recovered from the above definition.

The function $\phi : \mathbb{R} \to \mathbb{R}$ is said *differentiable* at $x$ if the limit

$$\lim_{h \to 0} \frac{1}{h} \left( \phi(x + h) - \phi(x) \right)$$

exists and is finite. That limit is called the *derivative* of $\phi$ at $x$, and is denoted by $\phi'(x)$. Its value $\lambda$ is both a number in $\mathbb{R}$ and a linear map in $\mathrm{lin}\,(\mathbb{R}, \mathbb{R})$ via the canonical isomorphism $\lambda \mapsto \lambda(1) = \lambda$, such that $y \mapsto \lambda y$.

Hence we may write for the ordinary derivative $\phi'(x) = D\phi(x)(1)$. This value is the *slope* of the tangent to the graph of $\phi$ at point $(x, \phi(x))$.

Because of the canonical isomorphism and the consequent identification of $\mathbb{R}$ with the dual space $\mathbb{R}^*$ of linear maps $\mathbb{R} \to \mathbb{R}$, we may also write, for $\phi : \mathbb{R} \to \mathbb{R}$

$$D\phi : \mathbb{R} \to \mathbb{R}; x \mapsto \phi'(x).$$

**Implementation**    The value of $\phi'(x)$ can be computed, according to its definition, by the function deriv0 of Script 5.2.1, with h a suitably "small" number. A *much* better numerical approximation to the slope of tangent to graph of $\phi$ at $x$ is given by the central difference implemented by function deriv1, as shown by the following approximations of $\sin' \frac{\pi}{3} = \cos \frac{\pi}{3} = \frac{1}{2}$:

```
deriv0:1E-4:SIN:(PI/3) ≡ 0.499956697895
deriv1:1E-4:SIN:(PI/3) ≡ 0.499999999166
```

---

**Script 5.2.1 (Derivation of $\phi : \mathbb{R} \to \mathbb{R}$ at $x$)**
```
DEF deriv0(h::IsReal)(f::IsFun)(x::IsReal) = (f:(x + h) - f:x)/h;
DEF deriv1(h::IsReal)(f::IsFun)(x::IsReal) = (f:(x + h) - f:(x - h))/(2*h);

DEF D11 (f::IsFun)(x::IsReal) = deriv1:1E-4:f:x;
```

---

The D11 operator is given to compute the derivative of functions $\mathbb{R} \to \mathbb{R}$ at a point $x$. Such specialized operator will be needed in Script 5.2.15 to implement a *generalized* derivation operator D, to be used to derive maps between spaces of any dimensions. Hence in the rest of the chapter we only make use of this generalized operator.

The differentiation operator D must be applied first to a function, and then to a real number, in order to return a real number. When it is applied only to a function, it returns the *derivative function* of its argument:

```
D:COS:0 ≡ 0.0
D:COS:(PI/2) ≡ -0.9999999983332231
D:COS ≡ An-Anonymous-Function
```

**Example 5.2.1 (Map of the derivate functions)**
In Figure 5.2 it is shown the graph of the cos function, together with the graph of the $D$ cos function. For this purpose we apply, in Script 5.2.2, the MAP primitive to function [ID, COS] $\circ$ $\sigma(1)$ and to function [ID, D:COS] $\circ$ $\sigma(1)$, respectively, and

then to a 1D polyhedral complex which defines a partition of the domain $[-\pi, \pi]$ with 60 subintervals.

Notice that the same approach is used to generate the graphs of $x$ and $y$ axes, by mapping the [ID, K:0] $\circ$ $\sigma(1)$ and [K:0, ID] $\circ$ $\sigma(1)$ functions, respectively. The generator interval of the domain partition is given in Script 5.1.1.

---

**Script 5.2.2**
```
STRUCT:<
    MAP:([ID, COS] ~ S1):(interval:<-:PI,PI>:60),
    MAP:([ID, D:COS] ~ S1):(interval:<-:PI,PI>:60),
    MAP:([ID, K:0] ~ S1):(interval:<-:PI,PI>:1),
    MAP:([K:0, ID] ~ S1):(interval:<-1,1>:1) >;
```

---

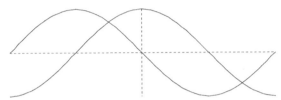

**Figure 5.2**   Graphs of cos and $D$ cos functions

## Higher-order derivatives

The differentiation operator $D$ can be applied repeatedly on a smooth function $\phi : \mathbb{R} \to \mathbb{R}$. In particular:

$$D^2 \phi := (D \circ D) \phi = D \phi' = (\phi')' =: \phi^{(2)}.$$

More in general, for each integer $n > 1$,

$$\phi^{(n)} := D^n \phi = D \phi^{(n-1)}.$$

## Example 5.2.2 (Polynomials)

The set of polynomial functions of degree $\leq n$ with coefficients in $\mathbb{R}$ is often denoted as $P_n[\mathbb{R}]$. Functions $\mu \in P_n[\mathbb{R}]$, where

$$\mu : \mathbb{R} \to \mathbb{R}; \quad x \mapsto \sum_{i=0}^{n} a_i x^i, \qquad a_i \in \mathbb{R},$$

are an important example of *smooth functions*, and constitute a vector space of dimension $n + 1$. In later chapters we will see that some special bases of such vector space play a very important role in defining *free-form* curves and surfaces used by CAD systems.

It is very easy to see that the derivative of a polynomial of degree $n$ is a polynomial of degree $n - 1$.

In other words, if $\mu \in P_n[\mathbb{R}]$, then $D\mu \in P_{n-1}[\mathbb{R}]$. This fact implies that

$$P_n[\mathbb{R}] \supset D(P_n[\mathbb{R}]) \supset \cdots \supset D^{n-1}(P_n[\mathbb{R}]) \supset D^n(P_n[\mathbb{R}]).$$

**Example 5.2.3 (Graph of derivatives of $\cos$)**
The graphs of functions $\cos$, $D\cos$, $D^2\cos$ and $D^3\cos$ on a partition of the domain $[-\pi, \pi]$ with 60 subintervals are produced by the last expression in Script 5.2.3, and are shown in Figure 5.3.

---

**Script 5.2.3**
```
    DEF dom = interval:<-:PI,PI>:60;

    STRUCT:<
       MAP:([ID, COS] ~ S1):dom,
       MAP:([ID, D:COS] ~ S1):dom,
       MAP:([ID, (D ~ D):COS] ~ S1):dom,
       MAP:([ID, (D ~ D ~ D):COS] ~ S1):dom >;
```

---

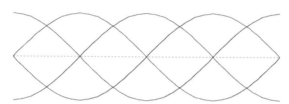

**Figure 5.3**   Graphs of cos function and of its first three derivatives

**Useful properties of derivatives**

Let us consider $E = F = \mathbb{R}$. The following properties hold for maps in $C^1(\mathbb{R}; \mathbb{R})$, in the following denoted as $C^1$. Actually, such properties hold also in more general settings.

**Linearity**   For all $a, b \in \mathbb{R}$ and all $\phi, \psi \in C^1$, the *linear combination* map $a\phi + b\psi \in C^1$, with

$$D(a\phi + b\psi) = aD\phi + bD\psi.$$

**Chain rule**   For all $\phi, \psi \in C^1$, the *compound* map $\phi \circ \psi \in C^1$, with

$$D(\phi \circ \psi) = (D\phi \circ \psi)D\psi.$$

**Leibnitz's rule**   For all $\phi, \psi \in C^1$, the *product* map $\phi\psi \in C^1$, with

$$D(\phi\psi) = (D\phi)\psi + \phi(D\psi).$$

**Example 5.2.4**

In Figure 5.4 we show the graph of $\sin \circ \cos$ function and of its three first derivatives $D(\sin \circ \cos)$, $D^2(\sin \circ \cos)$ and $D^3(\sin \circ \cos)$, as generated by Script 5.2.4.

---

**Script 5.2.4 (A few derivatives of** $\sin \circ \cos$**)**

```
STRUCT:<
    MAP:([ID, (SIN ~ COS)] ~ S1):dom,
    MAP:([ID, D:(SIN ~ COS)] ~ S1):dom,
    MAP:([ID, (D ~ D):(SIN ~ COS)] ~ S1):dom,
    MAP:([ID, (D ~ D ~ D):(SIN ~ COS)] ~ S1):dom
>;
```

---

The reader may check that the same graph generated by Script 5.2.4 and shown in Figure 5.4 can be produced by substituting the right-hand side of the following expressions to the left-hand side. The first equivalence is produced by the chain rule; the second equivalence is generated by using both chain and Leibnitz's rules.

```
D:(SIN ~ COS) ≡ (D:SIN ~ COS) * D:COS

(D ~ D):(SIN ~ COS) ≡
    D:(D:SIN ~ COS) * D:COS + (D:SIN ~ COS) * D:(D:COS)
```

An equivalent symbolic expression for `(D ~ D ~ D):(SIN ~ COS)` would produce several lines of code, as the diligent reader might check. Furthermore, it would require a longer computation and would produce a greater numeric error when evaluated on actual data.

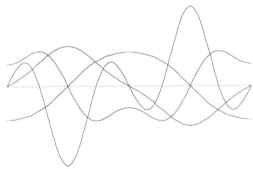

**Figure 5.4**   Graphs of $\phi = \sin \circ \cos$ and of its first three derivatives on $[-\pi, \pi]$

*5.2.2   Vector-valued maps of a real variable*

In this case we have $E = \mathbb{R}$, $F = \mathbb{R}^m$, and $\phi = (\phi_1, \ldots, \phi_m)$ is a vector-valued *continuous* map $\mathbb{R} \to \mathbb{R}^m$. In other words, $\phi \in C^0(\mathbb{R}; \mathbb{R}^m)$. Such a map is called a *curve* in $\mathbb{R}^m$.

At each $u \in \mathbb{R}$ the derivative $D\phi(u)$, if it exists, is a *linear* map $\mathbb{R} \to \mathbb{R}^m$.

By linearity it is, for all $s \in \mathbb{R}$:

$$D\phi(u)(s) = D\phi(u)(s1) = sD\phi(u)(1) = s\phi'(u) = s(\phi'_1(u), \ldots, \phi'_m(u))$$

**Implementation**   The function D1m, given in Script 5.2.5, which implements this derivative, is very easy to write down by considering that $D\phi(u)(s)$ is just a scalar multiple of the vector $(\phi'_1(u), \ldots, \phi'_m(u))$ whose components are the derivatives at $u$ of the scalar functions $\phi_1, \ldots, \phi_m \in C^1(\mathbb{R}; \mathbb{R})$.

Notice that the scalarVectProd operator, defined in Script 2.1.20 and normally used to multiply a scalar number times an ordered $d$-tuple of scalars, is here used to multiply a scalar function times an ordered $d$-tuple of functions. Such useful behavior of vector operators will often be found in this chapter.

---

**Script 5.2.5 (Derivative of $f : \mathbb{R} \to \mathbb{R}^m$ at $u$)**
```
DEF D1m (f::IsSeqOf:IsFun)(u::IsReal) =
   S1 scalarVectProd AA:K:((CONS ~ AA:D11): f: u);
```

---

In the following examples, according to Script 5.2.15, we use the generalized operator D instead of the specialized operator D1m.

Notice also that in the remainder of this chapter we usually implement in PLaSM a curve $\phi = (\phi_1, \ldots, \phi_m)$ as the *sequence*

$$< \phi_1, \ldots, \phi_m >$$

of its coordinate functions, and not as the vector-valued function

$$[ \phi_1, \ldots, \phi_m ]$$

given by their CONS. Such implementation choice allows for easier access and manipulation of the coordinate functions, and is a consequence of the discussion in Example 5.1.5.

### Example 5.2.5 (Circular curve)
The circular curve of unit radius centered at the origin may be given as a map

$$\texttt{circlemap} : \mathbb{R} \to \mathbb{R}^2; \quad u \mapsto (\cos u, \sin u), \qquad u \in [-\pi, \pi]$$

The derivative $D\texttt{circlemap}(u)$ at $u$ is a linear map. In Figure 5.5a we show both the image curve $\texttt{circlemap}[-\pi, \pi]$ and the line segment $D\texttt{circlemap}(\frac{\pi}{3})[-\frac{1}{2}, \frac{1}{2}]$. Notice that the point $D\texttt{circlemap}(\frac{\pi}{3})(0)$ clearly coincides with $(0,0)$.

The last expression of Script 5.2.6 produces Figure 5.5b, where the set $D\texttt{circlemap}(\frac{\pi}{3})[-\frac{1}{2}, \frac{1}{2}]$ has been translated to the tangency point $\texttt{circlemap}(\frac{\pi}{3})$. The part of tangent line there shown is exactly the point set

$$\texttt{circlemap}(\frac{\pi}{3}) + D\texttt{circlemap}(\frac{\pi}{3})[-\frac{1}{2}, \frac{1}{2}].$$

where, as usual, $f(A)$ stands for $\{f(a) \mid a \in A\}$, and $x + B$ stands for $\{x + b \mid b \in B\}$.

**Script 5.2.6 (Derivative at a circle point)**
```
DEF circlemap = < COS, SIN >;

STRUCT:<
    MAP:(CONS:circlemap ~ s1):(interval:<-:PI,PI>:60),
    T:<1,2>:(CONS:circlemap:(PI/3)),
    MAP:(CONS:(D:circlemap:(PI/3))):(interval:<-0.5,0.5>:1) >;
```

**Figure 5.5**   (a) Derivative of `circlemap` map $\mathbb{R} \to \mathbb{R}^2$ at $\frac{\pi}{3}$ (b) Corresponding affine map

## Example 5.2.6 (Circular helix)

The *circular helix* curve of radius $r$, pitch $h$ and $n$ number of $2\pi$ turns can be given as the map

$$\mathtt{helix}(r,h,n): \mathbb{R} \to \mathbb{R}^3 : u \mapsto (r\cos u, r\sin u, \frac{h}{2\pi}u), \qquad u \in [0, 2\pi n].$$

The corresponding variable-free formulation is

$$\mathtt{helix}(r,h,n) = \left( \; \underline{r}\cos \quad \underline{r}\sin \quad (\tfrac{h}{2\pi})\mathrm{id} \; \right)$$

The collection of helix curves with axis on $x = y = 0$, starting point on the $x$-axis, and prescribed radius, height and number of turns, may hence be generated by the PLaSM function

$$\mathtt{helix} : \mathbb{R}^+ \times \mathbb{R}^+ \times \mathbb{R}^+ \to (\mathbb{R} \to \mathbb{R}^3)$$

which is implemented in Script 5.2.7 as a sequence of three coordinate functions.

**Script 5.2.7 (Derivative at a helix point)**
```
DEF helix (r,h,n::IsRealPos) = < K:r*COS, K:r*SIN, K:(h/(2*PI))*ID >;

STRUCT:<
    MAP:(CONS:(helix:<1,0.5,4>) ~ s1):(interval:<0,8*PI>:180),
    T:<1,2,3>:(CONS:(helix:<1,0.5,4>):(2*PI/3)),
    MAP:(CONS:(D:(helix:<1,0.5,4>):(2*PI/3))):(interval:<-0.5,0.5>:1)
>;
```

The `STRUCT` expression gives both the helix image of the interval $[0, 8\pi]$ and the image of the tangent map in $\frac{2}{3}\pi$ on the interval $[-\frac{1}{2}, \frac{1}{2}]$. To be precise, the `STRUCT` expression of Script 5.2.7 produces (a simplicial approximation of) the sets

$$\texttt{helix}(r, h, n)[0, 8\pi] \qquad \text{and}$$

$$\texttt{helix}(r, h, n)(\frac{2}{3}\pi) + D\texttt{helix}(r, h, n)(\frac{2}{3}\pi)[-\frac{1}{2}, \frac{1}{2}]$$

with $r = 1$, $h = 0.5$ and $n = 4$. Both such sets are shown in Figure 5.6.

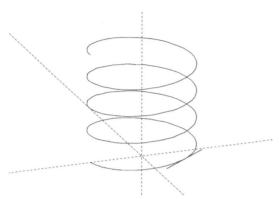

**Figure 5.6** Image of the tangent map to the $\texttt{helix}$ curve at the point $\frac{2}{3}\pi$

### 5.2.3 Real-valued maps of several real variables

In this case we have $E = \mathbb{R}^n$ and $F = \mathbb{R}$, where $\phi : \mathbb{R}^n \to \mathbb{R}$ is a real-valued function of $n$ real variables. The derivative $D\phi(\boldsymbol{a})$ at $\boldsymbol{a}$ (if it exists), is a *linear functional* $\mathbb{R}^n \to \mathbb{R}$, called the *gradient* of $\phi$ at $\boldsymbol{a}$, and often denoted by $\nabla\phi(\boldsymbol{a})$.

In order to compute $D\phi(\boldsymbol{a})$, notice that each $\boldsymbol{h} \in \mathbb{R}^n$ can be written, using the standard basis $(\boldsymbol{e}_1, \dots, \boldsymbol{e}_n)$, as $\boldsymbol{h} = h_1\boldsymbol{e}_1 + \cdots + h_n\boldsymbol{e}_n$, so that, by linearity

$$D\phi(\boldsymbol{a})(\boldsymbol{h}) = h_1 Df(\boldsymbol{a})(\boldsymbol{e}_1) + \cdots + h_n Df(\boldsymbol{a})(\boldsymbol{e}_n).$$

Each $Df(\boldsymbol{a})(\boldsymbol{e}_i)$ is the limit of the ratio of the function difference in two close points $\boldsymbol{a} - dx_i\boldsymbol{e}_i$ and $\boldsymbol{a} + dx_i\boldsymbol{e}_i$, over their distance $2\,dx_i$, but this limit of the "incremental ratio" is exactly the derivative of $f$ at $\boldsymbol{a}$ as a function of a single real variable, usually known as the *partial derivative* $\frac{\partial\phi}{\partial x_i}(\boldsymbol{a}) \in \text{lin}\,(\mathbb{R}^n; \mathbb{R})$, so that we can write:

$$D\phi(\boldsymbol{a})(\boldsymbol{h}) = h_1\frac{\partial\phi}{\partial x_1}(\boldsymbol{a}) + \cdots + h_n\frac{\partial\phi}{\partial x_n}(\boldsymbol{a}) = \nabla\phi(\boldsymbol{a}) \cdot \boldsymbol{h}.$$

**Implementation** To compute a partial derivative $\texttt{Dp}$ of $\phi$ at $\boldsymbol{a}$ in the $i$-th coordinate direction, it is necessary to compute the function difference in two points $\texttt{a1}$ and $\texttt{a2}$ which differ only for a suitably "small" amount $2\,dx$ of the $i$-th coordinate, if we choose a numerical scheme based on central differences.

The *gradient* at $\boldsymbol{a}$ of a function $\phi : \mathbb{R}^n \to \mathbb{R}$ is the column vector of the partial derivatives of $\phi$ at $\boldsymbol{a}$. It is easily implemented in Script 5.2.9.

Some examples of use of the $\texttt{grad}$ operator are given in Script 5.2.9. They may help to understand the semantics of the $\texttt{grad}$ implementation.

**Script 5.2.8 (Partial derivative of $f : \mathbb{R}^n \to \mathbb{R}$ at $a$)**

```
DEF Dp (i::isIntPos)(f::IsFun)(a::IsPoint)(h::IsVect) =
   (f:a2 - f:a1) / (2*dx)
WHERE
   a2 = CAT:<seq1, <SEL:i:a + dx>, seq2> ,
   a1 = CAT:<seq1, <SEL:i:a - dx>, seq2> ,
   seq1 = AS:SEL:(1..(i - 1)):a ,
   seq2 = AS:SEL:((i + 1)..n):a ,
   n = LEN:a ,
   dx = 1E-5
END;
```

**Script 5.2.9 (Gradient of $\phi : \mathbb{R}^n \to \mathbb{R}$ at $a$)**

```
DEF grad (f::IsFun)(a::IsPoint) = CONS:(DpVect:f):a
WHERE
   DpVect = (CONS ~ AA:Dp ~ INTSTO ~ LEN):a
END;

DEF f = SIN ~ S1 * SIN ~ S2;

grad:f ≡ An-Anonymous-Function
grad:f:<PI/3,PI/-2> ≡ < An-Anonymous-Function, An-Anonymous-Function >
CONS:(grad:f:<PI/3,PI/-2>):<1,1> ≡ <-0.4999999999921733, 0.0>
```

It may be also useful to show the variable-free representation of the map generated when using the Dn1 operator given in Script 5.2.10. Notice first of all, that such a function, like most PLaSM programs, is dimension-independent and works for any dimension $n$ of the domain space.

So, we have

$$\texttt{Dn1}(\phi)(a) := \frac{\partial \phi}{\partial x_1}(a)\sigma(1) + \cdots + \frac{\partial \phi}{\partial x_n}(a)\sigma(n),$$

where $\sigma(1), \ldots, \sigma(n)$ are the selector functions defined in Section 5.1.1, and

$$\texttt{Dn1}(\phi)(a)(u) = \frac{\partial \phi}{\partial x_1}(a)u_1 + \cdots + \frac{\partial \phi}{\partial x_n}(a)u_n = \nabla \phi(a) \cdot u.$$

**Script 5.2.10 (Derivative of $\phi : \mathbb{R}^n \to \mathbb{R}$ at $a$)**

```
DEF Dn1 (f::IsFun)(a::IsPoint) =
   (InnerProd ~ [AA:SEL ~ INTSTO ~ LEN, grad:f]):a ;
```

The reader should notice that the PLaSM expression

```
(AA:SEL ~ INTSTO ~ LEN):a
```

returns the sequence $< \sigma(1), \ldots, \sigma(n) >$ of selector functions, as well as the expression grad:f:a returns the sequence of partial derivatives of f at a. Also notice that the binary `InnerProd` operator, defined in Script 3.2.4, works with pairs of ordered $d$-tuples of either scalar numbers or scalar functions.

As always, we will use in the remainder of this chapter the generalized operator D of Script 5.2.15, instead of the specialized derivation operator `Dn1`.

**Directional derivative**   The weaker concept of *directional* (or *Gateaux*) *derivative* is defined as follows. Let $h \in \mathbb{R}^n$ be a unit vector and

$$\psi : \mathbb{R} \to \mathbb{R}; \ t \mapsto \phi(a + th).$$

Then the directional derivative of $\phi$ in the chosen direction $h$ is the scalar $\psi'(0) = D\psi(0)(1)$.

This directional derivative may be interpreted as the derivative along any curve passing for $a$ with $h$ as tangent vector at $a$:

$$D_h \phi(a) = \lim_{t \to 0} \frac{\phi(a + th)}{t}$$

The map $\phi$ is said to be *Gateaux-differentiable* at $a$ if $D_h\phi(a)$ exists for all $h \in \mathbb{R}^n$. When $D\phi(a)$ exists, $D_h\phi(a) = D\phi(a)(h) = \nabla\phi(a) \cdot h$.

**Example 5.2.7 (Graph of tangent space)**
The graphs of $\sin u \sin v$, i.e. of the function $\phi = (\sin \circ \sigma(1))(\sin \circ \sigma(2))$ on the set $U_1 = [0, \pi]^2$, and of the affine map $(\phi + D\phi)(\frac{\pi}{3}, \frac{\pi}{2})$ on the set $U_2 = [-\frac{1}{2}, \frac{1}{2}]^2$, is produced by Script 5.2.11 and is shown in Figure 5.7.

---

**Script 5.2.11 (Graph of tangent space)**

```
DEF f  = SIN ~ S1 * SIN ~ S2;
DEF U1 = interval2D:<0,0,PI,PI>:<20,20>;
DEF U2 = interval2D:<-0.5,-0.5,0.5,0.5>:<2,2>;

STRUCT:<
   MAP:[S1, S2, f]:U1 CREASE (PI/2),
   T:<1,2,3>:([S1, S2, f]:<PI/3, PI/2>),
   MAP:[S1, S2, D:f:<PI/3, PI/2>]:U2 COLOR RED
>;
```

---

Within the above PLaSM code two rendering-oriented language constructs are informally introduced. The CREASE binary operator, applied to a polyhedral complex and to an angle (in radiants), annotates the first argument with a rendering property checked by the VRML exporter. The resulting effect is the exporting of the surface with "indexed coordinates", so that a "Gouraud's shader" can be applied by the VRML browser in rendering the surface. Analogously, the binary operator COLOR applies the predefined RGB constant RED to its polyhedral argument. Both the CREASE and the COLOR operators require the loading of the PLaSM library named "colors". Such topics are discussed in detail in Chapter 10.

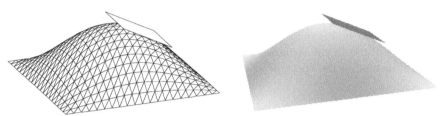

**Figure 5.7**  Graphs of map $\phi$ on $[0, \pi]^2$ and of map $(\phi + D\phi)(\frac{\pi}{3}, \frac{\pi}{2})$ on $[-1, 1]^2$, with $\phi = \sin u \sin v$: (a) polyhedral approximation (b) smooth rendering

In more precise terms, the STRUCT expresssion of Script 5.2.11 generates a simplicial approximation of the set:

$$(\sigma(1), \sigma(2), \phi)[0, \pi]^2 \cup \left((\sigma(1), \sigma(2), D\phi(\frac{\pi}{3}, \frac{\pi}{2}))[-1, 1]^2 + \phi(\frac{\pi}{3}, \frac{\pi}{2})\right)$$

*5.2.4  Vector-valued maps of several real variables*

In this case we have $E = \mathbb{R}^n$, $F = \mathbb{R}^m$ and $\phi : \mathbb{R}^n \to \mathbb{R}^m$. The derivative $D\phi(u)$ of $\phi$ at $u$ is a *linear map* $\mathbb{R}^n \to \mathbb{R}^m$, if it exists.

In other words, $D\phi(u)$ is a matrix in $\mathbb{R}^m_n$, called *Jacobian matrix* of $\phi$ at $u$.

By chosing bases $(e_i)$ in $\mathbb{R}^n$ and $(\epsilon_j)$ in $\mathbb{R}^m$, with $\phi = (\phi_1, \phi_2, \ldots, \phi_m)$ and each $\phi_i : \mathbb{R}^n \to \mathbb{R}$, we have

$$D\phi(u) = D\phi_1(u)\epsilon_1 + D\phi_2(u)\epsilon_2 + \cdots + D\phi_m(u)\epsilon_m,$$

The Jacobian matrix $D\phi(u)$ is often represented as

$$\frac{\partial(\phi_1, \phi_2, \ldots, \phi_m)}{\partial(x_1, x_2, \ldots, x_n)} = (\alpha_{ij}), \quad \text{with} \quad \alpha_{ij} = \frac{\partial \phi_i}{\partial x_j}(x).$$

The determinant

$$J = \left| \frac{\partial(\phi_1, \phi_2, \ldots, \phi_m)}{\partial(x_1, x_2, \ldots, x_n)} \right|$$

of the Jacobian matrix at $u$ is called the *Jacobian* of $\phi$ at $u$. When $\phi \in C^1(\mathbb{R}^n; \mathbb{R}^n)$ is a transformation of coordinates, $J(u)$ gives the ratio of the volume elements at $u$, with $dV' = J(u)dV$.

**Implementation**   Once again, this derivative is quite easy to implement in PLaSM. According to the functional character of the language, the easiest implementation of $D\phi(u)$ is as the sequence $(D\phi_1(u), \ldots, D\phi_m(u))$ of derivatives at $u$ of the coordinate functions of $\phi$. Such a derivative is denoted as Dnm in Script 5.2.12.

---

**Script 5.2.12 (Derivative of $f : \mathbb{R}^n \to \mathbb{R}^m$ at $a$)**
```
DEF Dnm (f::IsSeqOf:IsFun)(u::IsPoint) = (CONS ~ AA:Dn1):f:u;
```

---

As is usual at this point, we will refer to this operator as D, according to the generalized implementation of the derivative operator given in Script 5.2.15.

## Example 5.2.8 (Tangent plane at a point of a torus)

The parametric equations of the family of surfaces known as *toruses* can be seen as generated by a map

$$\phi : \mathbb{R}^+ \times \mathbb{R}^+ \to (\mathbb{R}^2 \to \mathbb{R}^3) : (r, R) \mapsto (\phi_x, \phi_y, \phi_z),$$

where $r, R$ are the *minor* and *major* radiuses of the surfaces, respectively, and

$$\phi_x, \phi_y, \phi_z : U \to \mathbb{R},$$

with

$$
\begin{aligned}
\phi_x &= (\underline{r}\cos \circ \sigma(1) + \underline{R})\cos \circ \sigma(2), \\
\phi_y &= (\underline{r}\cos \circ \sigma(1) + \underline{R})\sin \circ \sigma(2), \\
\phi_z &= \underline{r}\sin \circ \sigma(1),
\end{aligned}
$$

and

$$U = [0, 2\pi)^2 \subset \mathbb{R}^2.$$

Such equations can be easily derived from the general equation of rotational surfaces given in Chapter 12. They are directly translated into the PLaSM definition given in Script 5.2.13.

---

### Script 5.2.13 (Torus)

```
DEF torus (r1,r2::IsReal) = < fx, fy, fz >
WHERE
    fx = (K:r1 * COS ~ S1 + K:r2) * COS ~ S2,
    fy = (K:r1 * COS ~ S1 + K:r2) * SIN ~ S2,
    fz = (K:r1 * SIN ~ S1)
END;
```

---

Some preliminary check on the types of elementary expressions involving the torus function may be useful for a deeper understanding. In particular, we check that

1. the expression torus:<1,3> returns a triplet of (coordinate) functions;
2. such functions, evaluated at the same 2D point return a 3D point;
3. the derivative of torus:<1,3> at a point returns a triplet of (linear) functions,

as shown by the following examples:

```
torus:<1,3> ≡
    <An-Anonymous-Function, An-Anonymous-Function, An-Anonymous-Function>

CONS:(torus:<1,3>):<PI/3,PI/3> ≡
    <1.75, 3.031088913245535, 0.8660254037844386>

D:(torus:<1,3>):<PI/3,PI/3> ≡
    <An-Anonymous-Function, An-Anonymous-Function, An-Anonymous-Function>
```

**Figure 5.8**  Image of the affine map $(\phi + D\phi)(u)$ on the torus surface

In Figure 5.8 we show the image of the function `torus:<1,3>` on the domain $[0, 2\pi]^2$, i.e. the torus surface with radiuses $(1, 3)$, and the image of the affine map $\mathbb{R}^2 \to \mathbb{R}^3$ of type $(\phi + D\phi)(u)$ on the domain $[-\frac{1}{2}, \frac{1}{2}]^2$.

More formally, we can say that Figure 5.8 gives a picture of the set

$$\phi[0, 2\pi]^2 \ \cup \ (\phi(u) + D\phi(u)[-\tfrac{1}{2}, \tfrac{1}{2}]^2)$$

with $\phi = $ `torus:<1,3>` and $u = (\frac{\pi}{3}, \frac{\pi}{3})$.

---

**Script 5.2.14 (Image of the affine map $(\phi(u) + D\phi(u)v)$)**

```
STRUCT:<
    MAP:(CONS:(torus:<1,3>)):(interval2D:<0,0,2*PI,2*PI>:<24,48>) ,
    T:<1,2,3>:(CONS:(torus:<1,3>):<PI/3,PI/3>),
    MAP:(CONS:(D:(torus:<1,3>):<PI/3,PI/3>)):
        (interval2D:<-0.5,-0.5,0.5,0.5>:<2,2>) COLOR RGB:<1,0,0> >;
```

---

Actually, the implementation in Script 5.2.14 is based on the graphics approach of translating the image of the linear map $D\phi(u)$ with translation vector $\phi(u)$. A direct implementation of the affine mapping

$$v \mapsto \phi(u) + D\phi(u)v, \qquad u = \left(\frac{\pi}{3}, \frac{\pi}{3}\right), v \in \left[-\frac{1}{2}, \frac{1}{2}\right]^2,$$

should instead be written as

```
MAP:(vectSum
~CONS:([K~CONS:(torus:<1,3>), CONS~D:(torus:<1,3>)]:<PI/3,PI/3>)):
    (interval2D:<-0.5,-0.5,0.5,0.5>:<1,1>)
```

Notice that the greatest care was used in CONSing some sub-expressions, depending on whether they return either a single vector function or a sequence of functions. In fact a sequence *cannot* be applied to any argument nor composed with functions.

### 5.2.5   *Generalized implementation*

An implementation of a derivation operator

$$D : C^1(\mathbb{R}^n; \mathbb{R}^m) \to \text{lin}(\mathbb{R}^n; \mathbb{R}^m)$$

at point $\boldsymbol{u} \in \mathbb{R}^n$ is given in this section. This operator will work for arbitrary values of $n$ and $m$. To this purpose, there are four different cases that we need to manage, and for which we have already given specialized operators, respectively named D11, D1m, Dn1 and Dnm.

A cascaded IF sequence is just used to select the proper specialized operator, to be chosen depending on the type of input parameters f and u. Notice that the TT := K:True predicate returns *true* for any input.

---

**Script 5.2.15 (Generalized derivation operator)**
```
DEF D (f::TT)(u::TT) =
    IF:< AND ~ [ IsFun~S1, IsReal~S2 ], APPLY ~ [D11 ~ S1,S2],
    IF:< AND ~ [ IsSeqOf:IsFun~S1, IsReal~S2 ], APPLY ~ [D1m ~ S1,S2],
    IF:< AND ~ [ IsFun~S1, IsPoint~S2 ], APPLY ~ [Dn1 ~ S1,S2],
    IF:< AND ~ [ IsSeqOf:IsFun~S1, IsPoint~S2 ], APPLY ~ [Dnm ~ S1,S2],
ID >>>>:< f, u >;
```

---

### 5.3  Fields and differential operators

A *function* $\phi : \mathbb{E} \to F$ that maps points of an Euclidean space $\mathbb{E}$ into a linear space $F$ is called a **field**. When $F$ is the set of real numbers, or a vector or tensor space, $\phi$ is called a *scalar, vector* or *tensor field*, respectively.

#### 5.3.1  Gradient

The **gradient** $D\phi$ of a field $\phi : \mathbb{E} \to F$ is the map on $\mathbb{E}$ whose value at $x$ is the *derivative* $D\phi(x)$ of $\phi$ at $x$:

$$D\phi : \mathbb{E} \to \mathrm{lin}\,(\mathbb{E}, F) : x \mapsto D\phi(x)$$

In the remainder of the chapter, we identify the Euclidean $n$-space $\mathbb{E}^n$ with its linear support space $\mathbb{R}^n$, and denote the gradient of a field $\phi$ by $\nabla\phi$.

**Example 5.3.1 (Gradient of a scalar field $\mathbb{R}^m \to \mathbb{R}$)**
A vector field representation of gradient $\nabla\phi$ of a scalar field as a set of line segments is produced by the three expressions in Script 5.3.1. In particular, each expression aggregates the set of vectors on the vertices of the domain discretization named dom and the domain itself. The scalar fields shown in Figure 5.9 are, respectively:

$$
\begin{aligned}
(x,y) &\mapsto (x^2 + y^2)/a^2 &&\text{with } a = \sqrt{2}, \text{ and } \mathrm{dom} = [-1,1]^2 \\
(x,y) &\mapsto (x^2 - y^2)/a^2 &&\text{with } a = \sqrt{2}, \text{ and } \mathrm{dom} = [-1,1]^2 \\
(x,y) &\mapsto \sin x \, \sin y &&\text{with } \mathrm{dom} = [0,\pi]^2
\end{aligned}
$$

The first two fields correspond to the explicit representation of quadrics surfaces called *elliptic* and *hyperbolic paraboloid*, respectively. The function interval2D, to generate a cell decomposition of the Cartesian product of two line intervals, was given in Script 5.1.1.

**Script 5.3.1 (Vector field representation of the gradient of a scalar field)**

```
(STRUCT ~ [GradMap,s2]):<(s1*s1 + s2*s2)/K:2, interval2D:<-1,-1,1,1>:<7,7>>
(STRUCT ~ [GradMap,s2]):<(s1*s1 - s2*s2)/K:2, interval2D:<-1,-1,1,1>:<7,7>>
(STRUCT ~ [GradMap,s2]):<sin ~ s1 * sin ~ s2, interval2D:<0,0,PI,PI>:<7,7>>
```

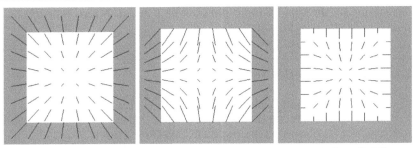

**Figure 5.9**   Graph of gradient of fields: (a) $\phi_1(x,y) = (x^2 + y^2)/a^2$
(b) $\phi_2(x,y) = (x^2 - y^2)/a^2$ (c) $\phi_3(x,y) = \sin x\ \sin y$

**Implementation**   As we already know, if $\phi$ is a scalar field $\mathbb{E}^n \to \mathbb{R}$, then $D\phi$ — in the following denoted as $\nabla\phi$ — can be seen as the vector field such that for each $\boldsymbol{u} \in \mathbb{R}^n$

$$D\phi(\boldsymbol{x})(\boldsymbol{u}) = \nabla\phi(\boldsymbol{x}) \cdot \boldsymbol{u}.$$

So, in Script 5.3.2 we give a function GradMap to generate a map of such a vector field for every scalar function f defined on an arbitrary (polyhedral) domain dom. In particular, an expression like GradMap:< f, dom > will generate a set of line segments attached to vertices of the cell decomposition of dom, where each segment at point $\boldsymbol{x}$ is a scaled image of the vector

$$\nabla f(\boldsymbol{x}) = \left(\ \frac{\partial f}{\partial x_1}(\boldsymbol{x})(1)\quad \cdots \quad \frac{\partial f}{\partial x_n}(\boldsymbol{x})(1)\ \right),$$

translated at $\boldsymbol{x}$. For this purpose a function segment is given in Script 5.3.2, that generates the image of vector b − a applied to a, and scaled with coefficient sx. The segment function makes use of the polyline primitive defined in Script 7.2.3.

---

**Script 5.3.2 (Graph of gradient of a scalar field)**

```
DEF Gradient (f::IsFun)(x::IsPoint) = CONS:(grad:f:x):(#:(LEN:x):1);

DEF Segment (sx::IsReal)(a,b::IsPoint) =
    (T:ind:a ~ S:ind:(#:n:sx) ~ T:ind:(AA:-:a) ~ polyline):<a,b>
WHERE
    n = LEN:a, ind = INTSTO:n
END;

DEF GradMap (f::IsFun; dom::IsPol) = (STRUCT
    ~ AA:(Segment:0.35 ~ [ID,vectSum ~ [ID,Gradient:f]])
    ~ S1 ~ UKPOL):dom
```

---

The simple algorithm used in implementing the GradMap function can be described as follows. The `vectSum` function was given in Script 2.1.19.

1. Compute the vertices of the cells of the polyhedral decomposition of `dom`, by "unpacking" its data structure and extracting their set with the `S1` selector.
2. Apply to all such vertices the function

    `segment:0.35 ~ [ID, vectSum ~ [ID, Gradient:f]]`

    which generates a sequence of segments — scaled with coefficient 0.35 — with first point in each cell vertex.
3. Aggregate all such segments in the output polyhedral complex.

**Gradient of a vector field**   The implementation of Script 5.3.2 works only for scalar fields. The gradient of a *vector field* $\phi : \mathbb{R}^2 \to \mathbb{R}^2$ would return a tensor (represented by the $2 \times 2$ Jacobian matrix) at each point. A graphical representation of the output tensor field would be much harder to devise. Anyway, a possible implementation of a function, which returns the gradient of a vector field in a point as the Jacobian matrix in that point, is given by function `Jacobian` in Script 5.3.3.

As a check on the implementation, we compute directly $\nabla \phi(0.25, 0.3)$, with

$$\phi(x, y) = \left( \frac{x^2 - y^2}{2}, \frac{x^2 + y^2}{2} \right).$$

In this case we have

$$\nabla \phi(x, y) = \begin{pmatrix} x & -y \\ x & y \end{pmatrix}, \quad \text{and} \quad \nabla \phi(0.25, 0.3) = \begin{pmatrix} 0.25 & -0.3 \\ 0.25 & 0.3 \end{pmatrix}.$$

As we are now used to doing, the field to be differentiated must be written using the variable-free notation

$$\phi = \left( \frac{\sigma(1)^2 - \sigma(2)^2}{2}, \frac{\sigma(1)^2 + \sigma(2)^2}{2} \right).$$

---

**Script 5.3.3 (Jacobian of a vector field)**
```
DEF Jacobian (f::IsSeqOf:IsFun)(x::IsPoint) = CONS:(AA:Gradient:f):x;

Jacobian:< (s1*s1 - s2*s2)/K:2, (s1*s1 + s2*s2)/K:2 >:<0.25,0.3> ≡
    <<0.24999999999995512, -0.2999999999999531>,
     <0.24999999999997247, 0.2999999999998837>> ;
```

---

*5.3.2   Divergence and Laplacian*

The divergence and Laplacian operators are defined for vector and scalar fields, respectively, and are both functions of the gradient.

The *divergence* of a vector field $\phi$ is defined as the *trace of the gradient*:

$$\text{div } \phi := \text{tr } \nabla \phi$$

Notice that the gradient of a vector field is a tensor field, whereas the divergence of a vector field is a scalar field.

The *Laplacian* $\Delta\phi$ of a scalar field $\phi$ is defined as the *divergence of its gradient*:

$$\Delta\phi := \text{div } \nabla\phi = \text{tr } \nabla\nabla\phi = \text{tr } \nabla^2\phi$$

Accordingly with the above remark, notice that the Laplacian of a scalar field is a scalar field.

### 5.3.3   Curl

Let $\phi$ be a smooth vector field. The *curl* of $\phi$, denoted curl $\phi$, is the unique vector field such that

$$(\text{curl } \phi) \times \boldsymbol{v} = (\nabla\phi - \nabla\phi^T)\boldsymbol{v}$$

for every vector $\boldsymbol{v}$. Unlike gradient and divergence, the usual setting of curl can be given only in $\mathbb{E}^3$. A more general definition of curl requires exterior calculus.

Let us remember that (a) a tensor $\boldsymbol{W}$ is said to be *skew* if $\boldsymbol{W} = -\boldsymbol{W}^T$, and (b) there is a one-to-one correspondence between skew tensors and vectors. In fact, for every skew tensor $\boldsymbol{W}$ there is one and only one vector $\boldsymbol{w}$ such that

$$\boldsymbol{w} \times \boldsymbol{v} = \boldsymbol{W}\boldsymbol{v}$$

for every vector $\boldsymbol{v}$. The one-dimensional space spanned by $\boldsymbol{w}$ is called *axis* of the tensor $\boldsymbol{W}$. It coincides with the null space of $\boldsymbol{W}$, i.e. with the subset of vectors that $\boldsymbol{W}$ maps to $\boldsymbol{0}$.

Clearly enough, curl $\phi$ is the axis of $\nabla\phi - \nabla\phi^T$, which is a skew tensor field.

### 5.3.4   Gradient, divergence and curl of a 3D field

In elementary vector calculus in $\mathbb{E}^3$ it is customary to use the operator

$$\nabla = \frac{\partial}{\partial x}e_1 + \frac{\partial}{\partial y}e_2 + \frac{\partial}{\partial z}e_3,$$

referred to as either *nabla* or *DEL*, as a sort of vector which follows the standard rules of vector calculus. Using this operator it is possible to give three simple and well-known formulas for gradient, divergence and curl, respectively.

**Gradient**   If $\phi$ is a differentiable scalar field, then the gradient of $\phi$ is defined by

$$\text{grad } \phi = \nabla\phi = \frac{\partial\phi}{\partial x}e_1 + \frac{\partial\phi}{\partial y}e_2 + \frac{\partial\phi}{\partial z}e_3$$

**Divergence**   If $\phi = \phi_1 e_1 + \phi_2 e_2 + \phi_3 e_3$ is a differentiable vector field, then the *divergence* of $\phi$ is given by

$$\text{div } \phi = \nabla \cdot \phi = \frac{\partial\phi_1}{\partial x} + \frac{\partial\phi_2}{\partial y} + \frac{\partial\phi_3}{\partial z}$$

**Curl**  If $\phi$ is a differentiable vector field, then the *curl* of $\phi$ is defined by

$$\text{curl } \phi = \nabla \times \phi = \det \begin{pmatrix} e_1 & e_2 & e_3 \\ \frac{\partial}{\partial x} & \frac{\partial}{\partial y} & \frac{\partial o}{\partial z} \\ \phi_1 & \phi_2 & \phi_3 \end{pmatrix}$$

$$= \left( \frac{\partial \phi_3}{\partial y} - \frac{\partial \phi_2}{\partial z} \right) e_1 + \left( \frac{\partial \phi_1}{\partial z} - \frac{\partial \phi_3}{\partial x} \right) e_2 + \left( \frac{\partial \phi_2}{\partial x} - \frac{\partial \phi_1}{\partial y} \right) e_3.$$

**Laplacian**  If $\phi$ is a differentiable scalar field, then the *Laplacian* of $\phi$ is given by

$$\Delta \phi = \nabla \cdot (\nabla \phi) = \frac{\partial^2 \phi}{\partial x^2} + \frac{\partial^2 \phi}{\partial y^2} + \frac{\partial^2 \phi}{\partial z^2} = \nabla^2 \phi$$

where $\nabla^2$ is called the *Laplacian operator*.

**Properties**  Some well-known statements relating gradient, divergence and curl say that, for every differentiable vector field $\phi$ and scalar field $\phi$:

1. the curl of the gradient is zero: $(\text{curl} \circ \text{grad}) \ \phi = \nabla \times (\nabla \phi) = \mathbf{0}$;
2. a vector field is (locally) a gradient if and only if its curl vanishes;
3. the divergence of curl is zero: $(\text{div} \circ \text{curl}) \ \phi = \nabla \cdot (\nabla \times \phi) = 0$;
4. a vector field is (locally) a curl if and only if its divergence vanishes.

**Implementation**  According to its definition, the `Divergence` of a vector field $\phi : \mathbb{R}^n \to \mathbb{R}^n$ is implemented in Script 5.3.4 as the `Trace` of Jacobian matrix of $\phi$. The `Trace` function, that returns the sum of diagonal elements of a square matrix, was introduced in Script 3.3.10.

The `Curl` operator is conversely defined here only for 3D fields, according to the formula $\nabla \times \phi$. Remember that `(S2~S3):M`, where M is a PLaSM matrix (stored by rows), returns the second element of the third row, i.e. $m_{32}$.

---

**Script 5.3.4 (Divergence and Curl)**

```
DEF Divergence (f::IsSeqOf:IsFun)(x::IsSeqOf:IsReal) =
    Trace:(Jacobian:f:x);

DEF Curl (f::IsSeqOf:IsFun)(x::IsSeqOf:IsReal) =
    [ S2~S3 - S3~S2, S3~S1 - S1~S3, S1~S2 - S2~S1 ]:(Jacobian:f:x)
```

---

**Example 5.3.2 (Checks on field operators)**
Some computational checks are done in Script 5.3.5, with the aim of showing both the usage and the result of some compound functional expressions involving curl, divergence and gradient.

The reader should notice that fields are written either as single functions (scalar fields), or as sequences of functions (vector fields), and using the variable-free notation.

In particular, f1 and f2 in Script 5.3.5 are two scalar fields in $\mathbb{R}^3$, and g is a vector field $\mathbb{R}^3 \to \mathbb{R}^3$.

According to our expectations, we can see that (curl $\circ$ grad) $\phi = \mathbf{0}$ and that (div $\circ$ curl) $\phi = 0$. Those checks are done in a single point, but it is reasonable to expect that they give the same result everywhere, as the reader may check.

Notice also the inefficiency involved in extracting the coordinate functions of the vector functions returned by expressions Gradient:f1, Gradient:f2 and Curl:g. At present, there is no way in PLaSM to deal efficiently with this kind of extraction.

---

**Script 5.3.5 (Some computational checks)**

```
DEF f1 = ( s1*s1 + s2*s2 )/K:2;
DEF f2 = ( s1*s1 + sin ~ s2 - s1*s3 )/ K:2;
DEF g  = < sin ~ s1, cos ~ s2, s1*s3 >;

Gradient:f1:<0.5,0.1> ≡ <0.49999999999994493, 0.10000000000010001>

Curl:< s1 ~ Gradient:f1, s2 ~ Gradient:f1, s3 ~ Gradient:f1 >:<0.9,8,0>
    ≡ <0.0, 0.0, 0.0>
Curl:< s1 ~ Gradient:f2, s2 ~ Gradient:f2, s3 ~ Gradient:f2 >:<1,0.5,1>
    ≡ <0.0, 0.0, 0.0>

Divergence:< s1 ~ Curl:g, s2 ~ Curl:g, s3 ~ Curl:g >:<0.5,110.5,1> ≡ 0.0
Divergence:< s1 ~ Curl:g, s2 ~ Curl:g, s3 ~ Curl:g >:<-8.5,0.5,-3> ≡ 0.0
```

---

Actually such a solution would exist, but it requires us to completely renounce the $\lambda$-style of writing PLaSM functions, and its somewhat static typing, and to adopt systematically a *pure* FL style, i.e. *without* formal parameters. Doing so, we would be able to write an expression like

```
Divergence:([s1,s2,s3] ~ Curl:g):<0.5,110.5,1>
```

This is not possible with the definition of Divergence operator given in Script 5.3.4, because the interpreter would expect to apply it to a *sequence* of functions, whereas [s1,s2,s3] ~ Curl:g is a single function.

Actually, there are some drawbacks in using only the pure FL style, including less self-documented and more intricate programs, and lack of any type checking. A carefully chosen compromise between $\lambda$-style and pure FL style is often preferable.

## 5.4  Differentiable manifolds

In some areas of geometric modeling, and in particular in solid modeling, the terms "manifold" and "differentiable manifold" are used quite frequently. A quick introduction to this concept may therefore be needed, and is given here. A manifold is a set where it makes sense to introduce coordinates, at least locally. Such coordinates locally behave like affine coordinates. Useful references are Crampin and Pirani [CP86], Jones, Gray and Hutton [JGH87], and Nakahara [Nak90].

### 5.4.1  Charts and atlases

The main concepts here are related to systems of coordinates, and are quite easy to understand. For several sets, for example the surface $S_2$ of the Earth, only one system of coordinates is not sufficient, because a single bijection between the $S_2$ points and 2-tuples of coordinates does not exist. Therefore the goal is to introduce coordinate systems on point *subsets* such that:

1. nearby points have nearby coordinates;
2. every point has unique coordinates in each system that contains it;
3. when two coordinate systems overlap, they must be related in a smooth way.

The last requirements guarantee that differentiable functions in one system are differentiable also in the other.

A *chart* for a set $M$ is a pair $(U, \phi)$, with $U \subset M$ and $\phi$ a bijective function from $U$ to an open set in $\mathbb{R}^n$. The subset $U$ is called the *coordinate neighborhood*, while $\phi = (\phi_1, \ldots, \phi_n)$ is the *coordinate map*, where $\phi_i : U \to \mathbb{R}$ $(1 \leq i \leq n)$ are the *coordinate functions*.

Two charts $(U, \phi)$ and $(V, \psi)$ for the set $M$ are said to be *compatible* if, provided that $U \cap V \neq \emptyset$, then:

1. the sets $\phi(U \cap V)$ and $\psi(U \cap V)$ are open subset of $\mathbb{R}^n$;
2. the map $\phi \circ \psi^{-1}$ is smooth with smooth inverse, i.e. is a *diffeomorphism*.

An *atlas* for the set $M$ is a collection $\{(U_i, \phi_i)\}$ of pairwise compatible charts such that $\cup_i U_i = M$.

### 5.4.2  Differentiable manifolds

Two atlases for the same set $M$ are *equivalent* if every chart in an atlas is compatible with every chart in the other atlas. This relation is reflexive, symmetric and transitive, i.e. is an equivalence relation.

Each equivalence class in the set of atlases of $M$ is said to be a *differentiable structure* for $M$. A *differentiable manifold* is a pair $(M, \mathcal{S})$, where $\mathcal{S}$ is a differentiable structure for $M$.

The one-chart atlas $(\mathbb{R}^n, \text{id} : \mathbb{R}^n \to \mathbb{R}^n)$ determines a differentiable structure for $\mathbb{R}^n$ as a manifold. This one is probably the most trivial example, where a single chart covers the whole space, and where the coordinate map is the identity map.

**Example 5.4.1 (Atlas for the circle $S_1$)**
Let us consider the one-dimensional circle $S_1 = \{ \boldsymbol{x} \in \mathbb{E}^2 |\ \| \boldsymbol{x} - \boldsymbol{o} \|^2 = 1 \}$, and choose two charts $(U_1, \phi_1)$ and $(U_2, \phi_2)$, with

$$U_1 = S_1 \backslash \{(1, 0)\}, \quad \phi_1 : U_1 \to (0, 2\pi) \subset \mathbb{R} : (\cos \alpha, \sin \alpha) \mapsto \alpha,$$

and

$$U_2 = S_1 \backslash \{(-1, 0)\}, \quad \phi_2 : U_2 \to (-\pi, \pi) \subset \mathbb{R} : (\cos \beta, \sin \beta) \mapsto \beta.$$

It this case it is easy to see that $U_1$ and $U_2$ are open sets and that $\phi_1$ and $\phi_2$ are smooth. Then, it can be seen that

$$\phi_1 \circ \phi_2^{-1} = \begin{cases} \text{id} & on \quad (0, \pi) \\ \\ \text{id} - 2\pi & on \quad (\pi, 2\pi) \end{cases}$$

is a diffeomorphism between $\phi_2(U_1 \cap U_2) = (0, 2\pi) \backslash \{\pi\}$ and $\phi_1(U_1 \cap U_2) = (-\pi, \pi) \backslash \{0\}$. The two charts are hence compatible, and $U_1 \cup U_2 = S_1$. Therefore we can conclude that $\{(U_1, \phi_1), (U_2, \phi_2)\}$ is an atlas for $S_1$.

**Manifold dimension**   Let $M$ be a differentiable manifold, and let $\mathcal{A} = \{(U_i, \phi_i)\}$ be an atlas for it. If all the sets $\phi_i(U_i)$ are contained in the same $\mathbb{R}^n$, then $n$ is called the *dimension* of the manifold. In other words, the dimension of a differentiable manifold is the (constant) number of coordinates of manifold points in all its charts. This number is the same for any atlas of the manifold.

   Not all differentiable manifolds have a dimension, since they may contain subsets covered by charts with different numbers of coordinates.

**Product manifold**   The *product* $M \times N$ of two manifolds $M$ and $N$ of dimension $m$ and $n$ respectively, with atlases $\{(U_i, \phi_i)\}$ and $\{(V_j, \psi_j)\}$, is a manifold of dimension $m + n$, whose atlas is $\{(U_i \times V_j, (\phi_i, \psi_j))\}$.

   In this case if $(p, q) \in U_i \times V_j$, then

$$(\phi_i, \psi_j)(p, q) = (\phi_i(p), \psi_j(q)). \tag{5.4}$$

**Spheres and toruses**   The $n$-dimensional sphere $S_n$ is defined as the set $\{x \in \mathbb{E}^{n+1} : \|x - o\|^2 = 1\}$.

   The 2-dimensional torus $T_2$ is the product manifold

$$T_2 = S_1 \times S_1.$$

Clearly it is $T_2 \subset \mathbb{E}^4$, since $S_1 \subset \mathbb{E}^2$. The product manifold called $m$-dimensional torus

$$T_m = S_1 \times \cdots \times S_1, \quad m \text{ times.}$$

with $T_m \subset \mathbb{E}^{2m}$, is an immediate generalization.

**Example 5.4.2 (Torus as Cartesian product of circles)**
Our aim in this example is to generate a 3D projection of

$$T_2 = S_1 \times S_1.$$

   In Script 5.4.1 we generate the 3D surface with the shape of a doughnut by translating and projecting against the subspace $\{x \in \mathbb{E}^4 | x_4 = 0\}$ the polyhedral complex `torus`, generated by Cartesian product of circle approximations `MAP:(cc:8):d1` and `MAP:(cc:2):d1`, where 8 and 2 are the radiuses, and `d1` is a

**Script 5.4.1 (Torus as product of circles (1))**
```
DEF cc (r::IsRealPos) = [ K:r * COS, K:r * SIN ] ~ S1;
DEF d1 = interval:< 0,2*PI >:24
DEF torus = (MAP: (cc:8): d1) * (MAP: (cc:2): d1);

VRML:((schlegel3D:2 ~ T:4:-11):torus CREASE (PI/2)):'out2.wrl' ;
```

partition of $[0, 2\pi]$ with 24 segments. The `schlegel3D` operator is given and discussed in Section 4.6.1. The `interval:` function is given in Script 5.1.1.

Notice that both circles, with $r = 8$ and $r = 2$ respectively, were produced by `MAP` operator as $\phi^{-1}[0, 2\pi]$, with a single chart $(U, \phi)$ depending on $r$, where

$$U = \{x \in \mathbb{E}^2 | (x - o)^2 = r^2\}, \quad \phi : U \to [0, 2\pi] : (r \cos \alpha, r \sin \alpha) \mapsto \alpha,$$

thus producing a singularity (a double coordinate value which results in the same point) in $\phi^{-1}(0) = (r, 0)$ and in $\phi^{-1}(2\pi) = (r, 0)$. This kind of singularity, i.e. double points at the boundary of charts of closed surfaces, will be accepted through the whole book, for the sake of implementation simplicity, in particular because the `PLaSM` kernel is currently able to manage only closed (i.e. with boundary) polyhedral complexes.

**Example 5.4.3 (Torus as manifold product of circles)**
Given the charts $(U_1, \phi_1)$ and $(U_2, \phi_2)$ of two circles $S_1(r_1)$ and $S_2(r_2)$ with different radiuses, we generate the torus

$$T_2(r_1, r_2) = S_1(r_1) \times S_1(r_2),$$

using the product chart $(U_1 \times U_2, (\phi_1, \phi_2))$.

A direct implementation of `torus` as the polyhedral approximation of a *product manifold* is hence given in Script 5.4.2, where `c1c2` implements the mapping $(\phi_1, \phi_2)^{-1}$ on $[0, 2\pi]^2$ using the *product chart* $(U_1 \times U_2, (\phi_1, \phi_2))$ described in equation (5.4). In particular, $(\phi_1, \phi_2)^{-1}$ is implemented by the `c1c2` function, whereas a cell decomposition of $[0, 2\pi]^2$ is given by the polyhedral complex `d1 * d1`, where `d1` is given in Script 5.4.1. The simplicial decomposition needed to take into account the double curvature of the doughnut surface is automatically provided by the `MAP` operator.

**Script 5.4.2 (Torus as product of circles (2))**
```
DEF c1c2 (r1,r2::IsRealPos) =
    [ K:r1 * COS~S1, K:r1 * SIN~S1, K:r2 * COS~S2, K:r2 * SIN~S2 ];
DEF torus (r1,r2::IsRealPos) = MAP: (c1c2:< 8,2 >): (d1 * d1);

VRML:((schlegel3D:2 ~ T:4:-11):(torus:<8,2>) CREASE (PI/2)):'out2.wrl' ;
```

The reader may try unbelievable variations of the generated 3D object by making small variations to the parameters of the expression, including the circle radiuses, the distance of the center of projection from the origin, the translation and the rotation parameters. For example, Figures 5.10a and 5.10c are respectively generated as

```
DEF rotations = (COMP ~ [R:<1,4>,R:<2,4>,R:<3,4>]):(PI/6);
VRML:((project:1):man CREASE (PI/2)):'out1.wrl' ;
VRML:((project:1 ~ rotations):man CREASE (PI/2)):'out3.wrl' ,
```

**Figure 5.10**   Different projections on $x_4 = 0$ of the manifold $T_2 = S_1 \times S_1 \subset \mathbb{E}^4$:
(a) standard projection gives a cylinder (b) central projection (c) multiple rotations
followed by projection produce a double self-intersection in the $\mathbb{E}^3$ embedding

Finally, let us notice that parametric equations of $T_2$ in $\mathbb{E}^4$

$$x_1 = r_1 \cos u, \quad x_2 = r_1 \sin u, \quad x_3 = r_2 \cos v, \quad x_4 = r_2 \sin v,$$

where $(u, v) \in [0, 2\pi]^2$, are simpler than equations (2.5) in $\mathbb{E}^3$.

### 5.4.3   Tangent spaces and maps

A *tangent vector* to $M$ at $x$ is an element of $\boldsymbol{T}_x\mathbb{R}^n$ of the form $(x, D\gamma(0)(1))$, where
$x \in M$ and $\gamma : I \to M$ is a smooth parametrized curve with $\gamma(0) = x$.

The **tangent space** to $M$ at $x$ is the set of all tangent vectors to $M$ at $x$. It is
denoted by $\boldsymbol{T}_xM$.

The tangent bundle of $M$ is the union of all its tangent spaces:

$$TM = \bigcup_{x \in M} \boldsymbol{T}_xM.$$

Let $f : M \to N$, with $M$ and $N$ submanifolds of $\mathbb{R}^m$ and $\mathbb{R}^n$, and $x \in M$. A tangent
map will send a small piece of curve through $x$ to a small piece of curve through $f(x)$.

The *tangent map* of $f$ at $x$ is the map:

$$\boldsymbol{T}_xf : \boldsymbol{T}_xM \to \boldsymbol{T}_{f(x)}N$$

such that

$$(x, D\gamma(0)(1)) \mapsto (f(x), D(f \circ \gamma)(0)(1))$$

for each differentiable curve $\gamma$ through $x$. The **tangent map** of $f$ is the map

$$Tf : TM \to TN : \boldsymbol{T}_xM = \boldsymbol{T}_xf, \quad \text{for each } x \in M.$$

## 5.5   Derivatives of a curve

An intrinsic representation of a curve, in the sense that it depends only on operations
carried out on the curve itself and does not rely on the ambient Euclidean space, is

obtained by repeated application of the derivation operator to the curve-generating function. It is only necessary that this function is (at least) twice differentiable for plane curves, and (at least) three times differentiable for space curves. Let us assume only smooth curves. This case is certainly the more frequent and useful one in CAD applications.

**Tangent**   The *tangent* $t$ vector field, also denoted as $c'$, to a curve $c : \mathbb{R} \to \mathbb{E}^d$, with $c = (c_i)$, is defined as the vector function $c' : \mathbb{R} \to \mathbb{R}^d$ such that:

$$t = Dc = c' = (c_i').$$

For each $u$ parameter value, $t(u)$ gives the tangent vector to the curve at $c(u)$.

If $u = t$ is the time $t$, then $v(t) = Dc(t)$ represents the *velocity* with which the point $c(t)$ describes the curve image. Analogously, $a(t) = Dv(t) = D^{(2)}c(t)$ represents the *acceleration*.

If $u = s$ is the curve length from $c(0)$, then $t(s)$ gives the unit tangent vector at curvilinear abscissa $s$. It is in fact easy to see that $\|t(s)\| = 1$ for every $s$.

**Normal**   Analogously, a *normal* to a twice derivable curve $c : \mathbb{R} \to \mathbb{E}^d$ is defined as the vector function field: $c^{(2)} : \mathbb{R} \to \mathbb{R}^d$ such that:

$$c^{(2)} = D^{(2)}c = (c_i^{(2)}).$$

For each $u$ parameter value, $c^{(2)}(u)$ gives one of normal vectors to the tangent vector for the corresponding point $c(u)$ of the curve.

It is important to notice that in Euclidean space a vector function $v(t)$ of constant norm has the property that $v(t)$ and $Dv(t)$ are orthogonal.

**Curvature**   The *curvature* $\kappa$ of a twice differentiable curve $c : \mathbb{R} \to \mathbb{E}^d : s \mapsto o + \alpha(s)$, where $s$ is the curve length from $c(0)$, is defined as the norm of the vector function $Dt$:

$$\kappa : \mathbb{R} \to \mathbb{R} : s \mapsto \|Dt(s)\| = \left\| D^{(2)}\alpha(s) \right\|.$$

In other words, the curvature $\kappa(s)$ is the magnitude of the acceleration vector to the curve $c(s)$, under the condition that this one is parametrized by the arc length $s$.

**Principal normal**   If $Dt(s) \neq 0$ for all $s$, then the unit vector function $n : \mathbb{R} \to \mathbb{R}^d$, such that

$$n = \frac{Dt}{\|Dt\|} = \kappa^{-1}Dt,$$

is called *principal normal* vector field.

**Binormal**   The plane which contains both $t$ and $n$ at $u$ is called the *osculating plane* at $u$. The word comes from Latin, for the plane which contains the osculating circle, i.e. the circle "kissing" the curve. The vector product of tangent and normal vector is called the *binormal* vector field:

$$b = t \times n$$

The norm of $Db$ gives the rate of variation of the osculating plane along the curve. If $u = s$ is the arc-length of the curve $c$, then it is possible to write

$$Db = -\tau n$$

where the function $\tau = \tau(s)$ is called *torsion* at $c(s)$.

The *fundamental theorem* of differential geometry of curves in $\mathbb{E}^3$ says that a curve is completely determined by its curvature and torsion functions within a congruence.

**The Serret-Frenet formulæ**   Let us study a space curve $c$ parametrized by the arc length $s$, also called the *natural parameter*.

The tangent $t$, the principal normal $n$ and the binormal $b$ vector functions are related to their derivatives by the curvature $\kappa$ and the torsion $\tau$, as shown by the Serret-Frenet formulæ:

$$D \begin{pmatrix} t \\ n \\ b \end{pmatrix} = \begin{pmatrix} 0 & \kappa & 0 \\ -\kappa & 0 & \tau \\ 0 & -\tau & 0 \end{pmatrix} \begin{pmatrix} t \\ n \\ b \end{pmatrix}$$

**Center of curvature**   For an arbitrary curve $a \in \mathbb{E}^n$, the curvature field $\kappa : \mathbb{R} \to \mathbb{R}$ is not constant. Where $\kappa(s) \neq 0$, the curve is approximated by a circle of radius $1/\kappa(s)$, which is tangent to $a$ in $a(s)$ and which is contained in the plane generated by $t(s)$ and $n(s)$.

This circle, called *osculating circle*, has the same tangent, curvature and principal normal of the curve in $s$. The center of the osculating circle is called *center of curvature* of $a$ in $a(s)$. It is a field $c : \mathbb{R} \to \mathbb{R}^d$ that can be written, using the variable-free notation, as:

$$c = a + \kappa^{-1} n.$$

## 5.6   Examples

**Helix**   The *circular helix* curve in $\mathbb{E}^3$ has vector equation $s = o + \beta(u)$, where the $u$ parameter denotes the angle between the $s$ projection in $z = 0$ and the $x$ axis. For a helix segment we have $\beta : U \to \mathbb{R}^3$, with $U \subset \mathbb{R}$, and

$$\beta(u) = \begin{pmatrix} a \cos u & a \sin u & bu \end{pmatrix} \tag{5.5}$$

where $a$ is the radius of the circular projection in $z = 0$ and $b$ is the ratio $pitch/2\pi$. The *pitch* of the helix is the vertical distance of two curve points differing for $2\pi$ in the parameter value.

**Figure 5.11**    Intrinsic triplet at a helix point

**Helix curvature and principal normal**  In Script 5.6.1 we have implemented
a curvature and principalNormal functions, by abstracting with respect to the
argument curve. The geometric object generated by evaluating the STRUCT expression
is shown in Figure 5.11. The helix curve domain is defined in Script 5.2.7. The
MKvector function is given in Script 6.5.2.

Notice that, according to the STRUCT semantics discussed in Chapter 8, the
translation operator is applied to all subsequent vector models. The intrinsic triplet
there generated is associated to the value $\frac{\pi}{2}$ of the curve parameter.

---

**Script 5.6.1 (Intrinsic triplet)**

```
DEF tangent (curve::IsSeqOf:IsFun) = UnitVect ~ CONS:(AA:D:curve);
DEF curvature (curve::IsSeqOf:IsFun) = VectNorm ~ CONS:(AA:(D ~ D):curve);
DEF principalNormal (curve::IsSeqOf:IsFun) = CONS:
    ((K:1 / curvature:curve) scalarVectProd (AA:(D ~ D):curve));
DEF binormal (curve::IsSeqOf:IsFun) =
    tangent:curve LIFT:vectProd principalNormal:curve ;

DEF curve = helix:<1,0.2>;
STRUCT:<
    MAP:(CONS:curve ~ s1):(interval:<0,4*PI>:60),
    T:<1,2,3>:(CONS:curve:(PI/2)),
    MKvector:<0,0,0>:(tangent:curve:(PI/2)),
    MKvector:<0,0,0>:(principalNormal:curve:(PI/2)),
    MKvector:<0,0,0>:(binormal:curve:(PI/2))
>;
```

---

**Helix parametrized by arc length**  Let us reparametrize the helix (5.5) as a
function of the arc length $s$. So we have:

$$D\beta(u) = \left(\begin{array}{ccc} -a\sin u & a\cos u & b \end{array}\right)$$

$$\frac{ds}{du} = \|D\boldsymbol{\beta}(u)\| = \sqrt{a^2 + b^2}$$

$$s = \int_0^s ds = \int_0^u \sqrt{a^2 + b^2}\, du = u\sqrt{a^2 + b^2}$$

and hence we can write $\boldsymbol{s} = \boldsymbol{o} + \boldsymbol{\alpha}(s)$, with $s \in [0, L]$ and

$$\boldsymbol{\alpha}(s) = \left( \ a\cos\tfrac{s}{\sqrt{a^2+b^2}} \quad a\sin\tfrac{s}{\sqrt{a^2+b^2}} \quad b\tfrac{s}{\sqrt{a^2+b^2}} \ \right)$$

Two helixes of the same length $L = 6\pi$ generated by $\boldsymbol{\alpha}(s)$ are shown in Figure 5.12.

**Figure 5.12**   Two helixes of the same length and different radius

**Osculating circle to the helix**   Our aim here is to produce the geometric construction shown in Figures 5.13 and 5.14, where a helix curve is displayed together with the curve of its centers of curvature (also a helix) and with the osculating circle at a point.

So, we start by computing the tangent vector field

$$\boldsymbol{t}(s) = D\boldsymbol{\alpha}(s) = \frac{1}{\sqrt{a^2 + b^2}} \left( \ -a\sin\tfrac{s}{\sqrt{a^2+b^2}} \quad a\cos\tfrac{s}{\sqrt{a^2+b^2}} \quad b \ \right)$$

which is a unit vector, and the second derivative

$$D\boldsymbol{t}(s) = \kappa(s)\,\boldsymbol{n}(s) = \frac{1}{a^2 + b^2} \left( \ -a\cos\tfrac{s}{\sqrt{a^2+b^2}} \quad -a\sin\tfrac{s}{\sqrt{a^2+b^2}} \quad 0 \ \right)$$

so that we get

$$\kappa(s) = \frac{a}{a^2 + b^2}$$

$$\boldsymbol{n}(s) = \left( \ -\cos\tfrac{s}{\sqrt{a^2+b^2}} \quad -\sin\tfrac{s}{\sqrt{a^2+b^2}} \quad 0 \ \right)$$

Let us note that the helix is a curve of constant curvature.

If $a \neq 0$ and $b = 0$, then the curve is a circle in $xy$ plane and $\kappa = 1/a$. In other words, the curvature is the reciprocal of radius.

If $a = 0$ and $b \neq 0$, then the curve is a segment of straigth line, with $\kappa(s) = 0$ and $\boldsymbol{n}(s)$ undefined.

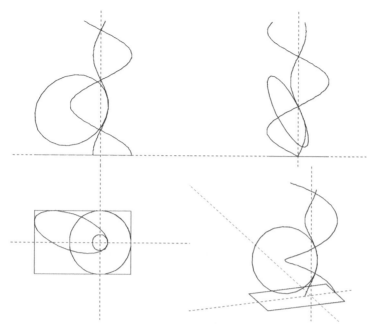

**Figure 5.13** Views of an "artistic" assembly including a helix, the locus of the centers of osculating circles and the osculating circle at a point

**Implementation** We start by implementing, in Script 5.6.2, the `helix` vector function $\alpha : \mathbb{R} \to \mathbb{R}^3$ and the intrinsic triplet of orthonormal vector functions $t$, $n$ and $b$. As always, we give a direct translation of the variable-free formulation of the $\alpha$ function, with

$$\alpha = \left( \underline{a}\cos \circ \frac{\mathrm{id}}{\mathrm{id}^{\frac{1}{2}} \circ \underline{a^2 + b^2}} \quad \underline{a}\sin \circ \frac{\mathrm{id}}{\mathrm{id}^{\frac{1}{2}} \circ \underline{a^2 + b^2}} \quad \underline{b}\frac{\mathrm{id}}{\mathrm{id}^{\frac{1}{2}} \circ \underline{a^2 + b^2}} \right)$$

Notice that, for the sake of abstraction and consistency with the contents of this chapter, we have used the derivation operator D in the definition of the `tangent` and `normal` functions, instead using the symbolic expressions previously given.

---

**Script 5.6.2 (Helix parametrized by arc length)**
```
DEF helix (a,b::IsReal) = <K:a * cos ~ u, K:a * sin ~ u, K:b * u>
WHERE
    u = ID / SQRT ~ K:(a*a + b*b)
END;

DEF helixtangent (a,b::IsReal) = AA:D:(helix:<a,b>);
DEF helixnormal (a,b::IsReal) =
    K:((a*a + b*b)/a) scalarVectProd AA:(D ~ D):(helix:<a,b>);
DEF helixbinormal (a,b::IsReal) = helixtangent:<a,b> VectProd helixnormal:<a,b>;
```

---

Notice also that in Script 5.6.2 we have redefined some function identifier already used with a more general meaning. So, in the remainder of this chapter the functions called `tangent`, `normal` and `binormal` uniquely refer to the unit vector triplet intrinsically related to the `helix` curve parametrized by the arc length.

In Script 5.6.3 it is first of all defined the `CurvatureCenter` $\mathbb{R} \to \mathbb{R}^3$ curve, generated as the vector sum of the `helix` $\mathbb{R} \to \mathbb{R}^3$ curve plus the `normal` $\mathbb{R} \to \mathbb{R}^3$ curve times the `K:((sqr:a + sqr:b)/a)` function $\mathbb{R} \to \mathbb{R}$. Actually the implementation produces a whole family of such curves, parametrized by the pair of real parameters $a, b$, corresponding respectively to the helix radius and to the $z$ interval between two helix points at unit curvilinear distance.

In the same script the `OsculCircle` function is also given, which generates the osculating circle at curvilinear ascissa $s$ for the curve `helix:<a,b>`. The image of such function in a concrete case is shown in Figure 5.13.

---

**Script 5.6.3 (Osculating circle)**

```
DEF helixcurvatureCenter (a,b::IsReal) =
    helix:<a,b> vectSum (K:((sqr:a + sqr:b)/a) scalarVectProd helixnormal:<a,b>)

DEF OsculCircle (a,b,s::IsReal) =
    (T:<1,2,3>:center ~ Rotn:<angle, axis>):circle
WHERE
    circle = MAP:((circle3D ~ radius):<a,b, s>):(interval:<0,2*PI>:24),
    angle = (- ~ ACOS ~ InnerProd):<ortho,<0,0,1>>,
    axis = CONS:(helixnormal:<a,b>):s,
    center = CONS:(helixCurvatureCenter:<a,b>):s,
    ortho = CONS:(helixbinormal:<a,b>):s
END;
```

---

Some utility functions needed to specify the geometric assembly of Figure 5.13 are given in Script 5.6.4. These include:

1. a function `circle3D` to produce a circle of radius `r` embedded in the coordinate subspace $z = 0$ and centered at the origin;
2. a function `radius` to compute the numeric value of the radius of the osculating circle at curvilinear abscissa $s$. Such a number is computed as the norm of the vector difference of two corresponding points on the `helix:<a,b>` and `curvatureCenter:<a,b>` curves;
3. a function `CurveGraph` to generate a simplicial approximation with 90 line segments of the image $f[0, 6\pi]$ of its vector function argument `f`;

---

**Script 5.6.4 (Utility functions)**

```
DEF circle3D (r::IsReal) = [K:r * COS, K:r * SIN, K:0] ~ s1;
DEF radius (a,b,s::IsReal) = (VectNorm ~ VectDiff):
    < CONS:(helix:<a,b>):s, CONS:(CurvatureCenter:<a,b>):s >;
DEF CurveGraph (f::IsSeqOf:IsFun) = MAP:(CONS:f ~ s1):(interval:<0,6*PI>:90);
```

---

Finally, in Script 5.6.5 we give the definition of an `assembly` object, whose geometric value is shown in Figure 5.14. Such an "artistic" assembly contains simplicial

approximations of the sets `helix:<1,2>[0,2π]` and `curvatureCenter:<1,2>[0,2π]`
and a "mat" (i.e. 2D) version of the osculating circle at $s = 2\pi$, as produced by
the `JOIN` primitive.

---

**Script 5.6.5 (Artistic assembly)**

```
DEF assembly = STRUCT:<
    (CurveGraph ~ helix):<1,2>,
    (CurveGraph ~ curvatureCenter):<1,2>,
    (JOIN ~ OsculCircle):<1,2, 2*PI>
>;

(STRUCT ~ [EMBED:1 ~ BOX:<1,2>, ID]):assembly;
```

---

**Figure 5.14**   "Artistic" assembly of: (i) a `helix` curve (ii) the locus of the centers
of its osculating circles (iii) the osculating circle at $s = 2\pi$

## 5.7   Intrinsic properties of a surface

According to the definition of curves, a surface can be defined as a *point-valued*
function $s$ of *two* real variables. So, a *surface* in $\mathbb{E}^d$ is generated as a set of points by
summing to the origin a vector-valued function $\beta : \mathbb{R}^2 \to \mathbb{R}^d$ of two real variables:

$$s(u,v) = o + \beta(u,v), \qquad (u,v) \in [0,1]^2 \subset \mathbb{R}^2.$$

The *image* of the surface is the set $s[0,1]^2$ of its $\mathbb{E}^d$ points. The *domain* of the surface
is the parameter interval $[0,1]^2$.

   A surface is said to be *regular* where the partial derivatives

$$s_1(u,v) = \frac{\partial s}{\partial u}(u,v) \quad \text{and} \quad s_2(u,v) = \frac{\partial s}{\partial u}(u,v)$$

are linearly independent. In the same way, it is regular (in $\mathbb{E}^3$) where

$$s_1(u, v) \times s_2(u, v) \neq \mathbf{0}.$$

In this case, $s_1(u, v)$ and $s_2(u, v)$ give a basis for the tangent space at $s(u, v)$.

Hence the tangent vector $c'(t)$ to a curve $c(t) = s(u(t), v(t))$ on the surface $s$ can be expressed as a linear combination of the partial derivatives of $s$:

$$c' = \frac{du}{dt}\frac{\partial s}{\partial u} + \frac{dv}{dt}\frac{\partial s}{\partial v} = u' s_1 + v' s_2.$$

**Normal to a 3D surface**   The *normal* field $n : \mathbb{R}^2 \to \mathbb{R}^3$ to a surface $s : \mathbb{R}^2 \to \mathbb{E}^3$ is given, where the surface is regular, by the normalized vector product of the partial derivatives:

$$n = \frac{s_1 \times s_2}{\|s_1 \times s_2\|}$$

**Implementation**   In Script 5.7.1 we give the function DS that, when applied to an integer i and to a surface map surf, defined as a *sequence* of coordinate functions $\mathbb{R}^2 \to \mathbb{R}$, returns the partial derivative field $\text{surf}_i : \mathbb{R}^2 \to \mathbb{E}^3$ ($1 \leq i \leq 2$). This result is obtained by suitably applying to each component of surfMap the Dp linear operator given in Script 5.2.8.

Also, a *normal field* operator N is defined, as the normalized vector product of the (tangent) fields generators DS:1 and DS:2. The vectorProd operator can be found in Script 3.1.3. Clearly, specific tangent or normal fields are returned when such operators are applied to a specific surface mapping.

---

**Script 5.7.1 (Partial derivatives and normal)**

```
DEF X(i::isIntPos)(f::IsFun)(a::IsPoint) = Dp:i:f:a:<1>;
DEF Norm3 (x,y,z::IsFun) = < x/den, y/den, z/den >
WHERE
    den = SQRT ~ + ~ AA:sqr ~ [x, y, z],
    sqr = ID * ID
END;

DEF DS (i::IsIntPos)(surfMap::IsSeqOf:IsFun) = AA:(X:i): surfMap;
DEF N = Norm3 ~ VectProd ~ [DS:1, DS:2];
```

---

**Example 5.7.1 (Graph of partial derivatives)**
We give in Script 5.7.2 an implementation of the geometric construction shown in Figure 5.15, where a graph is shown of both the tangent vectors DS:1$(\alpha)(\frac{\pi}{5}, \frac{\pi}{10})$ and DS:2$(\alpha)(\frac{\pi}{5}, \frac{\pi}{10})$, and of the normal vector N$(\alpha)(\frac{\pi}{5}, \frac{\pi}{10})$, for a surface $\alpha = (u, v, \sin u \sin v)$. in Figure 5.15 the two curves $\alpha(u, \frac{\pi}{10})$ and $\alpha(\frac{\pi}{5}, v)$ are also shown.

This geometric construction is produced by exporting the geometric value of the graph object in Script 5.7.2, for example as:

**Figure 5.15**  First partial derivatives and normal vector in $\alpha(\frac{\pi}{5}, \frac{\pi}{10})$ to a surface
$$\alpha(u, v) = (u, v, \sin u \sin v)$$

```
VRML:graph:'out.wrl';
```

Notice that the variable-free representation (see Section 5.1.1) of the studied surface is

$$\alpha := (\sigma(1), \sigma(2), (\sin \circ \sigma(1))(\sin \circ \sigma(2)))$$

which is directly translated into the surf sequence. The functions interval and interval2D, generating suitable decompositions of a 1D and 2D interval, respectively, are given in Script 5.1.1.

---

**Script 5.7.2 (Graph of partial derivatives)**

```
DEF surf = < S1, S2, SIN ~ S1 * SIN ~ S2 >;
DEF domain = interval2D:<0,0,PI,PI>:<10,10>;

DEF graph = STRUCT:<
  MAP:surf:domain CREASE (PI/2),
  MAP:surf:((T:2:(PI/10) ~ EMBED:1 ~ interval:<0,PI>):10),
  MAP:surf:((T:1:(PI/5) ~ R:<1,2>:(PI/2) ~ EMBED:1 ~ interval:<0,PI>):10),
  T:<1,2,3>:p,
  Segment:1:< <0,0,0>, CONS:(DS:1:surf):<PI/5, PI/10> >,
  Segment:1:< <0,0,0>, CONS:(DS:2:surf):<PI/5, PI/10> >,
  Segment:1:< <0,0,0>, CONS:(N:surf):<PI/5, PI/10> >
>
WHERE p = CONS:surf:<PI/5, PI/10> END;
```

---

**Example 5.7.2 (Sampling of normal field)**
A graphical representation of the normal field $n$ is produced by the N_Map function of Script 5.7.3, and displayed in Figure 5.16 for the normal field induced by the $\alpha(u, v) = (u, v, \sin u \sin v)$ surface, with $(u, v) \in [0, \pi]^2$.

In particular, Figure 5.16 is generated by graphically browsing the geometric value produced by the PLaSM interpreter when evaluating the last expression of Script 5.7.3.

The reader should notice that the N_Map function given here is very similar to the GradMap function of Script 5.3.2.

**Script 5.7.3 (Sampling of normal field)**

```
DEF N_Map (f::IsSeqOf:IsFun; dom::IsPol) = (STRUCT
    ~ AA:(Segment:0.35 ~ [CONS:f, vectSum ~ [CONS:f,(CONS ~ N):f] ])
    ~ S1 ~ UKPOL):dom;

N_Map:< surf, domain > STRUCT (MAP:surf:domain CREASE (PI/2))
```

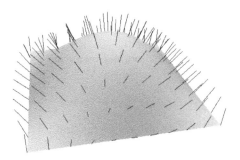

**Figure 5.16**   Sampling of the (scaled) normal field $n(u, v)$ to a surface
$\alpha(u, v) = (u, v, \sin u \sin v)$, over the domain $[0, \pi]^2$

*5.7.1   First fundamental form*

Let us consider a curve $c(t) = s(u(t), v(t))$ on the surface $s(u, v)$, with $a \le t \le b$, and let $s$ be the arc length:

$$s(t) = \int_a^t ds = \int_a^t \|c'(t)\| dt.$$

Hence we have:

$$
\begin{aligned}
\left(\frac{ds}{dt}\right)^2 &= \|c'\|^2 = c' \cdot c' = (u's_1 + v's_2) \cdot (u's_1 + v's_2) \\
&= (s_1 \cdot s_1)u' + 2(s_1 \cdot s_2)u'v' + (s_2 \cdot s_2)v'
\end{aligned}
$$

from where, by using the Gauss notation:

$$s_1 \cdot s_1 = E, \qquad s_1 \cdot s_2 = F, \qquad s_2 \cdot s_2 = G. \tag{5.6}$$

we have

$$\left(\frac{ds}{dt}\right)^2 = Eu' + 2Fu'v' + Gv',$$

and remembering that $u' = \frac{du}{dt}$ and $v' = \frac{dv}{dt}$, we get the intrinsic quantity called *First Fundamental Form* or also *Metric Form*

$$ds = E \, du + 2 \, F \, du \, dv + G \, dv,$$

in differential notation, which arises in computing the arc length of curves on surfaces, as well as the angle between tangent vectors on a surface.

In fact, let $v = as_1 + bs_2$ and $w = cs_1 + ds_2$ be tangent vectors to a surface $s$ in the same point. We can write

$$
\begin{aligned}
v \cdot w &= (as_1 + bs_2) \cdot (cs_1 + ds_2) \\
&= ac\,(s_1 \cdot s_1) + (ad + bc)\,(s_1 \cdot s_2) + bd\,(s_2 \cdot s_2) \\
&= ac\,\mathrm{E} + (ad + bc)\,\mathrm{F} + bd\,\mathrm{G} \\
&= ( a \quad b )\begin{pmatrix} \mathrm{E} & \mathrm{F} \\ \mathrm{F} & \mathrm{G} \end{pmatrix}\begin{pmatrix} c \\ d \end{pmatrix}.
\end{aligned}
$$

The matrix in the above formula is called *matrix of the first fundamental form* or also *metric tensor*.

Relabeling $s_i \cdot s_j = g_{ij}$, it is possible to write for the differential area element:

$$
\begin{pmatrix} E & F \\ F & G \end{pmatrix} = \begin{pmatrix} g_{11} & g_{12} \\ g_{21} & g_{22} \end{pmatrix}
$$

and, by labeling $du = du^1$ and $dv = dv^2$

$$
ds^2 = \sum_{i,j} g_{ij}\, du^i\, du^j, \qquad i, j \in \{1, 2\}.
$$

Another important property of the metric tensor is:

$$
\begin{aligned}
\|s_1 \times s_2\|^2 &= (s_1 \cdot s_1)(s_2 \cdot s_2) - (s_1 \cdot s_2)^2 \\
&= \mathrm{E\,G} - \mathrm{F}^2 \\
&= \det\begin{pmatrix} g_{11} & g_{12} \\ g_{21} & g_{22} \end{pmatrix} \\
&=: g
\end{aligned}
$$

**Example 5.7.3**
Let us try the forms $E$, $F$ and $G$ on the $(0,0)$ corner of the $[0,1]^2$ domain of the $s = (u, v, \sin u \sin v)$ surface map $[0,1]^2 \to \mathbb{E}^3$ given in Script 5.7.2.
In this case we have

$$
\begin{aligned}
s_1(u, v) &= (1, 0, \cos u \sin v) \\
s_2(u, v) &= (0, 1, \sin u \cos v),
\end{aligned}
$$

so that

$$
\begin{aligned}
E(s)(0,0) &= (s_1 \cdot s_1)(0,0) = ((1, 0, \cos u \sin v) \cdot (1, 0, \cos u \sin v))(0,0) = 1 \\
F(s)(0,0) &= (s_1 \cdot s_2)(0,0) = ((1, 0, \cos u \sin v) \cdot (0, 1, \sin u \cos v))(0,0) = 0 \\
G(s)(0,0) &= (s_2 \cdot s_2)(0,0) = ((0, 1, \sin u \cos v) \cdot (0, 1, \sin u \cos v))(0,0) = 1
\end{aligned}
$$

**Implementation**   The functional elements $E$, $F$ and $G$ of the metric tensor are easily computed in PLaSM as the functions E1, F1 and G1 of Script 5.7.4. According to their defining formulas (5.6), such functions are implemented as the composition of the innerprod operator (given in Script 3.2.4) with the appropriate CONS of partial derivation operators DS:$i$ given in Script 5.7.1.

**Script 5.7.4 (First fundamental form)**
```
DEF E1 = innerprod ~ [DS:1, DS:1];
DEF F1 = innerprod ~ [DS:1, DS:2];
DEF G1 = innerprod ~ [DS:2, DS:2];

E1:surf:<0,0> ≡ 1.0
F1:surf:<0,0> ≡ 0.0
G1:surf:<0,0> ≡ 1.0
```

*5.7.2   Second fundamental form*

The tensor of the *second fundamental form* is defined by the matrix:

$$\left( \begin{array}{cc} L & M \\ M & N \end{array} \right)$$

where the linear forms $L$, $M$ and $N$ of the tensor are respectively defined as:

$$L = \boldsymbol{n} \cdot \frac{\partial^2}{\partial u^2}$$

$$M = \boldsymbol{n} \cdot \frac{\partial^2}{\partial u \partial v}$$

$$N = \boldsymbol{n} \cdot \frac{\partial^2}{\partial v^2}$$

**Example 5.7.4**
Let us compute the values of the $L$, $M$ and $N$ forms on the $(0,0)$ corner of the $[0,1]^2$ domain of the $\boldsymbol{s} = (u, v, \sin u \sin v)$ surface.
  In this case we have

$$\begin{aligned} \boldsymbol{n} &= \boldsymbol{s}_1 \times \boldsymbol{s}_2 \\ &= (1, 0, \cos u \, \sin v) \times (0, 1, \sin u \, \cos v) \\ &= (-\cos u \, \sin v, \sin u \, \cos v, 1) \end{aligned}$$

and

$$\boldsymbol{s}_{11} = \frac{\partial^2 \boldsymbol{s}}{\partial u^2} = (0, 0, -\sin u \, \sin v)$$

$$\boldsymbol{s}_{12} = \frac{\partial^2 \boldsymbol{s}}{\partial u \partial v} = (0, 0, \cos u \, \cos v)$$

$$\boldsymbol{s}_{22} = \frac{\partial^2 \boldsymbol{s}}{\partial v^2} = (0, 0, -\sin u \, \sin v)$$

so that

$$
\begin{aligned}
L(s)(0,0) &= (n \cdot s_{11})(0,0) \\
&= ((-\cos u \sin v, \sin u \, \cos v, 1) \cdot (0,0,-\sin u \sin v))(0,0) = 0 \\
M(s)(0,0) &= (n \cdot s_{12})(0,0) \\
&= ((-\cos u \sin v, \sin u \, \cos v, 1) \cdot (0,0,\cos u \, \cos v))(0,0) = 1 \\
N(s)(0,0) &= (n \cdot s_{22})(0,0) \\
&= ((-\cos u \sin v, \sin u \, \cos v, 1) \cdot (0,0,-\sin u \sin v))(0,0) = 0
\end{aligned}
$$

**Implementation** In accordance with the implementation of the functional elements of the metric tensor, we give in Script 5.7.5 an implementation of the elements $L$, $M$ and $N$ of the second fundamental form, respectively denoted as L2, N2 and M2 in the implementation.

---

**Script 5.7.5 (Second fundamental form)**
```
DEF L2 = innerprod ~ [N, DS:1 ~ DS:1];
DEF M2 = innerprod ~ [N, DS:1 ~ DS:2];
DEF N2 = innerprod ~ [N, DS:2 ~ DS:2];

L2:surf:<0,0> ≡ 0.0
M2:surf:<0,0> ≡ 1.0
N2:surf:<0,0> ≡ 0.0
```

---

A computational check was also executed, by computing $L(s)(0,0)$, $M(s)(0,0)$ and $N(s)(0,0)$, and we found numerically the results already symbolically obtained in the above paragraph.

### 5.7.3 Gauss curvature

Let consider the normal $n(u,v)$ to a point $s(u,v)$ of a surface $S = s[0,1]^2$ in $\mathbb{E}^3$ and a unit tangent vector $v$ to such a surface in a point $s(u,v)$. Then consider the curve $\alpha_v$ generated by sectioning the surface with the normal plane passing for $n$ and $v$. The curvature of the osculating circle to $\alpha_v$ is called the *normal curvature of $S$ at $s(u,v)$ in the $v$ direction*, and is denoted as $k_n(v)$. This function varies between maximum and minimum values, which are reached at two orthogonal directions, called *principal directions*. The maximum and minimum normal curvatures at a point are called *principal curvatures* $k_1$ and $k_2$ at that point.

The product of the principal curvatures is called the *Gauss curvature* $K := k_1 k_2$.

The *Gauss curvature field* on a surface $s : [0,1]^2 \to S \subset \mathbb{E}^3$ can be defined as the ratio of determinants of the matrices of the second and first fundamental forms:

$$
K(s) : S \to \mathbb{R} : \frac{L(s)N(s) - M^2(s)}{E(s)G(s) - F^2(s)}
$$

**Implementation** We already used the symbol N to denote the normal field to a surface. Hence in Script 5.7.5, we used the symbols L2, M2 and N2 to denote the elements of the second fundamental form. In Script 5.7.6 we give the

$$\texttt{GaussCurvature} : ([0,1]^2 \to \mathbb{E}^3) \to (\mathbb{E}^3 \to \mathbb{R})$$

field operator which, when applied to a surface mapping, returns its curvature field. For the sake of readibility, we would like to write the GaussCurvature function using only infix operators, as, e.g., in

```
((L * N) - (M * M)) / ((E * G) - (F * F))
```

but this is not actually possible with the current PLaSM implementation, since the algebraic operators would be "raised" too many times. Hence, the standard FL prefix and CONSed form must instead be used.

---

**Script 5.7.6 (Gauss curvature)**
```
DEF GaussCurvature =
    / ~ [-~[*~[L2,N2], *~[M2,M2]], -~[*~[E1,G1],*~[F1,F1]]];

GaussCurvature:surf:<0,0>   ≡ -0.9999999999333331
GaussCurvature:surf:<PI/2,PI/2>  ≡  1.000000165454544
```

---

Clearly, the given computational examples are affected by approximation and round-off errors, as should be clear by remembering that we are using numeric derivation methods. Once again, the $\texttt{surf} = (u, v, \sin u \, \sin v)$ mapping, used for the two checks above, is the one given in Script 5.7.2.

## 5.8    Examples

An example of computation and presentation of the Gauss curvature field on a surface, generated by interpolation of two extreme curves with assigned extreme derivative fields, is given in this section. The surface generation by "transfinite" interpolation of curve maps, sometimes called *skinning* in CAD systems, is discussed in Chapter 12.5, but is anticipated here to work out a realistic example.

### 5.8.1    Color map of the Gauss curvature field

A very interesting application of many concepts studied in this book is discussed here. It allows experimentation with several features of the PLaSM language at the same time. In particular:

1. A smooth surface $s : [0,1]^2 \to S$, with $S \subset \mathbb{E}^3$, is generated by using transfinite interpolation methods. For this purpose two boundary curves

$$c_1 \quad : \quad [0,1] \to S : u \mapsto s(u,0) \tag{5.7}$$
$$c_2 \quad : \quad [0,1] \to S : u \mapsto s(u,1), \tag{5.8}$$

to be interpolated by $s$ are given, and are also assigned two fields of first derivatives along the images of such curves.

2. The field $K : S \to \mathbb{R}$ of Gauss curvature is *sampled* at the vertices of a cell decomposition defined upon the $s[0, 1]^2$ image of the surface. The result is represented as a polyhedral approximation, called `CurvatureField`, of the 2D manifold

$$(\mathrm{id}, K)(s)[0, 1]^2$$

embedded in 4-dimensional space $\mathbb{E}^3 \times \mathbb{R}$.

3. Finally, the 4-th coordinate of vertices of this object is checked for positivity/negativity and used to label each surface vertex with a color triplet in two different ranges of colors, thus transforming the 2-dimensional manifold `CurvatureField` in 4D space into the 2-dimensional manifold `colorGauss` in 6D space.

   (a) At exporting time into a VRML file, the first three coordinates are interpreted as position of points, the last three coordinates are interpreted as *color per vertex* (see for further details Section 10.7).

   (b) The resulting surface, shaded between *cyan* and *white* where the Gauss curvature is positive, and between *blue* and *cyan* where the curvature is negative, is shown in Figure 5.17.

Clearly, such a very simple computational solution to a quite complex scientific visualization problem, was possible because of the dimension-independent PLaSM approach to geometric modeling.

**Surface generation** First of all, we generate a surface mapping $s(u, v)$, with $(u, v) \in [0, 1]^2$, by Hermite[1] interpolation of two boundary curves

$$s(u, 0) = \texttt{c1} \quad \text{and} \quad s(u, 1) = \texttt{c2},$$

and two boundary fields of (constant) first derivatives

$$s_2(u, 0) = (\underline{1}, \underline{1}, \underline{1}) \quad \text{and} \quad s_2(u, 1) = (\underline{-1}, \underline{-1}, \underline{-1}).$$

It is not necessary to understand here how the $s$ mapping is generated. The used "transfinite" interpolation is discussed in Section 12.5. Anyway, we have:

$$s(u, v) = s(u, 0)h_0(v) + s(u, 1)h_1(v) + s_2(u, 0)h_2(v) + s_2(u, 1)h_3(v),$$

where $(h_0(v), h_1(v), h_2(v), h_3(v))^T$ is the Hermite's basis of cubic polynomials.

**Implementation** We are interested here to the `Surface` mapping, generated by the `CubicHermite` operator given in Script 12.5.5. Analogously, `c1` and `c2` are two cubic Hermite's curves generated by giving two extreme points and two extreme tangents. Finally, `dom` is a polyhedral complex partitioning the real interval $[0, 1]$ into 12 segments, and `CurvatureField` is the resulting polyhedral approximation of the 2D manifold $(\mathrm{id}, K)(s)[0, 1]^2$ embedded in 4-dimensional space.

---

[1] Discussed in Section 11.2.3 for the standard case of interpolation of points and tangent vectors, and in Section 12.5 for the transfinite interpolation of curves, surfaces and higher dimensional manifolds, together with assigned boundary derivative fields.

**Script 5.8.1 (Geometric data)**

```
DEF c1 = CubicHermite:S1:<<1,0,0>,<0,1,0>,<0,3,0>,<-3,0,0>>;
DEF c2 = CubicHermite:S1:<<0.5,0,0>,<0,0.5,0>,<0,1,0>,<-1,0,0>>;
DEF Surface = CubicHermite:S2:<c1,c2,<1,1,1>,<-1,-1,-1>>;

DEF dom = interval:<0,1>:12;
DEF CurvatureField =
    MAP: ((CONS ~ AR ~ [ID, GaussCurvature]):Surface): (dom * dom);

CurvatureField ≡ A-Polyhedral-Complex{2,4}
```

The transformation from the 2-manifold `CurvatureField` in 4D space, encoding the Gauss curvature as the 4-th coordinate, to the 2-manifold `colorGauss` in 6D space, encoding such curvature as a RGB color triplet, is performed in Script 5.8.2. For this purpose the maximum and minimum values of the 4-th coordinate of `CurvatureField` vertices are stored into `curvmax` and `curvmin`, respectively, and used to map the curvature values to the appropriate triples in the two color ranges used for positive and negative curvatures, respectively.

**Script 5.8.2 (Color map of curvature)**

```
DEF colorGauss = MAP:(IF:< IsRealPos ~ s4,
    [s1,s2,s3,/ ~ [s4,K:(curvmax - curvmin)],K:1,K:1],
    [s1,s2,s3,K:0,/ ~ [s4,K:(curvmin - curvmax)],K:1] >):CurvatureField
WHERE
    curvmax = MAX:4:CurvatureField,
    curvmin = MIN:4:CurvatureField
END;

VRML:(colorGauss CREASE (PI/2)):'out.wrl';
colorGauss ≡ A-Polyhedral-Complex{2,6}
```

**Figure 5.17** Gauss curvature field: (a) surface generated by Hermite's transfinite interpolation of two curves and two (constant) vector fields (b) subset of negative Gauss curvature (c) subset of positive Gauss curvature

# Part II

# Graphics

# 6

# Affine transformations

Transformations, i.e. linear invertible automorphisms, are used to map a picture or model into another one with different size, position and orientation. We will see that each useful geometric transformation may be reduced to an invertible linear transformation of a suitable linear space. Hence, given a basis, transformations are represented by means of squared invertible matrices, called *transformation matrices*. The main aim of this chapter is to study the structure and properties of matrices of "elementary" transformations. The interpretation of matrix multiplication as a geometric operator that maps a *point locus* (i.e. either a picture or model) into another one, is one of the great old ideas of computer graphics. In this chapter we first study the transformations of the 2D Euclidean space, then we see how they generalize to 3D and to greater dimensions. We also discuss how affine transformations are implemented as dimension-independent automorphisms by PLaSM. Several programming examples are given in the chapter.

## 6.1 Preliminaries

Some preliminary concepts needed in basic computer graphics are discussed in this section, including the definition of linear and affine transformations, the notation and conventions used for points, vectors, angles and positive rotations, and the important ideas underlying the use of homogeneous coordinates.

### 6.1.1 Transformations

A geometric transformation is defined as a one-to-one mapping of a point space to itself, which preserves some geometric relations of figures. For example:

1. *linear* transformations map lines *for the origin* to lines for the origin;
2. *affine* transformations map lines to lines preserving the *parallelism*;
3. uniform *scaling* transformations map point sets preserving the *similarity*;
4. translations and rotations, called *rigid* transformations, preserve the *congruence* of point sets.

*Geometric Programming for Computer-Aided Design*  Alberto Paoluzzi
© 2003 John Wiley & Sons, Ltd  ISBN 0-471-89942-9

**Linear transformations**  A linear transformation is an invertible linear map of a vector space to itself. Linear transformations of a vector space $\mathcal{V}$ earned this name because the transformed $\boldsymbol{p}^*$ of each $\boldsymbol{p}$ on the line segment joining $\boldsymbol{p}_1$ and $\boldsymbol{p}_2$ belongs to the segment joining the transformed images $\boldsymbol{p}_1^*$ and $\boldsymbol{p}_2^*$. In fact, let

$$\boldsymbol{p} = \alpha_1\boldsymbol{p}_1 + \alpha_2\boldsymbol{p}_2 \qquad 0 \le \alpha_1, \alpha_2, \qquad \alpha_1 + \alpha_2 = 1$$

and let $\boldsymbol{T} : \mathcal{V} \to \mathcal{V}$ be a linear transformation. By linearity of $\boldsymbol{T}$ we have

$$\boldsymbol{p}^* = \boldsymbol{T}\boldsymbol{p} = \boldsymbol{T}(\alpha_1\boldsymbol{p}_1 + \alpha_2\boldsymbol{p}_2) = \alpha_1\boldsymbol{T}\boldsymbol{p}_1 + \alpha_2\boldsymbol{T}\boldsymbol{p}_2 = \alpha_1\boldsymbol{p}_1^* + \alpha_2\boldsymbol{p}_2^*$$

This property is very important from a practical viewpoint, because it allows transformation of pictures or models, which are point loci with infinite elements, by just transforming a finite number of points, and in particular those called *vertices*, at the intersection of picture or model *edges*.

**Affine transformations**  An *affine map* is a map between two affine spaces which preserves the affine structure, i.e. maps lines to lines and preserves the parallelisms. Let $\mathcal{A}$ and $\mathcal{B}$ be two affine spaces with underlying vector spaces $\mathcal{V}$ and $\mathcal{W}$, respectively. Then a map $\boldsymbol{A} : \mathcal{A} \to \mathcal{B}$ is affine if, for each $x \in \mathcal{A}$ and $v \in \mathcal{V}$

$$x + v \mapsto \boldsymbol{A}(x + v) = \boldsymbol{A}(x) + \boldsymbol{T}(v),$$

where $\boldsymbol{T}$ is linear, and is called the *linear part* of $\boldsymbol{A}$.

An *affine transformation* is an invertible affine map of an affine space to itself. An affine map is invertible only if its linear part is invertible. The affine transformations of an affine space $\mathcal{A}$ form a group with respect to function composition, called the *affine group* of $\mathcal{A}$.

**Notation**  In the following sections we indifferently speak of either affine transformations — also called *tensors* in this book — and of their matrices, and normally we use the same notation. Tensor composition will occasionally be denoted by symbol concatenation, with the same notation used for matrix multiplication. An explicit denotation of functional composition is instead used within the PLaSM sources, where we need to distinguish between tensors, i.e. functions in the affine group, and their matrices.

### 6.1.2   Points and vectors

According to current practice, we give the coordinate representation of elements in a point space, e.g. of point $\boldsymbol{p} \in \mathbb{E}^2$, as a *column vector* $\begin{pmatrix} x \\ y \end{pmatrix}$. The coordinate representation of the point $\boldsymbol{p}^* = \boldsymbol{A}(\boldsymbol{p})$ generated by the action of a tensor $\boldsymbol{A}$ on a point $\boldsymbol{p}$ is hence given by *left-hand* multiplication by tensor matrix $[\boldsymbol{A}]$.

Actually, for sake of simplicity, we will often use the notation $\boldsymbol{A}$ to denote both the tensor and its matrix. We shall use the full notation $[\boldsymbol{A}]$ for a tensor matrix just occasionally, with the aim of remarking its use.

So, we have:

$$\boldsymbol{p}^* = \left( \begin{array}{c} x^* \\ y^* \end{array} \right) = \boldsymbol{A}\,\boldsymbol{p} = \left( \begin{array}{cc} a & c \\ b & d \end{array} \right) \left( \begin{array}{c} x \\ y \end{array} \right) = \left( \begin{array}{c} ax+cy \\ bx+dy \end{array} \right).$$

The convention of representing points with column vectors and transformations with left-hand matrix multiplication was adopted in graphics quite recently. Hence, several graphics books represent points as *row vectors* and transformations as *right-hand* matrix multiplications. E.g.:

$$\boldsymbol{p}^* = \left( \begin{array}{cc} x^* & y^* \end{array} \right) = \boldsymbol{p}\,\boldsymbol{A}^T = \left( \begin{array}{cc} x & y \end{array} \right) \left( \begin{array}{cc} a & b \\ c & d \end{array} \right) = \left( \begin{array}{cc} ax+cy & bx+dy \end{array} \right)$$

Notice the use of the transposed transformation matrix, and remember that the transposition of a matrix product is the product of transposed matrices, in the reverse order:

$$(\boldsymbol{S}_2\,\boldsymbol{S}_1\,\boldsymbol{p})^T = \boldsymbol{p}^T\,\boldsymbol{S}_1^T\,\boldsymbol{S}_2^T$$

### 6.1.3 Orientations and rotations

In studying the space transformations of 3D models, we need to first of all agree on orientation of rotations and angles.

In particular, the vectors $e_1, e_2, e_3$ in a Cartesian basis can be mutually oriented as the first three fingers of either the left or the right hand. The basis is called *left-hand* or *right-hand*, accordingly.

In most engineering and design disciplines, right-hand Cartesian bases are used, with the $x$ and $y$ axes contained on the image plane and the $z$ axes perpendicular and directed towards the observer. In a left-hand basis the $z$ axis has an opposite orientation, entering the image plane.

Given a basis $(e_i)$, the rotations are considered *positive* that move the basis vectors as follows:

$$e_1 \rightarrow e_2, \quad e_2 \rightarrow e_3, \quad e_3 \rightarrow e_1.$$

In right-hand bases the positive rotations (and positive angles) are counter-clockwise oriented, whereas in left-hand bases the positive rotations are oriented clockwise. In order to find the sign of rotation, the observer should look at as the rotation axis, see Figure 6.1.

### 6.1.4 Homogeneous coordinates

We know that several transformations of figures are linear. Linear transformations include scaling, rotation, reflection and shearing. They can be applied to some picture or model by matrix multiplication of picture (model) "vertices" times some suitable matrix. We also know that translations are conversely not linear, since they are applied by adding some constant vector to picture (model) vertices.

It is computationally inconvenient that the algebraic operation needed to apply different transformations is not always the same. This prevents from easy combining

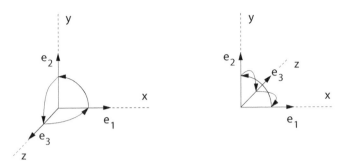

**Figure 6.1**	Basis orientation and positive rotations: (a) right-hand basis
(b) left-hand basis

different transformations to some object, by first multiplying the corresponding transformation matrices and by then applying the resulting product matrix to object vertices.

A solution to this problem was discovered by using *normalized homogeneous coordinates* rather than standard Cartesian coordinates. In particular, three-dimensional homogeneous coordinates are used for 2D pictures, whereas four-dimensional homogeneous coordinates are used for 3D models. More generally, $(n+1)$-dimensional coordinates are needed for $n$D models.

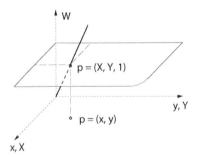

**Figure 6.2**	Homogeneous coordinates of 2D plane

Homogeneous coordinates define a bijective mapping between the set of points of Cartesian plane and the set of straight lines passing for the origin $o$ of the 3D space, see Figure 6.2. The origin is subtracted from such lines, considered as point sets, so that the mapping between plane points and space lines becomes one-to-one.

In this mapping $E^2 \rightarrow E^3$ each point $\begin{pmatrix} x \\ y \end{pmatrix} \in E^2$ is represented as a vector $\begin{pmatrix} X \\ Y \\ W \end{pmatrix} \in E^3$, with $W \neq 0$, such that $x = X/W, y = Y/W$. Notice that the same plane point is also represented by each vector $\lambda \begin{pmatrix} X \\ Y \\ W \end{pmatrix}$, where $\lambda \in \mathbb{R}$ and $\lambda \neq 0$.

The reverse mapping from lines to points is hence very simple. In order to return from an homogeneous point (or, better, vector)

$$p' = \begin{pmatrix} X \\ Y \\ W \end{pmatrix}$$

to its corresponding Cartesian point

$$p = \begin{pmatrix} x \\ y \end{pmatrix},$$

two divisions by the homogeneous coordinate $W$ are needed. In order to avoid such computation it is sufficient to associate the plane point $\begin{pmatrix} x \\ y \end{pmatrix}$ to the so-called *normalized* homogeneous representation $\begin{pmatrix} X \\ Y \\ 1 \end{pmatrix}$, for which it is

$$x = X, \qquad y = Y.$$

In the remainder of this book we use only lower-case letters for coordinates, so that the generic plane point will be denoted, in homogeneous normalized coordinates, as $\begin{pmatrix} x \\ y \\ 1 \end{pmatrix}$.

## 6.2   2D Transformations

In this section we discuss the properties of Cartesian plane $(\mathbb{E}^2, o, \{e_1, e_2\})$, and the structure of the *elementary* transformation matrices. In several figures the Cartesian axis are labeled both with $x, y$ and with $x^*, y^*$, in order to represent the coordinates of both the domain and range of the discussed mapping.

### 6.2.1   Translation

A plane translation is a mapping $T : \mathbb{E}^2 \rightarrow \mathbb{E}^2$ where a fixed vector $t = \begin{pmatrix} m \\ n \end{pmatrix}$ is added to each point $p = \begin{pmatrix} x \\ y \end{pmatrix}$, so that

$$p^* = T(p) = p + t = \begin{pmatrix} x \\ y \end{pmatrix} + \begin{pmatrix} m \\ n \end{pmatrix} = \begin{pmatrix} x + m \\ y + n \end{pmatrix}.$$

Notice that $t$ gives exactly the image of the origin in such a transformation. This movement of the origin implies that a translation is not a linear transformation, and hence that it cannot be directly represented by the product with some suitable matrix. We see here that the translation becomes linear when using homogeneous coordinates. In fact, the translation which maps a point $p$ in

$$p^* = p + t,$$

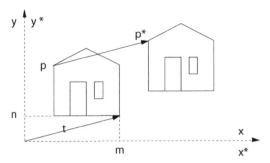

**Figure 6.3**   2D translation

with $\boldsymbol{t} = \left(\begin{array}{cc} m & n \end{array}\right)^{T}$, can be expressed by using homogeneous coordinates as:

$$\boldsymbol{p}^* = \boldsymbol{T}\,\boldsymbol{p} = \left(\begin{array}{ccc} 1 & 0 & m \\ 0 & 1 & n \\ 0 & 0 & 1 \end{array}\right)\left(\begin{array}{c} x \\ y \\ 1 \end{array}\right) = \left(\begin{array}{c} x+m \\ y+n \\ 1 \end{array}\right)$$

It is easy to see, looking at Figure 6.2 and to the structure of matrix $\boldsymbol{T}$, that by using three-dimensional homogeneous coordinates a translation of $\mathbb{E}^2$ is reduced to an elementary shearing (see Section 6.2.5) of $\mathbb{E}^3$.

**PLaSM representation of translation**   The elementary geometric transformations, i.e. translation, scaling, rotation and shearing, are defined in PLaSM by means of *higher level functions*, which require a double application to integer and real parameters to return the desired *transformation tensor*, which must be in turn applied to some geometric object to return the transformed object.

In particular, the application of a third-order transformation operator (say T, S or R) to either one or more integers, which *specify the coordinates* to be affected by the transformation, returns a more specific function, which must be applied to a suitable number of real parameters in order to return a tensor. The integer numbers are called *specificators*. The real numbers are called (transformation) *parameters*. Translation tensors are generated by PLaSM expressions:

    T: *specificators* : *parameters*

where *specificators* are either one integer or a sequence of integers and *parameters* are either one real or a sequence of reals, accordingly. Notice that *specificators* and *parameters* sequences of translations must have the same length. The token T is a PLaSM keyword, and cannot be redefined by the user.

According to their mathematical definition, transformation tensors are functions. Hence they can be composed with other functions, or applied to language expression that generate geometric objects, i.e. polyhedral complexes.

The translation tensors generated by such language expressions can be either composed by standard composition operator or applied to some language expression which evaluates to a polyhedral complex. E.g., in order to apply a translation with vector $\boldsymbol{t} = \left(\begin{array}{cc} 10.1 & 11.2 \end{array}\right)^{T}$ to the polyhedron `pol`, we write:

```
T:<1,2>:<10.1,11.2>:pol
```

In order to gain a full understanding, remember that multiple applications associate to left, so that the previous expression is evaluated as:

```
((T:<1,2>):<10.1,11.2>):pol;
```

As a further example, the translations $T(l, m), T(l, 0), T(0, m) \in Aff \; \mathbb{R}^2$ can be defined and applied as either:

```
T:<1,2>:<1,m>:pol        or      (T:1:1 ~ T:2:m):pol;
```

### Example 6.2.1 (2D house)
A very simple 2D polyhedral complex House2D, shown in Figure 6.4, is defined in Script 6.2.1. It is generated by aggregation of three 2D polyhedra respectively denoted wall, door and window. Each part is defined in local coordinates, with the local origin positioned in its lower left point. Two suitable 2D translation tensors are applied to door and window respectively, in order to relocate them in the Cartesian frame of wall.

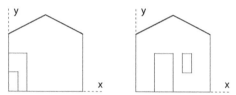

**Figure 6.4**   2D house: (a) without translations of parts (b) with translations

---

**Script 6.2.1**
```
    DEF House2D = STRUCT:< wall, T:1:2:door, T:<1,2>:<5,2>:window >
    WHERE
        wall = MKPOL:<<<0,0>,<8,0>,<0,6>,<8,6>,<4,8>>,<1..5>,<<1>>>,
        door = CUBOID:<2,4>,
        window = CUBOID:<1,2>
    END;
```

---

Two translation tensors are also applied to the second and third instances of the formal parameter Object, of polyhedral type, in the definition of function triplet given in Script 6.2.2. The value generated by evaluation of expression triplet:House2D is shown in Figure 6.5. The code is written with the aim of noting that the value generated by the evaluation of the expression T:1:12 is a transformation tensor, i.e. a *function*.

The triplet function could also be written more compactly, by using a proper FL style, as:

```
    DEF triplet = STRUCT ~ [ID, T:1:12, T:1:12 ~ T:1:12];
```

The triplet definition in Script 6.2.2 is said to use a λ-style, where formal parameters are given in the function *head* and referenced in the function *body*. The proper FL

**Script 6.2.2**

```
DEF triplet (Object::IsPol) = STRUCT:
   < Object, transl:Object, (transl ~ transl):Object >
WHERE
   transl = T:1:12
END;

triplet:House2D;
```

style is instead without parameters, as discussed in Section 2.1. The two definitions are equivalent. Clearly, to choose a programming style is not only a stylistic matter. There are good reasons for both choices, but a discussion of this topic is beyond the scope of this book.

**Figure 6.5**    Aggregation of three 2D houses

### 6.2.2   Scaling

A *scaling* $S$ is a transformation tensor represented by a diagonal matrix with positive coefficients, so that we have:

$$p^* = S\,p = \begin{pmatrix} a & 0 \\ 0 & b \end{pmatrix}\begin{pmatrix} x \\ y \end{pmatrix} = \begin{pmatrix} ax \\ by \end{pmatrix}, \qquad a, b > 0$$

If $a, b > 1$, then $S$ produces a *dilation* of pictures; conversely, if $a, b < 1$ then it produces a *compression* of pictures. A scaling with $a = b = 1$ is an *identity* mapping. Examples of 2D scaling on the first and second coordinate directions are given in Figures 6.6a and 6.6b, respectively.

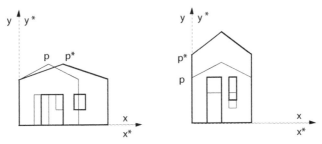

**Figure 6.6**   2D scaling: (a) about the $x$ coordinate (b) about the $y$ coordinate

The matrices of *uni-directional* scaling tensors, named $S_x$ and $S_y$, differ from the identity matrix for just one of the diagonal coefficients:

$$p^* = S_x\,p = \begin{pmatrix} a & 0 \\ 0 & 1 \end{pmatrix}\begin{pmatrix} x \\ y \end{pmatrix} = \begin{pmatrix} ax \\ y \end{pmatrix}$$

$$p^* = S_y\,p = \begin{pmatrix} 1 & 0 \\ 0 & b \end{pmatrix}\begin{pmatrix} x \\ y \end{pmatrix} = \begin{pmatrix} x \\ by \end{pmatrix}.$$

A generic scaling transformation (matrix) can be obtained by composition (product) of uni-directional scaling transformations (matrices):

$$\begin{pmatrix} a & 0 \\ 0 & b \end{pmatrix} = \begin{pmatrix} a & 0 \\ 0 & 1 \end{pmatrix}\begin{pmatrix} 1 & 0 \\ 0 & b \end{pmatrix}.$$

When $a = b$ the scaling is said to be *uniform*. The action of an uniform scaling is shown in Figure 6.7. In particular, the picture shows the action of a scaling matrix that doubles both the coordinates of picture points. We note that, in this transformation:

1. the size of all line segments is doubled;
2. the image $p^*$ of each point $p$ is located on the line joining $p$ to the origin;
3. the transformed picture is not only enlarged, but also moved away from the origin.

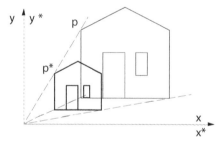

**Figure 6.7**   The action of a uniform scaling tensor

The normalized homogeneous matrix $S' \in \mathbb{R}_3^3$ of the 2D scaling tensor can easily be derived from the corresponding non-homogeneous matrix $S \in \mathbb{R}_2^2$, by adding a unit row and a unit column:

$$p^* = S'p = \begin{pmatrix} S & 0 \\ 0 & 1 \end{pmatrix}\begin{pmatrix} x \\ y \\ 1 \end{pmatrix} = \begin{pmatrix} a & 0 & 0 \\ 0 & b & 0 \\ 0 & 0 & 1 \end{pmatrix}\begin{pmatrix} x \\ y \\ 1 \end{pmatrix} = \begin{pmatrix} ax \\ by \\ 1 \end{pmatrix}$$

**PLaSM representation of scaling**   Scaling tensors are generated by the evaluation of PLaSM expressions

```
S:specificators:parameters
```

where *specificators* and *parameters* have the same type we discussed for translation tensors. The token S is a PLaSM keyword, and cannot be redefined by the user.

**Example 6.2.2 (2D trees)**

Example 6.2.1 is continued here, by adding a very schematic tree to the 2D house there developed. For this purpose we use the function `Circle` given in Script 1.6.1. This function generates a polygonal approximation of the circle of given radius centered in the origin.

Then the circle is translated and aggregated to a thin rectangle to generate an idealized tree shape, generated by `MyTree`. This one is a PLaSM function, parametrized on the shape height `h`, which generates a specific tree model when applied to an actual parameter value. Such a tree generator is instanced twice, using a translation, to give the `Trees` object.

Finally, the function `triplet` given in Script 6.2.2 is used to generate the model shown in Figure 6.8.

---

**Script 6.2.3**
```
DEF Leaves (radius::IsReal) = Circle:radius:<18,1>;

DEF MyTree (h::IsReal) = STRUCT:
   < T:1:(-:h/48):(CUBOID:<h/24,h/3>), T:2:(2*h/3):(Leaves:(h/3)) >;

DEF Trees = STRUCT:<MyTree:9, T:1:2:(MyTree:11) >;
DEF HouseTrees = STRUCT:< House2D, T:1:-0.75:Trees >;

triplet:HouseTrees;
```

---

Note that we could not use the token `TREE`, since this one is a reserved PLaSM keyword, which denotes a primitive operator with a semantics similar to that of `INSR` and `INSR` operators. See Section 2.1.2.

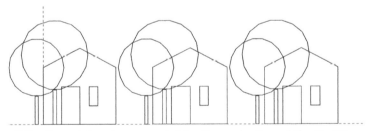

**Figure 6.8**  Geometric value generated by the evaluation of the PLaSM expression
`triplet:HouseTrees`

---

*6.2.3  Reflection*

The *reflection* — sometimes called *mirroring* in graphics — about a coordinate axis, is a linear transformation defined by a matrix generated by setting to $-1$ one of the diagonal coefficients of the identity matrix. Hence a reflection strongly resembles a scaling transformation. Two elementary reflections $\boldsymbol{M}_x$ and $\boldsymbol{M}_y$ can be given in the

$\mathbb{E}^2$ plane:

$$M_x = \begin{pmatrix} -1 & 0 \\ 0 & 1 \end{pmatrix}, \qquad M_y = \begin{pmatrix} 1 & 0 \\ 0 & -1 \end{pmatrix}.$$

As always, the normalized homogeneous representation of such transformations is obtained by adding a unit row and column to their matrices:

$$M'_x = \begin{pmatrix} M_x & 0 \\ 0 & 1 \end{pmatrix}, \qquad M'_y = \begin{pmatrix} M_y & 0 \\ 0 & 1 \end{pmatrix}.$$

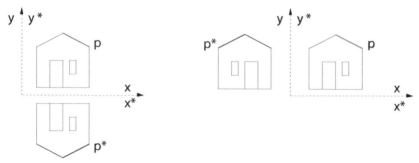

**Figure 6.9**   Elementary reflections of plane: (a) about the $x$ axis (b) about the $y$ axis

Clearly, the effect of a reflection tensor is to change the sign of just one coordinate of points. In Figure 6.9 is shown the action of both elementary reflections of the plane.

**PLaSM representation of reflection**   As we said, reflections resemble scaling. So it is easy to implement such tensors by using the predefined operator S:

$$M_x \equiv \texttt{S:1:-1}$$
$$M_y \equiv \texttt{S:2:-1}$$

The same implementation may be used for elementary reflections of 3D space.

**Example 6.2.3**
The previous example is continued here, by adding symmetry to the scene. This is done by reflecting the object HouseTrees and aggregating the original and the reflected object instances. The result of the evaluation of Script 6.2.4 is shown in Figure 6.10. A new implementation of the **triplet** function is given, where the $x$ size of the formal parameter Obj is used to compute the translation tensor.

*6.2.4   Rotation*

A rotation of the plane about the origin is a linear mapping that moves each point $p \in \mathbb{E}^2$ to a point $p^* = R(p)$ along an arc of circumference centered in the origin and with constant angle $\alpha$.

**Script 6.2.4**

```
DEF Mirror (d::IsIntPos)(Obj::IsPol) = (STRUCT ~ [S:d:-1, ID]):Obj;
DEF triplet (Obj::IsPol) = (STRUCT ~ [ID, T:1:x, (T:1:x ~ T:1:x)]):Obj
WHERE
    x = SIZE:1:Obj
END;

triplet:(Mirror:1:HouseTrees)
```

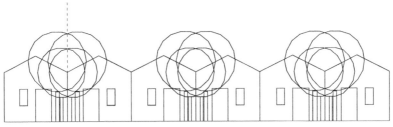

**Figure 6.10**   triplet of models generated by the expression
`triplet:(Mirror:1:HouseTrees)`

The matrix of a rotation tensor is easily computed by considering the mapping of basis vectors $\{e_i\}$. In particular, we can write that $e_1$ and $e_2$ are mapped to $e_1^*$ and $e_2^*$, respectively, where $R$ is the unknown rotation matrix:

$$\left( \begin{array}{cc} e_1^* & e_2^* \end{array} \right) = R \left( \begin{array}{cc} e_1 & e_2 \end{array} \right).$$

Looking at Figure 6.11 we can write, more explicitly:

$$\left( \begin{array}{cc} \cos\alpha & -\sin\alpha \\ \sin\alpha & \cos\alpha \end{array} \right) = R \left( \begin{array}{cc} 1 & 0 \\ 0 & 1 \end{array} \right),$$

from which $R$ is trivially derived.

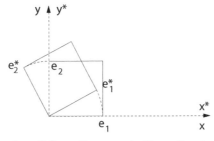

**Figure 6.11**   Rotation of the unit square built on the standard basis vectors

We note that the fixed point of this mapping is the origin, and that the rotation matrix depends on the rotation angle $\alpha$. The normalized homogeneous matrix $R' \in Lin\,\mathbb{R}^3$ of a plane rotation is obtained from the non-homogeneous matrix $R \in Lin\,\mathbb{R}^2$ in the standard way:

$$p^* = R'p = \begin{pmatrix} R & 0 \\ 0 & 1 \end{pmatrix} \begin{pmatrix} x \\ y \\ 1 \end{pmatrix} = \begin{pmatrix} x \cos\alpha + y \sin\alpha \\ -x \sin\alpha + y \cos\alpha \\ 1 \end{pmatrix}$$

**PLaSM representation of rotation**   A rotation is called *elementary* when the set of fixed points of this transformation is a coordinate subspace. Tensors of elementary rotations are generated by the evaluation of PLaSM expressions such as

R:<i,j>:$\alpha$

where <i,j> is a pair of integers that denotes the coordinate pair affected by the transformation, and the real $\alpha$ is the parameter of the transformation, i.e. the rotation angle, given in radians units.

The same syntax is used to specify elementary rotation tensors both in $E^2$ and in higher-dimensional spaces. Such specification of rotation is truly dimension-independent. Consider, in fact, that a rotation in $\mathbb{E}^n$, e.g. $R_{ij}(\alpha)$, is defined as one of the $\binom{n}{2}$ isometries of $E^n$ which keep fixed a coordinate subspace of dimension $n-2$ (and co-dimension 2), with equations

$$x_k = 0, \qquad 1 \le k \le n, \ k \ne i,j.$$

The two non-constant coordinates are changed by the tensor matrix according to the pattern of *sin* and *cos* functions previously seen in the 2D case.

Hence in $E^2$ we have the unique operator

R:<1,2> : $\mathbb{R} \to Lin\ \mathbb{R}^2$

such that, for each $\alpha \in \mathbb{R}$, the rotation tensor R:<1,2>:$\alpha$ is returned. Conversely, in $E^3$ there are $\binom{3}{2} = 3$ different operators

R:<1,2> : $\mathbb{R} \to Lin\ \mathbb{R}^3$,
R:<2,3> : $\mathbb{R} \to Lin\ \mathbb{R}^3$,
R:<1,3> : $\mathbb{R} \to Lin\ \mathbb{R}^3$,

which return a rotation tensor when applied to a real number, which is interpreted as the rotation angle. Analogously, in $E^4$ we have $\binom{4}{2} = 6$ different elementary rotation operators of this kind. Non-elementary rotations can be obtained by composition of suitable elementary rotations, as discussed in Section 6.3.2 for the 3D case, where the set of fixed points is an arbitrary axis.

### Example 6.2.4 (2D car)
In this example we generate a group of simplified 2D cars. We also rotate such a model with a variable angle. The single car model is generated by the PLaSM object named car in Script 6.2.5 and shown in Figure 6.12. The used Circle generating function is given in Script 2.2.5.

A row of integer length n of cars is generated by the function carQueue. Also a function rotatedCarQueue is given in Script 6.2.6, which generates a row of n cars on a "hillside" of any slope, specified by the formal parameter degrees. This function

**Script 6.2.5 (Car model)**

```
DEF car = (T:2:0.5 ~ STRUCT):
   < body, T:1:1.5:wheel, T:1:6:wheel >
WHERE
   body = MKPOL:<verts, cells, pols>,
   verts = <<0,0>,<3,0>,<7,0>,<6,2>,<4,2>,<3,1>,<1,1>>,
   cells = <<1,2,6,7>,<2,3,4,5,6>>,
   pols = <<1,2>>,
   wheel = S:<1,2>:<0.5,0.5>:(Circle:1:<18,1>)
END;
```

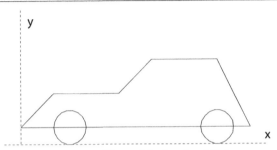

**Figure 6.12**   2D model of a simplified car

rotates the row of cars according to the hillside angle **alpha**. The scene generated by the expression **rotatedCarQueue:5:8** is shown in Figure 6.13.

A function **InclinedTriple**, where the mirrored pairs of houses given in previous examples are here translated also in the *y* direction, is given in Script 6.2.7. The 2D models produced by this function are easily combined with those produced by the function **rotatedCarQueue**. The resulting scene is shown in Figure 6.14.

**Script 6.2.6 (Rotated car row)**

```
DEF carQueue (n::IsInt) = (STRUCT ~ ##:n):< car, T:1:(1.2*SIZE:1:car) >;

DEF rotatedCarQueue (n::IsInt)(degrees::IsReal) =
   STRUCT:< basis, R:<1,2>:alpha:(carQueue:n) >
WHERE
   basis = MKPOL:<<<0,0>,<x,0>,<x,y>>,<<1,2,3>>,<<1>>>,
   x = (SIZE:1:(carQueue:n)) * (COS:alpha),
   y = (SIZE:1:(carQueue:n)) * (SIN:alpha),
   alpha = degrees * PI/180
END;

rotatedCarQueue:5:8
```

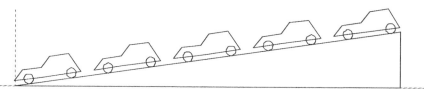

**Figure 6.13**   Car row on the hillside

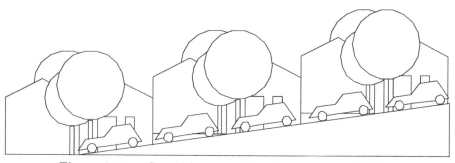

**Figure 6.14**    2D model generated by the expression STRUCT:<
InclinedTriple:8:(Mirror:1:HouseTrees), rotatedCarQueue:5:8 >;

---

**Script 6.2.7 (2D scene)**

```
DEF InclinedTriple (degrees::IsReal)(Object::IsPol) = STRUCT:
   < Object, transf:Object, (transf ~ transf):Object >
WHERE
   transf = T:<1,2>:<x, x * TAN:(PI*degrees/180)>,
   x = SIZE:1:Object
END;

STRUCT:<
   InclinedTriple:8:(Mirror:1:HouseTrees),
   rotatedCarQueue:5:8
>;
```

---

### 6.2.5   Shearing

Let us consider the plane as a bundle of straight lines perpendicular to a coordinate axis. An elementary 2D shearing is a tensor which maps line points to other points of the same line, in such a way that:

1. all points of a line translate by the same vector, i.e. the line translates by the vector;
2. only one line (the coordinate axis belonging to the bundle) is identically mapped, i.e. is not translated;
3. the translation of each line is proportional to its distance from the fixed line.

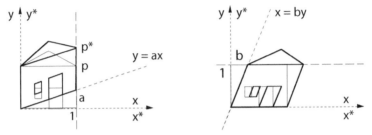

**Figure 6.15**   (a) Action of a shearing $H_x$ normal to $x$ axis (b) Action of a shearing $H_y$ normal to $y$ axis

In other words, a shearing tensor does not change a coordinate, whereas the other one is changed linearly with the fixed coordinate. Algebraically we can write:

$$p^* = H_x \, p = \begin{pmatrix} 1 & 0 \\ a & 1 \end{pmatrix} \begin{pmatrix} x \\ y \end{pmatrix} = \begin{pmatrix} x \\ y + ax \end{pmatrix}$$

$$p^* = H_y \, p = \begin{pmatrix} 1 & b \\ 0 & 1 \end{pmatrix} \begin{pmatrix} x \\ y \end{pmatrix} = \begin{pmatrix} x + by \\ y \end{pmatrix}$$

In particular, notice in Figure 6.15, that the line at unit distance from the axis translates of $a$ (respectively, of $b$). In other words the parameters $a$ and $b$ respectively represent the translations of lines $x = 1$ and $y = 1$.

**PLaSM representation of shearing**   A predefined shearing tensor does not currently exist in PLaSM. Anyway, this operator is very easy to give as a user-defined function, by using the standard language mechanism for tensor definition, i.e. the operator MAT, which accepts as input a normalized homogeneous invertible matrix and returns the corresponding tensor:

$$\texttt{MAT} : \mathbb{R}^3_3 \to \text{lin}^3$$

## Example 6.2.5 (Running car)

In order to define a parametrized tensor $\boldsymbol{H}_y(b)$ we can proceed as in Script 6.2.8, where the function MAT $\sim$ MatHom is applied to the non-homogeneous tensor matrix.

Then, two shearing tensor values — Hy:1 and Hy:-1, respectively — are applied to the 2D car model previously defined, in order to get three key-frames of a very simple animation storyboard.

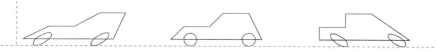

**Figure 6.16** Three key-frames of a simple storyboard

In particular, the model in Figure 6.16 is obtained by evaluating the symbol story, whereas the model in Figure 6.17 is obtained by evaluating the symbol story3D. Remember, from Section 3.3.6, that in PLaSM the homogeneous coordinate is the first one, so that we have:

MatHom:<<1, 5>, <0, 1>> ≡ <<1, 0, 0>, <0, 1, 5>, <0, 0, 1>>

---

**Script 6.2.8**
```
DEF Hy (b::IsReal) = (MAT ~ MatHom):<<1,b>,<0,1>>

DEF story = STRUCT:< Hy:1:car, T:1:12:car, (T:1:24 ~ Hy:-1):car >
DEF story3D = R:<2,3>:(PI/2):(Story * QUOTE:<3.5>);
```

---

The storyboard scenes can be easily transformed in 3D scenes by extruding the 2D images (see also Section 14.4) The extrusion operation is implemented in PLaSM as a Cartesian product with some 1D polyhedron. Also, we have to apply a rotation tensor of angle $\frac{\pi}{2}$ around the $x$ axis to the resulting object, in order to put the wheels upon the $xy$ plane.

**Figure 6.17** Three key-frames of the 3D storyboard ("My wife's car").

### 6.2.6 Generic transformation

We consider here the action of a generic tensor matrix $\boldsymbol{Q}$ on the unit square built on the basis vectors of a Cartesian frame $(\boldsymbol{o}, \boldsymbol{e}_i)$, with

$$\boldsymbol{Q} = \begin{pmatrix} a & c \\ b & d \end{pmatrix}.$$

Let $o^*, a^*, b^*, c^*$ be the images under $Q$ of points $o, a, b, c$, respectively, with $a = o + e_1$, $b = o + e_2$ and $c = o + e_1 + e_2$. We can either write

$$( \; o^* \quad a^* \quad b^* \quad c^* \; ) = Q( \; o \quad a \quad b \quad c \; ),$$

or, by using coordinates:

$$\begin{pmatrix} 0 & a & c & a+c \\ 0 & b & d & b+d \end{pmatrix} = \begin{pmatrix} a & c \\ b & d \end{pmatrix} \begin{pmatrix} 0 & 1 & 0 & 1 \\ 0 & 0 & 1 & 1 \end{pmatrix}.$$

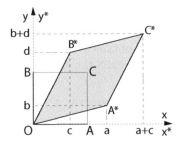

**Figure 6.18**    Action of a generic tensor on the standard unit square

Looking at Figure 6.18, it is easy to note that:

1. a linear mapping does not move the origin;
2. the parallelisms of lines is conserved by the mapping, i.e. mapped parallel lines are parallel;
3. the size of areas is, in general, not conserved.

### 6.2.7   Tensor properties

**Functional notation**   We remember, from previous sections, that plane rotations depend on one real parameter, whereas plane translation and scaling depend on two real parameters, and so on. Hence we write, with homogeneous coordinates and by using a mathematical notation to denote plane transformation tensors:

$$\begin{aligned} \boldsymbol{R}_{xy} &: \quad \mathbb{R} \to \mathrm{lin}^3 : \alpha \mapsto \boldsymbol{R}_{xy}(\alpha) \\ \boldsymbol{T}_{xy} &: \quad \mathbb{R}^2 \to \mathrm{lin}^3 : (m, n) \mapsto \boldsymbol{T}_{xy}(m, n) \\ \boldsymbol{S}_{xy} &: \quad \mathbb{R}^2 \to \mathrm{lin}^3 : (a, b) \mapsto \boldsymbol{S}_{xy}(a, b) \end{aligned}$$

The above notation gives a further explanation of the design choice for the syntax of PLaSM tensors, where rotation, translation and scaling are respectively denoted as R:<1,2>:α, T:<1,2>:<m,n> and R:<1,2>:<a,b>. In higher-dimensional spaces, the set of indices may clearly vary.

**Composition or product**   When a succession of tensors $Q_1, Q_2, \ldots, Q_n$ is applied to a point $p$, we can either write

$$p^* = (Q_n \circ \cdots \circ Q_2 \circ Q_1)(p), \quad \text{or}$$

$$p^* = Q_n \cdots Q_2\, Q_1\, p,$$

depending on the meaning (either tensor or tensor matrix) of the symbol $Q_i$.

**Associativity**   In the following expressions parentheses are not needed, since both tensor composition and product of matrices are associative operations. In fact:

$$Q_1 \circ Q_2 \circ Q_3 = (Q_1 \circ Q_2) \circ Q_3 = Q_1 \circ (Q_2 \circ Q_3)$$

$$Q_1 Q_2 Q_3 = (Q_1 Q_2)\, Q_3 = Q_1\, (Q_2 Q_3)$$

**Commutativity**   In general, tensor composition and matrix product are not commutative:

$$Q_1 \circ Q_2 \neq Q_2 \circ Q_1 \quad \text{and} \quad Q_1 Q_2 \neq Q_2 Q_1.$$

There are some important exceptions to this rule. The list is not exhaustive:

1. composition (product) of rotations about the same axis is commutative;
2. composition (product) of translations is commutative;
3. composition (product) of scaling is commutative;
4. composition (product) of rotations and uniform scaling is commutative.

A proof scheme of such statements is easier for their matrix versions. Write a matrix multiplication explicitly, and compute the resulting product matrix. The parameters of the compound mapping are expressed as either sum or product of parameters of component transformations.

**Product of scaling**   The statement follows from commutativity of number product.

$$S_2\, S_1 = \begin{pmatrix} a_2 & 0 & 0 \\ 0 & b_2 & 0 \\ 0 & 0 & 1 \end{pmatrix} \begin{pmatrix} a_1 & 0 & 0 \\ 0 & b_1 & 0 \\ 0 & 0 & 1 \end{pmatrix} = \begin{pmatrix} a_1 a_2 & 0 & 0 \\ 0 & b_1 b_2 & 0 \\ 0 & 0 & 1 \end{pmatrix} = S_1\, S_2$$

**Product of translations**   The statement follows from commutativity of number summation.

$$T_2\, T_1 = \begin{pmatrix} 1 & 0 & m_2 \\ 0 & 1 & n_2 \\ 0 & 0 & 1 \end{pmatrix} \begin{pmatrix} 1 & 0 & m_1 \\ 0 & 1 & n_1 \\ 0 & 0 & 1 \end{pmatrix} = \begin{pmatrix} 1 & 0 & m_1 + m_2 \\ 0 & 1 & n_1 + n_2 \\ 0 & 0 & 1 \end{pmatrix} = T_1\, T_2$$

**Product of rotations**  Trigonometric formulas of addition are used, together with commutativity of number summation.

$$
\boldsymbol{R}(\beta)\,\boldsymbol{R}(\alpha) \;=\; \begin{pmatrix} \cos\beta & -\sin\beta & 0 \\ \sin\beta & \cos\beta & 0 \\ 0 & 0 & 1 \end{pmatrix} \begin{pmatrix} \cos\alpha & -\sin\alpha & 0 \\ \sin\alpha & \cos\alpha & 0 \\ 0 & 0 & 1 \end{pmatrix}
$$

$$
= \begin{pmatrix} \cos\alpha\cos\beta - \sin\alpha\sin\beta & -(\cos\alpha\sin\beta + \sin\alpha\cos\beta) & 0 \\ \cos\alpha\sin\beta + \sin\alpha\cos\beta & \cos\alpha\cos\beta - \sin\alpha\sin\beta & 0 \\ 0 & 0 & 1 \end{pmatrix}
$$

$$
= \begin{pmatrix} \cos(\alpha+\beta) & -\sin(\alpha+\beta) & 0 \\ \sin(\alpha+\beta) & \cos(\alpha+\beta) & 0 \\ 0 & 0 & 1 \end{pmatrix}
$$

$$
= \boldsymbol{R}(\alpha)\,\boldsymbol{R}(\beta)
$$

**Composition and inverse**  From the statements proved above, one can conclude that:

1. Rotation and translation tensors have an *additive componibility*:

$$
\boldsymbol{T}_{xy}(m_1, n_1) \circ \boldsymbol{T}_{xy}(m_2, n_2) = \boldsymbol{T}_{xy}(m_1 + m_2, n_1 + n_2),
$$

$$
\boldsymbol{R}_{xy}(\alpha_1) \circ \boldsymbol{R}_{xy}(\alpha_2) = \boldsymbol{R}_{xy}(\alpha_1 + \alpha_2)
$$

2. Conversely, scaling tensors have a *multiplicative componibility*:

$$
\boldsymbol{S}_{xy}(a_1, b_1) \circ \boldsymbol{S}_{xy}(a_2, b_2) = \boldsymbol{S}_{xy}(a_1 a_2, b_1 b_2)
$$

3. Hence, it immediately follows for the inverse mappings that:

$$
(\boldsymbol{T}_{xy}(m, n))^{-1} = \boldsymbol{T}_{xy}(-m, -n)
$$

$$
(\boldsymbol{R}_{xy}(\alpha))^{-1} = \boldsymbol{R}_{xy}(-\alpha)
$$

$$
(\boldsymbol{S}_{xy}(a, b))^{-1} = \boldsymbol{S}\left(\frac{1}{a}, \frac{1}{b}\right)
$$

*6.2.8  Fixed point transformations*

Each invertible linear transformation $\boldsymbol{Q}$ of the plane has the origin of the Cartesian frame as the only fixed point, i.e. $\boldsymbol{Q}(\boldsymbol{o}) = \boldsymbol{o}$. To have a fixed point different from the origin, we need to compose three mappings, that respectively:

1. move $\boldsymbol{q}$ to the origin;
2. apply the desired transformation;
3. move the origin back to $\boldsymbol{q}$.

**Scaling with fixed point**   A scaling tensor with fixed point $q \neq o$, with $q = \begin{pmatrix} m & n \end{pmatrix}^T$, is given by:

$$\boldsymbol{S_q}(m, n, a, b) = \boldsymbol{T}_{xy}(m, n) \circ \boldsymbol{S}_{xy}(a, b) \circ \boldsymbol{T}_{xy}(-m, -n)$$

The succession of elementary transformations whose composition has the desired action, is graphically shown in Figure 6.19.

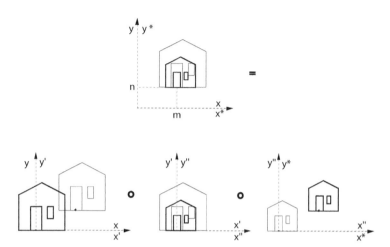

**Figure 6.19**   Decomposition of a scaling with fixed point into a product of elementary transformations

**Rotation with fixed point**   Analogously, for the rotation about a fixed point $q \neq o$, with $q = \begin{pmatrix} m & n \end{pmatrix}^T$, we have:

$$\boldsymbol{R_q}(m, n, \alpha) = \boldsymbol{T}_{xy}(m, n) \circ \boldsymbol{R}_{xy}(\alpha) \circ \boldsymbol{T}_{xy}(-m, -n)$$

The succession of elementary transformations, which give a rotation of angle $\alpha$ about a fixed point $q$, is graphically shown in Figure 6.20.

### 6.3   3D Transformations

*6.3.1   Elementary transformations*

The extension of transformations already discussed for the 2D case is very easy. Some more care is just needed for 3D rotation and shearing, so that we reserve most of this section to them. In the remainder, with the aim of unifying the management of both linear and affine transformations and of using the matrix product as the only geometric operator, we use normalized homogeneous coordinates and tensors in lin $\mathbb{R}^4$.

**Translation and scaling**   The *translation* tensor $\boldsymbol{T}_{xyz}(l, m, n)$ with parameters $l, m, n$ and the *scaling* tensor $\boldsymbol{S}_{xyz}(a, b, c)$ with parameters $a, b, c$ are represented, respectively, by matrices

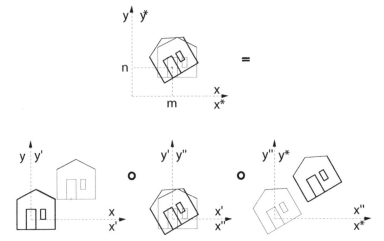

**Figure 6.20**    Decomposition of a rotation with fixed point into a product of elementary transformations

$$T_{xyz}(l,m,n) = \begin{pmatrix} 1 & 0 & 0 & l \\ 0 & 1 & 0 & m \\ 0 & 0 & 1 & n \\ 0 & 0 & 0 & 1 \end{pmatrix} \quad \text{and} \quad S_{xyz}(a,b,c) = \begin{pmatrix} a & 0 & 0 & 0 \\ 0 & b & 0 & 0 \\ 0 & 0 & c & 0 \\ 0 & 0 & 0 & 1 \end{pmatrix}.$$

**Shearing**    An elementary shearing of the 3D space is a tensor which does not change a coordinate and changes the other ones as linear functions of the non-transformed coordinate. We hence distinguish three elementary shearing tensors $H_{yz}(a,b)$, $H_{xz}(a,b)$ and $H_{xy}(a,b)$, whose matrices differ from the identity matrix just along the elements of one column. Such tensor matrices are easier to remember if denoted with the index of the invariant coordinate:

$$H_x(a,b) \equiv H_{yz}(a,b) = \begin{pmatrix} 1 & 0 & 0 & 0 \\ a & 1 & 0 & 0 \\ b & 0 & 1 & 0 \\ 0 & 0 & 0 & 1 \end{pmatrix}$$

$$H_y(a,b) \equiv H_{xz}(a,b) = \begin{pmatrix} 1 & a & 0 & 0 \\ 0 & 1 & 0 & 0 \\ 0 & b & 1 & 0 \\ 0 & 0 & 0 & 1 \end{pmatrix}$$

$$H_z(a,b) \equiv H_{xy}(a,b) = \begin{pmatrix} 1 & 0 & a & 0 \\ 0 & 1 & b & 0 \\ 0 & 0 & 1 & 0 \\ 0 & 0 & 0 & 1 \end{pmatrix}$$

In fact we have, respectively:

$$
\begin{aligned}
\boldsymbol{p}^* &= \boldsymbol{H}_x(a,b)\,\boldsymbol{p} = \begin{pmatrix} x & y+ax & z+bx & 1 \end{pmatrix}^T \\
\boldsymbol{p}^* &= \boldsymbol{H}_y(a,b)\,\boldsymbol{p} = \begin{pmatrix} x+ay & y & z+by & 1 \end{pmatrix}^T \\
\boldsymbol{p}^* &= \boldsymbol{H}_z(a,b)\,\boldsymbol{p} = \begin{pmatrix} x+az & y+bz & z & 1 \end{pmatrix}^T
\end{aligned}
$$

To visualize the action of such tensors, the 3D space should be considered as a bundle of planes parallel to a coordinate plane. The coordinate plane is invariant in this mapping; the other planes are moved by a translation on themselves. The translation of each plane is a linear function of its distance from the coordinate plane.

Consider, e.g., the tensor $\boldsymbol{H}_z = \boldsymbol{H}_{xy}(a,b)$. In this case:

1. the plane $z = 0$ is invariant;
2. the plane $z = 1$ translates by a translation vector $\boldsymbol{t} = \begin{pmatrix} a & b & 0 \end{pmatrix}^T$.
3. each plane $z = c$ translates by $\boldsymbol{t} = \begin{pmatrix} ac & bc & 0 \end{pmatrix}^T$;

**Elementary rotations**   Given a Cartesian frame in $\mathbb{E}^3$, we call *elementary rotations* $\boldsymbol{R}_x$, $\boldsymbol{R}_y$ and $\boldsymbol{R}_z$, also denoted as $\boldsymbol{R}_{yz}$, $\boldsymbol{R}_{xz}$ and $\boldsymbol{R}_{xy}$, respectively, three functions from reals to tensors in $\mathrm{lin}^4$, which return, for any given angle, the rotation tensor about the corresponding coordinate axis. We use equivalently either the notation $\boldsymbol{R}_z$ or $\boldsymbol{R}_{xy}$ to denote either the invariant coordinate or the varying coordinates. E.g.:

$$
\boldsymbol{R}_x : \mathbb{R} \to \mathrm{lin}^4 : \alpha \mapsto \boldsymbol{R}_{yz}(\alpha)
$$

The matrices of elementary rotation tensors defined above are obtained by suitably embedding the rotation matrix of 2D plane into the $4 \times 4$ identity matrix:

$$
\boldsymbol{R}_x(\alpha) \equiv \boldsymbol{R}_{yz}(\alpha) =
\begin{pmatrix}
1 & 0 & 0 & 0 \\
0 & \cos\alpha & -\sin\alpha & 0 \\
0 & \sin\alpha & \cos\alpha & 0 \\
0 & 0 & 0 & 1
\end{pmatrix},
$$

$$
\boldsymbol{R}_y(\beta) \equiv \boldsymbol{R}_{xz}(\beta) =
\begin{pmatrix}
\cos\beta & 0 & \sin\beta & 0 \\
0 & 1 & 0 & 0 \\
-\sin\beta & 0 & \cos\beta & 0 \\
0 & 0 & 0 & 1
\end{pmatrix},
$$

$$
\boldsymbol{R}_z(\gamma) \equiv \boldsymbol{R}_{xy}(\gamma) =
\begin{pmatrix}
\cos\gamma & -\sin\gamma & 0 & 0 \\
\sin\gamma & \cos\gamma & 0 & 0 \\
0 & 0 & 1 & 0 \\
0 & 0 & 0 & 1
\end{pmatrix}.
$$

**Example 6.3.1 (Stack of rotated elements)**
An assembly of rotated parallelepipeds is produced in this example. First a parallelepiped element is defined in Script 6.3.1, and is translated in $x, y$ by a tensor

T:<1,2>:<-5,-5>, in order to align the object center with the $z$ axis. Then the `pair` object is defined as an assembly of the untransformed element with a second element instance rotated about the $z$ axis (by tensor R:<1,2>:(PI/8)) and translated (by tensor T:3:2). The geometric value generated by evaluation of the `pair` symbol is shown in Figure 6.21a.

---

**Script 6.3.1**

```
DEF element = (T:<1,2>:<-5,-5> ~ CUBOID):<10,10,2>;
DEF pair    = STRUCT:< element, (T:3:2 ~ R:<1,2>:(PI/8)):element >;
DEF column  = (STRUCT ~ ##:17): < element, T:3:2, R:<1,2>:(PI/8) >;
```

---

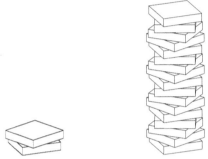

**Figure 6.21**   Rotated 3D elements: (a) `pair` (b) `column`

A fully equivalent but more elegant definition of the `pair` object can be given in proper FL style as follows:

DEF pair = (STRUCT ~ [ID, T:3:2 ~ R:<1,2>:(PI/8)]): element

To produce the `column` object shown in Figure 6.21b, both the combinatorial power of FL and the semantics of *hierarchical structures* (also called *hierarchical graphs* in graphics) are exploited. A wider discussion of hierarchical structures is given in Chapter 8.

### 6.3.2   Rotations

A 3D space rotation is a linear orthogonal transformation with a set of fixed points (called *autospace* in linear algebra) of dimension 1, known as the *rotation axis*. In such a transformation, every space point (outside the rotation axis) is mapped to the second extreme of a circle segment of constant angle with its center on the rotation axis, and belonging to the orthogonal plane passing for the point.

To compute the matrix of a rotation tensor $\boldsymbol{R}_{xyz}(\boldsymbol{n}, \alpha)$, with

$$\boldsymbol{R}_{xyz} : \mathbb{R}^3 \times \mathbb{R} \to \text{lin}^4 : (\boldsymbol{n}, \alpha) \mapsto \boldsymbol{R}_{xyz}(\boldsymbol{n}, \alpha),$$

where the rotation axis is parallel to the vector $\boldsymbol{n}$ and $\alpha$ is the rotation angle, we can proceed in several ways, two of which are discussed below.

**Composition of elementary rotations** A non-elementary 3D space rotation $R_{xyz}(n, \alpha)$ can be reduced to the composition of a suitable succession of elementary rotations.

First, a compound rotation $R_y(\gamma) \circ R_x(\beta)$ about the $x$-axis and $y$-axis is applied, with the aim of cancelling two components of the mapped $n$-axis, which is thus transformed onto the $z$-axis. A $z$-rotation tensor $R_z(\alpha)$ of angle $\alpha$ is applied at this point. Finally, the inverse rotation $(R_y(\gamma) \circ R_x(\beta))^{-1}$ is applied, with the aim of mapping the $n$-axis back to its original position. Hence we write:

$$\begin{aligned} R_{xyz}(n, \alpha) &= (R_y(\gamma) \circ R_x(\beta))^{-1} \circ R_z(\alpha) \circ (R_y(\gamma) \circ R_x(\beta)) \\ &= R_x(\beta)^{-1} \circ R_y(\gamma)^{-1} \circ R_z(\alpha) \circ R_y(\gamma) \circ R_x(\beta) \\ &= R_x(-\beta) \circ R_y(-\gamma) \circ R_z(\alpha) \circ R_y(\gamma) \circ R_x(\beta) \end{aligned}$$

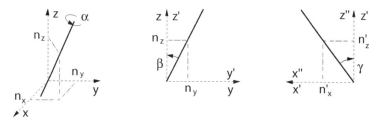

**Figure 6.22** Decomposition of a general rotation into elementary rotations: (a) the $n$-axis (b) the $x$-rotation (c) the $y$-rotation

We must finally compute the angles $\beta$ and $\gamma$, to draw out the elementary rotation tensors $R_x(\beta)$ and $R_y(\gamma)$. Looking at Figure 6.22 we can write:

$$\beta = \arctan\left(\frac{n_y}{n_z}\right) \qquad \gamma = -\arctan\left(\frac{n'_x}{n'_z}\right)$$

where $n' = R_x(\beta)\, n$.

**Transformation of coordinates** A rotation tensor $R_{xyz}(n, \alpha)$ can be derived very easily by composition of:

1. a coordinate transformation $Q(n)$ which maps the unit vector $\frac{n}{|n|}$ and two orthogonal unit vectors into the elements of a new basis;
2. a rotation $R_z(\alpha)$ about the $z$-axis of this new basis;
3. the inverse coordinate transformation $Q^{-1}(n)$.

Hence we write:

$$R_{xyz}(n, \alpha) = Q^{-1}(n) \circ R_z(\alpha) \circ Q(n). \tag{6.1}$$

To compute $Q(n)$ we choose an orthonormal vector triplet with an element directed as the rotation axis. Let $q_x, q_y, q_z$ be such a triplet, given in coordinates relative to the old basis $\{e_i\}$. We see they are transformed in a new basis $\{\hat{e}_i\}$ by the unknown matrix $Q(n)$:

$$( \ \hat{e}_1 \quad \hat{e}_2 \quad \hat{e}_3 \ ) = Q(n) \ ( \ q_x \quad q_y \quad q_z \ ).$$

But the left-hand side is the identity matrix, and hence:

$$Q(n) = ( \ q_x \quad q_y \quad q_z \ )^{-1} = ( \ q_x \quad q_y \quad q_z \ )^T = \begin{pmatrix} q_x^T \\ q_y^T \\ q_z^T \end{pmatrix}$$

where we set $Q^{-1}(n) = Q^T(n)$ since $Q(n)$, which maps an orthogonal unit triplet into an orthogonal unit triplet, is an orthogonal transformation.

Finally, we have to define the unit vectors $q_x$, $q_y$ and $q_z$. First we set

$$q_z = \frac{n}{\|n\|},$$

and also, provided that $n \neq e_3$, which would imply the trivial case $R(n, \alpha) = R_z(\alpha)$, we can write

$$q_x = \frac{e_3 \times n}{\|e_3 \times n\|}, \quad \text{and} \quad q_y = q_z \times q_x.$$

## Example 6.3.2

In this example we discuss the PLaSM implementation of rotation tensor $R_{xyz}(n, \alpha)$. For this purpose we first define a function Rot_xyz with a real alpha and a vector n as formal parameters. The function body, i.e. the expression used to compute its values, is a direct PLaSM translation of Formula (6.1).

The MatHom function, of signature $\mathcal{M}_n^n \to \mathbb{R}_{n+1}^{n+1}$, is given in Script 3.3.13; the functions UnitVect and VectProd are given in Scripts 3.2.4 and 3.1.3, respectively. Such functions homogenize a squared matrix by adding a unit row and column, normalize a vector and compute a vector product, respectively.

The higher-level function to compute the rotation tensor is called Rot_xyz. It is actually a filter which invokes either Rot_n or the predefined operator R:<1,2>, depending on the orientation of the n vector parameter. Two predicates IsZero and IsUp are defined for this purpose.

Notice that the tensor MAT:Q is defined by homogenizing the <qx, qy, qz> matrix, where the orthonormal vectors are directly accumulated by *row*, according to the discussed method. Remember in fact that a PLaSM matrix representation is a sequence of matrix rows.

The models of Figure 6.23 are respectively generated as:

```
STRUCT:<
    CUBOID:< 1, 1, 0.2 >,
    MKPOL:< <<0,0,0>, <1,1,0>>, <<1,2>>, <<1>> >
>;
```

**Script 6.3.2 (3D rotation about the _n_-axis)**

```
DEF Rot_n (alpha::IsReal; n::IsVect) =
   (MAT~TRANS):Q ~ R:<1,2>:alpha ~ MAT:Q
WHERE
   Q  = MatHom:<qx, qy, qz>,
   qx = UnitVect:(<0,0,1> VectProd n),
   qy = qz VectProd qx,
   qz = UnitVect:n
END;

DEF IsZero = AND ~ AA:(C:EQ:0);
DEF IsUp = AND ~ [C:EQ:0~s1, C:EQ:0~s2, NOT~C:EQ:0~s3];

DEF Rot_xyz = IF:< OR~[IsUp,IsZero]~s2, R:<1,2>~s1, Rot_n >;
```

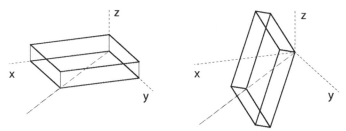

**Figure 6.23**   Action of a rotation tensor Rot_xyz:<PI/2,<1,1,0>> of angle $\pi/2$ about axis $\boldsymbol{n} = [1\ 1\ 0]^T$

```
STRUCT:<
   (Rot_xyz:<PI/2,<1,1,0>> ~ CUBOID):< 1, 1, 0.2 >,
   MKPOL:< <<0,0,0>, <1,1,0>>, <<1,2>>, <<1>> >
>;
```

### 6.3.3   Rotations about affine axes

A more general rotation tensor of $E^3$, with axis an *affine* subspace of dimension 1, i.e. a straight line in general not passing for the origin, is obtained by composition of transformations in lin $\mathbb{R}^4$:

$$\boldsymbol{R}^*_{xyz}(\boldsymbol{n},\boldsymbol{p},\alpha) = \boldsymbol{T}_{xyz}(\boldsymbol{p}-\boldsymbol{o}) \circ \boldsymbol{R}_{xyz}(\boldsymbol{n},\alpha) \circ \boldsymbol{T}_{xyz}(\boldsymbol{o}-\boldsymbol{p})$$

where $\boldsymbol{R}^*_{xyz}(\boldsymbol{n},\boldsymbol{p},\alpha)$ denotes the *rotation about the $\boldsymbol{n}$-axis passing for point $\boldsymbol{p}$*, and $\boldsymbol{o}$ is the origin of a Cartesian frame for $E^3$.

We note that the parameters of function $\boldsymbol{T}_{xyz}$ are vectors, since, from Section 3.2, the difference of points is a vector.

### 6.3.4   Algebraic properties of rotations

A rotation tensor $\boldsymbol{R} \in \text{lin}\,\mathcal{V}$ does not change the angles between vectors. This property can be written algebraically using the inner product.

For each $\boldsymbol{u}, \boldsymbol{v} \in \mathcal{V}$:

$$\boldsymbol{u} \cdot \boldsymbol{v} = \boldsymbol{R}(\boldsymbol{u}) \cdot \boldsymbol{R}(\boldsymbol{v})$$

We can write for the corresponding matrices:

$$[\boldsymbol{u}]^T [\boldsymbol{v}] = [\boldsymbol{R}\boldsymbol{u}]^T [\boldsymbol{R}\boldsymbol{v}] = [\boldsymbol{u}]^T [\boldsymbol{R}]^T [\boldsymbol{R}][\boldsymbol{v}]$$

so, we get

$$[\boldsymbol{R}]^T [\boldsymbol{R}] = [\boldsymbol{R}^T][\boldsymbol{R}] = [I],$$

and hence

$$\boldsymbol{R}^T \boldsymbol{R} = I = \boldsymbol{R}^{-1} \boldsymbol{R}.$$

We can conclude that

$$\boldsymbol{R}^T = \boldsymbol{R}^{-1}$$

i.e. that a rotation is an *orthogonal* tensor.

Some further properties of rotations are listed here:

1. In order to verify if a matrix is a rotation, it is sufficient to show that:

$$[\boldsymbol{Q}][\boldsymbol{Q}]^T = [\boldsymbol{Q}]^T [\boldsymbol{Q}] = [\boldsymbol{I}]$$

2. Since $[\boldsymbol{R}]$ is an orthogonal matrix, $det\ \boldsymbol{R}$ is either 1 or $-1$; a rotation with determinant 1 is called *proper*, with determinant $-1$ is called *improper*.
3. An improper rotation is the product of a proper rotation times a reflection.
4. The angle $\alpha$ of a rotation $\boldsymbol{Q}$ can be computed from the relation

$$tr\ \boldsymbol{Q} = 1 + 2\cos\alpha$$

5. The axis of a 3D rotation is given by the eigenvector associated with the real eigenvalue of its matrix.

**Reflections and improper rotations**   A *reflection* or *mirroring* is a tensor which reverses each vector of an axis for the origin and maintains fixed each vector of the orthogonal linear subspace.

For a reflection tensor $\boldsymbol{M}$ we have:

$$\boldsymbol{M}^2 = \boldsymbol{I}$$

$$\boldsymbol{M} = \boldsymbol{M}^T = \boldsymbol{M}^{-1}$$

The reflections which fix the coordinate planes are called *elementary* reflections or mirroring. They can be implemented as scaling with one coefficient equal to $-1$:

$$\begin{aligned}
\boldsymbol{M}_x &= \boldsymbol{S}_{xyz}(-1, 1, 1) \\
\boldsymbol{M}_y &= \boldsymbol{S}_{xyz}(1, -1, 1) \\
\boldsymbol{M}_z &= \boldsymbol{S}_{xyz}(1, 1, -1)
\end{aligned}$$

Tensors $Q$ with matrix determinant $-1$ are called either *improper rotations* or *rotational reflections*. They are given by the composition of a rotation about some axis and by the reflection with respect to the plane orthogonal to such axis.

Angle and axis of an improper rotation $Q$ are obtained from trace and eigenvector of its matrix, as for proper rotations. Exchanging $Q$ with $-Q$ exchanges the proper with the improper, and changes the sign of the rotation angle, but does not change the axis.

**Global scaling**  A uniform scaling tensor $S_{xyz}(a, a, a)$ can also be represented by a matrix $(s_{ij}) \in \mathbb{R}_4^4$, which differs from the identity just for the coefficient $s_{44}$:

$$S_{xyz}(a, a, a) \equiv \begin{pmatrix} 1 & 0 & 0 & 0 \\ 0 & 1 & 0 & 0 \\ 0 & 0 & 1 & 0 \\ 0 & 0 & 0 & \frac{1}{a} \end{pmatrix}$$

In fact, it is easy to verify that:

$$p^* = \begin{pmatrix} 1 & 0 & 0 & 0 \\ 0 & 1 & 0 & 0 \\ 0 & 0 & 1 & 0 \\ 0 & 0 & 0 & \frac{1}{a} \end{pmatrix} \begin{pmatrix} x \\ y \\ z \\ 1 \end{pmatrix} = \begin{pmatrix} x \\ y \\ z \\ \frac{1}{a} \end{pmatrix} = \begin{pmatrix} ax \\ ay \\ az \\ 1 \end{pmatrix}$$

**Structure of matrices**  Resuming what we said about the affine transformations of $E^3$, which are represented in homogeneous coordinates by $4 \times 4$ real matrices, we note they always have the structure:

$$Z = \begin{pmatrix} Q & m \\ 0^T & a \end{pmatrix}$$

where $Q$ is an invertible $3 \times 3$ matrix. If $m \neq 0$, then $Z$ contains a translational component. If $a \neq 1$, then we say that $Z$ is *not normalized*. In this case it contains a global scaling component with parameter $\frac{1}{a}$.

**Tensor action on covectors**  In both graphics and modeling applications it is sometimes necessary to apply a space transformation to face equations instead of to vertex coordinates. This often happens within the geometric kernel of PLaSM, where the linear equations of faces of polyhedral models are explicitly stored in memory.

Let, e.g.,

$$ax + by + cz + d = 0$$

be the Cartesian equation of a plane, and remember that this one is a point set mapped to zero by a linear function $\phi : \mathbb{R}^4 \to \mathbb{R}$, called *covector*, and represented in coordinates as the *row* vector

$$q = \begin{pmatrix} a & b & c & d \end{pmatrix}$$

of coefficients of the plane. We often need to compute the covector $q^*$ associated with the plane transformed by the action of a tensor $M$ on $E^3$.

If $p = \begin{pmatrix} x & y & z & 1 \end{pmatrix}^T$ is the homogeneous representation of $E^3$ points, then the points of the plane will satisfy the relation:

$$q\, p = 0. \tag{6.2}$$

Clearly, if we apply a tensor $M$ to $\mathbb{E}^3$, we also have:

$$q^*\, p^* = q\, T\, M\, p = 0, \tag{6.3}$$

where $T$ is the unknown tensor for the dual space, to be applied to $q$ covector. Since both identities (6.2) and (6.3) must hold, it is:

$$T\, M = I \qquad \text{and hence} \qquad T = M^{-1}$$

Therefore, in order to apply a tensor $M$ to a point space, we need to apply a left-hand matrix multiplication times $M$ to the underlying vectors, as well as a right-hand matrix multiplication times $M^{-1}$ to the underlying covectors.

## 6.4   PLaSM implementation

### 6.4.1   Pre-defined affine tensors

Some predefined higher-level PLaSM functions return either translation, scaling or rotation tensors, when applied to suitable parameters. Such functions are respectively denoted as T, S and R.

As is well known at this point, one major PLaSM characteristics is *dimensional independence*. This property allows definition of functions and evaluating expressions which are able to generate geometric objects of any dimension. A PLaSM object, seen as a point set, may in fact belong to spaces described by bases with any number of elements. In other words, object points may have any number of coordinates.

Affine transformation functions are accordingly designed to generate transformation tensors able to work on any user-specified subset of object coordinates.

**Translation**   Translation tensors are generated by the PLaSM operator denoted by symbol T. Hence, this symbol cannot be re-defined by the user, without generating an error at interpretation time. The signature of T operator is:

$$\text{T} : Z^d \to \mathbb{R}^d \to \text{lin } \mathbb{R}^*, \qquad 1 \le d$$

The dimension of the resulting tensor is not specified, because it is only determined at run-time — and not at interpretation time — depending on the dimension of the polyhedral expression it is actually applied to. For example, we can equally write:

```
(T:2:10.5 ∼ T:4:3):(CUBOID:<1,1,1,1,1>)  or
(T:<2,4>:<10.5,3>):(CUBOID:<1,1,1,1,1>)  or
T:<2,4>:<10.5,3>:(CUBOID:<1,1,1,1,1>)  or
(T:<2,4>:<10.5,3> ∼ CUBOID):<1,1,1,1,1>
```

where the evaluation of each such expression gives an instance of the 5-dimensional unit hypercube, translated on the second and fourth coordinates.

**Example 6.4.1**
Two very simple polyhedra are defined in Script 6.4.1, and designated as basis and pyramid. Then the assembly pair is given by using the STRUCT function, whose semantics is described in Chapter 8.

---

**Script 6.4.1**
```
DEF basis = CUBOID:<10,10,1>;
DEF pyramid = MKPOL:<
    <<0,0,0>,<8,0,0>,<8,8,0>,<0,8,0>,<4,4,4>>,<1..5>,<<1>> >;
DEF pair = STRUCT:<basis, T:<1,2,3>:<1,1,1>:pyramid>
```

---

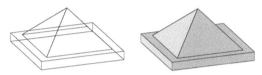

**Figure 6.24**   pair assembly with pyramid translation

In Figure 6.24 the object generated by evaluation of pair symbol is shown. A similar example is given in Script 6.4.2 where a transl tensor is defined and instanced more times. The triplet value is shown in Figure 6.25.

---

**Script 6.4.2**
```
DEF transl = T:<1,2,3>:<1,1,1>;
DEF pair    = STRUCT:<basis, transl:pyramid>;
DEF triplet = STRUCT: <basis, transl:basis, (transl ~ transl):pyramid>;
```

---

**Scaling**   Scaling tensors are generated by the higher-level PLaSM operator named S. The signature of this operator is:

$$\text{S} : Z^d \to \mathbb{R}^d \to \text{lin } \mathbb{R}^*, \qquad 1 \leq d$$

Also in this case the dimension of the resulting tensor is not specified, and is determined at run-time, as for translation tensors.

**Rotation**   The higher-level operator R generates elementary rotation tensors, i.e. space isometries which change two coordinates according to the pattern of plane rotations, and leave the other coordinates invariant. The R signature is:

$$\text{R} : Z^2 \to \mathbb{R} \to \text{lin } \mathbb{R}^*.$$

Once more, the dimension of the generated tensors is not specified, and is determined at run-time, as for translation and scaling. E.g., the tensor R:<1,2>:PI can be either applied to a 2D or to a 4D polyhedron.

**Figure 6.25**   More complex `triplet` assembly

## Example 6.4.2 (2D and 3D Clock)

We define here two PLaSM functions, named `clock2D` and `clock3D`, that generate simplified clock models with time set as specified by their integers parameters, corresponding to hours and minutes, respectively. The implemented code is given in Scripts 6.4.3 and 6.4.4. Some generated models are shown in Figures 6.26 and 6.27.

A 2-dimensional clock model is first given, by defining a circular `background`, the 12 hour `ticks`, and the `hour` and `minute` hands, each one given in a local coordinate frame. The `Circle` function is given in Script 1.6.1, and returns a polygonal approximation of circle of given radius. In this case it returns a 2D regular polygon with 24 sides.

---

**Script 6.4.3 (2D Clock)**

```
DEF background = Circle:0.8:<24,1>;
DEF minute = (T:<1,2>:<-0.05,-0.05> ~ CUBOID):<0.9,0.1>;
DEF hour = (T:<1,2>:<-0.1,-0.1> ~ CUBOID):<0.7,0.2>;
DEF ticks = (STRUCT ~ ##:12):< tick, R:<1,2>:(PI/6) >;
DEF tick = (T:<1,2>:<-0.025,0.55> ~ CUBOID):<0.05,0.2>;

DEF clock2D (h,m::IsInt) = STRUCT:<
   background,
   ticks,
   R:<1,2>:( PI/2 - (h + m/60)*PI/6 ):hour,
   R:<1,2>:( PI/2 - m*PI/30 ):minute
>;
```

---

The interesting part of Script 6.4.3 is constituted by the `clock2D` function, with integer parameters `h` and `m`, for hours and minutes to set, respectively. An $xy$ rotation of angle `PI/2 - (h+m/60)*PI/6` is there applied to the `hour` hand. The positive constant $\frac{\pi}{2}$ is summed to move the origin of angles on the vertical line. The negative term takes into account both the angles induced by integer parameters `h` and `m`. Such a term is negative, because the clock hand movements are (quite obviously!) *clockwise*, whereas positive angles are counter-clockwise. The definition of the `Q` function is discussed in Section 1.6.2. It is used in Script 6.4.4 as a short-hand for `QUOTE ~ LIST`.

**Figure 6.26**   Geometric values generated by evaluation of `clock2D:<2,35>` and `clock2D:<11,55>`

The clock3D function differs from clock2D by addition widths to objects in the $z$ direction, and by coloring red the solid background. The adding of VRML-like colors and textures to geometric models is discussed in Chapter 10. The generated 3D clock model is displayed in Figure 6.27.

Notice that both the Cartesian product of polyhedra * and the COLOR binary function are used infix in the 3D background transforming expression. They are evaluated correctly by the interpreter, because infix operators are left-associative in PLaSM, i.e.:

$$A \ op_1 \ B \ op_2 \ C \equiv (A \ op_1 \ B) \ op_2 \ C$$

Notice also that each tensor inserted as isolated element in the STRUCT sequence, e.g. as T:3:0.2, is applied to each geometric value which follows it, according to the semantics of hierarchical structures (Chapter 8). The Q operator, which is a shortcut for QUOTE working both on number sequences and on single numbers, is given in Script 1.5.5.

---

**Script 6.4.4 (3D Clock)**

```
DEF clock3D (h,m::IsInt) = STRUCT:<
    background * Q:0.2 COLOR RGB:<1,0,0>,
    T:3:0.2:(ticks * Q:0.01), T:3:0.2,
    R:<1,2>:( PI/2 - (h + m/60)*PI/6 ):(hour * Q:0.03), T:3:0.03,
    R:<1,2>:( PI/2 - m*PI/30 ):(minute * Q:0.03)
>;
```

---

**Figure 6.27**   3D VRML model generated by evaluation of clock3D:<2,35>

*6.4.2   User-defined affine tensors*

It may sometimes be useful to apply tensors not to polyhedra but to single points, i.e. directly to a set of coordinates (see, e.g. Script 3.3.15). This may be done by implementing the desired tensors as user-defined PLaSM functions. In the following the elementary rotations, translations and scaling in $E^3$, which depend on only one real parameter, are given.

It is interesting to note that, by using the standard composition of the language, such functions may be first partially specified, then freely composed, and only later applied

**Script 6.4.5 (User-defined 3D tensors)**

```
DEF Tx (a::IsReal)(x,y,z::IsReal) = < x + a, y, z >;
DEF Ty (a::IsReal)(x,y,z::IsReal) = < x, y + a, z >;
DEF Tz (a::IsReal)(x,y,z::IsReal) = < x, y, z + a >;

DEF Sx (a::IsReal)(x,y,z::IsReal) = < x * a, y, z >;
DEF Sy (a::IsReal)(x,y,z::IsReal) = < x, y * a, z >;
DEF Sz (a::IsReal)(x,y,z::IsReal) = < x, y, z * a >;

DEF Rx (a::IsReal)(x,y,z::IsReal) =
    < x, cos:a * y - sin:a * z, sin:a * y + cos:a * z >;
DEF Ry (a::IsReal)(x,y,z::IsReal) =
    < cos:a * x + sin:a * z, y, (- sin):a * x + cos:a * z >;
DEF Rz (a::IsReal)(x,y,z::IsReal) =
    < cos:a * x - sin:a * y, sin:a * x + cos:a * y, z >;
```

to the target points. For example, a rotation of angle $\alpha$ of the point $\boldsymbol{p} = (p_x, p_y, p_z)$ around a line parallel to the $y$-axis and passing for the point $\boldsymbol{q} = (0, h, k)$, i.e.

$$\boldsymbol{p}^* = \boldsymbol{R}_{xyz}(e_2, \boldsymbol{q}, \alpha)(\boldsymbol{p})$$

can be directly computed in PLaSM as:

```
DEF p_star =
    (Tz:k ~ Ty:h ~ Ry:alpha ~ Ty:(-:h) ~ Tz:(-:k)):< px,py,pz >
```

## 6.5   Examples

In this section we discuss some simple but quite realistic examples of geometric programming with affine transformations, whose implementation requires combining tensors in several ways with other PLaSM operators. The more interesting example, is probably the first one, where some functions MKframe and MKvector are given, to generate the geometric model of a Cartesian reference frame and of any applied vector.

### 6.5.1   Modeling applied 3D vectors and reference frames

Two useful functions MKframe and MKvector are given to generate the geometric model of the Cartesian frame, as well as of any *applied vector* in 3D. Several functions, including type predicates, vector and matrix functions, the rotation transformation around a given axis for the origin, and more, are given in previous Scripts.

In Script 6.5.1 the symbol MKversork generates a geometric model of the unit vector $e_3$ of the $z$ axis, as made by a cylinder of radius $1/100$ and height $7/8$ and by a cone of radius $1/16$ and height $1/8$.

**Script 6.5.1 (geometric model of the unit vector <0,0,1>)**

```
DEF MKversork =
    CYLINDER:<1/100,7/8>:3 TOP (Cone:<1/16,1/8>:8);
```

The MKvector function in Script 6.5.2 generates the geometric model of an applied vector with first extreme in point p1 and second extreme in point p2. The arrow model of the actual vector is produced by first scaling the object generated by MKversork to the proper size, then by rotating to make it parallel to the final model and then by translating the model to the final position. Finally, the optimize operator is applied, in order to make possible the VRML exporting of a polyhedral complex with a general transformation matrix inserted in the data structure. As already discussed elsewhere, the composite operator MKPOL ∼ UKPOL has the effect of flattening the hierarchical data structure of a polyhedral complex, by applying all the stored transformation matrices to the vertex data.

---

**Script 6.5.2 (geometric model of the applied vector p1−>p2)**
```
DEF optimize = MKPOL ∼ UKPOL

DEF MKvector (p1::IsPoint)(p2::IsPoint) =
   (optimize ∼ Tr ∼ Rot ∼ Sc):MKversork
WHERE
   Tr = T:<1,2,3>:p1,
   Rot = Rotn:< alpha, n >,
   Sc = S:<1,2,3>:<b,b,b>,
   b = VectNorm:u,
   u = p2 VectDiff p1,
   alpha = ACOS:(<0,0,1> innerProd UnitVect:u),
   n = <0,0,1> VectProd u
END;
```

---

In Script 6.5.3 the MKframe operator is given, which produces a model of the standard Cartesian frame, with labeling of axis, as shown in Figure 6.28.

---

**Script 6.5.3 (geometric model of 3D reference frame)**
```
DEF MKframe = STRUCT:<
   MKvector:<0,0,0>:<1,0,0>,
   MKvector:<0,0,0>:<0,1,0>,
   MKvector:<0,0,0>:<0,0,1>,
   (T:<1,2>:<1,1/8> ∼ S:<1,2>:<1/20,1/20>):XX,
   (T:<2,3>:<1,1/8> ∼ S:<2,3>:<1/20,1/20>):YY,
   (T:<3,1>:<1,1/8> ∼ S:<3,1>:<1/20,1/20>):ZZ >
WHERE
   XX = MKPOL:<<<-1,1,0>,<1,-1,0>,<1,1,0>,<-1,-1,0>>,
      <<1,2>,<3,4>>,<<1,2>>>,
   YY = MKPOL:<<<0,0,0>,<0,-1,1>,<0,1,1>,<0,0,-1>>,
      <<1,2>,<1,3>,<1,4>>,<<1,2,3>>>,
   ZZ = MKPOL:<<<-1,0,1>,<1,0,1>,<-1,0,-1>,<1,0,-1>>,
      <<1,2>,<1,4>,<3,4>>,<<1,2,3>>>,
END;
```

---

The following example shows the sum of a set of applied vectors in 3D, each given as an ordered pair of points. The VRML file exported by the language is displayed in Figure 6.28. Notice that the last vector, shown in red in Figure 6.28, is the sum of the previous three.

---

**Script 6.5.4 (Applied vectors modeling)**

```
STRUCT:< MKframe,
   MKvector:<0.5,-0.1,0>:<1.1,-0.7,0.3>,
   MKvector:<1.1,-0.7,0.3>:<2.1,-0.2,-0.3>,
   MKvector:<2.1,-0.2,-0.3>:<1.4,0.3,-0.5>,

   MKvector:<0.5,-0.1,0>:<1.4,0.3,-0.3> COLOR RED >;
```

---

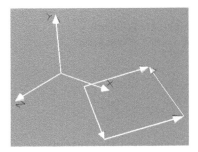

**Figure 6.28**   Geometric modeling of Cartesian frame and some applied vectors

**Example 6.5.1 (Linear ramp)**

First of all, we define a function Ramp in Script 6.5.5, which generates a parametrized linear stair as a complex of 2D polygons in $\mathbb{E}^3$.

In particular, this function accepts as input the three dimensions of a step, i.e. the *width*, *depth* and *height*, denoted as x,y,z, respectively, according to the Cartesian axes they are parallel to. The partial function generated by actual values of such parameters is then applied to an integer n, which specifies the number of steps of the ramp.

---

**Script 6.5.5 (Linear ramp)**

```
DEF Ramp (x,y,z::IsReal)(n::IsInt) = (STRUCT~##:n):<step, T:<2,3>:<y,z>>
WHERE
   step = STRUCT:<
      (T:3:z ~ EMBED:1):step_foot,
      (R:<2,3>:(PI/2) ~ EMBED:1):step_rise >,
   step_foot = CUBOID:<x,y>,
   step_rise = CUBOID:<x,z>
END;
```

---

We note the use of the PLaSM operator EMBED:$n$ which, when applied to a polyhedral complex of $E^m$, embeds it in the coordinate subspace of $E^{m+n}$ with equations

$$x_{m+1} = x_{m+2} = \cdots = x_{m+n} = 0.$$

The EMBED:1 function is hence used here to embed some $E^2$ rectangles into the $x_3 = 0$ subspace of $E^3$.

In Figure 6.29 we show the result of the evaluation of expression

```
Ramp:<0.9,0.28,0.16>:10;
```

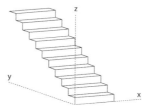

**Figure 6.29**   Model generated by function Ramp with 10 steps

## Example 6.5.2 (Multiple linear ramp)

The function Ramp is then used to generate an object theRamp which is multiply instanced and transformed, to generate the quite complex aggregation of stairs and landings shown in Figure 6.30.

The Landings body of Script 6.5.6 is a geometric expression which uses the Q operator, introduced in Script 1.5.5, to transform both numbers and sequences of numbers into 1D polyhedral complexes, and the Cartesian product * of polyhedral complexes (See Section 12).

The formal parameter n, in both MultipleStair and Landings generating functions, clearly denotes the number of floors.

---

**Script 6.5.6 (StairCase)**
```
DEF doubleRamp = STRUCT:< theRamp, (T:2:Y ~ S:<1,2>:<-1,-1>):theRamp > ;
DEF MultipleStair (n::IsInt) = (STRUCT ~ ##:n): < doubleRamp, T:3:Z > ;
DEF X = SIZE:1:theRamp;
DEF Y = SIZE:2:theRamp;
DEF Z = SIZE:3:theRamp;

DEF Landings (n::IsInt) = T:<1,2>:<-:X,-:X>:
   (Q:(2*X) * Q:<X,-:Y,X> * (@0 ~ Q ~ #:n):Z);

DEF StairCase = (STRUCT ~ [ MultipleStair, Landings ]):(n_floors - 1)
```

---

Two quite different values of the StairCase object are shown in Figure 6.30. In particular, the StairCase model associated with the definitions

```
DEF theRamp = Ramp:<3, 0.28, 0.16>: 8;
```

```
DEF n_floors = 2
```

is shown is Figure 6.30a. The one generated by changing such definitions to

```
DEF theRamp = Ramp:<0.95, 0.30, 0.15>: 10;
DEF n_floors = 5
```

is given in Figure 6.30b.

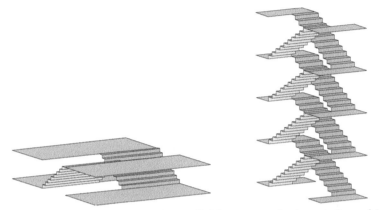

**Figure 6.30**   Two instances of the implicitly parametrized `stairCase` object

## Example 6.5.3 (Helix ramp)

The construction of a spiral stair ramp with squared basis and triangular steps is described here. Each step pair gives a turn of $\frac{\pi}{2}$ to the helix-centered angle, as shown by Figure 6.31.

In particular, the function L_Ramp of Script 6.5.7 depends on two positive reals x, z, and on a positive integer n_turns. The first two parameters correspond respectively to the half size of squared staircase and to the step height; the second one gives the number of $\frac{\pi}{2}$ turns, so that the number of steps is $2 \times$ n_turns.

---

**Script 6.5.7 (Parametric helix ramp)**

```
DEF L_Ramp (x,z::IsRealPos)(n_turns::IsIntPos) = (STRUCT ~ ##:n_turns):
    < step1, T:3:z, step2, T:3:z, R:<1,2>:(PI/2) >
WHERE
    step1 = STRUCT:<
        (S:1:-1 ~ T:1:(-:x) ~ T:3:z):step_foot,
        (R:<2,3>:(PI/2)) :step_rise >,
    step2 = STRUCT:<
        (S:2:-1 ~ T:2:(-:x) ~ T:3:z):step_foot,
        (R:<1,2>:(PI/4) ~ R:<2,3>:(PI/2)):step_rise >,
    step_foot = (EMBED:1 ~ S:<1,2>:<x,x> ~ SIMPLEX):2,
    step_rise = (EMBED:1 ~ S:<1,2>:<2**0.5,2**0.5> ~ CUBOID):<x,z>
END;
```

---

Notice that the primitive PLaSM function SIMPLEX, when applied to the integer 2, returns the 2-dimensional unit simplex of the plane, i.e. the triangle built on the basis vectors $e_1$ and $e_2$.

As in several previous examples, the body of L_Ramp function relies on the semantics of structures, where each tensor is applied to each following complex in the sequence order.

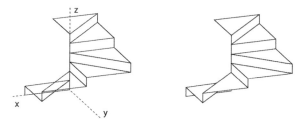

**Figure 6.31**  Squared helix ramp with turn of $\frac{3}{2}\pi$ angle

# 7

# Graphic primitives

This chapter is aimed at discussing the basic concepts of *graphic primitives* and *attributes*. Such concepts are first introduced from an historical perspective, starting with the ISO graphics standards *GKS* and *PHIGS*, respectively 2D and 3D. The set of basic primitives of *OpenGL*, the current *de facto* industrial standard, and those of *Open Inventor*, the first object-oriented 3D toolkit, are then described. The basic 3D primitives of the VRML language to experiment virtual reality on the World-Wide Web are also discussed, before introducing Java 3D, the platform-independent object-oriented 3D API. At the end of the chapter, a theoretical approach to polygonal lines is presented, where a quotient set of such objects is shown to be a vector space. This approach allows for a sound definition and implementation of shape *morphisms* and measures of shape *similarity*. According to the constructive character of this book, several primitives are quickly implemented in PLaSM in the main part of the chapter. In conclusion, we show here a set of basic and advanced geometric constructors, that will be found useful in later chapters, mainly when discussing geometric modeling.

## 7.1 Some background

The idea of graphics primitive refers to the early days of graphics standardization process. A primitive was conceived of as a basic operation performed by the graphics system in some well-defined as well as platform-, language- and device-independent manner. In the past two decades astonishing improvements have changed the field with increasing rapidity. Consequently, the set of basic primitives offered by graphics systems moved towards both greater efficiency and higher abstraction levels, particularly in the past few years, according also to the novel object-oriented approach to software development.

### 7.1.1 GKS

The 2D ISO graphics standard GKS (Graphical Kernel System), introduced in 1985 [ISO85, EKP87], was mainly concerned with *device-independence* and *portability* of graphics programs across different graphics devices and computing platforms.

*Geometric Programming for Computer-Aided Design*  Alberto Paoluzzi
© 2003 John Wiley & Sons, Ltd  ISBN 0-471-89942-9

In order to manage the complexity of specialized graphics devices, like refresh tubes, vector terminals, raster-scan monitors, graphic tablets, digitizers, plotters and so on, GKS identified a very limited number of *logical* graphic devices, able to perform a well-characterized set of basic operations, and implemented by very different physical devices.

Basic graphic operations were called *graphic primitives*. A strong distinction was introduced between *input* and *output* primitives. The set of parameters of primitives was standardized, as well the programming interface to use them. Some primitives are influenced not only by the actual value of their parameters, but also by other data stored in the graphics system, and defining its current state. Such external data were called *graphic attributes*.

For example, a picture can be constituted by several polygonal lines of different colors. They are traced by invoking the appropriate programming interface to the polyline primitive with actual sequences of coordinates for 2D points. Each such primitive is displayed on the graphics hardware by using the current LineColor value, e.g. red, stored as part of the state of the graphics system, i.e. as an attribute of polylines. Suitable procedures, e.g. SetLineColor, are available in the programming interface to change the value of graphics attributes.

GKS is a 2D system, and was used until recently, e.g. to implement GIS (Geographical Information System) applications. Subsets of output primitives are stored in 2D *segments* (see Chapter 8) which can be named, transformed, highlighted, picked and so on. Output primitives are defined in *world coordinates*, stored in *normalized device coordinates* and displayed in *device coordinates* (see Chapter 9). Conversely, input primitives enter the graphics system in device coordinates and are internally transformed into normalized and world coordinates, and thus returned to the programming application.

**Output primitives in GKS**  The list of output primitives defined by GKS is quite short:

1. polyline;
2. polymarker;
3. fill area;
4. text;
5. cell array;
6. generalized drawing primitive (GDP).

The polyline primitive is used to trace an open polygonal line by giving the ordered sequence of its vertices. The polymarker primitive is used to display an ordered sequence of points with some special graphics symbol, e.g. to trace the plotting of a sampled function. The fill area primitive is used to draw a plane polygon by giving the ordered sequence of its vertices. The text primitive is used to trace a graphics text in a specified position of the drawing area. The cell array primitive is used to define a rectangular pattern by specifying the number of rows and columns of a color array, the array of color indices, as well as the cell size and a reference point into the drawing area. Finally, the GDP primitive is offered to the application programmer as a general method to take into account the specialized characteristics of some graphics devices, such as the ability to generate circular arcs in hardware, and so on.

Among the output primitive attributes there are lineColor, lineWidth and lineStyle for the polylines; markerType and markerHeight for the polymarker; fillStyle (with values solid, hollow, hatch or pattern) for the fill area; charWidth, charHeight, charFont and several others for the text primitive, and so on.

**Input primitives in GKS** The list of input primitives is given below:

1. locator;
2. stroke
3. valuator;
4. choice;
5. pick;
6. string;

The locator primitive is used to enter a single 2D position with some input device such as a *mouse*, a *joystick* or a tablet *stylus*. The stroke primitive is conversely used to enter an ordered sequence of 2D points, e.g. by sampling the movement of an input device either at specified time intervals or at specified distances between subsequent entered points. The valuator primitive is used for entering a single real in a specified numeric interval. This abstraction emulates the physical potentiometers and allows the easy implementation of widgets like the *scroll-bar* of windows on the display. The choice primitive is an abstraction used to "make a choice", i.e. to enter a value of some enumerative type from an input device. It allows for easy implementation of interaction *menus*. The pick primitive is used to select a picture *segment* and/or an output primitive from the display area. It allows the easy implementation of graphical user interaction with the display content. The string primitive is used to enter some text string from the input device, e.g. a graphic tablet or even the keyboard.

### 7.1.2  PHIGS

PHIGS, the *Programmer's Hierarchical Interactive Graphics System* [ISO89, ANSI87, HHHW91, GG91, Gas92], allows the creation of models which may have a complex *hierarchical* structure and which produce pictures the user can *interact* with. As GKS, it was introduced in a language-independent way, together with *language bindings*, that defined the API to a highly portable library, implemented, e.g. in C, Fortran and Ada.

The main concepts of the standard (or better of its extension PHIGS+) concern the introduction of several new primitives for graphical output, the *style* of graphical output controlled by attributes external to the primitive, and the grouping of geometric information into lists called *structures*, which may invoke other structures in a hierarchical way, thus allowing use of *local coordinates* in the representation of parts, and multiple reusing of model parts into different contexts.

Several coordinate systems have been introduced to make the description, viewing, projection and rendering of complex scenes easier. Convenient local coordinate systems are used as *modeling coordinates*, which are combined together with *modeling transformation* to give *world coordinates*, which are obtained when a picture is *posted* to some workstation, by *traversing* the hierarchical *structure network*. Structure *editing* may change both the lists of primitives and the parameters of transformations, thus producing a change of the picture and/or an animation of it at next traversal of the structure network.

The list of PHIGS output primitives is very similar to the one on GKS primitives:

1. polyline 3;
2. polymarker 3;
3. text 3;
4. annotation text relative 3;
5. fill area 3;
6. fill area set 3;
7. cell array 3;
8. generalized drawing primitive 3.

Two new primitives fill area set and annotation text relative are introduced with respect to GKS. They allow description of multiply connected polygons, i.e. polygon with multiple cycles in the boundary, and attachment of descriptive annotations to graphics objects, respectively. All the primitives are defined as fully three-dimensional according to the main character of such 3D graphics standard.

The PHIGS+ extension was proposed very soon after the standard, in order to enrich the graphics system with illumination and shading techniques, as well as with various kinds of surface tessellations and with parametric curves and surfaces. The new primitives introduced with the PHIGS+ extension follow.

1. polyline set 3 with data;
2. fill area set 3 with data;
3. cell array 3 plus;
4. set of fill area set 3 with data;
5. triangle strip 3 with data;
6. quadrilateral mesh 3 with data;
7. non-uniform B-spline curve;
8. non-uniform B-spline surface with data;
9. compute fill area set geometric normal;

### 7.1.3   Open GL

*OpenGL* [Ope92, NDW92], the true Open Graphics Standard from Silicon Graphics, is the direct descendant of the IRIS Graphics Library, invented in 1982 and called IRIS GL. *OpenGL* provides a wide range of graphics abilities, from rendering a simple geometric point, line, or filled polygon, to rendering the most complicated lit, texture-mapped and trimmed NURBS surface.

The *OpenGL* library is truly platform-independent, and runs on top of several windows systems on all brands of UNIX and Linux, all versions of Windows (95/98/NT/2000) and recently on both the MacOS and the MacOS X.

*OpenGL* provides a great amount of control over the fundamental operations of 2D and 3D graphics, including transformations, viewing, texture mapping, rendering and pixel operations. All the commands are issued by means of function calls, which are executed in the calling sequence ordering. The nature of *OpenGL* is procedural more than descriptive, since it does not provide the means to describe or modeling complex geometric objects.

Primitives are defined by groups of vertices. Data, consisting of vertex coordinates, colors, normals, texture coordinates, and edge flags, are associated with a vertex and processed with it in the specified ordering. The set of *OpenGL* primitives can be summarized as follows:

1. points;
2. lines;
3. line strip and line loop;
4. triangles, triangle strip and triangle fan;
5. quads and quad strip;
6. polygon and polygon tessellation;
7. quadric object;
8. NURBS curve and NURBS surface.

Triangle strip and triangle fan create a connected group of triangles from an ordered set of points. Quads and quad stripe create a single quadrilateral or a connected set of quadrilaterals, respectively. The polygon primitive creates a single convex polygon. The polygon tessellation routines create a concave polygon with one or more contours. Quadric objects include sphere, cylinder and disk. An *evaluator* facility allows use of a polynomial mapping to produce vertices, normal, texture coordinates and colors. The domain values may be generated by either specifying a 1D or 2D evenly spaced grid, or by directly evaluating the mapping at some directly specified domain point. Such an evaluator is the basis of both NURBS curves and surfaces.

### 7.1.4   Open INVENTOR

In 1993 Silicon Graphics introduced *IRIS Inventor*, a proprietary environment for graphics development, which soon generated *Open Inventor* [WO94]. This object-oriented toolkit was designed to create interactive 3D applications, by taking advantage of powerful graphics hardware with minimal programming effort.

With respect to IRIS GL and *OpenGL*, *Open Inventor* allowed the graphics programmer and the developer of graphics applications to write code up to ten times more compact, by exploiting the economy and efficiency of a complete object system. In particular, *Inventor* introduced a conceptual graphics model based on *hierarchical graphs*, with nodes containing both geometric primitives and appearance properties, i.e. with definition of lighting and material properties of surfaces.

A hierarchical scene is defined as a network of several types of nodes. In particular, nodes of type geometry are containers of geometric primitives. When *traversing* (see Chapter 8) a hierarchical graph to produce a linear display list, several properties, including current appearance and geometric transformations, may be inherited by descendant nodes. The inheritance and composition of transformations are similar to that of other advanced graphics system, and may be primarily referenced to the model of structure network defined by the PHIGS graphics standard.

Geometric classes are all derived from class SoShape (where the prefix So stands for *space object*). The class SoShape derives from SoNode. The list of primitives made available by the *Open Inventor* library follows:

1. point set and indexed point set

2. line set and indexed line set
3. face set and indexed face set
4. triangle stripe set and indexed triangle stripe set
5. quad mesh;
6. NURBS curve and NURBS surface
7. linear profile
8. cone, cube, sphere, cylinder
9. text2,text3

Some simple shapes are predefined, including cone, cube, sphere and cylinder. Complex shapes are defined by a set of vertex coordinates and by a set of vertex normals, if the lighting model is set to PHONG (see Section 10.6). Both coordinates and normals are stored in separate nodes, so that they can be referred to by other nodes.

This library systematically uses the current state during the graph traversal. For example, a face set primitive generates a polygonal object by making use of the current coordinates, normals, materials and textures.

Indexed primitives are similar to the non-indexed ones, but are allowed to use current data in arbitrary ordering, specified by a set of indices. Triangle strip sets and quad meshes are generally faster to render than face sets. A quad mesh primitive uses the current coordinates in the order, arranged by row.

Graphics attributes, i.e. the properties which affect the different elements of the rendering state, are described by property classes, also derived from the class SoNode. Some examples of property nodes are SoMaterial, which sets the lighting properties of the current material, and SoDrawStyle, which tells the renderer about the drawing techniques to use.

### 7.1.5   VRML

In this section we briefly introduce the graphics primitives provided by the description language for 3D scenes named *VRML (Virtual Reality Modeling Language)* [ISO97, ANM97, Pes92], which was introduced in recent years to define, post and experiment virtual environments on the World-Wide Web.

When a VRML plug-in (SGI Cosmoplayer or Parallelgraphics Cortona, e.g.) is available within a web browser (Navigator or Explorer, say), then it becomes possible to download, render and visit a description of 3D virtual worlds developed for the more diverse aims. In particular, with VRML 2.0, it is possible to enjoy a really multimedia experience, where the generative 3D texture-mapped graphics is integrated with hyperlinks to video, sound, image and text objects which are available either locally on the client machine or remotely on the World-Wide Web.

The development of this description language started in 1994 with the preparation of the Draft Specification for VRML 1.0, based on the 3D Metafile format of Open Inventor, with enhancements to support networking. VRML 1.0 could only define static worlds navigable by the user without any real interaction with the virtual scene. In autumn 1995 discussion of the development of the new 2.0 version started, which conversely provided dynamic scenes, collision detection and integration with video and sound. VRML 2.0 became an ISO standard in 1997, with the name of VRML97.

As in *Open Inventor*, a scene is described as a hierarchical graph, which contains both branching nodes and other types of nodes, including geometry and appearance data. A scene graph is a sort of "family tree" containing scene data, where "children" are shapes, lights, sounds, etc., and "parents" are groups of children and other parents. This graph defines a hierarchical grouping of shapes and associated data.

Among the novelties introduced by VRML 2.0 to describe dynamic scenes and multimedia, we cite a node Sound to add sound and speech; a node Elevation grid for terrain modeling; a node Extrusion of type Geometry to produce translational and rotational extrusions; a node Background and Fog to define, e.g., a panorama with far mountains and plants, and with color graduations on both the sky and the ground. Also new node types Movie texture and Audio clip were introduced to define multimedia resources. In version 2.0 the node Shape encapsulates both an Appearance node and a Geometry node.

Also, it is remarkable that the Appearance properties are not inherited during the scene graph traversal (see Chapter 8), but defined locally to the node they refer. Such a characteristic makes the description more verbose, but allows for graph optimization and efficient rendering of dynamic scenes in both parallel and distributed environments.

The nodes of type Geometry in VRML are the following:

1. Box, Cylinder, Cone and Sphere;
2. IndexedFaceSet;
3. IndexedLineSet;
4. PointSet;
5. Text;
6. Texture;
7. Elevation Grid;
8. Extrusion;
9. PROTO.

Several types of geometric nodes are predefined in VRML 2.0. In particular, Box nodes define parallelepipeds parallel to the local frame, Cylinder, Cone and Sphere give the corresponding geometric objects; IndexedFaceSet defines a set of polygons either in the boundary of a solid or in some open faceted surface; IndexedLineSet is used to define sets of polylines used to generate "wire frame" models; the PointSet node type is used for various purposes, including the definition of the elementary geometric data needed to support other primitives; the Text node is used to generate graphical text; the Texture node allows definition of how to map 2D images upon various surfaces, often resulting in greater scene realism. The nodes Elevation Grid and Extrusion are used to model terrain and extrusion solids, respectively.

The PROTO node supports the creation of user-defined new *types of nodes*, by specifying the list of attribute names, their types and predefined values. Also, the root of a scene subgraph can be associated with a name by the DEF node and then instanced several times in the scene by just invoking the name in a USE node.

### 7.1.6  Java 3D

*Java 3D* [SRD00, SN99], by Sun Microsystems, provides a vendor-neutral, platform-independent API which integrates with other Java APIs, and in particular with image processing, fonts, 2D drawing, user interfaces, and more. In particular, *Java 3D* enables high-level application development, where authors may focus upon content, and not on rendering.

*Java 3D* performs rendering optimizations by using 3D graphics hardware acceleration and parallel processing where available. Also it gives high-level scene management based on concepts of virtual universe, locales and scene graphs, which are hierarchical groupings of shapes. The application builds a set of scene graphs using *Java 3D* classes and methods. *Java 3D* renders those scene graphs onto the screen. The library gives content culling based upon visibility (view frustum), efficient pipeline use and scene compilation to achieve high performance. The low-level rendering operations are demanded on *OpenGL*. No polynomial or rational curves or surfaces are currently included in the *Java 3D* API. The geometry primitives in the library are summarized in the following.

1. Simple and striped geometry array types:

   (a) points;
   (b) lines;
   (c) triangles;
   (d) quadrilaterals.

2. Simple and striped indexed geometry array types:

   (a) indexed points;
   (b) indexed lines;
   (c) indexed triangles;
   (d) indexed quadrilaterals.

3. 3D extruded text.
4. Raster image sprites.

*Java 3D* has multiple types of geometry that use 3D coordinates: points, lines, triangles, and quadrilaterals, 3D extruded text, and raster image sprites. Geometry constructors differ in what they build, and how you tell *Java 3D* to build them. The approach exploits full power of object-oriented design. All geometry types are derived from the class Geometry. The class GeometryArray extends it to build set of points, lines, triangles, and quadrilaterals. Generic methods on GeometryArray also set colors and texture coordinates of vertices.

A vertex describes a polygon corner and contains: a 3D coordinate and optionally a color, a texture coordinate and a lighting normal vector. Polygons, which are defined by vertex ordering, have a front and a back. By default, only the front side of a polygon is rendered.

There are 14 different geometry array types grouped into classes SimpleGeometry, StripGeometry, IndexedSimpleGeometry and IndexedStripGeometry.

A PointArray class builds points at each vertex. A LineArray builds lines between each pair of vertices. A TriangleArray builds triangles between each triplet of vertices. A QuadArray builds quadrilaterals between each quadruple of vertices. Point size, line width and style as well as triangle and quadrilaterals rendering may be controlled by shape Appearance attributes.

## 7.2   Basic primitives

In this section we aim to discuss a small set of basic geometric primitives. We also quickly implement the primitives and give use examples. As the reader already knows, the PLaSM language actually defines only one predefined geometry constructor, called MKPOL, which stands for MakePolyhedron. The MKPOL primitive provides a very powerful constructor of polyhedral complexes of arbitrary intrinsic dimension $d$ embedded in spaces of arbitrary dimension $n$, with $d \leq n$. Most of basic primitives we introduce in this section are therefore implemented using the MKPOL geometric operator.

### 7.2.1   Points

A set of points in $\mathbb{E}^n$ may be seen as a 0-dimensional polyhedral complex. This kind of complex is generated by enforcing the constraint that all convex cells in the complex are singletons, i.e. just contain a single point. Hence a points primitive may be defined as a function from point sequences to 0-dimensional polyhedra:

$$\text{points} : (\mathbb{E}^n)^m \to \mathcal{P}^{0,n}, \qquad 1 \leq n, m$$

and implemented in PLaSM as in the following Script 7.2.1. Some examples of use of this primitive with points in different spaces $\mathbb{E}^n$ are shown in Example 7.2.1.

---

**Script 7.2.1 (Points primitive)**
```
DEF points = MKPOL ~ [ID, cells, pols]
WHERE
    cells = AA:LIST ~ INTSTO ~ LEN,
    pols = cells
END;
```

---

**Example 7.2.1 (Convex hulls)**
The convex hull of a set of polyhedral complexes is generated by the primitive operator JOIN, which is a function from polyhedra to polyhedra. Hence, the convex hulls of the 0-dimensional polyhedra produced by the points operator may be generated as, e.g.:

```
(JOIN ~ points):<<-2>,<0>,<0.3>,<10>,<-4.2>>;
(JOIN ~ points):<<0,-0.23>,<20,0>,<5.77,11>,<20,-10>>;
(JOIN ~ points):<<1,1,1,1>,<0.1,0.1,0.2,3>,<4,5,6.78,0>,<1,0,0,0>>;
```

It is interesting to note that the first and second expressions generate polyhedral complexes of full dimensionality, i.e. *solid* results in $\mathbb{E}^1$ and $\mathbb{E}^2$, respectively. Conversely, the last expression generates a simplex of dimension 3 in $\mathbb{E}^4$, depending on the number of input points.

**Example 7.2.2 (Graph points)**
The 3D function graph displayed in Figure 7.1 is generated by the last expression of Script 7.2.1, where the function dom generates an uniform sampling with $n+1$ numbers of the interval $[0, a]$. E.g., we have:

```
dom:1:8 ≡ <<0>,<1/8>,<1/4>,<3/8>,<1/2>,<5/8>,<3/4>,<7/8>,<1>>
```

Notice that the function [ID, SIN] $\sim$ S1 is evaluated by the MAP operator on the 0-dimensional polyhedral complex in $\mathbb{E}^1$ given by dom_0D, so producing a 0D complex in $\mathbb{E}^2$. This one is finally multiplied (Cartesian product of polyhedra, discussed in Section 14.4) for the $(1, 1)$ dimensional polyhedron Q:0.5, thus producing the result displayed. The points primitive is defined in Script 7.2.1; the Q operator is given in Script 7.3.11; the SumSeqWithZero in Script 7.3.1.

We note that the space orientation of the resulting complex depends on the ordering and dimensions of the Cartesian product arguments.

---

**Script 7.2.2 (Points primitive)**

```
DEF dom (a::IsReal)(n::IsInt) = (AA:LIST ~ SumSeqWithZero ~ #:n):(a/n);
DEF dom_0D = (points ~ dom:(2*PI)):50;

Q:0.5 * MAP:([ID, SIN] ~ S1):dom_0D
```

---

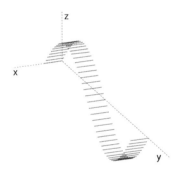

**Figure 7.1**   Polyhedral complex of dimension $(1, 3)$ generated by sampling the *sin* function with the points operator

### 7.2.2   Polyline

A polyline primitive is defined here as a function from sequences $(\mathbb{E}^n)^m$ of points in arbitrary Euclidean space $\mathbb{E}^n$, to the set of polyhedral complexes of intrinsic dimension 1 and embedded in $\mathbb{E}^n$:

$$\text{polyline} : (\mathbb{E}^n)^m \to \mathcal{P}^{1,n}, \qquad 1 \le n, 2 \le m.$$

The output is constituted by line segments $(\boldsymbol{p}_k, \boldsymbol{p}_{k+1})$, $1 \le k \le m - 1$, generated by pairs of subsequent points in the input sequence.

**Implementation**   A polyline function is given, starting from the operator MKPOL, which is the only geometric constructor defined as primitive in the PLaSM language. We remember from Section 1.5.1 that this operator accepts as input a triplet < points, cells, pols >, where points are the *vertices* of the output complex, cells are the vertex indices of each *convex cell* and pols are the convex cell indices of each *polyhedral cell*.

Two alternative definitions are given in Scripts 7.2.3 and 7.2.4, respectively, by using a $\lambda$-style and a proper FL style of functional programming. In the first case it is possible to use a predicate IsPointSeq to test the correctness of input data.

---

**Script 7.2.3 (Polyline: $\lambda$-style)**
```
    DEF IsPoint = IsVect;
    DEF IsPointSeq = AND ~ [IsSeqOf:IsPoint, EQ~AA:LEN];

    DEF polyline (points::IsPointSeq) = MKPOL:< points, cells, pols>
    WHERE
       cells = TRANS:< 1 .. (n - 1), 2 .. n >,
       pols = LIST:( 1 .. (n - 1) ),
       n = LEN:points
    END;
```

---

We like to note that this implementation is dimension-independent, i.e. that it works correctly with data points in Euclidean spaces $\mathbb{E}^n$ of arbitrary finite dimension $n$. In other words, the polyline function may produce polygonal lines in 1D, 2D, 3D, 4D, and so on.

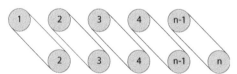

**Figure 7.2** Generation of a set of segments from the point sequence of a polyline

A graphical representation of the simple algorithm used in both the implementations of the function is shown in Figure 7.2. In particular, two sequences of indices, between 1 and $n - 1$ and between 2 and $n$, respectively, are generated and transposed, in order to produce the value of convex cells of the output.

---

**Script 7.2.4 (Polyline: proper FL style)**
```
    DEF polyline = MKPOL ~ [ID, cells, pols]
    WHERE
       cells = TRANS ~ AA:FROMTO ~ [[k:1, LEN - k:1],[k:2, LEN]],
       pols = LIST ~ INTSTO ~ (LEN - k:1)
    END;
```

---

**Example 7.2.3 (Multidimensional polyline)**
As we said, the output of such a function is a polyhedral complex of intrinsic dimension $d = 1$ embedded in $\mathbb{E}^n$, $d \leq n$, where $n$ is the (constant) number of coordinates of the

input points. For example, we may write in 1D, 2D and 3D, respectively:

```
polyline:<<1>,<2.5>,<3.999>,<4>>;
polyline:<<1,0,-5.1>,<1,1.2,0>,<0,2,-2>,<-1,-1.25,4>>;
polyline: <<0,0,0>,<0,1,0>,<0,1,1>,<1,1,1>,<1,0,1>,<1,0,0>,<0,0,0>>;
```

## Example 7.2.4 (Product of polylines)

The polyline operator is a first-class citizen in the world of functions. We show in Script 7.2.5 that a 2-dimensional grid of convex cells, as a single polyhedron decomposed into a complex of $10 \times 10$ connected quadrilaterals, may be generated as the Cartesian product of two 1D polylines. The coords_1D object contains a uniform sampling with 11 points of the interval $[0, \pi]$:

```
coords_1D ≡ <<0.0>, <0.3141592653589793>, <0.6283185307179586>,
    <0.9424777960769379>, <1.2566370614359172>, <1.5707963267948966>,
    <1.8849555921538759>, <2.199114857512855>, <2.5132741228718345>,
    <2.827433388230814>, <3.141592653589793>>
```

The polyhedral complex generated by grid_2D:coords_1D is shown in Figure 7.3.

We like to note here that the PLaSM language is dynamically typed. In fact the overloaded operator * is resolved only at run time, as a Cartesian product of polyhedral values.

A dimension-independent grid_nD generator operator, which may produce grids with hypercube $n$-cells of arbitrary finite n is finally given in Script 7.2.5.

---

## Script 7.2.5 (Polyline: multidimensional grid)

```
DEF coords_1D = (AA:LIST ∼ SumSeqWithZero ∼ #:10):(PI/10) ;
DEF grid_2D = polyline * polyline;
DEF grid_3D = polyline * polyline * polyline;

DEF grid_nD (n::IsInt) = (INSL:* ∼ #:n): polyline;
```

---

The 3d object displayed in Figure 7.3b is generated by evaluating either the expression (@2 ∼ grid_3D):coords_1D, or, by using the dimension-independent generator, as (@2 ∼ grid_nD:3):coords_1D.

## Example 7.2.5 (Non-uniform multidimensional grid)

The previous example produced a $n$-grid with a single set of coordinates in 1D. The obvious consequence is that all cells of such grids are $n$-cubes. To define a more flexible non-uniform $n$-grid where cells are $n$-parallelepipeds instead than $n$-cubes, we need to give as input to the generator function $n$ sequences of 1D points.

Notice the constraint that the coordinates of subsequent points $p_i = (x_i)$ in each 1D point sequence must be in increasing order:

$$x_1 \leq x_2 \ldots \leq x_{n-1} \leq x_n$$

Hence, in Script 7.2.6 the 1D point sequences are specified by giving the distance of each point from the previous one, and by using the Progressivesum function to compute the actual point coordinates.

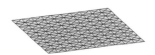
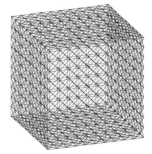

**Figure 7.3**  (a) Triangulation of the complex `grid_nD:2:coords_1D`
(b) Triangulation of the boundary of `grid_nD:3:coords_1D`

---

**Script 7.2.6 (Non-uniform grid)**

```
DEF nu_grid (data::IsSeq) =
   (INSL:* ~ AA:APPLY ~ DISTL):< polyline, data >;

DEF xcoods = (AA:LIST ~ Progressivesum):<0,1,1,1.5,0.9,0.1>;
DEF ycoods = (AA:LIST ~ Progressivesum):<0,0.5,1.5,1,1.5,0.2>;
DEF zcoods = (AA:LIST ~ Progressivesum):<0,0.5,2,1,1.5>;

nu_grid:< xcoods >;
nu_grid:< xcoods, ycoods >;
nu_grid:< xcoods, ycoods, zcoods >;
```

---

Notice also the dimension-independent use of the **nu_grid** operator. The last two expressions of Script 7.2.6 generate the 2D and 3D grids given in Figures 7.4a and 7.4b, respectively.

**Figure 7.4**  Triangulations of non-uniform grids: (a) 2D grid (b) boundary of a 3D grid

### 7.2.3  Polymarker

A 3D `polymarker` primitive is defined in this section. Such a primitive is similar to the one defined in the ISO GKS and PHIGS graphics standards. For the purpose of its definition, six different types of markers are given by using the MKPOL geometric primitive. The `polymarker` operator will simply instantiate the current marker type in each position of a given sequence of 3D points. The type of marker is defined by the actual value of the parameter `markerType`.

In a subsequent example the `polymarker` primitive is used to highlight a point sampling upon a helix curve. A `markerSize` attribute is also defined which is used to set the actual size of the graphics primitive.

**Marker attributes**  Six predefined marker shapes are given, as defined by the functions `Marker`$i$ in Script 7.2.7. The list of marker types is easily extensible with new markers. The shape of predefined markers is shown in Figure 7.5.

**Figure 7.5**   Geometric values associated to marker type 1 to 6, from left to right

---

**Script 7.2.7 (Definition of marker objects)**
```
DEF Marker1 (a,b::IsReal) = MKPOL:< <<a,0>,<0,a>,<b,0>,<0,b>>,
   <<1,2>,<2,3>,<3,4>,<4,1>>,<1..4> >;
DEF Marker2 (a,b::IsReal) = MKPOL:< <<a,a>,<b,a>,<b,b>,<a,b>>,
   <<1,3>,<2,4>>,<1..2> >;
DEF Marker3 (a,b::IsReal) = MKPOL:< <<a,a>,<b,a>,<b,b>,<a,b>>,
   <<1,2>,<2,3>,<3,4>,<4,1>>,<1..4> >;
DEF Marker4 = STRUCT ~ [Marker1, Marker2];
DEF Marker5 = STRUCT ~ [Marker1, Marker3];
DEF Marker6 = STRUCT ~ [Marker2, Marker3];
```

---

Only two main polymarker attributes are given here, and in particular the marker type and the marker size. The first one is implemented by the function `Marker` which depends on an input integer parameter. This function returns a 2D polyhedral output value. The second one is given by the constant `markerSize`. It can be easily abstracted, and given as a function depending on a real parameter. The definition of the `polymarker` primitive in script 7.2.9 should be updated accordingly. This is left as exercise to the reader.

---

**Script 7.2.8 (Polymarker attributes)**
```
DEF markerSize = 0.05;
DEF Marker (markerType::IsIntPos) = SEL: markerType:
   < marker1, marker2, marker3, marker4, marker5 >:<a,b>
WHERE
   a = markerSize, b = -:a
END;
```

---

**Definition**  The `polymarker` function constructs a hierarchical structure by translating an instance of the chosen marker type on each point contained in the sequence of points it is applied to. When used in a space of dimension $d \geq 3$, the markers are embedded, before translation, into the coordinate subspace $x_3 = \cdots = x_d = 0$.

---

**Script 7.2.9 (Polymarker primitive)**

```
DEF polymarker (markerType::IsIntPos) =
    STRUCT ~ AA:APPLY ~ DISTR ~ [AA:translation, embeddedSymbol]
WHERE
    translation = APPLY ~ [T ~ INTSTO ~ LEN,ID],
    embeddedSymbol = APPLY ~ [EMBED ~ (dim - K:2), K:(marker:markerType)],
    dim = LEN ~ S1
END;
```

---

The `polymarker` function is first applied to an integer defining the marker type, and then to the sequence of points where the marker must be mapped, e.g.:

```
polymarker:1:<<1,0>,<1,1>,<0,1>,<0,0>>
```

**Example 7.2.6 (Graph of a 2D function)**

It is easy to apply both a `polyline` and a `polymarker` to the same set of points. The graph, shown in Figure 7.2.6, of a sampling of the $\sin^2$ function in the interval $[0, 2\pi]$ may be produced as

```
graph:4:(SIN * SIN):abscissae;
```

where the `graph` function and the set of *abscissæ* (the word is Latin and plural) is given in Script 7.2.10. The `Progressivesum` function is instead given in Script 2.1.33. The geometric value generated by last expression as the graph of more function samplings is displayed in Figure 7.6. The `graph` function contemporary traces the `polyline` and `polymarker:2` relative to the same set of abscissae.

---

**Script 7.2.10 (Graph of function sampling)**

```
DEF abscissae = (C:AL:0 ~ ProgressiveSum ~ #:32):(2*PI/32);
DEF displaygraph (n::IsInt)(f::IsFun) =
    STRUCT ~ [polyline, polymarker:n] ~ AA:[ID,f];

(STRUCT ~ [displaygraph:1:SIN, displaygraph:2:COS, displaygraph:3:(SIN * COS)]):
    abscissae;
```

---

**Figure 7.6**    (a) Graph of $\sin^2$ in the interval $[0, 2\pi]$ (b) graphs of sin, cos and $\sin \cdot \cos$ functions in $[0, 2\pi]$

**Example 7.2.7 (Polymarker on 3D data points)**

The polymarker primitive is here applied to a set of points extracted from a 3D helix curve.

In particular, the helix symbol has as its value the simplicial complex in $\mathcal{P}^{1,3}$ generated by mapping the helix-generating function beta:<3,0.3> on the simplicial complex in $\mathcal{P}^{1,1}$ given by the expression intervals:(6*PI):90, i.e. on the partition with 90 segments of the real interval $[0, 6\pi]$.

Such complex is "unpacked", i.e. exported as a triplet of vertices, convex cells and polyhedral cells by the function UKPOL, and its vertices are extracted by S1 selector and given as input to the polymarker:1 primitive. The PLaSM code of the example is given in Script 7.2.11. The resulting object is shown in Figure 7.7.

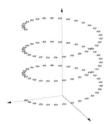

**Figure 7.7**   Application of polymarker:2 on a 3D helix curve

---

**Script 7.2.11 (3D polymarker example)**

```
DEF beta (a,b::IsReal) = [K:a * COS, K:a * SIN, K:b * ID] ~ S1;
DEF helix = MAP:(beta:<3,0.3>):(intervals:(6*PI):90);
DEF markerSize = 0.15;

(polymarker:1 ~ S1 ~ UKPOL):helix;
```

---

*7.2.4   Text*

A TEXT primitive is used to generate a 2D graphical text from a text string. In our geometric programming approach the output of the TEXT operator is a polyhedral complex, so that it can be subsequently handled by other geometric operators, as shown by various examples in the following paragraphs.

This primitive is normally enriched by several attributes. For example, the GKS graphics standard defines, among others, the following attributes:

1. The TextFont attribute is used to define the current font, i.e. the current set of definitions for character shaping. Fonts are actually classified into *vector* and *raster* fonts, depending on the type of representation of characters. In a raster font each character is represented as a properly dimensioned array of pixels, depending on the font size. In a vector font each character is codified as a subset of stroke primitives, and can be scaled to each desired dimension. Vector fonts (e.g. PostScript fonts) often use Beziér curves (see Section 11.2.4)

for this purpose.

2. The CharWidth and CharHeight attributes define the width and height of the grid which underlies the character design. They are given in world coordinates (see Chapter 9).

3. TextPrecision and TextAlignment respectively define the presentation precision (low, medium or high, with respect to the kind of text clipping[1] applied) and the type of text alignment (defined as left, centre or right).

4. The attributes TextAngle and TextDirection respectively control the *angle* of text presentation about an axis orthogonal to the text plane and passing for the text reference point, and the direction of vector *displacement* between subsequent characters. The possible values for TextDirection are left, right, up and down. The default value (normally used in printed text) is left.

5. A TextSlant attribute is used to italicize arbitrary character fonts, simply by applying a proper shearing matrix to each graphics text string.

6. A CharSpacing attribute is employed to control the spacing between pairs of adjacent characters in a string. A horizontal translation with CharSpacing + CharWidth parameter is hence inserted between character pairs.

7. A TextColor attribute clearly defines the current color to be used when drawing a graphics text string. The default value is black.

We will use a 1D vector font, given in Appendix A, denoted MyFont and defined as a sequence of $(1, 2)$-polyhedral complexes. Each character in the printable subset of the ASCII table, i.e. between ordinal numbers 32 and 126, is generated by one or more polylines. The definition of such a font should be considered only a graphics exercise. To generate an actual font would require both a better design of the font shape and a lot of optimizations. Anyway, this approach may be useful to quickly insert some annotation text into a geometric model generated by PLaSM.

**TEXT implementation** We discuss first a simpler implementation of the TEXT operator without taking into account text attributes. Notice that the predicate C:EQ can be used to compare both numbers and characters or strings.

The TEXT function must be applied to a string. The input is first transformed into its character sequence, then into the sequence of polyhedral characters extracted by selectPolChars function from the font. A suitable translation tensor is then DISTRibuted between the polyhedral characters, the output sequence is CATenated and aggregated by the STRUCT operator. The resulting hierarchical complex is finally "flattened" by the application of the optimize ≡ MKPOL ∼ UKPOL operator, whose result is that of destroying the internal hierarchy of data, and thus returning a more efficient representation of the generated polyhedral text.

The selectPolChars function transforms its input character sequence into the sequence of corresponding ordinal numbers, hence into a sequence of suitable selectors. A unique extractor function is then built by CONS, and this is APPLYed to the sequence MyFont of polyhedral characters given in Appendix A.

---

[1] The term *clipping* denotes a basic graphics operation used to cut the portions of a graphics primitive which (either totally or partially) fall outside the window area. A thorough discussion of clipping algorithms can be found in [Rog97].

Notice that the IF function is applied to each character in the input sequence, in order to filter the $'\sqcup'$ (*blank*) characters, which otherwise would give problems when applying further geometric operators to the polyhedral text, since the blank character does not contain valid geometric data.

---

**Script 7.2.12 (Text primitive)**

```
DEF selectPolChars = APPLY ~ [
    CONS ~ AA:(IF:< C:EQ:'⊔', (K ~ K):(T:1:0), SEL ~ (ORD - K:31) >) ,
    K:MyFont ]

DEF TEXT = optimize ~ STRUCT ~ CAT
    ~ DISTR ~ [ selectPolChars, K:(T:1:(1.25 * fontWidth)) ] ~ CHARSEQ;
```

---

A more complex implementation of the TEXT primitive is given in Script 7.2.13 by the function TextWithAttributes, which also takes into account the TextAlignment, as well as the TextAngle, TextWidth, TextHeight and TextSpacing. Its semantics may be understood by comparison with the TEXT function provided in Script 7.2.12, whose component functions are given *italicized* in the TextWithAttributes body. Therefore, let us discuss only the differences between them.

The first is in the size TextWidth + TextSpacing of the translation interposed between the (polyhedral translation) of characters. Then, the only polyhedra in the sequence are scaled with parameters TextWidth / FontWidth and TextHeight / FontHeight. Later, a suitable translation (computed by the SIZE:1 of the polyhedral text) is applied if the TextAlignment attribute is either $'right'$ or $'centre'$. Finally, a plane rotation of parameter TextAngle is applied to the output.

---

**Script 7.2.13 (Text primitive with attributes)**

```
DEF TextWithAttributes (TextAlignment::IsString;
    TextAngle, TextWidth, TextHeight, TextSpacing::IsReal) =
optimize ~ R:<1,2>:TextAngle
    ~ IF:< K:(TextAlignment EQ 'centre'),
        APPLY ~ [T:1 ~ / ~ [SIZE:1,K:-2],ID],
        IF:< K:(TextAlignment EQ 'right'),
            APPLY ~ [T:1 ~ - ~ SIZE:1,ID] , ID > >
    ~ STRUCT ~ CAT ~ DISTR
    ~ [ AA:(IF:<IsPOL, S:<1,2>:< TextWidth/FontWidth,
        TextHeight/FontHeight >, ID >)
        ~ selectPolChars, K:(T:1:(TextWidth + TextSpacing)) ] ~ CHARSEQ;

DEF TEXT = TextWithAttributes:< 'LEFT', 0, 1, 3/2, 1/2 >;

TextWithAttributes:< 'centre', PI/4, 1, 1, 0.5 >:'Hello, PLaSM World !';
TEXT:'Hello, PLaSM World !';
```

---

Furthermore, note that the TEXT operator was redefined, by using the TextWithAttributes function and by giving suitable default values for text attributes. In Figure 7.2.14 we shown the value produced by evaluation of Script 7.2.14. The

**Figure 7.8** The vector character design of `MyFont` font

`rotatedText` functions is an abstraction, parametrized respect to the TextAngle, and where the other attributes have fixed values. A sequence of angle values is generated by the last expression, and the corresponding set of rotated text strings is produced and displayed in Figure 7.9.

---

**Script 7.2.14 (Centered and rotated text)**

```
DEF rotatedText (alpha::IsReal) =
   TextWithAttributes:< 'centre', alpha, 1, 2, 0.25 >;

STRUCT:((CONS ~ AA:rotatedText ~ SumSeqWithZero ~ #:16):(PI/8):
   'Hello, PLaSM World !');
```

---

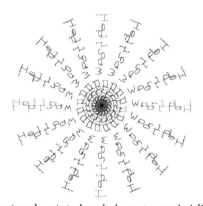

**Figure 7.9** The centered, rotated and character-scaled 'Hello PLaSM Word !'

**Example 7.2.8 (Hello, PLaSM World !)**

In Figure 7.10 we show how to use the TEXT primitive to obtain some modified font aspects. In particular, Figure 7.10 shows the VRML of the geometric value produced by evaluating the PLaSM expression given in the second part of Script 7.2.15. The Q function, given in Script 1.5.5, is used as a synonym of the QUOTE operator working both on numeric sequences and on single numbers. The Slanted function just produces a shearing tensor to be applied to the polyhedral output of the TEXT operator.

The EMBED:1 operator is required to mix in the same hierarchical output both 2D polyhedral complexes and 3D polyhedral complexes. Notice that each row of the generating expression (after the STRUCT row, say) produces one of the images in Figure 7.10.

---

**Script 7.2.15 (Hello)**

```
DEF Slanted = optimize ~ MAT:<<1,0,0>,<0,1,-0.25>,<0,0,1>>;

( STRUCT ~ [
    EMBED:1, K:(T:2:-2),
    EMBED:1 ~ OFFSET:<1/8,1/8>, K:(T:2:-2),
    EMBED:1 ~ SWEEP:<1/8,1/8>, K:(T:2:-2),
    EMBED:1 ~ Slanted ~ OFFSET:<1/8,1/8>, K:(T:2:-2),
    * ~ [ID, K:(Q:3)] ~ Slanted ~ OFFSET:<1/8,1/8> ]
  ~ TEXT ): 'Hello, PLaSM World !';
```

---

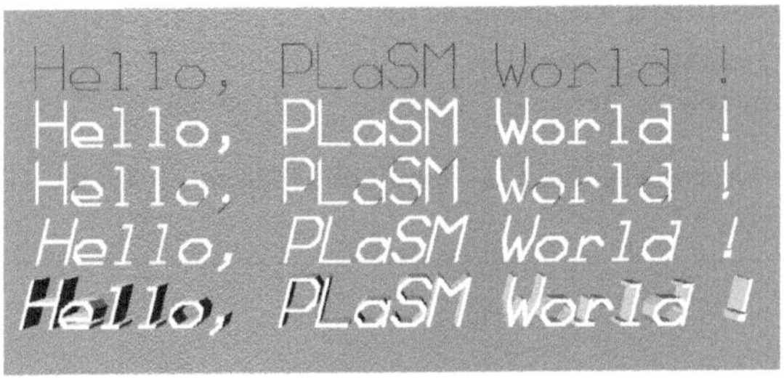

**Figure 7.10**    (a) Vector text (b) Offset text (c) Swept text (d) Slanted offset text
(e) Extruded slanted offset text

---

**Example 7.2.9 (String solidifier)**

It may be useful to transform a (multiline) text string into a solid polyhedral complex. This task is performed by the solidifier operator given in Script 7.2.16. The used algorithm is very simple:

1. The input string is transformed into the sequence of single line strings it is composed of, by the action of the operator StringTokens:< CHAR:13 >, defined in Script 2.1.25. Remember that CHAR:13 is the ASCII character CR (carriage return).
2. The sequence of line strings is reversed by the operator REVERSE.
3. Each string is transformed into a $(1,2)$–polyhedral complex by the TEXT operator and then a suitable thickness is given to characters by the operator OFFSET:<0.5,0.25>.
4. A vertical translation is distributed among the various solid text strings, then they are aggregated by the STRUCT operator, and finally an extrusion of depth 3 is applied by the operator resulting from the evaluation of the expression * ~ [ID, K:(Q:3)], where Q is the operator given in Script 1.5.5.

A funny example of this operator, entitled "the solidified solidifier", is shown in Script 7.2.16 and Figure 7.11, where the `solidifier` operator is applied to its own definition. Both the TEXT and the `solidifier` operators may be used to add textual annotations to drawings and geometric models.

---

**Script 7.2.16 (Solidifier)**
```
solidifier: 'DEF solidifier = * ~ [ID, K:(Q:3)]
   ~ STRUCT ~ CAT ~ DISTR
   ~ [ AA:(OFFSET:<0.5,0.25> ~ TEXT)
      ~ REVERSE
      ~ StringTokens:< CHAR:13 >,
   K:(T:2:8) ] ;'
```

---

**Figure 7.11**   The solidified `solidifier`

### 7.2.5   Triangle strip

The triangle strip primitive was first introduced by the PHIGS+ extension [ANSI87] of the ISO graphics standard. This primitive revealed to be very useful with 3D graphics, because (a) all surfaces are linearly approximated by triangulations; and (b) a set of $n - 2$ pairwise-adjacent triangles can be specified, using this primitive, by only $n$ ordered points. In particular, the $k$-th triangle is generated by points $p_k$, $p_{k+1}$ and $p_{k+2}$. A further computational benefit is obtained when some transformation is applied to such a primitive. Only $n$ points are in fact transformed, instead of $3(n-2)$ vertices.

We define the triangleStrip primitive in a dimension-independent way, as a function from sequences of points to polyhedra, where the points in the input sequence may belong to any $\mathbb{E}^d$, with $2 \leq d$. The primitive output is a 2-dimensional polyhedral complex embedded in $\mathbb{E}^d$. Hence we have

$$\text{triangleStrip} : (\mathbb{E}^d)^n \to \mathcal{P}^{2,d}, \qquad 2 \leq d,\ 3 \leq n$$

where $(\mathbb{E}^d)^n$ is the set of sequences of at least 3 $d$-points.

**Implementation**   The implementation given in Script 7.2.17 is done using the proper FL style, i.e. without using formal parameters. When the triangleStrip function is applied to some sequence of points, first the function [ID, cells, pols] is applied to points, then the resulting triplet is passed to the MKPOL function, thus generating the output polyhedral complex.

---

**Script 7.2.17 (triangleStrip: proper FL style)**
```
DEF triangleStrip = MKPOL ~ [ID, cells, pols]
WHERE
    cells = TRANS ~ AA:FROMTO ~ [[k:1, LEN-k:2],[k:2, LEN-k:1],[k:3, LEN]],
    pols = LIST ~ INTSTO ~ (LEN - k:2)
END;
```

---

The cells function works very similarly to the one we discussed in Script 7.2.4 to implement the polyline primitive. In this case its creates a sequence of triples of point indices, according to the scheme shown in Figure 7.12.

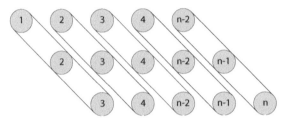

**Figure 7.12**   Generation of a set of triangles from the point sequence of triangleStrip

## Example 7.2.10 (Polygon with hole)

A multiply connected plane polygon is generated here by giving a well-formed triangulation of it, i.e. a simplicial complex (see Section 13.3.1) which partitions the polygon, and by describing this triangulation as a triangleStrip.

Notice that the description as a triangleStrip is quite efficient with respect to storage requirements. In this case the described shape has 8 vertices. The input point sequence is conversely made up of 10 vertices, in order to allow the "glueing" of first and last triangle. Notice in particular, from Figure 7.13, that we have:

$$p_1 = p_{n-1} \quad \text{and} \quad p_2 = p_n.$$

The polygon with hole is generated by the PLaSM expression

```
triangleStrip:
    <<0,3>,<1,2>,<3,3>,<2,2>,<3,0>,<2,1>,<0,0>,<1,1>,<0,3>,<1,2>>
```

## Example 7.2.11 (2D house front)

Two different triangulations of a simplified 2D house front are given in Scripts 7.2.18 and 7.2.19, respectively. The first triangulation is not a simplicial complex (see

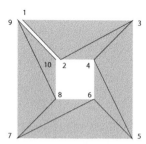

**Figure 7.13** The ordering of triangleStrip vertices which produces a 2D solid polygon with a hole

---

**Script 7.2.18 (House front triangulation)**
```
DEF house1 = triangleStrip: <
    <4,4>,<5,4>,<4,0>,<5,2>,<8,0>,<6,2>,<8,6>, <6,4>,<4,8>,
    <5,4>,<0,6>,<2,4>,<0,0>,<2,0> >;
```

---

Section 13.3.1), because two of triangles have an intersection which is not an edge of both, as shown by Figure 7.2.11a.

Conversely, the triangulation given in Script 7.2.19 is a simplicial complex, i.e. a well-formed triangulation, where each pair of triangles either do not intersect or share a common edge or vertex. To use a simplicial complex in a triangle strip may be more convenient, since it allows, for example, to correctly represent a multiply connected polygon. Look, for this purpose, at Figure 7.14.

---

**Script 7.2.19 (House front complex)**
```
DEF house2 = triangleStrip: <
    <5,4>,<4,4>,<5,2>,<4,0>,<6,2>,<8,0>,<6,4>,
    <8,6>,<5,4>,<4,8>,<4,4>,<0,6>,<2,4>,<0,0>,<2,0> >
```

---

**Example 7.2.12 (Multiply connected boundary)**
When a geometric object is defined in PLaSM by using a triangleStrip primitive with 2D input points, then the generated polygon in $\mathcal{P}^{2,2}$ is said to be *solid*.[2] In this case the geometric kernel of the language stores in the internal data structure all the adjacencies between the triangles of the strip. This fact allows extraction of the *boundary* of the polygon, both external and internal, by using the 1-skeleton extractor operator.

Hence in Script 7.2.20 we extrude the boundary of the **house2** polygon generated in Script 7.2.19 with a **triangleStrip** operator.

*7.2.6 Triangle fan*

The triangle fan primitive produces $n - 2$ triangles from an ordered sequence of $n$ points. In particular, the $k$-th triangle is generated as the convex hull of points $p_1$,

---

[2] I.e. fully-dimensional, since the *intrinsic* dimension is equal to the *embedding* dimension.

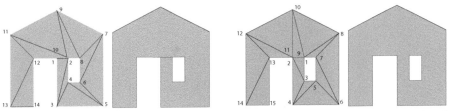

**Figure 7.14**    (a) Sequence of triangleStrip vertices not corresponding to a simplicial complex (b) Generated polygon (c) Sequence of triangleStrip vertices which correspond to a simplicial complex (d) Generated polygon

---

**Script 7.2.20 (House boundary complex)**
```
DEF object1 = @1:house2 * Q:1;
DEF object2 = STRUCT:< object1, EMBED:1:house2 >;
```

---

$p_{k+1}$ and $p_{k+2}$.

We define the triangleFan primitive as a function from sequences of points in any $\mathbb{E}^d$, with $2 \leq d$, to polyhedral complexes . The output is a 2-dimensional polyhedral complex in $\mathbb{E}^d$. More formally:

$$\texttt{triangleFan} : (\mathbb{E}^d)^n \to \mathcal{P}^{2,d}, \qquad 2 \leq d,\ 3 \leq n$$

where $(\mathbb{E}^d)^n$ is the set of sequences which contain at least 3 $d$-points.

The implementation of this primitive is given in Script 7.2.21.

**Example 7.2.13 (Star shaped polygons)**
In computational geometry the *kernel* of a polygon is the subset of points which see every polygon point. Two points see each other if the segment which connects them is contained in the polygon closure, i.e. in the union of polygon interior and boundary. A polygon is said to be *star shaped* if its kernel is non-empty.

A function star from integers to 2D polyhedral complexes, such that star:$n$ produces a star polygon with $n$ tips is given in Script 7.2.22.

The circlePoints function is used to generate n points on the circle of radius r centered on the origin and with initial angle startAngle.

The body of the star function is very simple. Two sets of n 2D points are generated, that correspond to the lower and upper vertices of the star tips. Their matrix is transposed and catenated, so generating the input sequence to the triangleFan primitive. The output of the last expression is shown in Figure 7.16a.

**Figure 7.15**    (a) object1 value: extruded boundary of a multiply connected triangleStrip (b) object2 value

**Script 7.2.21 (Triangle fan)**

```
DEF triangleFan (verts::IsSeq) = MKPOL:< verts, cells, pols >
WHERE
   row1 = #:(n - 2):1,
   row2 = 2..(n - 1),
   row3 = 3..n,
   cells = TRANS:< row1, row2, row3 >,
   pols = <1..(n - 2)>,
   n = LEN:verts
END;
```

**Script 7.2.22 (Star operator)**

```
DEF circlePoints (startAngle::IsReal)(r::IsReal)(n::IsInt) =
   AA:([K:r * cos, K:r * sin] ~ (ID + K:startAngle)):
      ((AA:* ~ TRANS ~ [K:(1..n), #:n]):(2*PI/n));

DEF star (n::IsInt) = (triangleFan ~ CAT ~ TRANS):<
   circlePoints:0:1:n,
   circlePoints:(PI/n):2.5:n >;

(STRUCT ~ [@1 * K:(Q:0.5), EMBED:1] ~ star):5
```

*7.2.7   Quadrilateral mesh*

The *quadrilateral mesh* primitive, often called quadMesh, is constituted by a 2D array of $(m - 1) \times (n - 1)$ quadrilaterals, defined by a grid $m \times n$ of vertices.

Four points in 3D are not guaranteed to be coplanar. Conversely, three points are always coplanar in any $\mathbb{E}^d$, with $2 \le d$. Hence each quadruple of adjacent points (which define a quadrilateral on the input mesh) is used to build two triangles, according to the fixed scheme shown in Figure 7.17a.

The QUADMESH operator, with

$$\text{QUADMESH} : \mathcal{M}_n^m(\mathbb{E}^d) \to \mathcal{P}^{2,d}, \qquad 2 \le d, m, n$$

where $\mathcal{M}_n^m(\mathbb{E}^d)$ is a space of matrices with $m$ row and $n$ columns of points in $\mathbb{E}^d$, $d$ is the number of coordinates of points, and $\mathcal{P}^{2,d}$ is the space of polyhedral complexes of intrinsic dimension 2 embedded in a $d$-dimensional space, is implemented in PLaSM by using the primitive geometry constructor MKPOL.

 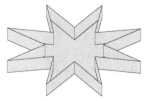

**Figure 7.16**   Polyhedral complexes generated by language expressions using the star:$n$ function

**QuadMesh implementation**   A predicate `IsPointMat` is first given, by using the predicate `IsPointSeq` already introduced in Script 7.2.3.

The implementation works by generating a value for the three components of the input to the operator `MKPOL`. The sequence `verts` of output vertices is easily generated by catenating the rows of input `points` matrix. Then the sequence of output convex `cells` is built by generating a sequence of triples of indices to adjacent vertices, following the scheme shown in Figure 7.17a. The sequence `pols` of polyhedral cells is given trivially.

Notice that a pair of triangular cells is associated with each point in the upper-left $(m-1) \times (n-1)$ submatrix of points. In particular, with each point $\boldsymbol{p}_{h,k}$, with $h \in \{1, \dots, m-1\}$ and $k \in \{1, \dots, n-1\}$, are associated two triangles

$$t^1_{h,k} = (\boldsymbol{p}_{h,k}, \boldsymbol{p}_{h+1,k+1}, \boldsymbol{p}_{h+1,k}), \qquad \text{and} \qquad t^2_{h,k} = (\boldsymbol{p}_{h,k}, \boldsymbol{p}_{h+1,k+1}, \boldsymbol{p}_{h,k+1}).$$

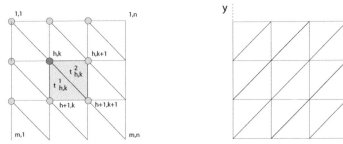

**Figure 7.17**   (a) Algorithmic scheme of `QUADMESH` (b) 2D grid generated by `QUADMESH` on a $4 \times 4$ grid of integer 2D points

**Algorithm**   The generative algorithm of the 2D output complex can be roughly decomposed into the following steps:

1. Compute the `m` and `n` numbers of rows and columns of the `points` matrix.
2. Compute the full sequence `pairSeq` of pairs of indices corresponding to the subset of $(m-1) \times (n-1)$ upper-left submatrix of input points. For example:

   `Cart:<1..2, 1..3> ≡ <<1,1>,<1,2>,<1,3>,<2,1>,<2,2>,<2,3>>`

   The implementation of the `Cart` operator is given in Script 2.1.17.
3. Define a function to transform any of such pairs to the index of the corresponding element stored into the 1-dimensional sequence `verts` of vertices. The standard function

$$\{1, \dots, m\} \times \{1, \dots, n\} \to \{1, \dots, mn\} : (h, k) \mapsto n \times (h-1) + k,$$

   for constant-time access to $(m \times n)$-array elements stored by rows, is used at this purpose, and named `address`. E.g., with respect to the example of previous point 2, we would have:

   `AA:address:<<1,2>,<1,3>,<2,3>> ≡ < 2, 3, 6 >`

4. The set of convex `cells` (as sequences of vertex indices) is hence generated by applying the function `[t1,t2]` to the `pairSeq` sequence.
5. The sequence `pols` of polyhedral cells is finally defined as constituted by a single element made by all the convex cells.

---

**Script 7.2.23 (Quadrilateral mesh)**
```
DEF IsPointMat = AND ~ [IsSeqOf:IsPointSeq, EQ~AA:LEN];

DEF QUADMESH (points::IsPointMat) = MKPOL:< verts, cells, pols >
WHERE
    m = LEN:points,
    n = (LEN ~ S1):points,
    pairSeq = Cart:<1..(m - 1), 1..(n - 1)>,
    address = K:n * (S1 - K:1) + S2,
    t1 = AA:address ~ [[S1,S2], [S1+K:1,S2+K:1], [S1+K:1,S2]],
    t2 = AA:address ~ [[S1,S2], [S1+K:1,S2+K:1], [S1,S2+K:1]],
    verts = CAT:points,
    cells = CAT:(AA:[t1,t2]:pairSeq),
    pols  = LIST:(1..((m - 1) * (n - 1) * 2))
END;
```

---

**Example 7.2.14 (Integer 2D grid)**
A simple use of the `QUADMESH` operator is demonstrated in this example. In this case a $4 \times 4$ matrix of 2D points with integer coordinates is given as input to the function `QUADMESH`, so generating a 2D polyhedral complex embedded in 2D plane. The 1-dimensional skeleton of this object is also extracted in Script 7.2.24, in order to highlight the pattern of triangles generated by the primitive, which is shown in Figure 7.17b.

---

**Script 7.2.24 (Integer grid)**
```
(@1 ~ QUADMESH):<
    <<0,0>,<1,0>,<2,0>,<3,0>>,
    <<0,1>,<1,1>,<2,1>,<3,1>>,
    <<0,2>,<1,2>,<2,2>,<3,2>>,
    <<0,3>,<1,3>,<2,3>,<3,3>>
>;
```

---

Notice in Figure 7.17 that the element $p_{1,1}$ of the input point grid is located, according to its coordinates, in the lower-left corner of the object. Conversely, in the algorithmic scheme of Figure 7.17a, that point is located in the upper-left corner, according to the standard ordering of the elements of a matrix.

**Example 7.2.15 (Fan object)**
The `QUADMESH` primitive is used here to generate the `fan` model shown in Figure 7.18. For this purpose a matrix < `row1`, `row2`, `row3` > of 3D points is built in Script 7.2.25.

In particular, each of the three rows contains 22 points. The first and second coordinates of each point are generated by applying an appropriate function to the `angles` sequence. E.g., the more external set of points (i.e. `row1`) has $x$ and $y$ coordinate generated by the expression

```
AA:[K:6*cos, K:6*sin]:angles;
```

The $z$ coordinates of points in each row are contained into the `z` sequence. The 3D sequences are generated by the action of infix binary operator `AA:AR~TRANS`.

---

**Script 7.2.25 (Fan object)**
```
DEF angles = (PI/-4) AA:+~DISTL (((PI/2)/21) AA:*~DISTL (0..21));

DEF fan = QUADMESH:< row1, row2, row3 >
WHERE
    row1 = AA:[K:6*cos, K:6*sin]:angles AA:AR~TRANS z,
    row2 = AA:[K:0.5*cos, K:0.5*sin]:angles AA:AR~TRANS z,
    row3 = AA:[K:0.5*cos - K:1, K:0.5*sin]:angles AA:AR~TRANS z,
    z = ##:11:<0.2,-0.2>
END;
```

---

Remember that `AR` (*append right*) has equational semantics:

$$< y_1, y_2, \ldots, y_n > \text{ AR } x \equiv < y_1, y_2, \ldots, y_n \ x > .$$

In order to fully understand the example, the reader should try to evaluate each sub-expression of the `angles` body. Notice that both `AA:+~DISTL` and `AA:*~DISTL` functions are used infix. As a further exercise, the reader should parametrize the example, by defining `fan` as a function of the opening angle.

**Figure 7.18**   Interesting use of the `QUADMESH` primitive: the `fan` object

## 7.3   Quotient set of polylines

Polygonal lines are the first and simplest geometric tool encountered by graphics users. Standard definition [FvDFH90] says that a polyline is a finite and ordered sequence (of arbitrary length) of points in the Euclidean space $\mathbb{E}^d$, $d = 2, 3$. Other representations are given as a piecewise-linear polynomial curve or as a finite sequence of tangent vectors, sometime defined in 2D using local circular coordinates (turned angle, length), as in the so-called "turtle-graphics". Similar representations, e.g. the "Freeman's code" [Hor89], can be found in vision and pattern recognition when encoding the shape of lines which live in a finite digital space.

**Linear space**   We show that if the attention is restricted to the set of polygonal lines with a given finite number of line segments, then a very useful algebraic structure can be given to them, by properly defining a commutative and associative addition and a scalar multiplication with the standard properties. In particular, the set of $n$-sided polylines can be partitioned into a set $S^n$ of equivalence classes with respect to a relation of parallelism, which actually reduces to translate the first vertex into the origin. It is easy to see that such a quotient set of $n$-shapes is a $n$–dimensional vector space where all the objects can be obtained as linear combination of $n$ generators in the set.

Such algebraic structure allows for a simple treatment of several questions concerning shapes. In particular, it can be shown that the various definitions of a polyline actually reduce to different choices of coordinates for such a space. One can also give a simple and sound algebraic formulation of some problems of current interest in graphics and pattern recognition. This is done here for the definition of both linear and curved *visual morphisms*, i.e. for the interpolation between a given set of "key" shapes, and for the computation of a *resemblance measure* between shapes. Other problems, e.g the finding the nearest relative "placement" of two polygonal curves, may also be approached in the same way.

### 7.3.1   Basic definitions

A set $R \subset S^2$ of pairs of elements of a set $S$ is called binary *relation $R$ on $S$*. If $R$ is reflexive, symmetric and transitive, it is called an *equivalence relation*. The elements of $S$ are divided by $R$ into classes of equivalent elements. If $a \in S$, the set

$$[a]_R := \{x \in S | (a, x) \in R\}$$

is called the *equivalence class* of $a$ with respect to $R$. The set

$$S/R := \{[a]_R | a \in S\}$$

is called the *quotient set* of $S$ by $R$. The equivalence classes $[a]_R$ give a partition of $S$, since they are pairwise disjointed, and their union is $S$. Therefore, a quotient set $S/R$ gives an abstract view of $S$ where equivalent elements are identified.

**Quotient set of polylines**   Let us consider the set $\mathcal{P}^n$ of $n$-sided *polygonal lines* or *polylines* of Euclidean plane $\mathbb{E}^2$. Each polyline $L \in \mathcal{P}^n$ is defined as an ordered sequence $(\boldsymbol{p}_i)$ of points $\boldsymbol{p}_i = (x_i, y_i)^T \in \mathbb{E}^2$, such that any pair of consecutive points defines a linear parametric curve $\boldsymbol{p}_i + \alpha(\boldsymbol{p}_{i+1} - \boldsymbol{p}_i)$, with $\alpha \in [0, 1]$, $0 \le i \le n - 1$.

Two $n$-sided polylines $L$ and $L'$ will be said to be *parallel* if there exists a vector $\boldsymbol{t} = (t_1, t_2)^T \in \mathbb{R}^2$ such that, for all $\boldsymbol{p}_i \in L$ and $\boldsymbol{p}'_i \in L'$:

$$\boldsymbol{p}'_i - \boldsymbol{p}_i = \boldsymbol{t}.$$

The relation of parallelism between two polylines $L$ and $L'$ will be written $L \parallel L'$. The relation of parallelism is an *equivalence relation*. The quotient set $S^n = \mathcal{P}^n / \parallel$ will be called the set of $n$-sided *polygonal shapes* or simply *n-shapes*.

**Characterization**   An $n$-shape $s$ can be represented as a pair of $n$-tuples of reals, so that $S^n$ is isomorphic to $\mathbb{R}^n \times \mathbb{R}^n$. In fact, consider any two shapes $[L]$ and $[L']$ in $\mathcal{P}^n$, with $L = (\boldsymbol{p}_i)$ and $L' = (\boldsymbol{p}'_i)$. $[L] = [L']$ implies that it is $\boldsymbol{p}'_i = \boldsymbol{p}_i + t$, i.e. $x'_i = x_i + t_1$ and $y'_i = y_i + t_2$, for each $i$.

In other words, the differences $X_i, Y_i$ of consecutive coordinates are invariant over the equivalence class:

$$\begin{aligned} X_i &= x_i - x_{i-1} = x'_i - x'_{i-1}, & 1 \le i \le n, \\ Y_i &= y_i - y_{i-1} = y'_i - y'_{i-1}, & 1 \le i \le n. \end{aligned}$$

Hence, the $n$-tuples $X = (X_i)$ and $Y = (Y_i)$ can be assumed as representative of the whole class $[L]$ of parallel $n$-sided polylines. The set of $n$-shapes is so defined as

$$S^n = \{s = (X, Y) \in \mathbb{R}^n \times \mathbb{R}^n\}.$$

Conversely, a representation of a shape $s = (X, Y)$ in $S^n$ as a polyline $L = (\boldsymbol{p}_i)$ in $\mathcal{P}^n$ such that $[L] = s$ is obtained by setting $\boldsymbol{p}_0 = (0, 0)$ and

$$\boldsymbol{p}_i = (x_i, y_i) = \left(\sum_{k=1}^{i} X_k, \sum_{k=1}^{i} Y_k\right) = \boldsymbol{p}_{i-1} + (X_i, Y_i), \qquad 1 \le i \le n.$$

We call *geometric support* $|s|$ or simply *support* of a shape $s = [L] \in S^n$, with $L = (\boldsymbol{p}_i)$, the set of points defined as

$$|s| = \{\boldsymbol{q} \in \mathbb{E}^2 : \boldsymbol{q} = (1 - \alpha)\,\boldsymbol{p}_{i-1} + \alpha\,\boldsymbol{p}_i,\ 1 \le i \le n,\ \alpha \in [0, 1]\}.$$

### Example 7.3.1 (Shape representation)

We give in Script 7.3.1 the implementation of some basic functions, useful to work with $n$-shapes.

A predicate `IsShape` is given as a synonym of the predicate `IsMat`, given in Script 3.3.3, since a shape is represented by a series of sequences of equal length of numbers.

Then some conversion operators are given. In particular, `points2shape` (to read *points-to-shape*) transforms a sequence of $d$-dimensional points into a $d$-dimensional shape, whereas `shape2points` executes the reverse operation. We note that, in general,

$$\texttt{shape2points} \sim \texttt{points2shape} \ne \texttt{ID},$$

since a shape $s = [L]$ is just represented by the representative $L$ for the origin of the class of parallel polylines which correspond to it.

The conversion operation `shape2pol` produces a polyhedral complex corresponding to the geometric support of the input shape.

The `Progressivesum` function is defined in Script 2.1.33; the `rtail`, `VectDiff` and `polyline` function are given in Scripts 4.2.5, 3.1.2 and 7.2.3, respectively.

**Script 7.3.1 (Points to shape)**
```
DEF SumSeqWithZero = C:AL:0 ~ Progressivesum;

DEF IsShape = IsMat;
DEF points2shape = TRANS ~ AA:VectDiff ~ TRANS ~ [TAIL, rtail];
DEF shape2points = TRANS ~ AA:SumSeqWithZero;
DEF shape2pol = polyline ~ shape2points;
```

**Operations on $n$-shapes**   Operations of *addition* (denoted by +) and *multiplication by a scalar* $\alpha \in \mathbb{R}$ (denoted by juxtaposition) are defined componentwise on $S^n$:

$$
\begin{aligned}
s + r &= (X, Y) + (U, W) = (X + U, Y + W) \\
&= ((X_i + U_i), (Y_i + W_i)) \quad\quad (7.1) \\
\alpha s &= \alpha(X, Y) = (\alpha X, \alpha Y) = ((\alpha X_i), (\alpha Y_i)) \quad\quad (7.2)
\end{aligned}
$$

It is noted that similar operations cannot be defined on the subset of polylines in $\mathcal{P}^{1,n}$, since addition of points as well as multiplication of a point times a scalar do not make sense.

A *join* operation $\oplus : S^n \times S^m \to S^{n+m}$, which allows appending a shape to another one, is defined as:

$$(X, Y) \oplus (U, W) \mapsto (S, T),$$

with

$$
\begin{aligned}
S_i = X_i, \quad\quad &T_i = Y_i, \quad\quad &1 \le i \le n \\
S_i = U_{i-n}, \quad\quad &T_i = W_{i-n}, \quad\quad &n + 1 \le i \le n + m
\end{aligned}
$$

This operation is linear and associative, but not commutative.

Two binary *swapping* operations $\wedge_{12}$ and $\wedge_{21}$ on the set $S^n$ will be useful in the remainder. Such operations combine two shapes, giving a new shape whose horizontal and vertical components are alternatively taken from the two arguments. In particular, the components of the arguments $s = (X, Y)$ and $r = (U, W)$ are combined as follows:

$$s \wedge_{12} r = (X, Y) \wedge_{12} (U, W) = (X, W),$$

$$s \wedge_{21} r = (X, Y) \wedge_{21} (U, W) = (U, Y).$$

For any $s = (X, Y) \in S^n$, two right-angled shapes with a double number of sides are defined as follows:

$$s^{inf} = \sigma_0(s) \wedge_{12} \sigma_1(s)$$

$$s^{sup} = \sigma_0(s) \wedge_{21} \sigma_1(s)$$

where

$$\sigma_0 : \mathbb{R}^n \times \mathbb{R}^n \to (\{0\} \times \mathbb{R})^n \times (\{0\} \times \mathbb{R})^n : ((X_i), (Y_i)) \mapsto ((0, X_i), (0, Y_i))$$

$$\sigma_1 : \mathbb{R}^n \times \mathbb{R}^n \to (\mathbb{R} \times \{0\})^n \times (\mathbb{R} \times \{0\})^n : ((X_i), (Y_i)) \mapsto ((X_i, 0), (Y_i, 0))$$

**Example 7.3.2 (Operations)**
The binary functions ShapeSum and ShapeProd in Script 7.3.2 implement the sum of
shapes and their product times a scalar, respectively.

---

**Script 7.3.2 (Algebraic operations)**

```
DEF ShapeSum (p,q::IsShape) = < VectSum:< X, U >, VectSum:< Y, W > >
WHERE
    X = s1:p, Y = s2:p,
    U = s1:q, W = s2:q
END;

DEF ShapeProd (alpha::IsReal; p::IsShape) =
    < ScalarVectProd:< alpha, X >, Scalarvectprod:< alpha, Y > >
WHERE
    X = s1:p, Y = s2:p
END;
```

---

Some other useful operations on shapes are given in Script 7.3.3. In particular,
the binary ShapeJoin appends two input shapes and produces an unique output
shape; the functions $\wedge 12$ and $\wedge 21$ implement the binary operations $\wedge_{12}$ and $\wedge_{21}$;
the functions Shape_0 and Shape_1 correspond to $\sigma_0$ and $\sigma_1$, respectively; the unary
operators ShapeInf and ShapeSup return the right-angled shapes associated to their
input.

---

**Script 7.3.3 (Other operations)**

```
DEF ShapeJoin (p,q::IsShape) = (AA:CAT ~ TRANS):<p,q>;
DEF ∧12 (p,q::IsShape) = [S1 ~ S1,S2 ~ S2]:<p,q>;
DEF ∧21 (p,q::IsShape) = [S1 ~ S2,S2 ~ S1]:<p,q>;
DEF Shape_0 (p::IsShape) = (AA:(CAT ~ DISTL) ~ [[K:0,S1], [K:0,S2]]):p;
DEF Shape_1 (p::IsShape) = (AA:(CAT ~ DISTR) ~ [[S1,K:0], [S2,K:0]]):p;
DEF ShapeInf (p::IsShape) = (∧12 ~ [Shape_0, Shape_1]):p;
DEF ShapeSup (p::IsShape) = (∧21 ~ [Shape_0, Shape_1]):p;
```

---

**Vector space of $n$-shapes** The set $S^n$ is a vector space. This result is
straightforward, since $S^n$ is identified with $\mathbb{R}^n \times \mathbb{R}^n$ and this one is isomorphic to
$\mathbb{R}^{2n}$, which clearly is a vector space. The dimension of the space is $2n$.

**Theorem** The set $S^n$ of $n$-shapes, together with the operations (7.2) and (7.2), is a
vector space over $\mathbb{R}$. In fact, the following conditions hold for all $s, r, t \in S^n$ and for
all $\alpha, \beta \in \mathbb{R}$:

1. $(s + r) + t = s + (r + t)$.
2. There exists $o$ in $S^n$ with the property that $s + o = s$.
3. There exists $-s$ in $S^n$ with the property that $s + (-s) = o$.
4. $s + r = r + s$.
5. $(\alpha + \beta)s = \alpha s + \beta s$.

6. $\alpha(s+r) = \alpha s + \alpha r$.
7. $\alpha(\beta s) = (\alpha\beta)s$.
8. $1s = s$.

It would be interesting to discuss the properties of some important subset of shapes. In particular, it is possible to shown that the subsets $C^n \subset S^n$ of *closed* shapes and $O^n \subset S^n$ of *right-angled* shapes are linear subspaces of $S^n$.

### Example 7.3.3 (Shape rotation)
The vector resulting from a rotation of angle $\alpha$ of $\boldsymbol{v} = (x,y)$ in a vector space $\mathcal{V}$ of dimension 2, can be computed as the linear combination of $\boldsymbol{v}$ and $\boldsymbol{v}^\perp = (-y,x)$, with scalars $\cos\alpha$ and $\sin\alpha$, respectively. Such implementation of shape rotation is given in Script 7.3.4 as a function

$$\texttt{ShapeRot} : \mathbb{R} \to S^n \to S^n.$$

---

### Script 7.3.4 (Shape rotation)
```
DEF ShapeNormal (p::IsShape) = [AA:- ~ S2,S1]:p;
DEF ShapeRot (alpha::IsReal)(p::IsShape) =
    (COS:alpha ShapeProd p) ShapeSum (SIN:alpha ShapeProd ShapeNormal:p);

DEF star = <<1.5,-0.5,1.5,1.5,-0.5,1.5,-2,-0.5,-0.5,-2>,
    <-1,-2,1.5,-1.5,2,1,0,2,-2,0>>;

(STRUCT ~ AA:Shape2pol ~ [ID, ShapeRot:(PI/4), ShapeRot:(PI/2)]):star;
```

---

The three configurations of the `star` shape defined by the last expression of the script are shown in Figure 7.19.

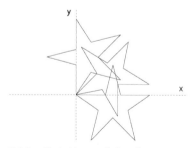

**Figure 7.19**   Rotations of the shape named `star`

**Closed shapes**   A shape $s = (X,Y) \in S^n$, with $X = (x_i)$ and $Y = (y_i)$, is said to be *closed* when both the $X$ and the $Y$ sequences have zero sum. In other words, the set $C^n \subset S^n$ is defined as

$$C^n = \{s = ((X_i),(Y_i)) \in S^n \mid \sum_i X_i = 0, \sum_i Y_i = 0\}$$

It is very easy to see that $C^n$ is a subspace of $S^n$, since it is closed with respect to the operations of addition and multiplication times a scalar.

A predicate `IsClosedShape` is given in Script 7.3.5 to test if a shape is closed. It works by computing if both coordinate sequences have zero sum. An operator

$$\texttt{ShapeClosed}: S^n \to C^n \cup C^{n+1}$$

is also given, which tests the closeness of the input shape and possibly appends one more number to each sequence, which equates the opposite of the sequence sum.

---

**Script 7.3.5 (Closed shapes)**

```
DEF IsClosedShape = AND ~ AL ~ [IsShape, AA:(C:EQ:0 ~ +)];
DEF ShapeClosed = IF:< IsClosedShape, ID, AA:(AR ~ [ID, - ~ +]) >;

ShapeClosed:<<5,3,-2.5,-2.5,-2.5,-2.5>,<0,4,-2,2,-2,2>> ≡
    <<5,3,-2.5,-2.5,-2.5,-2.5,2.0>,<0,4,-2,2,-2,2,-4>>;
```

---

**Orthogonal shapes**   A shape $r = (X, Y)$, with $X = (x_i)$ and $Y = (y_i)$, is said to be *right-angled,* or also *orthogonal,* when any pair of corresponding tangent vectors in $r$ is orthogonal. i.e. when

$$(x_i, y_i) \cdot (x_{i+1}, y_{i+1}) = x_i\, x_{i+1} + y_i\, y_{i+1} = 0$$

It is possible to show that the subset $O^n \subset S^n$ of right-angled shapes is a *linear subspace* of dimension $\frac{n}{2}\rceil$.

**Example 7.3.4 (Right-angled shapes)**
In Script 7.3.6 we give a predicate `IsOrthoShape` to test if a shape is either orthogonal or not. Then we show that a rotated instance of an orthogonal shape is orthogonal, and that a linear combination of two orthogonal shapes is also orthogonal. A predicate `IsCloseTo:x` is also given, to check the closeness of two real numbers within a predefined *precision*, in this case set to $0.0001$. The shape `ortho_2` is shown in Figure 7.20. The `rtail` function, to return a sequence without the last element, is defined in Script 4.2.5.

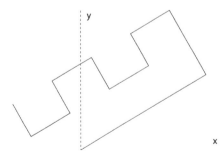

**Figure 7.20**   Orthogonal shape `ortho_2`

**Script 7.3.6**

```
DEF IsCloseTo (x::IsReal) = LT:0.0001 ~ (ABS ~ (ID - K:x));
DEF IsOrthoShape = AND ~ AA:(IsCloseTo:0 ~ +) ~ TRANS ~
    AA:(AA:* ~ TRANS ~ [rtail, TAIL]);

DEF ortho_1 = <<5,0,3,0,-2.5,0,-2.5,0,-2.5,0,-2.5,0>,
    <0,0,0,4,0,-2,0,2,0,-2,0,2>>;

DEF ortho_2 = ShapeRot:(PI/6): ortho_1;

IsOrthoShape: ortho_1 ≡ True;
IsOrthoShape: ortho_2 ≡ True;
IsOrthoShape: ((0.2 ShapeProd ortho_1) ShapeSum ortho_2) ≡ True;
```

## 7.3.2 Interpolation of shapes

In this section it is shown that $n$-shapes can be affinely and convexly interpolated as well as interpolated by polynomial curves in $S^n$, i.e. by vector-valued functions $[0,1] \to S^n$ (see Chapter 11 on curves and splines).

**Convex interpolation** It is quite interesting to note that any shape $s \in S^n$ has the same geometric support as the convex combination $s' \in S^{2n}$, with scalars 0.5 and 0.5, of the two right-angled shapes $s^{inf}$ and $s^{sup}$ uniquely associated with $s$, i.e.:

$$|s| = |s'| = \left| \frac{1}{2} s^{inf} + \frac{1}{2} s^{sup} \right|.$$

**Example 7.3.5 (Quasi-triangle)**
First, a triangular shape $t \in S^3$ is defined. Then, the two right-angled shapes $t^{inf}$ and $t^{sup}$ are computed. Finally, a 6-shape $r$ "close" to $t$ is derived as a convex combination of $t^{inf}$ and $t^{sup}$. The 6-shapes $t^{inf}$, $t^{sup}$ and $r$ are displayed in Figure 7.21.

$$
\begin{aligned}
t &= ((5, -2, -3), (3, 4, -7)), \\
t^{inf} &= (5, 0, -2, 0, -3, 0), (3, 0, 4, 0, -7, 0), \\
t^{sup} &= (0, 5, 0, -2, 0, -3), (0, 3, 0, 4, 0, -7, 0), \\
r &= 0.6\, t^{inf} + 0.4\, t^{sup}
\end{aligned}
$$

The shapes $t$ and $r$ are defined in Script 7.3.7 by the objects `triangle` and `quasi_triangle`. The polyhedral objects generated by expressions

```
Shape2Pol:triangle;
(Shape2Pol ~ ShapeInf):triangle;
(Shape2Pol ~ ShapeSup):triangle;
(STRUCT ~ AA:Shape2Pol ~ [ID, ShapeInf, ShapeSup]):quasi_triangle;
```

respectively, are shown in Figure 7.21.

**Script 7.3.7 (Quasi_triangle)**

```
DEF triangle = <<5,-2,-3>,<3,4,-7>>;

DEF quasi_triangle = (0.4 ShapeProd (ShapeInf:triangle))
    ShapeSum (0.6 ShapeProd (ShapeSup:triangle));

Shape2Pol:quasi_triangle;
```

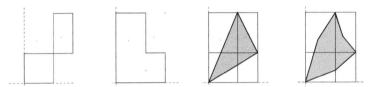

**Figure 7.21**  The right-angled shapes $t^{inf}$ and $t^{sup}$ associated with the triangle $t = ((5, -2, -3), (3, 4, -7))$, together with the interpolated "quasi-triangle" shape
$$r = 0.4\, t^{inf} + 0.6\, t^{sup}$$

**Sampled in-betweening**  As for any vector space, it makes perfectly sense to define the convex combination $\alpha_1 s_1 + \cdots + \alpha_m s_m$ of shapes $s_1, \ldots, s_m \in S^n$, with non-negative scalars $\alpha_1, \ldots, \alpha_m \in \mathbb{R}$, such that $\alpha_1 + \cdots + \alpha_m = 1$. In particular, the convex combination of two shapes in a same $S^n$ subspace lies in the subspace itself, since a linear subspace and a segment are both convex.

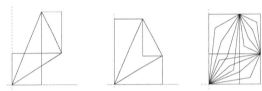

**Figure 7.22**  The triangle $t$ displayed with: (a) the associated $t^{sup}$ (b) the associated $t^{inf}$ (c) a family of convex combinations of such shapes

In Figure 7.22c a set of six 6-shapes on the segment between $p^{inf}$ and $p^{sup}$ in $S^6$ are given, obtained through

$$q(\alpha) = (1 - \alpha)\, p^{inf} + \alpha\, p^{sup}, \qquad \alpha \in \{0, \frac{1}{5}, \frac{2}{5}, \frac{3}{5}, \frac{4}{5}, 1\}.$$

Furthermore, the convex combination of an arbitrary number of elements in a subspace (e.g. of right-angled shapes) lies in the subspace. For example, consider Figure 7.23, where the segment between two shapes in the same subspace of $O^{10}$ is sampled.

Notice that $s = (X, Y)$ and $r = (U, W)$ lie in the same subspace of $O^n$ provided that any pair of corresponding tangent vectors $(X_i, Y_i)$ and $(U_i, W_i)$ are collinear. A sufficient condition for right-angled shapes $s = (X, Y)$ and $r = (U, V)$ to belong to the same linear subspace is that vectors $(X_1, Y_1)$ and $(U_1, V_1)$ are parallel,

**Implementation of in-betweening**  The binary in-betweening of shapes is implemented by the function **ShapeInBetweening** in Script 7.3.8. The function accepts

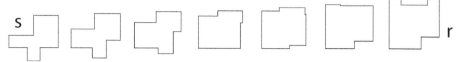

**Figure 7.23**    The convex interpolation of two orthogonal shapes $s$ and $r$

as input:

1. the real parameter `tx` of the translation to be interposed between any pair of subsequent interpolated shapes;
2. the integer number `m` of steps in $S^n$. The number of generated shapes, including the extreme ones, will be equal to $m + 1$;
3. the pair of input shapes `p` and `q` to be interpolated.

The function `ShapeComb` is applied to a quadruple of actual parameters, which must contain the two scalar combinators and the two shapes to be combined.

---

**Script 7.3.8 (Shape in-betweening)**
```
DEF ShapeComb (a,b::IsReal; p,q::IsShape) =
   (a ShapeProd p) ShapeSum (b ShapeProd q);

DEF ShapeInBetweening (tx::IsReal)(n::IsInt)(p,q::IsShape) =
   (STRUCT ~ transl ~ AA:(Shape2Pol ~ ShapeComb)): input
WHERE
   input = (AA:CAT ~ DISTR):< scalarPairs, <p,q> >,
   scalarPairs = (TRANS ~ [ID, REVERSE]):scalars,
   scalars = (SumSeqWithZero ~ #:n):(1/n),
   transl = CAT ~ DISTR ~ [ID, K:(T:1:tx)]
END;
```

---

**Example 7.3.6 (Interpolation of shapes)**
A convex interpolation of two 10-shapes is generated. Let us define two shapes, `star` and `spiral`. The segment in $S^n$ between these shapes is the curve $q : [0, 1] \rightarrow S^n$ such that:

$$q(\alpha) = (1 - \alpha)\,\mathtt{star} + \alpha\,\mathtt{spiral}$$

A sampling of this curve is displayed in Figure 7.24. The PLaSM implementation of the example is given in Script 7.3.9.

---

**Script 7.3.9 (In-betweening example)**
```
DEF star = <<1.5,-0.5,1.5,1.5,-0.5,1.5,-2,-0.5,-0.5,-2>,
   <-1,-2,1.5,-1.5,2,1,0,2,-2,0>>;
DEF spiral = <<0,1,0,-2,0,3,0,-4,0,5>,<-1,0,2,0,-3,0,4,0,-5,0>>;

ShapeInBetweening:0:5:< star, spiral >;
ShapeInBetweening:6:6:< star, spiral >;
```

---

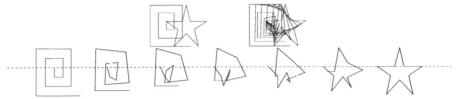

**Figure 7.24**   A sampling of the straight line in $S^{10}$ between the *spiral* and *star*
shapes

**Example 7.3.7**
A piecewise linear shape interpolation between the 10-shapes *spiral*, *quasi-circle* and
*star* is displayed in Figure 7.25, where *quasi-circle* is a regular polygon inscribed in
the circle of unit radius.

**Figure 7.25**   Two straight lines in $S^{10}$, visualized with interposed translations
between subsequent samples

Clearly, any kind of approximating or interpolating curve can be easily defined in
$S^n$. In particular, polynomial curves are defined as combinations of the elements of
some suitable basis of polynomials of degree less or equal to $d$ with a given set of $d+1$
shapes in $S^n$.

Notice that the shapes in such a morphism can be embedded in $\mathbb{E}^2$ in several ways
(i.e. according to an arbitrary pattern of translations, e.g. generated by using splines)
without affecting the "appearance" of any sampled shape, which does not depend on
its positioning in the Euclidean plane.

**Example 7.3.8**
A polynomial curve of degree 2 in $S^{10}$ is here defined as a Lagrange interpolation[3]
of the shapes *spiral*, *quasi-circle* and *star* defined in previous examples. A quadratic
vector-valued function morphism : $[0, 1] \rightarrow S^{10}$ is defined by combining the quadratic
Lagrange's basis of polynomials with the given shapes. So, a curve

$$morphism : \alpha \mapsto (2\alpha^2 - 3\alpha + 1)\,\text{spiral} + (-4\alpha^2 + 4\alpha)\,\text{quasi-circle} + (2\alpha^2 - \alpha)\,\text{star},$$

is given which interpolates the three given key shapes (for $\alpha = 0, \frac{1}{2}, 1$, respectively). A
sampling of such a curve in $S^{10}$ is displayed in Figure 7.26. A constant translation is
interposed between any pair of subsequent frames in order to make the picture easier
to understand. Notice, with respect to the piecewise linear interpolation displayed in

---

[3] The definition of polynomial curves as the combination of points or vectors with a suitable
basis of polynomials is discussed in Chapter 11. In particular, a polynomial curve in
Lagrangian form is the combination of a given set of vectors with the polynomials of the
Lagrange's basis.

Figure 7.25, that the shape transition between the three key shapes *spiral, quasi-circle* and *star* is now smoother.

**Figure 7.26**   Quadratic Lagrange interpolation in $S^{10}$ of three key shapes

### 7.3.3   Shape compatibility

One important question is how to combine $n$-shapes belonging to different spaces $S^n$, i.e. to spaces having a different number of generators. This can be readily done by defining a "compatibility" mapping, which associates an arbitrary pair of shapes with a new pair whose elements can be linearly combined. Such compatible new shapes must obviously have the same "support" of the old ones, i.e. must correspond to the same point sets in the Euclidean space. This can be done quite easily, by properly merging and then scaling back two similar instances (with unit length) of the given shapes. Such new operations, defined on the set $S^* = S^1 \cup S^2 \cdots \cup S^n \cup \cdots$ would result in a linear space of infinite dimension. A more useful way to combine any set of shapes in different spaces $S^{n_1}, \ldots, S^{n_p}$ would be obtained by always giving the result in the space $S^{\max(n_1, \cdots, n_p)}$ of highest dimension. Actually, the easiest implementation is obtained by associating a pair of spaces $S^n$ and $S^m$ with the space $S^{n+m-1}$.

Two shapes $s$ and $r$ will be said to be *compatible* when they lie in the same space $S^n$. So, only compatible shapes can be linearly combined. What to do when $s \in S^n$ and $r \in S^m$, with $n \neq m$? We give first a definition of two concepts that we used in the sequel.

**Partial shape**   We call *partial shapes* of a shape $s \in S^n$ any two shapes $p \in S^h$ and $q \in S^k$, with $1 \leq h, k$ and $h + k = n$, such that the *join* of $p$ and $q$ gives $s$:

$$p \oplus q = s.$$

**Shape length**   The *length* $\mu$ of a shape $s = ((X_i), (Y_i)) \in S^n$ is defined as the length of any one of the polylines that $s$ represents, i.e. as the functional

$$\mu : S^n \to \mathbb{R},$$

such that

$$\mu(s) = \sum_i \left( X_i^2 + Y_i^2 \right)^{\frac{1}{2}}.$$

An operator ShapeLen to compute shape lengths is given in Script 7.3.11. Clearly we have that:

$$p \oplus q = s \quad \text{implies} \quad \mu(p) + \mu(q) = \mu(s)$$

**Compatibility**   A mapping can be defined from any pair of non-trivial shapes $s \in S^n$ and $r \in S^m$ to a corresponding pair $\tilde{s}, \tilde{r} \in S^{n+m-1}$, such that both $s, \tilde{s}$ and $r, \tilde{r}$ have as image in $\mathbb{E}^2$ the same set of points, i.e. are associated to the same geometrical object. This mapping is defined as follows.

1. Normalize both $s$ and $r$ to their similar shapes of unit size $a = \frac{s}{\mu(s)}$ and $b = \frac{r}{\mu(r)}$.

2. Merge $a$ and $b$, thus building two "fragmented" shapes $\tilde{a}, \tilde{b} \in S^{n+m-1}$, such that:

   - $\tilde{a}, \tilde{b}$ have the same support of $a, b$, i.e. $|a| = |\tilde{a}|$ and $|b| = |\tilde{b}|$;
   - all pairs of partial shapes have the same size, i.e.:

$$\mu(\tilde{a}^h) = \mu(\tilde{b}^h), \qquad 1 \le h \le n + m - 2$$

3. Scale back $\tilde{a}$ and $\tilde{b}$ to the size of $s$ and $r$, so yielding $\tilde{s}$ and $\tilde{r}$.

Such a mapping associates a pair of compatible shapes $\tilde{s}, \tilde{r}$ with any pair of non-trivial shapes $s, r$, so allowing to make them combinable. More formally:

**Definition 7.3.1** A *compatibility mapping* is a function

$$MapShapes : S^n \backslash \{0\} \times S^m \backslash \{0\} \to S^{n+m-1} \times S^{n+m-1}$$

such that

$$(s, r) \mapsto (\mu(s)\, a, \; \mu(r)\, b),$$

with

$$\mu(a) = \mu(b) = 1, \qquad |a| = \left| \frac{s}{\mu(s)} \right|, \qquad |b| = \left| \frac{r}{\mu(r)} \right|,$$

and

$$\mu(a^h) = \mu(b^h), \qquad 1 \le h \le n + m - 2.$$

In such a mapping the (inversely scaled) fragmented shapes have the same support than the original shapes:

$$|\tilde{s}| = |\mu(s)\, a| = |s|, \quad \text{and} \quad |\tilde{r}| = |\mu(r)\, b| = |r|.$$

**Compatibility mapping implementation**   For sake of brevity, the PLaSM code which implements the compatibility mapping of shapes is given entirely in the following Scripts, but is not fully discussed. Anyway, it is not difficult to understand it by careful reading, and by checking the meaning of sub-expressions with a PLaSM interpreter.

According to its definition, the `MapShapes` function transforms a pair of shapes from spaces with different dimensions, into a pair of compatible shapes with the same support.

## Script 7.3.10 (Compatibility mapping)

```
DEF MapShapes (p,q::IsShape) = [
    AA:ComputeCoords ~ [[s2,s1,K:pSeq,K:<>],[s3,s1,K:pSeq,K:<>]] ~ S1,
    AA:ComputeCoords ~ [[s2,s1,K:qSeq,K:<>],[s3,s1,K:qSeq,K:<>]] ~ S2 ]:
        < ShapeTriple:p, ShapeTriple:q >
WHERE
    pqMerged = (rtail ~ TAIL ~ MERGE:IsLE):< norm:p, norm:q > ,
    pSeq = (PairDiff ~ AA:* ~ DISTL):< ShapeLen:p, pqMerged > ,
    qSeq = (PairDiff ~ AA:* ~ DISTL):< ShapeLen:q, pqMerged > ,
    norm = AA:/ ~ DISTR ~ [SumSeqWithZero ~ S1 ~ ShapeTriple, ShapeLen]
END;

DEF ShapeTriple (p::IsShape) = [LenSeq, CosSeq, SinSeq]:p
WHERE
    LenSeq = AA:VectNorm ~ TRANS,
    CosSeq = AA:/ ~ TRANS ~ [S1, LenSeq],
    SinSeq = AA:/ ~ TRANS ~ [S2, LenSeq]
END;
```

The ShapeTriple function returns a useful representation of the input shape, as a triplet of sequences of length $n$, that respectively contain the lengths, the *sin* and the *cos* of the angles with the horizontal line, for each vector $(X_i, Y_i)$ in the input shape $p = (X, Y) \in S^n$.

A small toolbox of auxiliary functions used in this section is given in Script 7.3.11. Some of the functions were already discussed elsewhere. They are collected here for the reader's convenience. The toolbox contains: the PairDiff function to transform a progressive sequence of $n + 1$ numbers into a sequence of $n$ differences; the VectNorm and ShapeLen operators to compute vector and shape lengths, respectively. The IsLE function, given in Script 2.1.29, is an uncurried version of the primitive LE (*Less or Equal*) predicate. A function of this kind is required by the semantics of the primitive function MERGE. An example of use of this function is also given. The Q operator to transform either a single number or a sequence of numbers into a 1D polyhedral complex is given in Script 1.5.5. The SQR function to compute the square of a number is given in Script 3.2.4.

## Script 7.3.11 (Function toolbox)

```
DEF PairDiff (p::IsSeq) = (AA:- ~ TRANS):< TAIL:p, rtail:p >;
DEF ShapeLen (p::IsShape) = (+ ~ AA:VectNorm ~ TRANS):p;

MERGE:IsLE:<<1,3,3,5,7>,<2,2,3,9>> ≡ <1,2,2,3,3,3,5,7,9>
```

The recursive function ComputeCoords, given in Script 7.3.12 in proper FL style, accepts as input the quadruple of sequences described below, and returns either the sequence $X$ or the sequence $Y$ of the fragmented $(X, Y)$ output shape.

This function is designed to work on quadruples <seq1, seq2, seq3, seq4>, defined as follows:

1. seq1 = sequence of $p$ trigonometric values (either $\sin \alpha$ or $\cos \alpha$), where $\alpha$ is

the angle between the vector $(X_i, Y_i)$ and the horizontal line;

2. seq2 = sequence of $p$ side measures (either $X$ or $Y$) before the subdivision;
3. seq3 = sequence of side measures (either $X$ or $Y$) after the subdivision;
4. seq4 = starting value equal to <> (basic case of recursion); when the procedure stops it contains the output sequence of signed ($X$ or $Y$) values.

---

**Script 7.3.12 (Computation of coordinates of fragmented shape)**

```
DEF ComputeCoords = IF:< stopTest, stop, ELSEIF >
WHERE
    stopTest = OR ~ AA:ISNULL ~ [s2,s3]
    stop = S4,
    ELSEIF = IF:< test, then, else >,
    test = OR ~ [IsCloseTo:0, GT:0] ~ value,
    then = ComputeCoords ~ [ S1,
        AL ~ [ value, TAIL ~ S2 ],
        TAIL ~ S3,
        AR ~ [ S4, * ~ [FIRST ~ S1, FIRST ~ S3]] ],
    else = ComputeCoords ~ [TAIL ~ S1, TAIL ~ S2, S3, S4],
    value = - ~ [FIRST ~ S2, FIRST ~ S3]
END;
```

---

**Example 7.3.9**

A linear interpolation between compatible shapes generated by

```
MapShapes:< star, triangle >;
MapShapes:< triangle, spiral >;
```

both lying in $S^{10+3-1}$, is shown in Figure 7.27, starting from a pair of key shapes with different numbers of sides. The key shapes are defined as follows, where the PairDiff and circlePoints functions are given in Scripts 7.3.11 and 7.2.22, respectively:

```
DEF star5 = <<1.5,-0.5,1.5,1.5,-0.5,1.5,-2,-0.5,-0.5,-2>,
    <-1,-2,1.5,-1.5,2,1,0,2,-2,0>>
DEF spiral = <<0,1,0,-2,0,3,0,-4,0,5>,<-1,0,2,0,-3,0,4,0,-5,0>>;
DEF triangle = <<5,0,-5>,<0,5,-5>>;
DEF quasi_circle = (AA:PairDiff ~ TRANS ~ circlePoints:(PI/-2):2):10;
```

**Figure 7.27**   Two linear curves in $S^{3+10-1}$, displayed with interposed translations

---

**7.3.4  *Shape resemblance***

Since each space of $n$-shapes is a linear space, a sound measure of resemblance between shapes $s$ and $r$ in $S^n$ may easily be given by the Euclidean norm of the difference $s - r$, where the difference operation is defined in the standard way. Hence we have

$$\text{Shapedist} : S^n \times S^n \to \mathbb{R} : (s, r) \mapsto \|s + (-1)r\|$$

where

$$\|\cdot\| : S^n \to \mathbb{R} : (X, Y) \mapsto \left( \sum_i X_i^2 + \sum_i Y_i^2 \right)^{\frac{1}{2}}$$

**Implementation** A very quick implementation of difference, norm and distance of shapes is given in Script 7.3.13. A ShapeZero generator of the zero element of $S^n$, for arbitrary value of $n$, is also given. The VectNorm function was defined in Script 3.2.4. The ShapeSum and ShapeProd operations were implemented in Script 7.3.2.

---

**Script 7.3.13 (Shape distance)**
```
DEF ShapeZero (n::IsInt) = [#:n, #:n]:0;
DEF ShapeDiff (p,q::IsShape) = p ShapeSum (-1 ShapeProd q);
DEF ShapeNorm (p::IsShape) = (VectNorm ~ CAT):p;
DEF Shapedist (p,q::IsShape) = (ShapeNorm ~ ShapeDiff):<p,q>;
```

---

**Example 7.3.10 (Distance properties)**
We exemplify here the standard distance properties for the space $S^{10}$. For this purpose we use the three shapes quasi_circle, spiral and star5, defined in Example 7.3.9. The distance properties obviously hold for arbitrary $n$ and for arbitrary triplet $p, q, r \in S^n$. The symbol $d$ is also used here to denote the distance function.

1. Zero distance: $d(p, p) = 0$ for each $p \in S^n$

   Shapedist:< star5, star5 > $\equiv$ 0

2. Symmetry: $d(p, q) = d(q, p)$ for each $p, q \in S^n$

   Shapedist:< spiral, star5 > $\equiv$ Shapedist:< star5, spiral >

3. Triangle inequality: $d(p, r) \leq d(p, q) + d(q, r)$ for each $p, q, r \in S^n$

   Shapedist:< quasi_circle, star5 > $\equiv$ 8.016730160686723
   Shapedist:< quasi_circle, spiral > $\equiv$ 10.598516851127517
   Shapedist:< spiral, star5 > $\equiv$ 12.186057606953941

## 7.4 Examples

A new primitive, based on quadrilaterals and called *quadrilateral array with holes*, is discussed here, that may be mainly useful in architectural design applications. In particular, the primitive may be mainly useful in the 2D case, where can be used (see Example 7.4.3) to quickly generate building fronts with several regular rectangular openings in the walls.

*7.4.1   Quadrilateral array with holes*

The QUADARRAY primitive accepts as input both a $m \times n$ array of points, and a $(m - 1) \times (n - 1)$ array of numbers in $\{-1, 0, 1\}$, used as flags that denote if the corresponding quadrilateral cell must be dropped from the output polyhedral complex.

The primitive implementation is very similar to the one of the QuadMesh primitive given in Script 7.2.23, and obviously uses the same algorithm described there, with the small variation of associating just one quad cell to each point instead than two triangles. The Cart function for Cartesian product of any collection of sets is given in Script 2.1.17.

---

**Script 7.4.1 (QuadArray primitive)**

```
DEF QUADARRAY (points,flags::IsSeq) =
   (optimize ~ MKPOL):<verts, cells, pols>
WHERE
   n = LEN:points,
   m = (LEN ~ S1):points,
   pairSeq = Cart:<1..(n - 1), 1..(m - 1)>,
   filteredSeq = (CAT ~ AA:(IF:<EQ~[K:-1,S2], K:<>, LIST~S1>) ~ TRANS):
      < CAT:pairSeq, CAT:flags >,
   quad = AA:address ~ [[S1,S2],[S1+K:1,S2+K:1],[S1+K:1,S2],[S1,S2+K:1]],
   address = K:m * (S1 - K:1) + s2,
   verts = CAT:points,
   cells = AA:quad:filteredSeq,
   pols = LIST:(1..((n - 1) * (m - 1)))
END;
```

---

**Example 7.4.1 (Architectural plan: automated input)**

We generate here the input data to the QUADARRAY operator developed in Script 7.4.1, starting from a simplified input, constituted by a sequence of side measures on the $x$ and $y$ directions. The two sets of measures are used to generate both a 2D matrix of points, named array_xy, and a 2D matrix of sign flags, named flags_xy, which is used to denote the quadrilateral cells to be dropped to the output complex generated by the final expression QUADARRAY:< array_xy, flags_xy >.

The QUADARRAY operator implementation is given in Script 7.4.1. The resulting polyhedral complex is shown in Figure 7.28a. Notice that, according to the semantics of the QUOTE operator (see Section 12), negative numbers are used to denote the side measure of empty cells.

**Example 7.4.2 (Architectural plan: direct input)**

The numeric values of the array_xy and flags_xy objects generated in the previous example are slightly modified here, to show that the CELLARRAY primitive accepts an arbitrary pattern of 2D points and of cell flags, and not only those generated by Cartesian product of linear sequences.

The 3D polyhedron generated by last expression of Script 7.4.3 is shown in Figure 7.28c. The actual shape editing should clearly performed by using some specific

**Script 7.4.2 (Input session)**

```
    DEF data_x = <2,-10,1,-15,1>;
    DEF data_y = <2,-12,-6,2>;

    DEF value_x = 0 AL (Progressivesum ~ AA:ABS):data_x;
    DEF value_y = 0 AL (Progressivesum ~ AA:ABS):data_y;
    DEF array_xy = Cart:< value_x,value_y >;

    DEF sign_x = AA:SIGN:data_x;
    DEF sign_y = AA:SIGN:data_y;
    DEF sign_xy = Cart:< sign_x,sign_y >;
    DEF flags_xy = (AA ~ AA):(SIGN ~ +):sign_xy;

    QUADARRAY:< array_xy,flags_xy >
```

**Script 7.4.3 (QUADARRAY: direct input)**

```
    DEF flags_xy = <
       <1, 0, 0, 1>,
       <0, -1, -1, 0>,
       <1, 0, -1, 1>,
       <0, -1, -1, 0>,
       <1, 0, -1, 1>>;

    DEF array_xy = <
       <<0, 0>, <0, 2>, <1, 14>, <0, 20>, <0, 22>>,
       <<2, 0>, <2, 2>, <3, 14>, <2, 20>, <2, 22>>,
       <<12, 2>, <12, 4>, <12, 14>, <12, 20>, <12, 22>>,
       <<13, 2>, <13, 4>, <13, 14>, <13, 20>, <13, 22>>,
       <<28, 0>, <28, 2>, <28, 14>, <28, 20>, <28, 22>>,
       <<29, 0>, <29, 2>, <29, 14>, <29, 20>, <29, 22>>>;

    QUADARRAY:< array_xy, flags_xy > * QUOTE:<10>;
```

GUI (Graphical User Interface) and not by symbolic text editing.


**Example 7.4.3 (Further abstraction)**

In the context of architectural design, it may be very useful to have available a geometric primitive which allows direct generation of quadrilateral shapes with several aligned quadrilateral holes, defined by giving only some small set of side information. A primitive of this kind is implemented in this example, by abstracting the code prepared for Example 7.4.1.

According to the semantic of QUADARRAY primitive, both an array of 2D points and a conformal array of integer flags are prepared internally to the XQUADARRAY function, by properly manipulating the two input sequences data_x and data_y. Such input sequences bring the lateral measures of the output, denoting its full and empty stripes with positive and negative numbers, respectively.

The 3D polyhedron produced by extrusion of a 2D square with many holes is generated by the last expression of Script 7.4.4.

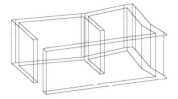

**Figure 7.28**    (a) Polygon generated by a quadArray primitive (b) Polygon generated by a quadArray primitive (c) Extruded solid

**Script 7.4.4 (XQUADARRAY)**

```
DEF XQUADARRAY (data_x,data_y::IsSeqOf:IsReal) =
    (QUADARRAY~[array_xy, flags_xy]):< data_x, data_y >
WHERE
    array_xy = Cart ~ AA:(AL ~ [K:0, Progressivesum ~ AA:ABS]),
    flags_xy = (AA ~ AA):(SIGN ~ +) ~ Cart ~ (AA ~ AA):SIGN
END;

XQUADARRAY:< ##:8:<1,-4> AR 1, ##:8:<1,-4> AR 1 > * Q:1
```

## 7.5    Annotated references

Various papers and some more references on orthogonal polygons can be found in the book [Tou88]. Several bilinear matrix forms for the area of both orthogonal and general polygons are given in [Pao96]. A linear time algorithm for the Hausdorff distance between convex polygons is shown in [Ata83]. A $O(n \log n)$ algorithm for the Hausdorff distance between general polygons is given in [AG92], in the framework of best matching of polygons. A measure of resemblance of polygonal curves using a Frechet metric is also defined in [AG95], where several algorithms for its computation are given. The beautiful and stimulating book [LD93] discusses several linear models which satisfy geometric postulates.

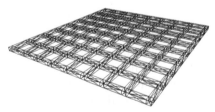

**Figure 7.29**    Single polyhedron of topologic genus 64 generated by XQUADARRAY:< <1,-4,1,-4,1,-4,1,-4,1,-4,1,-4,1,-4,1,-4,1>, <1,-4,1,-4,1,-4,1,-4,1,-4,1,-4,1,-4,1,-4,1> > * Q:1

# 8

# Hierarchical structures

Hierarchical models of complex assemblies are generated by an aggregation of subassemblies, each one defined in a local coordinate system, and relocated by affine transformations of coordinates. This operation may be repeated hierarchically, with some subassemblies defined by aggregation of simpler parts, and so on, until one obtains a set of elementary components, which cannot be further decomposed.

Two main advantages can be found in a hierarchical modeling approach. Each elementary part and each assembly, at every hierarchical level, are defined independently from each other, using a *local* coordinate frame, suitably chosen to make its definition easier. Furthermore, only *one* copy of each component is stored in the memory, and may be instanced in different locations and orientations how many times it is needed.

In the present chapter a graph-theoretical model of hierarchical assemblies is discussed, also making some reference to its concrete implementation in standard graphics systems. The chapter includes several worked examples of hierarchical structures, including the 2D and 3D design of the furniture of a living room, an anthropomorphic body modeling, the preliminary sketching of a parametric umbrella, an algorithm for drawing tree diagrams, and operators to make complex arrangments of 2D symbols.

## 8.1   Hierarchical graphs

A hierarchical model, defined inductively as an assembly of component parts [LG85], is easily described by an *acyclic directed multigraph*, often called a *scene graph* or *hierarchical structure* in computer graphics. The main algorithm with hierarchical assemblies is the *traversal* algorithm, which transforms every component from *local coordinates* to global coordinates, called *world coordinates*.

### Acyclic directed-multigraph

The standard definition of a *directed graph* $G$ states that it is a pair $(N, A)$, where $N$ is a set of *nodes* and $A$ is a set of directed *arcs*, given as ordered pairs of nodes. Such

*Geometric Programming for Computer-Aided Design*  Alberto Paoluzzi
© 2003 John Wiley & Sons, Ltd  ISBN 0-471-89942-9

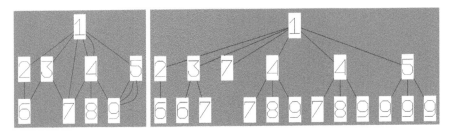

**Figure 8.1**   (a) Directed acyclic multigraph of an assembly (b) Tree of
sub-assembly instances generated when traversing the multigraph

a definition is not sufficient when more than one arc is to be considered between the
same pair of nodes.

In this case the notion of *multigraph* is introduced. A *directed multigraph* is a triplet
$G := (N, A, f)$ where $N$ and $A$ are sets of nodes and arcs, respectively, and $f : A \to N^2$
is a mapping from arcs to node pairs. In other words, in a multigraph, the same pair
of nodes can be connected by multiple arcs.

Directed graphs or multigraphs are said to be *acyclic* when they do not contain
cycles, i.e. when no path starts and ends at the same vertex. *Trees* are common
examples of acyclic graphs. Nodes in a tree can be associated with their integer *distance*
from the root, defined by the number of edges on the unique path from the root to
the node. A tree can be layered by *levels*, by putting in the same subset (level) all the
nodes with equal distance from the root. A tree, where each non-leaf node is the root
of a subtree, is the best model of the concept of *hierarchy*.

Acyclic graphs/multigraphs are also called *hierarchical graphs*, because they can be
associated to a tree, generated at run-time by visiting the graph with some standard
traversal algorithm, e.g. with a depth-first-search [AHU83]. The ordered sequence of
nodes produced by the traversal is sometimes called a *linearized graph*. Each node
in this sequence is suitably transformed from local coordinates to *world coordinates*,
i.e. to the coordinates of the root, by the traversal algorithm.

### 8.1.1   *Local coordinates and modeling transformation*

A hierarchical multigraph is used to model a *scene database* in the sense described
below. In particular, each *node* may be considered a *container* of geometrical objects,
where:

1. The geometrical objects contained in a node $a$ are defined using a system of
   coordinates which is *local* to $a$.
2. Each arc $(a, b)$ is associated with an affine transformation of coordinates. In
   simplest cases the identity transformation is used.
3. The affine mapping of the arc $(a, b)$ is used to transform the objects contained
   within the $b$ node to the coordinate system of the $a$ node.

The previous properties are extended inductively to the subgraphs rooted in each
node. In particular:

1. the subgraphs rooted in the $b_i$ sons of $a$, i.e., the geometrical data contained in such subgraphs, may be affinely mapped to the coordinates of $a$. The affine maps associated to $(a, b_i)$ arcs are used at this purpose;
2. a subgraph may be instanced in a node (i.e., in its coordinate space) more than once. As shown in Figure 8.1 and discussed in Example 8.3.1, the number of instances of a subgraph in a node equates the number of different paths that connect the subgraph to the node.

**Summary** The main ideas concerning *scene graphs* can be summarized as follows. Nodes are *containers* of geometrical data stored in *local* coordinates. They are also used as root of subgraphs, whose data are transformed to the node coordinates by a traversal algorithm. Arcs $(a, b)$ are associated with affine transformations, which map the data contained in $b$ from their local coordinates to the coordinates of $a$. More than one arc may exist between the same node pair. This allows storage in memory only of *one copy* of each container. The composite transformations of coordinates applied to the linearized graph generated at traversal time are collectively known as the *modeling transformation*.

## 8.2 Hierarchical structures

Various kinds of hierarchical assemblies are used in standard graphical systems, such as GKS, PHIGS and VRML, as well as in graphics libraries like Open Inventor[1] and Java 3D. The model of hierarchical structures adopted by PLaSM is inspired, even in the name of the operator used for this purpose, by the one introduced by PHIGS.

**GKS segments** In GKS (Graphical Kernel System) [EKP87, ISO85] the storage of graphical *segments* was introduced, which defines a two-level hierarchical system. More specifically: graphical *primitives* like polylines, polygons and text strings can be grouped into named collections, called *segments*. Segments are stored in a "normalized" coordinate space, and cannot be nested. Geometric transformations, including composite translation, rotation and scaling, can be applied to segments. Also, segments can be made visible/invisible, *picked* interactively and highlighted.

**PHIGS structure network** In PHIGS (Programmer's Hierarchical Interactive Graphics System) [HHHW91, ANSI87] *structure networks* are used, which can be visualized as acyclic graphs, where *structures* give the nodes of the graph, and *references* between structures give the arcs between nodes. Hierarchical assemblies of any depth can be modeled by such acyclic graphs. Structures are stored in a *centralized structure store* (CSS) independent of workstations, were structures can be *posted*. Structures can be interactively edited, by inserting, replacing and deleting *structure elements*.

---

[1] Inventor, later called Open Inventor, was developed and marketed by SGI (Silicon Graphics Instruments) and by TGS (Template Graphics Software). An *OpenSource* version for both Linux and Windows platforms has recently been released by SGI.

**Inventor's scene graphs**  In Open Inventor [WO94] scene *databases* are defined as collections of *scene graphs*. A scene graph is an ordered collection of *nodes*, which are basic building blocks holding shape descriptions, geometric transformations, light sources or cameras. In other words, each node represents a geometry, property, or grouping object. Hierarchical scenes are created by adding nodes as children of grouping nodes. This approach clearly results in building scene graphs as acyclic directed graphs. No properties or transformations are attached to graph arcs, which just represent the containment relation between nodes. Node kits are provided as C++ classes with a predefined behavior, which can be customized by the application programmer by subclassing.

**VRML scene graphs**  in VRML (Virtual Reality Modeling Language) [ANM97, ISO97] the same idea of scene graphs as ordered collections of nodes is used. The reader should notice that VRML originates from the File Format of Open Inventor. Such VRML files, written either in ASCII or gzipped binary format, can be used to import scene graphs into a scene database or even as an alternative to creating scene graphs programmatically. For example, scene graphs can be imported in Java 3D [SRD00] using VRML files. Some non-trivial differences exist between the semantics of scene graphs with versions 1.0 and 2.0 of VRML.

**Remarks**  The arcs of scene graphs are normally specified *implicitly* in real graphical systems. For example, an arc is actually specified when a node is contained or referred within another one. In particular, it is possible to specify a new container node together with either the matrix or the parameters of the transformation to be associated with the the arc that connects the new container to the current node.

### 8.2.1  *Hierarchical structures in* PLaSM

A *container* of geometrical objects is defined in PLaSM by applying the predefined operator STRUCT to the sequence of contained objects. The value returned from such application is of the *polyhedral complex* type. The coordinate system of the value returned from a STRUCT application is the one associated with the first object of the argument sequence. Also, the resulting geometrical value is often associated with a symbol used as the name of the container, as in

$$\text{DEF obj} = \text{STRUCT:} < \text{obj}_1, \text{obj}_2, \ldots, \text{obj}_n >;$$

The obj geometry can be pictorially described, using the previously discussed graph model of hierarchical structures, as shown in Figure 8.2a. Clearly, each component object may in turn be defined as a container of other objects, i.e. as the root of a subgraph, as shown in Figure 8.2b, according to the following definition:

$$\text{DEF obj}_2 = \text{STRUCT:} < \text{obj}_{21}, \ldots, \text{obj}_{2m} >;$$

Exactly the same geometric result[2] would be generated by direct nesting of STRUCT sub-expressions:

---

[2] Actually, using an internally-generated symbol to name the second son of the scene graph root.

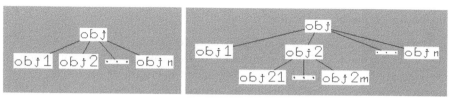

**Figure 8.2**   (a) Graph representation of a STRUCT assembly (b) Nested assembly

$$\text{DEF obj = STRUCT:} < \text{obj}_1, \text{ STRUCT:} < \text{obj}_{21}, \ldots, \text{obj}_{2m} >, \ldots, \text{obj}_n >$$

The sequence argument of the STRUCT operator may either contain or not affine transformations, together with polyhedral complexes. This fact results in generating an assembly either by using the same (global) coordinates for the various components or by using different (local) coordinate systems. The two cases are discussed in the two following subsections, respectively.

### 8.2.2   Assembly using global coordinates

Let us assume that the sequence argument of a STRUCT expression does not contain affine transformations. In other words we assume that the evaluations of the PLaSM expressions in the argument sequence return only polyhedral values.

In this case the output polyhedral complex is returned in the coordinate system of the first element of the input sequence, and no transformations of coordinates are applied to the assembly components, which are only aggregated within the same space, as shown by the following example.

### Example 8.2.1 (STRUCT assembly (1))

The PLaSM expression given below returns the object displayed in Figure 8.3a. Notice that the local origin and coordinate axes of the three component shapes coincide. The @1 operator is used with the only purpose of generating the wire-frame drawing shown in the figure.

$$(\texttt{@1} \sim \texttt{STRUCT}):< \texttt{CUBOID}:<2,2,2>, \texttt{CUBOID}:<1,1,1>, \texttt{SIMPLEX}:3 >$$

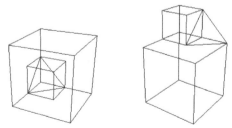

**Figure 8.3**   (a) Assembly without coordinate transformations (b) Assembly with coordinate transformations

### 8.2.3  *Assembly with local coordinates*

Let us conversely assume here that some affine transformations are contained within the sequence argument of a STRUCT expression. In this case, each transformation is applied to each polyhedral complex that follows it in the argument sequence.

From a user's viewpoint, the following equivalence holds, where $pol_1$, ... , $pol_n$ are polyhedral complexes and $T_1$, ... , $T_{n-1}$ are transformation tensors:

$$\text{STRUCT:} < pol_1, T_1, pol_2, T_2, pol_3, \ldots, T_{n-1}, pol_n > \equiv$$
$$\text{STRUCT:} < pol_1, T_1:pol_2, (T_1{\sim}T_2):pol_3, \ldots, (T_1{\sim}T_2{\sim}\cdots{\sim}T_{n-1}):pol_n >$$

Looking at the internal behavior of the geometric kernel of the language, the following transformation is applied to a STRUCT application at evaluation time:

$$\text{STRUCT:} < pol_1, T_1, pol_2, T_2, pol_3, \ldots, T_{n-1}, pol_n > \equiv \text{STRUCT:} <$$
$$pol_1,$$
$$(T_1 \sim \text{STRUCT}):< pol_2,$$
$$(T_2 \sim \text{STRUCT}):< pol_3,$$
$$\ldots$$
$$(T_{n-2} \sim \text{STRUCT}):< pol_{n-1}, T_{n-1}:pol_n >$$
$$\ldots \quad > > >$$

### Example 8.2.2 (STRUCT assembly (2))

Here we aggregate the same geometric components used in Example 8.2.1, but we also associate some transformations of coordinates, different from the identity, to the arcs of the graph representation of the resulting assembly.

In particular, let us describe their aggregation as done in the following.

$$(\texttt{@1} \sim \text{STRUCT}):< \text{CUBOID}:<2,2,2>, T:3:2, \text{CUBOID}:<1,1,1>, T:2:1, \text{SIMPLEX}:3 >$$

Notice, looking at the geometric result shown in Figure 8.3b, that:

1. the output assembly is represented in the coordinate system of first cube;
2. the second cube is translated in $z$ direction;
3. the unit tetrahedron is translated both in $y$ and in $z$ directions.

### 8.3  Traversal

The *traversal* of a hierarchical structure consists of a modified *Depth First Search* (DFS) of its acyclic multigraph,[3] where each arc — and not each node — is traversed only once. In particular, each node is traversed a number of times equal to the number of different paths that reach it from the root node.

The aim of the traversal algorithm is to "linearize" a structure network, by transforming all its substructures (i.e. all the subgraphs) from their *local coordinates* to the coordinates of the root node, assumed as *world coordinates*.

---

[3] Notice that the standard *dfs* graph traversal (see e.g. [AHU83]) visits all the nodes once, since it works by recursively visiting those sons of each node that it has not already visited.

For this purpose, a matrix denoted as the *current transformation matrix* (CTM) is maintained. Such a CTM is equal to the product of matrices associated with the arcs of the current path from the root to the current node. For the sake of efficiency, the traversal algorithm is implemented by using a stack of CTMs. When a new arc is traversed, the old CTM is pushed on the stack, and a new CTM is computed by (right) multiplication of the old one times the matrix of the arc. When unfolding from the recursive visit of the subgraph appended to the arc,[4] the CTM is substituted by the one popped from the stack. The TRAVERSAL algorithm is specified by some pseudo-language in Script 8.3.1.

---

**Script 8.3.1 (Traversal of a multigraph)**
**algorithm** TRAVERSAL $((N, A, f) : multigraph)$ {
   $CTM :=$ identity matrix;
   TraverseNode (*root*)
}

**proc** TRAVERSENODE $(n : node)$ {
   **foreach** $a \in A$ outgoing from $n$ **do** TraverseArc $(a)$;
   ProcessNode $(n)$
}

**proc** TRAVERSEARC $(a = (n, m) : arc)$ {
   Stack.push $(CTM)$;
   $CTM := CTM * a.\text{mat}$;
   TraverseNode $(m)$;
   $CTM := $ Stack.pop()
}

**proc** PROCESSNODE $(n : node)$ {
   **foreach** object $\in n$ **do** Process( $CTM *$ object )
}

---

The CTM is normally used to (left) multiply the vertices of geometric objects stored in the traversed containers. But the reader should remember that equations of hyperplanes and normal vectors must be conversely (right) multiplied for the inverse of the applied transformation, according to the mapping of covectors discussed in Section 6.3.4. A double stack of matrices, where to push/pop both the CTM and its current inverse, may therefore speed up the traversal. As a result of the algorithm, a linearized model in world coordinates is produced, which may be used, e.g., for rendering purposes, as discussed in the next chapter.

**Example 8.3.1 (Graph traversal)**
In Figure 8.1a a directed multigraph over the set of nodes $\{1, 2, \ldots, 9\}$ is shown.

---

[4] Using a pictorial image, we could say: when the arc is traversed in the opposite direction.

According to a standard convention of hierarchical graph drawing [DBETT99], each edge should be considered as downwards oriented. In Figure 8.1b the tree generated when traversing the previous multigraph is given. As the reader may notice, it contains a higher number of node instances. In particular, the ordered set of nodes produced by the traversal algorithm discussed above is:

$$(6, 2, 6, 7, 3, 7, 7, 8, 9, 4, 7, 8, 9, 4, 9, 9, 9, 5, 1).$$

We would like to emphasize the fundamental property that *the number of instances of a node equates to the number of different paths that reach it from the root.* Notice, e.g., there are five different paths in the hierarchical multigraph of Figure 8.1a from root 1 to node 9, so that five instances of the node 9 are produced in the *linearized graph* generated at traversal time.

## 8.4   Implementations

We briefly summarize here some main aspects of management of structured assemblies in PHIGS and in VRML, mainly because the first standard introduced the conceptual model of hierarchical structures adopted by PLaSM, whereas VRML is used as main exporting format by our design language.

### 8.4.1   *Structure network in PHIGS*

A *structure* is defined as an ordered collection of structure elements, where a *structure element* is either:

1. an *output primitive*, say, a polyline, polymarker, text, fill area, fill area set, cell array or generalized drawing primitive (see Section 7.1.2);
2. an *affine transformation*, either through by setting a transformation matrix or by invoking some elementary transformation (say, a $x$-, $y$- or $z$-rotation, a scaling or a translation);
3. a *reference* to other structures. A reference behaves exactly like a procedure invocation in a programming language. When such a reference is encountered at traversal time, the current state of the graphics system is saved on a stack; the invoked procedure is executed, i.e. displayed; the saved state is then restored and finally the control is returned to the following structure element;
4. an *attribute* specification for either primitives or structures, i.e. a setting of some appearance characteristic of primitives or collections of primitives;
5. a *label*, i.e. a symbolic name associated with a numbered position within a structure, used to make the process easier and speed up the structure editing at run-time.

A collection of structures referring to each other is called *structure network*. This one has the topology of a directed acyclic graph. The processing of a structure network for display on a workstation by stepping through its structure elements is called the *structure network traversal*. While traversing the structure network, a set of information called the *traversal state list* is maintained, including the current values of the *attributes* used to display the output primitives, and the current value of the *global modeling transformation*, that we called CTM, as well as the current value of the *local modeling transformation*, a sort of CTM internal to the current structure.

**Remarks**   We note that:

- A structure is defined by invoking a `openStruct(name)` procedure and ended by invocation of a `closeStruct()` procedure. Structure definitions cannot be nested. Conversely, *references* to external structures are allowed within a structure, as invocations of the `executeStruct(name)` procedure.
- *Attribute specifications* modify the current values of the appropriate attributes. Attributes are values of properties (like, e.g. polyline color, text height or width, etc.) used to determine the appearance of output primitives encountered during the traversal. Current values of attributes are maintained in the traversal state list, and are saved on the stack when an `executeStruct()` element is encountered.
- *Labels* as structure elements are used to make the editing of structures at run-time easier. Since changes to a posted structure network are immediately displayed on a workstation, the editing of structures (i.e. the insertion, deletion or modification of structure elements) often results in some animation of the posted structure network.

**Structure editing and animation**   As we already said, the animation of a posted structure network is obtained by editing the network, whose traversal is repeated several times at each time unit. Since changes of structure elements are immediately reflected on the workstation display, in order to animate a scene it will suffice to modify some element of posted structures, often by repeatedly changing some modeling transformation. In particular, a change to a modeling transformation may induce a change of the whole subgraph rooted on the edited node.

To obtain a continuous change of the scene appearance, i.e. a fluid animation, the frequency of traversal must exceed the latency of the perceived image on the observer's retina. The traversal frequency will clearly depend on the complexity of the posted structure network and, in particular, on the number of output primitives contained there. Modern graphics hardware available as add-on for personal computers nowadays provides an amazing computational power, and is able to display scene graphs with more that one million of multiply-textured and shaded triangles at a traversal rate of 80 times for second, or to traverse 2 million triangles 40 times/second, and so on.

### 8.4.2   *Hierarchical scene graph in VRML*

The definition of hierarchies in VRML is obtained by using *grouping nodes*, and in particular by using `Transform` and `Group` nodes. The *Group* node has a similar use to the *Transform* node, but without including a transformation. Both nodes may contain any number of children nodes:

```
Group {
    bboxCenter 0 0 0 # SFVec3f
```

```
      bboxSize -1 -1 -1 # SFVec3f
      children [ ... ] # MFNode
}
```

The *bboxCenter* (bounding box center) and *bboxSize* (bounding box size) attributes are optionally used to speed up the operations, and in particular the hierarchical graph culling (see Section 10.3.2) of VRML viewers. The *children* field may contain either a single node or any number of ordered nodes.

**Scene diagrams**   A useful tool for design and development of hierarchical assemblies is the drawing of scene diagrams, which help to visualize the structure of the scene. Nodes are shown as circles. In such diagrams dark circles are used for grouping nodes, i.e. for *Group* and *Transform* nodes, whereas light circles are used for the other types of nodes. According to a convention introduced by Open Inventor, the scene graph is drawn vertically, with children nodes aligned to the right of their father node, and connected to it by the same vertical line.

**Example 8.4.1 ( VRML scene graph)**
In this example we introduce the VRML scene graph of the *Living room* example fully implemented in PLaSM in Section 8.5.1, and shown in Figure 8.5b.

The reader may easily figure out that a complete linear description, i.e. a complete tree of the scene may be too verbose and redundant, and also difficult to read. In order to make the description more compact and readable, it is customary to adopt a bottom-up approach based on separating the definition and the instantiation of scene components.

Let us therefore start our VRML coding by independently defining, within "local" coordinate systems, the elementary parts of our scene, i.e. the *Table* and *Chair* nodes. The *ArmChair* node is defined by invoke a transformed instance of the *Chair*. Let us remember that a *Shape* node usually contains an *appearance* field and a *geometry* field. Also remember the VRML rule that nodes are capitalized, whereas fields are not.

---

**Script 8.4.1 (Table, Chair and ArmChair subgraphs)**
```
      DEF Table Shape {
          appearance Appearance  ...
          geometry Inline  url ...
      } #Table

      DEF Chair Shape {
          appearance Appearance  ...
          geometry inline  url ...
      } #Chair

      DEF ArmChair Transform {
          scale 1.2 1.2 1
          children USE Chair
      } #ArmChair
```

---

The diagram of *Table* node defined in Script 8.4.1 is given in Figure 8.4a.

Analogously, to define the *Couch* node (Figure 8.4b), it is sufficient to invoking three instances of the Chair node, each one suitably rotated and translated. The VRML coding of the *Couch* as a *Group* node (and the subgraph rooted on it) is given in Script 8.4.2.

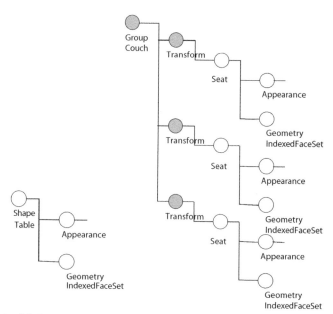

**Figure 8.4** (a) Scene diagram for the *Table* node (b) Scene diagram for the *Couch* node

---

**Script 8.4.2 (Couch subgraph)**

```
DEF Couch Transform {
    scale 1.2 1.2 1
    children [
        USE Chair ,
        Transform {
            children USE Chair
            translation 6 0 0 },
        Transform {
            children USE Chair
            translation 12 0 0 }
    ] #children
} #Couch
```

---

The *Dinner* node, given in Script 8.4.3, is defined by an instance of *Table* node, translated to position its center in the origin, and by four instances of the *Chair* node, properly translated and rotated. A *Transform* node is used for this purpose where a translated chair is defined, denoted as *TranslChair*, which is further accessed three times, using different rotations, in the coordinate system of the *Dinner* node.

**Script 8.4.3 (Dinner subgraph)**

```
DEF Dinner Transform {
   translation -5 -5 0 },
   children [
     USE Table,
     Transform {
        rotation 0 0 1 1.57
        children
          DEF TranslChair
            Transform {
               children USE Chair
               translation -8 -2.5 0 } },
     Transform {
        rotation 0 0 1 3.14
        children USE TranslChair },
     Transform {
        rotation 0 0 1 4.71
        children USE TranslChair },
     Transform {
        rotation 0 0 1 6.28
        children USE TranslChair }
   ] #children
} #Dinner
```

Analogously, a *Conversation* object is defined as a *Group* node, by using the local coordinates of its first child *Table*, and containing also a rotated and translated instance of the *ArmChair* node and a translated instance of the *Couch* node.

**Script 8.4.4 (Conversation subgraph)**

```
DEF Conversation Group {
   children [
     USE Table ,
     Transform {
        translation 0 9 0
        rotation 0 0 1 -0.523
        center 3.6 3.6 0
        children USE ArmChair },
     Transform {
        translation 10 0 0
        children USE Couch }
   ] #children
} #Conversation
```

Finally, we give the root node of the scene graph, called *LivingRoom*, using the same local coordinate system of the *Conversation* node, and containing also a translated instance of the *Dinner* node.

Let us finally notice that the above VRML description of the scene was developed using a *bottom-up* approach, i.e. by starting from the more elementary components,

**Script 8.4.5 (Living room subgraph)**

```
DEF LivingRoom Group {
    children [
        USE Conversation ,
        Transform {
            children USE Dinner
            translation 30 30 0 }
    ] #children
} #LivingRoom
```

and by iteratively assembling them into more complex components. The above is the common development method when using scene-graph-based 3D development environments. Conversely, in the PLaSM description of the same scene discussed in the next section, we are able to use a *top-down* approach, starting from a high-level design of the scene, and making modifications until we produce the model of the scene with the desired level of detail. To work with a similar approach, a graphics application developer would need the support of some quite sophisticated 3D authoring software.

## 8.5   Examples

We discuss here some examples of quite complex assemblies in different application domains. The first one concerns the modeling of a living room; the second example discusses the modeling of a simplified human body; then a first implementation of the opening mechanism of a simplified umbrella is discussed. The umbrella example will be worked out with more detail in the chapters on curves and on surfaces, respectively. Finally, some strategies for generating complex assemblies by suitably aligning their component parts are introduced.

### 8.5.1   Living room modeling

In this section a top-down development of a 3D model of a (simplified) "living room" is presented. Our aim is to discuss a step-wise PLaSM refinement of quite a structured assembly. The example was already introduced in the previous section using VRML, with the further aim of comparing the "flavors" of the two languages when describing a quite complex scene graph.

In particular, a *LivingRoom* object is again defined as the aggregation of a *Dinner* and a *Conversation* objects. The first one contains a *Table* and four *Chair* objects; the second one contains another *Table*, an *ArmChair* and a *Couch*. The *Couch* is obtained by assembling three transformed instances of the *Chair* object.

In Script 8.5.1 a first draft of such definitions is given, by associating a transformation matrix to each object instance within an assembly. The reader may notice that the definitions in Script 8.5.1 are nothing more, nothing less, than a linguistic description of the information coded by the scene graph shown in Figure 8.5.

The above definitions actually specify a hierarchical relation *part_of* between the components of the LivingRoom assembly, by naming both each node of the graph and the matrices to be associated with the arcs. According to the discussion in Section 8.1.1, such matrices transform the geometry data contained in the second

**Script 8.5.1 (Top-down design)**

```
DEF LivingRoom = STRUCT: < T1:Dinner, T2:Conversation >
DEF Dinner = STRUCT: < T3:Table, T4:Chair, T5:Chair, T6:Chair, T7:Chair >
DEF Conversation = STRUCT: < T8:Table, T9:ArmChair, T10:Couch >
DEF ArmChair = STRUCT: < T11:Chair >
DEF Couch = STRUCT: < T12, Chair, T13:Chair, T14:Chair >
```

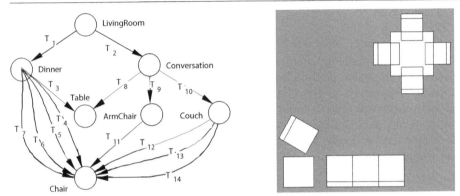

**Figure 8.5**   (a) Structure network (scene graph) of the LivingRoom design
(b) 2D preliminary LivingRoom

node, into the coordinates of the first node of the arc.

Next we go on to detail both the geometric content of the scene components and the transformation matrices. We may assume in this phase that the scene is 2D.

### Scene graph modeling

We start by setting, in Script 8.5.2, a first elementary specification of the basic parts of the scene; then we give a precise content, using local definitions, to the transformation matrices in Script 8.5.3.

**Script 8.5.2 (First version - Basic parts)**

```
DEF Chair = QUOTE:<1,5> * QUOTE:<5>;
DEF Table = CUBOID:<10,10>;
DEF ArmChair = S:<1,2>:<1.2,1.2>:Chair;
```

The higher-level assemblies in our scene are then fully detailed. The 1-skeleton of the resulting sketch of the scene, exported by the last expression of Script 8.5.3, is shown in Figure 8.5b.

**A better implementation**   A much better implementation of LivingRoom, Conversation and Dinner assemblies is given in Script 8.5.4, by exploiting the very powerful semantics of structures introduced by PHIGS and inherited by PLaSM (see Section 8.2.3). Look in particular at the definition of the Dinner structure, given as a sequence that contains various instances of the **seat** geometric object and of the Rxy

## Script 8.5.3 (First version - Assemblies)

```
DEF LivingRoom = STRUCT:< T1:Dinner, T2:Conversation >
WHERE
    T1 = T:<1,2>:<30,30>,
    T2 = T:1:0
END;

DEF Dinner = STRUCT:< T3:Table, T4:Chair, T5:Chair, T6:Chair, T7:Chair>
WHERE
    T3 = T:<1,2>:<-5,-5>,
    T4 = R:<1,2>:(1*PI/2) ~ T:<1,2>:<-9,-2.5>,
    T5 = R:<1,2>:(2*PI/2) ~ T:<1,2>:<-9,-2.5>,
    T6 = R:<1,2>:(3*PI/2) ~ T:<1,2>:<-9,-2.5>,
    T7 = R:<1,2>:(4*PI/2) ~ T:<1,2>:<-9,-2.5>
END;

DEF Conversation = STRUCT:< T8:Table, T9:ArmChair, T10:Couch >
WHERE
    T8 = S:<1,2>:<7/10,7/10>,
    T9 = T:2:9 ~ (T:<1,2>:<3.6,3> ~ R:<1,2>:(PI/-6) ~ T:<1,2>:<-3.6,-3>),
    T10 = T:1:10
END;

DEF Couch = STRUCT:< T12, seat, T13:seat, T14:seat >
WHERE
    seat = (R:<1,2>:(PI/2) ~ T:2:-5):Chair,
    T12 = S:<1,2>:<1.2,1.2>,
    T13 = T:1:5,
    T14 = T13 ~ T13
END;

VRML:((STRUCT ~ [ID,@1]):LivingRoom):'out.wrl';
```

transformation.

The associated multigraph would contain the Dinner, Table and seat nodes, an arc (with ID transformation) between Dinner and Table and four arcs between Dinner and seat. The transformation tensors associated with such four arcs would be ID, Rxy, Rxy~Rxy and Rxy~Rxy~Rxy, respectively.

The simplification obtained in Script 8.5.4 is partially due to the use of local modeling transformations even within the single structure and also partially due to a better positioning of the local origin within the elementary parts of the assembly. In particular, the new definitions given in Script 8.5.5 set the origin of local systems to the midpoint of containment boxes.

### 3D scene modeling

A quite detailed 3D modeling of the elementary parts of the scene is given in Script 8.5.6. The Chair object is decomposed into the assembly of a frame, a seat and a back, colored with black, yellow and white predefined colors, respectively. The Table object is decomposed into the assembly of four rotated instances of a

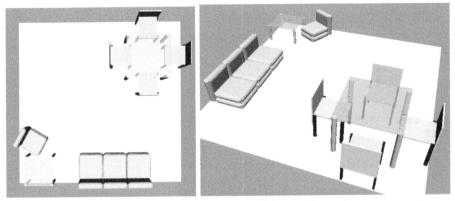

**Figure 8.6**   (a) Top view of the 3D version (b) View from the **dinner** angle

---

### Script 8.5.4 (Better assembly)

```
DEF LivingRoom = STRUCT:< Conversation, T:<1,2>:<27,27>, Dinner >;

DEF Conversation = STRUCT:< table2, T9:ArmChair, T10:Couch >
WHERE
    table2 = S:<1,2>:<0.7,0.7>:Table,
    T9 = T:2:9 ~ R:<1,2>:(PI/-6),
    T10 = T:1:10
END;

DEF Dinner = STRUCT:< Table, seat, Rxy, seat, Rxy, seat, Rxy, seat >
WHERE
    Rxy = R:<1,2>:(PI/2),
    seat = T:1:-5:Chair
END;
```

---

translated cylindrical **leg** and one superimposed tiny plane of colored **glass**. The more interesting model is associated with the *ArmChair* symbol, where a local **basis** produces a properly dimensioned instance of a "parametrized puff", i.e. a cushion parametrized by the sizes of its containment box.

As it possible to see in Figure 8.6b, the **ArmChair** assembly is made by three translated and rotated instances of the **cushion** located at the cushion angles. The **Q** version of the **QUOTE** operator was defined in Script 1.5.5. Script 8.5.7 provides the **puff** function, used to generating the component cushions of both the **ArmChair** and the **Couch**.

Notice that such parametrized cushion is generated by **JOIN** of four rotated instances

---

### Script 8.5.5 (Better parts)

```
DEF Couch = STRUCT:< seat, T:1:6, seat, T:1:6, seat >
DEF seat = R:<1,2>:(PI/2):ArmChair
DEF Chair = (T:<1,2>:<-3,-2.5>):(QUOTE:<1,5> * QUOTE:<5>);
DEF Table = (T:<1,2>:<-5,-5> ~ CUBOID):<10,10>;
DEF ArmChair = S:<1,2>:<1.2,1.2>:Chair;
```

**Script 8.5.6 (Detail modeling — parts)**

```
DEF Chair = STRUCT:< frame, seat, back >
WHERE
    frame = Q:<0.5,-4,0.5> * Q:<0.3,-4.4,0.3> * Q:4.5 COLOR BLACK,
    seat = Q:5 * Q:<-0.3,4.4> * Q:<-4.3,0.2> COLOR YELLOW,
    back = T:1:-0.2:(Q:0.2 * Q:5 * Q:<-3,5>) COLOR WHITE
END;

DEF Table =
    (T:<1,2>:<4.6,4.6> ~ STRUCT):< leg, Rz, leg, Rz, leg, Rz, leg >
    TOP (CUBOID:<10,10,0.2> MATERIAL glass)
WHERE
    leg = (T:<1,2>:<-4.6,-4.6> ~ Cylinder):<0.4,7,18> ,
    Rz = R:<1,2>:(PI/2),
    glasscolor = RGBCOLOR:<0.2,0.6,1>,
    glass = BASEMATERIAL:< glasscolor,glasscolor,0.2,BLACK,0.2,0.6 >
END;

DEF ArmChair = S:<1,2,3>:<5/8,5/8,5/8>:
    ((T:3:4 ~ R:<1,3>:(PI/2)):cushion RIGHT (cushion TOP cushion))
WHERE
    cushion = puff:<6,6,2> COLOR RGBCOLOR:<1,0.5,0>
END;

DEF Seat = ArmChair;
```

**Script 8.5.7 (Detail modeling — puff)**

```
DEF puff (a,b,c::IsReal) = (JOIN ~ STRUCT ~ ##:4):< theAngle, Rz >
WHERE
    Rz = R:<1,2>:(PI/2),
    cyl = (T:3:(c/-2) ~ cylinder):<c/2, c, 18>,
    corner = &:< cyl, R:<1,3>:(PI/2):cyl, R:<2,3>:(PI/2):cyl>,
    theAngle = T:<1,2>:<a/-2,b/-2>:corner
END;
```

of theAngle, a translated copy of corner generated by intersection of three rotated cylinders. The shape thus generated closely recalls at the corners the hand-made seams of real-world cushions, and gives more realistic results than using a small sphere — see Figure 8.6b.

**Storage comparison** It may be interesting to compare the storage used by the PLaSM description of the 3D LivingRoom discussed in this section, with the storage of the VRML file generated by it and displayed in Figure 8.6. On the Mac OS X file system, the first one needs 4KB, whereas the second one needs 112KB. The comparison between the number of characters contained in such files is even more unbalanced, going from $1,935$ to $103,621$ characters, with a ratio close to $\frac{1}{53}$.

### 8.5.2  Body model

A simplified model of the human body as a hierarchical assembly with rotational joints between parts is discussed in this section. A hierarchical structure is assumed as the basis of the modeling, where the Body symbol denotes the structure root. The body's main substructures, respectively called top_limb, upper_limb and lower_limb, are attached to it. The last two are clearly instanced twice. It is also assumed that all the degrees of freedom are rotational. In other words it is assumed that only rotations are allowed by body joints.

### Anthropomorphic robot

The upper level object, i.e. the root of the assembly, is given as a STRUCT expression named Body. The interesting part of the definition is how the joint conditions are defined, using the Tensor function. The particular shapes of the body components will be detailed in Script 8.5.13. The simplest shape for each part is a parallelepiped. The resulting object, resembling an anthropomorphic robot, is shown in Figure 8.7.

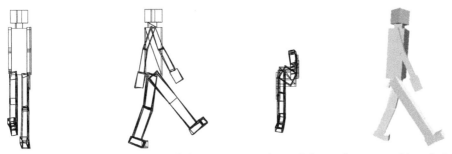

**Figure 8.7**   Front, side, top and dimetric projections of the anthropomorphic robot

The Tensor function is first applied to a sequence of integers, which specify the axes of rotations (either $x$, $y$ or $z$, respectively corresponding to input values 1,2 or 3) allowed by a joint, and the corresponding angles in degrees. The output of the function is a transformation tensor, generated by composition of elementary rotations. Notice that angles, entered in degrees, are transformed to convertedAngles in radians. The scalarVectProd operator is given in Script 2.1.20.

---

**Script 8.5.8 (Composite rotations)**
```
DEF Tensor (axes::IsSeqOf:IsInt) (angles::IsSeqOf:IsReal) =
   (COMP ~ AA:APPLY ~ TRANS): < rotations, convertedAngles >
WHERE
   rotations = AS:SEL:axes:< R:<2,3>,R:<1,3>,R:<1,2> >,
   convertedAngles = PI/180 scalarVectProd angles
END;
```

---

In Script 8.5.9 the Body structure is given, i.e. the root of the structure network discussed in this section. The children structures top_limb, upper_limb and lower_limb are invoked as functions, and applied to the actual values of the angles which determine their configuration. Notice that the rotations of each body's limb are about its local origin. Each joint which connects a limb to torso is then properly translated to its position in the body's coordinate system by a local joint$_i$ function.

---

**Script 8.5.9 (Assembly root)**

```
DEF Body = STRUCT:< torso,
    (joint1 ~ top_limb):<<0,0>,<0,0,-30>>,
    (joint2 ~ upper_limb):<<20,0,0>,<10,0>,<0>>,
    (joint3 ~ upper_limb):<<-20,0,0>,<10,0>,<0>>,
    (joint4 ~ lower_limb):<<40,0,-10>,<0>,<0>,<0>>,
    (joint5 ~ lower_limb):<<-10,0,10>,<-10>,<0>,<20>> >
WHERE
    torso = T:<1,2>:<-5,-5>:torso_shape,
    joint1 = T:3:30,
    joint2 = T:<1,3>:<6,30>,
    joint3 = T:<1,3>:<-6,30>,
    joint4 = T:1:4,
    joint5 = T:1:-4
END;
```

---

The top_limb structure, given in Script 8.5.10, contains a neck and a head object, respectively connected by two and three rotational degrees of freedom, which are passed via the dof (Degrees Of Freedom) formal parameter. Notice that the neck is allowed to rotate about its local $x$ and $y$ axes, whereas the head may rotate about $x$, $y$ and $z$.

---

**Script 8.5.10 (Neck and head)**

```
DEF top_limb (dof::IsSeqOf:IsSeq) = STRUCT:<
    rot1, pos1:neck, joint, rot2, pos2:head >
WHERE
    pos1 = T:<1,2>:<-2.5,-2.5>,
    pos2 = T:<1,2>:<-4,-4>,
    rot1 = Tensor:<1,2>:(S1:dof),
    rot2 = Tensor:<1,2,3>:(S2:dof),
    joint = T:3:3
END;
```

---

The upper_limb parametric structure given in Script 8.5.11 connects into a kinematic chain the upper_arm to the lower_arm and the latter to the hand objects, and connects them with three, two and one rotational degrees of freedom, passed as subsequences of the dof sequence, respectively. Notice, e.g., that the hand object is positioned with respect to its local origin by the pos3 tensor, then rotated about its origin by the rot3 tensor. Finally, the local origin, i.e. the position of the rotational joint, is translated within the local system of its father object (in this case lower_arm) by the joint2 tensor within the hierarchical assembly which models the kinematic chain of the body arm. A similar pattern of transformations is used for the subsequent subassemblies and joints, i.e. for `lower_arm` and `upper_arm`.

---

**Script 8.5.11 (Arm and hand)**

```
DEF upper_limb (dof::IsSeqOf:IsSeq) = STRUCT:<
    rot1 ~ pos1, upper_arm,
    joint1 ~ rot2 ~ pos2, lower_arm,
    joint2 ~ rot3 ~ pos3, hand >
WHERE
    rot1 = Tensor:<1,2,3>:(S1:dof),
    rot2 = Tensor:<1,3>:(S2:dof),
    rot3 = Tensor:<2>:(S3:dof),
    pos1 = T:<1,2,3>:<-1,-1.5,-15>,
    pos2 = T:<1,2,3>:<-1,-1.5,-15>,
    pos3 = T:3:-8,
    joint1 = T:<1,2>:<1,1.5>,
    joint2 = T:<1,2>:<0.5,-1>
END;
```

---

Analogously, the `lower_limb` function given in Script 8.5.12 is a parametric structure, joining a big `toe` to the `feet` and this one to the `lower_leg` and then to the `upper_leg`, which is finally positioned into the local reference system of the `lower_limb` by the transformation tensors named `pos1` and `rot1`.

---

**Script 8.5.12 (Leg and feet)**

```
DEF lower_limb (dof::IsSeqOf:IsSeq) = STRUCT:<
    rot1 ~ pos1, upper_leg,
    joint1 ~ rot2 ~ pos2, lower_leg,
    joint2 ~ rot3 ~ pos3, feet,
    joint3 ~ rot4, toe >
WHERE
    pos1 = T:<1,2,3>:<-2,-3,-20>,
    pos2 = T:<2,3>:<-3,-20>,
    pos3 = T:2:-1,
    rot1 = Tensor:<1,2,3>:(S1:dof),
    rot2 = Tensor:<1>:(S2:dof),
    rot3 = Tensor:<1>:(S3:dof),
    rot4 = Tensor:<1>:(S4:dof),
    joint1 = T:2:3,
    joint2 = T:3:-4,
    joint3 = T:2:9
END;
```

---

The sort of anthropomorphic robot depicted in Figure 8.7 is finally generated by assigning a parallelepiped shape to each Body part. The detailed definitions of all the component shapes are given in Script 8.5.13.

**Script 8.5.13 (Body components)**

```
DEF torso_shape = CUBOID:<10,10,30>;
DEF head = CUBOID:<8,8,8>;
DEF neck = CUBOID:<5,5,3>;
DEF upper_arm = CUBOID:<2,3,15>;
DEF lower_arm = CUBOID:<2,3,15>;
DEF hand = CUBOID:<1,5,8>;
DEF feet = CUBOID:<4,9,4>;
DEF toe = CUBOID:<4,3,4>;
DEF lower_leg = CUBOID:<4,6,20>;
DEF upper_leg = CUBOID:<4,6,20>
```

**Note**  The important part of the structured assembly discussed above is the hierarchical relationship between its parts, and the chains of transformations between the local coordinate systems induced by the joint conditions. The shapes of the elementary parts may easily be changed without requiring any change of the upper-level structures, as it is shown by the two variations of the body model given in Figure 8.8.

**Figure 8.8**  Two configurations of the Body model with different definitions for the elementary parts and same values for the joint angles

Actually, in order to be really invariant with respect to the dimensions and shapes of lower-level subassemblies and components, the $pos_i$ tensors should be moved on top of the children structures, and the $joint_i$ tensors should be written as parametric functions of the dimensions of the local root.

### 8.5.3  Umbrella modeling (1): structure

The goal of the geometric programming example given here is the generative modeling of a *parametric umbrella*, parametrized on the opening angle. In particular, we discuss the modeling from scratch of the kinematic mechanism, using wire-frame parts. In later chapters, this model will be step-wise refined by:

1. curving some rods as quadratic Bézier curves, depending on the opening angle of the umbrella (see Section 11.5.2);
2. modeling the umbrella canvas as Coon's patches delimited by polynomial curves of degrees 2, 1 and 0 (see Section 12.6.1);
3. modeling all the umbrella rods as solid parts, to substitute their previous

definitions as wire frames (see Section 13.6.1).
4. animating the various umbrella versions (see Section 15.6.1).

This example aims to demonstrate that the PLaSM language, conversely than other development environments for graphics programming and virtual reality, allows for progressive refinement of working models and *top-down development*. The authors believe this fact should be the very distinctive feature of a *design language*.

**Rod and axis modeling**    A 1D Rod of length len is defined along the $z$-axis in $\mathbb{R}^3$ by using the primitive constructor MKPOL. The core RodPair of the moving mechanism (shown in Figure 8.9a) is then described as a function depending on the height h and on the opening angle alpha. For this purpose two instances of the Rod primitive are properly combined with affine transformations. According to the semantics of standard ISO PHIGS structures, both Rod1 and Rod2 are defined in local coordinates and jointly transformed into world coordinates.

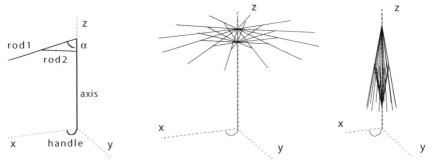

**Figure 8.9**    (a) Model generated by (STRUCT $\sim$ [Axis $\sim$ S1,Handle $\sim$ S1,RodPair]):<10,80>   (b) Value of Umbrella:<10,80> (c) Value of Umbrella:<10,15>

---

**Script 8.5.14 (Umbrella (1a))**

```
DEF Rod (len::IsReal) = MKPOL:<<<0,0,0>,<0,0,len>>,<<1,2>>,<<1>>>;
DEF Axis (len::IsReal) = Rod:len;

DEF RodPair (h, alpha::Isreal) = STRUCT:<
    T:3:h, R:<3,1>:(-:alphaRad), Rod1,
    T:3:(-:AB), R:<3,1>:(2*alphaRad), Rod2 >
WHERE
    alphaRad = alpha*PI/180,
    Rod1 = S:3:-1:(Rod:(2*AB)),
    Rod2 = S:3:-1:(Rod:AB),
    AB = h*4/10
END;
```

---

**Parametric umbrella**  The whole parametric `Umbrella` is then defined as a structure by catenating a sequence with one `Axis` and `Handle` and 12 pairs, each containing a rotation of $\pi/6$ around the $z$-axis and one instance of the `RodPair` model previously defined.

In particular, the `Handle` is defined as a properly positioned halfcircle linearly approximated with 12 segments. The whole `Umbrella` model at this stage is shown in Figure 8.9 for two different values of the opening angle.

---

**Script 8.5.15 (Umbrella (1b))**

```
DEF Umbrella (h, alpha::Isreal) = (STRUCT ~ CAT):
   <[Axis, Handle]:h, ##:12:< RodPair:<9/10*h,alpha>, R:<1,2>:(PI/6) > >;

DEF Handle (h::Isreal) = (T:1:Radius ~ S:<1,3>:<Radius,Radius>):
   (MAP:[COS ~ S1, K:0, SIN ~ S1]:dom )
WHERE
   dom = T:1:PI:(QUOTE:(#:12:(PI/12))),
   Radius = h/18
END;
```

---

*8.5.4   Tree diagrams*

In this section we develop and discuss a useful set of functions used to produce a graphical representation of a hierarchy, or, in other words, to perform some *tree drawing*. In particular, we assume here that every tree node is associated with a string. The given drawing approach can be slightly modified to produce a graphical representation of more general hierarchies, where a node may be associated to any kind of polyhedral complex of dimension 2 or 3. This approach could get useful to generate the hierarchical diagram of the *product model* in some industrial applications.

**Drawing strategy**

Very simple drawing rules are used, and no optimization of the drawing area is attempted. Two different styles for the drawing of the father-son relationship are alternatively implemented. The resulting diagrams of the same tree are shown in Figures 8.9a and 8.9b. The two simple style rules used in the following implementation may be summarized as follows:

1. the containment boxes of the subtrees rooted in a node (called brother subtrees in the following) are aligned with the top edges;
2. the containment boxes of brother subtrees are equally spaced.

Two more geometrical rules drive the whole drawing algorithm:

3. each node is defined in local coordinates, with the origin of the local system positioned in the centroid of the containment box of the node;
4. each subtree is defined in the local coordinates of its root node;

**Implementation**

In implementing the above drawing strategy, three main steps can be abstracted, concerning respectively (a) the drawing of a node; (b) the drawing of a subtree; and the (c) bottom up streaming aggregation of drawn subtrees, until one can draw or, better, generate a geometric model of the diagram of the whole input tree.

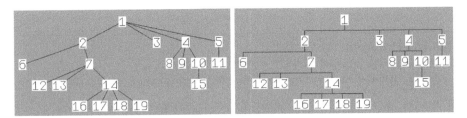

**Figure 8.10**    Two graphical representations of the same tree

**Tree input**    The tree shown in Figure 8.10, using two different drawing styles for the arcs outgoing from each node, is coded in Script 8.5.16.

In particular, a tree is defined as a *sequence of levels*, where each level is a sequence of sequences of nodes. There are as many elements (subsequences) in a level as there are nodes in the previous tree level, so to define a *one-to-one mapping* between *nodes* and sequences of their *children*. Therefore, a leaf node is associated with an empty sequence in the next level, a node with two children is associated with a sequence with two nodes, and so on. Also, each node is represented by a PLaSM string. Clearly, there are as many (top-level) sequences in this description as there are levels in the tree.

---

**Script 8.5.16 (Tree input)**

```
DEF tree = <
    <<'1'>>,
    <<'2','3','4','5'>>,
    <<'6','7'>,<>,<'8','9','10'>,<'11'>>,
    <<>,<'12','13','14'>,<>,<>,<'15'>,<>>,
    <<>,<>,<'16','17','18','19'>,<>>
>;

VRML:(drawTree:tree):'out.wrl';
```

---

Notice that the diagrams of Figure 8.10 were produced by the last expression of Script 8.5.16.

**Node drawing**    We assume here that each tree node is described by a label of type string, so that the TEXT operator defined in Script 7.2.13 can be applied to it. In Script 8.5.17 the drawNode operator is given for this purpose, which adds a properly scaled rectangle to the graphical text produced and centered about its midpoint by the centerLabel function.

## Script 8.5.17 (Node drawing)

```
DEF Label = STRUCT ~ [T:<1,2> ~ AA:- ~ MED:<1,2>, ID ] ~ TEXT;
DEF drawNode = STRUCT ~ [ ID, K:(S:<1,2>:<1.2,1.6>), BOX:<1,2> ] ~ Label;
```

More general assumptions about the nature of the nodes might be postulated and easily implemented, with the aim of generating the diagram as a polyhedral complex of suitable dimension.

**Subtree drawing**   The main design choices of the subtree drawing algorithm given in Script 8.5.18 concern the definition of each subtree in the local coordinate space of its own root node, with a local origin $(0, 0)$ coinciding with the center of the root's containment box.

Notice that the discussed drawing strategy is *bottom-up*, from leaf nodes in the lowest hierarchical level, up to the root node in the top tree level. The main algorithm is codified by the drawSubtree function, which is repeatedly called by the draw_level function in Script 8.5.19.

The drawSubtree algorithm just aggregates the two structures returned by the moved_sons function and by the drawEdges function. In particular, the last one returns a set of polylines between the local origin and the sonCenters. The moved_sons operator returns the structure produced by equispacing the subtree(s) of its son arguments. The translations to be applied between adjacent son pairs are computed on the fly, by analyzing the pairs of already modeled subtrees.

## Script 8.5.18 (Subtree drawing)

```
DEF pairs = CONS ~ AA:CONS
    ~ TRANS ~AA:(AA:SEL~FROMTO)~[[ k:1,len-k:1],[ k:2,len ]];
DEF size_pairs = APPLY ~ [pairs, ID] ~ AA:(SIZE:1);
DEF translations = AA:(T:1 ~ C:+:dx ~ /~[ID,K:2] ~ +)
    ~ AR ~ [ID, K:0] ~ size_pairs;
DEF last_transl (n::IsPol) = T:<1,2>
    ~ [(SIZE:1 / K:-2) + K:(SIZE:1:n / 2), K: dy];

DEF drawSubtree = STRUCT ~ [ moved_sons, drawEdges ];
DEF subtree = STRUCT ~ CAT ~ TRANS ~ [ ID, translations ];
DEF moved_sons (sons::isSeqOf:isPol) =
    (STRUCT ~ [ last_transl:(FIRST: sons), ID ] ~ subtree):sons;

DEF drawEdges (sons::isSeqOf:isPol) =
    (STRUCT ~ AA:Polyline ~ DISTL): < <0,0>, sonCenters >
WHERE
    sonTransl = (AL~[last_transl:(S1:sons)~subtree, translations]): sons,
    sonCenters = (S1 ~ UKPOL ~ STRUCT ~ CAT ~ DISTR):<sonTransl,MK:<0,0>>
END;
```

**Tree drawing**   The top-level operator, which is invoked to produce a diagram of a tree, is clearly named drawTree, and is given in Script 8.5.19. It is quite interesting, because does not use either explicit iteration or recursion to make its work, but instead a pure FL style based on a sort of stream processing. The drawTree behavior can be summarized as follows.

1. First, the input tree is preprocessed by "drawing" every node, i.e. by transforming every string into a 2D polyhedral complex.
2. Then, the $n$ levels in the input tree are paired bottom-up, and each level pair is repeatedly transformed into a single level, by reducing each corresponding (node, children sequence) into a single polyhedral complex, by using for this purpose the drawSubtree operator. This operation is repeated $n-1$ times.
3. Finally, some house-cleaning is performed, in order to extract the 2D output complex from the generated data structure.

---

**Script 8.5.19 (Tree drawing)**

```
DEF drawTree (levels::IsSeq) =
    (S1 ~ S1 ~ S1 ~ COMP:(#:(n - 1):reducePair AR preProcess)):levels
WHERE
    n = LEN: levels,
    preProcess = REVERSE ~ AA: draw_leafs,
    reducePair = AL ~ [structMapping, TAIL~TAIL]
        ~ AL~[ AA: pairing ~ TRANS ~ [draw_level ~ S1, CAT ~ S2], TAIL ]
END;

DEF draw_leafs = AA:(IF:< isVoid, K:<>, AA:drawNode >);
DEF draw_level = AA:(IF:< isVoid, K:<>, drawSubtree >);
DEF pairing = IF:< isVoid ~ s1, s2, STRUCT ~ [s2,s1] >;
DEF structMapping = APPLY ~ [CONS ~ AA:(AS:SEL) ~ select ~ S2, S1];
DEF select = AA:(FROMTO ~ [ + ~ [- ~[+ , LAST],K:1], + ])
    ~ APPLY
    ~ [CONS ~ AA:(AS:SEL ~ INTSTO)~INTSTO ~ LEN, ID]
    ~ AA:LEN;
```

---

**Drawing subtree forks**  The standard drawing style for a tree diagram puts a segment between non-leaf nodes and each of their children. More unusually, a single "fork" instead goes out from every non-leaf node, and enters each of the children of the node. The drawForks function given in Script 8.5.20 implements such a drawing style, and is intended to substitute the drawEdges call in the drawSubtree function of Script 8.5.18. An example of diagram with forks is given in Figure 8.10b. In this case a sort of "Manhattan" path is used when drawing edges between the starting point and the ending points. The mean function was given in Script 4.4.8.

*8.5.5  Array of aligned graphics symbols*

Our aim in this section is to discuss how to build complex arrangements of variously aligned graphics objects or symbols.

**Script 8.5.20 (Subtree forks)**

```
DEF drawForks (sons::isSeqOf:isPol) = (STRUCT ~ AA:Polyline ~ CAT):
    < LIST:middleExtremes, manhattan:<<0,0>, Meanpoint >,
      TRANS:< sonCenters, addedPoints >>
WHERE
    middleExtremes = DISTR:< [ S1~first, S1~last ]: sonCenters , dy / 2 >,
    Meanpoint = (AA: mean ~ TRANS): middleExtremes,
    addedPoints = AA:S1: sonCenters DISTR dy / 2,
    manhattan = [[S1, [s1~s1,s2~s2]], [[s1~s1,s2~s2], S2]]
    sonTranslations =
        (AL ~ [ last_transl:(FIRST: sons) ~ subtree, translations ]): sons,
    sonCenters = (S1 ~ UKPOL ~ STRUCT ~ TAIL ~ CAT ~ DISTL):
        < MK:<0,0>, sonTranslations >,
END;
```

For this purpose we first prepare a simplified 3D model of a house, given in Script 8.5.21, as a polyhedral complex assembling few 3D convex polygons. Such a house model is then projected in various ways, using methods discussed in Chapters 9 and 10, so generating several different 2D projections, shown in Figure 8.11. We do not discuss here how the projections are generated. An extensive discussion of standard projections may be found in Chapter 10. We are only interested here in the relative arrangements of the 2D projections.

**Script 8.5.21 (House model)**

```
DEF house = MKPOL:< verts,cells,pols >
WHERE
    verts = < <0,0,0>,<0,0,10>,<0,5,13>,<0,10,10>,<0,10,0>,
              <10,0,0>,<10,0,10>,<10,5,13>,<10,10,10>,<10,10,0>,
              <10,4,0>,<10,4,8>,<10,6,0>,<10,6,8>,
              <6,10,4>,<4,10,4>,<6,10,8>,<4,10,8> >,
    cells = < 15..18,<5,4,9,10>,11..14,6..10,<3,4,8,9>,
              <2,3,7,8>,<1,2,6,7>,1..5 >,
    pols  = < <1>,<2>,<3>,<4>,<5>,<6>,<7>,<8> >
END;
```

Each projection of the 3D house model generated (and assembled) by Script 8.5.22 produces a different 2D graphics object. In particular, a set of 15 different projections is organized in Script 8.5.22 as a 2D array of symbols with 5 rows and 3 columns. For this purpose the generating expressions (enclosed in round parentheses) are grouped into 5 subsets as STRUCT expressions, in turn assembled by an external STRUCT operator, together with translation tensors that relocate the graphics objects they refer to in proper locations of the 2D arrangement.

Notice that, according to the semantics of PHIGS structures, each T:1:28 tensor in Script 8.5.22 applies *only* to graphics objects which follow it within the argument sequence the tensor belongs to.

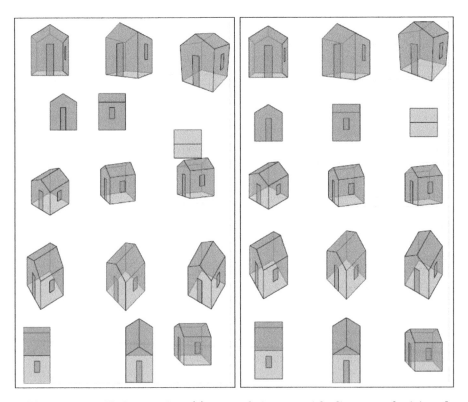

**Figure 8.11**  Flash exporting: (a) array of pictures, with alignment of origins of *local* systems (b) array of pictures *centered* around their (aligned) origins

## Script 8.5.22 (array of artworks)

```
DEF MxMy = STRUCT ~ [T:<1,2> ~ AA:- ~ MED:<1,2>, ID];

DEF out = STRUCT:<
  STRUCT:<
    MxMy:(projection: perspective: onepoint: house), T:1:28,
    MxMy:(projection: perspective: twopoints: house), T:1:28,
    MxMy:(projection: perspective: threepoints: house) > ,
  T:2:-25, STRUCT:<
    MxMy:(projection: parallel: orthox: house), T:1:28,
    MxMy:(projection: parallel: orthoy: house), T:1:28,
    MxMy:(projection: parallel: orthoz: house) > ,
  T:2: -22, STRUCT:<
    MxMy:(projection: parallel: isometric: house), T:1:28,
    MxMy:(projection: parallel: dimetric: house), T:1:28,
    MxMy:(projection: parallel: trimetric: house) > ,
  T:2: -28, STRUCT:<
    MxMy:(projection: parallel: leftCavalier: house), T:1:28,
    MxMy:(projection: parallel: centralCavalier: house), T:1:28,
    MxMy:(projection: parallel: rightCavalier: house) > ,
  T:2: -30, STRUCT:<
    MxMy:(projection: parallel: xCavalier: house), T:1:28,
    MxMy:(projection: parallel: yCavalier: house), T:1:28,
    MxMy:(projection: parallel: cabinet: house) >
>;
```

**Picture exporting**  The pictures shown in Figure 8.11 are produced by a web browser, e.g. *Microsoft Internet Explorer* or *Netscape Navigator*, equipped with a Flash plug-in, by loading the out.swf file exported by PLaSM at the evaluation of the expression given in Script 8.5.23. To successfully evaluate such expression, the PLaSM environment must have already loaded the library called flash.psm, where the definitions of the primitive functions FILLCOLOR, LINECOLOR and LINESIZE are contained. Notice that the argument sequence of FILLCOLOR and LINECOLOR contain 4 numbers in the interval $[0, 1]$, according to the *RGBα* (*Red, Green, Blue, Transparency*) color model used by Flash.

## Script 8.5.23 (Flash exporting)

```
flash:( out
  FILLCOLOR RGBAcolor:< 0,1,1,0.5 >
  LINECOLOR RGBAcolor:< 0,0,0,1 >
  LINESIZE 1 )
:300:'out.swf';
```

## Alignment operators

The picture shown in Figure 8.11b is generated by direct evaluation of the PLaSM code given above. The reader may find very instructive to re-evaluate the exporting expression 8.5.23 after some editing and re-evaluation of Script 8.5.22. In particular, the reader should cancel all the instances of the string "MxMy:", i.e. all the applications of the function MxMy — that stands for *Middle x, Middle y* — to the symbol generating expressions. The specific aim of this operator, defined in Script 8.5.22 as

```
DEF MxMy = STRUCT ~ [T:<1,2> ~ AA:- ~ MED:<1,2>, ID]
```

is to center a 2D object around its local origin.

This operation is accomplished as follows by the MxMy operator:

1. compute, by using the MED:<1,2> operator, the middle point $p$ of the containment box of the symbol;
2. then, generate the translation vector $o - p$, by just reversing the sign of all the $p$ components;
3. finally, produce a STRUCT expression that contains the T:<1,2>:$-p$ tensor as well as the symbol we want to relocate.

Several different *alignment operators* might easily be defined by substituting the MED:<1,2> operator with a different function, with the intent of suitably generating a different translation vector to be applied to the input symbol. For example, a graphics symbol can be usefully relocated by using one of the operators defined in Script 8.5.24.

---

**Script 8.5.24 (Alignment operators)**

```
DEF MxBy = STRUCT ~ [T:<1,2> ~ AA:- ~ [MED:1,MIN:2], ID]
DEF MxTy = STRUCT ~ [T:<1,2> ~ AA:- ~ [MED:1,MAX:2], ID]
DEF LxMy = STRUCT ~ [T:<1,2> ~ AA:- ~ [MIN:1,MED:2], ID]
DEF RxMy = STRUCT ~ [T:<1,2> ~ AA:- ~ [MAX:1,MED:2], ID]
```

---

Where:

1. MxBy stands for *Middle x, Bottom y*, and moves the center of the object baseline, clearly together with the whole object, to the origin of its local reference system.
2. MxTy stands for *Middle x, Top y*, and moves the center of the object topline to the origin of the local system.
3. LxMy stands for *Left x, Middle y*, and moves the center of left side of object's containment box to the origin of the local frame, thus preparing the graphics symbol for a "left-hand" alignment.
4. RxMy stands for *Right x, Middle y*, and moves the center of right side of object's box to the local origin, giving a "right-hand" alignment.

Other combinations of $x$ and $y$ alignments are clearly possible.

# 9

# Graphic pipelines

In this chapter we discuss the sequence of transformations that graphics data, including vertices, control points of curves and surfaces, normal vectors, etc., must undergo in order to be rendered on the screen or displayed on some other output device. Such sequence of transformations is denoted as *graphics pipeline* [FvDFH90]. It is customary to distinguish between 2D and 3D pipelines. The graphics pipelines defined by the GKS standard for 2D graphics and by the PHIGS standard for 3D graphics, respectively, are discussed in depth. Outlines of the graphics pipelines used by Open Inventor and Java 3D are also briefly introduced. A PLaSM implementation of the PHIGS pipeline and some examples of automatic insertion of viewpoints in PLaSM-generated VRML files are finally given.

## 9.1   2D pipeline

In the mid-1980s the vast majority of graphics systems and applications were two-dimensional. The situation has radically changed nowadays, but important classes of 2D applications remain, including Geographical Information Systems (GIS) and 2D drafting.

### 9.1.1   Coordinate systems

The pipeline of transformations between different coordinate systems was introduced by the ISO graphics standard GKS in order to achieve device independence, i.e. in order to display graphics data over devices with different dimensions and pixel addressing [ISO85, EKP87]. For this purpose three coordinate systems were defined:

1. world coordinates (WC);
2. normalized device coordinates (NDC);
3. device coordinates (DC).

*World coordinates* are used to define graphics data (parameters of graphics primitives and geometric attributes of primitives) in some suitable reference depending on the problem at hand; *normalized device coordinates* are employed to store and transform

*Geometric Programming for Computer-Aided Design*   Alberto Paoluzzi
© 2003 John Wiley & Sons, Ltd  ISBN 0-471-89942-9

data in a device-independent way; and, finally, *device coordinates* are used to display graphics data on some suitable subset of the current output device.

**World Coordinates** The so-called *world coordinates* (WC) define a reference system which coincides with a standard Cartesian system of two-dimensional Euclidean space. In such a reference system the more suitable coordinate values can be used for defining graphics primitives and attributes. Only a bounded rectangular subset of this space can be displayed on the graphics device. Such a user-defined subset is called a 2D *window*.

**Figure 9.1** (a) Graph of the function $f : \mathbb{R} \to \mathbb{R} : x \mapsto x + 3\sin x$, with $x \in [0, 6\pi]$, and *window* in WC (b) Normalized device coordinates and *viewport* in NDC (c) Rasterized picture in DC

**Normalized Device Coordinates** The standard 2D unit interval $[0,1] \times [0,1]$ in Euclidean space $\mathbb{E}^2$ is called the *normalized device coordinates* (NDC). This bounded subset gives a reference frame which is used to store and transform graphics data in a device-independent manner. The transformation from WC to NDC is given by defining a rectangular subset of NDC, called *viewport*, to be used as the target set where the window over graphics data must be mapped.

**Device Coordinates** Let us consider a device with $N_x \times N_y$ *pixels* (picture elements) which can be individually referenced in order to be, e.g., colored or displayed. The discrete 2D interval $[0, N_x - 1] \times [0, N_y - 1] \subset \mathcal{Z}^2$, corresponding to the address space of such a specific device, is called the *device coordinates* (DC). This discrete space clearly gives a "device-dependent" reference frame that can be regarded as a bijection with the set of device pixels. Notice that NDC is a square but DC is not necessarily so.

**Example 9.1.1 (Function graph)**
We want to generate the graph of the function $f : \mathbb{R} \to \mathbb{R} : x \mapsto x + 3\sin x$, shown in Figure 9.1. In particular, we are interested to the graph of $f$ restricted to the interval $[0, 6\pi]$, i.e. to the set of points

$$\{(x, f(x)) \in E^2 \mid 0 \le x \le 6\pi, f(x) = x + 3\sin x\}$$

In Script 9.1.1 this function graph is approximated by a `polyline` primitive connecting 91 sampled points in the $[0, 6\pi]$ interval. We remember that the function

`SumSeqWithZero`, given in Script 7.3.1, returns the cumulative sums of the elements of the sequence it is applied to, that is:

`SumSeqWithZero:< 1,1,1,1,1 > ≡ < 0,1,2,3,4,5 >`

---

**Script 9.1.1**

```
( polyline
    ~ AA:[ ID, ID + K:3 * sin ]
    ~ SumSeqWithZero
    ~ #:90 ): ( 6 * PI / 90 );
```

---

*9.1.2   Normalization and device transformations*

In this section we discuss how to transform a coordinate space into another coordinate space. The simple user-model of such kind of mapping, proposed by GKS, requires that two 2D intervals are defined in the domain and target spaces of the mapping, respectively. The mapping is then computed by ensuring that the first interval is affinely mapped onto the second one. The two intervals are called *window* and *viewport*, respectively. Such an approach to the computation of a coordinate transformation is called *window-viewport mapping*.

**2D Extent**   A *2D extent*, also called *2D box* or *2D interval*, is a rectangular domain $B$ of Euclidean space which is parallel to the reference frame. Such a box is represented by the ordered quadruple of real numbers that correspond to the coordinates of lower-left point $(b_1, b_2)$ and upper-right point $(b_3, b_4)$, so that:

$$B = (b_1, b_2, b_3, b_4) = [b_1, b_3] \times [b_2, b_4]$$

i.e.

$$B = \{\boldsymbol{p} = (x, y)^T \mid x \in [b_1, b_3], \ y \in [b_2, b_4]\} \subset \mathbb{E}^2$$

**Normalization transformation**   The bijective affine mapping $\boldsymbol{T}_N$ between a *window* $W_{wc}$ in WC and a *viewport* $V_{ndc}$ in NDC is called the *normalization transformation*:

$$\boldsymbol{T}_N : W_{wc} \to V_{ndc},$$

where

$$W_{wc} = [w_1, w_3] \times [w_2, w_4], \qquad V_{ndc} = [v_1, v_3] \times [v_2, v_4],$$

as shown in Figure 9.2a.

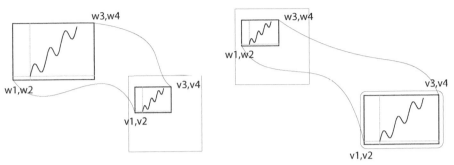

**Figure 9.2**   (a) Normalization transformation: WC → NDC;
(b) Device transformation: NDC → DC

**Device transformation**   Analogously, a *device transformation* $\boldsymbol{T}_D$ is a bijective affine mapping between a *workstation window* $W_{ndc} \subset NDC$ and a *workstation viewport* $V_{dc} \subset DC$:

$$\boldsymbol{T}_D : W_{ndc} \rightarrow V_{dc},$$

where

$$W_{ndc} = [w_1, w_3] \times [w_2, w_4], \qquad V_{dc} = [v_1, v_3] \times [v_2, v_4],$$

as shown in Figure 9.2b.

*9.1.3   Window-viewport mapping*

A *window-viewport mapping* is, by definition, a bijective affine transformation between 2D extents $W = [w_1, w_3] \times [w_2, w_4]$ and $V = [v_1, v_3] \times [v_2, v_4]$:

$$\boldsymbol{M} : W \rightarrow V : \qquad \boldsymbol{p} \mapsto \boldsymbol{M}(\boldsymbol{p}),$$

where $\boldsymbol{M}$ is a tensor in aff $\mathbb{E}^2$. Two methods are discussed below to compute such a transformation tensor, respectively by a direct approach and by the composition of elementary transformations.

**Direct Method**   We use here homogeneous coordinates. The two extreme points $(w_1, w_2, 1)^T$ and $(w_3, w_4, 1)^T$ of window $W$ are respectively mapped to the two extreme points $(v_1, v_2, 1)^T$ and $(v_3, v_4, 1)^T$ of viewport $V$. Also, the $\boldsymbol{M}$ tensor must transform a 2D extent, parallel to the reference frame, onto another one of the same kind. Hence, the matrix $[\boldsymbol{M}]$ will have a predictable structure, with only (unknown) coefficients of scaling and translation:

$$\begin{pmatrix} v_1 & v_3 \\ v_2 & v_4 \\ 1 & 1 \end{pmatrix} = \begin{pmatrix} a & 0 & b \\ 0 & c & d \\ 0 & 0 & 1 \end{pmatrix} \begin{pmatrix} w_1 & w_3 \\ w_2 & w_4 \\ 1 & 1 \end{pmatrix}$$

The previous matrix equation is equivalent to four scalar simultaneous equations in the unknown coefficients $a, b, c$ and $d$:

$$\begin{cases} a\,w_1 + b &= v_1 \\ c\,w_2 + d &= v_2 \\ a\,w_3 + b &= v_3 \\ c\,w_4 + d &= v_4 \end{cases}, \quad \text{and hence} \quad \begin{cases} a &= \frac{v_3 - v_1}{w_3 - w_1} \\ c &= \frac{v_4 - v_2}{w_4 - w_2} \\ b &= v_1 - \frac{v_3 - v_1}{w_3 - w_1} w_1 \\ d &= v_2 - \frac{v_4 - v_2}{w_4 - w_2} w_2 \end{cases}$$

**Composition of elementary transformations**   The window-viewport mapping tensor $\boldsymbol{M}$ can be derived easily by composition of some elementary transformations:

1. a translation $\boldsymbol{T}_1$ which maps the point $(w_1, w_2)$ into the origin $\boldsymbol{o}$ of the reference system;
2. a scaling $\boldsymbol{S}_1$ of $W$ onto the standard unit square;
3. a scaling $\boldsymbol{S}_2$ of the standard unit square onto $V$;
4. a translation $\boldsymbol{T}_2$ which maps $\boldsymbol{o}$ into $(v_1, v_2)$.

In other words we have:

$$\boldsymbol{M} : W \to V : \quad \boldsymbol{p} \mapsto (\boldsymbol{T}_2 \circ \boldsymbol{S}_2 \circ \boldsymbol{S}_1 \circ \boldsymbol{T}_1)(\boldsymbol{p}),$$

where

$$\begin{aligned} \boldsymbol{T}_1 &= \boldsymbol{T}(-w_1, -w_2), \\ \boldsymbol{S}_1 &= \boldsymbol{S}\left(\frac{1}{w_3 - w_1}, \frac{1}{w_4 - w_2}\right), \\ \boldsymbol{S}_2 &= \boldsymbol{S}\left(v_3 - v_1, v_4 - v_2\right), \\ \boldsymbol{T}_2 &= \boldsymbol{T}(v_1, v_2). \end{aligned}$$

**Non-isomorphic transformation**   The ratio $A_r$ between the horizontal and vertical measures of a box $B = [b_1, b_3] \times [b_2, b_4]$ is called the *aspect ratio* of the box:

$$A_r(B) = \frac{b_3 - b_1}{b_4 - b_2}$$

When $A_r(W) \neq A_r(V)$, the window-viewport mapping $\boldsymbol{M} : W \to V$ is said to be *non-isomorphic*, since it does not preserve the shape of figures. In general, a non-isomorphic mapping transforms squares into rectangles and circles into ellipses.

**Isomorphic transformation**   In order to preserve the shape of figures for every pair $W$ and $V$, it is customary that the graphics system substitutes a *computed viewport* $\widehat{V}$ of maximal area, such that

$$A_r(\widehat{V}) = A_r(W),$$

to the user-defined viewport $V$. Hence we may have, for the two different cases shown in rightmost part of Figure 9.3:

$$A_r(V) > A_r(W) : \begin{cases} \widehat{v}_1 = v_1, \quad \widehat{v}_2 = v_2, \quad \widehat{v}_4 = v_4, \\ \widehat{v}_3 = v_1 + (v_4 - v_2)\,A_r(W) \end{cases}$$

$$A_r(V) < A_r(W) : \begin{cases} \widehat{v}_1 = v_1, \quad \widehat{v}_2 = v_2, \quad \widehat{v}_3 = v_3, \\ \widehat{v}_4 = v_2 + (v_3 - v_1)\, A_r(W) \end{cases}$$

Different strategies can also be chosen, by imposing, e.g., that the computed viewport has the same center of the user-defined one, as shown in the central part of Figure 9.3.

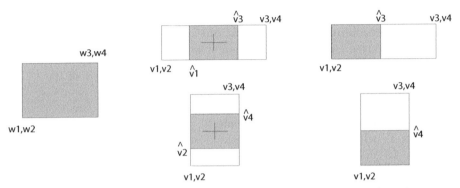

**Figure 9.3**  Computed viewports for preserving aspect ratio in window-viewport mapping. Two diverse strategies

**Device transformation**  Several device transformations may be associated in GKS with the same normalization transformation. This allows simultaneous connection of several devices in one graphics application.

The simplest example of device transformation is given by mapping the NDC space onto the discrete DC space, in the hypothesis of square pixels. In this case we have, for the isomorphic mapping:

$$\boldsymbol{T}_D^{iso} : NDC \to \widehat{DC}$$

that

$$\boldsymbol{T}_D^{iso} = \boldsymbol{S}(N-1, N-1),$$

with

$$N = \min(N_x, N_y),$$

where $N_x$ and $N_y$ are the numbers of columns and rows of discrete device space, respectively, and

$$\widehat{DC} = [0, N-1] \times [0, N-1] \subset DC.$$

**Rectangular pixel**  Some display devices (e.g. TV monitors) may have non-square pixels, usually with aspect ratio

$$\frac{d_x}{d_y} < 1,$$

where $d_x$ and $d_y$ are the pixel side measures. In this case, in order to mantain invariant the shape of figures, i.e. in order to map circles to circle, squares to squares, and so on, it is possible to define a *corrected* device transformation:

$$\boldsymbol{T}_D^{iso} : NDC \to \widehat{DC}$$

such that

$$\boldsymbol{T}_D^{iso} = \boldsymbol{S}_{pixel} \circ \boldsymbol{S}(N-1, N-1) = \boldsymbol{S}\left(\frac{d_y}{d_x}, 1\right) \circ \boldsymbol{S}(N-1, N-1)$$

where, as usual, $N = \min(N_x, N_y)$. If conversely $\frac{d_x}{d_y} > 1$, then we have $\boldsymbol{S}_{pixel} = \boldsymbol{S}\left(1, \frac{d_x}{d_y}\right)$.

**Reversed $y$ axis**  Some graphics monitors address the device space with encreasing $y$-coordinates from top to bottom of the screen. In this case the device transformation must combine a scaling tensor with a mirroring and vertical translation tensor:

$$\boldsymbol{T}_D^{iso} = \boldsymbol{T}(0, -N) \circ \boldsymbol{S}(1, -1) \circ \boldsymbol{S}_{pixel} \circ \boldsymbol{S}(N-1, N-1),$$

as shown in Figure 9.4. When displaying a graphics object on some reversed-axis device of such type, i.e. with origin of DC on its top-left point, we have the result shown in Figure 9.4b.

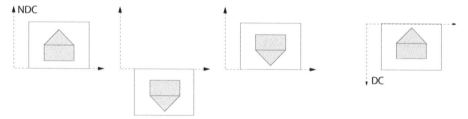

**Figure 9.4**  (a) Device transformation, with a reversed orientation of $y$ axis
(b) Display on a reversed $y$-axis device

## 9.2  3D pipeline

Every 2D picture of a 3D scene is obtained by *projection*, i.e., geometrically speaking, by intersection of a plane with the bundle of straight lines which project the scene vertices from some suitable projection center. Depending on the position of this center, there are two main classes of projections: *perspective* and *parallel*, with center in a finite point or at infinity, respectively. The various types of projections are thoroughly discussed in Chapter 10. A picture of a 3D scene on the output device is produced by applying several coordinate transformations to the scene data. Such a set of coordinate transformations is often called the 3D *pipeline*, and is discussed here.

*9.2.1   View model*

The mechanism of projection is very similar to that of human vision, where light's rays reflected from scene reach the observer's eye and are intercepted by the retina. This is a small portion of a spherical surface, which may be thought as locally approximated by the tangent plane. The image generated by light receptors on the retina is then transmitted to the superior brain centers, where it is suitably elaborated. In particular, from the small differences between the images perceived by the two eyes, due to the small difference between the positions of "projection centers", depth information about scene points is generated.

Actually, when using computers, the projection of scene points is not computed geometrically, but is derived algebraically by applying to the scene model a linear mapping of rank two which maps a three-dimensional space onto a two-dimensional one. This approach allows production of both parallel and perspective projections by using homogeneous coordinates. To preserve depth information, needed to generate pictures with hidden parts removed, the projection mapping is always generated by the composition of a linear mapping of rank three with an ortographic projection, which removes the third coordinate while leaving invariant the remaining ones.

**Camera model**   In the past two decades, 3D graphics systems have adopted a conceptual model of projection called the *camera model*, which is very easy to use and allows generation of both central and parallel projections with assigned geometric properties. This conceptual model of projection was developed in late 1970s by the Special Interest Group in Graphics of Association for Computing Machinery (ACM Siggraph), as a part of the more general 3D *Core system*, that became ANSI standard in those years. Subsequent graphics libraries and environments have introduced only small variations on this approach, that we are going to discuss in the following sections. In particular, we make reference to the PHIGS [ANSI87, ISO89, HHHW91, GG91, Gas92] specification of the camera model.

**View parameters**   Four 3D vectors, defined in WC, are called *view parameters* in ANSI Core. They completely specify the picture resulting from a specific projection, also called *view*, of the scene. The picture resulting from a projection is returned in a reference system linked to the projection plane. This system is called *uvn* or *view system* in ANSI Core, and *view reference* in PHIGS. A *view model* is a set of values for view parameters. The four vector parameters which specify the projection, i.e. the *view*, are the following:

1. *Center of Projection* (COP) is the common point of projecting lines. It coincides with the observer's position. It is substituted by the vector called *Direction of Projection* (DOP) for parallel projections, where the projection center is improper, i.e. is set at infinity.
2. *View Reference Point* (VRP) is the point targeted by the observer, at the intersection of the view axis and the view plane. It is assumed as the origin of the view reference system.
3. *View Up Vector* (VUV) is a vector used to orientate the projected picture. The *v* axis of view system is parallel to the projection of view up vector.

4. *View Plane Normal* (VPN) is a vector normal to the view plane. It is assumed as the direction of the $n$ axis of view reference system.

A further discussion and several examples of view parameters are given in Sections 10.1 and 10.2, where we discuss how to generate the more useful types of projections used in technical drawings.

### 9.2.2 Coordinate systems

In ISO graphics standard PHIGS, five different coordinate systems are used:

1. Modeling Coordinates (MC)
2. World Coordinates (WC3)
3. View Reference Coordinates (VRC)
4. Normalized Projection Coordinates (NPC)
5. Device Coordinates (DC3)

Such systems are connected by four coordinate transformations. The composition of such transformations is called the *3D pipeline*.

Each reference system, including device coordinates, in the PHIGS's 3D pipeline is fully three-dimensional. The acronyms WC3 and DC3 are used to distinguish them from the corresponding 2D coordinates of GKS.

**Modeling Coordinates (MC)** are coordinates which are *local* to each structure in the *structure network*. It is very useful and natural that each component substructure in a hierarchical model can be modeled by using a local coordinate frame. The local coordinates of each structure are called *modeling coordinates*.

A *traversal* algorithm, that we know (from Section 8.3) to be a *Depth First Search* (DFS), is used to linearize the structure network and transform all component substructures, i.e. the graphics primitives there contained, to the same coordinate frame, say, to world coordinates.

**World Coordinates (WC3)** are the global coordinates of the structure posted to a workstation, in order to be displayed or interactively modified. Often, world coordinates coincide with the local coordinates of the root (i.e. the initial structure) of some hierarchical structure network.

World coordinates are used as the common reference frame for all the graphics primitives (graphics data) contained in every component of a 3D scene. Such a reference frame is also used to define the camera position and orientation in a view model.

**View Reference Coordinates (VRC)** are used to establish the position of the observer in the scene, and the orientation of the view. With respect to the camera analogy, this view reference coordinates system is uniquely determined by the position and orientation of the camera.

The *view reference coordinate system*, or *uvn* system, has its origin in the view reference point (VRP), $n$ axis parallel to the view plane normal (VPN), and $v$ axis parallel to the projection of view-up vector (VUV), all given in WC3. The $u$ axis is then uniquely determined. The view plane normally coincides with the $n = 0$ subspace

The *projection reference point* (PRP) given in VRC, and the *type of projection* (either parallel or perspective) completely specify the projection. The 2D *window limits* on view plane in VRC and the *front, and back plane distances* (given as $n$ values in VRC) specify the *view volume* used to clip the scene to the desired portion.

**Normalized Projection Coordinates (NPC)** are used to describe the type of projection desired. In particular this is fixed by specifying the relative position to the observer and view plane, as well as some additional parameters which define what portion of the scene must be rendered on the output device.

The view mapping transformation first transforms the view volume given in VRC into a *canonical volume in NPC*, then into a 3D viewport contained in the 3D standard interval $[0, 1]^3$, where the transformed and clipped data are mantained in a device-independent manner.

Normalized projection coordinates are also used to compose different pictures. For example, a Monge projection (which is a composite orthographic projection where different views are composed simultaneously — see Section 10.2.2) is obtained by connecting different VRC systems to the same NPC. Different views can be composed in NPC by specifying different *projection viewports*.

The third coordinate of NPC system is the *perspective depth* of scene points and is used to compute the relative occlusion between scene parts. The actual projection of the scene is simply obtained by eliminating this coordinate, both in perspective and parallel cases.

**Device Coordinates (DC3)** are discrete 3D coordinates depending on the device. Such coordinates are three-dimensional in PHIGS, where advanced graphics devices are considered fully 3D.

Sometimes the device address space is bjiectively mapped onto the set of *voxels* (volume elements), really 3D, that allow for dynamic volume visualizations. More often a two-dimensional array of reals, called a *z-buffer*, is closely coupled to a 2D *frame buffer*, which accommodates a color index for each point displayed on the raster device. The $z$-buffer algorithm, which drives the rasterization of graphics primitives producing a hidden-surface removed picture of the scene, is discussed in Section 10.3.6.

### 9.2.3   Transformations of coordinates

A pipeline of four transformations of coordinates is associated with the five reference systems of PHIGS systems:

1. Structure Network Traversal
2. View Orientation
3. View Mapping
4. Workstation Transformation.

The Structure Network Traversal was already discussed in Section 8.3 and is only briefly recalled here; the other transformations are discussed in detail in the following subsections.

**Structure Network Traversal** is a composite algorithmic transformation from modeling coordinates that are local to the various hierarchical structures, to the global world coordinates:

$$MC \rightarrow WC3.$$

As we already know from Section 8.3, this algorithm clips the primitives certainly outside the view volume, while transforming the remaining ones to WC3 coordinates. The mapping from MC to WC3 is performed by traversing the structure network with a DFS, and multiplying each encountered primitive times the Current Transformation Matrix (CTM). The traversal algorithm returns the set of clipped primitives in the coordinates of the posted root stucture, assumed as WC3.

**View Orientation** is the mapping from world coordinates to view reference coordinates:

$$WC3 \rightarrow VRC.$$

This transformation is a rigid (possibly improper) transformation i.e. is composed by a translation, a rotation and possibly by an elementary reflection, to be considered only when WC3 and VRC systems have different orientation. In recent years world coordinates and view reference coordinates are both right-handed, so that the reflection coincides with the identity mapping.

**View Mapping** is the mapping from view reference coordinates to normalized projection coordinates:

$$VRC \rightarrow NPC.$$

This transformation maps the view volume in VRC onto a canonical volume $[-1, 1] \times [-1, 1] \times [-1, 0]$, then onto some NPC viewport. The first step is accomplished by composing a translation, a shearing, a scaling and possibly a perspective transformation (mathematically an affine homology). Such a transformation allows unification of the treatment of both parallel and perspective projections. A 3D window-viewport mapping, analogous to the transformation discussed in Section 9.1, is finally applied to transform the canonical volume onto some NPC viewport.

**Workstation Transformation** is the mapping from normalized projection coordinates to discrete 3D device coordinates:

$$NPC \rightarrow DC3.$$

It is used to transform a 3D workstation-window in NPC into a 3D workstation-viewport in DC3, both defined as 3D extents parallel to the coordinate frames. As in the 2D case, it is composed by translations and scaling transformations.

### 9.2.4   View orientation

The view-orientation transformation is a translation followed by a rotation, possibly improper, that moves the VRP to the origin, the VPN to the $z$ axis, the projection of VUV to the $y$ axis, and the cross-vector of the first two to the $x$ axis.

This roto-translation may be followed by a $z$-reflection if the WC3 system and the VRC system have different orientations, e.g. if the first is right-handed whereas the second one is left-handed, or vice versa.

Notice that the view-orientation transformation is exactly the same for both the parallel and the perspective case.

$$\boldsymbol{VO} = \boldsymbol{R}(VPN, VUV) \circ \boldsymbol{T}(-VRP)$$

where

$$\boldsymbol{T}(-VRP) = \begin{pmatrix} 1 & 0 & 0 & -vrp_x \\ 0 & 1 & 0 & -vrp_y \\ 0 & 0 & 1 & -vrp_z \\ 0 & 0 & 0 & 1 \end{pmatrix}$$

$$\boldsymbol{R}(VPN, VUV) = \begin{pmatrix} r_{ux} & r_{vx} & r_{nx} & 0 \\ r_{uy} & r_{vy} & r_{ny} & 0 \\ r_{uz} & r_{vz} & r_{nz} & 0 \\ 0 & 0 & 0 & 1 \end{pmatrix}$$

with

$$\boldsymbol{r}_n = VPN/\|VPN\|$$

$$\boldsymbol{r}_u = VUV \times \boldsymbol{r}_n/\|VUV \times \boldsymbol{r}_n\|$$

$$\boldsymbol{r}_v = \boldsymbol{r}_n \times \boldsymbol{r}_u$$

The transformation can also be seen as change of coordinates. The three vectors of the new basis, i.e., respectively, $\boldsymbol{VO}(\boldsymbol{r}_u)$, $\boldsymbol{VO}(\boldsymbol{r}_v)$ and $\boldsymbol{VO}(\boldsymbol{r}_n)$, denoted here as $x$, $y$ and $z$, are traditionally named $u$, $v$ and $n$ in graphics systems. Since we cannot invent new names for the basis of each coordinate system in the 3D pipeline, we will continue to use the standard names $x$, $y$ and $z$ for basis vectors of each pipelined reference frame.

**View Model**   We show here the great simplicity of the specification of a view model in a PHIGS-like graphics system. It may be useful to remember that VRP is the *target* point in the camera analogy, and that VPN is the normal to the view plane, so that it determines the *orientation* of the camera axis. Conversely, the VUV vector defines the vertical direction of the projected picture, i.e. the *rotation* of the camera about its axis. Let us remember also that PRP, the *window* limits and the *front* and *back* planes are given in VRC.

## Script 9.2.1 (View model)

```
DEF vrp = < 0, 2.0, 2 >;
DEF vpn = < 1, 0, 0 >;
DEF vuv = < 0, 1, 1 >;
DEF prp = < 0, 0, 25 >;
DEF front = 10;
DEF back = -1;
DEF window = < -4, -3, 4, 3 >;
```

## Example 9.2.1 (View model definition)

A set of values for the parameters described above will be called a *view model* in this book. An example of view model is given in Script 9.2.1.

**Implementation**  As we already know, the `ViewOrientation` tensor is composed of a translation followed by a rotation. The first one moves the origin to the PRP; the second one moves three unit normal vectors Ru, Rv and Rn, depending on VPN and VUV, in the unit vectors of reference frame. The implementation given in Script 9.2.2 directly translates the transformation formulas discussed in Section 9.2.4.

## Script 9.2.2

```
DEF ViewOrientation = RotVRC ~ TranslVRC;
DEF TranslVRC = T:<1,2,3>:(AA:-:vrp);
DEF RotVRC = (MAT ~ TRANS): <<1,0,0,0>,AL:<0,Ru>,AL:<0,Rv>,AL:<0,Rn>>
WHERE
    Ru = UnitVect:(vuv VectProd Rn),
    Rv = Rn VectProd Ru,
    Rn = UnitVect:vpn
END;
```

In Figure 9.5 we show the world positions of the house model and the view volume previously given.

In Figure 9.6 we show the result of application of tensor `ViewOrientation` to the WCscene model defined by Script 9.4.4. The generating expression of the model shown in Figure 9.6 is

```
ViewOrientation: WCscene;
```

Let us note that all the pictures of this section use both a Monge's and a dimetric projection. The direction of the $z$ axis in the dimetric projection is always vertical in the pictures. The Monge's images instead mantain the axis orientation typical of this kind of composite projection.

## 9.2.5  View mapping

The view mapping transforms the *view volume* in VRC onto the *canonical volume* in an intermediary coordinate system, and then maps this volume onto the *3D viewport* in NPC. The canonical volume is defined as the 3D interval $[-1, 1] \times [-1, 1] \times [-1, 0]$ in the parallel case, and the truncated pyramid with vertex in the origin, squared basis

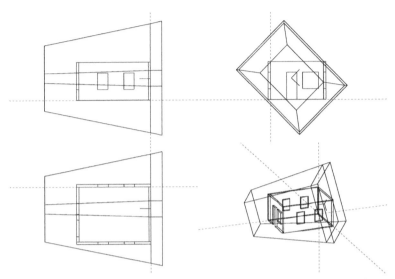

**Figure 9.5** House model and perspective view volume in world coordinates

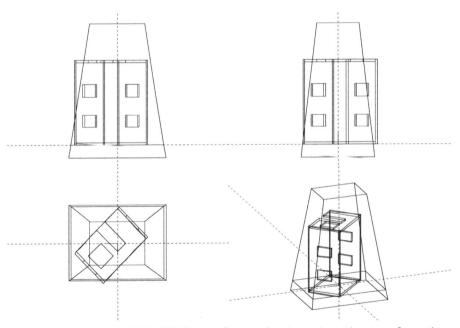

**Figure 9.6** House model in VRC according to the view orientation transformation

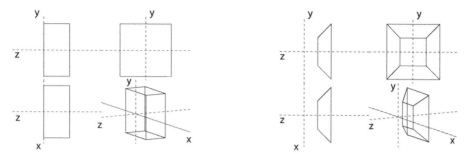

**Figure 9.7**   Canonical view volume: (a) parallel case (b) perspective case

in the plane $z = -1$ and side faces into the planes with unit slope, in the perspective case.

In perspective case an affine homology[1] is applied to the pyramidal canonical volume, which is transformed to the parallelepiped canonical volume, then mapped to the 3D viewport. In such canonical volume, two points aligned with the observer belong to the line of equations $x = a, y = b$, and differ only for their *perspective depth*, which coincides with the $z$ coordinate.

In the following we distinguish between the view mapping $\boldsymbol{VM}_{per}$ in the perspective case, from the view mapping $\boldsymbol{VM}_{par}$ in the parallel case.

**Parallel case**   The view mapping tensor $\boldsymbol{VM}_{par}$ is the composition of a shearing, a scaling and a translation:

$$\boldsymbol{VM}_{par} = \boldsymbol{T}_{par} \circ \boldsymbol{S}_{par} \circ \boldsymbol{H}_z.$$

The shearing $\boldsymbol{H}_z$ must shear the Direction Of Projection (DOP) vector in $(0, 0, dop_z, 1)^T$, thus shearing the possibly oblique view volume into a straight one. The DOP vector in VRC is defined in PHIGS as difference between the Center of Window (CW) and the Projection Reference Point (PRP):

$$DOP = CW - PRP = \begin{pmatrix} (u_{max} + u_{min})/2 \\ (v_{max} + v_{min})/2 \\ 0 \\ 1 \end{pmatrix} - \begin{pmatrix} prp_u \\ prp_v \\ prp_n \\ 1 \end{pmatrix}$$

So, it must be

$$\begin{pmatrix} 0 \\ 0 \\ dop_z \\ 1 \end{pmatrix} = \boldsymbol{H}_z \begin{pmatrix} dop_x \\ dop_y \\ dop_z \\ 1 \end{pmatrix} = \begin{pmatrix} 1 & 0 & sh_x & 0 \\ 0 & 1 & sh_y & 0 \\ 0 & 0 & 1 & 0 \\ 0 & 0 & 0 & 1 \end{pmatrix} \begin{pmatrix} dop_x \\ dop_y \\ dop_z \\ 1 \end{pmatrix},$$

and hence

$$sh_x = -\frac{dop_x}{dop_z}, \quad sh_y = -\frac{dop_y}{dop_z}.$$

---

[1] A bijective mapping of lines to lines and planes to planes that preserves the incidence relationship.

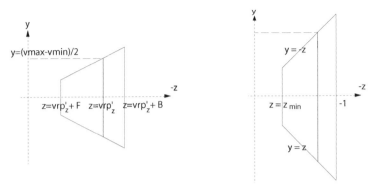

**Figure 9.8**  Scaling to canonical view volume of parallel case

After the action of such tensor, the bounds of view volume are

$$u_{min} \le x \le u_{max}, \quad v_{min} \le y \le v_{max}, \quad B \le z \le F$$

to be scaled and translated to the canonical volume

$$-1 \le x \le 1, \quad -1 \le y \le 1, \quad -1 \le z \le 0,$$

so that

$$\boldsymbol{T}_{par} = \boldsymbol{T}\left(-\frac{u_{min} + u_{max}}{2}, -\frac{v_{min} + v_{max}}{2}, -F\right),$$

$$\boldsymbol{S}_{par} = \boldsymbol{T}\left(\frac{2}{u_{max} - u_{min}}, \frac{2}{v_{max} - v_{min}}, \frac{1}{F - B}\right).$$

**Perspective case**    The view mapping tensor $\boldsymbol{VM}_{per}$ is the composition of a translation of PRP, that coincides with COP in this case, to the origin, followed by a shearing to make straight the view pyramid, and by a composite scaling to map the result into the canonical volume:

$$\boldsymbol{VM}_{per} = \boldsymbol{S}_{per} \circ \boldsymbol{H}_z \circ \boldsymbol{T}(-PRP),$$

where:

1. $\boldsymbol{T}(-PRP)$ moves the center of projection to the origin;
2. the shearing $\boldsymbol{H}_z$ tensor coincides with the one of parallel case;
3. the scaling tensor can be decomposed as: $\boldsymbol{S}_{per} = \boldsymbol{S}_2 \circ \boldsymbol{S}_1$.

where $\boldsymbol{S}_1$ maps the straight view pyramid onto a unit slope pyramid:

$$\boldsymbol{S}_1 = \boldsymbol{S}(\frac{-2\,vrp_z'}{u_{max} - u_{min}}, \frac{-2\,vrp_z'}{v_{max} - v_{min}}, 1)$$

and where $\boldsymbol{S}_2$ uniformly scales the three-space to move the $z = B$ plane (the Back plane) to the $z = -1$ plane:

$$\boldsymbol{S}_2 = \boldsymbol{S}(\frac{-1}{vrp_z' + B}, \frac{-1}{vrp_z' + B}, \frac{-1}{vrp_z' + B})^T$$

Notice that $vrp'_z$ is obtained by mapping the VRC origin by the translation to PRP and by the subsequent shearing:

$$VRP' = (\boldsymbol{H}_z \circ \boldsymbol{T}(-PRP))(0,0,0,1)^T$$

**Implementation**  The `ViewMapping` tensor maps the view volume from VRC to NPC. The NPC view volume must coincide, in the perspective case, with the pyramid centered in the origin and with squared basis $[-1,1] \times [-1,1]$ in the plane of equation $z = -1$.

As seen in Section 9.2.5, the view mapping tensor $\boldsymbol{VM}_{per}$ is composed of a translation tensor T_per, by a tensor shearing $H_z$ and by a scaling tensor S_per. Also in this case, the code given in Script 9.2.3 implement very directly the formulas given in Section 9.2.5.

Notice that `umin`, `vmin`, `umax` and `vmax` are generated by selecting the first, second third and fourth component of 2D `window`, and that the $z$ component of VRP is obtained by opening the polyhedral data structure and by extracting the origin of VRC exposed to the action of T_per and SH_per. The MK operator that transforms a point into a 0-dimensional polyhedron, so that tensors can apply to it, is given in Script 3.3.15.

---

**Script 9.2.3**

```
DEF ViewMapping = S_per ~ SH_per ~ T_per;
DEF T_per = T:<1,2,3>:(AA:-:prp);
DEF SH_per = MAT:
   << 1, 0, 0, 0 >,
    < 0, 1, 0, dopx / dopz >,
    < 0, 0, 1, dopy / dopz >,
    < 0, 0, 0, 1 >>
WHERE
    dopx = (umin + umax)/2 - s1:prp,
    dopy = (vmin + vmax)/2 - s2:prp,
    dopz = 0 - s3:prp
END;
DEF S_per = S:<1,2,3>:<sx,sy,sz>
WHERE
    sx = (2 * vrp_z)/((umax - umin)*(vrp_z + back)),
    sy = (2 * vrp_z)/((vmax - vmin)*(vrp_z + back)),
    sz = -1/(vrp_z + back)
END;


DEF umin = S1:window; DEF vmin = S2:window;
DEF umax = S3:window; DEF vmax = S4:window;
DEF vrp_z = (s3 ~ s1 ~ s1 ~ UKPOL ~ SH_per ~ T_per ~ MK): <0,0,0>;
```

---

In Figure 9.9 we show the result of application of `ViewMapping` tensor to the model generated by the previous step. The generating expression of the model shown is in this case:

```
(ViewMapping ~ ViewOrientation): WCscene;
```

### 9.2.6  Perspective transformation

The so-called *perspective transformation* [FvDFH90], mathematically an affine homology, maps the canonical pyramid volume of central projections onto the canonical parallelepiped volume of parallel projections.

Such a transformation moves the origin to the improper point of $z$ axis and the front plane to the plane $z = 0$, while keeping invariant the back plane, of current equation $z = -1$. Such a perspective tensor is associated with a matrix

$$
\boldsymbol{P} = \begin{pmatrix} 1 & 0 & 0 & 0 \\ 0 & 1 & 0 & 0 \\ 0 & 0 & \frac{1}{1+z_{min}} & \frac{-z_{min}}{1+z_{min}} \\ 0 & 0 & -1 & 0 \end{pmatrix}, \quad z_{min} \neq -1 \tag{9.1}
$$

### Example 9.2.2 (Perspective transformation)
Let us consider the vertices

$$
\boldsymbol{r} = \begin{pmatrix} -z_{min} \\ -z_{min} \\ z_{min} \\ 1 \end{pmatrix}^T \quad \text{and} \quad \boldsymbol{s} = \begin{pmatrix} 1 \\ 1 \\ -1 \\ 1 \end{pmatrix}^T
$$

of canical view volume of Figure 9.7b, where $\boldsymbol{r}$ is at the intersection of planes $x = -z$, $y = -z$ and $z = z_{min}$, and $\boldsymbol{s}$ is at the intersection of planes $x = -z$, $y = -z$ and $z = -1$. They are respectively mapped to

$$
\boldsymbol{P}(\boldsymbol{r}) = \begin{pmatrix} -z_{min} \\ -z_{min} \\ 0 \\ -z_{min} \end{pmatrix} = \begin{pmatrix} 1 \\ 1 \\ 0 \\ 1 \end{pmatrix} \quad \text{and to} \quad \boldsymbol{P}(\boldsymbol{s}) = \begin{pmatrix} 1 \\ 1 \\ -1 \\ 1 \end{pmatrix}
$$

**Perspective Transformation**   The perspTransf tensor, given in Script 9.2.4, maps the canonical view volume of central projections onto the canonical view volume of parallel projections, the 3D extent $[-1, 1] \times [-1, 1] \times [-1, 0]$.

In order to implement such a tensor it is necessary to remember that PLaSM, for the purpose of allowing for easy dimensional-independence of geometric operations, has conventionally chosen the first coordinate as the homogeneous one. Hence the matrix (9.1) of affine homology discussed in Section 9.2.6 must be accordingly modified. The desired result may be obtained by applying the cyclic permutation

$$
\begin{pmatrix} 1 & 2 & 3 & 4 \\ 2 & 3 & 4 & 1 \end{pmatrix}
$$

to the matrix rows and columns. The perspTransf tensor is hence defined as in the following Script.

**Script 9.2.4**

```
DEF perspTransf = (MAT ~ INV):<
    <     0,            0, 0,       -1>,
    <     0,            1, 0,        0>,
    <     0,            0, 1,        0>,
    <-:z_min/(1+z_min), 0, 0, 1/(1+z_min)> >
WHERE
    z_min = -:(vrp_z + front)/(vrp_z + back)
END;
```

The result of application of the `perspTransf` tensor to the model generated at the previous step is shown in Figure 9.10. The PLaSM expression which generates the model represented in such figure is

```
(perspTransf ~ ViewMapping ~ ViewOrientation): WCscene;
```

*9.2.7  Workstation transformation*

The workstation transformation maps a 3D workstation window in NPC onto a 3D workstation viewport in DC3. This mapping is similar to the 2D one defined by GKS and discussed in Section 9.1.2. It is composed of a translation that moves the NPC point of minimum coordinates to the origin, then by a scaling of the 3D extent to the size of the viewport and by a final translation of the origin to the DC3 viewport point of minimum coordinates. The device transformation is applied to the geometric data of primitives, including the control points of curves and surfaces (see Section 11.2). Such primitives are then rasterized in 3D, often using some variation of the $z$-buffer approximated algorithm for removing the hidden parts. Exact algorithms for hidden-surface removal would have already been applied in NPC coordinates.

So, if $W = [w_1, w_4] \times [w_2, w_5] \times [w_3, w_6] \subset NPC$, and $V = [v_1, v_4] \times [v_2, v_5] \times [v_3, v_6] \subset DC3$, then we have

$$T_D : NPC \to DC3$$

such that

$$T_D = T(v_1, v_2, v_3) \circ S\left(\frac{v_4 - v_1}{w_4 - w_1}, \frac{v_5 - v_2}{w_5 - w_2}, \frac{v_6 - v_3}{w_6 - w_3}\right) \circ T(-w_1, -w_2, -w_3)$$

**View volume clipping**   It is very convenient to perform in NPC the detail clipping of geometric primitives to the boundaries of the view volume. Remember that a fast culling of a hierarchical scene graph can already be performed in WC3 by pruning its covering tree at traversal time, on the basis of an intersection test between the containment box of current node (root of substructure) and the containment box of the view volume.

A clipping in NPC after perspective transformation is numerically convenient, because the intersection of primitives with a 3D extent parallel to the reference frame allows the use of very simple inequalities for boundary half-spaces, i.e.:

$$-x \le 1, \qquad x \le 1,$$

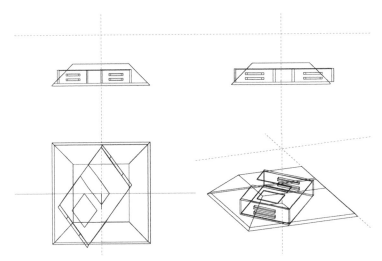

**Figure 9.9**   House model (in NPC) after the orientation and the view mapping transformation

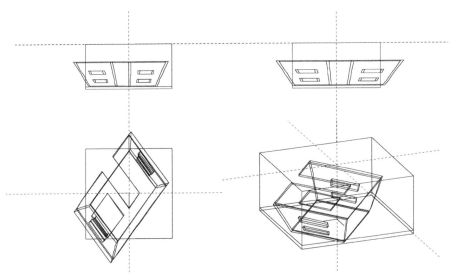

**Figure 9.10**   Canonical volume after perspective transformation

$$-y \leq 1, \qquad y \leq 1,$$

$$-z \leq 1, \qquad z \leq 0.$$

Such a clipping is easily microcoded on the graphics boards. The result of applying in NPC a clipping operation to the result of perspective transformation is shown in Figure 9.11. A possible PLaSM generating expression is given in Script 9.2.5.

---

**Script 9.2.5**
```
    DEF WCscene = < WCvolume, house >;
    DEF clipping = <1,2,3> && <1,2,3>;
    DEF perspPipeline = perspTransf ~ ViewMapping ~ ViewOrientation;


    (clipping ~ AA:perspPipeline): WCscene;
```

---

Some comments on the code in Script 9.2.5 are probably needed. First, notice that the `clipping` function is just an alias for the operator of intersection of polyhedral complexes of full dimensionality in 3D. The meaning of the `perspPipeline` function is straightforward.

**Window-viewport mapping**   Two window-viewport mappings are supported by PHIGS, between VRC and NPC as well as between NPC and DC3. The first one is slightly simpler, since the mapping domain is the canonical volume $[-1, 1] \times [-1, 1] \times [-1, 0]$, which is mapped onto a NPC viewport. As we know, this kind of mapping is a composition of a translation, a scaling and a further translation.

To finally obtain some realistic image from our example, we only need to scale our result to the size of VRC window. A further mapping to some NPC viewport should subsequently apply:

```
    (S:<1,2>:<(umax-umin)/2,(vmax-vmin)/2> ~ clipping
    ~ AA:perspPipeline): WCscene;
```

The geometric result of the previous expression is shown in Figure 9.12. The final 2D image algebraically generated by eliminating the third coordinate, is shown in Figure 9.13, where both a *wire-frame* image of projected model and a *hidden-surface removed* image are reported. We discuss in Section 10.3 how the insertion of perspective transformation in the 3D pipeline allows for a more efficient solution to the problem of removing the hidden parts of the scene.

## 9.3   Other implementations

A brief introduction to different models of 2D and 3D graphics approaches and pipelines is given in this section. Our aim is to help the reader to make connections and look at the similarities and differences between the different implementations of the same concept. According to the ancient Romans, we believe that history, even in the short run of two/three decades, is the best *magistra*.

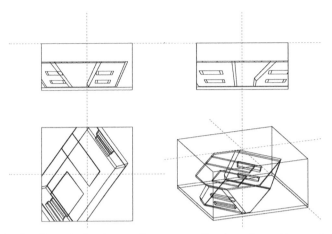

**Figure 9.11**   Canonical volume after perspective transformation and clipping

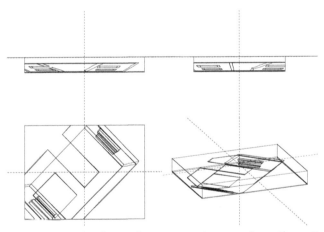

**Figure 9.12**   Canonical volume after perspective transformation, clipping and
scaling to the window 2D

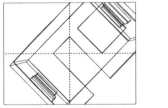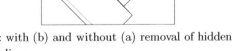

**Figure 9.13**   Final projected image: with (b) and without (a) removal of hidden
lines

## 9.3.1   Scalable vector graphics (SVG)

SVG is a recent standard for vector 2D graphics on the web defined by the *W3 Consortium* [Svg02]. When using the SVG format, a 2D graphics at vector precision will be created by the browser based on plain text instructions contained in a SVG file or directly embedded in a HTML document. No image files are necessary. A working draft specification was released on 2001 by the World-Wide Web Consortium, partly inspired by two earlier specifications by Microsoft, Macromedia, and others, and by Adobe, Netscape, Sun, and others.

When looking at the SVG specification document [Svg02], the authors were very impressed by the similarities with the 2D standard graphics codified by GKS, as a further signal of how pervasive and influential was the 1980s' movement for device-, platform-, application- and language-independent standardization of graphics methods.

The first thing we should note is that SVG is *plain text*. The code can live within an HTML document with no other files involved. This one is the main difference from Flash graphics, that is a binary format, that requires either ad hoc interactive tools or a dedicated API to create, i.e. much more than a plain text editor. The second thing to be aware of is that SVG is written in XML, that is a powerful and simple way to present structured information on the web.

**Primitives and attributes**   SVG offers several predefined primitives, and gives the user full control of their appearance, in particular by controlling the *Fill* and *Stroke* attributes. *Fill* means painting the interior of the shape by specifying the color and even making the inside of a shape partially transparent. *Stroke* means painting along the shape outline. Several built-in primitives are available, including:

1. rectangles (with optional rounded corners)
2. circles
3. ellipses
4. pie slices
5. polygons
6. paths

For example, `circle` may be defined as:

```
<circle style="fill: red; stroke: yellow"/>
```

The `<path>` element allows a combination of sequentially straight lines, cubic Bézier curves, elliptic or circular arcs, so that shapes can be made by any combination. And the user can have control over the color, width, antialiasing, and opacity of the stroke as well as how outlines end or come together. Also, it is possible to fill any shape with a GIF or JPEG image or make the image define a *pattern* tile to fill the space. And it is possible to create a pattern that would cover the stroke of a shape.

**Graphic text**   Graphic text can easily be inserted into a drawing. `<text>` is a new element for defining what your text is and what styling information you want to apply to it. The x and y attributes of a text elements, in particular, allow absolute positioning of text string on a web page. The text elements may be positioned along a `<path>`, as you can do, say, in *Adobe Illustrator*. Imagine drawing a curving path and then having the base line of your text follow that curve.

**Grouping and naming**   Multiple graphics elements can be grouped hierarchically and considered together enclosed in a `<g>` tag. A group or individual graphics element can be *named* and *instanced* several times in different positions and orientations and also stored for later use. Similarly, it is possible to define a set of characteristics in one part of the document and then apply those characteristics somewhere else, very much as is done with classes in CSS.

Each drawing can be positioned anywhere on a web page. SVG relies on Cascading Stylesheets (CSS) to take charge of positioning on the page as well as other visual parameters. Several graphics layers can be positioned over each other by any desired ordering, making use of the CSS property called `z-index`.

**Transformations and effects**   Furthermore, graphics elements, i.e. vector shapes, images, and text, can be subject to the following effects:

1. Clipping paths
2. Masks
3. Gradients
4. Visibility
5. Opacity
6. Transformations
7. Filter effects
8. Animation
9. Scripting

When a *clipping path* is applied to a region, only the area within that path will be visible. It is even possible to use a `<text>` as a clipping path. Is also possible to use any other graphic as an *alpha mask*, getting close to *Photoshop*-style techniques on the Web. Linear or radial *gradients* allow smooth transitions from one color to another within any shape. A *visibility* or *opacity* property for a single graphics element or a group may be set. *Transformations* include rotation, shearing, scaling, and translation. *Animations* are possible, because the language allows for JavaScript *scripting*, used to manipulate SVG graphics. In particular, any graphic, grouping, path, image, or text can be assigned any of the standard HTML *event handlers* (onclick, onmouseover, onmouseout, onload, and so on). Last but not least, it is possible to type in some code that would apply *filters* such as a *Gaussian blur* or *diffuse lighting* effects to SVG graphics or text.

**SVG exporting**   Some limited exporting to SVG files is possible for 2D PLaSM geometric objects. For this purpose the built-in SVG primitive is used. An example of exported SVG file is shown in Figure 9.14. The exporting syntax is given below.

```
SVG: object: width_cm: 'filename.svg'
```

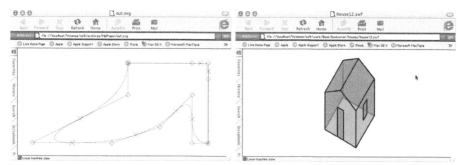

**Figure 9.14**   Rendering in a web browser of vector graphics exported by PLaSM:
(a) SVG graphics (b) Flash graphics

### 9.3.2   Open Inventor camera model

The conceptual model used by Open Inventor [WO94] to specify the view is no different
from the camera model adopted by ANSI Core and ISO PHIGS standards.

A camera node may be inserted anywhere in an Open Inventor scene graph. Such
a node generates a picture of every object situated after it in the graph. The camera
orientation is affected by the current geometric transformation. A node SoCamera is
provided at this purpose, with attributes

1. viewportMapping, associated with the type of treatment to apply in non-
   isomorphic camera-viewport mapping;
2. position, which is the location of viewport in local coordinates. It is affected
   by current geometric transformation;
3. orientation, of the camera viewing direction. Together with the current
   geometric transformation, this specifies the orientation of the camera in world
   coordinates;
4. aspectRatio, i.e. ratio of the camera width to height;
5. neardistance, farDistance, focalDistance, specify in VRC the distance
   of camera viewpoint from front and back clipping planes as well as from the
   point of focus, i.e. from the view plane.

Two subclasses SoPerspectiveCamera and SoOrthographicCamera are derived from
the SoCamera class. A new field heightAngle is added to SoPerspectiveCamera in
order to specify the vertical angle in radians of the camera view volume, i.e. of the
truncated pyramid volume specified by the camera. The horizontal angle of the view
volume is determined by heightAngle and by the camera's aspectRatio.

The new field height of SoOrthographicCamera derived class specifies the height
of the camera's parallelepiped view volume for parallel projections. A switch node (of
kind blinker, e.g.) may be used to choose between different predefined cameras of a
given scene.

### 9.3.3   Java 3D viewing model

Java 3D, the vendor-neutral 3D API based on Java platform, gives full support to
the creation of virtual worlds and to multiple interaction with them by using a plenty
of gadgetry. It hence must support the interaction of virtual and physical realities,

needing a much more complex viewing model that the standard camera's one.

Our main sources for the material in this section were [SN99, SRD00] by the chief architect of the Java 3D API and others.

In the Java 3D approach, a *VirtualUniverse* holds everything within one or more *Locales*. A Locale positions in a universe one or more *BranchGroups*, where each BranchGroup holds a *scene graph*. Scene graphs in Java 3D are typically divided into two types of branch graphs, called *Content branch* and *View branch*; the former contain scene modeling, including shapes, lights, and other content; the latter contain viewing information.

The *ViewPlatform* is a leaf node in a view branch of the scene graph which defines a viewpoint within the scene, by giving a frame of reference for the user's position and orientation in the virtual world. There can be many *ViewPlatforms* in a scene graph. Each such platform can be transformed by a *TransformGroup* parent node. User interface and animation features may modify such nodes to move the platforms under application control, like "magic carpets" [SN99] flying on the scene.

Many additional classes control how that scene is rendered, using either a *perspective* or a *parallel* projection. Support for *room-mounted* and *head-mounted displays* is provided, as well as for user's *head tracking*.

**Virtual vs physical worlds**   Shapes, branch groups, locales, and the virtual universe define the *virtual world*. A user co-exists in both this virtual world and in the *physical world*. In particular, s/he has a position and orientation in both worlds. The Java 3D view model handles *co-existence mapping* between virtual and physical worlds. A chain of relationships controls several mappings. In particular they map: the eye locations relative to the user's head; the head location relative to a head tracker; the head tracker relative to the tracker base; the tracker base relative to display (image plate), and so on.

A so-called *view policy* selects one of two constraint systems, associated with either *room-mounted displays*, whose locations are fixed, like CRTs, video projectors, multi-screen walls and portals, or to *head-mounted displays* (HMDs), whose locations change as the user moves.

When using room-mounted displays and head tracking, the constraint system uses the eye location relative to the image plate to compute a view volume (*view frustum*), where the eyepoint locations are computed automatically. To map from eye to image plate, the constraint system uses a chain of coordinate system mappings, linking *Eyes* to *Head* to *Head tracker* to *Tracker base* to *Image plate*. In particular, the constraint system uses the left and right eye locations relative to the left and right image plates to compute two view volumes.

Physical to virtual mappings are needed to allow the user to interact with the virtual scene. Recall that the user co-exists in the virtual and physical worlds. For this purpose consider that the user has both a physical and a virtual position and orientation. We have seen that room- and head-mounted display view policies handle mapping from the user's physical body to a tracker base and image plates. To map from this physical world to the virtual world, it is necessary to add to the constraint chain: a tracker base to coexistence mapping; a coexistence to view platform mapping; a view platform to locale mapping, and finally a locale to virtual universe mapping.

**Viewing model**  Summing up, the Java 3D viewing model is composed of: a *view policy* to choose a room- or head-mounted constraint system; a set of *physical body*, *physical environment*, and *screen configuration* parameters; a set of policies to guide the chosen constraint system, including the *view attach policy*.

The *view attach policy* establishes how the view platform origin is placed relative to the user (i.e., how it is attached to the user's view). Three such policies are possible:

1. *Nominal head* policy places the view platform origin at the user's head. It is convenient for arrangement of content around the user's head for a heads-up display. It is very similar to "older" view models.
2. *Nominal feet* policy places the view platform origin at the user's feet, at the ground plane. It is convenient for walk-throughs, where the user's feet should touch the virtual ground.
3. *Nominal screen* policy places the view platform origin at the screen center. It enables the user to view objects from an optimal viewpoint.

**Implementation**  The Java 3D viewing model is implemented through several classes. A `VirtualUniverse` defines the universe coordinate system. A `Locale` places a scene graph branch within that universe. A `ViewPlatform` (and a `Transform3D` above it) define a viewpoint within that locale. It defines a frame of reference for the user's position and orientation in the virtual world. A `View` is the virtual user standing on a `ViewPlatform`. There can be many views on the same view platform. A `PhysicalBody` describes the user's dimensions for use by a `View`. There is always one `PhysicalBody` for a `View`. A `PhysicalEnvironment` describes the user's environment for use by a `View`. There is always one `PhysicalEnvironment` for a `View`. A `Canvas3D` selects a screen area on which to draw a `View`. Every View has one or more Canvas3Ds. A `Screen3D` describes the physical display device (image plate) drawn on by a `Canvas3D`.

In conclusion: the 3D transformation pipeline in Java 3D is quite complex because it has to map a virtual world to several physical worlds, but it is quite easy to use because each kind of object has reasonable defaults. In the virtual world the `ViewPlatform` controls the user's virtual position and orientation, whereas a `View` sets a view policy. In the physical world a `PhysicalBody` describes the user, whereas the `PhysicalEnvironment` describes the user's environment. Finally, a `Canvas3D` selects a region to draw into, whereas a `Screen3D` describes the screen device.

### 9.4  Examples

#### 9.4.1  PHIGS pipeline display

In this section we develop some PLaSM functions which help to graphically display our implementation of the 3D pipeline for the central projection case. As already shown in Example 9.2.1, some functions without parameters are used to specify the view model.

The tensor $VO$, $VM_{per}$ and $P$ of view orientation, view mapping and perspective transformations are implemented by PLaSM tensors denoted as `viewOrientation`, `viewMapping` and `perspTransf`, in Sections 9.2.4, 9.2.5 and 9.2.6, respectively. Notice that such tensors implicitly depend on the view model parameters, i.e. they are implicit functions of such arguments.

**Figure 9.15** The model of the scene we have projected.

In particular, we generate here a geometric model of *view volume* starting from the parameters in view model. A geometric model of the *scene*, the *view volume* and a simplified model of the *view reference* system will be shown in world coordinates and then mapped by the component tensors of 3D pipeline in each intermediary reference frame.

**Geometric model of scene**   A sufficiently realistic 3D house model is given here to illustrate the various steps of 3D pipeline. Such a `house` model is quite simplified, and in particular is open at the top. The source code generating the model is given in Script 9.4.1; some projections of it are shown in Figure 9.15.

---

**Script 9.4.1**
```
DEF mesh = INSL:* ~ AA:QUOTE;
DEF house = T:2:-0.2:(walls - windows - door)
WHERE
    walls = STRUCT:<xWalls, yWalls>,
    xWalls = mesh:<<7>,<0.2,-5,0.2>,<3.5>>,
    yWalls = mesh:<<0.2,-6.6,0.2>,<-0.2,5>,<3.5>>,
    windows = STRUCT:
        < mesh:<<-1.5,1,-1.5,1>,<0.2,-5,0.2>,<-1,1.5>>,
          mesh:<<-6.8,0.2>,<-3,1.5>,<-1,1.5>> >,
    door = mesh:<<-6.8,0.2>,<-1.5,1>,<2.5>>
END;
```

---

**Computation of View Volume in WC**

In this section we show the computation of the view volume in WC3 starting from a given view model. The simplest method to generate such a volume probably consists in building the very simple pyramidal volume in NPC before of perspective projection, and then in getting its WC3 counterimage by applying the inverse 3D pipeline to it.

**Canonical View Volume in NPC**   The canonical volume before perspective transformation is a truncated pyramid with side faces $z = x, z = -x, z = y, z = -y$, back face $z = -1$, and front face $z = z_{min}$. The view plane is defined by the equation $z = z_{proj}$.

Therefore, in PLaSM the canonical volume in normalized projection coordinates may be generated by a MKPOL function which defines a polyhedral complex with 2 convex cells, each one given as convex combination of 8 vertices. In total, we need to explicitly give 12 vertices, situated by groups of 4 on the planes $z = z_{min}$, $z = z_{proj}$ and $z = -1$, as described by Script 9.4.2.

---

**Script 9.4.2**

```
DEF NPCvolume = MKPOL:< verts, cells, pols>
WHERE
    verts = < <z_min, z_min, z_min>, <z_min, -:z_min, z_min>,
        <-:z_min, z_min, z_min>, <-:z_min, -:z_min, z_min>,
        <z_proj, z_proj, z_proj>, <z_proj, -:z_proj, z_proj>,
        <-:z_proj, z_proj, z_proj>, <-:z_proj, -:z_proj, z_proj>,
        <1, 1, -1>, <1, -1, -1>, <-1, 1, -1>, <-1, -1, -1> >,
    cells = < <8, 7, 6, 5, 4, 3, 2, 1>, <12,11,10, 9, 8, 7, 6, 5> >,
    pols  = < <1, 2> >;

DEF z_min  = -:(vrp_z + front) / (vrp_z + back);
DEF z_proj = -:vrp_z / (vrp_z + back);
```

---

**View Volume in VRC**   In order to generate the geometric model of view volume in view reference coordinates, called VRCvolume in Script 9.4.3, it is sufficient to apply the inverse view mapping to the NPCvolume given in Script 9.4.2.

We also give as a polyhedral complex of dimension $(1, 3)$, a triplet of orthogonal segments of unit length, called ReferenceFrame, to be used as an image of the VRC system in the set of pictures dedicated to the discussion of the 3D perspective pipeline.

**View Volume in WC**   Finally, the view volume in world coordinates, called WCvolume, is obtained from the view model by applying the inverse view orientation mapping to the polyhedral complex VRCvolume given in Script 9.4.3. The scene used to produce several pictures in this example is defined as a structure that contains the WCvolume, the house model and the uvnSystem_in_WC.

*9.4.2   VRML camera implementation*

In this section we implement some simple operators to automatically generate viewpoints from the directions of the reference axes when producing a VRML output for PLaSM-generated models. For this purpose we will define, in Script 9.4.8, two functions called AxialCameras and CenteredCameras, respectively. The AxialCameras operator, when applied to some polyhedral complex, will insert in the output VRM hierarchical graph, three viewpoint nodes looking at the origin from the point on the $x$, $y$ and $z$ axis, respectively. The three viewpoints are labeled with strings 'x view', 'y view' and 'z view', and are searchable from the VRML interface of common web browsers. The CenteredCameras operator does something similar, but also it centers the viewpoints with respect to the orthogonal extent of the polyhedral scene or model it is applied to, so centering the produced views in the browsing

**Script 9.4.3**

```
DEF VRCvolume = (INV_T_per ~ INV_SH_per ~ INV_S_per): NPCvolume;
DEF INV_T_per = T:<1,2,3>:(prp);
DEF INV_S_per = S:<1,2,3>:<sx,sy,sz>
WHERE
    sx = ((umax - umin)*(vrp_z + back))/(2 * vrp_z),
    sy = ((vmax - vmin)*(vrp_z + back))/(2 * vrp_z),
    sz = -:(vrp_z + back)
END;
DEF INV_SH_per = MAT:
    <<1,0,0,0 >,
    <0,1,0,-:dopx / dopz>,
    <0,0,1,-:dopy / dopz>,
    <0,0,0,1 >>
WHERE
    dopx = (umin + umax)/2 - s1:prp,
    dopy = (vmin + vmax)/2 - s2:prp,
    dopz = 0 - s3:prp
END;
DEF uvnSystem = MKPOL:<
    < <0,0,0>,<1,0,0>,<0,1,0>,<0,0,1> >,
    < <1,2>,<1,3>,<1,4> >,
    < <1,2,3> > >;
```

viewport, as shown by Figures 9.18a, 9.18b and 9.18c.

**VRML viewpoint implementation** The PLaSM language and its underlying representation were recently extended by adding properties to nodes of the Hierarchical Polyhedral Complex (HPC) data structure. In such a way, graphics concepts such as appearance, lights, and viewpoints, that do not strictly depend on the geometry, can be inserted in the hierarchy in a simple and non-invasive manner. Furthermore, such properties are consistently retained after the evaluation of every PLaSM operators, including e.g. mapping, skeleton extraction, product and so on, and without any change in the implementation of the predefined language operators.

A camera is defined in PLaSM by making use of the semantics of the VRML viewpoint node. A viewpoint applies to the scene subgraph rooted on it, and is affected by the current value of transformation matrix. In PLaSM, a camera is joined to a polyhedral complex by an expression of this kind:

```
CAMERA:< pol_complex, camera >

camera ≡
< position, orientation, fieldOfView, focalDistance, description >
```

where position and orientation are a triplet and a quadruple of numeric expressions, respectively, according to the VRML semantics. We notice that a VRML orientation has the coordinates of a vector parallel to the orientation axis in the first three components, and an angle (in radiants) in the fourth component.

**Script 9.4.4**

```
    DEF WCvolume = invViewOrientation:VRCvolume;
    DEF invViewOrientation (volume::IsPol) = (invTransl ~ invRot): volume
    WHERE
        invTransl = T:<1,2,3>:vrp,
        invRot = MAT:< <1,0,0,0>, AL:<0,Ru>, AL:<0,Rv>, AL:<0,Rn> >,
        Ru = UnitVect:(vuv VectProd Rn),
        Rv = Rn VectProd Ru,
        Rn = UnitVect:vpn
    END;


    DEF uvnSystem_in_WC = invViewOrientation: uvnSystem;
    DEF WCscene = STRUCT:< WCvolume, house, uvnSystem_in_WC >;
```

**Toolbox**  First a small toolboox of auxiliary functions is given. It contains a non-raised version IsGT of the GT predefined operator, the greater selector of two argument numbers, which returns the greater of them. The MK function, used to transform a sequence of coordinates into a 0-dimensional polyhedron, is given in Script 3.3.15.

**Script 9.4.5 (Toolbox)**

```
    DEF IsGT (a,b::IsReal) = GT:a:b;
    DEF bigger  (a,b::IsReal) = IF:<IsGT,s2,s1>:<a,b>;
```

**Axial Camera**  Actually, several VRML browsers do not implement the full viewpoint semantics. In particular they implement the viewpoint position, and the angle value in the orientation field, as well the fieldOfView given in radians, but the result of using an orientation axis different from 0,0,1 is unpredictable, whereas the focalDistance field is unused.

Such browsers' implementation limits underlie our design choices of Script 9.4.6, where the MyCamera operator applies to a $(0,3)$-dimensional polyhedron, which coincides with the origin of 3D space, a camera with a variable prp and a variable description string. Any axialCamera:$i$ expression, with $i \in \{1,2,3\}$, will return a suitably oriented $(0,3)$-dimensional polyhedron, with attached camera in its local coordinate space, which may be rooted to the scene to display.

Let us remember that each binary PLaSM operator can be applied also in infix form, often increasing the code readability. In Figure 9.16 we show the display from the viewpoints in the VRML file generated by the STRUCT expression above, where MKframe is the 3D object described in Script 6.5.3. The last expression, where the AxialCameras operator given in Script 9.4.8 is used, produces exactly the same output.

**Centered Camera**  A useful camera operator, called centeredCamera:, is given is Script 9.4.7. The expression centeredCamera:i:obj puts a centered viewpoint on the $x_i$ direction, $i \in \{1,2,3\}$, in the polyhedral scene obj, at a distance suitably chosen, in such a way that the whole scene is gracefully accommodated into the VRML browser viewport, when the VRML file exported by PLaSM is loaded in the memory.

**Script 9.4.6 (Axial Camera)**

```
DEF prp = < 0,0,5 >;
DEF MyCamera (prp::Isseq)(string::IsString) = MK:< 0,0,0 >
   ASSIGNCAMERA < prp, < 0,0,1,0 >, <PI/4>, <>, string >;

DEF axialCamera  (i::IsIntPos) =
   IF:< C:EQ:3, K:(MyCamera:prp:'z view'), testxy >:i
WHERE
   testxy = IF:< C:EQ:1,
      K:((R:<2,3>:(PI/2) ~ R:<1,3>:(PI/2)):(MyCamera:prp:'x view')) ,
      K:((R:<1,2>:PI ~ R:<2,3>:(PI/2)):(MyCamera:prp:'y view')) >,
END;

STRUCT:< axialCamera:1, axialCamera:2, axialCamera:3, Mkframe >;
AxialCameras: MKframe;
```

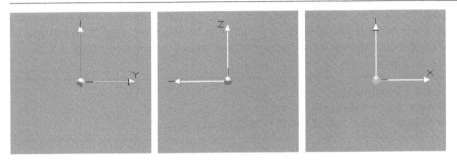

**Figure 9.16**  Scene display from viewpoints generated on the $x$, $y$ and $z$ axes, respectively

**Set of cameras**    Three axial cameras or three centered cameras on the directions of the reference axes are generated by the functions AxialCameras and CenteredCameras given in Script 9.4.8. An example of use of the last operator in displaying a quite complex 3D scene is shown in Figure 9.18. The inverse ordering <3,2,1> of axis indices is used in order to get the 'z view' as the first viewpoint on opening the VRML browser, as usual.

**Script 9.4.7 (Centered Camera)**

```
DEF centeredCamera (i::IsIntPos) (obj::IsPol) =
   (T:i:(trParam - S3:PRP) ~ T:<1,2,3>:objCenter):(axialCamera:i)
WHERE
   objCenter = MED:<1,2,3>:obj,
   trParam = 1.25 * bigger:(SIZE:(pair:i):obj) + (SIZE:i:obj)/2,
   pair = IF:< C:EQ:3, K:<1,2>, IF:< C:EQ:1, K:<2,3>, K:<1,3> > >
END;
```

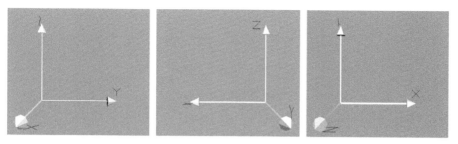

**Figure 9.17**    Scene display from viewpoints generated by `centeredCameras`
operator

---

**Script 9.4.8 (Set of cameras)**

```
DEF AxialCameras  (obj::IsPol) =
    STRUCT: (obj AL AA:AxialCamera:<3,2,1>);

DEF CenteredCameras  (obj::IsPol) =
    STRUCT: (obj AL (CONS ~ AA:centeredCamera):<3,2,1>:obj);
```

---

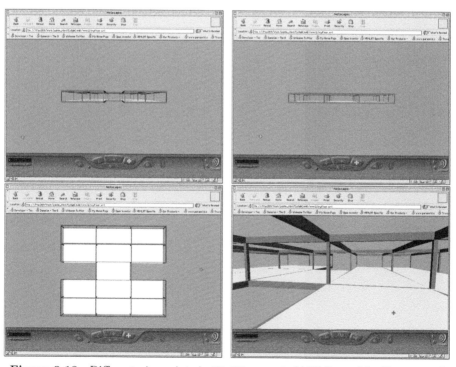

**Figure 9.18**    Different viewpoints in PLaSM-generated VRML model of beams and
pillars in a building fabric

# 10

# Viewing and rendering

This chapter is aimed at discussing the rendering process of a 3D scene on raster devices like display monitors and ink-jet printers. In the first part of the chapter we discuss how to choose the view models (i.e. suitable sets of parameters) in order to generate either realistic images or technical drawings of the modeled scene or object. For this purpose a detailed taxonomy of different types of projections is discussed, and several examples are given. Then the attention is shifted to the rendering process of realistic images, by discussing some main approaches to the hidden-surface removal (HSR) problem, i.e. to the removal of hidden parts of the scene. A short presentation is then given of lighting, shading and color models. Such techniques concern the computer treatment of light behavior of surfaces, and their rendering to produce realistic images. Some examples of VRML lighting, coloring and texturing PLaSM-generated models finally are discussed.

## 10.1 View-model

As we already know from the previous chapter, every 2D picture of a 3D scene is always obtained by *projection* from some *projection center* to some suitable *projection plane*, also called the *viewplane*.

1. The projection is said to be *perspective* when the projection center is *proper*.
2. The projection is said to be *parallel* when the projection center is *improper*, i.e. is set at infinity.

In the first case the bundle of lines that projects the scene points is a cone; in the second case it is a cylinder. In other words, the lines projecting the scene from a center at infinity are parallel.

Therefore, the first criterion used to distinguish between different types of projection is the kind, either proper or improper, of projection center. The projections of a 3D scene are then further classified depending on the position of center and on the attitude of the viewplane. The taxonomy of projections discussed in the following sections is summarized in Table 10.1.

*Geometric Programming for Computer-Aided Design*  Alberto Paoluzzi
© 2003 John Wiley & Sons, Ltd  ISBN 0-471-89942-9

**Table 10.1**　Taxonomy of projections

| Perspective | Central | (1-point) | |
|---|---|---|---|
| | Accidental | (2-point) | |
| | Oblique | (3-point) | |
| Parallel | Orthographic | Simple | |
| | | Multiple | |
| | Axonometric | Orthogonal | |
| | | Oblique | |

**Perspective machines**　The perspective as a projection from a point, already known to the Greek painters of theatrical backdrops, was rediscovered by the artists of the Italian Renaissance. In particular, Brunelleschi and Alberti were the main theorists of the new projection techniques. Some pictures of Dürer's drawing machines, which reproduce the geometric machinery of projection, are shown in Figure 10.1. They were already known to Brunelleschi and Alberti. The books by Panofsky [Pan91, Pan71] are the authoritative source for the history of perspective as well as for most later explanations of those machines.

**Figure 10.1**　Dürer's drawing machines

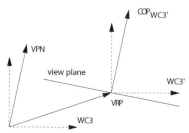

**Figure 10.2**  COP$_{\text{WC3}'}$ definition in a reference frame parallel to WC3, and with origin in VRP

### 10.1.1   View parameters

We are actually interested in computer-generated projections [CP78, Pao78, FvD82, FvDFH90] of some computer model of the scene. This section is therefore aimed at specifying how to produce some well-defined types of projection.

First we recall that the 3D scene is defined in world coordinates (WC3). The scene parts which are possibly defined in local modeling coordinate systems must be assembled in such a unique reference system before projecting.

The 2D picture of the scene is conversely generated with reference to a view reference coordinate system (VRC), called also *uvn* system, with two axes (*uv*) on the viewplane and the third axis (*n*) passing for the viewpoint.

We recall also, from Chapter 9, that such a VRC system is defined on the basis of few vector parameters given in WC3. As a matter of fact, it has:

1. its origin in *view reference point* (VRP);
2. *n* axis parallel to *viewplane normal* (VPN);
3. *v* axis (vertical, upwards) on the viewplane, and oriented as the projection of *view-up vector* (VUV);
4. *u* axis (horizontal, directed from left to right) normal to both *v* and *n*.

In Chapter 9 we have shown that, according to the PHIGS graphics standard, the *center of projection* (COP), for central projections, and the *direction of projection* (DOP), for parallel projections, may be derived from the *projection reference point* (PRP) given in VRC. In the present chapter, for this purpose of giving an easy way to define correct perspectives, we use a slightly different approach:

1. Define VRP in WC3, denoted as VRP$_{\text{WC3}}$, and use this point as the origin of a new system WC3' parallel to WC3.
2. Define COP$_{\text{WC3}'}$ in this parallel system, so that

$$\text{COP}_{\text{WC3}} = \text{VRP}_{\text{WC3}} + \text{COP}_{\text{WC3}'}.$$

3. Assume VPN$_{\text{WC3}}$ = COP$_{\text{WC3}'}$ .

This implies that the viewplane is orthogonal to the axis for VRP$_{\text{WC3}}$ and COP$_{\text{WC3}}$, as shown in Figure 10.2. This also implies, as shown by several examples in the remainder of this chapter, that *central, accidental* or *oblique* perspectives — or 1-, 2- and 3-point perspectives, according to computer graphics literature [CP78, FvD82, FvDFH90]— are produced by COP$_{\text{WC3}'}$ points with either 1, 2 or 3 non-zero coordinates, respectively.

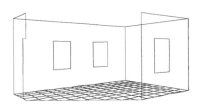 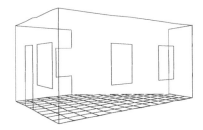

**Figure 10.3**   (a) Clipping at front plane (b) Clipping at back plane

Such an approach is clearly equivalent to the standard one, where the view orientation transformation is defined by giving VRP and VPN (and VUV), and where COP equates to the PRP in VRC. A set of "standard" PHIGS view models is given in Example 10.2.1, and the corresponding pictures are shown in Figure 8.11.

*10.1.2   View volume*

As we know from the previous chapter, the view volume is the bounded portion of WC3 which contains the subset of scene data which are seen in a specified projection. In particular, the subset of scene data which is outside the view volume must be *clipped* by the graphics system, whereas the subset of inside data must be *projected* and *rendered* on the output device.

**Perspective projection**   The view volume of a perspective projection is a truncated *pyramid* with the apex in COP, four side planes passing for COP and for the window edges in the viewplane, and with two sides parallel to the viewplane and contained in planes with VRC equations $n = f$ and $n = b$. Such parallel planes are the *front* and *back* planes, sometimes called *hither* and *yon* planes, respectively.

**Parallel projection**   The view volume is a *parallelepiped*, not necessarily straight, with four side edges parallel to DOP, four side faces for the window edges and front and back faces with VRC equations $n = f$ and $n = b$.

The view volume performs two different functions related to projection and clipping, respectively.

1. The shape of view volume actually specifies the *type of projection*, because the *view mapping* transformation must map this volume, as well as the inside content, onto the 3D viewport in NPC system.
2. The inside content of the view volume is projected and rendered to produce the actual picture of the scene. All the scene data that lie outside such a volume are instead clipped, i.e. not rendered, by the graphics system.

In Figure 10.3 we show the images generated by activating the clipping to the front and back planes, respectively, when the view volume intersects the scene model.

## 10.2    Taxonomy of projections

In this section we discuss in depth the classification of projections established in the military and engineering schools since the early times of descriptive geometry in the Napoleonic age.[1] In particular, we aim to discuss how to define the set of vector parameters that we collectively called *view model*, in order to obtain some well-specified kinds of projection.

### *10.2.1   Perspective*

As we already said, perspective projections are classified depending on the attitude of viewplane with respect to the reference frame. In particular, the viewplane can be either parallel to some coordinate plane, or parallel to some coordinate axes, or in a general position. Correspondingly, the generated projection is said to be either 1- or 2- or 3-point perspective. Some examples of such projections from the art history are given in Figure 10.4. The corresponding perspectives of the standard cube built on the vectors of the Cartesian basis are shown in Figure 10.5.

**Figure 10.4**    (a) Piero della Francesca, *The Baptism of Christ*, 1459, National Gallery, London (b) Raffaello, *The Carrying of Christ (Pala Baglioni)*, 1507, Borghese Gallery, Rome (c) Caravaggio, *The Crucifixion of Saint Peter*, 1600, Cerasi Chapel, Santa Maria del Popolo, Rome

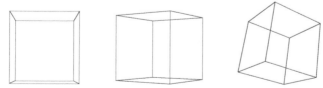

**Figure 10.5**    Central (1-point), accidental (2-point) and oblique (3-point) perspective

---

[1] Gaspard Monge (1746–1818) was a teacher at the military school of Mézières.

## One-point perspective

A *central* perspective is obtained when the viewplane is parallel to a coordinate plane. In such a projection only one of the improper points of coordinate axes has finite projection. In other words, the perspective has only one *accidental point*, also called a *vanishing point*, so it is often called *1-point perspective*.

Notice that in this projection the images of parallel straight lines which are also parallel to one of two coordinate axes remain parallel. The images of lines which are parallel to the coordinate axis perpendicular to the viewplane, conversely converge in the vanishing point. This effect is actually visible only when the scene to be projected is parallel to the reference frame.

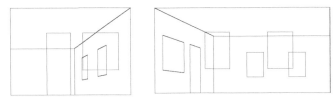

**Figure 10.6**    View models for one-point perspectives with center of projection set on the ground ($\text{VRP}_z = \text{COP}_z = 0$)

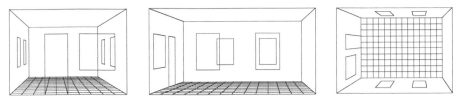

**Figure 10.7**    Central perspectives from the directions of coordinate axes

## Two-point perspective

When the viewplane is parallel to a coordinate axis we obtain an *accidental perspective*. In such a projection two of the improper points of coordinate axes have finite perspective. In other words, the accidental perspective has two vanishing points for the coordinate axes. This projection is also called *2-point perspective*.

The parallelism of the bundle of coordinate axis parallel to view plane is conserved by the projection. The images of lines in the two bundles parallel to the other two axes, instead converge in two finite vanishing points.

Such two vanishing points define the *horizon line* on the view plane. This line contains the perspective of the improper points of every bundle of lines parallel to the ground plane $z = 0$. The horizon line is the perspective of the line at infinity of the bundle of planes parallel to the ground.

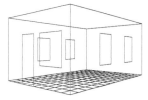

**Figure 10.8**  Accidental perspectives: (a) VRP on the ground (b) VRP above of the ground

### Three-point perspective

The more realistic type of perspective picture is obtained by the 3-point perspective, where all improper points of coordinate axes have finite projection.

Such a projection is also called "with sloping cadre" or *oblique* perspective or *photographic* perspective, since it reproduces the behavior of the camera, that can be placed in any position and with any orientation with respect to the scene when taking a picture.

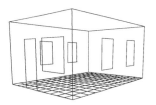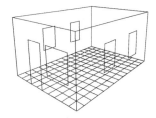

**Figure 10.9**  Two oblique (photographic) perspectives

**Remarks**  In order to generate well-specified types of perspective it may be useful to take into account the following points:

1. If the viewplane is vertical, i.e. parallel to the $z$-axes, and $VRP_z = COP_z = 0$, then the *horizon line* coincides with the *ground line* (see Figure 10.6). The first one is the image of the line at infinity of the plane bundle parallel to $z = 0$; the second one is the intersection of the viewplane with $z = 0$.
2. To force the non-coincidence of horizon and ground lines, it is necessary to put the camera's target above the ground, i.e. to have $VRP_z \neq 0$. Usually $VRP_z$ is set equal to the viewer's height.
3. It is very easy to specify the kind of perspective if COP is given in the WC3' system. In particular, the perspective is *central* if only one component of COP is not zero; it is *accidental* if two components are non-zero; it is *oblique* (photographic) if they are all non-zero.

**Interior perspective**  In Figure 10.10 we show two perspective pictures from outside and inside our usual scene. In order to obtain an image of the interior of the scene without inducing some overturning of the visual cone relative to the scene part on the viewer's back, it is necessary to activate the scene clipping at the front plane, often coinciding with the viewplane, or very close to it.

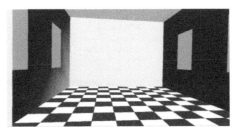

**Figure 10.10**   Perspective inside the scene, clipped to the front plane

*10.2.2   Parallel*

We remember that a projection is said to be *parallel* when the center of projection is improper. This implies that the projecting lines are a bundle of parallel lines. The parallel projections are classified as either orthographic or axonometric.

## Orthographic

A parallel projection is said to be *orthographic* when (a) the projection plane is a coordinate plane, and (b) the direction of projection is parallel to the orthogonal coordinate axis.

Clearly, there are only three different orthographic projections. The projection from the direction of $z$-axis is called the *plan view* or planimetry. The projections from the directions of $x$-axis or $y$-axis are called either *front view* or *side view* depending on the orientation of the scene with respect to the reference frame.

In every case, the viewplane normal must be parallel to the direction of projection. The easiest choice is to set VPN = DOP.

In all sorts of parallel projections, the generated image does not depend on the choice of the VRP. In fact, because the parallelism of projecting lines, the projected image is the same on each element of a bundle of parallel planes. For the sake of simplicity we choose VRP $= \begin{pmatrix} 0 & 0 & 0 \end{pmatrix}^T$.

## Multiple orthographic

A multiple orthographic projection, where either two or three orthographic projections are simultaneously generated and assembled, is known as Monge's projection, after Gaspard Monge, one of the inventors of descriptive geometry at the beginning of XIX century. In his work, every 3D geometric element, i.e. points, curves and surfaces, is described by two or more corresponding orthographic projections.

The reader should notice, from the view model of Figure 10.11c, that the plan view of a Monge's projection has the image of $y$-axis vertical but oriented downwards. Consequently, the image of $x$-axis is horizontal but oriented towards left. In 2D graphics we are conversely used to see such axes upwards and from left to right, respectively. This effect is obtained simply by setting VUV $= \begin{pmatrix} 0 & -1 & 0 \end{pmatrix}^T$.

In most graphical user interface of CAD systems, such multiple orthographic projections are used together with a further view of the scene or object at hand. Usually some orthogonal axonometric projection, described in the following sections, is used for this purpose, as shown in Figure 10.11. That picture, as well most of the images of this

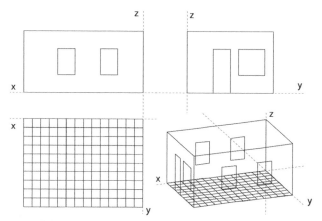

**Figure 10.11**   Monge's orthographic projections, and axonometric projection

section, was produced by using the solid modeler *Minerva*, developed at the University of Rome "La Sapienza" by the CAD Group in second part of 10980s [PRS89, PM89]. *Minerva* was, to the knowledge of the authors, the first solid modeler implemented on a personal computer, since it worked on the IBM PC in '86 and on the Apple Macintosh in '87.

## Axonometric

All the parallel projections that use projection planes which are not normal to a coordinate axis are called *axonometric projections*. They are classified into two main classes, depending on the existence or not of a parallelism between the direction of projection and the viewplane normal. The first ones are called *orthogonal axonometric projections*; the second ones are called *oblique axonometric projections*.

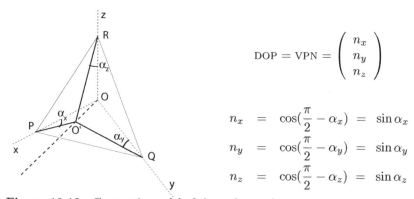

$$\text{DOP} = \text{VPN} = \begin{pmatrix} n_x \\ n_y \\ n_z \end{pmatrix}$$

$$n_x = \cos(\frac{\pi}{2} - \alpha_x) = \sin\alpha_x$$

$$n_y = \cos(\frac{\pi}{2} - \alpha_y) = \sin\alpha_y$$

$$n_z = \cos(\frac{\pi}{2} - \alpha_z) = \sin\alpha_z$$

**Figure 10.12**   Geometric model of the orthogonal axonometric projection

**Orthogonal axonometric**   When the direction of projection is orthogonal to the viewplane the projection is called *orthogonal axonometric projection*. In this case the DOP and VPN vectors are parallel by definition, and often are set equal each other. In the history of graphics techniques three standard orthogonal axonometric projections are well defined. They are called respectively:

1. isometric projection
2. dimetric projection
3. trimetric projection

depending on the relationship between the sizes of the projected images of the Cartesian basis of the WC3 system, as discussed in the following.

**Geometry of orthogonal projections**  In Figure 10.12 we give a conceptual model of geometry of orthogonal axonometric projections, where the axis $OO'$ is directed as the DOP vector, and where the projection plane is chosen as passing for points $P$, $Q$ and $R$. Notice that $O'$ is the projection of the origin, and that $O'P$, $O'Q$ and $O'R$ are the images of the reference system on the viewplane.

It is easy to verify that a unit vector $n$ parallel to $OO'$ has components $\begin{pmatrix} \cos\beta_x & \cos\beta_y & \cos\beta_z \end{pmatrix}^T$, where $\beta_x, \beta_y$ and $\beta_z$ are the angles between $n$ and the Cartesian axes. We remember from analytic geometry that such numbers are called *director cosines* of the plane. If we consider the right-angled triangles $OO'P$, $OO'Q$ and $OO'R$ and the angles $\alpha_x = \frac{\pi}{2} - \beta_x$, $\alpha_y = \frac{\pi}{2} - \beta_x$ and $\alpha_z = \frac{\pi}{2} - \beta_x$, that the projection plane makes with the axes, then we can conclude that in any orthogonal axonometric projection:

$$\text{DOP} \equiv \text{VPN} \doteq n = \begin{pmatrix} \sin\alpha_x \\ \sin\alpha_y \\ \sin\alpha_z \end{pmatrix}$$

**Isometric orthogonal projection**  This axonometric projection get its name from the fact that all the *images* of unit basis vectors have the same size (from *iso* = same, and *metric* = measure, size). The *image* of any pair of reference axes also includes the same angle of 120°.

We could actually distinguish between eight different orthogonal isometric projections, one for each octant where to choose the direction of projection. Anyway the standard isometric projection is that with $n_x = n_y = n_z > 0$. For this projection we have:

$$\alpha_x = \alpha_y = \alpha_z = 35°20',$$

but in this case it is certainly easier to choose DOP $=$ VPN $= \begin{pmatrix} 1 & 1 & 1 \end{pmatrix}^T$.

The orthogonal isometric projection is largely used both in mechanical and in architectural drawings. It may sometimes be a little confusing, because the projection of the standard cube appears as a regular hexagon. An example of isometric orthogonal projection is given in Figure 10.13.

**Dimetric projection**  The name *dimetric* is used because the projections of the unit basis vectors have two different sizes. From some handbooks of drawing techniques we

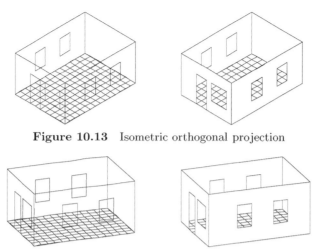

**Figure 10.13** Isometric orthogonal projection

**Figure 10.14** Dimetric orthogonal projection

get the values of the *director angles* of the projection plane, i.e. the angles between this plane and the coordinate axes, for the dimetric projection:

$$\alpha_x = 19°32', \quad \alpha_y = 61°50', \quad \alpha_z = 19°32'.$$

Actually there is an infinite number of different dimetric projections; the one given above should be more properly called the *standard dimetric projection*. An example is given in Figure 10.14.

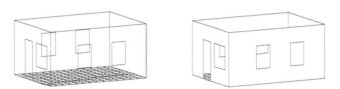

**Figure 10.15** Trimetric orthogonal projection

**Trimetric projection** The trimetric projection is so called because the projections of the unit basis vectors have three different sizes. Clearly, there are infinite trimetric projections, each one obtained by choosing any DOP and any non-parallel VPN. The *standard trimetric projection* is obtained by the following values of director angles:

$$\alpha_x = 27°30', \quad \alpha_y = 60°30', \quad \alpha_z = 9°50'$$

The trimetric projection of our usual scene model is shown in Figure 10.15.

**Oblique axonometric** The axonometric projections where the DOP vector is not normal to the projection plane are called *oblique projections*. As an obvious consequence of this definition, DOP and VPN cannot be equal nor parallel. Some special types of oblique projection are often used. In particular:

1. *cavalier*[2] *projections* are oblique projections where the view plane is parallel to a coordinate plane;
2. *military cavalier projections* are isometric cavalier;
3. *cabinet projections* are dimetric cavalier.

The cavalier projections are largely used by European architects. They are easy to draw with the traditional draftsman tools, since these projections do not change the geometric figures that lie on planes parallel to a coordinate plane. The cabinet projection is also quite realistic. Last but not least, such projections may be directly used in a workshop or building yard since they represent exactly the plan or front views of the artifact.

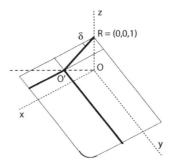

**Figure 10.16**    Geometric model of the cavalier projections

In every cavalier projection, the images of two Cartesian basis vectors have unit size and enclose a straight angle. This a consequence of the fact that a parallel projection on a plane of two parallel segments does not change either their sizes or their angle.

Hence, if we choose a projection plane at unit distance from the origin, then the number $|O'R|$, i.e. the size of the projection of the unit segment $OR$ (see Figure 10.16), determines the projection type. In particular, an isometric cavalier is generated when $|O'R| = 1$, otherwise a dimetric cavalier is obtained. This is called a *cabinet projection* when $|O'R| = \frac{1}{2}$.

Also, it becomes very easy to specify the DOP vector. Looking at Figure 10.16, we may assume

$$\text{DOP} = \begin{pmatrix} |O'R| \cos \delta \\ |O'R| \sin \delta \\ 1 \end{pmatrix},$$

where $\delta$ is the angle between the projections of $x$ and $z$ axes.

Notice that there are $\infty^2$ different cavalier projections, when the orientation of the projection plane is fixed, since they depend on the angle $\delta$ and on the number $|O'R|$. Both military cavalier and cabinet projections are parametrized by the $\delta$ angle.

**Military cavalier**    In this kind of projection the projection plane is parallel to a coordinate plane, usually the $z = 0$ plane.

---

[2] From the Italian mathematician Bonaventura Cavalieri (1599–1647), fellow of Galileo.

Here the DOP vector has an angle $\alpha_z = \frac{\pi}{4}$ to the $z$-axis, so that the projection of $e_3$ basis vector results of unit size. The images of $e_1$ and $e_2$ have also unit size because of their parallel projection on a parallel plane. Al we already said, a military cavalier projection is isometric.

The more common military projections, called *standard* and shown in Figure 10.17, have angle $\delta$ of the image of $x$-axis to the vertical line equal to 30°, 45° and 60°, respectively.

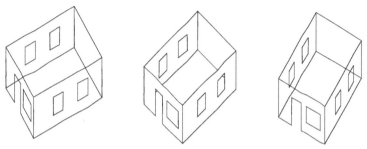

**Figure 10.17**   Left, centered and right standard military projections

Standard military projections are often used in architecture and interior decoration. In these applications an orientation of the picture different form the standard one may be needed. Such a requirement is easy to satisfy. The picture orientation of Figure 10.17 is given by VUV = $e_3$; the orientations in Figure 10.18 and Figure 10.19 are generated by VUV = $-e_2$ and VUV = $e_2$, respectively.

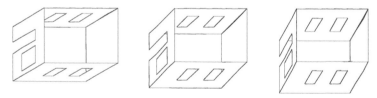

**Figure 10.18**   Standard military projections with VUV = $-e_2$

**Side and front cavalier**   Two very unusual and interesting military projections may be generated by choosing the DOP vector in a coordinate plane. The effect of such projections is a proper assembling of plan view and either front or side views, with no deformation or scaling. Such projections, shown in Figure 10.20, are sometimes used by architects, mainly in interior decoration drawings.

To understand the pictures generated by such projections we must look at the images of basis vectors. They appear as shown in Figure 10.20b. In particular, the image of $e_3$ is parallel to the image of either $e_1$ or $e_2$, respectively, but has opposite orientation. The images of $e_1$ and $e_2$ are neither scaled nor change their angle, since the projection plane is parallel to their plane.

It is interesting to notice, by looking at Figure 10.20a, that it is possible to reconstruct all the measures of our scene model from such projections, assuming that each one of the small squares on the ground plane has unit side. The PLaSM coding of

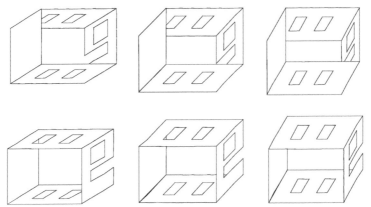

**Figure 10.19**  Standard military projections with VUV = $e_2$ and DOP in third and first octant, respectively

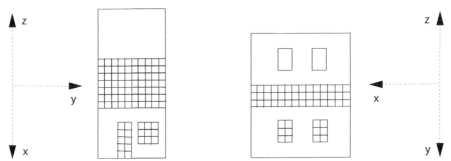

**Figure 10.20**  (a) Front and side military projections, with DOP in the $xz$ and $yz$ plane, respectively (b) Projected images of basis vectors

such a model is actually given in Section 10.8.

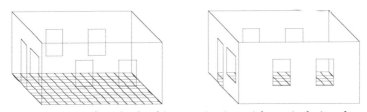

**Figure 10.21**  Standard cabinet projection with vertical viewplane

**Standard cabinet**   As we know, in every cavalier projection the viewplane is parallel to a coordinate plane. Hence the images of the two basis vectors spanning this plane have unit size. In a cabinet projection, the DOP vector is chosen in such a way that the image of the basis vector parallel to VPN gets size $\frac{1}{2}$.

For each given attitude of the viewplane there is an infinite number of different cabinet projections. The so-called *standard cabinet* has VPN = $e_2$, size $\frac{1}{2}$ of the $e_2$ image and angle $45°$ from this one to the horizontal line. A standard cabinet projection is shown in Figure 10.21.

### Example 10.2.1 (Standard view models)

A detailed definition of all significant standard viewmodels is given in Script 10.2.1, according to the PHIGS specification, i.e., with vrp, vpn, vuv given in WC3, and prp, window, front and back given in VRC.

Notice that the arc function produces an argument conversion from degrees to radians. The onepoint, twopoints and threepoints definitions produce perspective view models, whereas all the other definitions clearly produce parallel view models.

Use examples of such models and the display of produced projections, exported as Flash files, are given in Figure 8.11 and Script 8.5.22, respectively.

### Script 10.2.1 (Standard view models)

```
DEF ViewModel (vrp, vpn, vuv, prp, window::IsSeq; front, back::IsReal)
   = < vrp, vpn, vuv, prp, window, front, back >;

DEF arc (degrees, cents::IsReal) = (degrees + cents/60) * PI / 180;

DEF onepoint = ViewModel: <<0,5,4>, <1,0,0>, <0,0,1>, <0,0,35>,
   <-1,-1,1,1>, 0, -1 >;
DEF twopoints = ViewModel: <<0,0,4>,<3,2,0>,<0,0,1>,<0,0,35>,
   <-1,-1,1,1>, 0, -1 >;
DEF threepoints = ViewModel: <<0,0,4>,<3,2,1>,<0,0,1>,<0,0,35>,
   <-1,-1,1,1>, 0, -1 >;
DEF orthox = ViewModel: <<0,0,0>,<1,0,0>,<0,0,1>,
   <0,0,1>,<-1,-1,1,1>,1,-1 >;
DEF orthoy = ViewModel: <<0,0,0>,<0,1,0>,<0,0,1>,
   <0,0,1>,<-1,-1,1,1>,1,-1 >;
DEF orthoz = ViewModel: <<0,0,0>,<0,0,1>,<0,-1,0>,
   <0,0,1>,<-1,-1,1,1>,1,-1 >;
DEF isometric = ViewModel: <<0,0,0>, AA:(SIN arc):<<35,20>,<35,20>,
   <35,20>>, <0,0,1>, <0,0,25>,<-1,-1,1,1>,1,-1 >;
DEF dimetric = ViewModel: <<0,0,0>, AA:(SIN arc):<<19,32>,<61,50>,
   <19,32>>, <0,0,1>,<0,0,25>,<-1,-1,1,1>,1,-1 >;
DEF trimetric = ViewModel: <<0,0,0>, AA:(SIN arc):<<27,30>,<60,30>,
   <9,50>>, <0,0,1>, <0,0,25>,<-1,-1,1,1>,1,-1 >;
DEF centralCavalier = ViewModel: <<0,0,0>,<0,0,1>,<-1,-1,0><0,-1,1>,
   <-1,-1,1,1>,1,-1 >;
DEF leftCavalier = ViewModel: <<0,0,0>,<0,0,1>,<-1/2,SQRT:3/-2,0>,
   <0,-1,1>,<-1,-1,1,1>,1,-1 >;
DEF rightCavalier = ViewModel: <<0,0,0>,<0,0,1>,<SQRT:3/-2,-1/2,0>,
   <0,-1,1>,<-1,-1,1,1>,1,-1 >;
DEF cabinet = ViewModel: <<0,0,0>,<0,1,0>,<0,0,1>,
   <SQRT:2/-4,SQRT:2/4,1>,<-1,-1,1,1>,1,-1 >;
DEF xCavalier = ViewModel: <<0,0,0>,<0,0,1>,<0,-1,0>,
   <0,-1,1>,<-1,-1,1,1>,1,-1 >;
DEF yCavalier = ViewModel: <<0,0,0>,<0,0,1>,<-1,0,0>,
   <0,-1,1>,<-1,-1,1,1>,1,-1 >;
```

## 10.3   Hidden-surface removal

The photorealistic rendering of 3D scenes requires (a) the *hidden-surface removal* from the scene; (b) the *color shading* of visible surfaces depending on position, intensity, color, shape and orientation of lighting sources as well as on reflectance properties of surface materials; and (c) the *texture mapping* on 3D surfaces of a proper projective image of some 2D picture of material they are made. All such three points greatly enhance the realism of computer rendering of the modeled scene or object. Methods and algorithms for hidden-surface removal, illumination, color shading and texture mapping are the subject of this section and the subsequent sections of this chapter. Without loss of generality we suppose the geometry of the scene is described as a set of 3D polygons.

### 10.3.1   Introduction

The *hidden-surface removal* (HSR) is a major step in realistic graphics rendering of 3D scenes. It is usually assumed the the objects in the scene are *dull*, so that they cannot be traversed by light rays. As a consequence, not all parts of an object, as well as not all objects in the scene, are visible to the viewer. It is customary to distinguish between *direct* (or internal) and *indirect* (or external) *visibility*.

In recent years, when speaking of hidden-parts removal, we usually mean the removal of *hidden-surfaces*, more than the removal of *hidden lines*, i.e. of the portions of the boundary edges which are not seen by the viewer, depending on the greater practical importance of raster graphics with respect to vector graphics. Anyway, some algorithms used for removal of hidden-surfaces may be also used to remove their boundary edges.

Even the computation of *shades* generated by a given assignment of light sources may be reduced to the solution of a set of HSR problems.

**Taxonomy of algorithms**   The algorithms for HSR are usually classified, following the early survey [SSS74] by Sutherland, Sproull and Schumacker, into two classes:[3]

1. *object space* (or *exact*) algorithms, where the problem is solved using real coordinates, usually in NPC;
2. *image space* (or *approximated*) algorithms, where the computation is done in integer coordinates, usually in DC3, while rasterizing the picture with a resolution dependent on the available quantity of video RAM.

The first approach was used when using vector devices like pen plotters, which today have disappeared from the market. The second kind of approach is the standard nowadays with raster devices, and is usually implemented in firmware on graphics cards.

It is easy to see that a set of $n$ polygons may produce, in the worst case, a hidden-surface removed scene with $O(n^2)$ visible polygon parts. An optimal algorithm with quadratic complexity is given in [McK87].

---

[3] Foley *and others* [FvDFH90] refer to such two classes as *object-precision* and *image-precision* algorithms, respectively.

## 10.3.2 Pre-processing

Interactive visualization of large geometric data sets with high depth-complexity has long been a major problem within computer graphics. In particular, to efficiently solve the HSR problem always requires some pre-processing, including

- hierarchical graph culling;
- perspective transformation;
- view volume clipping;
- back-face culling;
- occlusion culling.

The word *culling* stands for something picked out from others, especially something rejected because of inferior quality. The root is from Latin *colligere*.

The aim of the above computations is to reduce the dimension of input, i.e. the number of processed polygons, while at the same time reducing the complexity of fundamental tests performed on each projected polygon.

**Graph culling and view-volume clipping**  If the viewpoint is close or inside the scene, so that only a data subset is actually visible, then it becomes highly useful to discard the scene portion outside the view-volume. This clipping is mandatory when the viewer is positioned *inside* the scene data, in order to prevent the projection of polygons on the viewpoint's back.

It is often possible to distinguish between a gross and a detailed clipping to the view volume.

A gross clipping is performed when traversing the hierarchical scene graph (or structure network — see Section 8.2), and is usually called *hierarchical graph culling*. It is implemented as an *intersection* between the *containment boxes* of the current subgraph and the view volume. If such boxes have an empty intersection, then traversal of the subgraph stops. Otherwise, recursive traversal continues. In order to perform a graph culling the containment box of subgraph data must be stored and maintained in each graph node.

The view-volume clipping is executed only on the data which passed the graph culling previously described. Such detailed clipping is performed using either NPC or DC3 coordinates, depending on the architecture of the whole rendering pipeline.

It may be useful to notice that the performance of a 3D browser of textscvrml data is strongly improved when the "world" description is enriched with information regarding the bounding boxes of world elements. Also, depending on the graph culling, the animation of a "walk-through" in a complex architectural scene may be much faster than the presentation of the whole scene from an external viewpoint.

**Perspective transformation**  To remove the hidden-surfaces of a scene requires discovering the polygons or their parts which are unseen from the viewpoint position. A *visibility test* on pairs of points must be often performed for this purpose. This may be defined as follows:

1. given two points $p$ and $q$, discover if they are aligned with the viewpoint $o$;
2. given three aligned points $p$, $q$ and $o$, determine if either $p$ or $q$ is closer to $o$.

A simple geometric approach to visibility test requires computing if

$$(\boldsymbol{p} - \boldsymbol{o}) \times (\boldsymbol{q} - \boldsymbol{o}) = \boldsymbol{0}, \tag{10.1}$$

i.e. verifying that three $2 \times 2$ determinants are zero, and then testing if $\boldsymbol{p}$ is closer to $\boldsymbol{o}$ than $\boldsymbol{q}$:

$$|\boldsymbol{p} - \boldsymbol{o}| < |\boldsymbol{q} - \boldsymbol{o}| \tag{10.2}$$

i.e., in components:

$$(x_p - x_o)^2 + (y_p - y_o)^2 + (z_p - z_o)^2 < (x_q - x_o)^2 + (y_q - y_o)^2 + (z_q - z_o)^2.$$

It is very useful, from a computational viewpoint, to perform the visibility test using NPC coordinates where the *perspective transformation*, already discussed in Section 9.2.6, has been included in the 3D pipeline.

Using such coordinates, the visibility test is algebraically reduced to the following much simpler formulation, where the condition

$$x_p = x_q \quad \text{and} \quad y_p = y_q$$

is tested rather than equation (10.1), and the condition

$$z_p < z_q,$$

is tested rather than equation (10.2).

Clearly, only two numeric comparisons are executed for the first point, rather than the computation of three determinants, and just one comparison is executed for the second point rather than 6 products, 6 differences and four additions.

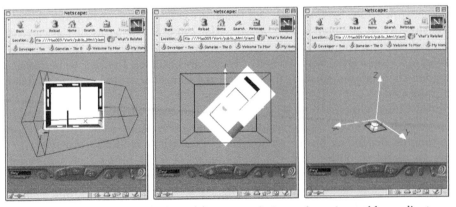

**Figure 10.22** Viewing pipeline: (a) scene and view volume in world coordinates (WC3); (b) in view reference coordinates (VRC); (c) in normalized projection coordinates (NPC) before perspective transformation

Hence, when using NPC or DC3 coordinates, the $z$ coordinate may correctly be called *perspective depth* of points and used to directly compare the relative position of two points respective to the viewer when they have the same $x$ and $y$ coordinates. Last but not least, this approach allows for a unified treatment of perspective and parallel projections when removing the hidden-surfaces of the scene. Some images from the viewing pipelines are given in Figure 10.22.

**Back-face culling**   This operation removes the surfaces of solids which cannot be seen because they reflect or diffuse the light rays in directions that cannot reach the viewer's eye. Such polygons are called *back-faces*. Their external normal gives an angle greater than $\frac{\pi}{2}$ to the DOP or COP vectors.

Let us consider that the viewpoint is mapped, by the perspective transformation, to the point at infinity of $z$-axis. Assuming a right-handed NPC system, the back-faces are easily recognized depending on the negative sign of the $z$-component of their *external* normal. This is a further computational benefit of perspective transformation.

The HSR problem is hence easy to solve for *single* and *convex* objects in NPC or DC3 coordinates. In such case it is sufficient to cull away the polygon faces whose external normal $n$ gives an angle greater than $\frac{\pi}{2}$ to the view direction, i.e. to the $z$-axes. It is easy to see that this condition is satisfied when $n_z \leq 0$.

Therefore, given a data set of complexity measured by the number $n$ of uniformly distributed faces, it is possible to assert that an average number $\frac{n}{2}$ of polygons is removed by back-face culling. If the scene contains only one convex object, then the back-face culling completely solves the visibility problem. Some examples of this fact are given in Figure 10.23.

### Example 10.3.1 (Back-face culling)

An example is given here of a PLaSM program generating a convex solid by intersection of three rotated instances of another convex solid. The generating function is called Jewel in Script 10.3.1. The three intersected instances are subject to a rotation of $\alpha = \frac{\pi}{4}$ about an axis of the reference frame. The Jewel operator is used twice, so generating the convex2 and convex3 objects, starting from the translated unit cube.

---

**Script 10.3.1 (Back-face culling)**
```
DEF Jewel (arg::IsPol) = arg1 & arg2 & arg3
WHERE
    arg1 = R:<2,3>:(PI/4):arg,
    arg2 = R:<3,1>:(PI/4):arg,
    arg3 = R:<1,2>:(PI/4):arg
END;


DEF convex1 = T:<1,2,3>:<-0.5,-0.5,-0.5>:(CUBOID:<1,1,1>);
DEF convex2 = Jewel:convex1;
DEF convex3 = Jewel:convex2;
```

---

The pictures resulting from hidden-surface removal by back-face culling of the geometric values obtained by evaluating the symbols convex1, convex2 and convex3 are shown in Figure 10.23.

**Occlusion culling**   Although graphics hardware has improved greatly in recent years, advances have not been able to keep up with the rapid growth of model complexity. *Occlusion culling* is a popular technique for reducing the number of polygons to be processed by the rendering engine by culling away those portions of the geometry which are hidden from the viewer by other geometry.

**Figure 10.23**  Hidden-surface removal via back-face culling

An interesting and simple approach to this problem was recently presented by Bernardini and others [BKES00]. In a pre-processing stage, they approximate the input model with a hierarchical data structure and compute simple view-dependent polygonal occluders to replace the complex input geometry in subsequent visibility queries. When the user is inspecting and visualizing the input model, the computed occluders are used to avoid rendering geometry which cannot be seen.

Their Directional Discretized Occluders (DDOs) approach, as most of techniques to accelerate the rendering, involves a pre-processing phase where an object-space hierarchical data structure — an octree in their current implementation, see Section 13.2.2 — is generated. The actual scene geometry is stored with the leaf nodes of the octree, and nodes are recursively subdivided so that a bounded number of primitives per leaf node is obtained. Each square, axis-aligned face is a view-dependent polygonal occluder that can be used in place of the original geometry in subsequent visibility queries.

When the user is inspecting and visualizing the input model, the rendering algorithm visits the octree data structure in a top-down, front-to-back order. Valid occluders found during the traversal are projected and added to a two-dimensional data structure. Each octree node is first tested against the current collection of projected occluders: if the node is not visible, traversal of its subtree stops. Otherwise, recursion continues and if a visible leaf node is reached, its geometry is rendered.

This method has several advantages which allow it to perform conservative visibility queries efficiently and it does not require any special graphics hardware.

### 10.3.3 Scene coherence

Before analyzing a few paradigmatic HSR algorithms in some detail, it is worth discussing the *scene coherence* relationship used to increase the efficiency of most object-space algorithms.

For this purpose, let consider a simple scene with two sole objects, i.e. two sole space polygons. We want to understand under what conditions the viewpoint may see both polygons, or better, under what conditions none of them may cover the other making it (or some its parts) non-visible from the viewpoint. The aim is to find some formal conditions allowing dividing the HSR problem into subproblems that can be solved *independently*.

**Visibility relation**  Given a pair of 3D polygons, every plane such that the polygons lie in different halfspaces is called *separation plane* of such polygons. We define as follows a binary *visibility* relation ◁ on the set of 3D polygons:

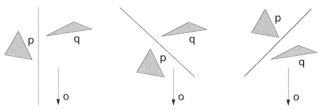

**Figure 10.24**    Three possible arrangements of two polygons and a separating plane

**Definition**    The notation $a \lhd b$, where $a$ and $b$ are polygons, means that *"a cannot cover b"* with respect to viewpoint. We state that

$$a \lhd b$$

if there exists a separation plane that either (a) contains the viewpoint or (b) has $a$ and the viewpoint in opposite halfspaces.

We can read the expression $a \lhd b$ as *"a not covers b"*, or better as *"a beyond b"* — clearly with respect to viewpoint. First of all, let remember that in NPC the viewpoint is coincident with the point at the infinity of the $z$-axis. Then consider that, given two polygons $p, q$ and a separation plane $\Pi$, there are three possible cases, as shown in Figure 10.24:

1. the plane $\Pi$ contains the viewpoint, i.e. is parallel to the $z$-axis;
2. the viewpoint lies in the same halfspace of $p$;
3. the viewpoint lies in the same halfspace of $q$.

Hence, in case (1) we have both $p \lhd q$, and $q \lhd p$; in case (2) we have $q \lhd p$; in case (3) we have $p \lhd q$.

**Visibility graph**    Let a scene description as a set of space polygons be given, and also suppose that a viewpoint position has been fixed. The graph of the visibility relation on a set of space polygons is called the *visibility graph*. Unfortunately the visibility relation *is not a partial order*. In fact, in general it is neither antisymmetric nor transitive. Anyway, the object-space algorithms must normally compute some partial ordering of polygons, according to such relation. To make the relation antisymmetric is easy. For any double pair $a \lhd b$ and $b \lhd a$ it is just sufficient to choose one pair. It is more difficult to make the relation transitive. For this purpose it is necessary to "open the cycles" of the kind $a \lhd b \lhd c \lhd a$. In this case it is sufficient to fragment a polygon within the visibility cycle, e.g. as shown by Figure 10.25.

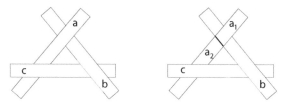

**Figure 10.25**    Opening a cycle in the *beyond* relation by fragmenting a polygon

A total ordering derived from the visibility graph is called *depth ordering*, and the relative constructive algorithm is called *depth sort*. It often constitutes an important point of exact solutions to HSR problem.

## Depth-sort

HSR algorithms in object-space are strongly based on the visibility relation, also called object coherence [FvDFH90], that is used to *depth-sort* [NNS72] or to *depth-merge* [SPGR93] the scene polygons, and on the subsequent rendering the polygons either in *back-to-front* or in *front-to-back* order, as discussed by the following subsections.

The so-called *depth-sort*, also known as *Newell's algorithm*, is actually due to Newell, Newell and Sacha [NNS72]. It is one of best known approaches to HSR problem.

On the set of polygons which results from pre-processing steps seen in Section 10.3.2, this algorithm computes a depth ordering and then generates the resulting picture by back-to-front rasterization.

Such a depth ordering is not exactly a sort on $z$, because each polygon is a set with infinite points, usually with variable $z$. More precisely, it is a total ordering compatible with the visibility relation previously discussed, so that it takes the name of *depth-sort*.

A black-box description of depth-sort follows:

1. (*Input*) culled, clipped and NPC-mapped but unordered scene polygons;
2. (*Output*) depth-ordered scene polygons.

Such an algorithm is based on a set of nested tests used to check the pairs of a preliminary total ordering of polygons produced by a $z$-sort. It may be described as constituted by two main steps, called *pre-sort* and *depth-sort*, respectively.

Let us denote with $s_x, s_y, s_z$ the $x$-, $y$- and $z$-extensions of the $s$ polygon, i.e. the polygon projections upon the coordinate axes, and with $h_s$ the plane of $s$.

**Sorting on** $z$   The polygons of the scene are preliminary ordered on the values of their minimal $z$ coordinate. Any kind of sorting algorithm may be used for this aim.

**Depth-Sorting**   The algorithm is a variation of a *bubble-sort*, where a quite complex test is used to compare if the generic pair of polygons is either already ordered or not.

Let $p$ be the polygon currently ordered, i.e. whose space position is currently compared against those of polygons in the already ordered subset, according to the usual strategy of bubble-sort. Let us also assume that $p$ must be currently compared against the $q$ polygon.

We formally describe in Script 10.3.2 the comparison test on the pair $(p, q)$ by using some pseudo-code.

The intersection tests on the coordinate projections of polygons are easily reduced to number comparisons. For example,

$$(p_z \cap q_z = \emptyset) \equiv (z_{max}(q) < z_{min}(p)) \vee (z_{max}(p) < z_{min}(q)), \qquad (10.3)$$

and so on for the other coordinates. When using a $z$-sort as pre-processing, the above test may be simplified to the rightmost clause.

**Script 10.3.2 (Depth-Test)**
**Algorithm** DepthTest $(p, q :: IsPolDim :< 2, 3 >)$
{
    if $p_z \cap q_z = \emptyset$, then $p \lhd q$
    else if $p_x \cap q_x = \emptyset$ then $p \lhd q$
    else if $p_y \cap q_y = \emptyset$ then $p \lhd q$
    else if $o$ and $p$ are into *opposite* halfspaces of $h_q$ then $p \lhd q$
    else if $o$ and $q$ are into the *same* halfspace of $h_p$ then $p \lhd q$
    else if If $p_{xy} \cap q_{xy} = \emptyset$ then $p \lhd q$
    else $Swap(p, q)$
}

The notation $p_{xy}$ and $q_{xy}$ stands for the projection of $p$ and $q$ in the $xy$ plane, respectively. To test if geometric objects $o$ and $p$ live in opposite halfspaces of the plane $h_q$, we may substitute a point into the plane, test for sign and multiply the signs generated by two substitutions. If the result is 1, then the two objects live in the same halfspace; if the result is instead $-1$, then they live in opposite halfspaces.

If the *DepthTest* also fails with respect to the converse pair $(q, p)$, then none of the two pairs may belong to the output ordering, because there is a cycle in the visibility relation. So, it is necessary to fragment one of the two polygons, e.g. by using the plane of the other for the cut.

**Implementation**

The depth-sort algorithm based on the Newell's visibility test is implemented here. As we know, the PLaSM language does its best when used in a declarative fashion. But it can be also usefully employed to quickly prototype complex geometric algorithms, as we show in this section.

There is a major difference between our implementation and the original formulation of the algorithm previously discussed. Instead of using the above variation of the *bubble-sort*, we make use of the SORT function already implemented in Script 2.1.30, which is a proper applicative implementation of the standard *merge-sort*.

It is well-known [AU92] that a bubble-sort has a worst case complexity $O(n^2)$, when its input is in reverse order. Conversely, the best behavior is reached when the input is already ordered. The pre-sort in the $z$-direction is hence performed with the aim of giving a quasi-ordered input to the proper depth-sort. Such pre-processing is not needed when a merge-sort algorithm is used, whose performance is $O(n \log n)$ for any possible input.

**Toolbox**   The geometric functions needed are given in Script 10.3.3:

1. mixedProd computes the mixed product $a \times b \cdot c$ of vectors $a, b$ and $c$;
2. box_int:$i$:<$p, q$> predicate computes the test of equation (10.3) between the projections of polygons $p$ and $q$ along the $i$-th coordinate axis;
3. three_points returns the first three points from the first convex cell of (the unique polyhedral cell of) its input polygon. Such points are used to make geometric tests against the affine hull of the polygon;

4. onPlane, given three points $p_1, p_2, p_3$ and a further point $q$, returns the signed value of the mixed product of vectors

$$p_2 - p_1, \ p_3 - p_1, \ q - p_1.$$

This value is zero when $q$ belongs to the affine hull of $p_1, p_2, p_3$; otherwise its sign characterizes the set-membership of $q$ to the affine halfspaces;

5. plane_vs_points returns the product of signs of numbers generated when checking two points for set-membership with a plane.

Few vector functions are also used, which are not collected here, including vectDiff, vectProd and innerProd. They were discussed in Chapter 3. The SORT function is defined in Script 2.1.30.

---

**Script 10.3.3 (Toolbox)**

```
DEF mixedProd (a,b,c::IsVect) = a vectProd b innerProd c;

DEF box_int (coord::IsInt) (p,q::IsPol) = OR:<
   GT:(MAX:coord:p):(MIN:coord:q),
   GT:(MAX:coord:q):(MIN:coord:p) >;

DEF three_points (polygon::IsPol) =
   (APPLY ~ [CONS ~ AA:SEL ~ [S1,S2,S3] ~ S1 ~ S2,S1] ~ UKPOL):polygon;

DEF onPlane (p1,p2,p3::IsPoint)(q::IsPoint) =
   (mixedProd ~ AA:vectDiff ~ DISTR): <<p2,p3,q>, p1>;

DEF plane_vs_points (a,b::IsFun;p::IsPoint) =
   * ~ AA:(SIGN ~ APPLY) ~ DISTL ~ [onPlane ~ a,[S1 ~ b, K:p]];
```

---

**Newell's pre-sort**   The pre-processing step is not mandatory in our implementation, but it is given anyway, to stress the pattern of use of the SORT operator with different predicates. In this approach the input polygons are paired with their minimum $z$ values, and the pairs are then sorted using the z_pred predicate to check if the generic couple of pairs is either already ordered or not.

---

**Script 10.3.4 (Pre-sort)**

```
DEF z_pred (a,b::ispair) = GT:(S2:a):(S2:b);

DEF presort (polygons::IsSeqOf:(IsPolDim:<2,3>)) = (S1
   ~ TRANS
   ~ SORT:z_pred
   ~ TRANS
   ~ [ID,AA:(MIN:3)] ): polygons;
```

---

**Visibility test**   The depth_test predicate given in Script 10.3.5 is a direct translation of the Newell's visibility test on 3D polygon pairs already discussed. It is written as a sequence of five cascaded tests, and works assuming that there are no cycles in the visibility relation. We also assume that there are no intersections between polygons. This assumption is certainly true when they came from the boundary of non-intersecting solid bodies.

For sake of numerical robustness we enforce the precondition that pairs of polygons cannot share any portion of their boundary. The satisfaction of this requirement is guaranteed from the application of an explosion transformation, with parameters slightly greater than 1, before the depth-sort. See the depth-sort definition in Script 10.3.6.

---

**Script 10.3.5 (Visibility test)**

```
DEF depth_test = IF:< step1, K:true, K:<> >
WHERE
    step1 = IF:< box_int:3, K:true, step2 >,
    step2 = IF:< box_int:1, K:true, step3 >,
    step3 = IF:< box_int:2, K:true, step4 >,
    step4 = IF:< (C:EQ:-1):(plane_vs_points:<q,p,o>), K:true, step5 >,
    step5 = IF:< (C:EQ: 1):(plane_vs_points:<p,q,o>), K:true, K:<> >,
    p = three_points ~ S1,
    q = three_points ~ S2,
    o = < 0, 0, 1E6 >
END;
```

---

**Depth-Sort**   A set of 3D polygons is extracted from the polyhedral scene by the extract_polygons function, defined in Script 10.8.4. Then, before depth ordering, such polygons are mutually disconnected by the function explode:< 1.001, 1.001, 1.001 > in order to put them in general position with respect to each other. The inverse explosion transformation is applied after the ordering has been produced by the depth_sort function.

The computational pipeline previously described is coded in Script 10.3.6 by the function called depth_sort, which is applied to the input scene. Notice that the pre-processing step is not mandatory in this approach. The explode function is given in Script 10.8.6.

---

**Script 10.3.6 (Depth-Sort)**

```
DEF depth_sort (scene::IsPol) =
    ( explode:< 1/1.001, 1/1.001, 1/1.001 >
    ~ SORT:depth_test
    ~ presort
    ~ explode:< 1.001, 1.001, 1.001 >
    ~ extract_polygons
    ): scene;
```

---

The algorithm has been written as above for sake of readability and compactness. A strong optimization of performance could be obtained, after the polygons extraction from the scene and their separation through the slight explosion, by pairing each polygon with its containment box and with the triplet of points used to construct its affine hull.

### 10.3.4 Back-to-front and front-to-back

The algorithms that are depth-sort based may be classified depending on the order of presentation of polygons on the output device. Both total orders generated from depth-sort, from furthest to nearest to the viewpoint, and its reverse, are used.

**Back-to-front presentation** When the input polygons have been depth-ordered, the Newell's algorithm generates the hidden parts removed picture by rasterizing the furthest polygon first. Then the second one in decreasing distance from the viewpoint is rasterized, where this one may cover some parts of the previous, and so on, until the polygon nearest to the viewpoint is presented on the device. When the presentation of depth-ordered polygons is finished, the only scene portions seen from the viewpoint are displayed. This strategy is called *back-to-front* presentation. Notice that a raster device is needed to execute this algorithm. Such a strategy, requiring drawing some picture areas more and more times, cannot be used on a vector device.

This method has some drawbacks. First, it can be used only with raster devices. Second, although the rasterization is very quick, when storing or moving a picture of a complex scene across a computer network, e.g. converted in *Postscript*, the size of data may become a problem, especially when we consider that most of polygons cannot be seen from the viewpoint.

**Front-to-back presentation** This name is given to the opposite strategy, where the picture of the scene is generated by drawing the depth-sorted polygons starting with the nearest polygon and ending with the furthest one.

In this case the whole first polygon is drawn and assumed as initial value of the so-called *apparent boundary* of the scene, i.e. the current boundary of the picture. Such an "occluder" is then subtracted from each following polygon in the depth-ordered sequence. Each non-empty result of such subtractions is drawn, since it is visible from the viewpoint. At the same time, the picture boundary is modified by union with each drawn polygon fragment. This procedure, repeated for each element in the *input* sequence, is described by using pseudo-code in Script 10.3.7.

This approach, which is perfect for vector devices, may also be used for presentations on raster devices. When used before a *Postscript* conversion of a vectorized scene picture, it may reduce some orders of magnitude the size of graphics data.

### 10.3.5 Binary Space Partition

The BSP algorithm removes the hidden parts of the scene by working in object space and does not require any specialized hardware. It was often used to generate animations in computer games (e.g. in the famous DOOM) as well as in real-time

**Script 10.3.7 (Front-to-back)**
**Algorithm** Front-to-back ($input :: IsSeqOf : (IsPolDim :< 2, 3 >)$)
{
    reverse the *input* sequence;
    $B := \emptyset$;   (initialize the apparent boundary)
    **for each** polygon $p \in input$:
    {
        $p := p - B$;
        draw or rasterize $p$;
        $B := B \cup p$;
    }
}

---

walks-through architectural models.

This algorithm builds in a pre-processing step a specialized data structure, which is a sort of spatial index. This binary tree is called *Binary Space Partition tree*, or simply *BSP-tree*. Using this data structure, for each possible viewpoint position a depth-ordering is generated in linear time with the number of polygons. Due to this performance, the algorithm is sufficiently fast to allow the animation of quite complex scenes using non-specialized graphics hardware.

It is worth noting — if the scene is static and only the observer is moving — that the same BSP-tree may be used for ordering the polygons in all the possible views. Furthermore, a new depth-order must actually be computed only when the viewpoint leaves the current cell of the space partition induced by the BSP-tree. Various subsequent frames of an animation can thus be rendered without computing a new polygon ordering. Such a major property of computer animations was discovered in the 1970s under the name of *scene coherence*.

**Approach** It may be useful to distinguish three main phases with the BSP-algorithm:

1. *construction* of the BSP-tree;
2. BSP-tree *traversal*, with generation of a depth-ordering;
3. *rendering* of the sorted list of polygons.

So, the BSP-tree construction step is needed only once when the scene is static. Conversely, a traversal of the BSP-tree is necessary for each space cell crossed by the viewpoint trajectory, if any. If such a trajectory is predefined, then all the tree traversals can be computed in advance with respect to the proper animation. The rendering of the scene is clearly demanded by the 3D pipeline, and is not considered part of the realm of HSR algorithms, because it is necessary to compute for each frame the position of data in device space.

The BSP algorithm can be described in a dimension-independent way. We choose this approach because it will allow us to discuss BSP-trees with reference to various applications, including HSR, solid modeling, and representation of polygons, polyhedra and geometric manifolds of higher dimensions.

**Definitions**

Given a set of hyperplanes in Euclidean space $E^d$, a *BSP-tree* defined on such hyperplanes establishes a hierarchical partitioning of the $E^d$ space.

A node $\nu$ of such a binary tree represents a convex and possibly unbounded region of $E^d$ denoted as $R_\nu$. The two sons of an internal node $\nu$ are denoted as *below*($\nu$) and *above*($\nu$), respectively. Leaves correspond to unpartitioned regions, which are called either *empty* (OUT) or *full* (IN) *cells*. Each internal node $\nu$ of the tree is associated with a *partitioning hyperplane* $h_\nu$, which intersects the interior of $R_\nu$. The hyperplane $h_\nu$ partitionates $R_\nu$ into three subsets:

1. the subregion $R_\nu^0 = R_\nu \cap h_\nu$ of dimension $d - 1$;
2. the subregion $R_\nu^- = R_\nu \cap h_\nu^-$ where $h_\nu^-$ is the negative halfspace of $h_\nu$. The halfspace $h_\nu^-$ is associated with the tree edge $(\nu, below(\nu))$. The region $R_\nu^-$ is associated with the *below* subtree, i.e. $R_\nu^- = R_{below(\nu)}$;
3. the subregion $R_\nu^+ = R_\nu \cap h_\nu^+$ where $h_\nu^+$ is the positive halfspace of $h_\nu$. The halfspace $h_\nu^+$ is associated with the tree edge $(\nu, above(\nu))$. The region $R_\nu^+$ is associated with the *above* subtree, i.e. $R_\nu^+ = R_{above(\nu)}$;

For any node $\nu$ in a BSP tree, the region $R_\nu$ is the intersection of the closed halfspaces on the path from the root to $\nu$. The region described by any node $\nu$ is:

$$R_\nu = \bigcap_{e \in E(\nu)} h_e$$

where $E(\nu)$ is the edge set on the path from the root to $\nu$ and $h_e$ is the halfspace associated with the edge $e$.

**Tree construction**

The BSP pre-processing consists of the scene tree construction. Such construction is executed in $O(n^3)$ in the worst case. Actually some heuristics are used to reach a near $O(n^2)$ complexity, to the cost of some sub-optimal increasing of scene storage.

**Algorithm**  The planes used are those which contain the scene polygons. The binary tree is built inductively. The root plane $\nu$ is suitably chosen and is associated with its polygon. Such a root polygon $p(\nu)$ is thus eliminated from the list of scene polygons. This list is then split into two sublists associated with the *above* and *below* subtrees. The first one contains the polygons in $R_\nu^+$; the second one contains the polygons in $R_\nu^-$. Polygons which are crossed by $\nu$ are split and their fragments are associated to the proper subtree. Such process is repeated on each subtree until each sublist contains just one element.

**Analysis**  It is essential for pre-processing efficiency that each root plane is chosen in such a way that (a) it crosses and splits the least possible number of polygons, so that their total number grows as small as possible, and that (b) the generated *above* and *below* subsets of polygons are relatively balanced, so that the subdivision process may continue over subsets of near half cardinality. If both such constraints are satisfied at each step, then the algorithm works efficiently.

When the number of output polygons equates the number $n$ of input polygons, such pre-processing has a cost variable between $O(n^3)$, for a completely unbalanced tree, and $O(n^2 \log n)$, for a perfectly balanced tree.

Actually, the total number of polygons may increase at each step depending on the choice of the root polygon, so that some satisfying compromise between the storage and time costs is heuristically searched.

Usually, each root plane is chosen in linear time, by comparing the size of the *above* and *below* sublists associated with some fixed number, usually between 4 and 8, of randomly chosen planes. Experimentally, this approach gives a pre-processing time between $O(n^2)$ and $O(n \log n)$, and a storage cost ranging between 1 and 4 times the size of input data.

The paper [PY90] by Paterson and Yao gives an algorithm for efficient binary space partitioning. It is efficient in the sense that, for an input space of $n$ polygons, a naïve partioning scheme will result in a BSP tree of size $O(n^3)$ while this algorithm yields paritions of size $O(n^2)$.

**Tree traversal**

Some kind of *inorder* traversal [AHU83] is used to traverse a BSP tree. Remember that, if a binary tree is a single node, then the node is added to the output list; otherwise one of its subtrees is first traversed in inorder, then the root is processed, then the other subtree is traversed in inorder.

The *node processing* consists in determining if the viewpoint is either in the above or below subspace of the current plane. Such a processing is done in constant time, by substituting the viewpoint coordinates in the plane equation, and looking for the sign of the resulting number. Since the node processing requires a constant time, the whole tree traversal requires a linear time.

---

**Script 10.3.8 (Traverse back-to-front)**
**Algorithm** TraverseB2F $(\nu : BSPtree)$ {
    if IsLeaf $(\nu)$ then Output$(\nu)$
    else {
        if $o \in R_\nu^+$ then {
            TraverseB2F $(below(\nu))$
            Output$(\nu)$
            TraverseB2F $(above(\nu))$ }
        else {
            TraverseB2F $(above(\nu))$
            Output$(\nu)$
            TraverseB2F $(below(\nu))$ }
    }
}

---

The descent ordering in the two subtrees may vary in each node, depending on the type of depth ordering to compute, which may be either *back-to-front*, say going from the plane which is further from the viewpoint to the closest plane, or *front-to-back*, say, going from the nearest to the more distant plane.

**Back-to-front ordering**    According to the inorder traversal, if the node is a leaf, then the associated polygon is put in the output list. Otherwise: (a) the viewpoint position with respect to the current plane is evaluated; (b) the subtree associated with the subspace which does not contain the viewpoint is traversed in inorder; (c) the node is put in the output list, and (d) the subtree corresponding to the subspace which contains the viewpoint is finally traversed in preorder.

The geometric idea used here concerns the visibility relation. As we already know, no one polygon in the subspace which does not contain the viewpoint may cover the polygons in the viewpoint subspace. The back-to-front traversal algorithm is given in Script 10.3.8.

**Front-to-back ordering**    If the node is a leaf, the polygon is put in the output list.

Otherwise: (a) the viewpoint position with respect to the current plane is evaluated; (b) the subtree associated with the subspace which contains the viewpoint is traversed in inorder; (c) the node is put in the output list, and (d) the subtree corresponding to the subspace which does not contain the viewpoint is traversed in preorder. The front-to-back traversal algorithm is described using pseudo-code in Script 10.3.9.

---

**Script 10.3.9 (Traverse front-to-back)**
**Algorithm** TraverseF2B ($\nu : BSPtree$) {
     if IsLeaf ($\nu$) **then** Output( $\nu$ )
     **else** {
         if $o \in R_\nu^+$ **then** {
            TraverseF2B (above($\nu$))
            Output( $\nu$ )
            TraverseF2B (below($\nu$)) }
         **else** {
            TraverseF2B (below($\nu$))
            Output( $\nu$ )
            TraverseF2B (above($\nu$)) }
     }
}

---

*10.3.6   HSR algorithms in image-space*

Image-space algorithms are traditionally classified according to the type of raster subset they focus on. Three main classes are usually considered, respectively with pixel-based algorithms (*z*-buffer and ray-casting), line-based algorithms (including various scan-line algorithms), and area-based algorithms (including Warnock's algorithm and others). In the following of this section we only discuss the *z*-buffer algorithm, because some variation of this algorithm is adopted today by the totality of 3D graphics accelerators.

## $z$-buffer algorithm

A main aspect of this algorithm is that it does not need any preliminary ordering of the scene polygons. The algorithm efficiency is strongly affected by this fact.

**Input/output**   The input to the algorithm is the unordered set of 3D polygons of the scene, already transformed in DC3 coordinates. The output is constituted by the final contents of the frame buffer, which contains a rasterized picture of the scene parts visible from the viewpoint.

**Storage structures**   Two storage arrays are used, respectively denoted as *frame-buffer* and *z-buffer*. Such arrays have the same number of rows and columns, and their elements are associated to the pixels of the viewport on the display device. The frame-buffer contains a color value, usually either a composite RGB value or an index to some color look-up table. The $z$-buffer contains the discrete value of the $z$ coordinate associated to the centroid of the polygon portion represented on a given pixel. Corresponding elements on the frame-buffer and on the $z$-buffer, say on the same row and column, are associated to the same polygon portion.

Notice that the $z$-buffer elements hold integer numbers, in a range of values depending on the number of bits per element, often equal to 24. Of course, the depth resolution of the algorithm depends on the quantity of RAM available for the $z$-buffer. This resolution may strongly affect the output quality when rastering 3D scenes of high geometric complexity.

**Algorithm**   The algorithm initialization can be distinguished from the algorithm core. In the initialization step the frame-buffer is set to the background color, and the $z$-buffer is set to the minimum representable value, in the hypothesis that a right-handed frame is used for the DC3 coordinates. The view direction is that of positive $z$ axis.

In the algorithm core the scene polygons are rasterized in any order. Let us consider the processing of the generic polygon. A covering with a discrete set of pixels at integer DC3 coordinates is produced, and the discrete $z$ for each pixel is also computed. Such set of pixels give a minimal covering of the polygon image, but only a pixel subset is usually stored, according to their current visibility from the viewpoint.

Each polygon is rasterized by rows. For each generated pixel we need to decide if either it must be stored in the frame buffer and in the $z$-buffer, or not. Such a decision is positive if the pixel already stored in memory at the same $xy$ address (i.e. at the same <column, row> pair) is further from the observer than the current pixel or vice versa. It is considered further when the integer value stored in the $z$-buffer is smaller than the $z$ of the current pixel.

When all the scene polygons have been rasterized, the frame buffer will contain the scene picture really perceived from the viewpoint.

The generic rasterization step requires the computation of the $z$ coordinate of the current pixel starting from the known $z$ of the previous pixel.

Let $\boldsymbol{p}_k = (x_k, y_k)$ be the current pixel, belonging to the $y_k$ row and to the $x_k$ column of the device space. The $z$ coordinate in $\boldsymbol{p}_k$ and $\boldsymbol{p}_{k+1}$ pixels may be computed by substituting the ordinate and abscissa of the two points into the plane equation of their polygon:

$$ax_k + by_k + cz_k + d = 0,$$
$$ax_{k+1} + by_{k+1} + cz_{k+1} + d = 0.$$

In other terms:

$$z_k = -\frac{1}{c}(d + ax_k + by_k),$$
$$z_{k+1} = -\frac{1}{c}(d + ax_{k+1} + by_{k+1}),$$

and hence

$$\Delta z = z_{k+1} - z_k = -\frac{a}{c}(x_{k+1} - x_k) - \frac{b}{c}(y_{k+1} - y_k).$$

But $y_{k+1} - y_k = 0$ and $x_{k+1} - x_k = 1$, so that

$$z_{k+1} = z_k + \Delta z = z_k - \frac{a}{c}. \tag{10.4}$$

By comparing $z_{k+1}$ with the value already stored in position $(x_{k+1}, y_{k+1})$ of $z$-buffer, it is possible to decide whether to store the pixel depth $z_{k+1}$ or not. If the $z$ value is stored, then the pixel color is also computed and stored. For this purpose other computations may be required, including normal interpolation and/or color shading, as discussed in the following sections.

**Analysis**   It may be interesting to note that, as shown by equation (10.4), the computation of the $z$ increment from the previous pixel only requires a subtraction by a constant number. This algorithm, which is extremely simple, is easily implemented in firmware on 3D graphics accelerators. Notice that the generation time of the hidden-surface removed picture depends linearly on the average area of polygons and on their number.

## 10.4   Illumination models

To generate realistic images by computer it is necessary both to remove the hidden-surfaces of the scene and to render the visible ones by taking into account the physical principles which regulate the diffusion and reflectance of light rays that incise on the external surfaces of bodies in the scene to be rendered. In particular, we need to take into account not only the geometry of the scene, but also some optical and physiologic aspects related to the diffusion, reflection and perception of light.

In this section we aim to discuss how the surfaces reflect and diffuse the incident light radiation. Let us first remember from optics that the light intensity incident on the exterior of a body may be

1. absorbed;
2. transmitted;
3. reflected, both diffusely and specularly,

in percentages that depend both on the body material and on the nature of the fixture of its exterior surface.

**Lighting models**   The terms "lighting" or "illumination models" are used to denote the choice of some particular equation to compute the light intensity in a space point, as a function of the intensity of the incident radiation and the geometric and physical properties of the surface the point belongs to. The goal when using lighting models is to compute the light intensity on the surfaces of the scene, given some assigned distribution and configuration of light sources and some assigned material properties of the surfaces.

**Sources**   When we model a scene, we have to give both its geometry and some suitable light sources. Such sources may be either set at infinity or at some finite position. As a consequence, light rays will be either parallel or divergent, respectively. Light sources may be geometrically shaped either as point sources or as distributed, i.e. extended, sources. Depending on requirements, we may have scenes with only one light source or with several sources. Also, we may imagine that the emitted light has the same intensity in all the directions, or that a source shines in a preferred direction. Such sources are called directional light sources.

**Absorbed radiation**   The portion of incident radiation which is absorbed by a body is transformed into heat and produces an increase in temperature. Notice that if the body had absorbed all the incident light, then it would be not visible. Such perfectly absorbent body is called "black body". The absorbed radiation is not interesting for our purposes, but it may be useful to note that different bodies do not absorb the different wave lengths in the same way. For this reason the different materials look as if they have different colors when exposed to the daylight.

**Transmitted radiation**   The incident radiation is partly transmitted inside the body when this is transparent. This case will not be considered in the remainder of the text. On this point we will only discuss how to set the percentage of transparency when stating the material properties in VRML.

**Diffusely reflected radiation**   The diffuse radiation can be thought to be due to the portion of incident radiation which is absorbed by the external layer of the body, and then is uttered in all directions allowed by the position and orientation of the external surfaces. We will see that, at least in computing the diffuse intensity using the simplest diffusion model, it is not necessary to consider the viewpoint position, since the body, in the case of perfect light diffusion, behaves exactly as an emitter body.

**Specularly reflected radiation**   We may imagine that the specularly reflected portion of the incident radiation does not traverse the external layer of the body, but is directly reflected in the plane defined by the direction of the normal to the surface in the considered point and by the direction of the incident light. In this case we need to compute how much reflected intensity may geometrically reach the viewpoint position.

### 10.4.1   Diffuse light

We know that the incident light on a opaque body may be partly diffused, partly reflected and partly absorbed by the body. Let us consider the simplest lighting model, where only the diffused light intensity is taken into account. The involved vector quantities are shown in Figure 10.26, where we have

1. $p$ = point on the body surface;
2. $n$ = normal unit vector to the surface in $p$;
3. $\ell$ = direction of incident light, given by the difference between the source position, supposed point-shaped, and $p$;
4. $\theta$ = angle between vectors $\ell$ and $n$.

**Lambert's diffuse intensity**   The physical phenomenon is regulated by the following *Lambert's cosine law*. If a body is a perfect diffuser, then the diffused intensity $I_d(p)$ from a point $p$ of its surface is proportional to the incident light intensity and to the cosine of the angle $\theta$:

$$I_d(p) = K_d I_\ell \cos \theta, \tag{10.5}$$

where $I_\ell$ is the light intensity incident in $p$. The factor $K_d$ is called *diffusion constant*. The $\theta$ angle must necessarily vary between 0 and $\frac{\pi}{2}$.

**Figure 10.26**   Lambert's cosine model of diffused reflection

The model described by equation 10.5 is the simplest lighting model, with a single light source which illuminates a single opaque body. For $\theta$ greater than $\frac{\pi}{2}$, we have $I_d(p) = 0$, where no light would be available since the $p$ point would not be visible from the source.

Such a single assumption is too strong, because it would render as *black* all the surface portions where $\frac{\pi}{2} \le \theta$. In other words, when using this simple model, we should render as black all the scene polygons which are not presently visible from both the viewpoint and the light source. Such a result would be actually unacceptable.

**Ambient diffuse intensity**   The problem of black surfaces discussed above may be easily solved by considering that in any scene there is some diffused lighting due to surrounding environment. For this purpose it is sufficient to assume that on each body surface there is also some, usually small, quantity of light not directly received from a light source but coming from the ambient surroundings of the scene. In other terms, it is assumed that each body will diffuse a constant portion of the ambient lighting.

An additive *ambient* term $K_a I_a$ is hence introduced in the diffusion equation 10.5, depending on the average *ambient lighting* $I_a$, characteristic of the ambient of the scene, and on the *ambient diffusion* constant $K_a$, characteristic of the body material:

$$I_d(\boldsymbol{p}) = K_d I_\ell \cos\theta + K_a I_a \tag{10.6}$$

Notice that black surfaces may appear again, as soon as either $K_a$ or $I_a$ are equal to zero. But also this simple model has some important drawbacks. Consider in fact two parallel polygons made with the same material and located at different distances from the viewpoint. By using the above equation they would have the some light intensity in each point (and hence exactly the same color), so that, in case of partial visual occlusion with respect to the viewpoint, it would be actually impossible for the observer to distinguish the first surface from the second surface.

**Depth attenuation of intensity**  To get more realistic results it is necessary to take into account the intensity attenuation as a function of depth. In particular, we should consider as appropriate physical parameter the *intensity flow*, defined as the energy which crosses the unit surface. This parameter would be measured at distance $d$ by the intensity diffused in $\boldsymbol{p}$, over the area $4\pi d^2$ of the spherical surface centered in $\boldsymbol{p}$. The intensity attenuation should be hence made proportional to the inverse of the squared distance.

But dividing the first term of equation (10.6) by the square of the viewpoint distance gives results which do not experimentally match the user experience. In particular it is possible to notice that by varying the intensity (i.e. the color) with the inverse of the square of the viewpoint distance produces a too strong variation between points belonging to surfaces located at relatively small distances from each other.

Conversely, some good visual results are given by the equation:

$$I_d(\boldsymbol{p}) = \frac{K_d}{d+K} I_\ell \cos\theta + K_a I_a \tag{10.7}$$

where $d$ is the viewpoint distance from $\boldsymbol{p}$ and $K$ is an additive constant which gives a "fine-tuning" of the lighting behavior of surfaces, until to make them look realistic. Notice that $d$ cannot be interpreted as the distance from viewpoint if this one is at infinity. In such a case $d$ is assumed as the $z$ difference between $\boldsymbol{p}$ and the scene point with maximum $z$.

### 10.4.2  Specular reflection

If a body is perfectly reflective, say, a perfect mirror, then all the radiation incident on $\boldsymbol{p}$, which is not absorbed or transmitted, is reflected along the symmetric direction of $\boldsymbol{\ell}$ with respect to $\boldsymbol{n}$, i.e. along the reflection vector $\boldsymbol{r}$. See Figure 10.27.

With a perfectly reflective body, the observer would see the considered point only if located along the reflection direction. Actually, real bodies do not behave like perfect ones, and do not reflect the light only along the reflection direction. Conversely, the reflected intensity is spatially distributed around $r$. Hence the viewer, located on the view direction $v$, may in any case get a perception of some portion of the reflected light, and can see $p$ when $\theta + \alpha < \frac{\pi}{2}$.

In particular, the reflected light intensity perceived along $v$ is a function of the angle $\alpha$ between $v$ and $r$, as shown in Figure 10.27. Notice that the view direction $v$ is not necessarily coplanar with the $\ell$, $n$ and $r$ vectors.

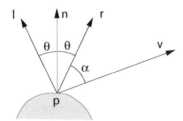

**Figure 10.27**   Specular reflection from a point source

The quantity of specularly reflected energy strongly depends in a quite complex way both on the wavelength $\lambda$ of the incident light and on the angle $\alpha$ between the reflection and view directions.

**Phong's reflection model**   A simplified description of the phenomenon is due to Phong Bui-Tuong [Pho75]. In this model it is assumed that the *specularly reflected intensity* $L_s(p)$ is proportional to (a) the incident radiation $I_\ell$ as well as to (b) the $n$-th power of cosine of angle $\alpha$ between the reflection and the view directions, through a function $w(\theta, \lambda)$ which depends on the incidence angle $\theta$ and on the wavelength $\lambda$.

$$L_s(p) = w(\theta, \lambda)I_\ell \cos^n \alpha$$

The $n$ parameter depends on the body material. In Figure 10.28 we show the graph of $\cos^n \alpha$ function, as generated by Script PLaSM 10.4.1.

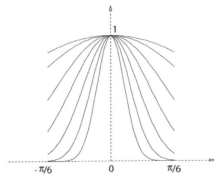

**Figure 10.28**   Graph of function $\cos^n \alpha$, for $-\frac{\pi}{6} \leq \alpha \leq \frac{\pi}{6}$, and with samples of $n$ between 1 and 80

In Figure 10.28 are shown the effects of various values of $n$ on $\cos^n \alpha$ and hence on the spatial distribution of energy. The exponent $n$ is low with no reflective material, e.g. paper, and can reach values between 50 and 100 with very reflective materials, such as metals with surface polished as a mirror.

---

**Script 10.4.1 (Graphs of $\cos^n \alpha$)**

```
DEF graph(n::IsIntpos) = MAP:[s1, ** ~ [cos ~ S1, K:n]]:
   ((T:1:(-:PI/6) ~ intervals:(pi/3):40);
DEF COSnGraphs = (STRUCT ~ AA:Graph):< 1, 2, 5, 10, 20, 40, 80 >;
```

---

**Simplified model of specular reflection**   The $w$ function of Phong's model, which takes into account both the incidence angle $\theta$ and the incident wavelength $\lambda$, is actually very complex, and can only be given empirically. It is usually substituted by a constant $K_s$, called the *specular reflection constant*, so that we have the simplified reflection model:

$$L_s(\boldsymbol{p}) = K_s I_\ell \cos^n \alpha.$$

The material properties are thus incorporated in the parameter $n$, whereas the geometric (incidence angle) and physical (wavelength) properties of the incident light are summarized by the $K_s$ constant. Since the aspects already discussed for the diffused intensity continue to hold, the following better expression is usually adopted for the specularly reflected intensity:

$$I_s(\boldsymbol{p}) = \frac{K_s}{d + K} I_\ell \cos^n \alpha + K_a I_a. \tag{10.8}$$

**Aggregated reflection models**   In summary, the expressions already seen for diffuse and specularly reflected intensities can be aggregated, since common bodies usually behave both as light diffusers and as mirrors. The aggregated model for the reflected light intensity is

$$I(\boldsymbol{p}) = \frac{I_\ell}{d + K} (K_d \cos \theta + K_s \cos^n \alpha) + K_a I_a \tag{10.9}$$

where $K_d, K_s$ and $n$ are material properties, $I_\ell$ depends on the light source, and $\alpha, \theta, K$ and $d$ are characteristics of the geometric configuration of the surface. The geometric parameters of the illumination model are better "highlighted" (!) by using inner products of unit vectors rather than cosines of angles:

$$I(\boldsymbol{p}) = \frac{I_\ell}{d + K} \left( K_d \boldsymbol{\ell} \cdot \boldsymbol{n} + K_s \left( \boldsymbol{r} \cdot \boldsymbol{v} \right)^n \right) + K_a I_a. \tag{10.10}$$

More in general, several light sources may appear on the stage, with different incident light intensities and properties. Hence, for the reflected intensity $I(\boldsymbol{p})$ in a point illuminated by various sources we can write

$$I(\boldsymbol{p}) = \sum_i \left[ \frac{I_{\ell_i}}{d + K_i} (K_d \, \boldsymbol{\ell}_i \cdot \boldsymbol{n} + K_s \, (\boldsymbol{r}_i \cdot \boldsymbol{v})^n) \right] + K_a I_a. \qquad (10.11)$$

**Geometry of reflection models** Vectors $\boldsymbol{\ell}, \boldsymbol{n}$ and $\boldsymbol{v}$ are independent variables of the geometric problem. In particular, $\boldsymbol{\ell}$ can be obtained by normalizing the point difference between the source location and the considered point $\boldsymbol{p}$. The $\boldsymbol{v}$ vector is computed analogously, by normalizing the point difference between the viewpoint and $\boldsymbol{p}$.

The normal vector $\boldsymbol{n}$ is constant on each planar surface. In a polygon it can be computed by the vector product of two consecutive edges with an internal angle less than $\frac{\pi}{2}$. Such a convex internal angle always exists, for both convex and concave polygons, where the common vertex of two edges is extremum with respect to one coordinate, e.g. is the point with either maximal or minimal $z$, provided that the polygon does not lie on a plane with equation $z = c$.

The computation of the direction of reflection $\boldsymbol{r}$ is a bit more complex. In this case it is necessary to compute a rototranslation tensor $\boldsymbol{Q}$ which maps $\boldsymbol{p}$ in the origin and the normal unit vector $\boldsymbol{n}$ in the basis vector $\boldsymbol{e}_3$ of the $z$ axis. So we have, in homogeneous coordinates:

$$\boldsymbol{r} = \boldsymbol{Q}^{-1} \boldsymbol{S}_{xy}(-1, -1) \, \boldsymbol{Q} \, \boldsymbol{\ell},$$

where $\boldsymbol{S}_{xy}(-1, -1)$ is the scaling tensor that reverses the sign of the $x$ and $y$ coordinates.

## 10.5 Color models

In this section we quickly present the more important concepts about color as individual perception of colored lights. We also discuss the additive and subtractive color theories, needed to understand the production of colored pictures done by computer monitors and printers, respectively, and some common models of color spaces.

**Additive and subtractive color** The term *color* stands for the cerebral sensation produced when the human eye is hit by electromagnetic radiation in the *visible spectrum*, i.e. in the range of wavelengths between 400 and 700 $nm$ (nanometers), with $1 \, nm = 10^{-9}$ meters.

When discussing the *perception* of color it is necessary to take into account both physical-optical and psycho-physiologic factors. In particular, some experimental apparatus is needed to define the concept of "visible color". In fact, the observer might get the same color perception even in the presence of sources emitting light radiations with different distributions of frequency.

Hermann von Helmholtz, a nineteenth-century German physiologist and physicist, proposed the well-accepted theory where he postulated that the human eye contains three physiologic structures which are able to perceive only the so-called fundamental colors *red*, *green* and *blue*.

Every different color is hence individually perceived as a proper summation of appropriate quantities of the three fundamental colors. The *additive theory* of perception of colored lights is built on such a very basic assumption. Conversely, to explain the color perceived by eyes/brain when receiving light reflected by materials which do not emit any radiation, such as e.g. press inks or colored clothes, the so-called *subtractive color* theory is used. In this case it is postulated that fabric material would subtract (by absorbing them) some part of fundamental colors from the incident daylight.

**Frequency distribution spectrum**   The *average daylight* is sometimes called *white* or natural *light*. This light, when observed through a prism or spectroscope, appears to be composed of some different colored lights, that we collectively call the *spectrum of visible light*, and is shown in Figure 10.29. To the extremes of the visible spectrum there are the minimum and maximum wavelengths perceivable by a human, corresponding to violet (400 *nm*) and red (700 *nm*).

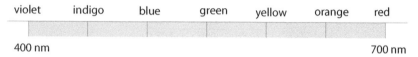

| violet | indigo | blue | green | yellow | orange | red |

400 nm                                                                      700 nm

**Figure 10.29**   Schematic representation of the visible spectrum

In the first half of the twentieth century several empirical experiments were done to define the concept of *visible color*, in particular by using an experimental machinery where a light of unknown color is compared with suitable triples of lights of fundamental colors. See Figure 10.30.

In particular, let us imagine red, green, blue light sources and a further source of light of an unknown color, where some potentiometers allow control of the intensity of fundamental lights. Such fundamental colors are summed and the observer may change their individual intensities until they "match" the unknown light. If such a match is possible, then it makes sense to state that

$$I(C) = I(R) + I(G) + I(B).$$

It is on the basis of several successful experiments that the additivity of fundamental color lights was postulated.

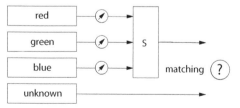

**Figure 10.30**   Experimental machinery for unknown color "matching" with fundamental colors

Actually, it is not always possible to sum three monochromatic lights and to match the unknown colored light. To understand why it is sufficient to consider that monochromatic lights, like any other light, have some distribution on the frequency spectrum, and hence they contain also some portion of the two other monochromatic lights. Another problem comes from the fact that the same subjective color perception might be obtained from totally different spectra. A frequency spectrum was hence considered not useful for color characterization.

**Normalized representation of color**   The *Comité Internationale de l'Éclairage* (CIE) in 1931 adopted the *additive* color theory, and the so-called *normalized representation* of color. The color system is assumed to be linear and purely additive. Three primary spectrum distributions, called $X$, $Y$ and $Z$, respectively, were substituted to red, green and blue in the "matching" process. Each other color intensity can be expressed as a sum of primary intensities $I(X), I(Y)$ and $I(Z)$. Three normalized ratios, called chromaticity values, are defined as

$$x = \frac{I(X)}{I(X) + I(Y) + I(Z)}$$
$$y = \frac{I(Y)}{I(X) + I(Y) + I(Z)}$$
$$z = \frac{I(Z)}{I(X) + I(Y) + I(Z)}$$

By definition, the sum of chromaticity values is hence unitary:

$$x + y + z = 1,$$

and each value is non-negative. Thus, two of such parameters are independent, and their values may be represented in a two-dimensional plane. In particular, each triplet $(x, y, z)$ can be represented as a point in the unit triangle with vertex $(0,0)$, $(1,0)$ and $(0,1)$, as shown in Figure 10.31. The chromaticity values $(x, y, z)$ can be considered to be the convex coordinates of points in such a triangle.

**Chromatic diagram**   The average experimental results of the matching process can be represented as points in the unit triangle of chromaticity values. Such points give a representation of how an average observer perceives the visible colors. Even the pure colors in the daylight spectrum become points in such a diagram, and are distributed along a curve which resembles the shape of a boot sole. We may orderly recognize *red*, i.e. the radiation at 700 nm, followed by *yellow, green, cyan, blue, violet*, i.e. the radiation at 400 nm. Since it is assumed that the phenomenon is linearly additive, it is worth considering each visible color as represented by a point on the segment which connects two component colors. Analogously, if any triplet of colors is fixed, their triangle gives all the visible colors which are obtainable by their combination. In particular, the *centroid* of the triangle of primary colors is the point where the intensities of primary colored lights are equal, and corresponds to the *white* color.

This diagram is called chromaticity diagram or *standard chromaticity diagram*. It is the result of a quite complex standardization work. In particular, a *standard*

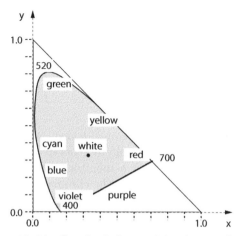

**Figure 10.31**   Standard chromaticity diagram by CIE

*distribution* was defined for three *primary lights*. The colors of the spectrum of daylight, called *pure* or *saturated* colors, are distributed on the boundary of the diagram. Each other *visible color* on this diagram, as an effect of the linearity assumption, can be considered to be obtained by mixing a saturated color with white. The corresponding coefficient is called the *degree of saturation* of the color. In particular, a color is saturated when it approximates to some pure color.

For each color $c$ let us trace the segment passing for it and the white $w$, until to encounter the pure color $p$ on the boundary of the chromaticity diagram. In this case we can write:

$$c = (1 - \alpha)\,w + \alpha\,p, \qquad 0 \le \alpha \le 1.$$

where the *saturation* of color $c$ is defined as the $\alpha$ coefficient of the convex combination of $p$ and $w$, or, in other words, as the ratio of distances of $c$ from $p$ and $w$. Usually, the color saturation is expressed as a percentage, so that a color saturated at 100% is pure, whereas one saturated at 0% coincides with white color.

**Complementary colors**   Take any color $c$. The color $b$ such that its summation with $c$ gives the white $w$:

$$b + c = w$$

is called the *complementary color* of $c$. The complementary color of $c$ is easily computed by considering the straight line for $c$ and $w$, and getting the color point at same saturation on the halfline opposite to $c$ with respect to $w$. Notice that the complement of a pure color is a pure color. The names of complementary colors of additive primaries are given in Table 10.2.

The standard chromatic diagram is closed by a segment joining the two extreme pure colors of daylight, thus enclosing the area shown as gray in Figure 10.31, where we have the pure colors. Such a "closure line", called the *purple line*, is only obtainable by convex combinations of the two extremes of the line, i.e. of *red* and *violet*. The internal points of such a diagram represent the set of *visible colors*, also called the *perceivable colors*.

**Table 10.2**  Mapping between primary additive colors and complementary colors

| Primary color | Complementary color |
|:---:|:---:|
| Red | Cyan |
| Green | Magenta |
| Blue | Yellow |

**Gamout of a monitor**   The screen of a monitor device cannot generate the whole set of visible colors. Actually each screen is able to generate only a triangular subset of colors. This set of colors realizable from a monitor screen is called the monitor *gamout*. For each monitor a triplet of points in the chromaticity diagram is assumed to be representative of *red*, *green* and *blue* lights. See Figure 10.32.

The design of a monitor screen is thus characterized by a triplet of pairs of chromaticity values in the CIE chromaticity diagram. This triangle is also called the RGB (*red*, *green*, *blue*) triangle of the screen. The area of this triangle is a good index of the screen quality. The wider is the area, the better is the quality.

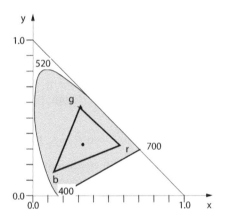

**Figure 10.32**   Typical monitor gamout, representative of the set of realizable colors

**RGB color model**   In the chromaticity diagram the light intensity is not taken into account. For this purpose a three-dimensional diagram is introduced and used as a model of realizable colors, where the intensity is explicitly considered. In particular, the intensities of primary colors, normalized between 0 and 1, are associated with the axes of a 3D reference frame. Each realizable colored light is thus associated with the points of the standard unit cube. This model is called the *RGB cube* or *RGB color model*.

In this model each color point is represented by a triplet in $[0, 1]^3$, by varying the intensities of primary colors. So, the point $R = (1, 0, 0)$ represents the *red* color at maximum intensity and analogously the point $G = (0, 1, 0)$ identifies the *green* color; the point $B = (0, 0, 1)$ gives the *blue* color. The origin $O = (0, 0, 0)$ with zero intensity for each primary light is associated with the *black* color. Analogously the point $W = (1,1,1)$ corresponds to the *white* color. Each other point on the line segment between *black* and *white* is a triplet of equal numbers. Such a segment is called *line of grays*.

Other interesting points of the RGB model are the vertices where two coordinates are unitary and one is null. They correspond to complementary colors *cyan* $C = (1,1,0)$, *magenta* $M = (0,1,1)$ and *yellow* $Y = (1,1,0)$. The RGB color model is quite important because it closely resembles the way color is stored in memory. Triples of integers corresponding to intensities of primary colors are usually stored, with a number of bits depending on the number of available colors. As we will see in Section 10.7.2, the RGB model is used in VRML to specify the values of type *SFColor*.

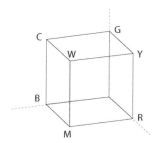

**Figure 10.33** RGB cube with both primary (*red, green, blue*) and complementary (*cyan, magenta, yellow*) colors in the cube vertices. The remaining vertices are associated with *black* and *white*

### Example 10.5.1 (RGB color cube generation)

An interesting example of color representation by embedding, written exploiting the dimension-independent geometry representation of the PLaSM language is given here. For this purpose it is sufficient to repeat each triplet of coordinates of vertices of the unit standard cube $[0,1]^3$ as coordinates in RGB color space.

---

**Script 10.5.1 (RGB color cube)**

```
DEF RGBcube = MKPOL:<<
   <0,0,0, 0,0,0>, <1,0,0, 1,0,0>, <0,1,0, 0,1,0>, <1,1,0, 1,1,0>,
   <0,0,1, 0,0,1>, <1,0,1, 1,0,1>, <0,1,1, 0,1,1>, <1,1,1, 1,1,1>
>,<1..8>,<<1>>>;

VRML:RGBcube:'out.wrl';
VRML:(@1:RGBcube):'out.wrl';
```

---

It may be interesting to note that the intrinsic dimension of RGBcube object generated by Script 10.5.1 is 3, whereas the dimension of its embedding space (i.e. the number of its coordinates) is 6. As a matter of fact, we have:

```
RGBcube ≡ A-Polyhedral-Complex{3,6}
```

Since the output object has a number of coordinates comprised between 3 and 6, the generated VRML file contains a *color per vertex* representation of the polyhedral parameter. According to the number of coordinates, the VRML file may contain either a representation with colors per vertex, or with normals per vertex, or both.

The results of exporting the geometric values generated by the expressions RGBcube and @1:RGBcube are shown in Figures 10.34a and 10.34b, respectively. Notice that the skeleton extractor function handles correctly a wire-frame model with color-per-vertex encoding.

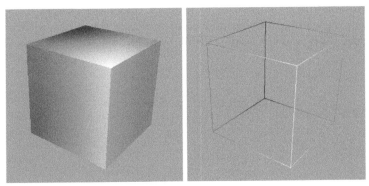

**Figure 10.34**   (a) VRML rendering of the 3D object RGBcube embedded in 6D space according to Script 10.5.1 (b) 1D skeleton of RGBcube

**Prismatic HSV color model**   For user interaction the so-called *hue, saturation, value* (HSV) color model is probably more interesting to the standard user. This color model is based on the saturation of a pure color (hue) with the white, and on the variation of intensity.

In particular, the intensity value (V) is associated with an axis labeled with numbers in $[0, 1]$. On the plane $V = 1$ is given a hexagon with a unit radius of the circumscribed circle. The hexagon vertices are orderly labeled with pure colors *red, yellow, green, cyan, blue* and *magenta*.

The edges of such a hexagon correspond to the colors which are generated by a convex combination of the two colors associated with the edge vertices. The angular parameter, called hue (H) (also called *tint* or *intrinsic color*), which clearly varies in the interval $[0, 2\pi]$, gives a description of the pure colors. By convention, the red color is associated with $H = 0$.

The radial parameter $S$ ranging in $[0, 1]$ is called *saturation*. The color point associated with $S = 0$ and $V = 1$ is the *white*; the one associated with $S = 0$ and $V = 0$ is the *black*. The segment between such points is called the *line of gray*, as in the RGB model.

### Example 10.5.2 (HSV color prism generation)

An embedding technique similar to that of Example 10.5.1 may be used to create a VRML model of the HSV color prism through the MKPOL primitive, as provided in Script 10.5.2. The generated VRML model is shown in Figure 10.36. Notice that in this case a polyhedral cell made of six tetrahedral cells is defined. A direct construction as a single convex cell made by either seven or eight $\mathbb{E}^6$ points is not possible, because the convex hull of such points would have intrinsic dimension 4.

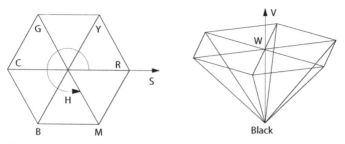

**Figure 10.35** HSV prism color model with labeled verticeso

---

### Script 10.5.2 (HSV color prism)

```
DEF HSVprism = MKPOL:<<
    < 0,0,0,                          0,0,0 >, % black    %
    < 0,0,1,                          1,1,1 >, % white    %
    < 1,0,1,                          1,0,0 >, % red      %
    < COS:(PI/3),SIN:(PI/3),1,        1,1,0 >, % yellow   %
    < COS:(2*PI/3),SIN:(2*PI/3),1,    0,1,0 >, % green    %
    < -1,0,1,                         0,1,1 >, % cyan     %
    < COS:(4*PI/3),SIN:(4*PI/3),1,    0,0,1 >, % blue     %
    < COS:(5*PI/3),SIN:(5*PI/3),1,    1,0,1 >  % magenta  %
>,<
    <1,2,3,4>, <1,2,4,5>, <1,2,5,6>,
    <1,2,6,7>, <1,2,7,8>, <1,2,8,3>
>,<1..6>>;

VRML:HSVprism:'out.wrl';
```

---

The HSV prism is often transformed into a cone, and sometimes into a cylinder. To generate such models may be an interesting exercise for the reader. *Hint:* use the `MAP` primitive to apply a suitable coordinate transformation to some properly decomposed 3D domain embedded in 6D.

**CMY color model** The *cyan, magenta, yellow* (CMY) model of *primary subtractive* colors is particularly suited to color management of printing devices, which do not use light sources, such as screen monitors, or print inks. Such materials reflect the incident daylight after having absorbed the frequencies of the complementary additive primary color. Hence, e.g., the *cyan* ink, which is the complementary color of *red* absorbs from the daylight, which is a mixture of *red*, *gree* and *blue*, its red frequencies, so reflecting a light which is a mixture of *green* and *blue*. Analogously, the *magenta* and *yellow* inks respectively reflect (a) a mixture of *red* and *blue* and (b) a mixture of *red* and *green*.

When two primary subtractive inks are blended together, their mixture will subtract the frequencies of two additive primaries from the white light, thus reflecting the remaining additive primary color. Therefore, the mix of *cyan* and *magenta* will subtract *red* and *green* from the daylight and reflect the only frequencies of *blue*. Analogously for the other combinations. Consequently, the mixing of all three subtractive primary inks will subtract all the frequencies from daylight, thus giving *black*.

**Figure 10.36** VRML color rendering: (a) object `HSVprism` generated in 6D space by PLaSM (b) view from below

The corresponding CMY color model is a cube analogous to the RGB model. But in this case we have $C = (1,0,0)$, $M = (0,1,0)$ and $Y = (0,0,1)$. Black and white clearly are exchanged: $W = (0,0,0)$ e $Black = (1,1,1)$. The transformation between the two color cubes is affine, and corresponds to a reflection with respect to the three coordinate planes, followed by a translation which moves the point $(-1,-1,-1)$ to the origin. Thus, in homogenous coordinates we have:

$$\begin{pmatrix} C \\ M \\ Y \\ 1 \end{pmatrix} = \boldsymbol{T}(1,1,1)\,\boldsymbol{S}(-1,-1,-1) \begin{pmatrix} R \\ G \\ B \\ 1 \end{pmatrix}. \tag{10.12}$$

And, in non-homogeneous coordinates:

$$\begin{pmatrix} C \\ M \\ Y \end{pmatrix} = \begin{pmatrix} 1 \\ 1 \\ 1 \end{pmatrix} - \begin{pmatrix} R \\ G \\ B \end{pmatrix}.$$

The inverse transformation from CMY to RGB is consequently derived:

$$\begin{pmatrix} R \\ G \\ B \end{pmatrix} = \begin{pmatrix} 1 \\ 1 \\ 1 \end{pmatrix} - \begin{pmatrix} C \\ M \\ Y \end{pmatrix}.$$

Such transformations between color models are clearly very easy to write in PLaSM. For this purpose we just have to write two lines of code, as given in Script 10.5.3. Notice that, according to textscvrml documentation, some virtual reality browsers, such as e.g. Cosmo Player, do not like the scaling transformations with negative coefficients, so that the result of the visualization is partly unpredictable, or better depends on the browser.

## 10.6 Shading models

In most practical cases the light intensity in a point of a visible surface is not computed for each pixel using the appropriate illumination model, but is computed only for a

**Script 10.5.3 (CMY cube)**
```
DEF CMYcube = (T:<1,2,3>:<1,1,1> ∼ S:<1,2,3>:<-1,-1,-1>):RGBcube;

VRML:CMYcube:'out.wrl';
```

suitable subset of points. Such points usually correspond either to the vertices of the surface (polygon) or to those of some triangulation of its interior. The computation of the intensities in other points is then done by convex interpolation of known values. This process is called either *color shading* or *normal shading* depending on the subject of the interpolation.

**Intensity interpolation**

For each RGB color component, the values on vertices of a triangle are interpolated in the discrete set of internal points, i.e. in the internal pixels. Such a method is called *Gouraud's shading*.

Let us consider as known the primary intensities $I_a, I_b, I_c$ of a color component given on vertices $a, b$ and $c$ of a triangle, as shown in Figure 10.38a. The intensity $I_p$ of a point $p$ on the horizontal line between two points $r$ and $s$ on the triangle boundary can be computed as:

$$I(p) = (1 - \gamma)I(r) + \gamma I(s), \qquad 0 \le \gamma \le 1, \qquad (10.13)$$

where

$$I(r) = (1 - \alpha)I_a + \alpha I_b, \qquad 0 \le \alpha \le 1, \qquad (10.14)$$
$$I(s) = (1 - \beta)I_a + \beta I_c, \qquad 0 \le \beta \le 1. \qquad (10.15)$$

**Example 10.6.1 (Color shading)**

In Script 10.6.1 two colored triangles are generated and exported as VRML using color per vertex representation. Their images as rendered by *Cosmo Player*© are shown in Figure 10.37. Notice that the centroid of the first triangle does not give the *white*, and the centroid of the second one does not give the *black*. Is something wrong here? The answer is no. The matter here is not the additive or subtractive theory, but the color shading. The interpolated RGB values for the two centroids are $(\frac{1}{3}, \frac{1}{3}, \frac{1}{3})$ and $(\frac{2}{3}, \frac{2}{3}, \frac{2}{3})$, i.e. darker and lighter gray respectively, according to Figure 10.37.

**Normal-vector interpolation**

We have seen the interpolation of color intensity of vertices, computed on those points by using a suitable illumination model. If, conversely, the interpolated entities are the normal vectors of surfaces computed on the vertices, then it is possible to use the illumination models pointwise, by using the appropriate model and the interpolated values of the normals. Such interpolation of normals per vertex, followed by a local use of illumination models to compute the lighting cnd color intensities, is called *Phong's shading model*.

**Script 10.6.1 (Color shading)**

```
DEF color_triangle (c11,c12,c13, c21,c22,c23, c31,c32,c33::IsReal) =
MKPOL:<<
    < 0,0, c11,c12,c13 >,
    < 1,0, c21,c22,c23 >,
    < COS:(PI/3),SIN:(PI/3), c31,c32,c33 >
>,<1..3>,<<1>>>;

DEF RGB_triangle = color_triangle:< 1,0,0, 0,1,0, 0,0,1 >;
DEF CMY_triangle = color_triangle:< 0,1,1, 1,0,1, 1,1,0 >;

VRML:RGB_triangle:'out.wrl';
VRML:CMY_triangle:'out.wrl';
```

**Figure 10.37**    VRML rendering of two color shaded RGB_triangle and
CMY_triangle

In this case some vector equations similar to equations (10.13–10.15) are used to compute the components of normal unit vector in the $p$ point:

$$n(p) \;=\; (1-\gamma)n(r) + \gamma n(s), \qquad 0 \le \gamma \le 1, \tag{10.16}$$

ove

$$n(r) \;=\; (1-\alpha)n(1) + \alpha n(2), \qquad 0 \le \alpha \le 1, \tag{10.17}$$

$$n(s) \;=\; (1-\beta)n(1) + \beta n(3), \qquad 0 \le \beta \le 1. \tag{10.18}$$

Clearly, the illumination point must be applied pointwise to compute the light intensity in each point. As we can see, Phong's shading is much more realistic by its precise rendering of specular reflection effects, but it is also considerably more computationally intensive.

**Example 10.6.2 (Normal per vertex)**

Gouraud's shading is used in VRML rendering when the user specifies a normal vector for each model vertex. In Script 10.6.2 we generate a polyhedral approximation of the sphere by the function Sphere_with_normals. It may be interesting to notice that the dimension-independent of the language is exploited to accommodate the components of the normal as added coordinates of each vertex. Notice on this point the dimensions of the generated object, which is a 2-manifold embedded in 6D space:

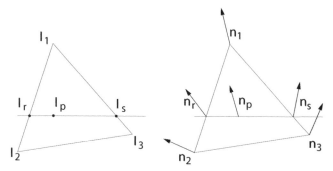

**Figure 10.38**   Bilinear interpolation: (a) Gouraud (b) Phong

```
Sphere_with_normals:1:<12,24> ≡ A-Polyhedral-Complex{2,6}
```

The VRML files exported by the two last expressions of Script 10.6.2 are shown in
Figures 10.39a and 10.39b, respectively.

---

**Script 10.6.2 (Color shading)**
```
DEF Sphere_with_normals (radius::IsRealPos)(n,m::IsIntPos)
  = MAP:[fx,fy,fz, fx,fy,fz]:domain
WHERE
    fx = K:radius * - ~ SIN ~ S2 * COS ~ S1,
    fy = K:radius * COS ~ S1 * COS ~ S2,
    fz = K:radius * SIN ~ S1,
    domain = dom1D:<PI/-2,PI/2>:n * dom1D:<0,2*PI>:m
END;

VRML:(Sphere_with_normals:1:<12,24>):'out.wrl';
VRML:(MAP:[s1,s2,s3,K:-1,K:-1,K:-1,s1,s2,s3]:
    (Sphere_with_normals:1:<12,24>)):'out.wrl';
```

---

**Example 10.6.3 (Crease angle)**
Gouraud's shading of model surfaces with average normal per vertex can be easily
generated by PLaSM programs, without actually generating the normal vectors, but
using the VRML attribute relative to the *crease angle*, as shown by Script 10.6.3. In
this case the `torus` function given in Script 5.2.13 with minor and major radiuses 1
and 3 is mapped on the domain $[0, 2\pi]^2$, thus giving the geometric value associated
with `myTorus` symbol.

The last two expressions of Script 10.6.3 produce the objects displayed in
Figures 10.40a and 10.40b, respectively. It is interesting to note that the polyhedral
approximation of the true surface is done at the same resolution in both cases!

**Example 10.6.4 (Color sphere)**
In this example we export a unit 3D sphere embedded in 6D space. A 3D
polyhedral approximation of such model is generated by the function `Sphere` given

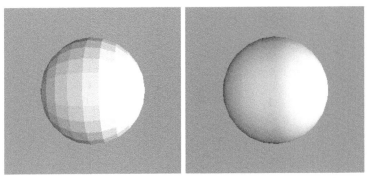

**Figure 10.39**   VRML rendering of spheres *at the same resolution*, without and with Gouraud's shading

---

**Script 10.6.3 (Color shading)**

```
DEF myTorus = MAP:(CONS:(torus:<1,3>)):(dom2D:<0,0,2*PI,2*PI>:<12,24>)

VRML:myTorus:'out.wrl';
VRML:(myTorus CREASE (PI/2)):'out.wrl';
```

---

in Script 10.6.4. The added coordinates are here used as RGB coordinates. This effect is obtained by suitably mapping the vector extractor function [S4,S5,S6] in Script 10.6.4.

The boundary polygons of the exported sphere are Gouraud shaded, using implicitly computed normal per vertex, because of the final invocation of the CREASE function. Figure 10.41 shows what happens when browsing the exsported VRML file with *Cosmo Player*©.

---

**Script 10.6.4 (Color sphere)**

```
DEF vect = [S1,S2,S3];
DEF out = MAP:(CAT ~ [vect,vect]):(Sphere:1:<12,24>)
VRML:(out CREASE (PI/2)):'out.wrl';
```

---

## 10.7   VRML rendering

As we have already seen in the previous examples, the rendering mechanism provided by VRML may be quite refined, since the language allows modeling of both point-shaped and directional lights with varying color and intensity, as well as the material properties of surfaces to be modeled quite carefully. Furthermore, the VRML language allows texture-mapping of 2D images on the 3D surfaces of the scene, thus greatly enhancing the realism of visual rendering. The present section is hence devoted to describing how lights, colors and textures may be specified in VRML, within the theoretical framework we discussed in the previous sections.

**Figure 10.40**   VRML rendering of toruses *at the same resolution,* without and with
Gouraud's shading

**Figure 10.41**   VRML shading of the unit spere, using the normals as color values

## 10.7.1   Illumination

First of all, let us remember that VRML describes the scene as a hierarchical graph,
where nodes may describe geometry, grouping, transformations, lights, textures,
sounds, videos and so on. As a general rule, let us remember that each node applies
its effect on the subgraph rooted in it.

An illumination node describes how the subscene rooted in it should be illuminated.
Such a kind of node, in particular, specifies the position and orientation of the light
source, the light color and other lighting characteristic, such as the contribution of
the source to the diffuse lighting of the ambient. Conversely, a VRML illumination
node does not specify a geometric shape of light source. If necessary, a Shape node
can be assigned to the source with a suitable geometry and a high value of the field
emissiveColor in the Material node of the appearance field.

VRML lights do not produce *shadows* in the scene, but only specify the
characteristics of the radiation which would incise on the scene surfaces, as if they
were isolated. If shadow rendering is needed, in order to give an appropriate level
of realism to the scene, shadows can be simulated by using colors and/or textures.
The simulation of shadows can be very refined, if performed according to suitable
HSR computations, polygon fragmentation and possibly according to global radiosity
algorithms, which may generate the detailed geometric data.

**Lighting nodes**   In particular, three types of *lighting nodes* are available:

1. node DirectionalLight;
2. node PointLight;
3. node SpotLight.

The *scope* of a light of type PointLight or SpotLight is spherical and specified by a field radius of SFFloat type. All the geometry outside the scope of a light is not illuminated by it. Conversely, a node of type DirectionalLight has a hierarchical scope: it will work only on nodes in the same group (i.e. with the same father node) and on their descendants. In other words, a DirectionalLight node will illuminate only the hierarchical subgraph rooted on its father.

**Common fields**   The three illumination nodes have some common fields, whose types and default values are given in the following.

```
on                  TRUE    # SFBool
intensity           1       # SFFloat
ambientIntensity    0       # SFFloat
color               1 1 1   # SFcolor
```

The Boolean field on modifies the status of the light source. This value may be modified at run time, by sending appropriate events to the node. The field color of RGB value defines the light color emitted from the source. It interacts with Material nodes to determine the color aspect of sources hit by light. The fields ambientIntensity and intensity have a real value between 0 and 1. The scalar field intensity is a scaling factor which multiplies the three color components to define the three intensity components of the light source. The product of color components times both the intensity fields is summated to color components of ambient light.

**Attenuation**   An attenuation field is used by PointLight and SpotLight nodes. It is a single valued real field between 0 and 1 used to multiply the intensity field as well as the distance of the considered point from the light source. The field attenuationField is conversely of SFVec3f type, i.e. is a single field with a 3D vector of reals. The first term is used as a multiplier for constant attenuation; it is functionally equivalent to the $K$ addendum at the denominator in the illumination model of equation (10.9). Second and third components are used for linear and quadratic attenuation, respectively.

**DirectionalLight**   The DirectionalLight node is used to define point-shaped sources which project parallel light rays, coming from the point at infinity of the direction vector. There is no attenuation field for directional lights, since it is not possible to compute the distance of a point from the light source. The default definition is the following:

```
DirectionalLight {
    on                  TRUE    # SFBool
    intensity           1       # SFFloat
    ambientIntensity    0       # SFFloat
```

```
        color                 1 1 1    # SFcolor
        direction             0 0 -1   # SFVec3f
}
```

The scope of a directional source is hierarchical. The source illuminates all the "brother" nodes and the subgraphs rooted in them. It can be used, e.g. to open a light in a room, where the adjacent rooms must remain in the dark. Not every browser supports a hierarchical scope for lights. In order to maximize the portability of models it is better to use directional lights at the root level of a VRML world.

**PointLight**   The PointLight node is used to define non-directional and point-shaped light sources. As for the other lighting nodes, it is defined in local coordinates by the location field, which is affected by the action of the current transformation matrix at the traversal of hierarchical scene graph.

```
PointLight {
        on                  TRUE     # SFBool
        intensity           1        # SFFloat
        ambientIntensity    0        # SFFloat
        color               1 1 1    # SFcolor
        location            0 0 0    # SFVec3f
        radius              100      # SFFloat
        attenuation         1 0 0    # SFVec3f
}
```

**SpotLight**   The SpotLight node is used to define point-shaped light sources with a preferred direction of light and an action cone. This is defined around the axis of the direction vector by two angles beamWidth and cutOffAngle given in radians. The source is assumed to emit at maximum intensity within the angle beamWidth, and is also assumed not to emit ouside the angle cutOffAngle. The types and default values of the node fields are the following:

```
SpotLight {
        on                  TRUE     # SFBool
        intensity           1        # SFFloat
        ambientIntensity    0        # SFFloat
        color               1 1 1    # SFcolor
        location            0 0 0    # SFVec3f
        radius              100      # SFFloat
        attenuation         1 0 0    # SFVec3f

        direction           0 0 -1   # SFVec3f
        beamWidth           1.5707   # SFFloat
        cutOffAngle         0.7853   # SFFloat
}
```

*10.7.2  Color*

The VRML language uses the the RGB color model to describe colors. Thus, when some node field has a value of type SFColor (Single Field Color), it must hold three real components in $[0, 1]$, to be interpreted as a point in the normalized RGB color cube. In other words, fields of SFColor type must be specified as normalized RGB triples.

Color information can be used both to assign a *global color* to some primitive or subgraph and to give a *local color* to some portion of a geometric primitive, respectively. The use of Color nodes is hence allowed within:

1. Material node;
2. DirectionalLight, PointLight and SpotLight nodes;
3. IndexedFaceSet, IndexedLineSet, PointSet and  ElevationGrid nodes.

**Material**   The Material node defines the material properties of surfaces in geometrical nodes associated with it. In particular, the diffuseColor field defines the diffusion constant $K_d$ for each of the three primary color components, the field specularColor defines the three constants of specular reflection $K_s$. The field emissiveColor is used to specify the color of light emitted from a luminous body. It can be useful to simulate the results of a radiosity computation, where some surfaces — e.g. the panes of a window — are considered as emitting light.

The shininess field, normalized between 0 and 1, has a meaning similar to the $n$ coefficient of cos of the angle between reflection and viewing directions in equation (10.8). Not all browsers actually support some partial transparency, as specified in the VRML document.

The various possible fields of Material node, their types and the default values are as follows:

```
Material {
    diffuseColor      0.8 0.8 0.8 #SFcolor
    ambientIntensity 0.2          #SFFloat
    specularColor     0   0   0   #SFcolor
    emissiveColor     0   0   0   #SFcolor
    shininess         0.2         #SFFloat
    transparency      0           #SFFloat
}
```

**Color per face**   In geometric primitives of type IndexedFaceSet and ElevationGrid it is possible to specify a field color of type SFnode bound to a Color node value, used to specify a set of colors as RGB triples:

```
Color {
    color    [
        0.8 0.8 0.8 ,    # 1
        0   0   1   ,    # 2
        .. .. .. .. .. .. ..
    ]
}
```

}

If in the geometric primitive the field colorPerVertex is FALSE, then such colors are used as *face colors*. Actually two different methods are available to make the association between faces and colors:

1. By specifying so many colors as many faces. In this case an explicit association is not necessary. The first face will be associated with the first color, the second face with the second color, and so on.
2. By specifying any number of colors, usually less than the number of faces. In this case the face colors must be explicitly given by using the field colorIndex, which contains a sequence of integer references to the values in the Color node, indexed by faces.

**Color per vertex**   The colors to use with geometric primitives IndexedFaceSet and ElevationGrid can be specified in greater detail. Such a detailed specification is used when the field colorPerVertex maintains the default value TRUE. In this case the set of polygons is rasterized by using the Gouraud's shading method. Three types of association of colors with vertices are possible here:

1. By giving as many colors as there are vertices specified in the field point of node Coordinate of field coord. In this case the explicit association between vertices and colors is not needed.
2. By giving colors of vertices as indices in field colorIndex, with reference to the triples contained in the Color node. Such references orderly correspond to vertex numbers.
3. As above, but with color references in colorIndex organized by faces. In this case there are as many lists in field colorIndex as there are faces. Each list will contain the reference to the color counterclockwise associated with the vertices of the associated face, and is terminated by an element with -1 value.

**Colored lines and points**   Both specification and rendering of colors with primitives IndexedLineSet and PointSet are absolutely similar to what as already been discussed for the IndexedFaceSet and ElevationGrid primitives. Gouraud's shading is used when colorPerVertex is TRUE (default). If colorPerVertex is FALSE, then a single color is used for each line, with color values assigned by using any one of the two specification methods seen for faces.

*10.7.3  Shading*

Without any light specification, the color of faces is assumed to be exactly equal to the one specified in their Color node. Also, without any Material specification, no lighting computations are executed at all. Conversely, if the geometric node is subject to the action of some lighting node, then the normal vectors of the faces are automatically generated and used to compute the face intensities, by using for this purpose the reflectance information stored in the Material node.

The default shading method, used when only colors per face are specified, is the *flat shading*. When specifying both normals and colors per face, a flat shading is again used. By giving normals per face and colors per vertices the *Gouraud's shading* is applied. Gouraud's shading is also used when normal per vertices are given, because Phong's shading was considered to be too computationally expensive for use with VRML browsers.

**Normals per face**   In nodes IndexedFaceSet and ElevationGrid the user may give a normal field of type SFnode, with value:

```
Normal {
    vector    [
        0.267 0.535 0.801 ,    # 1
        0     0     1     ,    # 2
        .. .. .. .. .. .. ..
    ]
}
```

Notice from previous example that normals should always be defined as unit vectors, i.e. as vectors with unit length. The node IndexesFaceSet has some specialized fields for normals, i.e.: normal, normalIndex and normalPerVertex. The normalIndex field is not acceptable within the ElevationGrid node.

Vectors in a Normal node are paired with faces if the normalPerVertex field is set to FALSE. Such normals are used for lighting computations if there exists a Material node acting on the geometric primitive. The methods that we have already seen to associate colors and faces may be used to pairwise associate normals and faces. In particular:

1. the simplest but also more verbose method consists in giving as many normals as there are faces. Remember that faces may be specified using the field coordIndex.
2. the more efficient method consists in giving the normals, using the field normalIndex, as references to the values in the Normal node.

**Shading with normals per vertex**   As we already said, normal vectors can be associated with vertex points. In this case the intensities of primary colors are computed on each vertex by using a complete reflectance model and the material properties. Such intensities are then interpolated on each polygon by using Gouraud's shading.

The same vertex may even have several normals associated with it. In particular, there can be as many normals on a vertex as there are faces incident on it. This association requires that the normalPerVertex field is set to the default value TRUE. As for the colors per vertex, there are three methods to specify the normals per vertex, by respectively giving:

1. the *same number* of normals and vertices;
2. the normals in the field normalIndex as references, indexed *on vertices*, to values in Normal node;
3. the normals in normalIndex as references, indexed *on faces*, to values in Normal node. In this case each list of normals in normalIndex must be terminated by -1, and must contain a reference to a normal vector for each vertex of the counter-clockwise oriented face.

## 10.7.4  Textures

The realism of 3D rendering may be greatly enhanced by using the texture mapping, a graphics technique available in the past only in top-level graphics workstations. Conversely, in the last few years graphics accelerators are common on the PC market with hardware support for advanced operations, including texture mapping, at the cost of few hundred dollars.

A Texture Map is a 2D raster image to be mapped on a 3D surface, and therefore subject to be processed in the 3D pipeline consistently with the supporting geometric data. In VRML 2.0 a texturing node allows specification of:

1. the texture, i.e. the raster picture (image) to map on the 3D surface;
2. the texture transformation, with a TextureTransform node;
3. some mapping rules and, in a certain sense, the type of mapping algorithm.

In VRML it is possible to choose between three types of textures, respectively associated with different types of nodes:

1. The ImageTexture node contains as attribute the url of either a JPEG or a PNG image file, so that it allows a photograph to be mapped on a surface. Such a *texture* may be generated in any way, even by using a scanner on the surface of a solid material. It becomes thus possible to visually simulate with extreme realism the surface aspect of solid models, and also to emulate geometric details that would be too expensive to model exactly.
2. The MovieTexture node contains the url of a MPEG-1 file, thus allowing mapping a movie on some surface of the scene, possibly with synchronized sound. In such a case a Sound node should be simultaneously used.
3. The PixelTexture node contains an explicit texture coding with hexadecimal values.

**Mapping algorithm**  Every geometric primitive, i.e. the Cube, Cylinder, Cone, IndexedFaceSet and ElevationGrid nodes, requires a specific *default algorithm* to map the texture on the surface of the primitive.

A mapping different from the default one may be specified by giving two corresponding sets of points on the 2D texture and on the 3D target surface. For this purpose, both the texture and the surface are triangulated using the corresponding points, and a piecewise affine map (i.e. a *simplicial map* — see Section 2.2.2) is accordingly built, that maps each texture triangle into the corresponding surface triangle.

**Texture components**  A texture is specified as an image defined in an $s, t$ bidimensional space, usually coincident with $[0, 1]^2$. There are four types of VRML textures:

1. With one component: the texture contains only intensity values. The only PNG file format is allowed.
2. With two components: there are both intensity and transparency values. The only PNG format is allowed.

3. With three components: the texture contains RGB values. Either JPEG or PNG or GIF file formats are allowed.
4. With four components: both RGB and transparency values are stored in this case. Either PNG or GIF formats are allowed.

### 10.7.5 PLaSM *lighting*

PLaSM makes direct reference to the VRML lighting model. In particular, it provides *point, directional* and *spot* light sources. The LIGHT binary operator must be used for this purpose, and applied to a *polyhedral complex* and to a PLaSM *object* of GenericLight type.

An object of this type is generated by applying the GenericLight function to a triplet < type, appearance, geometry >, where type $\in$ { 0,1,2 } stands for *pointSource, directionalSource* and *spotSource*, respectively. The appearance and geometry values are generated by GenericLightAppearance and GenericLight-Geometry functions, both built-in the 'colors' library.

**A generic light function**  In Script 10.7.1 we implement a generic light function TheLight, that is able to generate a coloured light source of every type, depending on the actual values of its parameters.

Notice that the parameters of GenericLightAppearance are color, intensity, ambientIntensity and isOn, according to the VRML lighting model. The fields of GenericLightGeometry are location, direction, attenuation, radius, beamWidth and cutOffAngle, also in accordance with the VRML model.

---

**Script 10.7.1 (Generic lights)**

```
DEF TheLight(type::isInt)(theColor::TT) =
   GenericLight:< type, appearance, geometry >
WHERE
   appearance = GenericLightAppearance:
      <color,intensity,ambientIntensity,isOn>,
   color = theColor,
   intensity = 1,
   ambientIntensity = 0.4,
   isOn = TRUE,

   geometry = GenericLightGeometry:
      <location,direction,attenuation,radius,beamWidth,cutOffAngle>,
   location = <0,0,0>,
   direction = <1,0,0>,
   attenuation = <1,0,0>,
   radius = 10,
   beamWidth = (PI/4),
   cutOffAngle = (PI/6)
END;
```

---

## Example 10.7.1 (Point, directional and spot lights)

In Script 10.7.2 we produce a visual comparison, shown in Figure 10.42, of the types of light source, by adding either a point, directional or spot MAGENTA light to a suitable decomposition of a unit cube. A decomposition of the cube, produced by grid3D:<10,10,10>:0.1, is used so that the VRML viewer may produce a better rendering of the illuminated surfaces.

**Figure 10.42**  Light sources: (a) *point* (b) *directional* (c) spot

---

## Script 10.7.2 (Point, directional and spot lights)

```
DEF cube = (T:1:1 ~ R:<1,2>:(PI/-6) ~ grid3D:<10,10,10> ):0.1;
DEF grid3D (m,n,p::IsIntPos)(a::IsRealPos) =
    ((Q ~ #:m) * (Q ~ #:n) * (Q ~ #:p)):a ;

DEF test1 = CenteredCameras:(cube LIGHT TheLight:0:MAGENTA);
DEF test2 = CenteredCameras:(cube LIGHT TheLight:1:MAGENTA);
DEF test3 = CenteredCameras:(cube LIGHT TheLight:2:MAGENTA);

VRML:test1:'/path/light1.wrl';
VRML:test2:'/path/light2.wrl';
VRML:test3:'/path/light3.wrl';
```

---

Notice that the three lit cubes test1, test2 and test3 are generated and exported with the associated *camera* nodes produced by the CenteredCameras operator discussed in Section 9.4.1. This operator allowed us to produce the three images of Figure 10.42 from exactly the same viewpoint. Notice also the color attenuation due to distance with point source in Figure 10.42a, whereas no distance attenuation is present with directional source in Figure 10.42b. Finally, notice that we set to *off* the *headlight* automatically set on the viewpoint by the VRML viewer.

## Example 10.7.2 (Colored spot lights)

RED, GREEN and BLUE spot lights are associated with a square without material properties in Script 10.7.3. The images produced by a vrml VIEWER, without and with a headlight, are shown in Figure 10.43. For this purpose a BASESPOTLIGHT operator is used. Analogous BASEDIRLIGHT and BASEPOINTLIGHT operators are also available in the 'colors' library. The unused fields, passed as null values <>, are suitably filled by the library itself.

**Figure 10.43**   Three spot coloured lights: (a) without headlight on the viewer
(b) with headlight

Notice that a useful Spot generator is defined in Script 10.7.3, depending only
on color, location and orientation parameters. It is *instanced* three times with
different colors and locations in our example. Notice also that the LIGHT binary
operator is used *infix* between its operands, and remember that binary operators
are *left-associative*.

---

**Script 10.7.3 (Spot lights)**
```
DEF grid2D (m,n::IsIntPos)(a::IsRealPos) = ((Q ~ #:m) * (Q ~ #:n)):a ;

DEF spot (color,location,orientation::TT) =
   BASESPOTLIGHT:< spotAppearance, spotGeometry >
WHERE
   spotAppearance = < color, <>, <>, <>>,
   spotGeometry = < location, orientation, <>, 100, PI/16, PI/4 >
END;

DEF object = grid2D:<30,30>:1
   LIGHT spot:< RED, <10,15,20>,<0,0,-1>>
   LIGHT spot:< GREEN, <20,10,20>,<0,0,-1>>
   LIGHT spot:< BLUE, <20,20,20>,<0,0,-1>>;

VRML:object:'out.wrl';
```

---

*10.7.6  PLaSM texturing*

The syntax and semantics of texturing operators used in PLaSM to easily export VRML
files are described in this section. The main goal in designing the PLaSM exporting
interface was to be as close as possible to the VRML semantics.

   In particular we have:

1. CREASE:< *pol*, $\alpha$ > $\equiv$ *pol*
   where $\alpha$ is the lower limit of the angle between adjacent faces of *pol* complex,
   used as the threshold value for the automatic computation of normals per

vertices;

2. TEXTURE:< *pol*, *texture* > ≡ *pol*, where

   > *texture* ≡ < url,
   >     < repeatS, repeatT >,
   >     < translationS, translationT >,
   >     < rotation >,
   >     < scalingS, scalingT >,
   >     < centerS, centerT >>

   with internal fields equivalent to the ones with the same name defined in VRML nodes ImageTexture and TextureTransform;

3. SimpleTexture:*'url'* ≡ *texture*

   where *'url'* is a string representing a local or web filename with extensions jpg or pnc.

### Example 10.7.3 (Textured Gioconda)

In this example we discuss the mapping of a jpeg image of Leonardo's Mona Lisa portrait (in the Louvre, Paris) over a cylinder, a sphere and a cube, respectively. The PLaSM code which generates the VRML files displayed in Figure 10.44 is given in Script 10.7.4.

First a mapping of "Gioconda" on the CYLINDER of radius 1 and height 2, approximated with 12 lateral facets is generated, by using a "crease angle" attribute with $\alpha = \frac{\pi}{2}$.

Notice that both the CREASE and the TEXTURE operations are binary operators, so that they can be used infix to their operands. Remember also that a multiple infix expression like arg1 op1 arg2 op2 arg3 is evaluated in leftmost order.

Figure 10.44c is obtained by mapping the jpeg file on the 2-skeleton of the cube. A direct mapping on a 3D object would give a different result, with a more "solid" appearance.

**Figure 10.44**   The Gioconda's image mapped on cylinder, sphere and cube, respectively

### Example 10.7.4 (Textured sun)

A 3D-textured model of the sun is produced in Script 10.7.5 and displayed in Figure 10.45. In this case a unit Sphere is used as the target surface of the image

**Script 10.7.4**
```
VRML:(CYLINDER:<1,2>:18
    CREASE (PI/2) TEXTURE SimpleTexture:'gioconda.jpg'):'out.wrl';

VRML:(Sphere:1:<12,24>
    CREASE (PI/2) TEXTURE SimpleTexture:'gioconda.jpg'):'out.wrl';

VRML:((@2 ~ CUBOID):<1,1,1>
    TEXTURE SimpleTexture:'gioconda.jpg'):'out.wrl';
```

texture contained in `sun.jpg` file. The `Sphere` generating function used here is that given in Script 2.2.7. Notice that the VRML standard mapping algoritm for `IndexedFaceSet` nodes with `creaseAngle` field (quite) correctly maps a circular texture on the two halves of the sphere.

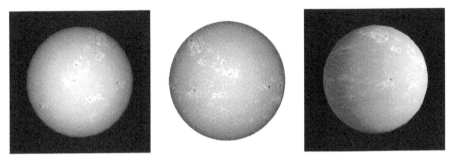

**Figure 10.45**   (a) and (c) 3D-textured model of the sun (b) 2D texture

**Script 10.7.5**
```
DEF mySphere = Sphere:1:<24,12>;

VRML:(mySphere CREASE (PI/2) TEXTURE SimpleTexture:'sun.jpg'):'out.wrl';
```

**Texture repetition and transformation**   The rules used for repeating a texture on a surface are not difficult, but are sometimes puzzling. Therefore, we discuss this point with some detail.

First of all, notice that `texture` and `textureTransform` are two fields of the node `Appearance`, of type `ImageTexture` and `TextureTransform`, respectively. The contents of such nodes and their default values follow.

```
appearance Appearance {
  texture ImageTexture {
    url "filename.jpg"
    repeatS FALSE
    repeatT FALSE
  }
```

```
textureTransform TextureTransform {
    translation 0.0 0.0
    rotation 0.0
    scale 1.0 1.0
    center 0.0 0.0
  }
}
```

**Aspect ratio of target surface**   First, the content of `ImageTexture` file is mapped on the standard unit interval $[0,1]^2$, giving a *normalized texture* in $(s,t)$ space. Then this is mapped onto the containment box of the *target surface*.

---

**Script 10.7.6 (Aspect ratio of target surface)**
```
DEF picture1 = CUBOID:<4,4> TEXTURE SimpleTexture:'gioconda.jpg';
DEF picture2 = CUBOID:<3,4> TEXTURE SimpleTexture:'gioconda.jpg';
DEF picture3 = CUBOID:<4,3> TEXTURE SimpleTexture:'gioconda.jpg';
```

---

**Figure 10.46**   Mapping of texture on surfaces with different aspect ratios

So, how does one generate a correctly sized model of Leonardo's masterpiece? The correct result is obtained by combining the normalized texture mapping on a square surface with a suitable modeling transformation, in this case a scaling in the $y$ direction:

---

**Script 10.7.7 (3D Mona Lisa)**
```
DEF aspectRatio = 404/600;
DEF MonaLisa = S:2:(1/aspectRatio):(CUBOID:<4,4>) * QUOTE:<0.5>
    TEXTURE SimpleTexture:'gioconda.jpg';
```

---

The `aspectRatio` parameter is the ratio of the number of horizontal pixels of the texture to the number of vertical pixels. The geometric value associated with the

MonaLisa symbol is shown in Figure 10.47.

**Figure 10.47**   The fascinating gaze of Leonardo's Mona Lisa in 3D

**Texture mapping on a polygon**   What happens when mapping a texture on a polygon? The mapping algorithm is substantially unchanged, and may be described as follows:

1. Texture is normalized.
2. Texture orientation and portion to be mapped are chosen with respect to the aspect ratio of the containment box of the target polygon.
3. The normalized texture is accordingly mapped and clipped.

The last point actually corresponds to the user view of the process. In practice, there is no texture clipping: at polygon rasterization time, for each rasterized pixel, a reverse mapping from device coordinates to the normalized texture space is performed, in order to compute the set of *texels* (i.e. texture elements) to map in that pixel, and to compute their averaged color.

The PLaSM mapping of Mona Lisa on a 2D `target` polygon is coded in Script 10.7.8. The geometric objects generated by the three last expressions are shown in Figures 10.48 a, b and c, respectively.

---

**Script 10.7.8 (Texture mapping on a polygon)**

```
DEF target = triangleStripe:
    <<0,0>,<1,4>,<1.5,2.5>,<3.5,4>,<3,2.5>,<4,0>,<3,1>,<1.5,1>,<1.5,2>>

target ;
target TEXTURE SimpleTexture:'gioconda.jpg' ;
target * QUOTE:<0.5> TEXTURE SimpleTexture:'gioconda.jpg' ;
```

---

**Figure 10.48** (a) Polygon generated by a `triangleStrip` (b) Texture mapping on polygon; (c) polygon extrusion followed by texture mapping

**Texture transformations** As we have already seen, a 2D transformation $X$ may be applied to the *normalized texture space* $s, t$. This transformation is composite by scaling and rotation about a fixed center, followed by translation. In formal terms, we may write, for the texture applied to the geometric surface:

$$X(t_s, t_t, \alpha, s_s, s_t, c_s, c_t) = T(t_s, t_t)\ T(c_s, c_t)\ R(\alpha)\ S(s_s, s_t)\ T(-c_s, -c_t)$$

where $(c_s, c_t)$ is the transformation center, i.e. the fixed point, $(s_s, s_t)$ are the scaling parameters, $\alpha$ is the rotation angle, and $(t_s, t_t)$ is the final translation.

It is important to understand that the fields of the VRML `TextureTransform` node actually contain the parameters of the inverse transformation $X^{-1}$. This is the true reason for the odd behavior of the `TextureTransform` VRML node, which makes its correct usage very difficult for the naïve user.

To give the correct values to the VRML `TextureTransform` node, it is actually very easy, by remembering that the inverse of a scaling tensor has reciprocal parameters, and the inverse of rotation and translation tensors have opposite parameters, according to the discussion in Section 6.2.8. Thus, within the `'colors'` library we have the following settings:

```
< centerS, centerT > = < -c_s, -c_t >
rotation = -α ,
< scalingS, scalingT > = < 1/s_s, 1/s_t >,
< translationS, translationT > = < -t_s, -t_t >,
```

and

```
repeatS, repeatT ∈ { FALSE, TRUE } .
```

At this point it is easy to understand how the transformed textures of Figure 10.49 were produced by the VRML viewer.

1. The first texture has a rotation of $\alpha = -\frac{\pi}{4}$ around the center $(c_s, c_t) = (0.5, 0.5)$ of normalized texture space, and no repetition.
2. The second one has same rotation and center, with a further scaling $(c_s, c_t) = (\frac{1}{2}, \frac{1}{2})$, and no repetition.
3. The third texture has the same transformation parameters of the previous one, but the repetition is activated in both coordinate directions.

The defining PLaSM code is given in Script 10.7.9.

**Script 10.7.9 (Texture transformations)**

```
DEF out1 = CUBOID:<1,1> TEXTURE FullTexture:<'gioconda.jpg', FALSE, FALSE,
   <0.5, 0.5>, PI/-4, <1,1>, <0, 0>>;

DEF out2 = CUBOID:<4,4> TEXTURE FullTexture:<'gioconda.jpg', FALSE, FALSE,
   <0.5, 0.5>, PI/-4, <1/2,1/2>, <0, 0>>;

DEF out3 = CUBOID:<4,4> TEXTURE FullTexture:<'gioconda.jpg', TRUE, TRUE,
   <0.5, 0.5>, PI/-4, <1/2,1/2>, <0, 0>>;
```

**Figure 10.49**    (a) Texture rotation with center of normalized space as fixed point (b) Rotation and scaling (c) Rotation and scaling with *repeatS = repeatT* = TRUE

**Texture mapping with repetition**    The texture may be repeated on the target surface by giving in VRML a TRUE value to Boolean fields repeatS and repeatT.

With the VRML approach to texture transformation previously described, the scalingS and scalingT fields of TextureTransform node have the role of *repetition parameters*, since their reciprocal values give the number of columns and rows, respectively, in the array of repeated texture instances within the normalized texture space.

In Script 10.7.10 we show how to obtain a repeated texture with $3 \times 2$ and $2 \times 3$ undeformed image instances, respectively. Both the results and the intermediate reasoning are displayed in Figure 10.50, which is produced by the STRUCT expression of the script. The aspectRatio parameter for the Mona Lisa's texture was defined in Script 10.7.7.

**Script 10.7.10 (Texture mapping with repetition)**

```
DEF repeatedTexture (scaleS,scaleT::IsReal) = CUBOID:<1,1> TEXTURE
   FullTexture:<'gioconda.jpg',TRUE,TRUE,<0,0>,0,<scaleS,scaleT>,<0,0>>;

DEF out = STRUCT:<
   repeatedTexture:<1/3,1/2>, T:1:1.2,
   repeatedTexture:<1/2,1/3>, T:1:1.2,
   S:2:(1/aspectRatio):(repeatedTexture:<1/2,1/3>), T:1:1.2,
   S:<1,2>:<aspectRatio, 1/aspectRatio>:(repeatedTexture:<1/2,1/3>)
   >;
```

**Figure 10.50**   Texture mapping with repetition

## 10.8   Examples

### 10.8.1   Orthogonal projection on any viewplane

We want to compute the view model that produces an orthogonal projection on the plane of the Cartesian equation $ax + by + cz + d = 0$. The solution is straightforward:

$$\text{VPN} = \text{DOP} = \begin{pmatrix} a \\ b \\ c \end{pmatrix}, \qquad \text{VRP} = \mathbf{0}.$$

Any vector value is feasible for VUV, provided that it is neither parallel to VPN nor equal to $\mathbf{0}$. In other words, we must just guarantee that

$$\text{VUV} \times \text{VPN} \neq \mathbf{0}.$$

### 10.8.2   Model of example house

---

**Script 10.8.1 (Walls and ground model)**

```
DEF front = MKPOL:< <<0,0>,<3,0>,<5,0>,<10,0>,<3,5>,<5,5>,
    <6,5>,<9,5>,<0,7>,<5.5,7>,<10,7>,<6,2>,<9,2>>,
    <<1,2,5,9>,<3,12,7,10,6>,<3,4,12,13>,<4,13,8,11>,
    <5,6,9,10>,<7,8,10,11>>, <1..6>>;

DEF side = MKPOL:< <<14,0>,<7,0>,<0,0>,<10,2>,<8,2>,<5,2>,<3,2>,
    <10,5>,<8,5>,<5,5>,<3,5>,<14,7>,<7,7>,<0,7>>,
    <<1,4,8,12>,<1,2,4,5>,<2,5,6,9,10,13>,<2,3,6,7>,
    <3,7,11,14>,<8,9,12,13>,<10,11,13,14>>, <1..7>>;

DEF pattern0 (n::IsInt) = (QUOTE ~ ##:n):<1,-1>;
DEF pattern1 (n::IsInt) = (QUOTE ~ ##:n):<-1,1>;

DEF ground = STRUCT:<
    STRUCT:<pattern0:7 * pattern0:5, pattern1:7 * pattern1:5> COLOR white,
    STRUCT:<pattern1:7 * pattern0:5, pattern0:7 * pattern1:5> COLOR blue >;
```

---

The PLaSM definition of the simplified house model used in this chapter to show the effects of different view models is given in Scripts 10.8.1 and 10.8.2. The front and side symbols return 2D polyhedral values corresponding to the house main walls. The ground symbol returns the 2D house floor with the checkerboard pattern.

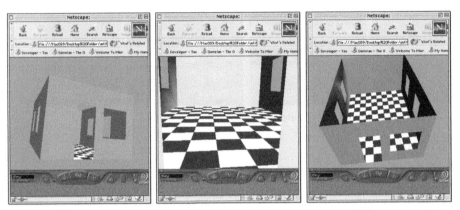

**Figure 10.51**  Browsing the VRML file produced when exporting the model value

---

**Script 10.8.2 (Model of house scene)**

```
DEF gold = RGBCOLOR:<0.73,0.6,0.1>;
DEF white = RGBCOLOR:<1,1,1>;
DEF blue = RGBCOLOR:<0,0,1>;

DEF house_model = STRUCT:<
    (T:1:14 ~ R:<1,2>:(PI/2) ~ R:<2,3>:(PI/2) ~ EMBED:1):front,
    (R:<1,2>:(PI/2) ~ R:<2,3>:(PI/2) ~ EMBED:1 ~ CUBOID):<10,7>,
    (T:2:10 ~ R:<2,3>:(PI/2) ~ EMBED:1):side,
    (R:<2,3>:(PI/2) ~ EMBED:1):side,
    EMBED:1:ground > COLOR gold;

house_model;
```

---

The 3D house_model is generated as an assembly of properly embedded and oriented front, side and ground instances. Notice in particular that the gold color is applied to the whole house_model, but does not modify the subassemblies (such as the ground) where specific colors were previously applied.

Some images taken from the screen during the browsing of the VRML model generated when exporting the polyhedral value of the house_model symbol are given in Figure 10.51.

It may be interesting to notice that exactly the same result is obtained by substituting the ground definition of Script 10.8.1, with the one given in Script 10.8.3, where pattern.jpg contains the tiled image shown in Figure 10.52.

**Script 10.8.3 (Textured ground)**
```
DEF ground = S:<1,2>:<14,10>:(CUBOID:<1,1> TEXTURE
    FullTexture:<'pattern.jpg', TRUE, TRUE, <0, 0>, 0, <7,5>, <0, 0>>) ;
```

**Figure 10.52**   Texture mapped on the **ground** of house model

*10.8.3   Cell extraction*

It can be quite important in various modeling problems to extract the cells of a polyhedral complex, in order to make possible some *ad hoc* handling of individual cells.

Therefore we show in Script 10.8.4 a SPLIT function from polyhedral complexes to *sequences* of polyhedral complexes, which takes a complex as input and gives as output the sequence of its convex cells, returned as isolated complexes. This function may be further specialized to extract the cells of the 1-, 2- or 3-skeleton of the input complex, as shown in the script.

The SplitCells implementation is quite simple. The input polyhedral **scene** is first decomposed into the **dataset** triplet; its vertices are moved into the **points** object; its **cells** are reconstructed as proper subsets of **points**. Finally, each element in the **cells** sequence is transformed into an individual complex by the combined action of functions [ID,[INTSTO ~ LEN],K:<<1>>] and MKPOL.

---

**Script 10.8.4 (Convex cells)**
```
DEF SplitCells (scene::IsPol) =
    AA:(MKPOL ~ [ID,[INTSTO ~ LEN],K:<<1>>]):cells
WHERE
    cells = ((CONS ~ AA:(CONS ~ AA:SEL) ~ S2):dataset):points,
    points = S1:dataset,
    dataset = UKPOL:scene
END;

DEF extract_wires (scene::IsPol) = (SplitCells ~ @1):scene;
DEF extract_polygons (scene::IsPol) = (SplitCells ~ @2):scene;
DEF extract_bodies (scene::IsPol) = (SplitCells ~ @3):scene;

extract_bodies:(ColRow:4);
extract_polygons:(ColRow:4);
```

---

The last two rows of Script 10.8.4 produce the geometric assemblies which are shown exploded in Figure 10.53. The generating expression ColRow:4 of the input complex was presented in Script 2.4.3 while discussing the Temple example.

The extraction of the components of a complex may usefully return the polyhedral

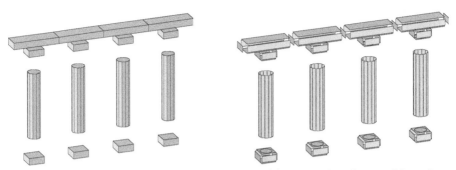

**Figure 10.53**  (a) $z$-exploded view of solid cells (b) $xyz$-exploded view of boundary
polygons

cells. For this purpose it is sufficient to slightly modify, as shown in Script 10.8.5,
the SplitCells operator previously given. Two pictures showing an exploded view
of either convex or polyhedral extracted cells from the hole object given below is
shown in Figure 10.54. The definitions of triangleStrip and Q operators are given
in Scripts 7.2.17 and 6.4.4, respectively.

---

**Script 10.8.5 (Polyhedral cells)**
```
    DEF SplitPols (scene::IsPol) =
        (AA:(MKPOL ~ [S1,S2,[INTSTO ~ LEN ~ S2]]) ~ DISTL):< points, pols >
    WHERE
        points = S1:dataset,
        pols = ((CONS ~ AA:(CONS ~ AA:SEL) ~ S3):dataset):(S2:dataset),
        dataset = UKPOL:scene
    END;

    DEF hole = (triangleStrip * K:(Q:1)):
        <<0,3>,<1,2>,<3,3>,<2,2>,<3,0>,<2,1>,<0,0>,<1,1>,<0,3>,<1,2>>;

    DEF extract_polygons (scene::IsPol) = (SplitPols ~ @2):scene;
    (STRUCT ~ explode:<1.2,1.2,1.5> ~ extract_polygons):hole;
```

---

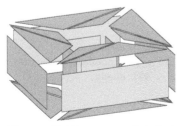
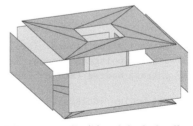

**Figure 10.54**  $xyz$-exploded view of boundary: (a) convex cells (b) polyhedral cells

### 10.8.4   Exploded views

In several applications of mechanical and architectural CAD it may be very useful to produce some *exploded view* of an assembly. The technique to use in this case is quite simple. First, choose a triplet of scaling coefficients $s_x, s_y, s_z \geq 1$ to apply to some assembly points; then, for each object $i$ in the input sequence do the following operations:

1. choose an internal point $\boldsymbol{p}_i$, e.g. the centroid of the containment box;
2. apply a scaling tensor $\boldsymbol{S}_{xyz}(s_x, s_y, s_z)$ to $\boldsymbol{p}_i$, so generating its image $\boldsymbol{p}_i^*$;
3. compute the vector $\boldsymbol{t}_i = \boldsymbol{p}_i^* - \boldsymbol{p}_i = \left( \begin{array}{ccc} t_{i_x} & t_{i_y} & t_{i_z} \end{array} \right)^T$;
4. finally apply the translation tensor $\boldsymbol{T}_{xyz}(t_{i_x}, t_{i_y}, t_{i_z})$ to the object.

In Script 10.8.6 we give, through the function explode, an implementation of the algorithm previously discussed. Such a function must be first applied to a triplet sx,sy,sz of scaling coefficients. The input scene in entered as a sequence of polyhedral complexes. The exploded views produced by the last two expressions of Script 10.8.6 are shown in Figure 10.53. Notice that a unit value of a scaling coefficient produces no mutual translation of parts along the corresponding direction.

The MK and UK functions, used to transform a point into a 0-complex, are given in Script 3.3.15; the function vectDiff, to compute the difference of two points or vectors, is given in Script 3.1.2.

---

**Script 10.8.6 (Exploded view)**

```
DEF explode (sx,sy,sz::IsReal) (scene::IsSeqOf:IsPol) =
   (AA:APPLY ~ TRANS):< translations, scene >
WHERE
   scalings = #:(LEN:centers):(S:<1,2,3>:<sx,sy,sz>),
   translVectors = (AA:vectDiff ~ TRANS):< scaledCenters,centers >,
   centers = AA:(MED:<1,2,3>):scene,
   scaledCenters = (AA:(UK ~ APPLY) ~ TRANS):< scalings, AA:MK:centers >,
   translations = AA:(T:<1,2,3>):translVectors
END;

(STRUCT ~ explode:<1,1,1.5> ~ extract_bodies ~ ColRow):4;
(STRUCT ~ explode:<1.2,1.2,1.5> ~ extract_polygons ~ ColRow):4;
```

---

### 10.8.5   Standard view models

In Figure 10.55 we show three examples of projections chosen from those discussed in Section 10.2. In particular we show a central (oblique) projection, an orthogonal (isometric) parallel projection and a oblique (cabinet) parallel projection, all generated by PLaSM and exported as Flash files. The PLaSM code is given in Script 10.8.7. A complete listing of the view models associated to standard projection types is given in Script 10.2.1. Clearly, in order to produce different projection it is sufficient to change the name of the view model in the generating line. Let us remember that the semantics of the flash exporting operator was discussed in Section 7.

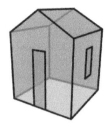 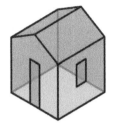 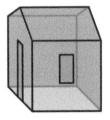

**Figure 10.55**  Projections exported as Flash files: (a) perspective oblique
(b) parallel isometric (c) parallel cabinet

The house model is defined in Script 8.5.21; the FILLCOLOR, LINECOLOR, LINESIZE
operators, to be used with FLASH exporting, are discussed in Section 15.3.2.

---

**Script 10.8.7 (View models)**

```
DEF house1 = projection: perspective: threepoints: house;
DEF house2 = projection: parallel: isometric: house;
DEF house3 = projection: parallel: cabinet: house;

DEF out (object::IsPol)(name::IsString) = FLASH:(object
    FILLCOLOR RGBAcolor:<0,1,1,0.5>
    LINECOLOR RGBAcolor:<0,0,0,1>
    LINESIZE 5):300:name;

out: house1: 'house1.swf';
out: house2: 'house2.swf';
out: house3: 'house3.swf';
```

---

## 10.9  Annotated references

Michael McKenna discussed in [McK87] a $O(n^2)$ worst-case optimal hidden-surface
removal algorithm. This was an improvement over the previous best worst-case
performance of $O(n^2 \log n)$. It was established that the hidden-line and hidden-surface
problems have an $O(n^2)$ worst-case lower bound, so the algorithm is optimal.

# Part III

# Modeling

# 11

# Parametric curves

Curves as *point loci* with a specific shape are often identified by a proper name, such as *circle, parabola, hyperbola, spiral, helix*, etc. For applications of computer-aided design, some classes of *free-form curves* are more interesting, because they are able to satisfy both geometric and esthetic constraints set by designers, depending on the shape design problem at hand. Even more useful, *splines* are piecewise-continuous composite curves used to either interpolate or approximate a discrete set of points. Various different representations of curves are in use. The present chapter is dedicated to discussing the *parametric* representation of *polynomial* and *rational* curves and splines, i.e. the main classes of free-form curves used by CAD applications, and also introduces a straightforward implementation of parametric curves and splines with PLaSM, together with several examples.

## 11.1   Curve representations

Curves may be represented by using different kinds of equations. In particular, it is possible to distinguish representations:

1. *explicit* or Cartesian, where the curve is given as the graph of a function;
2. *implicit*, as the zero set of one or more global algebraic equations;
3. *parametric*, associated with a vector function of one parameter;
4. *intrinsic*, where points locally satisfy differential equations.

### Explicit representation

An explicit or Cartesian representation of a plane curve is the graph $(x, f(x))$ of a function $f : \mathbb{R} \to \mathbb{R}$. We may also write, in this case:

$$y = f(x).$$

This representation is not particularly diffuse nor useful in geometric modeling, because it is unusable for closed curves nor, more in general, for curves where more than one value of the dependent variable, say, $y$, is associated with the same value of the independent variable, say, $x$. Also, it does not easily support affine transformations.

*Geometric Programming for Computer-Aided Design*   Alberto Paoluzzi
© 2003 John Wiley & Sons, Ltd   ISBN 0-471-89942-9

**Example 11.1.1 (Cartesian equation of a line)**

A simple example of explicit representation in the 2D plane is the well-known Cartesian equation of the line:

$$y = mx + c,$$

where $m$ is called the *angular coefficient* and coincides with the tangent of the angle that the line creates with the $x$ axis, and $c$ is the ordinate of the intersection point between the line and the $y$ axis. According with the previous remark, this representation cannot be used for vertical lines, for which we must conversely use the equation $x = a$.

### Implicit representation

The *implicit representation* denotes a plane curve as the locus of points that satisfy an equation, usually algebraic, of type:

$$f(x, y) = 0.$$

The simplest example of a plane curve is given by the implicit representation of the 2D line:

$$ax + by + c = 0.$$

A single equation in three variables instead denotes a surface in three-dimensional space, where a curve is given as the set of simultaneous solutions of two linear equations. More in general, a curve in $n$-dimensional space is the solution set of $n - 1$ algebraic equations of arbitrary degree. Its existence is always guaranteed only in a complex space.

**Example 11.1.2 (Conics curves)**

Another example of implicit representation is given by the curves of second degree, as the loci of points which satisfy the general equation

$$ax^2 + by^2 + cxy + dx + ey + f = 0.$$

Such curves are called *conics* because they describe the possible intersections of an indefinite 3D cone with the plane $z = 0$. In particular, the intersection is:

1. a *circle*, when such a plane is perpendicular to the cone axis;
2. an *ellipse*, when it crosses all the cone lines while cutting only one cone sheet;
3. a *parabola*, when the cutting plane is parallel to one line of the cone;
4. a *hyperbola*, when the plane is parallel to two such lines.

Such an intersection may also result in a (double) line or in two lines, in particular when the $z = 0$ plane contains one or two lines of the cone.

**Degrees of freedom**   The number of coefficients, called *degrees of freedom*, of the implicit equation and hence the number of different geometric objects it may represent, grows rapidly with the degree of the equation. As a consequence, the set of lines is a subset of conics, and conics are a subset of curves of degree three, and so on.

**Point-set membership**  The implicit equation of a plane curve enjoys the notable property of partitioning the plane into three subsets of points. They are the set of curve points, and two subspaces at the two sides of the curve, respectively corresponding to points that substituted into the curve equation and return either a positive or a negative number. Hence, to classify a point with respect to an implicit curve is a simple and efficient operation. It will suffice to substitute the point coordinates for the variables in the curve equation and compute the algebraic result. If this is zero, then the point belongs to the curve; otherwise, it belongs to one of the subspaces defined by the curve, depending on the resulting sign. The same property obviously arises for algebraic equations with three or more variables.

**Meaning and sensitivity of coefficients**  A negative aspect of implicit representation arises from small geometric significance of the coefficients of the implicit equations. Except in a few cases,[1] they do not have any explicit geometric meaning. Furthermore, there often exists a strong numerical sensitivity of the curve shape on even a small variation of some coefficients. In other words, a small variation of some coefficients of an implicit equation may produce a large and completely unpredictable variation of the curve geometry.

**Parametric representation**

With a *parametric* representation, a curve $c$ is given as a *point-valued map* of a single real parameter:

$$c : D \to \mathbb{E}^n \quad \text{such that} \quad c(u) = o + \left( \begin{array}{ccc} x_1(u) & \ldots & x_n(u) \end{array} \right)^T$$

where $o$ is the origin of the reference frame, and $D \subset \mathbb{R}$ often coincides with the standard real interval $[0, 1]$. When $n$ is either two or three, the curve is said to be a plane or a space curve, respectively. The component functions $x_i : \mathbb{R} \to \mathbb{R}$, $i = 1, \ldots, n$, are called the *coordinate maps* of the curve. The curve as a locus of points should be properly called the *image* of the curve. We would like to remind the reader that several differential concepts about parametric curves were already introduced in Chapter 5.

**Polynomial and rational curves**  When the coordinate maps are polynomial functions of a single variable the curve is called a *polynomial* (parametric) curve. When the coordinate maps are rational functions, i.e. ratio of polynomials, the curve itself is said *rational*. Both polynomial and rational curves are liked by shape designers, mainly because their coefficients have a precise geometric meaning and assess specific esthetic and geometric constraints on the generated free-form curves. By editing such coefficients, normally by using very simple and intuitive graphics tools, the designer is given strong control over shape generation. Metodology and algorithms to execute automatic parametrization of several classes of rational curves and surfaces from implicit representations is given in papers [BA87a, BA87b, BA88, BA89] by Bajaj and Abhyankar.

---

[1] E.g., in the linear equation in three variables, three of the coefficients are proportional to the "director cosines" of the plane, i.e. to the cosines of the angles between the represented plane and the coordinate axes.

**Polynomial and rational splines** It is necessary to distinguish between polynomial or rational *curves* and the so-called *splines* of the same kind. The former are single point-valued maps. The latter are composite maps, which can be thought of as piecewise-continuous curves, obtained by joining more curve segments with some proper degree of continuity at the extreme points. In particular, when we need to interpolate or approximate a long sequence of points, it is normally more useful to employ some low-degree spline, rather than using a single high-degree curve with sufficient degrees of freedom. The second alternative, other than requiring higher computational costs, may in fact generate unpredictable oscillations of the produced point set.

**Intrinsic representation**

Intrinsic representations are mainly used in differential geometry, and describe the curve locally, i.e. independent of its position and orientation with respect to some external reference frame. In particular, an *intrinsic representation* is a pair of relations

$$\frac{1}{\rho} = f(s)$$
$$\tau = g(s)$$

which express the *curvature* $\frac{1}{\rho}$, where $\rho$ is the radius of curvature, and the *torsion* $\tau$ as functions of *curvilinear abscissa* $s$, i.e. of the length of the curve arc. The *natural equation* of a curve is any equation

$$h\left(\frac{1}{\rho}, \tau, s\right) = 0$$

between curvature, torsion and arc length.

A natural equation characterizes a whole class of curves. For example, *plane curves* have the natural equation

$$\tau = 0.$$

Analogously, *straight lines* have the natural equation

$$\frac{1}{\rho} = 0.$$

Two natural equations determine a curve completely, except for position and orientation. This kind of representation of curves has only limited utility in geometric modeling applications, because in this case we are mainly interested in characterizing a curve as a subset of points of an affine space, showing where to apply geometric transformations such as translations and rotations, and also relative to positioning, intersection, blending, etc, of two of more curves.

## 11.2 Polynomial parametric curves

The use of parametric curves in graphics and CAD started at the end of the 1960s, first within the aerospatial and automotive industries, both in Europe and in the USA, and later in academia, where applied mathematicians were studying mathematical methods for computer-aided geometric design, actually by simulating the hand-crafting of physically modeled curves and surfaces. Previously, various instruments were used in the industry for this purpose, and in particular some mechanical and graphical "ad hoc" tools, from pantograph to a flexible ruler called a *spline*, whose name was soon extrapolated to denote the mathematical interpolation/approximation of sequences of points.

### Properties of parametric curves

We summarize below the main benefits of using a parametric representation of curves, by discussing some useful properties of such methods.

**Control handles**   A polynomial parametric curve may be seen as a linear combination, with vector coefficients, of the elements of a suitable polynomial basis.[2] The vector coefficients of such a combination normally have some geometric meaning useful for shape design and editing. In particular, depending on the choice of the polynomial basis, they may correspond either to points interpolated by the curve, or to approximated points, or to tangent vectors, etc. Such vector coefficients are collectively called *geometric handles* or *control handles*, since they are often implemented as handles to be dragged by the designer when interactively editing the shape of the curve.

**Multiple points**   When using explicit equations, it is not possible to represent curves where the same value of the independent variable is associated with multiple values of the dependent variable. No problems of this kind arise with parametric equations, which may easily represent curves which are self-intersecting, even more times. The presence of double or multiple points is not difficult to handle because every point instance is associated with a different value of the generating parameter. Conversely, when using implicit equations, such multiple points must be considered singular points, and a curve with singularities must be reduced to a set of curve segments without singularities.

**Affine and projective invariance**   A polynomial or rational parametric curve may be translated, rotated or scaled by just translating, rotating or scaling its geometric handles. The same property, called *affine invariance*, holds for polynomial and rational splines. Furthermore, a rational curve or spline can be projected by simply projecting its handles. The points of the projected curve can be later computed by just combining with proper rational functions the projected handles. Unfortunately, such a *projective invariance* property does not hold for polynomial curves and splines. The projective invariance is one of main reasons for the great success of rational splines like NURBS (see Section 11.4.2) in graphics libraries.

---

[2] Let us remember that the set of polynomials of degree less or equal to $n$ is a vector space of dimension $n + 1$.

**Local and global control**   The vector parameters of polynomial and rational curves are used for curve input and control, since they perfectly match the implementation of interactive tools for definition and editing of shape. Such control of shape is *global* for curves, because in this case every variation of one of vector coefficients (control handles) induces some variation of the whole curve point set. Conversely, for splines, shape control is *local*, because a variation of a control handle induces a variation of the only subset of curve segments which are influenced by the changed point or vector, whereas the images of other curve segments do not change. Such local control of shape is very important to the designer, who often wants to make only small local changes to a design profile whose shape otherwise is quite satisfactory to design constraints and/or esthetic criteria.

**Variation diminishing**   The possibility of unpredictable shape oscillations between interpolated points strongly increases with the growth of the degree of the interpolating polynomial. Some of the polynomial curves studied in this chapter, and in particular the Bézier curves, give a full control of this aspect, because they provide the so-called *variation diminishing* property. In particular, this property guarantees that the number of intersections of a curve with a hyperplane of its embedding space — i.e. a line in case of plane curves — is either less or equal to the number of intersections of the hyperplane with the polygon of control handles, also called the control polygon. In other words, this property states that a curve closely resembles its control polygon, which can be considered a linear approximation of the curve shape.

**Continuity order and degree elevation**   A polynomial curve of degree $n$ depends on $n + 1$ vector parameters, and has non-zero continuous derivatives until the order $n - 1$. If a curve is needed as a vector function with some fixed order of continuity, then it is sufficient to raise its degree as needed. The method for *degree elevation* of a polynomial curve, at least in the Bézier form, is quite simple. See the book by Farin [Far88]. Another reason to elevate the degree of a polynomial curve may arise when generating surfaces from curves. Several methods used for this purpose require the various input curves be of the same degree.

### 11.2.1   Linear curves

Let us start by discussing the polynomial curves of first degree. The matrix approach we use here, due to Jim H. Clark,[3] will be straightforwardly extended in later sections to polynomial curves of higher degree.

**Algebraic form**

We know that the line segment between points $p_1$ and $p_2$ can be written, in any $\mathbb{E}^d$, as:

$$(p_2 - p_1)u + p_1, \qquad u \in [0, 1],$$

---

[3] The founder of SGI and Netscape Corporations.

i.e. as a polynomial with vector coefficients in the $u$ indeterminate.

In general, let consider the polynomial curve of first degree, said *in algebraic form*:

$$C(u) = \boldsymbol{a}u + \boldsymbol{b}$$

and write it as a product of matrices:

$$C(u) = \begin{pmatrix} u & 1 \end{pmatrix} \begin{pmatrix} \boldsymbol{a} \\ \boldsymbol{b} \end{pmatrix} = \boldsymbol{U}_1 \, \boldsymbol{M}_1 \tag{11.1}$$

The row matrix $\boldsymbol{U}_1$ contains the elements of the standard *power basis* for the vector space $\mathbb{P}^1[\mathbb{R}]$ of polynomials of degree less or equal to 1, with coefficients in $\mathbb{R}$. The elements of this basis are $u^1$ and $u^0$, i.e. $u$ and 1, respectively. Notice that every other polynomial in $\mathbb{P}^1$ can be expressed as a linear combination of such basis elements.

### Geometric form

The matrix equation (11.1) contains two vector degrees of freedom, i.e. two "free" vector coefficients $\boldsymbol{a}$ and $\boldsymbol{b}$. In order to specify a given curve, we may specify two vector constraints to be satisfied by $\boldsymbol{a}$ and $\boldsymbol{b}$. We can, for example, require that the curve interpolates, at the extreme values of the parameter, two given points $\boldsymbol{p}_1$ and $\boldsymbol{p}_2$:

$$\begin{aligned} C(0) &= \boldsymbol{p}_1; \\ C(1) &= \boldsymbol{p}_2. \end{aligned}$$

By substituting 0 and 1 for $u$ in equation 11.1, we get, respectively:

$$\boldsymbol{p}_1 = \begin{pmatrix} 0 & 1 \end{pmatrix} \boldsymbol{M}_1$$

$$\boldsymbol{p}_2 = \begin{pmatrix} 1 & 1 \end{pmatrix} \boldsymbol{M}_1$$

The above vector equations can be collected into the following matrix equation:

$$\begin{pmatrix} \boldsymbol{p}_1 \\ \boldsymbol{p}_2 \end{pmatrix} = \begin{pmatrix} 0 & 1 \\ 1 & 1 \end{pmatrix} \boldsymbol{M}_1,$$

from which we have

$$\boldsymbol{M}_1 = \begin{pmatrix} 0 & 1 \\ 1 & 1 \end{pmatrix}^{-1} \begin{pmatrix} \boldsymbol{p}_1 \\ \boldsymbol{p}_2 \end{pmatrix} = \begin{pmatrix} -1 & 1 \\ 1 & 0 \end{pmatrix} \begin{pmatrix} \boldsymbol{p}_1 \\ \boldsymbol{p}_2 \end{pmatrix},$$

and, by substitution into equation 11.1, we get

$$C(u) = \begin{pmatrix} u & 1 \end{pmatrix} \begin{pmatrix} -1 & 1 \\ 1 & 0 \end{pmatrix} \begin{pmatrix} \boldsymbol{p}_1 \\ \boldsymbol{p}_2 \end{pmatrix} = \boldsymbol{U}_1 \, \boldsymbol{B}_1 \, \boldsymbol{G}_1. \tag{11.2}$$

Equation 11.2 is called the *geometric form* of the polynomial curve of first degree. In general, there can be several different geometric forms, corresponding to different sets of constraints, usually boundary conditions, on the coefficients of the algebraic form.

**Terminology** Let us compare some different ways of writing the parametric equation of a polynomial curve. Equation 11.1 is called the *algebraic form* of the curve. Conversely, equation 11.2 is called the *geometric form* of passage through two given points. In particular, the matrix $B_1$ is called the *basis matrix*, whereas the vector of points $G_1$ is called the *geometry vector* or tensor of *control handles* of the geometric form. Finally, the vector of polynomial functions given by

$$U_1 B_1 = ( \begin{array}{cc} u & 1 \end{array} ) \begin{pmatrix} -1 & 1 \\ 1 & 0 \end{pmatrix} = ( \begin{array}{cc} 1 - u & u \end{array} ) = ( \begin{array}{cc} b_1(u) & b_2(u) \end{array} )$$

defines the *polynomial basis* of the geometric form, i.e. its basis functions, called also *blending functions* of the curve. The reason for last name is quite obvious, when considering the generic curve point $C(u)$ written as a combination of blending function with control handles, i.e. as a sort of "blend" of such data:

$$C(u) = \sum_{i=0}^{1} b_i(u) \, p_i.$$

### 11.2.2   Quadratic curves

The approach discussed above is straightforwardly extended to polynomial curves of higher degree. For quadratic curves, we have what follows.

### Algebraic form

The algebraic form of the polynomial parametric curves of second degree depends on three free vector parameters:

$$\begin{aligned} C(u) &= a u^2 + b u + c \\ &= ( \begin{array}{ccc} u^2 & u & 1 \end{array} ) \, M_2 \\ &= U_2 \, M_2 \end{aligned} \tag{11.3}$$

### Lagrange's geometric form

The passage of the curve for three given points $p_1$, $p_2$ and $p_3$ can be imposed in order to specify the matrix $M_2$. In particular, by substituting in equation (11.3) for $u \in \{0, \frac{1}{2}, 1\}$, we can write:

$$\begin{pmatrix} C(0) \\ C(\frac{1}{2}) \\ C(1) \end{pmatrix} = \begin{pmatrix} 0 & 0 & 1 \\ \frac{1}{4} & \frac{1}{2} & 1 \\ 1 & 1 & 1 \end{pmatrix} M_2 = \begin{pmatrix} p_1 \\ p_2 \\ p_3 \end{pmatrix},$$

from which we get

$$M_2 = \begin{pmatrix} 2 & -4 & 2 \\ -3 & 4 & -1 \\ 1 & 0 & 0 \end{pmatrix} \begin{pmatrix} p_1 \\ p_2 \\ p_3 \end{pmatrix},$$

and hence

$$C(u) = U_2 M_2 = \begin{pmatrix} u^2 & u & 1 \end{pmatrix} \begin{pmatrix} 2 & -4 & 2 \\ -3 & 4 & -1 \\ 1 & 0 & 0 \end{pmatrix} \begin{pmatrix} p_1 \\ p_2 \\ p_3 \end{pmatrix} = U_2 B_2 G_2.$$

The previous interpolating form is called *Lagrange's geometric form* of the quadratic polynomial curve.

If we want to underline the meaning of this quadratic curve as a polynomial blending of three given points, then we may write:

$$C(u) = (2u^2 - 3u + 1)p_1 + (-4u^2 + 4u)p_2 + (2u^2 - u)p_3.$$

### 11.2.3 Cubic curves

Polynomial curves of third degree are largely used in CAD systems since they are sufficiently flexible for most applications. The *algebraic form* of their equation contains four vector parameters:

$$\begin{aligned} C(u) &= au^3 + bu^2 + cu + d \\ &= \begin{pmatrix} u^3 & u^2 & u & 1 \end{pmatrix} M_3 \\ &= U_3 M_3 \end{aligned} \tag{11.4}$$

Every set of four vector constraints that allow specification of the four degrees of freedom defines a different *geometric form* of the cubic curve. Such constraints may impose the passage of the curve through four assigned points, or through two points with assigned tangents (derivatives) in those points, and so on, as we see in the following sections.

### Lagrange's geometric form

A Lagrange cubic curve is defined by imposing the passage through four assigned points $p_1, p_2, p_3$ and $p_4$, with four equispaced values of the parameter in the unit interval, i.e. with $u \in \{0, \frac{1}{3}, \frac{2}{3}, 1\}$, respectively:

$$C(0) = p_1, \qquad C(\tfrac{1}{3}) = p_2, \qquad C(\tfrac{2}{3}) = p_3, \qquad C(1) = p_4,$$

so that, by substitution in equation (11.4) we have

$$\begin{pmatrix} p_1 \\ p_2 \\ p_3 \\ p_4 \end{pmatrix} = \begin{pmatrix} 0 & 0 & 0 & 1 \\ \frac{1}{27} & \frac{1}{9} & \frac{1}{3} & 1 \\ \frac{8}{27} & \frac{4}{9} & \frac{2}{3} & 1 \\ 1 & 1 & 1 & 1 \end{pmatrix} M_3,$$

and hence

$$M_3 = \begin{pmatrix} 0 & 0 & 0 & 1 \\ \frac{1}{27} & \frac{1}{9} & \frac{1}{3} & 1 \\ \frac{8}{27} & \frac{4}{9} & \frac{2}{3} & 1 \\ 1 & 1 & 1 & 1 \end{pmatrix}^{-1} \begin{pmatrix} p_1 \\ p_2 \\ p_3 \\ p_4 \end{pmatrix} = B_L G_L.$$

In conclusion, the Lagrange form of the cubic curve is defined as:

$$C(u) = U_3 \, B_L \, G_L \tag{11.5}$$

where $U_3$ is the cubic power basis, $B_L$ is the matrix of the cubic Lagrange's basis and $G_L$ is the Lagrange control tensor.

### Hermite's geometric form

In this case the cubic curve segment is forced to have assigned extreme points $p_1$ and $p_2$ and assigned extreme tangents $s_1$ and $s_2$, with $u \in [0,1]$. Such constraints are therefore:

$$
\begin{aligned}
C(0) &= p_1 \\
C(1) &= p_2 \\
C'(0) &= s_1 \\
C'(1) &= s_2
\end{aligned}
$$

From the algebraic form (11.4) of the curve we can compute the derivative with respect to the parameter, which gives the tangents to the curve:

$$C'(u) = \left( \begin{array}{cccc} 3u^2 & 2u & 1 & 0 \end{array} \right) M_3 \tag{11.6}$$

and, by substitution of $0,1$ for $u$ in equations (11.4) or (11.6), respectively:

$$
\begin{pmatrix} p_1 \\ p_2 \\ s_1 \\ s_2 \end{pmatrix} =
\begin{pmatrix}
0 & 0 & 0 & 1 \\
1 & 1 & 1 & 1 \\
0 & 0 & 1 & 0 \\
3 & 2 & 1 & 0
\end{pmatrix} M_3.
$$

So, we get

$$
M_3 =
\begin{pmatrix}
2 & -2 & 1 & 1 \\
-3 & 3 & -2 & -1 \\
0 & 0 & 1 & 0 \\
1 & 0 & 0 & 0
\end{pmatrix}
\begin{pmatrix} p_1 \\ p_2 \\ s_1 \\ s_2 \end{pmatrix}
$$

so that the Hermite geometric form for the cubic polynomial curves results

$$
C(u) = \left( \begin{array}{cccc} u^3 & u^2 & u & 1 \end{array} \right)
\begin{pmatrix}
2 & -2 & 1 & 1 \\
-3 & 3 & -2 & -1 \\
0 & 0 & 1 & 0 \\
1 & 0 & 0 & 0
\end{pmatrix}
\begin{pmatrix} p_1 \\ p_2 \\ s_1 \\ s_2 \end{pmatrix}.
$$

It can be written in matrix form as

$$C(u) = U_3 \, B_h \, G_h, \tag{11.7}$$

where $B_h$ is the matrix of the Hermite Basis and $G_h$ is the Hermite control tensor of cubic curves.

**Cubic Hermite basis** Let us rewrite the cubic Hermite curve as the polynomial combination of the elements of its control tensor. From equation (11.7) we get

$$C(u) = \begin{pmatrix} h_1(u) & h_2(u) & h_3(u) & h_4(u) \end{pmatrix} \begin{pmatrix} \boldsymbol{p}_1 \\ \boldsymbol{p}_2 \\ \boldsymbol{s}_1 \\ \boldsymbol{s}_2 \end{pmatrix}$$

where the Hermite basis polynomials are:

$$\begin{aligned} h_1(u) &= 2u^3 - 3u^2 + 1 \\ h_2(u) &= -2u^3 + 3u^2 \\ h_3(u) &= u^3 - 2u^2 + u \\ h_4(u) &= u^3 - u^2 \end{aligned}$$

In Figure 11.1 the graphs of such basis functions are shown. Let us notice that not all of them are nonnegative in the interval $[0, 1]$. This fact implies that some of the important properties which hold, e.g., for the Bézier form of a curve conversely do not hold for the Hermite form.

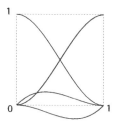

**Figure 11.1**   Graphs of the cubic polynomial Hermite basis

**Example 11.2.1 (Graphs of the Hermite basis)**
In Script 11.2.1 we produce the graph of the four polynomials of the Hermite basis in the $[0, 1]$ interval. A function `Intervals:a:n` produces a partition of the real interval $[0, a]$ into $n$ subintervals as a $(1, 1)$-dimensional polyhedral complex. The function `BaseHermite` then generates a polyhedral complex of dimension $(1, 2)$ made by the graphs of the four basis polynomials, that is shown in Figure 11.1. Notice that the Hermite polynomials are translated quite literally into variable-free functions `h1`, `h2`, `h3` and `h4`, using algebraic operators that work in function spaces. Notice also that, for this purpose, the constant multipliers of power terms are translated into constant functions.

**Example 11.2.2 (Examples of Hermite curves)**
A plane cubic Hermite curve may be written in scalar form, i.e. by giving its coordinate maps as:

$$\begin{aligned} x(u) &= x_1 h_1(u) + x_2 h_2(u) + t_{1x} h_3(u) + t_{2x} h_4(u) \\ y(u) &= y_1 h_1(u) + y_2 h_2(u) + t_{1y} h_3(u) + t_{2y} h_4(u) \end{aligned}$$

**Script 11.2.1**
```
DEF Intervals (a::IsReal) (n::IsIntPos) = (QUOTE ~ #:n):(a/n)

DEF BaseHermite =
    STRUCT ~ [ MAP:[u,h1], MAP:[u,h2], MAP:[u,h3], MAP:[u,h4] ]
    WHERE
        h1 = (k:2)*(u*u*u) - (k:3)*(u*u) + (k:1),
        h2 = (k:3)*(u*u) - (k:2)*(u*u*u),
        h3 = (u*u*u) - (k:2)*(u*u) + u,
        h4 = (u*u*u) - (u*u),
        u = s1
    END;

BaseHermite:(Intervals:1:20)
```

Direct implementation of such equations in given in Script 11.2.2, where a function Hermite2D is defined, that, when applied to a quadruple of 2D control handles $p_1 = (x_1, y_1)$, $p_2 = (x_2, y_2)$, $t_1 = (t_{1x}, t_{1y})$ and $t_2 = (t_{2x}, t_{2y})$, generates a vector function which can be mapped by the MAP operator over a 1D polyhedral partition of the unit segment.

**Script 11.2.2**
```
DEF Hermite2D (p1,p2,t1,t2::IsSeq) =
    [(x:p1 * h1) + (x:p2 * h2) + (x:t1 * h3) + (x:t2 * h4),
     (y:p1 * h1) + (y:p2 * h2) + (y:t1 * h3) + (y:t2 * h4)]
    WHERE
        h1 = (k:2*u*u*u) - (k:3*u*u) + (k:1),
        h2 = (k:3*u*u) - (k:2*u*u*u),
        h3 = (u*u*u) - (k:2*u*u) + u,
        h4 = (u*u*u) - (u*u),
        u = s1, x = (k~s1), y = (k~s2)
    END;

(STRUCT~[
    MAP:(Hermite2D:<<1,0>,<1,1>,<-:1,1>,<1,0>>),
    MAP:(Hermite2D:<<1,0>,<1,1>,<-:2,2>,<2,0>>),
    MAP:(Hermite2D:<<1,0>,<1,1>,<-:4,4>,<4,0>>),
    MAP:(Hermite2D:<<1,0>,<1,1>,<-:10,10>,<10,0>>)
]): (Intervals:1:20)
```

Four cubics generated by the PLaSM final expression of Script 11.2.2 are shown in Figure 11.2. Notice that the proportional growth of the extreme tangent vectors may produce a self-loop in the curve. This possibility is not actually loved by designers. Thus, Hermite curves are used very carefully in CAD systems.

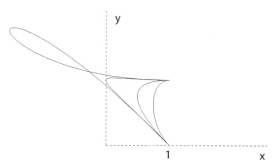

**Figure 11.2**  Four examples of Hermite curves through the same extreme points, and with proportional extreme tangents

### Bézier's geometric form

When the cubic curve is built by blending the ordered sequence of four control points, it is said to be in Bézier's geometric form, or also called the cubic Bézier curve. Such a curve interpolates the two extreme control points, and approximates the remaining two points.

Let us suppose the cubic arc is generated by points $q_0$, $q_1$, $q_2$ and $q_3$, and defined for $u \in [0, 1]$. To get its parametric equation we solve the set of constraints that impose (a) the passage through the extreme control points, and (b) the starting and ending tangent vectors parallel to the difference of two control points. Formally:

$$
\begin{aligned}
C(0) &= q_0 \\
C(1) &= q_3 \\
C'(0) &= s_0 = 3(q_1 - q_0) \\
C'(1) &= s_1 = 3(q_3 - q_2),
\end{aligned}
$$

so that, by using the equation of the Hermite's geometric form, we get:

$$
\begin{aligned}
C(u) &= U_3 \, M_3 \\
&= U_3 \, B_h \, G_h \\
&= U_3 \, B_h \begin{pmatrix} q_0 \\ q_3 \\ 3(q_1 - q_0) \\ 3(q_3 - q_2) \end{pmatrix} \\
&= U_3 \, B_h \begin{pmatrix} 1 & 0 & 0 & 0 \\ 0 & 0 & 0 & 1 \\ -3 & 3 & 0 & 0 \\ 0 & 0 & -3 & 3 \end{pmatrix} \begin{pmatrix} q_0 \\ q_1 \\ q_2 \\ q_3 \end{pmatrix} \\
&= U_3 \, B_h \, B_{hb} \, G_b \\
&= U_3 \, B_b \, G_b
\end{aligned}
$$

where $B_b$ is said matrix of the cubic Bézier basis, and $G_b$ is the Bézier control tensor.

**Transformations between geometric forms**  We have already computed the cubic Bézier form starting from the Hermite form:

$$U_3 \ B_h \ G_h = U_3 \ B_h \ B_{hb} \ G_b = U_3 \ B_b \ G_b$$

where we set

$$B_h \ B_{hb} = B_b$$

with $B_{hb}$ linear transformation from Hermite to Bézier forms. Analogously, we have

$$B_b \ (B_{hb})^{-1} = B_b \ B_{bh} = B_h$$

with $B_{hb}$ linear transformation from Bézier to Hermite.

More in general, every geometric form of a curve can be transformed into another form by a similar approach, since the choice of a new geometric form is simply using a different basis of polygons to blend the control handles of a curve. The transformation matrices discussed above are exactly the matrices of two linear *transformations of coordinates* (from one basis to another one) into the vector space of polynomials of proper degree.

**Cubic Bernstein/Bézier basis**  The cubic Bézier curve may be written as the blending of control points with the polynomials of the Bézier basis, also known as *Bernstein polynomials*:

$$C(u) = \begin{pmatrix} b_0(u) & b_1(u) & b_2(u) & b_3(u) \end{pmatrix} \begin{pmatrix} q_0 \\ q_1 \\ q_2 \\ q_3 \end{pmatrix}$$

where

$$\begin{pmatrix} b_0(u) & b_1(u) & b_2(u) & b_3(u) \end{pmatrix} = \begin{pmatrix} u^3 & u^2 & u & 1 \end{pmatrix} \begin{pmatrix} -1 & 3 & -3 & 1 \\ 3 & -6 & 3 & 0 \\ -3 & 3 & 0 & 0 \\ 1 & 0 & 0 & 0 \end{pmatrix}$$

and hence the Bernstein/Bézier cubic polynomials are

$$\begin{aligned} b_0(u) &= (1-u)^3, \\ b_1(u) &= 3u(1-u)^2, \\ b_2(u) &= 3u^2(1-u), \\ b_3(u) &= u^3. \end{aligned}$$

If we denote with $B_i^3(u)$, $0 \le i \le 3$, the elements of the cubic Bernstein basis, we can write:

$$B_i^3(u) = \begin{pmatrix} 3 \\ i \end{pmatrix} u^i (1-u)^{3-i}.$$

### 11.2.4   Higher-order Bézier curves

More in general, a Bézier curve of degree $n$ is a function $C : [0, 1] \to \mathbb{E}^d$ defined as a polynomial combination of $n + 1$ control points $q_i \in \mathbb{E}^d$:

$$C(u) = \sum_{i=0}^{n} B_i^n(u)\, q_i, \qquad u \in [0, 1] \tag{11.8}$$

where the blending functions $B_i^n : \mathbb{R} \to \mathbb{R}$ are the Bernstein polynomials:

$$B_i^n(u) = \binom{n}{i} u^i (1 - u)^{n-i}$$

**Bernstein basis of degree $n$**

In order to generate a curve or a function graph we need to map a suitable vector function over some partition of the unit interval $[0, 1]$. Such polyhedral decomposition of the unit interval is stored in the `Domain` object of Script 11.2.3, whereas the `Intervals` generating function was given in Script 11.2.1.

Then we need to compute the Bernstein basis of polynomials

$$B_i^n(u) = \binom{n}{i} u^i (1 - u)^{n-i} \qquad i = 0, \ldots, n$$

for any given $n$. This can be readily done in PLaSM. In particular, the `BernsteinBasis` function, when applied to an integer $n$, will return the ordered sequence of the $n + 1$ Bernstein polynomials of degree $n$.

In order to compute a `BernsteinBasis` of arbitrary degree $n$, a small toolbox of utility functions is needed. In particular, the applications `Fact:n`, `Choose:<n,i>` and `Bernstein:n:i` will respectively compute the factorial number $n!$, the binomial number $\binom{n}{i}$ and the Bernstein polynomial $B_i^n$. The definition of the `Bernstein` function in Script 11.2.3 may seem a little tricky, but the reader should consider that it actually computes a curried function with signature

$$B_i^n : \mathbb{Z} \to \mathbb{Z} \to (\mathbb{R} \to \mathbb{R}) : n \mapsto i \mapsto \left( u \mapsto \binom{n}{i} u^i (1 - u)^{n-i} \right)$$

where $\mathbb{Z}$ is the set of nonnegative integers.

---

**Script 11.2.3 (Bernstein/Bézier basis)**

```
DEF Domain = Intervals:1:30;

DEF Fact = IF: <C:EQ:0, K:1, * ~ INTSTO >;
DEF Choose = IF:< OR ~ [C:EQ:0 ~ S2, EQ], K:1, Choose ~ AA:(C:+:-1) * / >;
DEF Bernstein (n::IsInt)(i::IsInt) =
    *~[K:(Choose:<n,i>),**~[ID,K:i],**~[-~[K:1,ID],K:(n-i)]]~S1;

DEF BernsteinBasis (n::IsInt) = AA:(Bernstein:n):(0..n);
```

---

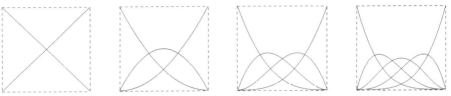

**Figure 11.3**   The graphs of Bernstein's bases of degrees 1, 2, 3 and 4

The functions `Fact` and `Choose`, for the factorial and the binomial numbers, were introduced in Scripts 2.1.6 and 2.1.10, respectively. They are recalled above for the reader's convenience. The graph of the `BernsteinBasis:4` basis shown in Figure 11.3d can be obtained by evaluating the expression:

```
STRUCT:<MAP:[S1, Bernstein:4:4]: Domain,
        MAP:[S1, Bernstein:4:3]: Domain,
        MAP:[S1, Bernstein:4:2]: Domain,
        MAP:[S1, Bernstein:4:1]: Domain,
        MAP:[S1, Bernstein:4:0]: Domain >;
```

More in general, a `PLaSM` function `BernsteinGraph`, that fully exploits the combinatorial power of the `FL` language, is given in Script 11.2.4. This function is used to generate the graph of the Bernstein's basis of arbitrary degree $n$.

---

**Script 11.2.4 (SVG exporting of Bezier basis graphs)**

```
DEF BernsteinGraph (n::IsIntPos) = STRUCT:(
   (CONS ~ AA:(MAP ~ CONS) ~ DISTL):< S1, BernsteinBasis:n >: Domain
   AR CUBOID:<1,1>
);

DEF out = (STRUCT ~ CAT ~ AA:[BernsteinGraph, K:(T:1:1.33)]):(1..4);
svg:out:10:'out.svg';
```

---

The graphs of the Bernstein/Bézier bases of degrees 1,2,3 and 4 shown in Figure 11.3 are produced by evaluating the `out` symbol of Script 11.2.4. Its geometric value is first exported to a `.svg` file by the last expression of the script, then imported in *Adobe Illustrator* for handling the line size, and finally exported into a `.eps` file to be included by the LATEX system used to typeset the present book. Most of pictures in this chapter are produced by a similar procedure.

**Bézier mapping of degree $n$**

We are finally ready to compute the Bézier mapping of degree $n$ from the parameter domain $[0,1]$ to the target space $\mathbb{E}^d$.

According to equation (11.8), we have to combine the sequence of `ControlPoints` with the `BernsteinBasis` of proper `degree`. For this purpose, the `ControlPoints` are transposed into the sequence `coordinateSeqs` of coordinate sequences, where each number is transformed into a constant function. Finally, each element in `coordinateSeqs`, i.e. each sequence of corresponding coordinates, is linearly combined with the basis polynomials returned by the expression `BernsteinBasis:degree`, resulting in a sequence of *coordinate maps*.

Let us remember that the `LEN` function returns the length of the sequence it is applied to, and that the `InnerProd` function for inner product of vectors (and function vectors) was defined in Script 3.2.4.

---

**Script 11.2.5**

```
DEF Bezier (ControlPoints::IsSeq) = (AA:InnerProd ~ DISTL):
    < BernsteinBasis:degree, coordinateSeqs >
WHERE
    degree = LEN:ControlPoints - 1,
    coordinateSeqs = ((AA ~ AA):K ~ TRANS):ControlPoints
END;
```

---

The `Bezier` function given above may be applied to an arbitrary sequence of control points, thus generating a Bezier's mapping of the appropriate degree, to be applied by the `MAP` function to some partition of the unit segment.

Notice in particular that the `Bezier` function may work for an *arbitrary* number of control points, including one. Furthermore, it can be used either in 2D or in 3D as well as for *every* other dimension of the target space, i.e. for arbitrary number of coordinates of curve points.

### Example 11.2.3 (Bézier curves of various degrees)

The curve examples of Figure 11.4 are produced by the `out` object defined in Script 11.2.6. Both the curves and the corresponding control polygons are displayed, for curve degrees increasing from 1 to 4. The four examples are generated by the control point sequences `pol1`, `pol2`, `pol3` and `pol4`. The generated polyhedral complex `out`, including the four curve images and the four control polygons, is finally exported as .svg file. The `polyline` primitive was defined in Script 7.2.3.

---

**Script 11.2.6 (Examples of Bézier curves)**

```
DEF pol1 = <<0,0>,<10,10>>;
DEF pol2 = <<0,0>,<10,0>,<10,10>>;
DEF pol3 = <<0,0>,<10,0>,<0,10>,<10,10>>;
DEF pol4 = <<0,0>,<10,0>,<10,10>,<0,10>,<0,0>>;

DEF out = STRUCT:<
    MAP:(Bezier:pol1):domain, polyline:pol1, T:1:15,
    MAP:(Bezier:pol2):domain, polyline:pol2, T:1:15,
    MAP:(Bezier:pol3):domain, polyline:pol3, T:1:15,
    MAP:(Bezier:pol4):domain, polyline:pol4
>;

svg:out:10:'out.svg'
```

---

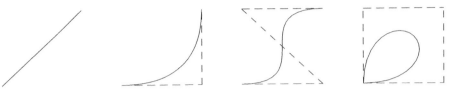

**Figure 11.4**   Bézier curves of degrees 1, 2, 3 and 4 with their control polygons

### Properties of Bézier curves

Bézier curves are greatly used by CAD systems because of their very useful properties, that we briefly summarize below:

1. *Affine invariance*
   A Bézier curve can be translated, rotated or scaled by simply translating, rotating or scaling its control points.
2. *Variation diminishing*
   The number of intersections of a Bézier curve with a hyperplane does not exceed the number of intersections of its control polygon.
3. *Interpolation of extreme points*
   A Bézier curve interpolates the first and last control points. Notice, in fact, that $B_0^n(0) = B_n^n(1) = 1$, whereas $B_i^n(0) = B_i^n(1) = 0$, for $0 < i < n$.
4. *Convex hull containment*
   A Bézier curve of arbitrary degree $n$ is contained in the convex hull of its control points $q_0, q_1, \ldots, q_n$. The proof is simple:

$$C(u) = \sum_{i=0}^{n} B_i^n(u)\, q_i$$

is a convex combination of $q_0, q_1, \ldots, q_n$, for every $u \in [0, 1]$.
The above statement is true because all polynomials $B_i^n(u)$ are non negative and sum to 1 for every $u \in [0, 1]$. Using Newton's formula for the power of binomials, we get in fact:

$$\sum_{i=0}^{n} B_i^n(u) = \sum_{i=0}^{n} \binom{n}{i} u^i(1-u)^{n-i} = (u + (1-u))^n = 1.$$

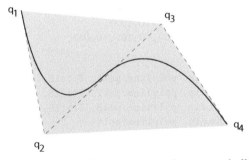

**Figure 11.5**   Containment of a Bézier curve in the convex hull of control points

## 11.3 Polynomial splines

A *spline* is a composite curve, defined by joining some adjacent curve segments with an appropriate order of continuity at the joints. We discuss in this section some useful classes of polynomial splines, largely diffused in most graphics and CAD systems, and in particular:

1. *cubic cardinal splines*, made by $C^1$-continuous Hermite cubic segments, which interpolate all the points in their control sequence;
2. *cubic uniform B-splines*, which only approximate the control point sequence, using cubic curve segments joined with $C^2$ continuity;
3. *non-uniform B-splines* of arbitrary degree, which are polynomial splines of great flexibility, that enjoy several useful properties.

### 11.3.1 Cubic cardinal splines

With *cubic cardinal splines*, also called *Catmull-Rom* splines [FvDFH90], each component curve segment is a Hermite cubic. In particular, a cubic cardinal spline is defined by a sequence $p_0, p_1, \ldots, p_m$ of $m+1$ control points ($m \geq 3$), that define $m-2$ adjacent cubic segments. The $i$-th curve segment $C_i(u)$ is defined by the interpolation of points $p_i$ and $p_{i+1}$, and by imposing that the tangent vector in a point $p_i$ is parallel to the vector difference between the adjacent points $p_{i+1}$ and $p_{i-1}$. Formally we have:

$$
\begin{aligned}
C_i(0) &= p_i \\
C_i(1) &= p_{i+1} \\
C_i'(0) &= h(p_{i+1} - p_{i-1}) \\
C_i'(1) &= h(p_{i+2} - p_i)
\end{aligned}
$$

As a consequence of such constraints, a cubic cardinal will interpolate all the points in the subsequence $p_1, \ldots, p_{m-1}$. In the intervals between $p_0$ and $p_1$ and between $p_{m-1}$ and $p_m$ the spline is not defined.

The equation of the segment $C_i(u)$ can be derived from the matrix form of Hermite curves as follows:

$$
C_i(u) = U_3 \, M_h \begin{pmatrix} p_i \\ p_{i+1} \\ h(p_{i+1} - p_{i-1}) \\ h(p_{i+2} - p_i) \end{pmatrix}, \qquad u \in [0,1].
$$

Thus, it is:

$$
\begin{aligned}
C_i(u) &= U_3 \, M_h \begin{pmatrix} 0 & 1 & 0 & 0 \\ 0 & 0 & 1 & 0 \\ -h & 0 & h & 0 \\ 0 & -h & 0 & h \end{pmatrix} \begin{pmatrix} p_{i-1} \\ p_i \\ p_{i+1} \\ p_{i+2} \end{pmatrix} \\
&= U_3 \, M_h \, M_{hc} \, G_i = U_3 \, M_c \, G_i
\end{aligned}
$$

where $M_{hc}$ is the matrix of the transformation from the Hermite to the cardinal form, $M_c$ is the matrix of the cardinal basis, and $G_i$ is the control tensor of the $i$-th spline segment.

**Cardinal basis**

As we know, the set of polynomials of the cardinal basis can be obtained from the product of the power basis $U_3$ times the matrix $M_c$ of the geometric form. Hence we have:

$$
C_i(u) = U_3\, M_c\, G_i = \begin{pmatrix} c_1(u) & c_2(u) & c_3(u) & c_4(u) \end{pmatrix} \begin{pmatrix} p_{i-1} \\ p_i \\ p_{i+1} \\ p_{i+2} \end{pmatrix},
$$

where

$$
\begin{pmatrix} c_1(u) & c_2(u) & c_3(u) & c_4(u) \end{pmatrix} = \begin{pmatrix} u^3 & u^2 & u & 1 \end{pmatrix} \begin{pmatrix} -h & 2-h & h-2 & h \\ 2h & h-3 & 3-2h & -h \\ -h & 0 & h & 0 \\ 0 & 1 & 0 & 0 \end{pmatrix}
$$

The expression of the cardinal cubic polynomial, whose graph is given in Figure 11.6, is:

$$
\begin{aligned}
c_1(u) &= -hu^3 + 2hu^2 - hu \\
c_2(u) &= (2-h)u^3 + (h-3)u^2 + 1 \\
c_3(u) &= (h-2)u^3 + (3-2h)u^2 + hu \\
c_4(u) &= hu^3 - hu^2
\end{aligned}
$$

It may be interesting to look at the shape of the four basis polynomials, shown in Figure 11.6, where the graph of each is separately given over the interval $[0,1]$. Notice that two such polynomials are not positive in the unit interval.

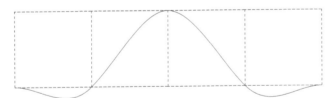

**Figure 11.6**   From left to right: graphs of polynomials $c_4(u)$, $c_3(u)$, $c_2(u)$ and $c_1(u)$ of the cubic cardinal basis

**Implementation**   The graph of Figure 11.6 is generated by evaluating the expression

```
CubicCardinalGraph:(Intervals:1:20)
```

where the function `CubicCardinalGraph` is given in Script 11.3.1, and defines a 2D structure containing the graphs of the single basis polynomials separated by a unit translation along the first coordinate axes.

Several examples of cubic cardinal splines will be discussed in Section 11.6.1, where a unified implementation of cardinal and uniform B-splines will be given. In that section we also discuss how to produce two more curve segments passing through the extreme points of the control segment.

**Script 11.3.1**

```
DEF CubicCardinalGraph =
    STRUCT ~ [MAP:[u,c4], k:(T:1:1), MAP:[u,c3], k:(T:1:1),
        MAP:[u,c2], k:(T:1:1), MAP:[u,c1]]
WHERE
    c1 = ((k:0 - h) * u3) + ((k:2 * h) * u2) - (h * u),
    c2 = ((k:2 - h) * u3) + ((h - k:3) * u2) + (k:1),
    c3 = ((h - k:2) * u3) + ((k:3 - k:2*h) *u2) + (h*u),
    c4 = (h * u3) - (h * u2),
    u = s1, u2 = u*u, u3 = u2*u, h = k:1
END;
```

### 11.3.2 Cubic uniform B-splines

Cubic uniform B-splines are composite curves used to approximate a sequence of $m+1$ control points $p_0, p_1, \ldots, p_m$, with $m \geq 3$. Such control points define $m-2$ adjacent segments of cubic polynomial curve. In particular, the $i$-th curve segment, denoted as $Q_i(u)$, is defined by imposing the geometric continuity and the continuity of first and second derivatives at the extreme points of the segment.

The discussion of cubic B-splines given in this section concerns the so-called *uniform* cubic B-splines, where each curve segment is obtained by a combination of four control points with the *uniform B-spline basis*. Each polynomial in this basis has the interval $[0, 1]$ as its domain. In a later section we discuss non-uniform B-splines, which are parametrized over different intervals of the real line.

### Uniform B-spline geometric form

The parametric equation of cubic segment $Q_i(u)$, with $u \in [0, 1]$, can be written in geometric form as follows:

$$Q_i(u) = U_3 \frac{1}{6} \begin{pmatrix} -1 & 3 & -3 & 1 \\ 3 & -6 & 3 & 0 \\ -3 & 0 & 3 & 0 \\ 1 & 4 & 1 & 0 \end{pmatrix} \begin{pmatrix} p_{i-1} \\ p_i \\ p_{i+1} \\ p_{i+2} \end{pmatrix}, \qquad 1 \leq i \leq m-2,$$

$$= U_3\, B_s\, G_i$$

where $B_s$, called the matrix of the cubic uniform B-spline, is derived in a later subsection. Therefore, the uniform cubic B-basis polynomials, given by the product $U_3 B_s$ and graphically shown in Figure 11.7, are

$$B_1(u) = \frac{1}{6}(-u^3 + 3u^2 - 3u + 1)$$

$$B_2(u) = \frac{1}{6}(3u^3 + -6u^2 + 4)$$

$$B_3(u) = \frac{1}{6}(-3u^3 + 3u^2 + 3u + 1)$$

$$B_4(u) = \frac{1}{6}u^3$$

## Uniform B-spline basis

The graph of Figure 11.7 is generated by evaluating the last expression of Script 11.3.2, where the function `UniformBsplineGraph` defines a 2D structure with the graphs of the single basis polynomials inserted within an empty unit box and separated by a unit translation on the first coordinate axis. Notice that all B-spline basis functions, unlike the cardinal case, are non-negative. They also sum to one for each $u$. According to such properties, each spline segment $Q_i(u)$ is contained in the convex hull of its geometry vector $G_i$.

---

**Script 11.3.2**

```
DEF UniformBsplineGraph =
    STRUCT ~ [Box, MAP:[u,B4], k:(T:1:1), Box, MAP:[u,B3], k:(T:1:1),
        Box, MAP:[u,B2], k:(T:1:1), Box, MAP:[u,B1]]
WHERE
    B1 = a * ((k:3*u2) - (k:1*u3) - (k:3*u) + (k:1)),
    B2 = a * ((k:3*u3) - (k:6*u2) + (k:4)),
    B3 = a * ((k:3*u2) - (k:3*u3) + (k:3*u) + (k:1)),
    B4 = a * u3,
    u = s1, u2 = u*u, u3 = u2*u, a = k:(1/6)
    Box = (K ~ @1 ~ CUBOID):<1,1>
END;

DEF out = UniformBsplineGraph:(Intervals:1:30)

SVG:out:10:'out.svg'
```

---

**Figure 11.7**    From left to right: graphs of polynomials $B_4(u)$, $B_3(u)$, $B_2(u)$ and $B_1(u)$ of the cubic uniform B-spline basis

## Global parametrization

When dealing with splines, it may be useful to maintain a bijective correspondence between spline points and parameter values. For this purpose a spline form is often used where the various curve segments are parametrized over subsequent real intervals of unit size.

In order to describe the whole spline and not the single spline segments, we change our notation, with respect both to the parameter and to the indexing of segments. This notation is adopted for the sake of uniformity with the one used in the following section for *non-uniform* B-splines.

As we know, a cubic B-spline approximates a sequence of $m + 1$ control points $\boldsymbol{p}_0, \boldsymbol{p}_1, \ldots, \boldsymbol{p}_m$, $m \geq 3$, with a sequence of $m - 2$ segments of cubic curves, which can be indexed as $\boldsymbol{Q}_3, \boldsymbol{Q}_4, \ldots, \boldsymbol{Q}_m$. With this choice of indices, a $\boldsymbol{Q}_i$ segment is a polynomial combination of points $\boldsymbol{p}_{i-4+k}$, $1 \leq k \leq 4$. Thus, the first segment $\boldsymbol{Q}_3$ is generated by points $\boldsymbol{p}_0, \ldots, \boldsymbol{p}_3$, and the last segment $\boldsymbol{Q}_m$ is generated by points $\boldsymbol{p}_{m-3}, \ldots, \boldsymbol{p}_m$.

The uniform cubic B-spline can be written as a function of a global parameter $3 \leq t \leq m + 1$, as

$$Q(t) = \bigcup_{i=3}^{m} \boldsymbol{Q}_i(t - i).$$

Each integer parameter value $t \in \{3, 4, \ldots, m+1\}$ is called a *knot*. The image $Q(t)$ of a knot, where $\boldsymbol{Q}_i(1) = \boldsymbol{Q}_{i+1}(0)$, is called a join point, or *joint*.

## Uniform B-spline matrix

We derive in this section the matrix of the cubic uniform B-spline, already given in Section 11.3.2. For this purpose we start from the boundary conditions imposed on pairs of cubic segments. In particular, a pair of adjacent spline segments $\boldsymbol{Q}_i(u)$ and $\boldsymbol{Q}_{i+1}(u)$, $0 \leq u \leq 1$, must be $C^2$-continuous, i.e. must satisfy the following conditions at the joint:

$$\boldsymbol{Q}_i(1) = \boldsymbol{Q}_{i+1}(0).$$
$$\boldsymbol{Q}'_i(1) = \boldsymbol{Q}'_{i+1}(0),$$
$$\boldsymbol{Q}"_i(1) = \boldsymbol{Q}"_{i+1}(0).$$

To be more explicit, we can write:

$$\sum_{k=1}^{4} B_k(1)\boldsymbol{p}_{i-4+k} = \sum_{k=1}^{4} B_k(0)\boldsymbol{p}_{i-3+k}$$

$$\sum_{k=1}^{4} B'_k(1)\boldsymbol{p}_{i-4+k} = \sum_{k=1}^{4} B'_k(0)\boldsymbol{p}_{i-3+k}$$

$$\sum_{k=1}^{4} B"_k(1)\boldsymbol{p}_{i-4+k} = \sum_{k=1}^{4} B"_k(0)\boldsymbol{p}_{i-3+k}$$

Such continuity equations can be written in matrix form as follows:

$$B \begin{pmatrix} \boldsymbol{p}_{i-3} \\ \boldsymbol{p}_{i-2} \\ \boldsymbol{p}_{i-1} \\ \boldsymbol{p}_i \\ \boldsymbol{p}_{i+1} \end{pmatrix} = \begin{pmatrix} \boldsymbol{0} \\ \boldsymbol{0} \\ \boldsymbol{0} \end{pmatrix} \tag{11.9}$$

with

$$B = \begin{pmatrix} B_1(1) & B_2(1) - B_1(0) & B_3(1) - B_2(0) & B_4(1) - B_3(0) & B_4(0) \\ B'_1(1) & B'_2(1) - B'_1(0) & B'_3(1) - B'_2(0) & B'_4(1) - B'_3(0) & B'_4(0) \\ B"_1(1) & B"_2(1) - B"_1(0) & B"_3(1) - B"_2(0) & B"_4(1) - B"_3(0) & B"_4(0) \end{pmatrix}$$

The matrix equation (11.9) states that 3 different linear combinations of 5 displacement vectors in general position must go to zero. This is only possible when all the coefficients, i.e. all the elements in the left-hand matrix, are zero.

Also, remembering that a blending function is the product of the power basis vector times a column of the unknown basis matrix $B = (b_{hk})$, we can write, for $1 \leq k \leq 4$:

$$B_k(u) = \begin{pmatrix} u^3 & u^2 & u & 1 \end{pmatrix} \begin{pmatrix} b_{1k} & b_{2k} & b_{3k} & b_{4k} \end{pmatrix}^T$$

$$B_k'(u) = \begin{pmatrix} 3u^2 & 2u & 1 & 0 \end{pmatrix} \begin{pmatrix} b_{1k} & b_{2k} & b_{3k} & b_{4k} \end{pmatrix}^T$$

$$B"_k(u) = \begin{pmatrix} 6u & 2 & 0 & 0 \end{pmatrix} \begin{pmatrix} b_{1k} & b_{2k} & b_{3k} & b_{4k} \end{pmatrix}^T$$

so that we get, respectively:

$$B_k(0) = b_{4k} \quad \text{and} \quad B_k(1) = b_{1k} + b_{2k} + b_{3k} + b_{4k},$$
$$B_k'(0) = b_{3k} \quad \text{and} \quad B_k'(1) = 3b_{1k} + 2b_{2k} + b_{3k},$$
$$B"_k(0) = 2b_{2k} \quad \text{and} \quad B"_k(1) = 6b_{1k} + 2b_{2k}.$$

By setting to zero each term of the matrix in equation 11.9, we get the following 15 equations among the 16 unknowns $b_{hk}$, with $1 \leq h, k \leq 4$:

$$B_1(1) = b_{11} + b_{21} + b_{31} + b_{41} = 0$$
$$B_2(1) - B_1(0) = b_{12} + b_{22} + b_{32} + b_{42} - b_{41} = 0$$
$$B_3(1) - B_2(0) = b_{13} + b_{23} + b_{33} + b_{43} - b_{42} = 0$$
$$B_4(1) - B_3(0) = b_{14} + b_{24} + b_{34} + b_{44} - b_{43} = 0$$
$$B_4(0) = b_{44} = 0$$
$$B_1'(1) = 3b_{11} + 2b_{21} + b_{31} = 0$$
$$B_2'(1) - B_1'(0) = 3b_{12} + 2b_{22} + b_{32} - b_{31} = 0$$
$$B_3'(1) - B_2'(0) = 3b_{13} + 2b_{23} + b_{33} - b_{32} = 0$$
$$B_4'(1) - B_3'(0) = 3b_{14} + 2b_{24} + b_{34} - b_{33} = 0$$
$$B_4'(0) = b_{34} = 0$$
$$B"_1(1) = 6b_{11} + 2b_{21} = 0$$
$$B"_2(1) - B"_1(0) = 6b_{12} + 2b_{22} - 2b_{21} = 0$$
$$B"_3(1) - B"_2(0) = 6b_{13} + 2b_{23} - 2b_{22} = 0$$
$$B"_4(1) - B"_3(0) = 6b_{14} + 2b_{24} - 2b_{23} = 0$$
$$B"_4(0) = 2b_{24}$$

A 16th equation can be obtained by ensuring that the basis polynomials sum to 1 for each $u$. So, we set

$$B_1(u) + B_2(u) + B_3(u) + B_4(u) = 1,$$

and, in particular, for $u = 0$ we get:

$$B_1(0) + B_2(0) + B_3(0) + B_4(0) = b_{41} + b_{42} + b_{43} + b_{44} = 1.$$

By solving the above system of equations for the unknown terms of the matrix of cubic uniform B-basis, we get

$$
B_s = \begin{pmatrix} b_{11} & b_{12} & b_{13} & b_{14} \\ b_{21} & b_{22} & b_{23} & b_{24} \\ b_{31} & b_{32} & b_{33} & b_{34} \\ b_{41} & b_{42} & b_{43} & b_{44} \end{pmatrix} = \frac{1}{6} \begin{pmatrix} -1 & 3 & -3 & 1 \\ 3 & -6 & 3 & 0 \\ -3 & 0 & 3 & 0 \\ 1 & 4 & 1 & 0 \end{pmatrix}
$$

### 11.3.3  Non-uniform polynomial B-splines

The B-splines discussed in this section are called *non-uniform* because different spline segments may correspond to different intervals in parameter space, unlike uniform B-splines. The basis polynomials, and consequently the spline shape and the other properties, are defined by a non-decreasing sequence of real numbers

$$
t_0 \le t_1 \le \cdots \le t_n,
$$

called the *knot sequence*. Splines of this kind are also named *NUB-splines* in the remainder of this book,[4] where the name stands for Non-Uniform B-splines.

The knot sequence is used to define the basis polynomials which blend the control points. In particular, each subset of $k + 2$ adjacent knot values is used to compute a basis polynomial of degree $k$. Notice that some subsequent knots may coincide. In this case we speak of *multiplicity* of the knots.

**Note**  In non-uniform B-splines the number $n + 1$ of *knot values* is greater than the number $m + 1$ of control points $p_0, \ldots, p_m$. In particular, the relation

$$
n = m + k + 1, \tag{11.10}
$$

where $k$ is the *degree* of spline segments, must hold between the number of knots and the number of control points. The quantity $h = k + 1$ is called the *order* of the spline. It will be useful when giving recursive formulas to compute the B-basis polynomials. Let us remember, e.g., that a spline of order four is made of cubic segments.

**Non-uniform B-spline flexibility**  Such splines have a much greater flexibility than the uniform ones. The basis polynomial associated with each control point may vary depending on the subset of knots it depends on. Spline segments may be parametrized over intervals of different size, and even reduced to a single point. Therefore, the continuity at a joint may be reduced, e.g. from $C^2$ to $C^1$ to $C^0$ and even to none (see Figure 11.10) by suitably increasing the multiplicity of a knot.

**Cubic non-uniform B-splines**

According to the previous statement, the knot sequence of cubic non-uniform B-splines can be given as

$$
(t_0, \ldots, t_3, \ldots, t_m, \ldots, t_{m+4}), \qquad t_i \le t_{i+1}.
$$

---

[4] Some authors call them non-uniform non-rational B-splines. We prefer to emphasize that they are polynomial splines.

In particular, the $Q_i(t)$ cubic segment is defined as

$$Q_i(t) = \sum_{\ell=0}^{3} p_{i-\ell} B_{i-\ell,4}(t) \qquad \begin{array}{l} 3 \le i \le m, \\ t \in [t_i, t_{i+1}) \end{array} \qquad (11.11)$$

where $B_{i,4}(u)$ is the B-basis polynomial of index $i$ and order 4, which is generated by the knot subsequence $(t_i, \ldots, t_{i+4})$.

For the spline as a whole, we can write:

$$Q(t) = \bigcup_{i=3}^{m} Q_i(t), \qquad t \in [t_3, t_{m+1}).$$

Outside the interval $[t_3, t_{m+1})$ a cubic non-uniform B-spline is not defined. Within this interval, each pair of adjacent knot values is associated with a spline segment. When a $t_i$ knot has multiplicity greater than one, i.e. when $t_i = t_{i+1}$, then the $Q_i(t)$ segment reduces to a point.

### Example 11.3.1 (Cubic Bézier)

Let us note that a cubic B-spline with a single curve segment needs 4 control points. As a consequence, the number of knots in this case must be 8, i.e. $4 + 3 + 1$. When parametrizing the spline in the interval $[0, 1]$, the knot sequence will therefore be:

$$(0, 0, 0, 0, 1, 1, 1, 1) \qquad (11.12)$$

The four basis polynomials to be combined with control points and the associated knot subsequences are: $B_{0,4}$ and $(0, 0, 0, 0, 1)$, $B_{1,4}$ and $(0, 0, 0, 1, 1)$, $B_{2,4}$ and $(0, 0, 1, 1, 1)$ and finally $B_{3,4}$ and $(0, 1, 1, 1, 1)$.

It is possible to show that the cubic non-uniform B-spline corresponding to the knot sequence (11.12) is the cubic Bézier curve.

### Geometric entities

In order to fully understand the construction of a non-uniform B-spline, it may be useful to recall the main inter-relationships among the 5 geometric entities that enter the definition.

**Control points** are denoted as $p_i$, with $0 \le i \le m$. A non-uniform B-spline usually approximates the control points.

**Knot values** are denoted as $t_i$, with $0 \le i \le n$. It must be $n = m + k + 1$, where $k$ is the spline degree. Knot values are used to define the B-spline polynomials. They also define the join points (or joints) between adjacent spline segments. When two consecutive knots coincide, the spline segment associated with their interval reduces to a point.

**Spline degree** is defined as the degree of the B-basis functions which are combined with the control points. The degree is denoted as $k$. It is connected to the spline order $h = k + 1$. The most used non-uniform B-splines are either cubic or quadratic. The image of a linear non-uniform B-spline is a polygonal line. The image of a non-uniform B-spline of degree 0 coincides with the sequence of control points.

**B-basis polynomials** are denoted as $B_{i,h}(t)$. They are univariate polynomials in the $t$ indeterminate, computed by using the recursive formulas of Cox and de Boor (see Section 39). The $i$ index is associated with the first one of values in the knot subsequence $(t_i, t_{i+1}, \ldots, t_{i+h})$ used to compute $B_{i,h}(t)$. The second index is called *order* of the polynomial.

**Spline segments** are defined as polynomial vector functions of a single parameter. Such functions are denoted as $Q_i(t)$, with $k \leq i \leq m$. A $Q_i(t)$ spline segment is obtained by a combination of the $i$-th control point and the $k$ previous points with the basis polynomials of order $h$ associated to the same indices. It is easy to see that the number of spline segments is $m - K + 1$.

**Non-uniform B-splines of arbitrary degree**

In this case the knot sequence may be written as

$$(t_0, \ldots, t_k, \ldots, t_{m+1}, \ldots, t_{m+h}), \qquad t_i \leq t_{i+1}.$$

with the spline defined in the interval $[t_k, t_{m+1})$. The first basis function $B_{0,h}(t)$ is defined by the knot subsequence $(t_0, \ldots, t_k, t_{k+1})$; the last function $B_{m,h}(t)$ is defined by $(t_m, t_{m+1}, \ldots, t_{m+h})$. Notice the bijection between basis polynomials and control points.

The equation of the non-uniform B-spline segment of degree $k$ with $m + 1$ control points may therefore be written as

$$Q_i(t) = \sum_{\ell=0}^{k} p_{i-\ell} B_{i-\ell,h}(t) \qquad \begin{array}{l} k \leq i \leq m, \\ t \in [t_i, t_{i+1}) \end{array} \qquad (11.13)$$

A global representation of the non-uniform B-spline as a whole can be given:

$$Q(t) = \bigcup_{i=k}^{m} Q_i(t) = \sum_{i=0}^{m} p_i B_{i,h}(t), \qquad t \in [t_k, t_{m+1}),$$

since each basis function $B_{i,h}(t)$ is zero outside the subinterval $[t_i, t_{i+h})$.

If the multiplicity of the first (last) knot value is equal to $h$, then the spline interpolates the first (last) control point. The interpolation is induced by the fact that such multiplicity induces $B_{0,h}(t_k) = 1$ $(B_{m,h}(t_{m+1}) = 1$, respectively).

**Example 11.3.2 (Degree elevation)**
In Figure 11.8 we show both a quadratic and a cubic spline interpolating the extreme control points. If we want to raise by one unity the degree of a non-uniform B-spline without changing the control polygon, then we have to:

1. decrease by one the parameter interval;[5]
2. increase by one the multiplicity of both extreme knots.

As a consequence of the degree elevation, the number $m - h$ of segments decreases of one. The PLaSM code that generates Figure 11.8 is given in Script 11.3.3. The DisplayAll operator, which displays both a spline and its control polygon and a polymarker to show the joints, is given in Script 11.6.4. The NUBspline function is given in Script 11.6.14.

---

**Script 11.3.3 (Degree elevation)**

```
DisplayAll:NUBspline:
   < <2,<0,0,0,1,2,3,4,5,5,5>>,
      <<1,3>,<-1,2>,<1,4>,<2,3>,<1,1>,<1,2>,<2.5,1>> >

DisplayAll:NUBspline:
   < <3,<0,0,0,0,1,2,3,4,4,4,4>>,
      <<1,3>,<-1,2>,<1,4>,<2,3>,<1,1>,<1,2>,<2.5,1>> >
```

---

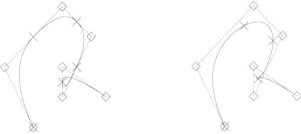

**Figure 11.8**   (a) Quadratic non-uniform B-spline with 7 control points and
$5 = 7 - 2$ spline segments (b) Cubic non-uniform B-spline with same control points
and $4 = 7 - 3$ segments

The reader may see, looking at Figure 11.8a, two interesting properties of quadratic non-uniform B-splines: (a) knots with multiplicity 1 are mapped to the middle point of a control polygon segment; (b) the spline is tangent there at the control polygon.

### Coox and de Boor formula

To compute the non-uniform B-spline basis polynomials $B_{i,h}(t)$ the recursive formulas derived by Coox [Cox71] and de Boor [dB72] are used. Their formulation was applied by Riesenfeld [Rie73, GR74] to curve definition in CAD. An interesting approach to B-splines can be found in Rogers and Adams [RA76].

   The computation of each basis function requires using a subset of knot values. In particular, the basis polynomial $B_{i,h}(t)$, called "with initial value $t_i$ and *order h*", is

---

[5] In case of knot intervals of integral size.

defined as:

$$B_{i,1}(t) = \begin{cases} 1 & \text{if } t_i \leq t \leq t_{i+1} \\ 0 & \text{otherwise} \end{cases} \tag{11.14}$$

$$B_{i,h}(t) = \frac{t - t_i}{t_{i+h-1} - t_i} B_{i,h-1}(t) + \frac{t_{i+h} - t}{t_{i+h} - t_{i+1}} B_{i+1,h-1}(t)$$

The above definition is recursive. A basis function of order $h$ and initial value $t_i$ is defined using two basis functions of order $h-1$ and initial values $t_i$ and $t_{i+1}$. In basic cases $B_{i,1}(t)$ of the recursion, concerning functions of order 1, *step functions* are used, whose value is 1 in the interval $[t_i, t_{i+1}]$, and 0 elsewhere.

**Dependence of basis functions on knots**   Let us develop a simple analysis of the dependence of basis functions on knot values. It is easy to see, from the Cox and de Boor formula, that $B_{i,h}(t)$ depends on the subsequence of knot values

$$(t_i, t_{i+1}, \cdots, t_{i+h}) \tag{11.15}$$

For example, $B_{1,3}(t)$ depends on the 4 knots $(t_1, \cdots, t_4)$, because it depends on $B_{1,2}(t)$ and on $B_{2,2}(t)$. In turn, $B_{1,2}(t)$ depends on $B_{1,1}(t)$ and on $B_{2,1}(t)$, and $B_{2,2}(t)$ depends on $B_{2,1}(t)$ and on $B_{3,1}(t)$. In conclusion, $B_{1,3}(t)$ is defined as a function of $B_{1,1}(t), B_{2,1}(t), B_{3,1}(t)$, and such functions depend on $(t_1, t_2, t_3, t_4)$, according to (11.15). In Figure 11.9 is shown the recursive dependence of a basis function $B_{i,4}$ on the knot values it depends on.

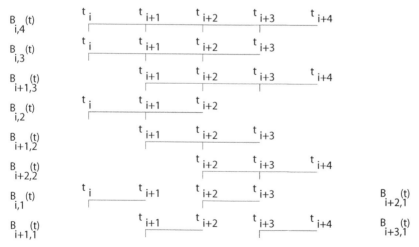

**Figure 11.9**   Representation of the dependence of $B_{i,4}(t)$ on lower order basis functions and on knot values

**Further remarks**   Let us summarize some properties of non-uniform B-splines.

1. The size of the parameter interval between two adjacent knots is *non-uniform*, i.e. may be variable. Often, integer intervals are used with size

either zero or one. In particular, non-integer knot values may arise when the parametrization of some spline segment must be more or less dense.

2. A non-uniform knot sequence implies that the basis functions may vary from a segment to another. This fact is negative, when considering the computational costs. The evaluation of B-basis polynomials in the general case is quite expensive. Most optimizations require integer knot values.

3. The continuity of segments at a join point may be reduced by raising the multiplicity of a knot value. Correspondingly, a spline segment is reduced to a single point. This fact also implies a reduction of the common subset of control points shared by two spline segments.

4. A control point may easily be interpolated, without introducing linear spline segments, simply by raising the multiplicity of a knot.

5. New control points and knots may easily be inserted, allowing for a powerful local editing and control of the spline shape.

**Example 11.3.3 (Continuity reduction at a joint)**
In Figure 11.10 an example is shown of reduction of the continuity at a join point by elevation of the multiplicity of a knot. The set of quadratic splines of the figure is generated by Script 11.3.4.

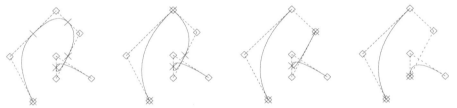

**Figure 11.10**   Quadratic non-uniform B-spline. Reduction of continuity, initially equal to $C^1$, by raising the multiplicity of the fourth knot

---

**Script 11.3.4**
```
DEF points = <<0,0>,<-1,2>,<1,4>,<2,3>,<1,1>,<1,2>,<2.5,1>>;

DisplayNUBspline:< 2,<0,0,0,1,2,3,4,5,5,5>>, points >;
DisplayNUBspline:< 2,<0,0,0,1,1,2,3,4,4,4>>, points >;
DisplayNUBspline:< 2,<0,0,0,1,1,1,2,3,3,3>>, points >;
DisplayNUBspline:< 2,<0,0,0,1,1,1,1,2,2,2>>, points >;
```

---

*11.3.4   Multiresolution Bézier and B-splines*

A new set of *multiresolution methods* is becoming popular which utilize a control polygon, as in the Bézier or B-spline case. Instead of using analytic methods to directly calculate points on the curve, such methods successively refine the control polygons into a sequence of control polygons that converge to a curve. Conceptually, multiresolution methods can be described as computing a succession of curves whose image converge to the desired point set. In practice, for a given $u$, they compute a succession of points that converges to $C(u)$.

## de Casteljau algorithm

A typical representative of multiresolution methods for curve generation, also called subdivision methods, is the de Casteljau algorithm for Bézier curves. We first present this method for curves of second degree (parabola), then we discuss its generalization to Bézier curves of arbitrary degree.

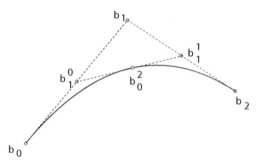

**Figure 11.11**   de Casteljau algorithm for a curve of second degree

**de Casteljau's parabola**   Let us consider three points $b_1, b_2, b_3 \in \mathbb{E}^d$ and a scalar $u \in [0, 1]$. Define the linear interpolations of point pairs:

$$
\begin{aligned}
b_0^1(u) &= (1-u)b_0 + ub_1 \\
b_1^1(u) &= (1-u)b_1 + ub_2 \\
b_0^2(u) &= (1-u)b_0^1(u) + ub_1^1(u)
\end{aligned}
$$

By substituting the first two equations into the third, we get

$$
\begin{aligned}
b_0^2(u) &= (1-u)\left[(1-u)b_0 + ub_1\right] + u\left[(1-u)b_1 + ub_2\right] \\
&= (1-u)^2 b_0 + 2u(1-u)b_1 + u^2 b_2
\end{aligned}
$$

which is the parametric equation of a *parabola*. By considering Figure 11.11, we can see with elementary geometric methods that

$$
\begin{aligned}
\mathrm{ratio}(b_0, b_0^1, b_1) &= \mathrm{ratio}(b_1, b_1^1, b_2) \\
&= \mathrm{ratio}(b_0^1, b_0^2, b_1^1) \\
&= u/(1-u)
\end{aligned}
$$

The linear interpolation is affinely invariant, i.e. is invariant with respect to rotation, translation and scaling. The above construction can be fully described by a triangular array of points:

$$
\begin{array}{ccc}
b_0 & & \\
b_1 & b_0^1 & \\
b_2 & b_1^1 & b_0^2
\end{array}
$$

**General case**   Consider points $\boldsymbol{b}_0, \boldsymbol{b}_1, \ldots, \boldsymbol{b}_n \in \mathbb{E}^d$ and $u \in [0, 1]$. Start by setting $\boldsymbol{b}_i^0(u) = \boldsymbol{b}_i$, and compute a succession of interpolations

$$\boldsymbol{b}_i^r(u) = (1 - u)\, \boldsymbol{b}_i^{r-1}(u) + u\, \boldsymbol{b}_{i+1}^{r-1}(u)$$

with $r = 1, \ldots, n$ and with $i = 0, \ldots, n - r$.

It is possible to show that $\boldsymbol{b}_0^n(u)$ will coincide with $\boldsymbol{b}(u)$, i.e. with the point which is the image of the Bézier curve of degree $n$ generated by the control polygon $\boldsymbol{b}_0, \boldsymbol{b}_1, \ldots, \boldsymbol{b}_n$.

### Example 11.3.4 (Cubic de Casteljau scheme)

The triangular array of points used for the generation of a cubic Bézier curve has four rows and four columns. The elements of the first column are the input data, i.e. the original control points. The other columns correspond to algorithm iterations. The element $(4, 4)$ of the array is the point generated on the curve for a given $u$ value, as shown below:

$$
\begin{array}{llll}
\boldsymbol{b}_0 & & & \\
\boldsymbol{b}_1 & \boldsymbol{b}_0^1 & & \\
\boldsymbol{b}_2 & \boldsymbol{b}_1^1 & \boldsymbol{b}_0^2 & \\
\boldsymbol{b}_3 & \boldsymbol{b}_2^1 & \boldsymbol{b}_1^2 & \boldsymbol{b}_0^3
\end{array}
$$

The de Casteljau scheme for a Bézier cubic is given graphically in Figure 11.12.

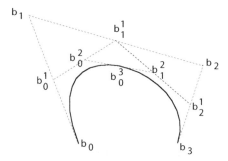

**Figure 11.12**   The de Casteljau algorithm for a Bézier cubic

## 11.4   Rational curves and splines

A rational function is a ratio of polynomial functions. A rational curve is a point-valued function of one real parameter, whose coordinate maps are rational. In particular, the coordinate maps of a rational curve or spline in $\mathbb{E}^d$ can be written as ratios of the coordinate maps of a corresponding polynomial curve in $\mathbb{E}^{d+1}$. For example, for a rational curve in $\mathbb{E}^3$ we have

$$\boldsymbol{Q}(u) = \begin{pmatrix} x(u) & y(u) & z(u) \end{pmatrix}^T,$$

with

$$x(u) = \frac{X(u)}{W(u)}, \quad y(u) = \frac{Y(u)}{W(u)}, \quad z(u) = \frac{Z(u)}{W(u)},$$

where $C(u) = \begin{pmatrix} X(u) & Y(u) & Z(u) & W(u) \end{pmatrix}^T$ is a polynomial curve in homogeneous space. The polynomials in homogeneous space are usually in Bézier or B-spline form, although any kind of curve or spline may be used. Non-uniform rational B-splines are called NURB-splines or simply NURBS.

### 11.4.1   Rational Bézier curves

Rational Bézier curves $Q(u)$ are defined as the projection from the origin on the hyperplane $x_{d+1} = 1$ of a polynomial Bézier curve $C(u)$ in $\mathbb{E}^{d+1}$ homogeneous space. The above hyperplane is easily identified by $\mathbb{E}^d$ by dropping the last coordinate. So, consider

$$C(u) = q_0 B_0^n(u) + \cdots + q_n B_n^n(u),$$

and

$$w(u) = w_0 B_0^n(u) + \cdots + w_n B_n^n(u),$$

where $q_i = (w_i b_i, w_i)^T \in \mathbb{E}^{d+1}$ and $w_i \in \mathbb{R}$. Notice that $b_i \in \mathbb{E}^d$ is the projection of the normalized $q_i$.

It is hence possible to write the rational curve $Q(u)$ of degree $n$, such that $C(u) = (w(u)Q(u), w(u))$, as a combination of control points $b_i \in \mathbb{E}^d$ with rational functions:

$$Q(u) = \sum_{i=0}^n b_i \frac{w_i B_i^n(u)}{w(u)}, \qquad b_i \in \mathbb{E}^d \tag{11.16}$$

The numbers $w_i$ are called *weights* of the control points. When the weights are all unitary, a rational curve coincides with its polynomial counterpart.

From the above it is possible to see that a rational Bézier function is a weighted average of the nonrational basis. It is easy to verify that the rational basis sum to 1 for each $u$. Rational Bézier curves hence continue to satisfy the properties of nonrational ones, i.e. the affine invariance, the variation diminishing and the containment in the convex hull of control points. Furthermore, rational Bézier curves enjoy also the projective invariance property, that makes them very useful for computer graphics.

### Rational Bézier mapping

In the remainder of this section we consider the control points as given in homogeneous space. In particular, for a rational curve in 3D of degree $n$, we have

$$q_i = (X_i, Y_i, Z_i, W_i)^T, \qquad 0 \le i \le n$$

so that we define a mapping $Q : \mathbb{R} \to \mathbb{E}^3$ as

$$Q(u) = \frac{1}{\sum_{i=0}^n W_i B_i^n(u)} \begin{pmatrix} \sum_{i=0}^n X_i B_i^n(u) \\ \sum_{i=0}^n Y_i B_i^n(u) \\ \sum_{i=0}^n Z_i B_i^n(u) \end{pmatrix} = \frac{1}{W \cdot B^n(u)} \begin{pmatrix} X \cdot B^n(u) \\ Y \cdot B^n(u) \\ Z \cdot B^n(u) \end{pmatrix} \tag{11.17}$$

where $\boldsymbol{B}^n(u)$ is a function vector having as a component the $n+1$ Bernstein basis polynomials, and where $\boldsymbol{X}$, $\boldsymbol{Y}$, $\boldsymbol{Z}$ and $\boldsymbol{W}$ are function vectors with $n+1$ constant functions corresponding to the coordinates of control points. So, we have, e.g.

$$\boldsymbol{X} := \big(\ X_i(u) = X_i\ \big), \qquad u \in [0,1],\ 0 \le i \le n.$$

**Implementation**    The PLaSM implementation of equation (11.17) is straightforward. It will suffice to combine, using a function `RationalBlend` given in the following Script 11.4.1, the sequence of basis functions generated by the expression

  `BernsteinBasis:degree`

with the sequence of *homogeneous* ControlPoints, being the **degree** of the curve equal to the number of control points minus one. The `BernsteinBasis` function is defined in Script 11.2.5.

---

**Script 11.4.1 (Rational Bézier curves)**
```
DEF RationalBezier (ControlPoints::IsSeq) =
   RationalBlend:(BernsteinBasis:degree): ControlPoints
WHERE
   degree = LEN:ControlPoints - 1
END
```

---

**Example 11.4.1 (Ellipse as rational Bézier)**
We get an exact representation of the quarter of ellipse as a quadratic rational Bézier curve, described [FP80] by homogeneous control points

$$(a,0,1), \quad \frac{\sqrt{2}}{2}(a,b,1), \quad (0,b,1),$$

where $a$ and $b$ are the two radii. Such an ellipse is generated with the center on the origin, the radius of size $a$ in the direction of the $x$ axis and the radius of size $b$ in the direction of the $y$ axis. In Script 11.4.2 the whole curve is generated by four symmetric instances of a quarter of curve.

 The ellipse quarter is obtained as a mapping of the rational Bézier quadratic on the interval $[0,1]$. The $n$ parameter establishes the number of segments in a polyhedral approximation of the image of curve quarter. The ellipse may be generated as a whole by a quadratic NURB-spline. See Example 11.4.2. The second order function `Intervals`, used to generate a partition of the interval $[0,a]$ with $n$ segments is given in Script 11.2.1.

 The plane ellipse of Figure 11.13a, with radii $\frac{1}{2}$ and 1, respectively, is combined in the last expression above with a 1D polyhedron of length $\frac{1}{2}$, thus generating the elliptical cylinder shown in Figure 11.13b.

---

*11.4.2  NURBS*

Rational non-uniform B-splines are normally denoted as NURB splines or simply as NURBS. These splines are very important for both graphics and CAD applications. In particular:

**Script 11.4.2**

```
DEF ellipse (a,b::IsReal; n::IsINtPos) = STRUCT:< half, S:1:-1, half >
WHERE
    half = STRUCT:< quarter, S:2:-1, quarter >,
    quarter = MAP: mapping: (Intervals:1:n),
    mapping = RationalBezier:<<a,0,1>,<a*c,b*c,c>,<0,b,1>>,
    c = SQRT:2/2
END;

ellipse:<1/2,1,10> * QUOTE:<1/2>
```

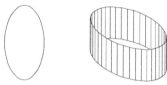

**Figure 11.13**   (a) Ellipse generated as Bézier curve (b) Surface generated by
Cartesian product with an interval

1. Rational curves and splines are invariant with respect to affine and projective transformations. Consequently, to transform or project a NURBS it is sufficient to transform or project its control points, leaving to the graphics hardware the task of sampling or rasterizing the transformed curve.
2. NURBS represent exactly the conic sections, i.e. circles, ellipses, parabolæ, iperbolæ. Such curves are very frequent in mechanical CAD, where several shapes and geometric constructions are based on such geometric primitives.
3. Rational B-splines are very flexible, since (a) the available degrees of freedom concern both degree, control points, knot values and weights; (b) can be locally interpolant or approximant; (c) can alternate spline segments with different degree; and (d) different continuity at join points.
4. They also allow for local variation of "parametrization velocity", or better, allow for modification of the norm of velocity vector along the spline, defined as the derivative of the curve with respect to the arc length. For this purpose it is sufficient to properly modify the knot sequence. This fact allows easy modification of the sampling density of spline points along segments with higher or lower curvature, while maintaining the desired appearance of smoothness.

As a consequence of their usefulness for applications, NURBS are largely available when using geometric libraries or CAD kernels.

### Rational B-splines of arbitrary degree

A rational B-spline segment $R_i(t)$ is defined as the projection from the origin on the hyperplane $x_{d+1} = 1$ of a polynomial B-spline segment $P_i(u)$ in $\mathbb{E}^{d+1}$ homogeneous space.

Using the same approach adopted when discussing rational Bézier curves, where $q_i = (w_i p_i, w_i) \in \mathbb{E}^{d+1}$ are the $m+1$ homogeneous control points, the equation of the rational B-spline segment of degree $k$ with $n + 1$ knots, may be therefore written as

$$R_i(t) = \sum_{\ell=0}^{k} w_{i-\ell} \, p_{i-\ell} \frac{B_{i-\ell,k+1}(t)}{w(t)} = \sum_{\ell=0}^{k} p_{i-\ell} N_{i-\ell,k+1}(t) \qquad (11.18)$$

with $k \leq i \leq m$, $t \in [t_i, t_{i+1})$, and

$$w(t) = \sum_{\ell=0}^{k} w_{i-\ell} B_{i-\ell,k+1}(t),$$

where $N_{i,h}(t)$ is the non-uniform rational B-basis function of initial value $t_i$ and order $h$. A global representation of the NURB spline can be given, due to the local support of the $N_{i,h}(t)$ functions, i.e. to the fact that they are zero outside the interval $[t_i, t_{i+h})$. So:

$$R(t) = \bigcup_{i=k}^{m} R_i(t) = \sum_{i=0}^{m} p_i \, N_{i,h}(t), \qquad t \in [t_k, t_{m+1}).$$

NURB splines can be computed as non-uniform B-splines by using homogeneous control points, and finally by dividing the Cartesian coordinate maps times the homogeneous one. This approach will be used in the NURBS implementation given later in this chapter. A more efficient and numerically stable variation of the Cox and de Boor formula for the rational case is given by Farin [Far88], p. 196.

### Example 11.4.2 (Circumference as quadratic NURBS)
A circumference may be generated exactly as a closed quadratic NURB spline [FP80] with 9 control points, where the last control point is equal to the first one. In this case the knot sequence must have $9 + 2 + 1 = 12$ elements. To guarantee the passage for the extreme control points the first and last knot must have multiplicity 3. Notice that to guarantee the passage for three other control points, three other knots must have multiplicity 2. As a consequence, using integral knots, the curve is globally parametrized on the $[0, 4]$ interval, with each one of the four nondegenerate spline segments parametrized over a unit interval. The `DisplayNURBspline` function is given in Script 11.6.20.

---

**Script 11.4.3 (Circumference)**

```
DEF knots = <0,0,0,1,1,2,2,3,3,4,4,4>;
DEF controlPoints = <
    <-1,0,1>, <-:c,c,c>, <0,1,1>, <c,c,c>,
    <1,0,1>, <c,-:c,c>, <0,-1,1>, <-:c,-:c,c>, <-1,0,1> >
WHERE
    c = SQRT:2/2
END;

DEF MarkerSize = 0.10;
DisplayNURBspline:<<2, knots>, controlPoints>;
```

---

A circumference implementation as a quadratic NURBS is given in Script 11.4.3. The resulting geometry, including a polyline through the control points and two polymarkers through the control and join points, respectively, is shown in Figure 11.14.

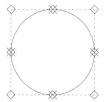

**Figure 11.14**   Circumference generated as a quadratic NURB spline

### Example 11.4.3 (Varying parametrization)

In Script 11.4.4 we vary the number of points sampled on a spline segment, by varying the size of the parameter interval associated with the segment. For this purpose it is sufficient to suitably modify the knot sequence, so that the size of the $[t_i, t_{i+1})$ interval becomes proportional to the number of points sampled on the curve. Let us compare the circumference samples in Figure 11.15. They are respectively produced by:

```
DEF knots = <0,0,0,1,1,2,2,3,3,4,4,4>,
DEF knots = <0,0,0,1,1,2,2,5,5,6,6,6>,
```

Notice that the symbol `splineSampling`, introduced for NURBS in Script 11.6.19, defines the number of sampling subintervals for unit in parameter space of the spline. The `markerSize` and the `markers` operator were defined in Scripts 7.2.8 and 5.1.3, respectively. The `NURBspline` operator will be given in Script 11.6.19.

---

### Script 11.4.4

```
[Polymarker on NURBS circle] DEF markerSize = 0.025;
DEF splineSampling = 6;

(markers ~ NURBspline:<2,knots>): controlPoints;
```

---

**Figure 11.15**   (a) Uniform parametrization of spline segments (b) Triply dense parametrization in the third segment (non-reduced to a single point)

## 11.5   Examples

A quite complex example of shape generation with a NURB spline is presented, and the design of various form features by knot insertion, control point duplication and weight variation is discussed. Then we bring a step further the "umbrella" example already introduced in Section 8.5.15, by substituting some linear rods with curved rods, with a curvature depending on the opening angle.

### 11.5.1   Shape design with a NURB spline

Let us build a NURB spline example in Script 11.5.1 by discussing the shape design of a sort of "shoe". The profile of Figure 11.16 is generated by evaluating the last expression of Script 11.5.1. The control points $p_0, p_1, \ldots, p_{11}$ are 12, and the spline has degree $k = 2$. Therefore the knots must be $12 + 2 + 1 = 15$, i.e $t_0, t_1, \ldots, t_{14}$.

The interpolation of first and last control points is enforced by setting $t_0$ and $t_{14}$ with multiplicity 3. Another interpolation constraint through point $p_4$, i.e. through the "heel tip" of the shoe, is enforced by setting $t_5 = t_6 = 3$. In this way the fourth spline segment $R_5(t)$, $t_5 \le t < t_6$, is reduced to a point. Since at the joints of this segment the continuity is reduced by one unit, and hence from $C^1$ to $C^0$, a sharp-cornered point is obtained.

---

**Script 11.5.1 (NURBS example)**

```
DEF splineSampling = 10;
DEF MarkerSize = 0.15;
DEF homCoord = 1;

DisplayNURBspline: < 2, <0,0,0,1,2,3,3,4,5,6,7,8,9,9,9>,
   < <0,5,1>,<4,5,1>,<5,5,1>,<5,4,1>,<5,0,1>,
    <4,0,1>,<4,3,1>,<2,1,1>,<-1,0,1>,<-6,0,homCoord>, <0,3,1>,<0,5,1> >
>;
```

---

First, remember that the numbering of spline segments $R_i(t)$ goes for $k < i < m$. To understand why $R_5(t_5) = R_5(t_6) = p_4$, i.e. why the 4-th spline segment reduces to the 5-th control point, consider what follows.

By continuity of spline segments, the last point of segment $R_4(t)$ is equal to the first point of segment $R_5(t)$, i.e. $R_4(t_5) = R_5(t_5)$, so that

$$R_5(t_5) \in \text{conv}\,\{p_3, p_4\} = (\text{conv}\,\{p_2, p_3, p_4\} \cap \text{conv}\,\{p_3, p_4, p_5\})$$

Analogously it is $R_5(t_6) = R_6(t_6)$, so that

$$R_6(t_6) \in \text{conv}\,\{p_4, p_5\} = (\text{conv}\,\{p_3, p_4, p_5\} \cap \text{conv}\,\{p_4, p_5, p_6\}).$$

As a consequence of $t_5 = t_6$ we have:

$$R_5(t_5) = R_5(t_6) \in (\text{conv}\,\{p_3, p_4\} \cap \text{conv}\,\{p_4, p_5\}) = \{p_4\}.$$

Summarizing: the spline segment $R_5(t)$, $t_5 \le t < t_6$, reduced to a single point when $t_5 = t_6$, must coincide with the control point $p_4$. This effect is achieved by simply duplicating a knot value. More in general: by raising the multiplicity of a knot, the spline is attracted towards an internal control point. This is interpolated when the knot multiplicity equals the degree. A multiplicity equal to the order is needed to interpolate the extreme control points.

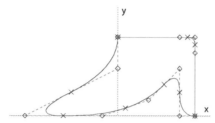

**Figure 11.16**   Quadratic NURB spline generated by 12 control points and by a suitable knot sequence

Also consider the segments $R_2(t)$ and $R_4(t)$ on the top and right of the shape, respectively, as generated by two *aligned* triples of control points. Since $R_2(t) \subset$ conv $\{p_0, p_1, p_2\}$ and $R_4(t) \subset$ conv $\{p_2, p_3, p_4\}$, they must necessarily be line segments.

**Example 11.5.1 (Attraction towards a control point)**
In Example 11.5.1 all the control points had unit $w_i$ weight. When a control point is edited from $p_i = (x_i, y_i, 1)$ to $q_i = (x_i, y_i, w_i)$, it is actually changed to $q_i = (\frac{x_i}{w_i}, \frac{y_i}{w_i}, 1)$.

The geometric effect of this editing on the homogeneous coordinate of a control point is shown in Figure 11.17, generated by Script 11.5.1 when to the homCoord parameter are assigned values $\frac{1}{2}, 1, 2$. Such weights produce the long, medium and short "shoe", respectively.

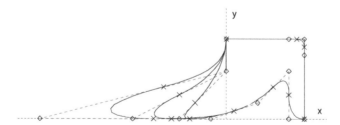

**Figure 11.17**   Three NURB splines that differ for the weights of a control point

**Points and knots insertion**   When editing a NURB spline it is often necessary to insert a new control point and a new knot without modifying the spline shape, in order to introduce some further degree of freedom in local editing of the shape.

This insertion is easily obtained, in a quadratic NURBS, by adding a new point corresponding to the middle point of a segment of the control polygon, and by doubling the corresponding knot value. Actually, this one is not a good way to add a new knot, as it affects the continuity by introducing a degenerate spline segment. A much better method is the Oslo algorithm [CLR80], or Boehm's method [Böh80]. Notice that, because the reelation between numbers of knots and control points must continue to hold, when a new knot is inserted, one more control point is generated. Actually, adding a knot causes two old control points to be replaced by three new control points.

### 11.5.2  Umbrella modeling (2): curved rods

We start in this section the step-wise refinement of the geometric modeling of a simplified umbrella already introduced in Section 8.5.3. In particular, the function RodPair is here redefined so that the previous Rod1 component is split into two components Rod10 and Rod11, where Rod11 is generated as a 1D polyhedral approximation with 4 segments of a quadratic Bézier curve. This one is tangent at the join point with Rod10 for every opening angle. The Bezier mapping generating operator is defined in Script 11.2.5. The definition of the Intervals function is given in Script 11.2.1. To fully understand the meaning of the RodCurve function, the reader should compare the code below with Script 8.5.14.

---

**Script 11.5.2 (Umbrella (2))**

```
DEF RodCurve (len,beta,n::IsReal) = MAP:
   (Bezier:<<0,0,0>,<0,0,len/2>,<len/2 * sin:beta,0,len>>):
      (Intervals:1:n);

DEF RodPair (h, alpha::Isreal) = STRUCT:<
   T:3:h, R:<3,1>:(-:alphaRad), Rod10, T:3:(-:AB): Rod11,
   T:3:(-:AB), R:<3,1>:(2*alphaRad), Rod2 >
WHERE
   alphaRad = alpha*PI/180,
   Rod10 = S:3:-1:(Rod:(AB)),
   Rod11 = S:3:-1:(RodCurve:<AB,-:alphaRad/4,4>),
   Rod2 = S:3:-1:(Rod:AB),
   AB = h*4/10
END;
```

---

Two different values of the geometric object resulting from the evaluation of the umbrella function for two different angles are shown in Figure 11.18. Notice that this function is defined in Script 8.5.15.

### 11.6  Splines implementation

The PLaSM language allows for fast prototyping of parametric curves and splines, for two main reasons.

1. First, since it allows the easy combination with algebraic operators of numbers, points and functions. As the reader knows, a parametric curve is a linear combination of polynomials with control points or vectors.
2. Second, the implementation of parametric curves may be based on the primitive operator MAP. For this purpose we only need to define a vector function of a real parameter, which is represented exactly, i.e. symbolically, by PLaSM, and a suitable decomposition of the spline domain. A polyhedral

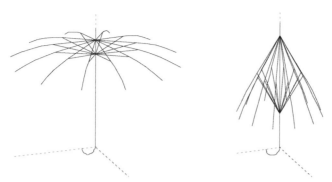

**Figure 11.18**   New values of `umbrella:<10,80>` and `umbrella:<10,30>` after the redefinition of the function `RodPair`

approximation of the curve image is thus automatically generated, based on a sampling of the curve points.

Indeed, the conceptual elegance of this approach has a trade-off in terms of computational costs. The evaluation of a spline in a functional environment, where the coordinate maps are computed by using algebraic operators in functional spaces, although closer to the mathematical definition of the spline itself, certainly requires higher computation times than its evaluation using imperative languages.

Conversely, the higher evaluation time in a functional environment has a positive revenue in terms of compactness, robustness and readability of the functional code. In particular, the authors believe that the proposed approach may be useful both to teach and fully understand the underlying mathematics of parametric geometry, and to quickly prototype new shape generation tools, as we show in next chapters.

### 11.6.1   *Cubic uniform splines*

A `PLaSM` implementation of cubic *cardinal splines* (see Section 11.3.1) and cubic *uniform B-splines* (see Section 11.3.2) is discussed in this section. As usual, our approach is dimension-independent, in order to generate spline images in arbitrary $\mathbb{E}^d$ space. Splines are more often used in 2D or 3D, but higher dimensional splines may be of great interest in some applications, e.g. in robotics, to model a motion as a curve in configuration space.

The design of the `PLaSM` code given in Script 11.6.1 has the specific aim of unifying the evaluation of cubic uniform splines, both cardinal and B-splines. In particular, the `domain` symbol contains a partition of the interval $[0,1]$ with a `splineSampling` number of subintervals, so that each spline segment is polyhedrally approximated with that number of linear segments. To modify the approximation precision it will suffice to redefine that parameter.

The `Blend` function is used to linearly combine a sequence of basis polynomials with a sequence of control points, thus generating the sequence of coordinate maps associated with a spline segment. The `CubicCardinal` and `CubicUBspline` functions generate a segment image, and are used as partial functions in the implementation of the `Spline` operator given in Script 11.6.2.

Script 11.6.2 defines two sequences of basis polynomials, named `CubicCardinalBasis`

**Script 11.6.1 (Cardinal and uniform B-spline maps)**

```
DEF splineSampling = 20;
DEF domain = (Intervals:1:splineSampling);

DEF Blend (Basis::IsSeq) (ControlPoints::IsSeq) =
    (AA:innerProd ~ DISTL):
        < Basis, (AA:(AA:K) ~ TRANS):ControlPoints >;

DEF CubicCardinal (domain::IsPol) (q1,q2,q3,q4::IsSeq) =
    MAP:(CONS:(Blend:CubicCardinalBasis:<q1,q2,q3,q4>)):domain;

DEF CubicUBspline (domain::IsPol) (q1,q2,q3,q4::IsSeq) =
    MAP:(CONS:(Blend:CubicUBsplineBasis:<q1,q2,q3,q4>)):domain;
```

and CubicUBsplineBasis, respectively. In both cases the arithmetics is strictly functional, so that all the sub-expressions produce a function. For this purpose it is necessary to convert each scalar coefficient of basis polynomials into a constant function.

---

**Script 11.6.2 (Cubic cardinal and uniform B-spline splines)**

```
DEF CubicCardinalBasis = < C0,C1,C2,C3 >
WHERE
    C0 = ((k:0 - a) * u3) + ((k:2 * a) * u2) - (a * u),
    C1 = ((k:2 - a) * u3) + ((a - k:3) * u2) + (k:1),
    C2 = ((a - k:2) * u3) + ((k:3 - k:2 * a) * u2) + (a * u),
    C3 = (a * u3) - (a * u2),
    u = s1, u2 = u * u, u3 = u2 * u, a = k:1
END;

DEF CubicUBsplineBasis = < B0,B1,B2,B3 >
WHERE
    B0 = a * ((k:3 * u2) - (k:1 * u3) - (k:3 * u) + (k:1)),
    B1 = a * ((k:3 * u3) - (k:6 * u2) + (k:4)),
    B2 = a * ((k:3 * u2) - (k:3 * u3) + (k:3 * u) + (k:1)),
    B3 = a * u3,
    u = s1, u2 = u * u, u3 = u2 * u, a = k:1/k:6
END;

DEF Spline (Curve::IsFun) = STRUCT ~ AA:Curve ~ subsets:4

DEF geometryVector =
<<-3,6>,<-4,2>,<-3,-1>,<-1,1>,<1.5,1.5>,<3,4>,<5,5>,<7,2>,<6,-2>,<2,-3>>;

Spline:(CubicUBspline:domain):geometryVector;
```

---

The Spline function given above has the purpose of generating a polyhedral approximation of a spline image, as the STRUCT aggregation of the $(1, d)$-polyhedra generated by the Curve vector function applied to all subsets of control points of length 4. Notice that Curve is the formal parameter of the Spline function, and is applied to all point quadruples generated by the subsets:4 function, in turn applied, at run time, to a control point sequence.[6] The definition of the `subsets` operator is given in Script 11.6.11.

**Computation and drawing of joints** In Script 11.6.3 we compute the join points between spline segments. The approach used may look interesting:

1. the `knotzero` symbol is loaded with the $(0,1)$-complex made by the single point $(0) \in \mathbb{E}$;
2. `knotzero` is used as domain of the formal parameter `TheSpline`;
3. the desired spline (ether `CubicCardinal` or `CubicUBspline`) is passed as actual argument of the `Joints` function; so that the expression `Spline:(TheSpline:knotzero)` computes the $(0,d)$-complex

$$\{Q_i(0)|1 \le i \le m-2\};$$

4. the internal data structure representing this complex is "unpacked" by the `UKPOL` primitive;
5. its vertices, i.e. the join points, are passed to the `polymarker:2` function.

---

**Script 11.6.3**

```
DEF knotzero = MKPOL:<<<0>>,<<1>>,<<1>>>;

DEF Joints (TheSpline::IsFun) =
    polymarker:2 ~ S1 ~ UKPOL ~ Spline:(TheSpline:knotzero);

Joints:CubicUBSpline:geometryVector;
```

---

The `Joints` function is used with a double application, as in Script 11.6.3.

**Display function** In Script 11.6.4 a function `DisplayAll` is given as user interface for uniform splines. It draws at the same time the spline, the control polygon and two polymarkers, respectively corresponding to control points and to the join point between spline segments.

Let us evaluate the last expression of the script. The generated geometric value is shown in Figure 11.19a. The reader might note that such a geometric result is too "bumped" when using as tangent vectors in $p_i$ the $s_i = p_{i+1} - p_{i-1}$ differences. In Figure 11.19b is shown the cubic cardinal spline generated with extreme tangents $s_i = \frac{1}{2}(p_{i+1} - p_{i-1})$. The `geometryVector` is the one given in Script 11.6.2. Notice that in a cardinal spline the joints coincide with the (internal) control points.

**Interpolation of extreme points** As we know, a cardinal spline is not defined at the extreme control points, and the uniform B-spline normally passes for none of control points. To force the passage for $p_0$ and $p_m$ it is necessary to set their multiplicity to 2 in case of cardinal, and to 3 for uniform cubic B-spline.

---

[6] A mixed programming approach is used here, with both a formal parameter in $\lambda$-style, and an implicit parameter, in proper FL-style.

**Script 11.6.4**

```
DEF DisplayAll (MySpline::IsFun)(points::IsSeq) = (STRUCT ~ [
    Spline:(MySpline:domain),
    Joints:MySpline,
    polyline,
    polymarker:1
]): points;

DisplayAll:CubicCardinal:geometryVector;
```

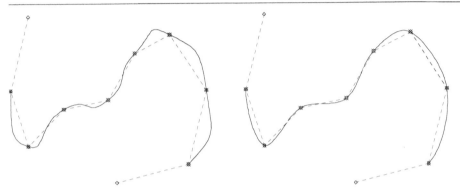

**Figure 11.19**  (a) Cubic cardinal spline with scalar $h = 1$ multiplying tangents at control points (b) Same spline with $h = \frac{1}{2}$

Therefore, in Script 11.6.5 we give a MultipleExtremes function which does the job. The two geometries generated by last expressions of the script are shown in Figure 11.20.

---

**Script 11.6.5**

```
DEF MultipleExtremes (multiplicity::IsIntPos) =
    CAT ~ [ Firsts, ID, Lasts ]
WHERE
    Firsts = #:(multiplicity - 1) ~ FIRST,
    Lasts = #:(multiplicity - 1) ~ LAST
END;

DEF geometryVector = <<3,0>,<6,0>,<7,3>,<6,6>,<3,7>,<0,6>,<0,3>>;
DisplayAll:CubicCardinal: (MultipleExtremes:2:geometryVector);
DisplayAll:CubicUBSpline: (MultipleExtremes:3:geometryVector);
```

---

**Example 11.6.1 (Closed cubic uniform B-spline)**
Two adjacent spline segments $Q_i(t)$ and $Q_{i+1}(t)$ share three common control points. So, to enforce a $C^2$-continuity between the first and last segments $Q_3(t)$ and $Q_m(t)$ of a cubic B-spline it is sufficient to set the first three points equal to the last three, i.e. , to require:

$$p_0 = p_{m-3}, \qquad p_1 = p_{m-2}, \qquad p_2 = p_{m-1}.$$

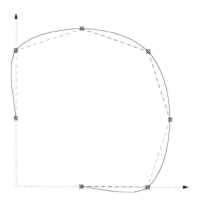

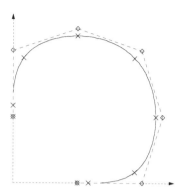

**Figure 11.20**    Interpolation of extreme control points: (a) cubic cardinal (b) cubic
uniform B-spline. Notice the presence of linear segments

The generated spline is shown in Figure 11.21a.

```
DisplayAll:CubicUBSpline:
   <<1,-1>,<-1,2>,<1,4>, <2,3>,<0,0>,<2.5,1>,<3,-1>, <1,-1>,<-1,2>,<1,4>>;
```

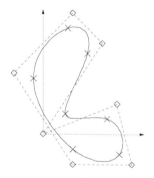

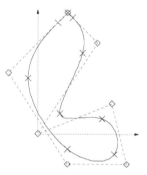

**Figure 11.21**    (a) Closed cubic uniform B-spline (b) Interpolation of a control
point

## Example 11.6.2 (Interpolation of a control point)

Consider the closed cubic uniform B-spline of the previous example, and enforce a
constraint of interpolation of an internal control point, e.g. $p_2$. This interpolation
is achieved by triplicating the point. Therefore, two new spline segments are created
(one for each new point instance). Since (a) both segments are generated by the triplet
point and by another point, and (b) they must be contained in the convex hull of their
control points, then it follows that they are line segments. A discontinuity on the
second derivative hence arises at their joints.

```
DisplayAll:CubicUBSpline:<<1,-1>,<-1,2>, <1,4>,<1,4>,<1,4>, <2,3>,
   <0,0>,<2.5,1>,<3,-1>, <1,-1>,<-1,2>,<1,4>>;
```

The generated spline is shown in Figure 11.21b.

## 11.6.2   Non-uniform B-splines

In this section we discuss a possible PLaSM implementation of non-uniform polynomial B-splines. In particular, we first approach the Cox and de Boor formula (11.14) for computation of B-basis functions up to order 4, then we abstract such implementation to B-bases of arbitrary order. Finally, the combinatorial power of a FL-like programming environment is exploited to combine control points and basis functions.

### Basis functions up to order 4

We start by giving explicit versions of Cox and de Boor recursive formula for orders $1, 2, 3$ and $4$. The implementation of such non-recursive approach will give the insight needed for a recursive implementation of arbitrary order. The explicit formulas to compute $B_{i,h}(t)$, with $1 \leq h \leq 4$, follow:

$$B_{i,1}(t) = \begin{cases} 1, & \text{if } t_i \leq t \leq t_{i+1} \\ 0, & \text{otherwise,} \end{cases}$$

$$B_{i,2}(t) = \frac{t - t_i}{t_{i+1} - t_i} B_{i,1}(t) + \frac{t_{i+2} - t}{t_{i+2} - t_{i+1}} B_{i+1,1}(t)$$

$$B_{i,3}(t) = \frac{t - t_i}{t_{i+2} - t_i} B_{i,2}(t) + \frac{t_{i+3} - t}{t_{i+3} - t_{i+1}} B_{i+1,2}(t)$$

$$B_{i,4}(t) = \frac{t - t_i}{t_{i+3} - t_i} B_{i,3}(t) + \frac{t_{i+4} - t}{t_{i+4} - t_{i+1}} B_{i+1,3}(t)$$

In Script 11.6.6 four B-basis functions respectively denoted Bi1, Bi2, Bi3 and Bi4 are given. To each $B_{i,h}$ implementation is associated as formal parameter the subsequence $(t_i, \ldots, t_{i+h})$ of knots it depends on. In particular, the $t_i, t_{i+1}, t_{i+2}, t_{i+3}, t_{i+4}$ parameters are denoted as ti0,ti1,ti2,ti3,ti4, respectively. The division is operated by a special-purpose myDiv operator, since we need to manage the division by zero, that arises when knots have a multiplicity greater then one.

**Special division**   An *ad hoc* functional division operator MyDiv is given in Script 11.6.7. In particular, MyDiv is applied to $a$ and $b$ parameters, where $a$ is a function and $b = (b_1, b_2)$ is a pair of numbers, applying the following rules when the denominator $\underline{b_1} - \underline{b_2}$ is zero: $a/\underline{0} = \underline{0}$ if $a \neq \underline{0}$, else $\underline{0}/\underline{0} = \underline{1}$.

### Example 11.6.3

The implementation of $B_{i,h}$ as a mapping $\mathbb{R} \to \mathbb{R}$ in Script 11.6.6 allows one to MAP each generated mapping over a polyhedral decomposition of the parameter interval. For this purpose it must be applied to domain points given as *sequences* of coordinates, actually with only one coordinate. So, we may write:

```
Bi4:< 0,0,1,2,2 > ≡ An-Anonymous-Function
Bi4:< 0,0,1,2,2 >:< 1.5 > ≡ 0.25
```

**Script 11.6.6**

```
DEF Bi1 (ti0,ti1::IsReal) =
   IF:< AND ~ [GE:ti0 ~ S1,LT:ti1 ~ S1], K:1, K:0 >;

DEF Bi2 (ti0,ti1,ti2::IsReal) =
   (((S1 - K:ti0) MyDiv <ti1,ti0>) * Bi1:<ti0,ti1>) +
   (((K:ti2 - S1) MyDiv <ti2,ti1>) * Bi1:<ti1,ti2>);

DEF Bi3 (ti0,ti1,ti2,ti3::IsReal) =
   (((S1 - K:ti0) MyDiv <ti2,ti0>) * Bi2:<ti0,ti1,ti2>) +
   (((K:ti3 - S1) MyDiv <ti3,ti1>) * Bi2:<ti1,ti2,ti3>);

DEF Bi4 (ti0,ti1,ti2,ti3,ti4::IsReal) =
   (((S1 - K:ti0) MyDiv <ti3,ti0>) * Bi3:<ti0,ti1,ti2,ti3>) +
   (((K:ti4 - S1) MyDiv <ti4,ti1>) * Bi3:<ti1,ti2,ti3,ti4>);
```

**Script 11.6.7**

```
DEF MyDiv (a::IsFun; b::IsSeq) =
   IF:< EQ ~ [s1,s2], StrangeValues, K:(a/c) >:b
WHERE
   StrangeValues = filter ~ a,  % precondition a/0        %
   filter =                     % if a = 0 then 1 else 0 %
      IF:<testOnZero, (K ~ K):1, (K ~ K):0>,
   testOnZero = (LT:precision) ~ (ABS ~ - ~ [ID,K:0]),
   precision = 1E-12,
   c = (K ~ -):b
END;
```

**Basis functions of arbitrary order**

Recursive formula (11.14) is implemented in Script 11.6.8 as a function named DeBoor, with a formal parameter knots which is a subsequence of knot values. The DeBoor function recognizes the basic case of order 1 from the length 2 of the input sequence. In such case a step function of constant value 1 is generated in the parameter interval, and 0 outside. Formula (11.14) is directly implemented for the recursive case.

**Example 11.6.4 (Linear and quadratics B-basis functions)**
We show in this example some non-uniform B-basis functions of order 2 and 3, i.e. of first and second degree, generated by the knot sequence $(0, 0, 0, 1, 2, 3, 4, 5, 5, 5)$. The domain of B-basis functions up to degree 2 generated by this knot sequence is $[0, 5]$. The graphs given in Figure 11.22 are generated by mapping these functions over a domain partition into 100 subintervals.

Let us first derive the second-order B-basis functions $B_{5,2}$ and $B_{6,2}$. The first one is generated by knot subsequence $(t_5, t_6, t_7) = (3, 4, 5)$; the second one by subsequence $(t_6, t_7, t_8) = (4, 5, 5)$. Their graphs (together with those of their first-order generating functions) are given in Figure 11.22a. The generating expressions of the graphs are given in Script 11.6.9.

In Figure 11.22b we show the graphs of third-order B-basis functions $B_{4,3}$, $B_{5,3}$ and $B_{6,3}$, together with those of their second-order generating maps. In particular, $B_{4,3}$

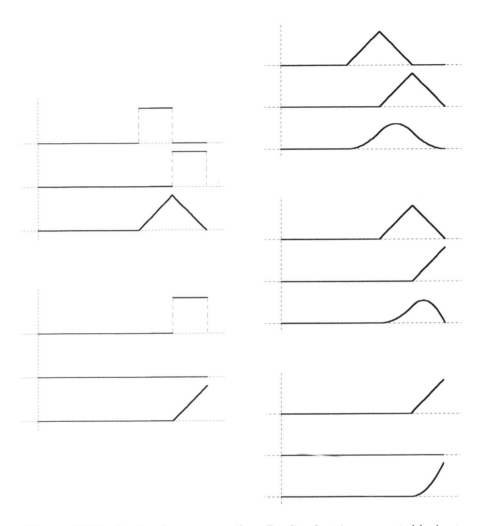

**Figure 11.22**   Graphs of some non-uniform B-spline functions generated by knot sequence $(0, 0, 0, 1, 2, 3, 4, 5, 5, 5)$. (a) Right, from top to bottom: graphs of $B_{5,1}(t)$, $B_{6,1}(t)$ and of $B_{5,2}(t)$ generated by them; graphs of $B_{6,1}(t)$, $B_{7,1}(t)$ and of $B_{6,2}(t)$ derived from them. (b) Left, from top to bottom: graphs of $B_{4,2}(t)$, $B_{5,2}(t)$ and of the generated $B_{4,3}(t)$; graphs of $B_{5,2}(t)$, $B_{6,2}(t)$ and of the generated $B_{5,3}(t)$; functions $B_{6,2}(t)$, $B_{7,2}(t)$ and $B_{6,3}(t)$ derived from them.

**Script 11.6.8**

```
DEF DeBoor (knots::IsSeqOf:IsReal) =
    IF:< C:EQ:2 ~ LEN, basicCase, recursiveCase >:knots
WHERE
    ui0 = S1:knots,
    ui1 = S2:knots,
    ui3 = (LAST ~ leftKnots):knots,
    ui4 = LAST:knots, u = S1,
    rightKnots = TAIL,
    leftKnots = REVERSE ~ TAIL ~ REVERSE,
    basicCase = K:(IF:<AND ~ [GE:ui0 ~ S1, LT:ui1 ~ S1], K:1, K:0>),
    recursiveCase = + ~ [
        K:((u - K:ui0) MyDiv <ui3, ui0>) RAISE:* (DeBoor ~ leftKnots),
        K:((K:ui4 - u) MyDiv <ui4, ui1>) RAISE:* (DeBoor ~ rightKnots)
    ]
END;
```

**Script 11.6.9**

```
DEF domain = Intervals:5:100;
STRUCT:<
    MAP:[s1,DeBoor:<3,4>]:domain, T:2:-1.25,
    MAP:[s1,DeBoor:<4,5>]:domain, T:2:-1.25,
    MAP:[s1,DeBoor:<3,4,5>]:domain >;
STRUCT:<
    MAP:[s1,DeBoor:<4,5>]:domain, T:2:-1.25,
    MAP:[s1,DeBoor:<5,5>]:domain, T:2:-1.25,
    MAP:[s1,DeBoor:<4,5,5>]:domain >;
```

is generated by the knot subsequence $(t_4, t_5, t_6, t_7) = (2, 3, 4, 5)$. $B_{5,3}$ corresponds to $(t_5, t_6, t_7, t_8) = (3, 4, 5, 5)$; $B_{6,3}$ is produced starting from $(t_6, t_7, t_8, t_9) = (4, 5, 5, 5)$. The generating expressions are in Script 11.6.10.

**Subsequences** In Script 11.6.11 a subsets operator is defined that, starting from every seq sequence, returns the set of subsequences of length h.

### Non-uniform B-basis of arbitrary order

The function BsplineBasis in Script 11.6.12 returns the set of basis functions $\{B_{i,h}(t)\}$, $0 \le i \le m$ for arbitrary order and knots sequence.

### Example 11.6.5 (Graphs of B-spline basis)

Let us build the graphs of B-bases of orders 3 (quadratics) and 2 (linear) generated by the $(0, 0, 0, 1, 2, 3, 4, 5, 5, 5)$ knot sequence, by evaluating the PLaSM code in Script 11.6.13. Notice that two B-basis functions of order 2 on the given knot sequence are identically zero.

**Script 11.6.10**

```
STRUCT:<
   MAP:[s1,DeBoor:<2,3,4>]:domain, T:2:-1.25,
   MAP:[s1,DeBoor:<3,4,5>]:domain, T:2:-1.25,
   MAP:[s1,DeBoor:<2,3,4,5>]:domain >;
STRUCT:<
   MAP:[s1,DeBoor:<3,4,5>]:domain, T:2:-1.25,
   MAP:[s1,DeBoor:<4,5,5>]:domain, T:2:-1.25,
   MAP:[s1,DeBoor:<3,4,5,5>]:domain >;
STRUCT:<
   MAP:[s1,DeBoor:<4,5,5>]:domain, T:2:-1.25,
   MAP:[s1,DeBoor:<5,5,5>]:domain, T:2:-1.25,
   MAP:[s1,DeBoor:<4,5,5,5>]:domain >;
```

**Script 11.6.11 (Subsequences)**

```
DEF subsets (h::IsIntPos)(seq::IsSeq) =
   (CONS ~ AA:(AS:SEL ~ FROMTO ~ [ID - K:h + K:1,ID])):(h..LEN:seq):seq;

subsets:5:<0,0,0,1,1,2,2,3,3,3> ≡ <<0,0,0,1,1>,<0,0,1,1,2>,
   <0,1,1,2,2>,<1,1,2,2,3>,<1,2,2,3,3>,<2,2,3,3,3>>
```

**Programming interface**

In this section we discuss the programming interface to non-uniform B-splines of arbitrary order. In particular, we give in Script 11.6.14 the function `Bspline`, which is the kernel of the implementation, and some user-callable functions. The `Bspline` function is a good summary of the theory discussed in the above sections. We illustrate its behavior by discussing the meaning of the symbols, both formal parameters and local functions, in its functional environment.

`points` is the sequence of control points $p_0, \ldots, p_m$;

`knots` is the knot sequence $t_0, \ldots, t_n$;

`degree` is the spline degree $k$. No check is performed to enforce the constraint $n = m + k + 1$, which is left to the user. This choice seems preferable to requiring the only input of control points and knots sequences;

`dom` is a polyhedrally-type parameter, usually a suitable partition of the interval $[0, 1]$, which is affinely transformed to provide the domain for the mapping of each spline segment;

`order` is the spline order $h = k + 1$;

`basis` is the non-uniform B-spline basis $\{B_{i,h}(t)\}$ of order $h$, $0 \le i \le m$. It is generated by invoking the `BsplineBasis` function;

**Script 11.6.12 (Non-uniform B-spline basis)**

```
DEF BsplineBasis (order::IsInt) (knots::IsSeqOf:IsReal) =
   (AA:DeBoor ~ subsets:(order+1)): knots;
```

**Script 11.6.13 (Graphs of quadratic and linear B-bases)**

```
DEF domain = Intervals:5:100;

(STRUCT ~ (CONS ~ AA:(MAP ~ CONS) ~ DISTL):
  <s1,BsplineBasis:3:<0,0,0,1,2,3,4,5,5,5>>):domain

(STRUCT ~ (CONS ~ AA:(MAP ~ CONS) ~ DISTL):
  <s1,BsplineBasis:2:<0,0,0,1,2,3,4,5,5,5>>):domain
```

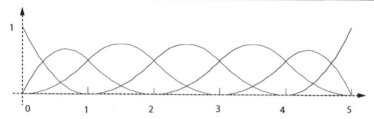

**Figure 11.23** B-spline basis functions of order 3 (quadratics) on the $(0,0,0,1,2,3,4,5,5,5)$ knot sequence

segments contains the sequence of polyhedral approximations of spline segments $Q_i(t)$, $t_i \leq t \leq t_{i+1}$, $k \leq i \leq m$. It is generated starting from a triplet of sequences. This triplet contains $m - k + 1$ copies of the MAP operator, $m - k + 1$ vector functions of one parameter (curves) stored in segmentmaps, and $m - k + 1$ polyhedral domains the curves must be applied on, stored in the poldoms sequence. This triplet of sequences is transposed into a sequence of triples; then the ones non-degenerating into a single point (when $t_i = t_{i+1}$) are selected and evaluated;

segmentmaps is the sequence of point-valued functions $Q_i : \mathbb{R} \to \mathbb{E}^d$ used to generate the spline segments. Each $Q_i$ is generated as product

$$\left( B_{i-k,h} \quad \cdots \quad B_{i,h} \right)\left( p_{i-k} \quad \cdots \quad p_i \right)^T.$$

by the Blend function given in Script 11.6.1. In particular, such sequence of maps is generated by transposing the <basis, points> pair, then by generating all the ordered subsets of order length, and finally by Blending all the generated pairs of subsets;

domain contains the subset of knots $(t_k, \ldots, t_{m+1})$. Externally to its extreme values, the spline is not defined;

subdomains is the sequence of all adjacent pairs of knots extracted from the spline domain, i.e. $((t_k, t_{k+1}), (t_{k+1}, t_{k+2}), \ldots, (t_m, t_{m+1}))$.

poldoms is the sequence of polyhedral domains generated by scaling the dom object with parameter $t_{i+1} - t_i$, and by translating with parameter $t_i$, for each pair in subdomains;

non-empty is a PLaSM function that, applied to a set pairs, returns as output a filter function that, when applied to another sequence of the same length,

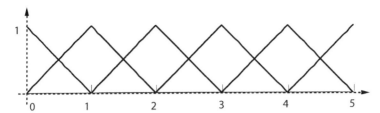

**Figure 11.24**  B-spline basis functions of order 2 (linear) on the
$(0, 0, 0, 1, 2, 3, 4, 5, 5, 5)$ knot sequence

returns the ordered subset corresponding to positions where the former
pair has no coincident elements;

nondegenerate is the filter function returned by the non-empty:subdomains
expression. It is used to filter out, i.e. to not compute the spline segments
reducing to a point, which otherwise would be produced in vain with a
multiplicity equal to the number of point samples in the segment domain.
We remember that a degenerate segment is produced by each pair of equal
subsequent knots in subdomains.

The intervals and knotzero function are given in Scripts 11.2.1 and 11.6.3,
respectively. Finally, NUBspline and NUBsplineJoints are two partial functions
derived from Bspline.

---

**Script 11.6.14**

```
DEF splineSampling = 10;
DEF NUBspline = Bspline:(intervals:1:splineSampling);
DEF NUBsplineJoints = Bspline:Knotzero;

DEF Bspline (dom::Ispol)(degree::Isint)(knots::IsSeq)(points::IsSeq) =
   STRUCT:segments
WHERE
   order = degree + 1,
   basis = BsplineBasis:order:knots,
   segments = (AA:(INSL:APPLY) ~ nondegenerate ~ TRANS):
      < #:(LEN:segmentmaps):MAP, segmentmaps, poldoms >
   segmentmaps = (AA:(INSL:APPLY ~ AL) ~ DISTL):
      < CONS ~ Blend, (AA:TRANS ~ subsets:order ~ TRANS):< basis, points >>,
   domain = AS:SEL:(order..(LEN:points+1)): knots,
   subdomains = subsets:2:domain,
   poldoms = AA:(STRUCT ~ [T:1~S1, S:1~(S2 - S1), K:dom]):subdomains,
   non-empty = AS:SEL ~ CAT ~ AA:(IF:< EQ~S1, K:<>, [S2] >)
      ~ TRANS ~ [ID,INTSTO ~ LEN],
   nondegenerate = non-empty: subdomains,
END;
```

---

**Display function**  A non-uniform B-spline may be displayed by using the
DisplayNUBspline function given in Script 11.6.15. The generated geometry contains

the spline, its control polygon and two polymarkers, marking both the control points and the join points among spline segments.

---

**Script 11.6.15**

```
DEF DisplayNUBspline (degree::Isint; knots::IsSeq ; points::IsSeq ) =
(STRUCT ~ [
   IF:< K:(GT:0:degree), NUBspline:degree:knots, polymarker:3 >,
   polymarker:2 ~ S1 ~ UKPOL ~ NUBsplineJoints:degree:knots ,
   polyline,
   polymarker:1
]): points;
```

---

**Example 11.6.6 (Nonuniform B-splines)**
An example of quadratic non-uniform B-spline in $\mathbb{E}^3$ is given below. The generated curve is shown in Figure 11.25. Notice that control `points` may be defined as a finite subset of $\mathbb{E}^d$, with arbitrary $d$.

```
DEF points = <<0.1,0>,<2,0>,<6,1.5>,<6,4>,<2,5.5>,<2,6>,<3.5,6.5>>;
DEF out = DisplayNUBspline:<2, <0,0,0,1,2,3,4,5,5,5>, points >;
SVG:out:10:'out.svg';
```

**Figure 11.25**   Non-uniform quadratic B-spline in $\mathbb{E}^2$

---

**Example 11.6.7 (Degree raising)**
We show in Figure 11.26 four non-uniform B-splines of different degrees defined by the same control polygon, generated by Script 11.6.16. It is required that all the splines interpolate the extreme control points.

Notice that the quadratic spline is tangent to the control polygon in the Meanpoint of each segment, but in the extreme segments. It can be shown (see Farin [Far88]) that such a spline, defined over knot intervals of size either 0 or 1, is a sequence of quadratics Bézier curves defined by a control polygon of type

$$\ldots, \boldsymbol{p}_i, \frac{\boldsymbol{p}_i + \boldsymbol{p}_{i+1}}{2}, \boldsymbol{p}_{i+1}, \ldots$$

**Script 11.6.16**

```
DEF MarkerSize = 0.15;
DEF points = <<0,0>,<-1,2>,<1,4>,<2,3>,<1,1>,<1,2>,<2.5,1>>;

DEF out = STRUCT:<
   DisplayNUBspline:< 0,<0,1,2,3,4,5,6,7>, points >, T:1:4,
   DisplayNUBspline:< 1,<0,0,1,2,3,4,5,6,6>, points >, T:1:4,
   DisplayNUBspline:< 2,<0,0,0,1,2,3,4,5,5,5>, points >, T:1:4,
   DisplayNUBspline:< 3,<0,0,0,0,1,2,3,4,4,4,4>, points >
>;
```

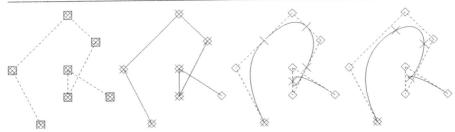

**Figure 11.26**   Non-uniform B-splines of degree $0, 1, 2$ with 7 points. Notice the reduction of number of segments $(6, 5, 4,$ respectively$)$ while raising the degree

**Example 11.6.8 (Continuity reduction at joints)**
We give finally an example of continuity reduction at a joint by reducing the multiplicity of a knot value. Let us use the same control `points` sequence defined in Example 11.6.7. It results that two adjacent B-spline segments of degree $k$ are $C^{k-r}$ at the image of a knot with $r$ multiplicity, as shown in Figure 11.27.

```
DisplayNUBspline:< <2,<0,0,0,1,2,3,4,5,5,5>>, points >;
DisplayNUBspline:< <2,<0,0,0,1,1,2,3,4,4,4>>, points >;
DisplayNUBspline:< <2,<0,0,0,1,1,1,2,3,3,3>>, points >;
```

*11.6.3   Non-uniform rational B-splines*

In this last section we quickly discuss a straightforward PLaSM implementation of NURB splines. As always, our approach is dimension-independent, so that the given operators may be applied to homogeneous control points with $d + 1$ coordinates, with

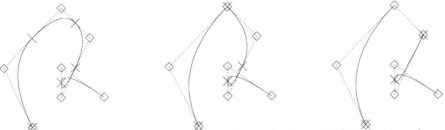

**Figure 11.27**   Non-uniform B-splines of degree 2 with multiplicity raising of a knot. Notice that the number of non-degenerate segments decreases

arbitrary $d$, so getting splines of dimension $(1, d)$. The user interface, as well as the implementation itself are extremely similar to those of non-uniform polynomial splines.

**NURB mapping** First define a `RationalBlend` operator to linearly combine a sequence of blending functions and a sequence of control points. The evaluation of the `RationalBlend` given in Script 11.6.17 returns a CONS-ed vector function of coordinate maps that is usable in mapping a partition of a real interval.

---

**Script 11.6.17**

```
DEF RationalBlend=
    Rationalize:( Blend:Basis:ControlPoints ) ;
```

---

Notice that the above `RationalBlend` operator differs from the `Blend` function of Script 11.6.1, only because the introduction of a `Rationalize` function, given below, in the computational pipeline.

**Rationalize operator** The `Rationalize` operator, given in Script 11.6.18, rationalizes a sequence of either numbers of functions, by dividing the other elements by the last element of the sequence , which is finally dropped out. The function `RTAIL` to eliminate the last element of a sequence, is given in Script 4.2.5.

---

**Script 11.6.18**

```
DEF Rationalize (functions::IsSeq) =
    (RTAIL ~ AA:NoExceptionDiv ~ DISTR):<functions,nth>
WHERE
    nth = LAST:functions,
    NoExceptionDiv = IF:<EQ ~ [S2,K:0], S1, (S1 RAISE:/ S2)>
END;
```

---

Notice that the division is performed in any case, even with zero denominator. In such cases the first components remain invariant by definition, as we show below.

```
Rationalize:<1, 2, 3, 4, 5> ≡ <1/5, 2/5, 3/5, 4/5>
Rationalize:<1, 2, 3, 4, 0> ≡ <1, 2, 3, 4>
```

**User interface** It is the same as in the non-rational case discussed in some sections above. Only the names of the given functions change slightly. The only difference in the coding of the implementation concerns the invoking of the function `RationalBlend` instead than the `Blend` operator in the `RationalBspline` function of Script 11.6.19. This would otherwise be a perfect copy of the `Bspline` function given in Script 11.6.14.

Analogous changes occur in the `DisplayNURBspline` function given below. Just notice that before be passed to the `polyline` or `polymarker` operators, the homogeneous control points of the NURB spline must be rationalized.

---

**Script 11.6.19**

```
    DEF NURBspline = RationalBspline:(intervals:1:splineSampling);
    DEF NURBsplineJoints = RationalBspline:Knotzero;

    DEF RationalBspline
     (dom::Ispol)(degree::Isint)(knots::IsSeq)(points::IsSeq) =
       STRUCT:segments
    WHERE
          ...
       segmentmaps = (AA:(INSL:APPLY ~ AL) ~ DISTL):
          < CONS ~ RationalBlend,
             (AA:TRANS ~ subsets:order ~ TRANS):<basis, points> >,
          ...
    END;
```

---

**Script 11.6.20**

```
    DEF DisplayNURBspline (degree::Isint; knots::IsSeq ; points::IsSeq ) =
    (STRUCT ~ [
       IF:< K:(GT:0:degree), NURBspline:degree:knots, polymarker:3 >,
       polymarker:2 ~ S1 ~ UKPOL ~ NURBsplineJoints:degree:knots ,
       polyline ~ AA:Rationalize,
       polymarker:1 ~ AA:Rationalize
    ]): points;
```

---

# 12

# Parametric surfaces and solids

Parametric curves can be combined to give parametric surfaces or solids or higher dimensional manifolds. This chapter is mainly aimed at introducing *generative methods* for parametric surfaces as vector functions of two real parameters, but also presents extensions to three-variate solids and to *n*-variate manifolds. In particular, some useful classes of surfaces are discussed, i.e. the *profile product* surfaces, including rotational surfaces; the *ruled* surfaces, including generalized cylinders and cones; the surfaces generated by *tensor product* of curves or splines. *Transfinite blending* is a powerful approach to dimension-independent generation of manifold maps by blending lower dimensional geometric maps, as univariate interpolation or approximation in functional spaces. Transfinite blending includes the *skinning* of curve or spline grids with *Coons' patches*, transfinite Bézier and B-splines. The transfinite approach is presented here in a simple functional framework, with the result that this powerful generative tool may be easily handled by the common graphics user. Once more, the simple combinatorial semantics of the language may give the reader useful insights into tensor operations and transfinite combinations.

## 12.1   Introduction

A surface as a point set in Euclidean space $\mathbb{E}^3$ can be defined *implicitly* as a level set, usually the zero set, of a continuous scalar field $s : \mathbb{E}^3 \to \mathbb{R}$, i.e. as the set $s^{-1}(0)$.

Often more usefully, a surface in $\mathbb{E}^n$ may be defined *parametrically* as the image of a function $\boldsymbol{S} : U \to \mathbb{E}^n$ of two real parameters, i.e. with $U \subset \mathbb{R}^2$.

In this chapter we are mainly interested in the surface generating map $\boldsymbol{S}$, which we call *surface map*, or even simply *surface*, thus denoting the Euclidean point set as the *surface image*. When the parametric domain $U$ is bounded, $\boldsymbol{S}(U)$ is called a surface *patch*. Surface points in $\boldsymbol{S}(U)$ are therefore associated with *coordinate pairs* $(u, v) \in U$. This association is mainly useful where it is one-to-one, i.e. where the surface is said to be *regular*.

*Geometric Programming for Computer-Aided Design*  Alberto Paoluzzi
© 2003 John Wiley & Sons, Ltd  ISBN 0-471-89942-9

### 12.1.1   Parametric representation

A surface as a point locus can be described, at least locally, as the image of a point-valued function

$$S : U \rightarrow \mathbb{E}^n, \qquad n \geq 2$$

defined on an open set $U \subset \mathbb{R}^2$. Therefore we have

$$(u, v) \mapsto \left(\ x_1(u, v) \quad x_2(u, v) \quad \cdots \quad x_n(u, v)\ \right)^T$$

and

$$S = \left(\ x_1 \quad x_2 \quad \cdots \quad x_n\ \right)^T$$

where the $x_i : \mathbb{R}^2 \rightarrow \mathbb{R}$, $1 \leq i \leq n$, are called the *coordinate functions* of the surface.

**Regularity**   The $S$ surface is said to be *regular* in $(u, v) \in U$ if

1. the coordinate functions have continuous partial derivatives in $(u, v)$;
2. the vectors

$$\begin{aligned}
S^u(u, v) &= \left(\ \partial^u x_1(u, v) \quad \partial^u x_2(u, v) \quad \cdots \quad \partial^u x_n(u, v)\ \right) \\
S^v(u, v) &= \left(\ \partial^v x_1(u, v) \quad \partial^v x_2(u, v) \quad \cdots \quad \partial^v x_n(u, v)\ \right)
\end{aligned}$$

are linearly independent. For a 3D surface this implies

$$S^u(u, v) \times S^v(u, v) \neq \mathbf{0}.$$

The $S$ surface is said *regular on* $U$ if it is regular for each $(u, v) \in U$.

**Example 12.1.1 (3D sphere)**
The parametric equation of the unit sphere in $\mathbb{E}^3$ can be derived starting from a half circumference in the $y = 0$ subspace, i.e. from the curve $c(u) = R_y(u)\, e_1$. By using, from Section 6.3.1, the matrix of the $R_y(u)$ rotation tensor about the $y$ axis, we have:

$$c(u) = \begin{pmatrix} \cos u & 0 & \sin u \\ 0 & 1 & 0 \\ -\sin u & 0 & \cos u \end{pmatrix} \begin{pmatrix} 1 \\ 0 \\ 0 \end{pmatrix} = \begin{pmatrix} \cos u \\ 0 \\ -\sin u \end{pmatrix}, \qquad -\frac{\pi}{2} \leq u \leq \frac{\pi}{2}.$$

So, the parametric equations of the sphere $S_2 = \{p \in \mathbb{E}^3 : \|p\| = 1\}$ can by generated as $R_z(v)\, c(u)$, i.e. by rotating $c(u)$ about the $z$ axis:

$$S(u, v) = \begin{pmatrix} \cos v & -\sin v & 0 \\ \sin v & \cos v & 0 \\ 0 & 0 & 1 \end{pmatrix} \begin{pmatrix} \cos u \\ 0 \\ -\sin u \end{pmatrix} = \begin{pmatrix} \cos u \cos v \\ \cos u \sin v \\ -\sin u \end{pmatrix}$$

with $-\frac{\pi}{2} \leq u \leq \frac{\pi}{2}$ and $-\pi \leq v \leq \pi$.
Let us consider where $S(u, v)$ is regular. We have

$$S^u(u, v) = \begin{pmatrix} -\sin u \cos v \\ -\sin u \sin v \\ -\cos u \end{pmatrix} \quad \text{and} \quad S^v(u, v) = \begin{pmatrix} -\cos u \sin v \\ \cos u \cos v \\ 0 \end{pmatrix},$$

so that

$$S^u(u, v) \times S^v(u, v) = \det \begin{pmatrix} e_1 & e_2 & e_3 \\ -\sin u \cos v & -\sin u \sin v & -\cos u \\ -\cos u \sin v & \cos u \cos v & 0 \end{pmatrix}$$

$$= (\cos^2 u \cos v)\, e_1 + (\cos^2 u \sin v)\, e_2 - (\sin u \cos u)\, e_3.$$

Since $\|S^u \times S^v\| = |\cos u|$, then $S$ is regular except where $\cos u = 0$, which holds only at the north and south poles.

## 12.2 Notable surface classes

A powerful approach to shape specification denoted as "generative modeling" was proposed by Snyder and Kajiya [Sny92, SK92]. As in other procedural methods of computer graphics,[1] shapes are described procedurally.

The power of the generative approach comes from the use of several operators to combine shapes, mainly parametric curves, to generate a great number of different kinds of surfaces and deformable solid models. Such a generative approach gives a natural, compact and symbolic representation to a large class of curved objects.

Some useful classes of surfaces are discussed in this section, and in particular *profile product* surfaces, *rotational* surfaces and *ruled* surfaces, including generalized *cylinders* and *cones*.

### 12.2.1 Profile product surfaces

The simplest generative method is perhaps the *profile product* [Bar81], where a surface $S(u, v) = (S_1(u, v),\ S_2(u, v),\ S_3(u, v))$ is generated in $\mathbb{E}^3$ by affinely transforming a *cross-section* plane curve according to a plane *profile* curve.

In particular, a surface $S$ is called the *profile product* of two plane curves $\alpha$ and $\beta$, embedded into two coordinate subspaces and respectively called *profile* and *cross-section* curve

$$\boldsymbol{\alpha}(u) = \begin{pmatrix} \alpha_1(u) & 0 & \alpha_3(u) \end{pmatrix}^T$$

$$\boldsymbol{\beta}(v) = \begin{pmatrix} \beta_1(v) & \beta_2(v) & 0 \end{pmatrix}^T$$

when it is of the form

$$\boldsymbol{S}(u, v) = \begin{pmatrix} \alpha_1(u)\, \beta_1(v) & \alpha_1(u)\, \beta_2(v) & \alpha_3(u) \end{pmatrix}^T$$

**Note**   We like to notice that the $\alpha_1$ coordinate function is actually used as a scaling coefficient, whereas $\alpha_3$ is used as a translation coefficient in the $z$ direction. In fact, the above equation can be generated as:

$$\boldsymbol{S}(u, v) = \begin{pmatrix} \alpha_1(u) & 0 & 0 \\ 0 & \alpha_1(u) & 0 \\ 0 & 0 & 1 \end{pmatrix} \begin{pmatrix} \beta_1(v) \\ \beta_2(v) \\ 0 \end{pmatrix} + \begin{pmatrix} 0 \\ 0 \\ \alpha_3(u) \end{pmatrix} = \begin{pmatrix} \alpha_1(u)\, \beta_1(v) \\ \alpha_1(u)\, \beta_2(v) \\ \alpha_3(u) \end{pmatrix}$$

---

[1] E.g., the POSTSCRIPT language [Ado85].

**Example 12.2.1 (Surface by profile product)**
In Script 12.2.1 we generate a surface as the profile product of two cubic Bézier curves, respectively defined as `alpha` and `beta`, that are both generated by the `Bezier` function, given in Script 11.2.5, as vector functions.

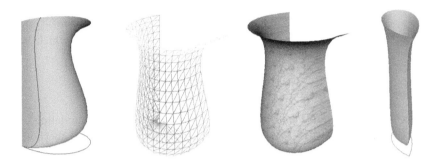

**Figure 12.1**   (a) Profile and section curve and generated surface (b) 1-skeleton (c) Texture-mapped surface (d) surface generated by same profile and different section curve

The reader should notice the composition of the components of the `section` function with the `[S2]` function, which allows application of the curve generating map `section` on the second coordinate of domain points.

---

**Script 12.2.1 (Surface by profile product)**
```
DEF ProfileProdSurface (profile, section::IsSeqOf:IsFun) = < fx, fy, fz >
WHERE
    fx = s1:profile * s1:section ~ [S2],
    fy = s1:profile * s2:section ~ [S2],
    fz = s3:profile
END;
```

---

Notice that the local definitions `fx`, `fy` and `fz` correspond to the three components of the parametric function $S(u, v)$.

The following Script 12.2.2 produces the assembly of both generating curves and their profile product surface shown in Figure 12.1a. The `intervals` generator of 1D polyedral complexes is given in Script 11.2.1.

**Example 12.2.2**
Two plane curves $\mathbb{R}^1 \to \mathbb{E}^3$ playing the role of a *cross-section* and a *profile* in a surface product are shown in Figure 12.2a. Such curves are modeled as Bézier functions, using the code given in Section 12.4.1. The cross-section is obtained grouping four patches (rotated by multiples of 90°) of the `cross_function`. The profile curve is also a Bézier function.

The surfaces shown in Figure 12.2(b)and 12.2(c) are respectively generated by the following PLASM expressions:

**Script 12.2.2 (Example of profile product surface)**

```
DEF alpha = Bezier:<<0.1,0,0>,<2,0,0>,<0,0,4>,<1,0,5>>;
DEF beta = Bezier:<<0,0,0>,<3,-0.5,0>,<3,3.5,0>,<0,3,0>>;

STRUCT:<
   MAP:alpha:(Intervals:1:20),
   MAP:beta :(Intervals:1:20),
   MAP:(ProfileProdSurface:< alpha, beta >):
      (Intervals:1:20 * Intervals:1:20)
   >;
```

**Script 12.2.3**

```
DEF section = (Bezier ~ TRANS):<<1,1,a,c,b,d,0>, <0,d,b,c,a,1,1>, #:13:0 >
WHERE
   a = 0.6, b = 0.6, c = 1.5, d = 0.2
END;

DEF profile = (Bezier ~ TRANS):
   < <b,b,d,da,f,h,l,n,p,r,a,a,a>, #:13:0,
   <0,c,e,ea,g,i,m,o,q,s, hh-(2*delta),hh-delta,hh> >
WHERE
   a = 1, hh = 19, delta = 1.5, b = 8, c = 6, d = -3, e = 5,
   da = -3, ea = 9, f = 14, g = 8, h = 12, i = 18, l = -7, m = 13,
   n = -2.5, o = 14, p = 5, q = 12.5, r = 5, s = 18.5
END;
```

where `domain` is a uniform partition of the $[0,1]^2$ interval, and `lines_domain` is a set of segments there contained.

## Rotational surfaces

When a smooth profile curve defined in $xz$ plane, i.e.

$$\boldsymbol{\alpha}(u) = \left(\begin{array}{ccc} f(u) & 0 & g(u) \end{array}\right)^T$$

is rotated about the $z$ axis, a *rotational surface* is obtained:

$$\boldsymbol{S}(u,v) = \boldsymbol{R}_z(v)\,\boldsymbol{\alpha}(u) = \begin{pmatrix} \cos v & -\sin v & 0 \\ \sin v & \cos v & 0 \\ 0 & 0 & 1 \end{pmatrix} \begin{pmatrix} f(u) \\ 0 \\ g(u) \end{pmatrix} = \begin{pmatrix} f(u)\cos v \\ f(u)\sin v \\ g(u) \end{pmatrix}.$$

In this case it is easy to see that:

**Script 12.2.4**

```
MAP:(ProfileSurface:< section,profile >):lines;
ProfileSurface:<cross_function,profile_function,trimmed_domain>;
MAP:(ProfileSurface:< section,profile >):domain;
```

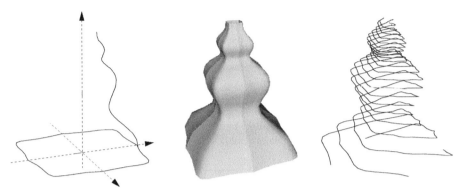

**Figure 12.2** ProfileSurface product of the two plane curves: (a) crossSection and profile curves (b) surface (c) surface mapping applied to a set of domain lines

1. the surface $S(u, v)$ is everywhere *regular* if $f(u) \neq 0$ and $\alpha'(u) \neq \mathbf{0}$ for each $u$;
2. where the surface is regular, the curves corresponding to constant values of parameters $u$ and $v$ intersect orthogonally each other.

**Note**   Notice that rotational surfaces are a special case of profile product surfaces, where the cross-section curve is a circle of unit radius, i.e. is defined as $\beta(v) = (\cos(v),\ \sin(v),\ 0)^T$.

**Implementation**   Rotational surfaces are generated by the RotationalSurface operator of Script 12.2.5, with formal parameter the ProfileCurve, given as a sequence of two coordinate functions.

---

**Script 12.2.5 (Rotational surface)**

```
DEF RotationalSurface (ProfileCurve::IsSeqOf:IsFun) =
    < f * cos ~ s2, f * sin ~ s2, g >
WHERE
    f = s1:ProfileCurve,
    g = s2:ProfileCurve
END;
```

---

**Example 12.2.3 (Rotational surface)**
A rotational surface is produced by Script 12.2.6 starting from a non-uniform B-spline profile curve. Both the profile curve and the generated surface are displayed in Figure 12.3.

Notice that the ProfileCurve symbol in Script 12.2.6 contains the pair of coordinate functions returned by Blend(ing) the BsplineBasis of order 4, generated by the knot sequence <0,0,0,0,1,2,3,4,4,4,4>, with the sequence of 2D control points <<0.1,0>,<2,0>,<6,1.5>,<6,4>,<2,5.5>,<2,6>,<3.5,6.5>>. The cellular decomposition of surface Domain is generated by Cartesian product of the 1D polyhedral complexes produced by the Intervals function given in Script 11.2.1.

**Figure 12.3**  Revolution surface: (a) profile curve (b) surface tessellation (c) smooth surface shading

The faceted polyhedral approximation `out` of the rotational surface is finally exported to the VRML file `out.wrl` by specifying also a *crease angle* $\frac{\pi}{2}$, so that some browsers may render it with Gouraud shading, as shown in Figure 12.3c.

---

**Script 12.2.6 (Example of rotational surface)**

```
DEF ProfileCurve = Blend:(BsplineBasis:4:<0,0,0,0,1,2,3,4,4,4,4>):
    <<0.1,0>,<2,0>,<6,1.5>,<6,4>,<2,5.5>,<2,6>,<3.5,6.5>>;

DEF domain = Intervals:4:19 * Intervals:(2*PI):32;
DEF out = MAP:(RotationalSurface:ProfileCurve):domain;

VRML:(out CREASE (PI/2)):'out.wrl';
```

---

### 12.2.2  Ruled surfaces

A surface is said to be *ruled* when each surface point belongs to a straight line, that is entirely contained in the surface. Ruled surfaces may be thought of as generated by the motion of a straight line.

A simple and general vector expression can be given for the parametric form of ruled surfaces. If $\alpha(u)$ is a curve that crosses all the surface lines, and $\beta(u)$ is a vector oriented as the line crossing $\alpha(u)$, then the ruled surface is

$$S(u, v) = \alpha(u) + v\,\beta(u) \tag{12.1}$$

**Implementation**  A PLaSM dimension-independent implementation of equation 12.1 is straightforward, and is given in Script 12.2.7, as a `RuledSurface` function of two parameter curves `alpha` and `beta`, passed as sequences of coordinate functions. Let us note that the vector operations defined in Chapter 3, i.e. `vectSum`, `vectDiff`, `scalarVectProd` and so on, were for this purpose defined as working between either vectors of numbers or vectors of functions.

---

**Script 12.2.7 (Ruled surfaces)**

```
DEF RuledSurface (alpha,beta::IsSeqOf:IsFun) =
    alpha vectSum (S2 scalarVectProd beta);
```

---

## Example 12.2.4 (Hyperbolic paraboloid)

The surface called *hyperbolic paraboloid* has implicit equation $x^2 - y^2 + 2z = 0$, and regular parametrization given by

$$\boldsymbol{S}(u,v) = \left(\begin{array}{ccc} u-v & u+v & uv \end{array}\right)^T,$$

so that we can write:

$$\begin{aligned}
\boldsymbol{\alpha}(u) &= \left(\begin{array}{ccc} u & u & 0 \end{array}\right)^T \\
\boldsymbol{\beta}(u) &= \left(\begin{array}{ccc} -1 & 1 & u \end{array}\right)^T \\
\boldsymbol{S}(u,v) &= \boldsymbol{\alpha}(u) + v\boldsymbol{\beta}(u) = \left(\begin{array}{ccc} u-v & u+v & uv \end{array}\right)^T
\end{aligned}$$

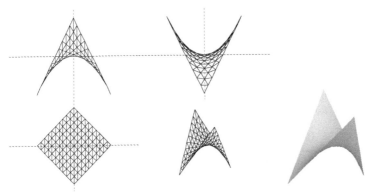

**Figure 12.4**   The patch $\boldsymbol{S}[-1,1]^2$ of hyperbolic paraboloid

The implementation of this ruled surface is given in Script 12.2.8. The surface patch resulting from the mapping $[-1,1]^2 \to \mathbb{E}^3$ is shown in Figure 12.4.

---

## Script 12.2.8 (Hyperbolic paraboloid)

```
DEF domain = T:<1,2>:<-1,-1>:((Intervals:2:10) * (Intervals:2:10));
DEF Paraboloid =
    MAP:(RuledSurface:< <S1, S1, K:0>, <K:-1, K:1, S1> >):domain

VRML:(Paraboloid CREASE (PI/2)):'out.wrl'
```

---

## Example 12.2.5 (Linear interpolation of curves)

In this example a ruled surface interpolating two arbitrary curves $\boldsymbol{c}_1$ and $\boldsymbol{c}_2$ is generated. In this case the direction of the rules is given by $\boldsymbol{c}_2 - \boldsymbol{c}_1$, so that we have:

$$\boldsymbol{S}(u,v) = \boldsymbol{\alpha}(u) + v\,\boldsymbol{\beta}(u) = \boldsymbol{c}_1(u) + v\,(\boldsymbol{c}_2(u) - \boldsymbol{c}_1(u)).$$

where, clearly, $\boldsymbol{c}_2(u) - \boldsymbol{c}_1(u)$ is the direction of the line passing for $\boldsymbol{c}_1(u)$.

In particular, In Script 12.2.9 we generate the ruled surface interpolating a 3D Bézier cubic c1 and a circle arc c2 embedded in $\mathbb{E}^3$. The resulting surface is shown in Figure 12.5. Notice that the circle generating function is reparametrized by the mapping $[0, 1] \rightarrow [0, \frac{3}{2}\pi]$ (see Section 5.1.2), and that the polyhedral domain $[0, 1]^2$ is partitioned into $20 \times 1$ subintervals.

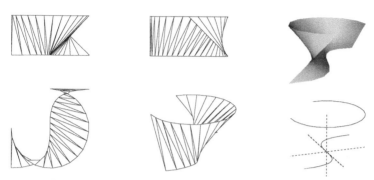

**Figure 12.5**   Linear interpolation of curves: surface connecting a portion of circle and a Bézier curve

A quite efficient and dimension-independent implementation of the ruled surface interpolating two arbitrary curves is given in Script 12.2.9, where v1 and v2 respectively denote the *sequences* of coordinate functions of the curves to be interpolated. The RuledSurface operator is given in Script 12.2.7.

---

**Script 12.2.9 (Linear interpolation of two curves)**

```
DEF v1 = Bezier:S1:<<1,1,0>,<-1,1,0>,<1,-1,0>,<-1,-1,0>>;
DEF v2 = < COS ~ (K:(3*PI/2) * S1), SIN ~ (K:(3*PI/2) * S1), K:1 >;

DEF domain = Intervals :1:10;
DEF out = MAP:(RuledSurface:< v1, v2 vectDiff v1 >):(domain * domain);

VRML:(out CREASE (PI/2)):'out.wrl';
```

---

*12.2.3  Cylinders and cones*

Cylinders and cones are subsets of the set of ruled surfaces. As such, they are characterized by vector equations that are special cases of equation 12.1. In particular, we denote as generalized cylinders and generalized cones the ruled surfaces whose lines either are all parallel or cross a single (proper) point, respectively.

**Generalized cylinders**

The generalized cylinders, simply called *cylinders* in the following sections, are ruled surfaces where the direction of the lines is given by a vector $\beta$ with constant components. Therefore, the general vector equation of cylinders is:

$$S(u,v) = \alpha(u) + v\,\beta.$$

It is easy to see that:

1. The special case of *straight circular cylinder* is obtained when $\alpha(u)$ is a circle and $\beta$ is normal to its plane.
2. $S(u, v)$ is not regular where $\alpha'(u) \times \beta = 0$.
3. $\alpha(\bar{u}) + v\beta$ and $\alpha(u) + \bar{v}\beta$, where $\bar{u}, \bar{v} \in \mathbb{R}$ are fixed numbers, are the two families of *coordinate curves*, i.e. the curves with one constant parameter.

**Example 12.2.6 (Cylindrical surface)**
In Script 12.2.10, the CylindricalSurface generating function is mainly an alias for the RuledSurface function given in Script 12.2.7, with the important difference that the beta parameter is here a vector of reals, that is transformed into a sequence of constant coordinate functions by the expression AA:K:beta.

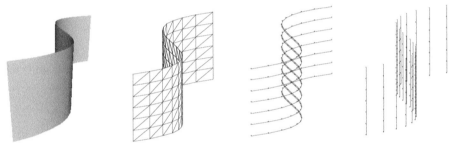

**Figure 12.6**   Polyhedral approximation of the cylindrical surface and some coordinate curves

---

**Script 12.2.10 (Cylindrical surface)**
```
DEF CylindricalSurface (alpha::IsSeqOf:IsFun; beta::IsSeqOf:IsReal) =
    RuledSurface:< alpha, AA:K:beta >;
```

---

The CylindricalSurface function given above clearly works in the hypotheses that:

1. the alpha section curve is three-dimensional;
2. the beta vector, parallel to the rules, is *non coplanar* with the section curve.

The example object generated by the Script 12.2.11 is displayed in Figure 12.6c. The geometric objects given in Figures 12.6a and 12.6b are produced by the other two definitions of the domain symbol.

At this point, the reader should write and test two different versions of a generating function for a circular and straight cylinder with arbitrary positive radius and height, by respectively using:

1. the CylindricalSurface given in Script 12.2.10, invoked with suitable values for actual parameters;

## Script 12.2.11 (Cylindrical surface example)

```
DEF alpha = Bezier:S1:<<1,1,0>,<-1,1,0>,<1,-1,0>,<-1,-1,0>>;

DEF Udomain = Intervals:1:20;
DEF Vdomain = Intervals:1:6;

DEF domain = Udomain * Vdomain;
DEF domain = Udomain * @0:Vdomain;
DEF domain = @0:Udomain * Vdomain;

DEF out = MAP:(CylindricalSurface:< alpha, <0,0,1> >):domain;
VRML:out:'out.wrl';
```

2. a standard Cartesian product of the 2D `circle` with positive `radius`, times a suitable 1D segment of positive `lenght`.

### Generalized cones

A *conical surface* is a ruled surface $S(u, v)$ according with the general equation

$$S(u, v) = \alpha + v\beta(u), \tag{12.2}$$

where the $\alpha$ point, that crosses all the rays $v\beta(u)$, is called the *apex* (or *vertex*) of the conical surface.

1. $S(u, v)$ is said to be an *half-conical surface* if either $v \geq 0$ or $v \leq 0$, for each $v$.
2. A *circular cone* results if, for each $u$, the vectors $\beta(u)$ give a constant angle $\theta$ with a fixed vector.
3. The surface $S(u, v)$ is *regular* almost everywhere. It is non-regular for $v = 0$, i.e. on the apex, and where $\beta \times \beta' = 0$.

**Implementation**   Once again, the PLaSM implementation of a *conical surface* is straightforward. It is given in Script 12.2.12, where the point `alpha` is the apex, and the curve `beta` describes the directions of the rays.

## Script 12.2.12 (Conical surfaces)

```
DEF ConicalSurface (alpha::IsSeqOf:IsReal; beta::IsSeqOf:IsFun) =
    RuledSurface:< AA:K:alpha, beta vectDiff AA:K:alpha >;
```

### Example 12.2.7 (Conical surface)

The conical surface patch generated by a cubic Bézier section on the plane $z = 0$ is given in Script 12.2.13 and displayed in Figure 12.7, where the $[0, 1]^2$ domain of the surface patch is decomposed into $20 \times 6$ convex cells (2D) and MAPped into $20 \times 6 \times 2$ triangles (3D).

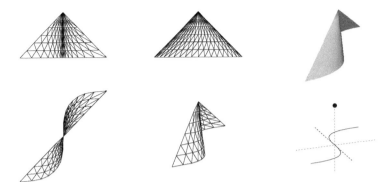

**Figure 12.7**   The conical surface generated by a Bézier curve in the $z = 0$ plane

---

**Script 12.2.13 (Conical surface example)**

```
DEF beta = Bezier:S1:<<1,1,0>,<-1,1,0>,<1,-1,0>,<-1,-1,0>>;
DEF domain = Intervals:1:20 * Intervals:1:6;

MAP:(ConicalSurface:< <0,0,1>, beta >):domain;
```

---

## 12.3   Tensor product surfaces

The parametric surfaces called *tensor product surfaces* are a bivariate generalization of parametric curves. As we know, polynomial curves can be seen as a linear combination of either points or vectors, called geometric handles, with a basis for polynomial functions of one variable, with appropriate degree. Analogously, polynomial surfaces are a linear combination of either points or vectors with a suitable basis of *bivariate* polynomial functions. Such a bivariate basis is obtained by *tensor product* of two univariate bases. The result of the linear combination of the bivariate basis with a set of geometric handles is a point-valued function of two real parameters, whose image set is the surface considered as a point locus. The properties of tensor product surfaces are a straightforward extension of properties of parametric curves. Rational surfaces in $\mathbb{E}^n$ are obtained from polynomial surfaces in $\mathbb{E}^{n+1}$.

**Geometric form of a curve**   We know, from Chapter 11, that the geometric form of a polynomial curve of degree $m$ can be written in matrix form as

$$c(u) = U_m \ B_m^m \ G^m = \mathcal{B}_m(u) \ G^m \tag{12.3}$$

where $U_m$ is the row vector containing the power basis of degree $m$, $B_m^m \in \mathbb{R}_{m+1}^{m+1}$ is the matrix of the geometric form, $G^m$ is a one-index column tensor of geometric handles, and $\mathcal{B}_m(u)$ is the polynomial basis, with degree $m$, of the geometric form.

**Geometric form of a surface**   Let us suppose that the geometric handles $G^m = (p^0, \ldots, p^m)^T$ are not constant points, but point-valued functions of the parameter

$v \in [0, 1]$, i.e. curves, all with the same geometric form and with the same degree $n$:

$$\boldsymbol{G}^m = \boldsymbol{G}^m(v) = \begin{pmatrix} \boldsymbol{c}^0(v) \\ \cdots \\ \boldsymbol{c}^m(v) \end{pmatrix},$$

so that we can rewrite equation (12.3) as

$$\boldsymbol{S}(u, v) = \boldsymbol{\mathcal{B}}_m(u)\, \boldsymbol{G}^m(v) = \boldsymbol{\mathcal{B}}_m(u) \begin{pmatrix} \boldsymbol{c}^0(v) \\ \cdots \\ \boldsymbol{c}^m(v) \end{pmatrix} \qquad (12.4)$$

where each $\boldsymbol{c}^i(v)$ can be written as

$$\boldsymbol{c}^i(v) = \boldsymbol{\mathcal{B}}_n(u)\, \boldsymbol{G}^n_i, \qquad 0 \le i \le m.$$

so that we have:

$$\begin{pmatrix} \boldsymbol{c}^0(v) & \cdots & \boldsymbol{c}^m(v) \end{pmatrix} = \boldsymbol{\mathcal{B}}_n(u) \begin{pmatrix} \boldsymbol{G}^n_0 & \cdots & \boldsymbol{G}^n_m \end{pmatrix}.$$

In order to get a column tensor of geometric handles, we can transpose the above expression:

$$\begin{pmatrix} \boldsymbol{c}^0(v) \\ \cdots \\ \boldsymbol{c}^m(v) \end{pmatrix} = (\boldsymbol{\mathcal{B}}_n(v) \begin{pmatrix} \boldsymbol{G}^n_0 & \cdots & \boldsymbol{G}^n_m \end{pmatrix})^T = \begin{pmatrix} \boldsymbol{G}^0_n \\ \cdots \\ \boldsymbol{G}^m_n \end{pmatrix} \boldsymbol{\mathcal{B}}^n(v)$$

And then it is possible to substitute in equation (12.4), getting finally

$$\boldsymbol{S}(u, v) = \boldsymbol{\mathcal{B}}_m(u) \begin{pmatrix} \boldsymbol{G}^0_n \\ \cdots \\ \boldsymbol{G}^m_n \end{pmatrix} \boldsymbol{\mathcal{B}}^n(v) = \boldsymbol{\mathcal{B}}_m(u)\, \boldsymbol{\mathcal{G}}^m_n\, \boldsymbol{\mathcal{B}}^n(v) \qquad (12.5)$$

where $\boldsymbol{\mathcal{B}}_m(u)$ and $\boldsymbol{\mathcal{B}}^n(v)$ are two univariate basis of polynomial (rational) functions of degrees $m$ and $n$, respectively, and $\boldsymbol{\mathcal{G}}^m_n = (\boldsymbol{G}^i_j)^{i=0,\dots,m}_{j=0,\dots,n}$ is a two-index tensor of control handles.

**Tensor product form** Making explicit the dependence of the surface on the degrees $n$ and $m$ of the polynomial (rational) bases in the $u$ and $v$ parameters, we can write in components:

$$\boldsymbol{S}(m, n)(u, v) = \boldsymbol{\mathcal{B}}_m(u)\, \boldsymbol{\mathcal{G}}^m_n\, \boldsymbol{\mathcal{B}}^n(v) = \sum_{i,j=0}^{m,n} B_i(u)\, B_j(v)\, \boldsymbol{p}_{ij} = \sum_{i,j=0}^{m,n} B_{ij}(u, v)\, \boldsymbol{p}_{ij}$$

The last expression is equal to the inner product of the bivariate basis times the control handles of the surface. In turn, the bivariate basis may be computed as tensor product of the univariate bases:

$$\boldsymbol{S}(m, n)(u, v) = \boldsymbol{\mathcal{B}}^n_m(u, v) \cdot \boldsymbol{\mathcal{G}}^m_n = \boldsymbol{\mathcal{B}}_m(u) \otimes \boldsymbol{\mathcal{B}}^n(v) \cdot \boldsymbol{\mathcal{G}}^m_n.$$

**Note**   The equivalent matrix form

$$S(m,n)(u,v) = U_m \, M_m^m \, \mathcal{G}_n^m \, M_n^n \, V^n$$

is often improperly called the "tensor product form". That denotation would be more appropriately used for the form given above.

**Implementation**   The *tensor product form* of surfaces will be primarily used, in the remainder of this chapter, to support the PLaSM implementation of polynomial (rational) surfaces. For this purpose, we start by defining some basic operators on function tensors.

In particular, a toolbox of basic tensor operations is given in Script 12.3.1. The ConstFunTensor operator produces a tensor of constant functions starting from a tensor of numbers; the recursive FlatTensor may be used to "flatten" a tensor with any number of indices by producing a corresponding one index tensor; the InnerProd and TensorProd are used to compute the inner product and the tensor product of conforming tensors of functions, respectively.

---

**Script 12.3.1 (Toolbox of tensor operations)**
```
DEF ConstFunTensor = IF:<IsSeq, AA:ConstFunTensor, K>;
DEF TensorInnerProd = InnerProd ~ AA:FlatTensor ;
DEF FlatTensor = IF:<IsSeqOf:IsFun, ID,CAT ~ AA:FlatTensor> ;
DEF InnerProd = + ~ AA:* ~ TRANS;
DEF TensorProd = AA:DistlTerm ~ DISTR;
DEF DistlTerm = IF:<IsFun ~ S2, FunProd, AA:DistlTerm ~ DISTL>;
DEF FunProd (f,g::IsFun) = f ~ [S1] * g ~ TAIL;
```

---

In Script 12.3.2 a TensorProdSurface dimension-independent generator is given, with input parameters the sequences Basis1 and Basis2 of univariate polynomial bases, and the conforming array of ControlPoints.

**Algorithm**   The algorithm implemented in Script 12.3.2 works as follows:

1. By suitably transposing the controlPoints parameter, a sequence $(X_i)$ of coordinate tensors, with $X_i \in \mathbb{R}_n^m$ and $1 \le i \le d$, is returned into CoordTensors. Notice that $d$ is the dimension of the target space of the $S(m,n) : \mathbb{R}^2 \to \mathbb{E}^d$ mapping.
2. Each such two-index array of numbers $X_i$ is transformed into a two-index array of constant functions by the expression

   AA:ConstFunTensor:CoordTensors

3. The bivariate basis $\mathcal{B}_m^n(u,v)$ is returned into BivariateBasis by applying the TensorProd operator on the univariate uBasis and vBasis.
4. The sequence of the $d$ coordinate functions of the $S(m,n) : \mathbb{R}^2 \to \mathbb{E}^d$ mapping is finally produced, by distributing the BivariateBasis over the sequence $(X_i)$, $1 \le i \le d$, and by applying to each pair the TensorScalarProd operator.

**Script 12.3.2 (Tensor product surface)**

```
DEF IsMatOf (IsType::IsBool) =
    AND ~ [AND ~ CAT ~ (AA ~ AA):IsType, EQ ~ AA:LEN, IsSeq];

DEF TensorProdSurface (uBasis,vBasis::IsSeq)(ControlPoints::IsMatOf:IsPoint) =
    (AA:TensorInnerProd ~ DISTL):
        < BivariateBasis, AA:ConstFunTensor:CoordTensors >
WHERE
    CoordTensors = (TRANS~AA:TRANS):controlPoints,
    BivariateBasis = TensorProd:< uBasis, vBasis >
END;
```

### 12.3.1  Bilinear and biquadratic surfaces

In this section we discuss some useful low-degree geometric forms of tensor product surfaces. A bilinear surface can be seen as both the Lagrange and the Bézier forms, interpolating four arbitrary control points, arranged as a $2 \times 2$ array. Biquadratic Lagrange forms interpolate a $3 \times 3$ array of control points.

### Bilinear surfaces

We know that the parametric equation of the line segment though two points $\boldsymbol{p}_1, \boldsymbol{p}_2 \in \mathbb{E}^d$ can be written as

$$\boldsymbol{\alpha}(u) = \boldsymbol{p}_1 + (\boldsymbol{p}_2 - \boldsymbol{p}_1)\, u \qquad u \in [0,1],$$

or, in matrix form, as

$$\boldsymbol{\alpha}(u) = \begin{pmatrix} u & 1 \end{pmatrix} \begin{pmatrix} -1 & 1 \\ 1 & 0 \end{pmatrix} \begin{pmatrix} \boldsymbol{p}_1 \\ \boldsymbol{p}_2 \end{pmatrix}.$$

If $\boldsymbol{p}_1, \boldsymbol{p}_2$ are linear functions of a $v$ parameter, or, in other words, are themselves *curves*, then the equation

$$\boldsymbol{S}(u,v) = \begin{pmatrix} u & 1 \end{pmatrix} \begin{pmatrix} -1 & 1 \\ 1 & 0 \end{pmatrix} \begin{pmatrix} \boldsymbol{p}_1(v) \\ \boldsymbol{p}_2(v) \end{pmatrix} \qquad (12.6)$$

will describe a *bilinear surface*. In fact, we have

$$\boldsymbol{p}_1(v) = \begin{pmatrix} v & 1 \end{pmatrix} \begin{pmatrix} -1 & 1 \\ 1 & 0 \end{pmatrix} \begin{pmatrix} \boldsymbol{p}_{11} \\ \boldsymbol{p}_{12} \end{pmatrix}$$

$$\boldsymbol{p}_2(v) = \begin{pmatrix} v & 1 \end{pmatrix} \begin{pmatrix} -1 & 1 \\ 1 & 0 \end{pmatrix} \begin{pmatrix} \boldsymbol{p}_{21} \\ \boldsymbol{p}_{22} \end{pmatrix}$$

so that

$$\begin{pmatrix} \boldsymbol{p}_1(v) & \boldsymbol{p}_2(v) \end{pmatrix} = \begin{pmatrix} v & 1 \end{pmatrix} \begin{pmatrix} -1 & 1 \\ 1 & 0 \end{pmatrix} \begin{pmatrix} \boldsymbol{p}_{11} & \boldsymbol{p}_{21} \\ \boldsymbol{p}_{12} & \boldsymbol{p}_{22} \end{pmatrix}.$$

By transposing both sides of the previous equation we have

$$\left( \begin{array}{c} p_1(v) \\ p_2(v) \end{array} \right) = \left( \begin{array}{cc} p_{11} & p_{12} \\ p_{21} & p_{22} \end{array} \right) \left( \begin{array}{cc} -1 & 1 \\ 1 & 0 \end{array} \right)^T \left( \begin{array}{c} v \\ 1 \end{array} \right)$$

whose right-hand side can be substituted for the left-side in equation (12.6). So, by setting

$$U_1 = \left( \begin{array}{cc} u & 1 \end{array} \right)$$

$$M_1 = \left( \begin{array}{cc} -1 & 1 \\ 1 & 0 \end{array} \right),$$

we can finally write the matrix form

$$S(u, v) = U_1 \, M_1 \, G_1^1 \, M^1 \, V^1 = B_1(u) \otimes B^1(v) \cdot G_1^1 \qquad (12.7)$$

of the bilinear surface, where

$$G_1^1 = \left( \begin{array}{cc} p_{11} & p_{12} \\ p_{21} & p_{22} \end{array} \right).$$

This kind of surface is called *bilinear* because it is linear both in the $u$ and in the $v$ parameter. Due to its construction, the surface patch $S[0, 1]^2 \subset \mathbb{E}^d$ clearly interpolates the four control points. Notice that such points belong to $\mathbb{E}^d$, with arbitrary positive integer $d$. Usually it is either $d = 3$ or $d = 2$.

**Implementation**   A *dimension-independent* bilinear patch defined by four extreme points can be generated by the `BilinearSurface` operator given in Script 12.3.3.

The reader may easily check from equation (12.7) that $B_1(u) = (1 - u, u)$ and that $B^1(v) = (1 - v, v)^T$. Such a basis is both Lagrange and Bernstein/Bézier, so that our implementation follows. The `BernsteinBasis` generator is given in Script 12.5.2.

---

**Script 12.3.3 (Bilinear surface)**
```
DEF BilinearSurface (ControlPoints::IsMatOf:IsPoint) =
    TensorProdSurface:< BernsteinBasis:S1:1, BernsteinBasis:S1:1 >:ControlPoints
```

---

**Example 12.3.1 (Bilinear surface patch)**
The bilinear patch produced by four 3D points given in Script 12.3.4 is shown in Figure 12.8. The `Intervals` constructor of 1D polyhedral complexes is given in Script 12.2.2.

**Biquadratic Lagrange form**

In this case the constraint is to require the surface passage for 9 arbitrary points, arranged as a $3 \times 3$ array.

As always, the tensor product form of the parametric vector equation is easy to obtain. Let us remember[2] that a quadratic polynomial curve through 3 points has the

---

[2] See Section 11.2.2.

**Figure 12.8**   Patch of bilinear surface defined by four extreme points

**Script 12.3.4 (Bilinear surface example)**
```
DEF Mapping = BilinearSurface:<<<0,0,0>,<2,-4,2>>,<<0,3,1>,<4,0,0>>>;

MAP:Mapping:(Intervals:1:10 * Intervals:1:10)
```

equation:

$$\alpha(u) = \left(\, u^2 \quad u \quad 1 \,\right) \begin{pmatrix} 2 & -4 & 2 \\ -3 & 4 & -1 \\ 1 & 0 & 0 \end{pmatrix} \begin{pmatrix} p_1 \\ p_2 \\ p_3 \end{pmatrix} = U_2\, M_2 \begin{pmatrix} p_1 \\ p_2 \\ p_3 \end{pmatrix},$$

so that

$$S(u,v) = U_2\, M_2 \begin{pmatrix} p_{11} & p_{12} & p_{13} \\ p_{21} & p_{22} & p_{23} \\ p_{31} & p_{32} & p_{33} \end{pmatrix} M^2\, V^2 = B_2(u) \otimes B^2(v) \cdot G_2^2.$$

Therefore, the Lagrange's basis of degree 2 is

$$B_2(u) = U_2\, M_2 = \left(\, u^2 \quad u \quad 1 \,\right) \begin{pmatrix} 2 & -4 & 2 \\ -3 & 4 & -1 \\ 1 & 0 & 0 \end{pmatrix} = \left(\, b_2(u) \quad b_1(u) \quad b_0(u) \,\right),$$

with

$$\begin{aligned} b_2(u) &= 2u^2 - 3u + 1, \\ b_1(u) &= -4u^2 + 4u, \\ b_0(u) &= 2u^2 - u. \end{aligned}$$

**Implementation**   A `BiquadraticSurface` generator function is given in Script 12.3.5 by using the the tensor product operations encoded within the `TensorProdSurface` operator defined in Script 12.3.2.

### Example 12.3.2 (Biquadratic patch)
The generation of a biquadratic surface patch using the Hermite's interpolating geometric form is exemplified in Script 12.3.6. The generated patch is shown in Figure 12.9. Once more, the `Mapping` sequence of coordinate functions is MAPped over a suitable partitioning of the $[0,1]^2$ domain, that is decomposed into $10 \times 10$ squared cells.

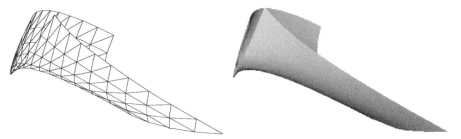

**Figure 12.9**   Biquadratic surface patch interpolating $3 \times 3$ assigned points

---

**Script 12.3.5 (Biquadratic surfaces)**

```
DEF BiquadraticSurface (ControlPoints::IsMatOf:IsPoint) =
    TensorProdSurface:< Basis, Basis >:ControlPoints
WHERE
    Basis = < u2, u1, u0 >,
    u2 = (k:2 * uu) - (K:3 * u) + K:1,
    u1 = (k:4 * u) - (k:4 * uu),
    u0 = (k:2 * uu) - u, uu = u * u, u = s1
END;
```

---

*12.3.2   Bicubic surfaces*

As already discussed in the previous chapter, cubic curves and bicubic surfaces are largely used by geometric modeling systems, since they provide a sufficient flexibility to define complex shapes by suitably connecting segments of curves or surfaces with $C^1$ continuity.

**Algebraic form**

The *algebraic form* of a bicubic polynomial surface is defined as

$$S(u,v) = \sum_{i=0}^{3}\sum_{j=0}^{3} a_{ij}u^i v^j, \qquad i,j \in [0,1]$$

where the 16 vector coefficients $a_{ij}$ are called *algebraic coefficients* of the surface, that results to have $16 \times 3 = 48$ *degrees of freedom* in $\mathbb{E}^3$. In matrix notation, the algebraic form of a bicubic surface is

$$S(u,v) = U_3 \ A \ V_3^T,$$

---

**Script 12.3.6 (example of biquadratic patch)**

```
DEF Mapping = BiquadraticSurface:<
    <<0,0,0>, <2,0,1>,<3,1,1>>,
    <<1,3,-1>,<3,2,0>,<4,2,0>>,
    <<0,9,0>, <2,5,1>,<3,3,2>> >;

MAP:Mapping:(Intervals:1:10 * Intervals:1:10)
```

---

where

$$U_3 = \begin{pmatrix} u^3 & u^2 & u & 1 \end{pmatrix}$$
$$V_3 = \begin{pmatrix} v^3 & v^2 & v & 1 \end{pmatrix}.$$

A more explicit vector form is

$$\begin{aligned}
S(u, v) = \ & a_{33} \, u^3 v^3 + a_{32} \, u^3 v^2 + a_{31} \, u^3 v + a_{30} \, u^3 \\
& a_{23} \, u^2 v^3 + a_{22} \, u^2 v^2 + a_{21} \, u^2 v + a_{20} \, u^2 \\
& a_{13} \, u v^3 + a_{12} \, u v^2 + a_{11} \, u v + a_{10} \, u \\
& a_{03} \, v^3 + a_{02} \, v^2 + a_{01} \, v + a_{00}.
\end{aligned}$$

As we already know from the study of parametric curves, the so-called *geometric forms* of the surface, defined by suitable polynomial bases, different from the standard power basis, and where the degrees of freedom have some explicit geometric meaning, are much more useful to the designer. Similarly to what we have seen for the curves, we can discover such useful bases for the bicubic surfaces by setting $4 \times 4 = 16$ vector constraints, and by solving their linear system.

**Lagrange's form**

As for curves, the passage of the surface is imposed for a set of $4 \times 4$ points $p_j^i \in \mathbb{E}^d$, arranged within a

$$G_{LL} = (p_j^i)_{j=0,\dots,3}^{i=0,\dots,3}$$

tensor, so that the surface mapping $S : [0,1]^2 \to \mathbb{E}^d$ is generated as

$$S(u, v) = U_3 \, M_L \, G_{LL} \, M_L^T \, V_3^T.$$

where the geometric Lagrange matrix $M_L$ is the same already computed in Section 11.2.3 for the cubic polynomial curves. The implementation of the bicubic Lagrange's mapping is left to the reader.

**Bicubic Hermite geometric form**

Let us consider that

$$S(u, v) = U_3 \, M_h \begin{pmatrix} p_1(v) \\ p_2(v) \\ s_1(v) \\ s_2(v) \end{pmatrix}$$

where $p_1(v), p_2(v), s_1(v)$ and $s_2(v)$ are cubic Hermite curves. So, we may write

$$\begin{pmatrix} p_1(v) & p_2(v) & s_1(v) & s_2(v) \end{pmatrix} =$$

$$\begin{pmatrix} v^3 & v^2 & v & 1 \end{pmatrix} M_h \begin{pmatrix} q_{11} & q_{21} & q_{31} & q_{41} \\ q_{12} & q_{22} & q_{32} & q_{42} \\ q_{13} & q_{23} & q_{33} & q_{43} \\ q_{14} & q_{24} & q_{34} & q_{44} \end{pmatrix}.$$

The resulting matrix and tensor forms for the bicubic Hermite surface mapping are:

$$S(u,v) = U_3 \, M_h \, G_{hh} \, M_h^T \, V_3^T,$$

$$S(u,v) = H_3(u) \otimes H_3(v) \cdot G_{hh},$$

where

$$H_3(u) = \left( \begin{array}{cccc} h_3(u) & h_2(u) & h_1(u) & h_0(u) \end{array} \right)$$

is the *cubic Hermite basis*, i.e.:

$$\begin{aligned} h_3(u) &= 2u^3 - 3u^2 + 1, \\ h_2(u) &= -2u^3 + 3u^2, \\ h_1(u) &= u^3 - 2u^2 + u, \\ h_0(u) &= u^3 - u^2. \end{aligned}$$

**Implementation**  Our standard format for the implementation of bicubic Hermite surfaces as tensor product surfaces is used in Script 12.3.7, where HermiteBasis just contains the PLaSM implementation with function algebra of the basis polynomials given above.

---

**Script 12.3.7 (Bicubic Hermite surfaces)**

```
DEF HermiteSurface (ControlPoints::IsMatOf:IsPoint) =
   TensorProdSurface:< HermiteBasis, HermiteBasis >:ControlPoints
WHERE
   HermiteBasis = < h3, h2, h1, h0 >,
   h0 = (uuu) - (uu),
   h1 = (uuu) - (k:2 * uu) + u,
   h2 = (k:3 * uu) - (k:2 * uuu),
   h3 = (k:2 * uuu) - (k:3 * uu) + (k:1),
   uuu = uu * u, uu = u * u,
   u = s1
END;
```

---

**Example 12.3.3 (Bicubic Hermite patch)**
A bicubic Hermite patch is generated by Script 12.3.8 and displayed in Figure 12.10, both as polyhedral approximation with $10 \times 10 \times 2$ triangles and with smooth rendering using a Gouraud shader. Notice that the only input is the $4 \times 4$ tensor of geometric handles, organized as a $4 \times 4$ matrix of 3D points, represented in PLaSM as sequences of coordinates.

**Coordinate functions**  It may be interesting to generate the graphs of the three coordinate functions of the mapping $S : [0,1]^2 \to \mathbb{E}^3$ produced in Example 12.3.3. The triplet of coordinate function graphs is generated by the out object of Script 12.3.9, and is shown in Figure 12.11.

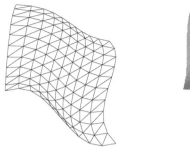

**Figure 12.10**   Bicubic Hermite's patch: (a) faceted approximation (b) smooth rendering

**Script 12.3.8**

```
DEF Mapping = HermiteSurface: <
    <<0,0,0>, <2,0,1>, <3,1,1>, <4,1,1>>,
    <<1,3,-1>,<3,2,0>, <4,2,0>, <4,2,0>>,
    <<0,4,0>, <2,4,1>, <3,3,2>, <5,3,2>>,
    <<0,6,0>, <2,5,1>, <3,4,1>, <4,4,0>> >;

MAP:Mapping:(Intervals:1:10 * Intervals:1:10);
```

**Meaning of Hermite's geometry tensor**   It is interesting to discuss the semantics of a decomposition into four submatrices of the bicubic Hermite's geometry tensor $\mathcal{G}_3^3$. Let us first remember that

$$S(u,v) = U_3 M_h\ \mathcal{G}_{hh}\ M_h^T V^3$$

where

$$\mathcal{G}_{hh} = \begin{pmatrix} q_1^1 & q_2^1 & q_3^1 & q_4^1 \\ q_1^2 & q_2^2 & q_3^2 & q_4^2 \\ q_1^3 & q_2^3 & q_3^3 & q_4^3 \\ q_1^4 & q_2^4 & q_3^4 & q_4^4 \end{pmatrix}$$

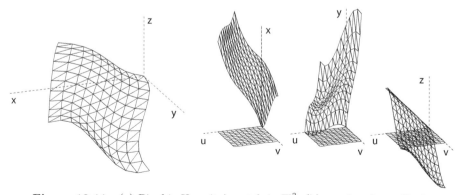

**Figure 12.11**   (a) Bicubic Hermite's patch in $\mathbb{E}^3$; (b) graphs of coordinate functions $[0,1]^2 \to \mathbb{R}$ from $(u,v)$ space

**Script 12.3.9**

```
DEF u = s1; DEF v = s2;
DEF x = s1; DEF y = s2; DEF z = s3;

DEF out = STRUCT:<
    (STRUCT ~ [MAP:[u, v, x:Mapping], EMBED:1]):domain, T:<1,2>:<-1.5,1>,
    (STRUCT ~ [MAP:[u, v, y:Mapping], EMBED:1]):domain, T:<1,2>:<-1.5,1>,
    (STRUCT ~ [MAP:[u, v, z:Mapping], EMBED:1]):domain
>;
```

If we look into the development process of the previous equation, it is easy to see that $\mathcal{G}_{hh}$ can be decomposed into four submatrices corresponding to the surface $S$, its first partial derivatives $S^u$, $S^v$ and its mixed second partial derivative $S^{uv}$, respectively evaluated in the four corners of $[0,1]^2$ domain:

$$\mathcal{G}_{hh} = \begin{pmatrix} S(0,0) & S(0,1) & S^u(0,0) & S^u(0,1) \\ S(1,0) & S(1,1) & S^u(1,0) & S^u(1,1) \\ \\ S^v(0,0) & S^v(0,1) & S^{uv}(0,0) & S^{uv}(0,1) \\ S^v(1,0) & S^v(1,1) & S^{uv}(1,0) & S^{uv}(1,1) \end{pmatrix}$$

**Example 12.3.4 (Effect of tangent vectors)**
By reversing the direction of the four vectors $S^u(0,0), S^u(0,1), S^u(1,0)$ and $S^u(1,1)$, as done in Script 12.3.10, we get the effect shown in Figure 12.12a.

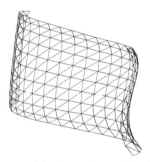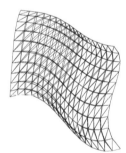

**Figure 12.12**   (a) Hermite's patch with reversed $S^u$ directions (b) Display of the differences between Hermite's and Ferguson's patches

**Script 12.3.10 (Reversing four partial derivatives)**

```
DEF ReversedExample = HermiteSurface:<
    <<0,0,0>, <2,0,1>, AA:-:<3,1,1>, AA:-:<4,1,1>>,
    <<1,3,-1>,<3,2,0>, AA:-:<4,2,0>, AA:-:<4,2,0>>,
    <<0,4,0>, <2,4,1>, <3,3,2>, <5,3,2>>,
    <<0,6,0>, <2,5,1>, <3,4,1>, <4,4,0>> >

MAP:ReversedExample:(Intervals:1:10 * Intervals:1:10)
```

### Example 12.3.5 (Ferguson's surfaces)

The geometric meaning of the second mixed partial derivatives $S^{uv}$, also called *twist vectors*, is not easy to understand. The easiest way to assign such derivatives at the patch corner points is by giving them a null value. In such a choice, the Hermite's surfaces are called Ferguson's surfaces, or else *F-patches*. An example of Ferguson's surface is produced by Script 12.3.11. The difference between a Ferguson's patch and an Hermite's patch with the same control tensor is displayed in Figure 12.12b.

---

**Script 12.3.11**

```
DEF FergusonExample = HermiteSurface:<
    <<0,0,0>, <2,0,1>, <3,1,1>, <4,1,1>>,
    <<1,3,-1>,<3,2,0>, <4,2,0>, <4,2,0>>,
    <<0,4,0>, <2,4,1>, AA:(k:0):<3,3,2>, AA:(k:0):<5,3,2>>,
    <<0,6,0>, <2,5,1>, AA:(k:0):<3,4,1>, AA:(k:0):<4,4,0>> >

MAP:FergusonExample:(Intervals:1:10 * Intervals:1:10)
```

---

### Bicubic Bézier geometric form

A derivation process, similar to the one leading to the bicubic Hermite's form, can be done for the bicubic Bézier surface, defined as the linear combination of the Bézier polynomial basis of degree three with four Bézier curves of the same degree:

$$S(u,v) = B_3(u) \begin{pmatrix} q_1(v) \\ q_2(v) \\ q_3(v) \\ q_4(v) \end{pmatrix},$$

where

$$B_3(u) = \begin{pmatrix} (1-u)^3 & 3u(1-u)^2 & 3u^2(1-u) & u^3 \end{pmatrix}$$

$$q_i(v) = B_3(v) \begin{pmatrix} q_{1i} \\ q_{2i} \\ q_{3i} \\ q_{4i} \end{pmatrix}, \qquad 1 \leq i \leq 4.$$

Hence it is possible to write

$$S(u,v) = B_3(u) \, G_{bb} \, B_3^T(v),$$

with

$$G_{bb} = \begin{pmatrix} q_{11} & q_{12} & q_{13} & q_{14} \\ q_{21} & q_{22} & q_{23} & q_{24} \\ q_{31} & q_{32} & q_{33} & q_{34} \\ q_{41} & q_{42} & q_{43} & q_{44} \end{pmatrix}.$$

Clearly, other possible forms for the Bézier bilinear surface are:

$$
\begin{aligned}
\boldsymbol{S}(u,v) &= \boldsymbol{U}_3 \, \boldsymbol{M}_b \, \boldsymbol{G}_{bb} \, \boldsymbol{M}_b^T \, \boldsymbol{V}_3^T, \\
&= \sum_{i=1}^{4} \sum_{j=1}^{4} B_i(u) B_j(v) \boldsymbol{q}_{ij}, \\
&= \boldsymbol{B}_3(u) \otimes \boldsymbol{B}_3(v) \cdot \boldsymbol{G}_{bb}.
\end{aligned}
$$

**Implementation**  The implementation of a dimension-independent `BezierSurface` generator of surface maps of arbitrary degrees $(m, n)$ is given in Script 12.3.12. It is simply defined by applying the `TensorProdSurface` operator to a pair of Bernstein/Bézier bases of degrees `m` and `n`, where `m` and `n` are related to the numbers of rows and columns of the `ControlPoints` matrix, respectively. The `BernsteinBasis` generator is given in Script 11.2.3.

The reader should notice that the `BezierSurface` operator is able to generate a Bézier surface of *arbitrary degrees*, embedded in a $\mathbb{E}^d$ space, with an *arbitrary dimension* d. For example, a bilinear surface though 4 points could be generated as a `BezierSurface` with a $2 \times 2$ `ControlPoints` array.

---

**Script 12.3.12 (Bézier surfaces)**

```
DEF BezierSurface (ControlPoints::IsMatOf:IsPoint) =
    TensorProdSurface:< BernsteinBasis:m, BernsteinBasis:n >:ControlPoints
WHERE
    m = LEN:ControlPoints - 1,
    n = (LEN ~ S1):ControlPoints - 1
END;
```

---

**Example 12.3.6 (Bicubic Bézier surface generation)**
Four quadruples of four control points needed to generate a bicubic surface, and called points$_i$, $1 \le i \le 4$, are given in Script 12.3.14. The surface generated by last expression is shown in Figure 12.13b. The BezierSurface generator is given in Script 12.3.12.

---

**Script 12.3.13 (Bicubic Bézier example)**

```
DEF points1 = <<0,0,0>,<0,3,4>,<0,6,3>,<0,10,0>>;
DEF points2 = <<3,0,2>,<2,2.5,5>,<3,6,5>,<4,8,2>>;
DEF points3 = <<6,0,2>,<8,3,5>,<7,6,4.5>,<6,10,2.5>>;
DEF points4 = <<10,0,0>,<11,3,4>,<11,6,3>,<10,9,0>>;

DEF pointArray = < points1, points2, points3, points4 >;

MAP:(BezierSurface:pointArray):(Intervals:1:10 * Intervals:1:10);
```

---

**Example 12.3.7 (Same surface from Bézier curves)**
We develop here an instructive variation of Example 12.3.6, where the same bicubic surface is generated starting from the 4 curves produced by the four rows of the $4 \times 4$

pointArray tensor given in Script12.3.13. The geometric construction we refer to is shown in Figure 12.13. We like to note that:

1. the biCubicBezier surface image interpolates only the first and last Bézier curves in primaryGrid;
2. both the second and third curve in primaryGrid are only approximated by the surface;
3. the secondaryGrid is constituted by $v$-curves (and their control polygons) corresponding to 0, 0.5 and 1 values of the $u$ parameter;
4. all the curves in secondaryGrid are interpolated by the surface, whereas their generating polygons have control points belonging to the curves in primaryGrid.

---

**Script 12.3.14 (Grid of control polygons)**
```
DEF curves = (CONS ~ AA:Bezier):pointArray;

DEF BezierAndPolygon (points::IsSeq) = STRUCT:<
  MAP:(Bezier:points):(Intervals:1:10),
  polyline:points
>;

DEF primaryGrid = (STRUCT ~ AA:BezierAndPolygon):pointArray;
DEF secondaryGrid = (STRUCT ~ AA:(BezierAndPolygon ~ curves ~ [ID])):
  < 0 , 0.5, 1 >;

DEF surfaceMap = BezierSurface:pointArray;
DEF biCubicBezier = MAP:surfaceMap:(Intervals:1:10 * Intervals:1:10)

STRUCT:< primaryGrid, secondaryGrid, biCubicBezier >;
```

---

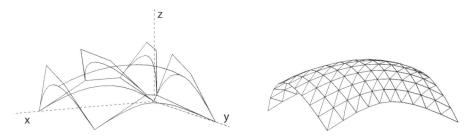

**Figure 12.13**  The geometric construction generated by STRUCT:< firstGrid, secondaryGrid, biCubicBezier >; Notice that the surface does not interpolate the two intermediate curves

### 12.3.3  Fixed-degrees tensor product surfaces

A quite common case of tensor product surface with different degrees in the $u$ and $v$ parametric directions is the linear/quadratic one. We show its equations as a further example. Hence, in this case we have:

$$S(u,v) = U_1 \; M_1^1 \; \mathcal{G}_2^1 \; M_2^{2^T} \; V^2$$

that can be rewritten as

$$S(u,v) = \mathcal{B}_2^1(u,v) \cdot \mathcal{G}_2^1 = \sum_{i=1}^{2} \sum_{j=1}^{3} B_j^i(u,v) \; p_j^i,$$

where

$$\mathcal{B}_2^1(u,v) = \mathcal{B}_1(u) \otimes \mathcal{B}_2(v)$$

$$B_1(u) = U_1 \; M_1 = \begin{pmatrix} B_1(u) & B_0(u) \end{pmatrix}$$
$$B_2(v) = V_2 \; M_2 = \begin{pmatrix} B_2(v) & B_1(v) & B_0(v) \end{pmatrix}$$

and

$$G_{12} = \begin{pmatrix} p_{11} & p_{12} & p_{13} \\ p_{21} & p_{22} & p_{23} \end{pmatrix}.$$

**Example 12.3.8 (Linear/quadratic Bézier surface)**
A simple example of implementation of a Bézier surface linear in $u$ and quadratic in $v$ is given in Script 12.3.15. The resulting ruled surface image is presented in Figure 12.14b. In this case the control tensor $\mathcal{G}_2^1$ is a $2 \times 3$ PLaSM matrix of 3D points.

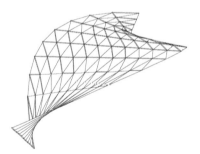 

**Figure 12.14**   Two polynomial surfaces of degrees $(1,2)$ generated by different bases in the $v$ direction

### 12.3.4  NURB surfaces

NURB surfaces are the tensor product bivariate extension of non-uniform rational B-spline curves. Due to their local control, the exact representation of quadrics, the containment in the local and global convex hulls of control points, and the other properties inherited from NURB curves, such surfaces are nowadays the industry standard representation for geometric modeling and boundary representation (see Section 13.5) of solids.

**Script 12.3.15**

```
DEF Mapping = BezierSurface:<
    <<0,0,0>, <1,1,-1>, <3,1,0>>,
    <<0,3,0>, <4,3,-2>, <5,4,-1>> >

MAP:Mapping:(Intervals:1:10 * Intervals:1:10)
```

**Tensor product NURBS**

As we know from Section 11.4.2, a NURB spline curve can be written as

$$R(t) = \bigcup_{i=k}^{m} R_i(t) = \sum_{i=0}^{m} p_i\, N_{i,h}(t), \qquad t \in [t_k, t_{m+1}).$$

where $N_{i,h}(t)$ is the non-uniform rational B-basis function of initial value $t_i$, order $h$ and degree $k$, that is zero outside the knot interval $[t_i, t_{i+h})$.

The tensor product NURB surface of orders $(h_1, h_2)$

$$S(u,v) = \bigcup_{i=k_1}^{m_1} \bigcup_{j=k_2}^{m_2} S_{ij}(u,v) = \sum_{i=0}^{m_1}\sum_{j=0}^{m_2} p_{ij}\, N_{i,j,h_1,h_2}(u,v),$$

with $u \in [u_{k_1}, u_{m_1+1})$, $v \in [v_{k_2}, v_{m_2+1})$, is clearly generated by a tensor product bivatiate basis of $(h_1, h_2)$ orders

$$N_{i,j,h_1,h_2}(u,v) = N_{i,h_1}(u)\, N_{j,h_2}(v), \qquad 0 \le i \le m_1,\ 0 \le j \le m_2,$$

combined with a two-index array $(p_{ij})$ of control points. The surface may be closed using repeated patterns of knots and control points at the extremes of the two sequences. Notice that, whereas control points are just repeated, extreme knots must be translated.

**Trimmed NURBS** When NURBS surface patches are joined together as the result of Boolean operations between boundary representations[3] of solid models, only portions of a tensor product surface are often used, that may be specified by giving a set of trimming curves in parameter $(u, v)$ space of the patch. Such curves, usually given as 2D NURB splines, are converted into a set of closed loops by a suitable combination with the boundary of parameter space. The used portions of the surface are those internal to the loops, according to some loop orientation. Notice that in order to have a meaningfull description, the loops must not intersect themselves or each other. The geometry representation of the boundary using trimmed NURB surfaces can represent objects of considerable complexity, as well as to exactly represent spheres, cylinders, cones and toruses, and their Boolean combinations. Trimmed NURBS are currently the industry stardard representation of surfaces within the kernel geometric libraries adopted by most CAD systems.

---

[3] See Section 13.5.

## 12.4  Higher-order tensor products

The bases of polynomials used to produce the generating maps of three-variate parametric solids can be generated by tensor product of 3 univariate bases. More generally, the same approach can be used to generate $d$-variate parametric manifolds.

### 12.4.1  Multivariate Bézier manifolds

In this section the standard tensor product approach for Bézier surfaces is extended to Bézier solids and to $d$-variate Bézier manifolds.

**Parametric curves and surfaces**   Let us remember that Bézier maps for curves and surfaces are respectively described, in form of combinations of control points with blending polynomials, as:

$$C(u) = \sum_{i=0}^{n} B_i^n(u) p_i$$

$$S(u,v) = \sum_{j=0}^{m} B_j^m(v) \sum_{i=0}^{n} B_i^n(u) p_{i,j}$$

$$= \sum_{i=0}^{n} \sum_{j=0}^{m} B_i^n(u) B_j^m(v) p_{i,j} = \sum_{i,j=0}^{n,m} B_{i,j}^{n,m}(u,v) p_{i,j}$$

**Parametric solids**   Analogously, for three-variate bodies we have:

$$B(u,v,w) = \sum_{k=0}^{l} B_k^l(w) \sum_{j=0}^{m} B_j^m(v) \sum_{i=0}^{n} B_i^n(u) p_{i,j,k}$$

$$= \sum_{i=0}^{n} \sum_{j=0}^{m} \sum_{k=0}^{l} B_i^n(u) B_j^m(v) B_k^l(w) p_{i,j,k} = \sum_{i,j,k=0}^{n,m,l} B_{i,j,k}^{n,m,l}(u,v,w) p_{i,j,k},$$

where the blending functions are the Bernstein's polynomials and $p_i, p_{i,j}, p_{i,j,k} \in \mathbb{E}^d$ can be seen as the elements of a tensor of points with 1,2 or 3 indices, respectively.

**Multivariate manifolds**   A $d$-variate Bézier Manifold map of integer degrees $n_1, n_2, ..., n_d$ is a map $M : \mathbb{R}^d \to \mathbb{E}^n$ such that

$$M(u_1, u_2, \ldots, u_d) = \sum_{i_1=0}^{n_1} B_{i_1}^{n_1}(u_1) \sum_{i_2=0}^{n_2} B_{i_2}^{n_2}(u_2) \cdots \sum_{i_d=0}^{n_d} B_{i_1}^{n_d}(u_d) \cdot p_{i_1,i_2,\ldots,i_d}$$

$$= \sum_{i_1,i_2,\ldots,i_d=0}^{n_1,n_2,\ldots,n_d} B_{i_1,i_2,\ldots,i_d}^{n_1,n_2,\ldots,n_d}(u_1, u_2, \ldots, u_d) \cdot p_{i_1,i_2,\ldots,i_d}, \quad (12.8)$$

where $p_{i_1,i_2,\ldots,i_d} \in \mathbb{E}^n$, and where

$$B_{i_1,i_2,\ldots,i_d}^{n_1,n_2,\ldots,n_d}(u_1, u_2, \ldots, u_d) = B_{i_1}^{n_1}(u_1) B_{i_2}^{n_2}(u_2) \cdots B_{i_1}^{n_d}(u_d). \quad (12.9)$$

A *d-variate Bézier manifold* can be seen as the image set $M(U) \subset \mathbb{R}^n$ of a $d$-variate Bézier map on a compact domain $U \subset \mathbb{R}^d$. Notice that $M$ depends only on the sequence of degrees $n_1, n_2, \ldots, n_d$ and on the tensor of control points $p^{i_1, i_2, \ldots, i_d}$.

**Tensor product** A tensorial formulation of this mapping can be given as follows. Let us denote with

$$\mathcal{B}^n = (B_i^n)_{i=0,\ldots,n}$$

the Bézier basis of order $n$, i.e. a one index tensor of functions $\mathbb{R} \to \mathbb{R}$. A left associative tensor product of such function tensors is

$$\mathcal{B}^{n_1 \cdots n_h} \otimes \mathcal{B}^m = \mathcal{B}^{n_1 \cdots n_h m} = \left( B_{i_1 \cdots i_h i_{h+1}}^{n_1 \cdots n_h m} \right)_{\substack{i_1 = 0, \ldots, n_1 \\ \cdots \\ i_{h+1} = 0, \ldots, m}}$$

where

$$B_{i_1 i_2 \cdots i_d}^{n_1 n_2 \cdots n_d} = B_{i_1}^{n_1} B_{i_2}^{n_2} \cdots B_{i_d}^{n_d} : \mathbb{R}^d \to \mathbb{R}$$

such that

$$(u_1, u_2, \ldots, u_d) \mapsto B_{i_1}^{n_1}(u_1) B_{i_2}^{n_2}(u_2) \cdots B_{i_1}^{n_d}(u_d).$$

It follows that the Bézier tensor $\mathcal{B}^{n_1 n_2 \cdots n_d}$ can be computed as

$$\mathcal{B}^{n_1 n_2 \cdots n_d} = \mathcal{B}^{n_1} \otimes \mathcal{B}^{n_2} \otimes \cdots \otimes \mathcal{B}^{n_d}.$$

**Tensor of control points** A similar notation is used for a tensor (depending on $d$ indices) of points of an Euclidean space $\mathbb{E}^n$

$$P^{n_1 \cdots n_d} = \left( p^{i_1 \cdots i_d} \right)_{\substack{i_1 = 0, \ldots, n_1 \\ \cdots \\ i_d = 0, \ldots, d}}, \qquad p^{i_1 \cdots i_d} \in \mathbb{E}^n$$

and for the corresponding tensors of coordinates, with $p = (x_1, \ldots, x_d)$

$$X_k^{n_1 \cdots n_d} = \left( x_k^{i_1 \cdots i_d} \right)_{\substack{i_1 = 0, \ldots, n_1 \\ \cdots \\ i_d = 0, \ldots, d}}, \qquad x_k^{i_1 \cdots i_d} \in \mathbb{R}$$

Two other concepts remain to be defined. The constant functional, which transforms a tensor of numbers in a tensor of constant functions, and the inner product of tensors. The constant functional $K$ from tensors of numbers to tensors of constant functions is defined as:

$$K(X_k^{n_1 \cdots n_d}) \equiv \mathcal{X}_k^{n_1 \cdots n_d} = (\chi_k^{i_1 \cdots i_d})$$

where

$$\chi_k^{i_1 \cdots i_d} : \mathbb{R}^d \to \mathbb{R} : (u_1, \ldots, u_d) \mapsto x_k^{i_1 \cdots i_d}$$

for any $(u_1, \ldots, u_d)$.

**Inner product of tensors**  Finally, the inner product of function tensors of the same order is defined as

$$\mathcal{B}^{n_1\cdots n_d} \cdot \mathcal{X}_k^{n_1\cdots n_d} = \sum_{i_1,\cdots,i_d=0}^{n_1,\cdots,n_d} B_{i_1\cdots i_d}^{n_1\cdots n_d} \, \chi_k^{i_1\cdots i_d}$$

where summation and product are between $\mathbb{R} \to \mathbb{R}$ functions.

**Implementation**  A bottom-up approach is assumed in implementing the `BezierManifold` generator function. First, a set of basic functions is defined, in order to compute factorials, binomial coefficients, the Bernstein function $B_i^n : \mathbb{R} \to \mathbb{R}$ and the Bernstein base $\mathcal{B}^n = (B_i^n)$. The `Bernstein` operator seems a little tricky, but it implements a functional with signature $\text{Int} \times \text{Int} \to (\text{Real} \to \text{Real})$.

Hence the most natural functional interface for the definition of a Bézier $d$-manifold is given in Script 12.4.1.

---

**Script 12.4.1 (Bézier manifolds by tensor product)**

```
DEF BezierManifold (degrees::IsSeq) (controlPoints::IsSeq) =
    (AA:TensorInnerProd ~ DISTL):<BezierTensor,CoordTensors>
WHERE
    BezierTensor = (INSR:TensorProd ~ AA:BernsteinBase):degrees,
    CoordTensors = AA:ConstFunTensor:controlPoints
END;
```

---

**Note**  It is very important to note that such an approach works correctly for an arbitrary polyhedral domain $U \subset \mathbb{R}^d$. In particular, domain may coincide both with a $d$-dimensional interval and with any $m$-dimensional polyhedral subset of it, $0 \le m \le d$. For instance, a 3-variate Bézier map can be applied either to a 3D interval, or to a 3D polyhedron, or to a (set of) polyhedral surface(s), or to a (set of) polyhedral curve(s) or even to a (set of) point(s). The only constraint is that both `controlPoints` and the Bézier manifold, i.e. $M(U)$, live in the same space, i.e. have the same number $n$ of coordinates. It may be useful to note that, in order to always correctly obtain a piece-wise linear result of any mapping, a simplicial decomposition of the domain is always performed by the `MAP` function.

**Example 12.4.1 (Bézier 3-manifold)**
The definition of a `BezierExample` can simply be the application of `Manifold` function on actual parameters `BezierMap` and `domain`. The specialized `BezierMap` is obtained by applying the `BezierManifold` operator of Script 12.4.2 to the degrees `<2,2,2>`, and to the tensor $\mathbb{P}^{3,3,3}$ of its control points. The result is a three-variate `BezierMap`: $\mathbb{R}^3 \to \mathbb{R}^3$ whose three parameters have all degree two.

In Figure 12.15 the results generated by the `Bezier_example` for different values of domain are reported. The four definitions of the polyhedral domain are referred to a 1-dimensional grid. Four polyhedral values generated by the function `Bezier_example` varying the definition of the domain are generated by Script 12.4.3.

**Script 12.4.2 (Bézier 3-manifold example (1))**

```
DEF BezierExample = MAP:BezierMap:domain

DEF BezierMap = BezierManifold:degrees:<Xtensor,Ytensor,Ztensor>
WHERE
    degrees = <2,2,2>,
    Xtensor = <<<0,1,2>,<-1,0,1>,<0,1,2>>,
              <<0,1,2>,<-1,0,1>,<0,1,2>>,
              <<0,1,2>,<-1,0,1>,<0,1,2>>>,
    Ytensor = <<<0,0,0.8>,<1,1,1>,<2,3,2>>,
              <<0,0,0.8>,<1,1,1>,<2,3,2>>,
              <<0,0,0.8>,<1,1,1>,<2,3,2>>>,
    Ztensor = <<<0,0,0>,<0,0,0>,<0,0,0>>,
              <<1,1,1>,<1,1,1>,<1,1,1>>,
              <<2,2,1>,<2,2,1>,<2,2,1>>>
END;
```

 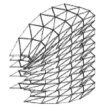  

**Figure 12.15**   (a) Three-quadratic Bézier solid (b), (c) and (d) Submanifolds of dimensions 2, 1 and 0, respectively

## 12.5   Transfinite methods

*Transfinite blending* stands for interpolation or approximation in *functional spaces*. In this case a bivariate mapping is generated by blending some univariate maps with a suitable basis of polynomials. Analogously, a three-variate mapping is generated by blending some bivariate maps with a polynomial basis, and so on. Transfinite methods are quite frequently used in CAD applications, mainly for automobile, ship and airplane shell design. It is sometimes called *function blending* [Gor68, LS86], or *transfinite interpolation* [Gor69, Gol87]. Gordon-Coons's patches were discovered [Coo67, Gor68] in the MIT project MAC at the end of the 1960s. The

**Script 12.4.3 (Bézier 3-manifold example (2))**

```
DEF grid1D = (QUOTE~#:step):(1/step) WHERE step = 5 END;

DEF domain = grid1D * grid1D * grid1D;
DEF domain = grid1D * grid1D * @0:grid1D;
DEF domain = grid1D * @0:grid1D * @0:grid1D;
DEF domain = @0:grid1D * @0:grid1D * @0:grid1D

MAP:(BezierManifold:degrees:controlPoints):domain
```

*skinning* of grids of curves used by high-end animation systems is a transfinite interpolation. Transfinite methods have recently been applied to interpolate implicitly defined sets of different cardinality [RSST01].

The implementation of transfinite blending with PLaSM consists in using functions without variables, that can be combined, e.g. multiplied and added, exactly as numbers. This approach seems both very powerful and simple. Several examples of such power are given in the following sections. Consider, e.g., that multivariate transfinite Bézier blending of *arbitrary degree* with both domain and range spaces of *arbitrary dimension* is implemented in Section 12.5.4 with only 11 lines (!) of quite readable source code.

### 12.5.1  Rationale of the approach

Transfinite blending is a strong generalization of standard parametric methods. For example, the standard Hermite generation of cubic curves, where two extreme points and tangents are interpolated, can be readily applied to surfaces, where two extreme curves are interpolated with assigned derivative curves, as well as to volume interpolation of two assigned surfaces with assigned derivatives fields.

**Definition**   A *d-variate parametric mapping* is a point-valued polynomial function $\Phi : U \subset X \to Y$ with degree $k$, domain $U$, support $X = \mathbb{R}^d$ and range $Y = \mathbb{E}^n$.

As commonly used in Computer Graphics and CAD, such point-valued polynomials $\Phi = (\Phi_j)_{j=1,\ldots,n}$ belong component-wise to the vector space $\mathbb{P}_k[\mathbb{R}]$ of polynomial functions of bounded integer degree $k$ over the $\mathbb{R}$ field.

**Polynomial coordinates**   Since the set $\mathbb{P}_k$ of polynomials is also a vector space $\mathbb{P}_k[\mathbb{P}_k]$ over $\mathbb{P}_k$ itself *as a field*, then each mapping component $\Phi_j$, $1 \leq j \leq n$, can be expressed uniquely as a linear combination of $k+1$ basis elements $\phi_i \in \mathbb{P}_k$ with *coordinates* $\xi_j^i \in \mathbb{P}_k$, so that

$$\Phi_j = \xi_j^0 \phi_0 + \cdots + \xi_j^k \phi_k, \qquad 1 \leq j \leq n.$$

Hence a unique coordinate representation

$$\Phi_j = \left( \xi_j^0, \ldots, \xi_j^k \right)^T, \qquad 1 \leq j \leq n$$

of the mapping is given, after a basis $\{\phi_0, \ldots, \phi_k\} \subset \mathbb{P}_k$ has been chosen.

**Choice of a basis**   If the basis elements are collected into a vector $\boldsymbol{\phi} = (\phi_i)$, then it is possible to write:

$$\boldsymbol{\Phi} = \boldsymbol{\Xi}\,\boldsymbol{\phi}, \qquad \boldsymbol{\phi} \in \mathbb{P}_k^{k+1}, \ \boldsymbol{\Phi} \in \mathbb{P}_k^n.$$

where

$$\boldsymbol{\Xi} = \left( \xi_j^i \right), \qquad 1 \leq i \leq n,\ 0 \leq j \leq k.$$

is the coordinate representation of a linear operator in $Lin[n \times (k+1), \mathbb{P}_k]$ that maps the $k+1$ basis polynomials of $k$ degree, into the $n$ polynomials which transform the vectors in the domain $U \subset \mathbb{R}^d$ into the $\mathbb{E}^n$ points of the manifold. A quite standard choice in computer-aided geometric modeling is $U = [0,1]^d$. As seen in previous sections, the *power* basis, the *cardinal* (or *Lagrange*) basis, the *Hermite* basis, the *Bernstein/Bézier* basis and the *B-spline* basis are the most common and useful choices for the $\phi = (\phi_i)$ basis. This approach can be readily extended to the space $\mathcal{Z}_k$ of rational functions of degree $k$.

**Blending operator**  The *blending operator* $\Xi$ specializes the maps generated by a certain basis, to fit and/or to approximate a given set of specific data (points, tangent vectors, boundary curves or surfaces, boundary derivatives, and so on). Its coordinate functions $\xi_j^i$ may be easily generated, as will be shown in the following subsections, by either

1. transforming the "geometric handles" of the mapping into vectors of constant functions, in the standard (non-transfinite) case. These are usually points or vectors $\boldsymbol{x}_j = (x_j^i) \in \mathbb{E}^n$ to be interpolated or approximated by the set $\boldsymbol{\Phi}(U)$;
2. assuming directly as $\xi_j^i$ the components of the curve (surface, etc.) maps to be fitted or approximated by $\boldsymbol{\Phi}$, in the transfinite case.

**Notation**  For the sake of readability, only Greek letters, either capitals or lower-case, are used in this section to denote functions. Latin letters are used for numbers and vectors of numbers. As usual in this book, bold letters denote vectors, points or tensors. Please remember that $B$ and $H$ are also Greek capitals for $\beta$ and $\eta$, respectively.

### 12.5.2  *Univariate case*

Let us consider the simple univariate case $\boldsymbol{\Phi} : U \subset X \to Y$, where the dimension $d$ of support space $X$ is one. To generate the coordinate functions $\xi_j^i$ it is sufficient to transform each data point $\boldsymbol{x}_i = (x_j^i) \in Y$ into a vector of constant functions, so that

$$\xi_j^i = \kappa(x_j^i), \quad \text{where} \quad \kappa(x_j^i) : U \to Y : u \mapsto x_j^i.$$

Using the functional notation with explicit variables, the constant function is such that

$$\kappa(x_j^i)(u) = x_j^i$$

for each parameter value $u \in U$. The PLaSM implementation clearly uses the constant functional K at this purpose.

### Example 12.5.1 (Cubic Bézier curve in the plane)
The cubic Bézier plane curve depends on four points p0,p1,p2,p3 $\in E^2$, which are given in Script 12.5.1 as formal parameters of the function Bezier3, that generates the $\boldsymbol{\Phi}$ mapping by linearly combining the basis functions with the coordinate functions. The local functions b0,b1,b2,b3 implement the cubic Bernstein/Bézier basis functions $\beta_i^3 : \mathbb{R} \to \mathbb{R}$ such that $u \mapsto \binom{3}{i} u^i (1-u)^{3-i}$, $0 \le i \le 3$.

The x and y functions, defined as composition of a selector with the constant functional K, respectively select the first (second) component of their argument

**Script 12.5.1**

```
DEF Bezier3 (p0,p1,p2,p3::IsSeqOf:isReal) =
    [ (x:p0 * b0) + (x:p1 * b1) + (x:p2 * b2) + (x:p3 * b3),
      (y:p0 * b0) + (y:p1 * b1) + (y:p2 * b2) + (y:p3 * b3) ]
WHERE
    b0 = u1 * u1 * u1,
    b1 = K:3 * u1 * u1 * u,
    b2 = K:3 * u1 * u * u,
    b3 = u * u * u,
    x = K ~ S1, y = K ~ S2, u1 = K:1 - u, u = S1
END;
```

sequence and transform such a number in a constant function. The reader should notice that + and * are used as operators *between functions* in the script above.

*12.5.3   Multivariate case*

When the dimension $d$ of the support space $X$ is greater than one, two main approaches can be used to construct a parametric mapping $\Phi$. The first approach is the well-known *tensor-product* method that we already know (see Sections 12.3 and 12.4). The second method is called *function blending*, also known as *transfinite blending*.

**Transfinite blending**   Let us consider a polynomial mapping $\Phi : U \to Y$ of degree $k_d$, where $U$ is $d$-dimensional and $Y$ is $n$-dimensional. Since $\Phi$ depends on $d$ parameters, in the following it will be denoted as $^d\Phi = (^d\Phi_j)$, $1 \le j \le n$. In this case $^d\Phi$ is computed component-wise by linear combination of coordinate maps, depending on $d-1$ parameters, with the *univariate* polynomial basis $\phi = (\phi_i)$ of degree $k_d$. Formally we can write:

$$^d\Phi_j = {}^{d-1}\Phi_j^0\,\phi_0 + \cdots {}^{d-1}\Phi_j^{k_d}\,\phi_{k_d}, \qquad 1 \le j \le n.$$

The coordinate representation of $^d\Phi_j$ with respect to the basis $(\phi_0, \ldots, \phi_{k_d})$ is thus given by $k_d + 1$ maps depending on $d-1$ parameters:

$$^d\Phi_j = \left( {}^{d-1}\Phi_j^0, \ldots, {}^{d-1}\Phi_j^{k_d} \right).$$

In matrix notation, after a polynomial basis $\phi$ has been chosen, it is

$$^d\Phi = \Xi\,\phi, \quad \text{where} \quad \Xi = ({}^{d-1}\Phi_j^i), \quad \phi = (\phi_i), \quad 0 \le i \le k_d, \; 1 \le j \le n.$$

**Example 12.5.2 (Bicubic Bézier)**

As an example of transfinite blending consider the generation of a bicubic Bézier surface mapping $B(u_1, u_2)$ as a combination of four Bézier cubic curve maps $B_i(u_1)$, with $0 \le i \le 3$, where some curve maps may possibly reduce to a constant point map:

$$B(u_1, u_2) = \sum_{i=0}^{3} B_i(u_1)\,\beta_i^3(u_2)$$

where

$$\beta_i^3(u) = \binom{3}{i} u^i (1-u)^{3-i}, \qquad 0 \leq i \leq 3,$$

is the Bernstein/Bézier cubic basis. Analogously, a three-variate Bézier solid body mapping $B(u_1, u_2, u_3)$, of degree $k_3$ on the last parameter, may be generated by univariate Bézier blending of surface maps $B_i(u_1, u_2)$, some of which may possibly be reduced to a curve map or even to a constant point map:

$$B(u_1, u_2, u_3) = \sum_{i=0}^{k_3} B_i(u_1, u_2)\, \beta_i^{k_3}(u_3)$$

**Note** The more interesting aspects of transfinite blending are *flexibility* and *simplicity*. Unlike the tensor-product method, there is no need for all component geometries to have the same degree, nor be all generated using the same function basis. For example, a quintic Bézier surface map may be generated by blending both Bézier curve maps of lower (even zero) degree together with Hermite and Lagrange curve maps. Furthermore, it is much simpler to combine lower dimensional geometries (i.e. maps) than to meaningfully assembly the multi-index tensor of control data (i.e. points and vectors) to generate multivariate manifolds with tensor-product method.

### 12.5.4 Transfinite Bézier

The full power of the PLaSM functional approach to geometric programming is used in this section, where dimension-independent transfinite Bézier blending of any degree is implemented in few lines of code, by easily combining coordinate maps which may depend on an arbitrary number of parameters.

We note that the `Bezier` : $[0,1]^d \to \mathbb{E}^n$ mapping given here can be used:

1. to blend points to give curve maps;
2. to blend curve maps to give surface maps;
3. to blend surface maps to give solid maps;
4. and so on ...

Notice also that the given implementation is independent on the dimensions $d$ and $n$ of support and range spaces.

**Implementation** For this purpose, first a small toolbox of related functions is needed, to compute the factorial function, the binomial coefficients, the $\beta^k = (\beta_i^k)$ Bernstein basis of degree $k$, and the $\beta_i^k$ Bernstein/Bézier polynomials.

Then the `Bezier:u` function is given in Script 12.5.3, to be applied on the sequence of `ControlData`, which may contain either control points $x_i = (x_j^i)$ or control maps $^{d-1}\Phi_i = (^{d-1}\Phi_j^i)$, with $0 \leq i \leq k$, $1 \leq j \leq n$. In the former case each component $x_j^i$ of each control point is first transformed into a constant function.

The body of the `Bezier:u` function just linearly combines component-wise the sequence $(\xi_j^i)$ of coordinate maps generated by the expression

**Script 12.5.2 (Transfinite Bézier toolbox)**

```
DEF Fact (n::IsInt) = IF:< C:EQ:0, K:1, * ~ INTSTO >;
DEF Choose = IF:< OR ~ [C:EQ:0 ~ S2, EQ], K:1, Choose ~ AA:(C:+:-1) * / >;
DEF Bernstein (u::IsFun)(n::IsInt)(i::IsInt) =
    * ~ [K:(Choose:<n,i>),** ~ [ID,K:i], ** ~ [- ~ [K:1,ID],K:(n-i)]] ~ u;
DEF BernsteinBasis (u::IsFun)(n::IsInt) = AA:(Bernstein:u:n):(0..n);
```

(TRANS~fun):ControlData

with the basis sequence $(\beta_i^k)$ generated by BernsteinBasis:u:degree, where degree equates the number of geometric handles minus one.

**Script 12.5.3 (Dimension-independent transfinite Bézier mapping)**

```
DEF Bezier (u::IsFun) (ControlData::IsSeq) = (AA:InnerProd ~ DISTR):
    < (fun ~ TRANS):ControlData, BernsteinBasis:u:degree >
WHERE
    degree = LEN:ControlData - 1,
    fun = (AA ~ AA):(IF:< IsFun, ID, K >)
END;
```

It is much harder to explain in few words what the actual argument is to pass (and why) for the formal parameter u of the Bezier function. As a rule of thumb let pass either the selector S1 if the function must return a univariate (curve) map, or S2 to return a bivariate (surface) map, or S3 to return a threevariate (solid) map, and so on.

**Example 12.5.3 (Bézier curves and surface)**

Four Bézier $[0,1] \rightarrow \mathbb{E}^3$ maps C1, C2, C3, and C4, respectively of degrees $1, 2, 3$ and $2$ are defined in Script 12.5.4.

It may be useful to notice that the control points have three coordinates, so that the generated maps C1, C2, C3 and C4 will have three component functions. Such maps can be blended with the Bernstein/Bézier basis to produce a cubic transfinite bivariate (i.e. surface) mapping:

$$B(u_1, u_2) = C0(u_1)\beta_0^3(u_2) + C1(u_1)\beta_1^3(u_2) + C2(u_1)\beta_2^3(u_2) + C3(u_1)\beta_3^3(u_2).$$

Such a linear combination of coordinate functions with the Bézier basis (here working on the second coordinate of points in $[0,1]^2$) is performed by the PLaSM function Surf1, defined by using again the Bezier function.

A simplicial approximation (with triangles) of the surface $B[0,1]^2 \subset \mathbb{E}^3$ is finally generated by evaluating the last expression of Script 12.5.4.

According to the semantics of the MAP operator, Surf1 is applied to all vertices of the automatically generated simplicial decomposition $\Sigma$ of the 2D product (Intervals : 1 : 20 * Intervals : 1 : 20) $\subset \mathbb{R}^2$. A simplicial approximation $B(\Sigma)$ of the surface $B([0,1]^2) \subset \mathbb{E}^3$ is finally produced and displayed in Figure 12.16c.

The four generating curves and the generated cubic blended surface are displayed in Figure 12.16. It is possible to see (Figure 12.16) that such surface interpolates the four boundary curves defined by the extreme control points, exactly as in the case of

**Script 12.5.4**

```
DEF C0 = Bezier:S1:<<0,0,0>,<10,0,0>>;
DEF C1 = Bezier:S1:<<0,2,0>,<8,3,0>,<9,2,0>>;
DEF C2 = Bezier:S1:<<0,4,1>,<7,5,-1>,<8,5,1>,<12,4,0>>;
DEF C3 = Bezier:S1:<<0,6,0>,<9,6,3>,<10,6,-1>>;

DEF Surf1 = Bezier:S2:<C0,C1,C2,C3>;

MAP: Surf1: (Intervals:1:20 * Intervals:1:20);
```

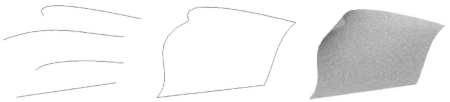

**Figure 12.16** (a) Graphs of four Bézier curve maps c0, c1, c2 and c3 (b) Graphs of c0 and c3 together with graphs of bicubic maps b0 and b1 generated by extreme control points (c) Graph of Surf1 surface

tensor-product method, but obviously with much greater generality, since any defining curve may be of any degree.

### 12.5.5 Transfinite Hermite

The cubic Hermite univariate map is the unique cubic polynomial $H : [0,1] \to \mathbb{E}^n$ which matches two given points $p_0, p_1 \in \mathbb{E}^n$ and derivative vectors $t_0, t_1 \in \mathbb{R}^n$ for $u = 0, 1$ respectively. Let us denote as $\eta^3 = (\eta_0^3, \eta_1^3, \eta_2^3, \eta_3^3)$ the cubic Hermite function basis, with

$$\eta_i^3 : [0,1] \to \mathbb{R}, \qquad 0 \le i \le 3,$$

and such that

$$\eta_0^3(u) = 2u^3 - 3u^2 + 1, \quad \eta_1^3(u) = 3u^2 - 2u^3, \quad \eta_2^3(u) = u^3 - 2u^2 + u, \quad \eta_3^3(u) = u^3 - u^2.$$

Then the mapping $H$ can be written, in vector notation, as

$$\begin{aligned} H &= \boldsymbol{\xi}_0\, \eta_0^3 + \boldsymbol{\xi}_1\, \eta_1^3 + \boldsymbol{\xi}_2\, \eta_2^3 + \boldsymbol{\xi}_3\, \eta_3^3 \\ &= \kappa(\boldsymbol{p}_0)\, \eta_0^3 + \kappa(\boldsymbol{p}_1)\, \eta_1^3 + \kappa(\boldsymbol{t}_0)\, \eta_2^3 + \kappa(\boldsymbol{t}_1)\, \eta_3^3. \end{aligned}$$

It is easy to verify, for the univariate case, that:

$$\begin{aligned} \boldsymbol{H}(0) &= \kappa(\boldsymbol{p}_0)(0) = \boldsymbol{p}_0, \quad \boldsymbol{H}(1) = \kappa(\boldsymbol{p}_1)(1) = \boldsymbol{p}_1, \\ \boldsymbol{H}'(0) &= \kappa(\boldsymbol{t}_0)(0) = \boldsymbol{t}_0, \quad \boldsymbol{H}'(1) = \kappa(\boldsymbol{t}_1)(1) = \boldsymbol{t}_1, \end{aligned}$$

and that the image set $\boldsymbol{H}[0,1]$ is the desired curve in $\mathbb{E}^n$.

A multivariate transfinite Hermite map $\boldsymbol{H}^n$ can easily be defined by allowing the blending operator $\boldsymbol{\Xi} = (\boldsymbol{\xi}_j) = (\xi_j^i)$ to contain maps depending at most on $d-1$ parameters.

**Implementation**  A transfinite `CubicHermite` mapping is implemented here, with four data objects given as formal parameters. Such data objects may be either points/vectors, i.e. sequences of numbers, or $1/2/3/d$-variate maps, i.e. sequences of (curve/surface/solid/etc.) component maps, or even mixed sequences, as will be shown in the following examples.

---

**Script 12.5.5 (Dimension-independent transfinite cubic Hermite)**

```
DEF HermiteBasis (u::IsFun) = < h0,h1,h2,h3 >
WHERE
    h0 = k:2 * u3 - k:3 * u2 + k:1,
    h1 = k:3 * u2 - k:2 * u3,
    h2 = u3 - k:2 * u2 + u,
    h3 = u3 - u2, u3 = u*u*u, u2 = u*u,
    fun = (AA ~ AA):(IF:<IsFun,ID,K>)
END;

DEF CubicHermite (u::IsFun) (p1,p2,t1,t2::IsSeq) =
    (AA:InnerProd ~ DISTL): < HermiteBasis:u, (TRANS ~ fun):<p1,p2,t1,t2> >;
```

---

### 12.5.6  Connection surfaces

The creation of surfaces smoothly connecting two given curves with assigned derivative fields by cubic transfinite blending is discussed in this section. The first applications concern the generation of surfaces in 3D space, the last concern the generation of planar grids as 1-skeletons of 2D surfaces, according to the dimension-independent character of the given PLaSM implementation of transfinite methods.

The curve maps $c1(u)$ and $c2(u)$ of Example 12.5.6 are here interpolated in 3D by a `Surf2` mapping using the cubic Hermite basis $\eta^3 = (\eta_j^3)$, $0 \le j \le 3$, with the further constraints that the tangent vector field $\mathtt{Surf2}^v(u,0)$ along the first curve are constant and parallel to $(0,0,1)$, whereas $\mathtt{Surf2}^v(u,v)$ along the second curve is also constant and parallel to $(0,0,-1)$. The resulting map

$$\mathtt{Surf2} : [0,1]^2 \to \mathbb{E}^3$$

has unique vector representation in $\mathbb{P}_3^3[\mathbb{P}_3]$ as

$$\mathtt{Surf2} = \mathtt{c1}\ \eta_0^3 + \mathtt{c2}\ \eta_1^3 + (\kappa(0),\kappa(0),\kappa(1))\ \eta_2^3 + (\kappa(0),\kappa(0),\kappa(-1))\ \eta_3^3.$$

**Example 12.5.4 (Surface interpolation of curves)**
Such a map is very easily implemented by the following PLaSM definition. A simplicial approximation $\mathtt{Surf2}(\Sigma)$ of the point set $\mathtt{Surf2}([0,1]^2)$ is generated by the `MAP` expression in Script 12.5.6, and is shown in Figure 12.17.

**Example 12.5.5 (Surface interpolation of curves)**
A different surface interpolation of the two plane curves c1 and c2 is given in Script 12.5.7, where the boundary tangent vectors are constrained to be constant

**Script 12.5.6 (Surface by Hermite's interpolation (1))**
```
DEF Surf2 = CubicHermite:S2:< c1,c2,<0,0,1>,<0,0,-1> >;
MAP: Surf2: (Domain:14 * Domain:14);
```

**Figure 12.17**   Some pictures of the surface interpolating two plane Hermite curves
with constant vertical tangent vectors along the curves.

and parallel to $(1,1,1)$ and $(-1,-1,-1)$, respectively. The resulting surface is given
in Figure 12.18. The same surface is used in Section 5.8.1 of the chapter on Differential
Geometry, to compute and display the Gauss' curvature field over a surface.

**Script 12.5.7 (Surface by Hermite's interpolation (2))**
```
DEF Surf3 = CubicHermite:S2:<c1,c2,<1,1,1>,<-1,-1,-1>>;
MAP: Surf3: (Domain:14 * Domain:14);
```

**Example 12.5.6 (Grid generation)**
Two planar Hermite curve maps c1 and c2 are defined, so that the curve images
c1$[0,1]$ and c2$[0,1]$.

Some different grids are easily generated from the plane surface which interpolates
the curves c1 and c2. For this purpose it is sufficient to apply the CubicHermite:S2
function to different tangent curves.

The grids generated by maps grid1, grid2 and grid3 are shown in Figure 12.19.
The tangent map dd is simply obtained as component-wise difference of the curve
maps c2 and c1.

It is interesting to notice that the map grid1 can be also generated as a linear
(transfinite) Bézier interpolation of the two curves, as given below. Clearly the solution
as cubic Hermite is more flexible, as it is shown by Figures 12.19b and 12.19c.

```
DEF grid1 = Bezier:S2:<c1,c2>;
MAP:(CONS:grid1):(Domain:8 * Domain:8);
```

**Example 12.5.7 (Wing section grid)**
A 2D grid for a computational problem is generated in a domain of $E^2$ bounded by
the four Hermite curves given in Script 12.5.9 and shown in Figure 12.20a.

First, a function Norm is defined in Script 12.5.10 to return the 2D unit normal vector
in $\mathbb{P}^2_k$ generated by a formal parameter fun2 $\in \mathbb{P}^2_k$. Remember that if $v = (x,y)$, then
$v^{\perp} = (-y,x)$. The Euclidean vector norm as squared root of the sum of squared
coordinates is used.

**Figure 12.18**    Some pictures of a new surface interpolating the same Hermite
curves with constant oblique tangent vectors.

---

**Script 12.5.8 (Examples of planar grids)**

```
DEF c1 = CubicHermite:S1:<<1,0>,<0,1>,<0,3>,<-3,0>>;
DEF c2 = CubicHermite:S1:<<0.5,0>,<0,0.5>,<0,1>,<-1,0>>;
DEF dd = (AA:- ~ TRANS):<c2,c1>;

DEF grid1 = CubicHermite:S2:<c1,c2,dd,dd>;
DEF grid2 = CubicHermite:S2:<c1,c2,<-0.5,-0.5>,dd>;
DEF grid3 = CubicHermite:S2:<c1,c2,<S1:dd,-0.5>,dd>;
```

---

Finally two different discretization of the interval $(0,1]$ are prepared in
Script 12.5.11, together with two functions to be used for abstracting the 1-variate
and the 2-variate simplicial mapping:

Then two bivariate (transfinite) cubic Hermite maps are generated between the wing
profile curves and the boundary curves, using normal univariate maps.

The geometry discretization shown in Figures 12.20a and 12.20b are respectively
generated by the last two PLaSM expressions. The approach shown here in 2D may be
readily applied to the volume discretization of much more complicated 3D domains.

*12.5.7  Coons' surfaces*

We know that a parametric surface is a function $S : U \subset \mathbb{R}^2 \to \mathbb{E}^n$. Let assign four
boundary curves, corresponding to the edges of the $U$ domain:

$$S(u,0), \quad S(u,1), \quad S(0,v), \quad S(1,v).$$

**Figure 12.19**    The simplicial complexes generated by the MAP operator on the
grid1, grid2 and grid3 maps given in Example 12.5.6.

## Script 12.5.9 (Wing profile)

```
DEF c1 = CubicHermite:S1:<<0,0>,<10,0>,<0,3>,<6,-1>>;
DEF c2 = CubicHermite:S1:<<0,0>,<10,0>,<0,-3>,<6,-1>>;
DEF b1 = CubicHermite:S1:<<-5,0>,<15,0>,<0,22>,<0,-22>>;
DEF b2 = CubicHermite:S1:<<-5,0>,<15,0>,<0,-22>,<0,22>>;
```

## Script 12.5.10 (Perpendicular to a 2D function vector)

```
DEF Norm (fun2::IsSeqOf:IsFun) = <- ~ yu/den, xu/den>
WHERE
    xu = S1:fun2, yu = S2:fun2, sqr = ID * ID,
    den = MySQRT ~ + ~ AA:sqr ~ [- ~ yu, xu],
    MySQRT = IF:<EQ ~ [K:0,ID], K:0, SQRT>
END;
```

A surface [Coo67] which interpolates the given curves is known as *Coons' patch*, that usually interpolates the four boundary curves by using linear blending functions as

$$\alpha_0(t) = 1 - t, \qquad \alpha_1(t) = t.$$

The vector expression of the Coons' surface patch is:

$$
\begin{aligned}
S(u, v) &= S_1(u, v) + S_2(u, v) - S_3(u, v) \\
&= \begin{pmatrix} \alpha_0(u) & \alpha_1(u) \end{pmatrix} \begin{pmatrix} S(0, v) \\ S(1, v) \end{pmatrix} + \\
&\quad \begin{pmatrix} S(u, 0) & S(u, 1) \end{pmatrix} \begin{pmatrix} \alpha_0(v) \\ \alpha_1(v) \end{pmatrix} - \\
&\quad \begin{pmatrix} \alpha_0(u) & \alpha_1(u) \end{pmatrix} \begin{pmatrix} S(0, 0) & S(0, 1) \\ S(1, 0) & S(1, 1) \end{pmatrix} \begin{pmatrix} \alpha_0(v) \\ \alpha_1(v) \end{pmatrix}
\end{aligned}
$$

The above equation can be interpreted as the sum of three signed bivariate vector functions, where

1. $S_1(u, v)$ is the ruled surface interpolating $S(0, v)$ and $S(1, v)$;
2. $S_2(u, v)$ is the ruled surface interpolating $S(u, 0)$ and $S(u, 1)$;
3. $S_3(u, v)$ is the bilinear surface interpolating the four corner points $S(0, 0)$, $S(0, 1)$, $S(1, 0)$ and $S(1, 1)$.

**Implementation** The implementation is very easy, and directly corresponds to the mathematical definition of equation (12.10). For this purpose two vector operations scalarVectProd and vectSum given in Script 2.1.19, for the product of a vector times

## Script 12.5.11

```
DEF dom1 = T:1:1E-8:(Domain:24);
DEF dom2 = T:1:1E-8:(Domain:12);
DEF graph1 (f::IsSeq) = MAP:(CONS:f):dom1;
DEF graph2 (f::IsSeq) = MAP:(CONS:f):(dom1 * dom2);
```

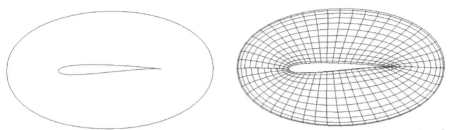

**Figure 12.20** (a) The plane domain bounded by the four curve maps c1, c2 and b1, b2 (b) Wire-frame picture of domain $\texttt{grid1}(\Sigma[0,1]^2) \cup \texttt{grid2}(\Sigma[0,1]^2)$.

**Script 12.5.12 (Domain discretization)**

```
DEF grid1 = CubicHermite:S2:<c1,b1,Norm:c1,Norm:b1>;
DEF grid2 = CubicHermite:S2:<c2,b2,Norm:c2,Norm:b2>;
(STRUCT ~ AA:graph1):<c1,c2,b1,b2>;
(STRUCT ~ AA:graph2):<grid1,grid2>;
```

a scalar and for the addition of vectors of any length are used. Notice that such operations are performed between function vectors and not between number vectors.

The 2D domain of the mapping is obtained as the polyhedral product of two partitions of the 1D segment.

### Example 12.5.8 (Coons' patch)

Let us suppose that the boundary curves are Bézier curves of degrees 1, 4, 3 and 2, respectively. The composition with the function [S2] is needed to reuse the Bézier PLaSM script when mapping from a 2D domain. The analogous composition with [S1] is given just for symmetry.

A Coons' patch which smoothly interpolates the four given curves is generated by the last expression of Script 12.5.14, and is displayed in Figure 12.21.

### Example 12.5.9 (Curve on surface mapping)

No constraints exist in PLaSM on the dimension and the topology of the domain of

**Script 12.5.13 (Coons' patches)**

```
DEF CoonsPatch (Su0,Su1,S0v,S1v::IsSeqOf:IsFun) =
    (vectSum ~ AA:scalarVectProd):
    <<a0u,S0v>,<a1u,S1v>,<a0v,Su0>,<a1v,Su1>,<-~a0v,b0u>,<-~a1v,b1u>>
WHERE
    b0u = (vectSum ~ AA:scalarVectProd):<<a0u,S_00>,<a1u,S_10>>,
    b1u = (vectSum ~ AA:scalarVectProd):<<a0u,S_01>,<a1u,S_11>>,
    S_00 = (AA:K ~ CONS:Su0):<0,0>, S_01 = (AA:K ~ CONS:S0v):<0,1>,
    S_10 = (AA:K ~ CONS:Su0):<1,0>, S_11 = (AA:K ~ CONS:S1v):<1,1>,
    a0u = K:1 - u, a1u = u,
    a0v = K:1 - v, a1v = v,
    u = S1, v = S2
END;

DEF Domain2D (n,m::IsIntPos) = Intervals:1:n * Intervals:1:n;
```

**Script 12.5.14**

```
DEF Su0 = Bezier:<<0,0,0>,<10,0,0>> ~ [S1];
DEF Su1 = Bezier:<<0,10,0>,<2.5,10,3>,<5,10,-3>,<7.5,10,3>,<10,10,0>> ~ [S1];
DEF S0v = Bezier:<<0,0,0>,<0,0,3>,<0,10,3>,<0,10,0>> ~ [S2];
DEF S1v = Bezier:<<10,0,0>,<10,5,3>,<10,10,0>> ~ [S2];

MAP:(CoonsPatch:<Su0,Su1,S0v,S1v>):(Domain2D:<12,12>)
```

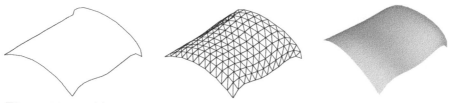

**Figure 12.21**    (a) Four assigned boundary curves (b) Polyhedral approximation of
the Coons' surface; (c) Smooth rendering

a parametric mapping, which can be any $d$-dimensional polyhedral complex, with
$d \leq n$ and $n$ the dimension of the mapping range. Thus, an example is given where a
spiral subset of 2D parameter space is mapped using the vector function CoonsPatch
previously defined.

In particular, let us consider the function SpiralMap : $[0, 6\pi] \subset \mathbb{R} \to \mathbb{E}^2$, such that
$t \mapsto (u, v)$, with

$$u = \frac{1}{2} + \frac{1}{2}\left(1 - 0.2\frac{t}{6\pi}\right)\sin t,$$

$$v = \frac{1}{2} + \frac{1}{2}\left(1 - 0.2\frac{t}{6\pi}\right)\cos t.$$

The 2D Spiral polyhedron in Figure 12.22a is mapped in $\mathbb{E}^3$ according to the last
expression of Script 12.5.15. The resulting curve image in 3D space is shown in
Figure 12.22b.

**Script 12.5.15**

```
DEF SpiralMap = [radius * COS, radius * SIN] ~ S1
WHERE radius = K:1 - (K:(0.2 / (6 * PI)) * ID) END;

DEF Spiral = (T:<1,2>:<0.5,0.5>~S:<1,2>:<0.5,0.5>):
    (MAP:SpiralMap:(Intervals:(6 * PI):100));

MAP:(CoonsPatch:<Su0,Su1,S0v,S1v>):Spiral;
```

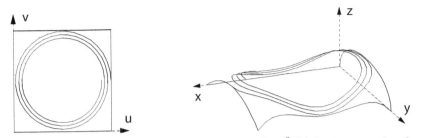

**Figure 12.22**   (a) Spiral in parametric domain $[0,1]^2$ (b) Its image under the
Coons' mapping defined by four 3D curves.

### 12.5.8   *Thin solids generated by surfaces*

A thin parametric solid described by a three-variate vector map $\boldsymbol{V}(u, v, w)$ generated
by a surface $\boldsymbol{S}(u, v)$ and with constant (small) thickness $\ell$ may be defined as

$$\boldsymbol{V}(\boldsymbol{S})(u, v, w) = \boldsymbol{S}(u, v) + w\ \boldsymbol{n}(u, v), \qquad u, v, w \in [0, 1]^2 \times [0, \ell] \qquad (12.10)$$

where

$$\boldsymbol{n}(\boldsymbol{S})(u, v) = \frac{\boldsymbol{S}^u(u, v) \times \boldsymbol{S}^v(u, v)}{\|\boldsymbol{S}^u(u, v) \times \boldsymbol{S}^v(u, v)\|}$$

is the unit vector function normal to the surface. Notice that, using the variable-free
notation (see Section 5.1.1) for functions, we have:

$$\boldsymbol{V} : (\mathbb{R}^2 \rightarrow \mathbb{E}^3) \rightarrow (\mathbb{R}^3 \rightarrow \mathbb{E}^3).$$

where

$$\boldsymbol{V}(\boldsymbol{S}) = \boldsymbol{S} + \sigma(3)\ \boldsymbol{n}(\boldsymbol{S}).$$

In other words, the $\boldsymbol{V}$ operator produces a *volume map* starting from a *surface map*.

**Implementation**   Luckily enough, it is very easy to write a PLaSM function
ThinSolid which implements in 3D the $\boldsymbol{V}$ operator described above. First, we
remember that the unit *normal* field $\boldsymbol{n}$ to a surface $\boldsymbol{S} : \mathbb{R}^2 \rightarrow \mathbb{E}^3$ is given by
the N operator defined in Script 5.7.1. So, by using our standard operators for
vector operations between function vectors, we can give the ThinSolid definition of
Script 12.5.16. As usual, S3 is the predefined selector of the $w$ coordinate of domain
points, and the formal parameter surface is a sequence of 3 bivariate coordinate
functions $\mathbb{R}^2 \rightarrow \mathbb{R}$, written using the selector functions S1 and S2, for $u$ and $v$,
respectively.

---

**Script 12.5.16 (ThinSolid operator)**
```
DEF ThinSolid (surface::IsSeqOf:IsFun) =
    surface vectSum (S3 scalarVectProd N:surface)
```

---

**Note**   We like to note the generality of the ThinSolid operator given above. It can be used to *solidify* every kind of parametric 3D surface discussed in this chapter, provided that the input to ThinSolid is a *triplet* of coordinate functions $\mathbb{R}^2 \to \mathbb{R}$. Even a 2D surface, namely surf2D, can be solidified into a triplet of coordinate functions of a solid map, by using a PLaSM expression like

      ThinSolid:(surf2D AR K:0);

The reader should notice that the ThinSolid operator cannot be used to transform a 2-manifold in $\mathbb{E}^n$ into a 3-manifold in $\mathbb{E}^n$, because the normal field is defined only in 3D as the vector product of partial derivatives. A more general definition would require exterior algebra, which is beyond the scope of this book, but is left as an interesting project for the mathematically skilled reader.

### Example 12.5.10 (Thin Coons' solid)

We conclude here our Coons' section by generating a thin solid slab from a 3D Coons' surface. Therefore, in Script 12.5.17, starting again from the 3D curves Su0, Su1, S0v and S1v defined in Script 12.5.14 and from the CoonsPatch and Domain2D generators given in Script 12.5.13, we first define a solidMapping sequence of coordinate functions of a volume map $\mathbb{R}^3 \to \mathbb{E}^3$. The thin solid *slab* of 0.5 thickness shown in Figure 12.23 is finally generated by the last script expression in the standard PLaSM way.

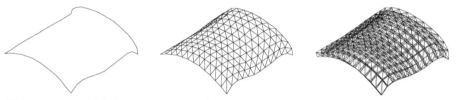

**Figure 12.23**   (a) Boundary curves (b) Interpolating surface (c) Thin Coons' solid generated by boundary curves

---

**Script 12.5.17 (Coons' slab)**

```
DEF solidMapping = (ThinSolid ~ CoonsPatch):<Su0,Su1,S0v,S1v>;
DEF Domain3D = Domain2D:<12,12> * Intervals:0.5:1;

MAP:solidMapping:Domain3D ;
```

---

## 12.6   Examples

Some non-trivial programming examples with parametric surfaces and solids are given in this section. In particular, we move one step further in the umbrella example of previous chapter, by generating the cloth canvas as surfaces depending on the opening angle; then we generate an helicoidal spiral volume resembling the Guggenheim Museum in New York City and a preliminary volume design of a sport building, and, finally, we model a free-form duct with cross-sections of constant area interpolating some given curves.

### 12.6.1   *Umbrella modeling (3): tissue canvas*

We continue here the step-wise refinement of the geometric modeling of the *parametric umbrella* introduced in Section 8.5.3 as a hierarchical assembly, already extended with curved rods in Section 11.5.2. A pair of cloth canvases is thus defined for the umbrella portion associated with the single instance of the `RodPair` object. The two canvases, shown in Figure 12.25a and Figure 12.25b, are defined as Coons' surfaces delimited by four Bézier curves of various degrees.

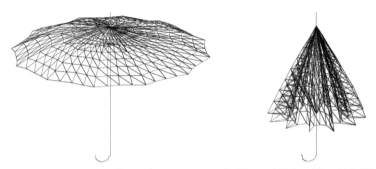

**Figure 12.24**   The new values of `Umbrella:<10,80>` and `Umbrella:<10,30>` after the redefinition of `RodPair`.

Before going on, our diligent reader should take another look at the previous implementation of the problem.

For `Canvas1`, two quadratic Bézier limiting curves (`ru0` and `ru1`) are generated by the same control points of `Rod11` and by their rotated instance (around the $z$ axis); the other two curves are obtained by taking respectively the first and the last points (`p1` and `p3`) of such curves, and by computing two more points (`p12` and `p22`) on the horizontal plane. The position of such control points is a proper function of the opening angle of the umbrella.

A function `MoveToWC` is needed to reproduce the pipeline of 3D transformations (discussed in Section 6.4.2) which must be applied to the extreme points of `rod11`. Notice that within the `Umbrella` generating function the same transformations are applied to polyhedra by using primitive PLaSM operators.

The second canvas just differs from the first one in the choice of the limiting curves. In particular, the functions `ru0` and `ru1` are now given as linear Bézier with two control points, and `r0v` is given as a Bézier function of degree 0 depending on a single control point.

**Figure 12.25**   (a) First canvas (b) Second canvas (c) Complex generated by `RodPair:<10,80>`

**Script 12.6.1**

```
DEF Canvas1 (h, alpha::Isreal) =
   MAP:(CoonsPatch:<ru0,ru1,r0v,r1v>):(Domain2D:<4,4>)
WHERE
   handles1 = MoveToWC:<<0,0,0>,<0,0,AB/2>,<AB/2 * sin:beta,0,AB>>,
   MoveToWC = AA:(Tz:h ~ Ry:(-:alphaRad) ~ Tz:(-:AB) ~ Sz:-1),
   handles2 = AA:(Rz:(PI/6)):handles1,
   ru0 = Bezier:handles1,
   ru1 = Bezier:handles2,
   r0v = Bezier:<p1, p12, Rz:(PI/6):p1> ~ [S2],
   r1v = Bezier:<p2, p22, Rz:(PI/6):p2> ~ [S2],
   p1 = FIRST:handles1,
   p2 = LAST:handles1,
   p12 = Rz:(PI/12):<S1:p1 - AB/2*COS:alphaRad, S2:p1, S3:p1>,
   p22 = Rz:(PI/12):<S1:p2 - AB*COS:alphaRad, S2:p2, S3:p2>,
   beta = -:alphaRad/4,
   alphaRad = alpha*PI/180,
   AB = h*4/10
END;
```

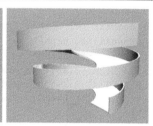

**Figure 12.26** (a) Helicoidal cylinder with vertical rules (b) Double helicoidal surface defined by two helix curves (c) Thin solid slabs generated by two surfaces

The function RodPair is thus defined again, by inserting in it a proper pair of canvases, shown in Figure 12.25. The new configurations of the whole umbrella for different opening angles are shown in Figure 12.24.

### 12.6.2 *Helicoidal spiral volume*

In this example we generate some curves and surfaces by using parametric affine transformations, and solids by linear transfinite interpolation of surfaces. Our goal is to make the reader acquainted with this kind of generative methods, which may offer useful shape modeling tools. In Figure 12.26 we show both intermediate and final results of our modeling session, i.e. a pair of spiral helix surfaces and solids with both horizontal and vertical rule directions.

In Figure 12.27 the design approach we are going to discuss is stepwise illustrated. The equations used and their PLaSM implementation are given below.

**Script 12.6.2**

```
DEF Canvas2 (h, alpha::Isreal) =
    MAP:(CoonsPatch:<ru0,ru1,r0v,r1v>):(Domain2D:<4,4>)
WHERE
    handles1 = MoveToWC:<<0,0,0>,<0,0,AB>>,
    MoveToWC = AA:(Tz:h ~ Ry:(-:alphaRad) ~ Sz:-1),
    handles2 = AA:(Rz:(PI/6)):handles1,
    ru0 = Bezier:handles1,
    ru1 = Bezier:handles2,
    r0v = Bezier:<p1> ~ [S2],
    r1v = Bezier:<p2, p22, Rz:(PI/6):p2> ~ [S2],
    p1 = FIRST:handles1,
    p2 = LAST:handles1,
    p22 = Rz:(PI/12):<S1:p2 - AB/2*COS:alphaRad, S2:p2, S3:p2>,
    beta = -:alphaRad/4,
    alphaRad = alpha*PI/180,
    AB = h*4/10
END;
```

**Script 12.6.3**

```
DEF RodPair (h, alpha::Isreal) = STRUCT:<
    Canvas1:<h, alpha>,
    Canvas2:<h, alpha>,
    T:3:h, R:<3,1>:(-:alphaRad), Rod10,
    STRUCT:<T:3:(-:AB), Rod11 >,
    T:3:(-:AB), R:<3,1>:(2*alphaRad), Rod2 >
WHERE
    alphaRad = alpha*PI/180,
    Rod10 = S:3:-1:(Rod:(AB)),
    Rod11 = S:3:-1:(RodCurve:<AB,-:alphaRad/4,4>),
    Rod2 = S:3:-1:(Rod:AB),
    AB = h*4/10
END;
```

## Planar spiral curve

This *curve* may be obtained by rotating the unit vector $e_1$ with parametric angle $u$, and then by uniform scaling the $\mathbb{E}^2$ plane with $R + \frac{d}{2\pi}u$ scaling parameter, where $R$ is the starting *radius* and $d$ is the *distance* between the two points reached by the curve before and after a $2\pi$ turn. Hence, we can write:

$$
\begin{aligned}
c(u) &= \begin{pmatrix} R + \frac{d}{2\pi}u & 0 \\ 0 & R + \frac{d}{2\pi}u \end{pmatrix} \begin{pmatrix} \cos u & -\sin u \\ \sin u & \cos u \end{pmatrix} \begin{pmatrix} 1 \\ 0 \end{pmatrix} \qquad 0 \le u \le 2\pi n \\
&= \begin{pmatrix} \left(R + \frac{d}{2\pi}u\right)\cos u & \left(R + \frac{d}{2\pi}u\right)\sin u \end{pmatrix}
\end{aligned}
$$

and, using the variable-free functional notation:

$$
c = \begin{pmatrix} (\underline{R} + \left(\frac{d}{2\pi}\right)\mathrm{id})\cos & (\underline{R} + \left(\frac{d}{2\pi}\right)\mathrm{id})\sin \end{pmatrix}
$$

**Figure 12.27**  (a) Planar spiral (b) Helicoidal spiral

**Implementation**  We can directly rewrite in Script 12.6.4 the previous notation, using the **radius** symbol for $R$. The curve shown in Figure 12.27a is produced with *Adobe Illustrator*© by importing the SVG file produced by the script. As always, the S1 selector is used rather than the ID function, because the coordinate functions must be applied to the domain decomposition vertices, that are represented as sequences.

---

**Script 12.6.4 (Planar spiral)**

```
DEF spiral (radius,d::isRealPos) = < rad * COS ~ S1, rad * SIN ~ S1 >
WHERE
    rad = K:radius + K:(d/(2*PI)) * S1
END;

DEF out = MAP:(spiral:<3,0.5>):(intervals:(2*PI*2):200);
svg:out:400:'out.svg'
```

---

### Helicoidal spiral

By adding a parametric translation in the $z$ direction, where $h$ is the *pitch*, i.e. the $z$ difference after one helix turn, we get the *helicoidal spiral curve* in $\mathbb{E}^3$, whose parametric equation as a function of the turning angle $u$ is:

$$c(u) = \begin{pmatrix} \left(R + \frac{d}{2\pi}u\right)\cos u \\ \left(R + \frac{d}{2\pi}u\right)\sin u \\ 0 \end{pmatrix} + \begin{pmatrix} 0 \\ 0 \\ \frac{h}{2\pi}u \end{pmatrix}$$

And, in variable-free notation

$$c = \left(\ (\underline{R} + (\tfrac{d}{2\pi})\mathrm{id})\cos \quad (\underline{R} + (\tfrac{d}{2\pi})\mathrm{id})\sin \quad (\tfrac{h}{2\pi})\mathrm{id}\ \right)^T$$

**Implementation**  In Script 12.6.5 the spiralhelix generator is given, as a function depending on **radius**, **d** and **h**, and producing a sequence of three coordinate functions. The produced curve is shown in Figure 12.27b. Notice that the * operator has a higher precedence than +.

**Script 12.6.5 (Helicoidal spiral (1))**

```
    DEF spiralhelix (radius,d,h::isReal) = < rad * COS~S1, rad * SIN~S1, z >
    WHERE
        rad = K:radius + K:(d/(2*PI)) * S1,
        z = K:(h/(2*PI)) * S1
    END;

    DEF out = MAP:(spiralhelix:<3,1,2>):(intervals:(4*PI):200);
    VRML:out:'out.wrl'
```

## Helicoidal cylinder

The *helicoidal spiral cylinder* surface shown in Figure 12.26a is obtained by bivariate transfinite interpolation of two curves. Such a Bézier surface of the *first degree* in the $v$ parameter is generated by two control (curve) maps. In particular, we execute the following steps:

1. the sequence of coordinate functions of a $c_1$ curve is generated;
2. a second curve $c_2 = c_1 + (0, 0, h)^T$ is defined;
3. the coordinate functions of the surface are produced as linear transfinite Bézier combination of the coordinate functions of $c_1$ and $c_2$;
4. finally, the surface coordinate functions are mapped over some suitable domain decomposition.

**Implementation**     Our helicoidal spiral cylinder is implemented in Script 12.6.6 by following the procedure discussed above. The c1 curve is a `spiralhelix`; the c2 curve is a translated copy of c1. Notice that the translation is given as a sum by a vector (sequence) of constant functions. The resulting sup surface is generated by the transfinite operator `Bezier:S2` given in Script 12.5.3. The reader should try some other generation method directly applicable to this case.

**Script 12.6.6 (Helicoidal spiral cylinder)**

```
    DEF c1 = spiralhelix:<3,1,2>;
    DEF c2 = c1 vectSum <K:0, K:0, K:1>;

    DEF sup = Bezier:S2:< c1, c2 >;
    DEF dom2D = intervals:(4*PI):100 * intervals:1:1;

    DEF out = MAP:sup:dom2D;
    VRML:(out CREASE (PI/2)):'out.wrl';
```

## Pair of connected surfaces

A pair of helicoidal spiral surfaces, connected on a common curve, with horizontal and vertical rules, respectively, is produced by Script 12.6.7 using three curves c0, c1 and c2. For this purpose the c0 curve is generated with smaller radius and d parameter equal to zero. The last expression of the script produces the model shown in Figure 12.26b.

---

**Script 12.6.7 (Pair of spiral surfaces)**
```
DEF c0 = spiralhelix:<1,0,2>;
DEF c1 = spiralhelix:<3,1,2>;
DEF c2 = c1 vectSum <K:0, K:0, K:1>;

DEF surf0 = Bezier:S2:< c0, c1 >;
DEF surf1 = Bezier:S2:< c1, c2 >;
(STRUCT ~ [MAP:surf0, MAP:surf1]):dom2D ;
```

---

### Double solid cylinder slab

A solid model of the two spiral slabs shown in Figure 12.26c is finally generated by assembling two helicoidal 3-manifolds, respectively generated by solid0 and solid1 $\mathbb{R}^3 \to \mathbb{E}^3$ maps, defined by transfinite Bézier blending of two surface maps in Script 12.6.8. Notice that dom3D is a suitable partition of the 3D interval $[0,1]^3$. Notice also that the objects named c1, c2, surf0 and surf1 are defined in Script 12.6.7. The spiralhelix generator is given in Script 12.6.5.

---

**Script 12.6.8 (Doppia superficie elicoidale)**
```
DEF c3 = spiralhelix:<3.15,1,2>;
DEF c4 = c3 vectSum <K:0, K:0, K:1>;

DEF surf01 = surf0 vectSum <K:0, k:0, K:0.15>;
DEF surf11 = Bezier:S2:< c3, c4 >;

DEF solid0 = bezier:S3:< surf0, surf01 >;
DEF solid1 = bezier:S3:< surf1, surf11 >;
DEF dom3D = dom2D * intervals:1:1;

DEF out = (STRUCT ~ [MAP: solid0, MAP: solid1]): dom3D ;
VRML:(out CREASE (PI/5)):'prove/out5.wrl';
```

---

**Suggestion** The reader is warmly invited to modify the scripts given above, in order to generate a lateral spiral wall belonging to a reversed conical surface, resembling the well-known design of the Guggenheim Museum in New York City. Finally, make the model solid by using again the transfinite Bézier approach.

### 12.6.3 Roof design for a sports building

Here we introduce a study project, shown in Figure 12.28, concerning the preliminary design of the roof of a building for indoor sport meetings. We suggest generating the building cover by using the same approach discussed in the previous section. The more interesting part of the project concerns the modeling of the lateral columns, linked to

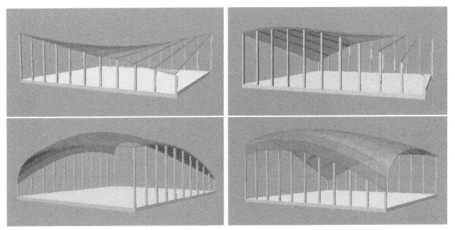

**Figure 12.28**   Some preliminary designs with roof covers of different geometry

the rhythm of the roof partitioning. We suggest using the curve maps interpolated to crate one of the roof surfaces as the generators of the data that produce and locate the columns, according to Figure 12.28.

No coding is given in this case. The reader is invited to reuse as much as possible of the implementation of the previous section. Notice that the authors' coding of this building is completely parametrized with respect to the degrees of the two roof directions and to the number of lateral columns. The roof's transparency effect can be obtained by loading the `colors` library, and by some statements like

```
DEF mycolor = RGBCOLOR:< 0.2,0.6,1 >;
DEF GLASS = BASEMATERIAL:< mycolor,mycolor,0.2,BLACK,0.2,0.6 >;
   roof MATERIAL GLASS;
```

where `roof` is a PLaSM object of polyhedral complex type.

### 12.6.4   Constrained connection volume

We discuss in this section the geometric design of curved ducts with a variable cross-section by transfinite interpolation with integro-differential constraints. This approach is based on piecewise multivariate transfinite interpolation of assigned cross-sections, via combination of section-generating functions with univariate cubic Hermite's polynomials. The volume mapping thus produced is composed of a local section scaling extracted from a one-parameter family of affine transformations, where the diagonal coefficients depend on the ratio between the areas of the starting and current sections. An appropriately chosen point sampling of the duct generated by the composition of volume mapping and section scaling may be used to generate the cell decomposition of the duct volume with tetrahedral elements. Such elements are used for numerical simulation of a fluid-dynamics problem.

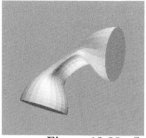

**Figure 12.29** Some views of the unconstrained interpolated duct.

**Problem statement**

Let two smooth parametric surfaces $S_0$ and $S_1$ be given, with

$$S_0, S_1 : [0, 1]^2 \to \mathbb{E}^3.$$

Let also two fields $N_0$ and $N_1$ of vectors normal to the surfaces $S_0$ and $S_1$ be assigned, with:

$$N_0 \quad : \quad [0,1]^2 \to \mathbb{R}^3 \quad : \quad N_0(u,v) = h(\partial_u S_0(u,v) \times \partial_v S_0(u,v)),$$
$$N_1 \quad : \quad [0,1]^2 \to \mathbb{R}^3 \quad : \quad N_1(u,v) = h(\partial_u S_1(u,v) \times \partial_v S_1(u,v)),$$

with $h \in \mathbb{R}$.

Our goal is to generate the solid obtained by cubic Hermite's interpolation of surfaces $S_0$ and $S_1$ with normal vector fields given by $N_0, N_1$. In other words, we want to generate the vector function $V$, depending on a triplet of real parameters $(u, v, w)$, and defined as:

$$V : [0, 1]^3 \to \mathbb{E}^3, \qquad \text{such that:}$$

$$V(u, v, 0) = S_0(u, v), \qquad V(u, v, 1) = S_1(u, v),$$
$$\partial_w V(u, v, 0) = N_0(u, v), \qquad \partial_w V(u, v, 1) = N_1(u, v),$$

under the constraint that the area of given "cross-sections" (for $w$ fixed) be constant and equal to the area of initial section:

$$\text{Area}(w) = \int_{V(U \times \{w\})} dS = \int_{S_0(U)} dS = \text{Area}(0), \qquad \text{for each } w \in [0, 1].$$

where $U = [0, 1]^2$. In the following we will refer to the function $V$ above as *volume map*.

**Approach** Of course, the more difficult part of the problem is given by the constraint of constant area for each cross-section of the solid generated by the volume map $V$. The volume map without such constraint would be constructed in a natural way as a cubic Hermite's transfinite blending of maps $S_0(u,v)$, $S_1(u,v)$, $N_0(u,v)$ and $N_1(u,v)$, according to the approach described in [BCP00]. The solution described here utilizes methods of transfinite blending, i.e., of interpolation in functional spaces.

The basic *volume map* is thus given by:

$$V(u, v, w) = \begin{pmatrix} h_0^3(w) & h_1^3(w) & \cdots & h_3^3(w) \end{pmatrix} \begin{pmatrix} S_0(u, v) \\ S_1(u, v) \\ N_0(u, v) \\ N_1(u, v) \end{pmatrix}$$

with

$$S_0, S_1, N_0, N_1 \in \mathbb{P}_2^n \subset \{\mathbb{R}^2 \to \mathbb{R}^3\}$$

$$V \in \mathbb{P}_3^n \subset \{\mathbb{R}^3 \to \mathbb{R}^3\}$$

Actually, the PLaSM implementation is a mapping of this kind:

$$M(u_1, \ldots, u_d) = \begin{pmatrix} h_0^3(u_d) & h_1^3(u_d) & h_2^3(u_d) & h_3^3(u_d) \end{pmatrix} \begin{pmatrix} S_0(u_1, \ldots, u_{d-1}) \\ S_1(u_1, \ldots, u_{d-1}) \\ N_0(u_1, \ldots, u_{d-1}) \\ N_1(u_1, \ldots, u_{d-1}) \end{pmatrix}$$

with

$$S_0, S_1, N_0, N_1 \in \mathbb{P}_{d-1}^n \subset \{\mathbb{R}^{d-1} \to \mathbb{R}^q\}, \qquad d-1 \leq q$$

$$M \in \mathbb{P}_d^n \subset \{\mathbb{R}^d \to \mathbb{R}^q\}, \qquad d \leq q$$

so it works in the general case of $d$-variate manifolds.

## Constrained Volume Map

In our approach the duct internal volume is generated by two surface interpolation steps, using three given surfaces. The desired volume map is thus obtained by the union of a first solid map interpolating the base section surface with a middle section surface, and a second solid map interpolating the middle section surface with the rotated and translated base section surface (see Figures 12.30b and 12.30c). An example of the final constrained duct interior is illustrated in Figures 12.32a, 12.32b and 12.32c, showing it from different points of view.

## Constant-area constraint

In the first phase of computation an initial sequence of interpolated sections is generated. Each section corresponds to one of the $w$ values of a user-specified uniform discretization. Successively, a proper affine transformation is applied to each section to satisfy the constant cross-section constraint.

First we get the solid $V([0, 1]^3)$ generated by the basic *volume map* applied to the standard 3-cube, to obtain an unconstrained duct. Then a family

$$Z : [0, 1] \to \text{aff}\{\mathbb{E}^3\} : w \mapsto Z(w)$$

**Figure 12.30** Input maps: (a) 2D curves (b) embedding in 3D (c) surfaces to be interpolated

of affine transformations, depending on a parameter $w \in [0,1]$, is properly applied to each cross-section. Each $\boldsymbol{Z}(w)$ is an *uniform dilatation* in the $x, y$ directions of a local frame $(\boldsymbol{e}_x(w), \boldsymbol{e}_y(w), \boldsymbol{e}_z(w))$, with

$$\boldsymbol{e}_x(w) = \frac{\boldsymbol{q}_x(w)}{\|\boldsymbol{q}_x(w)\|}, \qquad \boldsymbol{q}_x(w) = \boldsymbol{V}(\epsilon, 0, w) - \boldsymbol{V}(0, 0, w),$$

$$\boldsymbol{e}_y(w) = \frac{\boldsymbol{q}_y(w)}{\|\boldsymbol{q}_y(w)\|}, \qquad \boldsymbol{q}_y(w) = \boldsymbol{V}(0, \epsilon, w) - \boldsymbol{V}(0, 0, w),$$

$$\boldsymbol{e}_z(w) = \frac{\boldsymbol{q}_z(w)}{\|\boldsymbol{q}_z(w)\|}, \qquad \boldsymbol{q}_z(w) = \boldsymbol{V}(0, 0, \epsilon + w) - \boldsymbol{V}(0, 0, w),$$

and $\epsilon \to 0$. Notice that the local frame $\{\boldsymbol{e}_x(w), \boldsymbol{e}_y(w), \boldsymbol{e}_z(w)\}$ is extracted from the *tangent 3-manifold* to $\boldsymbol{V}[0,1]^3$ at $\boldsymbol{V}(0,0,w)$.

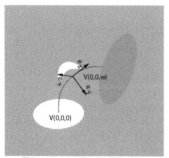 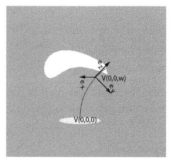

**Figure 12.31** Basis on the tangent 3-manifold at $\boldsymbol{V}(0,0,w)$ with the corresponding cross-sections $B(w)$ and $(\boldsymbol{Z}(w)(B(w)))$.

Each $\boldsymbol{Z}(w)$, $w \in [0,1]$, is applied to the point set $B(w) = \boldsymbol{V}([0,1]^2 \times \{w\})$. See Figures 12.31a and 12.31b to clarify this point.

The family of maps $\boldsymbol{Z}(w)$ is defined by composition of elementary affine transformations depending on the parameter $w$. In particular, as usual in graphics, translations $\boldsymbol{T}(t(w))$ and inverse $\boldsymbol{T}(-t(w))$, rotations $\boldsymbol{R}(w)$ and inverse $\boldsymbol{R}^T(w)$, and a scaling $\boldsymbol{S}(s(w), s(w), 1)$ are composed together:

$$\boldsymbol{Z}(w) = \boldsymbol{T}(-t(w)) \circ \boldsymbol{R}^T(w) \circ \boldsymbol{S}(s(w), s(w), 1) \circ \boldsymbol{R}(w) \circ \boldsymbol{T}(t(w))$$

with

$$\boldsymbol{R}(w) = \left( \begin{array}{ccc} \boldsymbol{e}_x(w) & \boldsymbol{e}_y(w) & \boldsymbol{e}_z(w) \end{array} \right)^{-1} = \left( \begin{array}{c} \boldsymbol{e}_x(w)^T \\ \boldsymbol{e}_y(w)^T \\ \boldsymbol{e}_z(w)^T \end{array} \right)$$

$$\boldsymbol{t}(w) = \boldsymbol{V}(0,0,0) - \boldsymbol{V}(0,0,w),$$

and where

$$\boldsymbol{S}(w) = \left( \begin{array}{ccc} s(w) & 0 & 0 \\ 0 & s(w) & 0 \\ 0 & 0 & 1 \end{array} \right)$$

with

$$s(w) = \sqrt{\frac{\mathrm{Area}(0)}{\mathrm{Area}(w)}} = \sqrt{\frac{\int \boldsymbol{S}_{0([0,1]^2)} \, dS}{\int \boldsymbol{V}_{([0,1]^2 \times \{w\})} \, dS}}$$

The surface integral is computed using a general polynomial-integrating algorithm described in [Ber91]. The algorithm allows an efficient computation of integrals of polynomial functions over polyhedral domains of any dimension. This is easily computed in PLaSM by a single primitive

```
INTEGRAL:pol_complex:<i₁,i₂,...,i_d>
```

which returns the value of the domain integral of the monomial

$$I_{x_1 \cdots x_d}^{i_1 \cdots i_d} = \int_{\texttt{pol\_complex}} x_1^{i_1} \, x_2^{i_2} \, \ldots, x_d^{i_d} \, dV.$$

The domain may not have a full dimensionality, e.g. a piecewise-linear curve or surface in $\mathrm{IR}^3$. In particular, when the expression is

```
INTEGRAL:pol_complex:0
```

the volume of the input complex is computed. When the input is the piecewise linear approximation of a curve or surface its length or surface area are computed.

## Maps composition

The *constrained volume map* $\boldsymbol{V}^*$ is now obtained by composition of the *volume map* $\boldsymbol{V}$ previously discussed with a family of affine transformations depending on one parameter. In particular, we have that

$$\boldsymbol{V}^* : [0,1]^3 \to \mathrm{IR}^3$$

is easily defined as:

$$\boldsymbol{V}^*(u,v,w) = (\boldsymbol{Z}(w) \circ \boldsymbol{V})(u,v,w)$$

with $\boldsymbol{V}$ cubic transfinite Hermite's interpolation of input maps, and $\boldsymbol{Z} : [0,1] \to$ aff $\{\mathrm{IE}^3\}$, the family of affine transformations previously given.

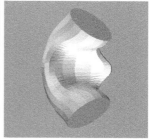

**Figure 12.32**   Some views of the final constrained duct

## Example

We aim to generate a duct interpolating two extreme circular sections lying on two orthogonal planes, and passing through any intermediate cross-section, defined by a closed Bézier curve. In this approach, we generate independently two duct segments by interpolating from both the extreme sections to the intermediate one. First, we give the plane curves defining the sections, then we build the 3D surfaces corresponding to the section interiors, and later we interpolate the section maps with assigned normal vector fields by using cubic Hermite interpolants. The pipeline of affine transformations that satisfy the constant cross-section area constraint is finally composed with the volume map.

**Note**   We have discussed a programming approach to the modeling of free-form ducts with cross-sections of constant area, based on the composition of transfinite volume maps with section scaling aiming to satisfy such integral constraint. The details of the implementation would require a quantity of code that is not reasonable to insert in a book section. Anyway, the authors found it interesting that the complete implementation amounts to three pages of PLaSM code, and that it was developed and tested in four days.

**Programming approach to features**   The geometric modeling of ducts with variable cross-section allowed us to evaluate the use of PLaSM in generating complex form features by a fully parametrized functional programming approach. The solid duct generation here described can in fact be completely parametrized with respect to number, position and orientation of the given key-sections, and even to their shape. Furthermore, this transfinite solution can also generate an optimal decomposition of the duct interior with tetrahedral elements. We like to emphasize that our geometric programming not only allows definition of geometric objects in a fully parametrized way, but also definition of compact new methods for geometric shape generation, even when subject to constraints of great mathematical complexity.

# 13

# Basic solid modeling

This chapter is dedicated to discussing the computer representation of mathematical models of physical bodies and some main algorithms on such so-called *solid models*. The attention of "classic" solid modeling is focused on representational issues for computer models of physical bodies. Its core topics concern Boolean operations and domain integration: the former allow the union, intersection or difference of solid models; the latter is used to compute volumes and inertial properties. Simulating numerically controlled (NC) machining [MV92] is another use of solid modeling technology. It also supports offsetting, reverse engineering from both physical and engineering models to computer models, and dimensional tolerancing analysis [RR86, VMJ97, Voe98]. We start this chapter by outlining Voelcker's and Requicha's theoretical approach, and their standard taxonomy of representation schemes. Then some main issues about boundary representations are introduced. Finally, we discuss two simple approaches to Boolean operations and volume integration over polyhedral objects by using a boundary triangulation. Our aim is to present a basic introduction to some classic notions in solid modeling. For an in-depth comprehensive review of both theoretical foundations and research directions, the interested reader is referred to the stimulating survey by Vadim Shapiro [Sha01].

## 13.1 Representation scheme

The concept of a *representation scheme*, located at the foundations of solid modeling, originates in the theoretical and applied research in design and manufacturing automation carried out by Project Automation Project (PAP) at the University of Rochester in late 1970s. In particular, the idea of a representation scheme was formalized by Aristides Requicha into his milestone paper [Req80]. A new interesting framework for both geometric and solid modeling and its practical implications are discussed by Rappoport in [Rap95].

*Geometric Programming for Computer-Aided Design*  Alberto Paoluzzi
© 2003 John Wiley & Sons, Ltd  ISBN 0-471-89942-9

*13.1.1   Definition and properties*

A *representation scheme* is defined as a mapping $s : M \to R$ between a set $M$ of mathematical *models* of solid objects and a set $R$ of computer *representations*, see Figure 13.1. In particular:

1. The set $M$ contains appropriate mathematical models of the class of solid object that the scheme is designed to represent.
2. The set $R$ contains symbolic representations, i.e. suitable data structures, built according to some appropriate computer grammar.

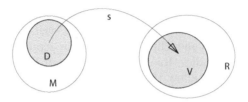

**Figure 13.1**   The representation scheme $s$ is a mapping between a set $M$ of
mathematical models and a set $R$ of computer representations

**Domain**   A representation scheme $s$ is usually defined only on a subset $D \subset M$ of mathematical models, that is called the *domain* of the scheme. In other words, not every element of a certain class of models might be represented in a given scheme, but this one could be designed to represent only a subset of the model collection. E.g., a scheme used to represent plane polygons should be able to filter *a priori* non-simple polygons (i.e. with self-intersecting boundary), because they are not interesting in most modeling problems.

**Validity**   Analogously, the codomain $V = s(D) \subseteq R$ of a scheme $s$ does not necessarily coincide with the target set $R$ of syntactically well-formed representations, i.e. built according to the given grammar. The set $V$ of representations which are not only syntactically correct, but also semantically significant, because they correspond to some model in the domain of the scheme, is called the *validity set* of the scheme.

When designing a representation scheme for a solid modeler it is important to device some *validity test* to check if a given representation really corresponds to some object in the domain of the scheme. As a matter of fact, syntactically correct representations may not be semantically significant.

Let us consider, e.g., the linked lists of vertices as representations of plane polygons. If the domain of the scheme is restricted to simple (non self-intersecting) polygons, then the statement appears false that every sequence of 2D points corresponds to some simple polygon. A typical validity test in this case should look for pair-wise intersection of boundary edges, given by couples of adjacent points.

**Completeness**  A valid representation $r \in V$ is said to be *complete* when it is associated by the scheme $s$ with just one model in the domain $D$ of the scheme. In formal terms, $r$ is said to be complete when

$$|s^{-1}(r)| = 1.$$

The scheme $s$ is also said to be *complete* when every representation in $V$ is complete. In other words, the scheme $s$ is complete when the inverse mapping $s^{-1}$ is a *function*.

The concept of completeness should be considered from an informational point of view. A representation which corresponds to more than one model is said non complete, because it captures some information which is common to all the associated models, and therefore is not sufficient to completely specify any one of them. A non complete representation is, in some sense, too general and not sufficiently specific. Conversely, a complete representation completely specifies the model that it represents.

**Unicity**  A representation $r \in s(m)$ is said to be *unique* when the set $s(m) \subset V$ contains just one element. Analogously, a representation scheme $s$ is complete when $|s(m)| = 1$, for each model $m \in D$.

When a scheme $s$ is both complete and unique, it establishes a one-to-one mapping between the domain and the validity set of the scheme. Such a kind of scheme is called *canonical*, and the associated representations are called canonical representations. A canonical scheme is quite unusual in solid modeling, depending on the high computational costs needed to guarantee the unicity of such kind of schemes.

With a canonical scheme the identity test between two representations $r, q \in V$ could be solved in a purely syntactical way, while conversely it requires serious semantical comparisons of the kind:

$$(s^{-1}(r) \cup s^{-1}(q)) - (s^{-1}(r) \cap s^{-1}(q)) \stackrel{?}{=} \emptyset.$$

Most representation schemes for geometric objects are not unique, because the same model may correspond to several representations. Typical reasons of non-uniqueness are of a *permutational* and *positional* nature.

An example of permutational non-uniqueness is given by the representation of a plane polygon as the linked list of its $n$ vertices. In this case, each one of the $n$ cyclic permutations of vertices gives one equivalent representation of the same polygon. A positional non-uniqueness is introduced when the representation is defined modulus a rigid transformation.

**r-sets**  In some sense, the usefulness of a scheme $s$ is measured by the size of its domain, i.e. by the number of mathematical models it is able to represent. The larger is the domain, the greater are the expressive power of the scheme and its usefulness for the purposes of a modeling system.

The Rochester group pointed out as a useful domain for a solid modeling representation scheme the collection of so-called *r-sets*, i.e. the collection of *regular, closed, bounded and semi-analytic subsets* of $\mathbb{E}^3$.

It may be useful to remember that a subset $S \subset \mathbb{E}^n$ is called:

1. *regular* when it is homogeneously $n$-dimensional, i.e. when each point $x \in S$ has a neighborhood $N(x) \subset S$ of dimension $n$;

2. *closed* when it contains its boundary. In other words, when

$$S = \text{clos}(S) = S \cup \partial S;$$

3. *bounded* when each point $x \in S$ has bounded coordinates. In other words, when the distance between every pair of points in $S$ is bounded;
4. *semi-analytic* when the set can be expressed as a Boolean combination of sets of type $\{x \in \mathbb{E}^n | f_i(x) \leq 0\}$, where each $f_i$ is an analytic function.

A function $f : \mathbb{E}^n \rightarrow \mathbb{R}$ is said to be *analytic* when it can be expanded into a convergent power series in the neighborhood of each point $x_0$ of its domain:

$$f(x_0) = \sum_{n=0}^{\infty} a_n (x - x_0)^n, \qquad \text{with } |x - x_0| \leq r, r > 0.$$

The sum, difference and product of analytic functions are again analytic. If $f(x)$ is analytic at $x_0$, then it is differentiable arbitrarily often in some neighborhood of $x_0$, and:

$$f(x_0) = \sum_{n=0}^{\infty} \frac{f^{(n)}(x_0)}{n!} (x - x_0)^n, \qquad (\textit{Taylor series}).$$

The concept of $r$-set played a very important role in the development of solid modeling as a discipline, since it seems to capture the more important aspects of the object's *solidity*.

**Manifolds**   A *manifold* object of dimension $n$ is defined as a point set where each point has some neighborhood homeomorphic to the $n$-disc. This means that there is some neighborhood of the point which may be bicontinuously transformed to such a disc.

Let us note that an $n$-dimensional $r$-set $S$ may have a *non-manifold* boundary (see Section 13.1), where some points in $\partial S$ do not have a neighborhood in $\partial S$ homeomorphic to the $(n-1)$-dimensional disc. See, e.g. Figure 13.2.

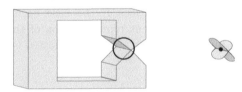

**Figure 13.2**   Non-manifold boundary points: they do not have a neighborhood homeomorphic to the 2-dimensional disc

It is very important to notice that a set of manifold models is not closed with respect to the property of manifoldness when considering Boolean set operations. For example, the union of two manifolds is not necessarily a manifold. Let us imagine, e.g., the union of two cubes touching along one edge or vertex. Thus, a representation scheme needs to take this point into careful account; in other words, it must be able to represent both manifold and non-manifold objects.

## 13.1.2   Taxonomy of representation schemes

A taxonomy of the more important representation schemes used in solid modeling and CAD systems developed in the 1970s was introduced by Ari Requicha in his milestone paper [Req80]. Such a classification continues to be valid more than 20 years later, and is very useful both in comparing systems existing today and in designing new ones. It is succinctly summarized in the following paragraphs. Several reviews of the state of art in solid modeling have been published in the last two decades. They include [Req80, RV83, Req88, RR92, Ros94, RR99, Sha01].

**Primitive instancing**   This is a sort of procedural approach. Each representation is a *tuple* with the name of a generating procedure or function as the first element, followed by the actual values of its parameters. Both the domain and the codomain of the scheme may be partitioned into non-intersecting classes. There is a one-to-one mapping between classes of models and classes of representations. This kind of approach was given new life with current object-oriented software development techniques, and is largely used with parametric and feature-oriented modeling systems. Some theoretically oriented recent approaches belong to this class of representations [Rag00, RS02]. It actually needs some underlying more abstract representation scheme where methods of general utility (like Boolean operations and integration operators) are really implemented.

**Enumerative schemes**   A solid model is described by enumerating the set of "full" cells in some partitioning of the embedding space. It is possible to distinguish between schemes using sparse Boolean matrices and schemes based upon hierarchical space decompositions, say *quadtrees* and *octrees*, in 2D and 3D case, respectively. In most cases such representations are approximations of the object's space occupancy, even for linear polyhedra.

**Decompositive schemes**   The object is represented as a set of cells, usually of a given topology. Unlike enumerative schemes, in this case the cell partition is induced by the represented object itself. The BSP (Boundary Space Partition) trees belong to this type of representation [NAT90]. As we have already seen, BSP trees are binary trees where each internal node is associated with one of the boundary hyperplanes of the object, and each leaf node represents a convex cell, either full or empty, of the space partition induced by such a set of hyperplanes. Decompositive schemes also support more abstract and generalized representations of topology [Lie89] and unifying approaches to both geometry representation and physical simulations [JS00].

**Boundary schemes**   These are the more common representation schemes used in computer graphics and in most modeling kernels. The interior of a body is represented by means of its external boundary, and in particular by a partition of it into shells, faces, edges and vertices. Each boundary representation stores in some way some of the binary adjacency relations between the various boundary entities. There is a notable difference between the boundary representations of *manifolds* and those of *non-manifold* objects.

**CSG schemes**   The acronym stands for *Constructive Solid Geometry*. In this scheme the representations are binary trees where internal nodes represent either regularized set operations or affine transformations, whereas leaf nodes represent either primitive solids or implicit halfspaces (usually linear or quadratic). An explicit representation of the boundary is obtained by suitably traversing the tree.

**Sweeping schemes**   In mechanical or civil applications, several solids may be defined as the result of properly moving a surface along an assigned profile curve. The representation in this case contains both the generating surface and curve. A sweeping scheme is particularly useful and simple with parametric representation of surfaces and curves. There are also approaches belonging to this class of schemes which can be reduced to some generalized version of the Cartesian product.

**Composite schemes**   Some commonly used schemes use multiple types of representations. Typically, in a composite scheme, a boundary representation is maintained together with another representation, often a CSG or decompositive or primitive instancing. There are some very interesting composite octree/boundary representations. The simplicial based representation [PBCF93], discussed in a following section, can be considered as a composite boundary/decompositive/sweeping representation.

The following sections are dedicated to discussing the more important types of representation schemes.

## 13.2   Enumerative schemes

In enumerative schemes each *model* is embedded in a space partition made with space cells of fixed topology and geometry, usually of either hexahedral or simplicial type. The enumerative *representation* is some kind of enumeration of material cells of the model, i.e. of full cells, as opposite to empty cells. Most enumerative representations are *approximate* representations, but they may have variable resolution, depending on the needs of the supported applications. This approach is particularly suitable to easy implementation of Boolean operations and computation of volume integrals.

Two different classes of enumerative schemes can be devised, which are respectively classified as:

1. *flat* enumerative schemes;
2. *hierarchical* enumerative schemes.

### 13.2.1   Flat enumerative schemes

A parallelepiped subset of the containment space of the model is subdivided into hexahedral (cubic) cells of size either constant or variable by rows, columns or planes. Such representation usually consists of a binary array with three indices in the 3D case, or with two indices in the 2D case. The resolution of this approach cannot be very small when representing objects of large size. Consider in fact, e.g., that a mechanical model with containment box of $1\,m^3$, represented with linear resolution of $10^{-4}m$, would require an array with $10^{12}$ cells. It is hence customary to store such a representation using sparse matrices, where only the boundary cells are explicitly memorized, relying on the fact that the transitions between empty and full cells are not frequent in a "solid".

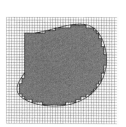
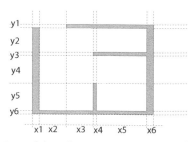

**Figure 13.3**   Enumerative representations: (a) with constant resolution (b) with variable resolution

**Constant resolution** In Figure 13.3 we give an example of flat enumerative representation of a curved 2D solid. The cells of plane partition may be labeled full when completely enclosed in the solid, and empty otherwise. A different choice, say with cells labeled empty when completely outside and labeled full otherwise, is equally acceptable, but clearly gives a different approximation of the solid. It is easy to see that such an approach works much better when the model is consistent with the cell grid, i.e. has orthogonal faces and their size is a multiple of the cell step. As we already pointed out, in order to get a good resolution, this approach must be implemented with sparse matrices, that are encoded by using some appropriate compression technique.

**Variable resolution** In this kind of scheme the *bounding box* of the model is partitioned by three sets of orthogonal planes, normally coplanar to the model faces. The resulting space decomposition into parallelepiped cells is encoded by using some appropriate array. Since the distances between pairs of adjacent cutting planes is generally non-constant, the partition is non-uniform, as shown in Figure 13.3b for the 2D case. An example of this representation, introduced in [Mit77], is given by the primitive QUADARRAY defined in Script 7.4.1.

The representation used in the 2D and 3D case, is respectively given by a pair (triplet) of real arrays, that contain the ordered distances between adjacent cutting lines (planes), and by a Boolean array with two (three) indices, which is used to encode the labels (empty/full) of the space partition cells. Such a representation can be encoded as follows, in the 2D and 3D case, respectively:

$$<< \texttt{Xarray}[i_1], \texttt{Yarray}[i_2] >, \texttt{BoolArray}[i_1, i_2] >$$
$$<< \texttt{Xarray}[i_1], \texttt{Yarray}[i_2], \texttt{Zarray}[i_3] >, \texttt{BoolArray}[i_1, i_2, i_3] >$$

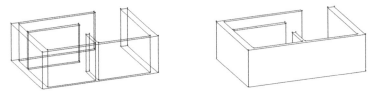

**Figure 13.4**   3D enumerative representation

*13.2.2   Hierarchical enumerative schemes*

The *hierarchical enumerative schemes* use a number of trees, which encode different partitioning schemes of the embedding space into cells of different type and size. The most important schemes of this type are $2^n$-trees and *bin*-trees, that are briefly discussed in the following subsections.

### $2^n$-Trees

The $2^n$-*trees* are *ordered trees* [AU92] characterized by the property that each non-leaf node has exactly $2^n$ son nodes, respectively denoted as first, second, etc., and as $2^n$-th son. When $n = 2$ and $n = 3$ such trees are called *quadtrees* and *octrees*, which are used to represent hierarchical decompositions of the 2D or 3D space, respectively [Sam88, Sam90b, Sam90a].

**Quadtrees**   When the model is embedded in 2D, i.e. when $n = 2$, the $2^n$-tree representation is called *quadtree*. Some useful properties of quadtrees follow:

1. a quadtree is a *quaternary* tree (i.e. each non-leaf node has exactly 4 sons);
2. the leafs are either *white* or *black* nodes (i.e. either empty or full);
3. the non-leafs are *gray* nodes (i.e. neither empty nor full);
4. the maximal *depth* of the quadtree is related to its *resolution*.

The number of arcs on the path from the root to a node is called *distance* of the node from the root. *Depth* of a tree is the maximal distance of its nodes from the root. The *resolution* of the quadtree with squared bounding box of size $L$ and depth $m$ is clearly equal to

$$r = L/2^m$$

**Example 13.2.1 (Quadtree encoding)**
In Figure 13.5 we show both a 2D object given as a hierarchical decompositive representation using the quadtree scheme, and its actual encoding as a labeled tree, where *black*, *white* and *gray* nodes respectively represent full and empty cells, and cells which are neither full nor empty. Note that the sons of a gray node are clockwise ordered, according to the scheme shown in the quadruple of small boxes in the middle top of Figure 13.5.

**Octrees**   When the model is embedded in 3D, i.e. when $n = 3$, the $2^n$-tree representation is called an *octree*. In this case the embedding space is subdivided by three pair-wise orthogonal planes, so giving $2^3$ cells (either white, black or gray) at each step (see Figure 13.6).

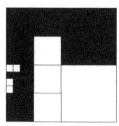
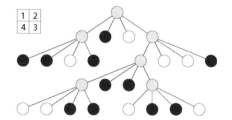

**Figure 13.5**   Quadtree encoding scheme: (a) 2D object (b) full cells (black), empty cells (white) and decomposed cells (gray)

## *Bin*-trees

The so-called *bin*-trees are *binary* trees representing solids in $\mathbb{E}^n$. In this case tree nodes contain hyperplanes equations of the kind $x_{(d_k \bmod n)} = c_k$, where $d_k$ is the (integer) distance of the node $k$ from the root. Hence, in 2D, *bin*-tree nodes at increasing distance from the root alternatively contain equations such as $x = a_i$ and $y = b_i$. In 3D, node equations will contain either $x = a_i$ or $y = b_i$ or $z = c_i$, alternatively. As in the case of quadtrees and octrees, leaf nodes are labeled either black or white, whereas non-leaf nodes can be considered as gray.

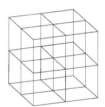

**Figure 13.6**   Octree: partition of a 3D cell into 8 sub-cells generated by three orthogonal planes

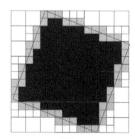
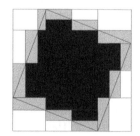

**Figure 13.7**   Quadtree vs bintree

## 13.3   Decompositive schemes

In a decompositive representation scheme, a solid object is represented as a set of cells, usually of a given topology. Unlike enumerative schemes, in this case the cell partition is induced by the represented object itself. Also in this case it may be useful to distinguish between non-hierarchical schemes and hierarchical schemes. Two very useful representations in such classes are the simplicial representations and the BSP-trees, respectively. Both are implemented within the PLaSM geometric kernel. They are used by the MAP primitive and by the Boolean operations, respectively.

The space of models of decompositive schemes is constituted by the so-called *cellular models*. They have been of increasing interest in recent years [BdB98, ES00]. In particular, the stratification of a solid model into cells provides a common theoretical framework to unify all representations [Sha01]. Furthermore, it also provides a basis for designing a representation-free standard API that is both formal and general [ABC+00].

### 13.3.1   Simplicial schemes

As we already know from Section 4.5, a *d-simplex* is a sort of *generalized triangle*, defined by the convex combination of a set of $d + 1$ affinely independent points. In particular, a 0-simplex is a point, a 1-simplex is a segment, a 2-simplex is a triangle, a 3-simplex is a tetrahedron, and so on. Analogously, a *simplicial complex* is a sort of *well-formed* generalized *triangulation*, where every two simplices either do not intersect or intersect along a common face, which is in any case a simplex of lower dimension, so that intersecting simplices are well-sticked together. It is possible to show that: (1) every solid may be triangulated by a simplicial complex; (2) every simplicial complex is transformed by a map of its vertices into another simplicial complex. For both such reasons, a representation scheme based on simplicial complexes may be very useful in a geometric modeling environment [PBCF93].

### 13.3.2   Convex-cell partitioning and covering

In recent years, several geometric environments for solid modeling have been offering the choice of working with either boundary or decompositive representations, by using some kind of convex cells. In particular, a very successful kind of decomposition uses BSP trees. Such trees were adopted as spatial indices for speed acceleration by several computer games, including DOOM and its successors.

When PLaSM was designed about one decade ago, a hierarchical scheme called *Hierarchical Polyhedral Complex* (HPC) was devised for it, with only a partial storage of topology of the cell complex. A HPC representation allows efficient representation of dimension-independent polyhedral complexes by using either a *covering* or a *partition* into convex cells of the associated point set, as discussed in Chapter 5.

Currently, PLaSM uses a composite scheme which combines both BSP-trees, mainly used for Boolean operations, the simplicial $\mathcal{W}$ representation, used with maps generating polyhedral approximations of curved objects, and the HPC representation, used for product and skeleton operations as well as to implement the hierarchical graph underlying a complex scene or assembly.

#### *BSP*-trees

A definition of BSP-trees has already been introduced in Section 10.3.5, when discussing the *hidden-surface removal* (HSR) of 3D scenes. The reader is in this case referred to that definition and discussion. The only difference introduced when using BSP-trees as a representation of solids is a labeling of leaf nodes. In fact, each leaf of such a tree is associated with a cell of the space partition induced by the hyperplanes stored with the non-leaf nodes of the tree. A label from the set {IN, OUT} is hence associated with each cell. The solid representation is given in this case by the *labeled* BSP-tree.

### Example 13.3.1 (BSP example)

A two-dimensional solid object is generated in Script 13.3.1 as the difference object between a ground rectangle and a polygonal hole. Both the object and its 1D skeleton are shown in Figure 13.8b, with the aim of displaying the underlying BSP representation, used by PLaSM to perform dimension-independent Boolean operations. The input hole is displayed in Figure 13.8a.

Notice that set *difference* between the geometric values stored in ground and hole symbols is denoted by the symbol "−" (minus). Analogously, set *union, intersection* and *symmetric difference* (also called *exclusive or*, i.e. XOR) are denoted by "+", "&" and "∧", respectively.

---

### Script 13.3.1 (BSP example)

```
DEF ground = CUBOID:<19,22>;

DEF hole = MKPOL:<
    <<9.8,4.2>,<3.2,5.8>,<1.6,12.5>,<12.4,18.2>,
    <16.5,8.6>,<9.8,12.5>,<6.2,10.4>>,
    <<1,2,3,7>,<3,4,6,7>,<4,5,6>>,<<1,2,3>>>;

DEF object = ground - hole;
DEF out = (STRUCT ~ [ID, @1]):object;
VRML:out:'out.wrl'
```

---

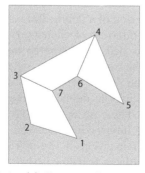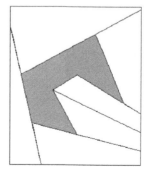

**Figure 13.8**   (a) Convex cells of the input (b) BSP representation of the difference object produced by Script 13.3.1

## Hierarchical polyhedral complexes (HPC)

The HPC representation scheme [PFP96] is the main representation used by the geometrical kernel underlying PLaSM, and is based on a hierarchical description of the object structure. In particular, the HPC representation scheme describes the geometric shapes as hierarchical collections of polyhedra, where each elementary polyhedron is decomposed in a set of convex cells. Each convex cell is in turn represented as a collection of either vertex vectors or facet covectors.

In such an approach an object is represented as a multilevel hierarchical structure. In particular, each object is represented as a decomposition in a set of objects, which are, in turn, either hierarchical decompositions or elementary polyhedra. For example, the plan of the building floor in Figure 13.9a is represented by the multigraph in Figure 13.9b. Each node with an outgoing arc is called *polyhedral complex*, and is decomposed in a set of disjoint elements. The outgoing arcs that compose the complex are called *polyhedral instances*, and relocate (affinely map) the pointed nodes in the proper position and orientation. The basic objects (associated with leaf nodes) are called *elementary polyhedra*, and are represented in a local coordinate frame as full dimensional complexes of convex cells.

So, a decompositive representation in convex cells is used in the representation of each elementary polyhedron. Along with each cell a rich symbolic description is maintained, and thus the use of numerical information is kept to a minimum. In this way the emphasis is shifted from numeric to symbolic information, with the first being considered less entrusting than the second, thereby increasing the robustness of the supported algorithms.

In PLASM and in several approaches to solid modeling [Bri89, RO90, Mau91, ES00, ABC⁺00] the reference representation is a cell decomposition. To represent the cells as an intersection of halfspaces has several advantages. In particular, with this representation the extrusion operation, which is of great importance in a dimension-independent approach, is simply a linear operator upon the space of linear functions (covectors) associated with the cell faces. Also, an affine transformation may be applied to this representation by just multiplying the face covectors by the inverse matrix of the transformation. Also, the computation of geometry and topology of the result of the generalized product described in Section 14.4 is very simple.

**Progressive difference**   A "complete" representation of a polyhedral complex must satisfy a quite difficult geometric constraint: the interiors of elementary polyhedra cannot intersect each other. This constraint is needed to guarantee unambiguous representations, but reduces the flexibility of the representation scheme, which cannot represent any design configuration where the design components are actually overlapping. Hence it becomes useful both to extend the domain of the scheme to the class of overlapping sets of polyhedra, and to define an operator PD (called the *progressive difference*) to automatically remove the intersections between elementary polyhedra, where they exist. In this way, i.e. by relaxation of the non-intersection constraint, a *weak* representation of hierarchical objects is defined, that we call the *polyhedral sequence*.

**Complete and weak representation** A *complete representation* of an object is a partitioning of its point set with an unordered set of (hierarchical) polyhedra, while a *weak representation* is simply a covering of the point set. An application of the PD operator to a weak representation returns a complete representation, since it subtracts each element of the polyhedral sequence from all the elements with higher position in the sequence. In such a way the ordering on the component instances is translated into a precedence rule on their point sets: points belonging to more than one component object are assigned to the first one in the polyhedral sequence which they belong to.

According to [Req80], we can distinguish between the representation of an object and its abstract model, and define the latter as an element of the set $\mathcal{M}$, which is the domain of both the complete and weak representation schemes. The set $\mathcal{R}$, which contains the complete representations, is the validity set of the scheme. Conversely, the set $\mathcal{R}^*$ of all weak representations is the range set of the scheme, with $\mathcal{R} \subset \mathcal{R}^*$. A more formal and detailed definition of the HPC scheme used in the PLaSM language can be found in [PFP96].

**Example 13.3.2 (Floor layout)**
Consider, e.g., the example in Figure 13.9, where the multigraph structure of the polyhedral complex (b) is represented. An equivalent polyhedral sequence (c) is obtained by replacing the `kitchen`, `living` and `bed2` rooms by their bounding boxes. Their sequence is a weak representation of the object (a) if `bed2` follows the `bath`, and both `kitchen` and `living` follow the `balcony`. An application of the PD operator to the weak representation (c) produces the complete representation (b).

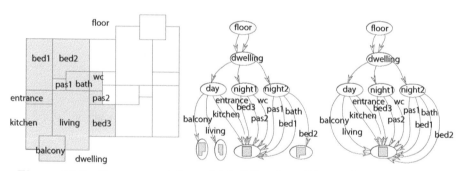

**Figure 13.9** Two representations: (a) building floor (b) *complete* representation (partitioning) (c) *weak* representation (covering)

In Script 13.3.2 we give the PLaSM definition of the `layout` of building floor shown in Figure 13.10, whose HPC representation is pictorially displayed in Figure 13.9.

The PLaSM definition of symbols `day`, `night1` and `night2`, which are the components of the 2D polyhedral complex `dwelling`, is given in Script 13.3.3. Notice that `floor_layout` is an assembly of two `dwelling` instances, where the second is flipped and translated both horizontally and vertically.

Notice also that the model embedded in 3D displayed in Figure 13.10 is generated by the last expression of the Script. This model is an assembly of the embedded `layout` object and of an extrusion of its 1D skeleton, generated by Cartesian product times a 1D interval.

**Script 13.3.2 (Layout as assembly)**

```
DEF floor_layout =
    STRUCT:< dwelling, T:<1,2>:<41,34>, S:<1,2>:<-1,-1>, dwelling >;
DEF dwelling = STRUCT:< day, T:<1,2>:<17,4>:night1, T:2:16:night2 >;

(STRUCT ~ [EMBED:1, @1 * K:(QUOTE:<6>)]):floor_layout;
```

All the sizes and the measures of length are given as multiples of a modular unit $1M = 30cm$. In particular, in Script 13.3.3 a `room` alias is given for the predefined PLaSM operator `CUBOID`. Then the three `dwelling` components called `day`, `night1` and `night2` are respectively defined.

**Script 13.3.3 (Layout components)**

```
DEF room = CUBOID;
DEF PD = STRUCT ~ PDIFFERENCE;

DEF day =
    PD:< T:<1,2>:<3.5,-3>:balcony, kitchen, T:1:7:living, T:2:12:entrance >
WHERE
    kitchen = room:< 7, 12 >,
    living = room:< 10,16 >,
    balcony = room:< 7, 7 >,
    entrance = room:< 7, 4 >
END;

DEF night1 = STRUCT:< bed3, T:2:8, pas2, T:2:4, wc >
WHERE
    bed3 = room:< 7, 8 >,
    pas2 = room:< 3.5, 4 >,
    wc = room:< 3.5, 6 >
END;

DEF night2 = PD:< bed1, T:1:7:pas1, T:1:10.5:bath, T:1:7:bed2 >
WHERE
    bed1 = room:< 7, 14 >,
    pas1 = room:< 3.5, 4 >,
    bath = room:< 6.5, 6 >,
    bed2 = room:< 10, 14 >
END;
```

**Note** In Script 13.3.3 a definition is also given for the PD operator, discussed in this section, which may transform a weak HPC representation into a valid complete representation, by executing a sequence of difference operations, called the *progressive difference*, upon the ordered sequence of polyhedral complexes the weak representation is composed of. Notice that `PDIFFERENCE` is a primitive PLaSM operator which maps a *sequence* of polyhedral complexes into a *complex* of (possibly empty) polyhedral complexes.

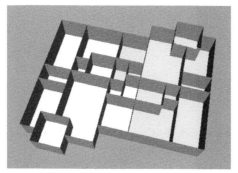

**Figure 13.10**   Assembly with `layout` embedded in 3D and the extrusion of its 1D
skeleton

A full implementation of the `PD` operator, with

$$\text{PD} : \mathcal{R}^* \to \mathcal{R}$$

would actually require a recursive implementation, so that it would be possible to apply the operator to any pair of hierarchical polyhedral sequences of whatever complexity. Such an approach would require, in practical cases, an intolerable amount of computation. So, we decided for a basic non-recursive implementation, with usage under direct user control, as shown by Script 13.3.3.

Notice also that, from a user viewpoint, the given `PD` implementation must apply to sequences of polyhedral complexes, and not to sequences of polyhedral complexes and affine transformations, as the `STRUCT` operator is allowed to do.

## 13.4   Constructive Solid Geometry

A *Constructive Solid Geometry* (CSG) representation scheme [RV77, Req80] has the set of 3D *r*-sets as domain and a set of binary trees as the validity set. In the standard definition, a *CSG tree* is a binary tree where non-leaf nodes are either regularized set operations (see below) or affine transformations, and where leaf nodes are either primitive solids or implicit halfspaces.

This kind of representation has a very useful semantics. It often models exactly the process of shape creation in the designer intentions, as well as in the manufacturing process. Complex objects are often assembled/manufactured by applying Boolean set operation on subassemblies or on elementary parts.

In most current systems CSG trees are used to capture the design intention, and are not generally used as the primary internal representation of the solid. In PLaSM a CSG representation is naturally expressed as a language expression involving polyhedral arguments, Boolean operations and affine transformations, as shown in Example 13.4.1. Efficient algorithms exist for converting a boudary representation of a solid into a CSG representation [SV93]. A CSG representation can be *optimized* by using algebraic rewriting rules [SV91]. An extention of the Constructive Geometry to representing *non-regularized* objects is discussed in [RR91].

### Example 13.4.1 (Boolean expression)
The solid `object` shown in Figures 13.11 and 13.12 is generated by Script 13.4.1.

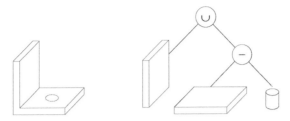

**Figure 13.11**  (a) Solid object (b) Constructive Solid Geometry (CSG)
representation

Notice that the PLaSM denotation for *union* and *difference* set operations is "+" and
"−", respectively. Set *intersection* and *symmetric difference* (XOR) are denoted as "&"
and "^", respectively. No special symbol is available for complement operation. Since
infix operators have the same precedence and are evaluated from left to right, it may
often be necessary to enclose some sub-expression between parentheses, in order to
correctly encode the desired CSG tree.

---

**Script 13.4.1**

```
DEF object = CUBOID:<2,10,10> +
    (CUBOID:<12,10,2> - T:<1,2>:<5,5>:(CYLINDER:<1,2>:24))
```

---

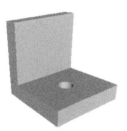

**Figure 13.12**  (a) Resulting solid object (b) Triangulation of the boundary of cells
of the generated space partition

## 13.5   Boundary schemes

Boundary representations are not used by PLaSM. Anyway, they are quite well discussed
in this section because they are used by most commercial solid modeling kernels and
systems. Boundary representations, at least as the output generated by some kind of
boundary evaluation algorithm, are also needed when graphically rendering any solid
model, with the unique important exception of volume rendering techniques.

**Definition**  A *boundary* representation scheme, often called *b-rep*, represents a *d*-
dimensional solid model through some representation of its $(d-1)$–dimensional
boundary [Bra75]. Such an approach is complete, i.e. unambiguous, because the

boundary of an orientable solid determines unambiguously its interior. In other words, two different solids cannot have the same boundary. A boundary representation is often defined inductively:

1. the boundary of a 3D solid is represented by a partition into bounded 2D pieces called *faces*;
2. each face is in turn represented by a partition of its 1D boundary into connected pieces called *edges*;
3. each edge is represented by its 0D boundary elements, i.e. by its extreme points, called *vertices*.

More in general, a boundary representation of a $d$-dimensional solid is given by the inductive subdivision of the elements of its $(d-1)$-dimensional boundary, thus generating a partition into cells of dimensions $d-1, d-2, \ldots, 1, 0$.

**Topology and geometry** In solid modeling literature the terms *topology* and *geometry* of a model usually refer to the set of incidence and adjacency relations between boundary elements, described below, and to the set of parametric equations of faces and edges, respectively.

When representing a linear $d$-polyhedron, all its geometry can be recovered by storing only the 0-dimensional elements, i.e. the vertices. Each $p$-dimensional boundary cell is in fact contained into the affine hull generated by $p+1$ affinely independent points.

For example, in 3D an edge is supported by the straight line generated by 2 vertices, and a face is supported by the plane generated by three non-collinear vertices. In the case of curved solids, the geometric information given by vertices is not sufficient, and the equations (either parametric or implicit) of the manifolds (say, curves and surfaces) supporting the boundary cells must be explicitly stored in computer's memory. A discussion of boundary representation with implicit algebraic surfaces can be found in [Hof89].

An important distinction concerns manifold and non-manifold b-reps. The kernel geometric libraries nowadays used in design environments with industrial strength are largely based on non-manifold boundary representations, whose study started with Weiler's thesis [Wei86].

**Boundary representations as hierarchical descriptions** As we have already seen, three main entities, i.e. *faces* $(F)$, *edges* $(E)$ and *vertices* $(V)$, are normally used in b-reps of 3D solids. Other useful entities, shown in Figure 13.13b, are often adopted in practical b-reps. In particular, it is customary to introduce also the following entities:

1. the set $B$ of connected components of the solid, called *bodies*;
2. the set $S$ of connected components of the body boundary, called *shells*;
3. the set $L$ of connected components of the face boundary, called *loops*.

It may be interesting to note that $B$, $S$ and $L$ are sets of geometric objects of dimension 3, 2 and 1, respectively. It may be also useful to remember that the arrow in a Bachman diagram stands for the *is-made-of* relationship. So, a solid is made of a subset of bodies, a body is made of a subset of shells, and so on.

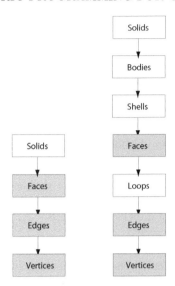

**Figure 13.13** (a) Bachman diagram of fundamental 3D boundary elements
(b) Extended hierarchy of 3D boundary elements

### 13.5.1  Adjacency and incidence relations

Let us consider the three main boundary entities $F$, $E$ and $V$. Clearly there will exist $3 \times 3 = 9$ binary relationships between, displayed in Table 13.1a. The diagonal elements of Table 13.1a are called *adjacency* relations; the others are called *incidence* relations. So we speak, e.g., about the adjacency of faces and about the incidence of faces and vertices.

Every relation in Table 13.1a is a subset of the Cartesian set product of the involved entities. For example:

$$FE \subset F \times E$$

In the remainder of this chapter we use a lower case letter to denote the cardinality, i.e. the number of elements, of a set. So, we set

$$f = |F|, \quad e = |E| \quad \text{and} \quad v = |V|.$$

It is possible to show quite easily [Woo85] that every binary relation, except $EE$, contains $2e$ elements. Conversely, it is $|EE| \geq 4e$, where the equality holds for solids with exactly 3 edges incident on each vertex, like, e.g., a cube, a tetrahedron or a polyhedral approximation of a circular cylinder.

### Example 13.5.1 (Cardinality of *VE*)

It is easy to verify, looking at Figure 13.14, that the pairs of incident vertices and edges in a double pyramid are exactly

$$|VE| = 24 = 2e.$$

as shown by Table 13.1b.

**Table 13.1**  (a) Binary relations between boundary entities (b) Cardinalities of boundary relations

|   | F | E | V |
|---|---|---|---|
| F | FF | FE | FV |
| E | EF | EE | EV |
| V | VF | VE | VV |

|   | F | E | V |
|---|---|---|---|
| F | $2e$ | $2e$ | $2e$ |
| E | $2e$ | $\geq 4e$ | $2e$ |
| V | $2e$ | $2e$ | $2e$ |

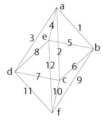

$$
\begin{aligned}
VE = \; & (\{a\} \times \{1,2,3,4\})\ \cup \\
& (\{b\} \times \{1,5,6,9\})\ \cup \\
& (\{c\} \times \{2,6,10,7\})\ \cup \\
& (\{d\} \times \{3,7,8,11\})\ \cup \\
& (\{e\} \times \{4,5,12,8\})\ \cup \\
& (\{f\} \times \{9,10,11,12\})
\end{aligned}
$$

**Figure 13.14**  Incidence relation $VE$ between vertices and edges

### 13.5.2  Euler equation

A fundamental equation due to Leonhard Euler (1707–1783) holds between the numbers of faces, edges and vertices of 3D polyhedra which are *homeomorphic* to the sphere, i.e. that can be bicontinuously transformed to the sphere. Such solids, like e.g. the cube or the tetrahedron, are said to have topological genus $g = 0$, and also to be *topologically equivalent* to the sphere. In this case it is

$$
v - e + f = 2 \tag{13.1}
$$

**Topological genus**  The number $g$ of handles of a "sphere with handles" topologically equivalent to a solid is called the *topological genus* of the solid. Such a topological invariant is used to classify solids into equivalence classes. Solids in the same class, i.e. with same genus, are said to be topologically equivalent. This statement actually means that such solids may bicontinuously transform into each other, i.e. that each can be continuously deformed into the other, and vice versa.

**Example 13.5.2 (Euler equation)**
In the case of a 3D cube, we have $v = 8$, $e = 12$, $f = 6$, so that

$$
8 - 12 + 6 = 2.
$$

Analogously, for a 3D tetrahedron, or 3-simplex, we have $v = 4$, $e = 6$, $f = 4$, and hence we have, as expected

$$
4 - 6 + 4 = 2.
$$

This demonstrates that the cube and the tetrahedron are in the same equivalence class with respect to the topological genus.

**Euler–Poincaré equation**   A strong generalization of the Euler equation (13.1) is due to Poincaré, French mathematician who started the study of algebraic topology at the end of the nineteenth and beginning of the twentieth centuries.

The so-called Euler–Poincaré equation holds between numbers of vertices, edges and faces of a connected polyhedral solid in 3D:

$$v - e + f = 2(s - g) + h, \tag{13.2}$$

where

1. $s$ is the number of connected components of the boundary of the solid body.
   In other words $s = |S|$, where $S$ is the set of shells of the body;
2. $g$ is the topological *genus* of the body;
3. $h$ is the number of *holes* (or internal loops) in body faces.

**Example 13.5.3 (Euler–Poincaré equation)**
We compute here the topological genus of the body in Figure 13.15, generated by subtracting two orthogonal parallelepipeds from a central cube. The $g$ genus is computed by counting the numbers of vertices, edges, faces and so on, and by substituting such values into equation (13.2), thus getting the unknown value of $g$. In particular, by substituting $v = 32$, $e = 48$, $f = 15$, $s = 1$ e $h = 4$ in (13.2) we get

$$32 - 48 + 16 = 2(1 - g) + 4$$

and hence $g = 3$. The solid is topologically equivalent to the sphere with 3 handles, as shown by Figure 13.15.

**Figure 13.15**   The Euler–Poincaré equation $v - e + f = 2(s - g) + h$ is specialized into $32 - 48 + 16 = 2(1 - g) + 4$, so that $g = 3$

### 13.5.3   Edge-based schemes

Boundary representation schemes can be classified in two main classes, that we call *edge-based* and *face-based*. The first class contains most of known representations, and is discussed in this section. In particular, we illustrate here the so-called *minimal* boundary representation, as well as Baumgart's *winged-edge* [Bau72] and Mäntylä's *half-edge* [Män88] representations.

### Minimal b-rep

It has been shown [Woo85] that the data structures which may implement every b-rep of 3D models are connected subgraphs of the complete oriented graph, shown in Figure 13.16a, defined by the sets $F, E, V$ of boundary entities.

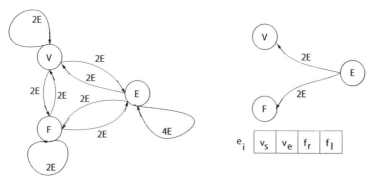

**Figure 13.16**  (a) Complete graph of topological relations between boundary entities (b) Minimal b-rep, given by two relations in normal form (Codd)

The smallest boundary representation, that stores two incidence relations in first normal form [Dat97], i.e. where each tuple has constant length, is given by the pair $(EV, EF)$.

The representation, shown in Figure 13.16b can be given as a table indexed on edges, where the tuple indexed by $e_i$ contains the two vertices and the two faces incident the edge $e_i$. This *minimal* boundary representation has size $4e$, because each edge-tuple contains 4 data items.

The minimal b-rep can only be used with manifold solids, where it is guaranteed that exactly two faces meet on each edge. The number of faces incident on an edge is, more in general, even for non-manifold solids. Clearly, the domain of minimal b-rep scheme is restricted to the subset of manifold models.

### *Winged-edge* representation

The so-called *winged-edge* representation, developed by B. G. Baumgart at the AI Laboratory of MIT in early 1970s [Bau72], is probably the more well-known and historically important boundary representation.

In this case we have a relational representation in normal form, based on two tables of indices and on a primary table indexed on edges. In particular, the tuple of the primary table indexed by $e_j$ contains 8 data items, including:

1. references to 2 incident vertices,
2. references to 2 incident faces and
3. references to 4 adjacent edges which also meet on the two adjacent faces.

The winged representation $WE$ is shown in Figure 13.17. The WE b-rep contains the minimal one, since it contains the two relations $EV$ and $EF$. Also it contains a subset of $EE$ with cardinality $4e$.

The tuple of the primary WE table, indexed by the $e_j$ edge, accommodates respectively the following fields:

$$(v_i, v_f, f_r, f_l, e_{ir}, e_{il}, e_{fr}, e_{fl})$$

where $v_i, v_f$ denote the references to the *initial* and *final* vertex of the edge $e_j$, $f_r, f_l$ are references to *right* and *left* incident faces on $e_j$, and $e_{ir}, e_{il}, e_{fr}, e_{fl}$ are references to:

1. the edge incident on the initial vertex and on the right face of $e_j$,
2. the edge incident on initial vertex and left face,
3. the edge incident on final vertex and right face,
4. the edge incident on final vertex and left face.

The name of this data structure probably derives from the picture of the tuple, that looks like the shape of a butterfly.

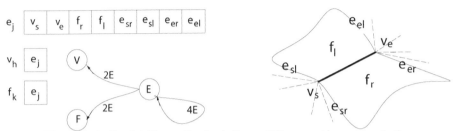

**Figure 13.17**   (a) Normalized relations of Baumgart's representation
(b) Incidence/adjacency relations stored in the primary tuple

**Optimality of *winged-edge* b-reps**   The $WE$ representation is very interesting, because it allows an answer to every topological query in time proportional to the size of the query output. This is generally impossible with the minimal b-rep previously discussed.

For example, in order to return the subset of vertices on the boundary of a face, it is possible to access, through the table of face indices, the tuple of one of incident edges, and then to navigate the only tuples of edges incident the face, thus accumulating, e.g., the first vertex of each tuple, until the starting tuple is accessed again. This approach results in a number of storage accesses equal to the number of boundary edges (and vertices). Conversely, an access to every tuple of the table would be needed when using the minimal b-rep.

**Multiply connected faces**   Like the minimal b-rep, the winged-edge scheme may only represent manifold solids with simply connected faces, i.e. with single-loop face boundaries. Two well-known variations of the $WE$ scheme, allowing representation of multiply connected faces, require either an explicit representation of the *face-loop* relation [Bra79] or the introduction of so-called *bridge-edges* [YT85] to reduce multiply connected face to simply connected ones, as shown by Figure 13.18. Bridge-edges are easily recognized in the primary $WE$ table, because they have $f_r = f_l$.

### *Half-edge* representation

The *half-edge* [Män86] representation by Martï Mäntylä is described by the Bachman diagram shown in Figure 13.19. In this representation the Edge entity is needed to implement the $FF$ relation. In particular, each instance of the Edge entity is linked to two instances of the HalfEdge entity. Clearly enough, a Loop entity is a linked list of HalfEdge instances.

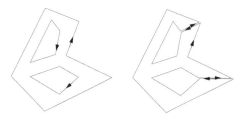

**Figure 13.18** (a) Multiply connected face (b) Simply connected face with inserted
*bridge-edges*

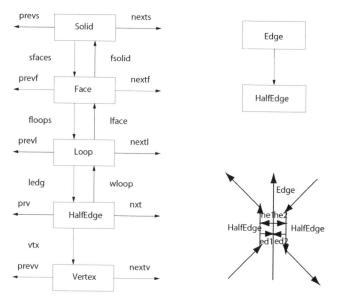

**Figure 13.19** (a) Mäntylä's *Half-Edge* representation (b) Diagram of topological
relations between edges and halfEdges

A typical characteristic of both this representation and of several other b-reps,
mainly when using very complex data structures, is the extensive use of so-called
*Euler operators* [Män88], used as middle-level access operations to the representation,
in particular when implementing very complex algorithms, like Boolean operations.
Such middle-level operations are used to step-wise modify the representation in a
consistent way, i.e. by always satisfying the Euler–Poincaré equation.

### 13.5.4 Facet-based schemes

Facet-based schemes are b-rep schemes where the main role is assigned to the 2D
elements of the partition of the object's boundary. We may classify here both the
*face-adjacency hypergraph* by L. De Floriani and B. Falcidieno [ADF85], and *the
winged-triangle b-rep* [PRS89] by A. Paoluzzi *et al.*, both discussed in this section.
We also discuss in this section, despite its name, the *quad-edge* representation [GS85]
by L. Guibas and J. Stolfi, because it fully exploits the duality relation between graphs
embedded on surfaces.

## Face Adjacency Graph

An interesting facet-based boundary representation was proposed by S. Ansaldi, L. De Floriani and B. Falcidieno [ADF85], and called *Face Adjacency Graph*, making use of some graph theoretical concepts described below, and in particular of the duality between embedded graphs. Their approach may be found very useful when describing and classifying geometric features in object design and manufacturing.

**Graph embedding**   The boundary of a 3D polyhedron of genus 0 can be represented as a *planar graph*, i.e. as a graph embedded — or "drawn" — on either the plane or the sphere, with an intersection of edges located only at vertices. More generally, the boundary of a solid of $g$ genus can be embedded as a planar graph on a surface of $g$ genus.

For example, the boundary of a 3D cube can be drawn on the plane as shown in Figure 13.20. Such *embedding* of the boundary graph contains 8 vertices, 12 edges and 6 faces. A *face* is here defined as a connected region of the plane partition generated when subtracting vertices and edges (as point sets) from the embedding surface. One of such regions, called the *external face*, is unbounded. Clearly, an external face does not exist when the graph is drawn on the sphere.

**Duality between planar graphs**   Let us consider an *abstract planar graph* as a triplet $G = (V, E, F)$, where $V$ is the set of vertices, $E$ is the set of edges and $F$ is the set of faces. It can be seen that *cycles* of edges constitute a group (the *cycle group*) with respect to an operation of cycle addition. All the cycles can be generated by a subset of independent generators, which constitute a basis for the group. There exists a bijective mapping between the set of *internal* faces of the graph embedding and a basis of cycles.

Given an abstract planar graph $G = (V, E, F)$ it is always possible to uniquely associate another planar graph, called the *dual planar graph*, $G' = (V', E', F')$ defined by three bijective maps $f$, $g$ and $h$, that associate vertices of primal with faces of dual, faces of primal with vertices of dual, and edges of primal with edges of dual, respectively:

$$f : V \to F', \qquad g : F \to V', \qquad h : E \to E'.$$

Clearly, the duality relation is idempotent, i.e. the dual of the dual is the primal.

The two edges $(v_i, v_j)$ and $h(v_i, v_j) = (v'_a, v'_b)$, associated by duality, must satisfy a mutual intersection constraint. In particular, both must be obtained by intersection of (the cycles of edges associated to) dual faces of the extreme vertices of the other. In formal terms:

$$(v_i, v_j) = g^{-1}(v'_a) \cap g^{-1}(v'_b),$$

and

$$(v'_a, v'_b) = f(v_i) \cap f(v_j),$$

so that

$$h(g^{-1}(v'_a) \cap g^{-1}(v'_b)) = f(v_i) \cap f(v_j).$$

**Example 13.5.4 (Boundary graphs)**
In Figure 13.20 we show two plane embeddings of the primal and dual graphs
associated to the boundary of a 3D cube.

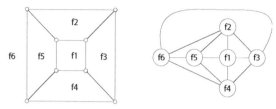

**Figure 13.20**  Primal and dual boundary graph of the cube

**Face-Adjacency Graph**  The *Face-Adjacency Graph* (FAG) representation [ADF85]
by Ansaldi, De Floriani and Falcidieno, represents a 3D solid through the non-directed
dual of the boundary graph, where the object faces are used as vertices and the
pairs of adjacent faces are used as arcs. The connectivity properties of this graph
are representative of the topological characteristics of the solid boundary. Variations
of this structure are often used to discover and reason with the geometric features
(pockets, slots, lumps, etc.) of the object.

### Quad-edge representation

A particularly elegant data structure for polyhedra is the *quad-edge* data structure,
invented by Guibas and Stolfi [GS85]. It is limited to closed manifolds, where edges
are always shared by two faces. In the quad-edge data structure, there are records for
vertices, edges, and faces, but the *Edge* record play the leading role. The edges store
complete topological information; all of the topological information stored by the faces
and vertices is redundant with respect to information in the edges.

Given a *directed* Edge, it is possible to find the immediately adjacent vertices,
faces, and edges, and the "symmetric" edge that points in the opposite direction. In
particular, for each edge, there are pointers to *next* edge around right face, with same
right face, *next* edge around left face, with same left face, *next* edge around origin,
with same origin, *next* edge around dest, with same destination. Similar pointers are
stored for *previous* elements.

### Winged-triangle representation

The so-called *winged-triangle* representation *WT*, by Paoluzzi, Ramella and
Santarelli [PRS89], is a b-rep based on vertices and triangles (0- and 2-simplices) of a
boundary triangulation, i.e. of a simplicial complex associated to the object boundary.
In particular, the *WT* representation is a table in first normal form [Dat97] where each
tuple, indexed by the $t_j$ triangle, contains:

1. 3 references to incident vertices;
2. 3 references to adjacent triangles.

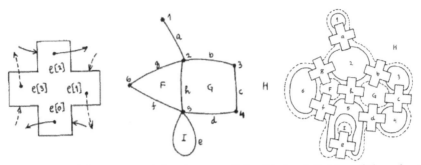

**Figure 13.21**   (a) **Edge** record showing **next** links (b) A subdivision of the sphere
(c) The data structure for the subdivision

This scheme is characterized by the design choice of making no use of Euler operators. This choice is allowed by the extreme simplicity of the data structure representing the triangulation of the boundary, and by the implementation of the Boolean algorithms, discussed in the following subsections, where the consistency of the boundary simplicial complex is easily maintained.

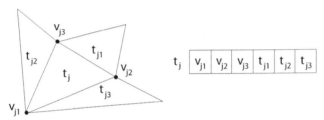

**Figure 13.22**   (a) Triangle $t_j$, with triplets of adjacent triangles and of incident vertices (b) Tuple associated to $t_j$

**Domain of the scheme**   The space of mathematical models represented by the $WT$ scheme is quite extensive. It coincides with the set of linear regular 3-polyhedra which are possibly:

1. unconnected;
2. unbounded (but with bounded boundary);
3. non-manifold ;
4. multishell;
5. with multiply connected faces.

**Range of the scheme**   A representation in this scheme is a quadruple $WT(\Sigma) = (V, T, \nu, \tau)$, where $V$ and $T$ are respectively the sets of 0-simplices and 2-simplices of a boundary complex $\Sigma$, and where

$$\nu \; : \; T \to V \times V \times V,$$
$$\tau \; : \; T \to T \times T \times T.$$

Hence, for the boundary triangle $t_j$, as displayed by the tuple in Figure 13.22, we have:

$$\begin{aligned} \nu(t_j) &= (v_{j_1}, v_{j_2}, v_{j_3}), \\ \tau(t_j) &= (t_{j_1}, t_{j_2}, t_{j_3}). \end{aligned}$$

**Validity set** A $WT(\Sigma)$ representation is *valid* if and only if the associated boundary simplicial complex $\Sigma$ is:

1. finite;
2. bounded;
3. closed (i.e. without boundary);
4. orientable.

The aims of such requirements are quite simple to explain. An infinite complex is intractable, because it cannot be stored in a computer memory. Also, an unbounded boundary complex is beyond the concept of a "solid" in the common experience. An open (i.e. with boundary) boundary complex does not satisfy the fundamental property which says that, for every body $B$, "the boundary of the boundary is empty":

$$\partial\partial B = \emptyset.$$

Finally, a boundary complex must be orientable in order to separate the interior from the exterior space.

When the above properties are satisfied, the support space $[\Sigma]$, i.e. the point set union of simplices in $\Sigma$, coincides with the boundary of some orientable 3-polyhedron. It may be also useful to note that such representation scheme is *complete*, but *not unique*. As a matter of fact, the boundary of a solid may support several different triangulations.

### Example 13.5.5 (Closed surfaces)
In Figure 13.23 we show the solid resulting from union of two translated parallelepiped solids. We remark that in every *valid* representation the boundary complex is closed, i.e. that every boundary triangle is always adjacent to *three* other triangles.

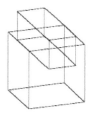 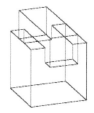 

**Figure 13.23** (a) Aggregation of solids $A$ and $B$ (b) $A \cup B$ (c) $A - B$

### Example 13.5.6 (Open surfaces)
What was noted above is not true for the winged-triangle representation of open (say with-boundary) polyhedral surfaces. Let consider the surface in Figure 13.24. Notice that the triangles which are adjacent to the boundary curves have only *two* adjacent

triangles. Anyway, a $WT$ representation, which is not valid as a solid representation, can be usefully exploited by adopting a special symbol, say either $-1$ or $\perp$, to read as "undefined", to denote the empty adjacencies in triangle tuples.

**Figure 13.24**   Open triangulated surface

**Non-manifolds as pseudo-manifolds**   Theoretically, the domain of the scheme should only embrace manifold solids. But, in order to make the domain closed with respect to Boolean operations, it is useful to represent non-manifold models in the same scheme. To give a pseudo-manifold $WT$ representation of a non-manifold solid is very easy and "natural". Let us consider for this purpose Figure 13.25. A *pseudo-manifold* complex can be defined as a simplicial complex with some *duplicated* simplices, and having a non-manifold support space.

No problems arise with duplicated *non-manifold edges*, if we choose from the various possible representations the one with the minimum number of shells. In this case the connection across the non-manifold edge is correctly preserved. Slightly more complex is the case of *non-manifold vertices*, where some auxiliary data structure, storing the shell-vertex incidence, is needed to track correctly the shell connection across such vertices.

Anyway, no management of this very special case is needed either for Boolean operations or for integration algorithms, as discussed in the following sections.

**Figure 13.25**   Pseudo-manifold representations of a non-manifold model

**Storage space of $WT$ representation**

For each surface triangulated by a simplicial complex the following useful properties hold. They have direct implications on the storage of the $WT$ representation in the computer memory.

**Theorem   (Storage space)**   The following relations between the numbers of triangles, edges and vertices of a boundary triangulation hold:

1. (Triangles-edges)
   The number $t = |T|$ of triangles and the number $e = |E|$ of edges satisfy the equation

$$t = \frac{2}{3}e. \tag{13.3}$$

2. (Triangles-vertices)
   In a polyhedron with a number $v = |V|$ of vertices, a number $s = |S|$ of boundary shells and $g$ genus, a minimal set of triangles $T$ which triangulates the boundary has size

$$t = 2v - 4(s - g). \tag{13.4}$$

3. (Storage respect to triangulation edges)
   The storage space $mem(WT)$ needed by a triangulated surface, where $e = |E|$ is the number of edges of the triangulation, is:

$$mem(WT) = 4e. \tag{13.5}$$

4. (Storage respect to polyhedron edges)
   For a 3D polyhedron, with $\hat{e}$ original edges, say non induced by the triangulation, $\hat{f}$ polygonal faces and $h$ holes in the faces (rings), we have:

$$mem(WT) = 12(\hat{e} - \hat{f} + h). \tag{13.6}$$

5. (Lower and upper bounds)
   The storage space $mem(WT)$, for any 3D polyhedron, is included between $\frac{1}{2}$ and $\frac{3}{2}$ of the storage required by $WE$ representation:

$$\frac{1}{2}mem(WE) \leq mem(WT) \leq \frac{3}{2}mem(WE). \tag{13.7}$$

**Proof** For point 1, since each triangle $t_i$ is incident to three vertices, all the subsets $t_i V$ of the incidence relation $TV \subset T \times V$ have the same number 3 of elements, so that $|t_i V| = 3$ for each $t_i \in T$, and hence

$$|TV| = \sum_{t_i \in T} |t_i V| = \sum_{t_i \in T} 3 = 3t.$$

Also we know that the incidence relation $VF$ has cardinality $2e$. For the $WT$ representation the boundary faces coincide with the triangles of the boundary complex, so that:

$$|VT| = 2e.$$

By the symmetry of incidence relation, we have $|TV| = |VT|$, so that equation (13.3) is proved. For point 2, the Euler–Poincaré equation [Poi53] (see Section 13.5.2) can be specialized for a triangulation as

$$v - e + t = 2(s - g),$$

since holes in the faces (rings) are not allowed ($h = 0$), so that

$$v - \frac{3}{2}t + t = 2(s - g)$$

and hence equation (13.4) is proved. For point 3, we can write for the primary table of the representation:

$$mem(WT) = 6t = 6 \left( \frac{2}{3} e \right)$$

For point 4, from Theorem (13.4) we have

$$t = 2v - 4(s - g), \tag{13.8}$$

and, from Euler–Poincaré equation

$$v = 2(s - g) + h + \hat{e} - \hat{f}. \tag{13.9}$$

So, by substituting the $v$ expression (13.9) into the $t$ expression (13.8) we get

$$t = 2(\hat{e} - \hat{f} + h)$$

and hence the statement is proved. The above properties can be combined, to get lower and upper bounds for the storage space of the $WT$ representation, as stated by point 5.

**Storage bounds**   Such results are quite interesting, because they give an upper bound for the $WT$ storage, depending either on the number of triangles or on the number of vertices. Notice in particular that the number of boundary triangles, and hence the size of the $WT$ primary table, is $O(v)$ and that, in particular, is bounded by $2v$. The lower bound of point 5 is obtained when all the original faces are triangular. This happens, e.g., when polyhedrally approximating solids with double curvature external surfaces. In this case the $WT$ representation is space-optimal, since it requires exactly the same space than the minimal b-rep discussed in Section 13.5.3. Conversely, the upper bound is approached when the original faces of the solid have an asyntotically increasing number of edges. In normal usage with linear polyhedra, the average size of a $WT$ representation is about 6 times the number of original edges of the object.

**Example 13.5.7**
A minimal triangulation of cube boundary is shown in Figure 13.26. The number of edges of such triangulation is $e = 12 + 6$, given by the original edges of cube, plus one edge for each face. From equation (13.3) we get, for the number of triangles, $t = \frac{2}{3}18 = 12$.

**Boolean operations on b-reps**

Several approaches to the computation of Boolean operators using a boundary representation can be found in the solid modeling literature (see, e.g. [Bra79, HHK88, LTH86, Män88]). The very simple Boolean algorithms defined with the $WT$ b-rep, that do not require the use of Euler operators, can be found in [PRS89].

**Figure 13.26**    *Winged-triangle* representation of cube boundary

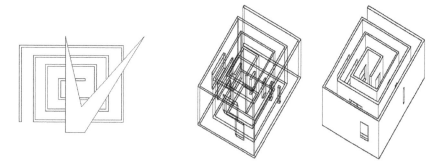

**Figure 13.27**    (a) 2D polygons (b) Boolean difference between extruded solids

**Regularized operations**    Set operations of union, intersection and difference, as
defined in solid modelers, are usually "regularized". Such modified operations are in
fact closed on the set of regular solids. In other words, the combination of regular
solids by means of a *regularized* set operation, always returns a regular solid. This
property is generally not true for standard set operations. In Figure 13.28 we show
that a standard set operation between regular arguments may produce a non-regular
result.

A *regularized set operation* is defined as the closure of the interior of the result of
the standard set operation. Let us denote the operation as op, with op $\in \{\cap, \cup, -\}$.
So, a regularized operation, denoted as op*, is defined as

$$A \text{ op}^* B = \mathbf{k}\,\mathbf{i}\,(A \text{ op } B),$$

where **k** and **i** denote the topological operations of *closure* and *interior*, respectively.
It may be useful to remember that $\mathbf{k}(S) = S \cup \partial S$.

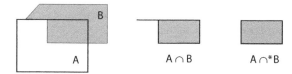

**Figure 13.28**    Standard set intersection and regularized set intersection

**Boolean algebra**    Several boundary representation schemes have as domain the set
of *bounded* manifolds (or non-manifolds). So, they do not allow for a complement
operator. Consequently, they must devise appropriate algorithms for each set
operation, i.e. for union, intersection and difference.

Conversely, the $WT$ representation scheme allows for a complement, and hence properly implements a Boolean algebra over the set of 3D polyhedra [PRS89], by explicitly enforcing the closure of the validity set of the scheme under the complement of representations. In this way, e.g., *intersection* and *difference* are reduced to the combination of *complement* and *union*, according to De Morgan's theorems of Boolean algebras. In particular, we have:

$$A \cap B = \neg(\neg A \cup \neg B),$$
$$A - B = \neg(\neg A \cup B).$$

Let us note that only two algorithms are needed in this case, to implement the basic operations of complement and union, respectively.

### 13.5.5  *Mass and inertia properties*

The evaluation of area, volume, centroid and moments of inertia of rigid homogeneous solids frequently arises in a large number of engineering applications, both in Computer-Aided Design and in Robotics. Hence, quadrature formulae for multiple integrals have always been of great interest in computer applications.

Many papers on integration methods were related to solid modeling, but as Lee and Requicha pointed out in [LR82] most computational studies in multiple integration often deal with calculations over very simple domains, like a cube or a sphere, while the integrating function $f(\mathbf{p})$ is very complicated. Conversely, in most of the engineering applications, the opposite problem usually arises.

**Definitions**  Mass and inertia properties of solid objects are defined as volume integrals of low-degree monomial fields $f(x, y, z)$, the integration being done over the space portion occupied by the object under consideration. If $B \subset \mathbb{E}^3$ is the set of body points, then the *mass* $M$, the *first moments* $M_x, M_y, M_z$, the *second moments* $M_{xx}, M_{yy}, M_{zz}$ and the *products of inertia* $M_{yz}, M_{xz}, M_{xy}$ are defined as

$$\iiint_B f(x, y, z)\, dM = \iiint_B f(x, y, z)\rho(x, y, z)\, dV,$$

where $\rho(x, y, z)$ is the local *density* of the body, and the scalar field $f(x, y, z)$ is respectively equal to 1 (mass); $x$, $y$ and $z$ (first moments); $x^2$, $y^2$ and $z^2$ (second moments); $yz$, $xz$ and $xy$ (products of inertia).

**Centroid**  The *centroid* $G = (G_x, G_y, G_z)$ of a body, also known as "center of mass", is defined by the ratios $G_x = \frac{M_x}{M}$, $G_y = \frac{M_y}{M}$ and $G_z = \frac{M_z}{M}$ of the first moments to the body mass. In *homogeneous* solids, where the density is constant, the centroid position does not depend on the density, but only on the geometry of the body.

**Moments of inertia**  The *moments of inertia* with respect to some axis are defined as the volume integrals of the squared orthogonal distances from the axis. Moments of inertia with respect to a coordinate axis are hence given, respectively, by

$$
\begin{aligned}
M_{r_x^2} &= M_{yy} + M_{zz}, \\
M_{r_y^2} &= M_{xx} + M_{zz}, \\
M_{r_z^2} &= M_{xx} + M_{yy}.
\end{aligned}
$$

The moment of inertia $M_{r^2}$ of body $B$ with respect to any axis $r$ is computed by first translating $r$ to the origin, then by rotating the translated axis $r'$ to some coordinate axis, say $z$, and finally by computing $M_{r_z^2}$, i.e.:

$$
M_{r^2}(B) = M_{r_z^2}(\boldsymbol{R}_{r' \to z} \boldsymbol{T}_{r \to r'} B).
$$

### Timmer-Stern's method

The volume integration problem can be stated as follows: *evaluate the volume integral*

$$
\iiint_B f(\boldsymbol{p})\, dV, \qquad \boldsymbol{p} \in B \tag{13.10}
$$

*where $f(\boldsymbol{p})$ is a scalar-valued field over $B \subset \mathbb{E}^3$.*

The integration method discussed in the following section may be considered as a specialization of Timmer and Stern's general method [TS80, Mor85], consisting of the transformation of a volume integral into a surface integral and then into a parametric line integral.

**Algorithm**  Timmer-Stern's integration procedure can be summarized as follows:

1. Search for a vector field $\boldsymbol{\Phi}$ such that:

$$
\iiint_B f(\boldsymbol{p})\, dV = \iiint_B \nabla \cdot \boldsymbol{\Phi}\, dV. \tag{13.11}
$$

2. Use the divergence theorem to transform the right-hand term of equation (13.11) into an integral on the closed boundary $S$ of the $B$ integration domain

$$
= \iint_S \boldsymbol{\Phi} \cdot \boldsymbol{n}\, dS. \tag{13.12}
$$

3. Use the property of domain-additivity of surface integrals over a partition of the boundary surface $S$ into a set $\{S_i\}$ of faces such that $\cup_i S_i = S$, and $S_i \cap S_j = \emptyset$ for each $i \neq j$ :

$$
= \sum_i \iint_{S_i} \boldsymbol{\Phi} \cdot \boldsymbol{n}\, dS_i. \tag{13.13}
$$

4. Transform each surface integral in a double integral in the parametric domain $S_{uv}^i$ of the face $S_i$ of the scalar field $\boldsymbol{\Psi}(u, v)$:

$$
= \sum_i \iint_{S_{uv}^i} \boldsymbol{\Psi}(u, v)\, du\, dv, \tag{13.14}
$$

where

$$\Psi(u, v) = \Phi(x(u, v), y(u, v), z(u, v)) \cdot n(x(u, v), y(u, v), z(u, v))|p_u \times p_v|.$$

5. Use again the divergence theorem in 2D to transform these last integrals into line integrals on the closed and simple boundary curves $C_i$ of domains $S_{uv}^i$. In other words, search for a vector field $\chi = (\chi_1, \chi_2)$ such that:

$$= \sum_i \iint_{S_{uv}^i} \Psi(u, v) \, du \, dv \qquad (13.15)$$

$$= \sum_i \iint_{S_{uv}^i} \nabla \cdot \chi \, du \, dv \qquad (13.16)$$

$$= \sum_i \oint_{C_{uv}^i} \chi \cdot \hat{n} \, ds. \qquad (13.17)$$

6. Then use the domain-additivity of curve integral to integrate over the set of curves associated with the boundary edges $C_{uv}^{ij}$ in parametric domain $uv$ of each boundary face:

$$= \sum_i \sum_j \int_{C_{uv}^{ii}} \chi \cdot \hat{n} \, ds. \qquad (13.18)$$

7. Finally, transform each term into a single integral in the parametric domain $C_t^{ij}$ of the trimming edge $C_{uv}^{ii}$:

$$= \sum_i \sum_j \int_{C_t^{ii}} \chi(t) \cdot \hat{n}(t) \, s'(t) \, dt. \qquad (13.19)$$

The Timmer's and Stern's method is specialized in the next subsection for when (a) the field $f(p)$ is a polynomial, (b) the integration domain $B$ is a 3D polyhedron and (c) a triangulation of $\partial B$ is available.

## Integration of polynomials over polyhedral domains

Here we summarize from [CP90] an exact and symbolic solution both to the surface and volume integration of polynomials, by using a triangulation of the volume boundary. The evaluation of surface and volume integrals is achieved by transforming them into line integrals over the boundary of every 2-simplex of a domain triangulation. A different approach to integration, using a decomposition into volume elements induced by a boundary triangulation is given in [ILK84] where a closed formula for volume integration over polyhedral volumes, by decomposing the solid into a set of solid tetrahedra, but such a method cannot be used for surface integrations.

**Problem statement**  A finite method [CP90] to compute double and triplet integrals of monomials over linear regular polyhedra in $\mathbb{R}^3$ is discussed. In particular, this method enables practical formulae for the exact evaluation of integrals to be achieved:

$$II_S \equiv \iint_S f(\mathbf{p}) \, dS, \qquad III_P \equiv \iiint_P f(\mathbf{p}) \, dV, \qquad (13.20)$$

where $S$, and $P$ are linear and regular 2- or 3-polyhedra in $\mathbb{R}^3$, $dS$ and $dV$ are the differential surface and the differential volume. The integrating function is a trivariate polynomial

$$f(\mathbf{p}) = \sum_{\alpha=0}^{n} \sum_{\beta=0}^{m} \sum_{\gamma=0}^{p} a_{\alpha\beta\gamma} x^{\alpha} y^{\beta} z^{\gamma},$$

where $\alpha, \beta, \gamma$ are non-negative integers.

Since the extension to $f(\mathbf{p})$ is straightforwardly given by the linearity of integral operator, we may focus on the calculation of integrals of monomials:

$$II_S^{\alpha\beta\gamma} \equiv \iint_S x^{\alpha} y^{\beta} z^{\gamma} \, dS, \qquad III_P^{\alpha\beta\gamma} \equiv \iiint_P x^{\alpha} y^{\beta} z^{\gamma} \, dV. \qquad (13.21)$$

**Algorithm preview**   Surface integrals are computed as a summation of integrals over a triangulation of the surface. Any triangle is mapped into the unit triangle in the 2-space of parameters, where integrals of monomials become particularly simple. Then formulae for integrals over polyhedral volumes are given. They are easily derived by transforming volume integrals in surface integrals. It is possible to show that such integrals are computable in polynomial time, and that inertia moments are computable in $O(E)$ time, $E$ being the number of edges of the solid model of the integration domain.

A very important feature of the integration formulae presented here is that they can also be used with a partial model of a polyhedron, consisting of the collection of its face loops. Loops are oriented counter-clockwise if external, clockwise if internal to another loop. Such a model, without explicit storage of face adjacencies, is very frequently adopted in Computer Graphics.

In this case it is sufficient to consider any $n + 1$-sided (also unconnected or multiply connected) face as topological sum of $n - 1$ oriented triangles $t_i$, with vertices $\langle v_0, v_i, v_{i+1} \rangle$, where $1 \leq i \leq n-1$. In applying formulae (13.31) or (13.34) to such a set of triangles, any edge that does not belong to the original polygon will be computed twice, in the two opposite directions. These contributions to the whole integral will mutually cancel each other out, as they correspond to pairs of line integrals evaluated along opposite paths.

**Surface integration**   We call *structure product* the integral of a monomial over a simplicial complex. Exact formulae for structure products over n-sided polygons in 2-space, the unit triangle in 2-space, and an arbitrary triangle in 3-space, are derived in the following. Structure products are a generalization of the usual products and moments of inertia, that can be obtained from (13.21) by assuming $\alpha + \beta + \gamma \leq 2$.

**Polygon integrals**   A structure product over a polygon $\pi$ in the plane $xy$ is

$$II_{\pi}^{\alpha\beta} = \iint_{\pi} x^{\alpha} y^{\beta} \, dS, \qquad \alpha, \beta \geq 0, integers. \qquad (13.22)$$

Such integrals can be exactly expressed, when $\pi$ is a polygon with $n$ oriented edges, as:

$$II_\pi^{\alpha\beta} = \frac{1}{\alpha+1} \sum_{i=1}^{n} \sum_{h=0}^{\alpha+1} \binom{\alpha+1}{h} x_i^{\alpha+1-h} X_i^h \sum_{k=0}^{\beta} \frac{\binom{\beta}{k}}{h+k+1} y_i^{\beta-k} Y_i^{k+1} \tag{13.23}$$

where $\mathbf{p}_i = (x_i, y_i)$, $X_i = x_{i+1} - x_i$, $Y_i = y_{i+1} - y_i$ and $\mathbf{p}_{n+1} = \mathbf{p}_1$. The derivation of the formula (13.23) is based on the application of Green's theorem and on Newton's expression for binomial powers.

**Unit triangle integrals**   The general formula (13.23) can be specialized for the unit triangle $\tau' = \langle \mathbf{w}_o, \mathbf{w}_a, \mathbf{w}_b \rangle$, with vertices

$$\mathbf{w}_o = (0,0), \qquad \mathbf{w}_a = (1,0), \qquad \mathbf{w}_b = (0,1), \tag{13.24}$$

getting a very simplified expression. With some algebraic manipulations, we obtain[1]

$$II^{\alpha\beta} = \frac{1}{\alpha+1} \sum_{h=0}^{\alpha+1} \binom{\alpha+1}{h} \frac{(-1)^h}{h+\beta+1}, \tag{13.25}$$

which reduces, for $\alpha = \beta = 0$, to the area of the triangle (13.24): $II^{00} = 1/2$.

**Triangle integrals**   In the following we derive the general expression for structure products evaluated on an arbitrary triangle $\tau = \langle \mathbf{v}_o, \mathbf{v}_a, \mathbf{v}_b \rangle$ of the 3-space $xyz$, defined by $\mathbf{v}_o = (x_o, y_o, z_o)$ and by the vectors $\mathbf{a} = \mathbf{v}_a - \mathbf{v}_o$ and $\mathbf{b} = \mathbf{v}_b - \mathbf{v}_o$. The parametric equation of its embedding plane is:

$$\mathbf{p} = \mathbf{v}_o + u\,\mathbf{a} + v\,\mathbf{b}, \tag{13.26}$$

where the area element is

$$d\tau = |J|\, du\, dv = \left| \frac{\partial \mathbf{p}}{\partial u} \times \frac{\partial \mathbf{p}}{\partial v} \right| du\, dv = |\mathbf{a} \times \mathbf{b}|\, du\, dv. \tag{13.27}$$

A structure product over a triangle $\tau$ in 3-space can be transformed by a coordinates transformation, as follows:

$$II_\tau^{\alpha\beta\gamma} = \iint_\tau x^\alpha y^\beta z^\gamma\, d\tau = |\mathbf{a} \times \mathbf{b}| \iint_{\tau'} x^\alpha(u,v) y^\beta(u,v) z^\gamma(u,v)\, du\, dv, \tag{13.28}$$

where $\tau'$ is the $uv$ domain that corresponds to $\tau$ under the coordinate transformation (13.26). In this case we have (the proof is given in [CP90]):

$$II_\tau^{\alpha\beta\gamma} = |\mathbf{a} \times \mathbf{b}| \sum_{h=0}^{\alpha} \binom{\alpha}{h} x_o^{\alpha-h} \sum_{k=0}^{\beta} \binom{\beta}{k} y_o^{\beta-k} \sum_{m=0}^{\gamma} \binom{\gamma}{m} z_o^{\gamma-m} \cdot$$

$$\cdot \sum_{i=0}^{h} \binom{h}{i} a_x^{h-i} b_x^i \sum_{j=0}^{k} \binom{k}{j} a_y^{k-j} b_y^j \sum_{l=0}^{m} \binom{m}{l} a_z^{m-l} b_z^l\, II^{\mu\nu}, \tag{13.29}$$

---

[1] $II_\pi^{\alpha\beta}$ is substituted, when referred to the unit triangle, by the symbol $II^{\alpha\beta}$.

where $\mu = (h + k + m) - (i + j + l), \nu = (i + j + l)$, and $II^{\mu\nu}$ is a structure product over the triangle (13.24), as given by formula (13.25). Of course the area of a triangle $\tau$ is:

$$II_\tau^{000} = \iint_\tau d\tau = |\mathbf{a} \times \mathbf{b}| \, II^{00} = \frac{|\mathbf{a} \times \mathbf{b}|}{2}. \qquad (13.30)$$

**Surface integrals** In conclusion, a structure product over a polyhedral surface $S$, open or closed, is a summation of structure products (13.29) over the 2-simplices of a triangulation $K_2$ of $S$:

$$II_S^{\alpha\beta\gamma} = \iint_S x^\alpha y^\beta z^\gamma \, dS = \sum_{\tau \in K_2} II_\tau^{\alpha\beta\gamma}. \qquad (13.31)$$

**Volume integration** Let $P$ be a three-dimensional polyhedron bounded by a polyhedral surface $\partial P$. The regularity of the integration domain and the continuity of the integrating function enable us to apply the divergence theorem, which can be briefly summarized, for a vector field $\mathbf{F} = \mathbf{F(p)}$ as:

$$\iiint_P \nabla \cdot \mathbf{F} \, dx \, dy \, dz = \iint_{\partial P} \mathbf{F} \cdot \mathbf{n} \, dS = \sum_{\tau \in K_2} \iint_\tau \mathbf{F} \cdot \mathbf{n}_\tau \, d\tau, \qquad (13.32)$$

where $\mathbf{n}$ is the outward vector normal to the surface portion $dS$, and hence $\mathbf{n}_\tau = \mathbf{a} \times \mathbf{b}/|\mathbf{a} \times \mathbf{b}|$.

As the function $x^\alpha y^\beta z^\gamma$ equates the divergence of the vector field $\mathbf{F} = (x^{\alpha+1} y^\beta z^\gamma / \alpha + 1, 0, 0)$, an expression for $III_P^{\alpha\beta\gamma}$ is easily derived, which depends only on the 1-simplices of a triangulation of the domain boundary and on the structure products over its 2-simplices.

As a matter of fact, we have:

$$\begin{aligned} III_P^{\alpha\beta\gamma} &= \iiint_P x^\alpha y^\beta z^\gamma \, dx \, dy \, dz \\ &= \iiint_P \frac{\partial}{\partial x} \left( \frac{1}{\alpha + 1} x^{\alpha+1} y^\beta z^\gamma \right) dx \, dy \, dz \\ &= \frac{1}{\alpha + 1} \sum_{\tau' \in K'_2} (\mathbf{a} \times \mathbf{b})_x \iint_{\tau'} x^{\alpha+1} y^\beta z^\gamma \, du \, dv. \end{aligned} \qquad (13.33)$$

Taking into account equations (13.27) and (13.28), we can substitute the integral in the previous equation, getting finally:

$$III_P^{\alpha\beta\gamma} = \frac{1}{\alpha + 1} \sum_{\tau \in K_2} \left[ \frac{(\mathbf{a} \times \mathbf{b})_x}{|\mathbf{a} \times \mathbf{b}|} \right]_\tau II_\tau^{\alpha+1,\beta,\gamma} \qquad (13.34)$$

where the surface integrals are evaluated by using the formula (13.29).

**Computation of inertia has linear complexity**   Surface and volume integrals over linear polyhedra are computable in linear time. In particular, *surface and volume integrals of a monomial $x^\alpha y^\beta z^\gamma$ over a linear 2-or 3-polyhedron are computable in $O(\alpha^3 \beta^2 \gamma^2 E)$ time, $E$ being the number of edges of the polyhedron.*

In fact for the surface and volume integrals it is very easy to see, from inspection of the given equations, that both integrals may be evaluated in $O(\alpha^3 \beta^2 \gamma^2 T)$ time, $T$ being the number of triangles of a minimal triangulation of the domain. It is easy to show that the relation $T = 2E - 2F < 2E$ holds between the number $T$ of triangles of a minimal triangulation of a polyhedron boundary and the numbers $E$ and $F$ of its original edges and faces respectively. When all triangle faces are triangular, the relation reduces to $T = \frac{2}{3}E$.

This property is very important for Computer-Aided Design and Robotics applications: it demonstrates that the inertia tensor of a linear polyhedral solid is easy to compute. It directly implies that *the inertia tensor of a linear polyhedron is computable in $O(E)$ time.* As a matter of fact the elements of the inertia matrix of a homogeneous object $B$, namely its *mass* $M$, *first moments* $M_x, M_y, M_z$, *products of inertia* $M_{xy}, M_{yz}, M_{zx}$, and *second moments* $M_{xx}, M_{yy}, M_{zz}$, can be all expressed as

$$\rho \int_B x^\alpha y^\beta z^\gamma \, dV, \tag{13.35}$$

where $\rho$ is the constant density, and where $0 \le \alpha + \beta + \gamma \le 2$. Being $\alpha, \beta, \gamma$ bounded, the assertion follows from the previous claim.

## 13.6   Examples

### 13.6.1   Umbrella modeling (4): solid parts

The 1D subcomplex with handle and rods defined in our last umbrella version with curve segments and surface patches (see Section 12.6.1) is refined with 3D solid parts in Script 13.6.1. In particular, the new handle is generated as a 3-variate mapping of the boundary Dom of a translated parallelopided D1 * D2 * D3 in parametric space, where D1 is a partition in 8 parts of the interval $[\pi, 2\pi]$, D2 is a partition in 1 parts of the interval $[0, r/3]$, where $r$ is the handle radius, and D3 = D2.

**Figure 13.29**   Some perspectives of the model generated by Umbrella:<10,80>, and Umbrella:<10,30>, where 80 and 30 (degrees) are the opening angles.

Finally, the curved tiny rods of the umbrella are generated from their initial wire frame definition, by using the primitive BezierStripe operator. Such a function will

## Script 13.6.1 (Umbrella modeling (4))

```
DEF Handle (h::Isreal) = T:<1,2>:<Radius*7/6,-:Radius/6>:
    (MAP:[S2*COS ~ S1, S3, S2*SIN ~ S1]:dom )
WHERE
    D1 = (T:1:PI ~ S:1:PI ~ Domain):8,
    D2 = (S:1:(1/3*Radius) ~ Domain):1,
    D3 = D2,
    Dom = @2:(T:2:Radius:(D1 * D2 * D3)),
    Radius = h/18
END;

DEF Axis (h::IsReal) = (@2 ~ STRUCT):<
    Handle2, T:3:(h/10), MetalRing, Rod, T:3:(2*AB), Tip >
WHERE
    Handle2 = T:<1,2>:<-1/6*Radius,-1/6*Radius>:
        (CUBOID:<1/3*Radius,1/3*Radius,h/10>),
    MetalRing = CYLINDER:<h/50, 0.5*h/10>: 12,
    Rod = CYLINDER:<h/90, 2*AB>: 12,
    Tip = Handle2,
    Radius = h/18,
    AB = h*4/10
END;

DEF Rod (len::IsReal) = T:<1,2>:<-2*a,-1/2*a>:((@2 ~ CUBOID):<2*a,a,len>)
    WHERE a = len/100 END;
```

generate a plane surface stripe depending on the 3 control points of a quadratic Bezier curve. The 3D solid rods are thus generated by the polyhedral product of the surface stripe times a 1D segment of size len/100.

## Script 13.6.2 (Umbrella modeling (4))

```
DEF RodCurve (len,beta,n::IsReal) =
    (R:<2,3>:(PI/2) ~ T:1:(2*len/100) ~ @2):
        ((T:1:(-2*len/(100 - 5)) ~ BezierStripe):
            <<<0,0>,<0,len/2>,<len/2 * sin:beta,len>>,2*len/100,n>
            * QUOTE:<len/100>);

Umbrella:<10,80>
```

Some projections of the refined model, for different values of the opening angle, are given in Figure 13.29.

# 14

# Dimension-independent PLaSM operators

The main geometric operations of the PLaSM language are discussed in this chapter, with the aim of presenting in some depth their dimension-independent algorithms. In fact, a basic understanding of the underlying computations may help in using the language in the best way, especially when the operations to be performed are intrinsically difficult. In particular, this chapter first gives some details about the internal representation HPC of the PLaSM language, then describes our implementation of Boolean algorithms with BSP-trees, and introduces dimension-independent integration techniques. Finally, some quite unusual but *very* important operations, such as *Cartesian product* and *Minkowski sum* of dimension-independent polyhedra, are discussed. All such operations were implemented for the first time, to the author's knowledge, within the PLaSM geometric kernel. After reading the last sections, the advanced user of the language may realize that s/he is now able to start exploring, like a fascinating new world, the homomorphism between the algebra of $d$-polyhedra and the algebra of FL programs.

## 14.1    Inside Hierarchical Polyhedral Complexes

Dimension-independent solid modeling requires representations and operations which uniformly apply to geometric objects of dimension $0, 1, 2, 3, \ldots, d$. This more abstract approach allows many different geometric problems in a uniform manner to be solved, such as modeling of articulated bodies, piecewise-linear approximation of curved manifolds, graphics representation of multidimensional data and motion encoding, and greatly contributes to the expressive power of the PLaSM language. We start this section by quickly summarizing some mathematical concepts needed to understand the HPC representation. A preliminary reading of Chapter 4 is strongly recommended.

**Summary**    The HPC representation scheme, already introduced in Chapter 13, is decompositive, where the cells are convex sets resulting from the intersection of linear halfspaces. A *polyhedron* is thus defined as the point set union of quasi-

*Geometric Programming for Computer-Aided Design*  Alberto Paoluzzi
© 2003 John Wiley & Sons, Ltd  ISBN 0-471-89942-9

disjoint bounded convex cells, i.e. of *polytopes* (see Chapter 4). This scheme allows representation of $d$-dimensional polyhedra, possibly non-regular, non-convex and unconnected. Each cell is represented as a set of simultaneous linear inequalities. The representation of a regular $d$-polyhedron is completed by the $(d-1)$-adjacency graph between pairs of $d$-cells. Two $d$-cells are adjacent when they have a common boundary *facet*. A *polyhedral complex* is also built up from polyhedral cells as a hierarchical graph, where nodes correspond either to polyhedral complexes or to polyhedra, and where transformation matrices are associated with arcs. The rationale for these design choices is given in Section 13.3.2; below the reader can find a more formal description of this representation.

**Facet covector and cell comatrix**    An affine hyperplane $ax = 0$, where $a = (a^0, a^1, \ldots, a^d)$ and $x = (x_0, x_1, \ldots, x_d)$, with $x_0 = 1$, can be seen as the subset of points $x \in \mathbb{E}^d$ which is mapped to zero by the linear function $a : \mathbb{E}^d \to \mathbb{R}$, i.e. as the kernel of the mapping. The space of linear functions like $a$ is a vector space of dimension $d$, which is called the *dual space* of $\mathbb{E}^d$, and denoted as $(\mathbb{E}^d)^*$. A convex set may either be defined as the convex combination of a convexly independent set of points, or as the set of simultaneous solutions of a set of linear inequalities. In this second case we represent a cell as a set of *face covectors* in dual space.

A cell of dimension $d$, or $d$-cell, is a convex set of $\mathbb{E}^d$; such a set is the intersection of the halfspaces defined by the affine hyperplanes which support the cell *facets*. A cell is therefore represented as an ordered set of face covectors, called *cell comatrix* in the sequel.

For each covector a normalized coordinate representation $f = (f^0, f^1, \ldots, f^d)$ is given, which is intended as a row vector where $|f| = 1$. For any point $x = (x_0, x_1, \ldots, x_d)$ internal to a cell, $fx < 0$ holds for any face covector $f$ of the cell. Conversely, for points on the cell boundary $fx = 0$ holds for some $f$. A point belongs to a face of codimension $k$ (or of dimension $d - k$) if it belongs to $h \geq k$ boundary hyperplanes ($k$ of which are affinely independent). Given the comatrix $C$, a cell $c$ as a set of points is defined as

$$c = \{x \in \mathbb{E}^d | \ x = (x_0, x_1, \ldots, x_d), x_0 = 1, Cx \leq 0\} \qquad (14.1)$$

A comatrix $C$ is *compatible* when the associated cell $c$ is non-empty. A covector $b$ is *implicated* by a compatible comatrix $C$ when both $C$ and $C$ augmented with row $b$ give the same cell. A comatrix is *non-redundant* when none of its rows is implicated by the others.

**Polyhedral cell**    A polyhedron of dimension $d$, or $d$-polyhedron, is the *union* of a collection of quasi-disjoint cells of dimension $\leq d$. The intersection of any pair of cells in a polyhedron is either empty or is a face ($i$-dimensional, $0 \leq i \leq d - 1$) for both cells. Note that with such a definition a polyhedron is regular, i.e. homogeneously $d$-dimensional, and may be non-convex and unconnected.

A face-based decompositive representation of a polyhedron $P$ is a pair $(F, C_F)$ where $F$ is the face covector database and $C_F$ is the cell database. For each cell a list of pairs (covector-pointer, sign) and a list of pointers to $(d-1)$-adjacent cells are stored. The presence of a sign is due to the opposite orientation for the face covector of the two cells $(d-1)$-adjacent along the face. Each vertex may be implicitly represented by the list of faces it belongs to. The solution of the linear system written using the incident covectors will give an explicit representation of the vertex, when necessary.

## Example 14.1.1 (Polyhedral complexes)

Some insight about the internal representation of polyhedral complexes is given in this example, by discussing the exported XML data corresponding to some extremely simple 2D objects. So, we generate geometric values for symbols square1, square2, doubleSquare1 and doubleSquare2 in Script 14.1.1 and export them to XML files with the same name. The XML code, discussed in the following, reflects quite closely the internal representation.

---

**Script 14.1.1 (PLaSM script)**
```
DEF square1 = CUBOID:<1,1>;
DEF square2 = MKPOL:<<<0,0>,<1,0>,<0,1>,<1,1>>,<<1,2,3,4>>,<<1>>>;
DEF doubleSquare1 = square1 STRUCT T:1:1:square1;
DEF doubleSquare2 = MKPOL: <<<0,0>,<1,0>,<2,0>,<0,1>,<1,1>,<2,1>>,
    <<1,2,4,5>,<2,3,5,6>>,<<1,2>>>;

SAVE: square1: 'square1.xml';
SAVE: square2: 'square2.xml';
SAVE: doubleSquare1: 'doubleSquare1.xml';
SAVE: doubleSquare2: 'doubleSquare2.xml';
```

---

The object square1 is a polyhedral complex with only one polyhedral cell made by one convex cell and represented by *faces*, i.e. by the cell comatrix. It is described in Script 14.1.2.

The <PolyhedralComplex> tag has attributes sdim, for the dimension of the embedding space, rep, for the kind of representation (either 'faces' or 'vertices') and the optional name. A <PolyhedralComplex> is a sequence of <PolyhedralNode>. This one is a container for a *pair*, where the first element is always a <mat>, i.e. a homogeneous representation of a matrix, and the second is either a <PolyhedralComplex> or a <Polyhedron>.

The <Polyhedron> tag has a further attribute pdim which denotes the intrinsic dimension of the polyhedral cell. The <mat> tag encloses a suitable representation of the transformation matrix to be applied to the <PolyhedralNode>. The <faces> tags enclose the set of covectors which are used to define the set of <ConvexCell> of the <Polyhedron>.

The <ConvexCell> tag is used to define each convex cell of the decompositive representation. For each cell, a set of indices to adjacent cells is given by the <adj> list. In our case the cell has 4 *facets*, and all the indices are set to -1 since on each facet there is no adjacent cell. In other words, the 4 cell facets are all boundary facets.

Finally, the <polfaces> and <fpoints> tags respectively denote the list of indices of covector faces, and the subsets of indices of covectors whose simultaneous resolution gives each cell vertex. To be concrete, the pair (3 0) states that the first cell vertex is generated by resolving the linear sistem of the fourth and first covector, i.e. by the intersection of affine supports of the fourth and first facet:

$$\begin{cases} c_3 x &= 0 \\ c_0 x &= 0 \end{cases}$$

---

**Script 14.1.2 (One polyhedral cell, one convex cell, on faces)**

```
<PolyhedralComplex sdim='2' rep='faces' name='square1'>
  <PolyhedralNode rep='faces'>
    <mat>((1 0 0)(0 1 0)(0 0 1))</mat>
    <Polyhedron rep='faces' pdim='2' sdim='2'>
      <faces>((1 0 -0) (-0.707107 0 0.707107)
        (-0 1 -0) (0 -0.707107 0.707107))</faces>
      <ConvexCell rep='faces' inpol='1' pdim='2' sdim='2'>
        <adj>(-1 -1 -1 -1)</adj>
        <polfaces>(0 1 2 3)</polfaces>
        <fpoints>((3 0) (3 1) (2 0) (2 1))</fpoints>
      </ConvexCell>
    </Polyhedron>
  </PolyhedralNode>
</PolyhedralComplex>
```

---

The dual representation *on vertices* is shown in Script 14.1.3 for the `square2` object of the PLaSM Script 14.1.1. Also in this case we have only one polyhedral cell, made of only one convex cell. The only difference is the kind `rep='vertices'` of representation of polytopes, as convex hull of the cell vertices. So, in this case, the `<points>` (vertices) of the 2D object are explicitly stored at the `<Polyhedron>` level, whereas `<polpoints>` and `<vfaces>` respectively give the list of vertex indices for each cell, and the subsets of affinely independent vertices whose affine combination generates the affine support (hyperplane) of each cell facet.

---

**Script 14.1.3 (One polyhedral cell, one convex cell, on vertices)**

```
<PolyhedralComplex sdim='2' rep='vertices' name='square2'>
  <PolyhedralNode rep='vertices'>
    <mat>((1 0 0)(0 1 0)(0 0 1))</mat>
    <Polyhedron rep='vertices' pdim='2' sdim='2'>
      <points>((1 1) (0 1) (1 0) (0 0))</points>
      <ConvexCell rep='vertices' inpol='1' pdim='2' sdim='2'>
        <adj>(-1 -1 -1 -1)</adj>
        <polpoints>(0 1 2 3)</polpoints>
        <vfaces>((1 3) (3 2) (0 1) (0 2))</vfaces>
      </ConvexCell>
    </Polyhedron>
  </PolyhedralNode>
</PolyhedralComplex>
```

---

The `doublesquare1` object of Script 14.1.1 is given in Script 14.1.4 as a polyhedral complex with two polyhedral cells, one convex cell for each polyhedron, represented *on faces.* In this case the `<PolyhedralComplex>` contains two `<PolyhedralNode>` container instances, where the `<mat>` object inside the second container is different from the identity, and implements the PLaSM tensor T:1:1. Notice that, according to the mathematics of transformations of dual space (see Section 3.2.5), the inverse matrix of that transformation is actually stored. No adjacencies are stored in both convex cells, because they belong to different polyhedral cells.[1]

---

**Script 14.1.4 (Two polyhedral cell, one convex cell, on faces)**
```
<PolyhedralComplex sdim='2' rep='faces' name='doublesquare1'>
  <PolyhedralNode rep='faces'>
    <mat>((1 0 0)(0 1 0)(0 0 1))</mat>
    <Polyhedron rep='faces' pdim='2' sdim='2'>
      <faces>((1 0 -0) (-0.707107 0 0.707107)
      (-0 1 -0) (0 -0.707107 0.707107))</faces>
      <ConvexCell rep='faces' inpol='1' pdim='2' sdim='2'>
        <adj>(-1 -1 -1 -1)</adj>
        <polfaces>(0 1 2 3)</polfaces>
        <fpoints>((3 0) (3 1) (2 0) (2 1))</fpoints>
      </ConvexCell>
    </Polyhedron>
  </PolyhedralNode>
  <PolyhedralNode rep='faces'>
    <mat>((1 0 -1)(0 1 0)(0 0 1))</mat>
    <Polyhedron rep='faces' pdim='2' sdim='2'>
      <faces>((1 0 -0) (-0.707107 0 0.707107)
      (-0 1 -0) (0 -0.707107 0.707107))</faces>
      <ConvexCell rep='faces' inpol='1' pdim='2' sdim='2'>
        <adj>(-1 -1 -1 -1)</adj>
        <polfaces>(0 1 2 3)</polfaces>
        <fpoints>((3 0) (3 1) (2 0) (2 1))</fpoints>
      </ConvexCell>
    </Polyhedron>
  </PolyhedralNode>
</PolyhedralComplex>
```

---

Finally, the `doublesquare2` object of Script 14.1.1 is shown in Script 14.1.5 as a polyhedral complex with one polyhedral cell made by two convex cells, and represented *on vertices.* As we already know, the vertex database is now available as `<points>` objects at `<Polyhedron>` level, so that the first (0-th) cell is defined by value (0 1 2 3) of `<polpoints>` object, whereas the second (1-st) cell is defined by (4 0 5 2).

The adjacency between the first and the second cell is codified inside the values (-1 -1 -1 1) and (0 -1 -1 -1) of `<adj>` objects, which tell us that the fourth facet of the first cell is adjacent to the first facet of the second cell, and vice versa, as it is possible to check by either looking for the common pair (0 2) in the two `<vfaces>` objects of Script 14.1.5, or by visual inspection of Figure 14.1.

---

[1] We have actually changed our mind on this design choice, so some future version of the geometric kernel will store, among other things, such kind of adjacency.

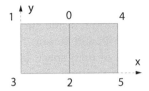

**Figure 14.1**  Polyhedral complex `doublesquare2`

---

**Script 14.1.5 (One polyhedral cell, two convex cell, on vertices)**

```
<PolyhedralComplex sdim='2' rep='vertices' name='doublesquare2>
  <PolyhedralNode rep='vertices'>
    <mat>((1 0 0)(0 1 0)(0 0 1))</mat>
    <Polyhedron rep='vertices' pdim='2' sdim='2'>
      <points>((1 1) (0 1) (1 0) (0 0) (2 1) (2 0))</points>
      <ConvexCell rep='vertices' inpol='1' pdim='2' sdim='2'>
        <adj>(-1 -1 -1 1)</adj>
        <polpoints>(0 1 2 3)</polpoints>
        <vfaces>((1 3) (3 2) (0 1) (0 2))</vfaces>
      </ConvexCell>
      <ConvexCell rep='vertices' inpol='1' pdim='2' sdim='2'>
        <adj>(0 -1 -1 -1)</adj>
        <polpoints>(4 0 5 2)</polpoints>
        <vfaces>((0 2) (2 5) (4 0) (4 5))</vfaces>
      </ConvexCell>
    </Polyhedron>
  </PolyhedralNode>
</PolyhedralComplex>
```

---

**Note**    As the reader should have guessed at this point, the more interesting aspects of the HPC scheme are dimension-independence and descriptive power, which allow to represent $d$-dimensional polyhedra, possibly non-regular, non convex, unconnected and non-manifold, and embedded in arbitrary $n$-dimensional space, for any $d \leq n$.

## 14.2    Boolean operations

Set operations of union, intersection and difference of polyhedral complexes are implemented in PLaSM by using a BSP representation. In Figure 14.2 both the result of a difference operation between two cubes, and the 1-skeletons of two alternative cell decompositions of the result are shown.

In this section we discuss quite deeply our implementation of BSP *tree merging*, defined by Naylor, Amanatides and Thibault [NAT90] at the beginning of the 1990s. It is implemented in a dimension-independent way within the PLaSM kernel, by using Linear Programming techniques. Our version of the BSP-tree merging is described here in some detail because it appears to be, to the knowledge of the authors, the first available dimension-independent actual implementation of this approach.

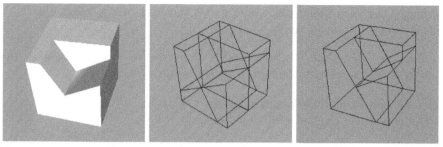

**Figure 14.2**   Difference between 3D cubes: (a) resulting object (b) set of solid cells of the space partition induced by the cube boundary planes (c) set of solid cells of the *pruned* BSP tree

*14.2.1   Algorithm*

According to Naylor [NAT90], the first step to perform in computing a set operation between two polyhedra represented as BSP trees, is to merge the space partitioning described by the trees into unique partitioning, as shown by Figure 14.3. The required set operation can be subsequently performed on the cells of such new partitioning. Actually, the two tasks are performed at the same time while *traversing* and *merging* the two input trees.

**Merging BSP trees**

The aim of merging two BSP trees is that of merging their associated space partitions. Imagine that two BSP trees generate two different partitions $P_1$ and $P_2$ of $\mathbb{E}^d$. Merging $P_1$ and $P_2$ creates a third partition $P_3$ of $\mathbb{E}^d$, whose cells $c_3$ are created by pairwise intersection of cells in $P_1$ and $P_2$:

$$P_3 = \{c_3 = c_1 \cap c_2 \neq \emptyset \mid c_1 \in P_1,\ c_2 \in P_2\}.$$

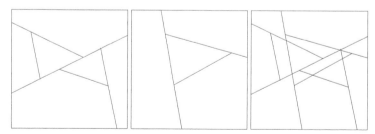

**Figure 14.3**   Two binary space partitions. To execute a set operation the two partitions must be *merged*

Let be given the BSP trees $t_1$ and $t_2$. The purposes of the algorithm given in Script 14.2.1 are:

1. subdividing the $t_2$ tree onto the $t_1$ tree to create a new tree $t_3$ which represents the new merged partition of the space;

2. performing a set operation while, during the traversal of the trees, the algorithm finds a leaf of the trees.

In particular, the algorithm PARTITION-BSP processes the tree $t2$ against the hyperplane $t1.h$ associated with the root of $t1$, and returns two trees:

- *InNegHs*, the part of $t2$ in the negative halfspace of $t1.h$;
- *InPosHs*, the part of $t2$ in the positive halfspace of $t1.h$.

At this point two problems similar to the original one are generated, so that the MERGE-BSP algorithm can be executed recursively. When a leaf node is found, the function MERGE-CELL is invoked, that indeed performs the requested set operation.

In Script 14.2.1, a variable of type `partitioned_tree` contains two different tree ( *InNegHs* and *InPosHs* ) after the invocation of function PARTITION-BSP. The variable *convex*, of *stack* type, gives the intersection of closed halfspaces on the path from the root to the currently visited node of the tree $t3$, that is generated during the execution of MERGE-BSP. From an algebraic viewpoint, this variable represents a system of simultaneous linear inequalities, whereas from a computational viewpoint it is a stack of objects.

---

**Script 14.2.1 (Merge-BSP algorithm)**

```
algorithm MERGE-BSP( t1, t2: bspt, op: operation, convex: stack ): bspt;

    t2_partitioned: partitioned_tree;

    if( t1 is a leaf or t2 is a leaf ) then
        return MERGE-CELL( t1, t2, op );
    else {
        t2_partitioned := PARTITION-BSP( t2, t1.h, convex );
        convex.push( t1.h, < );
        t1.below := MERGE-BSP( t1.below, t2_partitioned.InNegHs, op, convex );
        convex.pop();
        convex.push( t1.h, > ) ;
        t1.above := MERGE-BSP( t1.above, t2_partitioned.InPosHs, op, convex );
        convex.pop();
        return t1;
    }
end
```

---

### Partitioning a BSP tree against a hyperplane

The PARTITION-BSP algorithm, given in Script 14.2.2, has as input parameters a BSP tree $t$, a hyperplane $h$, called *binary partitioner*, and a *convex* cell where performing the computation. The output parameters, of BSP tree type, are called *InNegHs* and *InPosHs*, and respectively contain the $t$ part contained in the intersection of *convex* with the negative and the positive halfspaces of $h$.

More formally, the PARTITION-BSP algorithm can be seen as a map:

$$(t, h, \textit{convex}) \mapsto (\textit{InNegHs}, \textit{InPosHs})$$

where

$$\begin{aligned}
\textit{InNegHs} &= t \sqcup (h^- \cap \textit{convex}), \\
\textit{InPosHs} &= t \sqcup (h^+ \cap \textit{convex}).
\end{aligned}$$

The symbol $\sqcup$ indicates here the "intersection" of a BSP tree with a *convex* region of space. The result of such an operation is a BSP tree that describes the part of $t$ contained inside the *convex* region. The cells of *InNegHs* and *InPosHs* trees are:

$$\begin{aligned}
\text{cells}(\textit{InNegHs}) &= \{c^- \,|\, c^- = c \cap (h^- \cap \textit{convex}) \neq \emptyset, \; c \in \text{cells}(t)\} \\
\text{cells}(\textit{InPosHs}) &= \{c^+ \,|\, c^+ = c \cap (h^+ \cap \textit{convex}) \neq \emptyset, \; c \in \text{cells}(t)\}
\end{aligned}$$

The PARTITION-BSP algorithm must classify all hyperplanes of $t$, whose generic element is denoted as $t.h$, against the $h$ hyperplane into the *convex* region. There are seven possible cases. The correct choice is selected by using Linear Programming techniques, shortly described in the sections below.

In particular, *convex* codifies a system of simultaneous linear inequalities:

$$\begin{cases}
a_{0,0}x_0 + a_{0,1}x_1 + a_{0,2}x_2 + \cdots + a_{0,d}x_d \leq 0 \\
a_{1,0}x_0 + a_{1,1}x_1 + a_{1,2}x_2 + \cdots + a_{1,d}x_d \leq 0 \\
\quad\vdots \qquad \vdots \qquad \vdots \qquad \ddots \qquad \vdots \qquad \vdots \\
a_{r,0}x_0 + a_{r,1}x_1 + a_{r,2}x_2 + \cdots + a_{r,d}x_d \leq 0
\end{cases} \tag{14.2}$$

A standardized form of equations for $t.h$ and $h$ is thus added to this system. Then the solution of the augmented system is properly classified with respect to the seven cases discussed below, which are also displayed in Figures 14.4 and 14.5.

**Coincident**   (Figure 14.4) The two hyperplanes coincide, and have the same normal vector. In this case the two output trees are:

$$\begin{aligned}
\textit{InNegHs} &= \textit{t.below} \\
\textit{InPosHs} &= \textit{t.above}
\end{aligned}$$

**Opposite**   (Figure 14.4) The two hyperplanes also coincide, but with opposite normal vectors. In this case the two output trees are computed as:

$$\begin{aligned}
\textit{InNegHs} &= \textit{t.above} \\
\textit{InPosHs} &= \textit{t.below}
\end{aligned}$$

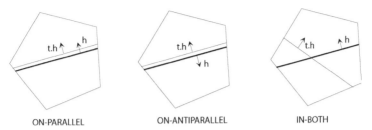

ON-PARALLEL        ON-ANTIPARALLEL        IN-BOTH

**Figure 14.4**   Two intersecting hyperplanes: (a) with same normal vector
(COINCIDENT) (b) with opposite normal vector (OPPOSITE) (c) intersecting within the
convex set (INTERSECT)

**Intersect**   (Figure 14.4c) The hyperplanes $t.h$ and $h$ intersect inside the *convex*
region. To discover this case, just add to *convex* system the equations of $h$ and $t.h$:

$$\begin{aligned} a_{h,0}x_0 + a_{h,1}x_1 + a_{h,2}x_2 + & \quad\cdots\quad + a_{h,d}x_d & = 0 \\ a_{t.h,0}x_0 + a_{t.h,1}x_1 + a_{t.h,2}x_2 + & \quad\cdots\quad + a_{t.h,d}x_d & = 0 \end{aligned}$$

and consider if the augmented system of equalities and inequalities has a solution.
If the first phase of the simplex method, performed on the augmented system, has
a solution, then the two hyperplanes intersect inside the *convex* region. In this case
*InNegHs* and *InPosHs* trees are given as:

$$\begin{aligned} InNegHs &= t \sqcup (h^- \cap S) \\ InPosHs &= t \sqcup (h^+ \cap S) \end{aligned}$$

Since the algorithm is recursive, it is just necessary to compute the two sons of the
node $t$. More specifically:

$$\begin{aligned} InNegHs.below &= t.below \sqcup (h^- \cap S) \\ InNegHs.above &= t.above \sqcup (h^- \cap S) \\ InPosHs.below &= t.below \sqcup (h^+ \cap S) \\ InPosHs.above &= t.above \sqcup (h^+ \cap S). \end{aligned}$$

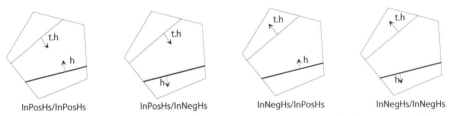

InPosHs/InPosHs        InPosHs/InNegHs        InNegHs/InPosHs        InNegHs/InNegHs

**Figure 14.5**   The hyperplanes $t.h$ and $h$ do not intersect inside the *convex* region

**Above-above**   (Figure 14.5) The hyperplane $h$ is contained in the positive halfspace
of $t.h$ (i.e. in the $t.above$ subtree) and $t.h$ is in the positive halfspace of $h$ into the
convex set. To check for this we add to *convex* system (14.2) first the equations:

$$\begin{aligned} a_{h,0}x_0 + a_{h,1}x_1 + a_{h,2}x_2 + & \quad\cdots\quad + a_{h,d}x_d & = 0, \\ a_{t.h,0}x_0 + a_{t.h,1}x_1 + a_{t.h,2}x_2 + & \quad\cdots\quad + a_{t.h,d}x_d & \geq 0, \end{aligned}$$

and then the equations:

$$a_{h,0}x_0 + a_{h,1}x_1 + a_{h,2}x_2 + \quad \cdots \quad + a_{h,d}x_d \quad \geq 0,$$
$$a_{t.h,0}x_0 + a_{t.h,1}x_1 + a_{t.h,2}x_2 + \quad \cdots \quad + a_{t.h,d}x_d \quad = 0.$$

If the two obtained systems have both solution and the case INTERSECT is not true, then this condition is true. In this case the *InNegHs* and *InPosHs* trees are defined as:

$$
\begin{aligned}
InPosHs &= t \\
InPosHs.below &= t.below \\
InPosHs.above &= t.above \sqcup (h^+ \cap S) \\
InNegHs &= t \sqcup (h^- \cap S)
\end{aligned}
$$

**Above-below**   (Figure 14.5) The hyperplane $h$ is contained in the positive halfspace of $t.h$ (i.e. in the $t.above$ subtree) and $t.h$ is in the negative halfspace of $h$ inside the *convex* region. To check for this case, we consider the convex (14.2) and respectively add to this system first the equations:

$$a_{h,0}x_0 + a_{h,1}x_1 + a_{h,2}x_2 + \quad \cdots \quad + a_{h,d}x_d \quad = 0$$
$$a_{t.h,0}x_0 + a_{t.h,1}x_1 + a_{t.h,2}x_2 + \quad \cdots \quad + a_{t.h,d}x_d \quad \geq 0$$

and then the equations:

$$a_{h,0}x_0 + a_{h,1}x_1 + a_{h,2}x_2 + \quad \cdots \quad + a_{h,d}x_d \quad \leq 0$$
$$a_{t.h,0}x_0 + a_{t.h,1}x_1 + a_{t.h,2}x_2 + \quad \cdots \quad + a_{t.h,d}x_d \quad = 0$$

If the two augmented systems have a solution and the case **intersect** is not true, this condition is true. In this case the *InNegHs* and *InPosHs* trees are defined as:

$$
\begin{aligned}
InPosHs &= t \\
InPosHs.below &= t.below \sqcup (h^+ \cap S) \\
InPosHs.above &= t.above \\
InNegHs &= t \sqcup (h^- \cap S)
\end{aligned}
$$

**Below-above**   (Figure 14.5) The hyperplane $h$ is contained in the negative halfspace of $t.h$ (i.e. in the $t.below$ subtree) and $t.h$ is in the positive halfspace of $h$ inside the *convex* region. To check for this case we add to convex set (14.2) first the equations:

$$a_{h,0}x_0 + a_{h,1}x_1 + a_{h,2}x_2 + \quad \cdots \quad + a_{h,d}x_d \quad = 0$$
$$a_{t.h,0}x_0 + a_{t.h,1}x_1 + a_{t.h,2}x_2 + \quad \cdots \quad + a_{t.h,d}x_d \quad \leq 0$$

and then the equations:

$$a_{h,0}x_0 + a_{h,1}x_1 + a_{h,2}x_2 + \quad \cdots \quad + a_{h,d}x_d \quad \geq 0$$
$$a_{t.h,0}x_0 + a_{t.h,1}x_1 + a_{t.h,2}x_2 + \quad \cdots \quad + a_{t.h,d}x_d \quad = 0$$

If the two systems have solution and the case INTERSECT is not true, then this condition is true. In this case the two trees *InNegHs* and *InPosHs* are defined as:

$$
\begin{aligned}
InNegHs &= t \\
InNegHs.below &= t.below \\
InNegHs.above &= t.above \sqcup (h^- \cap S) \\
InPosHs &= t \sqcup (h^+ \cap S)
\end{aligned}
$$

**Below-below**   (Figure 14.5) The hyperplane $h$ is contained in the negative halfspace of $t.h$ (in the $t.below$ subtree) and $t.h$ is in the negative halfspace of $h$ inside the *convex* region. Let us consider the convex (14.2) and add to this system first the equations:

$$
\begin{aligned}
a_{h,0}x_0 + a_{h,1}x_1 + a_{h,2}x_2 + \quad \cdots \quad + a_{h,d}x_d &= 0 \\
a_{t.h,0}x_0 + a_{t.h,1}x_1 + a_{t.h,2}x_2 + \quad \cdots \quad + a_{t.h,d}x_d &\le 0
\end{aligned}
$$

and then the equations:

$$
\begin{aligned}
a_{h,0}x_0 + a_{h,1}x_1 + a_{h,2}x_2 + \quad \cdots \quad + a_{h,d}x_d &\le 0 \\
a_{t.h,0}x_0 + a_{t.h,1}x_1 + a_{t.h,2}x_2 + \quad \cdots \quad + a_{t.h,d}x_d &= 0
\end{aligned}
$$

If both systems have solution and the case INTERSECT is not true, then this condition holds. In this case *InNegHs* and *InPosHs* trees are defined as:

$$
\begin{aligned}
InNegHs &= t \\
InNegHs.below &= t.below \sqcup (h^- \cap S) \\
InNegHs.above &= t.above \\
InPosHs &= t \sqcup (h^+ \cap S)
\end{aligned}
$$

A pseudo-coded but quite detailed description of the behavior of the Partition-BSP algorithm is given in Script 14.2.2.

**Script 14.2.2 (Partition-BSP algorithm)**

```
algorithm
PARTITION-BSP ( t: bspt, h: hyperplane, convex: stack ): partitioned_tree;
    partitioned_tree pt, pt1, pt2;
    if( t.type ≠ CUT ) pt.InNegHs = t; pt.InPosHs = t;
    else switch( CLASSIFY( t, h, convex ) )
        case COINCIDENT:
            pt.InNegHs = t.below; pt.InPosHs = t.above;
        case OPPOSITE:
            pt.InNegHs = t.above; pt.InPosHs = t.below;
        case INTERSECT:
            pt.InNegHs = t; pt.InPosHs = DUPLICATE(t);
            convex.push( t.h, < );
            pt1 = PARTITION-BSP( t.below, h, convex );
            convex.pop();
            convex.push( t.h, > ) ;
            pt2 = PARTITION-BSP( t.above, h, convex );
            convex.pop();
            pt.InNegHs.below = pt1.inNegHs; pt.InNegHs.above = pt2.inNegHs;
            pt.InPosHs.below = pt1.inPosHs; pt.InPosHs.above = pt2.inPosHs;
        case ABOVE-ABOVE:
            pt.InPosHs = t; pt.InPosHs.below = t.below;
            convex.push( t.h, > ) ;
            pt1 = PARTITION-BSP( t.above, h, convex );
            convex.pop();
            pt.InPosHs.above = pt1.inPosHs; pt.InNegHs = pt1.inNegHs;
        case ABOVE-BELOW:
            pt.InPosHs = t; pt.InPosHs.above = t.above;
            convex.push( t.h, < ) ;
            pt1 = PARTITION-BSP( t.below, h, convex );
            convex.pop();
            pt.InPosHs.below = pt1.inPosHs; pt.InNegHs = pt1.inNegHs;
        case BELOW-ABOVE:
            pt.InNegHs = t; pt.InNegHs.below = t.below;
            convex.push( t.h, > ) ;
            pt1 = PARTITION-BSP( t.above, h, convex );
            convex.pop();
            pt.InNegHs.above = pt1.inNegHs; pt.InPosHs = pt1.inPosHs;
        case BELOW-BELOW:
            pt.InNegHs = t; pt.InNegHs.above = t.above;
            convex.push( t.h, < ) ;
            pt1 = PARTITION-BSP( t.below, h, convex );
            convex.pop();
            pt.InNegHs.below = pt1.inNegHs; pt.InPosHs = pt1.inPosHs;
    return pt;
end
```

A function call such as CLASSIFY( $t$, $h$, *convex* ), with actual values for $t$, $h$ and *convex*, is used by the PARTITION-BSP algorithm to return a value of *classify_type*, i.e. a value in the set {*coincident, opposite, intersect, above-above, below-above, above-below, below-below*}, according to the computational strategies previously discussed. The CLASSIFY algorithm is given in Script 14.2.3.

---

**Script 14.2.3 (Classify algorithm)**
    **algorithm** CLASSIFY ( $t$: bspt, $h$: hyperplane, *convex*: stack ) : classify_type;

        *bresult*: bool;
        *pos*: position;

        **if**( $h$ and $t.h$ is the same hyperplane )
            **if**( $h$ and $t.h$ have same normal )
                **return** COINCIDENT;
            **else return** OPPOSITE;

        *convex.push*( $h$, = ); *convex.push*( $t.h$, = );
        *bresult* := SIMPLEX-METHOD( *convex* );
        *convex.pop*(); *convex.pop*();
        **if** *bresult* = TRUE
            **return** INTERSECT;

        *convex.push*( $h$, > ); *convex.push*( $t.h$, = );
        *bresult* := SIMPLEX-METHOD( *convex* );
        *convex.pop*(); *convex.pop*();
        **if** *bresult* = TRUE *pos* := above;
        **else** *pos* := below;
        *convex.push*( $h$, = ); *convex.push*( $t.h$, > );
        *bresult* := SIMPLEX-METHOD( *convex* );
        *convex.pop*(); *convex.pop*();
        **if**( *bresult* = TRUE )
            **if**( *pos* = above ) **return** ABOVE-ABOVE;
            **else return** BELOW-ABOVE;
        **else**
            **if**( *pos* = above ) **return** ABOVE-BELOW;
            **else return** BELOW-BELOW;
    **end**

---

The pseudocode of the algorithm is given in Script 14.2.2 and in Script 14.2.3.

### Classify a BSP subtree against a leaf

As shown by Script 14.2.1, the recursive merging process will continue until either $t1$ or $t2$ becomes a leaf node, i.e. a simple cell of the space partition. At this point the MERGE-BSP algorithm actually executes the required set operation between a leaf and a subtree by following the rules shown in Table 14.1. Complementing a BSP tree

**Table 14.1**      Rules to resolve a set operation between a leaf and a subtree. The ¬ symbol denotes the complement operator for BSP trees.

| Op1 | Op2 | ∪ | | ∩ | − | Δ |
|------|------|------|------|------|------|------|
| subtree | IN | IN | subtree | OUT | ¬ subtree | |
| subtree | OUT | subtree | | OUT | subtree | subtree |
| IN | subtree | IN | | subtree | ¬ subtree | ¬ subtree |
| OUT | subtree | subtree | | OUT | OUT | subtree |

is a simple task requiring to commute each IN label into an OUT label, and vice versa.

Let us remember, from Script 14.2.1, that the MERGE-CELL algorithm, given in Script 14.2.4, is invoked in the base case of the recursive algorithm MERGE-BSP, i.e. when either *t1* is a leaf **or** *t2* is a leaf. Notice that each of the four **switch** sections of Script 14.2.4 codifies one row of Table 14.1.

---

**Script 14.2.4 (Merge-Cell algorithm)**

    **algorithm** MERGE-CELL( *t1*, *t2*: bspt, *op*: operation ): bspt;
      **if**( *t1* is a IN cell )
        **switch** *op*
          **case** UNION: **return** *t1*;
          **case** INTERSECTION: **return** *t2*;
          **case** DIFFERENCE: **return** COMPLEMENT(*t2*);
          **case** SYMMETRICDIFFERENCE: **return** COMPLEMENT(*t2*);
      **else if**( *t1* is a OUT cell )
        **switch** *op*
          **case** UNION: **return** *t2*;
          **case** INTERSECTION: **return** *t1*;
          **case** DIFFERENCE: **return** *t1*;
          **case** SYMMETRICDIFFERENCE: **return** *t2*;
      **else if**( *t2* is a IN cell )
        **switch** *op*
          **case** UNION: **return** *t2*;
          **case** INTERSECTION: **return** *t1*;
          **case** DIFFERENCE: **return** *out*;
          **case** SYMMETRICDIFFERENCE: **return** COMPLEMENT*t1*;
      **else if**( *t2* is a OUT cell )
        **switch** *op*
          **case** UNION: **return** *t1*;
          **case** INTERSECTION: **return** *t2*;
          **case** DIFFERENCE: **return** *t1*;
          **case** SYMMETRICDIFFERENCE: **return** *t1*;
    **end**

---

In Script 14.2.4 we report the pseudocode of the algorithm MERGE-CELL, and in Figure 14.6 we show an example where *t1* is a subtree and *t2* is a IN cell.

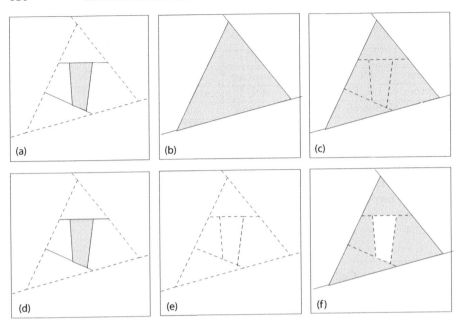

**Figure 14.6**    Combinations of a $t_1$ subtree *within* a $t_2$ leaf: (a) $t_1$ subtree (b) $t_2$ leaf
(c) $t_1 \cup t_2$ (d) $t_1 \cap t_2$ (e) $t_1 - t_2$ (f) $t_1 \wedge t_2$

*14.2.2  Optimizing by pruning and unpruning*

In this section we discuss two tree optimization algorithms. The *pruning* algorithm reduces the quantity of data, whereas the *unpruning* algorithm rebuilts the topological information, concerning the cell adjacency, which was lost during the execution of a Boolean operation.

In fact, the algorithm to perform a set operation automatically executes a first pruning of the resulting tree, but this process is not complete. The *pruning* algorithm, executed *a posteriori* on the result of a Boolean operation, glues two adjacent cells of the same type into a unique cell.

The recursive implementation is very easy. In particular, the algorithm discovers the pairs of brother leafs with the same label (say, either IN or OUT), deletes both such nodes from the tree, and assigns their label to the common father.

The algorithm PRUNE is given in Script 14.2.5. This operation may strongly reduce the size of a BSP tree. It is applied as the standard default in PLaSM after the execution of a Boolean operation.

Unfortunately, both the Boolean operations and the pruning process delete the topology of the cell complex, since two adjacent cells may not intersect on the whole common face, but generally only on a part of it. In order to reconstruct the topology, and store the adjacency information, we must first fragment the cells, so that each one becomes adjacent to another cell on a common face. This operation strongly increases the size of a BSP tree and forbids the use of the *pruning* algorithm. This reconstruction of the topology of the cell complex is called *unpruning*. The unpruning algorithm is given in Script 14.2.6.

**Script 14.2.5 (Prune algorithm)**

```
algorithm PRUNE( t: bspt );
    if t is an internal node
        PRUNE(t.below);
        PRUNE(t.above);
    else if t.below and t.above is the same type of leaf
        t = leaf of t.below type;
        delete t.below;
        delete t.above;
end
```

**Script 14.2.6 (UnPrune algorithm)**

```
algorithm UNPRUNE( t: bspt, convex: stack );
    if t is an internal node
        convex.push( t.h, < );
        UNPRUNE( t.below, convex );
        convex.pop();
        convex.push( t.h, > );
        UNPRUNE( t.above, convex );
        convex.pop();
    else if t is a in leaf
        UNPRUNEINLEAF( t, convex );
end

UNPRUNEINLEAF( t: bspt, convex: stack );
    Fragment the cell represented by the leaf t
    so that its faces are adjacent to the adjacent
    cells (eventually splitting these);
end
```

An easy way to find all the hyperplanes that cross a cell is to solve a linear programming problem, where the feasible set is given by the halfspaces that describe the cell and by the equation of one more hyperplane. If the problem has a solution then the hyperplane crosses the cell. The cell is split into two parts and the leaf of the tree which represents the cell becomes an internal node with two children of the same type.

### 14.2.3 Interface to PLaSM operators

The PLaSM user interface to Boolean operations hides the user from all algorithmic details. So, two alternate sets of keywords are offered for pruned operations — the standard default of the language — and for their unpruned counterparts. Both sets of keywords for standard operations of *union, intersection, difference,* as well as for less usual *symmetric* and *progressive differences* are shown in Table 14.2.

We note that symmetric difference, also called *exclusive or* (XOR), may be defined in PLaSM by the direct translation of the standard definition *union minus intersection,* as shown by Script 14.2.7.

---

**Script 14.2.7 (XOR definition)**
```
DEF XOR = OR DIFF AND;

A XOR B
```

---

Remember also that the PD operator, for the so-called *progressive difference*, was discussed in Section 13.3.2.

**Table 14.2**   Alternate PLaSM keywords for *pruned* and *unpruned* versions of Boolean operations

|          |     | union         | intersection     | difference        | simmetric diff     | progressive diff    |
|----------|-----|---------------|------------------|-------------------|--------------------|---------------------|
| pruned   |     | +             | &                | −                 | ∧                  | PD                  |
| unpruned |     | OR<br>union   | AND<br>intersection | DIFF<br>difference | XOR<br>sdifference | PDIFF<br>pdifference |

**Example 14.2.1**
In Script 14.2.8, we generate a 2D scheme of a building facade by subtraction of a set of rectangular windows from the external polygon, represented by the wall symbol.

---

**Script 14.2.8 (2D example)**
```
DEF wall = MKPOL:<<<0,0>,<10,0>,<0,22>,<10,22>,<5,25>>,<1..5>,<<1>>>;
DEF windows = QUOTE:<-1.5,2,-3,2,-1.5> * QUOTE:<-2,3,-2,3,-2,3,-2,3>;

DEF Front1 = wall DIFF windows;
DEF Front2 = wall - windows;

DEF Scene1 = STRUCT:< Front1, T:1:15, @1:Front >;
DEF Scene2 = STRUCT:< Front2, T:1:15, @1:Front >;
```

---

The results of the Boolean subtraction with and without unpruning, respectively returned when evaluating the symbols Front1 and Front2, are shown in Figure 14.7. The first one clearly requires more computation time and produces a quite bigger internal data structure. It should be generally used with some care by the language user.

### 14.2.4   Linear Programming implementation

The aim of this section is to describe the use of LP (Linear Programming) techniques in the PLaSM implementation of regularized Boolean set operations with BSP trees. In particular, the well-known *simplex method* is used to verify if a system of simultaneous linear equalities and inequalities has common solutions or not. To fully understand the material discussed here, some working knowledge of common LP techniques is needed.

**Figure 14.7** 2D object and 1-skeleton: (a) BSP *unprune* (b) BSP *prune* (standard default)

The interested reader is referred to [Chv83].

**Approach**  To answer the question if the convex set defined by the intersection of a finite number of hyperplanes and affine halfspaces is either empty or not, we first put the system of their linear equalities and inequalities in the so-called *standard form*, with only equality constraints and with non-negative variables. Then, an initial vertex of the polyhedral feasible region is found, if it exists, by putting the problem in *canonical form* with respect to an initial basic solution. This step is performed by using the simplex method on the tableau of the so-called *artificial problem*, which is in canonical form by definition. If the optimum value of the objective function of artificial problem is found to be equal to zero, then the original problem has a non-empty feasible region, i.e. our convex set is non-empty, and we have the answer to the query.

This algorithm is quite efficient in low dimensions, because the very limited number of variables and equations to take into account, and because the very good behavior of simplex method in actual computations. In the worst case, the algorithm complexity equates the number $O\binom{n}{m}$ of vertices of the feasible region defined by $m$ linear equations in $n$ variables.

**Emptiness test for a convex set**  So, a first computational step converts the stack (see the above section) of inequalities and equalities into a PL problem in standard form:

$$\min \left\{ w = \sum x_i \mid \boldsymbol{Ax} = \boldsymbol{b}, \boldsymbol{x} \geq \boldsymbol{0} \right\}. \tag{14.3}$$

Actually, the real $w$ does not matter, so that $w = x_1$ may work equally well. The second step consists of building the *artificial problem*

$$\min \left\{ w = \sum y_i \mid \boldsymbol{Ax} + \boldsymbol{Iy} = \boldsymbol{b}, \boldsymbol{x} \geq \boldsymbol{0}, \boldsymbol{y} \geq \boldsymbol{0} \right\}. \tag{14.4}$$

and of performing the second phase of the simplex method on it, i.e. in looking for an optimal solution. The simplex method always returns here an optimal solution because the objective function of the artificial problem (14.4) is inferiorly bounded on the feasible set [Chv83]. If such an optimal value is zero, then the convex set of the original problem is not empty, otherwise it is empty.

### 14.2.5   Boundary-to-interior operator

A very interesting algorithm is discussed in this section, which fully exploits the dimension-independence of the PLaSM language. In particular, we introduce [BP98] a *Boundary-to-interior* operator, in the following called `solidify`, that works between polyhedral complexes, and is defined as follows:

$$\texttt{solidify} : \mathcal{P}^{d-1,d} \to \mathcal{P}^{d,d} : \partial B \mapsto B.$$

This new operation may be very useful in a geometric modeling environment. For example, it can be used to easily generate a "solid" polygon $D \subset \mathbb{E}^2$ starting from the polyhedral complex $C \in \mathcal{P}^{1,2}$ whose support space is the boundary of the polygon, i.e. such that $[C] = \partial D$. But, it can be also used to generate a 3D solid polyhedron from the set of boundary polygons, in order, e.g., to add detail by using Boolean operations. Notice that the last one is the standard representation of geometric models in Computer Graphics.

**Algorithm**   A possible computational strategy [BP98] for the dimension independent *boundary-to-interior* `solidify` operator can be summarized as follows:

1. extract the $(d-1)$-cells $\mathcal{C} \subset \mathcal{P}^{d-1,d}$ of the input object $C \in \mathcal{P}^{d-1,d}$;
2. for each cell $c_i \in \mathcal{C}$

   (a) project $c_i$ on the hyperplane $H = \{\boldsymbol{x} : x_d = \alpha\} \subset \mathbb{E}^d$, with $\alpha \in \mathbb{R}$ a very large number, thus generating the cell *projection*

   $$p_i := \{\boldsymbol{x} + \lambda\boldsymbol{e}_1 : \boldsymbol{x} \in c_i, \lambda > 1\} \cap H;$$

   (b) compute the *stripe* cell

   $$s_i := (1 - \alpha)c_i + \alpha p_i, \qquad \alpha \in [0, 1].$$

   This operation is also called the *join* of $c_i$ with its projection $p_i$ on $H$;
3. compute the Boolean xor of the set of stripes $\{s_i\} \subset \mathcal{P}^{d,d}$.

The behavior of this algorithm is displayed in Figure 14.8 for a 2-dimensional example. For sake of comprehensibility, the XOR of stripe cells is displayed step-by step as ordered with respect to the input cells. Actually, for sake of efficiency, the PLaSM $n$-ary operator xor, denoted by the predefined symbol "∧", is implemented as acting recursively on two subsets of arguments of near equal lengths.

### Implementation

A very simple implementation, according to the PLaSM character, is given in Script 14.2.9.

**Figure 14.8**  The `boundary-to-interior` algorithm, based on the xor of stripes generated by boundary cells

In particular, the projection of a cell on the $H$ hyperplane defined above, is just obtained (a) by unpacking the internal representation; (b) by substituting the first coordinate of all cell vertices with the number $10^9$; and (c) by packing again the representation.

The extraction of cells of the $(d-1)$-dimensional input is performed by the SplitCells operator, whose definition is given in Script 10.8.4. The function StripePol, applied to the cell $c_i$, returns the *stripe polyhedran* $s_i = \operatorname{conv}(c_i, p_i)$.

The filter function, given in Script 1.3.1, is used to eliminate the lower-dimensional stripes generated by $c_i$ cells in special position. Remember, in fact, that DIM:$c_i$ gives the intrinsic dimension of the cell, whereas RN:$c_i$ returns the dimension of the embedding space. Also, notice that the xor operator $\wedge$, like the other Boolean operators, is $n$-ary and not binary.

---

**Script 14.2.9 (Boundary-to-interior operator)**

```
DEF StripePol = JOIN ~ [ID, InftyProject];
DEF InftyProject = MKPOL ~ [AA:(AL ~ [K:1E9, TAIL]) ~ S1, S2, S3] ~ UKPOL;
DEF Solidify =
    XOR ~ filter:(NOT ~ EQ ~ [DIM, RN]) ~ AA:StripePol ~ SplitCells;
```

---

**Example 14.2.2 (Solid polygon from boundary segments)**

The examples shown in Figure 14.9 are coded in Script 14.2.10. The input data are the p1, p2 and p3 closed polylines corresponding to the 3 cycles of Figure 14.9a, assembled together within the p123 structure.

The 3 definitions of the out symbol correspond to the geometric objects displayed in Figures 14.9a, b and c, respectively.

It is very interesting to notice that the geometric objects of Figure 14.10 are simply obtained by just substituting the definition of theo p2 cycle given in Script 14.2.10 with the following translated polyline:

```
DEF p2 = (T:1:-0.5 ~ polyline): <<0,3>,<0,1>,<2,2>,<2,4>,<0,3>>;
```

---

**Script 14.2.10 (2D solid polygon)**

```
DEF p1 = polyline: <<0,0>,<4,2>,<2.5,3>,<4,5>,<2,5>,<0,3>,<-3,3>,<0,0>>;
DEF p2 = polyline: <<0,3>,<0,1>,<2,2>,<2,4>,<0,3>>;
DEF p3 = polyline: <<2,2>,<1,3>,<1,2>,<2,2>>;

DEF p123 = STRUCT:<p1, p2, p3>;

DEF out = p123;
DEF out = (STRUCT ~ [Solidify, ID]): p123;
DEF out = Solidify:p123 * QUOTE:<0.5>;
```

**Figure 14.9** (a) Set of 2D polylines (b) 2D polygon generated by `Solidify` operator (c) Non-manifold solid generated by extrusion

**Figure 14.10** (a) 2D *Self-intersecting* polylines (b) Generated 2D polygon (3) Extruded solid. The results are always *valid* !

**Note** We like to remark, looking also at Figures 14.9 and 14.10, that the approach described above is extremely robust with respect to the *validity* (see Section 13.1.1) of the geometric result. The reader may notice in fact that the input polygons of Figure 14.9a are touching on vertices, thus generating a non-manifold polygon, whereas those of Figure 14.10 are even self-intersecting. The algorithm also works properly when generating an unconnected output whose components are not simply connected, i.e. have multiple boundary loops. This kind of geometric robustness clearly depends on the design choices underlying the PLaSM kernel, and in particular by the basic assumption of storing no topology in the HPC scheme and in using the BSP approach to Boolean operations.

## 14.3 Dimension-independent integration

Two algorithms were given by F. Bernardini in [Ber91] for the finite computation of the integrals of monomials

$$I_p^{d,n}(k_0, k_1 \ldots, k_{n-1}) = \int_P x_0^{k_0} \ldots x_{n-1}^{k_{n-1}} d\tau, \qquad (14.5)$$

where $P$ is a regular $d$-dimensional polyhedron, possibly non-convex, unconnected and non-manifold, embedded in a space of dimension $n$, with $d \leq n$, and where $d\tau$ is the infinitesimal volume element. The computational efficiency of the two algorithms strongly depends on the available representation of the polyhedral domain. The first algorithm fits well with a decompositive representation, whereas the second one is better suited with some b-rep, when either the boundary faces are known or their computation is easy. Both such algorithms are implemented in the geometric kernel of PLaSM language. The first one is a multidimensional generalization of the algorithm discussed in Section 13.5.5, when a simplicial decomposition of the domain boundary is given.

**Integration function in PLaSM**   The semantics of the integration function provided by PLaSM is the following. The expression

```
INT:pol_complex:<i₁,i₂,...,i_d>
```

returns the value of the domain integral of the monomial with integer exponents:

$$I_{x_1\cdots x_d}^{i_1\cdots i_d} = \int_{\texttt{pol\_complex}} x_1^{i_1} x_2^{i_2} \cdots, x_d^{i_d}\, dV.$$

In particular, this integral is computed as a summation of integrals associated with a simplicial decomposition of the `pol_complex` domain. The argument polyhedral complex may either have or not a full dimension. For example it may be a curve or a surface in $\mathbb{E}^3$. If the integration expression is

```
INT:pol_complex:0
```

the volume of the argument polyhedron is returned, or the surface area or the curve length, depending on the domain dimension.

**Example 14.3.1 (Integrals on 3D cube)**
We compute here explicitly some integrals on the cube with one vertex on the origin and with edges of size 10 parallel to the coordinate axes, as shown in Figure 14.11. In particular, we compute the volume $V$, the $y_G$ coordinate of centroid, the second moment $I_V^{0,2,0}$ and the product of inertia $I_V^{1,1,0}$.

1. **Volume**

$$V = I_{Dom}^{0,0,0} = \int\!\!\int\!\!\int_{Dom} dV = \int_0^{10} A\, dy = 100\,[\, y\,]_0^{10} = 1000$$

2. **Centroid**

$$y_G = \frac{I_{Dom}^{0,1,0}}{I_{Dom}^{0,0,0}} = \frac{A}{1000}\int_0^{10} y\, dy = \frac{1}{10}\left[\frac{y^2}{2}\right]_0^{10} = 5$$

3. **Second Moments**

$$I_{Dom}^{0,2,0} = \int\!\!\int\!\!\int_{Dom} y^2\, dV = A\int_0^{10} y^2\, dy = A\left[\frac{y^3}{3}\right]_0^{10} = 100 \times 333.\bar{3}$$

4. **Products of Inertia**

$$I_{Dom}^{1,1,0} = \int\!\!\int\!\!\int_{Dom} xy\, dV = \int_0^{10} y\int_0^{10} x\int_0^{10} dz\, dx\, dy = 10\int_0^{10} y\int_0^{10} x\, dx\, dy =$$

$$10\int_0^{10} y\left[\frac{x^2}{2}\right]_0^{10} dy = 500\int_0^{10} y\, dy = 500\left[\frac{y^2}{2}\right]_0^{10} = 25000$$

The same computations may be performed in PLaSM as shown in Script 14.3.1. Notice in particular that the expression INT:Dom:0, equivalent to INT:Dom:<0,0,0>, computes the volume of Dom, and that T:2:1000:Dom denotes a copy of Dom translated along the $y$ axis.

Two alternative definitions for the INT operator are given, which correspond to the two Bernardini's integration algorithms [Ber91]. A discussion of their relative performances may be found in [Ber91].

---

**Script 14.3.1 (Cube integrals)**
```
DEF INT = INTEGR_ON_S;
DEF Dom = CUBOID:<10,10,10>;

INT:Dom:0 ≡ 1000.0
INT:Dom:<0,1,0> / INT:Dom:0 ≡ 5.0
INT:(T:2:1000:Dom):<0,1,0> / INT:(T:2:1000:Dom):0 ≡ 1005.0
INT:Dom:<0,2,0> ≡ 33333.33333333333
INT:Dom:<1,1,0> ≡ 25000.0
```

---

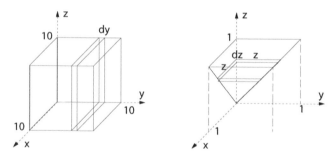

**Figure 14.11**   Reference volumes for the integration examples

**Example 14.3.2 (Integrals on reversed 3-simplex)**
A second numeric example is given here, where the integration domain is a mirrored and translated instance, shown in Figure 14.11b, of the standard unit 3-simplex. In particular, the volume, the first moment, the centroid coordinates and one of second moments are first computed by using standard integration techniques. Then, the same functionals are evaluated on the simplicial volume defined in Script 14.3.2, by using the predefined integration operators of the PLaSM language.

1. **Volume**

$$V = \iiint_V dV = \int_0^1 A(z)\,dz = \int_0^1 \frac{z^2}{2}\,dz = \frac{1}{2}\left[\frac{z^3}{3}\right]_0^1 = \frac{1}{6} = 0.1\bar{6}$$

2. **Centroid**

$$I_{Dom}^{0,0,1} = \int_0^1 zA(z)\,dz = \frac{1}{2}\int_0^1 z^3\,dz = \frac{1}{2}\left[\frac{z^4}{4}\right]_0^1 = \frac{1}{8}$$

$$I_{Dom}^{1,0,0} = \int_0^1 x A(x)\, dx = \frac{1}{2}\int_0^1 x(1-x)^2\, dx = \frac{1}{2}\left[ \frac{x^2}{2} + \frac{x^4}{4} - \frac{2}{3}x \right]_0^1 = \frac{1}{24} = I_{Dom}^{0,1,0}$$

$$(x_G, y_G, z_G) = \frac{1}{I_{Dom}^{0,0,0}}(I_{Dom}^{1,0,0}, I_{Dom}^{0,1,0}, I_{Dom}^{0,0,1}) = 6\left( \frac{1}{24}, \frac{1}{24}, \frac{1}{8} \right) = (0.25, 0.25, 0.75);$$

### 3. Second Moments

$$I_{Dom}^{2,0,0} = \iiint_{Dom} x^2\, dV = \int_0^1 x^2 \frac{(1-x)^2}{2}\, dx = \frac{1}{2}\left[ \frac{x^3}{3} + \frac{x^5}{5} - \frac{2}{4}x^4 \right]_0^1 = \frac{1}{60} = 0.01\bar{6}$$

---

**Script 14.3.2 (Reversed simplex integrals)**

```
DEF INT = INTEGR_ON_S;
DEF INT = INTEGR_ON_B;
DEF Dom = (T:3:1 ~ S:3:-1 ~o simplex):3;

INT:Dom:0 ≡ 0.16666666666666663
INT:Dom:<1,0,0> / INT:Dom:0 ≡ 0.2500000000000001
INT:Dom:<0,1,0> / INT:Dom:0 ≡ 0.2500000000000001
INT:Dom:<0,0,1> / INT:Dom:0 ≡ 0.7500000000000002
INT:Dom:<2,0,0> ≡ 0.01666666666666662
```

---

### 14.3.1  Tensor of inertia

It is useful in many ways to have the integrals described above for a body $B$ arranged into a $4 \times 4$ matrix, called the *tensor of inertia* of $B$, and denoted as $\boldsymbol{M}(B)$. Therefore we have:

$$\boldsymbol{M}(B) = \begin{pmatrix} M_{xx} & M_{xy} & M_{xz} & M_x \\ M_{yx} & M_{yy} & M_{yz} & M_y \\ M_{zx} & M_{zy} & M_{zz} & M_z \\ M_x & M_y & M_z & M \end{pmatrix}.$$

For homegeneous bodies, where the density field is a constant $\rho$, it is possible to write:

$$\boldsymbol{M}(B) = \rho\,\boldsymbol{I}(B)$$

where $\boldsymbol{I}(B) = [I_{ij}]$, with $i, j = 1, \ldots, 4$. This tensor denotes the geometric features of an homogeneous solid, and does not depend on the object's density or material.

**Affine transformations of inertia tensor**  Let $\boldsymbol{Q}$ be the matrix of an invertible affine transformation, and $B_Q$ the transformed body, with

$$B_Q = \boldsymbol{Q}\,B.$$

Then:

$$I(B_Q) = |\det \boldsymbol{Q}|^{-1} \, \boldsymbol{Q} \, I(B) \, \boldsymbol{Q}^T$$

This theorem, also known as Steiner's theorem, is a generalization of those given in Mechanics under the names of *Rotating axis* theorem and *Translating axes* theorem [Apo67], both valid only for rigid transformations. The previous formulation allows not only translation and rotation of space, but also stretching and shearing. Proof can be found in [Pao87].

**Inertia tensor computation**   The function INERTIA given in Script 14.3.3 uses the INT operator, and generates the matrix $4 \times 4$ of the inertia tensor computed on the 3-polyhedral argument. Such a tensor is defined as the table of second moments, first moments, products of inertia and volume:

$$\begin{pmatrix} I_x^2 & I_{xy} & I_{xz} & I_x \\ I_{xy} & I_y^2 & I_{yz} & I_y \\ I_{xz} & I_{yz} & I_z^2 & I_z \\ I_x & I_y & I_z & V \end{pmatrix}.$$

In PLaSM an INERTIA function from the set of 3-polyhedra to the set $\mathbb{R}_4^4$ of $4 \times 4$ real matrices

$$\text{INERTIA} : \mathcal{P}^3 \to \mathbb{R}_4^4$$

may be defined as given in Script 14.3.3.

---

**Script 14.3.3 (Inertia Operator)**

```
DEF INERTIA (pol::IsPol) = (AA ~ AA):(INT:pol):<
   <<2,0,0>,<1,1,0>,<1,0,1>,<1,0,0>>,
   <<1,1,0>,<0,2,0>,<0,1,1>,<0,1,0>>,
   <<1,0,1>,<0,1,1>,<0,0,2>,<0,0,1>>,
   <<1,0,0>,<0,1,0>,<0,0,1>,<0,0,0>> >;
```

---

**Dimension-independent inertia**   The inertia tensor can be defined in a dimension-independent way by using homogeneous coordinates, as:

$$I(Dom) = (I_{ij}(\Sigma)), \qquad 0 \le i, j \le n, \, Dom \subset \mathbb{E}^n,$$

where $\Sigma$ is a simplicial complex that triangulates the integration domain *Dom*, and

$$I_{ij}(\Sigma) = \int_\Sigma x_i x_j \, d\Sigma = \sum_{\sigma \in \Sigma} \int_\sigma x_i x_j \, d\sigma.$$

The PLaSM is very easy. Let us note that the matrix of triples of integer indices, used in the previous definition, can be generated by summing component-wise two matrices of triples, one obtained as the transpose of the other. For example, with $(i,j) \in \{0,1,2,3\}^2$, we have:

$$
\begin{pmatrix}
(2,0,0) & (1,1,0) & (1,0,1) & (1,0,0) \\
(1,1,0) & (0,2,0) & (0,1,1) & (0,1,0) \\
(1,0,1) & (0,1,1) & (0,0,2) & (0,0,1) \\
(1,0,0) & (0,1,0) & (0,0,1) & (0,0,0)
\end{pmatrix} =
$$

$$
\begin{pmatrix}
(1,0,0) & (0,1,0) & (0,0,1) & (0,0,0) \\
(1,0,0) & (0,1,0) & (0,0,1) & (0,0,0) \\
(1,0,0) & (0,1,0) & (0,0,1) & (0,0,0) \\
(1,0,0) & (0,1,0) & (0,0,1) & (0,0,0)
\end{pmatrix} +
\begin{pmatrix}
(1,0,0) & (1,0,0) & (1,0,0) & (1,0,0) \\
(0,1,0) & (0,1,0) & (0,1,0) & (0,1,0) \\
(0,0,1) & (0,0,1) & (0,0,1) & (0,0,1) \\
(0,0,0) & (0,0,0) & (0,0,0) & (0,0,0)
\end{pmatrix}
$$

At this point, the PLaSM implementation of a dimension-independent inertia tensor is quite direct:

---

**Script 14.3.4 (Dimension-independent inertia)**

```
DEF INERTIA (pol::IsPol) = (AA ~ AA):(INT:pol):
    (tensor tensorSum TRANS:(tensor))
WHERE
    n = RN:pol,
    tensor = (#:(n+1) ~ AR ~ [IDNT, APPLY ~ [#,K:0]]):n,
    tensorSum = (AA ~ AA):vectSum ~ AA:TRANS ~ TRANS,
    vectSum = AA:+ ~ TRANS
END;
```

---

where IDNT is a function, given in Script 3.3.5, that generates the identity matrix $n \times n$, and RN is the primitive function which returns the embedding dimension, i.e. the number of coordinates of points, of its polyhedral argument.

### Example 14.3.3 (Inertia of hypercuboids)

The generalized formulation of INERTIA operator allows the PLaSM to compute very easily the inertia tensor of polyhedral complexes of arbitrary dimension $d$, with $d$ quite low, because the dependence of complexity on dimension. Three examples of computation with unit cuboids of dimension 2,3 and 3, respectively, are given in Script 14.3.5.

### 14.4   Generalized product of polyhedra

In this section a powerful new solid operation on cell-decomposed and dimension-independent polyhedra is introduced [BFPP93]. This operation, that we call *generalized product* or simply *product* of polyhedra, takes two polyhedral arguments of possibly different dimensions and produces a polyhedral result of dimension greater or equal to both argument dimensions. The proposed operation is derived from the *Cartesian product* of cell complexes, and is reduced to it as a special case. It unifies several different operations which are often useful in solid modeling applications, such as the *extrusion*, the standard *intersection* and the *intersection of extrusions*. The

**Script 14.3.5 (Inertia of hypercuboids)**

```
INERTIA:(CUBOID:<1,1>) ≡
   <<0.33333333, 0.25,        0.5>,
    <0.25,        0.33333333, 0.5>,
    <0.5,         0.5,        1.0>>

INERTIA:(CUBOID:<1,1,1>) ≡
   <<0.33333333, 0.25,        0.25,        0.5>,
    <0.25,        0.33333333, 0.25,        0.5>,
    <0.25,        0.25,        0.33333333, 0.5>,
    <0.5,         0.5,        0.5,         1.0>>

INERTIA:(CUBOID:<1,1,1,1>) ≡
   <<0.33333333, 0.25,        0.25,        0.25,        0.5>,
    <0.25,        0.33333333, 0.25,        0.25,        0.5>,
    <0.25,        0.25,        0.33333333, 0.25,        0.5>,
    <0.25,        0.25,        0.25,        0.33333333, 0.5>,
    <0.5,         0.5,        0.5,         0.5,         1.0>>
```

various specialized products mainly differ in the way of embedding the arguments, of dimension $m$ and $n$, respectively, in the coordinate subspaces of the target space of dimension $p \geq \max(m, n)$.

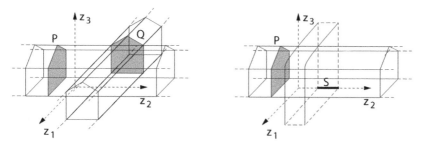

**Figure 14.12** Extrusion of two polyhedra in $\mathbb{R}^3$

*14.4.1 Definitions*

In this section, before giving a formal definition of the new operation, we describe three elementary computation steps (extrusion, permutation and intersection); their composition yields the desired product operator. The notation $\mathcal{P}^d$ is used to denote the set of regular polyhedra with dimension $d$ embedded in $\mathcal{A}^d$, the affine space associated to $\mathbb{R}^d$.

In the following a polyhedron $P \in \mathcal{P}^d$ will also be represented as a set of cells $\{c_i\}$, each cell $c$ being denoted as a pair $(C, \mathcal{AD}_c)$ where $C$ is the non-redundant cell comatrix, and $\mathcal{AD}_c$ is the ordered set of adjacent cells. Given two cells $c$ and $b$ of a polyhedron $P$, with $c = (C, \mathcal{AD}_c)$, then $\mathcal{AD}_c(i) = b$ means that the cell $b$ is adjacent to $c$ along the face with covector given by the $i$-th row of the matrix $C$. We will call this face the $i$-th face of $c$. We also write $\mathcal{AD}_c(i) = \perp$ to specify that there is no cell adjacent to $c$ along its $i$-th face, that is the $i$-th face of $c$ belongs to the boundary of the polyhedron $P$.

**Extrusion**  The (non-finite) extrusion is defined as a one-to-many mapping between affine spaces of different dimension:

$$\mathbb{E}^{p-d} : \mathbb{E}^d \to \mathbb{E}^p : x \mapsto x \times \mathbb{E}^{p-d}, \tag{14.6}$$

i.e. we have, using coordinate representations

$$x = (x_0, x_1, \ldots, x_d) \mapsto \{(z_0, z_1, \ldots, z_p) = (x_0, x_1, \ldots, x_d, w_1, \ldots, w_{p-d}), w_i \in \mathbb{R}\}.$$

It is not difficult to give a coordinate representation, i.e. a matrix representation, of the inverse extrusion mapping, which is a projection:

$$(\mathbb{E}^{p-d})^{-1} = (\ I \quad 0\ ),$$

where $I$ is a $(d+1) \times (d+1)$ identity matrix and $0$ is a $(d+1) \times (p-d)$ zero matrix, but it is not possible to give a similar representation of $\mathbb{E}^{p-d}$ if we remain in the affine spaces $\mathbb{E}^d$ and $\mathbb{E}^p$. A matrix representation of the extrusion operator is instead extremely easy to give if we move in their dual spaces, the spaces of the linear functions $\mathbb{E}^d \to \mathbb{R}$ and $\mathbb{E}^p \to \mathbb{R}$, as we show in Section 14.1.

**Permutation**  Let us denote as $\pi$ a permutation of the first $p$ integers, i.e. a bijective function on the finite set $\{1, \ldots, p\}$. The permutation mapping

$$\Pi : \mathbb{E}^p \to \mathbb{E}^p \tag{14.7}$$

such that

$$z = (z_0, z_1, \ldots, z_p) \mapsto \Pi z = (z_0, z_{\pi(1)}, \ldots, z_{\pi(p)})$$

is simply represented by the block matrix

$$\Pi = \begin{pmatrix} 1 & 0 \\ 0 & A \end{pmatrix}_{(p+1) \times (p+1)}, \tag{14.8}$$

where $A = [a_{i,j}]$ and $a_{i,j}$ is the element $(\pi(i), j)$ of the $p \times p$ identity matrix.

**Generalized product operator**  The two mappings previously defined can be combined, as the range set of the first coincides with the domain set of the second, so that a composite mapping can be defined:

$$\Theta^{p-d} = (\Pi \circ \mathbb{E}^{p-d}) \tag{14.9}$$

We are finally able to define the desired product operator as a mapping from pairs of polyhedra and pairs of permutations to polyhedra:

$$\otimes^p : \mathcal{P}^m \times \mathcal{P}^n \times \Pi^p \times \Pi^p \to \mathcal{P}^p \tag{14.10}$$

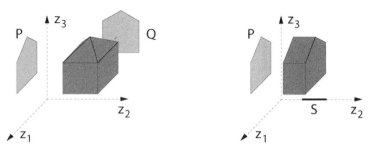

**Figure 14.13** Intersection of two extruded polyhedra: (a) $P_{102} \otimes_{012} Q$ (b) $P_{102} \otimes_{010} S$

where $\Pi^p$ denotes the set of permutations of the first $p$ integers. More useful, as discussed in the following, are the partial functions

$$_{\pi_1} \otimes^p_{\pi_2} : \mathcal{P}^m \times \mathcal{P}^n \to \mathcal{P}^p \tag{14.11}$$

such that

$$(P, Q) \mapsto (\Theta^{p-m} P) \cap (\Theta^{p-n} Q).$$

where $\Theta^{p-m} = \Pi_1 \circ \mathbb{E}^{p-m}$ and $\Theta^{p-n} = \Pi_2 \circ \mathbb{E}^{p-n}$. So, using the product symbol as an infix operator, we can write, by omitting the superscripts

$$P_{\pi_1} \otimes_{\pi_2} Q = \{z \in \mathbb{E}^p \mid z \in \Theta P, z \in \Theta Q\}.$$

where $\Theta$ means a proper extrusion and coordinate permutation in $\mathbb{E}^p$ space, depending on the embedding spaces of $P$ and $Q$ and on $\pi_1, \pi_2$, respectively. Notice that dropping the superscripts is allowed because the dimension $p$ of the result is given by the (common) length of permutations.

**Further notation** As usual in solid modeling we are mainly interested to the regularized version of the operator, defined as the closure of the interior:

$$P_{\pi_1} \otimes^*_{\pi_2} Q = \mathrm{clos}(\mathrm{int}(P_{\pi_1} \otimes_{\pi_2} Q)).$$

In the following we will drop the superscript $*$ symbol and the word "regularized", but we will always refer to the regularized operator.

In writing the permutations $\pi_1$, $\pi_2$, we will use the convention of substituting the indices corresponding to the added coordinates $w'$s with zeroes. E.g., when the point of coordinates $(x_0, x_1, x_2, x_3, w_1, w_2)$ maps to $(x_0, w_1, x_2, x_1, x_3, w_2)$, the corresponding permutation range (42135) is written as 02130. The first coordinate, $x_0$, never changes its position and is not taken into account in the permutations. The advantage of this notation is that it makes clear along which coordinates the extrusion is performed.

**Example 14.4.1**
In Figure 14.12 two examples of extrusion of two polyhedra are depicted. In

Figure 14.12a the resulting polyhedra $P'$ and $Q'$ are obtained as

$$P' \;=\; \Theta^1 P = (\Pi_1 \circ \mathbb{E}^1)P, \text{ with}$$
$$\mathbb{E}^1 \;:\; (x_1, x_2) \mapsto \{(z_1, z_2, z_3) = (x_1, x_2, w_1), w_1 \in \mathbb{R}\}$$
$$\Pi_1 \;=\; \begin{pmatrix} 1 & 0 & 0 & 0 \\ 0 & 1 & 0 & 0 \\ 0 & 0 & 0 & 1 \\ 0 & 0 & 1 & 0 \end{pmatrix},$$

with $\pi_1 = (132)$, written as 102. Analogously

$$Q' \;=\; \Theta^1 Q = (\Pi_2 \circ \mathbb{E}^1)Q, \text{ with}$$
$$\mathbb{E}^1 \;:\; (x_1, x_2) \mapsto \{(z_1, z_2, z_3) = (x_1, x_2, w_1), w_1 \in \mathbb{R}\}$$
$$\Pi_2 \;=\; \begin{pmatrix} 1 & 0 & 0 & 0 \\ 0 & 0 & 0 & 1 \\ 0 & 1 & 0 & 0 \\ 0 & 0 & 1 & 0 \end{pmatrix},$$

with $\pi_2 = (312)$, written as 012. Notice that it is also

$$P' = \Theta^1 P \cap \mathbb{E}^3 = P \;_{102} \otimes_{000} \; o$$
$$Q' = \Theta^1 Q \cap \mathbb{E}^3 = P \;_{012} \otimes_{000} \; o,$$

where $o \in \mathcal{P}^0$ is the 0-dimensional polyhedron which has homogeneous coordinate representation $(x_0)$, with $x_0 = 1$ ($\mathcal{P}^0$ is a singleton that contains only $o$). Similarly, in Figure 14.12b the polyhedron $P'$ is obtained as above, whereas $S'$ is given by

$$S' \;=\; \Theta^2 S = (\Pi \circ \mathbb{E}^2)S = S \;_{010} \otimes_{000} \; o, \text{ with}$$
$$\mathbb{E}^2 \;:\; (x_1) \mapsto \{(z_1, z_2, z_3) = (x_1, w_1, w_2), w_1, w_2 \in \mathbb{R}\}$$
$$\Pi \;=\; \begin{pmatrix} 1 & 0 & 0 & 0 \\ 0 & 0 & 1 & 0 \\ 0 & 1 & 0 & 0 \\ 0 & 0 & 0 & 1 \end{pmatrix},$$

with $\pi = (213)$, written as 010. In Figure 14.13 the results of the intersections of the extruded polyhedra are shown.

**Specialized products** The generalized product previously defined is able to unify several different operations which are often useful in modeling applications. The various operations mainly differ for the way of embedding the polyhedral arguments, of dimension $m$ and $n$, respectively, in the target space of dimension $p$:

1. If $p = m = n$ and both $\pi_1$ and $\pi_2$ are the identity permutation we obtain the usual intersection operation (see Figure 14.14a).
2. If $p > m = n$ and $\pi_1 = \pi_2$ we obtain the generation of an "indefinite cylinder", i.e. the intersection of the extrusions of $P$ and $Q$ (see Figure 14.14b).

3. If $p = m + n$ and $\pi_1(k) = 0$ if and only if $\pi_2(k) \neq 0, 1 \leq k \leq p$, we obtain the Cartesian product of polyhedra (see Figure 14.14c).

4. If $\max(m, n) < p < m + n$ we obtain the intersection of extrusions (see Figure 14.14d).

5. If $p = \max(m, n)$ and $m \neq n$ one polyhedral argument is intersected with the extrusion of the other.

6. If $p > m+n$ the kind of the result may vary, depending on the permutations. In general the result of the operation is an intersection of extruded solids.

**Dual extrusion mapping** In the previous section we defined the extrusion as the mapping (14.6), which we were unable to represent as a linear operator from the domain to the range space (remember that this was conversely possible for the inverse mapping). We give such a linear operator for the dual extrusion mapping, defined as a mapping between dual spaces:

$$E_{p-d} : (\mathbb{E}^d)^* \to (\mathbb{E}^p)^* : a \mapsto a \times \{0\}^{p-d}, \tag{14.12}$$

i.e., using coordinate representations

$$a = (a^0, a^1, \dots, a^d) \mapsto (a^0, a^1, \dots, a^p) =$$
$$= (a^0, a^1, \dots, a^d, 0, \dots, 0).$$

The dual extrusion mapping is a linear function that can be expressed as

$$E_{p-d} = ( \; I \quad 0 \; ),$$

where $I$ is a $(d+1) \times (d+1)$ identity matrix and $0$ is a $(d+1) \times (p-d)$ zero matrix. Note that

$$(E_{p-d}) = (\mathbb{E}^{p-d})^{-1}.$$

**Affine transformations** Let us consider how the hyperplane $ax = 0$ is transformed according to an affine transformation of the space $\mathbb{E}^d$ where the polyhedra live. As we use homogeneous coordinates, the transformation has a coordinate representation with a $(d+1) \times (d+1)$ invertible real $T$ matrix, so that we write $x^* = Tx$. Hence $x = T^{-1}x^*$, and by substitution in the hyperplane equation we have $aT^{-1}x^* = 0$, finally giving $a^* = aT^{-1}$ for the transformed covector. Notice that $a^*x^* = aT^{-1}Tx = 0$.

An affine transformation $T$ will therefore be applied to a polyhedron $P = (F, C_F)$ by right multiplication of each cell comatrix for $T^{-1}$, or better, by multiplication of each covector in the face database for $T^{-1}$. With the unusual but useful convention of using matrix multiplication to transform both polyhedra and sets of vectors or covectors, we can write

$$P^* = TP = (FT^{-1}, C_F).$$

### 14.4.2 Product of cell-decomposed polyhedra

In this section we discuss how to compute the generalized product previously introduced for cell-decomposed polyhedra. The following subsections discuss how to compute the geometry and the topology of the result, respectively.

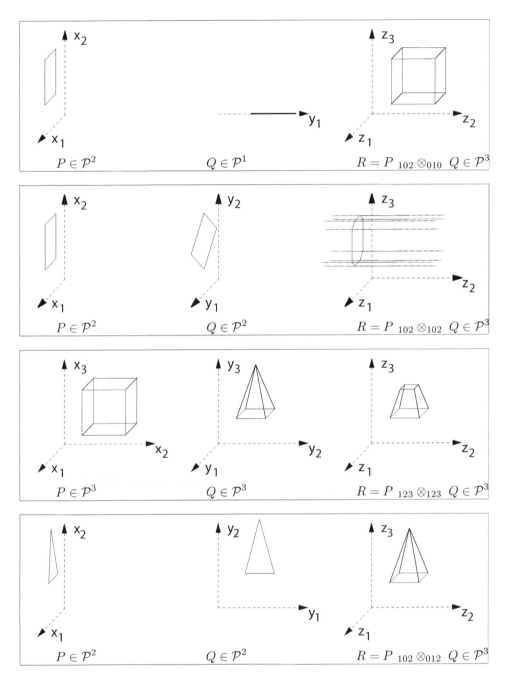

**Figure 14.14**  Some applications of the product operator: (a) Cartesian product
(b) intersection (c) and (d) intersection of extrusions

**Computation of geometry**   In Section 14.4.1 we saw that the generalized product of polyhedra can be computed as a sequence of three steps: an extrusion into the target space, a permutation of coordinates and an intersection. Both extrusion and permutation can be expressed as linear operators if we use a convex decomposition with face-based representation. The intersection of convex sets represented as intersection of halfspaces is simply the simultaneous resolution of their constraints. Hence we can easily express the result of the operation in matrix form, starting from the matrices associated with the cells of the operation arguments.

Let be given the polyhedra $P = \{p_h\}$ and $Q = \{q_k\}$, where $p_h = (P_h, \mathcal{AD}_{p_h})$ e $q_k = (Q_k, \mathcal{AD}_{q_k})$, where $P_h, Q_k$ are the cell comatrices of the cells $p_h, q_k$, respectively.

The product operation between the polyhedra $P$ e $Q$,

$$P \;_{\pi_1} \otimes_{\pi_2}\; Q,$$

gives a polyhedron

$$R = \{r_{hk}| \; r_{hk} = p_h \;_{\pi_1} \otimes_{\pi_2}\; q_k, \; (p_h, q_k) \in P \times Q\}.$$

The cell comatrix $R_{hk}$ of the cell $r_{hk}$ can easily be computed by extruding the argument comatrices in dual space (i.e. by computing $P_h E_{p-m}$ and $Q_k E_{p-n}$) and by applying the permutations $\Pi_1^T$ and $\Pi_2^T$ to the results, where $\Pi_1$ and $\Pi_2$ are matrices as defined in (14.8). The intersection of the extruded cells is then obtained by assembling the results in only one cell comatrix. Hence we have

$$R_{hk} = \begin{pmatrix} \tilde{P}_h \\ \tilde{Q}_k \end{pmatrix},$$

where

$$\tilde{P}_h = P_h E_{p-m} \Pi_1^T = P_h \Theta_1$$
$$\tilde{Q}_k = Q_k E_{p-n} \Pi_1^T = Q_k \Theta_2.$$

Notice that the same matrix $\Theta_1$ ($\Theta_2$) must be applied to all covectors of the polyhedron $P$ ($Q$), respectively, so that the covector database, seen as a set of covectors, of the resulting polyhedron is simply

$$F(R) = F(P)\Theta_1 \cup F(Q)\Theta_2. \tag{14.13}$$

The geometry computation of the product $P \otimes Q$ just requires $O(|F(P)| + |F(Q)|)$ matrix multiplications if implemented using the elegant but a bit too expensive linear algebra approach given here. The actual implementation requires only that the covectors database $F(R)$ is written copying covectors from $F(P)$ and $F(Q)$, after insertion of zeroes and a permutation of elements, a $O((|F(P)| + |F(Q)|)p)$ task.

A reduction step of the cell comatrix must be performed for each non-empty or less than $p$-dimensional cell of the result. In other words, all the $|P| \times |Q|$ comatrices $R_{hk}$ must be checked, to establish non-emptiness and full dimensionality of the associated sets (14.1). Then, all cells of dimension $p$ must be checked for non-redundancy, i.e. it is necessary to verify that no implicated covectors exist in a comatrix. The covectors in (14.13) which are not contained in some unredundant comatrix are discarded from the $F(R)$ database.

**Example 14.4.2**

In Figure 14.14d the generalized product of two single-cell polyhedra $P$ and $Q$ is displayed. In this case the name of the cell and that of its comatrix coincide. Let

$$Q = P = \begin{pmatrix} -12 & 4 & 1 \\ 36 & -4 & 1 \\ -8 & 0 & 2 \end{pmatrix}$$

and $\pi_1 = (132) \doteq 102$, $\pi_2 = (312) \doteq 012$. For sake of simplicity face covectors are not normalized. Then we have

$$\tilde{P} = P \begin{pmatrix} 1 & 0 & 0 & 0 \\ 0 & 1 & 0 & 0 \\ 0 & 0 & 1 & 0 \end{pmatrix} \begin{pmatrix} 1 & 0 & 0 & 0 \\ 0 & 1 & 0 & 0 \\ 0 & 0 & 0 & 1 \\ 0 & 0 & 1 & 0 \end{pmatrix}$$

$$\tilde{Q} = Q \begin{pmatrix} 1 & 0 & 0 & 0 \\ 0 & 1 & 0 & 0 \\ 0 & 0 & 1 & 0 \end{pmatrix} \begin{pmatrix} 1 & 0 & 0 & 0 \\ 0 & 0 & 1 & 0 \\ 0 & 0 & 0 & 1 \\ 0 & 1 & 0 & 0 \end{pmatrix}$$

$$R = \begin{pmatrix} -12 & 4 & 0 & 1 \\ 36 & -4 & 0 & 1 \\ -8 & 0 & 0 & 2 \\ -12 & 0 & 4 & 1 \\ 36 & 0 & -4 & 1 \\ -8 & 0 & 0 & 2 \end{pmatrix}$$

**Computation of Topology**   Two equivalent approaches can be taken to calculate the adjacency graph of a polyhedron resulting from the application of the product operator. The first way is to use a decision rule to recognize cell adjacency. For each cell of the result, the rule yields the appropriate set of edges for the associated graph node. Alternatively, the Cartesian product graph of the adjacency graphs for the operands is built, and then the subgraph describing the topology of lower-dimensional or empty cells, which do not belong to the representation of the result, is deleted and replaced by some suitable new arcs.

An obvious but important observation for this purpose of computing adjacencies for the resulting polyhedron is that the adjacency graphs of the extruded polyhedra are the same as for the operands. In fact, neither the number of cells, nor the number of highest-dimensional faces are affected by the extrusion operation. Moreover, it is easy to see that the extrusion operator can neither disjoint cells which were adjacent in the input polyhedron, nor can make adjacent cells which were not. A quite detailed discussion of the topology computation can be found in [BFPP93].

### 14.4.3   Intersection of extrusions

In the previous section we have introduced a general product operator which allows the unification of operations such as the extrusion, the standard intersection, the intersection of extrusions and the Cartesian product of cell-decomposed polyhedra. In particular, the *intersection of extrusions* is a useful tool to generate complex $pD$ models starting from two or more $m_i D$ ($m_i \le p$) cell complexes. This operation is particularly useful in the context of architectural design, where the 3D model of a building may be automatically generated starting from plan views and sections, both represented as 2D cell complexes [PS92]. A naïve implementation of such an operator is a hard task even in 3D, as it seems to require an extensive use of Booleans. In PLaSM a dimension-independent and efficient solution for this problem is given, using only some linear algebra and the Cartesian product of graphs.

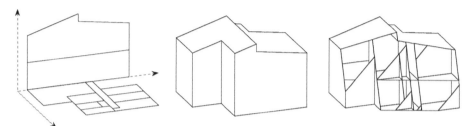

**Figure 14.15** The product operator used as an intersection of extrusions. The generating expression is @2($A$ $_{120}$ $\otimes_{102}$ $B$), where $A$ and $B$ are shown on the left and @2() is the extraction operator for the 2-skeleton.

The PLaSM denotation for this binary operator is &&, that is a second-order function, which must be first applied to a pair of integer sequences, which specify the kind of embedding of arguments in the space of the result, and then to the pair of polyhedral arguments, as discussed in the following section.

## Algorithm

As we have seen in the above section, the intersection of extrusion can be considered a special case of the generalized polyhedral product defined in [BFPP93]. But it can be also directly described in a easy way. In particular, the computational steps to perform in giving an algorithmic description of this operator can be summarized as follows:

1. Extrude each input polyhedron.
2. Properly embed each extruded polyhedron by a permutation of coordinates.
3. Generate a cells sequence for each polyhedron.
4. Compute the combinatorial Cartesian product of such sequences.
5. Apply a point set intersection to each tuple of cells.
6. Aggregate the generated intersection cells.

A dimension-indedpendent PLaSM implementation of the built-in operator && is given in Script 14.4.1. Since the predefined symbol && is protected by the interpeter environment, we use the alias XX for it. This operator, with signature

$$ \text{XX} : \Pi_1 \times \Pi_2 \times \cdots \Pi_d \to \mathcal{P}_1^{n-1,n} \times \mathcal{P}_2^{n-1,n} \times \cdots \times \mathcal{P}_d^{n-1,n} \to \mathcal{P}^{n,n}, \qquad d \le n, $$

takes as input a sequence of $d$ permutations $\pi_i : \{1, \dots, n\} \to \{1, \dots, n\}$ of the first $n$ integers, with $\pi_i \in \Pi$, and then a sequence of $d$ polyhedral complexes in $\mathcal{P}^{n-1,n}$, and returns a single polyhedral complex in $\mathcal{P}^{n,n}$.

**Implementation**  Each one of the input `pols` is *extruded* by using the `EX` operator given in Script 15.5.2. Also, a `maps` sequence of permutations of coordinates is prepared, in order to properly embed each extruded polyhedron in the target Euclidean space of dimension $n$. The two sequence of coordinate maps and of extruded polyhedra are then combined by the infix operator (`AA:APPLY` $\sim$ `TRANS`). Then, the cells of each polyhedron are extracted by the `SplitCells` operator given in Script 10.8.4.

---

**Script 14.4.1 (Intersection of extrusions)**
```
DEF XX (permutations::IsSeqOf:IsSeq) (pols::IsSeqOf:IsPol) =
    (fix ~ STRUCT ~ AA:& ~ CART ~ AA:SplitCells):
        (AA:MAP:maps (AA:APPLY ~ TRANS) AA:(EX:<0,1000000>):pols)
WHERE
    maps = AA:(CONS ~ AA:SEL):permutations
    fix = MKPOL ~ [S1,S2, AA:[ID] ~ CAT ~ S3] ~ UKPOL
END;
```

---

The (*combinatorial*) Cartesian product of the resulting set of $d$ sequences of cells is produced by the `Cart` operator defined in Script 2.1.17, and the (*point set*) intersection of each generated $d$-tuple is returned by the `&` built-in intersection operator. The resulting intersected cells are finally aggregated into a single polyhedral complex by the `STRUCT` operator. One more operation is actually needed to `fix` the data structure, by eliminating the empty polyhedral cells resuting from void intersections of extruded cells[2].

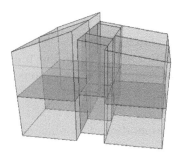 

**Figure 14.16**  (a) Variational house from an intersection of extrusions (b) Frame generated by offsetting the 1-skeleton

**Example 14.4.3 (Intersection of extrusions)**
A definition of the `house` section as a variational 2D complex of polyhedra is given in Script 14.4.2. A variational house is there defined as a binary intersection of extrusions. Notice that the expression:

---

[2] This one is actually a bug in the current implementation of the `STRUCT` operator.

```
&&:<<1,2,0>, <0,1,2>>:<Plan,Section>
```

which is syntactically equivalent to

```
Plan (<1,2,0> && <0,1,2>) Section
```

means that the `Plan` parameter, actually defined in 2D, is embedded in the subspace $z = 0$ so that its $x$ and $y$ axis are identified with $x, y$ in $\mathbb{E}^3$. Analogously, the `Section` parameter is embedded in the subspace $x = 0$ of $\mathbb{E}^3$ so that its $x, y$ axis are identified with $y, z$.

---

**Script 14.4.2 (Variational house)**

```
DEF plan (a,b::isRealPos) = IF:<K:ok, ID, ERROR>:ThePlan
WHERE
    ok = GE:b:a,
    ThePlan = STRUCT:<rooms, T:<1,2>:<a,-:b/2>:corridor>,
    rooms = QUOTE:<a,-:b,a> * QUOTE:<a, a>,
    corridor = QUOTE:<b> * QUOTE:<b, 2*(a-b), b>,
    ERROR = SIGNAL ~ [K:'no good plan ', ID]
END;

DEF section (a,b,h::IsRealPos)
    = STRUCT:<firstFloor, T:2:h, secondLeft, T:1:a, secondRight>
WHERE
    firstFloor = QUOTE:<a+b> * QUOTE:<h>,
    secondLeft = MKPOL:<<<0,0>,<a,0>,<a,h*5/4>,<0,h>>,<1..4>,<<1>>>,
    secondRight = MKPOL:<<<0,0>,<b,0>,<b,h>,<0,h*6/4>>,<1..4>,<<1>>>
END;

DEF House (Plan,Section::IsPol) = Plan (<1,2,0> && <1,0,2>) Section;
DEF House_1 = House:<plan:<4,2>, Section:<4+2, 4, 3> >;

DEF out1 = STRUCT:<
    House_1 MATERIAL
        Transparentmaterial:<green, 0.8>,
    @1:House_1
>;

DEF out2 = (OFFSET:<0.2,0.2,0.5> ~ @1):House_1;
```

---

The `out1` and `out2` objects are displayed in Figure 14.16. Remember that in order to use the `MATERIAL` and the `OFFSET` operators, the `'colors'` and `'offset'` libraries must be loaded.

## 14.5 Skeleton extraction

Consider a $d$-polyhedron $P$, and the relative decomposition in convex cells defined by the $d$-complex $\mathcal{K}$. A polyhedral complex $C_\partial$ associated $\partial P$ is defined by the collection of facets of cells in $\mathcal{K}$ along which no adjacent cell exists. More precisely, $C_\partial$ is composed of 0-order polyhedral instances, each corresponding to (the image of) a single $(d-1)$-polyhedron whose decomposition consists of one or more $(d-1)$-cells (facets of $P$).

**Figure 14.17**   1-skeleton of rotated 4D hypercube, projected in $\mathbb{E}^3$

The set of $k$-faces of $C_\partial$ is defined as the set of $k$-faces of cells contained in the polyhedral instances forming $C_\partial$, for $0 \le k < d$. Notice that the set of $k$-faces of $C_\partial$ is a polyhedral complex itself. The $k$-faces of a polyhedron $P$ are defined as the set of $k$-faces of $C_\partial$, where $C_\partial$ is the polyhedral complex associated to $\partial P$.

**Skeletons of polyhedra**   The $k$-*skeleton* @k of a polyhedron $P$ is the set of $k$-faces of $P$. Thus:

$$@\text{k} : \mathcal{P}^d \to \mathcal{C}^{k,d}, \qquad 0 \le k \le d,$$

where $\mathcal{P}^d$ is the set of $d$-polyhedra and $\mathcal{C}^{k,d}$ the set of polyhedral complexes of intrinsic dimension $k$ embedded in $E^d$.

Notice that the $k$-skeleton of $P$ is a polyhedral complex, and not a polyhedron. We conventionally assume that the $d$-skeleton of $P$ equals $P$ itself, and thus skeletons are defined for $0 \le k \le d$.

### Example 14.5.1 (Skeletons of a 3D cube)
The 2-skeleton of a 3D cube, which is 3-polyhedron, is the set of 2-faces of $C_\partial$, which is a polyhedral complex with 6 instances (the bounding squares). Hence, the 2-skeleton of the cube consists simply of these six squares, i.e. of its facets in the traditional sense. Similarly, the 1-skeleton is the set of its 12 edges (1-polyhedra), the 0-skeleton is the set of its 8 vertices (0-polyhedra).

### Example 14.5.2 (1-Skeleton of a 4D cube)
In Figure 14.17 we show a projection of the 1-dimensional skelon of a rotated 4D hypercube, projected in $\mathbb{E}^3$ by cutting the last coordinate. The `Project:`$n$ operator is given in Script 14.6.1.

---

**Script 14.5.1 (1-skeleton of rotated 4D cube)**

```
DEF cube4D = CUBOID:<1,1,1,1>;

(Project:1 ~ @1 ~ R:<1,4>:(PI/6) ~ R:<1,3>:(PI/7)):cube4D;
```

---

**Skeletons of polyhedral complexes**   The $k$-skeleton of polyhedral instances and complexes is defined as the set of $k$-skeletons obtained by applying the @k operator to the component elements, and we have:

$$\begin{aligned}\text{@k} : \mathcal{I}^{d,n} \to \mathcal{I}^{k,n}, \\ \text{@k} : \mathcal{C}^{d,n} \to \mathcal{C}^{k,n},\end{aligned} \qquad 0 \le k \le d \le n,$$

where $\mathcal{I}^{d,n}$ is the set of polyhedral instances of intrinsic dimension $d$ embedded in $E^n$.

Thus the @k operator remains defined on the whole set of mathematical models $\mathcal{M}$.

**Representation**  A $k$-skeleton, as every other polyhedral complex, is internally represented as a directed multigraph, where every leaf node contains some $k$-face, possibly decomposed in convex cells. The matrix associated with an arc performs the composite transformation that relocates the ending node to its affine hull, after an implicit embedding from $E^k$ to a coordinate subspace of $E^d$.

The @k operator produces an output multigraph which differs from the input multigraph only because the input leaves — $d$-polyhedra — are substituted by the graphs of their $k$-skeletons, and the $k$-skeleton of a $d$-polyhedron can be computed as the set of $k$-faces of $C_{\partial}$. Hence, we can concentrate without loss of generality on the basic problem of computing the $k$-skeleton of a single convex cell $c^d$.

Let the cell be represented by a non-redundant set of face covectors

$$c^d = \{f_1, \ldots, f_p\}$$

and let

$$\mathcal{V} = \{V_i \mid V_i \subset c^d, \ 1 \le i \le q\}$$

be its set of vertices, each represented as a subset of face covectors. Notice that $p \ge d+1$ and $q \ge d + 1$, where both equalities hold if and only if $c^d$ is an $d$-simplex. In this case the $k$-skeleton of $c^d$ is simply given by the $\binom{d+1}{d-k}$ cells obtained by choosing $d - k$ covectors as equalities and the remaining covectors as inequalities. E.g., the 1-dimensional skeleton of a 3-simplex (tetrahedron) is constituted by $\binom{3+1}{3-1} = 6$ edges. Unfortunately, this simple characterization does not hold for a general convex $d$-cell.

### 14.5.1   Algorithm

The computation requires only some linear algebra, and no optimization is discussed here. Rather, great care is dedicated to avoid numerical problems by using an implicit representation of geometric objects as much as possible. E.g., the numerical coordinates of a vertex are not explicitly calculated, but the vertex itself is implicitly represented as a set of face covectors associated with boundary hyperplanes which intersect in the vertex. Hence, the set membership of a vertex into an affine subspace, both represented as sets of covectors, is not solved numerically but tested as set inclusion.

**Preview**  In the general case, we need to check all the $k$-dimensional affine subspaces generated by intersection of face hyperplanes, in order to discover those sets of hyperplanes which are the support space of a boundary $k$-face. For each such set of hyperplanes we have to compute the $(k-1)$-dimensional boundary of the supported $k$-cell. Finally, an affine transformation is computed for each $k$-face that maps it into the subspace of the first $k$ coordinates. This final step is required to build the multigraph representation of the $k$-skeleton, where the inverse transformation matrix is associated with each directed arc.

The whole computation can be decomposed into 5 subsequent steps, which are described below.

**$k$-Dimensional affine subspaces**   First compute the set of $k$-dimensional affine subspaces generated by $c^d$.

Let $H \subset c^d$ be a subset of face covectors. Then:

$$\dim \operatorname{aff} H = k \iff \operatorname{rank} H = d - k,$$

where the symbol $H$ is used, depending on the context, to denote both a set of covectors and their matrix, and where $\operatorname{aff} H$ is the affine hull of $H$, i.e. the minimum affine subspace which contains the intersection of the hyperplanes $f_i \in H$. Thus, the collection of sets of hyperplanes which support affine sets of dimension $k$ can be written as:

$$\mathcal{H}^k = \{H \mid H \subset c^d,\ \operatorname{rank} H = d - k\}.$$

**Affine support of $k$-faces**   Given a $k$-dimensional affine subspace defined by a set $H \in \mathcal{H}^k$, test if a boundary $k$-face $c^k$ exists which is contained in $\operatorname{aff} H$:

$$c^k = c^d \cap \operatorname{aff} H.$$

In particular, verify if the vertices of $c^d$ which are contained in $\operatorname{aff} H$ span a $k$-dimensional subspace. Towards this end (a) find the vertices which are contained in $\operatorname{aff} H$, i.e. the hyperplane sets $V_i$ that contain $H$; (b) compute the rank of their intersection set $\overline{H}$.

The vertex $v_i \in E^d$, which is the intersection of elements of the hyperplane set $V_i$, will be contained in the affine subspace generated by $H$ if and only if $V_i \supset H$. Formally:

$$v_i \in \operatorname{aff} H \iff V_i \supset H.$$

Then, consider the set intersection of hyperplane subsets incident on the vertices contained in the affine hull of $H$:

$$\overline{H} = \bigcap_{V_i \supset H} V_i.$$

$\operatorname{aff} \overline{H}$ is the affine subspace spanned by the vertices of $c^d$ which belong to $\operatorname{aff} H$. If

$$\operatorname{rank} \overline{H} = \operatorname{rank} H = d - k,$$

then

$$\operatorname{aff} \overline{H} \equiv \operatorname{aff} H.$$

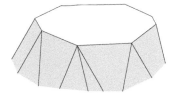 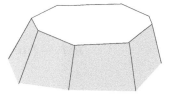

**Figure 14.18** (a) Hyperplanes incident on a $k$-face (in this case $k = 2$)
(b) Non-redundant representation of the face boundary

If $\overline{H}$ generates the same affine subspace generated by $H$, then it contains a $k$-face of $c^d$; otherwise $\overline{H}$ contains a cell of dimension less than $k$ and is of no interest for the computation of $k$-skeleton.

We can finally characterize the set $\overline{\mathcal{H}}^k$ of affine support spaces for the $k$-faces of a $d$-cell:

$$\overline{\mathcal{H}}^k = \{\overline{H} \mid \overline{H} = \bigcap_{V_i \supset H} V_i, \ H \in \mathcal{H}^k, \ \text{rank}\,\overline{H} = \text{rank}\,H\}.$$

**$k$-Faces boundary** Given the affine support $\overline{H} \in \overline{\mathcal{H}}^k$ of a $k$-face $c^k$, the next goal is to find the boundary hyperplanes of the cell. Consider the hyperplane set:

$$B = \left( \bigcup_{V_i \supset \overline{H}} V_i \right) - \overline{H},$$

which contains the hyperplanes of $c^d$ incident on the boundary of $c^k$, but not belonging to its affine support, and compute on the set $B$ an unredundant representation of $c^k$ as intersection of inequalities (see Figure 14.18). We look for the set $F \subseteq B$ of hyperplanes which intersect aff $\overline{H}$ in the support space of a face of $c^k$ of maximum dimension. Formally:

$$F = \{f_i \in B \mid \{f_i\} \cup \overline{H} \supseteq \overline{G}, \ \overline{G} \in \overline{\mathcal{H}}^{k-1}\}.$$

The pair $(\overline{H}, F)$, with the equalities set $\overline{H}$ and the inequalities set $F$, will give a representation of the $k$-cell associated to the covector subset $\overline{H} \in \overline{\mathcal{H}}^k$. A more compact equivalent representation is the pair $(H, F)$, with $H \subseteq \overline{H}$ any subset such that $|H| = \text{rank}\,\overline{H} = d - k$.

**Affine transformation** Affinely map each $k$-cell $c_j^k = (H_j, F_j)$ with affine hull aff $H_j$, where $H_j$ is used to denote both the set of face covectors $\{f_{j_1}, \ldots, f_{j_{d-k}}\}$ and their matrix, into the coordinate subspace

$$x_{k+1} = x_{k+2} = \cdots = x_d = 0.$$

This mapping can be performed by each transformation matrix $T_j$ that satisfies the condition:

$$H_j T_j = \left(\begin{array}{cc} 0 & I \end{array}\right)_{(d-k)\times(d+1)}$$

Since we have

$$T_j^T H_j^T = \left(\begin{array}{c} 0 \\ I \end{array}\right)$$

the $(d+1)\times(d+1)$ unknown matrix $T_j$ can be computed by applying the Gauss-Jordan pivotal method to the matrix $\left(\begin{array}{cc} H_j^T & I \end{array}\right)$, which is transformed into

$$\left(\begin{array}{cc} 0 & T_j^T \\ I & \end{array}\right)$$

from which we can extract $T_j$.

**Reduction to inequalities**   Finally, the transformation $T_j$ is applied to the set $F_j$ in order to map it into the coordinate subspace of the first $k$ coordinates. This makes it possible to store only the first $k$ coordinates of the transformed face covectors, as well as storing only the face covectors of a cell and not its affine support. Clearly, in the multigraph representation of the $k$-skeleton of $c^s$ the inverse matrices $T_j^{-1}$ will be associated with arcs that point to the $c_j^k$ cells.

## 14.6   Extrusion, sweep, offset and Minkowski sum

A multidimensional approach which unifies extrusion, sweeping and a subclass of offset and Minkowski sums is discussed in this section. This approach is given for linear, non-regular and non-manifold $d$-polyhedra embedded in a Euclidean $n$-space. The addressed operations are useful in several areas of CAD/CAM and robotics. Extrusion is used to generate 3D models from 2D sections. Sweeping is used to generate curves, surfaces and solids by moving points, curves, surfaces or solids along given paths. An inverted form of sweep is useful to plan inspection and manufacturing operations [IS99]. The Minkowski sum is referred to when planning collision-free motion of vehicles among obstacles. The subclass of offset operations studied here allows one to automatically generate solid models of buildings from polygon and wire-frame models.

### Introduction

An algorithmic construction is introduced in this section, that is based on the repeated execution of the Cartesian product of a point set in $\mathbb{E}^n$ times a unit interval, followed by a proper shearing. The partial or final results of a suitable sequence of such intermediate operations are projected back into $\mathbb{E}^n$. Some useful operations are obtained in this way. In particular:

1. *Extrusion* is defined as the Cartesian product of a polyhedral point set $A$ times the unit interval $[0,1] \subset E$.

2. *Sweeping* is defined as the union of joins of corresponding points in a polyhedral point set and in its translated image. An alternative definition of sweeping is introduced as the Minkowski sum with an interval. It is shown that sweeping can be computed as a composition of extrusion, shearing and projection.

3. If a convex $n$-cell $K$ is computable as a succession of sweeps from a single point, then the *Minkowski sum* of an arbitrary $d$-polyhedron $A$ with $K$ can be computed by applying the same sweeps to $A$.

4. An *orthogonal offset* operator is defined as the Minkowski sum of a polyhedral point set with a hyper-rectangle. A constructive definition of offset is given as the composition of suitable sweeps.

The given algorithm is limited to polyhedral domains, but it can be used with polyhedral complexes of arbitrary dimension $d$, with $0 < d < n$ (for arbitrary $n$, even greater than 3). Such point sets may be both solid and embedded, non-regular and non-manifold.

**References**   The operations considered and some of their parental relationships are not new. For example, the Minkowski sum of 2D polygons is referred by Schwartz and Sharir [SS90] to the early work of Lozano-Perez and Wesley [LPW79]. The novelty of the present approach relies on its close integration in a multidimensional computing environment. Among the ideas which made this approach possible: the representation of a point set by a *covering* with convex cells [GW89, Ede95, PPV95]; the representation of a convex set as an intersection of halfspaces [BFPP93], *no representation of topology* [Tak86, Tak91], a *multidimensional* approach to both data structures and algorithms, and a *functional* geometric environment [PPV95]. No topology representation implies simplicity, efficiency and robustness, beyond easy dimension-independence.

### 14.6.1   Background

Let us start by summarizing the main concepts needed to formalize the given algorithm. Some of them were previously given in this book, but it can be useful to briefly recall them here for the reader's convenience. According to the standard usage in modeling and graphics, normalized homogeneous coordinates $(x_0, x_1, \ldots x_n)$ are used, where $x_0 = 1$, to represent every point $p \in \mathbb{E}^n$.

**Polyhedron**   Polyhedra can be represented as coverings with convex sets. The polyhedra we deal with are non-convex, non-regular (i.e. may have parts of different dimension), non-connected and non-manifold. Any polyhedral point set $A \subset \mathbb{E}^n$ can be written as $\bigcup_i K_i$, where $\{K_i\}$ is a collection of relatively closed convex sets in $\mathbb{E}^n$, called *cells*. The dimension $d$ of a polyhedron is the maximum dimension of its convex cells. The set of polyhedra of dimension $d$ in $\mathbb{E}^n$ is denoted as $\mathcal{P}^{d,n}$.

**Product of polyhedra**   Polyhedral sets can be multiplied by pairwise Cartesian product of their cells. If $A_1 = \bigcup_i K_i$ and $A_2 = \bigcup_j K_j$, with $K_i \subset \mathbb{E}^n$ and $K_j \subset \mathbb{E}^m$, then

$$A_1 \times A_2 = \bigcup_{i,j}(K_i \times K_j), \quad \text{where} \quad A_1 \times A_2 \subset \mathbb{E}^{n+m}.$$

**Projection**  A *projection* $\Pi^r$ is here defined as a linear operator $\Pi^r : \mathbb{E}^n \to \mathbb{E}^{n-r}$ which maps a polyhedron $A = \bigcup_i K_i$, onto a polyhedron $\Pi^r(A) = \bigcup_i \Pi^r(K_i)$, where each $\Pi^r(K_i)$ is the convex hull of the projected vertices of $K_i$.

**Shearing**  This operation is defined as a special linear transformation $H$ of $\mathbb{E}^n$. The matrix representing such a transformation in a suitable basis differs from the unit matrix only for one column.

A shearing transformation produces a special deformation of the space which is applied to, considered as a bundle of hyperplanes parallel to a coordinate subspace of dimension $n - 1$. Under the shearing such coordinate subspace (let $x_n = 0$) is fixed, whereas all the parallel hyperplanes are translated linearly with $x_n$.

A shearing transformation along the $x_n$ coordinate is represented as a $(n+1) \times (n+1)$ matrix with the following structure:

$$H_v = \begin{pmatrix} 1 & 0 & \cdots & 0 & 0 \\ 0 & 1 & \cdots & 0 & v_1 \\ \vdots & \vdots & \ddots & \vdots & \vdots \\ 0 & 0 & \cdots & 1 & v_{n-1} \\ 0 & 0 & \cdots & 0 & 1 \end{pmatrix}$$

The matrix depends on a vector $v = (v_1, \ldots, v_{n-1}) \in \mathbb{R}^{n-1}$, which represents the translation acting on the points of the hyperplane $x_n = 1$. The application of the shearing $H_v$ to the point set $A$ is denoted as $H_v(A)$.

*14.6.2  Unified approach*

The Minkowski sum is usually defined [Sch93, Zie95] between convex sets in a vector space, so producing a location of the result which is different from that of both arguments. The definition in a Euclidean space given here follows [LPW79], and produces a "grown" version of the first argument.

**Minkowski sum**  Consider a polyhedron $A = \bigcup A_i$, where $A_i$ are convex cells, and another *convex* $K$. Choose a point $o \in K$ as the origin for a support vector space $\mathbb{R}^n$. Let $x = a - o$ and $y = k - o$ be the vectors spanning $A_i$ and $K$, respectively. For each convex cell $A_i$, consider the set

$$A_i + K = \{o + (a - k) \mid a \in A_i,\ k \in K\},$$

where $a - k = x - y$ is the vector (Minkowski) difference of the spanning vectors $x$ and $y$. The polyhedron obtained as the union of the expanded sets $A_i + K$ is called the *Minkowski sum* of $A$ with the convex $K$:

$$A + K = (\cup_i A_i) + K = \cup_i (A_i + K)$$

Notice that polyhedra are defined as point sets in an Euclidean space $\mathbb{E}^n$, while the difference of two points gives a vector in the underlying vector space, and the sum of a point and a vector gives a point.

In the following, it is supposed that an origin has been chosen once and for all, in order to identify the Euclidean space and the associated vector space.

**Sweeping**  The *sweeping* operation may be defined as the Minkowski sum of a polyhedral point set $A$ and the interval $[0, v]$

$$\text{Sweep}(v) : \mathbb{E}^n \to \mathbb{E}^n : A \mapsto A + [0, v].$$

If the set of vectors $\{v_1, v_2, \ldots v_k\}$ is linearly independent, then the set $\sum_{i=1}^{k}[0, v_i]$ is called the *parallelotope* spanned by those vectors.

Let us denote $[-v_i/2, v_i/2]$ as $[v_i]$. If $V_m = \{v_1, v_2, \ldots v_m\}$ is an arbitrary set of $m$ vectors, then the set $[V_m] = \sum_{V_m}[v_i]$ is called the *zonotope* spanned by the $v_i$. Any zonotope is symmetric: if $w \in [V_m]$, then $-w \in [V_m]$. This fact justifies the following definition.

**Offset]**  The *Offset* operator can be defined as the Minkowski sum of a polyhedral point set $A$ with a zonotope $[V_n]$.

An interesting special case, with applications to building design, is obtained when $V_n$ is an orthogonal basis. Because of the associative property of the Minkowski sum, a constructive definition of the offset operator is given as the composition of $2m$ sweeps:

$$A + [V_m] = (\text{Sweep}(-v_m/2) \circ \text{Sweep}(v_m/2) \circ \cdots \circ \text{Sweep}(-v_1/2) \circ \text{Sweep}(v_1/2))(A)$$

*14.6.3  Algorithms*

The Minkowski sum with an interval, i.e. a sweeping in $\mathbb{E}^n$, is reduced to computing a product times the unit interval, an affine transformation in $\mathbb{E}^{n+1}$ and a projection from $\mathbb{E}^{n+1}$ to $\mathbb{E}^n$. The Minkowski sum with either a parallelotope or a zonotope generated by $m$ vectors is reduced to a sequence of products (each associated with an affine transformation) and to a final projection from $\mathbb{E}^{n+m}$ into $\mathbb{E}^n$.

**Proposition:**  The *Minkowski sum with an interval* $[0, v]$ can be computed as the composition of extrusion, shearing and projection operators:

$$A + [0, v] = (\Pi \circ H_v \circ \text{Extr})(A) \tag{14.14}$$

**Proposition:**  A sequence of $m$ sweeps is equivalent to the alternate composition of $m$ extrusions and shearings, followed by a projection $\Pi^m$:

$$\text{Sweep}(v_m) \circ \cdots \circ \text{Sweep}(v_1) = \Pi^m \circ (H_{s_m} \circ \text{Extr}) \circ \cdots \circ (H_{s_1} \circ \text{Extr})$$

where the shearing vectors $s_i$ are obtained from the corresponding sweeping vectors $v_i$ by adding $i - 1$ more zero coordinates:

$$s_1 = v_1, \quad s_i = v_i \times \{0\}^{i-1}, \quad 2 \leq i \leq m.$$

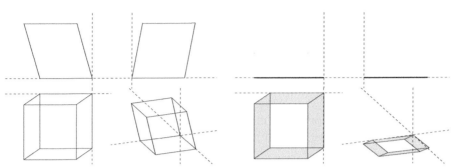

**Figure 14.19**  Extruded and sheared object $H(0.3, 0.2)(\partial I^2 \times I)$

**Figure 14.20**  Covering with convex cells of the point set $\text{Sweep}(0.3, 0.2)(\partial I^2)$

**Proposition:**  If a convex cell $K$ is computable by sweeps from a single point, i.e. if

$$K = (\text{Sweep}(r_m) \circ \cdots \circ \text{Sweep}(r_1))(p), \qquad p \in I\!E^n,$$

then the Minkowski sum $A + K$ of an arbitrary polyhedron $A$ with $K$ can be computed by applying the same sweeps to $A$. More precisely:

$$A + K = (\text{Sweep}(r_m) \circ \cdots \circ \text{Sweep}(r_1))(A)$$

### Example 14.6.1 (Extrusion and shearing)
Let $A = \partial I^2$, with $I^2 = [0,1] \times [0,1] \subset I\!E^2$. Notice that $\partial I^2 \in \mathcal{P}^{1,2}$. The result of the application of a shearing $H_v = H(0.1, 0.2)$ to the point set $\text{Extr}(A) = (\partial I^2) \times I$ is shown in Figure 14.19.

### Example 14.6.2 (Sweeping)
A simple example of sweeping can be given by applying the composite operator shown in Formula (14.14) to the point set $A = \partial I^2$. Let the sweeping vector $v$ be equal to $(0.3, 0.2)$. The swept object $\text{Sweep}(v)(A)$, computed as $(\Pi \circ H_v \circ \text{Extr})(A)$, is shown in Figure 14.20.

### Example 14.6.3 (Multiple sweeping)
A more interesting example can be given by first generating a 2D polyhedral complex embedded in 3D and then by repeatedly sweeping it in 3D. Suppose that

$$B = A \cup T(A),$$

where $A = \partial I^2 \times [0, 0.3]$ and $T$ is a translation of $I\!E^3$ with translation vector $t = (1, 0, 0)$. Let us compute the 3D object defined as:

$$(Sweep(v_3) \circ Sweep(v_2) \circ Sweep(v_1))(B)$$

where $v_1 = (-0.1, 0.2, 0)$, $v_2 = (0.1, 0, 0)$ and $v_3 = (0, 0.2, 0.3)$. Both the partial and the final results of the computation performed using Formula (14.14) are shown in Figure 14.21.

**Figure 14.21** Polyhedral complexes: (a) $B = A \cup T(A)$ (b)
$C = \mathrm{Sweep}(-0.1, 0.2, 0)(B)$ (c) $D = \mathrm{Sweep}(0.1, 0, 0)(C)$ (d) $E = \mathrm{Sweep}(0, 0.2, 0.3)(D)$

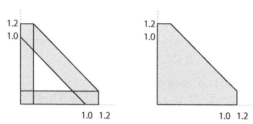

**Figure 14.22** Offset objects: (a) $\partial \sigma^2 + [V]$ (b) $\sigma^2 + [V]$, with
$V = \{(0.2, 0), (0, 0.2)\}$

**Example 14.6.4 (Offset with a parallelotope)**
Let $\sigma^2$ be the 2-dimensional standard simplex, i.e. the convex combination of points
$(0,0)$, $(1,0)$, and $(0,1)$, with $\sigma^2 \in \mathcal{P}^{2,2}$ and $\partial \sigma^2 \in \mathcal{P}^{1,2}$. In Figure 14.22 the polyhedra
$\partial \sigma^2 + [V]$ and $\sigma^2 + [V]$ are shown, where $V = \{(0.2, 0), (0, 0.2)\}$.

**Example 14.6.5 (Offset with a parallelotope)**
A more interesting example of offset is obtained by giving a 2-complex $A \subset \mathbb{E}^3$, which
models the vertical walls of a house, and by offsetting it with $[V]$. Both the starting
complex $A \in \mathcal{P}^{2,3}$ and the 3D solid result $A + [V]$ are shown in Figure 14.23.

**Example 14.6.6 (Offset with a parallelotope)**
A Minkowski sum with the cuboid of extreme point $(0.1, 0.2, 0.1)$ is given starting from
the 1-complex $B$ in $\mathbb{E}^3$ shown in Figure 14.24a. The "solid" result is in Figure 14.24b.

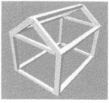

**Figure 14.23** (a) 2-complex $A$ in $\mathbb{E}^3$
(b) 3-complex $A + [(0.2, 0), (0, 0.2)]$

**Figure 14.24** (a) $B \in \mathcal{P}^{1,3}$
(b) $B + [(0.1, 0, 0), (0, 0.2, 0), (0, 0, 0.1)]$

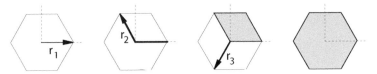

**Figure 14.25**    Tre three sweeping vectors which generate the hexagonal 2-cell

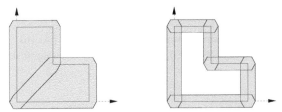

**Figure 14.26**    (a) Minkowski sum: (a) $A + B$. There are two convex cells in A
(b) $\partial A + B$

**Example 14.6.7 (Offset with a zonotope)**
In this example a convex 2-cell $B$ is generated and a Minkowski sum with $B$ is applied to both a 2-complex $A$ and a 1-complex $\partial A$. The convex $B$ is generated from $\{(0,0)\} \in \mathcal{P}^{0,2}$. The generation process is graphically shown in Figure 14.25.

$$
\begin{aligned}
B &= \{(0,0)\} + \left[ \left( -\frac{1}{2}, -\frac{\sqrt{3}}{2} \right), \left( -\frac{1}{2}, \frac{\sqrt{3}}{2} \right), (1,0) \right] \\
&= \left( \mathrm{Sweep}\left( -\frac{1}{2}, -\frac{\sqrt{3}}{2} \right) \circ \mathrm{Sweep}\left( -\frac{1}{2}, \frac{\sqrt{3}}{2} \right) \circ \mathrm{Sweep}(1,0) \right) \{(0,0)\}
\end{aligned}
$$

A polyhedral 2-complex $A = I^2 - K^2$ is then defined, where the minus denotes a Boolean subtraction, and $I = [0,1]$, $K = [0.5,1] \subset E$. The results of computing the expressions $A + B$ and $\partial A + B$ with this approach are shown in Figure 14.26.

**Analysis**    This approach is efficient. If the convex cells are represented as collections of a bounded number of intersecting halfspaces, then the Cartesian product times an interval is $O(m)$ in time and space, where $m$ is the number of convex cells in the input [BFPP93]. In fact, if a cell has a representation of bounded size $n$, after the product by an interval its representation has size $n + 2$, and is bounded also.

The shearing is linear in the size of the representation. The projection of convex cells is more costly, but the cell size is bounded. The actual cost is that of computing the convex hull of the projected cell vertices. This may imply the computation of vertices from face inequalities, and the number of vertices grows exponentially with the number of extrusions. With a bounded number of facets per cell, a better approach is based on the direct projection of face inequalities using the Fourier-Motzkin algorithm [TD97].

It follows that each linear sweep is $O(cm)$, where $c$ is the cost of the projection of a cell of bounded size, so that the Minkowski sum $A + K$ in $\mathbb{E}^n$ is $O(cpm)$, where $m$ is the cell number of $A$ and $p$ is the number of sweeps needed to generate the convex $K$.

## Implementation

An implementation of the algorithms discussed in this section is given in Script 14.6.1. First, some utility functions are given, followed, in Script 14.6.2 by the implementation of the main operators. The RTAIL function is given in Script 4.2.5, and the Project operator in Script 4.4.9, respectively.

---

**Script 14.6.1 (Minkowski toolbox)**

```
DEF vet2mat = (AA ~ AA):* ~ AA:TRANS ~ DISTR ~ [IDNT ~ LEN, ID];
DEF Scaling (s::IsReal) (v::IsVect) = (AA:* ~ DISTL):<s,v>;
DEF ExtrAndShear (v::IsVect) (pol::ISPOL) = Shear:v:(pol * QUOTE:<1>);
DEF Shear (v::IsVect) =
    (MAT ~ MatHom ~ TRANS ~ AR ~ [RTAIL ~ IDNT ~ LEN, ID] ~ AR):<v,1>
DEF MultipleExtr (v::IsVect) =
    (COMP ~ AA:ExtrAndShear ~ REVERSE ~ AppendZeros ~ vet2mat):v;
DEF AppendZeros (m::IsSqrMat) =
    (AA:CAT ~ TRANS ~ [ID, GenerateZeroSeqs]): m
WHERE
    GenerateZeroSeqs = AL ~ [ K:<>, APPLY ~ [
        CONS ~ AA:# ~ FROMTO ~ [K:1, - ~ [LEN,K:1]], K:0 ] ]
END;
```

---

In particular, the OffSet operator is implemented as a sum with an orthogonal parallelotope with extreme vertices 0 and $v$. The very compact PLaSM code gives also a quite readable documentation of the algorithmic approach used in implementing the Sweep, OffSet and Minkowski operators.

---

**Script 14.6.2 (Minkowski operators)**

```
DEF Sweep (v::IsVect)(p::IsPol) = (Project:1 ~ ExtrAndShear:v):p;
DEF OffSet (v::IsVect)(p::IsPol) = (Project:(LEN:v) ~ MultipleExtr:v):p;
DEF Minkowski (vects::IsMat)(p::IsPol) = (COMP ~ AA:Sweep):vects:p;
```

---

**Example 14.6.8 (Concrete frame from a wire model)**
In this example the wire-frame 3D model of a simplified house is defined by using the MKPOL primitive constructor. Then a translation in a 3D model with solid beams and columns is obtained by ortogonal OffSet. This operation corresponds to the Minkoswki sum with a 3D parallelepiped of size $0.1 \times 0.2 \times 0.1$. The implementation of the OffSet operator is given in Scripts 14.6.2 and 14.6.1.

**Example 14.6.9 (Minkowski sum with an hexagonal cell)**
In Script 14.6.4 a hexagonal 2-cell B is defined as the *zonotope* [Zie95] generated by three plane vectors of length 1 and forming angles of 120. The generation is executed starting from the 0D polyhedron p with the single point $(0,0)$ in 2-space. Then a 2D complex pol2D and its boundary pol1D are defined, and their Minkowski sum with B is stored in the objects Min1 and Min2, respectively. Min0 simply contains several

**Script 14.6.3 (Offset example)**

```
DEF House = MKPOL:< verts, cells, pols >
WHERE
    verts = <
        <0,0,0>,<3,0,0>,<3,2,0>,<0,2,0>,
        <0,0,1.5>,<3,0,1.5>,<3,2,1.5>,<0,2,1.5>, <0,1,2.2>,<3,1,2.2> >,
    cells = <
        <1,2>,<2,3>,<3,4>,<4,1>, <5,6>,<6,7>,<7,8>,<8,5>,
        <1,5>,<2,6>,<3,7>,<4,8>, <5,9>,<8,9>,<6,10>,<7,10>, <9,10> >,
    pols = <1..17>
END;

STRUCT:<
    House, T:1:(1.2 * SIZE:1:House),
    OffSet:<0.1,0.2,0.1>:House >;
```

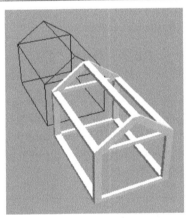

**Figure 14.27**   Solid model generated by `offset` operator from a wire model

instances of B translated at the positions of vertices of pol2D. Finally, an assembly of extruded instances, shown in Figure 14.28, of both Min0, Min1 and Min2 is generated.

## Example 14.6.10 (Variational building frame)

The concrete frame part of a building fabric of a *variational building* is defined by few lines of PLaSM code and given in Script 14.6.5. In particular, the concrete frame model is generated starting from the variational definition of the building layout plan and from its product times the inter-floor interval. The 1-skeleton of the generated assembly of 3D cells is then offset with a 3D interval having as linear dimensions the depth and width of the columns and the height of the beams. The resulting solid model is shown in Figure 14.29.

A quite realistic variational building generated by less than two pages of PLaSM code is given in Figure 14.29b.

**Figure 14.28** Minkowski sums with an hexagonal cell

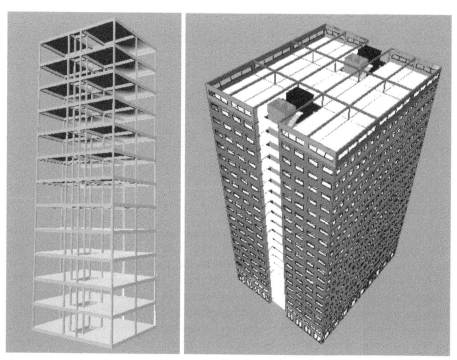

**Figure 14.29** (a) Concrete frame of a variational building; (b) schematic design of a short skyscraper. Views generated by a VRML viewer

**Script 14.6.4 (Minkowski example)**

```
DEF p = MKPOL:<<<0,0>>,<<1>>,<<1>>>;
DEF B = Minkowski : <<-1/2,SQRT:3/-2>,<-1/2,SQRT:3/2>,<1,0>> :p;
DEF vertices = <<0,0>,<1,0>,<1,0.5>,<0.5,0.5>,<0.5,1>,<0,1>>;

DEF pol1D = MKPOL:< vertices,
   <<1,2>,<2,3>,<3,4>,<4,5>,<5,6>,<6,1>>,
   AA:LIST:(1..6) >;
DEF pol2D = MKPOL:< vertices, <<1,2,3,4>,<4,5,6,1>>, <<1,2>>>;
DEF Min0 = STRUCT:(((CONS ~ AA:(T:<1,2>)):vertices):(S:<1,2>:<0.1,0.1>:B));
DEF Min1 = Minkowski:
   (AA:(Scaling:0.1):<<-1/2,SQRT:3/-2>,<-1/2,SQRT:3/2>,<1,0>>):pol1D;
DEF Min2 = Minkowski:
   (AA:(Scaling:0.1):<<-1/2,SQRT:3/-2>,<-1/2,SQRT:3/2>,<1,0>>):pol2D;

DEF Assembly = (Min2 * Q:0.05) TOP (Min0 * Q:0.7) TOP (Min1 * Q:0.05);
Assembly;
```

**Script 14.6.5 (Offset example)**

```
DEF plan (a,b::isRealPos) = STRUCT:<
   Q:<a,-:b,a> * Q:<a,a>,
   Q:<-:a,b> * Q:<a,-3*a/4,a/4> >;

DEF Block (a,b,h::isRealPos; n::IsIntPos) = STRUCT:<
   @1:(plan:<a,b> * (Q ~ #:n):h),
   plan:<a,b> * @0:((Q ~ #:n):h) >;

DEF SolidBlock (a,b,h::isRealPos; n::IsIntPos) = STRUCT:<
   OFFSET:<0.2,0.2,-0.4>:(@1:(plan:<a,b> * (Q ~ #:n):h) ),
   plan:<a,b> * @0:((Q ~ #:n):h) >;

DEF MyBlock = SolidBlock:<5,2,3,1>;

(STRUCT ~ ##:12):<MyBlock,T:3:3>
```

## 14.7  Annotated references

The point of view of performing geometric design and solid modeling without storing the topology is discussed by Takala [Tak86, Tak91]. An extensive overview and comparison of the more useful dimension-independent representations of geometry in geometric design can be found in [Fer95a]. The basic ideas underlying the representation of dimension-independent elementary polyhedra with simplicial decompositions and convex polytopes are discussed in [PBCF93, PFP96], respectively. Cell decompositions with hierarchical simplicial complexes, which could be used to gain efficiency when local refinements of polyhedral approximations of curved objects are required, can be found in [BFM95]. Products of polyhedra and skeletons of cell complexes are well known in algebraic topology [Poi53, Bro88] but only recently have been introduced in solid modeling [PS92, BFPP93, PPV95]. The present approach, where each elementary polyhedron is decomposed in a set of convex cells, also takes advantage of algorithms developed in different fields [Von78, Von81, Bur74, HdVT88].

# 15

# Motion modeling

This chapter is dedicated to discussing some geometric techniques for *animation modeling* and *motion planning*. In particular, the reader is introduced to the degrees of freedom of a moving system, and to the central issue of *configuration space* (CS), the set of numeric $k$-tuples that determine the placement and orientation of all the system components. A curve in configuration space, parametrized on the time domain, completely specifies the *motion* of the system. When the animated scene is too complex, it is necessary to project the configuration space onto coordinate subspaces related to the various actors, and to adopt a graph-theoretic approach to global *choreography*, allowing for motion coordination of interacting actors. The chapter also presents a general geometric technique to compute a polyhedral approximation of *free configuration space*, that encodes all the feasible motions of a mobile system in presence of obstacles. From a geometric programming viewpoint, the reader will learn that PLaSM provides FLASH animations based on 2D keyframes and gives a good support, based on CS sampling, to the symbolic generation of *animated* VRML of complex *storyboards*.

## 15.1 Degrees of freedom

Consider a moving system $R = \{R_i\}$, as a set of rigid bodies, either mutually constrained or not. The motion of $R$ is performed within a working space WS $\subset \mathbb{E}^d$, that contains an environment $E = \{E_j\}$, which is a set of rigid obstacles, that are either stationary or move along known trajectories. *Dimension* of the motion planning problem is the minimal dimension $d$ of an Euclidean space such that $R \cup E \subset \mathbb{E}^d$.

The moving system $R$ has also a number $k$ of *degrees of freedom* (DOFs) which is equal to the minimal number of scalar parameters that uniquely determine the *configuration* of $R$, i.e. the placement and orientation of all the $R$ elements with respect to a reference coordinate frame.

The degrees of freedom of a moving system are also called *generalized coordinates* [FL87], and constitute the main ingredient for the computation of the system dynamics using either the Lagrange-Euler or the Newton-Euler formulations. But system dynamics is beyond the scope of this book. The interested reader may

*Geometric Programming for Computer-Aided Design*  Alberto Paoluzzi
© 2003 John Wiley & Sons, Ltd  ISBN 0-471-89942-9

study a good Robotics book, for example [FL87]. A classical reading in Mechanics is [LCA26]. The realistic simulation of behavior of physical systems is one of the main achievements of computer graphics in the last decade [CS89].

**Rigid 2D body**   The *translational motion* of a planar body $B$ moving amidst a collection of polygonal obstacles has geometrical dimension 2 and 2 degrees of freedom, because the orientation of $B$ does not change, and the body position is determined by the position of one of its points, fixed in advance.

The more *general motion* of a single rigid planar figure has dimension 2 and 3 degrees of freedom, including two translational and one rotational degree. The rotational degree determines the orientation of the figure with respect to a reference coordinate frame. It is usually chosen as the angle between two corresponding axes from a fixed reference frame and from a frame attached to the object.

### Example 15.1.1 (2D body with 3 DOFs)
The simplest example is given in Script 15.1.1, where `body2D` is a rectangle. The x and y coordinates of its bottom-leftmost corner are assumed as the translational DOFs, whereas the `angle` between its bottom edge and the $x$ axis of the fixed frame in $\mathbb{E}^2$ is taken as the rotational DOF. The 2D cuboid configurations are generated as the images of the `body2D` function, depending on three real parameters. The four configurations produced by the last expression are displayed in Figure 15.1. The reader should notice that the object `CUBOID:<2,1>` is generated in a local frame centered on the bottom leftmost corner and aligned with the fixed reference frame. Notice also that the rotation tensor must be applied *before* the translation tensor.

---

**Script 15.1.1 (2D body with 3 DOFs)**

```
DEF body2D (x,y,angle::IsReal) =
    (T:<1,2>:<x,y> ~ R:<1,2>:angle): (CUBOID:<2,1>);

(STRUCT ~ AA:body2D):
    < <0,0,0>, <2,2,PI/4>, <4,2+2*SIN:(PI/4),0>, <6,0,3*PI/4> >
```

---

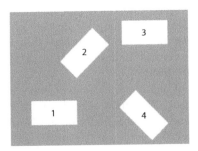

**Figure 15.1**   Four configurations of the 2D cuboid. The fixed reference frame is aligned with the bottom and left edges of configuration 1

**Rigid 3D body** The general motion of a single rigid body $B$ moving in a 3D space has 6 degrees of freedom. In this case there are 3 *translational* DOFs, corresponding to the position of a body point, and 3 *rotational* DOFs, corresponding to a triplet of *Euler angles*, that determine the orientation of a reference frame attached to the body, with respect to a fixed coordinate frame.

A common choice for the triplet of Euler angles $\phi, \theta, \psi$, in this case called *roll*, *pitch* and *yaw* angles, respectively, leads to a triplet of elementary rotation tensors $R_z(\phi)$, $R_y(\theta)$ and $R_x(\psi)$, where $R_z$, $R_y$ and $R_x$ respectively denote rotations about the $z$, $y$ and $x$ axes. Their composition in the order specified below gives to the general 3D rotation tensor that gives the body its orientation with respect to the fixed frame:

$$R(\phi, \theta, \psi) = R_z(\phi) \circ R_y(\theta) \circ R_x(\psi).$$

Some different choices for the Euler angles are quite common in Robotics, but are unusual in graphics and animation systems.

Our well-trained reader is certainly aware at this point that the above rotation tensor is applied to the moving system $B$ *before* the translation tensor, in order to get a given body configuration, i.e. the orientation and position corresponding to a 6-tuple of generalized coordinates.

### Example 15.1.2 (3D body with 6 DOFs)

The function body3D given in Script 15.1.2 produces a position and orientation of the CYLINDER with radius 0.2 and height 0.8, originally aligned with the $z$ axis and with the basis centered on the origin of the coordinate frame. The new configuration depends on the 6 generalized coordinates dx, dy, dz, roll, pitch and yaw.

---

**Script 15.1.2 (3D body with 6 DOFs)**

```
DEF body3D (dx, dy, dz, roll, pitch, yaw::IsReal) =
    (T:<1,2,3>:<dx,dy,dz> ~ R:<1,2>:roll ~ R:<1,3>:pitch ~ R:<2,3>:yaw):
    (CYLINDER:<0.2,0.8>:24);

STRUCT:< MkFrame, body3D:< 0.5,0.5,0, PI/2,0,PI/4 > STRUCT MkFrame,
    MKvector:<0,0,0>:<0.5,0.5,0> >;
```

---

The graphical assembly generated by the last expression, where MkFrame is the generator of the model of the standard 3D frame, and MKvector is the generator of the vector difference of two assigned points, is shown in Figure 15.2.

A given configuration of our cylinder, say, without reference frames, is clearly generated by the application of the generating function body3D to the 6-tuple of DOFs:

```
body3D:< 0.5,0.5,0, PI/2,0,PI/4 >
```

**Mechanical manipulators** A mechanical *manipulator*, more often called a *robot arm*, is an ordered set or rigid bodies, called *links*, pairwise connected by either revolute or prismatic *joints*. The first link is attached to a supporting basement, whereas the last link may handle a tool. A fixed reference frame is associated with the arm basement, and another reference frame is considered as rigidly attached to each link.

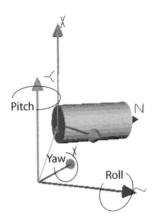

**Figure 15.2**  Position and orientation of a 3D body, depending on 6 degrees of freedom. Both the attached and the fixed frame are shown

**Joint transformations**  Various kinds of joints may allow for different combinations of rotational and translational DOFs. Usually, a *spherical* joint permits either 2 or 3 rotational degrees of freedom, a *cylindrical* joint allows for 1 rotational and 1 translational DOF, whereas a *prismatic* joint gives 1 translational degree. Notice that each joint is associated with a *link pair* and constrains the relative movement of the second link with respect to the first one.

A transformation tensor depending on the allowed degrees of freedom can hence be associated with each joint, i.e. to each ordered link pair $(R_i, R_j)$. This tensor will specify the position and orientation of the reference frame attached to the $R_j$ link with respect to the coordinate frame associated to the $R_i$ link.

**Kinematics chains and bones**  When analyzing the structure of a manipulator $R = \{R_i\}$ as a graph $G = (N, A)$, whose nodes are the links and whose arcs are the joints, i.e. with $N = R$ and $A \subset R^2$, the resulting graph is most often acyclic,[1] i.e. is a set of *open kinematics chains*.

Models of anthropomorphic robots also contain a tree made of links and joints. In computer animation a simplified representation and visualization of system links, used to visualize the degrees of freedom and to specify the *configuration space paths* that define the system motion, is usually given as a set of pairwise jointed *bones*.

**Example 15.1.3 (Plane robot arm)**
Let us consider a simplified 2D robot arm, as a kinematics chain with four links and three rotational joints. We also assume that (a) the links are rectangles; (b) they are equal to each other; (c) the first link is rigidly connected to the embedding space, i.e. it cannot move.

In Script 15.1.3 we give the `link` object as a rectangle with the main axis aligned with the negative $y$ axis, and with the position of the rotational joint positioned on the origin. The rotational `joint` is a function of a real parameter. When applied to an

---

[1] Or, even better, is a *tree*.

arbitrary value $\alpha$ of the argument in degrees, `joint:`$\alpha$ returns an affine transformation tensor. Finally, `arm` is a function of the three joint angles, respectively denoted `a1`, `a2` and `a3`.

To fully understand the meaning of the `arm` body expression, the reader should remember the semantics of hierarchical structures from Section 8.2.1. Two different configurations of the plane robot, produced by application of the `arm` generating function to different triples of actual parameters, are displayed in Figure 15.3.

---

**Script 15.1.3**

```
DEF link = (T:<1,2>:<-1,-19> ~ CUBOID):<2,20>
DEF joint (alpha::IsReal) = T:2:-18 ~ R:<1,2>:(alpha * PI/180);

DEF arm (a1,a2,a3::IsReal) = STRUCT:
    < link, joint:a1, link, joint:a2, link, joint:a3, link >;
```

---

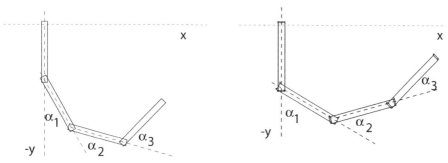

**Figure 15.3** Two plane robot configurations generated by `arm:<30,45,60>` and `arm:<60,45,30>`

## 15.2 Configuration space

Each one of the generalized coordinates $\xi_i$ of a moving system with $k$ degrees of freedom, may vary continuously within a real interval

$$\Xi_i = [\xi_i^{min}, \xi_i^{max}] \qquad 1 \le i \le k.$$

where $\xi_i^{min}$ and $\xi_i^{max}$ are often called *joint limits* in robotics applications.

The Cartesian product CS of the $k$ intervals $\Xi_i$ is called the *configuration space* of the moving system:

$$CS := \Xi_1 \times \Xi_2 \times \cdots \times \Xi_k \subset \mathbb{R}^k.$$

Each point $(\xi_1, \ldots, \xi_k) \in CS$ corresponds to a different *configuration* of the moving system, i.e. to a different placement and orientation of all its parts.

**Motion**  A continuous curve

$$\gamma : [0, 1] \to \mathbb{R}^k,$$

such that $\gamma[0,1] \subset CS$, completely defines a *feasible motion* of a mobile system.

The image of a smooth CS curve is also known as *configuration space path*. Clearly, $\gamma(0)$ and $\gamma(1)$ respectively correspond to the starting system configuration and to the goal configuration of the motion.

When reparametrized[2] in a time interval, such curve gives the configurations as a function of time, so that the curve itself and its first and second derivatives represent the configuration space *displacement, velocity* and *acceleration.*

Since a continuous acceleration is produced by a continuous force or torque, and standard actuators operate continuously, a feasible motion actually requires a configuration space curve at least of class $C^2$. More often, smooth CS curves are used to represent a motion, and in particular polynomial or rational curves. Non-uniform splines provide a very simple control of the motion acceleration.

### Example 15.2.1 (Configuration space path)

A continuous curve in configuration space for the 2D robot `arm` defined in Script 15.1.3 is produced in Script 15.2.1 by the cubic Bézier generating function `CSpath`, where the `intervals` generator of 1D polyedral complexes is given in Script 11.2.1. The curve image in CS with reference axes labeled as $\alpha_1, \alpha_2$ and $\alpha_3$, is displayed in Figure 15.4a. Notice that the sampling function produce the following values:

    Sampling:6 ≡ < 0 , 1/6 , 1/3 , 1/2 , 2/3 , 5/6 , 1 >

A motion representation by graphical aggregation of the robot placements corresponding to the generated CS sampling is given in Figure 15.4b.

---

### Script 15.2.1 (Bézier configuration space path)

```
DEF CSpath = (CONS ~ Bezier:S1):<<0,0,0>,<90,0,0>,<90,90,0>,<90,90,90>>;
DEF Sampling (n::IsInt) = (AA:/ ~ DISTR):< 0..n, n >;

(MAP:CSpath ~ Intervals):18;
(STRUCT ~ AA:(arm ~ CSpath ~ [ID]) ~ Sampling):18;
```

---

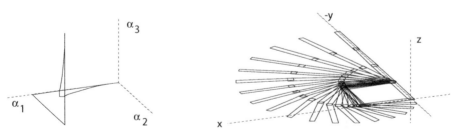

**Figure 15.4**   (a) Configuration space path produced as a cubic Bézier curve
(b) Set of configurations corresponding to a sampling of the path

---

[2] See Section 5.1.2.

**Example 15.2.2 (Different CS paths)**
Two different configuration space paths for the plane robot arm with 3 rotational
DOFs are given in Script 15.2.2 and displayed in Figure 15.5. Notice that both the
corresponding motions have the same start and goal configurations, whereas the two
intermediate control points of the configuration space path are different.

---

**Script 15.2.2**
```
DEF CSpath1 = Bezier:S1:<<0,0,0>,<90,0,0>,<90,90,0>,<90,90,90>>;
DEF CSpath2 = Bezier:S1:<<0,0,0>,<0,90,90>,<90,90,0>,<90,90,90>>;
```

---

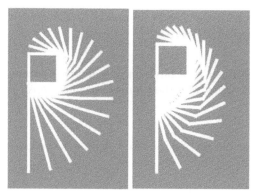

**Figure 15.5**   Two movements of the plane arm, corresponding to different
configuration space paths, i.e. to different behaviors

**Free configuration space**   The set FP of *free positions* for a moving system $B$
with $k$ degrees of freedom is the compact subset of $CS \subset \mathbb{R}^k$ constituted by all points
whose corresponding placement of the moving system is *free*, in the sense that $B$
neither intersects any obstacle in its working space WS nor self-intersects. The set FP
is more often known as *free configuration space*.

A goal configuration $r_2$ is reachable from a starting configuration $r_1$, i.e. there
exists a feasible motion between them, if they are both contained in a same connected
component of FP. To compute FP is therefore equivalent to deciding in advance all
the possible reachability problems for a mover $B$ and a set of obstacles $E$. Clearly, in
order to plan the motions from a given starting configuration $r_1$ of the mover, it is
sufficient to determine just the connected component of FP that contains $r_1$.

The reader interested to algorithmic robot motion planning is referred to the
Latombe book [Lat91].

**15.3   Animation with PLaSM**

In the last few years, PLaSM has been extended to support colors, textures, cameras
and animations. In particular, PLaSM was aimed at giving symbolic support to the
design of very complex animations.

For this purpose the language semantics were extended, and both an animation methodology and an animation server were developed [BBC+99]. The animation server, used only for display, was first implemented using *OpenInventor* as the animation engine. More recently, the language interpreter started to directly export *animated* VRML files, and some simple FLASH animations.

In this section we discuss the basic concepts of the PLaSM animation model, based on CS sampling, and give several simple examples. The design and implementation of complex animations with more than one animated *actor* are discussed in the next sections.

### 15.3.1   *Some definitions*

Let us start our discussion of the PLaSM approach to the generation of computer animations by giving some definitions.

**Scene**   A *scene* is here defined as a function of some real parameters, with values in some suitable data type, that we called *animated hierarchical polyhedral complex* (AHPC).

**Configuration**   Each feasible set of parameters defines a *configuration* of the scene.

**State**   A corresponding pair *<time, configuration>* is a *state* of the animation. The product of the time domain times the configuration space gives the *state-space* of the animation.

**Behavior**   The animation *behavior* is a curve in animation state-space. Each part of the scene may change in time with respect to position, orientation and modeling parameters, and may even change its internal assembly structure.

**Animation**   An animation is a pair <scene, behavior>.

### 15.3.2   *Generating* FLASH *animations*

The PLaSM language may give basic support to the generation of FLASH animations, exported as .swf files,[3] that are rendered by a FLASH viewer, usually embedded by default as a *plug-in* in web browsers.

Animations of this kind are based on the explicit generation of sequences of *frames* either by *inbetweening* of *key-frames* or by configuration space *sampling*.

The reader should remember that FLASH animations are, by definition, 2D only. The animation of a 3D scene would require a preliminary projection of the scene data base. Consequently, in the remainder of this section we assume we are dealing with 2D data only.

---

[3] Where the file suffix stands for *ShockWaveFlash* by Macromedia.

**Key-frame inbetweening** An important technique of computer generated animation, originating from traditional animation methods, consists in setting from scratch some pictures, called *key-frames*, with important postures of the characters in the scene, and in deriving a sufficient number of intermediate figures by interpolation, that in this context is called *inbetweening*.

With PLaSM, this animation technique may be instanced by defining the either open or closed polygonal contours of the objects in two or more subsequent keyframes, and by generating the intermediate postures by the *shape interpolation* or approximation methods defined in Section 7.3.2, that the interested reader is invited to review at this point.

Notice that a *shape* is there defined as an equivalence class of congruent figures, where the class representative is chosen with a vertex in the origin of the reference frame. Hence, in order to instance a shape in a plane configuration, two translational and one rotational parameter values are required. Such parameters, needed for placement and orientation of characters generated by shape interpolation, are equally derived by interpolation of the placements of two shape points, using 3D (three DOFs) curves or splines parametrized on the time domain.

**Configuration space sampling** When the shape as well as the placement of an actor may be generated by using a PLaSM generating function depending on actual parameters of numeric type, the easiest way to produce a FLASH animation consists of a variation of the CS sampling method used to export VRML animations.

The only difference in this case regards the need for explicit generation of a sequence of polyhedral complexes, one for each frame of each moving actor. As it is easy to understand, such an approach is quite space-inefficient, but is the only approach allowed by the *Macromedia* API to produce .swf files. It follows that only quite simple FLASH animations can be safely exported and efficiently rendered.

### PLaSM primitives for Flash animation

The PLaSM primitives that affect the FLASH rendering of an exported .swf file are listed and discussed in this section. To load a FLASH file in a web browser from an HTML page requires some specialized tags. They are given in Script 15.3.1 for the sake of user comfort, because the two more diffuse browsers require some horrible tag attributes. Below we give a solution for an HTML *anchor* that works on *both* browsers, at least at the time of this writing!

Notice that in Script 15.3.1 the filename is flashExample.swf, supposed to be in the same directory of the HTML page, and that the *anchor* name is flashExample.

A FLASH file may contain either a *movie* or a single static *picture*, that is also considered a movie. Hence we discuss here the primitives used to generate and export from PLaSM both single pictures and simple animations.

**RGBACOLOR** The RGBACOLOR primitive of the psmlib/flash.psm predefined library, applies to number quadruples in $[0,1]^4$, i.e. in RGBA space, where $\alpha \in A$, the last color coordinate, denotes (the opposite of) *transparency*, ranging from full transparency ($\alpha = 0$) to full opacity ($\alpha = 1$). Two examples follow:

**Script 15.3.1 (Embedding a flash file into html)**

```
<A NAME="flashExample">
<OBJECT CLASSID="clsid:D27CDB6E-AE6D-11cf-96B8-444553540000" WIDTH="100%"
CODEBASE="http://active.macromedia.com/flash5/cabs/
    swflash.cab#version=5,0,0,0">
<PARAM NAME="MOVIE" VALUE="flashExample.swf">
<PARAM NAME="QUALITY" VALUE="high">
</OBJECT>

<EMBED SRC="flashExample.swf"
WIDTH="100%" PLAY="true" LOOP="true" QUALITY="high"
PLUGINSPAGE="http://www.macromedia.com/shockwave/download/
    index.cgi?P1_Prod_Version=ShockwaveFlash">
</EMBED>
</A>
```

```
DEF darkGrey = RGBACOLOR:<0.1, 0.1, 0.1, 1>;
DEF trasparentDarkGrey = RGBCOLOR:<0.1, 0.1, 0.1, 0.7>;
```

**FILLCOLOR** is used to fill the object *interior* with the specified RGBACOLOR:

```
DEF name = pol2D FILLCOLOR RGBAcolor;
```

**LINECOLOR** is used to associate the given color property to the *boundary* edges of the object:

```
DEF name = pol2D LINECOLOR RGBAcolor;
```

**ACOLOR** is used to give a color property both to the edges and to the interior of the object:

```
DEF name = pol2D ACOLOR RGBAcolor;
```

**LINESIZE** is the operator used to specify the `lineWidth` in pixels of the object edges. In this case we have:

```
DEF name = pol2D LINESIZE lineWidth;
```

**Flash** is the exporting directive for single pictures, that exports the pol2D object, visualized in a display area of `areaWidth`, to the file with name `fileName.swf`

```
Flash:pol2D:areaWidth:'fileName.swf';
```

**ACTOR** is applied to the sequence `polComplexSequence` of frames related to the same object, and then to the `startingTime` integer, that specifies the ordinal time when the object must start being visible in the movie. The duration of the action of the actor in the movie will depend on the `frameRate` parameter specified in the exporting `FlashANIM` statement.

```
DEF name = ACTOR:polComplexSequence:startingTime;
```

**FRAME** is used to generate a given 2D polyhedral complex to be visible in the movie in the (ordinal) time interval [startingTime, endingTime].

```
DEF name = FRAME:polComplex:startingTime:endingTime;
```

**FlashANIM** is the statement used to export a movie. It must be successively applied to an *animation2D* value, that must be either (a) a sequence of sequences of 2D polyhedral complexes, or (b) a sequence of ACTOR and FRAME expressions. The resulting function is applied to the areaWidth parameter (in pixels), to the 'fileName.swf' string, and finally to the frameRate integer parameter:

```
FlashANIM:animation2D:areaWidth:'fileName.swf':frameRate
```

### Example 15.3.1 (A first example)
A very simple but complete example of generation and exporting of a FLASH animation is given in Script 15.3.2. In particular, a default colored square moves translationally over a background of a yellow rectangle with black borders. As stated by the FlashANIM primitive, the animation rendering is planned for a display area 300 pixel wide at a framerate of 10 frames per second. Also, the life cycle of the FRAME generated object (the yellow rectangle), corresponds to the ordinal time interval [1, 30], whereas the mover object (the cyan square) appears at ordinal time $t = 21$ and completes its motion at ordinal time $21 + 10$. The actual movie duration is 3.1 *sec*, depending on the given framerate.

---

### Script 15.3.2 (Translating square)
```
DEF mover (tx::isInt) = T:<1,2>:<tx,5>:(CUBOID:<1,1>);
DEF moverSequence = (AA:mover:(1..10));
DEF static_rectangle = (CUBOID:<10,20> fillcolor yellow);

DEF background = FRAME:static_rectangle:1:30;
DEF actor = ACTOR:moverSequence:21;

FlashANIM:< background, actor >:300:'animation1.swf': 10;
```

---

### Example 15.3.2 (Umbrella animation)
Here we animate the opening of the wire-frame umbrella with curved rods given in Script 11.5.2. So, in the following Script 15.3.3 we start by loading the flash, vector and viewmodels libraries. The latter is needed to set-up a proj projection of the 3D wire-frame umbrella in 2D space. Two *clips* to be displayed are then defined, corresponding to the opening umbrella, and to the same but reversed frame sequence. Finally, our FLASH animation, to be rendered at a framerate = 20 in a screen area wide 200 pixels, is exported to the umbrella.swf file.

**Script 15.3.3 (Animated umbrella)**

```
DEF proj = projection: parallel: dimetric;
DEF umbrellaFun = proj ~ t:1:5 ~ umbrella:10;
DEF umbrellaFrames= aa:umbrellaFun:(2 scalarVectProd 11..80);
DEF clip1 = ACTOR:umbrellaFrames:1;
DEF clip2 = ACTOR:(REVERSE:umbrellaFrames):41;

FlashANIM:< clip1, clip2 >:200:'umbrella.swf':20;
```

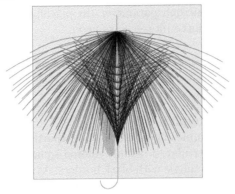

**Figure 15.6**   The set of frames used for the Flash umbrella animation

*15.3.3   Generating VRML animations*

Unlike FLASH animations, where only a basic support is currently given, to be possibly combined with the importing and editing of the generated .swf files within the FLASH interactive development environment (IDE), PLaSM offers quite sophisticated support to the design of complex VRML animations. The language may support the development of animations at three different levels:

1. by offering primitives resulting in a *hierarchical animation,* where movie clips may contain other movie clips, and are translated and scaled hierarchically on the time axis;
2. by supporting the *choreography* methodology discussed in the next section, that allows for automatical coordination of the time interaction of independently defined actors, by using network programming techniques, and by defining each clip *storyboard* as an oriented graph;
3. at a finer modeling level, a functional programming approach may define *actors as chains of operators* going from parameter spaces with smaller dimension, to spaces with higher dimension, up to the actor configuration space, even of very high dimension. The actor postures and motion can therefore be controlled at the more appropriate level, with the minimal animator effort.

Last but not least, the use of a scripting language in designing and implementing animations, allows for reuse of characters and for automatic generation of different behaviors. It is interesting to notice that the top-level animation systems contain a scripting language, like, e.g., *Maya* and *MEL*. Actually, *every* action performed in Maya runs based on *MEL* scripts. *MEL* is an integral part of Maya's overall design [LG02].

### Animation data structure

In order to insert an animation support into PLaSM, a new primitive data type *Animated Hierarchical Polyhedral Complex*, completely transparent to the user, was added to the language. We often refer in the following sections to such a data type using the abbreviation *AnimPolComplex*. We also call *clip* a data object of this type. An animated polyhedral complex is defined as a quadruple

    animpolc := < polc, id, $t_{start}$, $t_{end}$ >

where

1. polc := is a *hierarchical polyhedral complex* annotated with properties;[4]
2. id := is the unique *identifier* of the clip;
3. $t_{start}$ := is the clip *starting time*;
4. $t_{end}$ := is the clip *ending time*.

**Timeline**   A clip *timeline* is the interval $[t_{start}, t_{end}]$ of the clip representation as *AnimPolComplex*.

### Animation primitives

The set of specialized PLaSM primitives for animation modeling is introduced below. MOVE and FRAME are respectively dedicated to generating animated polyhedral complexes with a given behavior and to background objects on the scene in a specified time interval. ANIMATION is a container for non-linear editing of hierarchical animations. LOOP has the obvious meaning, SHIFT and WARP are used for hierarchical timeline translation and scaling, respectively.

**FRAME** is used for display of *static objects* is used for display of *static objects* $polc_i$ that are present on the scene only in a time interval $[t_i, t_{i+1}]$. Two patterns of usage are allowed:

    FRAME : polc : < $t_{start}$, $t_{end}$ >;
    FRAME : < $polc_1$, $polc_2$, ... , $polc_n$ > : < $t_1$, $t_2$ , ... , $t_n$ , $t_{n+1}$ >;

**MOVE**   must be orderly applied to (a) generator of *geometric data*, given as a function of real parameters (degrees of freedom); (b) *configuration data*, given as *n*-sequence of CS points; (c) *timing data*, given as an increasing sequence of *n* time values.

---

[4] In particular, annotated with the sequence of CS points to be pairwise linearly interpolated during the polyhedral complex animation, and with the name of the generating function.

```
MOVE : objfun : < par₁, par₂, ... , parₙ > : < t₁, t₂, ... , tₙ >
```

where the function `objfun` generates the object placement `objfun:par`$_i$ at $t_i$ time, and where the object configurations are linearly interpolated between the CS points `par`$_i$ and `par`$_{i+1}$ within the time interval $[t_i, t_{i+1}]$. Notice that PLaSM curves or splines can be used to generate a proper sampling of generic behavior curves.

**ANIMATION** is used as a *container* that allows *hierarchical* aggregation of both standard and animated polyhedral complexes, including nested `ANIMATION` invocations. It may also contain hierarchical operators over both standard and animated polyhedral complexes, say `STRUCT` operators and affine transformations, as well as `LOOP`, `SHIFT` and `WARP` operators discussed below.

```
ANIMATION : (pols::isseqof:(OR~[isanimpol,isfun,ispol])) → isanimpol
```

The reader should notice that the `STRUCT` operator is overloaded to the behavior of the `ANIMATION` operator, so that they are fully interchangeable. What to actually use may be mainly a matter of code self-documentation.

**LOOP and OUTERLOOP** are used to *repeat* `times` times the animated polyhedral complex `anim`. In particular, `LOOP` repeats the content of the timeline $[t_{start}, t_{end}]$, whereas `OUTERLOOP` works on $[0, t_{end}]$.

```
LOOP : (times::isint)(anim::isanimpol) → isanimpol
OUTERLOOP : (times::isint)(anim::isanimpol) → isanimpol
```

**SHIFT** applies a *timeline translation* to the animated polyhedral complex `anim` from $[t_{start}, t_{end}]$ to $[t_{start} + t, t_{end} + t]$.

```
SHIFT : (t::isnum)(anim::isanimpol) → isanimpol
```

**WARP and OUTERWARP** produce a *timeline scaling* of the `anim` parameter. In particular, `WARP` scales $[t_{start}, t_{end}]$ with the time origin as fixed point of the scaling, whereas `OUTERWARP` scales $[t_{start}, t_{end}]$ with $t_{start}$ as fixed point.

```
WARP : (t::isnum)(anim::isanimpol) → isanimpol
OUTERWARP : (t::isnum)(anim::isanimpol) → isanimpol
```

**Overloading of PLaSM primitives**

Some important predefined PLaSM geometric operators have been extended to work also with *animated* polyhedral complexes. They include:

1. affine transformation tensors: T, S, R;
2. hierarchical assembly: STRUCT
3. geometric constructors: CUBOID, MKPOL;
4. function mapping over polyhedral constructors: MAP.

The remainder of this section is dedicated to discussing some implementation details of the PLaSM animation subsystem. The standard reader may go directly to the next section for some easy animation examples.

**Animated behavior** The MOVE primitive is implemented by evaluating the geometry generation function objfun in a modified primitive PLaSM environment named *anim_env*. In such an environment a new type is defined:

$$\texttt{AnimBehaviour} := \; << \texttt{par}_1, \; \texttt{par}_2, \; \ldots \; , \; \texttt{par}_n >, \; < \texttt{t}_1, \; \texttt{t}_2, \; \ldots \; , \; \texttt{t}_n >>$$

This data type is used to manage (via the redefinition of the APPLY combinator) the parameter propagation in expression evaluation. In particular, a primitive redefined only in *anim_env*, in order to accept both its standard parameters and the ones of AnimBehaviour type, *absorbs* this parameter and creates some basic *AnimPolComplexes*. In particular, the primitive PLaSM *application*

```
f:a = APPLY:< f,a >
```

was redefined in such a way that:

$$\texttt{f} \; : \; <<\texttt{par}_1, \; \texttt{par}_2, \; \ldots \; , \; \texttt{par}_n>, \; <\texttt{t}_1, \; \texttt{t}_2, \; \ldots \; , \; \texttt{t}_n>> \; \to \; \texttt{AnimPol}$$

if the function f can accept AnimBehaviour values in *anim-env*; otherwise we have

$$\texttt{f} \; : \; << \texttt{par}_1, \; \texttt{par}_2, \; \ldots \; , \; \texttt{par}_n >, \; < \texttt{t}_1, \; \texttt{t}_2, \; \ldots \; , \; \texttt{t}_n >> \; \to$$
$$<< \texttt{f:par}_1, \; \texttt{f:par}_2, \; \ldots \; , \; \texttt{f:par}_n >, \; < \texttt{t}_1, \; \texttt{t}_2, \; \ldots \; , \; \texttt{t}_n >>$$

if f is a standard function. With this approach, the animation parameters are normally processed by all the standard PLaSM functions, until they encounter a function that supports the generation of animations, i.e. a function which can be applied to AnimBehaviour values.

**Specialized methods** Some specialized methods work with values of type Anim-Behavior:

1. anim-arg(arg::TT) returns arg if it is of AnimBehaviour type, else, if arg is a sequence <a1, ... , an>, then an AnimBehaviour with parameters <anim-arg:a1, ... , anim-arg:an> is returned; The purpose of this method is to homogenize AnimBehaviour with respect to sequences.
2. anim-pred(pred::IsFun)(arg::IsAnimBehaviour) is used to check if all arg parameters verify the pred predicate.
3. Finally we have:

$$\texttt{IsAnimBehaviourOf(pred::IsFun)(arg::TT)} \equiv \texttt{anim-pred:pred:(anim-arg:arg)}$$

**Affine transformations** The elementary affine tensors T, S and R are redefined as follows, so that they can be applied to standard polyhedral complexes as well as to animated polyhedral complexes:

```
{ T | S | R }(index::OR ~ [IsInt,IsSeqOf:IsInt])
   (par::IsAnimBehaviourOf:(OR ~ [IsNum,IsSeqOf:IsNum]))
   (pol::OR ~ [IsPol, IsAnimPol]) → IsAnimPol
```

**Geometric constructors**  The geometric constructor CUBOID may be animated by giving a value of type AnimBehaviour to its numeric parameters. Analogously, an animated behavior can be given to the points parameter of MKPOL constructor. Anyway, at least at the time of writing, the internal structure of a polyhedral complex can be animated only by animating the parameters of the embedded transformations.

> CUBOID (par::IsAnimBehaviourOf:(IsSeqOf:IsNum)) → IsAnimPol

> MKPOL (points::IsAnimBehaviourOf:(IsSeqOf:(IsSeqOf:IsNum)))
>     (cells::(IsSeqOf:(IsSeqOf:IsIntPos)))
>     (pols::(IsSeqOf:(IsSeqOf:IsIntPos))) → IsAnimPol

**Function mapping**  A (only internal) variation MAPC of the MAP primitive operator can be similarly animated, by ...

> MAPC (fun::((IsSeqOf:IsNum) → IsAnimBehaviourOf:(IsSeqOf:IsFun)))
>     (pol::IsPol) → IsAnimPol

## Simple examples

In this section we show some simple animation examples based on CS sampling. In each case the moving object must be defined as a *function* of its degrees of freedom. When some *animPolComplex* value is exported, an *animated* VRML file is appropriately generated. In particular, the VRML animation will produce a piecewise linear interpolation of adjacent configuration space points.

If a non-linear *behavior* is needed, i.e., if the object motion must correspond either to a non-linear CS path or to a non-uniform velocity, then it is always possible to linearly approximate the desired behavior with arbitrary precision by either generating a uniform point sampling of a nonlinear CS curve, or by using a non-uniform time sampling for equally spaced CS points, respectively.

### Example 15.3.3 (Rotated cube (1))

A very simple animation example is given in Script 15.3.4, where the standard unit cube is rotated about the $z$ axis. In this case we have only 1 rotational DOF, associated with the alpha parameter. In this case, the CS space is 1D, so that cube must be a function of one real parameter, and we have $(\alpha_i) = (0, \pi, 0) \subset CS$, and $(t_i) = (0, 3, 6)$. The animated VRML generated by the PLaSM interpreter gives a piecewise linear interpolation between such CS points.

---

### Script 15.3.4 (Rotated cube)

```
DEF cube (alpha::IsReal) = (R:<1,2>:alpha ∼ CUBOID):<1,1,1>;
DEF out = MOVE:cube:<0,PI,0>:<0,3,6>;

VRML:out:'out.wrl';
```

---

It is very hard to give an appropriate rendering of an animation sequence in a book. Figure 15.7 gives a frame sequence from a DV rendering of the animation of Script 15.3.4 left to right and top to bottom.

**Figure 15.7** A sequence of frames from the animated rotation of the unit cube about the $z$ axis

A rotation axis parallel to $z$ and passing for the cube centroid is used in Script 15.3.5. The reader should notice that standard tensor composition applies, where only one of the rotation parameters is used as an argument of the generating function `cube`, according to the fact that the animation has only 1 degree of freedom.

---

**Script 15.3.5 (Rotated cube (2))**

```
DEF cube (alpha::IsReal) =
    (R:<1,2>:alpha ~ T:<1,2>:<-1/2,-1/2> ~ CUBOID): <1,1,1>;
DEF out = MOVE:cube:<0,PI,0>:<0,3,6>;

VRML:out:'out.wrl';
```

---

**Example 15.3.4 (Planar robot arm)**

The planar robot arm with 3 DOFs defined in Scripts 15.1.3 and 15.2.1 is animated in Script 15.3.6 by using a CS path that is a piecewise approximation with 8 linear segments of a cubic Bézier curve defined by four CS points. Notice that:

1. the expression `Sampling:8` generates a sequence of 9 values in $[0, 1]$;
2. the `[ID]` function transforms each of them in a 1D vector;
3. the above vectors are finally mapped by the `CSpath` function into a sequence of CS points, according to the Bézier curve defined in Script 15.2.1.

---

**Script 15.3.6 (2D arm)**

```
DEF CSpoints = (AA:(CSpath ~ [ID]) ~ Sampling):8
DEF out = MOVE:arm:(CSpoints:(0..8));

VRML:out:'out.wrl';
```

---

**Example 15.3.5 (Planar motion of cube)**
A general planar motion with 3 degrees of freedom of the unit cube is produced by
Script 15.3.7, where the cube is translated along a circular path in 2D while rotated
about its own vertical axis. In particular, the CSpoints sequence used by the MOVE
primitive is generated by applying the function

$$\texttt{CScurve} : \mathbb{R} \rightarrow \mathbb{R}^3$$

to the elements of the number sequence in $[0, 2\pi]$ produced when evaluating
the expression 2*PI scalarVectProd Sampling:16. The scalarVectProd operator,
given in Script 2.1.21 returns the product of a scalar times a vector, i.e. in this case:

$$2\pi\,(0, 1/16, \dots, 15/16, 1).$$

Analogously, TimePoints contains a sampling with 17 elements of the interval $[0, 4]$,
so that the animation generated as value of the MOVE expression has a duration of 4
seconds. Notice, looking at the CScurve function, that

1. the circular path of the motion has radius $r = 2$;
2. the rotational parameter $\alpha$ is bound to the interval $\Xi_\alpha = [0, -4\pi]$.

---

**Script 15.3.7 (Planar motion)**
```
DEF movingCube (tx,ty,alpha::IsReal) = T:<1,2>:<tx,ty>:(cube:alpha);

DEF CScurve = [K:2 * COS, K:2 * SIN, - * K:2];
DEF CSpoints = AA: CScurve: (2*PI scalarVectProd Sampling:16);
DEF TimePoints = 4 scalarVectProd Sampling:16;
DEF WSpath = (polyline ~ AA:[S1,S2,K:0]): CSpoints;

DEF out = STRUCT:<
   MOVE: movingCube: CSpoints: TimePoints,
   WSpath >;

VRML:out:'out.wrl';
```

---

It is also important to note in this example that either STRUCT or ANIMATION
primitives could equally be used to define the *AnimPolComplex* out to be exported
to a VRML file.

**Example 15.3.6 (Clock animation)**
In Figure 15.9 we show four keyframes from the VRML animation generated by
Script 15.3.8.
   The *animPolComplex* movie is generated using the clock3D function defined in
Script 6.4.4. The animation *behavior* is described in this case by two <h,m> (*hour,
minute*) pairs corresponding to the starting and ending configurations, to be assumed
at 0 and 10 seconds, respectively. We note the *extreme ease* of the PLaSM approach to
animation definition.

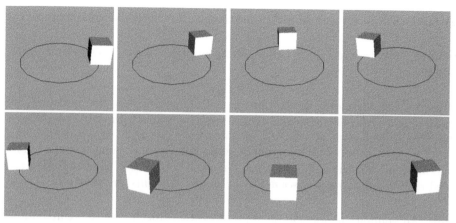

**Figure 15.8** A frame sequence from the rotating and translating cube animation

**Figure 15.9** Ten minutes in ten seconds ...

## 15.4 Motion coordination

The graph-theoretic model introduced in [BBC+99] for the design of complex animations is discussed in this section. It provides both a computer representation for the animation *storyboard* as an acyclic directed graph, and a computational technique for time coordination of independently defined animation *segments*. The graph representation and the timing algorithm make reference to the network programming method known as PERT (Program Evaluation and Revision Technique) [Rob63, Ste71] and to the CPM (Critical Path Method), respectively. Both are management techniques for complex projects that are well known to industrial engineers and production managers.

### 15.4.1 Non-linear animation

Let us start by giving some definitions of terms that are useful to connect the *choreography* approach for the control of very complex animations here presented to the methods currently used in computer animation.

---

**Script 15.3.8 (Clock animation)**

```
DEF movie = MOVE: clock3D:<<2,10>,<2,20>>:<0,10>

VRML:movie:'out.wrl';
```

---

**Background**   The scene part which is time-invariant is called the scene *background*.

**Foreground**   The time-varying portion of an animated scene is called the scene *foreground*.

**Storyboard**   The high-level description of the animation behavior is called the *storyboard*. It is represented as a hierarchical a-cyclic graph with only one node of in-degree zero (called *start* or *source* node) and only one node of out-degree zero (called *end* or *sink* node). The source node will represent the animation *start*. The sink node will represent the animation *end*. The nodes and arcs of the storyboard are also called *events* and *animation segments* (or simply *segments*), respectively.

**Segment**   An animation *segment* is an arc of the storyboard. It represents a foreground portion characterized by the fact that every interaction with the remaining animation is concentrated on the starting and ending events.

**Hierarchical animation**   Hence each segment may be modeled *independently* from the others, by using a *local* coordinate frame for both space and time coordinates. The concepts of storyboard and segment are interchangeable: each complex segment of an animation can be modeled by using a local storyboard, which can be decomposed into lower-level segments.

**Event**   An *event* is a storyboard node. Segments starting from it may begin only when *all* the segments ending in it have finished their execution.

**Segment**   The segment configuration space is defined as

$$XCS = T \times CS$$

where CS is the product space of the interval domains of segment DOFs, and $T = [0, \infty)$ is the time domain.

**Geometric model**   The *geometric model* of a segment is a description of both the assembly structure and the geometry of its elementary parts.

**Behavior**   A continuous curve in segment configuration space $XCS$ is called a *behavior* of the segment. Let

$$b : [0, 1] \to XCS, \quad \text{with } b(u) = (b_0(u), b_1(u), \dots, b_d(u))$$

be a behavior curve. Then it must be

$$b_0(u_k) > b_0(u_h) \qquad \text{for each } u_k > u_h.$$

The $d + 1$ dimension of XCS is related to the number $d$ of free parameters of the geometric model of the segment. In order to represent a behavior, sampled curves or splines of suitable degree, parametrized in the $[0, 1]$ interval, are used. A simple and

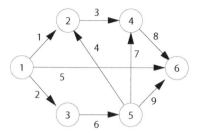

**Figure 15.10** Storyboard representation as oriented graph

often useful choice is to use Bézier curves to represent behaviors. In such a case the behavior is completely specified by a point subset in $XCS$. In particular, any Bézier curve interpolates the first and last points and approximates the other ones. The curve degree is defined by the number of points minus one. So a linear behavior will simply be described by giving two extreme points in $XCS$.

**Actor** We call an animation *actor* (or *character*) a connected chain of segments with the same geometric model and with different behaviors. So, at each given time each actor has a unique fixed set of parameters, i.e. a unique configuration.

**Choreography** In order to independently edit the developed animation segments as a whole, network programming techniques are used. In particular, the dynamic programming algorithm of critical path method is used to compute *minimal* and *maximal times* of events as well the *completing time* of the whole animation *clip*. Such an algorithm is used to compute the timing of actors in each animation segment.

*15.4.2 Network programming*

The PERT (Program Evaluation and Review Technique) [Rob63, Ste71], also known as *Critical Path Method*, is well-known for managing, i.e. programming and controlling, very complex projects and in particular for scheduling and optimum allocation of resources. Projects may have tens or hundred of thousands of activities and events.

Deterministic PERT for computation of critical activities is probably the most well known variation of network programming techniques, in which a bundle of inter-dependent activities is represented as a directed acyclic graph. Such a graph model is used as the computational basis for project analysis and forecasts.

**Storyboard representation** A storyboard is represented as a network, i.e. as a directed acyclic graph with only one source node and one sink node. The source node represents the animation start; the sink node the animation end. The arcs represent animation segments; the nodes represent the events of completion of *all* the entering arcs. Notice that segments (arcs) exiting from a node may start only when all the segments (arcs) entering that node have finished.

**Minimal and maximal spanning time** The *minimal spanning time* $(t_k)$ of a node $k$ is the *minimal* time for completing the segments entering the node $k$. Notice that

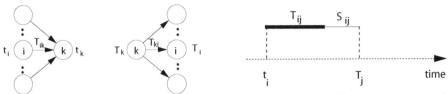

**Figure 15.11**     (a) Predecessors and successors of the $k$ event (b) Duration $T_{i,j}$ and slack $S_{i,j}$ of the $(i,j)$ segment

such segments *can* be completed into this time. The *maximal spanning time* $(T_k)$ of a node $k$ is the *maximal* time needed for completing the segments entering the node $k$. Notice that such segments *must* be completed into this time.

The algorithm to compute both minimal and maximal spanning times of nodes is very simple. The computational approach can be classified as an example of dynamic programming. Formally we have:

$$t_k = \max_{i \in \text{pred}(k)} \{t_i + T_{ik}\}, \qquad T_k = \min_{i \in \text{succ}(k)} \{T_i - T_{ki}\} \qquad (15.1)$$

The corresponding algorithm can be decomposed into a *forward computation* step and a *backward computation* step.

**Forward and backward computation**     Forward computation of minimal times $t_k$. Let 0 be the (unique) source node of the network. Set $t_0 = 0$. Then try to compute the minimal time $t_e$ of ending node, i.e. the completion time of the whole project. The recursive formula allows computing of the minimal times $t_k$ of all nodes.

Backward computation of maximal times $T_k$. Let $e$ be the (unique) sink node of the network. Set $T_e = t_e$. Then try to compute the maximal time $T_0$ of starting node. The recursive formula allows for computing the maximal times $T_k$ of all nodes.

**Segment slacks**     The *slack* $S_{ij}$ of the segment $(i,j)$ is defined as the quantity of time which may elapse without a corresponding slack of the completion time of the animation. The segment slack $S_{ij}$ is given by the formula

$$S_{ij} = (T_j - t_i) - T_{ij},$$

where $T_{ij}$ is the expected duration of segment $(i,j)$.

Notice that the so-called *critical segments* have null slacks, i.e. $S_{ij} = 0$.

## Implementation of CPM

A PLaSM implementation of CPM (Critical Path Method) is given in this section. We start (1) by preparing a small toolbox of basic functions and predicates in Script 15.4.1, then (2) we implement in Script 15.4.2 two operators `inarcs` and `outarcs` that return, respectively, the inward and outward arcs of a given node, then (3) we give in Script 15.4.3 two operators `tmin` and `tmax` to compute the minimum and maximum spanning times of nodes; and finally (4) we provide the computation of a small *storyboard* graph.

The graph is represented as follows. It is supposed that only one arc is allowed between each pair of nodes, so that the arc is identified by such ordered pair. We also suppose that the graph contains only one node of indegree 0 (the storyboard start) and only one node of outdegree 0 (the storyboard end).

The graph is here described as a set of triples, one-to-one associated with the arcs. Each triplet $(n_i, n_j, t_{ij})$ respectively contains the indices of the starting $n_i$ and ending $n_j$ node of the arc, and the scheduled duration $t_{ij}$ of the associated animation segment.

**Toolbox** Binary predicates `bigger`, `smaller`, `biggest` and `smallest` respectively return `true` if: (a) b is larger than a; (b) b is smaller than a; (c) b is the largest of `seq` elements; (d) b is the smallest of `seq` elements. They return `false` otherwise. Let us remember that the `TREE` primitive is a combinator that recursively applies a binary function over a sequence of arguments of any length.

---

**Script 15.4.1 (CPM toolbox)**
```
DEF bigger   (a,b::IsReal) = GT:a:b;
DEF smaller  (a,b::IsReal) = LT:a:b;
DEF biggest  (a,b::IsReal) = IF:< bigger, s2, s1 >:<a,b>;
DEF smallest (a,b::IsReal) = IF:< smaller, s2, s1 >:<a,b>;
DEF RMAX (seq::IsSeqOf:IsReal) = TREE: biggest: seq;
DEF RMIN (seq::IsSeqOf:IsReal) = TREE: smallest: seq;
```

---

**Operators** The partial function `inarc`:$n_i$, when applied to `arc` $\equiv$ $<n_k, n_i, t_{ki}>$ triplet, returns the sequence $<n_k, t_{ki}>$, denoting the arc as *entering* $n_i$, and the empty sequence `<>` otherwise. Analogously, partial function `outarc`:$n_i$, applied to `arc` $\equiv$ $<n_i, n_j, t_{ij}>$ triplet, returns the pair $<n_j, t_{ij}>$ for the *outgoing* arc, and `<>` otherwise. The subsets of `graph` arcs entering or leaving $n_i$ is returned by the `inarc`:$n_i$:`graph` and `outarc`:$n_i$:`graph` expressions, respectively.

The implementation in Script 15.4.2 was quick for the authors to write, but is pretty inefficient, since its complexity is $O(n^2)$, where $n$ is the number of graph nodes, so it makes sense to use only on small graphs. The reader trained in computer science may develop a more efficient solution.[5]

---

**Script 15.4.2 (Network analysis)**
```
DEF inarc (node::IsInt)(arc::IsSeq) =
   IF:< C:EQ:node ~ S2, [[s1,s3]], K:<> >:arc;
DEF outarc (node::IsInt)(arc::IsSeq) =
   IF:< C:EQ:node ~ S1, [[s2,s3]], K:<> >:arc;

DEF inarcs (node::IsInt)(graph::IsSeq) = (CAT ~ AA:(inarc:node)):graph;
DEF outarcs (node::IsInt)(graph::IsSeq) = (CAT ~ AA:(outarc:node)):graph;
```

---

[5] Hint for the other readers: just sort the arcs on either the second or first nodes, respectively.

**Algorithm**   The recursive algorithms coded in Script 15.4.3 are just a direct PLaSM translation of Formula (15.1) for the forward and the backward network computations.

---

**Script 15.4.3 (Algorithm)**

```
DEF tmin (graph::IsSeq)(node::IsInt) = RMAX:predecessorTimes
WHERE
   predecessors = inarcs:node:graph,
   predecessorTimes = IF:< C:EQ:0 ~ LEN,
      K:< Tstart >,
      AA:(+ ~ [tmin:graph ~ S1,S2]) >:predecessors
END;

DEF tmax (graph::IsSeq)(node::IsInt) = RMIN:successortimes
WHERE
   successors = outarcs:node:graph,
   successorTimes = IF:< C:EQ:0 ~ LEN,
      K:< Tstop >,
      AA:(- ~ [tmax:graph ~ S1,S2]) >: successors
END;
```

---

**Example 15.4.1 (Storyboard)**

The computation of the sequences of minimal and maximal spanning times $(t_k)$ and $(T_k)$ for the oriented graph coded by the storyBoard set of arc triples is provided by Script 15.4.4. The explicit statement of the lastNode is needed, as well as the statement of values for Tstart and Tstop times. Notice that there are some arcs with scheduled duration zero. They are called *dummy arcs* and are used to introduce coordination constraints. The reader should (1) draw the storyBoard graph; (2) label the arcs with their durations; and (3) annotate the nodes with the spanning times computed below. Notice that the total duration of our storyboard is 19 time units.

---

**Script 15.4.4 (Storyboard example)**

```
DEF storyBoard = <<0,1,2>,<1,2,5>,<2,3,3>,<3,4,4>,<1,5,0>,<6,2,0>,
   <2,7,0>,<8,3,0>,<5,6,10>,<6,7,5>,<7,8,2>>;

DEF lastNode = 4;
DEF Tstart = 0;
DEF Tstop = tmin:storyBoard:lastNode;

AA:(tmin:storyBoard):(0..8) ≡ < 0, 2, 12, 19, 23, 2, 12, 17, 19 >
AA:(tmax:storyBoard):(0..8) ≡ < 0, 2, 16, 19, 23, 2, 12, 17, 19 >
```

---

*15.4.3   Modeling and animation cycle*

Different clips can be edited (aggregated, time scaled and translated, looped, back-looped, etc.) on the movie *timeline* using the high level animation primitives discussed in Section 15.3.3. A simple but quite complete exercise with such editing primitives is given in Example 15.6.2.

The modeling and animation methodology summarized below concerns the single animation clip.

1. Clip decomposition into animation segments, and definition of the clip storyboard as a graph.
2. Modeling of geometry and behavior of the animation segments. Each segment will be modeled, animated and tested independently from each other.
3. Non-linear editing of segments by describing their events and time relationships. Segment coordination is computed by using the critical path method.
4. Simulation and parameter calibration of the animation as a whole.
5. Feedback with possible storyboard editing.
6. Starting a new cycle of modeling, editing, calibration and feedback, until a satisfying result is obtained.

### Animated lamps

In this section a complete example of scene modeling and animation is discussed. The example aims to resemble the famous *Luxo lamp* animation by Michael Kass and Andrew Witkin (see Foley *et al* [FvDFH90]). In our case two simpler lamps are moving together in animated VRML by describing a quite complex path in their configuration spaces.

The geometric models of the lamp components are generated, and the lamp assembly is defined in local coordinates. Then the storyboard of the animation is given, where the movements of the two actors are both specified and coordinated. The specification of a CS paths for one of animation segments is also given. Notice that the provided code is a quite complete working example, that runs under a PLaSM interpreter. If the reader provides the 6 missing CS curves, it may be exported to be displayed by a VRML plug-in supporting the rendering of animations.[6]

### Geometry modeling

First of all, some design parameters are defined in Script 15.4.5, in order to easily parametrize the resulting models with respect to some important design dimensions. The two lamps in our storyboard can be thus made different with respect to basis/head ratio, as happens for humans depending on age.

---

**Script 15.4.5 (Some design parameters)**
```
DEF rodHeight = 20;          DEF basisRadius = 20;
DEF rodSide = SQRT:2;        DEF basisHeight = 2;
```

---

A small toolbox of operators is given in Script 15.4.6. The function convert will transform a number sequence from degrees to radiants. The XCAT function is

---

[6] A complete coding may be found in the installed folder plasm/examples/anim/luxo.psm

a generalized version of the CAT concatenation operator. A further variation of the circle definition allows generation of *circle arcs* with variable angle a, radius r and number of approximating segments n. The truncated cone generator TrunCone depends on the bottom and top radiuses r1, r2 and on the height h, as well as on the number n of approximating facets. In addition, the Q generalized shortcut for QUOTE given in Script 1.5.5 is also used in the following scripts.

---

**Script 15.4.6 (Toolbox)**
```
DEF XCAT = CAT ~ AA:(IF:<IsSeq,ID,LIST>);
DEF convert (seq::IsSeq) = (AA:* ~ DISTL):< PI/180, seq >;
DEF circlesector (a::IsReal) (r::IsReal) (n::IsInt) =
    (S:<1,2>:<r,r>~JOIN):(MAP:([cos,sin]~s1): (intervals:a:n);

DEF TrunCone (r1,r2,h::IsReal)(n::IsInt) =
  MAP:[ x * cos ~ s2, x * sin ~ s2, z ]:
      (QUOTE:<1> * (QUOTE ~ #:n):(2*PI/n))
WHERE
    x = K:r1 + s1 * ( K:r2 - K:r1 ),
    y = K:0,
    z = s1 * K:h
END;
```

---

Then the geometric model of both the maleJoint and femaleJoint and the doubly JointedRod of the lamp are specified in Script 15.4.7, starting from the 2D halfcircular shape of halfHinge2D. Notice that the chain of infix operators in JointedRod is left-associative.

---

**Script 15.4.7 (Subcomponent modeling)**
```
DEF halfHinge2D = circlesector:PI:1:12;
DEF hinge2D = STRUCT:< halfHinge2D, T:<1,2>:<-1,-3>,Q:2 * Q:3 >;
DEF hinge = (MKPOL ~ UKPOL):(hinge2D * Q:0.5);
DEF DoubleHinge = STRUCT:<hinge, T:3:1.2, hinge>;
DEF hbasis = circle:1.2:<24,1> * Q:2;
DEF femaleJoint = STRUCT:<
    T:3:-5:hbasis, T:2:0.85,R:<2,3>:(PI/2):DoubleHinge>;
DEF maleJoint = STRUCT:< R:<2,3>:PI,
    T:3:-5:hbasis, T:2:0.25,R:<2,3>:(PI/2):Hinge>;
DEF rod = T:<1,2>:<rodSide/-2,rodSide/-2>:
    (CUBOID:<rodSide,rodSide,rodHeight>);
DEF JointedRod = maleJoint TOP rod TOP femaleJoint COLOR GREEN;
```

---

The basis object and the head generating function are given in Script 15.4.8. The function head depends on the integer parameter that specifies the number of approximating facets of TrunCone. The strange design choices of specifying basis and head so much differently, is motivated by the desire to show the great pervasiveness of AnimBehaviour type parameters (see Setion 15.3.3) through the language constructs.

And finally the Luxo generating function depending on three joint angles a1, a2

## Script 15.4.8 (Part modeling)

```
DEF basis =
    (circle:basisRadius:<32,1> * Q:basisHeight)
    TOP femaleJoint;

DEF head = STRUCT ~ [ K:maleJoint, K:(T:3:5),
    embed:1 ~ circlesector:(2*PI):4,
    TrunCone:<4,4,8>, K:(T:3:8),
    TrunCone:<4,20,20> ];
```

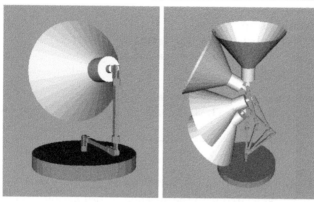

**Figure 15.12**   (a) The lamp configuration generated by (Luxo ~ convert):<-90,90,90>) (b) Some superimposed key-frames

and a3 and with red basis and white head is given in Script 15.4.9 and displayed in Figure 15.12. Remember that convert provides the degrees to radians numeric conversion.

## Script 15.4.9 (Lamp assembly modeling)

```
DEF Luxo (a1,a2,a3::IsReal) = STRUCT:<
    basis COLOR RED,
    T:3:(basisHeight+5), R:<1,3>:a1, JointedRod,
    T:3:(rodHeight+10), R:<1,3>:a2, JointedRod,
    T:3:(rodHeight+10), R:<1,3>:a3, head:32 COLOR WHITE
>;

DEF out = Luxo:(convert:<-90,90,90>);
VRML:out:'out.wrl'
```

## Motion modeling

**Actor definition**   As we know, a mobile object on the plane has 3 degrees of freedom: a rotation and two translations, to be applied in this order. The other 3 degrees of freedom are the internal joint angles. The two actors of our clip are defined in Script 15.4.10. Notice that the scaling tensor in LuxoSon is applied to the lamp model

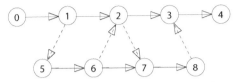

**Figure 15.13** Storyboard representation as oriented graph. Dummy arcs ($t_{ij} = 0$) are dashed

*before* applying the rotation and translation tensors.

---

**Script 15.4.10 (Mobile lamps)**

```
DEF LuxoFather (a1,a2,a3, a4,a5,a6::IsReal) = STRUCT:<
    T:1:a1, T:2:a2, R:<1,2>:a3, Luxo:<a4,a5,a6>
>;

DEF LuxoSon (a1,a2,a3, a4,a5,a6::IsReal) = STRUCT:<
    T:1:a1, T:2:a2, R:<1,2>:a3, S:<1,2,3>:<0.7,0.7,0.7>, Luxo:<a4,a5,a6>
>;
```

---

**Storyboard definition**  The clip storyboard is given as an oriented acyclic graph, with animation segments associated with the arcs and (coordination) events associated with the nodes. The expected duration of some animation segments are directly given as PLaSM definitions. In Figure 15.13 the storyboard representation as an abstract directed graph is given. A projection in $\mathbb{E}^2$ of the storyboard embedded in configuration space, corresponding to the 2 translational degrees of freedom, is given in Figure 15.13.

---

**Script 15.4.11 (Segment durations)**

```
DEF Time_0_1 = 3;        DEF Time_5_6 = 10;
DEF Time_1_2 = 5;        DEF Time_6_7 = 5;
DEF Time_2_3 = 3;        DEF Time_7_8 = 2;
DEF Time_3_4 = 4;
```

---

**Animation timing**  The minimal spanning times $t_i$ needed for starting and ending animation segments are denoted as t0, ... ,t8; The maximal spanning times $T_j$ are denoted as tt0, ... ,tt8.

Forward computation of minimal spanning times of coordination events is given in Script 15.4.12, where RMAX, RMIN are pre-defined PLaSM operators to compute maximum and minimum values of a set of reals, and are defined in Script 15.4.1. The maximal spanning times $T_i$ of nodes may be analogously computed by the functional environment of the language. The use of an explicit CPM implementation, given in Section 15.4.2, is not actually needed for moderately simple animation projects.

## Script 15.4.12 (Min forward and max backward times)

```
DEF t0 = 0;                          DEF tt0 = tt1 - Time_0_1;
DEF t1 = t0 + Time_0_1 ;             DEF tt1 = RMIN:<tt2 - Time_1_2, tt5>;
DEF t2 = RMAX:<t1 + Time_1_2, t6>;   DEF tt2 = RMIN:<tt3 - Time_2_3, tt7>;
DEF t3 = RMAX:<t2 + Time_2_3, t8>;   DEF tt3 = tt4 - Time_3_4;
DEF t4 = t3 + Time_3_4 ;             DEF tt4 = t4;
DEF t5 = t1;                         DEF tt5 = tt6 - Time_5_6;
DEF t6 = t5 + Time_5_6 ;             DEF tt6 = RMIN:<tt7 - Time_6_7, tt2>;
DEF t7 = RMAX:<t6 + Time_6_7, t2>;   DEF tt7 = tt8 - Time_7_8;
DEF t8 = t7 + Time_7_8 ;             DEF tt8 = tt3;
```

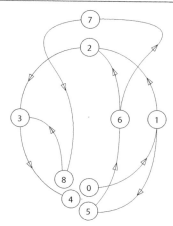

**Figure 15.14** Projection of CS paths in the coordinate subspace of basis translation parameters

**Fluidity constraint** A smooth and gracefully flowing of all animation segments in a clip is achieved if we use as starting and ending times of each MOVE expression the averages $tm_i$ of minimal and maximal spanning times of nodes. Such a fluidity constraint of the whole animation clip *holds for every possible choice of scheduled durations of animation segments* [BBC+99]. Such average times are computed explicitly in Script 15.4.13. This approach greatly helps in designing complex choreographies by using independently developed actors.

## Script 15.4.13 (Scheduled times)

```
DEF tm0 = (t0 + tt0) / 2;      DEF tm5 = (t5 + tt5) / 2;
DEF tm1 = (t1 + tt1) / 2;      DEF tm6 = (t6 + tt6) / 2;
DEF tm2 = (t2 + tt2) / 2;      DEF tm7 = (t7 + tt7) / 2;
DEF tm3 = (t3 + tt3) / 2;      DEF tm8 = (t8 + tt8) / 2;
DEF tm4 = (t4 + tt4) / 2;
```

**Segment's CS paths** For each animation segment the configuration space path must be given. This can be done, e.g., as a Bézier curve. One of them, for segment $(0, 1)$, is given in Script 15.4.14. The other CS paths can be specified similarly, by giving some points in 6-dimensional configuration space of the animation. The reader is challenged in giving by itself such paths for each non-dummy arc in animation graph, and by looking carefully at the clip results. Notice that the CS_0_1 object given below is a Bézier generating function of degree 3.

---

**Script 15.4.14 (CS paths)**

```
DEF CS_0_1 = AA:((Bezier:S1 ~ AA:XCAT):<
    <100,0, convert:<0, 0,0,0> >,
    <150,0, convert:<30, 30,0,-10> >,
    <200,50, convert:<-150, -20,90,0> >,
    <200,100, convert:<90+180, -60,105,60> >
    > );
```

---

**Clip definition**   Our Luxo's clip concerning both mobile lamps is exported to vrml by the last expression of Script 15.4.15. Notice that the xtime function is used to transform a sequence of time points into a sampling of the 1D Bézier curve generated by that points. Notice also that each non-dummy segment of the storyboard shown in Figure 15.13 corresponds to a MOVE expression in the ANIMATION container.

---

**Script 15.4.15 (Animation scripting)**

```
DEF xtime (tseq::IsSeqOf:IsReal) = (CAT ~ AA:(Bezier:(AA:LIST:tseq)));
DEF father = MOVE:LuxoFather;
DEF son = MOVE:LuxoSon;
DEF points = sampling:10;

DEF clip = ANIMATION:<
    father:(CS_0_1:points):(xtime:<tm0,tm1>:points),
    father:(CS_1_2:points):(xtime:<tm1,tm2>:points),
    father:(CS_2_3:points):(xtime:<tm2,tm3>:points),
    father:(CS_3_4:points):(xtime:<tm3,tm4>:points),

    son:(CS_5_6:points):(xtime:<tm5,tm6>:points),
    son:(CS_6_7:points):(xtime:<tm6,tm7>:points),
    son:(CS_7_8:points):(xtime:<tm7,tm7+0.6*(tm8-tm7),
        tm7+0.8*(tm8-tm7),tm8>:points)
    >;
```

---

The VRML exporting of the Luxo's clip mounted over a static and textured plane support is done in Script 15.4.16. Both TEXTURE and SIMPLETEXTURE operators are contained in the psmlib/colors.psm library. Some frames from the rendering of the exported VRML clip are given in Figure 15.15. The reader should notice that ANIMATION and STRUCT primitives may be freely nested into each other. The path of the file gioconda.jpg is relative to the plasm folder installed on the user machine. It should be suitably changed if the user has no writing permissions on the plasm folder, where the luxo.wrl is going to be exported by Script 15.4.16.

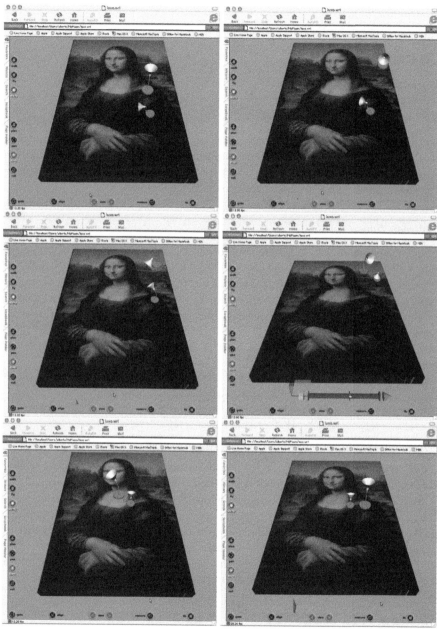

**Figure 15.15**  Some frames of our *Luxo*'s parody over Mona Lisa. In one on frames the widget for interactive control of the animation rendering is also shown. The animated VRML code generated by PLaSM is displayed using on *MacOS X* the *Cortona* plug-in by Parallelographics and Microsoft's *Internet Explorer*.

**Script 15.4.16 (VRML exporting)**

```
DEF Gioconda = SIMPLETEXTURE:'examples/color/img/gioconda.jpg';

DEF out = STRUCT:< clip,
   (T:<1,2,3>:<-8,-12,-1> ~ S:<1,2>:<16,24> ~ CUBOID):<1,1,1>
   TEXTURE Gioconda >;

VRML:out:'luxo.wrl';
```

## 15.5   Extended Configuration Space

In this section we discuss, implement and exemplify a general and simple geometrical method for solving a difficult problem: the computation of a polyhedral approximation of the *free configuration space* FP for a robot system $R$ moving in a working space containing obstacles $E$. This method was introduced in [Pao89].

### 15.5.1   Introduction

Let the *mobile system* $R \cup E \subset \mathbb{E}^d$ be composed of a set $R = \{R_i\}$ of mobile rigid parts with $k$ degrees of freedom, that we will call the *robot*, and a set $E = \{E_i\}$ of rigid *obstacles*. Both the robot and the obstacles are usually 2D or 3D. If the obstacles move along known trajectories, the whole system can be statically modeled taking time into account as an additional dimension, and by embedding the system in a 3D or 4D spacetime, respectively.

The symbol $P^d$ will be used to refer to both $R_i$ and $E_i$, being them represented as $d$–dimensional polyhedra.

Consider the configuration space $CS \subseteq \mathbb{R}^k$ and the working space $WS \subseteq \mathbb{E}^d$ of the robot. We define the *extended configuration space map* as a function

$$ECS : WS \to WS \times CS \subseteq \mathbb{R}^{d+k}.$$

The set FP of free positions of $R$ may be straightfardly computed when $ECS(R)$ and $ECS(E)$ are provided. The first term is a polyhedral encoding of all the possible placements of $R$ allowed by its degrees of freedom, whereas the second term is the result of a straight $k$-extrusion of obstacles, which do not depend on the degrees of freedom.

We like to remark that the distinction between robot and obstacles is softened in this approach. It does not make any difference if either the polyhedron $P^d$ is part of an articulated manipulator or it is an obstacle: the distinctive property is the association between objects in the scene and degrees of freedom.

### 15.5.2   Rationale of the method

The extrusion operations are defined in such a way that the point

$$q = (x_1, \ldots, x_d, t_1, \ldots, t_k) \in \mathbb{R}^{d+k}$$

belongs to $ECS(P^d) = P^{d+k}$ if and only if the projection of $q$ within the workspace, denoted as $\Pi_{\text{WS}}(q) = (x_1, \ldots, x_d)$, belongs to the placement of $P^d$ corresponding to the parameters value $(t_1, \ldots, t_k)$. We can write:

$$q \in P^{d+k} \iff \Pi_{\mathrm{WS}}(q) \in P^d \mid_{(t_1, \ldots, t_k)}$$

It follows that, if the ECS images $P_i^{d+k}$ and $P_j^{d+k}$ of $P_i^d, P_j^d \in R \cup E$ have a common point $q$, then $P_i^d$ and $P_j^d$ overlap or touch in the configurations corresponding to the last $k$ coordinates of $q$:

$$q \in P_i^{d+k} \cap P_j^{d+k} \iff \Pi_{\mathrm{WS}}(q) \in P_i^d \mid_{(t_1, \ldots, t_k)} \cap P_j^d \mid_{(t_1, \ldots, t_k)}$$

Imagine computing the intersection set of each pair

$$(P_i^{d+k}, P_j^{d+k}) \in \mathrm{ECS}(R \cup E) \times \mathrm{ECS}(R \cup E),$$

to project such sets onto CS and to take the union of the projections. This yields the *configuration space obstacles* CSO, i.e. the set of points in configuration space which correspond to prohibited configurations of the system. Recalling that *free configuration space* FP coincides with the difference between configuration space and configuration space obstacles, we conclude that FP can be computed by looking for intersections in ECS, and then by subtracting their projection from configuration space [Pao89].

In a single formula we can write:

$$\mathrm{FP} = \mathrm{CS} - \mathrm{CSO} = \mathrm{CS} - \bigcup_{i,j} \Pi_{\mathrm{CS}}(ECS(P_i^d) \cap ECS(P_j^d))$$

### 15.5.3 ECS algorithm

The conceptual skeleton of the ECS method for the computation of the free configuration space is summarized in Figure 15.16. A more detailed statement of the algorithm follows.

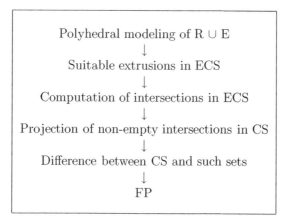

**Figure 15.16** Conceptual skeleton of the ECS method.

**Modeling step**   A suitable solid model of $R \cup E$ is given in the workspace WS. Convex decompositions are used to represent the system; this choice allows us to easily compute the ECS image of each part in the scene though the convex hulls generated by the JOIN operator.

**Extrusion step**   The image of each $P^d \in R \cup E$ in the Extended Configuration Space is computed. This results in a set of higher dimensional polyhedra $P^{d+k}$, where for each $P^{d+k}$ a convex decomposition within ECS is available.

**Intersection step**   The set intersection of each pair $P_i^{d+k}$, $P_j^{d+k}$ is computed. Such sets correspond either to auto-intersections of an articulated robot or to intersections of the latter with obstacles. Since a quasi-disjoint decomposition of the operands is given, intersection can be distributed and performed by pairwise intersecting convex cells. The intersection of convexes is a convex set, so that this step results in a set of quasi-disjoint convex cells, $\{c_i^{d+k}|c_i^{d+k} \subset \text{ECS}\}$.

**Projection step**   Each convex cell $c_i^{d+k} \subset \text{ECS}$ is projected onto CS. This process can be thought of as a sequence of $d$ elementary projections, each one performed along a coordinate direction. The result is the set

$$\{c_i^k|c_i^k = \Pi_{\text{CS}}(c_i^{d+k})\} \, .$$

Since the projection of a convex set is convex, a collection of convex sets in configuration space is obtained. Unfortunately, these are no longer quasi-disjoint, but give a set covering of configuration space obstacles.

**Difference step**   The free configuration space for the moving system $R \cup E$ is finally obtained as:

$$\text{FP} = \text{CS} - \bigcup_i c_i^k.$$

### 15.5.4   Encoding degrees of freedom

In this subsection it is discussed how to generate $ECS(R)$ and $ECS(E)$, i.e. how to encode the degrees of freedom of the mobile polyhedral system and the polyhedral scene itself within higher dimensional polyhedra.

Each one of the rigid parts which compose the robot, say $P^d$, may move according either to translational degrees of freedom only, or to rotational only, or to both translational and rotational degrees of freedom. If the position of $P^d$ depends on the value of a parameter $t_i$ ($\alpha_i$), we say that $P^d$ is *subject* to $t_i$ ($\alpha_i$). The representation $P^{d+k}$ of $P^d$, which encodes the whole set of $k$ degrees of freedom, is computed by performing an appropriate sequence of $k$ suitable extrusion operations.

### Types of extrusion

A definition of straight, linear and screw extrusions, recalled from [PBCF93], is given in the following. For each translational degree of freedom (with parameter $t_i$) and for each rotational degree of freedom (with parameter $\alpha_i$) in the scene, the following rules are applied:

1. If $P^d$ is subject to $t_i$, then an appropriate *linear extrusion* is required, which generates the whole set of positions corresponding to the translational degree of freedom (see Figure 15.17b).
2. If $P^d$ is subject to $\alpha_i$, an appropriate *screw extrusion* is performed, which generates the whole set of positions and orientations corresponding to the rotational degree of freedom (see Figure 15.17c).
3. If $P^d$ is subject neither to $t_i$ nor to $\alpha_i$, an appropriate *straight extrusion* is required, which encodes the independency of $P^d$ from the considered degree of freedom (see Figure 15.17a).

**Figure 15.17**   3D polyhedral encoding of a degree of freedom of a 2D object: (a) straight extrusion (independence on parameter) (b) linear extrusion (translational DOF) (c) screw extrusion (rotational DOF)

Notice that, according to the above rules, the sequence of extrusions to be applied to $P^d$ is partly determined by the degrees of freedom of $P^d$ itself, and partly by the degrees of freedom of other bodies in the scene.

Definitions of the straight, linear and screw extrusion operators ($E_h$, $LE_{\mathbf{v},h}$ and $SE_{\theta,i,j,h}$, respectively), are given below. As is shown, a linear extrusion can be computed by composition of a straight extrusion and of an affine transformation.

**Straight extrusion**   A *straight extrusion* is a mapping

$$E : \mathcal{P}^{d,d} \to \mathcal{P}^{d+1,d+1}$$

between polyhedral spaces, such that $P^d \mapsto P^d \times [0,1]$.

**Linear extrusion**   A *linear extrusion* is a mapping

$$LE : \mathcal{P}^{d,d} \times \mathbb{R} \to \mathcal{P}^{d+1,d+1}$$

such that $(P^d, t_i) \mapsto (\boldsymbol{H}_{d+1}(t_i) \circ E)(P^d)$, where $\boldsymbol{H}_{d+1}(t_i) \in \text{lin}\,(\mathrm{I\!R}^{d+1})$ is a *shearing* tensor with matrix $(\eta_{ij})$, where:[7]

$$
\eta_{ij} = \begin{cases} t_i, & i = 1, j = d + 1 \\ \\ \delta_{ij}, & \text{(Kröneker symbol) elsewhere} \end{cases}
\tag{15.2}
$$

**Screw extrusion**   A *screw extrusion* is a mapping

$$
SE : \mathrm{I\!R} \times N^+ \times \mathcal{P}^{d,d} \to \mathcal{P}^{d+1,d+1}
$$

where $N^+$ is the set of positive integers, and such that

$$
(\alpha, h, P^d) \mapsto SE(P^d) = P^{d+1},
$$

where $SE(P^d)$ is produced by the algorithm given below.

**Algorithm**   A sequence of computations needed to generate the dimension-independent *screw extrusion* $SE(P^d)$ of the $P^d$ polyhedron is discussed in the following.

First, the set of polyhedra

$$
\mathcal{S}^{d,d+1} = P^d \times \left\{ \frac{i}{h}, \ i = 0, \dots, h \right\},
$$

with $\mathcal{S}^{d,d+1} \subset \mathcal{P}^{d,d+1}$, called a set of *polyhedral d-slices* in $\mathrm{I\!E}^{d+1}$ space, is subject to the action of a discrete family of parametric rotation tensors

$$
\mathcal{R} = \left\{ \boldsymbol{R}_{d-1,d}\left( \alpha \frac{i}{h} \right), \ i = 0, \dots, h \right\}
$$

depending on the same parameter $i$, thus giving rise to the family of *rotated d-slices*

$$
\mathcal{RS}^{d,d+1} = \left\{ Q_i^d = \boldsymbol{R}_{d-1,d}\left( \alpha \frac{i}{h} \right) \left( P^d \times \left\{ \frac{i}{h} \right\} \right), \ i = 0, \dots, h \right\} \subset \mathcal{P}^{d,d+1}.
$$

Second, a *joinCells* operation is applied to each element of the set of pairs of rotated slices with adjacent indices, thus generating a set of *solid $(d + 1)$-dimensional layers* $S_i^{d+1}$ as the pairwise convex hulls of convex cells belonging to different hyperplanes:

$$
\mathcal{S}^{d+1,d+1} = \{ S_i^{d+1} = joinCells(Q_i^d, Q_{i+1}^d), \ i = 0, \dots, h - 1 \} \subset \mathcal{P}^{d+1,d+1}.
$$

Finally, the screw-extruded polyhedron $SE(P^d)$ is generated by quasi-disjoint union of solid $(d + 1)$-slices:

$$
SE(P^d) = \bigcup \mathcal{S}^{d+1,d+1} \in \mathcal{P}^{d+1,d+1}.
$$

---

[7] For the Kröneker symbol see Section 3.3.3.

**Implementation (1)** A dimension-independent implementation of the set of extrusion operators defined above is implemented in Scripts 15.5.1 and 15.5.2.

A slightly different strategy is used in the implementation of the $SE$ operator. In particular, the input `pol` is decomposed into a set $\{c_k\}$ of convex cells by the `SpliCells` operator given in Script 10.8.4, and a single

$$\texttt{slice} = \{c_k,\ k = 1, \dots, i_k\} \times \{0\}$$

is produced. Then a single solid `layer` is generated by pairwise `JOIN` of corresponding cells of `slice` and of a copy of it properly rotated and translated by a suitable `tensor`. Finally, the polyhedral result is obtained by `STRUCT` aggregation of properly rotated and translated copies of the single `layer`, exploiting at this purpose the `STRUCT` semantics.

The (homogeneous version of) shearing tensor $\boldsymbol{H}_{d+1}(t_i) \in \mathrm{lin}\,(\mathbb{R}^{d+1})$ described by equation (15.2), and needed to implement the $LE$ operator, is quite straightforwardly given by the `Shear` function. The `IDNT` operator, that yields the identity matrices of arbitrary dimensions, is given in Script 3.3.5.

---

**Script 15.5.1 (Extrusion toolbox)**

```
DEF Extrusion (angle::IsReal)(h::IsInt)(pol::Ispol) =
    (STRUCT ~ CAT ~ #:h):< layer, tensor >
WHERE
    slice = (AA:(EMBED:1) ~ SpliCells):pol,
    tensor = T:(d+1):(1/h) ~ R:< d - 1,d >:(angle/h),
    layer = (STRUCT ~ AA:JOIN ~ TRANS ~ [ID, AA:tensor]):slice,
    d = DIM:pol
END;

DEF Shear (t::Isreal)(pol::Ispol) = (MAT ~ Update ~ IDNT):(d+1):pol
WHERE
    update = < S1, newrow > (CONS ~ CAT) AA:SEL:(3..d+1),
    newrow = K:(<0,1> CAT #:(d - 2):0 AR t),
    d = DIM:pol
END;
```

---

**Implementation (2)** A revised definition of the *straight*, *linear* and *screw* extrusion operators is used for the implementation of EX, LEX and SEX operators given in Script 15.5.2. The purpose is to directly allow for encoding the degrees of freedom in a non-normalized fashion, using directly the *joint limits* associated with each feasibility interval $[\xi_i^{min}, \xi_i^{max}]$ of the $t_i$ or $\alpha_i$ parameters. Therefore we have:

$$EX : \mathbb{R}^2 \times \mathcal{P}^{d,d} \to \mathcal{P}^{d+1,d+1}$$

such that $((\xi_i^{min}, \xi_i^{max}), P^d) \mapsto (\boldsymbol{T}_{d+1}(\xi_i^{min}) \circ \boldsymbol{S}_{d+1}(\xi_i^{max} - \xi_i^{min}) \circ E)(P^d)$, where $\boldsymbol{T}_n(a)$ and $\boldsymbol{S}_n(b)$ respectively denote the translation and scaling tensors along the $n$-th coordinate direction. Analogously, for the linear extrusion we set

$$LEX : \mathbb{R}^2 \times \mathcal{P}^{d,d} \to \mathcal{P}^{d+1,d+1}$$

such that $((\xi_i^{min}, \xi_i^{max}), P^d) \mapsto (\boldsymbol{T}_{d+1}(\xi_i^{min}) \circ \boldsymbol{S}_{d+1}(\xi_i^{max} - \xi_i^{min}) \circ \boldsymbol{H}_{d+1}(\xi_i^{max} - \xi_i^{min}) \circ E)(P^d)$, where $\boldsymbol{H}_n(a)$ is the shearing tensor (15.2). Finally, the screw extrusion is redefined as:

$$\text{SEX} : \mathbb{R}^2 \times N^+ \times \mathcal{P}^{d,d} \to \mathcal{P}^{d+1,d+1}$$

such that $((\xi_i^{min}, \xi_i^{max}), h, P^d) \mapsto (\boldsymbol{R}_{d-1,d}(\xi_i^{min}) \circ \boldsymbol{S}_{d+1}(\xi_i^{max} - \xi_i^{min}) \circ SE)(\xi_i^{max} - \xi_i^{min}, h, P^d)$.

The above definitions of the EX, LEX and SEX operators are implemented very easily in Script 15.5.3. The reader should remember that a sequence of compositions is applied, as always, in reverse order.

---

**Script 15.5.2 (Extrusion operators)**

```
DEF EX (x1,x2::IsReal)(pol::Ispol) =
    ( T:(DIM:pol+1):x1
    ~ S:(DIM:pol+1):(x2 - x1)
    ~ Extrusion:0:1 ): pol;

DEF LEX (x1,x2::IsReal)(pol::Ispol) = ( MKPOL ~ UKPOL
    ~ T:(DIM:pol+1):x1
    ~ S:(DIM:pol+1):(x2 - x1)
    ~ shear:(x2 - x1)
    ~ Extrusion:0:1 ): pol;

DEF SEX (x1,x2::IsReal)(h::IsIntPos)(pol::Ispol) =
    ( R:<d, d - 1>:x1
    ~ S:(d + 1):(x2 - x1)
    ~ Extrusion:(x2 - x1):h ): pol
WHERE d = DIM:pol END;
```

---

**Example 15.5.1 (Straight, linear and screw extrusion)**
Three simple examples of straight, linear and screw extrusion of an empty square are produced by Script 15.5.3 and are displayed in Figure 15.18.

---

**Script 15.5.3**

```
DEF pol1 = (T:<1,2>:<-5,-5> ~ CUBOID):<10,10>;
DEF pol2 = S:<1,2>:<0.9,0.9>: pol1;
DEF pol3 = pol1 - pol2;

VRML:( EX:<0,10>: pol3):'out1.wrl';
VRML:(LEX:<0,10>: pol3):'out2.wrl';
VRML:(SEX:<0,PI>:16: pol3):'out3.wrl';
```

---

### 15.5.5 Computation of FP

In this section we discuss and implement some examples of FP computation where $\dim ECS = d + k$ is equal to 3, 4 and 5, respectively. In actual cases the embedding

**Figure 15.18**    Encoding of a DOF via straight, linear and screw extrusions
produced by EX, LEX and SEX operators

geometrical space has dimension $d \leq 4$, where $d = 4$ arises when modeling with a
spacetime approach. Conversely, $k = \dim CS$ may take an arbitrary (small) value,
depending on the structure of the moving system.

## 1D moving system ($d = 1$, $k = 2$)

Let us consider a one-dimensional moving system $R = \{R_1, R_2\}$, with both elements
equal to the unit segment $[0, 1] \subset \mathbb{R}$, and constrained to translate inside the interval
$\Xi = [0, 4]$ of the $x$ axis. Such a system has 2 degrees of freedom, defined by the
translations $t_1$ and $t_2$ of the first point of the segments.

**ECS representation**    A representation of this system in the extended space
$(x, t_1, t_2)$ is obtained as follows. The set of placements of the $R_1$ segment is given
on the plane $(x, t_1)$ by a parallelogram generated by linear extrusion of $R_1$. Since
it does not depend on $t_2$, its extended representation in $(x, t_1, t_2)$ space is given by
straight extrusion.

The computer representation with PLaSM is produced in Script 15.5.4 by applying a
suitable shearing tensor to the parallelepiped of size <1,4,4>. The dimetric projections
of the volumes $\mathcal{S}(R_1), \mathcal{S}(R_1) \subset ECS$ are produced by the last two expressions of the
script, having provided the loading of the viewmodels library.

---

**Script 15.5.4 (ECS example (1))**
```
DEF shear1 = MAT:<<1,0,0,0>,<0,1,3/4,0>,<0,0,1,0>,<0,0,0,1>>;
DEF shear2 = MAT:<<1,0,0,0>,<0,1,0,3/4>,<0,0,1,0>,<0,0,0,1>>;
DEF R1 = (shear1 ~ CUBOID):<1,4,4>;
DEF R2 = (shear2 ~ CUBOID):<1,4,4>;

projection:parallel:dimetric:R1;
projection:parallel:dimetric:R2;
```

---

A projected view of the polyhedral volume encoding the whole set of placements of
$R_1$ is shown in Figure 15.19a. The polyhedral encoding of the set of placements of $R_2$
is derived analogously, and is shown in Figure 15.19b.

A parallel projection of the set union and intersection of extended objects $\mathcal{S}(R_1)$
and $\mathcal{S}(R_2)$, produced by Script 15.5.5, respectively, is given in Figure 15.20.

Finally, in Script 15.5.5 a polyhedral representation of free positions FP is generated,
by set difference of configuration space CS and the intersections of extended obstacles

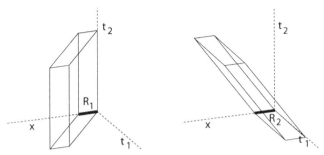

**Figure 15.19**  Representations $\mathcal{S}(R_1), \mathcal{S}(R_2) \subset ECS$ of the moving elements $R_1$ and $R_2$

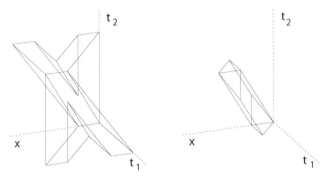

**Figure 15.20**  Set union and intersection of extended objects $\mathcal{S}(R_1)$ and $\mathcal{S}(R_2)$

projected in CS. The `project` operator, used to project a higher dimensional object onto the coordinate subspace defined by the `coords` subset of coordinate indices is also given in Script 15.5.6. The resulting FP is shown in Figure 15.21.

### 1D moving system with obstacle ($k = 2$)

Finally, we compute FP with the same approach in presence of a 1D obstacle in working space WS $= [0, 4]$. First, we assume as obstacle the interval $[2, 2.5] \subset$ WS, whose extended representation in WS $\times$ CS is given by the extended configuration space obstacle `ECSO` of Script 15.5.7. The union of intersections between the (extended representations of) mobile components and between them and `ECSO` is given by `UFP`. This extended representation of *unfeasible positions* is shown in Figure 15.22.

The FP set is finally computed in Script 15.5.7 and shown in Figure 15.23a for the $[2, 2.5]$ obstacle and in Figure 15.23b for the $[2.25, 2.75]$ obstacle.

---

**Script 15.5.5 (ECS example (2))**

```
projection:parallel:dimetric:(R1 + R2);
projection:parallel:dimetric:(R1 & R2);
```

---

**Script 15.5.6 (ECS example (3))**

```
DEF project (coords::IsSeq) =
    MKPOL ∼ [AA:((CONS ∼ AA:SEL):coords) ∼ S1, S2, S3] ∼ UKPOL;

DEF CS = CUBOID:<4,4>;
DEF FP = CS - project:<2,3>:(R1 & R2);

VRML:((STRUCT ∼ [ID, @1]):FP):'out.wrl';
```

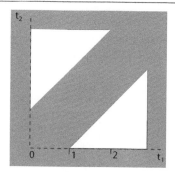

**Figure 15.21** Free configuration space FP (the white areas) for the unconstrained 1D example.

## 15.6    Examples

Some simple examples of animation and motion planning are given in this section. In particular we discuss: (a) a possible animation of or the umbrella modeling that we developed through the book; (b) a fast modeling of a *non-holonomic*, i.e. with non independent degrees of freedom, *planar motion* of a car; (c) the motion modeling of an *anthropomorphic robot* with several DOFs; (d) the *motion planning* problem that arises when solving a 2D labyrinth, by using the extended configuration space method;

### 15.6.1    Umbrella modeling (5): animation

An animation of the umbrella model defined in Script 8.5.14, and later refined in 11.5.2 and 12.6.1, is given in Script 15.6.1. Some keyframes from the generated movie are shown in Figure 15.24.

We believe it may be interesting to note that the animation effects of the umbrella model, including the extension of surface canvas and the changing curvature of rod curves, are obtained from the second line of the script, by animating *only* the umbrella opening angle, and *without any change* to the umbrella defining code given in the above

**Script 15.5.7 (ECS example (4))**

```
DEF ECSO = (T:1:2 ∼ CUBOID):<0.5,4,4>;

DEF UFP = (R1 & R2) + (R1 & ECSO) + (R2 & ECSO);
DEF FP = CS - project:<2,3>: UFP;

VRML:(FP):'out.wrl';
```

**Figure 15.22**   Extended configuration space representation of unfeasible
configurations: $UFP = ECS(CSO)$

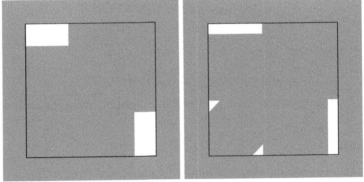

**Figure 15.23**   Free configuration space FP (the white areas) for the constrained
example: (a) 1D obstacle located at $x = 2$ (b) obstacle at $x = 2.25$

mentioned scripts. Such effects are due to the pervasiveness of values of *animBehaviour*
type trough the PLaSM code at evaluation time. We remember that the rods were
defined as Bézier curves depending on cortrol points depending in turn from the
opening angle, and analogously the canvas are Coons' patches defined by boundary
Bézier curves that are functions of the umbrella opening angle.

**Figure 15.24**   A sequence of frames from the animated umbrella opening

### 15.6.2   Non-holonomic planar motion

The example discussed in this section is aimed at illustrating a quite frequent case
of planar motion, where the degrees of freedom are non-independent. In this type of

**Script 15.6.1 (Singing in the rain)**

```
DEF clip = MOVE:(umbrella ~ [K:10, ID]):<10,50,70,80>:<0,1,2,3>;
DEF movie = (LOOP:10 ~ ANIMATION): < clip, SHIFT:3, WARP:-1:clip >;

VRML:movie:'out.wrl';
```

motion, typical of cars, the orientation of the moving body depends on the derivative of the displacement vector, i.e. on the direction of the velocity vector.

In other words, the orientation of the body, i.e. the rotational degree $\alpha(u)$ along the body's trajectory, depends on the derivative of the translational degrees $(c_x(u), c_y(u))$, seen as the smooth coordinate functions of a point-valued map $c(u)$ of a real parameter, i.e. as a smooth curve. In particular, we have:

$$c : [0,1] \to \mathbb{R}^2, \quad \text{with} \quad c(u) = (c_x(u), c_y(u)), \quad \text{and} \quad (\phi \circ c')(u) = \alpha(u)$$

where

$$\phi : \mathbb{R}^2 \to [-\pi, \pi], \quad \text{with} \quad \phi(c(u)) = \text{sign}\left(\frac{c'_y(u)}{\|c(u)\|}\right) \text{acos}\left(\frac{c'_x(u)}{\|c(u)\|}\right).$$

**Implementation** The PLaSM implementation of this kind of planar motion is quite easy, and is given in Script 15.6.2. The Vect2DToAngle operator is a direct implementation of the $\phi$ function above. When $\phi$ is applied to a vector in $\mathbb{R}^2$, it returns the angle that the vector gives with the $x$ axis. Notice that the UnitVect operator is given in Script 3.2.4, and that the ACOS predefined function returns the angle whose cosine is equal to the actual function argument.

The tangent operator, where D is the Fréchet derivative given in Script 5.2.15, when applied to a sequence of coordinate functions of a curve map, returns the sequence of coordinate functions of the derivate map.

Finally, the Curve2CSpath operator, which stands for *"from curve to configuration space path"*, when applied to a 2D curve generating sequence $c$, returns a function that, applied to some $u$ point in $[0,1]$, gives back the $(\alpha(u), c_x(u), c_y(u))$ configuration space point.

**Script 15.6.2 (From 2D curve to CS)**

```
DEF Vect2DToAngle = SIGN ~ S2 * ACOS~S1 ~ UnitVect;
DEF tangent (f::IsSeqOf:IsFun)(a::IsSeqOf:IsReal) = CONS:(D:f:a):<1>;
DEF Curve2CSpath (curve::IsSeqOf:IsFun) =
    AL ~ [Vect2DToAngle ~ tangent:curve, CONS:curve];
```

**Note** We note that the Curve2CSpath operator, when applied to some *arbitrary* 2D curve generating sequence $c$, returns the vector-valued function $(\phi \circ c', c) : \mathbb{R} \to \mathbb{R}^3$, such that $(\phi \circ c', c)(u) \in CS$ for each $u \in [0,1]$. In conclusion, we can say that the discussed planar non-holonomic motion is completely modeled by the map

Curve2CSpath given below, from the set of *trajectory* curves in working space[8] to the set of CS curves:

$$\texttt{Curve2CSpath} \equiv (\phi \circ \mathrm{D}, \mathrm{id}) : ([0,1] \to \mathbb{R}^2) \to ([0,1] \to \mathbb{R}^3),$$

where $D$ is the derivative operator.

### Example 15.6.1 (Our red "Ferrari")

A (very) simplified *dream car* is modeled and animated in Scripts 15.6.3 and 15.6.4, respectively. In particular, Ferrari is the mobile object generating function depending on three real parameters, where mover is a properly transformed instance of the extruded car defined in Script 6.2.5. In this case the reader is asked to give his/her own implementation of the mobile object, since the Curve2CSpath operator suitably applies to every planar motion of a rigid body. The background object is a container for the image of the trajectory, given in Script 15.6.4, and a supporting white rectangle.

---

**Script 15.6.3 (Ferrari example (1))**

```
DEF Ferrari (alpha,tx,ty::IsReal) =
    (T:<1,2>:<tx,ty> ~ R:<1,2>:alpha):mover
WHERE
    mover = (T:2:0.15~R:<2,3>:(PI/2)~S:<1,2>:<-1/8,1/8>~T:1:-1.5):car
END;

DEF background = STRUCT:<
    (T:<1,2>:<-1,-1> ~ CUBOID):<7,5> COLOR WHITE,
    MAP:trajectory:(Intervals:1:40)
>;
```

---

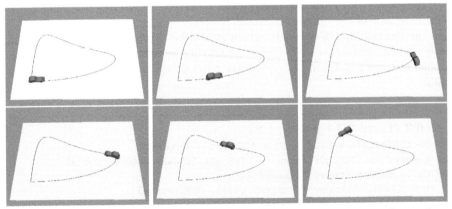

**Figure 15.25**   A frame sequence from the motion of a planar mover (our red "Ferrari") on a given trajectory

The motion of our red Ferrari is modeled in Script 15.6.4, where the *animated*

---

[8] Here we use the Robotics term for the space where the mover acts.

*polyhedral complex* produced by the evaluation of the out symbol is exported into the VRML file named out.wrl. A sequence of frames from the animation rendering produced by the *Cortona* Plug-in and *MS Internet Explorer* is shown in Figure 15.25.

The example trajectory is a Bezier curve of degree 5 generated by six 2D points. The CSpath is a piecewise linear approximation with 20 segments of the corresponding CS curve. The sampling operator is given and discussed in Script 15.2.1. Finally, the uniform timing of the animation is specified by the Timepath real sequence, for a total duration of 5 seconds. The scalarVectProd operator, for the product of a scalar times a vector, is given in Script 2.1.20.

---

**Script 15.6.4 (Ferrari example (2))**

```
DEF trajectory = Bezier:S1:<<0,0>,<8,0>,<5,5>,<2,-3>,<0,8>,<0,0>>;
DEF CSpath = (AA:(Curve2CSPath:trajectory ~ [ID]) ~ Sampling):20;
DEF Timepath = 5 scalarVectProd Sampling:20;

DEF out = STRUCT:< background,
   MOVE: Ferrari: CSpath: Timepath >;

VRML:out:'out.wrl';
```

---

**Project hint**  It might be interesting to note, as a project hint to the reader, that by reparametrizing the trajectory for $s \in [0, L]$, where $s$ is the *curvilinear abscissa* and

$$L = \int_{trajectory} ds$$

is the total length of the trajectory, the animation would linearly approximate the actual speed of the mobile object, for every arbitrary time sampling distribution into the increasing sequence Timepath.

### 15.6.3  *Anthropomorphic robot with* 29 *degrees of freedom*

The aim of this section is to show an easy strategy to reduce the number of parameters that an animation depends on, and to discuss the very high-level PLaSM operators used to develop a *hierarchical animation* (see Section 15.3.3). For this purpose we consider a 3D articulated moving system with several degrees of freedom, say the Robot object defined in Script 15.6.5, that we already introduced as the hierarchical body structure given in Script 8.5.9.

**Implementation**  The Robot function given in Script 15.6.5 is an explicitly parametrized version of the body object of Script 8.5.9. In this case, each formal parameter is a sequence of real numbers, denoting the subset of degrees of freedom associated with each body joint. The reader is referred to Section 8.5.2 for a discussion of the semantics of the articulated system. Just note here that the Torso is used as root of the tree of Robot links, and that there are 5 kinematics chains. The functions top_limb, upper_limb and lower_limb can be found in Section 8.5.2.

**Script 15.6.5 (Robot definition)**

```
DEF Robot( dofNeck, dofHead,
    dofShoulderR, dofElbowR, dofWristR,
    dofShoulderL, dofElbowL, dofWristL,
    dofHipR, dofKneeR, dofAnkleR, dofToeR,
    dofHipL, dofKneeL, dofAnkleL, dofToeL::IsSeqOf:IsNum ) =
STRUCT:< torso,
    (joint1 ~ top_limb):< dofNeck, dofHead >,
    (joint2 ~ upper_limb):< dofShoulderR, dofElbowR, dofWristR >,
    (joint3 ~ upper_limb):< dofShoulderL, dofElbowL, dofWristL >,
    (joint4 ~ lower_limb):< dofHipR, dofKneeR, dofAnkleR, dofToeR >,
    (joint5 ~ lower_limb):< dofHipL, dofKneeL, dofAnkleL, dofToeL >>
WHERE
    torso = T:<1,2>:<-5,-5>:torso_shape,
    joint1 = T:3:30,
    joint2 = T:<1,3>:<6,30>,
    joint3 = T:<1,3>:<-6,30>,
    joint4 = T:1:4,
    joint5 = T:1:-4
END;
```

**Interpolators** In some animation system the variables, defining a mapping from the standard unit interval to the interval of joint limits of some degree of freedom, are called *interpolators*.

Actually, an interpolator can be seen as a higher-level degree of freedom, and a complex motion, say a curve living in a high dimensional space $CS = \Xi^k$, can always be reduced to a curve living in a lower-dimensional configuration space $[0,1]^h$ defined by $h << k$ interpolators.

Two quite simple motions of our Robot with 29 degrees of freedom, specified by using a single interpolator, are defined in the following Example 15.6.2. Clearly, a finer control of the motion could be achieved by using an higher number of interpolators.[9]

**Example 15.6.2 (Gymnastic exercises)**
A function Exercise1 of a single real parameter cx is defined in Script 15.6.6 by referencing the Robot function given in Script 15.6.5 with actual parameters depending on cx, supposed to be in the interval $[0,1]$. It is clear that cx is an *interpolator* variable, as defined above. Notice that only 4 joint variables of Robot are affected by the cx interpolator, whereas the other 25 are set to some fixed values, and in this case are all set to zero. It is quite easy, by looking at Robot definition and at Figure 15.26 to recognize the type of motion.

Another gymnastic exercise of our Robot is defined in Script 15.6.7, where a single interpolator cx now defines a (linear) curve in a 16-dimensional CS subspace.

A hierarchical animation of the Robot generating function is defined bottom-up in Script 15.6.8:

---

[9] And, for the sake of animator' happiness, by connecting them to interactive widgets in the animation system interface.

**Script 15.6.6 (Exercise 1)**

```
DEF Exercise1(cx::IsNum) = Robot:<
    <0,0>,<0,0,0>,<0,150*cx,0>,<0,0>,<0>,<0,-150*cx,0>,<0,0>,<0>,
    <0,45*cx,0>,<0>,<0>,<0>,<0,-45*cx,0>,<0>,<0>,<0> >;
```

**Script 15.6.7 (Exercise 2)**

```
DEF Exercise2(cx::IsNum) = Robot:<
    <0,5*Cx>,<0,5*Cx,20 - 40*Cx>,<-30 + 60 * Cx,0,0>,<30 - 30*Cx,0>,<0>,
    <30 - 60 * Cx,0,0>,<30 * Cx,0>,<0>,
    <20 - 40 * Cx,0,0>,<-20 * Cx>,<-20 + 40 * Cx>,<20 * Cx>,
    <-20 + 40 * Cx,0,0>,<-20 + 20 * Cx>,<20 - 40 * Cx>,<20 - 20 * Cx> >;
```

1. By setting, at the deepest hierarchical level, two clips of `AnimPolComplex` type, called `clip1` and `clip2`, by using the `MOVE` animation primitive.
2. Defining, at a higher level, two more complex clips, produced by joining, within two adjacent *time segments* $[0,1]$ and $[1,2]$, one instance of `clip1` and one back-reversed copy of it, and analogously for `clip2`. The *reflection* of timeline is produced by the `WARP` primitive with $-1$ argument.
3. Each one of such double clips with timeline $[0,2]$ is looped 5 times, yielding two longer clips with timeline $[0,10]$.
4. At the highest hierarchical level, three clips with timeline $[0,10]$, $[0,1]$ and $[0,10]$, respectively, are mounted together. The second one is generated by the `FRAME` primitive, locking the `Robot` for 1 seconds in the configuration produced by `Exercise1:0`. The pasting of the three clips is performed by the timeline translations produced by the `SHIFT` primitive.

**Script 15.6.8 (Hierarchical animation)**

```
DEF clip1 = MOVE: Exercise1 :<0,1>: <0,1>;
DEF clip2 = MOVE: Exercise2 :<1,0>: <0,1>;

DEF movie = LOOP:10:(
    ANIMATION:<
        LOOP:5:(
            ANIMATION:< clip1, SHIFT:1, WARP:-1:clip1 >),
        SHIFT:10,
        FRAME:( Exercise1:0 ):<0,1>,
        SHIFT:1,
        LOOP:5:(
            ANIMATION:< clip2, SHIFT:1, WARP:-1:clip2 >)
    >);

VRML:movie:'out.wrl';
```

**Note**  It is important to remark that the semantics of the `ANIMATION` primitive closely resembles the one of the `STRUCT` primitive.

In particular, a *timeline transformation*, say a `SHIFT:`$t$ or `WARP:`$t$ tensor, can be either directly applied to a clip (*animPolComplex*), or inserted within the sequence argument of some `ANIMATION` primitive. In the latter case each timeline transformation applies to all clips that follow it in the sequence, exactly as done by affine transformations within a `STRUCT` sequence. The *animPolComplex* object called `movie` in Script 15.6.8 is a good example of this semantics.

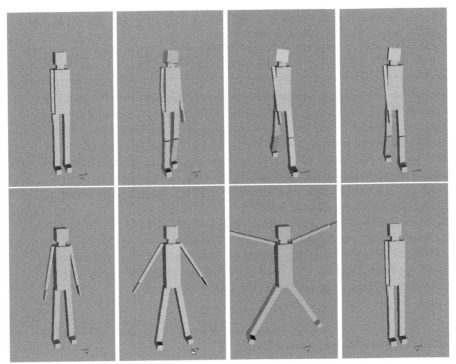

**Figure 15.26**   A frame sequence from robot's gymnastic exercises

### 15.6.4   *Solving a 2D labyrinth*

A 2D labyrinth, where a path connecting the entrance and the exit must be found, provides an interesting example for planning the motion of a mobile object moving amidst obstacles.

### Labyrinth modeling

In Script 15.6.9 we give a general method to produce geometric models of rectangular labyrinths by assembly predefined rectangular cells. In particular four cells models `c1`, `c2`, `c3` and `c4` are defined, that are displayed in Figure 15.27. A `coding` matrix using integers from $\{1, 2, 3, 4\}$ is then given, that codifies the desired labyrinth layout. The operators `Q` and `optimize` are defined in Scripts 1.5.5 and 6.5.2, respectively.

The transformation from the `coding` integer scheme to the 2D polyhedral complex

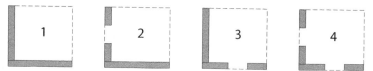

**Figure 15.27**   The four cells used for labyrinth assembly

**Script 15.6.9 (Labyrinth (1))**

```
DEF c1 = STRUCT:< Q:10 * Q:1, Q:1 * Q:<-1,9> >;
DEF c2 = STRUCT:< Q:10 * Q:1, Q:1 * Q:<-1,3,-3,3> >;
DEF c3 = STRUCT:< Q:<4,-3,3> * Q:1, Q:1 * Q:<-1,9> >;
DEF c4 = STRUCT:< Q:<4,-3,3> * Q:1, Q:1 * Q:<-1,3,-3,3> >;

DEF cellTypes = <c1,c2,c3,c4>;

DEF coding = <
  <1,1,4,2,4,1,2,1,2,2,3,1>,
  <3,2,2,3,3,4,4,4,3,4,3,2>,
  <2,1,2,2,2,3,3,1,2,1,2,1>,
  <1,2,1,2,2,2,3,3,2,4,2,2>,
  <3,4,2,4,3,4,1,1,4,3,3,2>,
  <1,1,4,3,3,3,3,4,3,1,2,2>,
  <2,2,2,3,3,3,2,3,3,1,4,2>,
  <1,1,2,1,2,1,2,1,2,1,2,1>>;
```

Labyrinth is given in Script 15.6.10. In this case, the coding matrix is first transformed into a CellArray matrix, whose elements are taken from the cellTypes set. Then, a polyhedral complex Assembly is generated from CellArray, by suitably inserting horizontal and vertical translation tensor generators T:1 and T:2 and STRUCT operators between CellArray elements. Finally, the Labyrinth model is completed by adding the topmost border1 and right-hand border2.

**Script 15.6.10 (Labyrinth (2))**

```
DEF CellArray = (CONS ~ AA:(CONS ~ AA:SEL)): coding: cellTypes;

DEF Assembly = (assemblyRows ~ AA:singleRow): CellArray
WHERE
    singleRow = STRUCT ~ CAT ~ AA:[ID, T:1 ~ SIZE:1],
    assemblyRows = STRUCT ~ CAT ~ AA:[ID, T:2 ~ - ~ SIZE:2]
END;

DEF border1 = Q:120 * Q:<-80,1>;
DEF border2 = Q:<-120,1> * Q:<34,-3,44>;
DEF Labyrinth = (optimize ~ STRUCT):< border1, T:2:70:Assembly, border2 >;

VRML:Labyrinth:'out.wrl'
```

The PLaSM code in Script 15.6.10 can easily be abstracted to give labyrinths of arbitrary dimensions starting from arbitrary sets of cells, with the only constraint that cells on the same row have the same height. We leave this task to the advanced

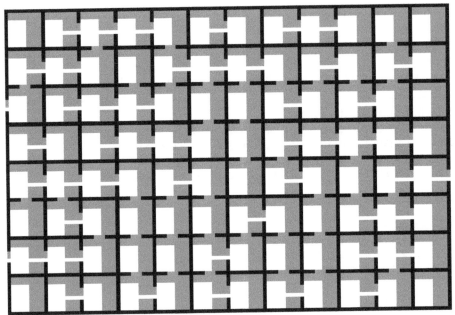

**Figure 15.28**  A 2D labyrinth (black) and the free configuration space (white) for a moving rectangle CUBOID:<4,2> with 2 translational DOFs *only*. The gray areas are the grown obstacles. The labyrinth's entrances are unconnected in FP, hence an admissible motion between them does not exist

reader of the book. We just note that the borders and the parameter of tensor T:2:70 must be suitably computed at this purpose.

### Translational motion

An early geometric technique, was developed by Lozano-Perez and Wesley [LPW79] for planning the collision-free motion of a 2D convex body translating amidst polygonal obstacles. Their approach reduces to planning the motion of a *single point* moving amidst a *grown* version of the obstacles, that is obtained as Minkowski sum of the obstacles and the moving body.

In Section 14.6 we defined the OFFSET operator as the Minkowski sum of a polyhedral complex with a rectangular parallelotope. Hence, if we suppose our mobile body to be defined as CUBOID:<4,2>, we can compute the *grown obstacles* and the free configuration space FP as done in Script 15.6.11.

---

**Script 15.6.11 (Labyrinth (2))**

```
DEF fp = (BOX:<1,2> - OFFSET:<-4,-2>):labyrinth ;

DEF out = STRUCT:< fp COLOR white, labyrinth COLOR black >;
VRML: out:'out.wrl';
```

---

The resulting out object is shown in Figure 15.28. As it is easy to see, FP is not path-connected, so that no solution exists for a translational motion of our horizontal rectangle with size $4 \times 2$. The reason is quite obvious: the width of the mobile body is larger than the passages between vertically adjacent labyrinth cells, so that only horizontal translations are allowed.

### General 2D motion

Let us suppose now that our mobile rectangle is also allowed to rotate about its local origin, with angle $\alpha \in [-\pi/2, +\pi/2]$, i.e. between $-45$ and $+45$ degrees. In this case it will be able to pass across both horizontal and vertical doors in the labyrinth.

In Script 15.6.12 we compute FP under this new assumption. First, we compute the extended representations ECSmover and ECSobstacles of the mobile body and the Labyrinth, respectively. Then we compute by intersection the set UFP of unfeasible positions. Finally, FP is given by subtracting from CS the projection of the unfeasible position set.

The EX, LEX and SEX operators, for straight, linear and screw extrusion, respectively, are given in Script 15.5.2. Every path in the path-connected FP component between the labyrinth entrances gives a feasible motion between the start and goal configurations of our mover object.

---

**Script 15.6.12 (Labyrinth (3))**

```
DEF ECSmover = (dof3 ~ dof2 ~ dof1): mover
WHERE
    dof1 = R:<1,2>:(pi/-2) ~ SEX:<pi/-2,pi/2>:6,
    dof2 = LEX:<0,121>,
    dof3 = LEX:<0,81>,
    mover = CUBOID:<4,2>
END;

DEF ECSobstacles = (dof3 ~ dof2 ~ dof1):Labyrinth
WHERE
    dof1 = EX:<pi/-2,pi/2>,
    dof2 = EX:<0,121>,
    dof3 = EX:<0,81>
END;

DEF UFP = ECSmover & ECSobstacles;
DEF CS = (T:3:(PI/-2) ~ CUBOID):< 121, 81, PI >;
DEF FP = CS - project:<3,4,5>: UFP;

VRML:(FP struct @1:CS):'out.wrl';
```

---

The reader should note that our result is only a polyhedral — and regularized — approximation of the true FP set. Also, as it is well known to computer scientists and computational geometers [HSS84, SS90], the FP computation is $PSPACE$ hard for an arbitrary number of moving rectangles. Thus, it remains tractable only for very simple settings, such as the one discussed in this section.

# Appendix A

# Definition of MyFont

The coding of our simplified vector font named `MyFont` is given in this appendix. Most characters are generated as a `struct` aggregation of polylines. Notice that only the printable ASCII subset between ordinal values 32 and 126 is given.

### Script A.0.13

```
DEF MyFont = <
    ascii32, ascii33, ascii34, ascii35, ascii36, ascii37, ascii38, ascii39, ascii40, ascii41,
    ascii42, ascii43, ascii44, ascii45, ascii46, ascii47, ascii48, ascii49, ascii50, ascii51,
    ascii52, ascii53, ascii54, ascii55, ascii56, ascii57, ascii58, ascii59, ascii60, ascii61,
    ascii62, ascii63, ascii64, ascii65, ascii66, ascii67, ascii68, ascii69, ascii70, ascii71,
    ascii72, ascii73, ascii74, ascii75, ascii76, ascii77, ascii78, ascii79, ascii80, ascii81,
    ascii82, ascii83, ascii84, ascii85, ascii86, ascii87, ascii88, ascii89, ascii90, ascii91,
    ascii92, ascii93, ascii94, ascii95, ascii96, ascii97, ascii98, ascii99,ascii100,ascii101,
    ascii102, ascii103, ascii104, ascii105, ascii106, ascii107, ascii108, ascii109, ascii110,
    ascii111, ascii112, ascii113, ascii114, ascii115, ascii116, ascii117, ascii118, ascii119,
    ascii120, ascii121, ascii122, ascii123, ascii124, ascii125, ascii126
>
WHERE
p = struct ~ AA:polyline ,
%   % ascii32 = (embed:1 ~ mkpol):<<<0>>,<<1>>,<<1>>>;
% ! % ascii33 = p:<<<1.75,1.75>,<1.75,5.5>>> struct T:2:0.5:ascii46;
% " % ascii34 = ascii39 struct T:1:1:ascii39;
% # % ascii35 = ascii61 struct p:<<<1.25,1.75>,<1.75,4>>,<<2.25,1.75>,<2.75,4>>>;
% $ % ascii36 = ascii83 struct p:<<<2,-0.5>,<2,6.5>>>;
% % % ascii37 = struct:<T:1:0.5:ascii46, T:2:5.5:ascii46, p:<<<1,0>,<3,6>>>>;
% & % ascii38 = p:<<<4,1>,<3,0>,<1,0>,<0,1>,<0,2>,<1,3>,<2,3>,<3,4>,<3,5>,<2,6>,<1,5>,<1,4>,<3,2>,<4,2>>>;
% ' % ascii39 = p:<<<1,4>,<2,5>,<2,5.5>>> struct T:2:5.5:ascii46;
% ( % ascii40 = p:<<<2,0>,<1,1>,<0.5,3>,<1,5>,<2,6>>>;
% ) % ascii41 = p:<<<2,0>,<3,1>,<3.5,3>,<3,5>,<2,6>>>;
% * % ascii42 = ascii43 struct (T:<1,2>:<2,3> ~ R:<1,2>:(PI/4) ~ T:<1,2>:<-2,-3>):ascii43;
% + % ascii43 = p:<<<1,3>,<3,3>>,<<2,2>,<2,4>>>;
% , % ascii44 = T:2:-5:ascii39;
% - % ascii45 = p:<<<1,3>,<3,3>>>;
% . % ascii46 = p:<<<2,0>,<2,0.5>,<1.5,0.5>,<1.5,0>,<2,0>>>;
% / % ascii47 = p:<<<1,0>,<3,6>>>;
% 0 % ascii48 = ascii79 struct p:<<<0,1>,<4,5>>>;
% 1 % ascii49 = p:<<<0,4>,<2,6>,<2,0>>,<<0,0>,<4,0>>>;
% 2 % ascii50 = p:<<<0,4>,<0,5>,<1,6>,<3,6>,<4,5>,<4,4>,<0,0>,<4,0>>>;
% 3 % ascii51 = p:<<<0,6>,<4,6>,<2,4>,<4,2>,<4,1>,<3,0>,<1,0>,<0,1>,<0,2>>>;
% 4 % ascii52 = p:<<<4,1>,<0,1>,<4,6>,<4,0>>>;
% 5 % ascii53 = p:<<<4,6>,<0,6>,<0,4>,<3,4>,<4,3>,<4,1>,<3,0>,<1,0>,<0,1>,<0,2>>>;
% 6 % ascii54 = p:<<<4,6>,<1,6>,<0,5>,<0,1>,<1,0>,<3,0>,<4,1>,<4,3>,<3,4>,<1,4>,<0,3>>>;
% 7 % ascii55 = p:<<<0,5>,<0,6>,<4,6>,<0,0>>>;
% 8 % ascii56 = (struct ~ [ID,T:2:3] ~ p):<<<1,0>,<3,0>,<4,1>,<4,2>,<3,3>,<1,3>,<0,2>,<0,1>,<1,0>>>;
```

*Geometric Programming for Computer-Aided Design* Alberto Paoluzzi
© 2003 John Wiley & Sons, Ltd  ISBN 0-471-89942-9

```
% 9 % ascii57 = p:<<<0,0>,<3,0>,<4,1>,<4,5>,<3,6>,<1,6>,<0,5>,<0,3>,<1,2>,<3,2>,<4,3>>>;
% : % ascii58 = (struct ~ [T:2:1,T:2:3]):ascii46 ;
% ; % ascii59 = (struct ~ [T:2:3 ~ S1,T:2:0.5 ~ S2]):<ascii46, ascii44> ;
% < % ascii60 = p:<<<3,6>,<0,3>,<3,0>>>;
% = % ascii61 = p:<<<1,2.5>,<3,2.5>>,<<1,3.5>,<3,3.5>>>;
% > % ascii62 = p:<<<1,6>,<4,3>,<1,0>>>;
% ? % ascii63 = ascii46 struct p:<<<1.75,1>,<1.75,2.75>,<3,4>,<3,5>,<2,6>,<1,6>,<0,5>,<0,4>>>;
% @ % ascii64 = p:<<<4,0>,<1,0>,<0,1>,<0,3>,<1,4>,<3,4>,<4,3>,<4,1>,<2,1>,<1,2>,<2,3>,<3,2>,<2,1>>>;
% A % ascii65 = p:<<<0,0>,<0,5>,<1,6>,<3,6>,<4,5>,<4,0>>, <<0,2>,<4,2>>>;
% B % ascii66 = p:<<<0,0>,<0,6>,<3,6>,<4,5>,<4,4>,<3,3>,<4,2>, <4,1>,<3,0>,<0,0>>,<<0,3>,<3,3>>>;
% C % ascii67 = p:<<<4,1>,<3,0>,<1,0>,<0,1>, <0,5>,<1,6>,<3,6>,<4,5>>>;
% D % ascii68 = p:<<<0,0>,<0,6>,<3,6>,<4,5>,<4,1>,<3,0>,<0,0>>>;
% E % ascii69 = p:<<<4,0>,<0,0>,<0,6>,<4,6>>,<<0,3>,<3,3>>>;
% F % ascii70 = p:<<<0,0>,<0,6>,<4,6>>,<<0,3>,<3,3>>>;
% G % ascii71 = p:<<<2,3>,<4,3>,<4,1>,<3,0>,<1,0>,<0,1>, <0,5>,<1,6>,<3,6>,<4,5>>>;
% H % ascii72 = p:<<<0,0>,<0,6>>,<<4,6>,<4,0>>,<<0,3>,<4,3>>>;
% I % ascii73 = p:<<<2,0>,<2,6>>,<<1,0>,<3,0>>,<<1,6>,<3,6>>>;
% J % ascii74 = p:<<<0,1>,<1,0>,<2,0>,<3,1>,<3,6>>,<<2,6>,<4,6>>>;
% K % ascii75 = p:<<<4,6>,<0,3>,<4,0>>,<<0,0>,<0,6>>>;
% L % ascii76 = p:<<<4,0>,<0,0>,<0,6>>>;
% M % ascii77 = p:<<<0,0>,<0,6>,<2,4>,<4,6>,<4,0>>>;
% N % ascii78 = p:<<<0,0>,<0,6>,<4,2>,<4,0>,<4,6>>>;
% O % ascii79 = p:<<<4,1>,<3,0>,<1,0>,<0,1>, <0,5>,<1,6>,<3,6>,<4,5>,<4,1>>>;
% P % ascii80 = p:<<<0,0>,<0,6>,<3,6>,<4,5>,<4,3>,<3,2>,<0,2>>>;
% Q % ascii81 = p:<<<4,1>,<3,0>,<1,0>,<0,1>, <0,5>,<1,6>,<3,6>,<4,5>,<4,1>>,<<3,1>,<4,0>>>;
% R % ascii82 = p:<<<0,0>,<0,6>,<3,6>,<4,5>,<4,3>,<3,2>,<0,2>>, <<3,2>,<4,0>>>;
% S % ascii83 = p:<<<0,1>,<1,0>,<3,0>,<4,1>,<4,2>,<3,3>,<1,3>,<0,4>,<0,5>,<1,6>,<3,6>,<4,5>>>;
% T % ascii84 = p:<<<2,0>,<2,6>>,<<0,6>,<4,6>>>;
% U % ascii85 = p:<<<0,6>,<0,1>,<1,0>,<3,0>,<4,1>,<4,6>>>;
% V % ascii86 = p:<<<0,6>,<2,0>,<4,6>>>;
% W % ascii87 = p:<<<0,6>,<0,3>,<1,0>,<2,3>,<3,0>,<4,3>,<4,6>>>;
% X % ascii88 = p:<<<0,0>,<4,6>>,<<0,6>,<4,0>>>;
% Y % ascii89 = p:<<<0,6>,<2,2>,<4,6>>,<<2,2>,<2,0>>>;
% Z % ascii90 = p:<<<0,6>,<4,6>,<0,0>,<4,0>>>;
% [ % ascii91 = p:<<<2,0>,<1,0>,<1,6>,<2,6>>>;
% \ % ascii92 = p:<<<1,6>,<3,0>>>;
% ] % ascii93 = p:<<<2,0>,<3,0>,<3,6>,<2,6>>>;
%   ^
%     % ascii94 = p:<<<1,5>,<2,6>,<3,5>>>;
% _ % ascii95 = p:<<<1,0>,<4,0>>>;
% ' % ascii96 = T:<1,2>:<0.5,4>:ascii46 struct p:<<<2,4.5>,<2,5>,<3,6>>>;
% a % ascii97 = ascii111 struct p:<<<4,0>,<4,3>>>;
% b % ascii98 = ascii111 struct p:<<<0,0>,<0,5>,<1,5>>>;
% c % ascii99 = p:<<<4,1>,<3,0>,<1,0>,<0,1>,<0,2>,<1,3>,<3,3>,<4,2>>>;
% d % ascii100 = ascii111 struct p:<<<4,0>,<4,5>,<3,5>>>;
% e % ascii101 = p:<<<4,0>,<1,0>,<0,1>,<0,2>,<1,3>,<3,3>,<4,2>,<4,1>,<0,1>>>;
% f % ascii102 = p:<<<4,3>,<4,4>,<3,5>,<2,5>,<1,4>,<1,0>>,<<0,1>,<2,1>>>;
% g % ascii103 = ascii111 struct p:<<<4,1>,<4,0>,<3,-1>,<1,-1>,<0,0>>>;
% h % ascii104 = p:<<<4,0>,<4,2>,<3,3>,<1,3>,<0,2>>,<<0,0>,<0,5>,<1,5>>>;
% i % ascii105 = T:<1,2>:<0.25,3.75>:ascii46 struct p:<<<1,0>,<3,0>>,<<1,3>,<3,3>>,<<2,0>,<2,3>>>;
% j % ascii106 = T:<1,2>:<0.25,3.75>:ascii46 struct p:<<<1,3>,<3,3>>,<<2,3>,<2,0>,<1,-1>,<0,0>>>;
% k % ascii107 = p:<<<0,0>,<1,0>,<1,3>,<0,3>>,<<4,0>,<2,0>,<1,1>,<3,3>,<4,3>>>;
% l % ascii108 = p:<<<2,0>,<2,5>,<1,5>>,<<1,0>,<3,0>>>;
% m % ascii109 = p:<<<4,0>,<4,3>,<2,2>>,<<2,0>,<2,3>,<0,2>>,<<0,0>,<0,3>>>;
% n % ascii110 = p:<<<3,0>,<3,3>,<1,2>>,<<1,0>,<1,3>>>;
% O % ascii111 = p:<<<4,1>,<3,0>,<1,0>,<0,1>,<0,2>,<1,3>,<3,3>,<4,2>,<4,1>>>;
% p % ascii112 = ascii111 struct p:<<<0,3>,<0,-1>>>;
% q % ascii113 = ascii111 struct p:<<<4,3>,<4,-1>>>;
% r % ascii114 = p:<<<0,0>,<2,0>>,<<1,0>,<1,3>>,<<1,2>,<2,3>,<3,3>,<4,2>>>;
% s % ascii115 = p:<<<0,0>,<4,0>,<3,1>,<1,1>,<0,2>,<1,3>,<3,3>,<4,2>>>;
% t % ascii116 = p:<<<1,0>,<3,0>>,<<2,0>,<2,5>>,<<2,4>,<3,4>>>;
% u % ascii117 = p:<<<0,3>,<1,3>,<1,1>,<2,0>,<3,0>,<4,1>,<4,3>>>;
% v % ascii118 = p:<<<0,3>,<1,0>,<3,3>,<4,3>>>;
% w % ascii119 = p:<<<0,3>,<0,2>,<1,0>,<2,2>,<3,0>,<4,2>,<4,3>>>;
% x % ascii120 = p:<<<0,3>,<1,3>,<4,0>>,<<1,0>,<4,3>>>;
% y % ascii121 = p:<<<0,3>,<1,3>,<2,5.1.5>>,<<0,0>,<1,0>,<4,3>>>;
% z % ascii122 = p:<<<0,2>,<0,3>,<3,3>,<0,0>,<3,0>,<4,1>>>;
% { % ascii123 = p:< <<2.5,6.5>,<2,6>,<2,3.5>,<1.5,3>,<2,2.5>,<2,0>,<2.5,-0.5>>>;
% | % ascii124 = p:<<<2,0>,<2,5>>>;
% } % ascii125 = p:<<<1.5,6.5>,<2,6>,<2,3.5>,<2.5,3>,<2,2.5>,<2,0>,<1.5,-0.5>>>;
```

```
%  ~  %  ascii126 = p:<<<1,5>,<1.75,5.5>,<2.75,5>,<3.5,5.5>>>
END;

DEF fontWidth = 4;
DEF fontHeight = 6;
DEF fontSpacing = 2;
DEF fontColor = MyFont (AA:COLOR ~ DISTR) RGBCOLOR:<0,0,0>;
```

# Appendix B

# PLaSM libraries

The set of predefined PLaSM operators is listed here, grouped by library and then alphabetically ordered. Functions are documented according to the format below. For sake of readability the preconditions are given using the same semantics of a PLaSM definition. The postcondition is a predicate that must be satisfied by the function output. Currently, all libraries are loaded at set-up by the interpreter. All visible symbols, i.e. those listed in this appendix, are protected and cannot be redefined by the user. It is easy to see when a symbol is protected: (a) it is colored blue by the XPLODE editor, and (b) a false value is returned by the interpreter when asking for the evaluation of a redefinition of some protected symbol. The user may easily change this behavior, by either preventing the loading of some libraries, or by loading them as non-protected at set-up, or by loading some needed library on request during the work session. Let us finally remember that the language is not case-sensitive.

| NAME short description of how the function works | |
| --- | --- |
| Pre/Post conds | function prototype $\rightarrow$ type of returned value |
| Example | function usage example |

## B.1  Standard

The standard library contains basic predefined combinators and functions providing backward compatibility with previous PLaSM versions.

| AA applies fun to each element of the args sequence | |
| --- | --- |
| Pre/Post conds | (fun::isfun)(args::isseq) $\rightarrow$ (isseq) |
| Example | aa:sqrt:<1,4,9,16> $\equiv$ <1,2,3,4> |

| ABS returns the absolute value of n | |
| --- | --- |
| Pre/Post conds | (n::isnum) $\rightarrow$ (isnum) |
| Example | abs:-5 $\equiv$ 5 |

| AC apply-in-composition. AC:fun:seq is equivalent to (COMP $\sim$ AA:fun):seq | |
| --- | --- |
| Pre/Post conds | (fun::isfun)(seq::isseq) $\rightarrow$ (isfun) |
| Example | AC:SEL:<1,2,3> $\equiv$ SEL:1 $\sim$ SEL:2 $\sim$ SEL:3 |

**ACOS** computes the closest to zero arc associated with a given cosine value **n**

| Pre/Post conds | (n::isnum) $\rightarrow$ (isnum) |
|---|---|
| Example | acos:1 $\equiv$ 0 |

**AL** append left. appends **elem** on the left of **seq**

| Pre/Post conds | (elem::tt; seq::isseq) $\rightarrow$ (isseq) |
|---|---|
| Example | al:<0,<1,2,3,4>> $\equiv$ <0,1,2,3,4> |

**ALIGN** aligns a pair of polyhedral complexes along any given subset of coordinates.
(see Scripts 2.3.1 and 2.3.3)

| Pre/Post conds | (constraints::iseqof:istriple)(pol1,pol2::ispol) $\rightarrow$ (ispol) |
|---|---|
| Example | align:<<1,min,min>,<2,min,max>>:<cuboid:<2,2>,cuboid:<1,1>> |

**AND** standard logical operation on an arbitrary sequence of logical expressions

| Pre/Post conds | (preds::isseqof:isbool) $\rightarrow$ (isbool) |
|---|---|
| Example | and:<true,eq:<1,cos:0>,lt:0:(cos:pi)> $\equiv$ true |

**ANIMATION** is a container for animation clips and/or polyhedra and/or affine trans.

| Pre/Post conds | (clips::isseqof:isanimpolc) $\rightarrow$ (isanimpolc) |
|---|---|
| Example | see Script 15.6.8 |

**APPLY** returns the result of the expression **fun:value**

| Pre/Post conds | (fun::isfun,value::tt) $\rightarrow$ (tt) |
|---|---|
| Example | apply:<cat, <<1,2>,<3,4>>> $\equiv$ <1,2,3,4> |

**AR** append right. appends **elem** on the right of **seq**

| Pre/Post conds | (seq::isseq; elem::tt) $\rightarrow$ (isseq) |
|---|---|
| Example | ar:<<1,2,3,4>,5> $\equiv$ <1,2,3,4,5> |

**AS** apply-in-sequence. **AS:fun:seq** is equivalent to(CONS $\sim$ AA:fun):seq

| Pre/Post conds | (fun::isfun)(seq::isseq) $\rightarrow$ (isfun) |
|---|---|
| Example | AS:SEL:<1,2,3> $\equiv$ [SEL:1, SEL:2, SEL:3] |

**ASIN** computes the closest to zero arc associated with a given sine value **n**

| Pre/Post conds | (n::isnum) $\rightarrow$ (isnum) |
|---|---|
| Example | asin:0 $\equiv$ 0 |

**ATAN** computes the closest to zero arc associated with a given tangent value **n**

| Pre/Post conds | (n::isnum) $\rightarrow$ (isnum) |
|---|---|
| Example | atan:0 $\equiv$ 0 |

**BOTTOM** locates the second argument bottom the first, by centering their $xy$ extents

| Pre/Post conds | (pol1, pol2 ::ispol) $\rightarrow$ (ispol) |
|---|---|
| Example | bottom:< simplex:3, cuboid:<1,1,1> > |

**BOX** generates the containment box of **pol** in the **coords** subspace

| Pre/Post conds | (coords::isseqof:isintpos)(pol::ispol) $\rightarrow$ (ispol) |
|---|---|
| Example | box:<1,2>:(simplex:4) |

**BSPIZE** converts the HPC representation to BSP and vice versa, thus producing a BSP
fragmentation of a non-convex **pol**

| Pre/Post conds | (pol::ispol) $\rightarrow$ (ispol) |
|---|---|
| Example | bspize:pol |

C curryfies a binary function, so that, for example, `fun:<a,b>`, can be evaluated as
   `c:fun:a:b`

| | |
|---|---|
| Pre/Post conds | `(fun::isfun)` $\rightarrow$ `(isfun)` |
| Example | `AA:(c:*:2)(1..10)` $\equiv$ `< 2, 4, 6, 8, 10, 12, 14, 16, 18, 20 >` |

CASE arguments are pairs `<pred`$_i$`, fun`$_i$`>` to be tested in sequence. If `pred`$_i$`:x` $\equiv$
   `true`, then `fun`$_i$`:x` is evaluated; otherwise the $(i+1)$-th pair is tested

| | |
|---|---|
| Pre/Post conds | `(conds::isseqof:(ispred` $\sim$ `s1, isfun` $\sim$ `s2)(x::t)` $\rightarrow$ `(isfun)` |
| Example | `CASE:<<LT:0,K:'1'>, <C:EQ:0,K:'2'>, <GT:0,K:'3'>>:22` $\equiv$ `'3'` |

CAT catenates a sequence of sequences, by eliminating a level of angled parenthesis

| | |
|---|---|
| Pre/Post conds | `(seqs::isseqof:isseq)` $\rightarrow$ `(isseq)` |
| Example | `cat:<<0>,<1,2>,<<3,4>>,<>,<5,6,7>>` $\equiv$ `<0,1,2,<3,4>,5,6>` |

CATCH is used to catch a raised exception (see SIGNAL)

| | |
|---|---|
| Pre/Post conds | `(and` $\sim$ `[ispair,isseqof:isfun])` $\rightarrow$ `(isfun)` |
| Example | `def nonzero = if:< c:eq:0, signal, id>;` |
| | `catch:<nonzero, k:'zero'>:0` $\equiv$ `'zero'` |
| | `catch:<nonzero, k:'zero'>:10` $\equiv$ `10` |

CEIL returns the nearest integer greater or equal than n.

| | |
|---|---|
| Pre/Post conds | `(n::isnum)` $\rightarrow$ `(isnum)` |
| Example | `ceil:2.3` $\equiv$ `3.0` |

CHAR maps an integer from $\{1,2, \ldots ,255\}$ into the corresponding ASCII character

| | |
|---|---|
| Pre/Post conds | `(n::(and` $\sim$ `[isint,ge:1,le:255]))` $\rightarrow$ `(ischar)` |
| Example | `char:99` $\equiv$ `'c'` |

CHARSEQ maps a string into a sequence of characters

| | |
|---|---|
| Pre/Post conds | `(str::isstring)` $\rightarrow$ `(isseqof:ischar)` |
| Example | `charseq:'plasm'` $\equiv$ `<'p', 'l', 'a', 's', 'm'>` |

CMAP version of MAP operator used for animations

| | |
|---|---|
| Pre/Post conds | `(fun::isfun)(pol::ispol)` $\rightarrow$ `(ispol)` |
| Example | `CMAP:[s1,s2,sin~s1 * sin~s2]:dom` |

COMP composition. Returns the composition of the functions in the argument
   sequence

| | |
|---|---|
| Pre/Post conds | `(funs::isseqof:isfun)` $\rightarrow$ `(isfun)` |
| Example | `comp:<sqrt,+>:<4,5>` $\equiv$ `(sqrt` $\sim$ `+):<4,5>` $\equiv$ `3` |

CONS construction. Applies a function sequence `<f`$_1$`, ... ,f`$_n$`>` to `x` producing the
   sequence of applications `<f`$_1$`:x, ... ,f`$_n$`:x>`. Notice the "syntactical sugar" [
   ... ]

| | |
|---|---|
| Pre/Post conds | `(funs::isseqof:isfun)(x::tt)` $\rightarrow$ `(isseq)` |
| Example | `cons:<+,->:<3,2>` $\equiv$ `[+,-]:<3,2>` $\equiv$ `<5,1>` |

COS computes the cos trigonometric function

| | |
|---|---|
| Pre/Post conds | `(n::isnum)` $\rightarrow$ `(isnum)` |
| Example | `cos:0` $\equiv$ `1` |

COSH computes the hyperbolic cosine function

| | |
|---|---|
| Pre/Post conds | $(n::isnum) \rightarrow (isnum)$ |
| Example | $cosh:0 \equiv 1.0$ |

**CUBOID** dimension-independent interval generator. dims is the sequence of projection sizes on coordinate directions

| | |
|---|---|
| Pre/Post conds | $(dims::isseqof:isnum) \rightarrow (ispol)$ |
| Example | $cuboid:<1,1,1,1> \equiv polcomplex\{4,4\}$ |

**DETERMINANT** evaluates the determinant of the m matrix

| | |
|---|---|
| Pre/Post conds | $(m::ismat) \rightarrow (isnum)$ |
| Example | $determinant:<<4,2>,<0,2>> \equiv 8$ |

**DIFFERENCE** computes the difference of a set of solids of the same dimension. The operator is dimension-independent

| | |
|---|---|
| Pre/Post conds | $(seq::isseqof:ispol) \rightarrow (ispol)$ |
| Example | $difference:<pol1,pol2,pol3> \equiv pol1 - pol2 - pol3$ |

**DIFFERENCEPR** returns the *progressive* Boolean difference of a polyhedral sequence

| | |
|---|---|
| Pre/Post conds | $(seq::isseqof:ispol) \rightarrow (ispol)$ |
| Example | $differencepr:<pol1,pol2,pol3> \equiv$ <br> STRUCT:< pol1, pol2 - pol1, pol3 - pol2 - pol1 > |

**DIM** returns the *intrinsic* dimension (number of coordinates in a *chart*) of pol

| | |
|---|---|
| Pre/Post conds | $(pol::ispol) \rightarrow (isint)$ |
| Example | $dim:(simplex:2) \equiv 2$ |

**DISTL** distribute left. Returns the pair sequence with x and the elements of seq

| | |
|---|---|
| Pre/Post conds | $(x::tt,seq::isseq) \rightarrow (isseqof:ispair)$ |
| Example | $distl:<x,<1,2,3>> \equiv <<x,1>,<x,2>,<x,3>>$ |

**DISTR** distribute right. Returns the pair sequence with the elements of seq and x

| | |
|---|---|
| Pre/Post conds | $(seq::isseq,x::tt) \rightarrow (isseqof:ispair)$ |
| Example | $distr:<<1,2,3>,x> \equiv <<1,x>,<2,x>,<3,x>>$ |

**DIV** *n*-ary left-associative division. It is an alias for "/"

| | |
|---|---|
| Pre/Post conds | $(nums::isseqof:isnum) \rightarrow (isnum)$ |
| Example | $/:<20> \equiv div:<20> \equiv 1/20$ <br> $20 / 2 \equiv 20 \; div \; 2 \equiv div:<20,2> \equiv 10$ <br> $20 / 5 / 2 \equiv /:<20,5,2> \equiv div:<20,5,2> \equiv 2$ |

**DOWN** locates the second argument down the first (along the $x_2$ coordinate). Equivalent to align:<<1,min,min>,<2,min,max>>

| | |
|---|---|
| Pre/Post conds | $(pol1, pol2 ::ispol) \rightarrow (ispol)$ |
| Example | $down:<cuboid:<1,1,1>, cuboid:<2,2,2>>$ |

**DUMP** prints a face-based representation of pol in the listener

| | |
|---|---|
| Pre/Post conds | $(pol::ispol) \rightarrow (isstring)$ |
| Example | DUMP:(CUBOID:<1,1,1>) |

**DUMPREP** prints a pol representation, face-based if rep = 1, vertices-based if rep = 0

| | |
|---|---|
| Pre/Post conds | $(pol::ispol)(rep::or \sim [c:eq:0, c:eq:1]) \rightarrow (isstring)$ |
| Example | DUMP:(CUBOID:<1,1,1>):0 |

**EMBED** embeds a *d*-polyhedron into the subspace $x_{d+1} = \cdots = x_{d+n} = 0$ of $\mathbb{E}^{d+n}$

| | |
|---|---|
| Pre/Post conds | (n::isintpos)(pol::ispol) → (ispol) |
| Example | ([dim,rn] ~ embed:1 ~ cuboid):<1,1> ≡ <2,3> |

EQ predicate, testing for equality of all values in the argument sequence

| | |
|---|---|
| Pre/Post conds | (or ~ aa:(or ~ [isnum,isbool,ischar,isstring,isfun])) → (isbool) |
| Example | 4 eq len:<1,2,3,4> ≡ eq:<4,len:<1,2,3,4>> ≡ true |
| | eq:<4, 5 - 1, 3 + 1, 2 * 2, 8 / 2> ≡ true |
| | eq:<char:56,'8'> ≡ true |
| | eq:<4> ≡ true |

EXP exponential. Computes the function $\mathbb{R} \to \mathbb{R} : x \mapsto e^x$

| | |
|---|---|
| Pre/Post conds | (x::isnum) → (isnum) |
| Example | exp:1 ≡ 2.718281828459045 |

EXPORT exports a geometric value to a VRML file

| | |
|---|---|
| Pre/Post conds | (pol::ispol)(filename::isstring) → (ispol) |
| Example | VRML:(cuboid:<2,2,2>):'out.wrl'; |

FALSE primitive logical value

| | |
|---|---|
| Pre/Post conds | → (isbool) |
| Example | and:<false,gt:0:1> ≡ false |

FIRST returns the first element of the sequence given as argument.

| | |
|---|---|
| Pre/Post conds | (seq::and ~ [isseq,not ~ isnull]) → (tt) |
| Example | first:<<1,2>,<3,4>,<5,6>> ≡ <1,2> |

FLASH exports a 2D pol within a drawing area of width pixels, in a .swf file

| | |
|---|---|
| Pre/Post conds | (pol::ispol)(width::isintpos)(filename::isstring) → (ispol) |
| Example | flash:(cuboid:<2,2>):200:'path/out.swf' |

FLASHANIM exports a 2D clip to a .swf file, with a given width and framerate

| | |
|---|---|
| Pre/Post conds | (clip::isseqof:ispol)(width::isintpos)(filename::isstring) (framerate::isintpos) → (ispol) |
| Example | see Script 15.3.3 |

FLOOR returns the nearest integer less or equal to x

| | |
|---|---|
| Pre/Post conds | (x::isnum) → (isint) |
| Example | floor:pi ≡ 3 |

FRAME creates a *static* object rendered within the [start,end] animation time

| | |
|---|---|
| Pre/Post conds | (pol::ispol)(start,end::isnum) → (isanimpol) |
| Example | FRAME:(CUBOID:<1,1,1>):<2,5> |

FROMTO returns the integer sequence from m to n. Empty if m > n. Alias for ..

| | |
|---|---|
| Pre/Post conds | (m,n::isint) → (isseqof:isint) |
| Example | fromto:<1,4> ≡ 1 .. 4 ≡ <1,2,3,4> |

GE predicate testing if the second argument n is *greater or equal* than m

| | |
|---|---|
| Pre/Post conds | (m::isnum)(n::isnum) → (isbool) |
| Example | ge:5.2:5.3 ≡ true |

GT predicate testing if the second argument n is *greater than* m

| | |
|---|---|
| Pre/Post conds | (m::isnum)(n::isnum) → (isbool) |
| Example | gt:2:pi ≡ true |

**HELP** prints a help screen within the listener

| | |
|---|---|
| Pre/Post conds | (a::tt) → (tt) |
| Example | help:0 |

**ID** returns the **arg** argument unchanged

| | |
|---|---|
| Pre/Post conds | (arg::tt) → (tt) |
| Example | id:7 ≡ 7 |

**IF** It is applied to a *triplet* of functions, where **pred** is a *predicate* specifying the conditional behavior with respect to x

| | |
|---|---|
| Pre/Post conds | (pred, then, else::isfun)(x::tt) → (tt) |
| Example | if:<gt:0, sqrt, k:0>:9 ≡ 3; if:<gt:0, sqrt, k:0>:-9 ≡ 0 |

**INSL** *insert left* combinator, allowing to apply a *binary* operator f to n arguments:
insl:f:<$x_1$, ... ,$x_{n-1}$,$x_n$> ≡ f:<insl:f:<$x_1$, ... ,$x_{n-1}$>, $x_n$>

| | |
|---|---|
| Pre/Post conds | (f::isfun)(args::and ∼ [isseq,not∼isnull]) → (tt) |
| Example | insl:**:<2,2,3> ≡ 4**3 ≡ 64 |

**INSR** *insert right* combinator, allowing to apply a *binary* operator f to n arguments:
insr:f:<$x_1$, ... ,$x_{n-1}$,$x_n$> ≡ f:<$x_1$, insr:f:<$x_2$, ... ,$x_n$>>

| | |
|---|---|
| Pre/Post conds | (f::isfun)(args::and ∼ [isseq,not∼isnull]) → (tt) |
| Example | insr:**:<2,2,3> ≡ 2**8 ≡ 256 |

**INTERSECTION** computes the intersection of a set of solids of the same dimension. The operator is dimension-independent

| | |
|---|---|
| Pre/Post conds | (seq::(and∼[isseqof:ispol,eq∼aa:dim,and∼aa:(eq∼[dim,rn])])) → (ispol) |
| Example | intersection:<cuboid:<0.8,0.8>, simplex:2> |

**INTSTO** integers to. The operator returns either the sequence 1 .. n if 0 < n, or the sequence -1 .. n if n < 0, or the empty sequence if n = 0

| | |
|---|---|
| Pre/Post conds | (n::isint) → (isseqof:isint) |
| Example | intsto:6 ≡ <1,2,3,4,5,6> |

**INV** matrix inversion returns the inverse matrix of m.

| | |
|---|---|
| Pre/Post conds | (m::(and∼[ismat, eq∼[len,len∼s1]])) → (ismat) |
| Example | inv:<<1,2>,<2,0>> ≡ <<0,1/2>,<1/2,-1/4>> |

**ISANIMPOL** predicate that tests if **arg** is an animated polyhedral complex

| | |
|---|---|
| Pre/Post conds | (arg::tt) → (isbool) |
| Example | isanimpol:(cuboid:<2,2,2>) ≡ false |

**ISBOOL** predicate that tests if **arg** is a Boolean expression

| | |
|---|---|
| Pre/Post conds | (arg::tt) → (isbool) |
| Example | isbool:(eq:<3+1,5-2>) ≡ true |

**ISCHAR** predicate that tests if **arg** is a character

| | |
|---|---|
| Pre/Post conds | (arg::tt) → (isbool) |
| Example | ischar:'a' ≡ true |

**ISEMPTY** predicate that tests if a geometric value is empty

| | |
|---|---|
| Pre/Post conds | `(pol::ispol)` → `(isbool)` |
| Example | `isempty:(-:<cuboid:<2,2>,<cuboid:<2,2>>)` ≡ `true` |

**ISFUN** predicate that tests if `arg` is a function

| | |
|---|---|
| Pre/Post conds | `(arg::tt)` → `(isbool)` |
| Example | `isfun:cons` ≡ `true` |

**ISINT** predicate that tests if `arg` is an integer

| | |
|---|---|
| Pre/Post conds | `(arg::tt)` → `(isbool)` |
| Example | `isint:10` ≡ `true` |

**ISINTNEG** predicate that tests if `arg` is a negative integer

| | |
|---|---|
| Pre/Post conds | `(arg::tt)` → `(isbool)` |
| Example | `isintneg:-7` ≡ `true` |

**ISINTPOS** predicate that tests if `arg` is a positive integer

| | |
|---|---|
| Pre/Post conds | `(arg::tt)` → `(isbool)` |
| Example | `isintpos:4` ≡ `true` |

**ISNULL** predicate that tests if `arg` is the empty sequence

| | |
|---|---|
| Pre/Post conds | `(arg::tt)` → `(isbool)` |
| Example | `isnull:<>` ≡ `true` |

**ISNUM** predicate that tests if `arg` is a number

| | |
|---|---|
| Pre/Post conds | `(arg::tt)` → `(isbool)` |
| Example | `isnum:pi` ≡ `true` |

**ISNUMNEG** predicate that tests if `arg` is a negative number

| | |
|---|---|
| Pre/Post conds | `(arg::tt)` → `(isbool)` |
| Example | `isnumneg:-12.7` ≡ `true` |

**ISNUMPOS** predicate that tests if `arg` is a positive number

| | |
|---|---|
| Pre/Post conds | `(arg::tt)` → `(isbool)` |
| Example | `isnumpos:12.7` ≡ `true` |

**ISPAIR** predicate that tests if `arg` is a pair (a sequence of exactly two elements)

| | |
|---|---|
| Pre/Post conds | `(arg::tt)` → `(isbool)` |
| Example | `ispair:<+,->` ≡ `true` |

**ISPOL** predicate that tests if `arg` is a geometric value

| | |
|---|---|
| Pre/Post conds | `(arg::tt)` → `(isbool)` |
| Example | `ispol:(simplex:1)` ≡ `true` |

**ISREAL** predicate that tests if `arg` is a real number

| | |
|---|---|
| Pre/Post conds | `(arg::tt)` → `(isbool)` |
| Example | `isreal:0.45` ≡ `isreal:4.5e-1` ≡ `true` |

**ISREALNEG** predicate that tests if `arg` is a negative real number

| | |
|---|---|
| Pre/Post conds | `(arg::tt)` → `(isbool)` |
| Example | `isrealneg:-5.4` ≡ `true` |

**ISREALPOS** predicate that tests if `arg` is a positive real number

| | |
|---|---|
| Pre/Post conds | `(arg::tt)` → `(isbool)` |
| Example | `isrealpos:pi` ≡ `true` |

ISSEQ predicate that tests if `arg` is a sequence

| Pre/Post conds | `(arg::tt) → (isbool)` |
|---|---|
| Example | `isseq:<id,cons> ≡ true` |

ISSEQOF second-order predicate that tests if `arg` is a sequence with all elements of pred type

| Pre/Post conds | `(pred::isfun)(arg::tt) → (isbool)` |
|---|---|
| Example | `isseqof:isint:<2,4,5.01> ≡ false` |

ISSTRING predicate that tests if `arg` is a string

| Pre/Post conds | `(arg::tt) → (isbool)` |
|---|---|
| Example | `isstring:'PLaSM' ≡ true` |

JOIN returns the *convex hull* of a sequence of geometric values in $\mathbb{E}^n$

| Pre/Post conds | `(seq::or ~ [isseqof:ispol, ispol]) → (ispol)` |
|---|---|
| Example | `join:< (embed:1 ~ cuboid):<1,1>, simplex:3 >` |

K constant functional that always returns the first argument, for any value of the second one

| Pre/Post conds | `(a::tt)(b::tt) → (tt)` |
|---|---|
| Example | `k:<1,2>:100 ≡ <1,2>` |

LAST returns the last element of the non-empty sequence argument

| Pre/Post conds | `(sequence::and ~ [isseq,not ~ isnull]) → (tt)` |
|---|---|
| Example | `last:<<1,2>,<3,4>,<5,6>> ≡ <5,6>` |

LE predicate that tests if the second argument `n` is *less or equal* than `m`

| Pre/Post conds | `(m::isnum)(n::isnum) → (isbool)` |
|---|---|
| Example | `le:2:(PI - 2) ≡ true` |

LEFT locates the second argument on the left of the first (along the $x_1$ coordinate)

| Pre/Post conds | `(pol1, pol2 ::ispol) → (ispol)` |
|---|---|
| Example | `left:<cuboid:<1,1,1>, cuboid:<2,2,2>>` |

LEN returns the *length* of the sequence given as argument

| Pre/Post conds | `(sequence::isseq) → (isint)` |
|---|---|
| Example | `len:<2,5,2,1> ≡ 4` |

LESS predicate that tests if the argument is a sequence of increasing numbers

| Pre/Post conds | `(nums::isseqof:isnum) → (isbool)` |
|---|---|
| Example | `less:<1,2,3> ≡ true` |

LESSEQ predicate that tests if the argument is a sequence of non-decreasing numbers

| Pre/Post conds | `(nums::isseqof:isnum) → (isbool)` |
|---|---|
| Example | `lesseq:<1,2,2,3> ≡ true` |

LIFT combining form with semantics `lift:f:<`$f_1,\ldots,f_n$`>` ≡ `f ~ [`$f_1,\ldots,f_n$`]`

| Pre/Post conds | `(f::isfun)(funs::isseqof:isfun) → (isfun)` |
|---|---|
| Example | `lift:+:<sin,cos> ≡ + ~ [sin,cos]` |

LIST returns the sequence containing `arg`. Alias for `[id]`

| Pre/Post conds | `(arg::tt) → (isseq)` |
|---|---|
| Example | `list:4 ≡ <4>` |

LN *natural logarithm* $\log_e$ of a positive real x

| Pre/Post conds | (x::isrealpos) → (isreal) |
|---|---|
| Example | DEF e = (+ ~ aa:(c:/:1.0 ~ fact)):(0..20); ln:1 = 0; ln:e = 1; |

LOAD loads a *script* file within the run-time PLaSM environment

| Pre/Post conds | (filename::isstring)) → (*side effect*) |
|---|---|
| Example | load:'~/Documents/example.psm' |

LOADLIB loads the *library* file passed as argument. Let us use no file extension

| Pre/Post conds | (filename::isstring) → (*side effect*) |
|---|---|
| Example | loadlib:'psmlib/curves' |

LOOP generates times repetitions of an animation

| Pre/Post conds | (times::isintpos)(anim::isanimpolc) → (isanimpol) |
|---|---|
| Example | def movie = loop:10:(animation:<clip1, clip2>); |

LT predicate that tests if the second argument m is *less than* n

| Pre/Post conds | (n::isnum)(m::isnum) → (isbool) |
|---|---|
| Example | lt:5:2 ≡ true |

MAP simplicial mapping. It maps a (possibly CONSed) sequence of coordinate funs over a polyhedral domain. A simplicial decomposition is automatically generated

| Pre/Post conds | (funs::or ~ [isseqof:isfun, isfun])(domain::ispol) → (ispol) |
|---|---|
| Example | map:<cos ~ s1,sin ~ s1>:((quote ~ #:32):(2*pi/32)) |

MAT generates a tensor (bijective transformation function) from its invertible matrix with first row and column homogeneous. Dimension independent operator

| Pre/Post conds | (m::issqrmat) → (isfun) |
|---|---|
| Example | def rot2d = mat ~ mathom ~ [[cos,- ~ sin],[sin,cos]]; rot2d:(pi/4):(cuboid:<1,1>) |

MAX returns the maximum values achieved by pol on coords coordinates

| Pre/Post conds | (coords::isseqof:isintpos)(pol::ispol) → (isseqof:isnum) |
|---|---|
| Example | max:<1,3>:(cuboid:<2,4,6>) ≡ <2.0,6.0> |

MED returns the medium values achieved by pol on coords coordinates

| Pre/Post conds | (coords::isseqof:isintpos)(pol::ispol) → (isseqof:isnum) |
|---|---|
| Example | med:<1,3>:(cuboid:<2,4,6>) ≡ <1.0,3.0> |

MERGE merging of two ordered sequences seqs using the binary predicate pred

| Pre/Post conds | (pred::isfun)(seqs::and ~ [isseq,not ~ isnull]) → (isseq) |
|---|---|
| Example | merge:less:<<1,3,4,5>,<2,4,6,8>> ≡ < 1,2,3,4,4,5,6,8 > |

MIN returns the minimum values achieved by pol on coords coordinates

| Pre/Post conds | (coords::isseqof:isintpos)(pol::ispol) → (isseqof:isnum) |
|---|---|
| Example | min:<1,2>:(cuboid:<2,4,6>) ≡ <0.0,0.0> |

MKPOL is a mapping from triples of number sequences to polyhedral complexes: mkpol:< verts, cells, pols >, where verts are *points* in $\mathbb{E}^d$ (given as sequences of coordinates); cells are convex *cells* (given as sequences of point indices); pols are *polyhedra* (given as sequences of cell indices). Each cell is the convex hull of its vertices, each polyhedron is the set union of its cells

| | |
|---|---|
| Pre/Post conds | `(verts::ismatof:isreal;` |
| | `cells,pols::AND ~AA:(isseqof:isintpos)) → (ispol)` |
| Example | `mkpol:<<<0,0>,<0,1>,<1,1>,<1,0>>, <<1,2,3,4>>,<<1>>>` |

`MOVE` basic primitive for configuration space (CS) sampling animation. Is applied to: (a) geometry generator function of real parameters (*degrees of freedom*); (b) sequence of CS points; (c) increasing sequence of *time* values, s.t. `len:cspoints ≡ len:timepoints`

| | |
|---|---|
| Pre/Post conds | `(geometry::isfun)(cspoints::or ~ [iseqof:isreal,ismatof:isreal])` |
| | `(timepoints::isseqof:isrealpos) → (isanimpol)` |
| Example | `def obj(x,a::isreal) = (t:1:x ~ r:<1,2>:a):(cuboid:<1,1>);` |
| | `def clip = move:obj:<<0,0>,<5,pi>,<5,0>>:<0,1,2>;` |

`NEQ` predicate, testing the non-equality of all values in the argument sequence

| | |
|---|---|
| Pre/Post conds | `(or ~ aa:(or ~ [isnum,isbool,ischar,isstring,isfun]))` |
| | `→ (isbool)` |
| Example | `neq:<4, 5 - 1, 3 + 1, 2 * 2, 8 / 2> ≡ false` |

`NOT` standard unary logical operation on logical values. Actually, it considers every PLaSM value as `true` but `<>`, thus returning, e.g., `not:'z' ≡ false` and `textttnot:¡¿ ≡ true`

| | |
|---|---|
| Pre/Post conds | `(a::tt) → (isbool)` |
| Example | `not:false ≡ true` |

`OPEN` restores a geometric object from a `.xml` file (see `SAVE`)

| | |
|---|---|
| Pre/Post conds | `(filename::isstring) → (ispol)` |
| Example | `def cube = open:'path/cube.xml';` |

`OR` standard logical operation between arguments with logical values

| | |
|---|---|
| Pre/Post conds | `(preds::isseqof:isbool) → (isbool)` |
| Example | `or:<false,(not ~ eq):<1,2>> ≡ true` |

`ORD` maps an ASCII character into its ordinal value, i.e. its index in the ASCII table

| | |
|---|---|
| Pre/Post conds | `(c::ischar) → (and ~ [isintpos,le:255])` |
| Example | `ord:'c' ≡ 99, ord:'\t' ≡ 9, ord:'⊔' ≡ 32` |

`PI` constant value. PLaSM denotation of $\pi$

| | |
|---|---|
| Pre/Post conds | `→ (isnum)` |
| Example | `pi ≡ 3.14159265358979` |

`PRINT` returns `arg` and prints its value in the listener. It may be used to debugging

| | |
|---|---|
| Pre/Post conds | `(arg::tt) → (tt)` |
| Example | `(@1 ~ print ~ embed:1 ~ print ~ simplex):2` |

`QUOTE` transforms non-empty sequences of non-zero reals into 1D polyhedra. Positive numbers produce solid segments; negative numbers are used as translations

| | |
|---|---|
| Pre/Post conds | `(nums::and ~ [isseqof:isnum, and ~ aa:(c:neq:0)]) → (ispol)` |
| Example | `quote:<2,-10,1,1,-10,2>` |

`R` dimension-independent rotation tensor. `coords` are the indices of the coordinate *pair* affected by the transformation. The rotation `angle` is given in radians

| Pre/Post conds | (coords::and ~ [ispair, isseqof:isintpos]) |
|---|---|
| | (angle::isnum)(pol::or ~ [ispol,isanimpol]) |
| | → (or ~ [ispol,isanimpol]) |
| Example | r:<1,2>:(pi/4):(cuboid:<10,10,10>) |

**RAISE** this combinating form is used to overload operators over both numbers and functions. In fact RAISE:f:seq ≡ IF:<IsSeqOf:IsFun, LIFT:f, f>:seq

| Pre/Post conds | (f::isfun)(args::isseq) → (isfun) |
|---|---|
| Example | raise:+:<+,*> ≡ + ~ [+,*] |

**RANGE** returns the integer sequence (possibly reversed) from m to n

| Pre/Post conds | (m,n::isint) → (isseq) |
|---|---|
| Example | range:<5,-1> ≡ <5,4,3,2,1,0,-1> |

**REVERSE** returns a sequence in reverse order

| Pre/Post conds | (seq::isseq) → (isseq) |
|---|---|
| Example | reverse:<<1,2>,<3,4>,<5,6>> ≡ <<5,6>,<3,4>,<1,2>> |

**RIGHT** locates the second argument on the right of the first (along the $x_1$ coordinate)

| Pre/Post conds | (pol1, pol2 ::ispol) → (ispol) |
|---|---|
| Example | right:<cuboid:<1,1,1>, cuboid:<2,2,2>> |

**RN** returns the *embedding dimension*, i.e. the number of coordinates of points

| Pre/Post conds | (pol::ispol) → (isintpos) |
|---|---|
| Example | (rn ~ embed:2 ~ simplex):3 ≡ 5 |

**S** dimension-independent scaling tensor. coords are the indices of coordinates affected by the transformation

| Pre/Post conds | (coords::or ~ [isintpos, isseqof:isintpos]) (params::or ~ |
|---|---|
| | [isnum, isseqof:isnum]) (pol::or ~ [ispol,isanimpol]) |
| | → (or ~ [ispol,isanimpol]) |
| Example | s:<1,2>:<0.5,-1.5>:(cuboid:<10,10,10>) |

**SAVE** stores a geometric value into an XML file

| Pre/Post conds | (pol::ispol)(filename::isstring) → (ispol) |
|---|---|
| Example | save:(cuboid:<1,1,1>):'/path/cube.xml' |

**SEL** returns the *i*-th element of seq sequence. An exception is raised if i > len:seq

| Pre/Post conds | (i::isintpos)(seq::isseq) → (tt) |
|---|---|
| Example | sel:2:<<1,2>,<3,4>,<5,6>> ≡ <3,4> |

**SHIFT** shifts the beginning of the animation clip of t seconds

| Pre/Post conds | (t::isnum)(clip::isanimpolc) → (isanimpol) |
|---|---|
| Example | shift:10:clip |

**SHOWPROP** returns the sequence of <property,value> pairs associated with obj

| Pre/Post conds | (obj::ispol) → (isseqof:ispair) |
|---|---|
| Example | showprop:(cuboid:<1,1> color red) ≡ <<'RGBcolor',<1,0,0>>> |

**SIGN** returns either 1 if x is positive, or -1 if x is negative, or 0 if x is zero

| Pre/Post conds | (x::isnum) → (isint) |
|---|---|
| Example | sign:-4.5 ≡ -1 |

**SIGNAL** raises an *exception*, to be captured by the CATCH primitive

| Pre/Post conds | $(\texttt{value::tt}) \to (\texttt{exception})$ |
| Example | $\texttt{def nonzero = if:<c:neq:0, id, signal>;}$ |
| | $\texttt{nonzero:0} \equiv \texttt{plasm exception: 0}$ (message in the listener) |
| | $\texttt{catch:<nonzero, k:'nonzero'>:0} \equiv \texttt{'nonzero'}$ |

**SIMPLEX** generator of the simplex $\sigma^d \equiv \text{conv}\left(\{e_i\} \cup \{0\}\right) \subset \mathbb{R}^d, 1 \le i \le d$

| Pre/Post conds | $(\texttt{d::isnat}) \to (\texttt{ispol})$ |
| Example | $\texttt{simplex:5}$ |

**SIN** computes the `sin` trigonometric function. The argument is in radians

| Pre/Post conds | $(\texttt{alpha::isnum}) \to (\texttt{isnum})$ |
| Example | $\texttt{sin:(pi/2)} \equiv \texttt{1.0}$ |

**SINH** computes the hyperbolic sine of `x`

| Pre/Post conds | $(\texttt{x::isnum}) \to (\texttt{isnum})$ |
| Example | $\texttt{sinh:0} \equiv \texttt{0.0}$ |

**SIZE** return the size of the `pol` projection/s on the specified coordinate direction/s

| Pre/Post conds | $(\texttt{coords::or} \sim \texttt{[isintpos,isseqof:isintpos]})(\texttt{pol::ispol})$ |
| | $\to (\texttt{or} \sim \texttt{[isrealpos, isseqof:isrealpos]})$ |
| Example | $(\texttt{size:2} \sim \texttt{cuboid}):\texttt{<2,4,6>} \equiv \texttt{4.0}$ |

**SQRT** square root operator. Negative arguments are allowed

| Pre/Post conds | $(\texttt{x::isnum}) \to (\texttt{isnum})$ |
| Example | $\texttt{sqrt:64} \equiv \texttt{8}$; $\texttt{sqrt:-64} \equiv \texttt{0+8i}$ |

**STRING** maps a sequence of characters into a string

| Pre/Post conds | $(\texttt{chars::isseqof:ischar}) \to (\texttt{isstring})$ |
| Example | $\texttt{string:<'c', 'a', 'd'>} \equiv \texttt{'cad'}$ |

**STRUCT** constructor of hierarchical assemblies

| Pre/Post conds | $(\texttt{args::isseqof:(or} \sim \texttt{[ispol, isanimpol, isfun])})$ |
| | $\to (\texttt{or} \sim \texttt{[ispol, isanimpol]})$ |
| Example | $\texttt{struct:<cuboid:<2,2>, t:1:3:, simplex:2>}$ |

**SVG** exporter of a 2D geometric value `pol` into a canvas of `width` pixels in a `.svg` file

| Pre/Post conds | $(\texttt{pol::ispol})(\texttt{width::isnum})(\texttt{filename::isstring}) \to (\texttt{ispol})$ |
| Example | $\texttt{svg:(cuboid:<1,1>):250:'out.svg'}$ |

**T** dimension-independent translation tensor. `coords` are the indices of the coordinates affected by the transformation

| Pre/Post conds | $(\texttt{coords::or} \sim \texttt{[isintpos,isseqof:isintpos]})$ |
| | $(\texttt{params::or} \sim \texttt{[isnum,isseqof:isnum]})$ |
| | $(\texttt{pol::or} \sim \texttt{[ispol,isanimpol]}) \to (\texttt{or} \sim \texttt{[ispol,isanimpol]})$ |
| Example | $\texttt{t:<1,2>:<-5,-5>:(cuboid:<10,10>)}$ |

**TAIL** returns the non-empty argument sequence but its first element

| Pre/Post conds | $(\texttt{seq::and} \sim \texttt{[isseq,not} \sim \texttt{isnull]}) \to (\texttt{isseq})$ |
| Example | $\texttt{tail:<<1,2>,<3,4>,<5,6>>} \equiv \texttt{<<3,4>,<5,6>>}$ |

**TAN** computes the `tan` trigonometric function. The argument is in radians

| Pre/Post conds | $(\texttt{alpha::isnum}) \to (\texttt{isnum})$ |
| Example | $\texttt{tan:(pi/4)} \equiv \texttt{1}$ |

**TANH** computes the hyperbolic tangent of the argument

| | |
|---|---|
| Pre/Post conds | `(x::isnum)` $\rightarrow$ `(isnum)` |
| Example | `tanh:0` $\equiv$ `0` |

---

**TIME** returns information about the execution time of the function argument

| | |
|---|---|
| Pre/Post conds | `(f::isfun)` $\rightarrow$ `(tt)` |
| Example | `time:cuboid:<1,1,1>` |

---

**TOP** locates the second argument over the first (z dir), by centering their xy extents

| | |
|---|---|
| Pre/Post conds | `(pol1, pol2 ::ispol)` $\rightarrow$ `(ispol)` |
| Example | `top:<cuboid:<1,1,0.5> color red, cuboid:<1,1,0.5> color blue>` |

---

**TRANS** transposes a sequence of sequences of the same length. The elements may be of arbitrary type

| | |
|---|---|
| Pre/Post conds | `(seq::ismat)` $\rightarrow$ `(ismat)` |
| Example | `trans:<<1,2>,<3,4>,<5,6>>` $\equiv$ `<<1,3,5>,<2,4,6>>` |

---

**TREE** recursively applies a binary function f to a sequence of arguments `arg`

| | |
|---|---|
| Pre/Post conds | `(f::isfun)(args::and` $\sim$ `[isseq,not` $\sim$ `isnull])` $\rightarrow$ `(tt)` |
| Example | `def bigger (a,b::isreal) = if:< greater, s1, s2 >:<a,b>;` |
| | `def biggest (seq::isseqof:isnum) = tree:bigger:seq;` |
| | `biggest:<8,2,4,2,3,11,-5>` $\equiv$ `11` |

---

**TRUE** a truth value. Primitive PLaSM value

| | |
|---|---|
| Pre/Post conds | $\rightarrow$ `(isbool)` |
| Example | `and:<true, gt:1:0>` $\equiv$ `false` |

---

**TT** constant predicate that returns `true` for every argument. Alias for `k:true`

| | |
|---|---|
| Pre/Post conds | `(arg::tt)` $\rightarrow$ `(isbool)` |
| Example | `tt:cons` $\equiv$ `true; tt:1000` $\equiv$ `true; tt:'aaa'` $\equiv$ `true;` |

---

**UKPOL** UnmaKe POLyhedron. Inverse operator of MKPOL (see). Returns `pol` represented as a *triplet* of vertices, convex and polyhedral cells

| | |
|---|---|
| Pre/Post conds | `(pol::ispol)` $\rightarrow$ `(isseqof:isseq)` |
| Example | `ukpol:(cuboid:<1,1>)` $\equiv$ `<<<0.0, 1.0>, <1.0, 1.0>, <0.0, 0.0>,` |
| | `<1.0, 0.0>>, <<1, 2, 3, 4>>, <<1>>>` |

---

**UKPOLF** unmake polyhedron *by faces*. Returns the internal representation by faces as a triplet `<covectors, cells, pols>`. Covectors are normalized

| | |
|---|---|
| Pre/Post conds | `(pol::ispol)` $\rightarrow$ `(iseqof:isseq)` |
| Example | `ukpolf:(cuboid:<1,1>)` $\equiv$ `<<<1.0, 0.0, 0.0>, <-0.7071, 0.0,` |
| | `0.7071>, < 0.0, 1.0, 0.0>, <0.0, -0.7071, 0.7071>>, <<1, 2,` |
| | `3, 4>>, <<1>>>` |

---

**UNION** of a set of solids of the same dimension. More expensive than the + operator, but produces a well defined cellular result

| | |
|---|---|
| Pre/Post conds | `(args::isseqof:ispol)` $\rightarrow$ `(ispol)` |
| Example | `(@1` $\sim$ `union` $\sim$ `[id, t:<1,2>:<0.5,0.5>]` $\sim$ `cuboid):<1,1,1>` |

---

**UP** locates the second argument over the first (along the $x_2$ coordinate)

| | |
|---|---|
| Pre/Post conds | `(pol1, pol2 ::ispol)` $\rightarrow$ `(ispol)` |
| Example | `up:<cuboid:<1,1,1>, cuboid:<2,2,2>>` |

**VRML** exports a geometric value into a vrml file with suffix `.wrl`

| | |
|---|---|
| Pre/Post conds | `(pol::ispol)(filename::isstring)` $\rightarrow$ `(ispol)` |
| Example | `vrml:(cuboid:<2,2,2>):'out.wrl';` |

**WARP** time scaling operator used for animations

| | |
|---|---|
| Pre/Post conds | `(s::isnum)(anim::isanimpol)` $\rightarrow$ `(isanimpol)` |
| Example | `(shift:10 ~ warp:-1):clip` |

**WITH** binary operator used to dynamically annotate a geometric value with pairs `<property,values>`, where `property` is a string

| | |
|---|---|
| Pre/Post conds | `(pol::ispol; prop_val:: and ~ [ispair, isstring ~ s1, tt ~ s2])` $\rightarrow$ `(tt)` |
| Example | `cuboid:<1,1> with < 'RGBcolor',<1,0,0> >` |

**XOR** Boolean XOR (union minus intersection) of a sequence of geometric values

| | |
|---|---|
| Pre/Post conds | `(args::isseqof:ispol)` $\rightarrow$ `(ispol)` |
| Example | `xor:<cuboid:<3,3,3>, t:<1,2>:<0.5,0.5>:(cuboid:<3,3,3>)>` |

---

**−** n-ary difference operator between (a) numbers, (b) functions, (c) matrices and (d) geometric values

| | |
|---|---|
| Pre/Post conds | `(args::lift:or:(AA:isseqof:<isnum, isfun, ismat, ispol>))` $\rightarrow$ `(or ~ [isnum,isfun,ismat,ispol])` |
| Example | `2 - 3.5 - 1 ≡ -:< 2, 3.5, 1 > ≡ 0.5` |
| | `(sin - cos):PI ≡ (- ~ [sin,cos]):PI ≡ 1.0` |
| | `idnt:2 - <<1,1>,<1,1>> ≡ <<0,-1>,<-1,0>>` |
| | `(id - t:<1,2>:<0.5,0.5>):(cuboid:<3,3,3>) ≡ PolComplex<3,3>` |

**#** repetition operator. Returns a sequence with `n` repetitions of `arg`

| | |
|---|---|
| Pre/Post conds | `(n::isintpos)(arg::tt)` $\rightarrow$ `(isseq)` |
| Example | `#:4:true ≡ <true,true,true,true>` |

**##** sequence repetition operator. `##:n:seq` is equivalent to `(cat ~ #:n):seq`

| | |
|---|---|
| Pre/Post conds | `(n::isintpos)(seq::isseqof:tt)` $\rightarrow$ `(isseq)` |
| Example | `##:3:<1,2> ≡ cat:(#:3:<1,2>) ≡ <1,2,1,2,1,2>` |

**&** n-ary Boolean intersection operator

| | |
|---|---|
| Pre/Post conds | `(seq::isseqof:ispol)` $\rightarrow$ `(ispol)` |
| Example | `&:<cuboid:<0.8,0.8,0.8>, simplex:3>` |

**&&** binary intersection of extrusions. The `args` are properly embedded into `coords` subspaces, indefinitely extruded and pair-wise intersected

| | |
|---|---|
| Pre/Post conds | `(coords::isseqof:isint)(args::isseqof: ispol)` $\rightarrow$ `(ispol)` |
| Example | |

**\*** n-ary product operator between (a) numbers, (b) functions, (c) matrices and (d) geometric values

| | |
|---|---|
| Pre/Post conds | `(args::lift:or:(AA:isseqof:<isnum, isfun, ismat, ispol>))` $\rightarrow$ `(or ~ [isnum,isfun,ismat,ispol])` |
| Example | `*:<20,5,2> ≡ 200` |
| | `(sin * cos):PI ≡ (* ~ [sin,cos]):PI ≡ 0.0` |
| | `<<4,2>,<2,1>> * <<1,1>,<0,2>> ≡ <<4,8>,<2,4>>` |
| | `simplex:2 * Q:1 ≡ PolComplex{3,3}` |

** power raising. Mathematical operator

| Pre/Post conds | (base,exp::isnum) → (isnum) |
|---|---|
| Example | **:<2,3> ≡ 8.0; 81 ** (1/2) ≡ 9.0 |

.. generator of the integer sequence from m to n. Alias for fromto

| Pre/Post conds | (m,n::isint) → (isseqof:isint) |
|---|---|
| Example | -1 .. 4 ≡ <-1,0,1,2,3,4> |

/ n-ary division operator between numbers and functions

| Pre/Post conds | (args::lift:or:(AA:isseqof:<isnum, isfun, ispol>)) → (or ~ [isnum,isfun,ispol]) |
|---|---|
| Example | /:<20,5,2> ≡ 2 |

∧ evaluates the Boolean XOR of a sequence of geometric values. It is less time-consuming than the xor operator, but returns a "weak" complex

| Pre/Post conds | (seq::isseqof:ispol) → (ispol) |
|---|---|
| Example | (@1 ~ ∧ ~ [id, t:<1,2>:<0.5,0.5>] ~ cuboid):<3,3,0.5> |

~ function *composition* operator. Alias for n-ary COMP

| Pre/Post conds | (funs::isseqof:isfun) → (isfun) |
|---|---|
| Example | (sqrt ~ +):<4,5> ≡ 3 |

+ n-ary addition operator between (a) numbers, (b) functions, (c) matrices and (d) geometric values (as union)

| Pre/Post conds | (args::lift:or:(AA:isseqof:<isnum, isfun, ismat, ispol>)) → (or ~ [isnum,isfun,ismat,ispol]) |
|---|---|
| Example | +:<5,2,1> ≡ 8 |
| | (sin + cos):PI ≡ (+ ~ [sin,cos]):PI ≡ -1.0 |
| | <<4,2>,<2,1>> + <<1,1>,<0,2>> ≡ <<5,3>,<2,3>> |
| | cuboid:<3,3,3> + t:<1,2>:<0.5,0.5>:cuboid:<3,3,3> |

@n returns the n-dimensional skeleton of a complex

| Pre/Post conds | (pol::ispol) → (ispol) |
|---|---|
| Example | @1:(cuboid:<0.8,0.8,0.8> & simplex:3) ≡ PolComplex{1,3} |

## B.2 animation Library

| Curve2cspath | Transforms a 2D point sequence into a CS path (3 DOFs) |
|---|---|
| Pre/Post conds | (curve::isseqof:isfun) → (isfun) |
| Example | (AA:(Curve2CSPath:trajectory ~ [ID]) ~ Sampling):20; |

| Inarcs | returns the inward arcs of a given node in a graph |
|---|---|
| Pre/Post conds | (node::isint)(graph::isseqOf:IsTriple) → (IsSeqOf:IsPair) |
| Example | inarcs:7:<<0,1,2>,<1,2,5>,<2,3,3>,<3,4,4>,<1,5,0>,<6,2,0>, <2,7,0>,<8,3,0>,<5,6,10>,<6,7,5>,<7,8,2>> ≡ <<2,0>,<6,5>> |

| Outarcs | returns the outward arcs of a given node in a graph |
|---|---|
| Pre/Post conds | (node::isint)(graph::isseqOf:IsTriple) → (IsSeqOf:IsPair) |
| Example | outarcs:7:<<0,1,2>,<1,2,5>,<2,3,3>,<3,4,4>,<1,5,0>,<6,2,0>, <2,7,0>,<8,3,0>,<5,6,10>,<6,7,5>,<7,8,2>> ≡ <<8,2>> |

Tmax computes the maximum spanning time of a given node in a graph

| Pre/Post conds | (graph::isseqof:istriple)(node::isint) → (isint) |
| Example | See p. 672 |

Tmin computes the minimum spanning time of a given node in a graph

| Pre/Post conds | (graph::isseqof:istriple)(node::isint) → (isint) |
| Example | See p. 672 |

## B.3   colors Library

The colors library makes large use of the recent OO extension of PLaSM described in [MMPP02]. In such a context *objects* are values belonging to classes; *classes* are sets generated by a CLASS constructor function; this one automatically generates a predicate in*classname* to test set-membership of objects.

---

Appearance the appearance property of pol is set by its mat material and fulltex

| Pre/Post conds | (pol::ispol; mat::isbasematerial; fulltex::isfulltexture) → (ispol) |
| Example | appearance:<pol,mat,fulltex> ≡ pol material mat texture fulltex |

Basecamera full detail definition according to the VRML specs of *camera* node

| Pre/Post conds | (position, orientation::or ~ [isvect, isnull]; fieldofview::or ~ [isreal, isnull]; description::isstring) → (isbasecamera) |
| Example | Basecamera:<<3,0,0>, <0,1,0,PI/2>, pi/4, 'x axis camera'> |

Basedirlight specialization of GenericLight with type ≡ 1 and various defaults

| Pre/Post conds | (dirappearance, dirgeometry::isseq) → (isbasedirlight) |
| Example | see psmlib/colors.psm |

Basematerial full detail definition according to the VRML specs of *material* node

| Pre/Post conds | (diffuse, specular::isrgbcolor; ambient::isinto:<0, 1>; emissive::isrgbcolor; shininess, transparency::isinto:<0, 1>) → (isbasematerial) |
| Example | basematerial:<rgbcolor:<1,0.85,0.85>,black,0.2,black,0.2,0.0> |

Basepointlight specialization of GenericLight with type ≡ 0 and defaults

| Pre/Post conds | (pointappearance, pointgeometry::isseq) → (isbasepointlight) |
| Example | see psmlib/colors.psm |

Basespotlight specialization of GenericLight with type ≡ 0 and defaults

| Pre/Post conds | (spotappearance, spotgeometry::isseq) → (isbasespotlight) |
| Example | see psmlib/colors.psm |

Basetexture specialization of Fulltexture with no texture transformation

| Pre/Post conds | (url::isstring; repeats, repeatt::isbool) → (isbasetexture) |
| Example | see psmlib/colors.psm |

Black plasm *object* of class rgbcolor and value <0,0,0>

| Pre/Post conds | → (isrgbcolor) |
| Example | cuboid:<1,1,1> color black |

Blue plasm *object* of class rgbcolor and value <0,0,1>

| Pre/Post conds | → (isrgbcolor) |
|---|---|
| Example | cuboid:<1,1,1> color blue |

Brown plasm *object* of class rgbcolor and value <3/5,2/5,1/5>

| Pre/Post conds | → (isrgbcolor) |
|---|---|
| Example | cuboid:<1,1,1> color brown |

Camera used to associate a camera to pol, to be inserted in a hierarchical graph

| Pre/Post conds | (pol::ispol; camera::isbasecamera) → (ispol) |
|---|---|
| Example | MK:<0,0,0> CAMERA BaseCamera:< prp, <0,0,1,0>, PI/4, string > |

Color returns pol annotated with col value for 'rgbcolor' property

| Pre/Post conds | (pol::ispol; col::isrgbcolor) → (ispol) |
|---|---|
| Example | cuboid:<1,1,1> color yellow |

Crease smooths pol by annotating it with angle value for 'VRMLcrease' property

| Pre/Post conds | (pol::ispol; angle::isreal) → (ispol) |
|---|---|
| Example | sphere:1:<12,24> crease (pi/2) |

Cyan plasm *object* of class rgbcolor and value <0,1,1>

| Pre/Post conds | → (isrgbcolor) |
|---|---|
| Example | cuboid:<1,1,1> color cyan |

Fulltexture generator of texture objects, including 2D texture transformations

| Pre/Post conds | (url::isstring; repeats, repeatt::isbool; center::ispoint; rotation::isreal; scale, translation::isvect) → (isfulltexture) |
|---|---|
| Example | fulltexture:<'img/glass.jpg',true,true,<0,0>,0,<1,1>,<0,0>> |

Genericlight used to switch between point, directional and spot lights

| Pre/Post conds | (type::isinto:<0, 2>; appearance, geometry::isgenericlightgeometry) → (isgenericlight) |
|---|---|
| Example | see examples/color/lights.psm |

Genericlightappearance returns objects embodying common params of light types

| Pre/Post conds | (color::or ~ [isrgbcolor, isnull]; intensity, ambient::or ~ [isreal, isnull]; ison::or ~ [isbool, isnull]) → (isgenericlightappearance) |
|---|---|
| Example | genericlightappearance:<magenta, 1, 0.4, true> |

Genericlightgeometry returns objects with common params of light geometries

| Pre/Post conds | (location, direction, attenuation::or ~ [isvect, isnull]; radius, beamwidth, cutoffangle::or ~ [isreal, isnull]) → (isgenericlightgeometry) |
|---|---|
| Example | GenericLightGeometry:<<0,0,0>,<1,0,0>,<1,0,0>,10,PI/4,PI/6> |

Gray plasm *object* of class rgbcolor and value <1/2,1/2,1/2>

| Pre/Post conds | → (isrgbcolor) |
|---|---|
| Example | cuboid:<1,1,1> color gray |

Green plasm *object* of class rgbcolor and value <0,1,0>

| | |
|---|---|
| Pre/Post conds | → (isrgbcolor) |
| Example | cuboid:<1,1,1> color green |

**Isinto** predicate to test set-membership of x into the [lower,upper] interval

| | |
|---|---|
| Pre/Post conds | (lower,upper::isnum)(x::isnum) → (isbool) |
| Example | isinto:<0,1>:0.5 ≡ true |

**Light** is used to apply a genericlight object to pol complex

| | |
|---|---|
| Pre/Post conds | (pol::ispol; light::isgenericlight) → (islight) |
| Example | (sqr ∼ q ∼ #:10):1 light spot:<red, <10,15,20>,<0,0,-1>> |

**Magenta** plasm *object* of class rgbcolor and value <1,0,1>

| | |
|---|---|
| Pre/Post conds | → (isrgbcolor) |
| Example | cuboid:<1,1,1> color magenta |

**Material** annotates pol with mat object value for 'VRMLmaterial' property

| | |
|---|---|
| Pre/Post conds | (pol::ispol; mat::isbasematerial) → (ispol) |
| Example | cuboid:<1,1,1> material Transparentmaterial:<green, 0.4> |

**Orange** plasm *object* of class rgbcolor and value <1,1/2,0>

| | |
|---|---|
| Pre/Post conds | → (isrgbcolor) |
| Example | cuboid:<1,1,1> color orange |

**Purple** plasm *object* of class rgbcolor and value <1/2,0,1/2>

| | |
|---|---|
| Pre/Post conds | → (isrgbcolor) |
| Example | cuboid:<1,1,1> color purple |

**Red** plasm *object* of class rgbcolor and value <1,0,0>

| | |
|---|---|
| Pre/Post conds | → (isrgbcolor) |
| Example | cuboid:<1,1,1> color red |

**Simplecamera** specialization of BaseCamera using defaults for common params

| | |
|---|---|
| Pre/Post conds | (position::or ∼ [isvect, isnull]; description::isstring) → (issimplecamera) |
| Example | (@1∼cuboid):<1,1,1> camera simplecamera:<<0.5,0.5,2.5>,'cam'> |

**Simplematerial** specialization of basematerial using defaults for common params

| | |
|---|---|
| Pre/Post conds | (color::isrgbcolor) → (issimplematerial) |
| Example | circle:1:<32,1> material simplematerial:blue |

**Simpletexture** specialization of basetexture with no repetitions

| | |
|---|---|
| Pre/Post conds | (url::isstring) → (issimpletexture) |
| Example | cuboid:<2,3> texture simpletexture:'path/monnalisa.jpg' |

**Spot** function that returns a plasm *object* of class basespotlight

| | |
|---|---|
| Pre/Post conds | (color,location,orientation::tt) → (isbasespotlight) |
| Example | (sqr ∼ q ∼ #:10):1 light spot:<red, <10,15,20>,<0,0,-1>> |

**Texture** annotates pol with tex value for the 'VRMLtexture' property

| | |
|---|---|
| Pre/Post conds | (pol::ispol; tex::isfulltexture) → (ispol) |
| Example | cuboid:<2,3> texture simpletexture:'path/monnalisa.jpg' |

**Transparentmaterial** specialization of basematerial with default values

| Pre/Post conds | (color::isrgbcolor; transparency::isinto:<0,1>)                    $\rightarrow$ |
| Example | (istransparentmaterial) |
|  | ndimsphere:3 material transparentmaterial:<red, 0.7> |

---

White plasm *object* of class rgbcolor and value <1,1,1>

| Pre/Post conds | $\rightarrow$ (isrgbcolor) |
| Example | cuboid:<1,1,1> color white |

---

Yellow plasm *object* of class rgbcolor and value <1,1,0>

| Pre/Post conds | $\rightarrow$ (isrgbcolor) |
| Example | cuboid:<1,1,1> color yellow |

## B.4   curves Library

---

Basehermite returns the graph of the cubic Hermite basis polynomials

| Pre/Post conds | (domain::ispol) $\rightarrow$ (ispol) |
| Example | basehermite:(intervals:1:20) |

---

Beziercurve generator of coordinate functions of Bézier curves of arbitrary degree.
    Alias for Bezier:S1

| Pre/Post conds | (controlpoints::ismat) $\rightarrow$ (isseqof:isfun) |
| Example | beziercurve:<<0,4,1>,<7,5,-1>,<8,5,1>,<12,4,0>> |

---

Bezierstripe generator of a 2D stripe generated by a Bézier curve of any degree

| Pre/Post conds | (controlpoints::ismat; width::isreal;n::isintpos) $\rightarrow$ (ispol) |
| Example | Bezierstripe:<<<0,0>,<7,5>,<8,5>,<12,4>>,1,20> |

---

Curve2mapvect coerces a vector function into a sequence of real maps

| Pre/Post conds | (curve::isfun) $\rightarrow$ (isseqof:isfun) |
| Example | curve2mapvect:[cos $\sim$ s1, sin $\sim$ s1] |

---

Derbernsteinbase derivative of the Bernstein/Bézier basis polynomials of degree n

| Pre/Post conds | (n::isintpos) $\rightarrow$ (isseqof:isfun) |
| Example | derbernsteinbase:2 |

---

Derbernstein derivative of Bernstein polynomial of degree $n$ and index $i$, $0 \leq i \leq n$

| Pre/Post conds | (n::isint)(i::isint) $\rightarrow$ (isfun) |
| Example | derbernstein:3:0 |

---

Derbezier generator of coordinate functions of the derivative of a Bézier curve

| Pre/Post conds | (controlpoints::ismat) $\rightarrow$ (isseqof:isfun) |
| Example | derbezier:<<0,0>,<7,5>,<8,5>,<12,4>> |

---

Hermite generator of the coordinate functions of a cubic Hermite curve

| Pre/Post conds | (handles::ismat) $\rightarrow$ (isseqof:isfun) |
| Example | MAP:(Hermite:<<0,0>,<1,1>,<-3,0>,<3,0>>):(Intervals:1:20) |

---

Norm2 generator of the coordinate functions of the normal unit field to a 2D curve

| Pre/Post conds | (curve::and $\sim$ [ispair,isseqof:isfun]) |
|  | $\rightarrow$ (and $\sim$ [ispair,isseqof:isfun]) |
| Example | (norm2 $\sim$ derbezier):<<0,0>,<1,1>,<-3,0>,<3,0>> |

`Rationalbezier` rational Bézier curves of arbitrary degree (weights on last coord)

| | |
|---|---|
| Pre/Post conds | `(controlpoints::ismat)` → `(isseqof:isfun)` |
| Example | `MAP:(RationalBezier:<<1,0,1>,[id,id,id]:(SQRT:2/2),<0,1,1>>):` |
| | `(Intervals:1:12)` |

---

`Rationalblend` linear comb. of basis with `controlpoints`, and normalization

| | |
|---|---|
| Pre/Post conds | `(basis::isseqof:isfun)(controlpoints::ismat)` → `(isseqof:isfun)` |
| Example | `rationalblend:(bernsteinbasis:s1:degree):controlpoints` |

---

`Rationalize` division of coordinate functions by the last element, then dropped out

| | |
|---|---|
| Pre/Post conds | `(coords::isseqof:isfun)` → `(isseqof:isfun)` |
| Example | `rationalize:(blend:(bernsteinbasis:s1:2):` |
| | `<<1,1,1>,<-3,0,1>,<3,0,1>>)` |

---

`Rev` reversing parametrization operator $[a,b] \mapsto [b,a]$

| | |
|---|---|
| Pre/Post conds | `(a,b::isreal)` → `(isfun)` |
| Example | `map:([cos,sin] ~ rev:<0,pi> ~ s1):(intervals:pi:24)` |

## B.5  derivatives **Library**

---

`Binormal` returns the coordinate functions of binormal vector function to a `curve`

| | |
|---|---|
| Pre/Post conds | `(curve::isseqof:isfun)` → `(isseqof:isfun)` |
| Example | `binormal:(beziercurve:<<-1,2,1>,<0,1.2,3>,<0,2,-1>,<3,2,2>>)` |

---

`Curl` returns the curl of a smooth vector field `f` computed at `x` point

| | |
|---|---|
| Pre/Post conds | `(f::isseqof:isfun)(x::ispoint)` → `(isvect)` |
| Example | `curl:<sin~s1,cos~s2,s1*s3>:<0,pi,pi/6>` ≡ `<0.0,-0.52359,0.0>` |

---

`Curvature` computes the scalar curvature function of the input curve

| | |
|---|---|
| Pre/Post conds | `(curve::isseqof:isfun)(a::ispoint)` → `(isfun)` |
| Example | `MAP:<s1, curvature:<cos ~ s1, sin ~ s1>>:(intervals:(2*pi):24);` |

---

`Divergence` returns the trace of Jacobian matrix of vector field `f`, evaluated at `x`

| | |
|---|---|
| Pre/Post conds | `(f::isseqof:isfun)(x::isseqof:isreal)` → `(isnum)` |
| Example | `def g = < sin ~ s1, cos ~ s2, s1 * s3 >;` |
| | `divergence:< s1 ~ curl:g, s2 ~ curl:g, s3 ~ curl:g >:` |
| | `<0.5,110.5,1>` ≡ `0.0` |

---

`Dp` partial derivative in the $i$-th coordinate direction of the real function `f` of several variables, at a point `x`

| | |
|---|---|
| Pre/Post conds | `(i::isIntPos)(f::IsFun)(x::IsPoint)` → `(isfun)` |
| Example | `dp:2:(sin ~ s1 * sin ~ s2):<pi/3, pi/6>:<1>` ≡ `0.75` |

---

`Ds` $i$-th partial derivative of a vector function `f` of several variables

| | |
|---|---|
| Pre/Post conds | `(i::isintpos)(f::isseqof:isfun)` → `(isseqof:isfun)` |
| Example | `MAP:(DS:1:<s1,s2,sin~s1,sin~s2>):((sqr ~ intervals:pi):12)` |
| | ≡ `PolComplex<1,4>` |

---

`D` derivative operator for scalar and vector functions of one or more variables

| Pre/Post conds | `(f::or~[isfun,isseqof:isfun])(u::or~[isnum,isseqof:isnum])` |
| | `→ (or~[isnum,isseqof:isnum])` |
| Example | `d:sin:pi ≡ -1` |
| | `CONS:(d:(beziercurve:<<-2,0>,<1,3>,<2,1>>):<1>):<0.5>≡<1,-2>` |

**Gausscurvature** returns the Gauss curvature of vector field f at point x

| Pre/Post conds | `(f::isseqof:isfun)(x::ispoint) → (isnum)` |
| Example | `gausscurvature:< s1, s2, sin~s1 * sin~s2 >:<0,0> ≡ -1.0` |

**Grad** gradient (linear map) of a scalar function f of several variables at point a

| Pre/Post conds | `(f::isfun)(a::ispoint) → (isseqof:isfun)` |
| Example | `cons:(grad:(sin~s1*sin~s2):<pi/3,pi/-2>):<1,1> ≡ <-0.5,0>` |

**Gradient** gradient (vector) of a scalar field point a

| Pre/Post conds | `(f::isfun)(a::ispoint) → (isvect)` |
| Example | `Gradient:(s1*s1 - s2*s2):<0.25,0.3> ≡ <0.5,-0.6>` |

**Jacobian** returns the Jacobian matrix at point a of a vector field f

| Pre/Post conds | `(f::isseqof:isfun)(a::ispoint) → (ismat)` |
| Example | `Jacobian:<(s1*s1 - s2*s2)/K:2, (s1*s1 + s2*s2)/K:2>:<0.25,0.3>` |
| | `≡ <<0.25,-0.3>,<0.25,0.3>>` |

**Normalmap** normal vector field map

| Pre/Post conds | `(f::isseqof:isfun; dom::ispol) → (ispol)` |
| Example | `normalmap:<s1,s2,sin ~ s1*sin ~ s2>:((sqr ~ intervals:pi):5)` |

**N** normal field operator, i.e. the normalized vector product of the (tangent) fields generators `DS:1` and `DS:2`

| Pre/Post conds | `(f::isseqof:isfun) → (isseqof:isfun)` |
| Example | `(cons~n):<s1,s2,sin~s1*sin~s2>:<0,0> ≡ <0,0,1.0>` |

**Principalnormal** intrinsic vector for a curve given by coordinate functions

| Pre/Post conds | `(curve::isseqof:isfun)(a::ispoint) → (isfun)` |
| Example | `MAP:(principalnormal:<cos ~ s1, sin ~ s1>):(intervals:(pi):12)` |

**Tangent** intrinsic vector for a curve given by coordinate functions

| Pre/Post conds | `(curve::isseqof:isfun)(a::ispoint) → (isfun)` |
| Example | `MAP:((tangent ~ bezier:s1):<<0,0,0>,<1,0,0>,<1,1,0>,<1,1,1>>):` |
| | `(intervals:1:20)` |

**X** $i$-th partial derivative of a scalar function f of several variables at point x

| Pre/Post conds | `(i::isintpos)(f::isfun)(x::ispoint) → (isnum)` |
| Example | `cons:(aa:(x:2):<s1,s2,sin ~ s1*sin ~ s2>):<0,0> ≡ <0,1.0,0>` |

## B.6   drawtree Library

**Drawtree** returns a 2D complex giving a picture of the input hierarchical structure

| Pre/Post conds | `(levels::isseqof:isseq) → (ispol)` |
| Example | `drawtree:<<<'1'>>,<<'2','3','4','5'>>, <<'6','7'>,<>,<'8','9','10'>,<'11'>>>` |

## B.7    flash Library

---

Acolor annotates the pol parameter with the color value, of rgba type

| Pre/Post conds | (pol::ispol; color::isrgbacolor) $\rightarrow$ (ispol) |
|---|---|
| Example | cuboid:<1,1> acolor rgbacolor:<0,1,0,0.5> |

---

Actor returns an animation level starting at time (timestop - len:framelist)

| Pre/Post conds | (framelist::isseq)(timestop::isintpos) $\rightarrow$ (isseqof:ispol) |
|---|---|
| Example | |

---

Fillcolor defines the rgba color to fill a 2D geometric object pol

| Pre/Post conds | (pol::ispol; col::isrgbacolor) $\rightarrow$ (ispol) |
|---|---|
| Example | cuboid:<1,1> fillcolor RGBAcolor:<1,0,0,1> |

---

Frame displays the obj object within the $[t_1, t_2]$ time interval

| Pre/Post conds | (obj::ispol)(t1::isintpos)(t2::isintpos) $\rightarrow$ (isseqof:ispol $\sim$ S1) |
|---|---|
| Example | frame:(cuboid:<1,1>):1:32 |

---

Linecolor used to define the color of 1-skeleton of a 2D geometric object pol

| Pre/Post conds | (pol::ispol; col::isrgbacolor) $\rightarrow$ (ispol) |
|---|---|
| Example | cuboid:<1,1> linecolor rgbacolor:<0,0.1,1,0.8> |

---

Linesize used to define the drawing size of 1-skeleton of a 2D object pol

| Pre/Post conds | (pol::ispol; pixelsize::isint) $\rightarrow$ (ispol) |
|---|---|
| Example | out fillcolor rgbacolor:< 0,1,1,0.5 > linecolor rgbacolor:< 0,0,1,1 > linesize 1 |

---

## B.8    general Library

---

Alias to return the data value paired with an integer key in an associative table

| Pre/Post conds | (key::isint)(table::isseqof:ispair) $\rightarrow$ (tt) |
|---|---|
| Example | alias:2:<<-1,35>,<2,1..3>,<5,41>,<7,43>,<18,44>> $\equiv$ <1,2,3> |

---

Assoc returns the pair whose key has smallest distance from the input key. Pairs are maintained in increasing key order

| Pre/Post conds | (key::isint) $\rightarrow$ (ispair) |
|---|---|
| Example | alias:2:<<-1,35>,<2,1..3>,<5,41>,<7,43>,<18,44>> $\equiv$ <2,1..3> |

---

Bigger is a binary operator that returns the greater of arguments

| Pre/Post conds | (pair::and $\sim$ [ispair, lift:or:(AA:isseqof:<isnum, ischar, isstring>)]) $\rightarrow$ (or $\sim$ [isnum,ischar,isstring]) |
|---|---|
| Example | bigger:<-122,22E2> $\equiv$ 2200.0<br>bigger:<'John','Robert'> $\equiv$ 'Robert' |

---

Biggest binary operator that returns the greatest of args values

| Pre/Post conds | (args::lift:or:(AA:isseqof:<isnum, isfun, ismat, ispol>)) $\rightarrow$ (or $\sim$ [isnum,ischar,isstring]) |
|---|---|
| Example | biggest:<'fred','wilma','barney','lucy'> $\equiv$ 'wilma' |

---

**Cart** returns the Cartesian product of two sequences

| Pre/Post conds | $(a,b::isseqof::tt) \rightarrow (isseqof:ispair)$ |
|---|---|
| Example | cart:<<1,2,3>,<'a','b'>> $\equiv$ |
| | <<1,'a'>,<1,'b'>,<2,'a'>,<2,'b'>,<3,'a'>,<3,'b'>> |

**Choose** is a generator of binomial numbers

| Pre/Post conds | $(n,k::isnat) \rightarrow (isintpos)$ |
|---|---|
| Example | 6 choose 2 $\equiv$ 15 |

**Fact** is a generator of the function $n \mapsto n!$

| Pre/Post conds | $(n::isnat) \rightarrow (isintpos)$ |
|---|---|
| Example | fact:5 $\equiv$ 120 |

**Filter** used for filtering a **sequence** according to a **predicate** on elements

| Pre/Post conds | $(predicate::isfun)(sequence::isseq) \rightarrow (isseq)$ |
|---|---|
| Example | filter:(LE:0):<-101,23,0,-37.02,0.1,84> $\equiv$ <23,0.1,84> |

**In** predicate to test the set-membership of **element** $\in$ **set**

| Pre/Post conds | $(set::isseq)(element::tt) \rightarrow (isbool)$ |
|---|---|
| Example | in:<'a','e','i','o','u'>:'z' $\equiv$ false |

**Iseven** predicate to test if **n** is an even number

| Pre/Post conds | $(n::isint) \rightarrow (isbool)$ |
|---|---|
| Example | iseven:13 $\equiv$ false |

**Isge** binary predicate to test if $b \geq a$ in some suitable ordering

| Pre/Post conds | $(a,b::tt) \rightarrow (isbool)$ |
|---|---|
| Example | isge:<'Fred', 'Wilma'> $\equiv$ true |

**Isgt** binary predicate to test if $b > a$ in some suitable ordering

| Pre/Post conds | $(a,b::tt) \rightarrow (isbool)$ |
|---|---|
| Example | isgt:<'Fred', 'Wilma'> $\equiv$ true |

**Isle** binary predicate to test if $b \leq a$ in some suitable ordering

| Pre/Post conds | $(a,b::tt) \rightarrow (isbool)$ |
|---|---|
| Example | isge:<'Fred', 'Wilma'> $\equiv$ false |

**Islt** binary predicate to test if $b < a$ in some suitable ordering

| Pre/Post conds | $(a,b::tt) \rightarrow (isbool)$ |
|---|---|
| Example | isge:<'Fred', 'Wilma'> $\equiv$ false |

**Isnat** unary predicate to test if a number **n** is a natural number. A natural number is any of the numbers $0, 1, 2, 3, \ldots$

| Pre/Post conds | $(n::isnum) \rightarrow (isbool)$ |
|---|---|
| Example | isnat:-1233 $\equiv$ false |

**Isodd** predicate to test if **n** is an odd number

| Pre/Post conds | $(n::isint) \rightarrow (isbool)$ |
|---|---|
| Example | isodd:13 $\equiv$ true |

**Mean** computes the arithmetic mean of a sequence **seq** of numbers

| Pre/Post conds | $(seq:isseqof:isnum) \rightarrow (isnum)$ |
|---|---|
| Example | mean:<10,22,5,16,4> $\equiv$ 57/5 |

**Mk** returns a 0D polyhedron starting from the coordinates of a point $x \in \mathbb{E}^d$, $d \geq 1$

| | |
|---|---|
| Pre/Post conds | `(x:ispoint)` $\rightarrow$ `(and` $\sim$ `[ispol,c:eq:0` $\sim$ `dim])` |
| Example | `(c:eq:0` $\sim$ `dim):(mk:<1,0,0,0>)` $\equiv$ `true` |

**Mod** binary operator that returns the remainder of the division of **a** by **b**

| | |
|---|---|
| Pre/Post conds | `(a,b::isnum)` $\rightarrow$ `(isnum)` |
| Example | `mod:<13.5,9.2>` $\equiv$ `4.3` |

**Pascaltriangle** returns the first $n + 1$ rows of the Pascal triangle of binomial numbers

| | |
|---|---|
| Pre/Post conds | `(n::isnat)` $\rightarrow$ `and` $\sim$ `aa:(isseqof:isintpos)` |
| Example | `pascalTriangle:3` $\equiv$ `<<1>,<1,1>,<1,2,1>,<1,3,3,1>>` |

**Permutations** returns the set of permutations of elements of the input **seq**

| | |
|---|---|
| Pre/Post conds | `(seq::isseqof:tt)` $\rightarrow$ `(and` $\sim$ `aa:(isseqof:tt))` |
| Example | `permutations:<1,2,3>` $\equiv$ |
| | `<<1,2,3>,<1,3,2>,<2,1,3>,<2,3,1>,<3,1,2>,<3,2,1>>` |
| | `permutations:<'a','b'>` $\equiv$ `<<'a','b'>,<'b','a'>>` |

**Powerset** returns the powerset $2^{\mathrm{set}}$ of the input **set**

| | |
|---|---|
| Pre/Post conds | `(set::isseqof:tt)` $\rightarrow$ `(and` $\sim$ `aa:(isseqof:tt))` |
| Example | `powerSet:<1,2,3>` $\equiv$ `<<1,2,3>,<1,2>,<1,3>,<1>,<2,3>,<2>,<3>,<>>` |

**Progressivesum** operator to compute the map $\{a_i \in \mathtt{Num}\} \mapsto \{b_i = \sum_{j=1}^{i} a_j\}$

| | |
|---|---|
| Pre/Post conds | `(input::isseqof:isnum)` $\rightarrow$ `(isseqof:isnum)` |
| Example | `ProgressiveSum:<1,3,5,7,9,11>` $\equiv$ `<1,4,9,16,25,36>` |

**Q** generalized alias for `QUOTE`, that is applicable to either numbers or sequences

| | |
|---|---|
| Pre/Post conds | `(params::and`$\sim$`[or`$\sim$`[isnum,isseqof:isnum],and`$\sim$ `aa:(c:neq:0)])` |
| | $\rightarrow$ `(and`$\sim$`[ispol,c:eq:<1,1>`$\sim$`[dim,rn]])` |
| Example | `ispol:(q:1)` $\equiv$ `true; (ispol` $\sim$ `q` $\sim$ `##:10):<1,-2>` $\equiv$ `true` |

**Rtail** returns the input **seq**, but the last element

| | |
|---|---|
| Pre/Post conds | `(seq::isseqof:tt)` $\rightarrow$ `(isseqof:tt)` |
| Example | `rtail:<'a','b','c','e'>` $\equiv$ `<'a','b','c'>` |

**Setand** set intersection between the argument sequences

| | |
|---|---|
| Pre/Post conds | `(set_a, set_b::isseqof:tt)` $\rightarrow$ `(isseqof:tt)` |
| Example | `<id,11,'Lucy',12,'Bart'> setand <'Bart','Homer',11,id>` $\equiv$ |
| | `<id,11,'Bart'>` |

**Setdiff** set difference between the argument sequences

| | |
|---|---|
| Pre/Post conds | `(set_a, set_b::isseqof:tt)` $\rightarrow$ `(isseqof:tt)` |
| Example | `<id,11,'Lucy',12,'Bart'> setdiff <'Bart','Homer',11,id>` $\equiv$ |
| | `<'Lucy',12>` |

**Setor** set union between the argument sequences

| | |
|---|---|
| Pre/Post conds | `(set_a, set_b::isseqof:tt)` $\rightarrow$ `(isseqof:tt)` |
| Example | `<id,11,'Lucy',12,'Bart'> setor <'Bart','Homer',11,id>` $\equiv$ |
| | `<'Lucy',12,'Bart','Homer',11,id>` |

**Setxor** symmetric difference (XOR) between the argument sequences

| | |
|---|---|
| Pre/Post conds | (set_a, set_b::isseqof:tt) $\rightarrow$ (isseqof:tt) |
| Example | <id,11,'Lucy',12,'Bart'> setxor <'Bart','Homer',11,id> $\equiv$ <br> <'Lucy',12,'Homer'> |

---

**Sort** merge-sort on numbers, characters and strings, with order depending on pred

| | |
|---|---|
| Pre/Post conds | (pred::isfun)(seq::isseqof:tt) $\rightarrow$ (isseqof:tt) |
| Example | sort:isgt:<'fred','wilma','barney','lucy'> $\equiv$ <br> <'barney','fred','lucy','wilma'> <br> sort:greater:<8,2,4,2,3,11,-5> $\equiv$ <11,8,4,3,2,2,-5> |

---

**Smaller** *binary* operator that returns the smaller argument (in a proper ordering!)

| | |
|---|---|
| Pre/Post conds | (args::or~[ispairof:isnum,ispairof:isstring]) <br> $\rightarrow$ (or $\sim$ [isnum,isstring]) |
| Example | smaller:<-122,22E2> $\equiv$ -122 <br> smaller:<'John','Robert'> $\equiv$ 'John' |

---

**Smallest** returns the smallest element of the args input sequence

| | |
|---|---|
| Pre/Post conds | (args::or~[isseqof:isnum,isseqof:isstring]) <br> $\rightarrow$ (or $\sim$ [isnum,isstring]) |
| Example | smallest:<'fred','wilma','barney','lucy'> $\equiv$ 'barney' |

---

**Sqr** unary operator that returns the *square* of the arg argument

| | |
|---|---|
| Pre/Post conds | (arg::or $\sim$ [isnum, isfun]) $\rightarrow$ (or $\sim$ [isnum, isfun]) |
| Example | sqr:sin:(PI/2) $\equiv$ (sin * sin):(PI/2) $\equiv$ 1.0 <br> sqr:4 $\equiv$ 16 |

---

**Uk** UnMaKe. Returns the point in $\mathrm{I\!E}^d$ corresponding to a 0D geometric object

| | |
|---|---|
| Pre/Post conds | (arg::and $\sim$ [ispol,c:eq:0 $\sim$ dim]) $\rightarrow$ (ispoint) |
| Example | (uk $\sim$ embed:2 $\sim$ mk):<1,1,1> $\equiv$ <1.0,1.0,1.0,0.0,0.0> |

## B.9  myfont **Library**

---

**Fontcolor** applies the col parameter to the polyhedral objects in myfont font

| | |
|---|---|
| Pre/Post conds | (col::isrgbcolor) $\rightarrow$ (iseqof:ispol) |
| Example | fontcolor:red |

---

**Fontheight** constant value, giving the height of characters in myfont. Default is 6

| | |
|---|---|
| Pre/Post conds | $\rightarrow$ (isnum) |
| Example | s:<1,2>:< textwidth/fontwidth, textheight/fontheight > |

---

**Fontspacing** constant value, giving the spacing of character boxes in myfont. Default is 2

| | |
|---|---|
| Pre/Post conds | $\rightarrow$ (isnum) |
| Example | t:1:(fontwidth + fontspacing) |

---

**Fontwidth** constant value, giving the width of characters in myfont

| | |
|---|---|
| Pre/Post conds | $\rightarrow$ (isnum) |
| Example | s:<1,2>:< textwidth/fontwidth, textheight/fontheight > |

---

**Myfont** is the name of the internal data structure where the character shapes are stored as geometric values. The drawable ASCII subset is [32, 126]

| | |
|---|---|
| Pre/Post conds | $\rightarrow$ (isseqof:ispol) |
| Example | sel:(ord:'a' - 31):myfont $\equiv$ PolComplex<1,2> |

## B.10   operations **Library**

---

Depth_sort returns a depth-sort ordering of the 2-faces of a polyhedral scene

| | |
|---|---|
| Pre/Post conds | (scene::ispol) → (isseqof:ispol) |
| Example | (depth_sort ~ @2 ~ r:<1,2>:(pi/6) ~ cuboid):<1,1,1> |

---

Depth_test is the Newell's binary predicate used to compare two 2-faces

| | |
|---|---|
| Pre/Post conds | (a,b::and ~ [ispol,c:eq:<2,3> ~ [dim,rn]]) → (isbool) |
| Example | (depth_test ~ [t:3:1, id] ~ embed:1 ~ simplex):2 |

---

Explode 3D "explosion" operator of the scene parameter

| | |
|---|---|
| Pre/Post conds | (sx,sy,sz::isreal) (scene::isseqof:ispol) → (isseqof:ispol) |
| Example | def hole = ((id - s:<1,2>:<0.5,0.5>) ~ mxmy ~ cuboid):<2,2,2>; |
| | (struct ~ explode:<1,1,1.5> ~ extract_polygons):hole |

---

Extract_bodies returns the 3D cells from the scene parameter

| | |
|---|---|
| Pre/Post conds | (scene::and ~ [ispol,ge:3 ~ dim]) → (isseqof:ispol) |
| Example | extract_bodies:(q:<1,-1,1,-1,1> * q:1 * q:10) |

---

Extract_polygons returns the 2D cells from the scene parameter

| | |
|---|---|
| Pre/Post conds | (scene::and ~ [ispol,ge:2 ~ dim]) → (isseqof:ispol) |
| Example | extract_polygons:(q:<1,-1,1,-1,1> * q:1 * q:10) |

---

Extract_wires returns the 1D cells from the scene parameter

| | |
|---|---|
| Pre/Post conds | (scene::and ~ [ispol,ge:1 ~ dim]) → (isseqof:ispol) |
| Example | extract_wires:(q:<1,-1,1,-1,1> * q:1 * q:10) |

---

Extrude with h displacement, the $n$-th convex cell in a pol complex

| | |
|---|---|
| Pre/Post conds | (n::isintpos; pol::ispol; h::isrealpos) → (ispol) |
| Example | extrude:<2,q:<1,-1,1,-1,1> * q:1,10> |

---

Extrusion *generalized* operator, with h steps and alpha angle, of pol parameter

| | |
|---|---|
| Pre/Post conds | (alpha::isreal)(h::isint)(pol::ispol) → (ispol) |
| Example | extrusion:(pi/18):1:(q:1 * q:1) |

---

Ex *right* extrusion, with x2 - x1 height and x1 starting

| | |
|---|---|
| Pre/Post conds | (x1,x2::isreal)(pol::ispol) → (ispol) |
| Example | ex:<0.5,1>:(q:1 * q:1) |

---

Lex *linear* extrusion, with x2 - x1 height and shearing, and x1 starting

| | |
|---|---|
| Pre/Post conds | (x1,x2::isreal)(pol::ispol) → (ispol) |
| Example | lex:<0.5,1>:(q:1 * q:1) |

---

Lxmy *left x, middle y* alignment operator. Moves the origin of the local frame

| | |
|---|---|
| Pre/Post conds | (ispol) → (ispol) |
| Example | lxmy:(cuboid:<5,5>) |

---

Mirror returns the obj parameter reflected on the $d$-th coordinate direction

| | |
|---|---|
| Pre/Post conds | (d::isintpos)(obj::ispol) → (ispol) |
| Example | (@1 ~ struct ~ [id, mirror:1] ~ simplex):2 |

---

Minkowski sum of p complex with the zonotope defined by vects sequence

| | |
|---|---|
| Pre/Post conds | `(vects::isseqof:isvect)(p::ispol) → (ispol)` |
| Example | `minkowski:<<-1/2, SQRT:2/-2>,<-1/2, SQRT:2/2>,<1, 0>>:` |
| | `((@1 ~ cuboid):<5,5>)` |

**Multextrude** a polyhedral complex, by associating the facets of p with the h heights

| | |
|---|---|
| Pre/Post conds | `(p::ispol) (h::isseqof:isreal) → (ispol)` |
| Example | `multextrude:(q:<1,-1,1,-1,1> * q:1):<1.0,2.0,3.0>` |

**Mxby** *middle x, bottom y* alignment operator. Moves the origin of the local frame

| | |
|---|---|
| Pre/Post conds | `(ispol) → (ispol)` |
| Example | `mxby:(cuboid:<5,5>)` |

**Mxmy** *middle x, middle y* alignment operator. Moves the origin of the local frame

| | |
|---|---|
| Pre/Post conds | `(ispol) → (ispol)` |
| Example | `mxmy:(cuboid:<5,5>)` |

**Mxty** *middle x, top y* alignment operator. Moves the origin of the local frame

| | |
|---|---|
| Pre/Post conds | `(ispol) → (ispol)` |
| Example | `mxty:(cuboid:<5,5>)` |

**Offset** geometric operator. Implemented as the composition of suitable extrusions, followed by projection

| | |
|---|---|
| Pre/Post conds | `(v::isvect)(pol::ispol) → (ispol)` |
| Example | `offSet:<0.1,0.2,0.1>:((@1 ~ cuboid):<1,1,1>)` |

**Optimize** is used to flatten the internal HPC data structure. The annotations of parts with properties are lost. Alias for `mkpol ~ ukpol`

| | |
|---|---|
| Pre/Post conds | `(ispol) → (ispol)` |
| Example | `(optimize ~ struct ~ [id, t:1:1, t:2:1]):(simplex:2)` |

**Planemapping** plane mapping through three points p0, p1 and p2

| | |
|---|---|
| Pre/Post conds | `(p0,p1,p2::ispoint) → (ispol)` |
| Example | `map:(planemapping:<<0,0,0>,<1,0,0>,<1,1,1>>):(cuboid:<1,1>)` |

**Polar** generator of the polar set of a n-dimensional convex

| | |
|---|---|
| Pre/Post conds | `(ispol) → (ispol)` |
| Example | `(polar ~ simplex):4 ≡ polcomplex<4,4>` |

**Presort** executes the preliminary z-ordering when depth-sorting a polygon sequence

| | |
|---|---|
| Pre/Post conds | `(pols::isseqof:(c:eq:<2,3> ~ [dim,rn])) → (isseqof:ispol)` |
| Example | `(presort ~ [t:3:1, id] ~ embed:1 ~ simplex):2` |

**Project** projection operator, that removes the last m coordinates of pol

| | |
|---|---|
| Pre/Post conds | `(m::isintpos)(pol::ispol) → (ispol)` |
| Example | `(Project:1 ~ @1 ~ R:<1,4>:(PI/6) ~ R:<1,3>:(PI/7)):` |
| | `(cuboid:<1,1,1,1>);` |

**Rxmy** *right x, middle y* alignment operator. Moves the origin of the local frame

| | |
|---|---|
| Pre/Post conds | `(ispol) → (ispol)` |
| Example | `rxmy:(cuboid:<5,5>)` |

**Schlegel2d** returns 2D Schlegel diagrams of 3-polytopes, projected from $(0,0,d)$

| | |
|---|---|
| Pre/Post conds | `(d::isreal)(pol::ispol) → (ispol)` |
| Example | `(@1 ~ schlegel2D:0.2 ~ T:3:2.5 ~ CUBOID):<1,1,1>` |

Schlegel3d returns 3D Schlegel diagrams of 4-polytopes, projected from $(0,0,0,d)$

| | |
|---|---|
| Pre/Post conds | (d::isreal)(pol::ispol) $\rightarrow$ (ispol) |
| Example | (schlegel3d:0.2 $\sim$ @1 $\sim$ t:<1,2,3,4>:<-1,-1,-1,1> $\sim$ cuboid):<2,2,2,2> |

Sex *screw* extrusion of pol, with h steps, x2 - x1 total angle, and x1 starting angle

| | |
|---|---|
| Pre/Post conds | (x1,x2::isreal)(h::isintpos)(pol::ispol) $\rightarrow$ (ispol) |
| Example | sex:<0,pi>:12:(q:1 * q:1) |

Solidify mapping boundary to interior; multidimensional operator

| | |
|---|---|
| Pre/Post conds | (and $\sim$ [ispol, c:eq:1 $\sim$ (rn - dim)]) $\rightarrow$ (ispol) |
| Example | Solidify $\sim$ STRUCT $\sim$ AA:polyline |

Splitcells extracts the convex $d$-cells of the $d$-dimensional scene

| | |
|---|---|
| Pre/Post conds | (scene::ispol) $\rightarrow$ (isseqof:ispol) |
| Example | (struct $\sim$ explode:<1,1,1.5> $\sim$ splitcells $\sim$ @2):hole |

Splitpols extracts the polyhedral $d$-cells of the $d$-dimensional scene

| | |
|---|---|
| Pre/Post conds | (scene::ispol) $\rightarrow$ (isseqof:ispol) |
| Example | (struct $\sim$ explode:<1.5,1.5,1.5> $\sim$ splitpols $\sim$ @2):hole |

Sweep returns the point set swept by pol when moved by a v displacement

| | |
|---|---|
| Pre/Post conds | (v::isvect)(pol::ispol) $\rightarrow$ (ispol) |
| Example | sweep:<10,0>:(circle:1:<24,1>) |

## B.11  primitives Library

Displaygraph graph generator for f : $\mathbb{R} \rightarrow \mathbb{R}$, where n is a marker index

| | |
|---|---|
| Pre/Post conds | (n::isint)(f::isfun)(sample::isseqof:isnum) $\rightarrow$ (ispol) |
| Example | (displaygraph:1:sin $\sim$ c:al:0 $\sim$ progressivesum $\sim$ #:32):(pi/16) |

Isclosedshape predicate to test if the arg shape is either closed or not

| | |
|---|---|
| Pre/Post conds | (arg::isshape) $\rightarrow$ (isbool) |
| Example | isclosedshape:<<5,3,-2.5,-2.5,-3>,<-2,4,-2,2,-2>> $\equiv$ true |

Iscloseto predicate to test is the arg distance from x is less than 1e-4

| | |
|---|---|
| Pre/Post conds | (x::isnum)(arg::isnum) $\rightarrow$ (isbool) |
| Example | iscloseto:0:0.001 $\equiv$ false; iscloseto:0:1e-6 $\equiv$ true |

Isorthoshape predicate to test if the arg shape is made by orthogonal segments

| | |
|---|---|
| Pre/Post conds | (arg::isshape) $\rightarrow$ (isbool) |
| Example | isorthoshape:<<5,3,-2.5,-2.5,-3>,<-2,4,-2,2,-2>> $\equiv$ false |

Isshape predicate to test if arg is a *shape* (see Section 7.3)

| | |
|---|---|
| Pre/Post conds | (arg::and $\sim$ [ispair,ismat]) $\rightarrow$ (isbool) |
| Example | isshape:<<5,3,-2.5,-2.5,-3>,<-2,4,-2,2,-2>> $\equiv$ true |

Mapshapes returns a sampling of segment between two shapes, made compatible

| | |
|---|---|
| Pre/Post conds | (p,q::isshape) $\rightarrow$ (isseqof:isshape) |
| Example | mapShapes:< <<5,0,-5>,<0,5,-5>>, <<0,1,0,-2,0,3,0,-4,0,0,5>,<-1,0,2,0,-3,0,4,0,-5,0>> > |

`Markersize` constant value used to define the marker size. Default value is 0.05

| | |
|---|---|
| Pre/Post conds | $\rightarrow$ (isnum) |
| Example | DEF MarkerSize = 0.10 |

---

`Mesh` returns a $d$-dimensional mesh with hyperparallelepiped cells

| | |
|---|---|
| Pre/Post conds | (seqs::and $\sim$ aa:(isseqof:isnum)) $\rightarrow$ (ispol) |
| Example | (@1 $\sim$ mesh):<<1,2,1,2,1>,<1,2,1,2,1,2,1>> |

---

`Points2shape` transforms a 2D point seq into a *shape* instance

| | |
|---|---|
| Pre/Post conds | (seq::and $\sim$ [ismat, ispair $\sim$ trans]) $\rightarrow$ (isshape) |
| Example | (points2shape):<<0,0>,<3,0>,<2,4>,<1,2>> $\equiv$ <<3,-1,-1>,<0,4,-2>> |

---

`Polypoint` point primitive generator

| | |
|---|---|
| Pre/Post conds | (points::ismat) $\rightarrow$ (ispol) |
| Example | (join $\sim$ polypoint):<<0,-0.23>,<20,0>,<5.77,11>,<20,-10>> |

---

`Polyline` generator of 1D connected complexes from the `points` sequence

| | |
|---|---|
| Pre/Post conds | (points::ismat) $\rightarrow$ (ispol) |
| Example | polyline:<<1,0,-5.1>,<1,1.2,0>,<0,2,-2>,<-1,-1.25,4>> |

---

`Polymarker` returns a complex of *markers* generated at specified `points`

| | |
|---|---|
| Pre/Post conds | (markertype::isintpos)(points::ismat) $\rightarrow$ (ispol) |
| Example | polymarker:3: |
| | ((aa:[id,sin] $\sim$ c:al:0 $\sim$ progressivesum $\sim$ #:24):(pi/12)) |

---

`Quadmesh` generator of a mesh of quadrilaterals from an array of `points`

| | |
|---|---|
| Pre/Post conds | (points::ismatof:ispoint) $\rightarrow$ (ispol) |
| Example | quadmesh:< <<0,0>,<1,0>,<2,0>>, <<0,1>,<1,1>,<2,1>>, |
| | <<0,2>,<1,2>,<2,2>> > |

---

`Shape2points` operator to return a point sequence from the `arg` shape

| | |
|---|---|
| Pre/Post conds | (arg::isshape) $\rightarrow$ (isseqof:ispoint) |
| Example | shape2points:<<1,2,3>,<0,1,0>> $\equiv$ <<0,0>,<1,0>,<3,1>,<6,1>> |

---

`Shape2pol` operator to return a polyhedral complex from the `arg` shape

| | |
|---|---|
| Pre/Post conds | (arg::isshape) $\rightarrow$ (ispol) |
| Example | shape2pol:<<1,2,3>,<0,1,0>> $\equiv$ polcomplex<1,2> |

---

`Shapeclosed` mapping from a $d$-shape to a $(d+1)$-shape, that adds a final tangent vector to close the `arg` shape

| | |
|---|---|
| Pre/Post conds | (arg::isshape) $\rightarrow$ (isshape) |
| Example | shapeclosed:<<1,2,3>,<0,1,0>> $\equiv$ <<1,2,3,-6>,<0,1,0,-1>> |

---

`Shapecomb` operator to linearly combine the input shapes, returning $ap + bq$

| | |
|---|---|
| Pre/Post conds | (a,b::isreal; p,q::isshape) $\rightarrow$ (isshape) |
| Example | shapecomb:<0.5,0.5,<<1,0,1>,<2,-1,3>>,<<0,2,2>,<-0.5,-1,0>>> |

---

`Shapediff` difference operator between p and q shapes

| | |
|---|---|
| Pre/Post conds | (p,q::isshape) $\rightarrow$ (isshape) |
| Example | <<1,0,1>,<2,-1,3>> shapediff <<0,2,2>,<-0.5,-1,0>> |

---

`Shapedist` Euclidean distance computation between p and q shapes

| | |
|---|---|
| Pre/Post conds | (p,q::isshape) $\rightarrow$ (isnum) |
| Example | <<1,0,1>,<2,-1,3>> shapedist <<0,2,2>,<-0.5,-1,0>> $\equiv$ 4.60977 |

**Shapeinbetweening** returns the polyhedral complex of n shapes on the s

Pre/Post conds    (tx::isreal)(n::isint)(p,q::isshape) $\rightarrow$ (ispol)

Example        ShapeInBetweening:0:4<<<1,0,1>,<2,-1,3>>,<<0,2,2>,<-0.5,-1,0>>>

---

**Shapeinf** returns the inferior shape of the p input shape

Pre/Post conds    (p::isshape) $\rightarrow$ (isshape)

Example        (shape2pol $\sim$ shapeinf):<<5,3,-2.5,-2.5,2.5>,<0,4,-2,2,-2>>

---

**Shapejoin** joins two shapes and returns a shape value

Pre/Post conds    (p,q::isshape) $\rightarrow$ (isshape)

Example        shapejoin:<<<1,0,1>,<2,-1,3>>,<<0,2,2>,<-0.5,-1,0>>>

---

**Shapelen** returns the sum of lengths of tangent vectors of p

Pre/Post conds    (p::isshape) $\rightarrow$ (isnum)

Example        shapelen:<<1,0,1>,<2,-1,3>> $\equiv$ 6.39834563766817

---

**Shapenormal** returns a shape whose tangent vectors are normal to those of p

Pre/Post conds    (p::isshape) $\rightarrow$ (isshape)

Example        (struct $\sim$ aa:shape2pol $\sim$ [id,shapenormal]):<<1,0,1>,<2,-1,3>>

---

**Shapenorm** returns the Euclidean norm of p as a vector in $\mathbb{R}^{2n}$

Pre/Post conds    (p::isshape) $\rightarrow$ (isnum)

Example        shapenorm:<<1,0,1>,<2,-1,3>> $\equiv$ 4

---

**Shapeprod** product of the p (shape) vector times the alpha scalar

Pre/Post conds    (alpha::isreal; p::isshape) $\rightarrow$ (isshape)

Example        shapeprod:<3,<<1,0,1>,<2,-1,3>>> $\equiv$ <<3,0,3>,<6,-3,9>>

---

**Shaperot** rotation of angle $\alpha$ of the p shape

Pre/Post conds    (alpha::isreal)(p::isshape) $\rightarrow$ (isshape)

Example        shaperot:(pi/6):<<1,0,1>,<2,-1,3>>

---

**Shapesum** addition operation between p and q shapes in their vector space

Pre/Post conds    (p,q::isshape) $\rightarrow$ (isshape)

Example        <<1,0,1>,<2,-1,3>> shapesum <<0,2,2>,<-0.5,-1,0>> $\equiv$
                 <<1,2,3>,<1.5,-2,3>>

---

**Shapesup** returns the superior shape of the p input shape

Pre/Post conds    (p::isshape) $\rightarrow$ (isshape)

Example        (shape2pol $\sim$ shapesup):<<5,3,-2.5,-2.5,2.5>,<0,4,-2,2,-2>>

---

**Shapezero** returns the neutral (zero) element of the vector space of $n$-shapes

Pre/Post conds    (n::isint) $\rightarrow$ (isshape)

Example        shapezero:4 $\equiv$ <<0,0,0,0>,<0,0,0,0>>

---

**Star** 2D star primitive with n tips

Pre/Post conds    (n::isintpos) $\rightarrow$ (ispol)

Example        (struct $\sim$ [@1 * k:(q:0.5), embed:1] $\sim$ star):5 $\equiv$
                 polcomplex<2,3>

---

**Trianglefan** multidimensional primitive with the first element of verts as pivot

Pre/Post conds    (verts::isseqof:ispoint) $\rightarrow$ (ispol)

Example        trianglefan:<<0,0,0>,<1,0,0>,<1,0,4>,<0,0,4>,<0,1,4>,<0,1,0>>

---

**Trianglestripe** multidimensional primitive giving a complex of oriented triangles

Pre/Post conds    (verts::isseqof:ispoint) $\rightarrow$ (ispol)

Example        triangleStripe:<<0,3>,<1,2>,<3,3>,<2,2>,<3,0>,<2,1>,<0,0>,
                 <1,1>,<0,3>,<1,2>>

## B.12 shapes Library

---

**Circle** returns on approx. with m×n quads/triangles of the 2D circle of r radius

Pre/Post conds    (r::isreal)(m,n::isintpos) → (ispol)

Example         circle:1:<24,1>

---

**Circumference** approx. with m segments of the 2D circle boundary of unit radius

Pre/Post conds    (m::isintpos) → (ispol)

Example         circumference:36

---

**Cone** approx. with m facets of the 3D cone with r radius and h height

Pre/Post conds    (r, h::isreal)(n::isint) → (ispol)

Example         Cone:<1,2>:24

---

**Convexhull** multidimensional operator returning the convex hull of points $\subset \mathbb{E}^d$

Pre/Post conds    (points::ismat) → (ispol)

Example         convexhull:<<0,0,0,0>,<1,0,0,0>,<0,1,0,0>,<0,0,1,0>,<0,0,0,1>>

---

**Crosspolytope** returns the $d$-dimensional crossPolytope

Pre/Post conds    (d::isintpos) → (ispol)

Example         crossPolytope:3

---

**Cube** generator of the 3D hexahedron of given side, with a vertex on the origin

Pre/Post conds    (side::isrealpos) → (ispol)

Example         mxmy:(cube:2)

---

**Dsphere** generator of $d$-sphere of unit radius, with boundary facets of $\pi$/m resolution

Pre/Post conds    (d::isnat)(m::isintpos) → (ispol)

Example         dsphere:3:24 material transparentmaterial:<red,0.7>

---

**Dodecahedron** constant value inscribed in the unit sphere

Pre/Post conds      → (ispol)

Example         VRML:dodecahedron:'path/out.wrl'

---

**Ellipse** approx. with $4 \times m$ segments of the ellipse boundary of a,b radiuses

Pre/Post conds    (a,b::isreal)(m::isintpos) → (ispol)

Example         ellipse:<1/2,1>:8 * quote:<1/2>

---

**Finitecone** $d$-dimensional cone with given basis and apex in $(0,\ldots,0) \in \mathbb{E}^d$

Pre/Post conds    (basis::ispol) → (ispol)

Example         finitecone:((t:<1,2,3>:<1,2,3> ~ cuboid):<1,1,1>)

---

**Fractalsimplex** generator of recursive $d$-simplex with $n$ levels

Pre/Post conds    (d::isintpos)(n::isintpos) → (ispol)

Example         fractalsimplex:3:5

---

**Hexahedron** constant value. 3D cube inscribed in the standard unit sphere

Pre/Post conds      → (ispol)

Example         VRML:hexahedron:'path/out.wrl'

---

**Icosahedron** constant value. 3D icosahedron inscribed in the standard unit sphere

Pre/Post conds      → (ispol)

Example         VRML:icosahedron:'path/out.wrl'

---

**Intervals** constructor of a uniform partition of 1D interval $[0, a]$ with m segments

| | |
|---|---|
| Pre/Post conds | (a::isrealpos)(m::isintpos) |
| | $\rightarrow$ (and $\sim$ [ispol,c:eq:<1,1> $\sim$ [dim,rn]]) |
| Example | intervals:(2*pi):24 |

---

**Ispolytope** predicate testing if **arg** is a polytope (bounded polyhedron) or not

| | |
|---|---|
| Pre/Post conds | (arg::ispol) $\rightarrow$ (isbool) |
| Example | ispolytope:(cuboid:<1,1,1,1>) $\equiv$ true |

---

**Issimplex** predicate testing if **arg** is either a simplex or not

| | |
|---|---|
| Pre/Post conds | (arg::ispol) $\rightarrow$ (isbool) |
| Example | issimplex:(simplex:3) $\equiv$ true |

---

**Mkframe** constant geometric value, returning a model of the 3D reference frame

| | |
|---|---|
| Pre/Post conds | $\rightarrow$ (ispol) |
| Example | struct:<mkframe, cuboid:<1,1,1>> |

---

**Mkvector** constructor of a 3D model of vector p2 - p1, with p1,p2 $\in \mathbb{E}^3$

| | |
|---|---|
| Pre/Post conds | (p1::ispoint)(p2::ispoint) $\rightarrow$ (ispol) |
| Example | mkvector:<1,0,0>:<1,1,1> |

---

**Mkversork** constant geometric value. Returns a 3D model of unit vector $e_3 \in \mathbb{E}^3$

| | |
|---|---|
| Pre/Post conds | $\rightarrow$ (ispol) |
| Example | struct:<mkversork, cuboid:<1,1,1>> |

---

**Ngon** constructor of 2D regular polygons with n sides

| | |
|---|---|
| Pre/Post conds | (n::and $\sim$ [isintpos, ge:3]) $\rightarrow$ (ispol) |
| Example | (struct $\sim$ cat):(aa:ngon:(3..8) distr t:1:2.5) |

---

**Octahedron** constant value. 3D Octahedron inscribed in the standard unit sphere

| | |
|---|---|
| Pre/Post conds | $\rightarrow$ (ispol) |
| Example | VRML:octahedron:'path/out.wrl' |

---

**Permutahedron** generator of the $d$-dimensional permutahedron

| | |
|---|---|
| Pre/Post conds | (d::isintpos) $\rightarrow$ (ispol) |
| Example | permutahedron:3 |

---

**Plane** generator of the 2-flat passing through 3 points in $\mathbb{E}^3$

| | |
|---|---|
| Pre/Post conds | (point0, point1, point2::ispoint) $\rightarrow$ (ispol) |
| Example | (s3 $\sim$ plane):<<0,0,0>,<1,0,0>,<1,1,1>> |

---

**Prism** generator of the $(d+1)$-prism with given **height** and $d$-dimensional basis

| | |
|---|---|
| Pre/Post conds | (height::isrealpos)(basis::ispol) $\rightarrow$ (ispol) |
| Example | prism:1:(crosspolytope:2) |

---

**Pyramid** complex of $(d+1)$-pyramids of h height, associated with the **basis** $d$-cells

| | |
|---|---|
| Pre/Post conds | (h::isreal)(basis::ispol) $\rightarrow$ (ispol) |
| Example | (struct $\sim$ aa:(pyramid:1) $\sim$ splitcells): (q:<3,3,3>*q:<3,3,3>) |

---

**Ring** difference of 2D circles with radiuses r1, r2, approximated with m×n steps

| | |
|---|---|
| Pre/Post conds | (r1,r2::isrealpos)(m,n::isintpos) $\rightarrow$ (ispol) |
| Example | (@1 $\sim$ Ring:<0.5,1>):<24,2> |

---

**Segment** scaled segment through two $d$-points a and b, with coefficient sx

| Pre/Post conds | (sx::isreal)(a,b::ispoint) $\rightarrow$ (ispol) |
|---|---|
| Example | segment:2:<<0,0,0>,<1,1,1>> |

**Simplexpile** extrusion operator for the $d$-simplex

| Pre/Post conds | (cell::issimplex) $\rightarrow$ (ispol) |
|---|---|
| Example | (struct $\sim$ [@1 $\sim$ simplexpile, id] $\sim$ simplex):2 |

**Sphere** generator of 3D sphere of r radius, approximated with m×n facets

| Pre/Post conds | (r::isrealpos)(m,n::isintpos) $\rightarrow$ (ispol) |
|---|---|
| Example | Sphere:1:<12,24> |

**Tetrahedron** constant value. 3D regular tetrahedron, inscribed in the unit sphere

| Pre/Post conds | $\rightarrow$ (ispol) |
|---|---|
| Example | VRML:tetrahedron:'path/out.wrl' |

**Torus** generator of 3D torus with radiuses r1,r2, approximated with m×n facets

| Pre/Post conds | (r1,r2::isreal) (n,m::isintpos) $\rightarrow$ (ispol) |
|---|---|
| Example | torus:<1,3>:<12,24> $\equiv$ PolComplex<2,3> |

**Truncone** 3D truncated cone, with h height, r1,r2 radiuses and n lateral facets

| Pre/Post conds | (r1,r2,h::isrealpos)(n::isintpos) $\rightarrow$ (ispol) |
|---|---|
| Example | truncone:<2,1,2>:24 |

**Tube** 3D empty tube with h height, r1,r2 radiuses and 2 × n lateral facets

| Pre/Post conds | (r1,r2,h::isreal)(n::isint) $\rightarrow$ (ispol) |
|---|---|
| Example | tube:<0.8,1,2>:24 |

## B.13   splines **Library**

**Blend** generator of the *coordinate functions* of a specific spline curve

| Pre/Post conds | (basis::isseqof:isfun) (controlpoints::ismat) $\rightarrow$ (isseqof:isfun) |
|---|---|
| Example | blend:(bsplinebasis:4:<0,0,0,0,1,2,3,4,4,4,4>): |
| | <<0.1,0>,<2,0>,<6,1.5>,<6,4>,<2,5.5>,<2,6>,<3.5,6.5>> |

**Bsplinebasis** non-uniform B-spline basis generator with assigned order and knots

| Pre/Post conds | (order::isnat) (knots::isseqof:isreal) $\rightarrow$ (isseqof:isfun) |
|---|---|
| Example | bsplinebasis:4:<0,0,0,0,1,2,3,4,4,4,4> |

**Bspline** non-uniform B-spline curve of assigned degree, knots and points

| Pre/Post conds | (dom::and $\sim$ [ispol,c:eq:<1,1> $\sim$ [dim,rn]])(degree::isnat) |
|---|---|
| | (knots::isseqof:isreal)(points::ismat) $\rightarrow$ (ispol) |
| Example | bspline:(intervals:1:10):3:<0,0,0,0,1,2,3,4,4,4,4>: |
| | <<0,0>,<-1,2>,<1,4>,<2,3>,<1,1>,<1,2>,<2.5,1>> |

**Cubiccardinalbasis** constant value. Cubic cardinal polynomial basis

| Pre/Post conds | $\rightarrow$ (isseqof:isfun) |
|---|---|
| Example | blend:cubiccardinalbasis:<<-1,0>,<-1,2>,<1,4>,<2,3>,<-4,2>> |

**Cubiccardinal** generator of the function argument to the spline operator, independent on the control points

| Pre/Post conds | `(segmentdomain::ispol) → (isfun)` |
| Example | `spline:(cubiccardinal:(intervals:1:10)):` |
| | `<<-3,6>,<-4,2>,<-3,-1>,<-1,1>,<1.5,1.5>,<3,4>>` |

`Cubicubsplinebasis` constant value. Cubic uniform b-spline polynomial basis

| Pre/Post conds | `→ (isseqof:isfun)` |
| Example | `blend:Cubicubsplinebasis:<<-1,0>,<-1,2>,<1,4>,<2,3>,<-4,2>>` |

`Cubicubspline` generator of the function argument to the `spline` operator, independent on the control points

| Pre/Post conds | `(segmentdomain::ispol) → (isfun)` |
| Example | `spline:(cubicubspline:(intervals:1:10)):` |
| | `<<-3,6>,<-4,2>,<-3,-1>,<-1,1>,<1.5,1.5>,<3,4>>` |

`Deboor` generator of a non-uniform b-spline basis polynomial

| Pre/Post conds | `(knots::isseqof:isreal) → (isfun)` |
| Example | `map:[s1,deboor:<2,3,4,5>]:(intervals:5:50)` |

`Displaynubspline` returns a non-uniform b-spline, with control polygon and joints

| Pre/Post conds | `(degree::isnat; knots::isseq ; points::isseq) → (ispol)` |
| Example | `displaynubspline:< 2,<0,0,0,1,2,3,4,5,5,5>,` |
| | `<<0.1,0>,<2,0>,<6,1.5>,<6,4>,<2,5.5>,<2,6>,<3.5,6.5>> >` |

`Displaynurbspline` returns a NURB spline, with control polygon and joints

| Pre/Post conds | `(degree::isnat; knots::isseq ; points::isseq) → (ispol)` |
| Example | `displaynurbspline:< 2,<0,0,0,1,2,3,4,5,5,5>, <<0.1,0,1>,` |
| | `<2,0,1>,<6,1.5,1>,<6,4,1>,<2,5.5,1>,<2,6,1>,<3.5,6.5,1>> >` |

`Joints` is used to apply a marker to each sampled point of the spline curve

| Pre/Post conds | `(thespline::isfun) → (isfun)` |
| Example | `joints:cubiccardinal:<<-3,6>,<-4,2>,<-3,-1>,<-1,1>,<1.5,1.5>>` |

`Nubsplineknots` returns the 0D complex of joints between nub-spline segments

| Pre/Post conds | `(degree::isnat)(knots::isseq)(points::isseq) → (ispol)` |
| Example | `(polymarker:2~s1~ukpol~nubsplineknots:2:<0,0,0,1,2,3,4,4,4>):` |
| | `<<0.1,0>,<2,0>,<6,1.5>,<6,4>,<2,5.5>,<2,6>>` |

`Nubspline` non-uniform B-spline curve of assigned `degree`, `knots` and `points`

| Pre/Post conds | `(degree::isnat)(knots::isseqof:isreal)(points::ismat)→(ispol)` |
| Example | `nubspline:2:<0,0,0,1,2,3,4,5,5,5>:` |
| | `<<0,0>,<-1,2>,<1,4>,<2,3>,<1,1>,<1,2>,<2.5,1>>` |

`Nurbsplineknots` returns the 0D complex of joints between NURB spline segments

| Pre/Post conds | `(degree::isnat)(knots::isseq)(points::isseq) → (ispol)` |
| Example | `(polymarker:2~s1~ukpol~nurbsplineknots:2:<0,0,0,1,2,3,4,4,4>):` |
| | `<<0.1,0,1>,<2,0,1>,<6,1.5,1>,<6,4,1>,<2,5.5,1>,<2,6,1>>` |

`Nurbspline` NURB spline curve of assigned `degree`, `knots` and `points`

| Pre/Post conds | `(degree::isnat)(knots::isseqof:isreal)(points::ismat)→(ispol)` |
| Example | `nubspline:2:<0,0,0,1,2,3,4,5,5,5>:` |
| | `<<0,0,1>,<-1,2,1>,<1,4,1>,<2,3,1>,<1,1,1>,<1,2,1>,<2.5,1,1>>` |

`Rationalbspline` NURB spline curve of assigned `degree`, `knots` and `points`

| Pre/Post conds | `(dom::and ~ [ispol,c:eq:<1,1> ~ [dim,rn]])(degree::isnat)` |
| --- | --- |
| | `(knots::isseqof:isreal)(points::ismat)` $\rightarrow$ `(ispol)` |
| Example | `rationalbspline:(intervals:1:11):3:<0,0,0,0,1,2,3,4,4,4,4>:` |
| | `<<0,0,1>,<-1,2,1>,<1,4,1>,<2,3,1>,<1,1,1>,<1,2,1>,<2.5,1,1>>` |

`Splinesampling` constant number of subintervals in the partition of unit interval

| Pre/Post conds | $\rightarrow$ `(isnum)` |
| --- | --- |
| Example | `intervals:1:splinesampling` |

`Spline` generator of uniform splines starting from a `curve` generator function

| Pre/Post conds | `(curve::isfun)` $\rightarrow$ `(isfun)` |
| --- | --- |
| Example | `spline:(cubicubspline:(intervals:1:splinesampling)):` |
| | `<<-3,6>,<-4,2>,<-3,-1>,<-1,1>,<1.5,1.5>,<3,4>>` |

## B.14 strings Library

`Nat2string` returns a binary representation of n, i.e. a string of binary digits

| Pre/Post conds | `(n::isnat)` $\rightarrow$ `(isstring)` |
| --- | --- |
| Example | `nat2string:19` $\equiv$ `'10011'` |

`Stringtokens` returns a sequence of tokens from the input string, given a set of separators

| Pre/Post conds | `(separators::isseqof:isstring)(input::isstring)` |
| --- | --- |
| | $\rightarrow$ `(isseqof:isstring)` |
| Example | `StringTokens:<'⊔','and',','>:'Fred, Wilma, Barney and Lucy'` |
| | $\equiv$ `<'Fred','Wilma','Barney','Lucy'>` |

## B.15 surfaces Library

`Beziermanifold` generator of Bézier $d$-manifolds in $\mathbb{E}^n$, for any dimensions/degrees

| Pre/Post conds | `(degrees::isseqof:isnat)(controlpoints::isseq)` |
| --- | --- |
| | $\rightarrow$ `(isseqof:isfun)` |
| Example | see `Script 12.4.1` |

`Beziersurface` generator of Bézier surfaces of arbitrary degree

| Pre/Post conds | `(controlpoints::ismatof:ispoint)` $\rightarrow$ `(isseqof:isfun)` |
| --- | --- |
| Example | `MAP:(BezierSurface:pointArray):((sqr ~ intervals:1):10)` |

`Bilinearsurface` generator of coord functions of a bilinear surface in $\mathbb{E}^n$

| Pre/Post conds | `(controlpoints::ismatof:ispoint)` $\rightarrow$ `(isseqof:isfun)` |
| --- | --- |
| Example | `def mapping = bilinearsurface:` |
| | `<<<0,0,0>,<2,-4,2>>,<<0,3,1>,<4,0,0>>>;` |
| | `map:mapping:((sqr~intervals:1):10)` |

`Biquadraticsurface` generator of coord functions of a biquadratic surface in $\mathbb{E}^n$

| Pre/Post conds | `(controlpoints::ismatof:ispoint)` $\rightarrow$ `(isseqof:isfun)` |
| --- | --- |
| Example | `biquadraticSurface:< <<0,0,0>, <2,0,1>,<3,1,1>>,` |
| | `<<1,3,-1>,<3,2,0>,<4,2,0>>, <<0,9,0>, <2,5,1>,<3,3,2>> >;` |
| | `map:mapping:((sqr~intervals:1):10)` |

**Conicalsurface** generalized cone, with apex a and curve `beta` crossing all the rules

| | |
|---|---|
| Pre/Post conds | `(a::isseqof:isreal; beta::isseqof:isfun)` → `(isseqof:isfun)` |
| Example | `map:(conicalsurface:<<0,0,1>,beta>):((sqr~intervals:1):10)` |

**Cylindricalsurface** generalized cylinder, with direction a and curve `beta` crossing all the rules

| | |
|---|---|
| Pre/Post conds | `(a::isseqof:isreal; beta::isseqof:isfun)` → `(isseqof:isfun)` |
| Example | `map:(cylindricalsurface:<<0,0,1>,beta>):((sqr~intervals:1):10)` |

**Hermitesurface** generator of coord functions of the *bicubic* Hermite surface

| | |
|---|---|
| Pre/Post conds | `(controlpoints::ismatof:ispoint)` → `(isseqof:isfun)` |
| Example | `map:(hermitesurface:< 4 × 4 matrix of points >):domain2d` |

**Profileprodsurface** returns the coord functions of a profile product surface

| | |
|---|---|
| Pre/Post conds | `(profile, section::isseqof:isfun)` → `(isseqof:isfun)` |
| Example | `map:(profileprodsurface:< alpha, beta >):domain2d` |

**Rotationalsurface** generates a surface by rotation of `profilecurve`. The opening angle of the rotational patch depends on the *2nd* domain parameter

| | |
|---|---|
| Pre/Post conds | `(profilecurve::isseqof:isfun)` → `(isseqof:isfun)` |
| Example | `map:(rotationalsurface:(bezier:s1:<<0,0>,<8,5>,<0,10>>)):` `(intervals:1:12 * intervals:(2*pi):24)` |

**Ruledsurface** surface from profile `alpha`($u$) and tangent vectors `beta`($u$)

| | |
|---|---|
| Pre/Post conds | `(alpha,beta::isseqof:isfun)` → `(isseqof:isfun)` |
| Example | `map:(ruledsurface:< c1, c2 vectdiff c1 >):domain2d` |

**Tensorprodsurface** tensor product surface generator

| | |
|---|---|
| Pre/Post conds | `(ubasis,vbasis::isseqof:isfun)(points::ismatof:ispoint)` → `(isseqof:isfun)` |
| Example | `(tensorprodsurface:< bernsteinbasis:s1:3,` `bernsteinbasis:s1:3>:controlpoints)` |

**Thinsolid** thin solid generated by a `surface`

| | |
|---|---|
| Pre/Post conds | `(surface::isseqof:isfun)` → `(isseqof:isfun)` |
| Example | `def solidmapping = (thinsolid ~ coonspatch):<su0,su1,s0v,s1v>` |

## B.16   text Library

**Rotatedtext** returns a 1D geometric text rotated by `alpha` radians

| | |
|---|---|
| Pre/Post conds | `(alpha::isreal)` → `(ispol)` |
| Example | `rotatedtext:(pi/4):'Hello Plasm!'` |

**Solidifier** operator to return an offset 3D geometric value for the `arg` string

| | |
|---|---|
| Pre/Post conds | `(arg::isstring)` → `(ispol)` |
| Example | `solidifier:'Hello, PLaSM World !'` |

**Textwithattributes** returns a 1D geometric text string with specified attributes

| | |
|---|---|
| Pre/Post conds | `(TextAlignment::IsString; TextAngle, TextWidth, TextHeight,` `TextSpacing::IsReal)(arg::isstring)` → `(ispol)` |
| Example | `TextWithAttributes:<'center',0,1,1,0.5>:'Hello, PLaSM World !'` |

**Text** returns some geometric text with default value for attributes

| | |
|---|---|
| Pre/Post conds | `(arg::isstring)` → `(ispol)` |
| Example | `text:'Hello, PLaSM World !'` |

## B.17  transfinite Library

---

**Bernsteinbasis** returns the Bernstein/Bézier polynomial basis of degree n

Pre/Post conds     (u::isfun)(n::isint) → (isseqof:isfun)

Example            bernsteinbasis:s1:3

---

**Bernstein** generator of the $i$-th Bernstein polynomial function of degree $n$

Pre/Post conds     (u::isfun)(n::isint)(i::isint) → (isfun)

Example            bernstein:s1:3:2

---

**Bezier** transfinite Bézier mapping of arbitrary dimension/degree

Pre/Post conds     (u::isfun) (controldata::isseq) → (isseqof:isfun)

Example            map(bezier:s1:<<10,0,0>,<10,5,3>,<10,10,0>>):dom1d

                       map(bezier:s2:<c1,c2,c3,c4>):dom2d

                       map(bezier:s3:<sur1,sur2,sur3,sur4>):dom3d

---

**Coonspatch** Coons′ patch interpolating four boundary curves su0, su1, s0v, s1v

Pre/Post conds     (su0,su1,s0v,s1v::isseqof:isfun) → (isseqof:isfun)

Example            MAP:(CoonsPatch:<Su0,Su1,S0v,S1v>):((sqr ~ Intervals:1):10)

---

**Cubichermite** transfinite cubic Hermite $d$-manifold generator

Pre/Post conds     (u::isfun) (p1,p2,t1,t2::isseq) → (isseqof:isfun)

Example            cubichermite:s2:< c1,v2,<0,0,1>,<0,0,-1> >

---

**Hermitebasis** returns the transfinite cubic Hermite basis

Pre/Post conds     (u::isfun) → (isseqof:isfun)

Example            hermitebasis:s1

---

## B.18  vectors Library

---

**Convexcoords** returns the convex coords of a point x w.r.t. a simplex p

Pre/Post conds     (p::issimplex)(x::ispoint) → (ispoint)

Example            convexcoords:(simplex:3):<1/3,1/3,1/3> ≡ <0.$\overline{3}$,0.$\overline{3}$,0.$\overline{3}$,0.0>

---

**Dirproject** directional projection of v vector in e direction

Pre/Post conds     (e::isvect)(v::isvect) → (isvect)

Example            dirproject:<1,1,0,0>:<10,15,20,25> ≡ <12.5,12.5,0,0>

---

**Idnt** identity matrix constructor

Pre/Post conds     (n::isintpos) → (ismat)

Example            idnt:4 ≡ <<1,0,0,0>,<0,1,0,0>,<0,0,1,0>,<0,0,0,1>

---

**Innerprod** inner product of vectors in $\mathbb{R}^n$

Pre/Post conds     (v,w::isvect) → (isnum)

Example            innerprod:<<11,12,13>,<4,5,6>> ≡ 182

---

**Isfunvect** predicate to test if arg is a sequence of functions or not

Pre/Post conds     (arg::tt) → (isbool)

Example            isfunvect:<id,k,sin> ≡ true

---

**Ismat** predicate to test if arg is a matrix (of either numbers or functions) or not

| Pre/Post conds | `(arg:tt)` $\rightarrow$ `(isbool)` |
|---|---|
| Example | `ismat:<<1.0,2.0,3.0>,<4.0,5.0,6.0>,<7.0,8.0,9.0>>` $\equiv$ `true` |

**Ismatof** to test if `arg` is a matrix of elements satisfying the `istype` predicate

| Pre/Post conds | `(istype::isfun)(arg:tt)` $\rightarrow$ `(isbool)` |
|---|---|
| Example | `ismatof:ispoint:<<<0,0,0>,<2,0,1>>,<<1,3,-1>,<3,2,0>>>` $\equiv$ `true` |

**Ispointseq** predicate to test if `arg` is a sequence of points in some $\mathbb{E}^d$

| Pre/Post conds | `(arg:tt)` $\rightarrow$ `(isbool)` |
|---|---|
| Example | `isPointSeq:<<0,0,0>,<2,0,1>,<1,3,-1.5>,<3,2,0>>` $\equiv$ `true` |

**Ispoint** predicate to test if `arg` is a point in some $\mathbb{E}^d$

| Pre/Post conds | `(arg:tt)` $\rightarrow$ `(isbool)` |
|---|---|
| Example | `ispoint:<0,0,0,1>` $\equiv$ `true` |

**Isrealvect** predicate to test if `arg` is a vector in some $\mathbb{R}^d$

| Pre/Post conds | `(arg:tt)` $\rightarrow$ `(isbool)` |
|---|---|
| Example | `isrealvect:<0,0,0,1>` $\equiv$ `true` |

**Issqrmat** predicate to test if `arg` is a square matrix in some $\mathcal{M}_d^d$

| Pre/Post conds | `(arg:tt)` $\rightarrow$ `(isbool)` |
|---|---|
| Example | `issqrmat:<<<0,0,0>,<2,0,1>>,<<1,3,-1>,<3,2,0>>>` $\equiv$ `true` |

**Isvect** predicate to test if `arg` is a vector in some $\mathcal{V}^d$ (of either numbers or functions)

| Pre/Post conds | `(arg:tt)` $\rightarrow$ `(isbool)` |
|---|---|
| Example | `isvect:<0,0,0,1>` $\equiv$ `true` |
| | `isvect:(beziercurve:<<0,0,0>,<1,0,0>,<1,1,1>,<0,1,0>>)` $\equiv$ `true` |

**Iszero** predicate to test if `arg` is the **0** element in some $\mathbb{R}^d$

| Pre/Post conds | `(arg:tt)` $\rightarrow$ `(isbool)` |
|---|---|
| Example | `iszero:<0,0,0,0>` $\equiv$ `true` |

**Matdotprod** binary inner product of matrix pair $\equiv$ ¡a,b¿ in some $\mathbb{R}_n^m$

| Pre/Post conds | `(pair::ismatof:isvect` $\sim$ `trans)` $\rightarrow$ `(isnum)` |
|---|---|
| Example | `<<1,2>,<3,4>,<5,6>> matdotprod <<10,20>,<30,40>,<50,60>>` $\equiv$ `910` |

**Mathom** matrix homogenization, i.e. adding of a unit *first* row and column

| Pre/Post conds | `(m::issqrmat)` $\rightarrow$ `(issqrmat)` |
|---|---|
| Example | `mathom:<<10,20>,<30,40>>` $\equiv$ `<<1,0,0>,<0,10,20>,<0,30,40>>` |

**Meanpoint** returns the point with middle coordinates from a `points` sequence

| Pre/Post conds | `(points::ispointseq)` $\rightarrow$ `(ispoint)` |
|---|---|
| Example | `Meanpoint:<<0,2,0>,<3,0,10>,<10,4,0>,<1,10,2>>` $\equiv$ `<7/2,4,3>` |

**Mixedprod** returns the mixed product $a \times b \cdot c$ of three vectors in $\mathbb{R}^3$

| Pre/Post conds | `(a,b,c::and` $\sim$ `[isvect, c:eq:3` $\sim$ `len])` $\rightarrow$ `(isnum)` |
|---|---|
| Example | `mixedprod:<<1,1,1>,<2,0,2>,<0,3,0>>` $\equiv$ `0` |

**Orthoproject** orthogonal projection of v vector in e direction

| Pre/Post conds | `(e::isvect)(v::isvect)` $\rightarrow$ `(isvect)` |
|---|---|
| Example | `orthoproject:<1,1,0,0>:<10,15,20,25>` $\equiv$ `<-2.5,2.5,20,25>` |

**Ortho** orthogonal component of a square `matrix`

| Pre/Post conds | (matrix::issqrmat) → (issqrmat) |
|---|---|
| Example | Ortho:<<0,1,0>,<0,0,2>,<1,1,1>> ≡ |
| | <<0,1/2,1/2>,<1/2,0,3/2>,<1/2,3/2,1>> |

**Pivotop** pivoting operation on the $(i,j)$ element of mat in some $\mathbb{R}^m_n$

| Pre/Post conds | (i,j::isintpos)(mat::ismat) → (ismat) |
|---|---|
| Example | (PivotOp:<2,2> * ID):<<1,2,0>,<0,-1,2>,<1,1,1>> ≡ |
| | <<1,0,4>,<0,1,-2>,<1,0,3>> |

**Rotn** rotation in $\mathbb{E}^3$ of $\alpha$ angle about an arbitrary axis $n$ for the origin

| Pre/Post conds | (alpha::isreal; n::isvect) → (isfun) |
|---|---|
| Example | rotn:<pi/4, <1,1,1>>:(cuboid:<1,1,1>) |

**Scalarmatprod** product of a scalar a times a matrix mat

| Pre/Post conds | (a::isnum; mat::ismat) → (ismat) |
|---|---|
| Example | 9 ScalarMatProd IDNT:3 ≡ <<9,0,0>,<0,9,0>,<0,0,9>> |

**Scalarvectprod** product of a scalar a times a vector v

| Pre/Post conds | (arg::ispair) → (isvect) |
|---|---|
| Example | 10 ScalarVectProd <1,2> ≡ <1,2> ScalarVectProd 10 ≡ <10,20> |

**Skew** skew component of a square matrix

| Pre/Post conds | (matrix::issqrmat) → (issqrmat) |
|---|---|
| Example | skew:<<0,1,0>,<0,0,2>,<1,1,1>> ≡ |
| | <<0,1/2,-1/2>,<-1/2,0,1/2>,<1/2,-1/2,0>> |

**Trace** returns the trace of the input matrix

| Pre/Post conds | (matrix::issqrmat) → (isnum) |
|---|---|
| Example | trace:<<1,2,3>,<4,5,6>,<7,8,9>> ≡ 15 |

**Unitvect** returns the unit vector of $\mathbb{R}^n$ parallel to $v \in \mathbb{R}^n$

| Pre/Post conds | (v::isvect) → (isvect) |
|---|---|
| Example | unitvect:<10,20,30> ≡ <0.2672612419, 0.534522483, 0.801783725> |

**Vectdiff** difference of vectors $v, w$ in a vector space $\mathcal{V}^d$ (of numbers or functions)

| Pre/Post conds | (v,w::isvect) → (isvect) |
|---|---|
| Example | vectdiff:<<11,12,13>,<4,5,6>> ≡ <7,7,7> |
| | beziercurve:<<0,0>,<1,0>,<1,1>,<0,1>> vectdiff <k:1,k:1> |

**Vectnorm** Euclidean norm of the vector v

| Pre/Post conds | (v::isvect) → (isnum) |
|---|---|
| Example | (vectnorm ∼ unitvect):<10,20,30> ≡ 0.9999999999999999 |

**Vectprod** vector product of vectors $u, v \in \mathbb{R}^3$

| Pre/Post conds | (u,v::isvect) → (isvect) |
|---|---|
| Example | vectProd:<<1,0,0>,<1,1,0>> ≡ <0,0,1> |

**Vectsum** addition of vectors $v, w$ in a vector space $\mathcal{V}^d$ (of numbers or functions)

| Pre/Post conds | (v,w::isvect) → (isvect) |
|---|---|
| Example | vectsum:<<11,12,13>,<4,5,6>> ≡ <15,17,19> |
| | beziercurve:<<0,0>,<1,0>,<1,1>,<0,1>> vectsum <k:1,k:1> |

**Vect2dtoangle** maps a vector $v \in \mathbb{E}^2$ to its signed angle with the $x$-axis

| Pre/Post conds | (v::isvect) → (isnum) |
|---|---|
| Example | vect2dtoangle:<1,1> ≡ vect2dtoangle:<2,2> ≡ 0.78539816339745 |

**B.19**  `viewmodels` **Library**

---

`Axialcameras` for VRML exporting. Centered on the reference frame axes

| | |
|---|---|
| Pre/Post conds | `(scene::ispol)` → `(ispol)` |
| Example | `Axialcameras:(cuboid:<1,1,1>)` |

---

`Cabinet` object; standard view model for parallel oblique projection

| | |
|---|---|
| Pre/Post conds | → `(isviewmodel)` |
| Example | `projection:parallel:cabinet:(cuboid:<1,1,1>)` |

---

`Centeredcameras` for VRML exporting. Centered on the `scene` containment box

| | |
|---|---|
| Pre/Post conds | `(scene::ispol)` → `(ispol)` |
| Example | `Axialcameras:(cuboid:<1,1,1>)` |

---

`Centralcavalier` object; standard view model for parallel oblique projection

| | |
|---|---|
| Pre/Post conds | → `(isviewmodel)` |
| Example | `projection:parallel:centralcavalier:(cuboid:<1,1,1>)` |

---

`Dimetric` object; standard view model for parallel orthogonal projection

| | |
|---|---|
| Pre/Post conds | → `(isviewmodel)` |
| Example | `projection:parallel:dimetric:(cuboid:<1,1,1>)` |

---

`Isometric` object; standard view model for parallel orthogonal projection

| | |
|---|---|
| Pre/Post conds | → `(isviewmodel)` |
| Example | `projection:parallel:isometric:(cuboid:<1,1,1>)` |

---

`Leftcavalier` object; standard view model for parallel oblique projection

| | |
|---|---|
| Pre/Post conds | → `(isviewmodel)` |
| Example | `projection:parallel:leftcavalier:(cuboid:<1,1,1>)` |

---

`Onepoint` object; standard view model for perspective projection

| | |
|---|---|
| Pre/Post conds | → `(isviewmodel)` |
| Example | `projection:perspective:onepoint:(cuboid:<1,1,1>)` |

---

`Orthox` object; standard view model for parallel orthographic projection

| | |
|---|---|
| Pre/Post conds | → `(isviewmodel)` |
| Example | `projection:parallel:orthox:(cuboid:<1,1,1>)` |

---

`Orthoy` object; standard view model for parallel orthographic projection

| | |
|---|---|
| Pre/Post conds | → `(isviewmodel)` |
| Example | `projection:parallel:orthoy:(cuboid:<1,1,1>)` |

---

`Orthoz` object; standard view model for parallel orthographic projection

| | |
|---|---|
| Pre/Post conds | → `(isviewmodel)` |
| Example | `projection:parallel:orthoy:(cuboid:<1,1,1>)` |

---

`Parallel` projection class, determining the type of 3D pipeline

| | |
|---|---|
| Pre/Post conds | `(vrp, vpn, vup, prp, window::IsSeq; front, back::IsReal)`<br>→ `(isfun)` |
| Example | `projection:parallel:orthoy:(cuboid:<1,1,1>)` |

---

`Perspective` projection class, determining the type of 3D pipeline

| | |
|---|---|
| Pre/Post conds | `(vrp, vpn, vup, prp, window::IsSeq; front, back::IsReal)` $\rightarrow$ `(isfun)` |
| Example | `projection:perspective:threepoints:(cuboid:<1,1,1>)` |

**Projection** top-level user interface operator

| | |
|---|---|
| Pre/Post conds | `(type::or` $\sim$ `[isparallel, isperspective])(view::isviewmodel)` `(scene::ispol)` $\rightarrow$ `(ispol)` |
| Example | `projection:parallel:orthoy` $\equiv$ `An-Anonymous-Function :` $\mathbb{E}^3 \rightarrow \mathbb{E}^2$ |

**Rightcavalier** object; standard view model for parallel oblique projection

| | |
|---|---|
| Pre/Post conds | $\rightarrow$ `(isviewmodel)` |
| Example | `projection:parallel:rightcavalier:(cuboid:<1,1,1>)` |

**Threepoints** object; standard view model for perspective projection

| | |
|---|---|
| Pre/Post conds | $\rightarrow$ `(isviewmodel)` |
| Example | `projection:perspective:threepoints:(cuboid:<1,1,1>)` |

**Trimetric** object; standard view model for parallel orthogonal projection

| | |
|---|---|
| Pre/Post conds | $\rightarrow$ `(isviewmodel)` |
| Example | `projection:parallel:trimetric:(cuboid:<1,1,1>)` |

**Twopoints** object; standard view model for perspective projection

| | |
|---|---|
| Pre/Post conds | $\rightarrow$ `(isviewmodel)` |
| Example | `projection:perspective:twopoints:(cuboid:<1,1,1>)` |

**Xcavalier** object; standard view model for parallel oblique projection

| | |
|---|---|
| Pre/Post conds | $\rightarrow$ `(isviewmodel)` |
| Example | `projection:parallel:xcavalier:(cuboid:<1,1,1>)` |

**Ycavalier** object; standard view model for parallel oblique projection

| | |
|---|---|
| Pre/Post conds | $\rightarrow$ `(isviewmodel)` |
| Example | `projection:parallel:ycavalier:(cuboid:<1,1,1>)` |

# Appendix C

**REFERENCES**

[ABC⁺00]    C. Armstrong, A.A Bowyer, S. Cameron, J. Corney, G. Jared, R. Martin, A. Middleditch, M. Sabin, J. Salmon, and J. Woodwark. *Djinn: A Geometric Interface for Solid Modeling.* Information Geometers, Winchester, UK, 2000.

[ABS97]    D. Avis, D. Bremner, and R. Seidel. How good are convex hull algorithms? *Computational Geometry: Theory and Applications,* 7(5–6): 265–301, April 1997.

[ADF85]    S. Ansaldi, L. De Floriani, and B. Falcidieno. Geometric modeling of solid objects by using a face adjacency graph representation. *Computer Graphics,* 19(3): 131–140, July 1985.

[Ado85]    Adobe Systems Inc. *PostScript Language Reference Manual.* Addison-Wesley, Reading, MA, 1985.

[AF92]    D. Avis and K. Fukuda. A pivoting algorithm for convex hulls and vertex enumeration of arrangements and polyhedra. *Discrete and Computational Geometry,* 8(5–6): 295–313, 1992.

[AG92]    H. Alt and M. Godau. Measuring the resemblance of polygonal curves. In *Proc. 8th Annu. ACM Sympos. Comput. Geom.,* pages 102–109, 1992.

[AG95]    H. Alt and M. Godau. Computing the Frechet distance between two polygonal curves. *Internat. J. Comput. Geom. Appl.,* 5: 75–91, 1995.

[AHU83]    A. V. Aho, J. E. Hopcroft, and J. D. Ullman. *Data Structures and Algorithms.* Addison-Wesley, Reading, MA, 1983.

[ANM97]    Andrea L. Ames, David R. Nadeau, and John L. Moreland. *The VRML 2.0 Sourcebook.* John Wiley & Sons, New York, 1997.

[ANSI87]    American National Standards Institute. *PHIGS+ Functional Description, Revision 2.0.* New York, July 1987.

[Apo67]    T.M. Apostol. *Calculus.* John Wiley, New York, 1967.

[Ars97]    H. Arsham. Initialization of the simplex algorithm: An artificial-free approach. *SIAM Review,* 39(4): 736–744, 1997.

[Ata83]    M. J. Atallah. A linear time algorithm for the Hausdorff distance between convex polygons. *Information Processing Letters,* 17(4): 207–209, November 1983.

*Geometric Programming for Computer-Aided Design*  Alberto Paoluzzi
© 2003 John Wiley & Sons, Ltd  ISBN 0-471-89942-9

[AU92]     A.V. Aho and J.D. Ullman. *Foundations of Computer Science*. Computer Science Press, W.H. Freeman and Co., New York, 1992.

[BA87a]    C. Bajaj and S. Abhyankar. Automatic parameterization of rational curves and surfaces I: Conics and conicoids. *Computer Aided Design*, 19(1): 11–14, 1987.

[BA87b]    C. Bajaj and S. Abhyankar. Automatic parameterization of rational curves and surfaces II: Cubics and cubicoids. *Computer Aided Desig*, 19(9): 499–502, 1987.

[BA88]     C. Bajaj and S. Abhyankar. Automatic parameterization of rational curves and surfaces III: Algebraic plane curves. *Computer Aided Geometric Design*, 5: 309–321, 1988.

[BA89]     C. Bajaj and S. Abhyankar. Automatic parameterization of rational curves and surfaces IV: Algebraic space curves. *ACM Transactions on Graphics*, 8(4): 324–333, 1989.

[Bac78]    J. Backus. Can programming be liberated from the Von Neuman's style? A functional style and its algebra of programs. *Communications of the ACM*, 21(8): 613–641, August 1978. ACM Turing Award Lecture.

[Bal61]    M.L. Balinski. An algorithm for finding all vertices of convex polyhedral sets. *Journal on Industrial Applied Mathematics*, 9: 72–78, 1961.

[Bar81]    A.H. Barr. Superquadrics and angle preserving transformations. *Computer Graphics*, 15(3): 11,23, August 1981.

[Bau72]    B.G. Baumgart. *Winged-Edge Polyhedron Representation*. Technical Report Stan-CS-320, Artificial Intelligence Laboratory, Stanford University, CA, 1972.

[BBC⁺99]   C. Bajaj, C. Baldazzi, S. Cutchin, A. Paoluzzi, V. Pascucci, and M. Vicentino. A programming approach for complex animations. Part I: Methodology. *Computer Aided Design*, 31(11): 695–710, November 1999.

[BCP00]    F. Bernardini, G. Cenciotti, and A. Paoluzzi. Transfinite interpolation of surfaces with integral and differential constraints using a geometric design language. In *Proc. of Seventh IFIP Workshop on Geometric Modeling: Fundamentals and Applications*, Parma, Italy, 2000. Kluever.

[BdB98]    R. Bidarra, K.J. de Kraker, and W. Bronsvoort. Representation and management of feature information in a cellular model. *Computer-Aided Design*, 30(4): 301–313, 1998.

[Ber91]    F. Bernardini. Integration of polynomials over n-dimensional polyhedra. *Computer Aided Design*, 23(1): 51–58, February 1991.

[BF89]     D. Ba Khang and O. Fujiwara. A new algorithm to find all vertices of a polytope. *Operations Research Letters*, 8: 261–2640, 1989.

[BFM95]    M. Bertolotto, L. De Floriani, and P. Marzano. Pyramidal simplicial complexes. In *Solid Modeling '95, Third ACM/IEEE Symposium on Solid Modeling and Applications*, Salt Lake City, Utah, 1995. ACM Press.

[BFM98]    D. Bremner, K. Fukuda, and A. Marzetta. Primal-dual methods for vertex and facet enumeration. *Discrete and Computational Geometry*, 20: 333–357, 1998.

[BFPP93]   F. Bernardini, V. Ferrucci, A. Paoluzzi, and V. Pascucci. A product operator on cell complexes. In J. Rossignac, J.Turner, and G. Allen, editors, *Proceedings of the $2^{nd}$ ACM/IEEE Symposium on Solid Modeling and Applications*, pages 43–52. ACM Press, May 1993.

[Bie94a]     H.-P. Bieri. Boolean and topological operations for Nef polyhedra. In *CSG '94 Set-Theoretic Solid Modelling Techniques and Applications*, pages 35–53, Information Geometers, Winchester, UK, 1994.

[Bie94b]     H.-P. Bieri. Nef polyhedra: A brief introduction. *Computing Supplementum*, 9(10), 1994.

[Bie95]      H.-P. Bieri. Nef polyhedra: A brief introduction. In H. Hagen, G.E. Farin, H. Noltemeier, and R. Albrecht, editors, *Geometric modelling, Dagstuhl, Germany 1993*, volume 10 of *Computing. Supplementum*, pages 43–60, Springer, New York, 1995.

[Bie98]      H.-P. Bieri. Representation conversions for Nef polyhedra. In Gerald Farin, Hanspeter Bieri, Guido Brunnett, and Tony DeRose, editors, *Geometric Modelling. 3rd Dagstuhl Workshop, Dagstuhl, Germany, 1996*, volume 13 of *Computing. Supplementum*, pages 27–38, Springer, New York, 1998.

[BKES00]     F. Bernardini, J. Klosowski, and J. El-Sana. Directional discretized occluders for accelerated occlusion culling. *Proc. of Eurographics*, 2000.

[BN88]       H.-P. Bieri and W. Nef. Elementary set operations with $d$-dimensional polyhedra. In H. Noltemeier, editor, *Computational Geometry and its Applications*, number 333 in Lecture Notes in Computer Science, pages 97–112. Springer Verlag, Berlin, 1988.

[Böh80]      W. Böhm. Inserting new knots into B-spline curves. *Computer Aided Design*, 12(4): 199–201, July 1980.

[BP98]       C. Baldazzi and A. Paoluzzi. Dimension-independent bsp (2): Boundary-to-interior mapping. *International Journal of Shape Modeling*, 4(1): 107–126, January 1998.

[Bra75]      I. Braid. The synthesis of solids bounded by many faces. *Communications of the ACM*, 18(3): 209–216, 1975.

[Bra79]      I. C. Braid. *Notes on a Geometric Modeler*. Technical Report 101, CAD Group Document, University of Cambridge, UK, 1979. (revised 1980).

[Bri89]      E. Brisson. Representing geometric structures in $d$ dimensions: Topology and order. In *ACM Symposium on Computational Geometry*, pages 218–227, ACM Press, New York, 1989.

[Bro83]      A. Brondsted. *An Introduction to Convex Polytopes*. Number 90 in Graduate texts in mathematics. Springer-Verlag, New York, 1983.

[Bro88]      R. Brown. *Topology*. Ellis Horwood, Chichester, UK, 1988.

[Bur74]      C.A. Burdet. Generating all the faces of a polyhedron. *SIAM Journal on Applied Mathematics*, 26: 479–489, 1974.

[BWW$^+$89]  J. Backus, J.H. Williams, E.L. Wimmers, P. Lucas, and A. Aiken. *FL Language Manual, Parts 1 and 2*. Technical Report RJ 7100, IBM Almaden Research Center, Almaden, CA, October 1989.

[BWW90]      J. Backus, J.H. Williams, and E.L. Wimmers. An introduction to the programming language FL. In D.A. Turner, editor, *Research Topics in Functional Programming*, Chapter 9, pages 219–247. Addison-Wesley, Reading, MA, 1990.

[Che65]      N.V. Chernikova. Algorithm for finding a general formula for the nonnegative solutions of a system of linear equations. *U.S.S.R Computational Mathematics and Mathematical Physics*, 5: 228–233, 1965.

[CHJ90]     P. Chen, P. Hansen, and B. Jaumard. *On-Line and Off-Line Vertex Enumeration by Adjacency Lists*. Technical Report RUTCOR 9–90, Rutgers Center for Operations Research, Rutgers University, New Brunswick, NJ, March 1990.

[Chv83]     V. Chvátal. *Linear Programming*. Freeman, New York, 1983.

[CLR80]     E.T. Cohen, T. Lyche, and R. Riensenfeld. Discrete B-splines and subdivision techniques in computer-aided geometric design and computer graphics. *Computer Grapics and Image Processing*, 14(2): 87–111, October 1980.

[Coo67]     S.A. Coons. *Surfaces for Computer-Aided Design of Space Forms*. Technical Report MAC-TR-41, MIT, Cambridge, MA, 1967.

[Cox71]     M.G. Cox. *The Numerical Evaluation of B-Splines*. Technical Report DNAC 4, National Physical Laboratory, August 1971.

[CP78]      I. Carlbom and J. Paciorek. Planar geometric projections and viewing transformations. *Computing Surveys*, 10(4): 465–502, December 1978.

[CP86]      M. Crampin and F.A.E. Pirani. *Applicable Differential Geometry*. Number 59 in London Mathematical Society Lecture Note Series. Cambridge University Press, Cambridge, UK, 1986.

[CP90]      C. Cattani and A. Paoluzzi. Boundary integration over linear polyhedra. *Computer Aided Design*, 22(2): 130–135, March 1990.

[Cro97]     P.R. Cromwell. *Polyhedra*. Cambridge University Press, Cambridge, UK, 1997.

[CS89]      J. Cremer and A. Steward. The architecture of Newton, a general-purpose dynamics simulator. In *IEEE International Conference on Robotics and Automation*, pages 1806–1811. IEEE Press, 1989.

[Dan51]     G.B. Dantzig. Maximization of a linear function of variables subject to linear inequalities. In T.C. Koopmans, editor, *Activity Analysis of Production and Allocation*, Chapter 21, pages 339–347. Wiley, New York, 1951.

[Dan63]     G.B. Dantzig. *Linear Programming and Extensions*. Princeton University Press, Princeton, 1963.

[Dat97]     C.J. Date. *An Introduction to Database Systems*. The Systems Programming Series. Addison-Wesley, seventh edition edition, 1997.

[dB72]      C. de Boor. On calculating with B-splines. *Journal of Approximation Theory*, 6: 50–62, 1972.

[DBETT99]   G. Di Battista, P. Eades, R. Tamassia, and I.G. Tollis. *Graph Drawing: Algorithms for the Visualization of Graphs*. Prentice-Hall, Upper Saddle River, New Jersey, 1999.

[DC73]      G.B. Dantzig and B. Curtis Eaves. Fourier-motzkin elimination and its dual. *Journal of Combinatorial Theory*, 14: 288–297, 1973.

[DP77a]     C.T.J. Dodson and T. Poston. *Graphs, Surfaces and Homology*. Pitman Publ., London, 1977.

[DP77b]     M.E. Dyer and L.G. Proll. An algorithm for determining all extreme points of a convex polytope. *Mathematical Programming*, 12: 81–96, 1977.

[Dye83]     M.E. Dyer. The complexity of vertex enumeration methods. *Mathematics of Operation Research*, 8(3): 381–402, 1983.

[Ede87]     H. Edelsbrunner. *Algorithms in Combinatorial Geometry*. Number 10 in EATCS Monographs on Th. Comp. Sci. Springer-Verlag, New York, 1987.

[Ede95]    H. Edelsbrunner. Algebraic decomposition of nonconvex polyhedra. In *Procs. of 36th Symposium on Foundations of Computer Science*, pages 248–257, October 1995.

[EKP87]    G. Enderle, K. Kansy, and G. Pfaff. *Computer Graphics Programming. GKS — The Graphics Standard.* Springer-Verlag, New York, second edition, 1987.

[ES00]     R. Egli and N.F. Stewart. A framework for system specification using chains on cell complexes. *Computer-Aided Design*, 32(9): 447–459, 2000.

[Far88]    G. Farin. *Curves and Surfaces for Computer Aided Geometric Design.* Academic Press, San Diego, CA, 1988.

[Fer95a]   V. Ferrucci. Dimension-independent solid modeling. PhD thesis, Dip. di Informatica e Sistemistica, Università "La Sapienza", Rome, June 1995.

[Fer95b]   V. Ferrucci. Representing Nef polyhedra. In *Pacific Graphic Conference*, 1995.

[FFFK98]   M. Felleisen, R.B. Findler, M. Flatt, and S. Krishnamurthi. The DrScheme project: An overview. *ACM Sigplan Notices*, 33(6), 1998.

[FH92]     M. Friedman, D.P. Wand and C.T. Haynes. *Essentials of Programming Languages.* The MIT Press and McGraw-Hill, Cambridge, MA, 1992.

[FL87]     R.C. Fu, K.S. Gonzales and C.S.G. Lee. *Robotics: Control, Sensing, Vison and Intelligence.* McGraw-Hill, New York, 1987.

[FP80]     I.D. Faux and M.J. Pratt. *Computational Geometry for Design and Manufacture.* Halsted, Chichester, England, 1980.

[FP91]     V. Ferrucci and A. Paoluzzi. Extrusion and boundary evaluation for multidimensional polyhedra. *Computer Aided Design*, 23(1): 40–50, February 1991. Special issue entitled 'Beyond Solid Modeling'.

[FvD82]    J.D. Foley and A. van Dam. *Fundamentals of Interactive Computer Graphics.* Addison-Wesley, Reading, MA, 1982.

[FvDFH90]  J.D. Foley, A. van Dam, S.K. Feiner, and J.F. Hughes. *Computer Graphics, Principles and Practice.* Addison-Wesley, Reading, MA, 1990. Second edition.

[Gas92]    T. Gaskins. *PHIGS Programming Manual: 3D Programming in X.* O'Reilly, Sebastopol, CA, 1992.

[GG91]     W.A. Gaman and W.A. Giovinazzo. *PHIGS by Example.* Springer-Verlag, New York, 1991.

[Gib77]    P.J. Giblin. *Graphs, Surfaces and Homology.* Chapman and Hall, London, 1977.

[GLS88]    M. Grötschel, L. Lovász, and A. Schrijver. *Geometric Algorithms and Combinatorial Optimization.* Springer-Verlag, Berlin and Heidelberg, 1988.

[Gol87]    R.N. Goldman. The role of surfaces in solid modeling. In G.E. Farin, editor, *Geometric Modeling: Algorithms and New Trends.* SIAM Publications, Philadelphia, Pennsylvania, 1987.

[Gor68]    W.J. Gordon. *Blending Function Methods of Bivariate and Multivariate Interpolation and Approximation.* Technical Report GMR-834, General Motors, Warren, Michigan, 1968.

[Gor69]    W.J. Gordon. Spline-blended surface interpolation through curve networks. *Journal of Mathematical Mechanics*, 18: 931–952, 1969.

[GR74]     W.J. Gordon and R.F. Riesenfeld. Bernstein-Bézier methods for the computer-aided design of free form curves and surfaces. *Journal of the ACM*, 21: 293–310, 1974.

[Grü67]     B. Grünbaum. *Convex polytopes.* J. Wiley, London, UK, 1967.

[GS85]      L. Guibas and J. Stolfi. Primitives for the manipulation of general subdivisions
            and the computation of Voronoi diagrams. *ACM Transactions on Graphics,*
            4(2): 74–123, 1985.

[GT87]      J.L. Gross and T.W. Tucker. *Topological Graph Theory.* John Wiley, New
            York, 1987.

[GW89]      O. Günther and E. Wong.  Convex polyhedral chains: a representation for
            geometric data. *Computer Aided Design,* 21(3): 157–164, March 1989.

[HdVT88]    R. Horst, J. de Vries, and N.V. Thoai. On finding new vertices and redundant
            constraints in cutting plane algorithms for global optimization. *Operations
            Research Letters,* 7: 85–90, 1988.

[HHHW91]    T.L.J. Howard, W.T. Hewitt, R.J. Hubbold, and K.M. Wyrwas. *A Practical
            Introduction to PHIGS and PHIGS PLUS.* Addison-Wesley, Wokingham, UK,
            1991.

[HHK88]     C.M Hoffmann, J.E. Hopcroft, and M. Karasick.  Towards implementing
            robust geometric computations. In *Fourth ACM Symposium on Computational
            Geometry,* pages 106–117, ACM Press, New York, 1988.

[Hof89]     C.M. Hoffmann. *Geometric and Solid modeling.* Morgan Kaufman, New York,
            1989.

[Hop83]     H. Hopf. *Differential Geometry in the Large.* Springer-Verlag, Berlin, 1983.

[Hor89]     B. Horn. *Robot Vision.* McGraw-Hill, New York, 1989, seventh edition.

[HSS84]     J.E. Hopcroft, J.T. Schwartz, and M. Sharir. On the complexity of motion
            planning for multiple independent objects; pspace hardness of "warehouseman's
            problem". *Internat. J. Robotics Res.,* 3(4): 76–88, 1984.

[IS99]      H. Ilies and V. Shapiro. The dual of sweep. *Computer Aided Design,* 31(3):
            185–201, 1999.

[ISO85]     International Organization for Standardization. *The Graphical Kernel System
            (GKS): ISO 7942.* International Organization for Standardization, Geneva,
            Switzerland, 1985.

[ISO89]     International Organization for Standardization. *The Programmer's Hierarchi-
            cal Interactive Graphics System (PHIGS): ISO 9592.* International Organiza-
            tion for Standardization, Geneva, Switzerland, 1989.

[ISO97]     International Organization for Standardization. *The Virtual Reality Modeling
            Language: ISO/IEC 14772-1.* International Organization for Standardization,
            Geneva, Switzerland, 1997.

[JGH87]     A. Jones, A. Gray, and R. Hutton. *Manifolds and Mechanics.* Number 2 in
            Australian Mathematical Society Lecture Series. Cambridge University Press,
            Cambridge, UK, 1987.

[JS00]      A.C. Jeffrey and V. Shapiro. A multivector data structure for differential forms
            and equations. *IMACS Transactions Journal, Mathematics and Computers in
            Simulation,* 54(1): 33–64, 2000.

[Lat91]     J.C. Latombe. *Robot Motion Planning.* Kluwer Academic Publishers, Boston,
            MA, 1991.

[LCA26]     T. Levi-Civita and U. Amaldi.  *Lezioni di meccanica razionale.* Zanichelli,
            Bologna, 1926.

[LD93]      J. Loustau and M. Dillon. *Linear Geometry with Computer Graphics*, volume 170 of *Pure and Applied Mathematics Series*. Marcel Dekker, New York, 1993.

[Lef49]     S. Lefschetz. *Introduction to Topology*. Princeton University Press, Princeton, NJ, 1949.

[LG82]      R. Light and D.C. Gossard. Modification of geometric models through variational geometry. *Computer-Aided Design*, 14(4): 209–214, 1982.

[LG85]      K.W. Lee and D.C. Gossard. A hierarchical data structure for representing assemblies: Part 1. *Computer Aided Design*, 17(1): 15–19, 1985.

[LG02]      J. Lammers and L. Gooding. *Maya 4 Fundamentals*. New Riders, Indianapolis, Indiana, 2002.

[Lie89]     P. Lienhardt. Subdivisions of $n$-dimensional spaces and $n$-dimensional generalized maps. In *ACM Symposium on Computational Geometry*, pages 228–236, New York, 1989. ACM Press.

[lLK84]     S. Ling Lien and J.T. Kajiya. Symbolic method for calculating the integral properties of arbitrary nonconvex polyhedra. *IEEE Computer Graphics and Applica- tions*, 4(10): 35–41, 1984.

[LPW79]     T. Lozano-Perez and M. Wesley. An algorithm for planning collision-free paths among polyhedral obstacles. *Communications of the ACM*, 22: 560–570, 1979.

[LR82]      Y.T. Lee and A.A.G. Requicha. Algorithms for computing the volume and other integral properties of solids i: known methods and open issues. *Communications of the ACM*, 25(9): 635–641, 1982.

[LS86]      P. Lancaster and K. Salkauskas. *Curve and Surface Fitting. An Introduction*. Academic Press, London, UK, 1986.

[LTH86]     D.H. Laidlaw, W.B. Trumbore, and J.F. Hughes. Constructive solid geometry for polyhedral objects. *ACM Siggraph '86, Computer Graphics*, 20(4): 161–170, August 1986.

[Lue84]     D.G. Luenberger. *Linear and Nonlinear Programming*. Addison-Wesley, Reading, MA, 1984.

[LW69]      A.T. Lundell and S. Weingram. *The Topology of CW Complexes*. Van Nostrand Reinhold, New York, 1969.

[LZ88]      P. Lucas and S.N. Zilles. *Applicative Graphics Using Abstract Data Types*. Technical Report RJ 6198, IBM Almaden Research Center, February 1988.

[Män86]     M. Mäntylä. Boolean operation of 2-manifold trough vertex neighborhood classification. *ACM Transactions on Graphics*, 5(1): 1–29, 1986.

[Män88]     M. Mäntylä. *An Introduction to Solid Modeling*. Computer Science Press, Rockville, Maryland, 1988.

[Man88]     Benoit B. Mandelbrot. *Fractal Geometry of Nature*. W.H. Freeman & Co., 1988.

[Mau91]     A. Maulik. An efficient intersection algorithm for polyhedral cellular decompositions. In J. Rossignac and J. Turner, editors, *ACM Symposium on Solid Modeling Foundations and CAD/CAM Applications*, pages 109–118, Austin, TX, 1991. ACM Press.

[McK87]     M. McKenna. Worst-case optimal hidden-surface removal. *ACM Transactions on Graphics*, 6(1): 19–28, January 1987.

[Mit77]     W.J. Mitchell. *Computer-Aided Architectural Design*. Van Nostrand Reinhold, New York, 1977.

[MMPP02]   M. Cialdea Mayer, G. Marzano, A. Paoluzzi, and S. Portuesi. Representing and exporting design knowledge. Submitted paper, November 2002.

[MN68]     M. Manas and J. Nedoma. Finding all vertices of the convex polyhedron. *Numerische Mathematik*, 12: 226–229, 1968.

[Mor85]    M.E. Morteson. *Geometric Modeling*. John Wiley & Sons, New York, 1985.

[MR77]     T.H. Matheiss and D.S. Rubin. *Comments on Dyer and Proll's Vertex Generating Algorithm*. Technical Report 11, Curriculum in Operations Research, University of North Carolina at Chapel Hill, September 1977.

[MR80]     T.H. Matheiss and D.S. Rubin. A survey and comparison of methods for finding all vertices of convex polyhedral sets. *Mathematics of Operation Research*, 5(2): 167–185, 1980.

[Mun84]    J.R. Munkres. *Elements of Algebraic Topology*. Addison Wesley, Reading, MA, 1984.

[Mur83]    K.G. Murty. *Linear Programming*. Wiley & Sons, New York, 1983.

[MV92]     J. Menon and H. Voelcker. Toward a comprehensive formulation of nc verification as a mathematical and computational problem. In *1992 Winter Annual Meeting of ASME*, volume 59, pages 147–164, Anaheim, CA, 1992.

[Nak90]    M. Nakahara. *Geometry, Topology and Physics*. Graduate Student Series in Physics. Adam Hilger, Bristol, UK, 1990.

[Nak91]    M. Nakahara. *Geometry, Topology and Physiscs*. Graduate Student Series in Physiscs. Adam Hilger, Bristol, UK, 1991.

[NAT90]    B.F. Naylor, J. Amanatides, and W. Thibault. Merging BSP trees yields polyhedral set operations. *Computer Graphics*, 24(4): 115–124, August 1990. Proc. of ACM Siggraph'90.

[NDW92]    J. Neider, T. Davis, and M. Woo. *OpenGL Programming Guide*. Addison-Wesley, Reading, MA, 1992.

[Nef78]    W. Nef. *Beiträge zur Theorie der Polyeder — mit Anwendungen in der Computergrafik*. Herbert Lang, Bern, 1978. In German.

[Neg70]    N. Negroponte. *The Architecture Machine: Towards a More Human Environment*. MIT Press, Cambridge, MA, 1970.

[Nem96]    G.L. Nemhauser. Branch-and-price for solving integer programs with a huge number of variables: Methods and applications. Number 1118 of *Lecture Notes in Computer Science*, Springer Verlag, Berlin, 1996.

[NNS72]    M.E. Newell, R.G. Newell, and T.L. Sancha. A solution to the hidden surface problem. In *Proceeedings of the ACM National Conference*, pages 443–450, 1972.

[Ope92]    OpenGL Architecture Review Board. *OpenGL Reference Manual*. Addison-Wesley, Reading, MA, 1992.

[Pan71]    E. Panofsky. *The Life and Art of Albrecht Durer*. Princeton University Press, Princeton, NJ, 1971.

[Pan91]    E. Panofsky. *Perspective as Symbolic Form*. Zone Books, New York, 1991. (1927).

[Pao78]    A. Paoluzzi. *Disegno Automatico di Solidi Poliedrici*. Quaderni di Architettura Tecnica 16, Istituto di Architettura, Edilizia e Tecnica Urbanistica, Università "La Sapienza", Rome, May 1978. In Italian.

[Pao87]     A. Paoluzzi. *Integration Constraints in Parametric Design of Physical Objects.*
            Techn. Rep. 87-804, Dept. of Computer Science, Cornell University, Ithaca,
            NY, January 1987.

[Pao89]     A. Paoluzzi. *Motion Planning + Solid Modeling = Motion Modeling.* Techn.
            Rep. 17.89, Dip. di Informatica e Sistemistica, Università "La Sapienza", Rome,
            November 1989.

[Pao96]     A. Paoluzzi. Bilinear matrix forms for the area of polygons. *Computer Aided
            Design*, 28(4): 301–306, 1996.

[PBCF93]    A. Paoluzzi, F. Bernardini, C. Cattani, and V. Ferrucci.  Dimension-
            independent modeling with simplicial complexes.  *ACM Transactions on
            Graphics*, 12(1): 56–102, January 1993.

[Pes92]     M. Pesce. *VRML Browsing and Building Cyberspace.* New Riders, London,
            UK, 1992.

[PFP96]     V. Pascucci, V. Ferrucci, and A. Paoluzzi. Dimension-indipendent convex-cell
            based hpc: Skeletons and product. *International Journal of Shape Modeling*,
            2(1): 37–67, January 1996.

[Pho75]     B.T. Phong. Illumination for computer generated pictures. *Communications
            of the ACM*, 18(6): 311–317, June 1975.

[PM89]      A. Paoluzzi and M. Masia. The geometric modeler Minerva. *Wheels for the
            Mind*, Apple Europe, 3(2): 14–32, April 1989.

[Poi53]     H. Poincaré. *Oeuvres*, volume 6. Gauthier-Villars, Paris, 1953.

[PPV95]     A. Paoluzzi, V. Pascucci, and M. Vicentino.  Geometric programming: a
            programming approach to geometric design. *ACM Transactions on Graphics*,
            14(3): 266–306, July 1995.

[PRS89]     A. Paoluzzi, M. Ramella, and A. Santarelli.  Boolean algebra over linear
            polyhedra. *Computer Aided Design*, 21(8): 474–484, October 1989.

[PS85]      F.P. Preparata and M.I. Shamos. *Computational Geometry.* Springer-Verlag,
            Berlin, 1985.

[PS92]      A. Paoluzzi and C. Sansoni.  Programming language for solid variational
            geometry. *Computer Aided Design*, 24(7): 349–366, July 1992.

[PY90]      Michael S. Paterson and F. Frances Yao. Efficient binary space partitions
            for hidden-surface removal and solid modeling. *Discrete and Computational
            Geometry*, 5: 485–503, 1990.

[RA76]      D.F. Rogers and J.A. Adams. *Mathematical Elements for Computer Graphics.*
            McGraw-Hill, New York, 1976.

[Rag00]     S. Raghothama. Models and representations for parametric family of parts.
            PhD thesis, Department of Mechanical Engineering, Univeristy of Wisconsin-
            Madison, September 2000.

[Rap95]     A. Rappoport. Geometric modeling: a new fundamental framework and its
            practical implications. In *Solid Modeling '95, Third ACM/IEEE Symposium
            on Solid Modeling and Applications*, Salt Lake City, Utah, 1995. ACM Press.

[Req77]     A.A.G. Requicha. *Mathematical Models of Rigid Solid Objects.* Technical
            Report 28, Production Automation Project, Univ. of Rochester, NY, November
            1977.

[Req80]     A.A.G. Requicha.  Representations for rigid solids: theory, methods and
            systems. *ACM Computing Surveys*, 12(4): 437–464, December 1980.

[Req88]     A.A.G. Requicha. Solid modeling: A 1988 update. In B. Ravani, editor, *CAD Based Programming for Sensory Robots*, number 50 in Nato ASI Series, pages 3–22. Springer-Verlag, Berlin, 1988.

[Rie73]     R.F. Riesenfeld. *Application of B-Spline Approximation to Geometric problems of Computer Aided Design*. Technical Report 126, University of Utah, 1973.

[RO90]      J. Rossignac and M. O'Connor. SGC: A dimension-independent model for pointsets with internal structures and incomplete boundaries. In M.J. Wozny, J. Turner, and K. Preiss, editors, *Geometric Modeling for Product Engineering*, pages 145–180, Rensselaerville, NY, 1990. North Holland.

[Rob63]     F.D. Robinson. The background of the PERT algorithm. *The Computer Journal*, 5(4): 297–300, January 1963.

[Rog97]     David F. Rogers. *Procedural Elements for Computer Graphics*. McGraw-Hill, New York, 1997, second edition.

[Ros94]     J.R. Rossignac. Through the cracks of the solid modeling. In S. Coquillart, W. Strasser, and P. Stucki, editors, *From Object Modelling to Advanced Visualization*. Springer-Verlag, 1994.

[RR86]      J.R. Rossignac and A.A.G. Requicha. Offsetting operations in solid modeling. *Computer Aided Geometric Design*, 26(2): 129–148, 1986.

[RR91]      A.A.G. Requicha and J.R. Rossignac. Constructive non-regularized geometry. *Computer-Aided Design*, 23(1), 1991.

[RR92]      A.A.G. Requicha and J.R. Rossignac. Solid modeling and beyond. *IEEE Computer Graphics and Applications*, 12(9): 31–44, September 1992.

[RR99]      A.A.G. Requicha and J.R. Rossignac. Solid modeling. In J. Webster, editor, *Encyclopedia of Electrical and Electronics Engineering*. John Wiley & Sons, New York, 1999.

[RS72]      C.P. Rourke and B.J. Sanderson. *Introduction to Piecewise-Linear Topology*. Springer Verlag, Berlin, 1972.

[RS89]      J. Ruppert and R. Seidel. On the difficulty of tetrahedralizing 3-dimensional non-convex polyhedra. In *ACM Symposium on Computational Geometry*, New York, 1989. ACM Press.

[RS02]      S. Raghothama and V. Shapiro. Topological framework fo part families. In K. Lee and N.M. Patrikalakis, editors, *Seventh ACM Symposium on Solid Modeling and Applications*, pages 1–12, Saarbrücken, Germany, 2002. ACM Press.

[RSST01]    V.L. Rvachev, T.I. Sheiko, V. Shapiro, and I. Tsukanov. Transfinite interpolation over implicitly defined sets. *Computer Aided Geometric Design*, 18: 195–220, 2001.

[RV77]      A.A.G. Requicha and H.B. Voelcker. *Constructive Solid Geometry*. Technical Report TM-25, PAP, University of Rochester, Rochester, NY, November 1977.

[RV83]      A.A.G. Requicha and H.B. Voelcker. Solid modeling: Current status and research directions. *IEEE Computer Graphics and Applications*, 3(7): 25–37, October 1983.

[Sam88]     H.S. Samet. An overview of quadtrees, octrees, and related hierarchical data structures. In R.A. Earnshaw, editor, *Theoretical Foundations of Computer Graphics and CAD*, Nato ASI Series, pages 51–68. Springer-Verlag, Berlin, 1988.

[Sam90a]    H.S. Samet. *Applications of Spatial Data Structures: Computer Graphics, Image Processing, and GIS.* Addison Wesley, Reading, MA, 1990.

[Sam90b]    H.S. Samet. *The Design and Analysis of Spatial Data Structures.* Addison Wesley, Reading, MA, 1990.

[San70]     R.J. Sandor Ritz. *The temple of Santo Stefano Rotondo in Rome, the new Jerusal of Revelation.* Tipografia PUG, Rome, 1970. in Italian.

[Sch86]     A. Schrijver. *Theory of Linear and Integer Programming.* John Wiley, London, 1986.

[Sch93]     R. Schneider. *Convex Bodies: The Brunn-Minkowski Theory.* Cambridge University Press, Cambridge, UK, 1993.

[Sei81]     R. Seidel. *A Convex Hull Algorithm Optimal for Point Sets in Even Dimensions.* Technical report, University of British Columbia, Dept. of Computer Science, 1981.

[SF97]      J. Springer and D.P. Friedman. *Scheme and the Art of Programming.* The MIT Press and McGraw-Hill, New York, 1997.

[Sha01]     V. Shapiro. Solid modeling. In G. Farin, J. Hoschek, and M.S. Kim, editors, *Handbook of Computer Aided Design.* Elsevier Science Publishers, Oxford, 2001.

[SK92]      J.M. Snyder and J.T. Kajiya. Generative modeling: a symbolic system for geometric modeling. *Computer Graphics*, 26: 369–378, 1992. SIGGRAPH '92 Proceedings.

[SN99]      H.A. Sowizral and D.R. Nadeau. *An Introduction to Programming AR and VR Applications in Java3D.* ACM Siggraph Tutorial, 1999.

[Sny92]     J.M. Snyder. *Generative Modeling for Computer Graphics and CAD.* Academic Press, San Diego, CA, 1992.

[Sob89]     C. Sobhanpanah. Extension of a boundary representation technique for the description of $n$ dimensional polytopes. *Computers & Graphics*, 13(1): 17–23, 1989.

[SPGR93]    S. Scopigno, A. Paoluzzi, S. Guerrini, and G. Rumolo. Parallel depth merge: A paradigm for hidden surface removal. *Computers & Graphics*, 14(2), 1993.

[SRD00]     H.A. Sowizral, K. Rushforth, and M. Deering. *The Java 3D API Specification.* Addison-Wesley, Reading, MA, 2000.

[SS90]      J.T. Schwartz and M. Sharir. Algorithmic motion planning in robotics. In Jan Van Leeuwen, editor, *Handbook of Theoretical Computer Science*, volume A, Algorithms and Complexity. Elsevier and The MIT Press, Amsterdam, 1990.

[SSS74]     I.E. Sutherland, R.F. Sproull, and R.A. Schumacker. A characterization of ten hidden-surface algorithms. *ACM Computing Surveys*, 6(1): 1–55, March 1974.

[Ste71]     K.A. Steele. CPM/PERT. In *Second Canadian Man-Computer Communications Conference*, pages 81–84, May 1971.

[Sug93]     K. Sugihara. Resolvable representation of polyhedra. In J. Turner, J. Rossignac, and G. Allen, editors, *Second ACM/IEEE Symposium on Solid Modeling and Applications*, pages 127–135, Montreal, CA, 1993. ACM Press.

[SV91]      V. Shapiro and D.L. Vossler. Construction and optimization of CSG representations. *Computer-Aided Design*, 23(1): 4–20, 1991.

[SV93]      V. Shapiro and D.L. Vossler. Separation for boundary to csg conversion. *ACM Transactions on Graphics*, 12(1): 35–55, 1993.

[Svg02]   SVG Working Group. *Scalable Vector Graphics (SVG) 1.1 Specification.* Technical report, W3 Consortium, 2002. URL http://www.w3.org/TR/2002/PR-SVG11-20021115/.

[Tak86]   T. Takala. Geometric boundary modeling without topological data structures. In A.A.G. Requicha, editor, *Eurographics '86.* North-Holland, Amsterdam, 1986.

[Tak91]   T. Takala. A taxonomy of geometric and topological models. In *Proc. Eurographics Workshop on Mathematics and Computer Graphics,* S. Margherita, Genova, Italy, October 1991.

[TD97]    M.N. Thapa and G.B. Dantzig. *Linear Programming 1: Introduction.* Springer series in Operation Research. Springer-Verlag, Berlin, 1997.

[Tou88]   Godfried T. Toussaint. *Computational Morphology.* North Holland, Amsterdam, 1988.

[TS80]    G.H. Timmer and J.M. Stern. Computation of global geometric properties of solid objects. *Computer Aided Design,* 12(6), 1980.

[Van91]   G. Vaněček, Jr. Brep-index: A multidimensional space partitioning tree. *International Journal of Computational Geometry and Applications,* 1(3): 243–261, 1991.

[VMJ97]   T. Varady, R. Martin, and J. Cox. Reverse engineering of geometric models: an introduction. *Computer-Aided Design,* 29(6): 255–268, 1997.

[Voe98]   H.B. Voelcker. The current state of affairs in dimensional tolerancing: 1997. *Integrated Manufacturing Systems,* 9(4): 205–217, 1998.

[Von78]   B. Von Hohenbalken. Least distance methods for the scheme of polytopes. *Mathematical Programming,* 15: 1–11, 1978.

[Von81]   B. Von Hohenbalken. Finding simplicial subdivisions of polytopes. *Mathematical Programming,* 21: 233–234, 1981.

[Wei86]   K.J. Weiler. Topological structures for geometric modeling. PhD thesis, Rensselaer Polytechnic Institute, Albany, NY, 86.

[Wen71]   M.J. Wenninger. *Polyhedron Models.* Cambridge University Press, Cambridge, UK, 1971.

[Wil82]   J.H. Williams. Notes on the FP style of functional programming. In P. Henderson, J. Darlington, and D.A. Turner, editors, *Functional Programming and its Applications,* pages 219–247. Cambridge University Press, Cambridge, UK, 1982.

[WO94]    J. Wernecke and Open Inventor Architecture Group. *The Inventor Mentor.* Addison-Wesley, Reading, MA, 1994.

[Woo85]   T. Woo. A combinatorial analysis of boundary data structure schemata. *IEEE Computer Gaphics & Applications,* 5(3): 19–27, March 1985.

[WW91]    J.H. Williams and E.L. Wimmers. *An Optimizing Compiler Based on Program Transformation.* Technical report, IBM Almaden Research Center, March 1991. Internal IBM report.

[Yao90]   F.F. Yao. Computational geometry. In J. Van Leeuwen, editor, *Handbook of Theoretical Computer Science,* Chapter 7, pages 364–374. Elsevier, Amsterdam, 1990.

[YT85]    F. Yamaguchi and T. Tokieda. Bridge edge and triangulation approach in solid modeling. In T.L. Kunii, editor, *Frontiers in Computer Graphics.* Springer Verlag, Berlin, 1985.

[Zie95]    G.M. Ziegler. *Lectures on Polytopes*. Number 152 in Graduate texts in mathematics. Springer-Verlag, New York, 1995.

[ZLL+88]   S.N. Zilles, P. Lucas, T.M. Linden, J.B. Lotspiech, and A.R. Harbury. The Escher document imaging model. In *ACM Conference on Document Processing Systems*, 1988.

# Index

*Geometric Programming for Computer-Aided Design* Alberto Paoluzzi
© 2003 John Wiley & Sons, Ltd ISBN 0-471-89942-9

Printed and bound by CPI Group (UK) Ltd, Croydon, CR0 4YY

paramet 27/10/2024 , 369